The Institutions of France under the
Absolute Monarchy, 1598–1789

Translated by Brian Pearce

Roland Mousnier

The Institutions of France under the Absolute Monarchy 1598-1789

Society and the State

The University of Chicago Press

Chicago and London

This work first appeared in French under the title *Les In-stitutions de France sous la monarchie absolue, 1598–1789*. Volume 1: *Société et Etat*. Copyright ©1974 by Presses Universitaires de France.

The University of Chicago Press, Chicago 60637
The University of Chicago Press, Ltd., London
©1979 by The University of Chicago
All rights reserved. Published 1979
Printed in the United States of America
84 83 82 81 80 79   5 4 3 2 1

Roland Mousnier has been a professor of modern history at the Sorbonne since 1955. Since 1958 he has been the director of the Center for Research on Modern European Civilization. Some of his publications in English are *Peasant Uprisings in Seventeenth-Century France, Russia, and China; Social Hierarchies;* and *The Assassination of Henri IV*.

Contents

Introduction: What Are Institutions? How Can
They Be Studied?   xiii

1   *The Social Structure of France under the
Absolute Monarchy*

1   The Social Structure as Seen by Some
Contemporaries   3

Charles Loyseau and the society of orders   4

The duc de Saint-Simon and the transition   16

Domat and the transition   29

The transition to class society completed: Barnave   36

2   The Society of Lineages   48

Lineage, marriage, lineal property   48

Lineage, house, family   48   The *livre de raison*   50
Some great lineages   51   Problems of marriage: Mis-
alliance, abduction by seduction. The decrees of the
Council of Trent   58   Lineage and property   66
(*Propres*, lineal property   66   The *retrait
lignager*   67   Customary reservation   70
Primogeniture   72   Fiduciary substitutions   74
Parage and *frérage*   77   Customary laws of property
in southern France   78)

v

The domestic communities   78

Tacit communities   79   Other types of community   81   The decline of the communities   82   The
ménage breaks free from the lineage   83

The *ménage*   84

The omnipotence of the paterfamilias   85

The *maison*   91

3   The Society of Fealties   99

The relationship between master and *fidèle*   99

The relationship between *protecteur* and *créature*   105

**From fealties to the relationship between subject and
state   107**

Fealty and feudalism   108

4   The Society of Orders: The Nobility   112

Armorial bearings   113

The order of the nobility   120

The quality of being noble   121   The degrees of
nobility   122   The privileges of the nobility   124
Ennoblements   126   Derogation   131   Investigations of claims to noble status   135   "Point of
honor" and the duel   139   The Tribunal du point
d'honneur   141

The social standing of the nobility   147

How many nobles?   147   The social degrees of the
nobility   152   The court nobility   153   The provincial higher nobility   158   The *noblesse de robe*   159
The middle and petty *gentilhommerie*   165

The nobles' means of living   166

The fortunes and incomes of the nobles   173   A
commercial nobility and a military nobility   190

The unity of the order of the nobility   198

The divisions in the order of the nobility   202

5   The Society of Orders: The Ennobled and the
         Bourgeois "Living like Nobles"   214

Traitants, partisans, financiers   216

The "men of talent," officeholders   221

Minor officials   227

The "noblemen of letters"   227

The wholesale merchants   229

The holders of decorations   232

6   The Society of Orders: The Common
       People   236

The "*bourgeois*"   236

The "estates" of the *bourgeoisie*   239

The manual workers   253

In the towns   255   In the countryside   264

The poor   274

7   The Society of Orders: The Order of the Catholic
       Clergy   281

The law of the ecclesiastical order   283

The ecclesiastical hierarchy: The secular clergy   283
The ecclesiastical hierarchy: The regulars   291   The
privileges of the clergy   294   Ecclesiastical jurisdiction   296   The property of the Church   302
(Tithes   303   Benefices   304   Collation to benefices   305   Patronage   306   Conditions for obtaining
a benefice   307   The financial obligations borne by
benefices   309)   The liberties of the Gallican
Church   311

The relations between the clerical order and society   316

The numbers of the clergy   319   The relation between the degrees of the clerical order and the hierarchy of orders and estates in society as a whole   320
The recruitment of bishops   322   The recruitment of
abbots and abbesses   325   The recruitment of vicars
general   326   The recruitment of canons   327   The
recruitment of parish priests   328

The income of the clerical order   331

The bishoprics   331   The monasteries   332   The income of the parish priests   333   The poor
priests   335   The hermits   335   Financial obligations   336

The life-style of the clerical order   337

The first half of the 17th century   338   The recovery,
from the middle of the 17th century to the middle of
the 18th   340   (The seminaries   340   Results of
training   351)   From Christocentrism to anthropocentrism (from the end of the 17th century to
the end of the 18th century)   353   Conflicts between
ecclesiastical "estates"   356

**The political organization of the clergy in
France   358**

The origin of the system of representation   359   The
General Assembly   361   The agents general   367
The receiver general of the tenths   368   The diocesan
and provincial organs   369   (The financial functioning of these organs   371   The political functioning of
these organs   372)   The Assembly's participation in
royal acts   374

8   The Society of Orders: The Protestant
       Order   383

Religious organization   383

Organization of justice and administration   388

Political and military organization   389

**The demolition of the political and military or-
ganization   391**

The destruction of the Protestant order   393

From the Revocation to the Revolution   402

9   The Society of Orders: The Jews   413

10   The Society of Corporations   429

The corporations of royal officials   431

The corporations of auxiliaries of justice   437

The advocates before the Paris *parlement*   439   The
advocates before the king's Council   442   The attorneys (*procureurs*) before the Paris *parlement*   445
The notaries attached to the Paris Châtelet   447   The
tipstaffs (*hussiers*) and bailiffs (*sergents*)   448

The *"officiers de police"* or domanial officials   449

The universities   450

The Académie française and other royal academies   455

The medical corporations   458

Physicians   458   Surgeons   459   Apothecaries   462

The communities of arts and crafts   463

The different categories of craft   463   The organization and functioning of the sworn crafts   466

The commercial corporations: The East India and other joint-stock companies   473

11   The Territorial Communities:
     The *Seigneuries*   477

The legal position of *seigneuries*   477

The hierarchy of the *seigneuries*   479   The law of fiefs   482   The law of *censives*   492   The forms of ownership surviving from serfdom: *Domaine congéable (convenant), quevaise, complant*   499   Leases for ground rent   501   The law of seignorial powers of justice   504

The actual situation of the *seigneuries*   514

The number and extent of the *seigneuries* and the presence of the *seigneurs*   514   The functioning of the seignorial courts   517   The relations between the *seigneur* and his men   528   Seignorial and feudal exactions   531   The seignorial reaction   534   The king and the *seigneuries*   540   *Seigneurie* and society   544   Individual property and state property   547

12   The Territorial Communities Treated as
     Corporations: Villages and Parishes   551

The community   551

The parish   557

The types of agent of the communities of inhabitants   558

The evolution of the communities of inhabitants   559

13   The Territorial Communities Treated as
       Corporations: The Towns   563

Three kinds of towns: "Seignorial" towns, *villes de
"bourgeoisie,"* and communes   564

A *ville de "bourgeoisie"*: Bordeaux   565

The evolution of institutions in Bordeaux   570

A "seignorial" town: Paris   574

The *"police"* powers of the king's officials   574   The
"police" powers of the Bureau de la Ville   579
Functions of the municipal officials   582   Privileges
of the municipal magistrates   584   The recruitment of
municipal magistrates   585

A commune town: Beauvais   590

The municipal reform of 1764–65   598

14   The Territorial Communities Treated as
       Corporations: The Provinces   606

The meaning of the word "province"   606

The contractual nature of the kingdom   607

The personality of the provinces   608

An example: The provincial estates of Languedoc   612

The provincial assemblies   627

Conclusion to Part One: The Need for a Strong State
to Arbitrate and Coordinate in the Interest of the
Common Good   640

2   *The State and the State's Resources*

15   The State   645

The statute of the French state: The fundamental
laws   649

The mystic body of the monarchy   653

The anointed king   654   The king as miracle-worker 655 The "mystery of the monarchy" 656 The king by divine right 656

The king's sovereignty 659

The royal supremacy 659 The royal sovereignty 659 Absolutism and tyranny 663

The concentration of powers 665

Personal rule 666 Delegation of powers 668

The absolute monarchy and the conception of the universe 670

The royal mythology 670 The destruction of the royal mythology 674

16   The State's Resources 681

The territory of the state 682

The dimensions of the territory 682 The speed of travel 686

Knowledge of the territory 689

Cartography 689 Statistics 698

The population 704

Changes in the number of inhabitants 704 (Short-term changes 705 Long-term changes 709) The quality of the population 710

Intellectual training for political and other leadership 713

The humanities 713 Law 719 Engineering 720 Summary 721

Construction methods 722

Building the fortress of Ath 723

The state's financial resources 729

How the French viewed taxation 730 The margin offered by production 731

A state with extensive political powers but only feeble resources 740

Glossary 745

Index 765

Introduction: What Are Institutions?
How Can They Be Studied?

Historians talking among themselves know very well what they mean by institutions. Where 17th- and 18th-century France is concerned, what is meant are the royal household, the *parlements,* and corporations, the *seigneuries,* and so on. But this word has been used by sociologists in so many different senses that the philosopher-sociologist Georges Gurvitch was no longer able to make any sense of it and wanted to ban its use completely. It would be a pity, though, to lose the word. Let me, then, make clear the meaning it bears in the present work.

An institution is, first and foremost, a guiding idea, the idea of a definite purpose of public good which is to be realized, by way of procedures that have been provided for and laid down, through an obligatory form of behavior. This idea has been accepted by a group of persons who have undertaken to apply these procedures and realize this purpose. It is the guiding idea and the procedures that make of this group of persons an *institution.* They cause this group to differ completely from a mere accidental coming-together or or from a set of individuals who happen to possess common characteristics. The guiding idea and the procedures dominate the persons who join this group, molding them to a certain degree, giving them common forms of behavior and similar

xiii

attitudes. They make this group an entity. Individuals leave the group through death, retirement, resignation, dismissal, or promotion, but their places are taken by other individuals, and the group itself persists. It endures like an organism, with its specific features and distinctive life. Because of the guiding idea and the procedures, what exists is not merely a group of persons but an institution—a state council and not merely state councilors, a judiciary and not merely judges, a landed estate and not merely estate owners. It is therefore pointless to argue about whether "duration" is requisite for the existence of an institution. A few days or a few hours are enough, provided that the guiding idea has made its appearance, together with some procedures, and that a group of persons has undertaken to apply these procedures.

However, the group of persons does form an integral part of the institution. By simplifying and stretching the terms, one could almost say that an institution *signifies* a group of persons. An institution exists only if the idea and the procedures find embodiment in men who apply them, give them obligatory force, and in this way impose certain kinds of action upon other persons. The institutional group is thus at the same time a social group. One therefore should have a good knowledge of the guiding idea of an institution and its procedures, such as can be obtained, on the one hand, from various customaries, edicts, ordinances, and regulations and, on the other, from administrative correspondence, official registers, and all sorts of evidence of practical activity. The idea, the rules, and the procedures determine in advance the motions to be performed, the words to be spoken, the ways in which problems are to be tackled; and all this is imposed by society and the state upon the institutional group and by this institutional group upon the individuals who join it. The idea, rules, and procedures mold the individuals in a certain fashion, creating a common mentality and mode of behavior, a common outlook, a standard of values, and even a way of feeling—without, of course, annihilating their individual personalities, characters, and reactions. In order to obtain exact knowledge of all this, we should have to study the day-to-day activity of the members of the institutional group, their day-to-day relations and behavior among themselves, within the institutional group, and also their behavior outside this group, both with persons belonging to other institutional groups and with the general public in its various social groupings. In other words, an institutional study can never be restricted to the examination of laws and regulations but must be extended to take in everything that can enable us to grasp the actual relations between the persons concerned, from one day to the next.

But these persons, while belonging to this social group, their own institutional group, also belong to other social groups—families, existence groups, social strata, parishes, cities, *seigneuries,* provinces, and so on. They have taken over from these groups, to a greater or lesser extent, certain ideas, value judgments, attitudes, and forms of conduct, and all this is not without influence on the pursuit of a particular public interest by the institutional group which exists to realize it. The way in which laws, regulations, customs, and usages are applied is found to be affected by this circumstance, and the entire functioning of a given institution, in practice, may be modified as a result. Consequently it is essential to carry out a thorough *social* study of the members of an institutional group.

One would like, first of all, to know the collective psychology or mental structures of all these individuals and all these social groups, that is to say, in the first place, the way their minds worked, the way in which they became aware of things, drew inferences, and established the existence of facts and drew general conclusions from these—and so, what sort of education they had had, their notions of logic, the influence upon them of scientific progress in the age they lived in, what they regarded as being established and certain, what they considered to constitute proof. It would be good to know what their opinions and ideas were concerning man, their conception of his place and role in the universe, his purposes and his destiny, and so their religion, their general knowledge, their religious practices, their spiritual life and notions of morality. We ought to know their ideas and opinions on political and social themes, what they thought about the social structure of their age and about monarchy and monarchical government. We should ascertain those unavowed, often unconscious assumptions, those unexpressed value judgments, which lie at the root of a whole series of opinions, ideas, judgments, and reasonings. In tracing these assumptions to their sources, we ought, since man is guided in grave situations and moments of crisis more by reactions that spring from the depths of his being than by ideas, reflections, and reason, to discover what the feelings of these men were, their emotions and desires, their satisfactions and dissatisfactions, their attitudes—that is, their disposition to react in a certain way to external stimulation or to adopt a certain kind of behavior—and to discern the values, images, symbols, and myths which activated emotion, "inner movement," in these men, determining their ideas and dictating their actions.

Then, in the case of all these individuals and social groups, we ought to know their social status, meaning the degree of social esteem—the honor, dignity, rank, and prestige—that they enjoyed. Indications of these are provided by social functions, occupations, careers, kinds of work, and by associations, the chief of which is marriage. And so we ought to know whom the members of the various social groups married, who their relatives were, what family they belonged to, what type of family theirs was, what family connections they formed; their friends, their relations of fealty and clientage; the coteries they belonged to; their membership in religious confraternities, learned societies, political groups, factions, sects; the social conduct of their group—its values, ceremonies, etiquette, forms of politeness; the role of this group, or what one was supposed to do as a member of it in all the circumstances of life; the pattern of conduct prescribed for all members of the group—its social symbols, life-style, recreations, education, speech, manners, etiquette, and conduct, from the time of getting up in the morning to that of going to bed at night, and from the cradle to the grave; the passing of the given individual, family, or social group into higher or lower strata—in other words, their upward or downward social mobility; finally, the group's social myths; and for each of these points, the conscious value attached to it by contemporaries and its real value as demonstrated by actual behavior.

We should know the economic situation of all these individuals and all these social groups and, in the first place, the nature of their resources (which is more important than the amount): the share contributed by salaries, by allowances, by pensions; the resources obtained through fees and commissions or through participation in banking, tax-farming, or army-supplying activities and those drawn from rent of land or *seigneuries* or even, perhaps, from profits. Next, we should know how much of their fortune was derived from each of these sources (something which is of greater importance than the overall amount): the relative weight of their public offices and that of their landed properties, which in turn must be analyzed according to their legal situation (alods, *seigneuries*, fiefs, *censives*) or in relation to mode of exploitation—direct cultivation, sharecropping, tenant farms; the way in which they exploited these properties and how much they invested in them; the contribution made by *rentes* of various kinds, derived from loans, bills of exchange, promissory notes, bank deposits; the proportion represented by jewelry, silverware, coins, furniture, works of art, books. Possibly, also, the element furnished by industrial, commercial, or craft enterprises, with their buildings, their equipment, their stocks of raw materials and finished products, or the proportion of the individual's wealth resulting from participation in such enterprises. Then the total, the level of wealth possessed, which is, after all, not something to be ignored, along with the division of this between what remained the man's "fortune," his means of consumption, and what became capital, means of production. Then, too, the tendency, the history, of these resources, of the man's fortune and capital. Finally, the social value ascribed by contemporaries to each particular type of resource and fortune, regardless of what it amounted to.

Furthermore, we should determine what power was possessed by these individuals and these institutional groups: in other words, the means that a person or a group had at his disposal to compel the wills of others to go the way he or it wanted. Besides the power resulting from their functions inside the given institution, it would be appropriate to find out what influence the members of an institutional group could draw from their membership in it *in everyday life,* in their current dealings with other individuals or other social groups: how and to what extent their functions or their associations enabled them to influence opinion, and how and to what extent their resources and fortune enabled them to form clientages made up of persons who owed them money, or were in their pay, or were employed by them, and of suppliers, persons engaged in various lines of buying and selling.

Clearly, these questions constitute only a brief summary of what we should need to know in order to carry out a thorough study of an institution. Such a study will not be found here, for neither research on the institutions concerned and their personnel nor research on the relevant social structures, mental structures, and social movements is sufficiently advanced for that to be possible. There are still too many special studies lacking. But this book has been written with all these questions in mind (and others as well), and perhaps it may help to stimulate the necessary research.

Every study of institutions must include political, administrative, and social institutions. The state cannot be separated from the society which has produced it but which, in its turn, it informs and shapes. The state is a natural and spontaneous organism, produced by the needs inherent in societies at a certain degree of development. In social milieus which have reached a certain level of civilization there are many collective needs and interests which can be provided for only by a state. At that moment men create the state by what they do, without being fully aware of what they are doing, and the state exists for a long time before men become conscious of its existence. Out of the social groups that make up society there emerges a public corporation or collectivity possessing organs that will and act on behalf of society and in its name. This public corporation, this moral and legal person, is the state, an organization which realizes the unity of a plurality of individuals. The state, raised by society above itself in order to look after its common concerns and interests, in its turn continuously acts to give shape to society as a whole, to the social groups and their mutual relations—that is, to the social structures. Thus there is a constant reciprocal relation between state and society, so that study of the one cannot be separated from study of the other but is essential to it. For convenience of exposition, however, I shall begin with the makeup of society before going on to consider the state.

Guide to further reading

A bibliography of sources and old works is conveniently available in:

Lavisse, Ernest: *Histoire de France depuis les origines jusqu'à la Révolution* (Hachette, 1911): vol. 6, part ii, *Henri IV et Louis XIII*, by J. H. Mariéjol; vol. 7, parts i and ii, *Louis XIV, 1643–1685*, by E. Lavisse; vol. 8, part i, *Louis XIV, 1685–1715*, by A.-R. de Saint Léger, A. Rebelliau, P. Sagnac, and E. Lavisse, and part ii, *Le règne de Louis XV, 1715–1774*, by H. Carré; vol. 9, part i, *Le règne de Louis XVI, 1774–1789*, by H. Carré, P. Sagnac, and E. Lavisse, and part ii, *Tables alphabétiques*.

Old textbooks of legal history are also useful; see, for example, those by Chénon, Declareuil, and Brissaud, and the following two works:

Esmein, Adhémar. *Cours élémentaire d'histoire du droit français.* 15th ed. Edited by R. Génestal. Sirey, 1925.
Olivier Martin, François. *Histoire du droit français des origines à la Révolution.* Domat-Montchrestien, 1948.

The *Bibliographie annuelle de l'Histoire de France,* published by the Comité français des Sciences historiques, Editions du Centre National de la Recherche scientifique, lists both French and other publications on France, beginning in 1953. Eighteen volumes have so far appeared, that for the year 1972 having been published in 1973.

The standard periodicals enable one to keep up with the progress of publications. The most important of these periodicals are: *Revue historique* (P.U.F.), *Revue d'Histoire moderne et contemporaine* (Armand Colin), *Revue d'Histoire économique et sociale* (Marcel Rivière), and *Revue historique de Droit français et étranger* (Sirey). The major journals and periodicals dealing with particular regions must not be forgotten: *Paris et Ile-de-France, Revue du Nord, Revue d'Alsace, Normania, Provence historique, Annales du Midi, Annales de Bretagne, Annales de Bourgogne,* etc.

The reader can easily find the royal edicts and the *arrêts* of the king's Council (Conseil du roi) thanks to:

Jourdan, Decrusy, and Isambert. *Recueil général des anciennes lois françaises,* vols. 15–29. (This work is usually referred to below as "Isambert.")
Guyot. *Répertoire universel et raisonné de jurisprudence civile criminelle, canonique et bénéficiale.* 17 vols. 1874–85.
Catalogue général des livres imprimés de la Bibliothèque nationale: Actes royaux. Edited by Albert Isnard and Mme. S. Honoré. 6 vols. Imprimerie Nationale, 1910–57.

In the Archives nationales there are the series of printed documents: ADIA, Série chronologique; ADIB, Série méthodique; AD +. Fonds Rondonneau.
Numerous sources are mentioned by Louis André, *Les sources de l'histoire de France, XVIIe siècle,* 8 vols. Picard, 1913–35.

The *Dictionnaire universel de la France* by Saugrain (Paris, 1726), in three folio volumes, giving all the provinces, towns, market centers *(bourgs),* and villages, and the *Dictionnaire géographique, historique et politique des Gaules et de la France,* by the Abbé Expilly, in six folio volumes (Paris 1762–68), are indispensable.
The guides to further reading at the end of each chapter have been deliberately restricted to a few basic works, preferably those containing bibliographies.

1

The Social Structure of France
under the Absolute Monarchy

1 The Social Structure as Seen by Some Contemporaries

We need to distinguish between two aspects of "social structure." On the one hand, there is the way that contemporaries perceived the French society of their time, and, on the other, there is the way that men's actual behavior shaped that society. We cannot avoid studying the first aspect, because the view taken by contemporaries always contains an element of the truth, and, moreover, this view serves for contemporaries as one of the motives governing their actions. But contemporaries never have more than partial knowledge of the society of their time, and what they know is defective, especially insofar as it is based on hearsay or on observations that are interpreted inadequately and with prejudice. Besides, there are certain realities which society's members prefer not to admit and which they avoid discussing. It is therefore necessary to go beyond expressed opinions to examine, by way of what men actually did, what their real relations were among themselves and to distinguish clearly between the two pictures of one and the same society which we thus obtain. Too many historical writings consist of a mosaic constructed from contemporary opinions *and* the observations actually made by scholars, which, when juxtaposed, present a composite and misleading picture. Nevertheless, we must *begin*

3

with what was believed by contemporaries, since this provides us with an approach that we cannot do without, with a part of reality, and with hypotheses for subsequent investigation.

If it were possible to proceed in a thoroughly methodical manner, we should have to classify the views expressed by contemporaries regarding the society of their time first of all according to the type of evidence given; to study in systematic fashion the theoretical treatises on society and the state, the dissertations on public law, the collections of *arrêts* made by the *parlements* and other courts of justice, the remonstrances presented by the sovereign courts and by other official bodies, the *cahiers* of the Estates General and those of the provincial estates, the programs of rebel movements, pamphlets, memoirs, letters, diaries, administrative correspondence, sumptuary laws, registers of coats of arms, local chronicles—and so on and so forth. Since this mass of material is too great to be fully explored, we should need to take samples, decide on the parameters of inquiry, apply the methods of quantitative semantics and content analysis, and weigh the results obtained, distinguishing between different geographical regions, territorial communities, occupations, qualities or estates, existence groups, religious or philosophical denominations, political tendencies or parties, sexes and ages. This task has never been carried out, even in the form of sampling in selected test areas, and it cannot be undertaken here. I shall confine myself to singling out a few good observers who tried to elaborate a theory of the society in which they lived and will then seek to discover what, in successive periods, their conceptions of French society were.

Charles Loyseau and the society of orders

I shall begin with the view of French society held by Charles Loyseau. He was born in 1564 and died in 1627, and the first edition of his works appeared in 1610, being reissued in 1614, 1640, 1666, and 1678. His Complete Works were to be found in many libraries belonging to magistrates and men of letters. Even as late as the middle of the 18th century he was held in high esteem by jurists, and writings of his were used by publicists like Boutaric and Jousse—mainly, at that time, his *Traité des seigneuries,* which was still important for experts on the feudal law of French society. The Paris *parlement* continued to invoke his authority in defense of the ancient constitution of French society. However, his ideas about society lost their influence in proportion as the French turned away from the ideal of the society of orders, which he described, and toward the society of classes.

Charles Loyseau possessed all the means needed for becoming well informed about French society. He belonged to a family which was on its way up in the social scale. His grandfather was a *laboureur* (a well-to-do cultivator who owned a plough team) at Nogent-le-Roi. His father had been an advocate before the Paris *parlement* and later had entered the service of persons of distinction: he became the advocate of Diane de Poitiers and of the duc d'Aumale. Charles was born in Paris and was proud to call himself a Parisian. He studied in Paris and became a petty official, a minor magistrate, in a provincial town: *lieutenant royal* in the *bailliage* of Sens, which was the seat of a presidial court. Later he became a seignorial official. From 1600 onward he exercised the function of *bailli* of the county of Dunois, having been appointed by Catherine de Gonzague, duchesse de Longueville, and resided for a long time in Châteaudun, the chief town of the county. It was while performing his studies as a judge that he wrote most of his works—the *Traité des seigneuries,* the *Discours sur l'abus des justices de village,* the *Traité des Offices,* the *Traité des Ordres*—employing "those few hours that were left to me by my regular occupations to give form to the studies which I had dedicated and devoted to my country."

Subsequently he came to Paris to practice as an advocate, living in a house on the corner of the rue d'Hautefeuille. In 1620 he became president of the Order of Advocates, and he died in Paris in 1627.

His son and grandson continued the social ascent achieved by this former peasant family. The son became a counselor in the Paris *cour des aides,* and the grandson, at last, a counselor in the Paris *parlement,* one of a group entitled to be addressed as "Messieurs," thus crowning his family's rise in the world by entry into one of the highest posts of the magistracy.

In his *Traité des Ordres et simples dignités* Charles Loyseau presents French society to us as part of a universe ruled and arranged by the mind of God, all in ranks and degrees, in which man, free and made in the image of God, plays an essential role between the celestial realm and the realm of matter.

> There must be order in all things . . . . The world itself is so-named for that reason in Latin . . . The inanimate creatures are all placed in it in accordance with their higher or lower degree of perfection. Their times and seasons are certain, their properties regulated,

their effects assured. As for the animate creation, the heavenly in-
telligences have their hierarchical orders, which are changeless;
and, with regard to men, who are designated by God to rule over
the other animate creatures of this world, though their order may be
changeable and subject to vicissitude, owing to the particular capacity and freedom that God has given them to choose between
good and evil, it is the case that they cannot survive without order,
for we should not be able to live together in a state of equality, but
of necessity some must command and others obey. Those who
command have many orders and ranks . . . Thus, through these
manifold divisions and subdivisions, out of many orders a general
order is established . . . so that, in the end, by means of order, a
number numberless achieves oneness.

For Loyseau, French society is therefore not a society made up of
castes—that is, one in which social stratification is determined, not in
accordance with its members' riches and their consuming capacity or
with their role in the production of material goods, but in hereditary
fashion, on the basis of their degree of religious purity or impurity, with
strict rules separating social groups through fear of defilement. But
neither is it a society made up of classes, one in which, in a market
economy, social groups are arranged hierarchically according to the
role played by each in the production of material wealth. A class consists of persons who have the same source of income—profit, rent,
salary, or wages—and who, within this basic category, possess income or wealth of the same approximate amount and share the same
life-style and common interests. A class attains perfection if, to all this,
it adds consciousness of all that is common to its members and carries
out action in common. For Loyseau, however, French society is a
society of orders; that is, the arrangement of social groups in hierarchical social strata is effected in accordance with the social esteem, honor,
and dignity attached by society to different social functions, without
there being any direct link between this and the production of material
goods—for example, the honor and esteem attached to the profession
of arms, with the fitness for command and the protection of others
resulting from this; or, in the China of the Ming dynasty, to the condition of the graduate scholar, with eligibility to fulfill public duties and
enjoy the status of magistrate.

For Loyseau, the whole of French society is divided into hierarchical
orders. An order signifies "a rank, with a particular fitness for public
authority," and "in French it has the special name of Estate, since it is

the rank and quality which is a man's most stable and most inseparable feature." A rank, "of the same kind and bearing the same name, is held by many (plusieurs) persons."[1] (Plusieurs, in those days, meant not "several" but "many.")[2] An order is, therefore, indeed a social group.

French society is officially divided into three principal orders. At the top is the ecclesiastical order, the clergy, since, by rights, the "ministers of God" should possess "the first place of honor."[3] Then the nobility, both the "gentlefolk," ancient and "immemorial," descended "from old families," and also those nobles who owe their rank to the offices and seigneuries they have acquired, which confer upon them the same privileges.[4] Last, the third estate, embracing all the rest of the people.[5]

Each of these main orders, however, is subdivided into "particular orders," hierarchically arranged in "ranks," "degrees," or subordinate orders."[6] The ecclesiastical order consists of a hierarchy, from the top downward, of cardinals, primates or patriarchs, archbishops, bishops; the three holy orders of priests, deacons, and subdeacons; the four minor orders of acolytes, exorcists, readers, and porters; and, finally, those who have merely taken the tonsure, since "the tonsure ... is the entrance into all the orders of the church, that which makes a man a cleric and distinguishes the clergy from the people."[7] The order of the nobility is subdivided, from above downward, into princes of the blood; princes who are more distantly related to the sovereign;[8] the higher nobility of the chevaliers, distinguished among themselves by their fiefs of rank, from dukes at the top down through marquises, counts, and barons to castellans;[9] and, finally, the ordinary nobility of gentilshommes de race, engaged in the profession of arms.[10] The third estate actually includes the officials administering justice and government finance, though some of these men are ennobled by their offices, so that they are of noble rank.[11] In principle, this order is headed by the "learned men" (gens de lettres)—doctors, licentiates, bachelors of the faculties of theology, law, medicine, and arts (grammar, rhetoric, philosophy). Then come the advocates. After them follow the financiers, meaning "all those who concern themselves with the management of finance, that is, of the king's revenues." Next, the "practitioners or men of business," those of the "long robe," clerks of the courts, notaries, attorneys; then those of the "short robe," bailiffs, trumpeters, valuers, and sellers of confiscated property. Then the merchants, "both because of the utility and even necessity of trade ... and because of the wealth these men usually possess, which brings them esteem and respect, together with the fact that the means they enjoy of employing craftsmen and laborers gives them a great deal of power in the towns"; accordingly, the merchants are the lowest group of the common people that possess the quality of honor, being called "honorable men" or "worthies" (*honnêtes personnes*) and *"bourgeois* of their towns." Grouped with them are the crafts of apothecary, goldsmith, jeweler, *mercier-grossier,* draper, hosier, and furrier, men who are engaged in trade rather than in manual work. All these can be styled *bourgeois* if they live in privileged towns, which have the right to constitute corporations and communities, provided that they participate in the assemblies of these towns. Next below the merchants come all those who in their occupations "depend more upon manual labor than on trading activity or on the sharpness of their wits, and those occupations are the basest." This means, first and foremost, the *laboureurs,* "those whose normal occupation is ploughing the land for others, as tenant farmers." They, like all villagers, or "peasants," are "base persons." Beneath even them, however, are the craftsmen "who practice the mechanical arts, which are so called in contrast to the liberal arts . . .We give the name mechanical to whatever is base and contemptible." They have their several ranks of master craftsmen, journeymen, and apprentices. Still lower stand "those who have neither craft nor trade but earn their living by the strength of their arms, the people whom we therefore call hands or hired men, such as porters, builder's laborers, carters, and other workers hired by the day, who are all the basest of the humble folk" of town and country. Finally, at the very bottom of the social scale is the order of "sturdy beggars," "vagabonds and tramps," who live "in idleness and without care, at the expense of others."[12]

Each order has "its special mark, sign, or outward ornament," that is, its social symbol. The members of the ecclesiastical order wear the long robe and the tonsure. In addition, those who belong to the four minor orders wear the surplice or the alb; subdeacons have the maniple, worn on the left arm; deacons have the stole; priests, the chasuble; bishops, the miter, crozier, gloves, and ring; cardinals, the hat and the scarlet robe. Among the nobles, "the mere *gentilshommes* have their crested coats of arms, the knights have their spurs and gilded armor . . .The princes have their princely mantles." Among the commoners, "the doctors, licentiates, and bachelors have their different kinds of hood, corresponding to the different faculties, besides the long robe or gown, which they share with the churchmen; the advocates have their distinctive hats, while the attorneys have only the long robe, which marks them off from the mere legal practitioners, who have no status in court."

The orders possess "two other prerogatives of honor, namely, title and rank." Titles are those of *chevalier* (knight) for the great nobles, the great officers of the Crown, the members of the State Council (Conseil d'Etat), the *présidents* and "king's men" (*gens du roi*) of the Paris *parlement,* and the *premiers présidents* of the other sovereign courts; of *noble homme* for the officers of justice and advocates who are not noblemen, with that of *demoiselle* for their wives; of "king's counselor" (*conseiller du roi*) for a number of officials, members of the *parlements, baillis,* and *sénéchaux,* with their *lieutenants,* and the *trésoriers généraux de France.* There are "honorific epithets": "illustrious and excellent" for princes, "high and mighty lord" for *chevaliers* and *grands seigneurs,* "most illustrious" for cardinals, "most reverend" for bishops, "reverend father in God" for abbots, "venerable and discreet person" for other minor ecclesiastics, *noble homme* for officials, *honorable homme* or *honneste personne* for burgesses.

There are "forms of address": "Sire" for the king, "Monseigneur" for princes, "Messire" for *chevaliers,* "Monsieur" for ordinary nobles, "Maistre" for *gens de lettres,* "Sire so and so" for merchants or craftsmen, "Madame" for wives of *chevaliers,* "Mademoiselle" for ordinary noblemen's wives, "Dame" so-and-so (or, by usurpation, "Madame") for burgesses' wives.[13]

Each order has its "rank, that is to say, its particular place of precedence in sitting and walking: . . . to wit, the ecclesiastical order is the first, that of the nobility second, and the third estate last—though there is no ordinance to this effect," and the order of precedence is observed through "voluntary respect." Thus, the humblest of priests should precede the greatest of ordinary *gentilshommes.* "But because the ecclesiastical order is regarded as standing outside secular affairs, our Redeemer Himself having said that His Kingdom is not of this world . . . it is commonly seen nowadays that those who possess some secular rank do not choose to give way to priests unless the latter hold some high rank in the church." The least of the *gentilshommes* must go before the richest and most honorable member of the third estate if the latter holds no royal office. Should he hold such office, the princes "do not yield precedence to any official, whoever he may be; *chevaliers* and other members of the higher nobility give way only to those officials who are, ex officio, *chevaliers* themselves" ("since the latter belong to the same order as they do and, in addition, have their offices"), such as the chancellor of France, the councilors of the State Council, the heads of the sovereign courts; ordinary nobles, *gentilshommes,* and *écuyers* (esquires) give way to royal officials who are magistrates, that is, to the principal officers of government and justice, "in the area where they have jurisdiction," even if those officials happen to be commoners.[14]

The orders as such have no authority, no public administrative organization of their own. Some of them, though, "have corporations and colleges, which sometimes possess the right to make regulations and elect higher officers who have power over the whole body," or else they include a number of corporations and colleges of this kind, as in the case of the crafts.[15]

The orders have their specific privileges. Only *gentilshommes* hold the right to bear coats of arms that are crested, that is, surmounted by a helmet or other "head armor," and a certain number of offices are, in principle, reserved for them: the headships of the offices of the royal household, many military offices, positions as gentlemen of the bedchamber, gentlemen of the bodyguard, waiting-gentlemen, equerries of the royal stables, gentlemen of the stag hunt and the falcon house: "all the principal military appointments, whether in command of fortresses or of companies, and in particular all cavalry commands; and even for the mere command of *compagnies d'ordonnance* and infantry companies, *gentilshommes* are given preference."

As for ecclesiastical appointments, *"plusieurs"* cathedrals and abbeys have their positions of rank, canonries, and monks' places reserved for *gentilshommes*. In general, the *gentilshommes* are favored in the church by being given dispensations that privilege them as regards age limits, pluralism, or length of studies required.

As regards *seigneuries,* fiefs are reserved for *gentilshommes*. Commoners may acquire them only if given a dispensation to do so, and then only on payment to the king of the due of frank fee. But only *gentilshommes* may hold "great" *seigneuries*—duchies, marquisates, counties—and also middle-ranking ones—viscounties, baronies, appointments as *vidame* or castellan. Commoners are allowed to acquire only ordinary *seigneuries,* with rights of high, middle, and low justice.

Gentilshommes, to the exclusion of nobles of the gown, or long robe, alone have the right to wear the sword, "this being the sign and ornament of nobility, and in France they wear it even in the king's study." All members of the higher nobility have the right to be saluted by commoners. Since they risk their lives for the defense of the state, *gentilshommes* are "exempt from paying the *taille* or other personal taxes levied for war purposes . . . and from having men-at-arms billeted on them." "*Gentilshommes* furthermore possess the privilege of hunting . . . so that in peacetime they may exercise themselves in a way that resembles the practice of war."

For an ordinary crime, gentlemen are not punished so severely as commoners and are never condemned to shameful punishments, such as whipping or hanging. While they are punished more leniently as far as corporal penalties are concerned, they are punished more severely when it is a matter of fines; they also incur harsher punishment for crimes which are repugnant to their quality as nobles and which are therefore aggravated by the rank of the offender—crimes such as treason, theft, perjury, and fraud.

Gentilshommes enjoy the privilege of seeking satisfaction for an insult by fighting a duel. Dueling is reserved to the members of their order. They are not obliged to fight duels with commoners.[16]

The third estate has the benefit of an enormous general privilege, namely, that *gentilshommes* (with the exception of glassmakers and a few others) are not allowed to engage in gainful activity in any trade or craft and so cannot compete with members of the third estate.[17]

Membership in an order is acquired. The ecclesiastical order is entered by way of the tonsure, which is the public acknowledgment that a man is dedicating himself to God. The noble order is entered either at birth or by letters patent from the king, "the distributor ordained by God of the tangible honors of this world,"[18] or by appointment to, and acceptance and installation in, offices, royal or municipal, which confer nobility on the holder. Knighthood, and thereby membership in the higher level of the nobility, is conferred upon the great officers of the Crown, the heads of the offices of the royal household, the heads of the sovereign courts, and the king's governors and lieutenants in the provinces. Since they belong to the higher nobility, their children are automatically ordinary *gentilshommes*. "Secretaries to the king, the royal household, and the Crown of France" have the status of nobles of four generations, and their nobility descends to their children, provided they bequeath their offices to sons or sons-in-law. The counselors of the sovereign courts are personally noble, and if grandfather, father, and son have held office without a break, then their descendants are ipso facto noble. By royal privilege, the municipal offices of certain towns confer nobility on their holders. Finally, anyone can claim nobility, by virtue of a decision of the *cour des aides,* if he can prove that he, his father, and his grandfather have all lived "like nobles," preferably on a *seigneurie,* or fief, exercising the profession of arms, and without committing any base action or one that would entail forfeiture of their rank. Later on, these conditions were to be tightened up. The royal declaration of 22 June 1664 made it necessary to prove by incontestable evidence that one's family had been noble since before 1560.[19]

Membership in the different sections of the third estate is acquired by the obtaining of university degrees; by appointment to, and acceptance and installation in, various offices; by registration as an advocate or as an attorney in the various courts of justice; or by acceptance into one of the craft guilds.[20]

Membership in an order can be lost. One ceases to be a priest if (as rarely happens) one is unfrocked for infamous conduct.[21] Membership in the nobility of office is forfeited as a result of ignominy entailing removal from office. Nobility of blood is lost if one is guilty of *lèse-majesté* or treason, when a *gentilhomme* is declared infamous and deprived of his nobility by the sentence passed on him. Other crimes, and the practice of base or mechanical arts for gain, do not, however, annul the noble quality of the *gentilshommes* concerned but merely suspend it for the time being, since nobility of blood is "as though part of a man's nature." If a *gentilhomme* who has "derogated" resumes the noble way of life, he only needs to obtain letters of rehabilitation from the king, who never refuses to grant them. The *gentilhomme* could even manage without them, for "it is a point of common law that rights deriving from blood and nature cannot be lost by civil means."

> The employments incompatible with nobility are those of attorney acting for another, clerk of the court, notary, bailiff, clerk, merchant, and craftsman . . . other than glassmaking . . . This is understandable, since all these employments are carried on for gain: for it is the pursuit of gain, a base and sordid thing, that takes away nobility, the characteristic of which is to live on one's *rentes* or at least not to sell one's labor power. And yet, judges, advocates, doctors, and professors of the humanities do not forfeit any nobility they may possess, even though they earn their living by means of their occupation: this is because, besides the fact that their occupation involves mental rather than manual work, it is honorary rather than mercenary . . . Agricultural work is not incompatible with nobility . . . since nothing that a gentleman does for himself, and without receiving money from others for doing it, is derogatory . . . Nobles are not forbidden to take up sharecropping leases (*métairies*) in perpetuity, for long periods or for life, since in such

leases the *dominium utile* of the land is transferred to the tenant . . . so that the gentleman is then said to be cultivating his own land and not that of another.[22]

This is the picture that Loyseau draws for us of the stratification of French society into orders. This lawyer describes to us, above all, whatever had been given legal significance, whether by custom, edict, ordinance, or *arrêt* of the king's Council (Conseil du Roi) or the *parlements*. Though his book is scattered with observations taken from real life, things this penetrating observer has noted in everyday experience, Loyseau does not furnish us—and why, indeed, should he?—with a complete sociological description. He does not dwell upon the endogamous tendencies that existed at every level of the two lay orders, offset by cases of hypergamy; the general tendency to heredity in a given order or estate, and the caste tendencies that showed themselves among the *gentilshommes;* the restrictions on social mobility resulting from the manners and customs of society, since it often required several generations of "living like *gentilshommes*" for the families of ennobled persons to be accepted by *gentilshommes* as belonging to their social group. We must not be surprised if Loyseau does not lay stress on an essential principle, for to him that principle is obvious: namely, that a family cannot acquire a place in the higher levels of this hierarchy by virtue of money obtained in activities aimed at the production of material wealth (whether in agriculture, industry, or trade) if these are carried on for the purpose of selling the product. The order to which one belongs is what decides the quantity of riches of this world that one receives, and, in the case of the clergy and the nobility, together with the higher strata of the third estate, this income is received in the form of feudal dues, land rents, interests on state bonds, pensions, emoluments, salaries, honoraria (including magistrates' fees), and proportional allowances or *"taxations."* The income obtained even from productive activities was sometimes regulated by custom rather than by the state of the market. There were, as a matter of fact, *gentilshommes*, graduates, and magistrates who were poor; nevertheless, they were, as a rule, held in higher respect than the richest of merchants.

Normally, the officials remained within their own order. But there was a steady and stubborn struggle (revealed by the attitude and declarations of the third estate in the Estates General of 1614–15, by the policy of the Paris *parlement,* and by the role that it and the other *parlements* played during the Fronde) not to transform the society of orders into a class society but to change the hierarchy of orders so that the order of magistrates, the "gentlemen of pen and ink," might be recognized as constituting the first order—to alter the principle of society and cause to be acknowledged as most worthy, not the service of arms, but the civil service of the state: the magistracy *über alles,* the magistracy as the true highest rank of the nobility. Amplifying one of the tendencies at work in French society, Loyseau explains this idea very simply. He arranges everything in accordance with fitness to exercise public authority. Accordingly, he divides society into two parts, those who command and those who obey. Those who command are the king and the magistrates, his officials. Those who obey, "the people," are all the rest: ecclesiastics, nobles, and third estate.

> The sovereign has close to his person his officials of general competence, who convey his orders to the magistrates of the provinces, who in turn convey them to those of the towns,[23] and these magistrates cause them to be carried out by the people. So much for those who command; and as for the people who obey, they, being a body with many heads, are divided into orders, estates, and particular occupations. Some are dedicated especially to the service of God, others to the defense of the state by force of arms, yet others to nourishing and maintaining the state by the labors of peace. These are our three orders, or Estates General of France—the clergy, the nobility and the third estate.[24]

And in Loyseau's thinking it is not just a matter of the magistrates' authority in the exercise of their functions, by virtue of powers delegated to them by the king, but of a claim on their behalf to social preeminence. Loyseau stresses the fact that the princes do not take second place to any official—which is to be expected, since the princes are related, more or less closely, to the king—*except* when these officials are exercising their functions. Here we see a clear distinction between what is political and administrative and what is social. But all the other members of the higher nobility—the *chevaliers,* in other words—must give way to those officials who possess the rank of *chevalier* by virtue of their offices, and they must do so even when the latter are *not* exercising their functions; this applies to the chancellor of France, the *premiers présidents* of the sovereign courts, *présidents,* and the king's attorneys and advocates before the Paris *parlement.* And all ordinary *gentilshommes* must give way to all magistrates, even if they be commoners, in the area where the latter have authority, even when they are not actually exercising their functions.[25]

Loyseau attacks the claims of the *gentilshommes* to superiority of family and purity of blood, an obstacle that the claims of the officials could not overcome.

> Man's rational soul, deriving as it does directly from God, who creates it specially when he sends it into a human body, has no natural participation in the qualities of the seed that has generated the body in which it is placed. I am therefore amazed that almost all the most distinguished philosophers and poets . . . should have given credence to the idea that there are certain secret principles of quality which are transferred from fathers to the children they beget, as, for example, the sorites or induction of Socrates, who concluded that just as the best-bred apple or wine or horse was the best of its kind, so also the man of noble origin was the best of men. And Aristotle says, in the eighth chapter of the third book of his *Politics,* that, in all nations, the nobles are held in honor and esteem because it is likely that he who is born of excellent parents will himself be excellent, and therefore he defines nobility as . . . a quality which is inherited.

Loyseau denies the validity of this theory:

> We see often enough that the children of worthy folk are themselves worthless persons and that those of learned men are ignoramuses . . . And that if sometimes the characters of children prove to be like those of their fathers, this happens not through their engendering, which contributes nothing to men's souls, but rather through their upbringing—in respect of which, indeed, the children of worthy folk are at a great advantage in acquiring quality—and owing to the careful instruction they are given, and by means of the continual and impressive example set them by their fathers, and, again, on account of the obligation placed upon them not to degenerate and fail to live up to their origins, and, finally, because of the credit and good reputation that the memory of their ancestors ensures for them.[26]

Everything depends, therefore, upon upbringing, example, and inherited status, not upon blood. Everything depends upon what a man can acquire for his children, not upon that which cannot be acquired.

Finally, Loyseau makes use, in favor of the officials, of the old myth that explains French society by reference to a conquest. The origin of the social stratification existing in France lies, he says, in the Frankish conquest. The victorious Franks became the nobles, while the conquered Gauls were the commoners. The Franks, having conquered the

Gauls, "reserved this prerogative over them, that they sought to keep for themselves all public offices, the use of arms, and possession of fiefs, without any obligation to make payments, either to the lords of particular places or to the king, for the state's needs; instead of this they remained bound exclusively to serve in the wars." The conquered Gauls were treated as being incapable of holding office, bearing arms, or possessing fiefs and were obliged to pay *cens* to the lords and taxes to supply the state's needs. As time passed, the two nations merged; the Gauls obtained the rights previously confined to the Franks and, together with them, formed the *gentilhommerie,* who preserved the privileges of the conquerors. Gaulish commoners were no longer absolutely excluded from offices, from the bearing of arms, or from possession of fiefs. However, they continued to be excluded from the principal offices of the Crown and of the royal household, from governorships, from the command of *compagnies d'ordonnance,* and from the principal fiefs and *seigneuries,* and they remained subject to payment of frank fee for ordinary fiefs.[27]

Loyseau does not think of rejecting this myth, since for him, as for his contemporaries, it was the very stuff of history. But he does not draw the usual conclusion, namely, that the social stratification existing in France was just and reasonable because derived from right of conquest. The conclusion he draws is quite different: it is that nobility is born of "public and general law," that it belongs to the realm of "common law," that it originates not "from natural law, like freedom, but from the ancient law and disposition of the state."[28] One can see what this reflection suggests: something that is a natural right is unchangeable, but something that is a right established by the state may be changed. Accordingly, if it was a law of the state that made the warrior noble, then another such law can make the magistrate a noble, and this not only alongside the warrior but even above him. In a society which was still a society of orders, with the same forms of nobility, even a slight change, spreading upward from society to the state, could make the magistrate the noble *par excellence* in place of the warrior.

The duc de Saint-Simon and the transition

It is helpful to pass straight from Charles Loyseau, at the beginning of the 17th century, to the duc de Saint-Simon, at the end of the period that historians treat as the 17th century, which ends with the death of Louis XIV in 1715, early in what is chronologically the 18th century.

Saint-Simon gave expression mainly to ideas of social and political reform; but from his proposals themselves and also, of course, from many of the observations he makes regarding these proposals, there emerges a view of French society which suggests that profound changes have taken place since Loyseau's time.

Saint-Simon's ideas are certainly personal; that is, they bear the mark of his own arrogant aspirations, his morbid sensitivity, his chimerical imagination, and also that insight and perspicacity that he drew from his hatred of the age he lived in. But these ideas are not, in the main, peculiar to him. The principles underlying them are those of a whole group, the duc de Bourgogne and his circle, which existed toward the end of Louis XIV's reign. The duc de Bourgogne was Louis XIV's grandson, the son of the dauphin, and was born in August 1682. After the campaign of 1708 he lived in semi-disgrace. In that year, when he was twenty-six, Louis XIV saw fit to send him into the army, the command of which was to be shared between him and the duc de Vendôme. The duc de Bourgogne failed to support Vendôme during the Battle of Oudenarde, on 11 July 1708, so that half of the French forces there present took no part in the fighting. Nevertheless, the outcome was uncertain, and Vendôme wanted to remain on the field and join battle again the next day. But Bourgogne obliged him to withdraw. What is difficult about a withdrawal is ensuring that the troops carry it out in orderly fashion. Bourgogne prevented Vendôme from exercising command, and himself commanded very badly. The retreat turned into a rout and a disaster. France was invaded and Lille besieged. The duc de Bourgogne, hesitant and indecisive, allowed Lille to fall. Public opinion turned violently against him. He was charged with incapacity and cowardice and was made the theme of songs that ridiculed him. There was even anger against him, for it was put about that when he was told of the surrender of Lille he was playing shuttlecock and did not so much as interrupt his game.

On 14 April 1711, Bourgogne's father, the dauphin, died of smallpox, so that Bourgogne was now heir-presumptive. Louis XIV was showing his age very markedly, going downhill fast, and everyone perceived that in all likelihood there would soon be a change of monarch. Although not a brilliant soldier, Bourgogne took an interest in affairs of state. Louis XIV had had him prepared for a governing role. It was for the duc de Bourgogne that the duc de Beauvillier had drawn up in 1697 the well-known questionnaire that was sent out to the intendants so that an inquiry might be undertaken that would result in a description and statistical survey of the whole realm. This produced, between 1697 and 1702, forty-two intendants' reports. Bourgogne had taken part in composing the questionnaire. Louis XIV had given him the right to attend all of the king's councils, and he did in fact attend the Conseil d'en haut, the Conseil des Dépêches (assiduously), and the Conseil des Parties, though he was hardly ever present at the Conseil des Finances, a branch of government he disliked. After the dauphin's death, Louis XIV ordered his ministers to confer with the duc de Bourgogne; and regularly thereafter the secretary of state for foreign affairs, Torcy, together with Voysin and the comptroller general of finance, Desmarets, reported to the duke, who also, like the king himself, instigated the writing of memorials, addresses, and recommendations for reform of the kingdom. He received these documents from all quarters and read them with attention. He gave audience to numerous persons who had proposals to put forward. He drew up projects, in consultation with his political advisers, until he, too, died, of measles, on 18 February 1712.

First among Bourgogne's political advisers was the duc de Beauvillier, third son of the duc de Saint-Aignan—a younger son for whom the death of his two elder brothers had opened the path to honors. He was first gentleman of the king's bedchamber. Louis XIV appointed him head to the royal Conseil des Finances in 1685, and he was a minister of state from 1691 onward. He was one of Louis XIV's chief confidential advisers and was among the most influential members of the Council. Having formerly been tutor to the duc de Bourgogne, he was also in the confidence of his ex-pupil, to whom he was devotedly attached.

Another of Bourgogne's advisers was the duc de Chevreuse, grandson of the famous duchess and brother-in-law to Beauvillier, both of them being sons-in-law of Colbert. Captain of the king's Light Horse, governor of Guyenne since 1687, Chevreuse often visited Beauvillier at the château of Vaucresson and was often host to him in his own château of Dampierre. With Louis XIV's permission, Beauvillier kept Chevreuse informed about the business coming before the Conseil d'en haut and, on the king's behalf, very frequently asked for his views on the most important matters, so that Chevreuse played a highly influential role as a "secret minister." Chevreuse's mind was that of a great political and social reformer, and he wrote numerous projects for reform.

Chevreuse and his wife were disciples of the duc de Bourgogne's

one-time preceptor, Fénelon, who had been condemned for adherence
to the Quietist heresy and banished to his archbishopric of Cambrai,
under a sort of administrative internment. He continued to act as director of conscience to the duke and duchess, corresponded with them,
and, in dealing with problems of conscience, touched upon political
affairs. Chevreuse often visited a *seigneurie* he possessed in Picardy, in
the small town of Chaulnes, which he wanted to have made into a
dukedom for his second son, the *vidame* of Amiens. Fénelon went
secretly every year to Chaulnes in order to meet Chevreuse. In October 1711 they conferred together for a month and drew up the well-
known "Tables de Chaulnes, or Plan of Government Devised together
with the Duc de Chevreuse, for Presentation to the Duc de Bourgogne," which were actually put before Bourgogne.

Finally, the fourth adviser was the duc de Saint-Simon. The duchesse
de Saint-Simon was a friend of the duchesse de Bourgogne. In the opinion of Beauvillier and Chevreuse, Saint-Simon ought to become a
member of the Prince's Council when the time arrived for the duc de
Bourgogne to ascend the throne of France. Meanwhile, after the
dauphin's death, Bourgogne summoned Saint-Simon very discreetly to
discuss with him the reform of the kingdom. They had a number of
conversations, at Marly, Versailles, and Fontainebleau. Saint-Simon
brought along dossiers and talked about the contents with the duke. He
recast all the proposals in the form of a memorandum entitled "Plans
of Government Decided upon by Monsieur le Duc de Bourgogne,
Dauphin, after Mature Consideration." The original of this memorandum was not to be found among Saint-Simon's papers deposited in the
ministry of foreign affairs. Under the Second Empire, Paul Mesnard
discovered an unsigned copy in the Bibliothèque Nationale (in the
Supplement français 1260). He identified the style of this document and
the ideas it contained, without difficulty, and left no doubt as to its
authenticity. He fixed the date when it was written as falling between
March 1714 and August 1715, because the comte de Toulouse is
mentioned in the memorandum as holding the office of master of the
royal hunts, and the count was given that office in March 1714, while
Louis XIV us referred to as though still alive, and he died on 1 September 1715. The document had therefore not been dictated by the duc de
Bourgogne, who was already dead by then. Had Saint-Simon added
much of his own? Probably. We can, indeed, compare these proposals
with those of Saint-Simon himself and with the basic ideas of the duc de
Bourgogne. On the one hand, comparison of this text with Saint-

Simon's writings, published by Faguère, especially the *Refutation of the Idea That the Parlement Is the First-Ranking Institution of State,* the *Proposals for the Reestablishment of the Kingdom of France* (January 1712), and the *Draft of a Plan for Reestablishing the Three Estates of the Kingdom of France*[29] shows similarity between them and the "Plans of Government of the Duc de Bourgogne." On the other hand, Bourgogne had composed plans on his own. His papers passed to his descendants. In 1782 the Abbé Proyart set about writing a *Life of the Dauphin, Louis XV's Father.* The Abbé Soldini, confessor to Louis XVI, supplied him with a large number of documents which had been left by the king's mother, the Dauphine Marie-Josèphe de Saxe. Among them were writings by the duc de Bourgogne. Louis XVI gave permission for these to be published. Unfortunately the Abbé Proyart confined himself to the duc de Bourgogne's principles and maxims, without giving any practical conclusions, whereas Saint-Simon's memorandum swarms with practical conclusions. Comparison is, therefore, not always easy to effect. Nevertheless, it seems clear that while the two series of writings have a common inspiration and possess an undoubted common basis, Saint-Simon's contains many personal ideas of his which he placed under the name of the duc de Bourgogne in order to secure a wide hearing for them. It is therefore the "Plans of Government Decided upon by Monsieur le Duc de Bourgogne, Dauphin, after Mature Consideration," a work much fuller and more systematic than Saint-Simon's other political writings, that we should analyze in order to find, together with his plans for reform, his view of French society as it was in his time.[30]

Saint-Simon's proposals are not revolutionary but reactionary. Their purpose is not to introduce innovations but to restore traditional French society. In that society of orders and "estates," down to the 16th century the greatest degree of social honor had been attached to the hereditary profession of arms, although the role of the magistrate, who as dispenser of justice held the power to command, had always enjoyed high prestige. But it seems clear that, since Henri IV's time at the latest, a silent revolution had come about, which continued under Louis XIV: the profession of magistrate had been gradually accorded no less honor than that of the fighting man. The gown sought to achieve social equality with the sword and even to supplant it in the service of the state. The king's Council (Conseil du Roi) was now filled with officials, whereas that of François I had been made up of sword-wearing *gentilshommes.* And everything pointed to the preparation by Louis

XIV of a further revolution, which would not merely ennoble artists, men of letters, and members of the liberal professions but would proclaim the dignity of large-scale trade by land and by sea. Saint-Simon loathed with all his heart this *"règne de vile bourgeoisie."* His aim was to bring back the old French society of orders and "estates," or at least what he imagined this to have been—in other words, to reestablish a strict hierarchy of dignities and qualities, with rigorous respect shown to titles, ranks, precedences, and all other social symbols. Their importance is indicated in his work by the long and detailed prescriptions he gives on the subject of who is to have *"la main,"* that is, to stand on the right, the place of honor, and on the use of carriages, coats of arms, and costumes, and also by his proposal to establish a new branch of the king's Council, the "Council of Orders."[31] The purpose of this council was to remedy the "confusion" which "disfigures the court and all the orders and particular institutions of state," the prevailing "deformity."[32] It was to be made up, first, of a head, who must always be a duke-and-peer, clothed with the new title, created specially for the purpose, of *grand maréchal de la Cour;* of four other dukes-and-peers; of two dukes, not peers, "verified" by the Crown in *parlement;* and of two marquises, two counts, a viscount, and a baron. The competence of this council was to extend to "all matters of rank, distinctions, honors, inscriptions on arms, titles used in deeds, protocols, tables of precedence, disputes, contested names, claims in respect of these matters, and regulations to be laid down." It would have, in particular,

to regulate the qualities mentioned in the transactions entered into with each other by persons of all estates, addresses and subscriptions of letters, coats of arms and their ornamentation (so that no one may adopt any that do not belong to him), the wearing of arms by *bourgeois* and servants (forbidden to both categories), the permissible and impermissible forms of funerals and of the deep mourning to be worn by different persons (ensuring that members of every estate, right down to the lowest, never appear otherwise than in the dress assigned to their estate); to prevent foreigners from wearing on their coats of arms ornaments which they would not wear in their own countries; to check on the abuse of inscriptions upon town houses and the employment of gate porters by persons not entitled to have them; to prevent liveried servants, without exception (apart from gate porters), from carrying arms or canes and to ensure that no liveried servant appear otherwise than in livery or, in the case of servants of those below the rank of baron, without some recognizable mark.

This council was to have supreme power of decision on matters within its competence. It would be given jurisdiction over claims and offenses and the right to inflict punishments.

Saint-Simon devotes the greatest attention to the topmost group in French society, the *Grands* ("grandees"), a group whose chief members were the dukes-and-peers, both ecclesiastical and lay, but which also included the other dukes and the "great officers of the Crown." These "grandees" are, "by virtue of their rank and the offices they hold, *laterales regis,*" at the king's side. They have the right to accompany him to the theater, at the foot of the throne, and in the assemblies of the Estates General. "These persons are the born and natural counselors of the king and of the state." After them "we come to the three orders of which the state is particularly formed and composed." The distance separating Saint-Simon and Loyseau can be measured if we recall that the latter placed the royal officials at the summit of society, before the three orders, and, in particular, before the nobility.

But Saint-Simon is interested first and foremost in the dukes-and-peers, the category to which he belonged. There were to be forty hereditary dukes-and-peers and fifteen "verified" dukes, who were not peers and held no office or function but were also hereditary. The eldest sons of these fifty-five persons were to be dukes "by special appointment," so as not to remain without rank or distinction while they waited for their fathers to die or retire in their favor. Consequently, there would, in all, be one hundred eleven (*sic*) persons in this group. As there were seven peers who were bishops, and therefore unmarried, the wives of one hundred four of these persons would possess the right to sit on a stool in the presence of the queen, like the wives of eldest sons of dukes in England and of eldest sons of grandees in Spain.

Louis XIV had raised his bastard sons above all the dukes-and-peers. The duc du Maine, comte de Toulouse, had been received in the *parlement,* on 8 May 1694, as the comte d'Eu, peer of France; then, in 1695, the duc d'Aumale had been received as a peer and, in 1697, had been given the titles of comte de Toulouse and duc de Penthièvre, peer of France. By an edict of May 1711 Louis XIV had seated his legitimized offspring in the *parlement,* immediately behind the princes of the blood and in front of the dukes-and-peers, even those whose dukedoms-and-peerages were the oldest-established. He gave them the right to represent the former, now-extinct, peers, at the coronation of kings of France, to the exclusion of the other peers of France.

Saint-Simon was keen to put Louis XIV's bastards in their place among the peers. He planned to have revoked by edict, the day after the coronation of the new king, all the privileges which had been given them, reducing the duc du Maine and the comte de Toulouse to their rank as peers and to their seniority in that category. Later, in 1717, he was behind a petition calling for the reduction of the bastards to the ranks, honors, and seniority of their peerages. At a *lit de justice* held on 26 August 1718 Louis XV did indeed cause to be registered an edict which reduced the bastards to their rank as peers.

Saint-Simon wanted the peers to be reestablished in a position superior to that of the chancellors of France. He noted that it was Séguier, chancellor to Louis XIII and Louis XIV, who was the first to be made a duke "by special appointment" (as duc de Villemor) and who first among chancellors bore a coronet on his coat of arms. In the head of the judiciary was symbolized the social ascent of the whole body of magistrates. A chancellor who was a duke seemed to Saint-Simon something monstrous. But all the succeeding chancellors copied Séguier in putting a coronet on their arms, even though none of them became a duke and keeper of the seals. "This ornament of rank of the highest nobility is inappropriate for an officer of the Crown who is a *lawyer* and a *plebeian* and the only one of the officers of the Crown who sits on a lower seat at a *lit de justice,* whereas all the rest sit on the high seats, along with the king and the peers, and the only one, too, who, for the same reason, the king does not address as 'cousin.' " Chancellors, according to Saint-Simon, were to display their arms with all the ornaments appropriate to a chancellor, but *without* any coronet.[33]

Peers should take precedence over all dukes who were verified as being older-established than themselves, "since they possess not only a fief like the others but also an office with capital functions." The dukes-and-peers should have the exclusive right to escort ambassadors to their ceremonial audiences, and the duke escorting an ambassador should keep his hat on, like a prince of the blood. Dukes and officers of the Crown were to take precedence over governors, *lieutenants généraux,* and provincial commanders-in-chief even in their provinces. Steps must be taken to restore the military honors and dignities of state to dukes-and-peers and to enable them to take part in all the councils. Indeed, places should be specially reserved for them therein. The head of the Conseil des Finances should always be a duke-and-peer, as should also be the case with the Conseil de Dépêches and Conseil d'Ordres, in which there ought, in addition, to be four other dukes-and-peers.[34]

The fact that Saint-Simon was himself a duke-and-peer, and had suffered greatly from the futility to which this rank had been reduced, certainly counted for much in the meticulousness and asperity of his demands. But it needs also to be appreciated that in a society of orders, based on a hierarchy of honors and dignities, establishing firmly the situation of the *first* order of society—an example and ideal for all the rest, and different from the legally defined "order of the nobility" as a whole—meant ensuring the organizational principle of society, its stability and lastingness.

As regards the ecclesiastical order,[35] Saint-Simon's attitude is resolutely Gallican. The most important consideration for him is defense of the liberties of the Gallican Church against the enterprises of the Roman Curia and application of the Gallican declaration of 1682. He reveals constant distrust of the clergy. There must be no French cardinals: they are "a leprosy." They are useless. They live in France, know little of the Roman Curia, and are in the dark when they attend a conclave. They are too greedy for splendor and money and church benefices. Being legally inviolable, they all too often act the traitor. So let the king nominate *Italian* cardinals, living in Rome, who will be delighted with the gift of an abbey in France and, knowing as they do how Rome is governed, will serve the king well—not to mention thirty or forty Italian prelates whose fidelity to the king will be guaranteed by their hope of receiving a similar benefice.

After the grandees, the archbishops and bishops will take precedence over everyone else. They will hold the rank of marquis. When they write to the officers of the Crown, they will address them merely as "Monsieur," even in the case of chancellors and keepers of the seals, whom at present they address as "Monseigneur." They will not bear a coronet on their coats of arms. They will have no dealings with the papal nuncio, who is merely an ambassador like any other. They will never enter the Conseil d'Etat. In other words, Saint-Simon grants them great honors while depriving them of all political influence.

Saint-Simon considers it indispensable to reduce the number of monks and nuns—"persons who can be called deserters of the people of this realm," "incapable of providing posterity," compelled "to live at the expense of the community without rendering it any service." Their celibacy "dries up the kingdom," so that there are no more men available in the countryside or for the militia, "whereas Germany and the northern countries are swarming with men, to such an extent that our enemies take no account of their losses of them in war and do not even maintain hospitals."[36] The remedy would be to forbid anyone to enter the novitiate before the age of twenty-five instead of the existing age limit of fifteen.

On the other hand, the numbers of the secular clergy need to be increased so that they may properly carry out their duties in the parishes. The seminaries, from which at present priests emerge knowing nothing, ought to be reformed. The inadequate emoluments of parish priests should be increased by equalizing benefices. Collegiate churches and monastic benefices should be abolished. In order that bishops may carry out their functions properly, the territorial extent of dioceses must be redistributed, enlarging the small and reducing the big ones.

But it is to the restoration of the order of the nobility that Saint-Simon devotes his full attention, regarding this as the essential order of French society.[37] His first point is that the nobility must be given back their military character, becoming once again a *gentilhommerie*. It is arms that make nobility, so that "the general officers commanding armies and provinces are considered noble without even having to bear any other title." Conversely, it is henceforth to be made impossible to become noble through the exercise of any craft or profession but that of arms. Saint-Simon calls for the ending of "mechanical ennoblements," by which expression he contemptuously refers to the ennobling of doctors, surgeons, apothecaries, chemists, botanists, painters, sculptors, inventors, and architects, many of whom were granted noble status by Louis XIV. Ennoblements must "no longer be allowed except for feats of arms or long service in the wars, which is the only thing that can and must confer nobility and is how, in fact, many noble families have originated." Thus, the sons of marshals of France are to become hereditary barons.

As for the "secretaries to the king," whose office, which conferred nobility, was a *"savonnette à vilain"* (literally a means of washing the dirt from a peasant), they must be reduced in number from three hundred to forty, and the privilege of automatic ennoblement of themselves and their progeny must be done away with. Apart from anything else, this privilege has meant too many people being exempted from paying the *taille*. Similarly, ennoblement through the exercise if the offices of mayor and alderman in certain towns must be ended. The decorations proper to nobles, notably the Order of Saint Michael, which have been "prostituted to scholars, doctors, surgeons, painters, architects," must be taken away from all such and reserved to *gentilshommes*.

These reform proposals by the duc de Saint-Simon suggest that French society had changed profoundly by the end of Louis XIV's reign. There is still a nobility, but it seems to be not the same as before—it is no longer a category made up of gentlemen of the sword. Not only magistrates, those "plebeian lawyers," but also scholars, artists, and members of the liberal professions have become noble *through the exercise of their professions.* Society is still a society of orders, since social placing is still determined by the honor and dignity accorded to social functions for reasons other than the role played in the production of material wealth. Saint-Simon does not have in mind what would be for us a *class* society, since he does not include merchants or manufacturers in his list, although some of these, too, were in fact ennobled. But the society of his day was evolving toward a "society of talent," in which one's placing in the social hierarchy was determined increasingly by the role one played in intellectual work—in creation, teaching, and practice in the judicial, scientific, artistic, and literary spheres. The fundamental principle of society seems to have altered profoundly. To placing by reference to the hereditary profession of arms had been added, since the 16th century, placing by reference to the magistrate's profession, which tended to become hereditary; and then, under Louis XIV, there appeared placing by reference to intellectual work, to talent. A slow, silent revolution was under way, which Saint-Simon sought to throw into reverse.

Saint-Simon strove to restore a rigorous hierarchy within the nobility. First, there must be the hierarchy of the upper nobility, in the descending order of marquises, counts, viscounts, and barons—"titles that were not created as a joke, as might appear from most of those one sees now, but were actual dignities, with particular ranks and distinctions." Use of the coronet on coats of arms would be reserved for them. Their number would be restricted in order to enhance their dignity. The king would name these members of the higher nobility on lists of *gentilshommes.* In this way, emulation would restore to the nobility the qualities they had lost.

These higher nobles would occupy positions in the Order of the Holy Spirit not in accordance with the seniority of their titles but according to their rank and according to their seniority within each rank. In this way the reestablishment of families in accordance with their respective qualities would be ensured. The Order of Saint Michael would be reserved for one hundred fifty of them.

Counts, marquises, and dukes would be permitted to dine with the king and to ride in his carriages, and their wives to dine with the queen and to ride in her carriages. Viscountesses and baronesses would be presented to the queen and received in full court dress, and their marriage contracts would be signed by Their Majesties.

The authority of the higher nobility over the lesser would be restored, for the nobles would no longer all be equally subordinate to the secretaries of state and obliged to address them as "Monseigneur." Also, it would be forbidden to non-dukes to wear the coronet and mantle of a duke. Similarly, the "Order of Promotion" would be abolished: generals would be permitted to give command of units not necessarily to the most senior, when his turn came round, but to the most valiant; thus there would be selection and emulation, good leaders would be formed, and generals and colonels would be able to promote these officers without regard to seniority. Finally, the higher nobility, having recovered the monopoly of political power, would by its political and military influence fully restore its authority over the lower nobility.

Hierarchy would be reestablished among the lower nobility. Certain fiefs and *seigneuries* would be raised above the rest, with rights of precedence in relation to seating, processions, and the distribution of holy water and consecrated bread.

"Quality" and "merit" would everywhere be restored, at the expense of money. All payments made by governors of provinces, fortresses and towns, *lieutenants généraux* of provinces, and minor provincial *lieutenants du roi* for *brevets de retenues et de survivances* of their offices would be reimbursed. Appointments as *lieutenants généraux* of provinces would be given to lieutenant generals of armies when they retired, and appointments as *lieutenants du roi* in the provinces would be given similarly to *maréchaux de camp*. The venality and inheritability of all appointments would be abolished, including those of regimental commanders and *baillis d'épée* (so as to reaccustom the nobility to living in the provinces), those in the royal and princely household, and those of the officers of the Crown.

The magistrates, the *noblesse de robe*, those rivals of the *gentilshommes* (the only true nobility), would be pushed back into the third estate: "a *gentilhomme*, even a man of quality, who is also a magistrate, cannot, owing to his position as a magistrate, be a deputy to the Estates General otherwise than in the third estate."[38] They must therefore be compelled to wear the gown and forbidden to practice "the fairly recent abuse of putting helmets and coronets on their coats of arms." No magistrate whatsoever should take precedence over any baron. In order to reduce the importance of money, the venality of the offices of *premiers présidents, procureurs généraux,* and *avocats généraux* in the "higher" courts would be abolished. Furthermore, all the "higher" courts would give way to the king's Council, "the Council with which the Grand Conseil would merge." Magistrates would be reduced to the dispensing of justice and deprived of their administrative functions. Through administrative reform a considerable number of offices would be abolished: the *trésoriers de France,* the *élus,* the officials concerned with the *gabelle* and the salt storehouses, the inspectors of highways, all those "petty tyrants of the provinces" who get relief from taxation for their relatives, their farmers, their friends, and their hirelings and whose offices are the chief means whereby men rise into the magistracy and thence into the nobility, thus perverting the social constitution of France. For the same reason, Saint-Simon wished to abolish the principal financial auxiliaries of the state, the farmers general, treasurers, and *fermiers particuliers,* who derive a certain luster from their role as state servants and are able by means of this, and by the wealth they acquire as auxiliaries in public finance, to raise themselves in the social hierarchy and drag down the nobility. There must also disappear those enemies of the nobility, those commissioners recruited by the king from among the magistrates, the famous intendants of the provinces. In this way, the magistracy and the financiers having been brought down and put back in their proper place, the right hierarchy will be reestablished and French society will be restored.

For Saint-Simon it is the state that bears the main responsibility for the corruption and decline of the French society of orders and estates. It is the king's ministers, "plebeian lawyers," who have multiplied their like, the intendants, in the provinces and used them to destroy, bit by bit, the power of the provincial governors, the commanders-in-chief, and the *lieutenants généraux* of the provinces, and also the power of the great lords and that of the bishops in the temporal affairs of their dioceses, along with the power of the *parlements* and municipalities. The intendants—with their authority over financial matters, "their power *ex officio* to levy taxes, their constantly available means of either protecting or harassing both great and small, and of stirring up and supporting the latter against the former," of relieving or oppressing parishes and private persons—have left the lords and individual gentlemen without any authority whatsoever, depriving them of all prestige and thereby forcing them to abandon their lands and their home districts and come to live in Paris and at the court, so as to try and obtain there such influence and protection as may cause them to be treated with consideration by the intendants. In this way, grandees, lords, nobles, corporations, and individuals have been ruined by nobodies acting as agents of the king's ministers. The degradation of the social hierarchy has been brought about by the despotic and arbitrary state, with its commissioners and financiers.[39]

Domat and the transition

Domat's work was written at the important turning point of social and political thought in the nineties of the "Great Century." Domat, an *avocat du roi* in the presidial court of Clermont, in Auvergne, published *Les Lois civiles dans leur ordre naturel* and *Le Droit public* between 1689 and 1697, during the War of the League of Augsburg. He was, in the first place, a mechanistic deist, probably a Stoic. For him, man was created in order to know God and to love Him. Man was made in the image and resemblance of God, and man's first law is to seek out and love that sovereign good which is God. This law is common to all men. It thus includes a second law: men should love one another and unite together, because they are all brothers. They must therefore form themselves into a society.

Every society is based on a set of natural obligations entered into between men. These are of two kinds. The first kind consists of the natural ties of marriage, between men and women, and those of birth, between parents and children, together with the obligations of kinship by blood or marriage which result therefrom, embracing all the collateral relatives—uncles, aunts, cousins, nephews, and nieces.

> The second kind takes in all other forms of obligation which bring all sorts of persons into association, and which take different forms, either in the various relations between men in their work, their industry, and all manner of offices, services, and other ways of helping each other, or in relations concerning the way things are used, which embraces all the various uses of the crafts, employments, and occupations of every nature and everything that can link persons together according to the different needs of life, either by gratuitous communications or by trade.

Thus society is constituted, not only by natural links, but also by relations of service between men, some of which are relations are concerned with things. Society is an aggregate of relations between men.

Society is ruled by an order which God has willed.

> This is constituted by the way He has arranged people in society, wherein He has assigned to everyone his place, so as to show each man, by the situation he finds himself in and the relations linking him with others, what the duties are which are proper to the rank he holds; and *He* places everyone in his proper rank, by birth, upbringing, inclination, and the other effects of a man's behavior which place him, subjecting all men to the general obligations that affect conditions, occupations, and employments, and fixing everyone in a certain state of life.

Society is thus a hierarchy of levels of social status, into which one enters through birth and heredity, through the upbringing that results from one's parents' status, and, lastly, through inclination and personal choice.

> These obligations, then, involve the state. First, there are obligations between citizens, and then the state arises from these, because such obligations call for the functioning of a government that will keep everyone in his proper place. It is in order to ensure this government that God has established the authority of those powers which are needed so as to maintain society.

Thus social relations are anterior to the formation of the state and the state's laws. The state exists only for the purpose of ensuring the working of obligations spontaneously entered into and to guarantee these obligations. It operates like a policeman.

God is always present in Domat's system, but this system could function without God, for there is present in all individuals

> that light of reason which, discovering to all men a sense of the common rules of justice and equity, serves them as a law which has remained in all minds, amidst the darkness that self-love has spread over them. Thus all men have in their minds an impression of the truth and authority of these natural laws: that one ought not to do harm to anyone, that one must render to everyone his due, that one should be sincere in fulfilling one's obligations and faithful in carrying out one's promises, and other like rules of justice and equity ... Reason reigns in all of us in such a manner that the most unjust of men are so far in love with justice as to condemn injustice in others and hate it ... And it is through this awareness of the natural

laws that those nations which have had no knowledge of religion have enabled their societies to survive.

A society made up of atheists would be a possibility; at any rate, Domat's society is a society of Cartesians and mechanists.

"All men are equal by their nature, that is, in the humanity that constitutes their essence." Domat refers to the Bible (Wisdom of Solomon 7:1, 3, 4, 5, and 6), but it may be that the source of his idea is to be found in Stoicism and Roman law.

> Within this natural equality men are distinguished from each other by other principles which render their conditions unequal and form among them relations and dependences that regulate the different duties of each man toward the rest .... We give the name "orders" of persons to the different conditions and occupations which, by placing each man among his own people (in his order) and giving to everyone his rank, make up the general order.[40]

At this point Domat warns us that he does not employ the division of all conditions into three orders—the three estates of the nobility, the clergy, and the third estate. "I do not take account of this; first, because I have to go into greater detail than this division into three orders allows...If one were to follow this division, one would be obliged to include in the third estate the leading magistrates of the kingdom, many officials of the king's Council, and other persons who should be accorded a distinguished rank." The division into three orders is thus only political and legal in character and is, so to speak, overridden by the spontaneous organization of society into orders.

For Domat a "condition" means "the situation of each person in one or other of the different orders of persons that constitute and make up the general order of society and which give everyone therein a distinct rank, placing some higher than others, whether they are engaged in some employment or profession or have none." Social function thus includes occupation but is not confined to it. There are social functions which are not occupations. The quality of "duke" is a condition that corresponds to a social function without an occupation. This social function consists in providing the model, the social ideal, in this type of society. A *bourgeois* of Paris or elsewhere, a *rentier* who lives "like a noble," without "practicing craft or trade," has no occupation, but he does have a social function: as head to a family, he governs it and regulates the way his children are brought up; he administers a patrimony; he fulfills the important function of taxpayer; he is capable of assuming voluntary public responsibilities, as alderman, administrator of poor relief, hospital governor, and so on.

"Qualities" are the features which determine individuals' "estates in life"—"features that fix them in a certain mode of life and occupation and place them above or beneath others in the social order, depending on the differences between these qualities: from the very first—those of prince, duke-and-peer, count, marquis, officer of the Crown, and so on—down to the meanest—those of craftsman, ploughman, and the rest, the least of the people."

These features are honor, dignity, authority, necessity, and utility. Honor means the special consideration that the public accords to those who possess a certain social condition. Advocates and doctors enjoy honor only, without either dignity or authority. "Even in the conditions of trade and the crafts, as there are some which are more creditable than others, one may consider in them a sort of honor which distinguishes them and sets them higher than the others." Dignity adds to mere honor, and to the consideration or esteem it may bring, an elevation which confers, over and above honor, the dignity of *office,* which must be respected. Those possessing dignity are the princes of the blood, the knights of the royal orders of chivalry, the dukes, counts, and marquises, the *présidents* and counselors of the sovereign courts, and so on. Authority is "the right to exercise some public function with a power to compel obedience by those upon whom this function is to be exercised, so that all authority implies an honor and a dignity proportionate to the office to which it is attached." Those who possess authority, honor and dignity, all three, are officers of the Crown, governors of provinces, marshals of France, military officers, officers of the judiciary, administration, and finance, mayors and aldermen of towns, judges in mercantile courts, and, in general, all those who have some jurisdiction or exercise some public function that puts other persons under their command. Necessity refers to

> those occupations without which we could not live, such as agriculture and the various crafts which serve to feed us and to provide clothing, shelter, and remedies for our ills. Likewise necessary are the occupations without which government would fall into disorder, namely, all those concerned with arms, justice, and revenue, and finally, those which seem necessary for many profitable and convenient uses, such as printing, painting, embroidery for church ornaments, and so on . . . . The character of utility is common to all occupations.

"Certain conditions" combine all five of these features and thereby possess the highest "quality," namely, the conditions of prelates,
magistrates, and military commanders. Others possess honor without
dignity, namely, ordinary *gentilshommes,* teachers, advocates, doctors, engineers (that is, those whose crafts depend on principles and
rules derived from mathematics, geometry, optics, or astronomy, like
architecture, the art of fortification, and the art of mapmaking). All
these are in the same category as *gentilshommes.* Finally, there are
others who possess only utility and necessity, such as those who practice the mechanical arts—tailors, carpenters, shoemakers, bakers,
locksmiths, and so on. Honor and dignity can come "first from birth,
then from offices and other employments, and, finally, from the bare
will of the Prince."

For Domat, the social hierarchy corresponds to society's needs.
There are two main types of need, spiritual and temporal. Spiritual
needs are the affair of the clergy, temporal ones the affair of laymen.
Society's primary temporal need is public tranquillity, the maintenance of peace, defense against an enemy or against rebel subjects.
The first of the secular orders is, therefore, "that of the profession of
arms, the practice of which constitutes the Prince's glory; this forms a
body of which he is the head, and which has for members the princes of
the blood, those officers of the Crown who wear a sword, the governors of provinces," and so on. The second need of society is good
order in government, and the second secular order is "that of the
ministers and other persons whom the Prince honors with a place in his
Privy Council." The third need of society is that justice shall reign, and
so the third order is that of those "persons who exercise the functions
of administration and justice, either in the Prince's Council or in the
various judicial corporations, and also those officials who judge on
their own, and, further, the various servants of the judiciary—
advocates, attorneys, clerks of the courts, and so on."

Domat notes that there is a dispute about rank and precedence between the profession of arms and that of justice, between the gown and
the sword. Regarding that matter, he says, there is no law or rule but
merely usage. Most people consider that the sword should precede the
gown, that soldiers should go before magistrates. The point is that the
Prince is the supreme justiciar. When he makes war, he is merely
implementing God's justice and correcting the injustices committed by
other princes. In such cases, soldiers are directly enforcing God's justice, and, embodying as they do that supreme justice, they take precedence over all magistrates.

The fourth of society's temporal needs is that all things which the public uses should be in good order, meaning rivers, bridges, ports, highways, lakes and forests, hunting and fishing facilities, and, of course, the public purse, the revenue. Consequently, the fourth order comprises the officials who look after all that, especially those concerned with finance, the magistrates of the *chambre des comptes,* the *cours des aides,* the *trésoriers de France,* the *élus,* and so on.

Society's fifth need is to have the use of the sciences, "so called because of the dignity of the knowledge which enters into these arts." In descending order these are divinity, canon law, civil law, medicine, and the liberal arts, that is, logic, rhetoric, grammar, mathematics, and physics. The fifth order is therefore made up of university teachers, doctors, advocates, and "engineers."

The sixth need of society is trade, "causing the things needed for life to be conveyed into all parts of the kingdom." The sixth order consists of merchants, with a higher stratum, the wholesalers, and a lower, the retailers.

Society's seventh need is to fit for use all things necessary for men's needs by transforming them through various crafts and techniques. The seventh order therefore comprises all craftsmen.

The eighth of society's needs is to get from the soil the crops, fruits, and timber needed for the feeding, clothing, and housing of mankind. The last of the orders—although "the first in terms of necessity for man's life"—is that of the persons engaged in agriculture and stockbreeding.

Within each of these orders there are different degrees and ranks. In the first of them are to be found, below the marshals of France, the generals, colonels, and captains. In the second, beneath the ministers of state, there are the secretaries of state, and so on. In the third, after the chancellor, there are the Conseil des Parties, the judicial corporations, the officers of the *bailliages* and *sénéchaussées,* and the judges in the service of *seigneurs.*

There is overlapping between the orders.

Many members of an order which is as such less honorable have much more dignity than some belonging to a higher order which takes precedence over them . . . The rank of the highest officials who have the direction of the revenue is above that of the lowest officials of the judiciary . . . If we take a receiver of *taille,* who, as being a member of the order of finance, is inferior to a clerk of the court, who belongs to the order of the administration of justice in a

presidial court, we find that the advantages of the office and functions of this receiver, and the rank he holds in his order, will give
him precedence over the clerk of the court.

Loyseau grouped people in accordance with power and fitness for
public functions. Domat groups them in accordance with public needs.
Although he evaluates these needs in relation to the criteria characteristic of the society of his time, which was still very military, the
result is that, practically speaking, the clergy vanish and the nobility
fade away. Considerable importance and relatively high ranks are accorded by Domat to the magistrates and men of the law. The ordinary
gentilhomme, who is the nobleman *par excellence,* if he comes of an
old family, is merged with the advocates, doctors, and "engineers." It
seems as though the importance acquired by "talent" and "technique"
has proved too much for Domat and has compelled him to modify the
arrangement of society. "Technicians," "specialists," "men of talent" play an increasing role in this society. For Domat it is men's
occupations that place them and no longer, essentially, a hereditary
quality they possess, an "estate" which is inherent in their person.
Another change we observe is that, for Loyseau, the ploughman
ranked above the craftsman, whereas for Domat the craftsman takes
precedence over the agriculturalist—perhaps because manufacture,
everything concerned with the making of goods, was growing in importance even in the depths of the countryside, where craftsmen steadily increased in both numbers and relative importance throughout the
18th century.

Domat's work reveals that a change had occurred, one that heralds a
new world. Basically, his view of society lines up with Saint-Simon's
critique. He was prophetic. The doctrine and spirit of Domat reappear
in d'Aguesseau, from his youthful writings of about 1694 to his *Essai
d'une institution du droit public,* in the works of Pothier, which appeared between 1776 and 1778, and Guyot's *Traité de jurisprudence
civile et criminelle,* which began publication 1784. In the course of the
18th century, although Loyseau was still being invoked in 1776 by the
Paris *parlement,* Domat's influence came to replace the earlier theo-
rist's.

All that was needed was to modify Domat's criterion of utility, to take
as the most useful of functions that of producing the material goods
needed for life, in order to find in him the doctrine of a society dominated by landowners, merchants, industrialists, and bankers—a bourgeois society, capitalist and liberal. Domat was reissued between 1828

and 1830 by the advocate Rémy, who inserted under the original headings and numbers the legislation and regulations which made up the administrative law of the Restoration and which people had been uncertain how to arrange. Domat provided a convenient framework of classification for this society of classes and for the spirit of the doctrines of liberalism and of the state as policeman.

The transition to class society completed: Barnave

Let us move on to the last quarter of the 18th century. Our documents have so far suggested to us that in the first half of the 16th century there existed a society of orders and estates based on the principle of the superiority of the hereditary profession of arms; then, in the second half of the 16th century and the first half of the 17th, a society in which the magistracy was coming into rivalry with the *gentilshommes,* the gown with the sword; and then a society in which the magistracy—in the shape of those men who had emerged from that milieu to form the ruling circle of ministers, secretaries of state, state councilors, masters of requests, and intendants—was getting the upper hand of the *gentilshommes* and leveling out the social hierarchy to its own advantage but in which, at the same time, men of "talent" were entering the ranks of the nobility, by the will of the king, who was thus introducing a third principle of social stratification, capable of changing French society into a different variety of society of orders and estates and perhaps even opening the way for a society made up of *classes.* In the last quarter of the 18th century a whole movement of ideas manifested itself which was aimed at sweeping away the ancient constitution of French society in orders and estates and replacing it by a class society—not without opposition from the order of the nobility and of certain corporations. This movement and the opposition to it are known to us from numerous documents, for example, the remonstrances of the Paris *parlement,* on 2 and 4 March 1776, regarding Turgot's edict abolishing compulsory labor service for the upkeep of the main roads and replacing this by a levy assessed on real property.[41] The *parlement,* a corporation of magistrates who were nobles *ex officio* and in many cases integrated into the hereditary nobility, recalls the ancient constitution of French society, quoting Loyseau with approval, but at the same time shows us the significance of the attack leveled against it, which aims to replace a society arranged hierarchically in orders and "estates" by a society based on a "baneful equality" of rights. "The kingdom of France," says the *parlement*,

> is by its constitution made up of a number of distinct and separate estates. This distinction between conditions and persons goes back to the origin of the nation; it was born with the nation's way of life; it forms the precious chain binding the sovereign to his subjects ...In the assembly of persons made up of these different orders, all the people in your realm are subject to you, and all are obliged to contribute to the state's needs. But in this contribution itself, the general order and harmony is still present. The personal service rendered by the clergy consists in fulfilling all the functions connected with instruction and with religious worship and in bringing, by means of alms, relief to the unfortunate. The nobleman gives his blood for the defense of the state and helps the sovereign with his advice. The lowest section of the nation, which cannot render the state such distinguished services as these, does its duty thereto by paying tribute, by industry, and by manual labor ... Although all are equally faithful subjects, their varying conditions have never been confounded, and the nature of their services is linked essentially with the nature of their estate. The service rendered by the nobles is noble like themselves; the nobleman is not obliged to pay the *taille* or to perform base labor service, but only to serve in the wars and perform other noble deeds.[42] These institutions are not such as are formed by accident and which time can change. To abolish them, one would have to alter the entire constitution of France. It is possible to change by legislation that which legislation has established. But that which the spirit, the way of life, and the general will of a nation have made characteristic of it, in the course of its formation and throughout the whole duration of the kingdom, cannot be changed.

"Distinctions," "conditions," "estates," a whole hierarchy of right, imposed by the nature of things and consequently no less lasting than French society itself—this is, for the *parlement*, "the ancient rule," which must not be touched.

And what Turgot's edict has brought against this is a ruinous equality, destructive of society as a whole.

> Any system which, under a seeming humanity and beneficence, would tend, in a well-ordered kingdom, to establish between men *an equality of duties* and to destroy these necessary distinctions would soon bring about disorder, the *inevitable consequence of absolute equality,* and accomplish the overthrow of civil society, the

harmony of which is maintained only *through* this gradation of powers, authorities, preeminences, and distinctions which keeps everyone in his place and safeguards all estates against confusion.

Moreover, this gradation conforms to the divine plan of the universe, which has bestowed strength and genius unequally. "What dangers, then, are not inherent in a project derived from an *unacceptable system of equality,* the first effect of which is to confound all the orders in the state by imposing upon them the uniform burden of a land tax?" It is this that the *parlement* sees as alarming and unacceptable: the destroying of distinctions and gradations, of orders and estates, the approach to a society based on equality of rights and duties.

But a society of that kind was now desired by an increasingly large number of persons; or, rather, so far as they were concerned, it already existed *de facto,* and what was needed was to have it recognized and proclaimed by public law. This was the meaning of the attitude taken by the third estate at the opening of the Estates General in 1789.[43] For the deputies of the third estate the essential purpose of the Estates General was to provide not only the French state but French society as a whole with a new constitution. What was required was to put an end to the structuring of society in orders and corporations, to reduce the *gentilshommes,* the priests, and the members of corporations to the condition of ordinary citizens. As one of the deputies wrote, on 10 May 1789: "If we prescribe a different costume for the deputies of the different orders, will this not mean reinforcing that unfortunate distinction between orders *which can be regarded as our nation's original sin,* and from which it is absolutely necessary that we purge ourselves if we want to be regenerated?" "The essence of the assembly lies in equality," that is, "equality of right and power," in the expectation that this will be proclaimed as the essential character of the nation. Equality of rights and powers instead of distinctions and the hierarchy of orders and "estates": that was the significance of the third estate's struggle against ceremony and etiquette, against everything that might preserve, through external forms, the distinctions between orders and the organization of society into corporations. This was the aim of their efforts to alter the procedure to be followed, substituting, for deliberation by orders, in separate rooms, deliberation in common in a single room, as an "assembly," since "the essence of the assembly lies in equality." A hiatus left in the royal organization of the Estates General played into the hands of the third estate. No special room had been provided for *this* order, which therefore sat in the great hall where all three orders met together for the sessions to be presided over by the king. The third estate gave this room the name of "The Hall of the Nation" and admitted the public to it. To the public, the third estate soon came to incarnate the entire Estates General. This circumstance helped the third estate to advance from the system of orders to the system of classes, which was accomplished when, on 17 June 1789, the deputies of the third estate proclaimed themselves the National Assembly; when, after the royal session of 23 June, the members of the other orders came and joined the third estate; and when, on 9 July, the National Assembly was able to proclaim itself the Constituent Assembly. With the transformation of the Estates General into the National Assembly there was made manifest the will to transform the society of orders into a society of classes. The doubling of the number of deputies of the third estate, the majority acquired in the third estate by those deputies who were engaged in the liberal professions or in occupations concerned with the production of material wealth, at the expense of royal or seignorial officials, showed what the basis of this society was going to be: domination by the bourgeois class, the class of wealth and talent, which was taking over sovereignty.

Barnave gives us the philosophy of this revolution in his *Introduction à la Révolution française* (1792),[44] where he says that France had changed before the Revolution from a society of orders to a class society, and this change made it necessary to proceed by way of the Revolution from a state of orders to a class state.

Barnave's thought presents far-reaching differences from that of Loyseau. For the latter, the society of orders and "estates" is a natural organism, willed and imposed by God and forming part of a cosmos ordained by God. It is something arranged by Divine Providence, and all that men have to do is to recognize it and conform to it, on pain of disaster—certainly not to try and change it. But they are, of course, free to choose woe by setting themselves against God's will. The essence of Loyseau's thought is a theological spiritualism. The essence of Barnave's thought is a deterministic materialism: "Man's will does not make the laws; it can have little or no influence on the form to be taken by governments. It is the nature of things—the social stage which a people has reached, the territory wherein it lives, its wealth, needs, habits, and customs—that decides how power is distributed." It is causes bound up with the nature of things, the constant and regular action of which predominates, that end by bringing about, "almost of necessity," their effect, regardless of men's passions and men's will. There are three sources of power: armed force, property, and the strength of public opinion. Those who possess power in society make the laws. They dominate the state and the government.

For Loyseau, the social order is static. He knows about the Germanic invasions, and he thinks that French society results from the Frankish conquest. In his view, the conquering Franks became the nobles and the conquered Gauls became the commoners. He does not overlook the subsequent merging of conquerors and conquered in the social structure resulting from the conquest. On the whole, however, he sees, since then, only changes of a limited character, oscillations rather, which do not modify the unchangeable nature of society. Loyseau's thought is fixist. For Barnave, however, a veritable evolution takes place in the foundations of power, and especially in property. This evolution determines a succession of societies which differ essentially from each other, with corresponding forms of state. What exists at present is the culmination of a "general movement" which must be traced to its beginnings if one is to understand the current epoch. Every political theory is therefore a *history*, the description of a movement. Studying societies and states means discovering a historical movement. Barnave's theory is based on a conception of becoming. His thought is evolutionist.

Finally, Loyseau describes and analyzes only a society of orders and "estates." These terms have almost vanished from the vocabulary of Barnave, who never uses them without adding the epithet "privileged," as though an order or "estate" were only a group of persons sharing the same privileges.[45] Barnave employs almost always the word "class." This is no mere difference of terminology. Barnave has clearly in mind the notion that it is the forms of property, of wealth, and consequently the role played in relation to the production of material goods, that modify social stratification and the nature of society. He therefore has the idea of class society in clear-cut form. As often happens with many historians (or, rather, with many politicians who write history), he projects into the past the social relations of the society of his own time and presents all societies as being class societies—a mistake imitated by Karl Marx.[46]

For Barnave the driving forces of history are size of population, wealth, and capacity to form independent judgments correctly. If these three factors increase, then civilization advances. If they decrease, then there is retrogression. "There are three things which are connected and which together accompany the progress of civilization among men, namely: population, wealth, and independence of opin-

ion." These things, "population, wealth, customs, and enlightenment," are the "substance" forming the body of society. "Laws and
government" are "the fabric that contains and envelops them" Thus
the state is what maintains unity and order in society. But it varies as
this society varies.

In accordance with these principles, Barnave studies the universal
and necessary succession of the forms of society and the forms of
state and of government that correspond to these. This succession
corresponds to the levels of an increasing capacity for production.

The simplest societies are those of the hunting peoples. Property is
hardly known among them. The whole of the land is common to everyone. The only personal possessions are bows and arrows, game and
skins. Their political organization is a pure democracy. Independence
and natural equality are complete. However, the principle of monarchy
has already made its appearance, for it is necessary to have a war
leader, and the principle of an aristocracy of knowledge has appeared
too, with the elders, the priests, the augurs, and the doctors.[47]

As the population increases, more food, and a more regular supply of
food, becomes necessary. The people apply themselves to stockbreeding and become pastoral. The land remains common, but property
develops in the form of ownership of herds, But this property becomes
increasingly unequal in distribution. Property has to be protected.
Consequently, military and civil authority are increased, in the form of
monarchy or aristocracy. Those who wield authority "gain wealth by
means of power, and by means of wealth increase their power, con-
solidating this in their own hands." The most widespread form of state
is monarchy, for, to defend the people against attack by other pastoral
peoples, a leader or general is required.[48]

The population continues to increase, and so also the need for food,
and the people are obliged to become settled cultivators. The soil becomes subject to individual ownership. But these landed properties are
very unequal. If what happens is merely occupation of an uninhabited
territory, the soil is divided in accordance with ranks, powers, and size
of herds. If what happens is a conquest, the leaders receive a much
larger share than the soldiers. Inequality between landed properties
continues to increase, for the unreliability of the seasons compels the
poor man to borrow from the rich one, who takes advantage of the debt
to get possession of the property of the debtor. The large properties absorb the small ones. On the other hand, this now settled mode of life is
more peaceful, and there is less need of a leader or general. Accordingly,

"a few citizens acquire with ease, over the many, the threefold empire of wealth, force, and education and consolidate in their own
hands the government of the state, jurisdiction, military command, and
priesthood." What we have here, then, is an aristocratic type of state,
and, thanks to the prevailing peace, every large proprietor is able to
maintain order in his lands and ensure security for them: there is therefore great fragmentation, and the state takes a federal form. "The basis
of aristocracy is ownership of land." This was the only form of property at the height of the feudal period, and at that time the monarchy
was still weak. Characteristic of the feudal period, therefore, were:
property only in land, an all-powerful landed aristocracy, federalism,
and a weak monarchy. This was the kind of society and state that
France had known in the 10th and 11th centuries.[49]

When trade began, or revived, "a numerous class of citizens came
into being who, accumulating much wealth from their industry, had the
greatest interest in maintaining internal order and, by means of the
taxes they paid, gave the public authority the strength needed in order
to enforce general laws and bind together all parts of the realm." The
increase in movable property became a factor promoting an increase in
democracy as against aristocracy and cementing the unity of the state.
But it is necessary to distinguish between several stages and several
cases.[50]

If movable property remains inconsiderable, the aristocratic and
federal forms of feudal government continue to prevail. Society and
government merely become firmer and more regular in form.

If movable property undergoes increasing development, but this
happens in a *small* state, then the form assumed by the state is that of a
republic; for there is no army, or not much of one, this being contrary
to the principle of trade, which is peace. The democratic republic is
based on simplicity in way of life and equality in wealth. If, however, a
few families acquire excessive riches, they usurp public authority, render the magistracy hereditary, and constitute a "bourgeois aristocracy," usurping the title of "nobles." The nature of this aristocracy is,
however, quite different from that of a military aristocracy. It consists
of a group of "rich capitalists" with nobody above them, as in Venice
and Holland. The state's unity is centered on a city and on the extent
of territory that a city can dominate without the help of an army, which
is always odious to big merchants.[51]

If movable property develops increasingly in a *large* state, but one
where the countryside retains greater influence than that of the towns,

then the power center, the center of the state's unity, can exist only in the form of the leader of an army. The state is therefore monarchical. But an alliance is established between the monarch and the "rich capitalists," who remain, in this setting, a democratic factor, because there is an aristocracy present and they are opposed to it. Having responsibility for protecting, against the aristocracy and against anarchy, the civil rights of his subjects and, in particular, their property, the monarch receives from his people the major share in the exercise of political authority and concentrates political power in his own person. With the taxes he receives from his people the king withdraws from the grandees' control military power, the administration of justice, and part of the legislative authority. This was what happened in France, where, with the help of the militias of the communes, the kings had taken over the great fiefs in the 12th and 13th centuries. The monarchy became strong. Major wars with external enemies, like the Hundred Years' War, favored the prince's power. They made taxation permanent and arbitrary and enabled the king to form and maintain a regular standing army. This regular army was a powerful bond of union. The transition from the militias to the paid standing army was the great agent of a revolution, the transition to absolute monarchy, for the basis of monarchy and of absolutism is the public armed forces. The absolute monarchy in France grew steadily from the times of Charles VII and Louis XI, along with the growth of capitalist trade and the army. Richelieu laid low the last of the great lords. After his time, the aristocracy, which alone until the middle of the 18th century had fought against the throne, continued to exist only through corporations, bodies of nobles, the provincial estates, the clergy, and the judicial bodies. Owing to the venality of offices, "the magistracy was independent; it had been bourgeois and royalist, it became noble, feudal, refractory." The ruling power became obliged to struggle against the judicial order, which had been its strength and which ought to have continued to support it, by means of annulments of court decisons, the setting up of extraordinary tribunals, commissions, *lettres de cachet*. During this period, "a knightly nobility still succeeds in making its principles prevail, after the real foundation of its power has gone." This was a precarious and transient state of affairs. It inspired Montesquieu to propound the erroneous maxim: "No monarchy without a nobility"—erroneous, because a despotic government, in which the prince's power is greatest in intensity, cannot allow an aristocracy to exist.[52]

But if, in a large state, movable wealth ends by outweighing wealth in land, owing to peace and the increase of trade, then, since movable wealth is the basis of democracy, a true democracy will establish itself. The people lay down conditions for allowing the prince to tax them, and they check on what is done with the tax revenue. The people themselves engage in those state activities which they are capable of conducting and check on the exercise of those which are beyond their powers. "Then a free and limited monarchy will be organized, the happiest and finest of governments ever to reign upon earth," with "two predominant powers, that of the people and that of the king. Owing to the extent of territory involved, the people will have to be drawn into participation in the government of the country through the agency of representatives." This was what was going on in France in Barnave's period: "with the strength of the people increasing all the time, while the aristocracy was declining, the democratic explosion took place at the end of the 18th century." "While the crafts, trade, and luxury enrich the industrious part of the people, impoverish the great landowners, and bring the classes closer together, as regards wealth, the sciences and education bring them closer together in way of life and recall men to original ideas of equality." "The two privileged orders who still formed the machinery of government had ruined themselves by their luxury and degraded themselves by their way of life: the third estate, on the contrary, had acquired much enlightenment and immense riches." In the Estates General there came face to face, "on the one hand, the commons and, on the other, the privileged orders . . . two powers, one of which had only just been born while the other was already on the point of death."[53] Provided we keep in mind that, for Barnave, the "people," the "power of the people," and "democracy" included the wealthy merchants, the "rich capitalists," and even that these formed the essential part of it—the upper stratum of the people and of the "democratic" element, in which persons are placed primarily in accordance with the wealth and property they own—it will be realized that, in his thinking, it was indeed a class society that had been formed in France and that was expressing itself in the political movement called the French Revolution, putting an end officially and legally to the ancient society of orders and "estates" and to the absolute monarchy which corresponded to it, replacing the latter with a limited monarchy under the control of the "people."

This was the movement of French society in the 17th and 18th centuries, as contemporaries saw it and as they suggest to us that it was happening. Already at the beginning of the 17th century the old society that still existed under François I and Henri II had been left behind—the society dominated by the principle of the social superiority of the hereditary profession of arms. Already in Henri IV's time the principle of the social superiority of the magistracy had appeared, alongside the earlier principle; and at the end of Louis XIV's reign the magistracy was indeed another nobility, equal (at least), in its pretensions, to the gentlemen of the sword. However, by the second half of Louis XIV's period of personal rule, at the latest, the growing number of ennoblements of persons of "talent" and of merchants and manufacturers was introducing a new principle of social placing: the superiority of the artist, the scholar, the inventor, the producer. The spirit of the society of orders and estates still reigned; but with the tremendous advance of trade and industry during the 18th century, the general prosperity, the growth of the towns, the increasing interest shown in the material conditions of life, in production and well-being, together with the belief spread by the *philosophes* that man is naturally good and that his individual interest coincides with the general interest, and with the actual formation of the class society of which contemporaries gradually became conscious, the idea spread wider and wider, in a variety of forms, that the society of orders and corporations ought to be replaced by an open class society, whose members, free and equal before the law, should no longer be distinguished from one another except by wealth, talent, and mode of life. These were the "pictures" and this the development that have to be verified and tested in the course of the present book.

Notes

1. Loyseau, *Traité des Ordres,* chap. 1, p. 3.
2. Furetière, *Dictionnaire.*
3. Loyseau, *Ordres,* chap. 3, par. 2.
4. Ibid., chap. 4, pars. 27, 28.
5. Ibid., chap. 8, par. 1.
6. Ibid., chap. 1, par. 39; chap. 3, par. 5.
7. Ibid., chap. 3, pars. 6, 7, 8.
8. Ibid., chap. 7.
9. Ibid., chap. 6.
10. Ibid., chap. 5.
11. Ibid., chap. 4, par. 27; chap. 8, par. 6. See also Roland Mousnier, *The Assassination of Henri IV* (London: Faber, 1973), pt. 3, chap. 10.
12. Loyseau, *Ordres,* chap. 8.

13. Ibid., chap. 11, pars. 10–11, 27–29, 37–38.
14. Ibid., chap. 1, pars. 26–39.
15. Ibid., par. 40.
16. Ibid., chap. 5, pars. 71–87.
17. Ibid., par. 102.
18. Ibid., chap. 4, par. 44.
19. Ibid., chap. 5, pars. 38–48. See also L. N. H. Chérin, *Abrégé chronologique sur la noblesse* (1788), pp. 139, 140; François Bluche and Pierre Durye, "L'anoblissement par charges avant 1789," *Les Cahiers nobles,* nos. 23 and 24 (1962) (with bibliography).
20. Loyseau, *Ordres,* chap. 8.
21. Ibid., chap. 9, pars. 26–55.
22. Ibid., chap. 5, pars. 88–110.
23. This means the king's officers residing in towns, the *lieutenants généraux de bailliage* and the *lieutenants particuliers,* for instance, as against governors of provinces. It does *not* mean municipal magistrates.
24. Loyseau, *Ordres,* Foreword, pars. 6–7.
25. Ibid., chap. 1, pars. 33–35.
26. Ibid., chap. 4, pars. 1–3.
27. Ibid., pars. 38–40.
28. Ibid.
29. *Ecrits inédits de Saint-Simon,* ed. P. Faugère (Hachette, 1880), vol. 3, p. 399; vol. 4, pp. 191, 217.
30. *Projets de gouvernement du duc de Bourgogne (1714–1715),* ed. Paul Mesnard (Hachette, 1860).
31. Ibid., p.57.
32. Ibid., p. 55.
33. Ibid., p. 127.
34. Ibid., pp. 50, 54.
35. Ibid., pp. 15, 78–79, 102–7, 132.
36. Ibid., pp. 15–16.
37. Ibid., pp. 42–44, 80, 92–93, 116, 130, 140, 142, 149, 150, 153.
38. Ibid., pp. 10, 91, 153, 154, 155.
39. *Parallèle des trois rois Bourbons,* in *Ecrits inédits de Saint-Simon,* ed. P. Faugère, vol. 1, pp. 285–87.
40. Jean Domat, *Droit public,* p. 64.
41. *Remontrances du Parlement de Paris au dix-huitième siècle,* ed. Jules Flammermont (Imprimerie Nationale, 1898), vol. 3: *1768–1788,* pp. 279–80.
42. Loisel, vol. 1, vi, no. 8 (quoted in the remonstrance; the reference is to Antoine Loisel, 1536–1617).
43. Georges Lefebvre and Anne Terroine, *Recueil de documents relatifs aux séances des Etats généraux, mai–juin 1789* (Editions du Centre National de la Recherche Scientifique, 1953), vol. 1, pp. 47–78.
44. Antoine Barnave, *Introduction à la Révolution française,* ed. Fernand Rudé, *Cahiers des Annales,* no. 15 (Armand Colin, 1960).
45. Ibid., p. 57.
46. Ibid., pp. 5–6.
47. Ibid., p. 5.
48. Ibid., p.6.

49. Ibid., pp. 8, 9, 13, 37, 47, 49.
50. Ibid., pp. 10, 14.
51. Ibid., pp. 29, 33.
52. Ibid., pp. 22, 36, 37, 39, 40, 47, 48.
53. Ibid., pp. 37, 38, 49, 51, 57.

2

The Society of Lineages

Lineage, marriage, lineal property

Lineage, house, family

The fundamental social group is the family,
"source and origin of every commonwealth and
principal constituent thereof," as Jean Bodin put
it.[1] In the 17th and 18th centuries French society
was still a society of lineages, even though
Furetière was already observing in 1690 that "the
word [*lignage*] is becoming archaic."[2] A lineage
is "a succession of kinfolk, related in different
degrees, who descend from the same stock or
common progenitor. The direct line is that which
runs from father to son. The collateral line is that
to which uncles, aunts, cousins, and nephews belong." In place of the word *lignage*, contemporaries were more frequently using the term *maison*
("house" or "household") when the persons
involved were distinguished by birth or were
illustrious through valor or office and raised high
by their positions of dignity, although this word
sometimes tended to be restricted to the direct
line or even to a *ménage*, that is, to the persons
constituting a family, inhabiting the same building, and living on the same income. It was in this
latter sense that contemporaries spoke of the
royal household as *la Maison du Roi*. When per-

48

sons from the world of the judiciary, or that of the bourgeoisie and business, were concerned, the world *famille* was used instead of *maison,* although *famille,* too, could also signify merely a *ménage,* made up of the head, his wife, and his children, together with his servants and all other associates living with him (*domestiques*). It was as the bourgeois equivalent of the words *maison* or *lineage* that the ennobled Racine used the term *famille* when, on 27 February 1698, he reproached his eldest son Jean-Baptiste for not keeping accounts: "We, good people of family (*bonnes gens de famille*), behave more simply and consider that it is not beneath the dignity of a person of worth (*honnête homme*) to know exactly where he stands financially."[3]

The social function of lineage is to define the group of kinfolk with whom the individual is linked, those with whom he enters into relations of mutual aid. This definition is governed by the rule of descent, which is less a biological relationship than a cultural principle, characteristic of each society, according to which an individual is socially allocated to a definite set of blood relations. The term "lineage" is only approximately exact as regards French society. Actually, what it designates is a kinship group of unilinear descent which includes those persons who can trace their common relationship through a genealogy that follows the line of preponderant descent—through males in patrilineal, through females in matrilineal, descent. The pseudolineage of the France of the *ancien régime,* however, included not only the father's blood relations *or* those of the mother, as alternatives, but the blood relations on both sides. The individual was linked with a group made up of a fairly large number of blood relations of both of his parents. Consequently, descent in France was bilateral. Nevertheless, the custom of passing on the father's name—that is, patrilineal inheritance of the family name—gave this kinship group the look of a lineage. All persons born with the same name and able to trace their genealogy in the male line to a common ancestor constituted a sort of patrilineage. The French solution to the problem of kinship combined advantages of bilateral descent, the form closest to biological descent, with the solidity of a group of unilineal kinship, in which everyone knows from whom he can expect help and to whom he owes it.

The French form of lineage fulfilled its social role perfectly. The individual found within it all the help he needed. As a member of his lineage he could cooperate in a common task. A lineage functioned as a unit for the conquest of social advantages. The head of a lineage could count on backing from his kinfolk—brothers, uncles and aunts, nephews and nieces, first and second cousins, and so on to the furthest degrees of relationship by blood or marriage. Every member of a lineage could rely on receiving the protection and patronage of the head of the lineage. Every member could be sure of help from every other.

The livre de raison

For great families of the sword or of the gown it is obvious that the lineage still played an important role in the two centuries preceding the Revolution. Was this also true of families belonging to social strata that were not so high in the social scale? Yes, indeed, if we are to judge by the frequency of *livres de raison* and by what they contained.[4] A *livre de raison* was a *liber rationum,* an account book, and was sometimes called, characteristically, *liber domus meae,* "the book of my household." A *livre de raison* usually comprised three sections. First, there was the origin and history of the family, its genealogy, kindred, and marriage connections, with dates of marriage, children's birthdays, and dates of deaths. Next, everything to do with the patrimony and with the management of property, income, expenses, savings, and investments. Finally, counsels concerning religion, morals, behavior—great basic principles, duties to God, one's neighbor, and oneself; the respect, honor, and obedience due to one's mother; the affection and deference to be shown to parents; and the unity to be maintained between brothers.

Implicit in the *livre de raison* is the idea of lineage. A son could, as soon as he married, start a *livre de raison* of his own, but often he continued the one his father had kept. The father's *livre de raison* passed to the eldest son, but the younger sons had the right to know what was in it and, if need be, to make a copy. In Provence, it is said, all the coheirs even had the right to require that their father's *livre de raison* be produced when he died, so as to gain full knowledge of the family property for which he was responsible. Whole series of *livres de raison* extend over five, six, or even ten generations. In Brittany there are dynasties of *livres de raison,* from about 1400 down to 1789, and the same is true of other areas as well. The Curières of Castelnau kept *livres de raison,* from father to son, from 1346 to 1879. The primary purpose was to prove the antiquity and maintain the tradition of the lineage. Among noblemen of the sword, De Saulx-Tavannes declared: "Children, nephews, cousins, I write from duty to our father, to furnish examples and precepts to you, my kindred, and not from vain-glory." Henri de la Tour d'Auvergne, duc de Bouillon, did likewise, and so also, among the *noblesse de robe,* did Chancellor Hurault de Cheverny at the end of the 16th century. But these were also the purposes of more modest persons. Jean Etienne Gautier, canon and vicar general to the bishop of Cavaillon, kept his *livre de raison* from 1634 to 1704 for the benefit of his nephews and grand-nephews. He restricted himself to recording his genealogy for eight generations and no more, "since this is pointless in the case of a family which *has no need to prove nobility,* and which is known in this town as one of the worthiest and most ancient, having provided canons in this cathedral for more than four hundred years."

These *livres de raison* were kept by *gentilshommes,* by *bourgeois,* by merchants, by artists (such as Joseph Vernet, who kept his from 1735 to 1788), and also by peasants, owners of their land and share-croppers alike. Many families of small landowners preserved in this way their genealogies and their family traditions, in Burgundy, Dauphiné, and Provence. Claude Jaunet, a vine-growing landowner established at Demigny (now in Saône-et-Loire), kept his *livre de raison* from 1735 to 1756; mingled with accounts and details concerning wine harvests and the quality of wines we find a chronicle of the princi-pal events concerning his family, the day when his daughter began attendance at the school at Marsanges (for a monthly fee of ten livres), and some beautiful forms of prayer. Small traders, draftsmen, weavers, all did the same. We ought to find out the "density" of *livres de raison* by period, region, and social category and to ascertain whether this practice, which reflects the social ideal of the lineage, was still being kept up, was declining, or was changing as the Revolution drew near.

Some great lineages

All the families of the grandees and high nobility, and those of the ministers, secretaries of state, state councilors, and *présidents* of the sovereign courts, provide us with examples of lineages. Let us recall some of these.

The Richelieus originated from the Du Plessis family, established on the borders of Brenne and Poitou. These soldiers, subvassals of the bishops of Poitiers, *archers* and *écuyers* who were sometimes in the service of the great lords of their neighborhood, sometimes in that of the kings of France or the kings of England, appear in records as early as 1201, in the reign of Philip Augustus. At the end of the 14th century,

Sauvage du Plessis initiated the junior branch of the family, which subsequently adopted the name Du Plessis de Richelieu. Sauvage's son Geoffrey married Perrine Clérambault, whose brother Louis, lord of Richelieu, was *major domo* to Queen Marie of Anjou, wife of King Charles VII. Louis Clérambault died about 1490 without issue and left his estate of Richelieu to his nephew François du Plessis, who assumed its name. Thereafter the Du Plessis de Richelieu family intermarried with families occupying offices at court and in the army, as well as ecclesiastical appointments, and, through the backing these marriage connections gave them, themselves entered such posts. Another François du Plessis de Richelieu, grandson of the first, as a page to King Charles IX and lieutenant in the company commanded by the prince de Dombes, heir of the Montpensiers, attached himself to the fortunes of the duc d'Anjou and accompanied him to Poland, where the duke was elected king. When Anjou left Poland in order to take up the crown of France under the name Henri III, François followed him. King Henri III appointed him *prévôt de l'hôtel,* then *grand prévôt de France* in 1578, and in 1585 made him a knight of the Order of the Holy Spirit. It was he who arrested Jacques Clément after the assassination of the king on 1 August 1589 and who investigated the affair. This loyal companion of Henri III declared in favor of Henri IV, was maintained by him in his functions as grand provost, and became his comrade-in-arms in the struggle for the conquest of France. After fighting at Arques and at Ivry, he died during the great siege of Paris, on 10 July 1590. Although a *gentilhomme,* he had married Suzanne de la Porte, daughter of an advocate before the Paris *parlement,* who was president of the Order of Advocates. It was his third son, Armand-Jean, who became Cardinal de Richelieu and Louis XIII's chief minister. His example enables us to appreciate clearly what the French system of patrilineage amounted to, for the cardinal became the head of his lineage although he was not the eldest son. His elder brother, Henri du Plessis de Richelieu, who was, like his father, a faithful adherent of Henri IV, became one of the seventeen *seigneurs* who set the tone at court, ruled the changes of fashion, and was devoted to Queen Marie de Médicis. He always willingly helped in the advancement of his younger brother. Henri de Richelieu enjoyed the support of his brother-in-law, Du Pont de Courlay, captain of the king's guards, who had married, on 23 August 1603, Françoise du Plessis, the sister of Henri and Armand. The Richelieu family had at their disposal the bishopric of Luçon, a favor which Henri III had granted to his grand provost. The Richelieus received the consistorial revenues of Luçon through the mediation of *"confidentaire"* bishops, who lent their names to the arrangement. For fifty years the bishopric was handed down in this way, at the family's discretion. Some members of the family sacrificed themselves in order to play the role of bishop at certain times: there was the grand provost's uncle, Jacques de Richelieu, the king's chaplain, and, later, a young brother of the future cardinal, until Armand was appointed bishop of Luçon in 1606 (before he had taken his degrees and five years before reaching the canonical age), by grace of King Henri IV; for this, Armand was indebted to his elder brother. Subsequently, Richelieu, having become cardinal, chief minister, and duke, favored his family in every way and also made use of them. He obtained from Louis XIII the appointment of his brother Alphonse, a Carthusian, as archbishop of Aix-en-Provence in 1625, then as archbishop of Lyon in 1629, grand almoner of France, cardinal, and, eventually, in 1634, ambassador to Rome. As governor of Brittany in 1631, Richelieu arranged to be represented there by three *lieutenants généraux,* two of whom were his own cousins-german, the duc de la Meilleraye and the marquis de Coislin. His elder brother, Henri, *maréchal de camp* in the army of the duc de Nevers, was killed in a duel by the marquis de Thémines and left no children. The Richelieus were on the point of dying out at the very moment when they were reaching their apogee. They were saved by their nephews. Françoise du Plessis, sister of Henri, Alphonse, and Armand and wife of René de Vignerod, *seigneur* of Pont-Courlay, had two children, François and Marie-Magdeleine. The latter, having become Madame de Combalet, was by favor of the cardinal-minister made duchesse d'Aiguillon in 1638. François de Vignerod, marquis de Pont-Courlay, her brother, the cardinal's nephew, became governor of Le Havre and general of the galleys in 1635. His son Armand-Jean, born on 2 October 1631, the grand-nephew of the cardinal-minister, duc de Richelieu, was given the names and arms of the Du Plessis de Richelieu family, so saving the lineage. Armand-Jean became duc de Richelieu et de Fronsac, peer of France, prince de Mortagne, marquis de Pont-Courlay, comte de Cosnac, a knight of the royal orders, and gentleman-in-waiting to Madame la Dauphine. He succeeded his father as general of the galleys, taking the oath in January 1643 at the age of fifteen. He resigned from this post in 1661 and died in 1715, aged eighty-four. He left four children, one of whom was Louis-François-Armand du Plessis, duc de Richelieu (1696–1788). From 1710 onward the spoiled child of the court and most gallant of courtiers, a witty and a brave man, the duc de Richelieu, who became a peer of France in 1721, won himself a reputation as diplomat and as soldier. He was a triumphant ambassador to Vienna in 1725 and to Dresden in 1746, *maréchal de camp* and royal *lieutenant général* in Languedoc in 1738, an intimate friend of Louis XV as first gentleman of the bedchamber in 1744, *lieutenant général* of the king's armies and brilliant leader of the charge of the household troops at Fontenoy in 1745, savior of Genoa, marshal of France in 1748, governor of Guyenne and Gascony in 1755, conqueror of Minorca in 1756. Remarried at the age of eighty, he would have become a father again but for an unfortunate miscarriage. Louis XVIII's minister was his grandson.

The Nicolaï family were a famous lineage who held the post of *premier président* of the Paris *chambre des comptes* without interruption from 1506 until the abolition of that court during the Revolution. This family, probably of Italian extraction, established themselves at Saint-Andéol, a small town in Vivarais. It was Jean II Nicolaï, *seigneur* of Saint-Victor, who brought the post of *premier président* into the family. As a counselor in the *parlement* of Toulouse, he accompanied Charles VIII on that expedition into Italy which was to have been the prelude to a crusade to free Jerusalem and restore the Eastern Empire. He became chancellor of the Kingdom of Naples during the French occupation. Louis XII made him a master of requests, and then, two years later, in 1506, *premier président* of the Paris *chambre des comptes*. Jean II resigned in favor of his son Aimar in 1518. Thereafter, the eldest sons of the Nicolaï family married daughters of *présidents* of the *parlement, présidents* of the *chambre des comptes,* treasurers of the central treasury (*Epargne*), and state councilors—all, that is, except Jean-Nicholas II, who married Marie de Billy, daughter of the baron de Courville—and all of them, from father to son, were *premiers présidents* of the *chambre des comptes,* while, in the 17th century, their younger brothers entered the military profession, becoming a cornet in the *gendarmes du roi,* a lieutenant in the artillery, and even, at the end of the century, in the person of Nicholas (brother to Jean-Aimar I, marquis de Goussainville, appointed *premier président* on 5 March 1626), marquis d'Ivor, colonel of the regiment of Auvergne, a *brigadier* in the king's armies. The sisters of these *premiers présidents* were married without difficulty to *gentilshommes*—professional soldiers, marquises, governors of towns. Through the eldest sons the lineage remained by choice in the *noblesse de robe,* and among the higher nobility they did not rise higher than the rank of *chevalier* which went with their office, except by virtue of the marquisate bestowed on different branches of the family at the end of the century. Jean-Baptiste-Antoine-Nicholas Nicolaï, son of Jean-Aimar I, who became *premier président* by reversion in 1717, left no heir capable of succeeding him. However, he had a half-brother, Aimar-Jean, offspring of Jean-Aimar I's second marriage, to Françoise-Elisabeth de Lamoignon, daughter of Lamoignon de Basville, intendant of Languedoc. Aimar-Jean, like a good younger son, first went into the army. Having attained the rank of *mestre de camp* in the dragoons, he left the service in order to keep the office of *premier président* in his family, assuming its responsibilities in 1734, while his brother Antoine-Chrétien, faithful to the profession of arms, became a count and marshal of France in 1775, and his remaining brother, Aimar-Chrétien, became bishop and count of Verdun in 1754. Once more, in the absence of the elder son, it was Aimar-Jean's second son who saved the situation by abandoning the sword for the gown. Aimar-Charles François de Nicolaï, marquis d'Osny, colonel of dragoons in 1761, colonel of the Royal Legion in 1764, left the service and became *président à mortier* in the Paris *parlement* in 1771, *président* in the Grand Conseil in 1774, and eventually, in November 1776, the tenth member of his family to be *premier président* of the *chambre des comptes*. He was also the last of the Nicolaïs to hold this office, being sentenced to death on 27 April 1794 by the revolutionary tribunal for having attempted to leave the country; he was guillotined on the following day. His brother, the bishop of Béziers, had had to flee from France in 1792. His fourth son, Aimar-Charles-Marie-Théodore, was raised to the peerage by Louis XVIII on 17 August 1815.

The Phélypeaux family, who retained for nearly two centuries the office of secretary of state, hailed from Blois, where their presence is recorded as early as the 14th century. In the 16th century Louis Phélypeaux, *seigneur* of La Vrillière, was counselor in the presidial court of Blois. Married in 1557, he had five sons, two of whom—the fourth, Paul, and then the eldest, Raymond—became secretaries of state, while the others became, respectively, a *maître* in the Paris *chambre des comptes,* an advocate before the Paris *parlement,* and a state councilor. His three daughters married, respectively, a *secrétaire du roi,* a treasurer of the central treasury (Paul Ardier), and a counselor in the presidial court of Blois.

Paul Phélypeaux, born in 1569, was the founder of the Pontchartrain branch of the family. Of his nephews (the sons of his elder brother Raymond, born in 1560, *seigneur* of Herbaut and of La Vrillière), the eldest, Balthasar Phélypeaux, *chevalier* and *seigneur* of Herbaut, founded the senior branch of the Phélypeaux d'Herbaut; the second, Louis, *seigneur* of La Vrillière and of Châteauneuf-sur-Loire, baron d'Hervy, founded the branch of the Phélypeaux de la Vrillière; and the third, Antoine, *seigneur* of Le Verger, founded the branch of the Phélypeaux du Verger.

After Balthasar, the eldest sons of the Phélypeaux d'Herbaut were state councilors and counselors of the *parlement,* and one of them, Antoine-François, became intendant general of the navy; in this capacity he received a mortal wound at Malaga on 24 August 1704. The younger sons became ecclesiastics, sometimes rising to be bishops, or else, occasionally, they were soldiers, officers in the king's armies.

The Du Verger branch rose into the *noblesse d'épée* but died out toward the end of the 17th century. Antoine, a counselor in the *parlement* of Paris in 1629, intendant of justice in Bourbonnais, and then a state councilor, died in 1665. He had married the daughter of a *maître d'hôtel du roi,* who gave him two sons. The elder of these, Raimond-Balthasar Phélypeaux, *seigneur* of Le Verger, lieutenant general in the king's armies, state councilor with rank as a *noble d'épée,* became viceroy of Canada, where he died, unmarried, in December 1713. The younger, Jacques-Antoine, became bishop of Lodève in 1690.

Paul Phélypeaux, *seigneur* of Pontchartrain, was the one who brought the office of secretary of state into his lineage. Clerk to Secretary of State Louis Revol in 1588, and then to Villeroy in 1594, he became *secrétaire des Commandements* to Marie de Médicis in 1600; on 21 April 1610 he was granted an office as secretary of state, and he died in harness, during the siege of Montauban, on 21 October 1621. His brother, Raimond Phélypeaux, *sieur* of Herbaut, succeeded to the office and also died still holding it, on 2 May 1629, at Susa, during the expedition into Italy. The office then passed to a second son, Paul's nephew Louis, *seigneur* of La Vrillière and Châteauneuf-sur-Loire, baron d'Hervy, who functioned as secretary of state for Protestant affairs and for a certain number of *généralités* from 1629 to 1681. His second son, Balthasar Phélypeaux, marquis de Châteauneuf-sur-Loire et de Tanlay, *seigneur* of La Vrillière, comte de Saint-Florentin, baron d'Hervy, having been granted the reversion in 1699, took up the office in 1681 and died in possession of it on 27 April 1700. Balthasar's eldest son, Louis Phélypeaux, marquis de La Vrillière, comte de Saint-Florentin, succeeded to the office of secretary of state and died still holding it on 7 September 1725. His son Louis Phélypeaux, comte de Saint-Florentin, who had been granted the reversion in 1723, took up the office on his father's death and remained secretary of state until 1775, when he was dismissed, and died childless on 27 February 1777. The marriage connections made by the La Vrillière branch of the family demonstrate its rise up the social ladder. The first Louis married Marie Particelli, daughter of the superintendent of finance, a dubious parvenu; Balthasar made an honorable marriage, to the daughter of a councilor of the Grand Conseil; but the second Louis found his wife among the *noblesse d'épée*—Françoise de Mailly, daughter of Louis, comte de Mailly, *maréchal de camp* in the king's army; and the third Louis's bride was Amelie-Ernestine von Platen, daughter of Ernst-August von Platen, count of the Holy Roman Empire, lord chamberlain and minister of state to His Britannic Majesty and hereditary grand postmaster of the states of Brunswick-Lüneburg.

In the Pontchartrain branch, Paul's eldest son, Louis I Phélypeaux, was eight years old when his father died. Nevertheless, he was granted the office of secretary of state, though subject to the condition that during his minority it was to be exercised by his uncle Raymond, in whose favor he subsequently resigned, contenting himself with the presidency in the *chambre des comptes* in 1650. His son, Louis II Phélypeaux, born in 1643, was made a counselor of the Paris *parlement* in 1661, became in 1677 *premier président* of the *parlement* of Brittany, intendant of finance in 1687, comptroller general of finance in 1689, the minister and secretary of state for the affairs of the royal household, the clergy, and the navy on 6 November 1690. He gave up the last-mentioned office in 1699 to become chancellor of France, in which office he remained until 2 July 1714.

His son Jérôme Phélypeaux, comte de Pontchartrain et de Maurepas, who had possessed since 1693 the reversion of the secretaryship of state held by his father, took up this office in September 1699 and resigned it in November 1715. His son, Jean-Frédéric Phélypeaux, comte de Maurepas, then became secretary of state for the affairs of the royal household and of the clergy. He strengthened the ties between the Pontchartrain and La Vrillière branches of the family by marrying, in 1718, Marie-Jeanne Phélypeaux, daughter of Louis, marquis de la Vrillière, minister and secretary of state, and of Françoise de Mailly. In 1723 Maurepas added the department of the navy to that of the royal household, and in 1738 he became minister of state. On 24 April 1749 he was ordered to retire but was recalled in 1774 by Louis XVI to serve as minister of state; he died on 21 November 1781 without issue.

Thus, from 1610 to 1715 there was always, in the house of Phélypeaux, at least one office of secretary of state (two from 1690 to 1749), and it also attained the office of chancellor of France, as well as the function of minister of state and the dignities of honorary member of the Academy of Sciences and the Academy of Inscriptions and Belles-Lettres. It survived from the 14th century (at least) until the end of the 18th.

How many other lineages would repay study—those of Ormesson, Le Tonnelier de Breteuil, Voyer d'Argenson, for instance, not to mention, of course, the Colberts and the Louvois!

Our *livres de raison* suggest that the lineage was still in being at the end of the 18th century in all strata of the French population, but this needs to be established, especially where the humblest workers and peasants are concerned, and the proportion of survival needs to be determined.

Problems of marriage: Misalliance, abduction by seduction. The decrees of the Council of Trent

Lineage was vitally important, and this was why marriage was accorded such importance. Marriage between members of a lineage was a way of strengthening its solidarity. Canon law forbids marriage between kindred up to the seventh degree of kinship (as reckoned by civil law), but social pressure compelled the church authorities to grant numerous dispensations. Marriage was a means of increasing the extent and influence of a lineage through ties with other lineages, and it was also a way of integrating *fidèles* in a lineage. For ambitious persons it was a way of ensuring the "protection" required for social advancement. By marrying the grand-niece of a great lord, one made certain that thenceforth the patronage of this great lord could be relied on, since it entailed vowing fealty to him. In the 17th century, André d'Ormesson, doyen of the Council of State, wrote about his father, Olivier Lefèvre, *seigneur* of Ormesson, born in 1525, who became treasurer for extraordinary war expenditure:

> My father, realizing (in 1557), as a result of the setbacks and the acts of charity he had experienced, how hard it was to live for any length of time at court without support or assistance, resolved to

marry, linking himself with some family that might uphold and defend him. At that time Messire Jean de Morvilliers, bishop of Orléans and state councilor, was held in great esteem and reputation and could do much, owing to the good services he had rendered and was rendering to France. My father sought a connection with him and married Damoiselle Anne d'Alesso (grand-niece by marriage of M. de Morvilliers, through his sister). In this way my father came to be greatly loved and always favored by M. de Morvilliers ... On 16 July (1559) my father was married, and he received ten thousand livres as his bride's dowry. He had sought support and alliance more than riches.

The calculation proved sound. In 1566 the king ordered an inquiry into embezzlement by the officials in charge of the state finances.

All the officers of the royal household were removed from their posts. There was need of a reliable man who could take over these posts by commission, and my father was chosen on the recommendation of M. de Morvilliers, who said at a meeting of the Council that he was going to propose a man for whom he would answer with his own body. The queen mother said, as she left the Council: "M. de Morvilliers must like M. d'Ormesson very much and consider him a reliable man, for it has not been his custom to put himself forward so much on another's behalf."[5]

But then, Ormesson was a member of his lineage! This revealing passage concerns events in the 16th century, but the customs did not change in these matters in the 17th century, and not greatly in the 18th, until about 1750. When a man married, he was espousing, in fact, not so much a woman as the social situation of her father or, rather, that of her lineage. This explains the reply given by a gentleman who was to have married a certain kinswoman of Richelieu's. Some time after this had been agreed, the cardinal told him that he had had to dispose of the lady to someone else and offered her younger sister instead. "I accept," was the gist of the gentleman's reply; "I am not much concerned about the girl. It is Your Eminence I am marrying."

When good marriages were made, the lineage rose in the social hierarchy, while bad marriages dragged it down. Consequently, families lived in terror of a "misalliance"—a marriage between a man and a woman so unequal in social position and wealth that a factor was thereby introduced into the socially superior family which might spoil its homogeneity and drag it down. In his declaration of 26 November 1639 Louis XIII denounced misalliances, which had "disturbed the serenity of so many families and stained their honor through marriages that were unequal and often shameful and infamous," and which added to the offense given to private persons "that which is given to the public laws." The provisions of the ordinance were binding, moreover, upon all social strata and all persons, "even though they be of humble condition." In 1780 an application to a court for authority to make approaches with a view to marrying a miller's son still referred to the "equality of fortune, birth, and status" between the couple concerned. According to judgments by the Paris *parlement* during the 17th and 18th centuries, cases of misalliance included the marriage of a big grain merchant with a servant; a man who possessed the quality of *"seigneur de"* some *seigneurie* with the daughter of a sailor; a tipstaff in the Paris *parlement* with the daughter of a tailor; the son of a clerk in the civil registry of the *parlement* with a girl whose father was a tipstaff in the Tribunal des Consuls and whose mother was a servant; a *secretaire du roi* with a prostitute; a duke with the daughter of a magistrate; the daughter of a *seigneur* who was a *brigadier* in the king's army, with a lackey; the daughter of a *président* in the *élection* of Senlis with a musician who was a pensioner of the king's own orchestra. We thus see that some persons of good family were willing to marry an attractive woman or man without worrying about their family background. The thoughtless might in this way, on the vain pretext of love, sully the honor and compromise the position of a lineage.

Canon law offered insufficient safeguards to lineages. Marriage, indeed, is the union of mutual consent of a man and a woman, upon conditions they have put to each other. For the Roman Catholic Church, marriage is one of the seven sacraments. It is therefore contracted upon conditions laid down by the Church. It is indissoluble, by positive divine law (Genesis 2:23–24) and because it is symbolic of the union between Christ and the Church. Divorce is, accordingly, forbidden, but separation from bed and board is possible. One of the purposes of marriage being to foster charity among men through kinship and affinity, marriages are not allowed between persons related up to the fourth degree, by canonical computation. But the officialities can grant dispensations for charitable reasons. A previous marriage constitutes an impediment to a marriage, for monogamy is the rule. Other impediments are created by a person's being in holy orders above the degree of subdeacon or by having taken a vow of chastity; by a mistake concerning a person's identity (or condition, if a slave); and by the spiritual relationship of godparenthood. The sacraments are the source of grace, so that access to them must be easy. As a sacrament, marriage is a source of grace, enabling the married couple to accomplish fittingly the purposes of marriage. It must therefore be easy of access, and especially so since it is the remedy for concupiscence. All persons who have attained puberty (boys at fourteen, girls at twelve) are capable of contracting a marriage without the consent of their parents. Clandestine marriages, though disapproved of, are valid, for a marriage results from mere consent freely given by the man and the woman. The substance is the consent of the couple, and the form is the words in which this consent is expressed. The priest receives the expressions of consent and records the marriage, but it is not he who effects it. If there is an abduction, that is, if a girl is carried off by force, she may make a valid marriage with her abductor by her own free will. In every case it is the mutual consent of the man and the woman that alone constitutes a marriage. No formality is required, nor is any witness necessary. The most clandestine of marriages is valid and indissoluble.

Abductions and clandestine marriages, without parents' knowledge and against their will, occurred very frequently. Protests by fathers of families became so numerous that the ambassadors of the king of France asked the Council of Trent to rule that there must be witnesses to marriages and to declare null and void marriages contracted by persons under the age of twenty-five without the consent of their parents. Since marriage is a sacrament, the Council refused to nullify clandestine marriages; it even proclaimed them, by the decree called *Tametsi,* to be true and regular marriages and anathematized the contrary view. Its decision, with the accompanying anathema, thus formed a canon, and whoever rejected it was not merely a schismatic but even a heretic.

However, the Church had always disapproved of clandestine marriages, and the Council of Trent set about making them more difficult. To this end it introduced a new impediment by declaring invalid any marriages not concluded in the presence of the couple's parish priest, or of a priest authorized by him or by his bishop, and in the presence of two witnesses. Parish priests were advised to ascertain the parents' opinion. Three publications of banns in the parish church, to be made by the couple's own priest, were required (thereby repeating a decision of the Lateran Council of 1215), though the bishop could grant dispensation from this requirement. The Council ordered parish priests to keep registers and to record therein the names of the spouses, with those of the witnesses also, and the date and place of the marriage. It declared the nullity of any marriage concluded following an abduction, on the presumption that the consent of the abducted girl had not been given freely; before a valid marriage could be made, she must be separated from her abductor and taken to a place of safety, in which circumstances she might give her free consent. All these arrangements were to come into force thirty days after the Council's decisions had been published in a given parish.

But the disciplinary decrees of the Council of Trent were not accepted in France. The king's government regarded them as infringing the rights of the temporal power and the liberties of the Gallican Church. Consequently, in France the old law continued to prevail. Marriages were validated by the mere consent of the man and woman, even if this was expressed only before a notary, who certified its genuineness, without a priest having any part in the proceedings. The fathers of families, who would, in any case, have been given only partial satisfaction by the decisions of the Council, received none at all.

They intervened through their representatives at the Estates General held at Blois in 1576. At the request of the Estates General, the king issued the Ordinance of Blois, 1579, which remained the basis of law and jurisprudence on this point until 1789. Articles 40–44 of this ordinance, which repeated some of the decisions of the Council of Trent, annulled all marriages for which banns had not been published, which had not been solemnized in public, at which four witnesses had not been present, or which had not been entered in a register. The ordinance gave priests the exclusive right to celebrate marriages; article 44 forbade notaries, on pain of corporal punishment, to receive the declarations of the two parties expressing their mutual and formal consent to a marriage.

The ordinance imposed the penalty of death for abduction, even if the person abducted should subsequently consent to it, and this was to apply to the abduction of boys as well as girls, whereas the Council had considered only the abduction of girls. Marriage entered into without the consent of parents or guardians was to be treated as equivalent to the crime of abduction and so punishable by death. Furthermore, the ordinance notably expanded the concept of abduction. For the Council, it had meant the removal of a girl by force. According to the Ordinance of Blois (article 42), however, "suborning" also amounted to abduction. "Suborning" someone signified leading them, by means of words, to act against their duty, to perform some bad action: seducing them, in fact—committing the act which was later to be called "abduction by seduction."

Thus the king did not create a new impediment to marriage. He did not say that the absence of parental consent rendered a marriage invalid, which would have gone against the decree *Tametsi* and made him a heretic. But he achieved the same result by making marriage without parental consent equivalent to abduction, which *did* constitute an impediment.

Subsequent law and jurisprudence merely developed the principles contained in the Ordinance of Blois. The *parlements* substituted their jurisprudence for that of the Church authorities by way of the procedure of *appel comme d'abus*. Any marriage at which a priest had not been present was to be considered invalid. But what priest? Nineteen decisions by the *parlement* of Paris, adopted between 1591 and 1640, answered: the priest of the parish where the couple were living. An ordinance of 1639 required that permission from the parish priest to another priest to take his place as witness to the marriage must be given in writing and attached to the marriage register. Jurisprudence remained firm on this point: a marriage was not valid if the right priest was absent. The ordinance of 1639 confirmed article 40 of the Ordinance of Blois and interpreted it. The banns must be published by the parish priest of each of the contracting parties, with the consent of their parents or guardians. Four witnesses worthy of confidence were required "in addition to the priest who is to receive the consent of the parties and join them in marriage." A priest was to marry only his own parishioners, except where permission in writing had been given by the parish priest of the party or parties concerned. Registers of marriages and dispensations must be kept.

But the Council of Trent had merely required the *presence* of the priest, since what constituted the sacrament was mutual consent, with the priest being no more than a passive witness. On this point the ordinance of 1639 was not applied properly. The practice arose of marriages *à la Gaulmine,* named after Gaulmin, doyen of the masters of requests, who used it in the days of the Fronde—though he was only following a procedure that already had a long history. The parties would arrive unexpectedly before the priest, accompanied by a notary. They would exchange their consents, and the notary would formally record both this fact and the presence of the priest. If the latter wanted to go away, he would be restrained, by force if necessary. This practice made clandestine marriages possible, and their numbers grew considerably.

Therefore, in 1674, the *parlements* annulled marriages at which the priest had not been present voluntarily and to which he did not give his consent. The edict of March 1697 required that "the appropriate priest" be present, and assigned him an active role. He it was who had to "join in marriage" the betrothed persons, questioning them, receiving their expressions of consent, and proclaiming their union. The edict did not actually annul marriages effected by the mere consent of the parties, which would have violated the Council's decrees, but it obtained the same result by depriving such marriages of civil significance: they could not provide authority for payment of dowry, community of property, or inheritance. The "appropriate" priest was defined as the priest of the parish in which each party had actually resided for six months, or a year. The parish priest of only *one* of the two parties was at first regarded as sufficient, but it was found that this enabled the parties to apply to a priest who might be unaware of a possible irregularity in the position of the party who was not one of his parishioners. From 21 February 1732 onward the courts required the concordance of both priests if the parties lived in different parishes and, in addition, written authorization from the one who was not celebrating the marriage.

"Abduction by seduction" received attention from the beginning of the 17th century. Upon a father's *appel comme d'abus* against the celebration of a marriage, the Paris *parlement,* on 13 June 1626, and subsequently the *parlements* of Aix, Grenoble, Rouen, and Toulouse, annulled marriages to which parents had not consented—not because of the absence of parental consent, which would have been a breach of the decree *Tametsi,* but because this lack of consent gave grounds for presuming that there had been subornation, that is, seduction, and therefore abduction. Marriages resulting from "abduction by seduction" were annulled. Even an underage girl could be accused of seduction and abduction, and this even if the alleged victim was a boy who was no longer a minor. Even in cases where the spouses were both adults, their marriage could be annulled if the "seduction" had begun when one of them was a minor. Moreover, abduction being a crime that disturbed public order, magistrates proceeded against it *ex officio,* without any complaint by parents being required; and if deception or violence was involved, they punished this crime with severe penalties, even with death.

The ordinance of 1639 was inspired by the *parlements*. For several

years the king's advocates general before the Paris *parlement,* Bignon
and Talon, had been arguing the need for an ordinance against abduction and clandestine marriages. The occasion was provided by the
marriage projected between Cinq-Mars, the *grand écuyer,* and the
courtesan Marion de l'Orme. Madame d'Effiat, Cinq-Mars's mother,
complained to the *parlement,* which accused Marion de l'Orme and her
accomplices of subornation, ordered their arrest, and forbade the parties to proceed with the marriage. King Louis XIII entrusted Bignon,
premier avocat général, with the drawing-up of a declaration, which
the *parlement* registered "with one voice." This declaration of 1639
confirmed Henri II's edict of 1556, which permitted the fathers and
mothers of persons still of minor status—which meant aged up to thirty
in the case of boys, twenty-five in that of girls—who had married
without their consent, to disinherit them and revoke any gifts they had
made to them. The guilty would be deprived, as regards inheritance, of
all benefit of the laws and customs of the realm and could be punished
as the judges saw fit. The declaration of 1639 also confirmed articles
41–44 of the Ordinance of Blois and added to them. The penalty for
abduction was to be incurred even if, subsequently, consent was given
by parents and guardians. Widows, sons, and daughters of minor status
(up to twenty-five years old) who married without their parents' consent were to be deprived of all right of succession, whether direct or
collateral, and of all rights established by the customs or laws of the
realm, even of their legitim. Sons over thirty and daughters over
twenty-five had to obtain the written approval and consent of their
fathers and mothers before they could marry without incurring dis-
inheritance; but if the parents refused consent, they were free to go
ahead. Marriages contracted after abduction by sons, daughters, and
widows were declared to have been "contracted invalidly," even if the
adult person concerned, after being set free as prescribed by the Council, should give consent to the marriage. A victim of abduction, and any
children born of such a marriage, were to be incapable of any succession, whether direct or collateral, and this applied likewise to "persons
abducted by subornation" and their children. Secret marriages were
forbidden, and the children born of such marriages were declared incapable of any succession. Princes and *seigneurs* were forbidden to
make representations for the king to rehabilitate persons rendered incapable of succession. The secretary of state was forbidden to sign
letters of rehabilitation in such cases, and the chancellor was forbidden
to seal them.

The term "abduction by seduction" was first introduced into royal legislation by the Edict of Marly, 22 November 1730, which, in connection with some muddles committed by judges in Brittany, ordered article 42 of the Ordinance of Blois and the declaration of 6 November 1639 to be enforced "throughout our kingdom and all the lands and lordships subject to us." Abductors and suborners were to be punished by death, without permission to marry the abducted person, even if she should ask for this, whether before or after the sentence had been passed. Those who were guilty only of "illicit dealings" were to be punished, but not capitally.

The theory of "abduction by seduction" was elaborated during the 18th century and set forth by the jurist Pothier in his *Traité du mariage* in 1768. There was to be irrefragable presumption of seduction whenever the marriage of a minor took place without parental consent, and seduction was equivalent to abduction and therefore entailed the invalidity of the marriage.

Thus, without ever introducing in principle a fresh impediment, without apparently violating the rights claimed by the Church and the decrees of the Council of Trent, jurisprudence and law did, in practice, introduce a fresh impediment to marriage and gave effective protection to lineages.

Lineage and property

Propres, lineal property

The perpetuity and rank of a lineage were ensured, not simply by good marriages, but also by the durable property transmitted, which provided the means for maintaining the style of life appropriate to the status, rank, and condition of the given lineage. It was a question of possessing the "means to sustain one's name and house" (René de Voyer d'Argenson). Without hereditary property there could be no lineage. Hence the importance ascribed to lineal property, that which was "proper" to the members of a lineage—to the extent that many jurists, such as Bacquet, considered that, while the prime function of the state, its principal *raison d'être,* was to maintain peace and order, its second function was to safeguard everyone's possessions, in particular those which were "proper" to him. What were "proper" were the possessions that had to remain within the lineage, ensuring its material strength and contributing to its perpetuity. These possessions were kept within the lineage because they were excluded from the community of goods between spouses and were subject to restrictions on freedom of disposal and to special measures affecting successions. These possessions consisted of fixed, "real" property, that is, lands and houses. They were not the possessions with the highest value or producing the biggest annual returns in money, but they were the most secure and also the most honorable, especially when they took the form of *seigneuries* or fiefs. Treated as equivalent to real property were those possessions which were the most certain, after "immovable" property, namely, perpetual and utilizable rights: seignorial justice, *cens,* rents, and seignorial or royal offices. The income arising from such rights was sometimes treated as real property. Flocks of sheep were classed as real property by certain "customs" in the southwestern part of France.

All these possessions were "proper" heritages when they had come by way of succession, direct or collateral, or when they had been identified as such by convention. The marriage contract distinguished, among the belongings contributed by the husband and those in his wife's dowry, between what was made common to both and what remained "proper" to the husband or the wife, respectively. The husband could enjoy only the usufruct of what was "proper" to his wife. He could not dispose of it without her consent; and, if he obtained this, he was obliged to use the money he got for it to buy real property, which could be added to the property which was heritable. If children were left when the couple died, there would be no difficulty: the possessions of both parties passed to their offspring. If, however, there were no children, the possessions "proper" to the husband went to his kindred—brothers, sisters, cousins of his "side and line"—while those of his wife went, similarly, to her kindred. If there were children but these died without issue, the possessions "proper" to their mother also passed to her "side and line." All this was in accordance with the rules *paterna paternis, materna maternis,* and *"propres ne remontent,"* that is, that the possessions "proper" to one line ought not to pass to persons belonging to ascendants of another line. In actual usage and interpretation, however, the rule *paterna paternis* was subject to serious variations, and the customs observed fell into five classes, similar to those of the *retrait lignager*—the right to redeem lineal property.

The *retrait lignager*

One of the spouses might be forced to sell the possessions "proper" to him or her. In that case, however, any one of the kindred of this spouse's "side and line" always had the right to invoke his kinship and recover the property from the purchaser, on reimbursing him for the price paid and any costs incurred in making the acquisition. This was the *retrait lignager,* which prevented possessions "proper" to a lineage from leaving it. It was still operative, and much in use, at the end of the 18th century. It existed in all the regions where customary law prevailed and also in ten "customs" of the area subject to written law (Marsan, Bayonne, Soule, Labourt, Bragerac, Acs, Saint-Sever, Bordeaux, and both the duchy and county of Burgundy); in the counties of Provence and Forcalquier after 1472; in two districts of Dauphiné (the *bailliage* of Briançon and the town of Romans); in Quercy and Rouergue, in the area under the jurisdiction of the *parlement* of Toulouse; and in those regions subject to written law which were under the jurisdiction of the *parlement* of Paris, in Mâconnais and the written-law part of Auvergne, but not in Lyonnais or in Forez.

The customs of Paris, Orléans, Calais, Artois, Hainault, Brittany, and others subjected to the *retrait lignager* only what were called *"héritages,"* that is, landed property, to the exclusion of offices, *rentes,* and the like. The customs of Sens, Meaux, Auxerre, Normandy, and other places made it applicable to all "real property." The custom of Sedan and some others applied it even to movable property if this was all that there was in an inheritance or if it was sold by the same contract as the "real property." The customs of Paris, Orléans, Calais, Artois, Hainault, Boulonnais, Ponthieu, Amiens, and some other places restricted the *retrait lignager* to possessions "proper" to a lineage, whereas those of Normandy, Touraine, Poitou, Angoumois, Saintonge, Bordeaux, Saint-Sever, and elsewhere extended it to embrace acquests as well.

The right of *retrait lignager* was accorded by the various customs to members of the seller's family, sometimes so remotely related as in the twentieth degree. In Franche-Comté, however, it extended only to the tenth degree, in Brittany to the ninth, in the area subject to the customs of Sens and Bourbonnais to the seventh, and in Nivernais to the sixth degree. The custom of Paris and most of the others confined the right to members of "the side and line," that is, it could be exercised by the family of the seller on the "side and line" from which descended the possessions which had been sold—those who were akin, at least collaterally, to the person by whom the *"héritage"* in question had been brought into the family. The customs of Metz and Sedan, however, extended the right to those of "side alone," that is, it could be exercised by *all* kindred of the seller, on the side from which the possessions had come, even if they did not belong to the line of the person who first acquired them. The customs called *souchères* (from *souche,* meaning "stock") allowed the right of *retrait* to be exercised only by the posterity of the person who had brought the property into the family; these were the customs of Bayonne, Melun, Montargis, Orléans, and Nivernais. The name of *coutumes de tronc commun* (from *tronc,* also meaning "stock") was given to those customs under which the only kindred allowed to exercise the right were those who shared with the seller a common stock down through which the inheritance had passed, as in Besançon. In the areas subject to the *coutumes de simple parenté* ("customs of mere kinships")—Burgundy, Franche-Comté, Luxembourg, and all those which brought acquests within the scope of the *retrait lignager*—all the seller's kindred without discrimination were allowed to exercise the right, even if they were not related to him on the side from which the inheritance had descended. In those customs, however, where, if there were no linear kindred to inherit, the possessions "proper" to the lineage were confiscated, the right to exercise *retrait* was limited to the kindred of the person who had brought these possessions into the family. In Touraine, Maine, Anjou, and Brittany, *retrait* could be effected by all these relatives, whether on the father's or on the mother's side. In Normandy, however, it was necessary to be one of the person's agnates, that is, related to him on his father's side, and the *parlement* of Rouen confirmed this requirement by its *arrêt* of 20 December 1655. In general, in the areas subject to the customs of Paris, Maine, Anjou, Touraine, Loudunois, etc., "whoever cannot inherit cannot exercise the right of *retrait.*"

Retrait became possible as soon as a deal had been fully concluded. In most of the custom areas this possibility remained open for a year; in the case of the customs of Paris, Orléans, and Normandy, for a year and a day; for three months under the customs of Auvergne and Bourbonnais; for sixty days in Berry; for forty days under many of the customs in the Lille region and in some towns in Normandy; for a month in Provence; for ten days in Briançonnais. Elsewhere the possibility of *retrait* remained open until the purchaser had "published the banns" of the contract; in Flemish-speaking Flanders this period was closed when the purchaser had made two or three such announcements at intervals of a fortnight.

Customary reservation

Similar in tendency to the *retrait lignager* was the "customary reservation." This meant those possessions, or portions thereof, which custom rendered inalienable and reserved for inheritors. Freedom to dispose of one's entire fortune, by way of gifts or by making a will, existed in the regions of written law and also in those subject to the customs of Lille, Douai, Hesdin, Arras, Bayonne, Luxembourg, Bassigny, and Burgundy. But, even there, "reservation" applied to the legitim—that portion guaranteed by law, to certain heirs-presumptive, of the possessions they would have inherited in entirety but for the liberalities indulged in by the deceased to their detriment. The legitim was also recognized by the majority of those customs which did not allow freedom to alienate, notably the custom of Paris (article 298). However, there was a difference between the legitim and "customary reservation." The legitim was taken exclusively from the possessions of the deceased, as a certain proportion of these. But no one could claim the right of "customary reservation" unless he accepted the status of heir, that is, without assuming his share of the deceased's liabilities as well as of his assets. The "reservation" safeguarded the retention of possessions within families, whereas the legitim merely ensured that "alimony" was paid to those individuals who had a right to it. A claimant to legitim had to deduct from his legitim all the gifts he had received from the deceased, these being regarded as so many "payments on account." An heir, however, made no deductions when he exercised his right of reservation. The right to legitim applied to the deceased's children and grandchildren; if there were none of these, to his ascendants; and, if there were none of these, then to his collateral relatives. According to the written law, when there were four children or less, the legitim amounted to one-third of what they would have had among them if their father had died intestate; if there were five or more, it was to be one-half of this sum. Some customs adopted a fixed proportion independent of the number of persons with a claim to legitim: the custom of Paris provided for one-half, that of Bordeaux for one-third. Other customs, such as those of Berry, Rheims, and Vermandois, followed the rules of the written law. The amount of legitim was to be determined, in relation to each variety of possessions making up an inheritance, in accordance with the custom or law of the region where the property in question was situated.

Only possessions "proper" to the lineage were subject to the "customary reservation" in the areas covered by the customs of Paris, Orléans, Senlis, Valois, Clermont-en-Beauvaisis, Dourdan, Montfort, Etampes, Nivernais, Mantes, Auxerre, Melun, Grand-Perche, Amiens, and Ponthieu, which fixed the proportion at four-fifths. The customs of Péronne, Chauny, Saint-Quentin and Ribémont distinguished between those possessions "proper" to a lineage that were feudal in character and those which were not, being *roturier* ("commoner"), and fixed a reservation of four-fifths in the case of the former and two-thirds for the latter. The customs of Montargis, Blois, and Dreux made the same distinction but increased the reservation applicable to nonfeudal possessions to three-quarters. The customs of Dreux, Châteauneuf, and Chartres added to this a right for the testator to bequeath one year's income from his "proper" possessions, and the customs of Boulonnais and Montreuil, which fixed the reservation at four-fifths of these possessions (whether feudal or not), added to this the right to alienate the income therefrom for three years, etc. Other customs—those of the castellany of Lille, of the Langle district in Artois, and of Metz, Marsal, Brussels, Nivelle, Tournai, and Tournésis—made reservation applicable to acquests as well as to "proper" possessions. Other customs went further, including movable property within the scope of reservation; for example, those of Auvergne and Bourbonnais, which fixed the reservation at three-quarters, those of Marche and Flemish Flanders, which fixed it at two-thirds, various customs in Flanders and the customs of Normandy and Labourt, which provided different treatment for "proper" possessions and acquests and distinguished between the latter and movable property. Finally, thirteen customs provided that, if there were no "proper" possessions, reservation was applicable to acquests and, in the absence of such, to movable property; these were the customs of Touraine, Anjou, Maine, Loudunois, Poitou, Angoumois, La Rochelle, Saintonge, Brittany, Bar-le-Duc, Sens, Abbeville, and Rue-en-Picardie. Some customs restricted the "customary reservation" in favor of heirs by blood to wills, codicils, and gifts at death, but others made it apply also to gifts *inter vivos*. Among the former were those of Paris and most of the customs which, like Paris, restricted reservation to "proper" possessions, but also in this category were Lille, Auvergne, Bourbonnais, Bar-le-Duc, Sens, etc. Among the latter were the customs of Lorraine, Saint-Michel, Rheims, Vermandois, Calais, Saint-Omer, Marche, Touraine, Anjou, Poitou, Angoumois, La Rochelle, Saintonge, and Brittany.

Primogeniture

The possessions "proper" to a lineage could grow. A family's acquests, if in the form of real property, became, on inheritance,
"proper" to the children and entered into the property of the lineage.
But, without decreasing in number, extent, or value, and even if they
actually grew, the possessions "proper" to a lineage could cease to be
adequate to support this lineage if they were fragmented among an
increasing number of heirs. The risk of this happening was great, for
common law provided for equal division of inherited property, with
all the children of one father having equal rights to his estate (see article
302 of the custom of Paris). The remedy was to concentrate the
"proper" possessions in the hands of one heir, who could then play the
leading role and win social advantages for the rest. To this end, in
regions where customary law obtained, lineages made use of an old
provision of feudal law prevailing there, relating to noble property, fiefs
or noble freeholds, the original purpose of which had been to guarantee
the service of the fief to the lord to whom it belonged: namely, the right
of primogeniture. For example, according to the custom of Paris, articles 15 and 16, the eldest son might, *par préciput,* select from a fief of
his inheritance, chosen by him, the château or principal manor house,
with all its dependencies—courtyard, moats, and bailey—and also the
enclosed area adjoining the manor house, to the amount of one arpent.
The privilege of annexing this piece of feudal land was sometimes
referred to as "the capon's flight." If the area taken was larger than an
arpent, the eldest son could keep the whole of it, provided he compensated his juniors for their loss. If the inheritance consisted of a single
fief made up merely of a château and its dependencies, the entire fief
passed to the eldest son, with provision that the younger children could
take from it their legitim or dowry, whether fixed by custom or decided
beforehand. The *préciput,* or preference legacy, of the eldest son included the right to present to the church livings attached to the fiefs. He
had the right to call himself *seigneur* of the fief, as though he were its
sole owner. This was the common law of France. As for the younger
children, they might call themselves *seigneurs en partie* of the fief in
question. Whether fiefs of rank—dukedoms, marquisates, counties,
and baronies—might be retained in their entirety by the eldest son, on
condition that he compensated his juniors for the share they would
have been able to claim, was a disputable question. In the 17th century
the jurists Loisel and Brodeaux, as, in the 16th, Tiraqueau and Chopin

(though the latter died in 1606, his work appeared in the second half of
the 16th century), held that it did. But by the end of the 18th century
this rule had fallen into desuetude in several custom areas, notably that
of Paris. The sole case in which the eldest son might keep a fief for
himself alone, compensating his juniors with money payments, was
when the inheritance included only this one fief and when there were
no other possessions included in the inheritance from which the juniors
could receive compensation (article 17). The jurists of the 18th century
generally held (repeating an opinion given by old Dumoulin) that this
applied to fiefs of rank just as it did to ordinary ones. The only exception was the fief of a duke-and-peer—by its very nature, since the office
was bound up with the land, and also by virtue of the edict of 1711.
When, included in one and the same inheritance, there were fiefs
situated in different custom areas, the eldest son took a *préciput* in
each of them. Besides this, the eldest son took a larger share than fell to
his juniors of the fiefs included in the inheritance. This was his
"privileged portion." If there were only two children entitled to inherit, he took two-thirds of the noble lands and the rights derived from
these; if there were more, the eldest son took half, the remainder being
divided among his juniors. On the other hand, the eldest son was liable
to pay the debts of the deceased only to the same extent as his
brothers; that is, the responsibility for these debts was divided equally.

The right of primogeniture descended in the direct line. Certain customs, however, such as those of Amiens, Poitou, Maine, and Angoumois, allowed it also in the case of the collateral line. The right of
primogeniture also applied to fiefs deriving from the mother. It was an
absolute right. Parents could neither alienate their fiefs to younger sons
nor order that they be shared out equally; judgments to this effect were
given by the Paris *parlement* on 14 March 1600, 8 March 1612, 26
March 1628, and 8 March 1638. But on 18 March 1749 that same *parlement,* basing itself this time not on the custom of Paris but on article
133 of the custom of Artois, ruled that two spouses domiciled at Hesdin
had been within their rights in stipulating, in the contracts whereby
they acquired a number of fiefs, that these were to be shared equally
among their children and, consequently, in providing in their will that
the fiefs in question be divided equally, to the detriment of their eldest
son's right of primogeniture. When a father reduced his eldest son's
inheritance to his legitim, this had, by the custom of Paris, to consist of
the *préciput* together with the "privileged portion" of the fiefs and
noble freeholds, plus half of his share in the rest of the property.

The custom of Paris allowed the right of primogeniture to commoners as well as nobles, where fiefs and noble freeholds were concerned, and this custom constituted common law for all the custom areas where no contrary arrangement was in force. However, the custom of Champagne, and some others too, restricted this benefit to nobles.

The customs differed greatly in the share they allotted to the eldest son. Those of Troyes and Auxerre restricted it to the *préciput,* without any additional "privileged portion." The custom of Grand-Perche, on the contrary, added to the *préciput* and the "privileged portion" all the chattels and personalty and, in the case of the noble eldest son, a *préciput* from the rest of the property. The customs of Brittany, Anjou, Touraine, and several other places reserved considerable privileges to eldest sons belonging to the nobility. The custom of Chauny accorded to girls the right of primogeniture in relation to fiefs if male children were lacking.

Fiduciary substitutions

Another means of keeping property within a lineage and ensuring that the head of the lineage had sufficient property to live in accordance with his rank and condition and so maintain the social standing of his family, was the use of *substitutions fidéicommissaires* (fiduciary substitutions). This involved "substituting" one person for another as recipient of an inheritance. It could be done through wills, codicils, or gifts at death. It was necessary to lay down an order of succession such that the person "substituted," after receiving the inheritance left by the person who nominated him, was obliged to preserve this inheritance for the benefit of those indicated as his successors, one after the other, from one degree of relationship to the next—either from one male person to the next male in line or from eldest son to eldest son. A fiduciary substitution could be created so as to continue forever in favor of a family, a line, or the male members only of a line. A man who had only daughters could save his property for his family by "substituting" a nephew, his brother's son, and this nephew's male descendants, to receive this property when he died, and providing, in the event that this nephew should have no male descendants, that the male descendants of another nephew, his brother's son, were to take over. A man who feared that an excessive number of descendants might break up the economic foundation of the lineage could "substitute" an eldest son and the eldest sons descending from him, or, in the event of a failure of this line, the eldest sons descending from a younger son.

This right of creating fiduciary substitution was allowed to anyone who had the right to make gifts *inter vivos* or at death. The aristocratic ordinance of 1629, drafted by chancellor de Marillac, the so-called "Code Michaud," in its article 125 forbade "rustic persons" to create these entails. This article was observed until 1747 by the *parlement* of Burgundy and down to 1789 so far as entails registered before 1747 were concerned. Rustic persons, of base condition, meant those who lived in the country and worked on the land. The category embraced tenant farmers and large-scale peasants, who in most cases chose to call themselves "merchants" if they worked someone else's land, themselves ploughing the fields attached to the farms they leased. *Not* included in this category, even though they lived in the country, were *gentilshommes* or *bourgeois* who cultivated their land, or had it cultivated for them, on the grounds that "the plough is not incompatible with a man's rank when he is working his own inheritance." Similarly excluded from this category were rural merchants who were engaged only in trade, cultivating their land by the hands of laborers who worked under their orders. A village craftsman was a "rustic": he was considered to be of base condition. However, urban craftsmen were not, even if they were illiterate, for in the king's "good towns" they were able to find counsel to explain to them the procedure of substitution, and three *arrêts* of the *parlement* of Dijon, dated 18 July 1658, 16 June 1665, and 3 January 1678 ruled that "craftsmen living in towns are allowed to create substitutions in their wills." The ordinance of 1747 (I,1) gave the right of creating substitutions indiscriminately to "all persons capable of disposing of their property, regardless of the their estate and condition." By the Ordinance of Orléans, 1560 (article 59), substitutions could not range further afield than two degrees of relationship, excluding the first-named inheritor. The Ordinance of Moulins, 1566 (article 57), limited previously made substitutions to the fourth degree of relationship, after the first-named inheritor. A faulty reading of this ordinance led to the belief that it fixed this limit for *future* substitutions as well. This was how it was understood by the *parlements* of Toulouse and Bordeaux and, at first, by the Paris *parlement,* which, however, soon dropped this interpretation. The *parlements* of Grenoble, Aix, and Dijon interpreted the ordinance correctly, as limiting substitutions created after 1560 to two degrees of relationship after the first-named inheritor. The ordinance of 1747 confirmed this interpretation as applicable throughout the realm. Nevertheless, in the areas subject to the *parlements* of

Besançon and Pau and to the *conseils supérieurs* of Roussillon and Alsace, all entails were allowed to go on forever.

Substitution had to be "published in court on a day when hearings are being held, and registered at the seat of royal authority nearest to the residences of those who have created the said substitutions." This was provided by an edict of Henri II, May 1553, by the Ordinance of Moulins, 1566 (article 57), and by the declaration of 17 November 1690. However, the Ordinance of Moulins was not observed by the *parlements* of Toulouse, Bordeaux, and Aix or by the *conseil supérieur* of Alsace. Louis XIV therefore issued the declaration of 18 January 1712, which confirmed the need to publish and to register entails and added that this must be done "both in the seat of royal authority nearest to the residence of the creator of the substitution and in that nearest to the property entailed." The ordinance of August 1747 made it clear that this meant "the *bailliage, sénéchaussée,* or other seat of royal authority immediately under the jurisdiction of our *parlements* or *conseils supérieurs."* The *parlement* of Grenoble had not observed the Ordinance of Moulins. Though it registered, on 27 February 1691, the declaration of 17 November 1690, it ruled that substitutions created before 27 February 1691 did not have to be either published or registered. By a declaration of 22 April 1739 the king ordered that all substitutions, old and new, created in the province of Dauphiné must be published and registered. Louis XIV had made the same decision in an edict of July 1707 applying to Franche-Comté, which was confirmed by a declaration of 14 September 1721. In the French Netherlands the *placard* of 6 December 1586 and article 15 of the perpetual edict of the archdukes Albrecht and Isabella (similar to the Ordinance of Moulins) were no better observed. The provincial council of Artois sought to revive them by means of a regulation introduced on 5 October 1661, but only for substitutions created after that date. The Paris *parlement,* however, declared substitutions created in Artois before 5 October 1661 null and void because they had not been registered; this it did in several *arrêts,* beginning with one dated 30 April 1683—but also issued some *arrêts* to the contrary. The declaration of 18 January 1712 gave fixity to the law. A pronouncement by the Council of Artois, 31 January 1715, and two *arrêts* of the Paris *parlement,* dated 4 July 1726 and 16 May 1743, confirmed it: all substitutions, old and new alike, must be published and registered in Artois and French Flanders, just as in the rest of the kingdom.

Freedom to create substitutions was subject to a variety of restrictions in ten custom areas: Bourbonnais, Marche, Auvergne, Sedan, Montargis, Bassigny, Nivernais, Brittany, Normandy, and Hainault. In Brittany only substitutions authorized by royal letters patent and registered by the *parlement* of Rennes were allowed validity.

In some French provinces which had formerly been under Spanish rule—Flanders, Artois, Cambrésis, and Franche-Comté—the majorat had been in use, and substitutions were created under this title. "It is a gradual, successive, perpetual, and indivisible entail created by the testator in order to preserve the name, arms, and splendor of his house and destined forever for the benefit of the eldest sons of the testator's family." The "regular" form of majorat appointed as trustee the eldest person nearest related to the last possessor of the property, following the order of legitimate succession. The *majorat salutaire* appointed as trustee the eldest member of the family, whoever he might be, even if he were *not* the nearest relative of the last possessor. Unless a special arrangement was made, the majorat was permanent and included all the substitutions that might be needed, even though they were not explicitly mentioned. French jurisprudence decided that, in future, no majorat might be created without royal authority and that every majorat already in being must be subject to the same rules as other forms of entail.

Parage and *frérage*

Connected with the desire to preserve the patrimony of a lineage, avoiding the detrimental results of division among inheritors, were two surviving institutions called *parage* and *frérage*. By *parage,* in the case of any fief which did not fall completely within his *préciput* or his "privileged portion," the eldest son did homage to the *seigneur* of this fief for the whole of it and was solely responsible for it to him, even though each of his juniors received a share of the fief. The eldest son was the *chef parageur,* or *miroir de fief.* By *frérage,* the eldest son did homage to the lord for the whole of the fief, but the share given to each junior inheritor was subinfeudated to the eldest son, and each of them had to do homage to him. These institutions became increasingly rare. They were still to be found, however, in the Paris region, in Beauvaisis, Normandy, Champagne, Hainault, Franche-Comté, Touraine, Anjou, Poitou, Maine, and Loudunois, and a few cases are to be observed even on the eve of the Revolution.

Customary laws of property
in southern France

The reader will be tempted to object that all the institutions described as testifying to the existence and power of lineages are peculiar to the north of France, for the jurists of the 17th and, more especially, those of the 18th century have long accustomed historians to making a sharp distinction between the areas subject to customary law and those where written law prevailed. After the 17th century, writers do not mention the customs which obtained in the south of France. Actually, even the custom of Toulouse was still being observed, in part, in 1789. The triumph of Roman law was not ensured until after 1670, the written law was often a compromise between customs and Roman law, and, if we turn away from the Mediterranean lands, from the ancient Gallia Narbonensis, Provence, the Comtat, and Languedoc, to look at the southwest of France, we find that there customs were surviving and being observed, with the same institutions governing inheritance as in the regions of customary law: the *paterna paternis* rule, the reserving of "proper" possessions, unequal shares, exclusion of dowered girls, the *retrait lignager*—everything that might serve to ensure the preservation of property, especially ancestral property, within the same lineage. Evidence of this is found throughout Gascony, Guyenne, Saintonge, Quercy, and Rouergue, at Bayonne, in Béarn, and in the valleys of the western Pyrenees. Some of these customs, moreover, had been formulated in the 16th century: namely, those of Bordeaux, Marsan, Dax, Saint-Sever, Labourt, and Soule.

The *retrait lignager* survived in those parts right down to the Revolution. The records of notaries of the region of Cahors and Montauban reveal very many deeds that mention exercise of the right of *retrait,* especially in the final years of the *ancien régime*. Generally speaking, the *cahiers* of 1789 called for abolition of the *retrait lignager,* but those of the third estate of Agenais and those of Lauzerte and Puy-l'Evêque in Quercy favored retention of the *retrait* for the direct line of succession.

The domestic communities

Above all a society of lineages, French society was also a society composed of domestic communities, although these were steadily declining and giving place to the conjugal family, the *ménage*.

Tacit communities

In the 17th century the jurist Papon, in his *Arrêts notables,* published in 1610,[6] distinguished carefully between two extreme types: the tacit community (*communauté tacite ou taisible*) of family life, and the conventional associations. He expressed his idea like this:

> The one called tacit is formed and contracted when two adult brothers, cousins, or other related persons, having the use of their rights and not being in the power of anyone else, have remained together for a year and a day, meeting their expenses jointly, sharing pot, salt, fire, and expenses, keeping only one table, without rendering accounts to each other, and sharing their gains and losses . . . and then they are regarded as having acquired community of all chattels and *héritages* that shall have been acquired by them and by each of them during such common life and association . . . We have many such communities in Berry and Nivernais, mainly in the houses of the Mages [village elders] which, in accordance with the constitution of these regions, all consist of groupings of several persons to form a community. In these communities the head is called "master." He is usually the eldest . . . The contracts made by these masters are binding on the other members of the community, provided they are made for the advantage and concerns of the community . . . and such contracts are enforceable against members of the community who are declared to be such, equally as against the masters of the community; payments made to the master are valid, and the debtor is discharged. The master may also act alone in the name of the community, and as a master and author thereof, without being given power of attorney by his fellow members, in matters concerning the community . . . There is another sort of community, called an explicit community (*communauté expresse*), which is formed between kindred and strangers, as between merchants for purposes of trade or tenancy, and which should therefore be given the form of a written contract, owing to the provision of article 54 of the Ordinance of Moulins, although in the eyes of the law such contracts are regarded as complete *sine scriptura cum solo consensu* . . .

Papon indicated precisely the characteristic features of the tacit community. It is a community of natural kinship but one which could also be formed by adoption or *affrèrement*—that is, when kindred or strangers resolve to pool their possessions and live together "like brothers." It is a community which is formed by living together for a year and a day. It involves pooling possessions so as to make a common stock, which may include houses and lands belonging to the family and also common chattels and acquisitions. The common property and common interests are in principle looked after collectively but in fact are managed by a representative, a master, who may be the father, a son, a brother, the father-in-law, or an elected "master," as in Nivernais. The master's authority is not patriarchal, for within the community each head of a family exercises authority over his own wife and children. The members of the community live together in the same home, at common expense, in a house called in Valais *hospice,* in Auvergne *communauté,* in Nivernais *maison,* in Burgundy *meix,* in Bresse *auberge.* It is "a truly integral alliance... formed in order the better to resist the dangers and bear the burdens of a hard life" (J. Gaudemet).

Tacit communities, which seem to have reached their highest point of development in France in the 14th and 15th centuries, were widespread in Franche-Comté, Burgundy, Nivernais, Berry, Orléanais, Auvergne, Limousin, Périgord, Quercy, and Guyenne. They were not unknown in Provence, in Roussillon, or even in the Paris region. In the 16th century some customs still took account of them: the old custom of Perche (1505), the old and new customs of Poitou, the old and new customs of Bourbonnais, the custom of Nivernais (1534), the old and new customs of Sens, the custom of Chaumont-en-Bassigny (1509), the custom of Montargis (1531), and the old custom of Orléans (1509), though not in the new one (1583). Some customs required an expression of will to establish the community, that is, they misunderstood the essential nature of tacit communities and transformed a natural grouping into a conventional one. This was the case with the old and new customs of Touraine (1507 and 1559), those of Loudunois, Maine, and Anjou, the old custom of Bourges, the new custom of Mantes (1556), and those of Melun, Auxerre, Bar, and Bassigny. Actually, during the 17th and 18th centuries tacit communities declined in number and importance. They survived above all in regions with enclosed and irregular fields—places like Nivernais, Limousin, and Poitou, characterized by a fragile economy, frequent revolts and, above all, by insecurity. But they gradually declined. Community between spouses did not, in principle, exist there, but this conjugal community gradually emerged. In Nivernais in the 16th century, if a *ménage* left the community, it lost what it had brought into the community and had no claim to a share of the common property. In the 17th century, if a *ménage* left the community, the woman was allowed to take her dowry with her and to retain a right to inherit from her parents. This tendency was more advanced in the towns than in the countryside. According to the custom of Nivernais, 1534, the conjugal community was predominant among the urban population, though it was only beginning to make its way among the country folk.

Tacit communities might embrace many persons: grandfather, father, son, grandson, uncles, cousins, with their spouses, and strangers who had become "brothers," with theirs. They might be confined to a grandfather with his sons and grandsons and their wives. They might embrace merely a group of brothers, with their wives and children, who, having formed a community with their father, had continued it after his death. Where tacit communities survived, it would be interesting to know what proportion of the inhabitants they included, in how many villages they existed, how many of them there were in a given village, and what proportion of the villagers were members of them.

Other types of community

Other types of communities also survived. There were communities formed between a new *ménage* and their parents: the wife brought her dowry into the household of her new family, the husband's father gave up part of his property to the young couple but reserved his right to enjoy the benefit of this and stipulated that the new *ménage* must remain in community with him and under his authority; or else, contrariwise, and more rarely, the husband went to live with his parents-in-law and gifts made to the couple were accompanied by reservations of usufruct and requirements of community in favor of the bride's parents.

Right to the end there lasted communities that were continued between a surviving member of a *ménage* and his children and sometimes, if this survivor remarried, together with the second spouse, who might have children from a previous marriage. Numerous customs accepted this form of community: those of Bourges, Châlons, Senlis, Bassigny, Paris, Bouillon, Etampes, Dourdan, Montfort-l'Amaury, Mantes, Melun, Sens, Auxerre, Meaux, Troyes, Maine, Orléans, Poitou, Montargis, Sedan, and others.

The decline of the communities

During the 18th century, however, all these types of community were on the downgrade. Family communities were decaying fast in most regions. They barely survived except in the form of the continued community formed by the surviving partner of a marriage with the children of the marriage. Jurists had, in general, become hostile to these communities. Pothier deals with them only in an appendix to his *Traité de la société* (1765). He discusses the continued communities, the only form of such communities which he is still willing to recognize. He sees in them, moreover, "a kind of quasi-contract," for he no longer has any feeling for the nature of communities. He emphasizes all their disadvantages, being deeply inimical to them. At Clamecy, family groupings seem to have almost vanished during the 18th century. In Paris, a partial examination of the records of six notaries, between 1650 and 1780, revealed that out of 400 deeds, only 8 referred to cases of joint ownership, and 2 concerned communities continued with the children after the death of one parent; one of these was a "composite community," involving a widow who had remarried, and was due to the lack of an inventory of property at the death of her first husband, so that this community was a punishment for negligence. The six other cases concerned temporary joint ownership of inheritances, due to the presence in the common stock of a piece of real property difficult to allot. They mainly involved craftsmen. There is no instance of either a tacit community or an *affrèrement,* that is, a contract concluded between "brothers," whether kindred or strangers, who decide to pool their possessions and live together "like brothers," or of a *compagnie d'héritage,* a community formed by inheritors around a particular heritage: rights of justice, a mill, an oven, a wine press, a fishery.

Instead of the community, what becomes predominant is joint ownership, as provided for by Roman law, between legatees of a single piece of property or coheirs of one inheritance or, by agreement between married persons, associates, or members of a chapter, commune, or trade guild. The reciprocal obligations are no longer based on a bond of brotherhood and mutual affection but on the idea of quasi-contract and personal contributions (Domat, *Lois civiles,* II, V, 2); each co-owner possesses a proportion of the undivided inheritance which he can alienate freely, and the common property must be divided whenever one of the co-owners requires this to be done; gains are shared out in proportion to each person's share in the property, and each person is responsible to the others for any damage or loss he may cause. There is thus a contrast between the tacit community and joint ownership.

Other forms of community seem to have been more numerous. Frequently, marriage contracts stipulate that the young couple are to remain for a year, or for two years, with the bride's parents and are to be maintained in their home during this period, sometimes in accordance with their rank, with a manservant, a maidservant, a carriage, two horses, and a coachman. In such cases, their temporary maintenance forms part of the bride's dowry.

In other cases, parents and their married children, along with *their* children, live together in one household, without our knowing what their financial arrangements were. In principle, so long as the children have not grown up and married and continue to live in their father's home, they form a community with their parents. Once they are grown up and married, it seems that, in the eyes of the law and the courts, the community no longer exists. From that standpoint the young *ménages* are independent, masters of their own property, and the husband in each of them retains his full legal authority. But there does exist here a common life, a social community, which is important. The family groups three generations under one roof. It is, in fact, an *enlarged family*. This social group in many cases ensures, in practice, the authority of the grandfather and the indefinite continuity of the family and its tradition; for the son continues to live with his own original family, his *nuclear family* (father, mother, and children), which is the family in which he was brought up and given his direction in life, but he lives there with his wife and children, his procreative family, which is the family that will guide the development of *his* children. In this way a greater continuity is ensured and also a greater degree of cooperation among the members of the family.

With the enlarged family, however, we are moving from the community to the *ménage*.

The ménage *breaks free from the lineage*

Thus, in the 17th and 18th centuries a change was completed which had begun in the 13th: the transition from the family community to the conjugal family or *ménage,* just as, to a greater and greater extent, the *ménage* was emerging and liberating itself from the lineage. The reason for this gradual change was, seemingly, in the first place, the growth in the power of the public authority, which favored the emancipation of the individual. The latter tried, as soon as he could, to escape from family constraints. He preferred the remote authority of the state, which left him greater freedom, to the too close discipline of the family. The revival and advance of Roman law, with its highly individualistic emphasis, favored the breakup of family communities. The Church gave its backing to Roman law, so as to make possible the alienation of property, freed from communal ownership, to the advantage of churches and monasteries. Merchants were restive under collective obligations, and their needs harmonized with the individualism of Roman law. Finally, in the Age of Enlightenment, there developed, under the influence of Roman law and Roman Stoicism, an individualist philosophy, one which had unbounded respect for the rights of private property. Consequently, lineage and community steadily declined in favor of *ménage*. The Civil Code was careful of equality between inheritors, and it regulated divisions of property with meticulous care. It knew not the tacit community, the continued community, or the community of inheritors. It declared that "no one can be forced to remain under a regime of joint ownership" (article 815). Co-ownership was no longer anything but an incidental provision in article 2205. Individualism had triumphed.

The *ménage*

The 17th and 18th centuries saw the gradual triumph of the *ménage*—the conjugal or nuclear family—which gradually separated out from the communities and lineages. Strictly speaking, the term *ménage* can signify several types of family, which, though similar, are not identical. In the first place, it signifies the conjugal (or nuclear) family, consisting of father, mother, and children and usually, in this period, domestics as well, even if only a maidservant. But the term can also signify the enlarged family, consisting of a grandfather, together with some of his sons and their wives, some of his daughters and their husbands, the grandchildren, sometimes uncles, aunts, and cousins, and *domestiques*. The latter include all who, without being blood relations of the head of the family, live in his house in various capacities—as "clients" (in the Roman sense), secretaries, paid companions, manservants, and maidservants. The term *ménage* can be replaced by *maison*, though this applies, above all, in the case of nobles or those who sought to imitate them.

The *ménage* already seemed to be the essential cell of the lineage in the second half of the 16th century. Jean Bodin wrote in his *Traité de la République* in 1576: "A commonwealth may be defined as the rightly ordered government of a number of families (*ménages*), and of those things which are their common concern, by a sovereign power" (book I, chapter 1), and, later: "A family (*ménage*) may be defined as the right ordering of a group of persons owing obedience to a head of a household, and of those interests which are their proper concern." It is notable that this great observer, political thinker, and sociologist speaks of the *ménage,* not of the lineage. The *ménage* already seems to him to be the more important of the two.

The omnipotence of the paterfamilias

An essential feature of the *ménage* is the increasing power of the paterfamilias over his wife and children, and in practice also over his *domestiques,* as the 17th and 18th centuries advanced. This development kept pace with the growth in the power of the king. It originated in the world of "the gown," the magistrates and all those who revolved around them—advocates, attorneys, notaries, tipstaffs, bailiffs. It was enforced by the practice of the courts. Then the state turned it to account, through the law, for it was in the king's interest to be able to wield absolute authority over the heads of families who were themselves all-powerful in imposing their will, and so the will of the state. This prepared the way for the situation consecrated by the Civil Code and the administrative reorganization and carried out under the Consulate: an omnipotent state reigning over a large number of authoritarian heads of families who act as its instruments.

The *ménage* fulfilled basic social functions: the reproduction of society through the procreation of children; the continuity of society, through their upbringing; the maintenance of life, through economic cooperation, even if only in the form of the bride's dowry, put to use by the husband; mutual aid, moral and spiritual, between the spouses; satisfaction of needs for affection and tenderness.

The importance of the nuclear family was often reinforced by change in place of residence. The young *ménage* ceased immediately, or after a certain time, to live with the parents, and established a new home, where the spouses, and especially their children, were able to escape to some extent from the influence of the family. This influence still remained great, but a move to a new place of residence nevertheless served as a factor favoring relative autonomy and change. In the *ménage* it was the husband and paterfamilias who was to wield complete authority over his wife and children, like the king over his subjects in the state. Jean Bodin affirmed this: "The government of all commonwealths, colleges, corporate bodies, or households whatsoever, rests on the right to command on one side and the obligation to obey on the other" (I, 3). "The well-ordered family is a true image of the commonwealth, and domestic authority is comparable with sovereign authority. It follows that the right ordering of the household is the model of right order in the commonwealth" (I, 2).

In the "commonwealth," public authority is entrusted to the sovereign, who lays down the law and is personified in the magistrates, who themselves obey the law and have rule over other magistrates and over private persons. "The private right to command is vested in heads of households (*ménages*) or in the collective authority which colleges and corporate bodies exercise over their particular members." Authority in *ménages* is exercised by the husband over his wife, the father over his children, the master of the house over those who serve him.

King Louis XIII echoes this view in his declaration of 26 November 1639:

> Whereas marriages are the seed plot of states, the source and origin of civil society, and the basis of the families which make up commonwealths, which serve to form their organization, and in which the natural reverence of children toward their parents is the bond of legitimate obedience of subjects in relation to their sovereign: therefore the kings our predecessors have considered it worthy of their concern to make laws to govern their public ordering, their outward decency, their worthiness and dignity.[7]

In principle, Christianity proclaims the equality of man and woman (Saint Paul, 1 Cor. 7; Lactantius; Saint Jerome).[8] *Una lex de mulieribus et viris.* In the 13th century every woman was considered capable in law almost on a level with a man. She was *dame de soi* ("her own woman"). She could manage her fortune, alienate her property, enter into undertakings on her own behalf and that of others by giving sureties, and go to court to maintain her rights. She could even hold a fief and take her seat in a feudal court. She could stand in for her husband when he was absent or ill, and her legal instruments were recognized as valid. She could operate freely as a public trader, her husband's authorization being presumed to be given if he said nothing against it.

On the other hand, Saint Paul proclaims the husband "the head of the wife" (Ephesians 5:22–23); it is necessary, where two people are living together, that one of them shall have the last word; and, finally, Roman law, convinced of the frailty and frivolity of woman, continually tended to whittle away her rights. Very soon, consequently, when a woman married, she came under the authority of her husband, who was the head of their association or community. The husband chose the conjugal domicile, and the wife had to follow him there. He could compel her to look after him and his *ménage*. He could compel her to engage in gainful work of an honorable kind, the gains from it to come to him. He could inflict corporal punishment on her, provided this was not severe. The husband administered both his own property and his wife's. He had full power over the chattels she brought with her, though he was only the usufructuary of her real property and needed to get his wife's agreement before alienating it. The wife could authorize no legal instrument without her husband's permission, neither an alienation, nor the incurring of a liability, nor a gift, nor the initiation of proceedings in court; for all these she needed her husband's agreement, explicit or tacit, depending on the given case. When a husband was away or was prevented from acting, his wife had to get permission from a judge before she could act in his stead. A husband's authorization of his wife's legal instruments had to be given in a formal way, with express consent and special approval at the time when the instrument was authorized by his wife.

The paterfamilias had the right to correct his children. He could call upon the courts for support by having a rebellious son imprisoned. He could exclude him from the family, driving him from the house. However, he had no right to kill him. Infanticide and abortion were punishable by banishment. The father was not allowed to inflict correction in too harsh a form; he could himself be punished by the courts for doing so. He had no right to sell his children, even in cases of extreme poverty, but could only hire out their services. On the other hand, in the regions where customary law prevailed, he was responsible for any crimes and misdemeanors committed by his sons.

The paterfamilias had some right to the property of his children, so long as they resided with their parents, legally forming a single community with them. However, this right was limited, for the customs allowed children to retain ownership of inheritances, gifts, and legacies that came their way. And the father was obliged to use the family's patrimony in the interest of his children.

All this, which was established fact as early as the beginning of the 16th century, seemed insufficient. With the advance of Roman law and the magistracy's rise in the social hierarchy, three restrictions which canon law imposed upon paternal authority became odious to fathers of families, namely: the freedom of children to enter religious orders at the age of fourteen without their father's consent; the freedom of sons to marry as they pleased at the age of fourteen; and the freedom of daughters who had been abducted to marry their abductor. In general, any restriction on their power was becoming hateful to these men. Jean Bodin demanded that fathers of families be given power of life and death over their children. Pierre Ayrault, *lieutenant criminel* in the presidial court of Angers, in his treatise *De la puissance paternelle* (written in 1587 and included in the 1615 edition of his works) said: "Domestic discipline, in which the father is in the position of a dictator, requires that all who are under him—wife, child, servant —shall depend upon what he says, that none shall have any will but that of the father and master of the house."[9] In the works of Guillaume du Vair, keeper of the seals, which were published in 1636, we find: "We must look upon our fathers as gods upon earth, who are given to us not only to furnish us with life but also to make life blessed for us through good upbringing and wise instruction." Thus, a father was to be regarded like the king, as an earthly god, and, like the king, he should wield absolute power, comparable to that of God.

For these magistrates, absolute paternal authority had been instituted by God. It was based on the fourth of his commandments. Furthermore, God had willed that parents should cooperate with him in the engendering of children. God gave the soul and the parents the body, with its passions and affections, and so they were "visible gods." A father was always to be revered and thanked, even if he was a bad father. Most fathers, though, provided upbringing and possessions, and the duty of gratitude obliged children to obey them. The example of Jesus Christ is binding upon children. What proves that Jesus Christ is God the Son is his obedience to God the Father, to the very point of death. Natural law also requires total obedience by children, because their parents, in giving them life, have furnished them with the greatest and finest of gifts. Public necessity, finally, justifies paternal absolutism. The "commonwealth" is an assemblage of private households. If the father of a family is obeyed, he provides the "commonwealth" and the sovereign with citizens who are docile and habituated to living peaceably and respecting the rights of others. Otherwise, the children, allowed to become used to doing as they please, grow up into wasteful and ruinous citizens, debauchees, murderers, rebels, and sedition-mongers, and the "commonwealth" is doomed to destruction.

The magistrates succeeded in convincing most of the people of France. The national *mores* upheld the authority of the paterfamilias. Stage comedies provide evidence of this, since in them a paterfamilias is hoaxed by his daughter, and by the lover who seeks her hand, only by their using forms which acknowledge absolute paternal authority and alliance between families. Consider *Monsieur de Pourceaugnac* (act 2, scene 7). Eraste, who wants to get permission to marry Julie from her recalcitrant father Oronte, pretends to withdraw: "Farewell, Sir. I had all the desire in the world to ally myself with you; I did all in my power to obtain that honor; but I have proved unlucky, and you have not judged me worthy of this favor. That will not prevent me from preserving the sentiments of esteem and veneration for you to which your person binds me; and if I have not succeeded in becoming your son-in-law, at least I shall forever be your servant." Oronte, touched by this, says he will let him marry Julie. In order to fix her father more firmly in the decision he has taken, Julie pretends to jib at it. Oronte then says, in his capacity as sovereign father: "It is for her to obey me, and I know how to show that I am master." Eraste, acting the obedient son-in-law, loyal and devoted, says to Julie: "Do not suppose that it is for love of you that I take your hand in mine. It is only *Monsieur votre père* that I love, and it is he that I am marrying."

Jurisprudence is no less significant. The paterfamilias exercises his rights of custody and correction and his rights over the children's property with the support of public authority and under its supervision. He exercises them even over sons who are more than thirty years old. He can request the detention of his sons under the age of twenty-five, given the permission of the lieutenant of police in Paris. By the *arrêts* of 9 March 1673 and 26 October 1697 the guilty youngsters could be sent to the prison of Villeneuve-sur-Gravois, where the Lazarists taught the prisoners and looked after them. By the ordinance of 20 April 1684, issued for the benefit of the craftsmen and poor people living in the town and suburbs of Paris, if a complaint was lodged by a father, mother, or guardian with the office of the Hôpital Général, against boys or girls less than twenty-five years old who did not want to work and led wanton lives, the boys could be locked up at Bicêtre and the girls in the Salpêtrière. A father could, moreover, always secure the detention of a son or daughter by obtaining a *lettre de cachet* from the king.

The Ordinance of Compiègne, 15 July 1763, authorized the deportation to the island of La Désirade (in the West Indies) of "young persons of family . . . who have fallen into ways of disorderly conduct likely to endanger the honor and tranquillity of their families, or for which they have come into the hands of the police, without, however, having been guilty of crimes for which the laws provide punishment," this deportation to be carried out if their parents applied to the secretary of state for war and for the navy.

The rights of parents to have custody of their children was strengthened. By an *arrêt* of 7 May 1653, François Brun obtained letters of emancipation and had them ratified by the *sénéchaussée* of Poitiers despite his father's opposition. His father appealed, and the Paris *parlement* pronounced that the son not be entitled to these letters and ordered him to go back to the family home.

Serious insults to one's parents were treated as a public crime. Judges took action on their initiative against those accused of it, though respecting paternal authority. In 1648 a son was condemned on this charge. The father appealed against the sentence to the *parlement* of Paris, claiming that he alone had the right to bring such a charge. Honoring the father's authority, the *parlement* annulled the sentence, but it nevertheless ordered the son to pay a fine and to apologize to his father publicly, on his knees, and warned him that if he offended in this way again he would incur the penalty of death.

Mores and jurisprudence even retained in existence a kind of domestic jurisdiction. In Dauphiné in 1663 a son was sentenced by his father, with the rest of the family's approval, to twenty years in the galleys for having tried to kill him. The king's *procureur général* before the *parlement* of Grenoble gave notice of appeal *a minima*. The *parlement* sentenced the son to the galleys for life. As a rule parricide was punished by death.

While all jurisprudence and legislation concerning marriage had the aim and result of preserving the lineage, they also had the aim and result of strengthening paternal authority in the lineage. The ordinances of Orléans 1560 (article 19), Moulins (article 55), and Blois, 1579 (article 18) forbade fathers, mothers, guardians, and kindred to allow their children or wards to become monks or nuns before the age of twenty-five in the case of boys, and twenty, in that of girls, a prohibition that had been asked for by the fathers of families. The edict of March 1768 changed the age limits to twenty and eighteen, respectively. The courts always annulled entry into a religious order by anyone under the age of sixteen; but where persons between sixteen and twenty-five years old were concerned, the judges took account of the circumstances, since the vows, once spoken, were canonically valid.

The *maison*

It was the concern of fathers of families to ensure the continuity of generations and of family tradition. The case of the state councilor René de Voyer d'Argenson (1596–1651) is instructive. His great preoccupation was to give his eldest son "the means of keeping up name and house (*maison*) by a just design of a good father of a family who wishes to preserve them so that God may be served by those who follow him in the same way as He has been served by those who preceded him, and who loved God and their kings without ever departing from good religion and the obedience due from all true Christians."[10] D'Argenson concerned himself, therefore, with three matters: property, careers, family tradition. As regards property: "It is enough for a father to have the wherewithal to live simply and to leave his children the means of living in the same way, while serving God according to their conditions." A will of 1651 shows that the fortune that d'Argenson needed in order to "live simply" amounted to at least 536,100 livres (not counting the silver plate), half of this, if not more, being made up of lands, *seigneuries,* and houses, most of the lands and *seigneuries* being long-standing possessions "proper" to his family. "The most effective way to preserve *maisons* is to promote the advantages of the eldest son." René d'Argenson, therefore left his eldest son, René II de Voyer d'Argenson, property to the value of 300,000 livres, including the old family *seigneuries* in Touraine and Blésois.

The second means of sustaining the name and honor of the family consisted in the careers of its members and the dignities they acquired. D'Argenson considered that the father of a family was sole judge of these and solely responsible for them:

Although a father is not obliged to account for what he has done
for his children, of whom he must dispose, and their estate with
them, in the sight of God, just as he thinks best, after having considered their temperaments and inclinations and whatever their
callings may be, I have thought it appropriate to leave behind in
writing the motive that inspired me to give early to my eldest son
that which might be his, without waiting to leave it at my death.

The services of fathers being regarded as a good reason why the king
should shower favors upon sons, who were supposed, moreover, to be
impregnated with the good examples set by their sires, René d'Argenson succeeded in obtaining for René II, born in 1624, the office of
counselor in the *parlement* of Normandy in 1642, when this son of his
was only eighteen. He arranged for the young man to accompany him
on his missions as intendant for justice, administration, and finance in
Angoumois, Aunis, and Saintonge in 1644, as commissioner for the
pacification of Guyenne and Bordeaux in 1649, and as ambassador to
Venice in 1651. He secured for him a commission as subdelegate to his
father in the *élections* of Saintes and Cognac in 1644, a function which
he exercised at the age of twenty, and the intendancy of the *élections* of
Saintes and Cognac, in his father's absence, in 1646, when he was
twenty-two. In 1649, at twenty-five, René II became master of requests
and councilor of state. In 1651, at twenty-seven, he was councilor of
state in ordinary and took his father's place as ambassador to Venice.

But the other members of the family were not overlooked. René II
had received the major part of his father's property with the charge "to
help his brothers, as I order him to do," imitating his uncle, René I's
younger brother, Claude de Voyer, *écuyer, seigneur* of Chartres,
priest, and chaplain in ordinary to the king, "who let me enjoy the
entire property of my *maison,* so as to sustain its honor," and in 1659
gave his nephew René II the sum of 99,970 livres, which he had acquired during his lifetime. René I advanced the fortunes of this younger
brother of his, while making use of his help. Claude de Voyer went with
him, probably into Catalonia in 1641, certainly to the intendancy of
Poitou in 1644, and became prior of Saint-Nicolas de Poitiers in 1648
and abbot of Chartres-lès-Cognac. René I's second son, Louis de
Voyer, churchman, prior, and abbot, became provost of Saint-Laurent
de Parthenay in 1651, when his uncle Claude resigned. René I's third
son, Pierre de Voyer, a gentleman in ordinary of the king's bedchamber, received the office, which was an old one in his family, of

grand bailli of the district and duchy of Touraine. It was a young cousin of René I's, René de Paulmy, *chevalier* and *seigneur* of Dorée, who acted as his second-in-command in the intendancy of the army in Italy in November 1638 and helped him with the victualing of the troops and of the fleet of Catalonia, taking over from him on 12 November 1641. Everything proceeded as though the family was to some extent a sort of clique, the members of which were bound together by relations of protection and service in the conquest and exercise of public functions.

The third means of sustaining the name and the *maison* was preserving a good tradition in it. The d'Argensons had a tradition of loyalty to the king and to the Catholic Church. This tradition René I strove to uphold, through the way he brought up his children and through his maxims and instructions. He wrote in his will:

> I affirm that I shall spend what remains of my life in that same faith in Jesus Christ and his Catholic, Apostolic, and Roman Church in which I was baptized, and I repudiate all contrary views—in particular those which are nowadays called "Jansenist" and which have been condemned by the sacred councils and by the popes. I pray my children, and, so far as in me lies, I enjoin them, in God's name, never to give ear to any new or curious proposition prejudicial to the purity and simplicity of the true Catholic, Apostolic, and Roman religion, outside of which there is no salvation.

René II followed in his father's footsteps. His father had been a very active member of the Compagnie du Saint-Sacrement. René II joined its ranks in 1656 and wrote its *Annales*. Father Rapin testifies to René II's attachment to his father's tradition in connection with the visit paid to him, as ambassador in Venice, by Desmares and Manessier, the Jansenist delegates, on their return from Rome:

> It was in vain that they tried to win him over and bring him into their party. He was too clever to let himself be caught by their tricks and was too set against their doctrine, for family reasons, to listen to them. I learned from his own lips that besides the aversion he felt for these 'innovations,' by the will of the count, his father, to whom he had succeeded in this embassy, he had been expressly ordered to hold aloof from the opinions of the bishop of Ypres.

René II obeyed his father's orders and kept up the tradition of his *maison*.

The term *maison* often indicates a branch of a lineage. Very often,

too, however, it signifies all who are living under one roof with the
father of a family: in the first place his wife, and perhaps all those who
are linked with him by blood—children and grandchildren, brothers,
sisters, nephews, nieces, and cousins—or who are allied to him by
marriage—the husbands and wives of members of his family; then, his
familia—his *domestici*, as the Romans said—that is, not only the
servants of every category who looked after his necessities of life, but
also all those who, for whatever reason, had attached themselves to the
master of the house and associated themselves with his fortunes. Over
all of these, even if they were in no way related to him, the paterfamilias had to exercise a paternal authority analogous to that of God
the Father and Creator over His creatures and also to treat them with
God's goodness and act as a Providence toward them, watching over
all their needs and their futures. All the *domestiques* owed him that
total obedience, that unlimited service, and that affection, even that
respectful and infinite love, which a father is entitled to expect from his
children, and God, "Our Father," to expect from His creatures. This
paternalism and these filial feelings were supposed to prevail, according to the conceptions of the time, in all the hierarchical relations of
society and everywhere, even in professional life, in public offices, and
in the state. The ideal relationship of father and son was the fundamental hierarchical relationship and the model for all others.

The royal household (*Maison du Roi*) was the model for all private
maisons. The great lords imitated it more or less, depending on their
rank and fortune. They could not fall below a certain limit of seemli-
ness. Audiger, in *La maison réglée*, fixed the lowest limit permissible
for a great nobleman at thirty-six *domestiques*, not counting the household of his wife, which was distinct from his own. Eight *domestiques*
sufficed for a foreign person of quality or a provincial *gentilhomme*,
and four for lesser *seigneurs* or *bourgeois*. The makeup of a domestic
staff was fairly uniform: a chaplain, a steward, an equerry, a secretary,
a butler, and persons responsible for food and drink. A *gentilhomme*
needed a kitchen, an office, and a stable, with the necessary staff. In
the very great houses there would also be serving gentlemen, pages,
musicians, a doctor, a barber-surgeon, and, in the houses of princes or
governors of provinces or towns, there would be guards.

Richelieu reformed in 1636 the excessively extravagant household of
his nephew Du Pont de Courlay. He dismissed the chaplain, steward,
and butler and retained only twenty-nine *domestiques* who were considered indispensable:

Three gentlemen, including his equerry, who will use the lackeys of M. Le Général des Galères and the horses in his stable. If there are more gentlemen than this, he is to find them employment in his regiment or in the galleys. Two secretaries, with no other scribes. Three *valets de chambre,* including the tailor and the laundryman. Two pages. Four or five lackeys, at most. A purveyor, with his manservant. A cook, with his kitchen boy. A cellarman, with his assistant. A coachman and a postilion. Two stablemen. One mule-driver. One hall porter.[11]

The children of the family had their own households, too. The prince de Condé's son, later the duc d'Enghien, was given a complete household as soon as he was of an age to be taken out of the hands of the womenfolk: a *gentilhomme,* La Bussière, as his governor, and two Jesuits as his teachers; a doctor, a surgeon, and an apothecary; a head for each department of the household; a comptroller, two *valets de chambre,* a page, and two footmen; a carriage, and some saddle horses. When his father sent him to Paris, to the Académie de Benjamin, at the age of fourteen, he gave him a gentleman of his bedchamber, an equerry, two pages, a comptroller, a chaplain, four footmen, two *valets de chambre,* a coachman and a postilion, six carriage horses, some saddle horses, and a head for each department of his household. The great officials imitated the princes. Catherine, daughter of Antoine Nicolaï, *premier président* of the Chambre des Comptes, had, "at the age of fifteen, two little lackeys, with whom she amused herself, playing and jesting all day long."[12]

Everyone imitated the king, the princes, and the grandees: not only the *gentilshommes* and the *seigneurs,* the officials, the lawyers, the doctors, the big merchants, but also the master craftsmen and the well-to-do peasants. Many a poor craftsman had his *familia,* in which, along with his own kindred, a journeyman or a maidservant was included; they, too, were closely linked with their master and associated with his fortunes, for in that type of society, where a comparative scarcity of goods prevailed, where the great problem was to find some work to live by, and where many manual operations were required for all the needs of a household and a workshop, there were few who could not find some poor girl or boy whom they had need of and who was willing to become a member of their *maison.*

This paternalism appears to have gradually declined.

Notes

1. Jean Bodin, *De la République*, edition of 1576, book 1, chap. 2.
2. Furetière, *Dictionnaire* (1690).
3. Quoted by Charles de Ribbe, *Une grande dame dans son ménage au temps de Louis XIV*, page 3 note 1.
4. Charles de Ribbe, *Les familles et la société en France avant la Révolution*, 4th ed. (1879), vol. 1, chap. 1, pp. 3 ff.
5. Memoirs of André d'Ormesson, in "Journal d'Olivier Lefèvre d'Ormesson," ed. M. Chéruel, in *Collection de documents inédits sur l'Histoire de France* (1860), vol. 1, Introduction, pp. vii–ix.
6. Papon, *Arrêts notables* (1610), book XV, chap. 29, pp. 884–86.
7. Le Ridant, *Code matrimonial* (1770), vol. 1, p. 121.
8. What follows applies to the regions where customary law prevailed. Qualifications need to be made where the regions subject to written law, and also Normandy, are concerned. See G. Lepointe (works cited in the bibliography, below).
9. Pierre Ayrault, *De la puissance paternelle* (1615), pp. 718–19.
10. Roland Mousnier, ed., *Lettres et mémoires adressés au Chancelier Séguier*, vol. 1, pp. 104–9.
11. *Lettres...de Richelieu*, ed. Avenel, vol. 5, p. 502.
12. Tallemant de Réaux, *Historiettes*, ed. Monmerqué, vol. 3, p. 396.

Guide to further reading

—On the subject as a whole: Gabriel Lepointe, *Droit romain et ancien droit français: Régimes matrimoniaux, liberalités, successions* (Montchrestien, 1958) (with a bibliography); Gabriel Lepointe, *La famille dans l'ancien droit*, 4th ed. (Domat-Montchrestien, 1953); Pierre Guyot, *Répertoire universel et raisonné de jurisprudence*, 17 vols. (Visse, 1784–85).

—On the lineage: P. Petot, *Le Lignage* (lectures for the doctor's degree course, 1949–50); P. C. Timbal, "L'esprit du droit privé au XVIIᵉ siècle," *XVIIᵉ siècle* 58–59 (1963): 34–39; Charles de Ribbe, *Les familles et la société en France avant la Révolution*, 2 vols. (Tours: Mame, 1879); Charles de Ribbe, *Le livre de famille* (Tours: Mame, 1879).

—On marriage: Pierre Le Ridant, *Code matrimonial*, 2d ed. (Hérissant Fils, 1770); Pierre Le Ridant, *Examen de deux questions importantes sur le mariage* (1753) (B.N.: F 5506, E 2869); *Conférences ecclésiastiques de Paris sur le mariage établies et imprimées sur l'ordre de S. S. M. le Cardinal de Noailles, archevêque de Paris*, 2d ed., 5 vols. (1715); *Journal des Audiences du Parlement de Paris, 1751–1754*, 7 vols., by Dufresne, de La Guessière, Nupied, and Duchemin; Pothier, *Traité du contrat de mariage*, 2 vols. (Orléans and Paris, 1768–71); Adh. Esmein, *Le mariage en droit canonique*, 2d ed., revised by R. Génestal and Jean Dauvillier, 2 vols. (Sirey, 1929–35) (B.N.: E 10595); J. Basdevant, *Des rapports de l'Eglise et de l'Etat dans la législation du mariage du Concile de Trente au Code Civil* (Law thesis, Paris, 1900) (B.N.: 8° F. 12109) (bibliography); V. Martin, *Le gallicanisme et la réforme catholique: Essai historique sur l'introduction en France des décrets du Concile de Trente* (Paris Faculty of Letters thesis, 1919); Abbé Alexandre Vantroys, *Etude historique et juridique sur le consentement des parents au mariage de leurs enfants* (Rousseau, 1889) (B.N.: 8°F 5435); L. Beauchet, "Etude historique sur les formes de la célébration du mariage dans l'ancien droit français," *Nouvelle Revue historique de Droit français et étranger* 6 (1882): 351–92, 631–83; Duguit, "Etude historique sur le rapt de séduction," *Nouvelle Revue historique de Droit* (1886), pp. 587 ff; G. Pacilly, "Contribution à l'histoire de la théorie du rapt de séduction," *Tijdschrift voor Rechtgeschiedenis* 13 (1934): 309 (B.N.: 8°F 232); E. Bertin, *Les mariages dans l'ancienne société française* (Faculty of Letters thesis, 1879); J. Ghestin, "L'action des Parlements contre les mésalliances aux XVIIe et XVIIIe siècles," *Revue historique de Droit* (1956), pp. 74–110, 196–224 (B.N.: P. 251.8).

—On lineage property: P. Petot, *Les propres* (lectures for the doctor's degree course, 1941–42); Emile Jarriand, "La succession coutumière dans les pays de droit écrit," *Revue historique de Droit* 14 (1890): 30–69, 222–268 (B.N.: P. 251.8); Emile Jarriand, "L'évolution du droit écrit dans le Midi de la France depuis le IXe siècle jusqu'en 1789," *Revue des questions historiques* n.s. 4 (58) (1890–91): 204–16 (B.N.: P. 199.8); L. Falletti, *Le retrait lignager en droit coutumier français* (1923); P. Ourliac, "Le retrait lignager dans le sud-ouest de la France," *Revue historique de Droit* (1952), pp. 328–55 (B.N.: P. 251.8); A. Soubie, "Le retrait lignager dans la coutume de Bordeaux," *Revue juridique et économique du Sud-Ouest* (1961) (B.N.: P. 4796.8); J.-F. Le Calonnec, *Etude sur le régime des biens entre époux dans la coutume d'Anjou (1508–1789)* (Angers, 1963) (Travaux de la Société d'Histoire du Droit et des Institutions des Pays de l'Ouest de la France, vol. 2); R. Génestal, *Le parage normand* (1911); H. Legoherel, "Le parage en Touraine-Anjou au Moyen Age," *Revue historique de Droit français et étranger* 4th ser., 43 (1965): 222–46.

—On domestic communities: Jean Gaudemet, *Les communautés familiales* (Marcel Rivière, 1963) ("Petite bibliothèque sociologique internationale") (B.N.: Z 29^a [8] 12); Fr. Olivier-Martin, *Histoire de la coutume de la prévôté et vicomté de Paris*, 3 vols. (1922–30); Pothier, *Traité de la communauté entre époux*, ed. Bugnet (1861); M. Nicolle, *Les communautés de laboureurs dans l'ancienne droit* (Law thesis, Dijon, 1902); M. Blanc, *Les communautés familiales dans l'ancien droit et leurs survivances en Limousin* (Law thesis, Paris, 1905); P. Dardel, *Les communautés de famille en France et en Suisse* (Law thesis, Paris, 1905); G. Bloch, *De la communauté entre époux en Bourgogne* (Law thesis, Dijon, 1910), pp. 95–100; P. Bastid, *De la fonction sociale des communautés taisibles* (Law thesis, Paris, 1916); Th. Prieuret, *Une association agricole en Nivernais: Histoire de la grosse communauté du Jault (1580–1847)* (Nevers, 1930); J. Gay, *Les effets pécuniaires du mariage en Nivernais du XIVe au XVIIIe siècle* (Law thesis, Dijon, 1952); Simone Galliot, *Le régime matrimonial en droit franc-comtois de 1459 à la Révolution* (Law thesis, Paris, 1954); G. Chevrier, "L'originalité du droit franc-comtois," *Tijdschrift voor Rechtgeschiedenis* 27 (1959): 9, 30, 172, 180 (Sorbonne: P. 3399); A. Vandenbossche, "Note sur la notion de propre de succession en Béarn au XVIIIe siècle," *Etudes de droit privé offertes à Pierre Petot* (1959); Moreau de Bellaing, *L'indivision familiale dans la région parisienne au XVIIIe siècle* (memoir for the diploma of advanced studies in the history of law, Paris, 1961).

—On the *ménage*: Pierre Ayrault, *Plaidoyers et arrêts, opuscules et divers traictez de maistre Pierre Ayrault* (L. Sormins, 1615); Pierre Ayrault, *Conclusion de l'ordre, formalité et instruction judiciaire, de P. Ayrault lieut. crim. d'Angers, à René Ayrault son fils qu'il ne luy est pas licite de faire voeu, sans le vouloir et consentement de ses père et mère* (1588); Estienne Pasquier, *Epistres (Lettres)* (Lyon: J. Veyrat, 1597) (B.N.: fols. 73v–80r); Taudiére, *Traité de la puissance paternelle* (Pédone, 1898); J. Du Plessis de Grenedan, *Histoire de l'autorité paternelle dans l'ancien droit français depuis les origines jusqu'à la Révolution* (Rousseau, 1900); Léon Abensour, *La femme et le féminisme avant la Révolution* (Faculty of Letters thesis, Paris, 1922); G. Fagniez, *La femme et la société française dans la première moitié du XVIIᵉ siècle* (Gamber, 1929); P. Gide, *Etude sur la condition privée de la femme,* 2d ed., ed. A. Esmein (Larose, 1885); Dufau, *La puissance paternelle du XVIᵉ au XVIIIᵉ siècle* (Law thesis, Paris, 1953, typescript); J. Le Lièvre, *Pratique du contrat de mariage chez les notaires au Châtelet de Paris, de 1769 à 1804* (Law thesis, Paris, 1965, typescript); J. Hilaire, *Le régime des biens entre époux dans la région de Montpellier du début du XIIIᵉ à la fin du XVᵉ siècle (et sur régions voisines)* (Montpellier: Caux, Graille & Castelnau, 1957); Claude Lehmann, *Personnalité ou réalité de la puissance paternelle sur les biens au début du XVIIᵉ siècle* (Law thesis, Paris, 1958); A. M. Petit, "Mariages et contrats de mariages à Agen en 1785 et en 1786," *Annales du Midi* 72 (1960); Claude Aboucaya, *Le Testament lyonnais de la fin du XVᵉ au milieu du XVIIIᵉ siècle* ("Annales de l'Université de Lyon," 3d ser., Law, fasc. 21) (Sirey, 1961).

—On the *maison:* Father Jean Cordier, *La famille sainte* (1644); Pierre Fortin, Sieur de la Hoguette, *Testaments ou conseils fidèles d'un bon père à ses enfants* (1661); Raymond Poisson, "Le baron de La Crasse" (1662), in *Oeuvres de M. Poisson* (J. Ribou, 1679); Maximin Deloche, *La maison du cardinal de Richelieu* (Champion, 1912); Roland Mousnier, ed., *Lettres et mémoires adressés au chancelier Séguier (1633–1649)* ("Publications de la Faculté des Lettres et Sciences humaines de Paris," Série Textes et Documents, vol. 6; Travaux du Centre de Recherches sur la Civilisation de l'Europe moderne, fasc. 2, 1964).

3

The Society of Fealties

The relationship between master and *fidèle*

From the top to the bottom of society, men were
bound together by bonds of fealty, a man-to-man
relationship between *maître* and *fidèle* which became more important under Henri IV and Louis
XIII than feudalism itself. These relationships
have been little studied and are not well known
so far as our period is concerned. What we have
here is a world of feelings and ideas completely
alien, it would seem, to Frenchmen of the 19th
and 20th centuries, and it calls for an effort on
our part today if we are to make them live again
and enter into them. Some examples are needed.

When Du Bourg surrendered the Bastille to
Henri IV on 27 March 1594, he was "required to
recognize the king and to acknowledge him as a
good prince, and he replied that he did not doubt
this but that he was in the service of M. de
Mayenne, to whom *he had plighted his faith*."
The royalists were thus asking this Leaguer to
admit that Henri IV was indeed the legitimate
king, that he was not a tyrant, and that he therefore had the right to command obedience. This
the Leaguer did not deny; but there was an
obedience which had priority for him over the
obedience he owed to the king, namely, the
loyalty he had promised to a master whose

servant he was, the duc de Mayenne, to whom he had given his word to be faithful. Consequently, fealty implies obedience to a master, carried so far as to take precedence of the obedience due to the head of state, the incarnation of France.[1]

Bassompierre, a *gentilhomme* of Lorraine, coming from one of the territories of the Empire, cared neither for the duke of Lorraine, who was his natural sovereign and to whom, according to our notions, he should have owed his entire service, nor for the emperor, head of the Holy Roman Empire of the German nation, of which the duchy of Lorraine formed part. He hesitated between serving the king of France and serving the king of Spain. He decided to go and see each of them and then make his choice. At the court of France, however, he was swept off his feet and told Henri IV that

> he had so charmed me that, without *seeking further for a master*, if he wanted *my service, I would devote myself to him, until death.* He then embraced me and assured me that I could have found no *better master* than himself, none who would be fonder of me or would do more to contribute to my good fortune and advancement. *That happened on a Tuesday, 12 March (1599). From that time onward I considered myself a Frenchman.*[2]

The date when he made his vow is carefully recorded. Almost all that was involved in fealty is exhibited here. Fealty means the free choice of a master by a servant, without regard to nationality. The servant thenceforth devotes himself to this master, to the point of considering that he has changed his nation, adopting that of his master. Thus, he has embraced all the sentiments, opinions, inclinations, and intentions of this master and has devoted himself to him to the point of readiness to give his life for his sake. In return, the master promises him affection, advancement, and prosperity. It is therefore not a mere service relationship, a mere exchange of services and rewards, but a total devotion, a gift of oneself, on the one side, and a pledge of affection on the other. The bond that binds *maître* and *fidèle* is an emotional one.

Arnauld d'Andilly in 1623 defended the *surintendant des finances* Schomberg against the charge of embezzlement and observed: *"as I was not M. de Schomberg's man, but his Majesty's, attached to M. de Schomberg,* if he had given cause for the bad allegations made against him, His Majesty would have known of that . . . through my breaking with M. de Schomberg."[3] Thus, if Schomberg had embezzled and acted dishonorably, Arnauld d'Andilly would have broken with him, not at all because Schomberg had in this way violated his obligations toward the state and society, but because Arnauld d'Andilly was the king's man and not M. de Schomberg's. The *fidèle*, then, belonged, body and soul, to his master. The implication is plain to see, though: if Arnauld d'Andilly had been Schomberg's man, had he belonged in this way to Schomberg, the latter might have embezzled as much as he liked and Arnauld d'Andilly would have stayed with him and served him in his thieving. Fealty implies, therefore, service to an individual before service to the state, to the detriment of the state, and even without concern for God's commandments.

Pontis was urged in 1627 by Father Joseph to give up his lieutenancy in the king's guards and enter the cardinal's service. "He (Richelieu) wants officers who will be *faithful to him and will be his men, without exception or reservation* ...This is what has caused him to cast his eyes upon you, because he knows that when *you have given yourself to a master,* you think only of him and *serve him alone, after God."* Thus, fealty implies the total surrender of the *fidèle* to his master, becoming his master's man without any reservation, serving him alone, under God—that is, serving him before the king or even the state. Pontis refused: "Would not he (the Cardinal) be the first to reproach me with *infidelity* if, after *the honor which it has pleased the king to do me by placing me near his person and himself giving me* a lieutenancy in his guards, I should thereupon quit his service *to give myself to another?"* [4] Pontis does not refer, in his refusal, to his position as the king's subject and does not seem concerned about his duty to the state; he merely refers to the fealty which he is obliged to maintain because of the benefits and favors the king has seen fit to grant him. Here we see another source of fealty besides the gift of himself made by the *fidèle*, namely, the benefits conferred by a master and, in the case of the king, his royal favors, which possess a constraining power, namely, that of gratitude. The devotion of the *fidèle*, the favors of the *maître*—these are the two sources of fealty, binding one man to another.

The cardinal wanted to surround the king with men devoted to himself and to get rid of the king's own *fidèles*. The king would have ended by being practically isolated, lacking any real power in face of his minister; for the latter would have become the master of the best swordsmen, and the king would no longer have been able to make himself obeyed in his kingdom otherwise than through the agency of his chief minister and that minister's *fidèles*. Toward the end of the reign, Richelieu was coming to resemble a mayor of the palace. Louis XIII had promised to give Puységur the guards company of Pauillac, which was vacant through the death of its commander. In December 1640, however, the cardinal caused this company to be assigned to someone else and told the king that Puységur was too greatly needed in the army in Piedmont. "This courteous refusal had been engineered by M. le Cardinal, who wanted to have in the guards and in the governorates only persons *who were his men and who had promised fealty to him.*" Puységur had remained, indeed, loyal to the king despite all solicitations. In January 1641,

> M. le Comte de Soissons, who had taken refuge in Sedan, and who had much consideration and friendship for me, came every day to the gate of the camp and asked for me. I never wanted to go out and meet him, for fear lest it be thought that I had some understanding with him; because I was always unbreakably attached to the king's service, and *I knew the honor he did to me in loving me,* I was far from thoughts of taking any side but the king's.[5]

An essential reason for Puységur to remain attached to the king's service was that his master loved him, that between them there was that bond of affection which was an essential element in the bond of fealty.

These feelings were very powerful. But the most powerful feelings sometimes weaken and die. Pontis tells us how, in 1642,

> when I was with the king one day, His Majesty beckoned me to follow him into his dressing room . . . and, sitting down on a chest, in very pensive mood, he began asking, showing much confidence in me, how it happened that the captains he had appointed were all leaving him, so that hardly one was left attached to his person . . . how it happened that a certain man, whom he named, had left him to enter M. le Cardinal's service . . . I could not understand . . . how anyone could be so dastardly as to *prefer to the king's service that of one of his subjects,* however powerful that subject might be.[6]

Thus, for these *gentilshommes,* the king was only one of many possible masters, and everyone had the right to choose his master and become the *fidèle* of that man, even instead of the king and even against the king, the head of state. Some deserted their master for no other reason than pursuit of their own interests. However, opinion severely condemned such acts of infidelity, seeing in them a sort of betrayal. This is shown by the efforts made by Montrésor to justify himself for having deserted the service of the duc d'Orléans: *"When I was a child I had the honor to give myself* to M. le duc d'Orléans, and I will dare say . . . that I had no other object, while I was *in his service,* but *his glory* and *my duty . . .* In this discourse, in which I seek to justify my conduct, I will out of respect to M. le duc d'Orléans, refrain from mentioning any but those grievances which must be cited in order to show clearly that I *did not fail in my duty."* He recalls his fealty: "His first discourse related to the credence he gave to my *fealty,* which, as he put it to me, I had observed so completely *that it was impossible for him to conceal his affairs and his sentiments from me."* He mentions the hardships he has undergone, the dangers he has incurred, how he followed his master in the latter's disgrace, even beyond the frontiers of the realm—how, in fact, he has performed all the duties of a *fidèle.* The duc d'Orléans, however, has on several occasions deserted him, left him without support, not including him in his treaty of 1637 with Louis XIII and not stipulating his immunity therein. Consequently, the master having plainly failed in his obligations, being clearly guilty of betrayal of his *fidèle,* the latter is released from *his* obligations: "I decided . . . to seek in a retired and private life *the security that had been denied me in the protection of a master* to whom I had devoted myself so completely.[7] Thus, to the total giving of himself, the unlimited devotion on the part of the *fidèle,* there ought to correspond the total trust, the unlimited confidence, and the protection of the master. If one of these conditions is lacking, then either the *fidèle* or his master has let the other down; a serious fault has been committed, a sort of betrayal, which breaks the bond between the two men and entails the reproaches of public opinion.

All these quotations demonstrate that we have to consider as faithful pictures of the *mores* of the time—allowing for the abridgment of caricature—certain passages in the fictional writings of those days. Baron de Foeneste sets out from home to seek his fortune in Paris.

We arrived at Aigre, both of us ill with fever and having no longer so much as a single *raquette*[8] . . . When the comte de Merle came by, he was pleased, being in love, to take us along with him, to add to his retinue, and at Poitiers he had a splendid surcoat made for each of us . . . (In Paris) Monsieur le Comte provided me with good clothes . . . He handed me over to Monsieur de Montespan . . .[9]
When I was left on my own, I frequented the town house of

Monsieur de Guise through the favor of Monsieur de Loux, who often asked me if I would help him to kill some duke, a task for which I freely offered myself.[10]

Charles Sorel's Francion gives us an example of an offer of service:

Monseigneur, the very great desire that I feel to serve you, together with my desire to be released from the persecutions of certain of my kinfolk, has caused me to come here and ask you to take me under the wing of your protection by including me among your subjects. I ask of you neither wages nor reward; provided I have my livelihood, that is enough, and, given that, I undertake to render you good service, such as you may not hope for from many men. I am a licentiate of laws, Monseigneur, and have as much instruction as I need for any occasion; and furthermore I have courage, and should it be necessary to wield a sword, I will acquit myself as well as any *gentilhomme* of your train.

Francion is in a similar situation in the house of Clérante. Clérante feeds him and gives him "good maintenance." Francion amuses him, composes verses, makes fun of people, reprimands their foolish acts, humbles their vanity. He has comrades who gain a great deal from Clérante's protection. One of them strikes a man. Some townsfolk come to the man's aid. The friends of the *fidèle* say: "*Messieurs*, this rascal insulted Clérante's gentlemen, whom you see here. 'Yes, indeed,' says Collinet, 'I am one of Clérante's gentlemen.' At the name of this highly respected *seigneur* they hesitate, and his men slip away quietly."[11] We could write Orléans, Guise, Condé, or Soissons in place of Clérante: the novel here merely reflects historical reality.

To recapitulate: fealty is a bond of sentiment, based on mutual affection, which links two men together totally, by their free choice, independently of duty toward nation, king, law, or society. The *fidèle* gives himself completely to the master. He espouses all the latter's ideas, inclinations, ambitions, and interests. He devotes himself to him utterly. He serves him in every way possible: he accompanies him, entertains him, speaks, writes, intrigues, and argues for him, fights, plots, and rebels for him, follows him into exile, helps him against everyone else, even against the king, against the state; if necessary, he gives his life for his master. In exchange for all this, the master owes the *fidèle* first and foremost his friendship, his absolute trust, his confidence. He owes him food, clothing, maintenance, and protection in all the circumstances of life, even against justice, even against the head of state. He must see to the advancement of his *fidèle*, arrange a marriage for him, obtain offices and functions for him. If the master has rebelled and is making terms with the king, he must include stipulations on behalf of his *fidèles* in any treaty he signs. Although there is a hierarchical relationship, the master standing higher than the *fidèle*, the two belong to each other and are almost one man in two bodies.

The relationship of the master and *fidèle* is found first of all among the *gentilshommes*. It starts with the first *gentilhomme* of the realm, the king himself, who is master of many *fidèles*. The relationship between Louis XIII and Richelieu is that of a master and his *fidèle*, and Richelieu himself writes "that he has given himself to the king and the queen mother."[12] (Later, he gave himself to the king alone.) From the king, the relationship of master and *fidèle* extends gradually down to the humblest *gentilhomme*, forming a long chain of mutual ties. The relationship of master and *fidèle* becomes multiplied through the practice of *gentilshommes* giving their sons as *fidèles* to personages who are in a position to ensure a career for them. Monsieur le Prince "gives" his son, the duc d'Enghien, to *Monsieur le Grand Maître*, the cardinal's cousin. Madame de Liancourt "gives" her son, the comte de Rocheguyon, to marshal de Gassion.[13] It frequently happens that a *fidèle* marries into the lineage of his master, and this additional link strengthens the bond of fealty.

The relationship between *protecteur* and *créature*

A similar relationship, that of protector and *créature*, became dominant, in the sphere of government, around the king, between chancellor, state councilors, secretaries of state, *surintendant des finances*, intendants of finance, masters of requests, and so on, in the spheres of offices and finance, among poets, writers, secretaries, *argentiers* (household treasurers), comptrollers, *valets de chambre;* and, in general, it linked those *"domestiques"* who were not *nobles d'épée*, those of the *"famille"* who were not *gentilshommes*, with the head of a household. Richelieu called himself Louis XIII's *créature*, while Pierre Séguier, the keeper of the seals and chancellor of France, secretaries of state such as the Bouthilliers, Sublet de Noyers, and Chavigny, and *surintendants des finances* like Claude Bouthillier and Claude de Bullion called themselves the *créatures* of Richelieu, who was their "protector." In their turn, these ministers were the "protectors" of state councilors, masters of requests, and intendants of the army or of provinces, who declared themselves their *créatures* while being themselves the protectors of other *créatures,* and so on. The *créature* gives himself to his protector just as the *fidèle* gives himself to his master. The writer Costar gave himself to the abbot of Lavardin, who later became bishop of Le Mans.[14] Pellisson was first the poet and then the secretary of the *surintendant des finances* Fouquet, who said of him: "M. Pellisson has done me the honor of giving himself to me."[15] Just as a master can hand over his *fidèle* to another master, so Richelieu, as protector, one day "gave" to Bautru the viola-player Maugars, who was his man. The relationship between protector and *créature* was very similar to that between master and *fidèle.* Like the latter, it implied reciprocal affection and trust, total devotion and unlimited service on the part of the *créature,* protection and social advancement on the part of the protector. However, there were some differences. Usually, the protector was expected to appoint his *créature* to an office or other public function and ensure his career in the world of the gown and the sphere of government. His *créature* was really his creation: as regards his career, the protector did, indeed, "create" him. The *créature* had, in the fulfillment of his functions, to serve the interests of his protector, even in preference to, or actually against, those of the king and the state, if need be. It is probable that this relationship was derived from that of master and *fidèle,* being an adaptation of it to the world of the magistracy and the government.

It would be worth investigating the extent to which these two relationships had penetrated society and whether they were to be found low down in the hierarchy of the third estate or were peculiar to the nobility and the higher levels of the third estate. We know of other fealties—that of the *censitaire* (copyholder) to his lord, and that, similar in kind, of the vassal to his suzerain—and these survived in the 17th and 18th centuries. But they were essentially different from the two relationships under consideration, since they originated in the ownership of land, did not result from free choice by the persons concerned, and implied reciprocal obligations that were in fact less extensive. They were essentially feudal, which the relationships of master and *fidèle,* protector and *créature,* were not. *These* fealties did not involve any act of "faith and homage." The commitment did not require any oath, any ritual, any agreement in writing. The remuneration never took the form of a fief, any more than it was a fief or a *censive* that imposed the rendering of reciprocal services. These ties were of a different order: that of the gift of himself that one person makes to another, the order of love.

From fealties to the relationship between subject and state

We know little about how these fealties changed, whether and to what extent they declined, what strength they still possessed on the eve of the Revolution. It would appear that they had become weaker. Perhaps Louis XIV contributed to this process during his personal government, before the philosophy of the Enlightenment turned men's hearts away from such relationships, while the spirit of capitalism, accustoming everyone to translate everything into figures, gradually dried them up. Louis XIV had seen during the Fronde how important fealties were. It was thanks to them that the princes and grandees in revolt had been able to gather around themselves thousands of the nobility of both sword and gown; but it was also thanks to them that the king had retained, even at the worst moments, a few hundred loyal *gentils-hommes* to furnish officers for his army and vanquish the rebels. Louis XIV appreciated very well that it was impossible to launch a direct attack upon such powerful feelings and social relations, to which Frenchmen were so deeply attached. But he sought to make use of this custom by attaching all Frenchmen to himself, to his own person, by a personal bond of fealty. A master could create *fidèles* by means of grace and favor. Louis XIV made use of royal favor; he wished to be the sole source of favor in order to make *fidèles* for himself. In his *Mémoires pour l'instruction du dauphin* he says, speaking of himself as king:

> All eyes are fixed upon him alone. To him alone are all petitions addressed. He alone receives all respect, he alone is the object of all hope. Nothing is pursued, nothing expected, nothing done but by him only. His favors are seen as the exclusive source of all good things. No one supposes himself able to rise in the world otherwise than in proportion as he draws closer to the king's person or the king's esteem. All else is fruitless.

This passage assumes its full significance in the setting of fealties. The king is here putting himself in the situation of a "master." He wants to get all Frenchmen to give themselves to him as *fidèles,* with all that this relationship implies. This is why he has insisted that all favors be asked directly of him, so that he may be the universal benefactor, at once the universal "master" and the universal "protector," and so that all Frenchmen may be bound to him by a master-*fidèle* or protector-*créature* relationship or by the hope of entering into such a relationship.

In his endeavors to achieve this aim, Louis XIV sometimes showed touching delicacy. The comte de Béthune was in need of money to pay for his office as *chevalier d'honneur* to the queen. When the king heard that he was in difficulties, he sent him "six thousand *louis d'or* of his own money,...and told him that, having heard that the comte had turned to his friends for help, the king was surprised not to have been included among them." The king of France, spontaneously calling the count his friend and making a fine gesture of friendship, using his own money and not resorting to the state's coffers, manifested that sentiment of affection, source of protection or of service, which was the basic condition for the relationship between master and *fidèle.*

Louis XIV succeeded in his plan to a large degree, but his very success was perhaps one of the causes of the decline of fealties. Since favors could no longer be expected otherwise than from him personally, since the "master" *par excellence* was the king, other fealties lost their reason for existence. He reduced all fealties to fealty to himself. Yet he was the embodiment of the state: "l'Etat, c'est moi." Consequently, he brought together the bond of fealty and subjection to the state. Confounding fealty with subjection to the state, he caused the latter to benefit from all the power of love, devotion, and service that was included in fealty. The state became the master and the state's subjects the *fidèles.* By making use of the bond of fealty in this universal and permanent fashion, Louis XIV actually destroyed it, through integrating it in a relationship which the feelings of fealty were supposed to strengthen, namely, the relationship between a subject and the state.

Fealty and feudalism

The fealties engendered by feudalism were of a different nature. This is not the place to discuss fiefs and *censives,* which deserve separate treatment. But it is necessary to recall the nature of the relationships between men which arose from these forms of property. The feudal regime was, in the 17th and 18th centuries, still intact in law and seems from time to time to have renewed its vigor. There was still a hierarchy of fiefs. The holder of one of these fiefs still owed to the holder of the fief on which his own was dependent "faith, homage, and an oath of fealty." He became "his man," his vassal, and he owed to his suzerain the performance of noble service—service in connection with the lord's court actions, service of counsel, military service, financial help in certain cases; and, if the suzerain should sell the fief, the vassal owed *quint et requint*, while, should it pass to someone else by succession, gift, or marriage, *relief* or *rachat* must be paid. In every fief the lord reserved a demesne for himself, which he caused to be cultivated either by hired men or by tenant farmers, and he often exercised rights of justice and administration; but he put out most of the arable land as "commoner" fiefs or *censives*. The lord of the fief retained the *directe seigneuriale* over the *censives*, that is, his right to fealty on the part of the *censitaire*, with rendering of services and payment of *cens, lods, et ventes* and certain dues. The *censitaire* acquired the *seigneurie utile*, with the right to use the land and take crops from it, consuming or selling these, together with the right to sell, give away, pledge, bequeath, or transmit by inheritance the *seigneurie utile*. He owed fealty to the *seigneur direct* and became his "subject," his "man," to the extent that the *seigneur direct* could still require armed service from the *seigneur utile* in order to arrest malefactors and protect the fief against soldiers (if need be, too, against tax collectors); however, the *seigneur utile* could not be obliged to render any form of *noble* service but only to cultivate the land. The *seigneur utile* owed a variety of services and forms of work and many dues.

The *seigneurs directs* were far from despising the material benefits they obtained from their fiefs, but they perhaps saw as still more important the social superiority they derived either from the act of faith and homage or from the levying of a *cens*. This superiority is implicit in all the documents, but it is actually expressed in the contract of sale of two arpents of arable land at Sens on 16 April 1616.[16] The contract notes that these two arpents are subject to the payment of two *sols tournois, as a sign and mark of superiority,* payable each year to the said prior of Saint-Denis, and, in addition, a sum of twelve deniers to whom it shall belong, for *all right of superiority."* Fief and *censive,* as sources of fealty, were symbols of rank and authority. Rights of justice, too, were the sign of power to command.

These feudal fealties were very different from the relationships of master and *fidèle* and protector and *créature*, and, in my opinion, they were less important. In the first place, they were derived from the hierarchy of rights of property in land; and the acquisition of land, even if consideration of the fealties involved in it was taken into account in the choice made, often inevitably took place without regard to the persons who were to become vassals or *censitaires* of the acquirer. The choice made applied to land and to a set of rights but not to persons, and, reciprocally, the vassals and *censitaires* in occupation did not choose their suzerain or lord—unlike what applied in the relationships of master and *fidèle* and protector and *créature*. The bond between persons was derivative, not principal, a consequence and not a cause. Protection, on the one hand, and services, on the other, were determined by law and custom and by written undertakings and were strictly limited, whereas in the relationships between master and *fidèle*, protector and *créature*, neither protection nor services was defined but remained unlimited. Actually, protection and services in feudal fealties were highly variable and in certain areas, such as the Paris region, fell far short of what law, custom, and undertakings provided for, whereas, in fealties defined by the master-*fidèle* and protector-*créature* relationships, regional variations appear to have been of little importance, and the reciprocal obligations involved appear to have been really fulfilled, apart from a comparatively small number of cases of failure. Accordingly, without underestimating the feudal fealties, we ought to regard the fealties governed by the master-*fidèle* and protector-*créature* relationships as being much more important in the two centuries we are studying and characteristic of them, so that these centuries should be included in the epoch of fealties and no longer the epoch of feudalism.

Notes

1. Lestoile, *Mémoires-journaux,* ed. Michaud and Poujoulat, p. 210.
2. Bassompierre, *Mémoires* (Société de l'Histoire de France), vol. 1, p. 69.
3. Arnauld d'Andilly, *Mémoires,* ed. Michaud and Poujoulat, p. 442.
4. Pontis, *Mémoires,* ed. Michaud and Poujoulat, pp. 525–26.
5. Puységur, *Mémoires,* ed. Tamizey de Laroque, vol. 1, pp. 250–54.
6. Pontis, *Mémoires,* p. 629.
7. Montrésor, *Mémoires,* ed. Michaud and Poujoulat, pp. 215, 216, 218.
8. A small coin current in Béarn.
9. Captain of Henri IV's guards in 1610.

10. D'Aubigné, *Le Barong de Foeneste* (1630) (Cologne: Marteau, 1729), vol. 1, chap. 3, pp. 23, 27, 28.

11. Charles Sorel, *Histoire comique de Francion*, ed. Roy (Société des Textes français modernes), vol. 2, pp. 137, 138, 156.

12. Avenel, *Lettres*, vol. 3, p. 213.

13. Tallemant de Réaux, *Historiettes*, vol. 3, p. 385.

14. Ibid., vol. 4, p. 141.

15. Ibid., vol. 5, p. 404.

16. Archives départementales de Sens, série E, famille Balthazar.

Guide to further reading

Mousnier, Roland. *La vénalité des offices sous Henri IV et Louis XIII.* 2d ed. P.U.F., 1970.

——. "Les concepts d''Ordres,' d''états,' de 'fidélité,' et de 'monarchie absolue' en France de la fin du XVᵉ siècle à la fin du XVIIIᵉ," *Revue historique,* April–June 1972, pp. 289–312.

Ranum, Orest. *Richelieu and the Councillors of Louis XIII.* Oxford: Clarendon Press, 1963.

4 The Society of Orders
The Nobility

French society in the 17th and 18th centuries was not only a society of lineages and a society of fealties but also a society of "orders" and "estates." "Orders are dignities which are permanent and belong for their lifetime to those men who have been honored with them, provided they be not lost by forfeiture."[1] Persons were distinguished from each other in accordance with their dignities and were divided into hierarchically arranged social categories, social strata, in accordance with the nature and degree of their dignities. In France it was traditional, for the king's political requirements when he wished to communicate with his subjects, that government personages and jurists should recognize the three official orders of the Estates General of France: the clergy, the nobility, and the third estate. Actually, there were more than three estates. The clergy was composed of two orders, which each included a hierarchy of degrees or "estates." The first of these orders consisted of the cardinals, archbishops, and bishops; the second, of the abbots, deans, canons, and other ecclesiastics. The order of the nobility was likewise divided into secondary orders, with degrees or "estates" inside each of these, and the same was true of the third estate. But the real orders, the

social orders, did not coincide simply with the

divisions of the three political orders. Many of them transcended the limits of those three, breaking through the official classification. The fact is that orders are engendered spontaneously by the social body. They result from a certain social esteem which is tacitly accorded, through a sort of consensus, more or less conscious, to groups of persons who are sometimes possessed of very different juridical status. The edicts, *arrêts,* and declarations issued by the king usually recognized only part of this consensus—this already existing social situation—and often the less important part at that.

It is almost impossible to define the boundaries between the orders. We move from one to the other through imperceptible transitions. Moreover, cases of overlapping occur: the highest levels of the lower orders may prove to be, in everyday social reality, above the lowest levels of the order immediately above it. The best way of finding one's bearings in this matter is therefore to locate some social nuclei and observe the hierarchy that governs them. Each of these nuclei is surrounded by a sort of nebula of individuals, becoming more and more rarefied, and the frontiers between one nebula and the next are found to fade and then vanish.

Any stratification of society based on a set of value judgments is relative to a group of circumstances. In a sense, every town, every district, had its own stratification. That of Châteaudun, a small town with a dying industry, which lived mainly on the judiciary, was not that of Beauvais, a still important center of trade and manufacture, or that of Toulouse or Bordeaux, which were commercial towns that also had *parlements.* The upper bourgeoisie of Châteaudun would find its place only in the lowest levels of the middle bourgeoisie in Bordeaux or Toulouse. It would certainly be possible to select a few typical towns and parts of provinces and give an overall description of the social stratification in each of these. But while, in a given order, the various "estates" were not always the same, regardless of place and time, there were some which played similar and corresponding roles, so that a general view does become possible.

Armorial bearings

The most characteristic social symbols of this type of society of orders are armorial bearings. Having first appeared in the 12th century as a means by which fighting men might recognize each other in battle, armorial bearings soon became the symbol of a rank occupied in a hierarchical society. Armorial bearings were colored emblems peculiar to a family, community, corporation, or college, almost always depicted on a shield, and subject, as regards their arrangement and form, to the special rules of "coats of arms." The totality of usages relating to armorial bearings formed the science of heraldry. This system of rules was a matter of value judgments and spontaneous social behavior. Some of these usages were recognized by jurisprudence and sanctioned by law, but what was essential was "usage." When the Paris *parlement* rejected Louis XV's ordinance of 29 July 1760 regulating the wearing of coats of arms, it grounded its decision on a claim that the ordinance was contrary to the laws, maxims, and usages of the kingdom.

According to the jurist Charles Loyseau, "it is only the nobles who in France have the right to armorial bearings." But he gives no proof of this statement, and indeed he could not have proved it. For five centuries the usages of the kingdom had allowed all its inhabitants without exception, commoners included, to wear armorial bearings. This was why the Paris *parlement* rejected the ordinance of 1760, for the king was seeking to restrict the right to heraldry to the nobles and a small number of privileged commoners: army officers, magistrates, farmers general, receivers general, the subdelegates of the intendants, mayors, aldermen, municipal judges, and city consuls—all persons distinguished by service to the king or the public. Louis XIII's declaration of 8 August 1635, directed against officers who had left the army without leave from the king's lieutenant generals, ordered that the nobles among them be deprived of their armorial bearings and their noble status and that the commoners be deprived of their armorial bearings and sent to the galleys. Thus the king was acknowledging that both nobles and commoners were in their rights in having coats of arms. We see in 1668 an ordinary rich peasant of Flanders, one Martin Cattel, decorating his seal with a shield that shows a chevron charged with three roses, accompanied by three birds, and surmounted by a helmet with a bird upon it. Everyone was free to adopt armorial bearings if he chose and to devise them as he pleased. The usage of armorial bearings was indeed a general right, arising from the very constituent principle of French society.

Armorial bearings were emblems which were hereditary in families, or else they were emblems of corporations, permanent moral persons. In families, complete armorial bearings were hereditary for agnates, in the line of primogeniture, exactly like the Crown of France. Cognates and relations by marriage could wear them, but only as a "quartering," in one quarter of their shield. Heralds divided the shield, in some cases, into as many as sixteen "quarters." Junior members of a family wore its arms "with a difference"; that is, while retaining the major part of the arms, so that these were perfectly recognizable, they modified some detail, so as to constitute a distinctive sign for themselves.

The shield (or "escutcheon") was often "timbred" or "crested," that is, surmounted by a helmet. For a long time this usage was freely allowed to members of all orders. But in this type of society two tendencies were constantly manifest: a tendency for the higher orders to refine and intensify the frontiers between the orders, strengthening the hierarchical situation, and a tendency for the lower orders to usurp the symbols of the higher ones, so as to raise themselves in rank and dignity. In the 16th century the right to surmount a coat of arms with a helmet was restricted to the nobles. After the *arrêt* of the *parlement* of Paris dated 2 March 1556, the Ordinance of Orléans, in January 1561, in its article 110, forbade commoners to adopt or to wear crested armorial bearings on penalty of discretionary fines. This was confirmed by the ordinance of May 1579 (article 257) and the edict of March 1583 (article 1). Two *arrêts* of the Dijon *parlement* condemned those who usurped the helmet (October 1607 and 11 December 1608). The edict of January 1634, on the *taille,* in its article 2 inflicted a fine of 2,000 livres on commoners who wore arms surmounted by a helmet. This decision was confirmed by the declarations of 30 December 1656, 8 February 1661, and 26 February 1665, which were strictly enforced for several years. Between 1662 and 1665 the *cour des aides* passed sentence by royal commission upon a large number of commoners who had put a helmet on top of their escutcheons. However, it appears that these sanctions were invoked only against persons who usurped both noble status and helmet-surmounted arms. Those commoners who, without claiming to be nobles, stuck helmets on their coats of arms out of mere swank were probably not disturbed.

In Franche-Comté, which was conquered in 1674 and annexed by the Peace of Nijmegen, the edict of Philip IV of Spain, dated 4 July 1650, remained in force. This forbade commoners the use of timbred arms. Louis XIV confirmed this ban by his declaration of 3 March 1699.

Actually, commoners often timbred their arms in all the territories ruled by the king of France, and it was the same with the use of coronets. Though commoners were forbidden to include them in their arms, they did so nevertheless.

In Artois and in the parts of Flanders and Hainault annexed after the treaties of the Pyrenees and Nijmegen, the regulation of 14 December 1616, issued by Archduke Albrecht and the Infanta Isabella, remained in force. It provided for a fine of 300 florins for unauthorized use of helmets shown full face and of the coronets appropriate to princes, dukes, counts, and marquises.

Despite all this, in the second half of the 17th century, throughout the lands ruled by the king of France, the count's coronet was in current use among commoners. Oval escutcheons having come into general use in the 18th century, the possessors of armorial bearings often surmounted them with a coronet, which formed a very suitable "heading" for this type of escutcheon. In 1779 Mirabeau wrote to Sophie de Monnier to ask for a signet ring with an escutcheon surmounted by a ducal coronet, because "persons of quality are all adopting the duke's coronet, since every solicitor now has a count's or a marquis's."

Every possessor of armorial bearings had the right to have these depicted on objects belonging to him, and they became a sign of ownership. They appeared on crockery, books, tapestries, firebacks, seals, ships, real property. If the last-mentioned took the form of buildings, the arms were carved over the door. If it was land, the owner had his arms cut on a boundary stone or post. On the boundary between two estates, each owner had his arms shown on one face of a flat stone marking the line of division. Where fiefs were concerned, the face of the stone turned toward the vassal's fief was not supposed to show any arms; only the reverse side bore the *seigneur*'s arms. Those *seigneurs* who possessed the power of high justice enjoyed the exclusive privilege of displaying their arms in the places that were under their jurisdiction. Even the king himself might not affix his own there. Under Louis XIII the royal officials of Brignoles caused the arms of France to be set up in a number of neighboring localities where the prior of La Celle held the powers of high, middle, and low justice. Acting on his complaint, the *parlement* of Provence, by an *arrêt* of 24 November 1634, condemned the king's action and ordered that his arms be everywhere replaced by those of the prior. The royal arms were taken down, with great show of honor, and conveyed to the office of the court amid marks of veneration by the people; but, all the same, they were taken down.

The *seigneur* who held the power of high justice or, in his absence, the *seigneur* who held the patronage of a church living had the right to a *litre,* or mourning-band, in that church. This meant "a mark of black paint, a foot and a half or two feet wide, drawn around the fabric of a church, inside and out, as a sign of mourning after the death of the patron or the *seigneur justicier,* and on which were depicted, at intervals, the arms of the deceased.'' The *litre* was distinct from the "funeral sashes," or hangings of black material, that were placed in the church during the actual funeral ceremony and on which the dead man's arms were shown. As late as 1743 the Paris *parlement* gave a ruling on disputes concerning a *droit de litre.*

An individual could remove someone else's arms if they had been improperly affixed to his property; but if he did this anywhere else, he would be liable to an action for tort.

When a family was on the point of dying out, its last representative could appoint a distant relative or even a friend to be the inheritor of all his possessions, on condition that he adopted his name and arms. This was called *relèvement de nom et d'armes.* Marriage contracts provided for the bridegroom to take over the bride's coat of arms. Individuals of their own volition adopted the name and arms of a relative—for example, those of their grandmother—or the name and arms that their family had borne earlier and had abandoned when they took over the name and arms of another family.

As a member of this society the king shared in all the usages related to armorial bearings. The royal arms appeared on public buildings above the arms of the persons—governors or whoever else they might be—who had built them. The royal arms were shown on the gates of towns situated on the royal demesne. When affixed in any place or on any symbolic object, the royal arms signified that the population of that place or the bearer of that object was under the king's protection. This was why the king's bailiffs (*sergents royaux*) had fleurs-de-lis on their staffs. In 1739 Louis XV gave the inhabitants of Spa a warrant of protection and therewith authorized them to set up, wherever they thought best, his "arms, signs, and royal staffs, so that no one might have any pretext for not knowing" the situation. Breach of royal protection constituted a crime of *lèse-majesté,* as did also the tearing-down or breaking of the royal arms.

In the 17th century the king, the princes of the blood, and the peers of France started to give their escutcheons the backing of an ermine-lined mantle. The great officers of the Crown each had emblems of his particular office, which he placed behind his escutcheon.

As sovereign, responsible for the good order of society, it behooved the king to know everything about armorial bearings, the fundamental social symbol of this society.

The royal tribunals took cognizance of usurpation of arms, of the right to complete arms, of conditions included in wills regarding the adoption of name and arms, of the *relèvement* of arms, of the affixing of arms in churches, of the right to bear arms surmounted by helmets, and of the removal and destruction of the arms of others, which constituted tort. The courts with competence in these matters were the ordinary judges, the *lieutenants généraux* in *bailliages* and *sénéchaussées*, with right to appeal to the *parlements;* the extraordinary jurisdictions—the Conseil privé (the Conseil des Parties) and the tribunal of the constable and the marshals of France—which dealt with cases involving defectors, deserters, and officers guilty of surrendering a town without a fight and which, after 1615, heard appeals in heraldic cases within the competence of the *juge d'armes de la France;* and the Cour des Aides, which dealt with usurped titles of nobility and timbred arms.

The king granted by favor to individuals or communities, civil or religious, either complete coats of arms (*concessions d'armoiries*) or particular heraldic features (*augmentations d'armoiries*). Louis XIII gave the Augustinians of Paris an azure escutcheon with a representation of Our Lady wearing a silver crown accompanied by three golden fleurs-de-lis, and the young Louis XIV, in March 1644, at the instigation of Anne of Austria, gave the abbey of Val-de-Grâce "the arms of France quartered with those of Austria, with a coronet."

Despite the freedom that existed in principle in the matter of armorial bearings, jurists from the 16th century onward considered that any change in one's arms, or any *relèvement*, ought to be submitted for approval to the sovereign before becoming valid, but there was no law to this effect, and many people never sought such approval.

The king placed at his subjects' disposal a group of experts and a specialized jurisdiction, his officers of arms. From 1407 onward they were organized in the College of Heralds. There were three grades: pursuivants, heralds, and kings of arms, the last-named being elected by the heralds and pursuivants assembled in chapter and appointed by the king. After 1615 the heralds were attached to the Grande Ecurie and were appointed by the king on presentation by the *grand écuyer.* Experts in "noble lore," they prepared armorial bearings, determined the form and construction of new escutcheons, corrected imperfect ones, composed coats of arms granted by the king, checked the validity of letters of ennoblement and grants of arms (this was confirmed by the ordinance of the Grand Ecuyer Louis de Lorraine, 29 September 1687), and reported on questions of heraldic law when called upon to do so by the judges. After 1615 they played a mainly honorific role in public ceremonies.

The complexity and importance of heraldic questions led to the creation, by an edict of January 1615, of an office of *conseiller du roi, juge général d'armes de France*. In principle he was to be a magistrate with exclusive competence in heraldic affairs, apart from the power of *prévention* possessed by the sovereign courts and the right of appeal to the Tribunal of the Marshals of France. He was to give judgment on the basis of the reports of heralds who acted as assessors in his court. Actually, however, this court was never organized. The *juge d'armes* had no office or clerk, no courtroom or usher. What he did was to approve armorial bearings granted by the king and those of newly ennobled persons. He issued "confirmations" and "regulations" to families who wished to have documents proving their right to the arms they bore.

The *juge d'armes* had to be "a *gentilhomme* of old family." He was appointed by the king on presentation by the *grand écuyer*. The first was François de Chevrier de Saint-Maurice, appointed on 11 January 1615. Later the office became hereditary in the d'Hozier family. Pierre d'Hozier was made *juge d'armes* on 25 April 1641. His sons Louis and Charles succeeded him on 3 January 1666. Louis-Pierre, Charles's nephew, became *juge d'armes* on 2 November 1710, being followed by his son Antoine-Marie on 12 October 1734; after him came his nephew, Ambroise-Louis-Marie, who took office on 26 October 1788.

The office of *juge d'armes* was abolished by the edict of November 1696 which established the Armorial Général, but it was reinstituted by the edict of April 1701. In the interval, Charles d'Hozier performed the functions of officer in charge of the Armorial Général, and fresh letters of appointment to the office of *juge d'armes* were sent to him on 23 August 1701.

By an *arrêt* of the Council of 9 March 1706 it was laid down that the *juge d'armes* was to approve timbred arms, register them in the Armorial Général, and affix his deed of approval under the counterseal on letters conferring nobility or confirming it, changes of name or arms, and grants of arms, before these were registered by the courts of justice. Generally speaking, the practice was observed.

The edict of November 1696 established "a grand mastership and special masterships consisting of officers who are to take cognizance of differences and disputes arising in connection with the said armorial bearings and blazons," ordered the establishment of an Armorial Général, and laid down a scale of fees for the registration of arms. This edict, which was purely fiscal in purpose, being issued during the War of the League of Augsburg, was to have brought nearly six million livres into the royal treasury. Actually, despite a number of *arrêts* by the Council, many persons neglected or refused to register their arms. Many others were angered by the fantasies indulged in by clerks who carried out the registration. After the war, in August 1700, an edict issued from Versailles abolished the various masterships—since no office had been sold—and registrations in the Armorial Général ceased after 1709, the earlier practices being resumed. What was left of this episode was sixty-nine authentic registers of the Armorial Général, which were deposited in the Cabinet des Titres that the king formed in his library in 1711. The Cabinet was in the care, first of Guiblet, then of Delacour, who died in 1779 and was succeeded by the Abbé de Gevigney, who was still there in 1789. The Armorial Général contains 180,000 names from the whole of France, 30,000 of these being from Paris and Versailles, and provides descriptions and pictures of blazons for persons ranging from the dauphin to innkeepers and fishmongers.

The king employed the social degradation entailed by loss of the right to wear armorial bearings as a means of keeping his subjects dutiful. In the event of desertion or *lèse-majesté*, nobles were deprived of their noble status and their arms, while commoners lost their arms. When this happened, the coats of arms were blackened and publicly smashed, being torn down from all the places where they had been affixed. By Henri IV's edict of April 1602, duelists were treated as criminals guilty of *lèse-majesté*. The Edict of Fontainebleau, June 1609, prescribed degradation and loss of armorial arms for duelists and loss of arms for their seconds. The Edict of Saint-Germain-en-Laye, August 1679, inflicted deprivation of arms upon duelists who had involved seconds in their quarrel. Their arms could not be transmitted to their children, who would have to put in for a new blazon. By virtue of the Edict of Versailles, February 1723, the Tribunal of the Marshals of France, which dealt with affairs of honor between *gentilshommes,* was empowered to sentence to deprivation of noble status and of arms any nobleman who struck another.

The order of the nobility

Armorial bearings concerned all the orders in the kingdom. In addition, however, each order had its own dignities, ranks, and other special privileges. In law, owing to reverence for religion, the first-ranking order, with precedence over both the others, was the order of the clergy. But in fact, socially speaking, the first order was the order of the nobility; it even obtained most of the highest ecclesiastical appointments, and it was the ideal of all Frenchmen—the order into which nearly everyone tried to bring his family, the model to which nearly everyone tried to conform. We shall therefore begin with the nobility.

The quality of being noble

The nobility of France had a juridical status derived from a number of royal edicts and *arrêts* of the Council of State and the sovereign courts and also from custom. All writers are agreed on a prime feature of nobility: it is a quality inherent in the person. But the writers of the 17th century emphasized the quality of blood and hereditary transmission. The true nobility was one of race:

> Nobility is a quality which makes generous whoever possesses it and which privily disposes the soul toward worthy things. It is the virtue of a man's ancestors that confers this excellent imprint of nobility. There is in the seed I know not what power or principle which transmits and continues the inclinations of fathers among their descendants. And everyone who issues from great and illustrious personages feels increasingly at the bottom of his heart a certain impulse that urges him to imitate them, while their memory incites him to seek glory and great deeds.[2]

Nobility which has been acquired is not true nobility, although it may *become* that. Eighteenth-century writers, on the contrary, especially those of the latter part of the century, such as Chérin and Guyot (1784, 1788), emphasized the role of the state, embodied in the king, in the formation of the nobility, its nature as a reward for services rendered to the state, and, consequently, the unity of the nobility and the possibility of everyone's claiming this status.

> Nobility is defined as a *quality that the sovereign power imprints upon private persons,* so as to raise them and their descendants above the other citizens. Three attributes constitute the essence of nobility, of that real, perfect, universal, sole, unique quality common to all nobles. These attributes are universality of prerogatives; inherence in the person, regardless of domicile or occupation; and transmission to descendants in perpetuity.

This section of jurisprudence is of interest to commoners because *"under our fortunate constitution, all citizens can aspire to nobility."*

This idea meant a transition from the concept of a society of orders based partly on biological characteristics—on race and blood and the inheritance of these characteristics, mitigated by a relatively weak dose of social nobility resulting from service—to that of a society of orders based on qualities resulting from talent and consolidated by heredity.

Seventeenth-century authors agree on the point that men are everywhere of the same species and the same condition as regards natural principles. Those of the 18th century go further: "All men are born equal." Whence, then, come the distinctions that exist among them? For the 17th century their origin is to be found in military valor, in bravery and fine deeds, the honor resulting from these having been transmitted by inheritance. Nobility is the more perfect in proportion to length of ancestry. At the end of the 18th century Guyot records the opinion of the comte du Boulainvilliers and the *président* de Montesquieu, for whom the nobility had "an origin as ancient as the gathering of men in society" and for whom, in particular, "the Frankish nobility is the stem of the great houses that exist today." But Guyot espouses the theory of the abbés Dubos and Mably, according to whom it was the perpetuity of fiefs that gave rise to transmissible nobility, so that it was the exercise of high employments and the will of kings that lay at the origin of this nobility. In short, the 17th century saw the nobility as a spontaneous social creation, an acknowledgment by society of an honor which subsequently became an inherited characteristic, whereas the late 18th century regarded the nobility as no more than a creation of the state's.

The degrees of nobility

The nobles enjoyed a certain number of privileges, consisting partly of social symbols, honorific titles indicating their rank, and partly of useful rights. In the 17th century and the first half of the 18th, however, these privileges were divided into degrees. The order of the nobility was subdivided into "estates." There were two main estates—the *gentilshommes* and the other nobles. Each of these was made up of a hierarchy of degrees. In the second half of the 18th century, however, the jurists tended to unify the order into a single undifferentiated nobility.

The lowest title was that of *écuyer* (esquire), for "the nobles have always borne *écus* (shields), bucklers, and armorial bearings, which are the oldest marks of nobility." This title was held by all nobles and was the ordinary qualification of mere nobility.

"Noble homme," which was a title of nobility in the first half of the 16th century, had ceased to be this by the beginning of the 17th. It was then a title for *bourgeois,* one with which "the worthiest of the townsfolk" adorned themselves. The *règlement* issued by the king's Council on 4 June 1668 provided that the quality of *noble homme* mentioned in contracts before and after 1560 was not to constitute proof of nobility.

The title of *gentilhomme* was reserved for those "whose ancestry has never included a commoner" and who were therefore truly noble. An ennobled person was not a *gentilhomme.* However, it was accepted in practice that the fourth generation of a family succeeding an ennoblement began to be *gentilshommes.* At the end of the 18th century Guyot considered that the title of *gentilhomme* was "a generic denomination belonging to all nobles." He tended to merge together the degrees of the nobility and to treat it as a single entity. But he had to admit that "some people" in his own day "make exception of the ennobled person, to whom they refuse to allow the qualification of *gentilhomme.*"

Among the *gentilshommes* there was an élite, the *gentilshommes de nom et d'armes,* "those whose family is so old that their beginning is unknown," a "kind of nobility that was formed when fiefs, surnames, and armorial bearings began and which has been made notable by warlike watchwords and military exploits." "The ennobled man may indeed, given time, become a *gentilhomme* but never a *gentilhomme de nom et d'armes,* since he does not possess the antiquity of race required for that." "This nobility *de nom et d'armes* stands at the highest point of human greatness and at the summit of the hierarchy of all who are down here on earth" (La Roque).

At a lower level, but also higher than mere *gentilshommes,* was the *gentilhomme de quatre lignes,* "symbols of an excellent nobility": a person whose parents, grandparents, and great-grandparents were all *gentilshommes* or *gentilsfemmes* had four quarters, or lines, of nobility.

Lower down came the *noble de race,* whose father, grandfather, and great-grandfather were *gentilshommes.* This nobleman counted his noble degrees on his father's side, without considering the maternal line. "The ennobled person acquires *noblesse* but not *race.*"

The king's commissioners investigating the nobility of Languedoc under Louis XIV divided it into four kinds: *noblesse illustre,* meaning the holders of great dignities, the barons; *noblesse d'ancienne race; noblesse de robe,* those who possessed offices in the *parlement;* and *noblesse de cloche,* the *capitouls* who had governed the city of Toulouse, with their descendants. All these distinctions tended to fade away toward the end of the 18th century, when the idea of the equal status of all nobles came to prevail.

The title of *"très haut et très puissant seigneur"* belonged to the princes of the blood royal and the *gentilshommes* whose families were connected by marriage with the royal house. That of *haut et puissant seigneur* was given to the *gentilshommes* whose proofs of nobility went back at least to the first ten years of the 15th century and whose houses had been "made illustrious by great marriages, considerable services, and important employments."

A *gentilhomme* could describe himself as a *"bourgeois"* of such and such a place without compromising his noble status, as the word *bourgeois* was here being used merely to define where he lived and did not relate to his personal quality.

A certain number of titles were common to *gentilshommes* and other nobles, since they corresponded to positions that even nobles who were not *gentilshommes* could attain. The higher nobility adorned itself with the title of *chevalier,* which was reserved to those possessing great *seigneuries* and high offices. Thus a mere noble like the chancellor of France could call himself *chevalier,* since the title went with his office.

Similarly, nobles who were not *gentilshommes* could, like *gentilshommes,* bear the titles of baron, count, marquis, or duke if they held fiefs of dignity corresponding to one of those degrees of the higher nobility.

Below the *gentilshommes* came the mere nobles. What these had in common was the fact that the date when their nobility began was known and was not far in the past, going back no further than three generations and resulting from an ennoblement which had raised them out of the commonalty through an action by the sovereign. Socially they were less highly regarded than the *gentilshommes,* but from the juridical standpoint they shared all their privileges—the privileges of the nobility.

The privileges of the nobility

Besides titles, the nobles possessed the right to bear distinctive emblems. In the first place, there were the armorial bearings, which were the hereditary signs of the noble status of a family, regulated in accordance with the science of heraldry and approved by the sovereign. It was no more permissible to change them than to change one's name. "The form and timbre of armorial bearings serve to distinguish between the different classes of the nobility." The wearing of coats of arms was general in this spontaneously hierarchical society and free to all—it had never been denied even to *bourgeois* and peasants. But the kings tried to bring it under regulation.

Next, the nobles had the right to possess weapons. They could keep them in their houses and could wear swords wherever they saw fit, even in the king's study. They possessed the right to hunt and to fire harquebuses, these rights being confirmed by the ordinance of 1601, article 4. The nobles also had distinctive forms of behavior; these were governed mainly by the system of precedence. It was for nobles to precede members of the third estate, unless the latter were magistrates. They took precedence over everyone on their own lands who was subject to their power of justice and over all ecclesiastics, unless these held some high rank in the church. They even took precedence over certain magistrates. The judges who administered "high seignorial justice" in Lower Poitou took precedence over *gentilshommes*. The latter protested, and the king's Council issued an *arrêt* on 1 September 1685 by which the *gentilshommes* were to enjoy throughout the year precedence over the judges of the *seigneurs hauts justiciers* in processions, presentations of offerings, distributions of consecrated bread, and other great church occasions and in assemblies and public ceremonies, except on the feast day of the saint to whom the relevant parish church was dedicated, this exception being made in order to do honor to the *seigneur haut justicier* of that place.

Gentilshommes and other nobles possessed in common a certain number of other privileges which were both marks of rank and useful rights. They were exempt from paying the *taille,* except on "commoner" lands they owned in Dauphiné and Provence, where the *taille réelle* prevailed, and were also exempt from paying *crues, aides,* and *subsides.* They were exempt from performing *corvée* for the king and from all forms of personal bondage, such as the obligation to use a certain *seigneur's* bake oven. They had to be given preference in appointments to civil dignities and to ecclesiastical dignities and benefices. Indeed, certain of the latter were expressly reserved for them. A number of chapters, such as those of Lyons, Brioude, Mâcon, Saint-Claude, and Strasbourg, admitted only nobles to membership. They were given preference where offices in the royal household were concerned, and several of these were assigned to them exclusively.

They alone could possess fiefs, *seigneuries,* and noble property in general, commoners being merely tolerated in possession of them, by dispensation. Nobles were privileged in the universities in respect of the period for which they were required to study. Exhibitions were reserved for them, such as those of the Collège Mazarin, the Collège des Quatre-Nations, in Paris; by a royal declaration of 21 August 1724, the nobles of Bresse, Bugey, and Gex were given the right to share in these exhibitions. Places at the Ecole royale militaire were given to nobles alone. Above all, *gentilshommes* and other nobles enjoyed substantial privileges in matters of justice; they were never flogged or hanged but were beheaded, unless they had committed treason, theft, or perjury or had been guilty of bearing false witness—for "a man's condition aggravates and increases his crime." They had the privilege of being more severely punished by fines and other financial penalties. By virtue of the Ordinance of Roussillon, all nobles were exempt from the jurisdiction of the lower royal courts, being subject in first instance to the *baillis* and *sénéchaux;* but they remained subject to the judges of the *seigneurs* who possessed powers of justice, since these powers were patrimonial. According to the ordinance of 1673 (article 10, heading 12), they could not be brought before the (commercial) courts of the consuls, though they were free to have summoned before these courts persons to whom they had sold grain, wine, cattle, or other products of their lands. By a royal declaration of 5 February 1731, in the event of their being charged with a crime, they were exempt from the jurisdiction of the provost marshals and from that of the presidial courts of last resort. At any time, in any case involving criminal charges, they could ask to be tried by the Grand-Chambre of the *parlement* of Paris and by its criminal division, the Tournelle. Peers of France were to be tried only by the *parlement* of Paris, with, moreover, a sufficient number of peers present. This whole set of privileges that were common to all the different "estates" of *gentilshommes* and nobles placed the order of the nobility above the rest of society.

Ennoblements

Nobility could be acquired. "It is for the Prince alone to declare noble those who deserve this quality." The right of ennoblement was a royal right, which went with the Crown, and ennoblement depended on the king's mere favor. But while no condition was *sufficient,* certain conditions were *necessary*. One had to be of legitimate birth and free condition, and of virtuous conduct, to have rendered services, and not to exercise, or to have exercised, any "mechanical art," that is, any manual trade. The ennobled person received the privileges, rights, and advantages of the *nobles de race* but did not acquire their "quality," their *race*: "The man who is ennobled acquires *noblesse* but not *race*." According to Henri III's letters patent of 5 May 1583, *noblesse de race* meant nobility going back at least four generations, to one's great-grandfather. The ennobled person was a noble but not a *gentilhomme*.

The king ennobled a commoner in the first place by acknowledging his right to possess a "fief of dignity"—a barony, viscounty, county, marquisate, or duchy—which he had acquired. To do this, the king received in person the new owner of the "fief of dignity," to accept his faith and homage. Ordinary fiefs did not bring ennoblement with them.

The king might also ennoble a man by means of letters of ennoblement. These had to be sealed with the Great Seal and checked by *maîtres des comptes,* whose job it was to assess the money lost to the king as a result of the immunities, franchises, and exemptions accorded to the grantee and involving a diminution of the king's rights. They had to be checked also by the *cours des aides,* which dealt with all the taxes imposed on commoners. These letters conferred on the grantee and on his posterity, born and yet to be born in lawful wedlock, enjoyment of the privileges of nobility which the other nobles of the kingdom had and were accustomed to enjoy.

Letters of ennoblement were usually granted as a way of rewarding merit. In moments of financial difficulty, however, the king sold them. Louis XIV justified the expedient by saying that financial services deserved to be rewarded no less than others. This explanation, which was somewhat insulting to the *noblesse de race,* was given in the preamble to his edict of March 1696:

> Unless noble origins and antiquity of family, which confer so much distinction among men, are merely the gift of blind fate, the title which is the source of nobility is a gift from the Prince, who knows how to reward appropriately the important services which subjects render to their homeland. These services, so deserving of the gratitude of sovereigns, are not always rendered arms in hand. Zeal is shown in more ways than one; and there are occasions when, by devoting one's possessions to the upkeep of the troops defending the state, one becomes worthy, to some degree, of the same reward as is given to those who shed their blood to defend it.

Actually, once the emergency had passed, all that was left was the disadvantage of having increased the number of privileged persons, and from time to time the king would cancel ennoblements he had granted. This was, besides, a way of obliging the beneficiaries to pay a second time, to ensure maintenance of their noble status.

Thus, the edict of January 1598 revoked all ennoblements granted in return for money during the previous twenty years; but in 1606 these were all reinstituted, against payment. In January 1634 all the ennoblements of the previous twenty years were revoked, except for the twelve which had been granted to the associates of the Compagnie de la Nouvelle France by the edict of May 1628. In November 1638 nobility was conferred on various persons in celebration of the birth of the dauphin. By the Edict of Saint-Germain, November 1640, all the ennoblements effected in the previous thirty years, whether for payment or otherwise, were revoked, and this decision was confirmed by the declaration of 16 April 1643.

However, in May 1643 Louis XIV issued an edict granting two ennoblements in each *généralité* to celebrate his "happy accession" (*joyeux avènement*) to the throne. In October 1645 the Edict of Fontainebleau created fifty nobles in towns in Normandy which were exempt from the *taille*—an excellent way of getting some money out of them. By a declaration of 30 December 1656 all ennoblements effected since 1606 were confirmed, on payment of 1,500 livres in each case. In January 1660 an edict celebrating the treaty concluded on 7 November 1659, the Peace of the Pyrenees, granted nobility to two persons in each *généralité*, against payment. In August and September 1664, two edicts revoked all the ennoblements granted in the previous thirty years, though the king reserved his right to confirm those granted for signal services rendered in the army or in other functions. On 13 January 1667 two *arrêts* by the Council extended the retroactive effect of this revocation to 1 January 1614 in Normandy and to 1 January 1611 in the other provinces. All the ex-nobles had to start paying *taille* again.

During the great wars of the last phase of the reign, between 1689 and 1713, letters of ennoblement were granted several times in return for money and were then revoked when peace came. Thus, an edict of December 1692 and a declaration of 17 January 1696 imposed payments on ennobled persons who had been reinstated after the revocation of 1664, and men who had been ennobled since 1664 had to make a fresh payment as a substitute for an increase in the services rendered. All letters of ennoblement for which no money had been paid were called in. The edict of March 1696 ordered the ennoblement of 500 persons, from among those most distinguished by their merits, virtues, and good qualities, in return for payments of 6,000 livres. With the same conditions, the edict of August 1702 ordered the ennoblement of 200 persons. The decree of October 1704 canceled half of these and imposed on persons ennobled in 1696 and 1702 an extra payment of 3,000 livres. The edict of December 1711 launched a hundred more letters of ennoblement. When peace came, the edict of August 1715 revoked all ennoblements granted since 1 January 1689 and put all those who had been ennobled back on the list of persons obliged to pay *taille*. However, at the beginning of Louis XV's reign, all who had been ennobled by letters issued between 1643 and 1715 were confirmed in their noble status on payment of a confirmation fee.

The performance of certain functions gave the right to ennoblement, but this situation was of recent date, for in 1582 Henri III's edict on the *taille* recognized only two sorts of nobles—those of noble origin and those who had been ennobled by royal letters. After that time, however, it had become accepted that the performance of certain functions ennobled a man. All the same, a distinction must be made: in principle, men ennobled by their offices—such as holders of military appointments in the *compagnies d'ordonnance* and the royal bodyguard; certain civil officers in the royal household; the counselors of the sovereign courts and the clerks of these courts; the *trésoriers généraux de France,* who were treated as being officers of the sovereign courts; and so on—possessed only a personal and temporary nobility. Such men were allowed to assume the style of "noble" or "esquire" and to enjoy the privileges of the nobility. But they were merely occupying places belonging to nobles, who in former times had had the exclusive right to hold these positions, and the proof that this nobility of theirs was not genuine was that it did not pass to their descendants.

Gradually, though, the children of these officials could acquire nobility; and after the edict of March 1600 on the *taille,* article 25, when a father and grandfather had both died while in the exercise of such offices, or if they had held them for at least twenty years and had done nothing that derogated from noble status, then a grandson of whom the same was true acquired a nobility that was transmissible to his heirs. The great-grandson was a hereditary noble and could even call himself a *gentilhomme.* In Normandy an extra generation was required—great-grandfather, grandfather, father, and son—in a similar exercise of these functions.

Certain offices conferred full nobility at once and even put a man among the higher nobility—those who could bear the title *chevalier* and had to be addressed as "Messire." These were the offices of chancellor, *présidents* of the sovereign courts, the highest positions in the armed forces and the royal household, and, in the provinces, governors, *commandants*, and *lieutenants du roi*.

Finally, the office of *secrétaire du Roi, Maison, et Couronne de France* conferred on those who held it a *noblesse de race* that was transmissible to their posterity just as if they had held it for four generations, that is, as if they were *gentilshommes*, according to letters patent of Charles VIII dated February 1484 and confirmed by the Declaration of Blois, 29 March 1577 and the edict of April 1673; in this case, however, there was a condition that letters of honor were granted after at least twenty years' service.

In numerous towns the functions of mayor, consul, alderman (*échevin*), or *capitoul* conferred a kind of nobility that was called *noblesse de cloche* or *noblesse municipale*. In Paris, the provost of the merchants, the four aldermen, and their children, born and yet to be born in lawful wedlock, were noble by virtue of letters patent issued from Blois in January 1577 and confirmed by an *arrêt* of the *parlement* of Paris on 30 March 1624. A charter of 9 August 1370 was supposed to have given all the *bourgeois* of Paris the privileges of nobility, with permission to have timbred armorial bearings and to hold fiefs and freeholds anywhere in the kingdom without payment. At Poitiers the mayor and aldermen were ennobled, with their posterity, by letters patent of Charles V on 8 January 1372. At La Rochelle and Saint-Jean-d'Angély the mayors, aldermen, and town councilors enjoyed the same privilege, but this was revoked by Louis XIII in 1628. Ennobled in the same way, along with their descendants, were the mayor and aldermen of Angoulême, the two administrators of Saint-Maixent, the annual mayor and the twenty-four life aldermen of Tours; the mayor, the twelve aldermen, and the twelve sworn councilors of Niort; and the eight *capitouls* of Toulouse, who were proclaimed *nobles de race, gentilshommes*, and heads of the local nobility; the consuls and aldermen of Lyons, who were allowed to carry on trade and business without derogation, provided they did not openly "keep shop"; the eighteen aldermen, the thirty-six councilors, the attorney, and the town clerk of Angers; the four aldermen of Bourges—though their noble status was canceled if they engaged in trade or became notaries or attorneys. Also ennobled were the municipal magistrates of Cognac, Abbeville, Péronne, and Nantes.

Without actually being ennobled, the *bourgeois* of Orléans, Troyes, Rheims, Autun, Dijon, and Chalon-sur-Saône enjoyed exemption from frank fee and from the *ban et arrière-ban*.

According to the general custom of Champagne and Brie, "the womb ennobles." A mother passed her noble status on to her children even if her husband, their father, lived like a commoner, as a merchant. The customs of Troyes, Châlons-sur-Marne, Chaumont-en-Bassigny, Vitry, Sens, and Meaux confirmed this arrangement.

The edict of 1600 on the *taille* declared that the right to "assume the quality of esquire and join the ranks of the nobility" belonged to those "whose grandfather and father had followed the profession of arms and had committed no action that was base or derogatory to their quality." By the Edict of Fontainebleau, November 1750, registered by the *chambre des comptes* on 4 February 1751, in response to a current of ideas regarding the warlike origin of the nobility, the king created a military nobility which could be acquired by right through military service, without any special letters of ennoblement being needed. All army officers were to be exempt from paying *taille* while they were officers. All officers of nonnoble origin whose rank was below that of *maréchal de camp,* who were *chevaliers* of the Royal and Military Order of Saint-Louis, and who had thirty years of unbroken service were to be exempt from *taille* for the rest of their lives. The qualifying period of service was shortened to twenty years for captains, eighteen for lieutenant colonels, sixteen for colonels, and fourteen for *brigadiers*. Captains who were *chevaliers* of the Order of Saint-Louis and who had left the service owing to wounds were to be exempt from *taille*. "Every officer, born in lawful wedlock, whose father and grandfather acquired exemption from paying *taille* by virtue of the above articles shall be noble by right," after becoming a *chevalier* of the Order of Saint-Louis and fulfilling the conditions previously set out. This noble rank passed by right to legitimate offspring and was then regarded as being four-generation nobility, so that the children were *gentilshommes*. All general officers were ennobled, along with all their posterity born and to be born in lawful wedlock.

Derogation

New nobility, meaning that possessed by the first holder of letters of ennoblement or by someone holding an office that carried nobility with it, was lost either by the holder's leaving office or by his committing actions incompatible with nobility and derogatory to it. But derogation did not entail loss of *noblesse de race*. Though this might lie dormant, it was never extinguished. "He who possesses that nobility which we call natural and 'of the blood' can never lose or alienate it, since its original essence survives even those who have been condemned, and passes to their children. In short, rights of blood are inviolable and civil ordinances are incapable of violating them" (La Roque). Even three consecutive generations of derogation did not bring loss of nobility. The *cour des aides* of Paris ruled in May 1601 that children could be relieved of the consequences of actions derogatory to nobility which had been committed by their fathers and grandfathers. An *arrêt* of the same court, in March 1684, ruled that one hundred years of derogation extinguished nobility for good. However, the line taken by these magistrates was not followed by the jurists. At the end of the 18th century Guyot was still saying that "nobility, once acquired, constitutes the condition of a family, and not merely of its existing members but also of all those yet to be born." Consequently, the *noble de race* who gave up his derogatory way of living became noble again without need of any formality. Nevertheless, it was customary for him to announce his intention by obtaining letters of rehabilitation from the king. The regulation of 1661 confirmed this practice. Letters of rehabilitation were addressed to the *parlement* and the *chambre des comptes,* for them to check whether the grantee was indeed of noble race and then to ratify them.

Generally speaking, what derogated from nobility was any activity aimed at making money, especially trade, and any manual labor which was held to be base and "mechanical." These activities were, for the nobleman, the equivalents of original sin for men at large. The nobleman was supposed to live on his rents. "*Gentilshommes* wish only for the riches of glory; merchants, on the other hand, always aim at profit and usually employ all sorts of tricks in order to get what they want." "Nobility is engendered in war and increased through the practice of war; and it seems that this quality cannot survive in mercenary persons, who spend their lives in a continual striving to become rich."

This was how it was that farming someone else's land for profit became an action that derogated. In general, nobles were forbidden to take leases of lands, tithes and other church revenues, *champarts,* and *agrières,* even if they used another person's name, nor could they stand surety for farmers, participating in the profits of their farms (ordinances of François I, 1540; of Orléans, 1560; of Blois, 1567, article 48; of Blois, 1588; *arrêts* of the Council of State, 13 January 1667 and 10

October 1668). But a noble could, without derogating, farm parts of the king's revenue, for royal service was always honorable and elevated the rank and quality of whoever engaged in it. After the *arrêt* of the Council dated 25 February 1720, nobles were also allowed to farm without derogation the lands and *seigneuries* of the princes and princesses of the blood.

Trade entailed derogation for whoever engaged in it. But it was retail trade and shopkeeping that the jurists considered forbidden by the Ordinance of Aumale, April 1540, by the ordinance of 1567, and by the ordinance of 15 January 1629, article 451. Wholesale trade was *not* derogatory, and this applied especially to maritime trade. As early as 1566 Charles IX had given permission to the inhabitants of Marseilles, because of the small amount of cultivable land available to them, to call themselves nobles and merchants at the same time. The customs of Brittany and Normandy and the privileges of the city of Lyons held that nobility and wholesale trade were compatible. The edicts of May and August 1664, establishing trading companies for the East and West Indies, authorized any nobleman to join them. By the Edict of Saint-Germain-en-Laye, August 1669, verified by the Paris *parlement,* the *chambre des comptes,* and the *cour des aides,* nobles could engage in maritime trade without derogation and could take shares in merchant vessels and their cargoes, provided they carried on no retail trade. The edict of December 1701 established the point that all nobles other than magistrates could freely engage in wholesale trade and at the same time take precedence over merchants, retaining all the privileges of nobility. Nobles were not required to obtain membership in any corporation of merchants or submit to any apprenticeship. The status of wholesale merchant was accorded to "all who carry on their trade in warehouses, selling their goods in bales and crates or as undivided units and who do not keep an open shop or have any display or sign at their doors or before their houses." But the edict of September 1706 confirmed an old rule: *magistrates* were not permitted to engage in any trade, either wholesale or retail, on pain of losing their privileges and exemptions.

A base and derogatory character was assigned to a certain number of occupations connected with the enforcement of justice: all bailiffs (*sergents*), considered *vils et abjects,* all tipstaffs, all clerks of seignorial and municipal courts, all clerks of royal courts except those of the sovereign courts, and those attached to the *bureaux des finances,* whose offices were never regarded as derogatory until 1666 but were so regarded after the judgment of the commissioners investigating the nobility in the *généralité* of Châlons in that year; all notaries other than those of the Châtelet of Paris (to the latter the edict of August of 1673, registered by the *parlement* and the *chambre des comptes,* attributed the quality of *conseillers du roi* and confirmed their power to record contracts, inventories, and other deeds throughout the realm "without the title and functions of *notaire garde-note* being taken as derogatory to those who at present possess the title of nobles or who shall acquire that title in time to come"). The occupation of attorney derogated those who practiced it, with the possible exception of attorneys employed in the *parlements.* Advocates who pleaded in the lower courts where there were no attorneys did not suffer derogation, by virtue of *arrêts* of 1 August 1618 and 13 June 1665. In Brittany neither attorneys nor notaries suffered derogation.

Minters suffered derogation, because they were manual workers, but the keepers and masters of the mint, who were magistrates, did not.

Doctors of medicine did not suffer derogation, for their gains, like those of advocates, were honorary rather than mercenary; but apothecaries did, owing to the manual nature of their work.

Work as a servant—as lackey, *valet de chambre,* waiting-man—was derogatory unless performed in the service of the king or the princes of the blood.

Bankruptcy and insolvency were derogatory; even the aldermen of Paris, if they became insolvent, were deprived of their nobility (edict of June 1716).

Cultivating one's own land in order to consume the crops, or even to sell them, was never derogatory. It was an occupation "no less worthy for a *gentilhomme* in peacetime than that of bearing arms in wartime is glorious" (La Roque).

Glassmaking was not derogatory, by virtue of the *arrêt* of the *cour des aides* of Paris in 1582, that of 1597 in favor of the *gentilshommes* of Melun who were glassmakers, and that of April 1601 for the benefit of the glassmakers of Charleu, Fontenay, Thiérache in Picardy, and Princeaux near Nevers. Nobles were allowed, without derogation, to direct work in mines, associating themselves with or involving themselves in the digging and exploitation of such mines and the smelting of the ore produced (letters patent of Henri II, 30 September 1548 and 10 October 1552; edict of June 1601, article 17; edict of February 1722, article 12).

To sum up, nothing to do with the exploitation of a *gentilhomme's* own land or its subsoil was derogatory, nor were any functions, even the humblest, which were exercised in the king's service or near his person or that of a prince of the blood. Derogation bore the ancient mark of a highly hierarchical society of the military and agrarian type. Little by little the expansion of trade and credit and a mercantilist policy caused juridical exceptions to be made in favor of large-scale trade, but these entered only slowly into general acceptance.

Investigations of claims to noble status

Nobility was the ideal of all members of the society. Consequently there were many who usurped noble status. The state did not accept these spontaneous social elevations, which reduced the number of tax-payers and debased the social hierarchy. The *cours des aides* often, acting on complaints by parishes or private persons, required alleged nobles to prove their noble status. The King in Council from time to time resolved to carry out investigations of the nobility, who were invited to show their title deeds.

Henri II's Ordinance of Amboise, 26 March 1555, forbade common-ers to usurp noble status on pain of a fine of 1,000 livres. By articles 3 and 110 of the Ordinance of Orléans, judges could impose discretionary fines on usurpers of titles of nobility and timbred armorial bearings. These provisions were repeated by the edicts of July 1576 and Septem-ber 1577, by the Ordinance of Blois (article 257), and by the edicts of 1600 and 1632.

In order to prove his nobility, a person claiming this status did not have to produce a title deed: publicly known possession of this status for a century or more was sufficient for presumption of its validity. A hundred years sufficed to establish presumption but did not constitute a term of prescription, for "nobility is not acquired by any lapse of time whatsoever." Authenticated contracts that were mere family deeds, in which a man's father and grandfather assumed the quality of noblemen, were not sufficient; what was needed was external and public evidence (declaration of 22 June 1664). What had to be produced, therefore, were deeds recorded by a notary or extracts from registers of church membership, marriage contracts, certificates of baptism, sharings of inheritances, wills, tonsurings, and other public documents in which mention of descent was made, the "qualities" derived from fiefs held by one "race" of nobles after another and mentioned in contracts, court rulings about "condition," inscriptions and epitaphs in public places, or the continuity of the same armorial bearings in one family. Nobility was further verifiable through dignities held, by showing the letters of appointment and acts of reception, or through military responsibilities, by showing extracts from muster rolls and the accounts submitted to the *chambre* by the *trésoriers ordinaires ou extraordinaires des guerres*. Finally, evidence for nobility was to be found in the acts of faith and homage performed for fiefs and in histories and chronicles.

Facts of genealogy and nobility could be verified by documents but also by witnesses, following a number of *arrêts* of the *cour des aides* in Paris, such as that of June 1599. Four witnesses had to be produced who would affirm that they had known the grandfather and father of the alleged noble and that they had seen him live like a noble and perform actions characteristic of nobles, without ever having derogated and without ever having been subjected to payment of the *taille* (except the *taille réelle*). By the edict of March 1600 on the *taille,* a man being investigated had to prove nobility over three generations, including his own, everywhere in the kingdom. In Normandy, proof covering four generations, back to the great-grandfather, had to be provided, according to letters patent of 8 May 1583, and this also applied in Brittany, Dauphiné, and Lorraine. By an *arrêt* of the Council dated 19 March 1667, nobles had to show how they, their fathers, and their grandfathers had assumed the quality of *chevalier* and *écuyer* since 1560. "Living like a noble means bearing arms and serving the Prince in time of war, exercising the responsibilities of captain, lieutenant, or ensign, and performing other actions of a true *gentilhomme,* without doing anything derogatory."

Investigations aimed at exposing pseudo-nobles were resolved upon on 15 March 1655, for Normandy; 30 December 1656, for the areas covered by all the *cours des aides;* 8 February 1661 for the area covered by the Paris *cour des aides;* 20 June 1664 for the whole kingdom; 20 January 1668 for Brittany; 4 September 1696 for the whole kingdom.

Usurpations of noble status had been numerous owing to the wars, both civil and foreign. Inspired by complaints from nobles and from payers of *taille,* royal declarations of 30 December 1656 and 8 February 1661 obliged all who claimed enjoyment of the status of nobleman to furnish their proofs. *Règlements* of 15 March 1655, 10 December 1656, 8 February 1662, and 5 July 1664 authorized the *cours des aides* to look for pseudo-nobles in the areas subject to their jurisdiction. But the judicial procedures involved were slow and expensive.

The declaration of 22 June 1664 ordered those who claimed the qualities of *chevalier* and *écuyer* to show the originals of their titles and, in conformity with the *arrêts de vérification* of the declaration of 1661, to "produce the original engrossings or records of the titles justifying their nobility since the year 1560." Those who could produce only titles and contracts that were later in date than that would be declared commoners and taxpayers and sentenced to pay fines. The *arrêt* of the Council, in the form of a *règlement* dated 19 March 1667, confirmed these provisions and set out the proofs required.

The *arrêts* of the Council of 8 August 1664, 22 March 1666, and 5 May 1667 put an end to prosecutions by the *cours des aides* and gave authority to the commissioners sent into the provinces, the intendants, to seek out pseudo-nobles. Article 17 of the Council's *arrêt* of 22 March 1666 ordered that, when this inquiry had been completed, a catalogue should be compiled containing the names, surnames, arms, and residences of those *gentilshommes* who had been recognized as such. These catalogues should be registered in their respective *bailliages*. *Arrêts* by the Council on 15 March 1669 and 2 June 1670 ordered these catalogues, together with the lists of individuals found guilty of usurpation, to be deposited in the king's library. The commission of 14 May 1666 appointed other commissioners to be attached to the king's Council and ready to act upon its orders. The views of the intendants would be reported to these commissioners, who would have the last word. This commission was revoked by the Council's *arrêt* of 6 January 1674.

During the War of the League of Augsburg and the War of the Spanish Succession, usurpations of nobility multiplied, even on the part of those who had already been found guilty of this offense. Furthermore, the king created 500 new nobles. In order to relieve the burden on the taxpayers, the royal declaration of 4 September 1696 directed that the commissioners sent into the provinces were to seek out both those usurpers who had already been caught once and those who had never been prosecuted. The *arrêt* of the Council dated 26 February 1697, issued as a *règlement,* laid it down that *arrêts* of the higher courts and judgments in which the parties had assumed the quality of *noble homme, écuyer, messire,* or *chevalier* should not constitute titles justifying a claim to nobility and that, for this purpose, only marriage contracts would be acceptable, along with divisions of inheritances, transactions between members of the same family, and other authentic documents, *arrêts* of the Council, and ordinances and judgments by the intendants issued since the Council's *règlement* of 22 May 1666.

The declaration of 30 January 1703 ordered that the investigation be pursued. The usurpers did their best to drag out the inquiries, so the

Council's *arrêt* of 15 May 1703 laid down an accelerated form of procedure.

Toward the end of the War of the Spanish Succession, and after it was over, the declaration of 16 January 1714 directed the intendants and commissioners sent into the provinces and the general commissioners assigned to investigate usurpers of titles of nobility to continue and complete their work. The alleged nobles were called upon to prove their possession of noble status for a period of one hundred years, counting back from the day when the declaration was registered. A Council *arrêt* of 12 February 1715 prescribed that all the supposed usurpers involved in the investigation of the nobility before the declaration of 1714 had to submit authentic titles going back to 1560, inclusive. The investigation of the nobility persisted until 1 July 1718, by virtue of Council *arrêts* of 1 May and 18 December 1717.

The commission for investigating usurpers of nobility was abolished by a Council *arrêt* of 26 June 1718. As regards cases left pending, it was decided that those persons who had been summoned before the commission and those whose cases had not been decided should be declared noble, while those who had been found guilty and had appealed against this verdict should be declared usurpers. By a declaration of 8 October 1729, undecided cases were referred to the *cours des aides,* though the *parlements* and the ordinary judges might deal with questions of nobility which were incidental to matters and disputes that fell within their competence.

After 1718 no further measures were taken against usurpers of noble status, but toward the end of the century Guyot wrote in his *Répertoire:*

> Such measures are more needful than ever, for usurpers are operating without restraint; unqualified *gentilshommes* and even ennobled persons are boldly assuming the quality of *hauts et puissants seigneurs* and even of *très hauts et très puissants;* mere *écuyers* are assuming that of *chevalier;* and persons well known to be commoners are having themselves announced as marquises, counts, barons, and viscounts and are giving themselves these titles, if they are not satisfied with that of *écuyer,* in the documents they sign.

It would be interesting to know how frequently such acts occurred. They would seem to show both the continuing success of the conception of the noble hierarchy, men's frenzy to lift themselves up into it, and, at the same time, the debasement of titles and the leveling that resulted from this, a *de facto* equalization brought about before the legal abolition of this hierarchy took place.

"Point of honor" and the duel

Gentilshommes set great store by their "point of honor" and its sanction, the duel, as a social symbol marking them off from the other estates of society. Honor was what attracted esteem and consideration among the people. "Point of honor" was the point wherein honor was most involved and where the man of honor was most sensitive and touchy. For the *gentilhomme* this meant his honor as a warrior—or, rather, as a knight—whose primary characteristic was bravery, courage in facing any danger and confronting all enemies, without tricks or evasions; and so his second characteristic was total truthfulness, rejection of that shirking of risks and difficulties which constitutes a lie; and his third characteristic was absolute loyalty to his pledged word regardless of the consequences. Any expression of doubt, any appearance of doubt, as to the courage, truthfulness, or loyalty of a *gentilhomme* was an insult, casting a stain upon the warrior's honor which could be wiped out only with blood, on pain of infamy. Honor indeed, was what must be given priority over everything else—over the laws of God and those of the king, over life, over the strongest and dearest feelings—so that, even if the author of an insult was his own father, the insulted man had to kill him. Honor had become a deity to which the *gentilhomme* must sacrifice everything; it had become a cult—an object of idolatry.

It was nature that gave *gentilshommes* this honor of theirs. They inherited it from their fathers at birth; the blood of their ancestors brought them honor and the duty to keep this honor spotless, like their blood, so as to transmit both, perfectly pure, to their posterity. But it followed that their honor could be truly insulted only by one in whose veins the blood of a *gentilhomme* ran and that an insult could be wiped away only with that man's blood. The *gentilhomme* should fight duels only with his peers, with other *gentilshommes*. An affront to the honor of a *gentilhomme* coming from a commoner was a disturbance of the social order rather than an insult, and in such cases the courts were available—or else, quite simply, the stick.

Since the duel was a symbol of men's belonging to one of the higher orders, the number of duels fought was very great. In the course of the

17th and 18th centuries the king's government strove constantly to prevent duels by obliging *gentilshommes* to have recourse to a court in order to safeguard their honor. By doing this, the king dragged the *gentilshommes* down to the same level as the commoners, thus narrowing the distance between the orders and tending to wipe out the frontiers between them.

The preamble to the "Declaration on the Matter of Duels and Encounters," dated May 1634, expresses clearly what the king's motives were.

> This crime, which offends gravely against God's majesty and in a detestable form of sacrilege destroys his living, breathing temples, violates the laws of nature, which seek to keep everyone in being, desolates the noble families of our kingdom, and, finally, weakens the state through the loss of the blood of so many *gentilshommes*, who could have used it so much more valuably and honorably for the state's defense and security. Furthermore, contempt is shown to our authority, which is greatly injured by the fact that each private individual not only disposes of his life contrary to our intention but also presumes to take justice into his own hands and finds satisfaction in shedding the blood of his enemy on the pretext of safeguarding his honor: which honor, however, obliges him above all else to show respect to his sovereign prince and obedience to his laws.

Thus the king blamed the duel for violating positive divine law by ignoring God's fifth commandment, "Thou shalt not kill"; for violating the natural order created by God; for laying waste the second juridical estate (and first social estate) of the realm; for depriving the king's army of a great number of officers; and, finally, for diminishing the authority of the king, the embodiment of the state, through contempt of his laws and commandments.

The Roman Catholic religion provided very strong arguments for combating the duel. The edict of 1634 appeared at the moment when the Catholic renaissance was creating a movement of opinion in favor of the suppression of this crime. It was the period when Jean-Jacques Olier, the *curé* of Saint-Sulpice, helped or inspired by the Compagnie du Saint-Sacrement, formed an association opposed to dueling; it was composed of *gentilshommes* possessing the most brilliant military honors, so there could be no doubt as to their courage. On 28 May 1651, Whitsunday, some *gentilshommes* made public declaration and solemn protestation, in the chapel of the seminary of Saint-Sulpice, that they would never fight duels with each other. On 1 July 1651 the Tribunal of the Marshals of France approved their initiative and asked for their proposals regarding satisfactions that could take the place of the duel. On 10 August 1651 more than fifty doctors of divinity of the Paris faculty expressed the view that *gentilshommes* who did not resolve to renounce dueling ought to be barred from the sacraments of the Church and that those who died of their wounds in the place where they had fought a duel ought to be refused a religious burial, declared infamous, and excommunicated. A few weeks later a score of bishops publicly congratulated the *gentilshommes* who had signed the declaration against dueling and once more hurled their anathema against the barbarity of this practice.

As part of this same drive, the kings issued numerous edicts against dueling—in June 1609, February 1626, May 1634, June 1643, March 1646, September 1651, and August 1679, 1704, and 1711. These edicts in many cases merely repeated and confirmed each other, so that it will perhaps suffice to recall their general provisions.

The edicts made dueling a crime in law. When it occurred, it had to be punished, like any other crime, by the ordinary courts, with appeal to the *parlements*.

The Tribunal du point d'honneur

It was better to prevent duels from occurring, and so the edicts organized a whole system of arbitration and of friendly satisfactions and amends, with, if need be, legal punishment for insults.

These preventive measures and legal sanctions were the responsibility of a special tribunal, made up of persons well equipped to deal with "point of honor": the Tribunal of the Marshals of France, high dignitaries whom the king addressed as "cousins" and whom even the dukes-and-peers had to address as "Monseigneur" when they wrote to them.

The tribunal was very ancient. Since early times the constable of France had tried, together with the marshals, all the cases of crime and misdemeanor committed by soldiers and all disputes between *gentilshommes* when these concerned military service. The Ordinance of Anet, 26 June 1547, declared that the marshals of France were "members, joined and united together, forming a college, under one head, the constable." The marshals of France thus constituted one of the great corporations of the kingdom. The constable's office had been abolished in 1627, but his place in jurisdiction was taken by the doyen of the marshals, presiding over the college of the marshals of France.

It is necessary to distinguish between the Tribunal de la Connétablie and the Tribunal du Point d'honneur. The former was the supreme organ of the *maréchaussée* (marshalsea), the body charged with maintaining order on the highways and, in particular, with policing the behavior of the soldiery. This tribunal, which met around the marble table in the Palace of Justice, consisted of royal judges, *lieutenants généraux*, and *lieutenants particuliers*, who dispensed justice in the name of the marshals of France. The latter had at their disposal, in Paris, the Compagnie de la Connétablie, the colonel's troop of the *maréchaussée*, whose grand provost held the title of first colonel of the light cavalry. In the provinces the *maréchaussée* was represented by thirty-three provincial provostships, which were organs of both justice and police. Each of them included a provost general, a lieutenant, a sublieutenant, a sergeant, corporals, and *archers*.

The Tribunal du Point d'honneur was made up of marshals of France, who heard cases in person, under the chairmanship of their doyen, and not through the mediation of delegated magistrates. The competence of this tribunal extended to all *gentilshommes* and all soldiers, even foreign ones, when what was involved between them were insults, assaults, threats, and excesses committed by word of mouth, in writing, or by means of blows with fist or stick, and also *promesses stipulées d'honneur,* that is, gambling debts acknowledged orally, which were very frequent phenomena. This tribunal did not try cases of actual dueling, which came within the competence of the ordinary judges, but took all measures necessary for preventing such cases from occurring.

The edicts against dueling promulgated by Henri IV and Louis XIII did not produce the results hoped for. The swordsmen feared to be thought cowards, and they clung to a privilege that set them high above the commonalty. The king, first *gentilhomme* of the kingdom, often granted an *abolition,* an amnesty for persons guilty of dueling.

Louis XIV therefore took up the struggle anew. His edicts, which confirmed all the earlier legislation and completed it, prescribed penalties first and foremost for *combat actuel,* that is, for duels that were actually fought. In these cases the guilty men incurred the death penalty, with confiscation of property. A new provision was that the "unforeseen encounter" was to be treated in the same way as the premeditated duel and punished with the same penalties. In this way a means of getting round the previous edicts was eliminated.

If the duel had not yet taken place but an *appel au combat* had been issued, the appellant was liable to a sentence of three years' banishment and confiscation of half his property, with sentence of death in case of a renewed offense.

Recel du coupable (harboring of the criminal) after a duel was frequent, especially on the part of the great ones of the kingdom. It was henceforth to be punishable by a year's exile from the court. The royal officers were authorized to mobilize the town militias by sounding the alarm bell, in order to break into the castles of the grandees and arrest the guilty men—a supreme humiliation.

If *ignobles,* that is, commoners, challenged *gentilshommes* to a duel, were refused, and incited other *gentilshommes* to fight on their behalf, these *ignobles* were also to be sentenced to death.

Lackeys and servants who carried challenges or who guided anyone, whether a principal or a second, to the place of encounter were liable, on the first occasion, to be whipped and have a fleur-de-lis branded on the shoulder and, in the event of a second offense, to be sent to the galleys for life.

Thus the king tried to see that neither dueling nor actions likely to facilitate it should escape repression. He also organized preventive measures more and more firmly, notably by his edict of September 1651, which confirmed all the powers of "our cousins, the marshals of France"; by the Declaration of Saint-Germain, August 1679; and by the regulations which the marshals of France laid down in consequence of this.

The marshals took in hand the supervision of the provinces. They were able to commission, in every *bailliage* and *sénéchaussée,* certain *gentilshommes* who were qualified to take cognizance of disputes and try to reconcile the parties. If these commissioners did not succeed in this, they then referred the cases to the marshals. The procedures became sufficiently long drawn out for time to soothe the parties' anger.

When the War of the League of Augsburg constrained the king to seek all possible sources of finance, in March 1693 these commissions were made into venal offices, with the name of *lieutenants des maréchaux de France en province.* The organization was completed during the War of the Spanish Succession, when, in October 1702, similar lieutenancies were created in each of the judicial areas constituted by the *duchés-pairies* and in all those that came directly under the *parlements*. The edict of November 1707 created a second lieutenancy in the *bailliages* and *sénéchaussées*, in the judicial areas of the *duchés-pairies*, and in "others coming directly under the courts."

Anyone who had knowledge of a dispute between *gentilshommes* was duty-bound to inform these commissioners and these lieutenants of the marshals of France. He also had to warn the governors, the *lieutenants généraux* of the provinces, and the marshals of France. It was everyone's duty to intervene to stop a fight.

The preventive measures also included penalties for insults of a kind that might give rise to duels. After 1651, if one *gentilhomme* called another a fool, a coward, or a traitor, he risked a month's imprisonment and the painful obligation to apologize. In 1679 the punishment was increased to two months in prison. Whereas in 1651 an accusation of lying, or threats, meant two months' imprisonment and an apology, in 1679 it meant four months' imprisonment and an apology. In a case where a *coup de main* had been struck (a slap in the face, for instance), in 1651 the offender incurred six months' imprisonment and had to submit to receiving a similar blow; if the insulted person did not hit him, the insulter had to thank him humbly for his forbearance in not exacting the reparation to which he was entitled and to apologize to him. These provisions were retained in 1679, but the six months' imprisonment was doubled if the blow had been provoked by a charge of lying and, if it had not, then quadrupled. If a blow with a stick had been given, in 1651 the penalty was a year's imprisonment, with the obligation to ask pardon, on one knee, of the insulted person and to submit to a similar blow; and if the *lex talionis* was not applied, the offender had to thank the other man humbly and offer his apologies. In 1679 the penalties were increased to two years' imprisonment if a *coup de main* had provoked the blow with a stick and to four years if this mitigating circumstance was absent.

The Paris *parlement* applied these edicts with vigor, passing sentences of ever greater severity. The king insisted firmly on execution of the *parlement*'s *arrêts* and enforced the authority of the Tribunal of the Marshals of France. For example, in 1662 an encounter occurred, involving the prince de Chalais, in which eight men fought each other, with three seconds on each side. One of the combatants was killed; the others fled. The *parlement* sentenced all the survivors to death in their absence. A pardon for them was begged of the king, but he stubbornly refused to grant it, and the men remained in exile for twenty years. In 1713 the duc d'Estreés, a peer of France, and the comte d'Harcourt, a prince of the House of Lorraine, quarreled while visiting the duchesse d'Albret, in the presence of a numerous company. Their mutual hostility was very strong. The marshals of France assigned to each of them a guard from the *prévôté,* who was instructed to accompany them wherever they went, to eat at their tables and sleep in their bedrooms, so as to prevent them from coming to blows. The noblemen suspected of criminal intention refused to accept these guards, claiming—one as a duke-and-peer and the other as a prince—that they were not subject to the jurisdiction of the marshals of France but were answerable only to the king. Marshal de Villeroi, doyen of the Tribunal du Point d'honneur, reported this to Louis XIV. At once, by *lettre de cachet,* the king dispatched the recalcitrants to the Bastille, with an order to the governor to hand them over to the Tribunal of the Marshals of France whenever the latter should require to question them and try their case. The two men then made a pact together that neither would answer the tribunal's questions. But Louis XIV made them aware that that decision was quite the worst they could have come to, and this he did to such effect that they conformed without resistance to all the orders given them by the marshals of France.

It appears that duels became much less frequent. At any rate, Louis XIV congratulated himself that this was so. In the preamble to the Edict of Versailles in 1704 he declared himself pleased that *"ces funestes combats"* had almost entirely ceased. Was this official optimism justified? Doubtless it was, since, for once, Saint-Simon agrees with Louis XIV. In volume 16 of his *Additions au journal de Dangeau,* under date 7 April 1716, he writes: "In the time of the late king, who granted no pardons, even when the *parlement* exonerated an accused man, duels were extremely rare and were always kept very secret." The phrase implies, moreover, that the number of duels increased afresh under the Regency.

All these measures contributed to depriving the *gentilshommes* of a social symbol which they regarded as essential. The edict of 1634 had already altered the conception of honor, equating this—for the *gentilshommes,* in the first place—with respect shown to the sovereign and obedience to his laws. The honor of the subject and the citizen was to replace that of the warrior and the knight. The 1704 Edict of Versailles appears to tend in the same direction, effacing frontiers and distinctions among subjects of the king and the state. This edict provided for a case which had not been covered until then (perhaps it was something new in society) and which would be significant of the pretensions being asserted by the *robins:* the case of *"des officiers qui font profession de la robe"* so far forgetting themselves as to insult in some way *"gentilshommes et autres personnes qui font profession des armes."* Such persons were thenceforth to incur the penalties laid down by the edict of 1679 and the regulation of the marshals of France dated 22 August 1679, but they would be dealt with by ordinary judges, not by the Tribunal du Point d'honneur. The ordinary judges, themselves *robins,* were thus made judges in matters of "point of honor." It could be said, of course, that in a sense this edict still set the *gentilshommes* apart from and above everyone else, since it gave them special protection. But if we consider that, for the first time, the *robin,* whether ennobled by his office or still a commoner, was now being treated like the *gentilhomme,* subject to the same *prévention* as regards dueling and preserved from the risk of being purely and simply beaten up, and that in this connection the *robin*—a mere ennobled person or even a commoner—might himself become a judge of "point of honor," then perhaps we may conclude that, basically, the edict consecrated a sort of equivalence between the magistrate and the *gentilhomme,* reflecting a change in the social hierarchy.

The last major 18th-century legislative document directed against dueling was the edict which Louis XV, having come of age, promulgated at Versailles in February 1723. It confirmed all the previous edicts, and the king added the provision that any *gentilhomme* who struck another, in any circumstances, was to be punished by deprivation of armorial bearings and personal nobility, together with fifteen years' imprisonment. The king took a solemn oath and made a public declaration that he would never grant a pardon or amnesty for dueling, even on the occasion of the marriage of a prince or princess of the blood or the birth of a member of the royal family. Duels nevertheless continued to take place frequently, though chiefly between young officers. Insults were not unusual, and the insulted man would reply by giving the insulter the lie; that would lead to an exchange of blows, and that in turn would lead to a duel. But feelings were changing. The *gentilshommes,* taken as a whole, no longer brought to dueling the same passion, keenness, and fury as in former times. Dueling still occurred but was no longer the devouring malady that it had been in the previous century.

The social standing of the nobility

How many nobles?

It is hard to estimate the total number of nobles in the kingdom as a whole; even if we include, however, the ennobled and those whose nobility went with their offices, it was without doubt relatively small. The number had probably increased since the end of the Hundred Years' War, during the 16th century and until the middle of the 17th, through usurpation, prescription, purchase of noble lands and fiefs, military service, the acquiring of offices which carried noble status, and the granting of letters of nobility. The government strove to cut down the number of nobles, both in order to preserve the social order, by restoring to the old nobility their former luster, and out of fiscal interest, so as to oblige usurpers to resume paying *taille,* thus relieving the burden borne by others who were subject to this tax. It was especially after the Fronde, after 1655, and, above all, after 1664, during Colbert's period as minister, that the major efforts in this direction were undertaken.

In 1710 d'Hozier's *Armorial* registered the names of 58,000 nobles. In the places where lists of nobles enable us to check, it has been noted that d'Hozier recorded about three names out of ten. There would therefore seem to have been 190,000 nobles. Many of these, however, were heads of families, so that the total numbers of the nobility must have been much greater. Vauban in 1707 estimated the number of nobles at 52,000 families, made up of 260,000 individuals, which appears to be an underestimate. Coyer in 1756 thought there were 400,000 of them, which seems more likely. If, then, the population of France was about 20 million, there would have been two nobles for every hundred inhabitants.

Let us take Brittany as an example. In 1668 Colbert had the titles of nobility in that province checked by a Chambre de la Réformation de la Noblesse, made up of magistrates of the *parlement* of Brittany, all of them nobles themselves. The papers of this commission were burned in 1792 as "feudal deeds," but we still possess the notes taken by Father Toussaint de Saint-Luc in 1691. He reckoned that there were at that time about 1,500 noble families, forming 6,000 households or *ménages.* Given an average of five persons per *ménage,* the Breton nobility would then have numbered about 30,000 persons. The population of

Brittany was at that time approximately 2 million, so that the nobility must have constituted about 1.5 percent of it.

The investigation of impostor nobles was resumed by an *arrêt* of the Council dated 30 October 1696. Since 1688 an intendancy had been established in Brittany. The intendant, Béchameil de Nointel, was made responsible for carrying out the investigation. He used, among other documents, the poll-tax (*capitation*) rolls which had been started in 1695, in which nobles were listed on separate rolls. Entry on these separate rolls he considered to constitute proof of nobility. By applying this criterion, he found only 4,000 noble households, which meant about 20,000 nobles. In 1710 the poll-tax rolls furnished no more than 3,200 noble households, or about 16,000 nobles, and in 1750 these figures fell to 2,800 households and 14,000 individuals.

What was happening? Not a natural process of the dying-out of families but a change in the criteria of social classification. The commission of 1668 had upheld in their claim to noble status many poor men, even those who practiced trades, such as painters, innkeepers, tavern-keepers, or brothel-keepers. It had thus treated nobility as a feature that was inherent in the race and blood and could never be extirpated. After 1695, however, the king's agents were willing to regard as nobles only those who were capable of figuring in the special tax rolls of the nobility. The intendants thrust poor nobles down into the third estate. By order of the intendant, certain nobles were to be inscribed among the third estate, "even though they be *gentils-hommes*," "because they were without any property" or because they were exercising the functions of attorney, advocate, or bailiff (*sergent*). Thus, the royal exchequer made noble status depend no longer upon the quality of a man's blood but on his possession of a certain minimum income. The state's taxation system began to identify nobility with riches. The state began to alter the social constitution and the principle on which society was organized. Since the poll tax was levied everywhere in the kingdom, it is probable that the same method of proof of noble status was used elsewhere and that this tendency prevailed throughout France. It would be useful to find out what the attitude of the people was toward nobles who had been degraded in this way by the state.

The diminution in the number of nobles as a result of fiscal policy does not appear to have been balanced by the number of ennoblements. There were a number of paths to ennoblement. One was that of offices which conferred nobility. The offices of the magistrates of the sovereign courts brought with them "gradual" nobility. Holders of these offices enjoyed all the noble privileges, and when a grandfather and a father had each held one of these offices for at least twenty years or had died in office, a grandson also holding such an office was established in the nobility and passed this status on to his descendants. But custom allowed only a narrow gate of ennoblement through office. In Provence, and in Brittany after 1672, recruitment to the *parlements* was effected exclusively from among persons already noble. In Brittany, where there was no *cour des aides*, entry into the nobility via offices was possible only through those of the *chambre des comptes* (to which the *trésoriers généraux de France* belonged) and those of the chancellery "attached to the *parlement* of Brittany." In that province edicts of 1644 and 1645 had granted first-degree nobility to the members of all the sovereign courts. As a result of a remonstrance by the Chambre de la Réformation de la Noblesse, an edict of 13 August 1669 revoked that of 1644. The consequence was that while the *présidents, maîtres,* and *correcteurs* of the *chambre des comptes* of Brittany continued to enjoy the privileges of nobility, the auditors had to wait for confirmation in this "gradual" nobility until the *arrêt* of the Council of State dated 7 July 1693. In 1736 the deputies of the *procureur général* in the *chambre des comptes,* and in 1754 the chief tipstaff, were allowed to enjoy the same privileges. After 1711 the *chambre des comptes* offered a total of ninety-four offices, which were very tempting, because no examination or legal training was required, and, since the *chambre* sat "semestrially," the holder of one of these offices could spend half the year "living like a noble" on his estates. However, opportunities were restricted by the fact that there were families who perpetuated their occupation of certain offices, such as the Becdelièvres, who monopolized the office of *premier président* from 1678 to 1689, or the La Tullayes, who similarly installed themselves in the office of *procureur général.* Nevertheless, from 1700 to 1789 there were 365 changes of officeholder: 31 *présidents,* 125 *maîtres,* 40 *correcteurs,* 138 auditors, 10 *avocats généraux,* and 21 *trésoriers de France.* If we deduct 70 offices which were purchased during the twenty years preceding the Revolution, which had not had the time to produce their "gradual" effect, we are left with 280 cases in which offices changed hands—offices which conferred "gradual" nobility, 140 of these ennobling their holders definitively.

The *conseillers secrétaires du roi* employed in the chancellery of Brittany enjoyed the same privileges as those in Paris. They were recognized as possessing hereditary nobility. A declaration of August 1669 required, in order that their descendants might be accepted as noble, that they hold office for twenty years and obtain certificates of long service. But a declaration issued in the following month confirmed the rights of members of the Breton chancellery. An edict of July 1724 and an *arrêt* of the Council issued in August allowed the holders of these offices to retain only personal nobility, but they and their descendants were reestablished as hereditary nobles by the edicts of October and December 1727. By these means about seventy-one families attained nobility.

In principle, the holding of municipal offices in Nantes conferred a *noblesse de cloche*. After 1559 the mayor and aldermen, and after 1668 the mayor alone, were ennobled by office. But all of them found their nobility challenged in the latter part of Louis XIV's reign. Aldermen who had been ennobled before 1668 were subjected to a multitude of confirmation dues. Mayors had to obtain letters authorizing them to practice division of inheritances in the noble fashion, like true Breton nobles. Between 1693 and 1789 Nantes had nineteen mayors, but in the end only one of them was confirmed as possessing old-established nobility.

The second channel by which ennoblement could be obtained was that provided by letters of nobility granted by the king. Between 1696 and 1714, impelled by war needs, Louis XIV sold letters of nobility, though he reserved them for persons "who have most distinguished themselves by their merits and good qualities." In Brittany thirty-one such letters were sold, twenty-five of them to persons of dubious nobility who were in danger from the investigation of 1696. They were canceled in 1715, but their holders subsequently secured confirmation of their noble status.

Other letters were issued liberally for "special merit," with a view to fostering "emulation." As Descazeaux du Hallay, of Saint-Malo, put it in his memoir of 1700, they were issued to persons who had "discovered new channels of trade, caused many ships to be built, taken prizes from the enemy, established habitations in foreign countries, increased colonial settlements, brought specie into the kingdom, discharged through their commercial activity the kingdom's surplus, brought in plenty for those in want, given the people the means of existence through the movement and circulation of trade, and caused millions of dues to be paid into the royal coffers." Between 1696 and 1715 letters of nobility were granted to persons of this kind. They were canceled in August 1715, but in fact the beneficiaries did not suffer any disadvantage. Between 1715 and 1754 about ten letters were issued on similar grounds. Thereafter the number grew—twelve between 1754 and 1774, twenty-five between 1775 and 1788—in proportion as large-scale overseas trade progressed.

All together, though, between 1700 and 1788 there took place in Brittany only about 300 real and unquestioned ennoblements, effected by all the means available. Furthermore, these ennobled persons were far from being all of them accepted by noble society and integrated into the old nobility. The increase in the number of nobles therefore amounted to little and did not compensate for the decrease brought about by the agency of the fiscal system.

The density of the noble element in the population varied greatly from place to place. In Brittany one-fifth of the nobility lived in the towns; there were 75 noble families in Rennes, not including those connected with the *parlement,* and 93 in Nantes. Most of the nobility lived in the country. Some villages were well stocked with nobles; there were 16 families at Flélo, 25 at Pordic, 46 at Plouha. In other places nobles were very thin on the ground; in yet others, they were completely absent, and, though the peasants must have known that a nobility existed, they may never have set eyes on a noble. This was true elsewhere than in Brittany, too. The province of Maine had, in March 1789, 458 nobles whose names were registered for the elections to the Estates General, 279 of them being in the *élection* of Le Mans. However, the poll-tax rolls for this constituency show only 140, which means that nearly half of the 279 were *not* resident there, these being all members of the higher nobility. If we confine our attention to the petty nobles resident in the constituency, we find that, in the 261 parishes it contained, there were 129 nobles subject to the poll tax, of whom we know that 83 were men and 44 were women (widows, wives separated from their husbands, or spinsters). Seventy-nine lived in towns and *bourgs,* 71 of these in Le Mans itself, and only 50 in the country. There was therefore not even one noble to five parishes, and sometimes there were even fewer than that. The distribution of the nobility was indeed very uneven. There were 19 nobles concentrated in the northern sector, at Bourg-le-Roi, Courgains, Fresnay, La Fresnaye, and Vivoin. Elsewhere, dozens of parishes contained not a single noble.

Nearer to Paris, in the valley of the Essonne, between La Ferté-Alais and Corbeil, on the borders of Hurepoix and Gâtinais, during the second half of the 17th century, resident nobles accounted for no more than 0.5 percent of the population. The higher nobility, owners of the land in this district, lived at Versailles or in Paris—for example, the duc de Villeroy, peer and marshal of France, head of the king's Conseil des Finances; there were many nobles or ennobled persons who held offices in the *parlement,* which kept them in Paris. Moreover, most of the petty nobles themselves spent most of their time with the army, leaving their wives to look after their estates.

In other areas the presence of noblemen was episodic or marginal. Although Châteaudun was the chief town of the county of Dunois, belonging to the ducs de Longueville, it had not one member of the nobility among its inhabitants throughout the two centuries we are considering. As a judicial center, however, it must have seen *gentils-hommes* from the countryside, coming in as litigants, and in the 18th century some cavalry regiments of distinguished name were stationed there. How many inhabitants of the kingdom were there who knew the nobility only through hearsay, or a brief visit, or the passage or stationing of the king's armed forces?

The social degrees of the nobility

The works on economic and social history written by historians of the 19th and 20th centuries show us a social hierarchy within the nobility which is expressed in the way that both nobles and commoners behaved toward different members of that order. But we cannot know whether this picture we receive from their books actually corresponds to reality. On the one hand, all these historians derived inspiration from Loyseau and La Roque and included in their descriptions views propounded by these theoreticians which ought to have been checked against facts. On the other hand, they used mainly fiscal sources, and when they did use notaries' records they concentrated mainly, in studying postmortem inventories and divisions of inheritances, upon the wealth and income of the nobles. This means that what they give us is mainly economic hierarchies, hierarchies of wealth and income, rather than true social hierarchies. No one, so far as I know, has yet directed his main attention to what is strictly social in character, namely, associations of all kinds, including the most important of these: marriages. We still lack, so far as most of our towns and country districts are concerned, a systematic examination of marriage contracts and sociological discussion of the data resulting from this, which would enable us to perceive what the "existence groups" were and what their real hierarchy was. Moreover, while using Loyseau and La Roque, historians have not always seen fit to observe those writers' criteria of nobility—the gulf they set between *gentilshommes* and ennobled persons and, within the group of *gentilshommes,* the different levels they established—so that it is sometimes difficult, when reading their books, to make out whether they are really dealing with nobles, and, if so, what sort of nobles, and whether the levels theoretically existing among the *gentilshommes* actually corresponded to social realities.

With these reservations made, here is, provisionally, the social hierarchy of the nobility which seems to have been common to France as a whole in the given period, leaving aside many provincial peculiarities.

The court nobility

Standing at the head of the nobility were the court nobles. These were the *gentilshommes* who lived continually near the king, fulfilling functions in the royal household and in the households of the princes, together with those who, though they did not live continually near the king, had been, like them, "presented" to the king at his court. Presentation took place as a rule in the Cabinet du Roi, with someone already "presented" acting as sponsor. The men so presented might be invited to ride in the king's carriages, to go hunting with him, and to ride the king's own horses when they did so. The women were permitted to offer their cheeks to be kissed by the king, the queen, the dauphin, and the princes of the blood. They might also be admitted to the royal carriages. Entrée to these vehicles constituted the essential court honor. For the most favored, there might also be admission to the *"cercles de la cour,"* attending balls and receptions. Those "presented" at court thus fell into three hierarchical ranks: persons who had merely been presented, those who were allowed entry to the king's carriages, and those who were admitted to the *"cercles de la cour."*

In order to be presented, one had, in principle, to belong to an old family of *gentilshommes*. After 1732 it was necessary to prove 300 years of military nobility, without any known starting date. According to the regulation of 1760 one had to belong to a family going back to before 1400. Exempted from this rule were the chancellors and the keepers of the seals, the ministers and secretaries of state, the marshals of France, and the *chevaliers* of the Order of the Holy Spirit, with their descendants in the male line. Actually, the king's decision was absolute.

A relatively large number of presentations took place. Even quite a lot of petty provincial *gentilshommes* were presented to the king. It was a means whereby he could recruit *fidèles*. The number of presentations increased during the 18th century. By about 1789, 4,000 families had been "presented," which meant about 20,000 persons.

"Court honors" made possible the contracting of advantageous marriages and facilitated careers. By the second half of the 18th century they had become the proof *par excellence* of one's belonging to the higher nobility.

Only nobles who had been presented could aspire to a brilliant career in the army. They alone could rise above the rank of colonel, and high military appointments were their monopoly. Only presented persons could hope to obtain high offices at court, ambassadorships, and royal pensions.

Those presented at court constituted a superior social group. Chérin, the genealogist, wrote in his book entitled *La noblesse considérée dans ses divers rapports* (published in 1788): "In some circles they make a point of being at home only to persons who have been presented at court and so pitilessly shut their doors upon good and worthy *gentilshommes*."

This group, increasing through cooptation by its members, subject to the king's approval, possessed the largest fortunes in the kingdom.

The category of the "presented" had as its crown a narrower group, that of the dukes-and-peers and the ordinary dukes. These were a set of the king's *fidèles*, an élite, serving as a model for all members of this society of orders. The royal letters of 1621 which made of the county of Chaulnes a *duché-pairie* for the benefit of marshal de Cadenet, brother to the duc de Luynes, exalted this "highest dignity," granted in order to encourage others to "imitate" the virtues of the recipient and to "serve as a stimulus." The dukes-and peers occupied the front rank in the state and possessed the highest dignity among the nobility of France. This supreme honor was accorded by the king on account of the merit of the person so promoted or that of his ancestors. The merit in question consisted in love of warlike glory, notable deeds of arms, constant fidelity to the king, fervent love for the honor and independence of France. Letters of promotion to this honor were usually given to great and ancient military families distinguished in war. The only exception was Chancellor Séguier, who, to the scandal of contemporaries, was made duc de Villemor in 1650; but he had no male issue, and when his dukedom was raised in 1651 to a *duché-pairie*, the advantage went to his grandson, Armand du Cambout, marquis de Coislin, who came of an old family of *noblesse d'épée*. No other chancellor ever became either a duke or a duke-and-peer, and so the claim of the gown to equality with the sword remained without this sanction.

The group in question possessed, as such, no power or political authority. Its preeminence was exclusively social. But this was affirmed by a number of privileges. The dukes-and-peers enjoyed the honors of the court. They were permitted to enter the courtyards of the royal palaces on horseback or in carriages. Their wives had the right to sit on a stool in the queen's presence. They ranked immediately after the royal family and the princes of the blood in respect of marriages, funerals, baptisms, royal and princely banquets, and Te Deums. The king addressed them as "cousin." In the marriage contracts of the king's children, they signed their names just below those of the princes of the blood. They were entitled to be called "Monseigneur" and "Votre Grandeur." The ducal coronet and mantle were reserved for them. In the *parlement* they came in wearing their swords, occupied the high seats, and spoke standing up. They possessed consultative voice and gave their opinions before the *présidents à mortier*. Their own powers of justice came directly under the *parlement,* and cases affecting them personally were heard by the *parlement,* except when the security of the state was involved. Until 1667 they were, by right, members of the Conseil des Parties; thereafter they joined it only when invited to do so, and after 1673 they disappeared from its meetings— the *règlement* of that date does not mention them.

There were degrees among them. Since the edict of December 1576, members of the royal family and princes of the blood were peers by birth. They had precedence over all the other peers. At the ceremonies of the Order of the Holy Spirit they could use a hassock, whereas, after 1688, the other dukes-and-peers were not allowed to. The princesses of the blood were allowed to have two carriages when they traveled—one for themselves, the other for their equerries—whereas the other peeresses were restricted to one. In 1711 the princesses of the blood received the privilege of having their sunshades carried for them in a procession of the Blessed Sacrament, whereas the other peeresses had to carry theirs themselves. After 1643 the *premier président* of the *parlement,* at an ordinary session, asked, hat in hand, the princes of the blood for their opinion, whereas, when he asked the other peers for theirs, he kept his hat on. After 1650 the princes of the blood took to themselves the privilege of walking across the well of the court to their seats. By an edict of May 1711 it was the princes of the blood who, with the legitimized princes of the royal family, represented the peers of olden times at the anointing of the kings of France.

The other peers ranked according to the date on which their dukedom had been raised to the status of a peerage. At the royal anointment and in the *parlement* they sat in the order of the registration of their peerage in the name of its first holder. But these were not the only distinctions. First after the princes of the blood came the "foreign" dukes-and-peers, descended from eight great families which were described as "foreign" but *fidèles* of the king of France: Clèves, Savoy-Nemours, Gonzague (Mantua), Luxembourg, Lorraine, Grimaldi (Monaco), La Tour d'Auvergne (Bouillon-Sedan), and Rohan.

Next came the dukes-and-peers who were descended from families of *gentilshommes* distinguished by having "long lineages of valiant and illustrious officers of war, devoted to the service of the kings and of France, rewarded in certain of their descendants by the title of duke-and-peer." There seems to have been no difference between dukes-and-peers and counts-and-peers; the latter, in any case, became fewer and fewer.

After the dukes-and-peers came the "brevet dukes" (those whose peerages had not been registered by the *parlement* of Paris) and the plain dukes, who formed a single social group.

That what was involved was social degrees and not mere juridical differences is clearly indicated by the record of marriages. Of 205 marriages which have been studied, 100 united two families of dukes-and-peers; 76 took place between dukes-and-peers and daughters of the higher *noblesse d'épée;* and 29 joined dukes-and-peers to daughters of the higher *noblesse de robe*—ministers or secretaries of state—among whom we observe the Colberts and the Louvois. To an increasing extent the princes and princesses of the blood married among themselves, forming a superior group which gradually became exclusive. The "foreign" princes showed the same tendency. It was the same with the dukes-and-peers and the dukes from the ranks of the *gentilshommes.* As the 17th century advanced, the number of marriages made *within* each of the three groups increased.

The court nobility was represented in all the provinces. It did not reside there, as a rule, with any continuity, but it owned property in the country and exercised power and influence there, favorable to the king. In Brittany, for example, the court nobility included, in the first place, the king himself, who was *seigneur direct* of 409 rural parishes (out of 1,278) and of several towns, including Lorient; also the princes of the blood—the prince de Condé and the prince de Conti; members of the great houses of France, related to Breton families and holding property in Brittany, such as the duchesse d'Elbeuf, baroness of Rostrenen by her first marriage, and great Breton families integrated in the court, like the Rohan-Soubises and the Rohan-Guéménées, or the duc de Penthièvre; families of the higher nobility which, though not of the province, held property there, having been implanted in Brittany in the second half of the 17th century in order to control it, such as the duc de Mazarin and the duc de Rochechouart-Mortemart. Altogether, there were thirty-eight of these families. The group was reinforced by integration of members of the local higher nobility; the number of presentations at court increased during the 18th century, and families developed the habit of spending the winter at Versailles and the summer in Brittany.

A similar set of members of the higher nobility whose responsibilities kept them in Paris or at the court were to be found in the province of Maine: marshal de Balincourt, *seigneur* of Bouloire; the marquis Angrand de Fonpertuis, councilor in the Paris *parlement, seigneur* of Challes; the marquis de Villier, the marquis de Fontenailles, the marquis de Montbrun, the comte de Tessé; not to mention the Choiseuls, the Chevreuses, the Luynes, and the Richelieus.

In Beauvaisis the higher group of the nobility was made up of very great personages, attached to the king's service and residing habitually in Paris, who possessed fiefs and *seigneuries* in Beauvaisis, where some of them spent the most pleasant part of the year, or at least the months of hunting, harvesting, and *vendange*. Among them were the prince de Conti and the marshal de Noailles and, at a lower level, some state councilors and members of the Paris *parlement*.

In Picardy and at Amiens the high court nobility possessed extensive estates; there were the comtes de Noailles and d'Estrades de Clermont-Tonnerre, the Gontaut-Birons, the La Motte-Houdancourts, and the Chevreuses. But the most important role was played by great personages who spent part of their time in the province. The de Chaulnes, Créquy, and d'Aumont families dominated the country by virtue of their wealth, their clientages, and their offices and brought to it the customs and ostentation of the court. The Créquys were princes de Poix. The ducs de Chaulnes were barons de Piquigny, *vidames* of Amiens, and holders of 1,100 fiefs at the end of the 17th century. Governors of Picardy since 1633 and lieutenants general in the king's armies, the ducs de Chaulnes were accustomed to make solemn entries into Amiens, accompanied by a train of relatives, *fidèles*, officers, and vassals. The municipality came as a body to do homage to them. The de Chaulnes family had difficulty in concealing the fact that they looked upon *robins* and merchants as persons of little account.

Around Paris, in Beauce, Brie, and the Ile-de-France, representatives of this higher nobility were plentiful. Examples were the Villeroys, descendants of a family of *secrétaires du roi* but integrated into the high *noblesse d'épée,* whose castellany of Villeroy had been elevated in 1615 into a marquisate and then, in 1663, into a duchy. The duc de Villeroy, peer of France, marshal of France, governor of Lyons and Lyonnais, head of the royal Conseil des Finances established by Louis XIV, was one of the greatest personages at the court of the Great King.

In Burgundy, too, we find members of the high court nobility, such as, in 1666, Louis-Antoine Duprat, marquis de Vitteaux, who lived in great style when at court; and many others.

A higher nobility in the king's service, whether owners of property in the region or else residing in it at intervals, fulfilling functions there and integrated in its life, seems to have been represented in most of the provinces of the kingdom.

The provincial higher nobility

Below the court nobility in both functions and wealth, yet respected and envied because of its ancient origins and what remained of its past splendor, there was a provincial higher nobility who furnished an ideal for all society and whose way of life and fashions at least a large section of the nobles, the *robins*, and the merchants tended to imitate, adopting their moral values and prejudices.

In Beauvaisis it was the *chevaliers* and *écuyers* of the old nobility who mostly resided in the country: the Rouvroy de Saint-Simon family, the Gouffiers, in their two famous branches of Bonnivet and Crèvecoeur, the Gaudecharts, the families of François de l'Epinay, du Piez, de Canisy, de Boissy, d'Hécourt, de Bonburs, de Comberelle, de Cressy, and de la Hérelle, and the comte d'Auteuil. These were families whose importance was on the decline. They had been ruined by the Wars of Religion, by their elimination from royal offices, and, still more, by the noble way of life. However, while deeply in debt and forced to sell off fiefs and *seigneuries,* these *gentilshommes* retained the highest sense of their quality. M. de Malinguehen, *lieutenant général* in the *bailliage* of Beauvais, having charge of the roll of the *arrière-ban* between 1674 and 1697, taxed the marquis de Saint-Rémy, despite the latter's declarations. He found himself rebuked for not having believed the marquis on his word as a *gentilhomme*—he, who was only a *robin*—and the marquis wrote to him: "I thought that people were quite sure that when persons of our sort say something is so, it can be believed." The chevalier du Metz d'Hécourt wrote to this *robin*: "It is rather extraordinary that a judge should take so miserable a side as that of a wretched cad like Limermont against persons of quality, for whom you ought naturally to show more consideration, not to mention the duty of your office." Perrot de Fercourt, whose farmer had been given an order to do something, recalled his "dignity and prerogatives... I observe, too, that there is an insult in the term *'fermier judiciaire'*: that looks to me like a trick played by your *procureur du roi*. But as you are his superior, you should take care what you put your name to... Take order for that."

This old provincial nobility seems likewise to have existed everywhere. Often on the decline and sometimes needy, it nevertheless also included many rich families, who cultivated their estates with care. In Picardy in 1698, out of 500 noble families, 86 of whom were in the *élection* of Amiens, there were a good many of these higher nobles, such as the marquis de Tiercelin and the comte de Thoury, who were among the 28 living in Amiens itself; and among the majority who lived in the country were the old families of the comtes de Mailly, at Toutencourt and Rubempré, the marquis de Lameth, at Hénancourt, the Boufflers at Remiencourt, and the Rouaults at Gamaches.

These great nobles set the tone. The marquis de Tiercelin lived in a fine house in Amiens and held a salon in a "high chamber," seated on a couch of yellow damask hemmed with gold, in front of tapestries depicting the life of Solomon. Both town and country families held receptions, the middle-ranking and petty nobles as well as the others, and even the *robins*. The country-dwelling nobility continually visited Abbeville and Amiens, attending salons and balls and gambling with fervor. A common "society" way of life united them. From the early years of the 18th century onward, these country nobles came in ever greater numbers to reside in the towns, or at least to spend the winter there. The constitution of the commune of Amiens in 1726 gave a majority on the municipal council to the representatives of the nobility living in the town and to the officials of the judicature.

The noblesse de robe

Next, at a lower social level, came the nobility composed of *grands robins*, the members of the king's Council and the *parlement* of Paris;

below them came the members of the provincial *parlement* and, at a slightly lower level still, the members of the other sovereign courts. In principle, nobles who owed their noble status to their offices were supposed to give precedence to all *gentilshommes d'épée*. But what complicated the actual social classification was the number of genuine *gentilshommes,* and even of members of great families, who were to be found among the officeholders. Besides, the magistrates, as representatives of the king, derived a luster from that position which sustained their claim to be the equals of at least the *noblesse d'épée* if not the higher branch of the nobility. Though obliged to give precedence to the most illustrious families of the sword, they succeeded, through the prestige of their offices and through their wealth, in placing themselves above the middle and lesser groups of the *noblesse d'épée.*

The situation of the Paris *parlement* was special in the sense that its members formed, as a whole, part of a large social group of higher civil servants which embraced the masters of requests and the state councilors, presenting the same characteristics as the magistrates of the *parlement*. It was necessary to have been a counselor in the *parlement* or in the Grand Conseil in order to become a master of requests and then a state councilor. Numerous families who gained access to the Council of State subsequently consolidated their positions in the Paris *parlement*, that "august senate," venerated by the people, into which they sent their eldest sons for generation after generation, with only some of the younger sons following ecclesiastical or military careers. The social composition of the officialdom of the Council remained for two centuries amazingly stable and remarkably similar to that of the Paris *parlement*. Here were lineages that lasted for between six and nine generations, sometimes more. At the moment when they attained the office of master of requests and the dignity of state councilor, the members of these lineages were usually already nobles, having been ennobled, sometimes long since, by their holding of royal offices. For most of them, their accession to the corporation of masters of requests and to the Council constituted not only the apogee of their career but also the culmination of their family's social ascent. Their lineages had often begun, long before, in the commercial *bourgeoisie* and had climbed the ladder of the social hierarchy by means, first, of financial offices, then judicial offices in the *bailliages* and *sénéchausées,* then offices in the *parlements* and other sovereign courts, to reach, finally, the summit, the king's Council (Conseil du Roi). Once they had reached the Council, some families maintained their positions there for several generations before they left the scene. The lineage, while represented in the Council, also had members in the *parlement*, in the Grand Conseil, and in the other sovereign courts and higher judicial bodies. Its members found their wives in the world of the masters of requests, state councilors, officials of the court, either *robins* or *financiers,* or of the *parlement* and other sovereign courts, with which they formed a single social group that was, nevertheless, divided into two political groups, distinct and opposed to each other. On the one hand were the king's *fidèles* in the Council and at court, and, on the other, the men of the sovereign courts, officials who were often in opposition to the king, being wedded to a particular conception of the monarchy. The world of the gown, the Council, and the sovereign courts gave some of its daughters to great nobles of the sword, but these were cases of hypergamy on the women's part, which, although procuring useful connections, did not put the *robins* on the level of the *grande gentilhommerie d'épée.* The latter did not, with few exceptions, give their daughters in marriage to men of the gown; for them the latter were merely *bourgeoisie*. Similarly, though the world of the gown sent some of its younger sons into the world of the sword, it is important to note that the eldest sons as a rule remained *robins* and that, also as a rule, the younger sons failed to rise very high either in the ranks of the army and navy or in their "quality" as *gentilshommes* and did not really create families belonging to the *noblesse d'épée.* A few families from the world of the gown did become transformed into families of the *grande noblesse d'épée,* but these were few and far between. The world of the gown remained a world apart and distinct, despised by the men of the sword, for whom it consisted of *bourgeois*. The historian is therefore justified in calling this world and its inhabitants *bourgeois*. He must not forget that, juridically and socially, these men were a nobility exercising on the king's behalf and in his service, though sometimes against him, the essential elements of power (even over the *noblesse d'épée*): a nobility claiming to remain itself, socially, and to attain, socially, equality with or even superiority over the *noblesse d'épée*. It seems that, in the second half of the 18th century, a merging of conditions took place in proportion as the conception of the society of orders grew vaguer in men's minds, to the advantage of the conception of the society of classes—and this even where the society of orders seems to have remained liveliest, namely, in the *parlement*, to perhaps an even greater extent than in the king's Council.

The magistrates of the *parlement* of Paris—*présidents* and counselors of the various chambers—constituted a nobility. Between 1716 and 1771, 563 magistrates joined the *parlement*—between 9 and 11 each year. Including those who were already members in 1715, the *parlement* consisted of 951 magistrates belonging to 590 lineages. In 1715, out of 303 persons about whom we are well informed, 247 (81.5 percent) were already noble when they joined the *parlement*, 28 were sons of members of the privileged orders, and 28 were commoners when they took office, becoming endowed with the privileges of nobility by doing so. All the *présidents à mortier* were noble before they took office, together with all the *procureurs du roi* and *avocats généraux* and the six honorary counselors, and also twenty-two out of the twenty-three *présidents* of the various chambers—in other words, nearly all the most important magistrates, and especially those holding the posts of greatest responsibility. In 1771 89.9 percent of the magistrates were already noble before becoming members of the *parlement*. The "noble" character of the *parlement* had been intensified.

Nobles of very ancient origin—those whose noble status went back to before the 15th century, without any record of ennoblement—were not very numerous in these circles. Among such were the d'Argouges, nobles since 1223; they enjoyed the honors of the royal court, had members in the king's armies, the episcopate, and the Order of Malta, and were connected by marriage with such distinguished families as the d'Harcourts and the La Rochefoucaulds. In the 18th century, seventeen families of the Paris *parlement*, including those of Barrin de la Galissonière, Mesgrigny, and Testu de Balincourt, held the right to ride in the king's carriages. Magistrates from these very old families made up only 7 percent of the whole *parlement*—but then, such *gentilshommes* made up only 5 percent of the nobility as a whole.

Many magistrates of the *parlement* had three, four, or five generations of nobility behind them. One out of every two counselors who joined the *parlement* after 1716 represented at least the fourth noble generation of his family. Consequently, all of these men could be classified as *nobles de race*, nobles by blood, and considered to be *gentilshommes*.

Nevertheless, this was a special sort of nobility, a nobility of *civil* service. Out of 477 families ennobled before their entry into the *parlement*, 58, or less that 10 percent, had received *lettres de noblesse*. Sixteen of these were already *robins*—officers of the sovereign courts or of the *bailliages, trésoriers de France;* 14 were financial officials in the king's service—farmers general, receivers general; 9 were royal

physicians. Two hundred forty-one (41 percent) had been ennobled
through obtaining offices as *notaire et secrétaire du Roi, Maison, et
Couronne de France*. One hundred thirty-two lineages (nearly 23 percent) had acquired nobility through an ennobling office in the judiciary
of the financial apparatus. Five and a half percent belonged to the
noblesse de cloche, owing their nobility to municipal offices. There
remained only 13 percent belonging to families that were of commoner
status when they entered the *parlement.*

These commoners belonged to lineages that were close to the nobility. The abbé René Pucelle was descended from a great-grandfather
and a grandfather who were attorneys, but his father was already a
famous advocate. When he became a counselor in 1684, his uncle,
Pierre, was already noble by virtue of being a *secrétaire du roi*, his
elder brother had been a counselor of the *parlement* since 1675, and, on
his mother's side, he was related to 21 members of the *parlement,*
masters of requests, and state councilors. Most of the commoners who
became members of the *parlement* were sons of counselors or *procureurs du roi* in the *bailliages* and presidial courts, sons of advocates,
or, less frequently, sons of farmers general or receivers general. Two
councilors alone came from families engaged in trade: Claude Glucq,
who joined in 1710, and who was the son of a master dyer, the manager
of the Gobelins works, and Gayet de Sansale, son of a Lyons merchant
who was the administrator of the city's hospitals. Even in their cases,
their fathers must have enjoyed a certain luster due to the administrative functions they performed in a public service.

Out of the 590 families, 106 noble families had entered the *parlement*
in the 16th century, and 289 noble families, more than half of the total,
in the 17th. The Paris *parlement* was thus tending to become a closed
corporation, with the same families perpetuating themselves in it. After
1660 the *parlement* made it more difficult for sons of *traitants,* or tax
farmers, to be accepted into its ranks, however high in dignity they
might already have risen through their dealings in the royal finances
and despite the king's own orders. The 17th century seems to have
been the great period of both the renewal of this body's composition
and its fixation.

In Brittany *gentilshommes* occupied most of the offices in the *parlement* of Rennes, and after 1678 only nobles were accepted as members.
In 1671, though *gentilshommes* whose nobility went back to the Middle
Ages accounted for 69 percent of the magistrates who were natives of
the province and 38 percent of the others, and ennobled persons

accounted for 19 and 37 percent, respectively, of these categories, 11 and 24 percent came from the *bourgeoisie*. But the Chambre de la Réformation de la Noblesse de Bretagne, itself drawn from the *parlement*, ennobled all the members of the *parlement* who were of *bourgeois* origin. It then closed the *parlement* to commoners, so as ⫫ preserve the "purity" of this court, issuing an *arrêt* on 9 January 1678 which declared: "subject to His Majesty's pleasure, no *présidents*, counselors, or *gens du roi* will be accepted in this court who are not of noble extraction or excellent condition." In its application of this rule, which in itself did not shut the door upon ennobled persons, the *parlement* was even stricter, rejecting nobles of recent origin, sons of presidial judges or royal secretaries. The noble character of the *parlement* of Brittany became an unquestionable dogma. In 1764 the intendant Le Bret wrote: "Offices ... can be held only by *gentilshommes* who furnish proof of the their nobility before being admitted." Most of the oldest families were concentrated in the *parlement*. Sixty-three percent of the families represented in it possessed nobility going back to the Middle Ages, before the end of the 15th century, while 20 percent had been ennobled in the 16th century and 17.5 percent in the 17th; by contrast, among the Breton nobility generally, only 28 percent were of medieval origin, with 55 percent dating from the 16th century and 17 percent from the 17th century. Certain families formed dynasties in the *parlement*. Of 984 officeholders, 293, or 30 percent, were provided by 45 families. The families of La Bourdonnaye and de Furcy furnished 24 of these, and the Becdelièvre, Boylesve, and de Cornulier families 11 each. But these magistrates found only 30 percent of their wives in families of *parlement* members: 46 percent of these ladies came from the *non-parlementaire* nobility and 21 percent from families of ennobled persons or rich *bourgeois*. In the case of the last-mentioned, the attraction of the large dowries brought by daughters of merchants and shipowners certainly counted. On the other hand, however, the court nobility and even, to a large extent, the old higher nobility of the province refused to give their daughters' hands to members of *parlement*. There was a gulf between the two sorts of nobility.

The *parlement* of Aix offers comparable features, though its noble families were on the whole less ancient. Some were genuine *gentilshommes*, whose noble status dated from the 15th century, though more often from the 16th. In the 18th century, however, a large number of them were of more recent origin. They came either from the commercial community—especially from the merchants of Marseilles—or from the world of law, from among minor officers of justice and advocates. Nearly all, though, passed through the stage of being *notaires et secrétaires du Roi, Maison, et Couronne de France* or else *trésoriers généraux de France*. They formed, moreover, a group apart, maintaining its distinction from the *noblesse d'épée* and stubbornly loyal to *la robe*. Very few were the families who disappeared from the *parlement*. When this did happen, and it was not due to natural extinction or an exclusively female issue, there were very special reasons, which usually did not have to do with social climbing. The Forbin-Maynier family sold their office in the *parlement* owing to financial difficulties; the Langier family sold theirs as a result of unpleasantness with their colleagues in connection with the affair of the Jesuits. Few of them sought to enter the *gentilhommerie d'épée*. Among such were the Roux de Bonneval family, who sold their office in the *parlement* in order to purchase a *seigneurie*, and the Félix du Muy and Valbelle families, who transferred to exalted military functions which obliged the holder to be present at court and integrated them into the highest nobility. Most of the magistrates of the *parlement*, however, persisted in passing their offices on to their eldest sons, or at least to some member of their family, so that this family stayed *parlementaire*. The nobility of the *parlements* thus constituted a distinct level of the nobility.

The middle and petty gentilhommerie

At a social level that was not so high as the nobility of the *parlements* stood a middle-ranking and petty *gentilhommerie* whose precise situation and different levels of honor and dignity have as yet been little studied. Historians have been struck above all by the mediocrity of their wealth and income, frequently even by their poverty, which, however, seems to have been the reflection of their social status rather than its cause. All that still needs investigation. It seems possible to state the following characteristics: the middle and petty *gentilhommerie* included some families which, though very old, had never held very high appointments near to the king or the grandees; most of these *gentilshommes* lived on their estates as countrymen, but quite a few of them left home for long periods to serve in the king's armies. Nearly all of them carried out their duties as *fidèles* either of the king or, more often, of his representatives, the governors, or else of the grandees, the princes of the blood, members of the high court nobility, or members of the higher nobility of their own provinces. These *gentilshommes* might complete their education as pages, serve as *fidèles* attached to the person of a higher-ranking nobleman, or, on the occasion of great ceremonies, help to swell the escort of one of the grandees and, during the troubles, join his forces, to serve either for or against the king. It was only the very poorest who did not fulfill such duties. Many of these petty *gentilshommes* spent their lives on their estates, as country dwellers.

In Beauvaisis, out of 109 nobles, 70 *gentilshommes* possessed incomes of not more than 1,000–2,000 livres, and 23 had only 500 livres—27 sous a day, less than the income of a country priest. It was this category which has left us letters written in a clumsy hand, with phonetic spelling, for its members could no longer afford to employ a tutor. Some families of the petty *gentilhommerie* ended by disappearing, in some cases, certainly, through biological extinction but in others probably because, being unable to continue to "live like nobles," members of the family took to practicing a trade and so vanished from the records of the nobility.

In Brittany the middle and petty nobility belonged to the clientage of the court nobles, the great provincial nobles, and, especially, the *noblesse parlementaire*, all of whom held great *seigneuries* and powers of high justice and to whom the middle and petty *gentilshommes*, holders of the smallest fiefs, with powers of middle and low justice, owed "faith and obedience," with *aveux et dénombrements* and very heavy feudal dues, *quints et requints, lods et ventes*, and so on. A suzerain could make life impossible for one of his vassals by insisting on returns of *aveux*; each time this happened it meant heavy expenses and long and burdensome journeys, which easily swallowed up 10 or 15 percent of the income of a middle or petty *gentilhomme*.

On the borders of Hurepoix and Gâtinais, between La Ferté-Alais and Corbeil, around 1690, the middle and petty nobility were usually in the king's service, in the army, either in fortresses or on campaign.

The nobles' means of living

Among the 400,000 persons who made up the nobility of France, there were many differences in wealth and style of living. It is difficult to express a general opinion regarding the situation of the nobility from this standpoint. We have to distinguish, first, between, on the one hand, the nobility who lived in areas where large-scale trade was carried on, with relatively easy communications, and where grain and wine were produced in great quantity for substantial markets—Ile-de-France, Beauce, Brie, and, in general, the Paris basin, for the feeding of Paris; Bordelais and neighboring areas, for the export of wine to England; Lauragais, for the sale of grain in the market of Toulouse; and the Rennes basin, for the export of grain either to the Mediterranean or to the Baltic—areas where even middle and petty *gentilshommes* could enjoy a comfortable living; and, on the other, the nobility whose homes lay in remote areas, where travel was difficult and, often, the soil was less productive, such as Auvergne, Limousin, and most of the interior of Brittany, where the nobles were, as a rule, much poorer. We next have to distinguish between the nobles living in towns, who were able to reside there precisely because their country estates provided them with higher rents, and the country-dwelling *gentilshommes*, who were obliged to remain in the country by a poverty which sometimes approached the level of want. We have to distinguish, further, between the nobles who held appointments and were usually better-off, and those who did not, who were less well situated and might even be poor. And we must distinguish between eldest sons and younger sons. Almost everywhere, the need to ensure a firm economic basis for the family, and so the possibility of keeping up the style of living appropriate to their rank, entailed the attribution to the eldest son of the major share in inheritances. The younger sons had to be content with a small share, often resigning themselves to bachelorhood, a mediocre career, and an early retirement, usually to the country; and it was they, probably, who gave the *gentilshommes* their reputation for poverty. We must doubtless also distinguish between two periods: first, the period which runs from the end of the Wars of Religion to the middle years of the 18th century, after the War of the Austrian Succession and before the Seven Years' War (1748–56), when, following ruinous civil strife and in an epoch of climatic disasters, of *"mortalités"* with a cumulative effect, and of wars, especially foreign wars, the situation of the landed nobility must have tended to worsen and when, doubtless, the only ones to improve their lot were those who were able to secure offices, pay, and pensions from the king; and, second, the period, after the middle of the 18th century, when, with recovery from the demographic and economic disasters, real economic growth took place and a large section of the landed nobility retrieved their losses and became rich.

The poll tax (*capitation*) of 8 January 1695, the regulations for which divided the population of France into twenty-two categories, grouping, without regard to social status, the persons considered to be approximately equal in capacity to pay, enables us to form a notion of the relative economic position of the nobles.

In the top category, taxed at 2,000 livres, were the dauphin, the other princes and princesses of the blood, the ministers, and the farmers general. The second category, obligated to pay 1,500 livres, included the princes, dukes, marshals of France, the great officers of the Crown, the *premier président* of the *parlement* of Paris, and the intendants. In the third category (1,000 livres) were the *lieutenants généraux* of the provinces, the *chevaliers* of the Order of the Holy Spirit, and some *robins*: the *présidents à mortier* of the *parlement* of Paris, the *premiers présidents* of the other sovereign courts of Paris, and the *premiers présidents* of the provincial *parlements*. The fourth category (500 livres) included the state councilors, the *procureurs généraux* and *avocats généraux* of the Paris *parlement*, and the *présidents* of the other sovereign courts of Paris. In the fifth and sixth categories (400 and 300 livres) were a whole series of magistrates, mainly provincial, of the rank of *président*. In the seventh category (250 livres) were the marquises, counts, viscounts, and barons. In the eighth category (200 livres) were the counselors of the five sovereign courts of Paris and, in the ninth (150 livres), those of the sovereign courts in the provinces. In the tenth category (120 livres) were the higher stratum of the rural nobility, the *gentilshommes* who were patrons of Church livings. In the fifteenth category (40 livres) were the nobles who possessed a fief and occupied a château. In the nineteenth category were the *gentilshommes* who had neither fief nor château; they had to pay six livres, the same as "craftsmen in second-grade towns who have a shop and employ journeymen." There was thus a hierarchy of wealth in which we perceive the presence of a whole body of *gentilshommes* of mediocre fortune or even poor.

In the 17th century the nobility seem to have been big spenders. A *gentilhomme* had to *"faire largesse"*—it was one of his social characteristics. Furthermore, he must do nothing for gain, *"vile et servile,"* but live on his rents. *Gentilshommes* often lived up to this ideal. Ennobled persons sought, more or less cautiously, to approximate to it. For many of them, the noble life-style led to ruin. In Beauvaisis in 1593 Gouffier maintained fifty-seven persons, of whom forty were *domestiques*. The nobles of the region spent their time hunting, feasting, riding about the countryside, fighting in the wars; they spent without reckoning what they spent, and while, in principle, there was nothing to stop them from supervising the administration of their estates and the collection of their seignorial and feudal dues, in fact many of them did not bother to. They gradually fell into debt and were ruined, selling their fiefs and *seigneuries* to their creditors, who were usually officeholders. What demonstrates clearly that it was the noble life-style that was chiefly responsible for the impoverishment of the *gentilshommes* is the fate experienced by the ennobled. Let us take the Tristan family, who were, from father to son, *élus* in the *élection* of Beauvais. Their great prosperity began with Maître Tristan, who died in 1647, *président* in the *élection* and *bailli* of the town, *bailliage*, and *comté-pairie* of Beauvais. The Tristans discreetly grew rich from the income derived from their offices and the loans they made to *gentilshommes*. The latter, finding themselves unable to repay these loans, had to yield their fiefs and *seigneuries* to the Tristans. Having become *seigneurs*, the Tristans remained, none the less, economical commoners, sharp in their dealings with farmers and *censitaires*. At the beginning of the 18th century, the purchase of an office of *notaire et secrétaire du roi* transformed them juridically into *gentilshommes*. One of them, Nicolas Tristan, *seigneur* of Hez, Juvignies, and Verderel, undertook to become a *gentilhomme* socially. He abandoned the gown for the sword, became a lieutenant in Louville's regiment, and adopted the noble life-style. On 7 September 1762 his debts forced him, in his turn, to sell the family property.

The trouble was that the careers available to a *gentilhomme* were not numerous and were generally ruinous. In the army or the navy, the careers that were truly worthy of him, or at court, in high government appointments, the *gentilhomme* spent more than he received. Some *gentilshommes*, belonging to the middle or petty nobility, entered the judicial magistracy of the *bailliages, sénéchaussées,* and presidial courts and sometimes the *élections*. They formed only a small proportion of the nobility as a whole, for all these functions, even when associated with the dignity of the king's justice and service, were tainted with something *"bourgeois."*

Some *gentilshommes* suffered derogation, for nobility of blood could never be lost, only suspended. In Brittany, according to article 561 of the custom of the province, if, from father to son through several generations, *gentilshommes* engaged in trade, carried out the functions of attorney in the lower courts, or practiced a purely "mechanical" trade, they thereby caused their rights and privileges, which they ceased to enjoy, to become dormant. Their noble status was not destroyed, only put to sleep: this was *noblesse dormante*. In order to reawaken it, they had only to make declaration at the clerk's office of the royal court in the place where they lived that they no longer wished to pursue these derogatory activities. Thus, poor *gentilshommes* and the younger sons of families could invest their money in ships' cargoes, in the commissioning of ships, in exchange business, bottomry, or insurance; they could embark on careers in the merchant marine, take employment in the administration of the farms of the Estates of Brittany, become supernumeraries, comptrollers, or clerks engaged in the collection of taxes; or they could become teachers or surgeons in the parishes. In this way they could recover the means to "live like nobles" and obtain the restoration of all their rights. In other provinces it was necessary, besides making the declaration mentioned, to obtain *lettres de relief de dérogeance* from the king. But *noblesse dormante* actually set the nobleman, for a time, in the third estate, and it always left a blemish, since the *gentilhomme par excellence* was one who had been such from time immemorial, without any of his ancestors ever having followed an activity that was *ignoble*.

The proper means of living of a *gentilhomme*, then, were the rents from his *"héritages,"* his real property, which he ought to manage carefully and use economically. Some *gentilshommes* did this very well. In Picardy some of the rich nobles exploited their property with rigor. Louis d'Allencourt, comte de Dromesnil, possessed an annual income of between 7,000 and 8,000 livres in 1649. The marquis de Tiercelin was in receipt, around 1644, of 3,000 livres of income from land and 3,000 livres in *rentes* and had 35,000 livres in ready money. Petty *gentilshommes* kept a careful eye on all that was due to them and integrated themselves into the life of their district, where they cut a fine figure. According to a *livre de raison*, between 1708 and 1728 François-Joseph Le Clerc, *seigneur* of Bussy, kept precise accounts, personally exacted his *censives* and *champarts*, pursued poachers, and thrashed a peasant whose cow was found in cornfields belonging to the château; but he also organized the *corvée* to maintain the roads, went on pilgrimage with the local crowd, took part in the jay-shooting contest, joined in games of battledore and shuttlecock in the village, and danced with the village girls.

Many heads of families showed special care in ensuring the economic basis of their lineage, being aided in this by the local customs. All of these, and that of Paris in the first place, provided that, in the case of nobles, there should be right of primogeniture, so that the eldest son, responsible for perpetuating the lineage, should be guaranteed the lion's share of the inherited property. Some customs went very far in this direction. In Brittany the right of primogeniture was all the more important because this was the only province of France in which "noble" division of inheritances constituted the very foundation of the juridical definition of nobility, according to article 23 of the custom of 1580 ("of successions and their apportionment"), which was confirmed and explained by the *Maximes de la Chambre de Réformation de la Noblesse* (1668) and the *Consultation des avocats au Parlement* (April 1770): three successive "noble" divisions of inheritances provided proof of nobility. According to the right of primogeniture as observed in Brittany, the eldest son took, first, a *préciput* of 5 percent of the lands, houses, and woods. Then he took two-thirds of the noble lands, leaving a third to be divided among the younger sons. (Noble lands were fiefs which owed military service. Many tracts of land were "ennobled" during the 17th and 18th centuries.) The eldest son further enjoyed the "right of increment," which meant that he took the share of the inheritance that would have been due to his brothers and sisters who had entered religion (provided that he paid for their upkeep) and also the share that would have been due to a sister who had married a person of her own condition, who had to be content with her dowry. The eldest son chose for himself the items making up his share. The eldest son had seisin of the family's titles, deeds of ownership, and archives until the inheritance was divided. On the other hand, the eldest son had to assume liability for two-thirds of the debts of the estate.

If there was no son, the noble right of primogeniture applied to the eldest daughter; and, if there were no direct descendants, it passed to the collateral branches.

This right of primogeniture resulted in considerable differences of wealth. In 1778 the *partage noble* of the Le Cornulier family left, all together, 391,588 francs to the eldest son and 148,530 francs to be divided among five younger sons, or 29,706 francs each. Since the *partage noble* had to be applied, in their turn, by the younger sons, many nobles became extremely poor. We can follow them for two or three generations; they then disappear from view, having descended to the plough or to some trade.

Differentiation was all the more intensified in Brittany because the court nobility, the greatest Breton families, and the *noblesse parlementaire*—in fact, all those whose wealth was substantial—adopted for their own families the custom of Paris. But the middle and petty nobility, with their more limited resources, clung to the Breton custom; this in many cases made it possible for the eldest son to "live like a noble" and for the family to retain its noble status, but it sacrificed the younger sons.

The custom of Poitou was the same as that of Brittany. The customs of Maine, Anjou, and Touraine worsened still further the lot of the younger sons, for there the eldest son took all the movable property. In Bordelais the right of primogeniture was similar to that in Brittany, with, in addition, the eldest son alone succeeding to the baronies, viscounties, and counties held by his family.

The customs of Paris, Orléans, and Berry went part of the way toward the rules of that part of the country where written law prevailed. The eldest son took a house, held as a fief, which he chose as his principal manor house, and half of all the other properties held as fiefs, while all the other children shared the remaining half. Similarly, in Saintonge and Angoumois the eldest son took one-fifth, and in Aunis, Marche, and Auvergne he retained the principal manor house *en préciput*. There was no extension of the *partage noble* to collateral branches.

The nobleman was a rent-drawer and also, in the most favored cases, the recipient of a salary or a pension (another form of rent), but rarely a producer, though he might become this by directly cultivating part of his estate. Until the end of the 16th century the noble enjoyed almost complete exemption from payment of *taille*. This exemption was increasingly encroached upon, in the areas of *taille personnelle*, by the *règlement* of 1634, the declaration of 1663, and, especially, the declaration of 1664. The nobles remained exempt from *taille* for an arable farm of four *charrues* (ploughlands) in a single parish. The noble might cultivate this farm himself, employing as wageworkers men who had not been tenant farmers for the three preceding years. His other arable lands in the same parish, or in other parishes, he had to lease out to tenants who were subject to the *taille;* they had to pay only the *taille d'exploitation*, which was always lighter than the *taille de propriété*, borne by those peasants who held land *en censive*, possessing the *seigneurie utile* of it, which meant effective ownership. A *charrue* meant, depending on the region, between 90 and 120 arpents, or about 45 to 60 hectares. Four *charrues* thus covered about 180 to 240 hectares, which meant a big estate. The exemption was without limit as far as woods, meadows, ponds, and vineyards were concerned. In the regions of *taille réelle*, the nobles had to pay *taille* on their "commoner" land, and their *domaine proche* always included a certain amount of this.

The fortunes and incomes of the nobles

The *haute gentilhommerie* of the court and the higher nobility of office possessed vast estates. The Villeroy family offers an example. The duc de Villeroy—a peer, a marshal of France, head of the king's Conseil des Finances—had a property in the valley of the Essonne, the duchy of Villeroy, which was made up of forty "noble lands," twenty-four of which were fiefs belonging to the duchy, while sixteen were held directly by the duke in twelve parishes. The *domaine proche* embraced ten farms, five mills, and wine presses that the peasants were obliged to use (*banaux*) and several barns for storing *champart;* there were between 2,000 and 2,500 arpents of arable land and between 500 and 700 arpents of copses.

The duke held the right of tithe in several parishes—one of the biggest tithes in the kingdom, "the eleventh sheaf." He had the power of *banalité*, with the right to take the grain crops and grind them. He had the right to levy a tithe on wine, the right to charge *forage, persage, et rouage* on wine, rights to fishing and to the exploitation of warrens, the right of *placeage, pesage, mesurage, et aulnage* in relation to cattle, and the right to exact a due for the game of stick-skittles played at Mennecy during fairs.

The duke held powers of justice—high, middle, and low—in the *bailliage* of Villeroy and profited from the costs incurred by litigants and the fines levied. He maintained for this purpose about ten attorneys, tipstaffs, and bailiffs at Mennecy, adjoining the château of Villeroy. In addition, he received "*relief, aubaine, confiscation, déshérence, et bâtardise.*"

In a region where the land was fragmented into tiny plots, the duke's domain was the only case of large tracts of land belonging to one owner, grouped in large farms of 200, 250, 400, and 450 arpents, exploited by rich peasants who were also merchants—big semicapitalist tenant farmers. And yet this property brought the duke an income of only about 20,000 livres a year. The trouble was that the "commoner" lands that were included in the *seigneuries* of the duchy were subject only to a light *cens* or to a small *champart* with a very light *cens:* fifteen deniers of *cens* per arpent, a sou and a quarter, or else a *champart* of four sheafs per arpent, which brought an average of seventy, with, in addition, a *cens* of one denier.

Above all, too, the duke, who was kept busy at court or with the army, could not personally administer his *domaine proche* or levy his dues through his own agents. He farmed everything out—arable land, tithes, *banalités,* sundry feudal and seignorial dues—either to rich peasants who were also merchants; or to local day laborers; or to townspeople of Corbeil, merchant tanners or *rentiers;* or to Parisians, advocates, attorneys with the Paris *parlement,* or nobles of recent date, men who had become *écuyers* by being *notaires et secrétaires du roi*—all of whom, in their role as *amodiateurs,* became the real beneficiaries of the feudal and seignorial system. The ducs de Villeroy would not have been able to survive without the salaries and pensions paid them by the king.

This was the situation, too, of the prince de Conti, governor of Languedoc after 1650. Castellan of La Grange-aux-Prés, Cessenon, and Cabrières, comte de Pézenas, owner of Montagnac, Secrian, and Saint-Thibéry, he derived from these properties not less than 100,000 livres in rent. But the abbeys given him by the king brought him in about 120,000 livres, and he received a pension of 100,000 livres from the king and 80,000 livres from the provincial estates, as governor.

The dukes-and-peers and the mere dukes all watched carefully over their fortunes—the "means of consumption" they needed in order to honor their social obligations. In general they kept exact accounts and devoted careful attention to their sources of income. Usually, after marriage, their principal ranged from 1 to 3 million livres. There were, of course, some fortunes that were greater. Condé had 10 million livres in 1651; Richelieu, in 1642, had 22 million. The main part consisted of landed property in the form of *fiefs de dignité* and ordinary fiefs. The *duchés-pairies,* which extended over two or three of today's cantons (and the capitals of which have in many cases become administrative centers of cantons) were worth between 200,000 and 500,000 livres. Of Condé's fortune, 88 percent was accounted for by landed property. Richelieu enjoyed an income of 872,511 livres, to which his emoluments as a minister contributed 20,000 livres and his salary as a state councilor 2,000 livres. The duc de Beauvillier, however, received 86,000 livres a year as first gentleman of the bedchamber, minister of state, and commander of the King's Orders, and 95,000 as head of the Conseil des Finances; and Sully, in 1611, had an income of 202,900 livres, to which his lands contributed only 60,000 livres. In terms of the principal, the value of the high offices of state surpassed that of landed property. In 1675 the post of first gentleman of the bedchamber was worth 800,000 livres. The dukes-and-peers were sensitive to the social aspect of their fortunes. They maintained with vigor the rights and privileges of their *seigneuries.* Though they farmed out their fiefs and *seigneuries* to farmers general, they kept the château and its grounds for the sake of their social prestige.

The same was usually true of the men of the *grande robe,* in the king's councils and the great sovereign courts. Let us take as an example Louis Boucherat, chancellor from 1685 to 1699. While he was in office, he had an income of about 165,000 livres, of which 120,000, or nearly three-quarters, came from his salary as chancellor (70,000 livres) and the profits of the Seal—in other words, a deduction from state tax revenues. The remainder was provided by the rents of his houses and lands (129,000 livres); by the interest on his loans to various private persons—men of both the sword (marquises, counts) and the gown (officials of the Council of State and of the *parlement*) (25,000 livres)—and loans to the king (about 5,000 livres); and by the farm of the boat service (the "water coaches") plying between Joigny and Auxerre (probably 1,500 livres). Everything that he possessed that was not a salary or a due taken from the royal finances furnished a good income. His *seigneurie* of Sainte-Mesmes, valued at 56,000 livres, brought in 3,300 livres a year (5.8 percent), and his Compans estate, valued at 71,000 livres, brought 6,600 livres (9.5 percent). His loans to private persons returned interest at 5 percent. Even so, in relation to the considerable amount of the principal—469,808 livres for loans to private persons, 265,600 livres for houses in Paris—this income fell far short of what he obtained from salaries and dues derived from the king's revenues. And all that consisted entirely of money that was turned into consumer goods, the chancellor's salary and dues being indirectly deducted from production, in which he played no part in any way.

Louis II Phélypeaux, *seigneur* of La Vrillière, secretary of state from 1629 to 1678, inherited in 1630 his post of secretary of state, the *seigneurie* of La Vrillière, and a whole series of minor offices and dues in the Blois area. His main livelihood was what his office brought him. But in 1635 he married Marie Particelli, the daughter of Michel Particelli, *seigneur* of Hémery and intendant of finance, and, bit by bit, down to 1678, the entire fortune of the Particelli family came to him through inheritance. The dowry and inheritances of his wife brought La Vrillière nearly 2 million livres. Of this amount, nearly 1 million was accounted for by the *seigneurie* of Châteauneuf-sur-Loire; the house and grounds of La Chevrette, near Paris; the estates of Vaulay and Avreuil in Champagne; the viscounty of Saint-Florentin in Champagne; and the estates of Tanlay and Thoré in Burgundy. La Vrillière further acquired, with his own money, the barony of Ervy-le-Châtel, in Champagne, and the *seigneurie* of Le Hallier, in Orléanais, and steadily enlarged Châteauneuf-sur-Loire until this estate, now embracing three castellanies, could be raised to the status of a marquisate in 1659. La Vrillière obtained from the king in 1660 letters patent authorizing him to compile a terrier of his *seigneuries;* he rendered and received "faith and homage" for his fiefs, some of his estates were made fiefs, and his sons applied the right of primogeniture to these lands which had become fiefs. The secretary of state had integrated himself into the seignorial and feudal order.

La Vrillière had a new château built at Châteauneuf-sur-Loire, and in Paris he built the Hôtel de La Vrillière, at the end of the rue Neuve-des-Petits-Champs, together with four houses adjoining it.

In 1678 his total wealth in real estate reached 1,850,000 livres; with the furniture and collections of pictures and statues, it exceeded 2,100,000 livres. Since his offices as *secrétaire du roi* and secretary of state were valued in 1670 at 300,000 livres, La Vrillière's total fortune amounted to 2,400,000 livres—and he had given his daughter a dowry of 400,000 livres. To be sure, against this figure must be set debts totaling 400,000 livres.

Yet this *seigneur* of many estates, baron d'Hervy, vicomte de Saint-Florentin, marquis de Tanlay et de Châteauneuf, drew from his estates an income that was proportionately rather slight: 35,000 livres a year. From his infrequent loans he derived very little. La Vrillière obtained the main part of his resources from his court functions and the king's favors—the salary and emoluments of his posts as secretary of state and *secrétaire du roi et de la Chambre de Sa Majesté;* the king's permission to accept gratuities from the Estates of Languedoc, Normandy, Burgundy, Bresse, and Bugey; and a 10 percent levy on the coal mines opened, or to be opened within thirty years, in the provinces of Lyonnais, Forez, and Beaujolais. In short, La Vrillière must have had an income of about 100,000 livres a year, of which at least 65 percent was derived from his offices and only about 35 percent from his lands—four hundred times the earnings of a building worker of the period. The predominance of the income from offices over that from land, both in proportion of the whole and in rate of interest on investment (over 20 percent for the former, 1.9 percent for the latter), was

due to the fact that his acquisitions of land were conceived as an
element in his life-style as a nobleman and a support for his social
standing; they were not aimed at constituting a mass of capital invested
in real estate.

We find the same attitude in another secretary of state, Charles
Colbert, marquis de Croissy, who was in charge of foreign affairs from
1680 to 1696. After being a master of requests, a state councilor, an
intendant, and, on several occasions, from 1663 to 1680, an ambassador and minister plenipotentiary, including a period as ambassador to
London, his salary and emoluments, amounting to more than 59,000
livres, accounted for 98 percent of his total income. In 1690 he received
106,000 livres in emoluments and pension (80 percent of his income),
15,000 livres from his house in the Place des Vosges and from the
marquisate of Croissy (10 percent), and between 12,000 and 13,000
livres in interest on money lent to the state (about 8 percent). His
offices brought him a dividend of more than 20 percent, his lands only 6
percent.

It seems that this was the case of all those men—state councilors,
masters of requests, magistrates of the sovereign courts—who saw in
service to the king, the exercise of public office, their main activity and
chief concern in life.

In approximately the same situation as the chancellors and secretaries of state were the magistrates who had been obliged to work in
order to pay for their offices. A *noble homme* named Jean-Baptiste
Chotard, *sieur* of La Loierie, son of a counselor in the presidial court of
Angers and intendant for Monseigneur le Prince in Anjou and Brittany,
who was married to the marquise de Cornulier, himself married in 1743
Marie-Françoise Trochon, who brought him a dowry of 40,000 livres.
Thanks to this, Chotard was able in 1745 to buy a post as *maître* in the
chambre des comptes of Brittany, at Nantes, for 49,000 livres, plus
7,439 "expenses," a total of 56,439 livres. He put down 36,439 livres
on purchase and paid off the rest in eighteen years, starting in 1748, at 5
percent interest, which meant 12,856 livres all together. By 1763 he had
cleared his debt, thanks to the income derived from the office, which
gave a small surplus over the annual installments. This income, in
salary, *épices,* perquisites, and various *droits et avantages* in kind,
amounted in 1766 to 2,939 livres—a little more than 5 percent of the
principal. During all that time the family had lived on the income derived from a *seigneurie,* 1,000 livres a year; from an apartment at
Nantes, 500 livres; from the interest on a loan of 20,000 livres at 5

percent, 1000 livres—all together, 2,5000 livres a year. Their total income came to nearly 5,500 livres, of which about 55 percent originated from Chotard's office, 28 percent from his estates, and 18 percent from payments by private individuals.

By 1774 the principal initially invested had been recovered, and the income from the office began, after twenty-nine years, to constitute a net profit. It is noteworthy that during all that time Chotard's family had lived mainly on the moneys they received from ground rent and redeemable bonds. The office, which brought with it ennoblement, here appears as having been, to start with, essentially something to "place" the man socially.

Others, however, *always* saw their offices above all as dignities which conferred a social rank upon them; these concerned themselves less with their duties, and the proportion between the elements making up their fortune and income was never the same.

Messire Charles Pinon, master of requests from 1637 to 1666, intendant of justice, police, and finance in Berry from 1637 to 1641 (and perhaps again in 1655), seems to have been content with a relatively modest career in the middle-ranking offices of the Council of State, and he settled his family in the same offices and in those of the sovereign courts. One of his sons was a counselor in the Paris *parlement* to the end of his life (1670–77); another, after a period in a similar office, became a *président* in the Grand Conseil in 1690 and then a master of requests; and his daughter married a counselor in the *parlement*. Charles Pinon's principal activity seems to have been that of a moneylender who chose his debtors with a view to both the security of the money he lent and the creation of a network of persons under obligations to him in the sovereign courts and the Council of State and at court; between 1661 and 1671 he lent considerable sums to dukes, marquises, secretaries of state, masters of requests, *présidents* of the *cour des aides,* and counselors of the *parlement.* His loans totaled 314,733 livres and brought him 15,021 livres annually in interest; his total wealth in 1672 was 815,240 livres, and his total income about 30,000 livres. His second-string activity was collecting real property; he got together some ten houses and three shops in Paris, worth 188,000 livres and bringing in 7,500 livres a year, and the noble fief of Quincy, in Berry, purchased in 1643. This, after being increased by the addition of various other fiefs, was transformed into a viscounty with the power of high justice; it was worth over 109,000 livres in fiefs and *seigneuries* and doubtless brought in about 4,000 livres a year. His emoluments from the Council of State made up only a very small part of his annual income.

The magistrates of the *parlement* of Brittany often behaved like this unambitious master of requests. They were frequently absent from their duties. Out of 110 or 120 counselors, only 40 or 50 were ever actually sitting. Some *chambres* did not sit at all, for lack of members. They did little work. In 1672 five counselors dealt on their own with 940 cases, 60 percent of the total. For most of them, *épices* amounted to very little. Their offices brought them in hardly anything: 1.2 percent until about 1750, thereafter 5 percent—but only because their prices had collapsed. "The acquisition of an office in the *parlement* is first and foremost a question of social standing and importance." The *parlementaires* of Brittany were more interested in the large *seigneuries* of their province, of which they held 40 percent in 1700 and 56 percent in 1788. They managed their landed property strictly, with regularity and thrift. From it they derived both the main part of their resources and a heightened social prestige. They therefore defended vigorously the custom of Brittany, with its feudal spirit—the privileges of their province. They fought for the most anachronistic kind of seignorial and feudal property rights and, being opposed to any change, put themselves forward as protectors from the fiscal and bureaucratic policy of the central government, a rampart against ministerial despotism.

It was the same with many members of the sovereign courts. In 1641 Messire Jacques Pinon, *seigneur* of Donssy and Vitry, with power of high justice, a councilor in the Council of State and the Conseil Privé, doyen of the counselors of the *parlement* of Paris, left a fortune of 635,425 livres. This was made up as follows: his office contributed 80,000 livres; his *seigneurie*, valued chiefly for its social significance, contributed 34,920; nine houses in Paris, eight of which were tenements, contributed 314,000; and there were also 241,025 livres 9 sols from loans to individuals and *rentes sur l'Hôtel de Ville*. (His debts account for the difference in the totals.) His eldest son, Jean Pinon, counselor in the *parlement* of Metz, had leisure enough to be able to reside in Paris and there to look after the properties of the widows and ecclesiastics in his family, from whom he received, as his reward, gifts of fiefs in Brie and some *rentes*.

The *premier président* of the *parlement* of Normandy, Claude Groulart, left in 1602 about 376,000 livres (471,000 days' wages of a building worker) and had an income of about 30,000 livres. Of his wealth, 288,200 livres were contributed by landed property (baronies, castellanies, farms), which accounted for 13,100 livres of his annual income. He had 73,500 livres in *rentes* at 10 percent, which brought in 7,350 livres. His 16,000 livres in demesne offices and tax farms provided about 1,600 livres. Claude Groulart's office of *président*, with a commission as *premier président*, was worth 1,800 livres a year to him, or 6 to 7 percent of his income.

In Burgundy, about 1650, nearly all the families holding offices in the *parlement* possessed extensive country estates, with fiefs and *seigneuries*, about fifty of these being in the neighborhood of Dijon. The *président* Desbarres inherited from his father the *seigneuries* of Echirey and Ruffey, and when he married Antoinette de Beauclerc d'Achères, she brought him as her dowry the marquisate of Mirebeau and seven other fiefs or *seigneuries*. Other *grands seigneurs* included the Bouhier family, the *président* Claude Fremyot, and the *président* of the *chambre des comptes,* Jacques Legrand. Similarly situated were all the counselors of the *parlement*, many officers of the *chambre des comptes,* and the *trésoriers de France.* Among them they held hundreds of fiefs and *seigneuries* all over Burgundy.

In the regions where cash crops were raised and large-scale capitalist trade was carried on, some of these *nobles de fonctions* even drew the greater part of their income from selling the produce of their lands—an activity not regarded as incompatible with their noble status. In 1663 de la Tresne, *président* in the *parlement* of Bordeaux, had an income of 36,576 livres. Of this, 2,500 livres were contributed by the salary of his office (2.5 percent, for an office valued at 100,000 livres). We do not know what the *épices* amounted to. His feudal and seignorial dues produced 1,494 livres. But 66 percent of his income—22,848 livres— came from the sale of the products of his estates (wheat, beans, hemp, flax, sheep), with 40 percent (13,934 livres) accounted for by the sale of 118 casks of wine from La Tresne and Graves.

We do not possess sufficient figures to establish the relative frequency of these different types of cases.

The provincial nobility of all levels lived mainly on the rents they drew from their lands. However, it is necessary to distinguish between provinces. In many of them—for example, those in the Paris basin— seignorial and feudal dues represented a very small proportion of the *rentes.* From the economic standpoint, the important "noble property" was not the *mouvance* but the *domaine proche,* exploited either directly or, more often, through tenancies and sharecropping leases.

Picardy included among its old noble families many who were rich, exploiting their estates with care. But there were also some needy *gentilshommes,* like the *seigneur* of Sailly, whose sole income in 1645 came from a crop of 200 *septiers* of grain. Cases of that sort were not rare. The records of the *ban* and *arrière-ban* of 1675 enable us to discern the situation in which 386 nobles found themselves. Of these, 30 were with the army; 62 had served, or had a son serving; 51 paid 300 livres in *taxe de remplacement* and therefore must have had more than 2,000 livres a year; 89 were taxed at 40 livres, which meant they had an income from their land of less than 300 livres, or about 16 sous a day—almost the same as a workman's wages; and 40 were exempted altogether, owing to their poverty.

In Burgundy the situation was similar. The higher nobility of the province still included some families of *gentilshommes* who owned fiefs and *seigneuries*. In the 17th century the comte de Tavannes and his cousin, the marquis de Mirebel, held between them, as fiefs, twenty-one villages in the lowlands and three in the hilly area (*côte*), and each possessed between 25,000 and 30,000 livres in rents. But their visits to the royal court meant ruin for this provincial higher nobility. They, and the middle and petty nobility along with them, were impoverished by the costs of military service; decimated by the wars, their property passed to orphans who were infants or adolescents, who were despoiled of it. Finally, idleness and poor management, the noble way of life, completed the disaster. In the du Châtelet family, Erard VI, marquis de Tréchâteau, retired to his château of Til-Châtel, where he maintained a household of twenty children, together with a staff made up of a *gentilhomme écuyer,* a tutor, a *valet de chambre,* a head lackey, a lady companion, two chambermaids, a cook, a nurse, two footmen, a coachman, two ploughmen, a poultry keeper, and two women to look after the cattle. He lived in "gilded poverty." In 1662 his heir, Antoine du Châtelet, had his property sold off at the instance of his creditor, Claude Potet, counselor of the *parlement* of Dijon. The purchaser of the barony of Til-Châtel was Claude Housset, *trésorier des parties casuelles,* who paid 198,000 livres for it. All the *gentilshommes* were sunk in debt, improvident, without experience in legal proceedings, and were eventually forced to sell up. The transfer of fiefs and *seigneuries* to members of the "official" nobility or to *bourgeois* of Dijon, which had begun in the 15th century, became widespread in the 16th, by the end of which the majority of the old nobility had been dispossessed, and the process was completed during the 17th century. By 1700 the *gentilshommes* held no more than forty-seven rural *seigneuries*.

In the 17th century nobles found themselves situated on different levels of the hierarchy of incomes, in an order which did not necessarily correspond to their social rank. The social hierarchy and the hierarchy of incomes were two different realities. In Amiens between 1625 and 1645, judging by a sample of 5 percent of the marriages celebrated in that town, there was, at the top, with more than 50,000 livres for the couple getting married, a group made up of officeholders (*trésoriers de France, présidents, procureurs du roi, lieutenants généraux,* and *lieutenants particuliers* in the presidial courts, the *bailliages,* the *élections,* and the salt storehouses, most of whom were not noble) and of noble families established in the town; next, with between 10,000 and 50,000 livres, came more nobles and lower-ranking officeholders—*élus,* counselors in the *bailliage* and the presidial court of Amiens, or in the *sénéchaussée* and presidial court of Ponthieu, and counselors at the salt storehouse; then, at the level of 8,000–10,000 livres, nobles disappear (while merchants appear)—but this is because most of the nobles lived in the country, and these included (along with some rich families) the least well-off among them.

In the 18th century many of the characteristic features of the 17th were still present. The court nobles were still, generally speaking, in the forefront of the great fortunes of the realm. In their circle, incomes of 100,000 to 150,000 livres were common, corresponding to 2 or 3 million livres of principal. Some, though, were even richer. In Louis XVI's reign the house of Orléans, joined with that of Penthièvre, possessed 8 million livres of rent annually; the house of Condé had 1,500,000 livres; the house of Conti, at a more modest level, 600,000 livres, corresponding to about 12–15 million livres of principal. Besides these rents, the court nobility enjoyed large annual pensions from the king: 260,000 livres for the prince de Condé, 700,000 livres for the Polignac family. From time to time they received substantial gratuities; the king's brothers, the comte d'Artois and the comte de Provence, were on one occasion given 37 million and 29 million, respectively, to pay off their debts.

All of these people were in debt. When Choiseul died, in 1785, he left debts amounting to six million livres. The trouble was that the court nobility remained faithful to the tradition of *largesse.* Under Louis XVI they still wore clothes made of gold or silver, each garment being worth a small fortune. The most ordinary ball dress cost at least 2,000 livres. The court nobles competed with each other to see who would have the finest horses and the richest carriages, upholstered in velvet and decorated with painted panels. A large staff of servants seemed indispensable: thirty or forty valets, plus chambermaids, stewards, and so on. A great part of their time was spent in receptions, dinners, balls, attending the theater, going to suppers, hunting, and frequenting parties of every kind. It was considered good form to keep two or three mistresses or even more. When they were not at the court or in town, the court nobles lived in their country houses. But *la vie de château* was no less sumptuous than life at Versailles or in the nobles' town houses in Paris. The duc de Choiseul, when in disgrace, kept open house in his retreat at Chanteloup. Every evening he received, gave concerts, had guests for supper. His 800,000 livres of rent were far from adequate for all this. The château of the Brienne family included a dining room for "intimate dinners" with places for eighty people. This château also had a billiard room, a room devoted to natural history, and another to experimental physics; there was also a theater, which was transformed into a ballroom when the floor and the stage were brought to the same level by means of a lift. There was another ballroom for use by the domestic staff.

As a rule, the provincial nobility have been considered poor, with most of them looked upon as being "embarrassed or even poverty-stricken" (Carré), "doomed to impoverishment" because they did not know how, or did not even want, to become rich (Georges Lefebvre). That was what was said in the 18th century, and historians have gone on repeating it. It would appear, however, that, in the second half of the century, in the areas of large-scale trade, matters were frequently otherwise. Many provincial nobles, it seems, behaved as landed proprietors and entrepreneurs who were extremely active and well-to-do, managing their estates and looking after their fortunes with discipline, strictness, and thrift and adapting their *domaine proche* to a growing market for agricultural produce. They applied new methods of management and exploitation and new techniques in the spheres of business accounting or of actual cultivation. They carried out rearrangements of their fields, brought wasteland under the plough, provided storage for the crops, and even engaged in speculation. They undertook political activity directed toward the *parlements*, the provincial Estates, and the *chambres de commerce*, with a view to obtaining improvements in communications, abolishing common lands, and securing "a good price for grain."

Some provincial *gentilshommes* reshaped their estates and enlarged their *domaines proches* by buying up outlying plots, which they exchanged for plots close to their châteaux so as to form more extensive farms, cultivated by a single tenant. In the Toulouse area, between 1750 and 1790, fourteen noble families enlarged their *domaines proches* from 3 to 70 hectares. Fifteen families in Bordelais enlarged theirs from 3 to 130 hectares. Enlargement of the *domaine proche* was also achieved by bringing brush land under cultivation in the southeast, heath in Brittany, and *lande* and fen in the Médoc area, at the expense of the commons.

The *domaines* which had thus been enlarged were, in part, exploited directly. In one Médoc village, after 1740, the *gentilshommes* who had purchased the land got rid of the tenant farmers and planted vines, which they cultivated, using workers paid at 12 sous a day (or, what came to the same thing, on a piecework contract for between 20 and 32 livres per hectare) or else, in some cases, sharecroppers. In the Toulouse area, the wheat fields of the domain, close to the château, were cultivated, for a yearly wage, by workers known as *maîtres-valets* or again, in some cases, by sharecroppers.

The *gentilshommes* did not do much to imitate their English contemporaries as regards rotation of crops, catch crops, selective breeding of animals, or introduction of new crops. Some of them experimented with artificial meadows, applied some of the ideas of Jethro Tull on row planting, repeated cultivation, not letting the land lie fallow, and so on; these included the marquis d'Escouloubre[3] and the comte de Villèle, in the Toulouse area, and the marquis de Caradeuc and the marquis de Montluc in the neighborhood of Rennes. But nearly all of them improved their methods of selling. Instead of disposing of the crop on the domain itself to *blatiers* (grain brokers), who dictated their own price, the *gentilshommes* took to selling it directly in the market, at the moment when prices were highest. In Toulouse, Bordeaux, and Rennes they did not behave at all like passive receivers of feudal dues but as entrepreneurs, endeavoring to make the most out of their domains, and shrewd sellers in an expanding market.

Now, the nobility held a big proportion of the land. In Lauragais, if we take into account only the *domaine proche,* that is, the land for which the nobles possessed both *seigneurie directe* and *seigneurie utile*—in other words, full ownership—and leave aside the *mouvances,* we find that these nobles—who made up one-hundredth of the population and included 226 families—held 455 estates, covering 24,672 hectares, or 44.4 percent of the land, with an average size of 54 hectares. The greater part was held by members of the older nobility, of sword and gown, numbering 95 families, and the rest by 131 ennobled families.

The clergy held 132 properties, covering 3,629 hectares, 6.5 percent of the land; the *bourgeoisie* held 820 properties, 14,136 hectares, 25 percent of the land, with the average size of a property 17 hectares; the peasants and craftsmen, who made up about 80 percent of the population, held 5,355 properties, 12, 535 hectares, 22.5 percent of the land, with the average of one of their properties 2.3 hectares. Common land covered 1.2 percent of the total.

The average village contained one or two *gentilshommes* who each owned between 200 and 300 arpents; three or four petty nobles and *bourgeois,* each of whom had 40 to 50 arpents; and a mass of petty *bourgeois* and peasants, each of whom had between 12 or 13 hectares and 1.5 hectares.

The nobles were not everywhere so well placed as this. In the province of Maine, out of 580,000 hectares, noblemen's estates covered only 120,000, or about 21 percent of the territory. One of these estates was 2,700 hectares in size, six were between about 400 and 700 hectares; many of them exceeded 40 hectares. The nobles held not more than 15 percent of the cultivable land. The marquis de Courtanvaulx held 665 hectares of cultivable land, spread over five parishes covering 7,000 hectares. He thus held less than 10 percent of the land, and what he held was cultivated in large farms by well-to-do big peasants. Not one cultivator in fourteen was connected with the nobility by occupational ties. The nobles' direct economic control over the peasants was weak. So also was their influence in general. The majority of the estates of the *gentilshommes* were in the east of the province, where they accounted for 33 (or even 32) percent of the land. This area proved resistant to the Chouan movement.

The importance of the nobles in this area was due to their ownership of most of the forests. The largest of these belonged to *grands seigneurs.* The forest of Vibraye, 1,350 hectares in size, belonged to the marquis Hurault de Vibraye. He leased it for cutting, at intervals of eighteen years, to the ironworks at Champerond for 18,000 livres a year. This forest made up half of the estates of the Vibraye family. The comte de Tessé, *seigneur* of fifteen *seigneuries* covering twenty-nine parishes, possessed 1,552 hectares of woods, which constituted 52 percent of his domain.

Although seignorial and feudal dues were greatly increased in the second half of the 18th century, they formed a large proportion of the nobles' income only where the *domaine proche* was small. In Upper Maine the *seigneurie* of Le Fresnay, belonging to the comte de Tessé, included very little by way of *domaine proche.* Seignorial and feudal dues therefore amounted to nearly 50 percent of the income: 706 livres out of 1,566. In the northern part of Gâtinais the duchy of Nemours included hardly any *domaine proche,* and so seignorial and feudal dues represented 90 percent of the duke's income.

In regions that were poor and remote from large-scale trade, seignorial and feudal dues usually formed at least a third of the nobles' income. In the duchy of Penthièvre, these dues were 44 percent of total income; in the case of the Chateaugiron family, who held 25 *seigneuries* and lands in the present department of Ille-et-Vilaine, seignorial and feudal dues constituted 34 percent and the product of the *domaine proche* 64 percent of their livelihood. Similarly, in Upper Auvergne, about 1789, seignorial and feudal dues formed, on the average, 34 percent of the income of those nobles who possessed them.

Where, however, the *domaine proche* was fairly extensive (and where there were also opportunities for trade), the income derived from it greatly exceeded that derived from seignorial and feudal dues. In Upper Maine the largest landowner, the comte de Tessé, obtained 54,899 livres from twelve *seigneuries.* Of this, seignorial and feudal dues accounted for 5,406 livres, or 10.8 percent. For the whole of his fifteen *seigneuries,* which brought him, on the eve of 1789, an income of 81,899 livres, the *cens* and *lods et ventes* produced no more than 6,112 livres, while the *champarts* and *terrages* had fallen into desuetude and produced nothing, but tenancies produced 49,127 livres and the Antoigné ironworks produced 25,000 livres. In the northern part of Gâtinais the *seigneur* of Caumartin held nine *seigneuries.* From his *domaine proche* of 910 hectares he derived 10,700 livres; from his seignorial and feudal dues from 3,680 hectares he got 1,000 livres—less than a tenth of the income from his lands. In the *seigneurie* of Varennes, 33 hectares of *domaine proche,* mostly consisting of meadows, brought in 1,600 livres, while the seignorial and feudal dues from 72 hectares brought 58 livres. At Vieillevigne, about 30 kilometers southwest of Toulouse, the marquis d'Escouloubre supervised the cultivation of a *domaine proche* that provided him with 6,000 livres a year; from his seignorial and feudal rights he got 520 livres, or barely 7.5 percent of his income.

Taxation took relatively little of this income. In the regions of *taille réelle* the nobles had to pay tax on their "commoner" lands, but they made composition with the fiscal authorities. Escouloubre paid 240 livres in *taille.* In the regions of *taille personnelle* the nobles paid *taille* only indirectly, what their tenant farmers paid being deducted from the rents paid by the latter. The nobles were also exempt from the joint-obligation system.

The nobles paid the poll tax (*capitation*), which, instituted in 1695, was greatly increased during the Seven Years' War. Escouloubre paid 136 livres. The nobles had to pay the "twentieth," a 5 percent income tax which began to be levied in 1750; it was doubled in 1756 and then tripled between 1760–64 and 1780–86. However, the nobles managed to make arrangements with the fiscal authorities, as a result of which they paid less than 15 percent. Escouloubre paid 209 livres. His total taxes amounted to 585 livres and absorbed 8 percent of the income from his *domaine proche*. He was particularly fortunate. On the average, the nobles of Toulouse paid in taxes about 15 percent of the income from their estates. (In addition, they paid indirect taxes.) In Picardy, however, peasant landholders paid 40 percent of their income, and, in Limousin, according to Turgot, they paid as much as 80 percent. The greater part of the nobles' income thus escaped taxation.

It would appear that in the second half of the 18th century most of the nobles had abandoned the tradition of *largesse* and lived in a sober, even frugal, manner, thriftily. A provincial nobleman with an income of 10,000 or 12,000 livres would have been poor in Paris, but in the provinces he was, economically speaking, a very important person. He might possess several residences, in town and country, four to six servants, carriages, and a library and be able to take the cure at some spa. In the Toulouse region most of the nobles lived in their châteaux, on their estates, not hunting much, but supervising the work done on their farms and checking their accounts. Their recreations were of a modest order: family dinners, occasional visits to their neighbors. When winter came, they would spend three or four months—from November to March, say—in Toulouse. The town was small, everybody knew everybody else, and old families had no need to indulge in ostentatious spending. Their recreations—salons, the theater, the academies—were not very costly. These nobles tended to get richer.

The nobles avoided fragmentation of their fortunes by means of careful drafting of marriage contracts and wills. The right of primogeniture maintained family properties in being. Law and public opinion concurred in reserving for the eldest son the greater part of a family's fortune and the bulk of its estates.[4] In Provence a young member of the Mirabeau family wrote to his eldest brother, the Physiocrat marquis: "I have known from childhood that you must have everything except what is absolutely necessary for me to live on, because you are the *chef de la race,* because you are in charge of everything, and it is my duty to contribute and not to appropriate.'' The *parlement* of Toulouse laid it down that ''a son is obliged to take his legitim (in his share of the inheritance from his father) in cash when, for the honor of his illustrious family, the lands of the inheritance should remain together, since this dignity cannot be kept up if the lands are divided.'' Half of the inheritance should go to the eldest son if there were five or more children; two-thirds if there were four or fewer. The eldest sons gave the younger ones their share in cash—if necessary, as an annual *rente.* Moreover, the younger children usually refrained from marrying. Most of them went into the army or the church. The girls became nuns or stayed spinsters. The sons who went into the army did not, as a rule, rise higher than the subaltern ranks, and after twenty to twenty-five years' service they would retire, with the Cross of Saint-Louis and a modest pension.

The eldest son married, so as to ensure the continuity of the family—and married as rich an heiress as he could find.

If it was necessary to secure husbands for the girls of the family, arrangements were made to spread the payment of their dowries over the longest possible period and to pay as much of the total sum as possible by transferring claims on individual debtors or public institutions.

The provincial nobility thus included some of those whose fortunes were large. In Toulouse in 1789 the magistrates of the *parlement* were mostly *gentilshommes.* They accounted for only 5.58 percent of those who made declarations at the *enregistrement,* but they held 43.66 percent of all the wealth in Toulouse, with 23 percent of the value of dwelling houses, 45 percent of the value of rural property, 60 percent of loans to individuals, and 70 percent of loans to the state and public bodies. After this group came the nobles who occupied civil or military offices other than those in the sovereign courts. These made up 0.83 percent of the declarants and possessed 2.77 percent of all the wealth. Their total fortune was constituted in much the same proportion as that of the *parlement* men. Last came the unemployed nobles. They were 5.46 percent of the declarants. They possessed 16.66 percent of all the wealth, with 11.70 percent of the value of dwelling houses, 22.44 percent of that of rural property, 15.91 percent of loans to individuals, and 11.72 percent of loans to the state or public bodies.

All together, the nobility possessed 63 percent of the total wealth in Toulouse.

If we take the livre *tournois* as being more or less equivalent to the

franc *de Germinal,* then the average fortune of the *présidents* of the
Toulouse *parlement* was 435,156 francs, that of the counselors of the
parlement, 289,869 francs, that of the nobles who were generals or high-
ranking officers in the army, 256,889 francs, that of the unemployed
nobles 128,140 francs—and that of the workmen and laborers of Toulouse, 389 francs.

If we construct a scale of Toulouse fortunes with sixteen rungs, the
first being the lowest and the sixteenth the highest, we find in the
sixteenth section (over 1 million francs) 2.11 percent of the nobles; it is
one of these, a *parlementaire,* who has the largest fortune, 1,287,993
francs. In the fifteenth section (between 398,109 francs and 1 million),
there are 10.56 percent of the nobles; in the fourteenth (158,469–
398,109 francs), 28.16 percent of the nobles; in the thirteenth (63,036–
158,469 francs), 29 percent; in the twelfth (25,000–63,000 francs), 15
percent; in the eleventh (10,000–25,000 francs), 7 percent; in the tenth
(4,000–10,000 francs), 2 percent; and in the ninth (1,585–4,000 francs),
0.70 percent.

Almost 75 percent of the nobles of Toulouse owned between 63,000
and 398,000 francs and were therefore comfortably off. Twenty-four
percent of them owned between 63,000 and 3,745 francs, the latter
figure being the smallest fortune recorded for a nobleman.

It certainly seems to emerge from these figures and qualitative
analyses that the nobility, and, in particular, the provincial *gentilhommerie,* played in the second half of the 18th century a much more
important role in production than historians used to think. We can
relate this fact to the participation of the *gentilshommes* of the provinces in the exploitation of mines of coal, iron, copper, etc. In this
period they not only intensified their exploitation of small mining units,
but the large mining companies were usually established on the initiative of nobles and *gentilshommes;* an example is the Anzin company,
founded in 1756, which in 1789 employed 4,000 workers in its mines
and was already a sort of large-scale capitalist industrial concern. It
was the same with the Carmaux mines, which were mostly owned by
the marquis de Solage.

In all these cases the *gentilshommes* were exploiting either the soil or
the subsoil of their lands. It had always been permissible for a *gentilhomme* to exploit his lands and sell the product without in any way
compromising his noble status. Perhaps there was nothing new in principle in what was happening at this time—merely greater activity in a
period of economic upsurge.

But when we consider the efforts made by the great nobles of the provinces to improve their techniques, so as to produce for sale in expanded markets and penetrate into commercial circuits with a capitalistic aspect to them, we are justified in wondering whether this does not point to a new spirit among these *gentilshommes,* a new scale of social values, and whether the highest social value for them was not becoming, more or less consciously, the production of material goods and the money to be gained by this production. To be sure, these *gentilshommes* did not give up their old ideal. They vigorously defended their rights, exemptions, and immunities. They wanted to remain *gentilshommes.* But an entire "section" of their behavior was becoming that of the capitalist landowners and *bourgeois* of the 19th century—to such an extent that there are grounds for asking whether these *gentilshommes* were not on the way to becoming *bourgeois* and whether the *order* was not in the process of being transformed into a *class.*

A commercial nobility and a military nobility

A large proportion of the *gentilshommes* were still very poor. There were even some extreme cases. In 1787 the military college of La Flèche opened its gates to a descendant of the comtes de Limoges, one of the most illustrious of the old families of France, who was wearing peasant's dress, with clogs on his feet and a woolen cap on his head. Without sinking quite so far, there were in the province of Maine, around 1789, many petty *gentilshommes* who owned hardly any land. Half of the 129 nobles subjected to the poll tax in the *élection* of Le Mans at the beginning of 1789 had neither fiefs nor *seigneuries.* Fifty of the country *gentilshommes* were poor, their average poll-tax assessment not exceeding 35 livres per year. The châteaux were deserted. In Upper Auvergne a third of the *gentilshommes* enjoyed only a small income, 300 to 500 livres per year, and half of them had no benefit from seignorial or feudal dues. Such cases were sufficiently numerous for contemporaries to consider that, in general, the *gentilshommes* were poor. Thoughtful folk applied their minds to the question of providing them with resources.

This idea was not new. It had been one of Richelieu's aims. He wished to give the nobility the material means for fulfilling military, judicial, and ecclesiastical functions, for, "good morals being taken for granted, then quality, together with the authority which normally accompanies it, should be preferred even to very great learning."[5] The establishment of pawnshops was authorized so that poor nobles might obtain the money they needed, in accordance with their request made at the Estates General of 1614. Richelieu opened up the great enterprises of overseas trade to the nobility by allowing them, through a provision in the relevant edicts, to enter the companies without losing their noble status. The ordinance of January 1629 made it easier for *gentilshommes* to obtain positions in the royal household and the household of the queen mother and the duc d'Orléans and in military offices, *capitaineries,* and governorships of provinces, fortified towns, and fortresses by abolishing the venality of these offices. The ordinance confirmed the exclusive right of nobles of noble descent to the prebends and places as canons and monks that were reserved for them in cathedral churches. Finally, it allotted to the *gentilshommes* two positions as *conseillers de robe courte* in each of the *parlements.* In 1636 Richelieu set up a fund of 22,000 livres in *rente* to establish a military school for young *gentilshommes.* Situated in the rue Vieille-du-Temple, this school accommodated twenty-two pupils, who spent two years there. When they graduated, the young *gentilshommes* proceeded to serve the king for two more years in his Guards regiments or on his ships. However, this institution did not survive Richelieu. The cardinal also proposed to form, from among the poor *gentilshommes,* companies of light horse, to be maintained by the provinces. But the question of what to do about the poor *gentilshommes* became acute in the second half of the 18th century. Persons influenced by the ideas of the *philosophes* considered that commerce ought to serve as the nobles' means of existence. They came up against vigorous opposition. The starting point of the controversy was furnished by a little book written by the abbé Coyer, called *La noblesse commerçante,* published in 1756. A large number of writings, both for and against the idea, appeared between 1756 and 1760. Later the excitement died down, but even on the eve of the Revolution economists and political writers did not fail to give some attention to the question, in passing.

From the legal standpoint there was no problem. The edict of December 1701 opened up large-scale trade, on sea and land alike, to the nobility, and this was confirmed by the edicts of 1765 and 1767. Socially, however, the problem remained what it had been, for, though there were some ennobled persons engaged in trade (not many, in fact), there were very few *gentilshommes* so engaged before 1756.

The abbé Coyer's book seems to have resulted from a change in the social values held by French society between 1750 and 1760. Interest shifted gradually from military honor and religious devotion to the wealth obtainable from trade and industry. "The nation, bored with poetry, set itself to reasoning about the crops." The subject of trade gave occupation to a number of good writers and began to compete with religion. Books on political economy multiplied and were analyzed in the newspapers and commented on in the salons. Discussion about agriculture, commerce, navigation, and finance became widespread. Producing goods, and the making of money thereby, became a social value that was in process of ousting other values.

To the abbé Coyer it seemed that most of the nobility were poverty-stricken. They were watching their fathers' châteaux fall into ruins. The nobleman's tears mingled with those of the farmer. The seignorial lands failed to support their *seigneurs*, the *métairies* lacked cattle, the fields were poorly cultivated, the harvests languished. The miserable *gentilhomme* saw with terror the approach of his creditor, a court order in his hand, to wrest from him his ancestral lands. His family were short of clothes and education. This was a social catastrophe.

But the nobility could save itself through engaging in commerce. There was nothing disgraceful about this. It was service to the king, a source of dignity no less than military service. "Commerce has become the soul of political interest and of the balance of power . . . The balance of trade and the balance of power are now one and the same." Commerce was indeed an affair of state, worthy of the attention of a *gentilhomme*. Commerce ought to be given the first place in the kingdom, and every noble should engage in it "for the good of commerce itself, which means for the good of France." He should even engage in retail trade, "for one form of commerce leads to another—small-scale trade leads to middling, and middling to large-scale trade."

Through commerce the nobility would become busy and rich. It would accumulate resources, and, thanks to this, it would be able to develop its estates, acquiring great flocks and herds that would make possible the expansion of textile factories and tanneries. Thirty thousand *gentilshommes* made wealthy by commerce would each spend, on the average, 3 livres more every day. Consumption would be increased by over 109 million a year. The craftsmen and farmers would earn wages and make profits as a result of this extra consumption. The kingdom would be enabled to support three or four million more people, and the king's armies would thus become all the more numerous and formidable. Shipping would increase. Gold and silver would pour into the country. The colonies would develop, and the navy would be strengthened to the point that it could vanquish the maritime powers, England and Holland. France would extend her hegemony over the whole world.

However, the *gentilshommes* did not follow the abbé Coyer's advice. In Brittany, at Morlaix, only fifteen nobles became merchants after 1750, five of these after 1772. In Nantes a few families of the old nobility produced some very notable shipowners; these were the Espivent de Villesboisnet, Luynes, and Belloneau families. At Saint-Malo the Sébires, an old noble family, were highly respected shipowners. René-Auguste de Chateaubriand, the writer's father, fitted out forty-four ships between 1758 and 1775; he thereby restored his family's fortune and was able to acquire the château of Combourg. In Nantes, out of seventy-nine noblemen engaged in trade, only five were of noble extraction or sons of ennobled persons.

In Bordeaux, out of forty-seven noblemen engaged in trade, only one was of noble extraction and seven were sons of ennobled persons. In Toulouse, of thirteen noblemen engaged in trade, only two were of noble extraction or sons of ennobled persons, and in Lyons, out of fifty-six, only seven. At the end of the 18th century 80 percent of the nobility engaged in trade consisted of traders who had been ennobled but remained semi-commoners; barely 20 percent were nobles, of whom some were genuinely of noble origin but the majority were sons of ennobled persons, not *gentilshommes*. The *gentilshommes*, whose resources were slender or who were even poor, remained loyal to the ideal of the warrior and landowner.

In principle, the true occupation of a *gentilhomme* was still that of arms. The nobility of France remained essentially military, a real *gentilhommerie*. However, in the army the middling and petty *gentilshommes* found themselves faced with competition from three sources: commoners, sons of *financiers*, and nobles "presented" at court.

Commoners risen from the ranks could attain the rank of lieutenant. They sometimes made up half the total number of lieutenants, but it was unusual for them to advance any further; a captain who was a commoner was a rarity. The *gentilshommes* therefore did not resent them, since these commoners were real soldiers, worthy of respect, and since they did not compete with them for the higher ranks.

Much more serious was the competition from sons of *financiers*, farmers general, *receveurs*, and *trésoriers*. As the colonels were usually in debt through following the noble way of life, the *financiers* were able to buy from them, for their sons, either a company, with the rank of captain, or sometimes even a whole regiment, with the rank of colonel. The *gentilshommes* could then hope, at best, to rise to lieutenant colonel; they saw the ranks of colonel and general closed to them. They were furious in their hostility to the *financiers* and waged a veritable social war against them.

Finally, the most redoubtable competition was that coming from the young nobles who had been "presented" at court and were consequently destined for the command of regiments, with, thereafter, the highest ranks of lieutenant general and marshal of France open to them. The middling and petty *gentilshommes* had to wage a conflict of "estates," within their own order, against the "presented" nobility.

The last problem was that of resources. In the army, the *gentilshommes* carried to extremes the traditon of *largesse*. Being an officer could mean financial ruin. Many *gentilshommes* were forced to leave the service and live in the country, in discomfort and sometimes in poverty.

In order to solve this social problem, the chevalier d'Arc proposed that France be transformed into a warrior society, living, like the Spartans, in the worship of honor. This was the theme of his book, published in 1756, *La noblesse militaire, ou le patriote français*.

Philippe-Auguste de Sainte-Foix, chevalier d'Arc, was a Bourbon, a grandson of Louis XIV, and a bastard of two degrees, since he was the natural son of the comte de Toulouse, himself the natural son of Louis XIV and Madame de Montespan.

He considered the France of his time to be rotted by luxury and commerce. The kingdom must consecrate itself to austerity of life and manners and find its happiness in the pursuit of greatness by way of military honor. The prejudices known by the name of "honor" must have their value restored to them. The military way of life must become society's ideal. The king and the court should set the example, illustrating the military virtues, whose foundation is self-sacrifice, even unto death, in the interest of the state and the nation. The king and his courtiers should be models of austerity, always wearing the uniform of their rank and receiving at court the rank-and-file of the *gentilhommerie*, themselves clad in their soldiers' uniforms.

This ideal of honor and grandeur should be entrusted to a nobility that was wholly military, a *gentilhommerie*. On the one hand, the hereditary *gentilshommes* would all be obliged to follow the military career. When young they would join cadet companies, there to serve as ordinary soldiers subject to all the servitudes of the soldier's trade.

Any who refused would, on reaching the age of thirty, be deprived of the privileges of nobility. On the other hand, officers who rose from the ranks would be given personal nobility and regarded as *gentilshommes*. The army and the nobility would henceforth be one.

This military nobility would take the lead in a country given new life. Trade and industry, harmful activities since they favored luxury, would not be encouraged. Agriculture, however, would be developed, with the king setting the example of interest in this pursuit by ploughing fields and milking cows in person. He would award distinctions to the best cultivators. Thus there would always be a good supply of cheap foodstuffs. In years of plenty the king would stock up the public granaries so as to be in a position to relieve the poor in times of dearth. Families would therefore be able to have many children. The king would favor heads of large families with honorific privileges, tax exemptions, bounties, and pensions. The population would increase and provide so many soldiers that the French army would become irresistible.

The ideas of the chevalier d'Arc did not remain without influence, but they were distorted in their application by the pressure of the "presented" nobles and the *financiers*, who kept their monopoly hold on higher ranks, and that of the traditionalist *gentilshommes*, who strove to bar commoners from access to officer rank. The exclusivist outlook of this second group, which was strengthened by the circumstance that the army did not expand sufficiently to absorb all the *gentilshommes*, was well expressed in 1781 by François-Philippe Loubert, baron de Bord, colonel of dragoons and major general of the *gendarmerie*, in his *Examen critique du militaire français:*

> The nobility complains, with good reason, that it does not have the sole right to military appointments. It is often humiliated by being refused positions which its ancestors held and cemented with their blood. The wealth that corrodes everything and breaks down all the barriers that honor and glory have raised between citizens has today become a sufficient title for claims to every position. We see the sons of clerks putting on uniform, contesting precedence, and trying to level themselves with men of quality. If anyone should dare to say that the nobility is not large enough to fill all the appointments, I should reply that the provinces are full of *gentilshommes* who have not been able to obtain appointments.

What was achieved fell very far short of what the chevalier d'Arc had dreamed of. January 1751 saw the creation of the Ecole Royale Militaire in Paris, for the benefit of the poor nobility, at the instigation of the secretary of state for war, D'Argenson. This school was open to all nobles who could prove four quarterings of nobility on their fathers' side, on condition that they were indigent and in accordance with their fathers' merits. After 7 April 1764 the former Jesuit college of La Flèche was transformed into a military college to serve as a preparatory school for the Paris establishment. Two hundred fifty sons of poor noblemen were to be educated at La Flèche, and the best of these, at the age of fourteen, after being found physically fit for service and having passed an examination, were to enter the Paris Ecole Militaire.

However, it was extremely difficult for poor provincial *gentils-hommes* to prove their noble descent through four generations by means of authentic documents. It was the sons of the "presented" nobility and the sons of the *financiers* who entered the Ecole Militaire. They brought into it their habits of luxury and the "noble style of living," which had to be changed. Therefore, the comte de Saint-Germain in February 1776 abolished the Paris Ecole Militaire and replaced it with twelve military colleges in the provinces (La Flèche being one of these) for the benefit of the poor *gentilshommes*. When they left these colleges, the young *gentilshommes* were to enter cadet companies. Despite its official abolition, the Paris Ecole Militaire was kept in being and received the most outstanding pupils of the provincial colleges.

Other measures were taken for the benefit of the hereditary *gentils-hommes*. After the *règlements* of 1718 and 1727, the *règlement* of 22 May 1781 obliged all who were put forward for the rank of second lieutenant to prove four quarterings of nobility on their fathers' side by means of evidence from registers of baptism, marriage contracts, extracts from *taille* rolls, *arrêts,* and court judgments on questions of nobility, and so on, and to present certificates to this effect, confirmed by *le sieur* Chérin, the genealogist. Excepted from this requirement were the sons of commoner officers who had been made *chevaliers* of the Order of Saint-Louis for their deeds on the battlefield. Commoners who were already officers retained their rank, but promotion of non-commissioned officers was almost completely blocked. The army was to become the monopoly of the hereditary *gentilhommerie*.

The reforms of 1788 tended in the same direction. The Assembly of Notables in 1787 had called for economies. The army alone cost 114 million a year. The comte de Brienne, secretary of state for war, set up a Conseil de la Guerre whose *rapporteur* was colonel comte de Guibert, and he inspired the ordinances of 1788.

The reforms made were more in the spirit of the baron de Bord than in that of the chevalier d'Arc. In the royal household the *gendarmerie* (900 men), which had been wide open to the sons of *financiers* and rich *bourgeois*, was purely and simply abolished. The *gardes du corps*, however, recruited exclusively from *gentilshommes*, were maintained, though their numbers were reduced from 1,300 to 1,000 or 1,200.

The "presented" nobles kept their privilege of arriving very quickly at the rank of colonel. They had actually to serve as acting second lieutenant, acting captain, and major second-in-command. But they were to pass through all these ranks in the short space of four years. The comte de Guibert had desired to respect "the privileges of that part of the nobility which is more especially called to the command of regiments," namely, the nobles who had been presented at court.

Guibert tried, however, to let it be possible for the middling and petty nobility, "who form the foundation of the army," to attain the rank of general. Most of them did not get further than captain, and the best-favored remained stuck at the level of major or lieutenant colonel. It was decided that these nobles could be made second lieutenants after passing an examination; they could then rise to lieutenant and captain, either by seniority or by promotion. After that they could advance— but by promotion only—to major and lieutenant colonel. However, every lieutenant colonel was sure of becoming a *maréchal de camp* after twenty years' service, with war service counting double, and every *maréchal de camp* could aspire to the rank of lieutenant general.

For the commoners the reforms meant a step back from the *règlement* of 22 May 1781, for the exception in favor of sons of *chevaliers* of the Order of Saint-Louis was retained only in respect of men whose fathers had served with substantive rank of captain, and there were very few of these.

On the eve of the revolution of 1789 the 35,000 officers of the army were divided into four social categories. At the very top of the scale were the "presented" nobles and the sons of *financiers*. Then came the mass of the provincial *gentilshommes* of four quarterings, confined for the most part to subaltern ranks. Next, the ennobled and the commoners who had become officers before the ordinance of 1781—a small group tending to become even smaller. Finally, a few officers who had come up from the ranks, who owed their good fortune to the fact that their fathers had been both substantive captains and *chevaliers* of the Order of Saint-Louis.

The middling and petty hereditary *gentilshommes*, who saw themselves as the backbone of the army, conceived a violent hostility to the privileged position of the "presented" nobles and to the Conseil de la Guerre and the comte de Guibert, who had upheld it. Guibert was compelled to leave the assembly of the *bailliage* of Bourges, held for the purpose of elections to the Estates General, on 18 March 1789, under a hail of insults from the nobles present. The mass of the hereditary *gentilshommes* who were in the army were deeply discontented and wanted an overhaul of institutions. A good many of them were Freemasons. In 1789 there were sixty-nine regimental Masonic lodges, officially frequented by a thousand officers, though in fact there were many more. These hereditary *gentilshommes,* members of the provincial nobility, obeyed the king's orders only reluctantly during the troubles of 1788 and often disregarded them, refusing to suppress disturbances and themselves giving their men their first lessons in insubordination.

The unity of the order of the nobility

The order of the nobility possessed a sense of its own unity and singularity. It considered that, of the three orders, it alone formed, together with the king, a mystical body, of which the king was the head, while the *gentilshommes* were the members. From this resulted a "quality" that was inherent in their persons and was hereditary, involving "rights," and "prerogatives," "exemptions," and "immunities" which the *gentilshommes* grew angry to hear called "privileges," since they were not granted in order to facilitate the exercise of social functions but were of the essence of their quality, the essence of an "estate" that resulted from race and blood. The *gentilshommes* therefore believed that they had the right to decide, together with the king, all matters concerning the state—which, moreover, was military in its very foundation. In particular, they saw as coming within their province everything that related to the succession to the throne and to regencies, for it was the nobles who had made the family of Hugues Capet the ruling dynasty, the nobles who had caused the "Salic Law" to triumph, the nobles who had bestowed the kingdom on Henri IV. The *gentilshommes,* moreover, ought to exercise the responsibilities and fulfill the functions that were of highest importance for the king's service, since, as *gentilshommes,* they were incapable of doing anything unworthy of their birth, and it was their blood, shed in so many wars, that ensured the survival of the kingdom and the grandeur of the king.

The *gentilshommes* thought that they should be judged only by persons of their own rank. Yet the provost marshals and the presidial courts were given by commission the power to prosecute members of the nobility. Thus, a *gentilhomme,* being liable to be judged by commoners, was worse off than a mere priest, who could be tried only by ecclesiastical judges, or a commoner, also tried by persons of his own condition.

The *gentilshommes* considered that it was part of their "quality" that they should be exempt from taxation. Yet, they claimed, the king subjected them to the *taille,* since, because their tenant farmers had to pay it, the income obtainable from leasing their lands was correspondingly reduced. In places where it was hard to find tenants, *gentilshommes* had been authorized to have their land cultivated by their stewards and domestic servants, without paying the *taille.* But the regulations governing the *taille* restricted this tolerance to a tract of land not exceeding the limits of a parish; the *gentilshommes* wanted this right to apply to *all* their lands. In order to prevent salt-smuggling, the farmers of the *gabelle* obtained commissions entitling them to look for "unauthorized salt," using armed men who were empowered to search houses, in particular those of *gentilshommes,* if necessary storming their way in, using assault ladders, petards, and cannon. The *gentilshommes* protested against the obligation to serve, at their own expense and in person, in the *bans et arrière-bans* or else to pay a compensating tax. For them, this feudal service was equivalent to an imposition offensive to their "quality."

Finally, they complained of the excesses committed by the soldiers, who plundered and sacked crops, farm buildings, and dwelling houses. They complained of the blank requisition orders that certain governors supplied to officers in command of troops, which these officers used for exactions even from the property of *gentilshommes.* They denounced the royal treasury, the burden of taxes, and the costs incurred in the levying of taxes. The conduct of the soldiers and tax collectors was such that sometimes the *gentilshommes* were unable to find tenants any longer and that, often, farmers and *censitaires* ceased to be able to pay their rents or their seignorial or feudal dues. The *gentilshommes* considered themselves worse dealt with than the peasants.

The *gentilshommes* therefore desired to obtain the political means to form a corporation, that is, for their order to be recognized as a moral person, with an organ for expressing their collective will. This was why they continually called for convocation of the Estates General, in which, when it met, the nobility undoubtedly constituted a corporation. This was why, too, they participated fully in the surviving provincial Estates and called for convocation of such assemblies in the provinces where they had ceased to exist; for in each of these estates the nobility constituted a corporation. After 1615, however, though the Estates General were convoked in 1649 and 1651, they never actually met again, and the number of provinces in which the estates were no longer convoked kept on increasing. A considerable number of *gentils-hommes* (three to four thousand of them in 1651, for example), mostly from the countryside, therefore tried, in times of crisis, to form representatives of the noble order into an "estate" assembly, in other words, a corporation, so as to take part in the government. The nobility regarded such an assembly as constituting the most natural kind of intermediate authority, without which France would have not a monarch but a despot and without which, also, the monarch would find it difficult to secure obedience; for "in general assemblies, the spirit of the corporation, which is wholly noble and, consequently, wholly royal, is dominant and enters into all the individuals present, some of whom may not, taken separately, have the same feeling." It is possible that in some districts of Burgundy and Auvergne the nobles ordinarily elected a permanent representative of their corporation; but it was in the time of the Fronde that assemblies of the nobility made their appearance—in 1649, 1651, and 1652 and then, afterwards, in 1658 and 1659. These assemblies, which were open to all the *gentilshommes* of France or to their representatives, and which therefore spoke in the name of nobility as a whole, represented mainly the *gentilshommes* of the rural areas of Orléanais, Beauce, Anjou, Blésois, Normandy, Sologne, and the borders of Brittany, though they also invited participation by those of Berry, Aunis, Saintonge, and Guyenne. Assemblies of the nobility were held again in 1716 and 1717, during the minority of Louis XV, but these actually consisted of only a few courtiers.

In the assemblies that were held in the time of the Fronde the *gentils-hommes* adumbrated the institutions of a "corporation of the nobility." This was to be constituted by an act of union signed by every member, according to which each committed himself to support all the rest, "on our faith and honor"—that is, by swearing an oath. Any *gentilhomme* could join the union, provided he was independent, that is, not a *serviteur domestique* of any prince of the blood or grandee. A commission of *gentilshommes,* elected by the assembly, checked on the noble status of those who sought to join. A member could nominate someone to act as his proxy, voting on his behalf in the assemblies and informing him of the decisions adopted. The assemblies circulated *pro formas* for proxy arrangements. There was to be one proxy for fifty or for two hundred *gentilshommes.*

The chief organ of the corporation was the General Assembly. Actually, any *gentilhomme* who chose could attend at any time. Since, however, it was difficult to bring a large number of persons together for purposes of deliberating and voting, the assembly in 1652 was made up, in principle, of two deputies from each *bailliage*. In 1658 the organization was further improved. The basis for the General Assembly was to be cantonal assemblies, with each canton grouping fifteen parishes. Representatives chosen by these assemblies met in groups based on *élections* or *bailliages* to choose representatives to go forward to a provincial assembly, and the latter sent delegates to the General Assembly.

The General Assembly elected a chairman and secretaries. It met periodically and when convoked by the chairman. During its deliberation anyone might speak and explain why he intended to cast his vote in a particular way. Voting was by individuals, and decisions were adopted by a simple majority.

The assembly communicated with its supporters by means of circular letters. It appointed agents in the provinces to carry on propaganda and recruitment. It initiated a military organization in each canton, with a captain, a lieutenant, and an ensign. It invited parishes and communities to link up with the union, and in 1652 it asked the king for permission to utilize the communes to compel the soldiers to obey its decisions. The corporation of the nobility would thus have been using a rural militia to counter the professional army. The entire countryside would have been organized hierarchically under the command of the country *gentilshommes*.

The assembly elected deputies to negotiate with the king, the ministers, the secretaries of state, and the princes of the blood and to present lists of grievances.

The king, his secretaries of state, and his *parlement* considered that the nobility formed a corporation in France only during meetings of the Estates General, whereas the nobility considered that they were a permanent corporation. The king and his Council declared that the nobles could act as a body and sign common petitions only if the king gave his express permission (1717). The *procureur du roi* stated in the *parlement* that assemblies of the nobility, like other assemblies, could be convoked only by formal act of the king, through letters patent registered by the *parlement* (1652). And the king and his ministers, Richelieu and Mazarin, had no intention of assembling the nobility. When gathered together, the nobles might become dangerous, with the turbulent spirits among them infecting the others. The king's government put up with gatherings it was unable to prevent and even treated some of them—in 1649, 1652, and 1716—as lawful assemblies. Still, whenever it possessed the military means to do so, it ordered the governors and intendants to disperse them and had the ringleaders prosecuted and sentenced—showing itself capable, however, of timely clemency and pardoning those who had gone astray.

The Fronde, that great effort of aristocratic reaction, saw the last true assemblies of the nobility to be held before 1788. The nobles of certain areas nevertheless continued to group themselves corporatively, outside the provincial estates, maintaining a permanent representation to express their will in the form of either an individual (called "deputy" in Hainault and "syndic" in Dauphiné) or a body (a "syndicate" in Provence and a "directory" in Lower Alsace).

The divisions in the order of the nobility

The order of the nobility thus possessed unity. But it included social and political diversities which sometimes led to antagonism and conflict between strata. In the first place, there was a great antagonism between the *gentilshommes* and the ennobled. As the former saw it, the latter contaminated the purity of an order based on race and blood. They did not make it easy for ennobled persons to become integrated into the nobility. Though ready enough to open their ranks to men who had been ennobled for their merit and their distinguished services to the state, they rejected those whose nobility was bought with money, through purchase of letters of ennoblement or acquisition of offices which conferred noble status or of fiefs and *seigneuries* which facilitated the usurping of noble names. Here are some examples additional to those already given.[6] In their *cahier* of 1652 the *gentilshommes* demanded the revocation of all letters of ennoblement which had been granted without inquiry into the circumstances and for payment, and they called on the king to declare "null all possessions usurped or purchased by many individuals, by virtue of which they enjoy our exemptions and immunities, to the dishonor of our corporation and the burdening of your people." Ennobled farmers general, even though admitted to the society of persons of condition, did not succeed in marrying daughters of the higher nobility and were regarded by the court nobles and the old families as so many *bourgeois*. The peasants themselves made distinctions between the ennobled and the *gentilshommes*. Even in 1789, in many areas, when elections to the Estates General were held, the ennobled were excluded from the lists of the nobility and entered on those of the third estate.

Cases of usurpation of nobility were combated even more vigorously by the nobles. In 1755, in Burgundy, Jean Benoist, a wood merchant who was M. de Paulmy's farmer, bought the little fief of Vaubuzin. He swore fealty and homage to his suzerain in accordance with the traditional forms used by vassals. "The said *sieur* Benoist, having presented himself as a vassal without sword or spurs, bareheaded and kneeling on one knee, placed his hands between those of the said *seigneur* comte Duban, saying: 'Monsieur, I become your man and pledge to you faith and loyalty.' " A few months later he was behaving like an enfeoffing nobleman, claiming the title of *seigneur* of Vaubuzin. He had an inscription put on the bell and on his pew in the choir of the local church, included in his *dénombrement* the labor services and eating-chickens due from his *censitaires*, and called himself "Benoist de Vaubuzin." His *seigneur*, the comte, who held the power of high justice, regarded these usurpations as insufferable: "This merchant must be brought down to his proper level." The title of *seigneur*, though not conferring nobility, did at least cause its holder to be presumed noble. At most this man could be allowed to style himself "*sieur* of a fief at Vaubuzin." The *parlement*, to which the comte referred this matter, dismissed Benoist's claims and, in particular, refused to allow him use of the title of *seigneur*.

Among the *gentilshommes* themselves there were different strata, with conflicts between these. We have already encountered the conflict between the middling and petty *gentilshommes* and the "presented" nobles over ranks in the army.[7] But these *gentilshommes* also combated the political pretensions of the higher section of the "presented" nobles, the dukes-and-peers. The assemblies of the nobility held in 1649 and 1716 declared that the dukes-and-peers ought not to constitute a separate and superior body in the state; that they were not like the peers of olden times and so had no right to govern; and that they did not constitute a corporation and so should possess neither syndics nor commissioners. The dukes-and-peers resisted these attacks with vigor.

The dukes-and-peers also came into conflict with the higher levels of the "presented" nobility. All of the former group paid very close attention to problems of rank and precedence. The peers who were *gentilshommes* by origin set up in 1661 a permanent agency to inquire into titles, having as its general secretary the learned Jean Le Laboureur, the king's almoner, who died in 1675. After 1704 the same functions were carried out by the abbé Joachim Le Grand. The dukes-and-peers who were *gentilshommes* often met together, notably between 1662 and 1664 and in 1715 and 1716. They spoke in their collective name, as though constituting a corporation and college. They asserted their continuity with the original peers, the dukes of Normandy, Burgundy, and Aquitaine, the counts of Flanders, Champagne, and Toulouse, the archbishop of Rheims, and the bishops of Laon, Langres, Noyon, Châlons, and Beauvais. They defined their role as that of "guardians of the king and of the Crown," "high judges of the kingdom and of the Salic Law," "upholders of the state," with "a share in royalty," entrusted with "the spreading of the royal authority." Being heirs of the grandees of Merovingian and Carolingian times, the electors of Hugues Capet, they should exercise the powers of those grandees.

Within their group they successfully opposed the pretensions of the legitimized bastards of the king of France, bringing them down to the same level as other peers (1717–18). They engaged in numberless disputes about precedence. Outside their group, they attacked the privileges of the "foreign" princes who were not peers—Rohan, La Tour d'Auvergne, Grimaldi. They denied them their status as princes and the privileges they claimed: the *tabouret* for their daughters-in-law; the right to remain covered at audiences for ambassadors, with the latter to be escorted only by the House of Lorraine; precedence over dukes-and-peers at the ceremonies of the Order of the Holy Spirit; the *"pour,"* meaning the privilege of having, during official journeys, the words "pour le duc de X" written by the harbingers on the doors of their lodgings instead of merely "monsieur le duc de X"; the exclusive right of the "foreign" princesses to take up the collection at religious services held in the presence of the king.

The *gentilhommerie d'épée* as a whole set themselves against the *noblesse de robe*. This antagonism has been questioned by some historians, who have noted that members of the second group made their way into the first, that some branches or members of families of the *noblesse de robe* belonged to the *noblesse d'épée;* that marriages occurred between families of the two groups; and that there were many *gentilshommes* in the *parlements*. They overlook the fact that, generally speaking, in a family of the *noblesse de robe*, the eldest son remained in that category, with only the younger sons (and not all of them) entering the *noblesse d'épée* or the Church. Through the eldest sons and the senior branch the family remained *"de robe."* It was known for a family of the *noblesse de robe* actually to pass over into the *noblesse d'épée;* when this happened, it entered a social category which it regarded as superior. *Gentilshommes* did indeed marry daughters of *robins* who already held many titles, when these ladies brought big dowries with them. But they were not so ready to let their own daughters marry *robins*. Hypergamy by women—marrying into the rank immediately above their own—takes place in all societies, for reasons of dowry and economic cooperation and also because of beauty; but it does not alter the social hierarchy. The facts, correct though partial, quoted by the historians mentioned do not affect the feeling which the *noblesse d'épée* possessed that it constituted the true nobility, whereas the *robins* were only *"bourgeoisie."* They do not affect the aspiration of the *robins* to raise themselves to the same level as the *noblesse d'épée* while remaining essentially different and even claiming that they were the true nobility, superior to the *noblesse d'épée*. The conflicts between the two "estates"—at the Estates General of 1614–15, for instance—testify to this tension within the nobility, this struggle between social strata.[8]

Besides the examples given in earlier works, here are some more examples of this differentiation and this antagonism. On the death of his father, the marquis de Châteauneuf, secretary of state, in 1700, Louis III, marquis de La Vrillière, was obliged, in order to obtain this place for himself, to offer to "marry Mademoiselle de Mailly for nothing." Françoise de Mailly, great-niece of Madame de Maintenon, was the eldest daughter of an old family of *gentilshommes*. Her father had recently died, in the rank of *maréchal de camp* in the king's armies and *maître de camp général* of the French dragoons, leaving numerous children but so little property that La Vrillière was obliged discreetly to furnish his fiancée with her dowry. Chancellor de Pontchartrain, Madame de Maintenon, and the king were well satisfied with the arrangement. But the girl "set herself to weeping and crying that she was very unhappy, saying that they could marry her to a poor man, if they liked, *provided he was a gentilhomme and not a petit bourgeois out to make his fortune.*" She never got used to being Madame de La Vrillière and often made this plain to those around her. She was always complaining that people of her own social group whispered that her husband was *"a petit bourgeois." That* was what a La Vrillière still was, in the eyes of the nobility, despite the family's four generations as secretaries of state; even though officially styled *chevalier* and *marquis,* he was not regarded as a *gentilhomme*. The "bourgeoisie" and the "nobility" were two races perpetually distinct from each other. For Louis III, moreover, what made things worse was the fact of the marriage of his grandfather, Louis II, in 1635, to Marie Particelli, daughter of an intendant of finance with a bad reputation; this marriage had brought wealth but also a big stain of "commonness," which the courtiers still spoke of in 1700.

Louis III's sister, Charlotte-Thérèse, had married in 1692, at the age of seventeen, Louis d'Aubusson, duc de La Feuillade, peer of France, governor and lieutenant general for the king in Dauphiné, son of marshal de La Feuillade—thanks to her dowry of 400,000 livres and the indebtedness of the bridegroom. It was an unhappy marriage for the young woman, whose husband "always got on badly with her . . . and showed complete contempt for her family." The duke despised the low origins of his father-in-law, for the D'Aubussons belonged to a very old family in Marche, and this *gentilhomme de race et d'armes* could not hide his disdain for the "gentleman of pen and inkhorn," the *"bourgeois."*

This is what accounts for the zeal shown by high-placed families of the *noblesse de robe* to associate themselves with old families of the *gentilhommerie,* even by means of the gravest falsifications. Charles Colbert, that is, Croissy, the minister and secretary of state for foreign affairs, younger brother of the "Great" Colbert, a *chevalier* since his marriage in 1664 and, since 1680, "the high and mighty *seigneur* Monseigneur Charles Colbert, marquis de Croissy," was able to marry only a *robin*'s daughter, Françoise Béraud, described by the Venetian ambassador as "a lady of base origin." He worked, with the other Colberts, at forging a myth concerning a Scottish ancestor: the Colberts were said to be directly descended from one James Colbert, baron of Castlehill, who settled in Rheims in the 13th century. Learned men, even including a Jesuit, wrote folios to prove this descent. The Scottish Parliament formally confirmed it in 1686. Croissy did not shrink from forging the marriage contracts of his family so as to get his son Louis-Henri into the Order of Malta by proving that he had four quarterings of nobility.

The dukes-and-peers were constantly embattled against the *noblesse de robe*. For them the magistrates were not nobles at all but, at best, "honorable *bourgeois* who enjoy noble privileges" (Saint-Simon, *Papiers ducs et pairs,* Assemblies of 1716). The magistrate's profession was noble, but not the persons exercising it. Still less was it true that the *robe* was higher than the nobility, despite its claim that the laws were higher than the sword: for laws emanated from the monarch, the first gentleman of the kingdom. In order to be able to pronounce judgment, the nobles had attached to themselves jurists sprung from the people, but these were only the servants of the nobles. The latter were a race descended from the Frankish conquerors, whereas the magistrates belonged to an inferior race, descended from the Gauls, who had been conquered and reduced to serfdom.

Hence the importance of the *question du bonnet* in the Paris *parlement*. At ordinary sessions of this body the *présidents à mortier* represented the king, and so they gave their opinion even before the princes of the blood or even the dauphin; and though the *premier président* removed his hat when he asked their opinion, he kept it on when addressing the dukes-and-peers other than the princes of the blood. (That had been so since 1643.) At a *lit de justice,* however, when the king was present, the dukes-and-peers were the first to be consulted, and the *premier président* took off his hat to them and not to the *présidents à mortier.* The latter protested against this procedure in 1662 but were rebuffed by an *arrêt* of the Council in 1664. They raised the question again in 1683, 1713, 1714, September 1715 (after Louis XIV's death), and 1716, but always unsuccessfully. So far as the dukes-and-peers were concerned, the *parlement* was merely the highest corporation of the third estate. At most, in 1721 and after, a group of peers inspired by the duc de Luxembourg seems to have considered supporting the political claims of the Paris *parlement, provided* that it was dominated and led by the peers. The latter had perhaps found in it a means of political expression and action. But this intention of theirs had no bearing on the social question.

In the same way, from the beginning of the 17th century and increasingly under the personal rule of Louis XIV, the dukes-and-peers challenged the political power and social rank of the chancellor or the keeper of the seals, of the *surintendant* or *contrôleur général des finances,* and of the secretaries of state. To dukes-and-peers the position of minister meant nothing. The chancellor himself was a jurist, a plebeian, *bourgeois, peuple.* Finally, the dukes-and-peers refused to address secretaries of state as "Monseigneur."

Everything goes to confirm the antagonism between "gown" and "sword." This was a conflict not only between two levels in the hierarchy but also between two types of profession and two different ways of life.

There were other antagonisms, too, between different degrees of the noble hierarchy within the same categories. The members of the Paris *parlement,* despite their marriage connections, actually comprised different social degrees which were not free from mutual conflict. In the 18th century this *parlement* was mostly made up of "dynasties" of magistrates linked together by marriage, for unions with families of the *financier* or merchant category were rare. The Gilbert de Voisins family were related by marriage to sixteen families, among which figured the names Fieubet, d'Aguessau, Bochart, Camus, Lamoignon, and Petit de Villeneuve. Through these connections they were linked with seventy-one other families represented in the *parlement*. They were all each other's cousins. The most powerful families intermarried: Lamoignon with d'Aguesseau, d'Aligre, Bullion, Feydeau, Gourgues, Le Peletier, Longueil de Maisons, Maupeou, Molé, and Potier de Novion. The nobles of old stock, the new nobles, and the ennobled were all connected by marriage and kinship. One's first impression is therefore one of a social group that was united and homogeneous.

But the actual relationships reveal many different social degrees and much contempt on the part of the old noble families for the new ones. The *premier président* was always chosen from among those families which could pride themselves on their "birth, large property, and standing at court." De Mesmes, who was appointed in 1712, represented the seventh generation of nobility in his family. The nomination of Portail in 1724 caused something of a scandal, for he was only the grandson of a man ennobled by office. The advocate Barbier wrote: "M. Portail's birth is not proportionate to the position of *premier président*." In 1753 Jean-Baptiste Bochart de Saron presented himself as candidate for the office of *avocat général*. His family had been noble since 1466. His rival for the post, Claude-Louis Aubert de Tourny, *avocat général* in the Grand Conseil, was the son of the well-known intendant Tourny. In the eyes of public opinion, however, he was the grandson of Colbert's *valet de chambre*. Everyone considered his degree of nobility inadequate, and the government rejected him. Another man, Jacques II Frécot de Lanty, failed in 1751 to obtain the office of *président aux enquêtes* because his father, though endowed with the equivalent of four generations of nobility by his post as *secrétaire du roi*, had been a banker. Often candidates for the office of counselor were turned away politely, as soon as they began their round of visits, because they were sons of suppliers to the army or of merchants. In 1757 the *premier président* was Mathieu-François Molé, comte de Champlâtreux. Owing to his high birth he looked down on all the other counselors. Insufficiently high birth was the reason why more than a quarter of all the counselors were ostracized by the others. If the magistrates of the Paris *parlement* formed a single social group, it was one that included many antagonistic levels. There might even be cases of "overlapping," with that quarter of the total number of counselors who were looked down on for their low birth finding themselves socially outside the corporation and at the level of another, lower, "estate."

The *chambre des comptes* in Brittany presents the same phenomena of internal social stratification and conflict between strata, even though its members were ennobled by their offices. The *présidents* usually came from the nobility, and they married women of noble family. The background of the *maîtres* was trade, and they married into the upper ranks of the commercial bourgeoisie of Nantes. The *correcteurs* and auditors were sons of petty court officers, doctors, notaries, and merchants of middling and lower rank, and they married daughters of notaries, doctors, and sea captains. A social tension, a veiled rivalry, set one group against another, especially the auditors against the *maîtres* and *présidents*. The Revolution brought this struggle between ranks into the open, with the *présidents* and *maîtres* showing hostility to it, while the auditors were mostly favorable, some being genuine revolutionaries.

The higher nobility as a whole were opposed by the middling and petty nobility. During the Fronde this opposition of interests was openly expressed. The middling and petty nobility compelled the princes of the blood and the grandees to accept a General Assembly of the noble order. The nobles of the different provinces sent their deputies to this assembly. Their aim was to restore the privileges of the nobility: a certain proportion of offices should be reserved for *gentilshommes* so as to provide them with resources and influence, and the nobles should exercise supervision over the government. The assembly wished the Estates General to meet. The princes of the blood and the grandees, however, wanted to keep the absolutist regime in being so as to make use of it to their own advantage. They arranged matters so that the Estates General, though convoked, never actually met and so that the assembly of the nobles should make as few decisions as possible and that even these should not be put into effect.

In every province such hidden conflicts between the court nobles and the higher provincial nobility, on the one hand, and the middling and petty nobility, on the other, continued to be waged, with various ups and downs. In Brittany the entire local nobility slyly combated the king, their supreme *seigneur,* and the high court nobles. As the latter fell heavily into debt, one form taken by the struggle against them was the purchase of their fiefs and *seigneuries* in Brittany by the higher provincial nobles and the *parlementaire* nobles. All of them, however, mainly carried on their fight by encroachments on the royal domain and the domains and rights of the high court nobility. As vassals of the latter and the king, they rendered false *aveux,* built mills of their own, to which the peasants had to bring their corn, established their own markets, and appointed seignorial notaries, who drew up documents in which the rights of the suzerain were ignored. The law courts protected the Breton nobles, the lead being given by the *parlement* of Brittany itself, which issued *arrêts* in their favor and annulled those of the *chambre des comptes* for Brittany.

Gradually the noble magistrates of the *parlement* of Brittany ousted the court nobles as *seigneurs* and granters of fiefs. But the middling and petty nobles, hard pressed by the feudal and seignorial system, in turn fought against them, by means of encroachments. They usurped honorific rights and levels of jurisdiction, and they cheated in reporting the real extent of their *seigneuries.* In their *aveux* they claimed to hold rights of middle or high justice; they omitted some of the rights of the *seigneur* above them; they mentioned lands or rights which had never formed part of their fief or *seigneurie.* Or else some of these middling or petty nobles became *sergents féodés* on behalf of the higher *seigneur,* which meant that they were entrusted with collecting rents and feudal and seignorial dues for him. The peasants came to look on the nobleman to whom they actually paid their rent as their *seigneur,* entering into feudal dependence upon him and rendering *aveu* to him and no longer to the higher *seigneur*—whose place was eventually taken by this petty noble. The middling and petty nobles annexed the heaths and wastelands normally treated as part of the superior fief. They created new fiefs. They nibbled away at the great fiefs of the court and *parlementaire* nobles, quietly and steadily.

The different degrees, the different "estates," of the French nobility were in constant struggle, one against the other.

Notes

1. Charles Loyseau, *Offices,* book 1, chap. 9, no. 33.
2. La Roque, *Traité de la noblesse* (1735 edition), preface.
3. Escouloubre is a very good example. See Robert Forster, *The Nobility of Toulouse in the 18th Century,* Johns Hopkins University Studies in Historical and Political Science, ser. 78, no. 1 (Baltimore, 1960).

4. See above, pp. 170–72.
5. *Testament politique* (1764 edition), vol. 1, p. 106.
6. See above, pp. 158–59, 161.
7. See above, pp. 193–94.
8. See Roland Mousnier, *La vénalité des offices sous Henri IV et Louis XIII; The Assassination of Henri IV;* and *Lettres et mémoires adressés au chancelier Séguier.*

Guide to further reading

Ambrosi, Christian. "Aperçu sur la répartition et la perception de la taille au XVIe siècle," *Revue d'Histoire moderne et contemporaine* 8 (1961): 282–300.

Aulard, F. A. *La Révolution française et le régime féodal.* Armand Colin, 1919.

Baehrel, René. *Une croissance: La basse Provence rurale (XVIe siècle à 1789).* S.E.V.P.E.N., 1961.

Behrens, Betty. "Nobles' Privileges and Taxes in France at the End of the Ancien Régime," *Economic History Review* 2d ser. 15 (1962–63): 451–75.

Belleguise, A. *Traité de la noblesse et de son origine suivant les préjugés rendus par les commissaires députez pour la vérification des titres de noblesse.* 1700.

Bluche, François. *L'origine des magistrats du Parlement de Paris au XVIIIe siècle.* Daupeley-Gouverneur, 1956. (Originally published in *Paris et Ile-de-France* 5–6 [1953–54].)

———. *Les honneurs de la Cour.* Les Cahiers Nobles, nos. 10–11. 1957.

———. *Les magistrats du Parlement de Paris au XVIIIe siècle.* Annales Littéraires de l'Université de Besançon, vol. 35. Besançon: Jacques & Demontrand, 1960.

———. *Les magistrats de la Cour des Monnaies de Paris au XVIIIe siècle, 1715–1790.* Annales Littéraires de l'Université de Besançon, vol. 81. Paris: Les Belles-Lettres, 1966.

———. *Les magistrats du Grand Conseil au XVIIIe siècle, 1690–1791.* Annales Littéraires de l'Université de Besançon, vol. 82. Paris: Les Belles-Lettres, 1966.

———, and Durye, Pierre. "L'anoblissement par charges avant 1789," in *Les Cahiers nobles,* nos. 23 and 24. 1962.

Bois, Paul. *Paysans de l'Ouest.* Le Mans: Vilaire, 1960.

Brocher, Henri. *Le rang et l'étiquette sous l'Ancien Régime: A la cour de Louis XIV.* Alcan, 1934.

Bruley, Edouard. "Nobles et paysans picards à la fin de l'Ancien Régime," *Revue d'Histoire moderne et contemporaine* 16 (1969): 606–11.

Carré, Henri. *La noblesse de France et l'opinion publique au XVIIIe siècle.* 1920.

Chérin, L. N. H. *De la noblesse.* 1788.

Cobban, Alfred. *The Social Interpretation of the French Revolution.* Cambridge, Eng.: At the University Press, 1964.

Cole, Hubert, *First Gentleman of the Bedchamber.* New York: Viking Press, 1965.

Coyer, Abbé. *La noblesse commerçante.* London and Paris, 1756.

Depitre, Edgar. "Le système et la querelle de la noblesse commerçante," *Revue d'Histoire économique et sociale* 6 (1913): 137–76.

Deyon, Pierre. *Amiens, capitale provinciale.* Paris and The Hague: Mouton, 1967.

Durand, Yves. *La maison de Durfort à l'époque moderne*. Fontenay-le-Comte: Imprimerie Lussaud, 1975.

Egret, Jean. *La Prérévolution française, 1787–1788*. P.U.F., 1962. (English trans. by Wesley D. Camp, *The French Prerevolution, 1787–1788*. Chicago: University of Chicago Press, 1977.)

Foisil, Madeleine. *Mémoires du Président Alexandre Bigot de Monville*. Vol. 1. A. Pedone, 1976.

Fontenay, Michel. "Paysans et marchands ruraux de la vallée de l'Essonne dans la seconde moitié du XVIIᵉ siècle," *Paris et Ile-de-France* 10 (1958): 157–282.

Ford, Franklin L. *Robe and Sword: The Regrouping of the French Aristocracy after Louis XIV*. Cambridge, Mass.: Harvard University Press, 1953.

Forster, Robert. *The Nobility of Toulouse in the 18th Century*. Johns Hopkins University Studies in Historical and Political Science, series 78, no. 1. Baltimore: Johns Hopkins University Press, 1960.

———. "The Noble Wine-producers of the Bordelais in the 18th Century," *Economic History Reveiw* 2d ser. 14 (1961).

———. "The Provincial Noble," *American Historical Review* 68, no. 3 (1962–63): 681–89.

———. *The House of Saulx-Tavannes. Versailles and Burgundy, 1700–1830*. Baltimore and London: Johns Hopkins University Press, 1971.

Goodwin, A. "The Social Origins and Privileged Status of the French 18th-Century Nobility," *Bulletin of the John Rylands Library* 47 (1964–65): 382–403.

Goubert, Pierre. *Beauvais et le Beauvaisis de 1600 à 1730*. S.E.V.P.E.N., 1960.

Gresset, Maurice. *Le monde judiciaire à Besançon de la conquête par Louis XIV à la Révolution française (1674–1789)*. 2 vols. University of Lille III: Service de Reproduction des Thèses, 1975.

Guyot, P. J. J. G. *Répertoire universel raisonné de jurisprudence civile, criminelle, canonique et bénéficiale*. 17 vols. 1784–85.

Halgouet, Hervé du. "Gentilshommes commerçants et commerçants nobles aux XVIIᵉ et XVIIIᵉ siècles," *Mémoires de la Société d'Histoire et d'Archéologie de Bretagne* 16 (1935): 147–88.

Jacquart, Jean. *Société et vie rurales dans le sud de la région parisienne 1540–1660*. Sorbonne Faculty of Letters thesis, 1971. (Typescript.)

Jouanna, Arlette. "L'idée de race en France aux XVIᵉ et XVIIᵉ siècles." 4 vols. University of Paris-Sorbonne, Centre de Recherches sur la Civilisation de l'Europe Moderne, 1975. (Typescript.)

Labatut, Jean-Pierre. *Les ducs et pairs de France au XVIIᵉ siècle: Etude sociale*. P.U.F., 1972.

La Roque, G. A. de. *Traité de la noblesse*. 1735 edition.

Laulan, Robert. "Pourquoi et comment on entrait à l'Ecole royale militaire de Paris," *Revue d'Histoire moderne et contemporaine* 4 (1957): 141–50.

Lefebvre, Georges. "Le mythe de la Révolution française," *Annales historiques de la Révolution française* 28 (1956): 337–45.

Léonard, E.-G. *L'armée et ses problèmes au XVIIIᵉ siècle*. Plon, 1958. (Series "Civilisations d'hier et d'aujourd'hui.")

Lévy-Bruhl, Henry. "La noblesse de France et le commerce," *Revue d'Histoire moderne* 8 (1933): 209–35.

Mathieu, Rémi. *Le système héraldique français*. J.-B. Janin, 1946.

Merle, Louis. *La métairie et l'évolution agraire de la Gâtine poitevine de la fin du Moyen Age à la Révolution.* S.E.V.P.E.N., 1958.

Meurgey de Tupigny, Jacques. *Armorial de la généralité de Paris.* 4 vols. Mâcon, 1965.

Meyer, Jean. *La noblesse bretonne au XVIIIe.* S.E.V.P.E.N., 1966.

Mousnier, Roland, ed. *Lettres et mémoires adressés au chancelier Séguier, 1633–1649.* 2 vols. P.U.F., 1964.

————. *Le Conseil du Roi de Louis XII à la Révolution.* P.U.F., 1970.

————. *La vénalité des offices sous Henri IV et Louis XIII.* 2d ed. P.U.F., 1970.

————. *La stratification sociale à Paris aux XVIIe et XVIIIe siècles.* Vol. 1: *L'echantillon de 1634–1635–1636.* A. Pedone, 1976.

————; Labatut, Jean-Pierre; and Durand, Yves. *Deux cahiers de la noblesse pour les Etats-Généraux de 1649–1651.* P.U.F., 1965.

Poitrineau, Abel. *La vie rurale en basse Auvergne au XVIIIe siècle (1726–1789).* P.U.F., 1965.

Richard, Guy. "Les corporations et la noblesse commerçante en France au XVIIIe siècle"; "La noblesse commerçante à Bordeaux et à Nantes au XVIIIe siècle"; "A propos de la noblesse commerçante à Lyon au XVIIIe siècle," *Information historique* 19 (1957): 85–189; 20 (1958): 185–90; 21 (1959): 156–61.

Roupnel, Gaston. *La ville et la campagne au XVIIe siècle: Etude sur les populations du pays dijonnais.* 2d ed. Armand Colin, 1955.

Sagnac, Philippe. *Quomodo jura dominii aucta fuerint regnante Ludovico XVI.* 1898.

Saint-Jacob, Pierre de. *Les paysans de la Bourgogne du Nord au dernier siècle de l'Ancien Régime.* Dijon, 1960.

Sée, Henri. *Les classes rurales en Bretagne du XVIe siècle à la Révolution.* 1906.

Sentou, Jean. *Fortunes et groupes sociaux à Toulouse sous la Revolution, 1789–1799.* Toulouse: E. Privat, 1969.

Soboul, Albert. "Le prélèvement féodal au XVIIIe siècle," in *L'abolition de la féodalité dans le monde occidental.* Colloques internationaux du C.N.R.S., Sciences humaines, Toulouse, 1968. Editions du C.N.R.S., 1971.

5

The Ennobled and the Bourgeois "Living like Nobles"

Those who "lived like nobles" were bourgeois who lived in the noble style, on their *rentes*, "without practicing any craft or engaging in any commerce." This condition was the ideal aimed at by persons who wished to draw closer to the nobility, prepare the way for their own ennoblement, or open the road to noble status for their descendants. The sons of fathers "living like nobles" were sure that they would not be rejected on grounds of unworthiness when they offered themselves as candidates for royal offices. Otherwise there was a serious risk of not being accepted by the members of the corporation concerned. A merchant tanner was at the same time an innkeeper at Avallon. He became rich. One fine day he tried to buy for his son the office of *procureur du roi* in the jurisdiction of Avallon. The young man was flatly turned down despite his father's money. If only the father had had the inspiration to give up his trade and live "like a noble" on his *rentes* for a few years before attempting to buy the office, the son would have stood a chance of getting accepted. The category of persons "living like nobles" had long been recognized by jurists. The *arrêt* of the king's Council dated 30 October 1767 still used the expression (in connection with wholesale merchants). The social importance of "living like nobles," together with the Catholic ideal of moderation in one's use of the good things of this world, accounts for the frequency of early retirements. A wholesale merchant or a lawyer often retired very early and with very limited resources. In Orléans in 1789 3,000 livres of *rente* was sufficient to support a modest and regular way of life. The highest value was not getting rich but the consideration acquired by a style of living which resembled that of a nobleman insofar as it was remote from any commercial or mercenary activity, even if it resembled that of a bourgeois in the importance accorded to the simple pleasures of family life, friendship, and intellectual activity.

It was among those "living like nobles" that the king chose the persons he wanted to turn into nobles, especially by means of letters of ennoblement. The ennobled were legally nobles, enjoying the principal privileges of the nobility. Socially, however, the nobles treated them as a different set of people. The farmers general, for example, were mostly nobles. In 1774 only 17 percent of them were commoners, and this proportion was down to 11 percent in 1786. Forty-three percent of them even had three generations of nobility, and 15 percent had four generations, which meant that they could be regarded as *gentils-hommes* if their origins were forgotten. They were accepted in good society, in the salons, and even supped with the high court nobility. They were received politely, even courteously. For the princes, the marshals of France, and the entire high court nobility, however, they remained *"bourgeois."* What furnishes good proof of this is the fact that, with very rare exceptions, they did not marry daughters of the nobility. Their wives were daughters of merchants, of Paris *bourgeois* who were *rentiers,* of employees of the tax farms, of farmers general, of *receveurs généraux des finances,* of doctors and surgeons. Despite their wealth, fewer than 8 percent of them succeeded in marrying women of quality. It is true that this wealth enabled them to marry half of their daughters to very high-ranking nobles. But marriages like these were examples of female hypergamy, which do not "place" the farmers general as a group. In this patrilineal society it was the marriages of the *menfolk* that defined the social rank of a family. The marriages made by the farmers general show that, despite the opinion of contemporaries who saw them as husbands of daughters of the higher nobility and kinfolk of the court nobility, they were not integrated into the nobility. They remained "ennobled persons"—a superior stratum of the upper *bourgeoisie.*

All the ennobled were in the same boat. Saint-Simon said: "Kings create ennobled persons but not nobles." Even at the end of the 18th century usage distinguished very clearly between the ennobled and the noble. For the population generally, an ennobled person still lacked the essential thing: condition, quality, birth. At Caen an ennobled person was put forward by the intendant for the position of *premier échevin noble*. All the nobles were furious. What sort of respect for the nobility could he have if he did a thing like that? It was necessary to withdraw the proposal. In the provincial assembly of Upper Normandy in 1787 and 1788 an ennobled person, Le Couteu de Canteleu, represented the third estate, and it was he who composed a memorandum demanding that the deputies of the third estate be neither nobles nor ennobled persons—distinguishing the latter clearly from the former. In the elections to the Estates General of 1789 the ennobled persons had to vote along with the nobles; in some cases the nobles tolerated them, in others they made them go away. At Arles the ennobled were joined with the advocates and doctors, that is, with those who "lived like nobles." The *cahier* of Vie-le-Comte, in Auvergne, contained this contemptuous phrase: "It is a very bad use of words to describe as noble this factitious nobility, which is nothing but what is bought with gold and the result of good luck." In Orléans in 1789, of thirty-four sugar refiners "living like nobles," seventeen were nobles; of ninety-six wholesale merchants considered as "living like nobles," thirty-five were nobles. But these ennobled persons remained distinct from the *gentilshommes*. They had to find their brides among the daughters of wholesale merchants and industrialists, while the *gentilshommes* usually married daughters of *nobles d'épée*. The fusion of the ennobled with the old nobility was still a very slow process. The old nobility of Orléanais did not conceal its feelings either. The vicomte Alès de Corbet in his *Recherches sur l'ancienne gendarmerie* (1759) and his *Origines de la noblesse* (1766) repeated the old theory that the *gentilshommes* were a race, descendants of the Teutonic warriors who in early times had subjugated the Gauls, while the commoners were also a race, a crowd of descendants of the conquered. Office or royal letters patent could not change a man's race. The ennobled were still inferiors.

Traitants, partisans, financiers

The ennobled and the persons "living like nobles" embraced, first, those who were called in the 17th century the *traitants* and *partisans* and in the 18th century, as a superior group, the *financiers,* especially those of Paris. These were the men who handled the king's money, either by farming the collection of the royal revenues (typical of these were the corporation of farmers general), by actually collecting these revenues (as in the case of the companies of *receveurs généraux des finances, régisseurs généraux des aides,* or general administrators of the royal domain), or by making payments as treasurers (*trésoriers de l'Epargne, trésoriers des Parties Casuelles,* miscellaneous treasurers of the royal household, treasurers general of the war department and the navy, etc.). All of them were obliged to have recourse to borrowing in order to carry out their functions, and at the end of the 18th century some of them—Claude Baudard de Saint-James, treasurer general of the navy (1738–87), Antoine de Mégret de Sérilly, treasurer general of the war department from 1772 to 1788—even had to engage in commercial and industrial undertakings of a capitalist character. These men must be distinguished from the bankers, who were only businessmen, even when they lent money to the king.

The *financiers* had some characteristics in common. At the end of the 18th century, public opinion accorded them a very high position. When the Revolution came, they were treated the same as the aristocrats. But, to an increasing extent as the century progressed, they came to be regarded as belonging to Parisian "good company," in which, from the standpoint of contemporaries, all estates, ranks, and fortunes were mixed together and what mattered was not so much one's birth as one's *savoir-vivre,* education, wit, and culture. "The grandee forgets that he is a *seigneur.* Everyone mingles in the salons and in the conversation that takes place there." What won a man consideration in this "good company" was "good tone." In the salons,

> everything tended to level out, manners as well as fortune. What reigned there was that tone of which I have already frequently spoken. It was a constant habit of not violating in any way the rules of decorum and the most exquisite politeness, of showing oneself, in relation to persons of different ranks and ages, respectful without servility, gay without abuse of freedom, gallant without presumption, witty without affectation, of avoiding the use of any excessively vulgar expression or any excessively common style of behavior, of allowing oneself only seldom to speak too plainly of delicate matters, concealing them behind the modesty of one's language, and of blunting the arrows of one's pleasantries so as not to let them shock anybody.[1]

According to contemporaries, the consideration acquired by "good tone" could be given equally well to a courtier, a soldier, a bishop, a *robin,* or a *financier.* The differences between grandees, nobles, and bourgeois still existed, but they were often reduced to mere nuances. A sort of fusion took place, produced by the common enjoyment of the same pleasures and the same way of enjoying them.

Writers included all the *financiers* in this "good company," but they were unanimous in excluding businessmen. The latter were strangers to the world of the salons. The *financiers* belonged to it, coming immediately after the men of the sword and the gown, as a sort of third division of the nobility. They also adopted the title of *écuyer*, had the right to wear swords, enjoyed other privileges, such as that of making their payments of poll tax on a roll of their own, provided for by an *arrêt* of the king's Council, exemption from the burdens of guardianship, from the collection of taxes, from collective responsibility for taxes, from having soldiers billeted on them, from duties of watch and ward, from drawing lots for the militia, and from being taken to court, except before the *cour des aides* in Paris, for matters connected with their occupation. In many cases they assumed, instead of their family name, the name of their principal *seigneurie*. They modeled themselves on persons of condition. Contemporaries thought, too, that they often married daughters of the high nobility. They therefore had their place among the persons of condition; and for high society the social hierarchy consisted of only two sorts of people: at the top, the persons of condition, and then, below, all the rest.

They were indeed received as supper guests of the high court nobility, along with composers, singers, poets, and economists. In this respect they were in a quite different position from the *noblesse de robe,* The *robins* came to dinner but not to supper.

The *financiers* themselves held salons and had guests to supper. Until 1762 the farmer general Leriche de La Pouplinière held a musical salon which became famous, and he left behind him a reputation as one of the principal music lovers and collectors of music of his day. The farmer general Philippe-Guillaume Tavernier de Boulongne de Préminville, who farmed between 1750 and 1787, received personages of the court and of Paris in his château of Magnanville, near Mantes. Paulze held a philosophical salon, where the talk was mainly of plans for fiscal, financial, and political reform and where the guests included Turgot, Trudaine, Malesherbes, Condorcet, Dupont de Nemours—a majority of high-ranking *robins*. His son-in-law, Lavoisier, made a specialty of being at home at the Arsenal to foreigners like Arthur Young and Benjamin Franklin; *grands seigneurs* interested in science like the duc de la Rochefoucauld, d'Ayen, de Chaulnes, and de Liancourt; and also *robins* or men from government circles like Malesherbes, Turgot,

Dupont de Nemours, and Necker. Jean-Joseph de Laborde, a farmer general and court banker, received almost exclusively members of the high court nobility. Laurent Grimot de La Reynière even received the intimates of Marie-Antoinette, and when the future Czar Paul, Catherine II's son, came to Paris under the name of "Comte du Nord," he asked to visit this salon, which was known all over Europe.

Another social symbol was the opera. There the boxes of the farmers general were situated among those of the high court nobility. Just like *grands seigneurs,* some of the farmers general kept mistresses who belonged to the opera.

Yet another social symbol was a town house in Paris, with material luxury in the form of marble, crystal, lacquer, damask, gilding, luxury of design, and the luxurious character of the quarter where one's house was situated. In the 17th century the *financiers* lived in the Marais. At the beginning of the 18th century they moved to the Place des Victoires. After 1750 most of them were in the quarters of the Palais-Royal (rues Saint-Honoré, Neuve-des-Capucines, Sainte-Anne, and de Richelieu, and Place Vendôme) and Montmartre (rues Vivienne, Neuve-des-Petits-Champs, Gaillon, d'Antin, and Louis-le-Grand). In 1789 they were tending to move to the north of the Boulevards. Jean-Joseph de Laborde had two houses there, one in the rue Neuve-Grange-Batelière and the other in the rue d'Artois. A dozen farmers general lived in the rue de la Chaussée d'Antin, the rue Cadet, and the rue Caumartin. Saint-James, the treasurer general of the navy, lived after 1777 in a house in the Place Louis-le-Grand (soon to be renamed the Place Vendôme), where the general staff of the king's financial service were concentrated—farmers general, *receveurs généraux des Finances,* and treasurers. At Neuilly he possessed the Folie Saint-James, with a park, a river, a Chinese pavilion, groves, and statues.

The *financiers* played a role as patrons and collectors. Collections served as a sign of one's belonging to the same social group: the same feelings experienced before the same objects. The *financiers* had cabinets of mineralogical curiosities and precious stones, paintings, sculptures, large libraries. They took writers and artists under their wing and gave them commissions to perform. The edition of La Fontaine's *Contes et Nouvelles,* called the *"édition des Fermiers Généraux,"* published in 1762, is well known. Saint-James had his cabinet of natural history. He commissioned Houdon to make a bust of him. For his gardens he purchased two groups of statuary by Lemoyne.

The *financiers* had enjoyed the same education as the *nobles de robe* and the better-educated court nobles. They had spent seven years at school, usually with the Jesuits, at the Collège de Clermont, later named Louis-le-Grand, that seedbed of the sovereign courts, the secretariat of state, the bar, medicine, and the army, where court nobles rubbed shoulders with *robins*. Others had attended the Collège de Juilly, under the Oratorians. Lavoisier had studied at the Collège Mazarin, winning in 1760 the second prize for a speech in French in a general competition. After their school years they had studied law, usually with a coach rather than at a university, and had been called to the bar. Some of them had at the same time attended one of the four royal academies, where they had been educated as young *gentilshommes,* in riding, combat, dancing, mathematics, and drawing. Only after all that had they gone to work in the finance offices. Most of them, moreover, held advanced ideas, like the young *gentilshommes* who were officers. While Helvétius was frankly materialistic and atheistic, the majority were Deists and Freemasons, belonging either to the lodges of the Grand Orient de France, which were rationalist, or to others which were occultist and mystic in tendency. Saint-James was a member, from 1773 onward, of the lodge of "Friends-Met-Together," which held its gatherings in the rue de Clichy and later in the rue Royale, and where he met many personages with whom he had business dealings.

Finally, the *financiers* were *seigneurs.* If they did not inherit *seigneuries* from their parents, they lost no time in purchasing them. They do not seem to have troubled much about the income from these *seigneuries,* for, generally speaking, what they got from them was between 1.1 and 2.8 percent, whereas the average income from *seigneuries,* taking France as a whole, was 3.3 percent. The *financiers* wanted to be *seigneurs* for the sake of the social prestige it gave them. They quickly assumed the title of their principal *seigneurie* and even sometimes falsified matters a little, calling themselves "comte de X" or "vicomte de Y" when they ought to have said merely "seigneur du comté de X" or "seigneur du vicomté de Y." They had magnificent genealogies constructed for them, in which their ancestry was traced back to the Crusaders, or almost.

Here, then, were men whom one might suppose to be integrated into the nobility, even into the high court nobility. Yet the same recreations, the same style of outward show, the same way of consuming part of their income, meeting in the same places to enjoy the same pleasures—all that is not enough to allow us to speak of social integration. The court nobility tolerated such encounters because these *financiers* were in the service of the king, which was always a source of dignity, luster, and consideration. Furthermore, the nobles drew part of their income from the profits of the *financiers* by acting as silent partners, by way of pensions and sureties, and even, in the case of petty *gentilshommes*, by being given jobs in the offices of the General Farm or in those of other *financiers*. The great nobles did not despise the dowry that the daughter of a great *financier* could bring. They kept their contempt for the daughter herself and her father. But the higher nobility always regarded the *financiers* as being to one side of and beneath them. We have already noticed the most important point, namely, that they normally declined to let their daughters marry them, and how often the documents show that they regarded them as *bourgeois*. A few further strokes may be added to the picture. Public opinion looked on the *financiers* as persons of very low origin, even as sons of lackeys. That was not in fact the case. In general they came from the middle ranks of Parisian society. Half of them were sons of men engaged in credit operations, and the rest were sons of wholesale merchants, finance officials, officers of justice of middling and petty rank, notaries, doctors, advocates. But the mere existence of this disparaging myth testifies to a desire to denigrate the *financiers* socially, a refusal to integrate them properly. It should further be noted that, while the *financiers* grouped themselves, along with the rest of the "good company," around the Palais-Royal, the Tuileries, and the Boulevards, the members of the sovereign courts, the *noblesse de robe*, stayed loyal to the Marais, while the high court nobility moved to the Faubourg Saint-Germain. Whatever their importance, the *financiers* remained below the level of the nobility. They formed, one may say, the topmost level of the ennobled and those "living like nobles."

The "men of talent," officeholders

Beneath the *financiers*, among those "living like nobles," we find the "persons of talent." These were, in the first place, members of what we might call "the public services."

To begin with, there were those officials whose offices did not confer nobility. Some of these, of course, might be nobles by birth and, before entering upon their offices, even *gentilshommes*, and in that case they ranked among the nobility. The officials ennobled by their offices were the chancellor, the *maîtres des requêtes de l'Hôtel du Roi*, the *notaires et secrétaires du Roi, Maison, et Couronne de France,* the *présidents* and counselors of the sovereign courts, the Grand Conseil, the *parlements,* the *chambre des comptes,* the *cours des aides,* the *cours des monnaies,* and the *bureaux des trésoriers de France.* The other offices did not confer nobility.

In Normandy between 1620 and 1650 the officials who were not ennobled by office but who were regarded as "living like nobles" were, in the first place, the magistrates of the various royal courts—the presidial courts, the *bailliages,* and the *vicomtés* (these last playing the same role as the *prévôtés* and *vigueries* in other parts). These magistrates possessed the "quality" of *conseillers du roi.* At their head were the *présidents* of the presidial courts, then came the *lieutenants généraux* of the *baillis,* then the counselors in the *bailliages* and presidial courts, the *lieutenants particuliers, civils, et criminels,* of the secondary centers of the *bailliage.* They often assumed the style of *écuyer,* though it seems probable that this was in most cases a usurpation of nobility. A certain number of them married daughters of their colleagues, while others married daughters of minor officials, *élus,* clerks of the court, or even daughters of *bourgeois* "living like nobles."

Under them came the magistrates of the department of waters and forests and of the admiralties, the higher magistrates of the royal fiscal organization, the *présidents* and *avocats du roi* in the *élections* and the salt storehouses. These, when they did not marry daughters of colleagues, married into families of petty rural nobles or lower-ranking officials of the royal household who were doubtless actually merchants or former merchants.

Under them, but in a similar situation, were most of the magistrates of the *élections—lieutenants, élus,* and, already, officials who belonged not to the law courts but to the financial system: some receivers of *taille.* Some of them had purchased the title of *conseiller du roi;* they married daughters of *"nobles hommes,"* of *secrétaires du roi,* and even of petty rural nobles. Others remained *"honorables hommes"* and married into families of merchants or *bourgeois rentiers.* These latter, despite their functions, were no longer in the category of persons "living like nobles" but in that of mere *bourgeois.*

In the same debatable zone were the minor law officers and finance officers attached to the sovereign courts who received a certain luster from the "Messieurs" with whom they worked: the *huissier du roi audiencier* in the *parlement* of Rouen, the *greffier hérédital* of the *bureau des finances,* the *receveurs* and payers of salaries of the "Messieurs" of the *cours des aides,* who married daughters of *"nobles hommes,"* attorneys or merchants.

In Beauvais and Beauvaisis in the 17th century, according to M. Goubert, the officials who were not ennobled by their office were not separated from the merchants by any great gulf. They were all brothers, brothers-in-law, or cousins of merchants. Together with the latter they formed a group which Goubert calls "the Families"— forty-six families whose names (Borel, Pocquelin, Danse, Motte, Foy, etc.) are found everywhere: in the presidial court, the *élection,* the salt storehouse; in the lists of aldermen, mayors, administrators of the Hôtel-Dieu and the Bureau des Pauvres, and churchwardens; and likewise in the chapter, canonries, monasteries, and priories, which they monopolized. All these families intermarried and met together in family ceremonies—baptisms, marriages, funerals.

Possession of the same surname does not always mean close family ties; for belonging to the same family did not rule out differences in social level, and the strength of the lineages in the 17th century did not prevent the existence of diversities of social status among their members. In Beauvais the magistrates were separate from and higher than the merchants. At the Estates General of 1614, Beauvais did not present one *cahier* for the third estate but two: a *cahier du bailliage* for the officials and a *cahier de la ville* for the merchants. Gradually, as the 17th century progressed, the officials ousted the merchants from their places as aldermen. The fortunes possessed by the officials reveal a style of living different from that of the merchants and superior from the standpoint of the epoch. Much less large (between 60,000 and 100,000 livres, as against 400,000 to 500,000), these fortunes were derived, to the extent of one-half, from *seigneuries* and fiefs, while a quarter was contributed by money lent to petty nobles and peasants and the other quarter by the value of offices, houses, and furniture— instead of stocks of goods and credit. The homes of the officials contained libraries in which humanists, jurists, and theologians were represented. The Beauvais officials appear as *seigneurs, rentiers,* men of classical intellectual culture, not as producers and speculators. They were persons "living like nobles," differing from the ordinary merchants of their town and their period.

In 17th-century Amiens the officials comprised, in descending order of rank, first, the *trésoriers de France* in the *bureau des finances,* who were, in principle, *nobles de robe* (eight in 1578; twelve in 1621; fourteen in 1626; eighteen in 1628; twenty-three in 1635). Beneath them came the *présidents, lieutenants,* and counselors and the *avocat du roi* and the *procureur du roi* in the *bailliage* and the presidial court, who were undoubtedly among the persons "living like nobles." At the end of the century they numbered thirty-one all together, of whom twenty-four were counselors, four of these having been created under Louis XIII and four between 1689 and 1696. Several aldermen were recruited from among them, and they almost always provided the leading aldermen. After them came officials about whom we do not know to what extent they were classed among the persons "living like nobles": the *maîtres* of the department of waters and forests, the magistrates of the *prévôté royale,* the provost marshal of Picardy, the *présidents* and *élus* in the *élection,* the magistrates of the salt storehouse, the judges of the *traites foraines,* the wardens of the mint. Clearly inferior in rank to them, and probably to be classed among the mere *bourgeois,* were the accounting officials, comptrollers, and receivers in the financial system.

In the town the *trésoriers de France* and the *présidents* and counselors of the presidial court, even if they were commoners, took precedence, as individuals, over ordinary *gentilshommes.* As a body they yielded precedence only to members of the higher nobility, the governor, and the lieutenant général du roi.

Some of them were nobles, and even nobles of old family. The Piquet de Douries family went back to the 14th century and contributed, between the 16th century and the 18th, seven generations of *lieutenants particuliers* in the *bailliage* and the presidial court. Three or four other families had been noble since the beginning of the 16th century. But the majority were not noble. All of them aspired to noble status, but some were only in the first generation of *noblesse graduelle,* and the majority were still plain, ordinary commoners who had emerged during the 16th century from families of merchants, master craftsmen, even well-to-do peasants. Certain families had high destinies before them, such as the d'Aguesseau, Louvencourt, Pingré, and Trudaine families. Jean Trudaine, who died in 1539, was a merchant goldsmith. His son Jean became a *seigneur* and a finance official; he was *sieur* of Oissy and Dreuil and *receveur des tailles* in Amiens. His grandsons, Antoine and Jean, were able to enter the magistracy as *trésoriers de France;* they were considered members of the sovereign courts and possessed personal nobility by virtue of their offices.

During the 17th century the social ladder to be climbed remained the same: first trade; then, in the next generation, finance, meaning the tax farms; in the third generation, offices in the financial system, as *receveurs* or *contrôleurs;* and, in the fourth generation, officers in the law courts. But the ascent grew harder. The world of the law courts became a closed one. Dynasties of officials came into being: the De Herte family were for three generations, between 1625 and 1707, *présidents* in the presidial court; the Morel de Cresmery family held, from father to son, through four generations, the fifteenth office of counselor in the presidial court; the Lequieu de Moyenneville family had five successive representatives who sat for 130 years in the *bureau des finances.* Some candidates who had received letters of appointment to an office from the king were not accepted by the body of officials because they were sons of merchants and so had to withdraw. The magistrates urged their kinfolk to abandon trade. Since this was happening at the same time as the intendants were increasing in importance, with the result that the functions, power, and prestige of these officials were decreasing, one may speculate that they were perhaps seeking social compensation by "living like nobles," they and their whole lineage with them.

The magistrates consolidated a situation of *de facto* heredity for themselves. This corresponded to the idea that an official dispensed justice, or administered the royal finances or the royal domain, "by virtue of the honorable character of his family and almost by the quality of his blood." Function tended to be derived from social rank rather than the other way round. Accordingly, in the thinking of the officials, their offices gave them rights even more than it gave them duties. Each body of officials considered that it possessed corporate rights, some of which were common to the whole order of officials. From this resulted some very tightly closed social groups. Marriages took place between families of officials except where large dowries furnished an outside attraction. Among the counselors in the *bailliage* and in the presidial court, endogamy was even quite strict.

The officials possessed fortunes which played no role at all in production but consisted of a vast accumulation of consumer goods. They were made up predominantly of *rentes*—seignorial and feudal rents, bonds secured on the Hôtel de Ville of Paris, the *gabelles* and the Cinq Grosses Fermes, and, increasingly in the second half of the century,

private mortgage loans. Their offices made an ever more modest contribution to their fortunes, for their prices declined, and the officials did
not derive the main part of their incomes from them. The salaries of
officials in the law courts were very low, bringing in between 0.5 percent and 1.5 percent of the purchase price of their office. The salaries of
finance officials were a little higher, bringing in 5 percent after 1664. It
was not the income to be derived from their offices that was the attraction for officials, at least in the case of those in the law courts. "The
exercise of their profession becomes for them a kind of vocation of
honor."[2]

Many officials had two residences, one in town and one in the country, and also a *pied-à-terre* in Paris. The finance officials were often
recruited from Parisian families and had their principal residence in the
capital.

In Amiens the development of social life was reflected in the arrangement of houses, which comprised a reception room, bedrooms,
kitchen, and office, and especially by the presence of a *lit de salle,* a
sort of grand daybed on which the lady of the house lay to receive her
visitors. The house was decorated with tapestries, chairs covered with
embroidery, beautiful cabinets, and collections of pictures, books, and
coins. It was all as though the Counter-Reformation was being succeeded by a revival of the Renaissance. In the first half of the century
the subjects of the pictures were religious, but in the second half they
were secular, and antique and pagan subjects appeared as well. The
books reflected a culture which was classical (secular literature in Latin
and Greek), juridical, and Christian, with a touch of Jansenism, and
also a taste for history and erudition (Du Cange was a *trésorier de
France* in Amiens) and, in the second half of the century, an increasing
taste for modern French literature (the French classics—Corneille,
Molière, Racine, and so on).

At Châteaudun, trade was on the downgrade after the revocation of
the Edict of Nantes. Before 1685 there had been lively tanning and
textile industries there, but all the persons engaged in trade and industry were Protestants, and most of them emigrated. Consequently, in
the 18th century the higher "estate" of the population was made up of
persons whose quality was that of *noble homme,* that is, *bourgeois* who
"lived like nobles." Here the *nobles hommes* were officials whose
offices did not confer nobility—seignorial officials of the *bailliage* and
county of Dunois, who paid the *taille,* or the royal magistrates belonging to the *élection.* These magistrates who were *nobles hommes* formed
a separate "estate," since they married the daughters of their col-

leagues, the group being 95 percent endogamous. They could not find enough women to marry in Châteaudun itself, of course, and therefore sought them in Orléans, Blois, and Chartres—but always in the same circle of families of the magistracy. Their fortunes were made up mainly of landed property: *métairies*, vineyards, and houses of various kinds. These fortunes were extremely diverse and not always the largest in the town. It was not the size or the nature of their fortunes that set them apart but their own desire, as is shown by their endogamy.

Minor officials

Below the officials "living like nobles" came a sort of bureaucracy which developed steadily through the 17th and 18th centuries: clerks to the ministers and secretaries of state; subdelegates to the intendants of the provinces; consuls, chargés d'affaires at the papal court, embassy secretaries; functionaries in the strict sense—inspectors general of commerce, military engineers, engineers in the department of bridges and highways. Some of these received letters of ennoblement. Between 1750 and 1788 about a hundred such letters were granted to persons like the clerks of the secretariat of state for the royal household, Dodin and Reineval; the chief clerk in the finance department, Le Harivel; the brothers Bottignies de Saint-Romain, one of whom was chief clerk for the provinces administered by the secretary of state, Vergennes, while the other was chief secretary to the keeper of the seals; the chief clerk of the royal household, Silvestre Jurien; the chief clerk in the war department, Séjean; Chérin, genealogist of the royal orders; Perronet, creator of the corps of civil engineers and founder and director of the Ecole des Ponts et Chaussées. It was a foreshadowing of that nobility of functionaries that Napoleon I tried to establish.

The "noblemen of letters"

Among the "men of talent" there was a "nobility of letters," a sort of social nobility of the mind, made up of literary men and scholars, which Loyseau already acknowledged and which expected to receive letters of ennoblement from the king. "Even without letters of ennoblement, genius is always noble."[3] Members of this "nobility of letters" were some university professors and some advocates who were ennobled for services rendered in public affairs. Not all of the advocates were classified as "living like nobles": it was not the profession as such that counted but one's success in the profession. Many advocates were mere *bourgeois*. Examples of the type who "lived like nobles" were, in Paris, the advocates before the Conseil d'Etat or the king's Conseil d'Etat et Privé, who, moreover, were law officials (*officiers ministériels*). They numbered 160 in 1644, and their office was worth 400 livres. These advocates married their colleagues' daughters, or daughters of *notaires et secrétaires du roi*, nieces of priors or of counselors in the *parlement*, daughters of *élus* in the Paris *élection*, and sometimes daughters of merchants, *bourgeois* of Paris, who brought with them dowries of between 20,000 and 30,000 livres. Among those "living like nobles" in Paris must be included the advocates before the *parlement*, who, without being officeholders, formed part of that corporation and were to be found in all the law courts within the area of jurisdiction of the *parlement*. All of them licentiates, all of them *nobles hommes*, often *seigneurs* of somewhere or other, sometimes calling themselves *écuyers* and possibly being such, they were great lenders of money and owners of land, even in the provinces. They willingly married daughters of their colleagues—sometimes the daughter of some *"honorable homme, marchand, bourgeois de Paris,"* sometimes the daughter of some provincial *écuyer*. There were doctors and surgeons (three of whom were ennobled between 1738 and 1750 and thirty-one between 1750 and 1785), especially those who were attached to the royal household or the households of the princes. There were technicians whose inventions were recognized as useful, such as Pierre Morat, ennobled because, according to his letters of ennoblement, "he devoted himself from youth onward to the study of mechanics" and organized in Paris a group of firemen, efficient enough to have dealt with the fire at the Hôtel-Dieu, and because reward was properly due to an "outstanding talent to which the country is indebted for inventions of recognized utility." As for the savants whom society acknowledged as members of this "nobility of letters," they were only rarely ennobled by the king, doubtless because strictly scientific discoveries had no practical applications and so possessed, as a rule, only long-term "usefulness." Neither Monge, the inventor of descriptive geometry, nor Berthollet, the chemist, nor Bailly, the mathematician, nor Borda, the navigator, nor the mathematicians and astronomers Lalande and Laplace, nor the abbé Nollet, the physicist, received letters of ennoblement. If the mathematician Leblond was ennobled, it was as teacher of the king's children; if Quesnay, it was as Louis XV's doctor, not as founder of the Physiocratic school of political economy; and his disciples Dupont de Nemours and Abeille were ennobled in 1783 and 1787 as inspectors general of commerce. Writers and artists belonged to the "nobility of letters." But writers, always a dangerous lot, were hardly ever ennobled. Few of the Encyclopedists were so honored. Artists, on the contrary, were ennobled to the number of twenty-five between 1750 and 1785: architects, like Lassurance, Soufflot, and Mique; painters, like Van Loo, Natoire, Lemoyne, Vien; engravers, like Reutier and Cochin; sculptors, like Pigalle and Coustou; and one musician, Rameau. All together, the "nobility of letters" received, between 1750 and 1785, about sixty ennoblements.

The wholesale merchants

Among those "living like nobles" who were candidates for ennoblement were also some merchants, namely, the wholesalers. The edict of 1701 defined them as "all those who carry on their business in warehouses, selling their goods by bales, crates, or entire pieces, and who have no shops opening on the street or any displays or signs on their doors or houses." The king, anxious to encourage Frenchmen to engage in this activity of first importance, on the one hand exempted from derogation those *gentilshommes* who went in for wholesale trade and, on the other, sought to ennoble the wholesale merchants who were commoners. The ordinance of 1629 conferred the enjoyment of the privileges of nobility, though not nobility itself, upon those persons who had maintained for a period of five years a trading vessel of between 200 and 300 tons burden. They were to continue to enjoy these privileges as long as they maintained such a vessel. They could take part in all municipal assemblies, sitting immediately behind the *lieutenants généraux* and the counselors of the presidial courts. Those who had been aldermen, consuls, or wardens of their corporation were authorized to assume the quality of nobles.

The intention of all this was fine, but the ordinance in question, the "Code Michau," was not registered by the Paris *parlement* and does not appear to have come into force.

The edict of 1701 brought the wholesale merchants and the *gentilshommes* notably closer together. The *gentilshommes* were relieved of the risk of compromising their noble status by engaging in wholesale trade. Those wholesalers who also possessed offices as *secrétaires du roi* or *trésoriers de France,* and were thus on their way to ennoblement, were allowed to continue in their business without being obliged to obtain letters of compatibility; their commercial activity was not derogatory and did not affect their acquisition of gradual nobility through their offices. They were allowed, while continuing as wholesale traders, to occupy all the municipal offices—mayor, alderman, *capitoul, jurat,* first consul—and all the levels of consular jurisdiction. A wholesale merchant could become a noble while remaining a wholesale merchant.

The *arrêt* of the Council dated 30 October 1767 went further still. It aimed at forming the wholesalers into a new privileged order in the kingdom—and one that would be a seedbed of nobles, for two of them were to be ennobled each year. To belong to this order, wholesalers had to obtain special letters patent and have them registered.

> His Majesty wishes and intends that they shall be regarded as living like nobles and that they shall be given rank and precedence in this quality in municipal and other assemblies and enjoy all the honors and advantages that are associated particularly with exemption from militia service for themselves and their sons, that they shall have the privilege of wearing swords in the towns and, when traveling, the weapons needed for their safety, regardless of the ban on the carrying of arms, from which His Majesty has excepted and excepts them; His Majesty reserves the power to grant each year two special letters of ennoblement to those of the said wholesale merchants *who have distinguished themselves* in their profession and, preferably, to those whose *fathers and grandfathers* have exercised this profession with the *honor* that it demands and who continue to *distinguish themselves* in it.

Honor, distinction, heredity—this is almost the definition of an order. From the pen of Turgot, in a letter written in the same period, there came quite naturally the expression "wholesale merchants of a higher order."

This *arrêt* increased considerably the ennoblement of wholesalers. In the sixteen preceding years only seven letters of ennoblement had been granted to various wholesale merchants. After the *arrêt* they became numerous. Candidates for ennoblement presented their request to the secretary of state. He asked the intendant of the province to carry out an investigation and present a report, on the basis of which the secretary of state would make his decision. The investigations were strict and the refusals many. The king ennobled large-scale wholesalers who possessed numerous vessels and had a very high turnover, men like Gourlade, who fitted out thirty ships in the port of Lorient and was responsible for imports and exports exceeding 40 million livres in value, thereby contributing 4 million to the royal treasury. Also favored were wholesale merchants who opened up new markets, men like Feray, in Rouen and Le Havre, Sahuc, who maintained a business house in Cadiz, and Isaac Couturier, of Bordeaux. The slave trade was a basis for ennoblement. The letters that ennobled Laffon-Ladébat in 1773 specified as the grounds for his honor that "since 1764 he has transported more than 4,000 [Negroes to the West Indies], in fifteen shipments." In this way, at Saint-Malo in 1789, out of 34 nobles engaged in commerce, 32 were ennobled wholesalers (2 of these being of noble extraction). At Nantes, out of 79 nobles engaged in commerce, 64 were ennobled businessmen (5 of these being of noble extraction, while 49 were sons of ennobled persons). At La Rochelle the corresponding figures were 10 out of 17 (7 being sons of ennobled persons), at Bordeaux 39 out of 47, and at Bayonne 5 out of 6. Ennoblements through purchase of the office of *secrétaire du roi* are included in these figures.

The *arrêt* of 1767 dealt in a special way with Lyons, where the position of alderman already gave, every year, to two of the notables a nobility that was complete and transmissible. These notables were usually great silk merchants or bankers. The *arrêt* of 1767 introduced *lettres de banquiers* for Lyons. Those who received them were to be regarded as "living as nobles" and given preference in the annual ennoblement by letter of two businessmen. Thus, before 1789, 56 wholesale merchants of Lyons were ennobled, 40 of these through serving as aldermen.

Industrialists were ennobled relatively often. Their activity was, indeed, a source of trade; they gave work, and thereby livelihood, to a considerable number of persons, and in particular to many women, children, and old men; they brought foreign workers into France, some as better technicians than the natives, others as strikebreakers. Thus, Abraham Poupart received letters of ennoblement because he employed 1,500 workers in Sedan, the brothers Dugas because they provided means of existence for 2,000 families at Saint-Chamond, Papion because he supported 800 families in Tours, Cadot for employing 500 workers in his factory in Rheims, Faucompre for setting up spinning mills and linen factories near Moulin and providing work in them for 200 foundlings, Labauche for his strikebreaking activities at Sedan and Châteauroux.

Foreign industrialists were ennobled, even if they were Protestants. The Englishman Holker, ennobled in 1775, had brought in English machinery and technology and also English workmen and had established spinning factories and training centers in most of the *généralités*. According to his letters of ennoblement, 80,000 of the king's subjects had found work thanks to him. Oberkampf, ennobled in 1787, was congratulated in his citation for having provided work, in his factories for making printed cloth, for numerous children aged five and six.

All together, by 1787, fifty letters of ennoblement may have been granted by virtue of the *arrêt* of 1767; it is certain that thirty-one were so granted, and such grants were made in 1775, 1776, and 1785.

The holders of decorations

Among those "living like nobles" must doubtless be included persons who had been decorated—meaning not the holders of the Order of the Holy Spirit, which was reserved for *gentilshommes de nom et d'armes,* but those who held the order of Saint-Louis and Saint-Michel.

The Order of Saint-Louis was intended as a reward for merit which was not associated with birth. It was a military decoration, created in 1693 by Louis XIV. To be eligible for it, one had to be a good Catholic and to have performed outstanding feats of arms, or else to have served in the army for at least twenty-five years. The order was restricted to forty holders of the Grand Cross and eighty commanders, but the number of knights was unlimited. Its emblem was a red ribbon. By 1785 even Protestants were being awarded it. Protestant officers were also eligible for the Order of Military Merit, created in 1759 for the officers of foreign regiments recruited in Protestant countries but eventually opened to French Protestant officers as well. The holders of these two orders formed a category halfway between the officers who were nobles and those who were commoners. It was among them that the king chose grantees for letters of ennoblement for military services.

The Order of Saint-Michel was mainly for civilians. It had been established by Louis XI in 1469, to consist of thirty-six members, all *chevaliers* and all with a long noble ancestry. Soon, however, it was opened to men of the *robe* and to "men of learning" and seemed to become especially associated with them. Louis XV purged the order in 1661, reducing it to one hundred members, who had to be either nobles or distinguished by their military services and who must never have exercised occupations incompatible with nobility. After the creation of the Order of Saint-Louis in 1693, however, the Order of Saint-Michel was in practice reserved for artists and then, in the second half of the 18th century, for functionaries, doctors, and wholesale merchants. "Men of talent" were exempted from the requirement to show proof of noble origin on both sides which had been laid down in principle for this order. It served either as a complement to ennoblement or else, more frequently, as a preliminary to ennoblement. Those who were awarded it were usually persons "living like nobles" who were marked out by receipt of this decoration for the grant of letters of ennoblement at a future date.

Thus, the ennobled formed a social stratum which was inferior to that of the true nobility, and persons "living like nobles" formed a stratum inferior to the ennobled but superior to the mere *bourgeois*. In Orléans in 1789, among the 40,000 inhabitants there were 34 sugar refiners, of whom 17 were ennobled and 17 "living like nobles." Out of 200 wholesale merchants, 35 appear to have been ennobled and 61 were regarded as "living like nobles." Belonging to the same category were about 100 *rentiers* and pensioners, about 30 holders of offices in the *bailliage*, the *maîtrise* of the department of waters and forests, the *élection*, the salt storehouse, and the mint. Out of 500 higher-ranking families, comprising about 2,500 persons and so forming more than 16 percent of the population of Orléans, there were thus some 50 to 60 ennobled persons, 200 to 250 "living like nobles," and 200 families of the upper *bourgeoisie*.

The most noted of the persons "living like nobles" were town dwellers. These had their counterparts, however, in the countryside, in the villages and market centers. They were usually not so well off as the townsmen and would have enjoyed less consideration if they had come to live in the towns, but they played a similar role in the villages and market centers. In Burgundy there were in the 18th century in every village, below the *gentilshommes,* one or two *bourgeois* "living like nobles." Their houses, with their tiled roofs, stood out among the thatched roofs of the other inhabitants. They had neither profession, craft, nor office but were content to supervise those who looked after their land or managed their money. They lent money and were creditors of a great number of people. In 1782 Jean Parison was a *bourgeois* of Aubigny. He owned a domain consisting of a house surrounded by four *journaux* of orchard and pasture (1 hectare); 16 *journaux* (5 hectares) of land, 8 *soitures* of wheat, a *journal* and a half of vineyard, and about 10 hectares of land sown to grain crops, worked by a servant of his and some jobbing ploughmen, etc. He owned some small farms, spread out over a total of 150 *journaux* (less than 40 hectares), leased out to seven peasants at 12 livres *tournois* per *journal* (600 livres *tournois*), and one farm leased for an amount of corn equivalent to 194 livres *tournois*. His farms thus brought him in an income of 800 livres. He leased out a cow and twenty-one ewes, receiving half of their increase. He leased out the local toll for 8 livres. He held the farm of the poorhouse for 2,410 livres and dealt in this connection with various subfarmers for 2,224 livres. All together, his income must have come to more than 3,000 livres. He was assessed for the *taille* at 234 livres. He was typical of the *bourgeois* "living like a nobleman."

In the Bocage area of Maine there were a few *"bourgeois"* or *"propriétaires"* who "lived like nobles" in this way. In forty-eight parishes, 123 have been found. As a rule, they lived on the income they drew from one or more *métairies* or *bordages* and some other *rentes*. They were in many cases former merchants who had retired from business. They were not very rich—often less so than the *laboureurs*, the big farmers. But they were held in higher consideration than the latter, were socially on a higher level. Although they lived in the country, they were related to townsfolk in their way of life and interest—and to those townsfolk who "lived like nobles."

The persons "living like nobles" resembled the nobility in their horror of every form of activity that was incompatible with noble status, in their esteem for birth, their repugnance for marriage with persons of a category lower than their own, and in their disdain for persons of lower rank, especially the manual workers, to which they added a parvenus' arrogance that the *gentilshommes* usually lacked. But they retained a great deal of the *bourgeois* style of living.

Notes

1. Comte d'Allouville, *Mémoires secrets* (published between 1770 and 1780).
2. Deyon, *Amiens, capitale provinciale* (Mouton, 1967), p. 279.
3. Robespierre.

Guide to further reading

To the works mentioned at the end of Chapter 4, add the following:

Barber, Elinor G. *The Bourgeoisie in 18th-Century France.* Princeton: Princeton University Press, 1955. 2d ed., 1968.

Bosher, J. F. *French Finances, 1770–1795: From Business to Bureaucracy.* Cambridge, Eng.: At the University Press, 1970.

Boutruche, Robert. *Bordeaux de 1453 à 1715.* Bordeaux: Fédération historique du Sud-Ouest, 1966.

Dent, Julian. *Crisis in Finance: Crown, Financiers, and Society in 17th-Century France.* New York: St. Martin's Press, 1973.

Dessert, D., and Journet, J. L. "Le lobby Colbert: Un royaume ou une affaire de famille?" *Annales E.S.C.* 30 (1975): 1303–36.

————. "Pouvoir et finance au XVIIᵉ siècle: La fortune de Mazarin," *Revue d'Histoire moderne et contemporaine* 23 (1976): 161–81.

Durand, Yves. *Les fermiers-généraux en France au XVIIIᵉ siècle.* P.U.F., 1971.

Hurt, J. "Les offices au Parlement de Bretagne sous Louis XIV: Aspects financiers," *Revue d'Histoire moderne et contemporaine* 23 (1976): 3–31.

Jacquard, Andrée (Mme Chauleur). *Le rôle des traitants dans l'histoire et l'administration de la France de 1643 à 1653.* 3 vols. Paris: Université de Paris-Sorbonne, Centre de Recherches sur la Civilisation de l'Europe Moderne, 1962. (Typescript.)

Jullian, Camille. *Histoire de Bordeaux.* Bordeaux: Féret & Fils, 1895. (This has not been superseded by Boutruche's work.)

Lefebvre, Georges. *Etudes orléanaises, I: Contribution à l'étude des structures sociales à la fin du XVIIIᵉ.* Commission d'Histoire économique et sociale de la Révolution, Mémoires et Documents, vol. 15. 1962.

Mousnier, Roland. *Stratification sociale à Paris.*

Ozanam, Denise. *Claude Baudart de Saint-James, Trésorier Général de la Marine et brasseur d'affaires (1738–1787).* Librairie Droz, 1969.

Pariset, François-Georges. *Bordeaux au XVIIIᵉ siècle.* Bordeaux: Fédération historique du Sud-Ouest, 1968.

Reinhard, Marcel. "Elite et noblesse dans la seconde moitié du XVIIIᵉ siècle," *Revue d'Histoire moderne et contemporaine* (1956): 5–37.

6

The Society of Orders
The Common People

The *bourgeois*

Beneath the *bourgeois* who "lived like nobles" came the ordinary *bourgeois*. The term "*bourgeois*" had several meanings in the language of the 17th and 18th centuries.

In some documents the "*bourgeois*" are all the inhabitants of a town, all the townsfolk in contrast to the countryfolk. In others, they are the third estate of a town in contrast to the *gentilshommes* and the clergy. Sometimes the word is a juridical title, designating persons who reside in a town which constitutes a corporation and community, who contribute to the town's financial obligations, serve in the militia, and have been accepted as *bourgeois* by the municipality. Such a person is a "*bourgeois* of Paris," a "*bourgeois* of Bordeaux," or whatever. In this sense, a *gentilhomme* may be a *bourgeois:* a "*bourgeois* of Bordeaux," for example. But a very humble craftsman, a mere cobbler, may also be a *bourgeois* of a particular town. In some towns, to be one of their *bourgeois* it was necessary also to fulfill certain conditions regarding fortune, income, and residence, and it could happen that, in fact, only the merchants and the principal master craftsmen were considered *bourgeois*.

The *bourgeois* may be specifically a man who "lives like a noble," on his *rentes,* without practicing any craft or carrying on any kind of commerce, and who participates in the honors and privileges of the city, with the right to a seat in its assemblies and the possibility of becoming a municipal magistrate. Numerous chroniclers use the word in this special, restricted sense.

For Loyseau the *bourgeois* are the merchants, together with those master craftsmen who are occupied more with commerce than with manual labor—the apothecaries, goldsmiths, jewelers, and wholesale mercers, drapers, hatters, and furriers. These last are the lowest-ranking of the men who bear an honorable quality, being described as *"honorable homme"* or *"honnête personne."* They have a share in the honors of the town and its rights and privileges. They sit and vote in the municipal assemblies and are eligible for municipal functions.

In certain documents the *bourgeois* is a man who has a workman working for him.

Here I am going to use the term in a sense which corresponds to the way the people of the epoch behaved toward each other. For me, therefore, the *bourgeois* is a man who is not noble and who lives mainly by his work, but by a kind of work in which mental effort is more important than physical effort. The *bourgeois* is distinguished by a horror and contempt of manual work. Tolerance is extended, in this connection, only to artists, whether sculptors or painters, and to certain crafts which are ennobled by their artistic character or by the value of the material with which they work, such as those of the engraver, the goldsmith, or the jeweler. The *bourgeois* devotes himself to mental work; this may be intellectual work in the strict sense, such as that of the university professor, the savant, the advocate, or the doctor, or it may be work in the fields of organization, command, management, correspondence, accounting, or bookkeeping, performed by members of the public services, court officials, merchants, traders, and entrepreneurs of various kinds. For the *bourgeois,* however, this work often becomes the supreme value, an end in itself, the first and foremost of worldly activities. The *bourgeois* is proud of putting work first and treating this as the most important activity in which he spends his time. In Bordeaux, rich and well-reputed merchants like the Bethmans, Texiers, and Bonnaffés worked from six in the morning to eight at night, with short breaks for meals, and went to bed directly after dinner. It was the master's sons themselves who swept out the place of business.

When Bonnaffé gave a ship to one of his sons, it was his wife and daughters who sewed the new master's monogram on the sailcloth.

Next to work, the second *bourgeois* value and virtue was economy. True, some of the large-scale traders "living like nobles" resembled the *gentilshommes* in their ostentation. There were such persons in Bordeaux among the big merchants enriched by the boom in the second half of the 18th century. In 1782, 310 ships set out from Bordeaux for the West Indies and brought back about 130 million in goods. There was a turnover of 250 million, a figure not attained again by Bordeaux until the Second Empire; this constituted, before the Revolution, one-quarter of France's maritime trade. Between 1785 and 1789 the merchants of Bordeaux received more than a milliard's worth of goods. Out of 400 wholesalers in Bordeaux, over half had, between 1782 and 1784, more than 200,000 livres when they married, taking the bride's dowry and the bridegroom's contribution together, at a time when a laborer's wage was about 200 livres a year. François de La Rochefoucauld wrote in 1783: "The way of life of the merchants of Bordeaux is extremely luxurious. Their houses and commercial premises are on a very grand scale. Great dinners are often served on silverware." Formerly, the big merchants of Bordeaux had lived in the Quarterons district, where their houses had plain façades. Under Louis XVI some of them swarmed all through the town, both in the suburbs, where the château of Peixotto the Proud rose at Talence, or along the new Chapeau-Rouge and Intendance streets and in the Place de la Comédie, where the Saige and Bonnaffé residences were established. Some of these merchants went in for gambling in a big way, while others kept dancers and singers from the theater. They imitated the governor, the maréchal de Richelieu, striving to assume the style of living of the court nobility.

But these were, after all, exceptions among those who "lived like nobles." Most of them, even when they possessed a big house of their own, made a point of living well below their means. The rule for them was always simplicity, sobriety, severity in morals—at least outwardly. Only the very large-scale merchants had big houses (*hôtels*). In most cases, the merchants' houses were fairly small. Even among rich people it was normal to find several beds in the same bedroom. It was exceptional to have a bedroom to oneself. Houses in the country were modest. Recreations were simple and relatively inexpensive: family dinners with a few friends invited, which did not cost much, even when the table was well laden and the guests well waited on; exchanges of visits, conversation, some time spent in the country, and, for the better educated, the pleasures of the intellect.

The third of the *bourgeois* values was the family. Whereas the court nobles pretended not to be interested in their wives, the *bourgeois* lived at home with theirs, as a family, with mutual affection between the spouses and between parents and children, in good understanding and harmony (outwardly and in principle, at any rate), and the family was surrounded by a ring of cousins and friends which was fairly narrow but within which exchanges were frequent, warm, and cordial.

All this made up what could be called the *bourgeois* style of living. Those who "lived like nobles" retained something of this, even while adopting some aspects of the noble life-style.

The *"estates"* of the bourgeoisie

Social climbing at Châteaudun enables us to form some idea of the way in which the *bourgeoisie* was divided into hierarchical "estates." Social mobility was slow in this little town during our two centuries, perhaps because economic activity was relatively slight there, and even slighter after the revocation of the Edict of Nantes in 1685. Seven or eight generations were needed for a family to make its way up the rungs of the social ladder—sometimes even ten or eleven. The families in question would start out, at the beginning of the 17th century, in some branch of commerce—for instance, tanning or textiles. One of the tanner's sons, say, would begin studies in law which he did not manage to complete but which enabled him to become a "practitioner," a "legal adviser." One of the practitioner's sons completes *his* studies and becomes a licentiate in law. This degree defines a certain social level, separating two categories of persons, a higher and a lower. Our licentiate becomes an advocate. He has changed his social nature. Another son does the same by becoming a doctor of medicine. The advocates and doctors form an endogamous group in the district where they live. Their sons may enter the service of the princes and the king, either in minor offices of the princes' households or in the tax farms, or in the receiverships of the *taille*. One of the sons of these men crosses a new threshold, that of the persons who "live like nobles." He becomes a magistrate, either seignorial (as *procureur-fiscal* in the *comté* and *bailliage*) or royal (as *élu* in the *élection*). The family's rise in society culminates when one of its members attains the supreme office of *lieutenant général* in the *bailliage*.

In Paris there was an official classification according to the dignity of one's social function. First, officially, there ranked the "six corporations": the drapers, the wholesale mercers, the hatters, the furriers, the grocers, and the goldsmiths. The wholesale wine merchants fought to the very end to secure recognition as the seventh of the great corporations. According to the *règlement* of 1582 the merchants and master craftsmen of Paris were arranged in five "ranks." In the first rank were the "best," namely, the apothecaries, the grocers, the refiners of gold and silver, the drapers, the wholesale mercers, the "jewelers who sell rings, silk cloth, square-headed nails, hardware in the form of weapons, and andirons," tawers, tanners, and dyers of cloth. The second rank, "between the best and the middling," embraced the barbers, the butchers, the drapers, the hosiers, and the dyers of silk, cotton, and wool. The third rank, "the middling crafts," comprised the shoemakers, the beltmakers, the pork butchers, the cartwrights, the carpenters, the blacksmiths, the makers of pewter pots, the carpetmakers, the glassmakers. In the fourth rank, "the crafts between the middling and the minor," were the "mercers selling small wares" (haberdashers), the cookshop keepers, the cobblers, and the stonemasons. Finally, in the fifth rank, that of the "minor crafts," were the ropemakers, the wool carders, the makers of wreaths, the gardeners, and the inspectors of pigs.

We do not know how much weight was given in this classification to the dignity attributed in this society to each of those social functions, to their real economic role, and to the amount of profits and wages involved in each.

The actual stratification of society seems to have differed from this hierarchy, either because things had changed since 1582 or because social criteria were no longer the same. It is clear that, in fact, many of the members of the "six corporations" were rather petty *bourgeois*. While there was undoubtedly a hierarchy of the crafts, not always easy to make out, the role a man played within his craft was perhaps even more important—whether he was engaged in direction, organization, or execution, each of which had its different levels. Thus there were tailors at every level of the *bourgeoisie* and the craftsmen, from the tailor working for the court—directing an entire workshop, conceiving the idea of a garment, trying it on a client, conducting fittings, never cutting or sewing himself any more, or only exceptionally, a sort of artist on the fringes of the upper *bourgeoisie*—to the little local tailor working for the practitioners and shopkeepers of the neighborhood, a humble craftsman who carried out all the operations himself, with, if need be, the help of a breeches maker and an alterations hand. We must also note that there was a difference between Paris and the provinces. A social level in Paris might be higher in reality than one in the provinces that was in principle higher. An advocate before the Paris *parlement* who was merely a *noble homme* might succeed in marrying the daughter of a provincial *gentilhomme*. Some son of a *"noble homme, conseiller du Roy, juge, lieutenant en la prévôté de Tours,"* rose in the world when he became a *"marchand, bourgeois de Paris"* and married the daughter of a Parisian grain merchant, although the "judicature" was, in principle, very much higher in the social scale than "commerce."

With these reservations, it would appear that there existed in Paris in the period of the Fronde an upper *bourgeoisie* of wholesale merchants who bore the title of *"honorable homme, marchand, bourgeois de Paris"* or simply *"honorable homme, marchand."* They belonged to families with members in the law courts and in the finance offices. They married among themselves. Such a one was Georges Aubert, an apothecary and grocer, *bourgeois de Paris,* who married Catherine Cuperly, daughter of a tailor who made coats, who brought him a dowry of 8,000 livres. One first cousin of Georges Aubert's was a *trésorier ordinaire des guerres,* while another was a tipstaff for the *chambre des comptes,* and a third worked as clerk in the department which received the taxes paid by the clergy. Such also were the grain merchants around the quays of the Grève, who were often also wine merchants, and, at a more modest level, nearer to the middle *bourgeoisie,* the wood merchants and hay merchants, who also had dealings with the nobles and the high officials. These men were substantial businessmen who in Brie, Beauce, and Champagne bought grain and timber wholesale from the collectors of rents and dues in the *seigneuries*. In 1649 one of them bought 400 *setiers* of wheat at Vitry-le-François, in one transaction, for 6,000 livres in cash; another, in 1654, bought 60,000 bundles of wood for 1,900 livres and 4,000 logs for 5,600 livres. They resold their goods in small quantities on the Paris market, often on credit, to small retail traders, carpenters, joiners, keepers of hostelries and taverns, bakers and pastry cooks. They mainly married daughters of their colleagues, with dowries of between 7,000 and 16,000 livres, but also daughters of tipstaffs and notaries. They gave their own daughters in marriage either to merchants like themselves or to *procureurs* before the *parlement*. One of them assumed the title of *gendarme de la Compagne de la reine* in order to marry the daughter of a *secrétaire de la reine,* who was himself, perhaps, only a merchant. Their fortunes, which ranged between 35,000 and 110,000 livres, consisted predominantly of cash and IOUs. They and their wives were not always uneducated persons or without concern for religion. Jean-Baptiste Aubert, a grain merchant who died at the age of thirty-five, left two theorbos and a guitar, sixteen quarto volumes dealing mainly with history, ancient and modern, and seven little octavo volumes bound in calf: *Spiritual Counsel, The Conduct of a Confession, The Christian's Guide, The Religious Writings of Granada, Meditations on the Mystery of Faith,* and *The Sinner's Guide.*

A little below these merchants were the booksellers, who bought their goods from the printers. Some printers were also booksellers. All held the rank of *honorable homme.* As a rule they married daughters of merchants of the "six corporations," but the dowries were low, ranging from 1,600 to 3,000 livres. They set their sons to study and oriented them toward the advocate's profession and the office of advocate before the Grand Conseil.

On the same level were the minor officers of the law courts, the tipstaffs of the *parlement,* the *bailliage* of the Palace of Justice, and the Châtelet, who also held the rank of *honorable homme.* Also on this level, though perhaps a little lower, were the notaries of the Châtelet and the attorneys, who were very numerous (there were 400 of them attached to the Paris *parlement* alone), and who bore the title of *maître.* They were generally themselves sons of attorneys and had brothers who were attorneys, practitioners, or advocates and, in exceptional cases, an *écuyer,* a waiting-gentleman in the royal household. They usually married daughters of their colleagues but sometimes married merchants' daughters.

Close to these merchants may be ranked the domain officials, who were grouped in communities—the sworn wine brokers, the sixty sworn "sellers and controllers" of wine, whose task it was to sell the wine brought to the Paris market by itinerant merchants. They were responsible to the merchant for the price of his wine and guaranteed this. Their community's funds could be used for advances to the merchant to meet the costs of carriage, the dues to be paid for entering Paris, and the expenses of his stay in the capital. Their offices, which in 1628 were worth 8,900 livres, were worth as much as 38,000 livres in 1647, but their emoluments amounted in 1647 and 1648 to 7,599 livres each. Their fortune came to about 60,000 livres. All the same, they were only middle-ranking *bourgeois* living in modest houses.

At a still lower level of the *bourgeoisie* were other domanial officials working at the same quays—the sworn carriers of grain, the sworn carriers of coal, the sworn "measurers and controllers" of grain, the sworn "measurers and controllers" of hay, the sworn *mouleurs, compteurs, et mesureurs de bois*—who, of course, employed for the actual handling of the goods a great number of coalporters and laborers. They were close socially to some master craftsmen—saddlers and coachmakers, tailors who made coats, carpetmakers, wheelwrights, masons, who were perhaps becoming *entrepreneurs*—and married into their families and those of the tipstaffs and catchpoles of the Châtelet or into that of some commissioner of the *bureau des aides*.

In Normandy, in Rouen, between 1620 and 1650, it is surprising to find below those who "live like nobles," in the mere *bourgeoisie*, some members of the sovereign courts—counselors of the *parlement* and *maîtres* and auditors of the *cours des comptes*—even though they enjoyed the privileges of nobility. The point was that they were "new men," sons of attorneys or even merchants. Though they could call themselves *noble homme* and *conseiller du roi*, they were looked down upon by the families of their colleagues. They managed to marry only daughters of merchants, advocates, attorneys, or *rentiers*, all with the rank of *honorable homme*. Only their sons, after the family had been made respectable by a phase of at least one generation in offices, were looked on by the others as being truly on an equality with themselves.

The marriages made by these "new men" put them on a lower level than some magistrates in the *élections* and some minor officials and finance officers attached to the sovereign courts, although most of the latter were classifiable, owing to their marriage connections, as mere *bourgeois* and therefore as ranking, all the same, *after* these "new men."

Finally we come to the great mass of those entitled to be called *honorable homme,* in which officeholders form existence groups along with merchants and *rentiers*. First, at the top of this category, are the finance officers of the *élections* and the salt storehouses, the *receveurs* and *contrôleurs* of the *taille,* the *receveurs* of the *taillon* and those of the salt storehouses; the *maîtres particuliers* of the Rouen mint; some of the *seigneurs'* financial officials, such as the *receveur* of the barony of Monville; and, finally, some attorneys in the sovereign courts. They married daughters of wholesale merchants. The dowries varied between 4,000 and 12,000 livres.

We find ranking below them, although the "judiciary" was superior to "finance," some petty magistrates of the secondary centers of *bailliages,* presidial courts, and *vicomtés: conseillers assesseurs, enquêteurs et examinateurs, procureurs du roi* in the *vicomtés,* and also *procureurs du roi* in the *élections* and in the department of waters and forests; officials of the salt storehouses—*contrôleurs* and *grènetiers.* They married daughters of men with the rank of *"honorable homme"*—merchants, advocates, and even master craftsmen—and their daughters married such men. The dowries ranged from 4,000 to 6,000 livres.

Only then do we come upon the bulk of the advocates before the *parlement* of Rouen and the presidial courts and the doctors of medicine and university professors—all those among them, that is, who were not either *écuyer* or *noble homme* but only *honorable homme.* They married mainly the daughters of their colleagues or daughters of attorneys, hereditary registrars, and clerks employed in the registry of the *parlement.* They gave their daughters' hands to colleagues or to *rentiers* with the rank of *"honorable homme."* The dowries ranged from 2,000 to 7,000 livres.

Below them again is a social group which marks the transition from the petty *bourgeoisie* to the craftsmen. This is made up of minor court officials (tipstaffs in the *parlement,* the *bureaux des finances,* and the presidial courts, royal notaries, and clerks of the court), domanial officials (brokers and measurers of cloth, etc.), surgeons, and small-scale manufacturers and entrepreneurs—printers and booksellers, painters and sculptors, clothiers, goldsmiths, dyers, grocers, tinsmiths and plumbers, and so on. Their families intermarried, the dowries being in the 2,500–4,500-livre range.

A little lower still, perhaps, were the registrars of the *cours des aides,* the *bureaux des finances,* and the *traites foraines,* together with the chief clerks of the civil register office of Rouen and the chancellery of Normandy.

We gradually quit the company of the men with the rank of *honorable homme,* passing through the grade of *honnête personne,* and it is to be wondered whether perhaps we ought to exclude from the *bourgeoisie* and place with the manual workers such men as the royal bailiffs who distrained on goods and sold them in the *bailliages* and *vicomtés;* the clerks in the salt storehouses, the department of waters and forests, and the *vicomtés;* most of the attorneys in the *parlement;* and the wine brokers.

In Beauvais and Beauvaisis in the 17th century we find among the *bourgeois* "living like nobles" and among the upper *bourgeoisie* some wholesale merchants, like the Danses and the Mottes. They did not manufacture anything and possessed no looms. They obliged the clothmakers to agree to make the types of cloth required by their clientele, even if these did not conform to the regulations. They supplied the serge-makers of the countryside with wool from Soissonnais, Brie, Beauce, and Berry, on credit. At the *bureau forain* they received lengths of cloth made by the small producers of the countryside and attached a leaden seal to them. They bought all the cloth unbleached and undertook to get it finished by fullers, shearers, nappers, launderers, and dyers. They carried on trade by means of "barter, reciprocal commerce, and payments in kind." They dominated the manufacturing process and were the moving spirits and leaders in it. They were aware of this and proud of the fact. They demanded freedom for themselves but regulation for those who actually made the goods.

Their fortunes were bigger than those of the officials "living like nobles." They ranged from 400,000 to 500,000 livres. That of one of the Danse family at the beginning of the 18th century came to a million livres. But these fortunes were even more different as regards their composition. Movable property predominated—all those things that could be used in business, stocks of cloth, IOUs, and, in the last quarter of the 17th century, bills of exchange. These wholesalers owned fine houses but not much land. Their libraries contained only a few works of piety.

When these men became integrated with families that "lived like nobles," the composition of their fortunes underwent a change. The principal factors of growth were speculations in foodstuffs and loans on mortgage. Their property in land, ownership of which always gives a certain dignity, increased to make up at least half of their total fortune and to contribute nearly half of their income. This landed property embraced a manor house and farms. One farm would be assigned the task of maintaining the owner's family, which was fed, kept warm, and clothed with the products of rent paid in kind. Sundays were spent staying at this farm.

Below the upper *bourgeoisie* of the wholesale merchants comes a middle *bourgeoisie* of merchants; they played a similar role, but on a smaller scale, and they were less wealthy.

Below them are a petty *bourgeoisie* of "merchant manufacturers" or "merchant drapers." These owned looms, or "*ostilles.*" Twenty of them each had between six and twelve of these. Two of them, in 1633, had nineteen. Their workplaces included big rooms full of the means of production—looms, spinning wheels, bales of wool, rods for beating it, thistles, combs, reeling machines for rolling it up, warping frames, oil for greasing the yarn, presses, shearing tables, spring shears, tables for folding and packing cloth. They employed workmen (*ouvriers*), a certain number of whom had the legal status of *maître de métier* (master craftsman); among these were weavers, nappers, shearers, combers, and so on. Some of these lived at the workplace, while others came to work in the morning and returned home in the evening. The manufacturers bought wool in bales—in Castile, England, and Beauce—and had it spun and combed in their manufactories and by the workers at home in Beauvais and the countryside. They had the pieces of cloth woven in their manufactories and at the homes of master weavers, to whom they lent a loom, and each of whom worked at home with the help of a boy. They put the cloth out to be dyed and fulled and had it finished in the manufactory. They employed a permanent staff of about twenty workmen. They sent their goods to Troyes or Paris, either through Beauvais merchants or else directly to the merchants or brokers. Some of them gave up manufacturing and rose in the social hierarchy by becoming exclusively merchants.

In 17th-century Amiens the upper *bourgeoisie* consisted of a score of families of big merchants who held a monopoly of wholesale trade in drysaltery and textiles. They formed an endogamous group and built up some fine fortunes. Jacques Morgan, who dealt in dyestuffs, spices, and cloth, possessed, in 1646, 10,000 livres and, in 1688, 80,000 livres. His son, Jean-Baptiste, was master in 1695 of 400,000 livres. The greater part of their patrimony was invested in commerce, for capital circulated very slowly. Land accounted for no more than 15 to 20 percent of their fortune. They lived in the center of the town in modest houses without porches. Their life was a simple one. They did not own carriages. Merchants, in any case, used to travel in groups on horseback, to guard their cartloads of goods.

For a long time this group was highly unstable. The Catholic Church was inimical to mercantile activities, to the lending of money at interest, which it called usury, and to the unlimited accumulation of wealth. The Counter-Reformation and Jansenism strengthened these tendencies. The *gentilshommes* respected only the sword. Merchants were encouraged to arrange a spiritual retirement for the saving of their souls by giving up business early in life in order to live on their *rentes* or, still better, on the income from a *seigneurie* or a fief, or else to take up an office. Many sons of rich merchants abandoned their fathers' occupation to "live like nobles" on their *rentes* or to take up an office, adopt the profession of arms, or become priests. In the course of the 17th century the composition of the merchant families was almost entirely renewed, for less than a sixth of the original families remained in the occupation.

But ideas were changing. In 1700, while the Assembly of the Clergy reaffirmed the condemnation of usury, the Conseil de Commerce proposed that noble status be granted to wholesale merchants in the fourth generation. Jean-Baptiste Morgan, ennobled in 1709 as *secrétaire du roi,* nevertheless continued in business. His sons and grandsons, though legally assimilated with the *gentilshommes,* behaved likewise and introduced the making of velvet into Amiens. The Damien family, ennobled in 1696, continued in the clothing business for two generations. The Jourdains were, all through the 18th century, both *écuyers* and wholesalers. At the end of the 17th century the rich merchants conceived a new sense of dignity, just as the world of offices was becoming a closed shop and the value of offices was diminishing, together with their power and prestige. In 1708 the merchants organized themselves in a special community. This movement coincided with a change in their religious attitude. At the beginning of the 17th century, religion had been the chief concern of their lives. Their Catholicism had been uncompromising. The books they owned were works of piety— lives of the saints and the works of Luis de Granada and Saint François de Sales. They allowed themselves to read the Stoics, Seneca, Plutarch, on account of Christian Stoicism. They formed the great strength of the Church. To it they gave their sons, as priests and monks. They themselves were parish churchwardens, hospital administrators, members of the Confraternity of the Blessed Sacrament. At the opening of the 18th century their piety was still sincere and deep, but it was no longer the same. The world exerted a greater attraction than before. They showed more attachment to their children and their families generally. They showed more taste for literary culture and classical beauty and a love of nature and of reverie. They surrounded themselves with more books, tapestries, and pictures than before. The sensations and pleasures of life were acquiring greater value for them.

Amiens had also a middle and petty *bourgeoisie* of smaller merchants, grocers, mercers, clothiers, entrepreneurs in weaving and dyeing, merchant craftsmen specializing in luxury trades and the manufacture of expensive articles, goldsmiths, apothecaries, brewers, dyers, and tanners, whose techniques required the use of relatively costly equipment. They lived in houses that included a living room, some small rooms, bedrooms, a wood yard, a corn loft, heaps of linen, gold, and silver plate, and ledgers—but few books. In the course of the century they became further and further separated from the rank-and-file of the crafts. They no longer served in the town guard but had their servants take their places or else bought themselves out of the obligation to serve. They became hostile to the popular festivals and public dances and to the *jeu de Mahon,* which was played with fisticuffs. In this attitude they were imitated by a certain number of shopkeepers.

At Châteaudun in the 18th century the upper *bourgeoisie* embraced, beneath the magistrates "living like nobles," advocates and doctors, who formed an endogamous existence group. There was a middle *bourgeoisie,* consisting of wine merchants, wholesale cloth merchants, and masters of enterprises. Owing to the economic decline of the town, however, their number was small. They were compelled to find some of their wives among the daughters of minor officials of the *comté* and the *élection* and even the daughters of surgeons and apothecaries. This middle *bourgeoisie* was not to be compared with that of bigger and more prosperous towns like Orléans or Toulouse. The petty *bourgeoisie* consisted of shopkeepers, especially secondhand-clothes dealers, who were relatively quite numerous and were the only traders whose numbers increased during the century in this town. Their prosperity was due to the obligation to sell by auction the clothes that underage children inherited. The minor in question was assigned a guardian, who had to sell the movable property in his inheritance and invest the money obtained, so that the minor could be supported by the interest on it and recover the principal when he came of age. For this reason, secondhand clothes were available in plenty and found a ready market among a rather poor population. This petty *bourgeoisie* also included boarding-school keepers and the crowd of clerks attached to the various courts.

In Orléans, as 1789 approached, the upper *bourgeoisie,* below the level of those who "lived like nobles," embraced about two hundred families of wholesale merchants, manufacturers, and *rentiers*. The middle *bourgeoisie* included about thirty doctors, twenty-one advocates, thirty-four notaries, some registrars, attorneys, clerks to the intendant (the three, four, six, or eight persons whom an intendant usually maintained in his office), collectors for the various tax farms, employees of the *régies* and the General Farm, its regional managers, *contrôleurs* and collectors, finance officials "of the second grade," printers and booksellers, and entrepreneurs of various sorts. Enthroned at the summit of this middle *bourgeoisie* sat a group of advocates, some of whom were also professors of law at the University of Orléans. Beneath these advocates was a group embracing members of a number of professions, each of which constituted a corporation and was, for that reason, more highly esteemed: doctors, printers, booksellers, notaries. Still further down came a stratum of attorneys and *huissiers-audienciers* distinct from the rest because, when the *cahiers* were being drawn up in 1789, they were allowed to meet separately, being described as *corps libéraux*. Finally, the lowest rank of the middle *bourgeoisie* was made up of thirty or so merchants who sold cloth or linen at retail and about a hundred small manufacturers who belonged to the craft corporations but who, owing to the size of their enterprises and the small amount of manual work they performed themselves, can be classified as forming part of the *bourgeoisie*—as part, even, of its middle section. This middle *bourgeoisie* numbered in all about 500 families. The interests of some of the lawyers were closely bound up with those of the nobles and with the seignorial and feudal form of property: five advocates and two notaries held as *baillis* the twenty-one seignorial judgeships which were located in the town, and eleven attorneys and one notary were procurators-fiscal in seignorial courts. Some of these men held a great many offices. One advocate, Pierre Perche, was an officeholder in nine courts in Orléans and four in the surrounding country, at Châteauneuf, Ingré, Saint-Cyr-en-Val, and Cléry. Another, Jean Coston, was at one and the same time a professor at the university, *bailli* of two courts in Orléans, and *bailli* of Jargeau.

The petty *bourgeoisie* of Orléans consisted of small shopkeepers, who were well described, along with the lowest rank of the middle bourgeoisie, by the deputy Lecointre in his speech of 30 April 1793 in the Convention: "I include in this number all those who have an annual turnover of between 6,000 and 30,000 livres ... this numerous class of merchants who are always dependent on the wholesalers and capitalists, always their slaves. Formerly, competition between wholesalers enabled all the small traders to secure the means and benefits of their labors.''

The petty *bourgeoisie* also included the commissaries of police, lodging-house keepers, teachers, employees of the stagecoach companies and the postal service, five or six hundred clerks of the *basoche* (working as assistants to advocates and notaries)—all together about 4,000 persons out of a total of 40,000. Georges Lefebvre considered that this category ought to be extended to include craftsmen working for a wholesaler but themselves employing workmen. However, contemporaries did not categorize them like this, because these men's activity involved so much manual work. Take, for example, the man who made knitted goods at home. Though employing three workmen, he worked all day with his hands, side by side with his men. He was no *bourgeois*. Besides, when he had paid for his raw materials, given his men their wages, and met various overheads, all he had left was about 50 sous a day. Even though *that* aspect was quite secondary, the sum was, nevertheless, rather little for a *bourgeois*.

In Toulouse on the eve of 1789 the upper *bourgeoisie* consisted of a small group of wholesale merchants and manufacturers, hardly more numerous than the nobles. The economic activity of this great provincial capital was very slight compared with Bordeaux, Lyons, or Marseilles. In the case of 72 percent of these big *bourgeois,* three-quarters of their fortune consisted of real estate, mainly in the country. Their fortunes were mainly in land, in which respect they resembled the *gentilshommes* and the officials of the *parlement.* Merchandise and movable property made up only a small part of their fortunes. However, they were markedly less well off than the nobility: 70 percent of the nobles possessed a total fortune of more than 63,000 francs; 55 percent of the big *bourgeois* had a total fortune of more than 25,000 francs.

In a town which lived chiefly by its *parlement,* the middle *bourgeoisie* was made up essentially of advocates and minor court officials, notaries, attorneys, and *huissiers,* together with doctors and surgeons and a whole series of "men of talent"—professors, architects, surveyors. Nearly all of them had this in common, that they got their livelihood not in the form of wages or salaries but in private honorariums, paid in return for private services. Their fortune when they married was only one-twelfth that of an unemployed nobleman but was one-fourth of it when they died, which shows that they had more opportunities for bettering their financial situation and preparing for a change of life-style. The liberal professions belonging to the realm of the law accounted for nearly 70 percent of all the members of this category, and the average fortune of their members was 50 percent higher than that of those in the health service, the doctors and surgeons. The Toulouse law faculty attracted many students and included some notable teachers. In the composition of their fortunes, landed property formed a large element (in half of the cases it was larger than all the rest). Their fortunes as a rule were in excess of 25,000 francs— close to those of the big *bourgeoisie;* yet, in spite of this fact, the members of the liberal professions remained socially inferior to that group. The less-well-off among them, with between 10,000 and 25,000 francs, were advocates who worked as experts in feudal land law and earned less than the others, some of the doctors and surgeons, and, in general, the engineers, men of letters, teachers, and surveyors.

The petty *bourgeoisie* of Toulouse included tipstaffs and bailiffs, attorneys, legal practitioners, fencing masters, teachers of music and dancing, and those merchants, shopkeepers, and retailers who were listed in the *petit tableau* (whereas the wholesalers were listed in the *grand tableau*) and whose trade was confined to Toulouse (whereas the wholesalers operated over the entire south of France). Their average fortune at death was 16,000 francs—less than the figure for the liberal professions (30,000), the big businessmen (42,000), or the *rentiers* (49,000) but twice that for the craftsmen (8,000). Sixty-five percent of their fortune consisted of real estate, mainly in the city.

The *bourgeoisie* was not an exclusively urban phenomenon. Just as there were, in the country, persons who "lived like nobles," so also were there persons who played there the role that the *bourgeois* played in the towns and who must be regarded as *bourgeois*. In the Bocage region of Maine in the 18th century the market centers and larger villages contained quite a few of these: notaries, *huissiers,* attorneys, both royal and seignorial, some doctors, and a few *financiers,* who acted as agents for the farmers general or for noblemen. Taken as a whole they corresponded to the petty *bourgeoisie* of the towns. The merchants and manufacturers can be considered as belonging to the same category. The linen and flax merchants were much richer than the other *bourgeois*. Owning their own horses, they transported lengths of linen made in the countryside to the markets of Alençon, La Ferté-Bernard, and Le Mans. Some of them procured linen in these markets in order to sell it in faraway provinces or to export it to Spain or the West Indies. Some undertook the finishing process; among these were the Pérard family at Ponthieu, near Le Mans, who employed forty workmen and were on the fringe of the middle *bourgeoisie*. Also *bourgeois* were the manufacturers of linen who owned a dozen looms, employed a score of workmen, and no longer worked with their own hands but managed their enterprises.

These *bourgeois* were the biggest purchasers of land in the countryside of Maine. They owned more than 50 percent of all the land in the region, more than either the nobility or the clergy. They owned some farms and a larger number of *bordages*, and it was with them more than anyone else that the bulk of the peasantry had dealings. It was they who mainly dominated that countryside on the eve of 1789.

In the rural districts of northern Burgundy there was also, in the 18th century, a petty *bourgeoisie* consisting of notaries and legal practitioners, who were often at the same time *procureurs fiscaux* for the *seigneuries*, lenders of money or hirers-out of farm animals, *greffiers*, surgeons, and parish priests. The priests were sons of well-to-do rural families. They received 700 livres by way of stipend, together with tithes and perquisites, and also benefited from endowments. They were very comfortably off. They were exempt from the *taille* and from the "twentieth," and the declaration of 1698 associated them with the *seigneurs* and the judiciary in what it laid down regarding forms of respect and ceremony to be observed in relation to them, providing for penalties against those who disregarded these. Such priests retained the enterprising spirit of their families. They acted as moneylenders and were very grasping; they were also very active as leaders of opinion in the village assemblies, prominent in opposition to the local *seigneurs*.

Should we regard as *bourgeois* the big *laboureurs-marchands*, well-to-do peasants who also acted as merchants—the minority of rich tenant farmers? Some historians have thought so, among them Georges Lefebvre, who wrote about northern France on the eve of the Revolution: "The village formed a little community, which had its dominant class, the big tenant farmers and well-to-do cultivators, who made up the very small rural *bourgeoisie*."[1] These big farmers certainly formed a dominant group, and certainly also a group that was very much richer than the rural *bourgeois* already described. They owned a great deal of equipment—plough teams, ploughs, carts, various tools—a capital which they set to work by means of their servants and agricultural laborers. Many of them acted as collectors of seignorial and feudal dues for the *seigneuries*, and sometimes they lived at the manor house, seeming to the peasants to be the actual *seigneurs*. But did their activity not still consist more of *manual* labor than of the other kind? And their way of life, wearing smocks and clogs, a hard and poor life—was it really that of even a *petty* bourgeois? Contemporaries placed them on a lower social level than the craftsmen in the towns. *They* did not see them as being *bourgeois,* and it would seem that the historian's view should be the same.

The manual workers

The different "estates" of the manual workers are not yet well known, especially where the towns are concerned. The descriptions of them that have been written are mainly prolongations of economic studies of urban industry and trade in which attention is give to the wages, food, clothing, and housing of these workers, their organizations, and their revolts, all this being looked at more often than not, by 19th- and 20th-century historians, either from the standpoint of the *bourgeois* society of their own time or from that of one form or another of socialism. We possess hardly any strictly social studies, based on systematic research into the existence groups of these workers through investigation of their various associations, especially that fundamental association, marriage. The few social studies we do possess have usually not been carried out in a sufficiently scientific way, that is, in accordance with the type of society under consideration. It has been assumed that the social hierarchy and social mobility of the manual workers corresponded exactly with the hierarchy of their wages and earnings and that these in turn were governed only by economic factors; but the question has not been asked whether the wages themselves were not determined as a function of a value judgment concerning the social dignity of the service rendered by the product of their labor. For a society of orders and "estates," any social investigation must be guided by a search for social value judgments, explicit or implicit, resulting in the construction of a scale of dignities. This work has not been done in the case of French society as it then was. The social hierarchy of the manual workers which can be set out here is therefore only rudimentary and provisional.

To meet the needs of the state, part of the social organization of the manual workers was given a legal formulation which reality overflowed in all directions. This will be examined as a whole in the chapter on corporations and communities. Here let it suffice to mention a few features which are immediately relevant. In this legal hierarchy the topmost position was occupied by the crafts which "have the right to form corporations and communities," with the "free" crafts ranking below them. The former group were known as "sworn crafts," or "*maîtrises et jurandes.*" The *jurande* was the group of "jurors" elected by the master craftsmen and forming the governing body of the craft. Each "sworn craft" was a moral person, fulfilling public responsibilities. There was an official hierarchy among these crafts, indicated by the rank assigned to each in public ceremonies—the state entry of a king or queen, a Te Deum, processions, and so forth—which defined, in principle, their dignity in the eyes of the state and the society.

Inside each craft there was also an official hierarchy among its members. At the top were the members of the *jurande*, the jurors or syndics elected by the assembly of master craftsmen. Former jurors retained from the function they had fulfilled a sort of social superiority over the other members of the community. Below the *jurande* came the council, elected by the general assembly, whose members and former members also enjoyed a kind of special dignity. Below the council, the general assembly brought together all the master craftsmen of the "sworn craft," who formed a "political," an "aristodemocratic," corporation. In most cases the general assembly was confined to the master craftsmen, the journeymen and apprentices being excluded. The term "master craftsman" (*maître de métier*) covered many different realities. Wholesale merchants, manufacturers, artisans, workmen, all might bear this title.

Under the master craftsmen came the journeymen, grouped in *compagnonnages,* which were periodically banned, and in religious confraternities, which formed pressure groups. Below them were the apprentices, who might have their own *compagnonnages* and confraternities.

After Turgot's abolition of the *maîtrises et jurandes,* and of all corporations and communities of merchants and craftsmen, by the Edict of Versailles of February 1776, the edict of August of the same year regrouped a certain number of crafts in new corporations and communities within the area of jurisdiction of the Paris *parlement,* this reform being extended, between 1777 and 1780, to the areas covered by the *parlements* of Normandy, Grenoble, and Metz and the sovereign council of Roussillon.

At a lower level of the legally recognized hierarchy stood the crafts called "free," which meant, probably, all the crafts practiced in the countryside and the majority of those practiced in the towns. Their members were free in the sense that they did not belong to a corporation and were not subject to the obligations imposed on the members of such a corporation. They were, however, regulated and supervised by magistrates—the royal judge, the seignorial judge, the municipal magistrate—who watched over their conduct and checked on wages and proper prices, on the safety, hygiene, and good quality of products, and on observance of all the relevant administrative regulations.

This legally recognized hierarchy does not precisely express all the social differences that existed. It seems that we need to distinguish, in the first place, between the hierarchy of the "industrial" crafts and that of the "artisan" crafts. The industrial crafts were those which, even if they retained an artisan form, actually produced goods, such as cloth or iron, which served in their turn as raw materials for the manufacture of objects of prime necessity and everyday use, such as clothes or tools; or they produced objects of prime necessity, in large quantities, for large-scale markets and for export—goods such as stockings, caps, etc. The artisan crafts were those which satisfied the public's immediate short-term wants, particularly in food, clothing, adornment, transport, and so on.

In the towns

In these artisan crafts in Paris, in the period of the Fronde, the interplay of matrimonial alliances and associations reveals a hierarchy based on the dignity resulting from social value judgments. At the top is the group of craftsmen who work to meet the luxury and prestige requirements of the great and the rich: master beltmakers, master corset-makers, master glovemakers and perfumers, some of the master tailors, master saddlers, master burnishers and decorators of swords, master bakers of rolls, and so on. We have here an indubitable existence group, for they are all linked together by marriage. It appears that one can add to them surgeons, butchers, master cooks, and suppliers to the gentlemen of the royal household, who were also the persons who usually lent money to the latter, being not merely creditors for the supplies furnished but also advancing loans.

Below them comes another stratum which is also an existence group, bound together by intermarriage. These are the craftsmen concerned with transport, with horses and carriages, and the auxiliaries of travel and large-scale trade, such as the makers of means of transport and the hotelkeepers. They included master harness-makers, master saddlers, some master carpenters occupied in making boats, and some men engaged in traffic by water—those who owned their boats and hired them out for carrying purposes or who themselves transported goods on behalf of merchants of goods which they themselves were selling, thus taking a step in the direction of vertical concentration. At this level also are the master coopers, closely linked with the carriers, and many hotelkeepers and innkeepers. In the case of Toulouse at the end of the 18th century, it has been sought to classify the innkeepers in the petty *bourgeoisie,* since their average fortune at death was 20,553 francs, thus exceeding that of the petty *bourgeois* engaged in trade. Socially, however, they were nonetheless *below* the latter, since they had to marry craftsmen's daughters. The daughters of the small traders did not want them; hotel business was not sufficiently honorable, for it involved too much manual work and too many tasks similar to those of servants.

Finally, below them, we find a third stratum of craftsmen, concerned only with satisfying the elementary needs of everyday life, especially in the middle and lower sections of the population: master butchers, master bakers, master cooks, master pastry-makers, master pork-butchers, master cobblers, master shoemakers, master tailors, master sheath-makers (for knives), and so on.

The hierarchy of these three strata seems to result from a value judgment regarding the social quality of the services rendered rather than the economic value of the product. This value judgment, which engenders a social differentiation, also engenders, as a consequence, an economic differentiation: the glovemaker-perfumer of the Ile de la Cité who works for persons of elegance stands higher than the master cobbler who mends the footwear of the craftsmen of the Faubourg Saint-Antoine.

In the Paris of the first third of the 17th century, 40 percent of the master craftsmen married daughters of master craftsmen; 31 percent married daughters of unqualified craftsmen or of servants; 15 percent married daughters of "merchants," who could be either persons above the level of master craftsman or, on the contrary, persons who had not succeeded in getting a mastership; 5 percent married daughters of *bourgeois de Paris,* very modestly situated *rentiers,* perhaps retired master craftsmen; 6 percent married daughters of men described as *"honorable homme, marchand, bourgeois de Paris"*—these were marriages that meant social ascent. Finally, we find various marriages with daughters of soldiers and noncommissioned officers and with the daughters of a *fruitier* or a *fauconnier* of the royal household, a sworn town crier, a *procureur fiscal* of a *seigneurie,* and a royal bailiff (*sergent*).

Among the journeymen, a few who were master craftsmen's sons and destined for masterships married into a world of superior master craftsmen, on the fringe of the merchants. Thirty percent of the sons of journeymen, craftsmen, or *laboureurs* married daughters of master craftsmen, while 48 percent took as brides the daughters of unqualified craftsmen or else servants.

Among the service personnel, the *maîtres d'hôtel* were sons of merchants, *bourgeois de Paris,* or royal bailiffs (*sergents*). They married daughters of *bourgeois de Paris,* of men described as *"noble homme, maître avocat au parlement," "lieutenant pour le roi"* or *"sergent des tailles."* They should be grouped with the merchants.

The cooks and secretaries married daughters of master craftsmen and should be grouped with them.

The *valets de chambre,* kitchen hands, and hotel servants, who were sons of tenant farmers, tinkers, coachmen, and ostlers, married housekeepers, servants, and daughters of vinegrowers and craftsmen who were not masters.

Unqualified craftsmen, who were sons of men like themselves or of peasants, vinegrowers, or gardeners, married daughters of men belonging to the same categories or else servants. Many of them were persons who had recently arrived from the surrounding country or from the provinces. Some found wives from the families of master craftsmen, with the prospect of rising in the world.

To this stratum must be added those persons who, though they called themselves "merchants," were actually very petty retailers—old-clothes men or food-sellers—and married into the same circles as the unqualified craftsmen.

In the "industrial" crafts, if we take for example the silk business in Lyons, we need to distinguish three categories of master craftsmen. First, at the top, came the *"maîtres-marchands," "le grande fabrique,"* some of whom were in fact master craftsmen. These merchants, owners of capital, undertook to supply silk and patterns to the *"maîtres-ouvriers"* and to market their products. Such *maîtres-marchands* were *bourgeois* and are mentioned here so that they should not be lost sight of.

Under them, in the category of manual workers, were the *"maîtres-ouvriers-marchands," "la petite fabrique."* These were independent workers. They bought the raw material, wove it on looms which were their own property, and themselves sold the cloth they made. They worked with their hands but were helped by two or three journeymen and apprentices. However, their economic positon declined steadily as a result of competition from the *maîtres-marchands*. The latter eventually secured the consular ordinance of 1731, which, on the one hand, forbade these men to work for the *maîtres-marchands* and, on the other, and most important, obliged them to possess no more than two looms and to work them personally, together with their children, without journeymen or apprentices. The *maîtres-ouvriers-marchands* were thus reduced to practicing their craft on a family basis, and to a very precarious existence. They were often poorer than the *maîtres-ouvriers;* but since they did not work for anyone else, but were independent, they ranked socially above them.

The third category was that of the *maîtres-ouvriers*. They generally owned their own looms, but "they make the cloth as the merchants pay them to do this." They received the raw material and the pattern from the *maître-marchand*. The latter called on them in order to collect what they had made and to pay them the agreed price, which was a mere wage. The *maître-marchand* saw to the selling of the goods; the *maître-ouvrier* no longer had any contact with either the market or the clientele at the retail stage. He was only a workman. He worked with his hands, but he was allowed to have as many as four looms and to hire journeymen and apprentices.

The fourth stratum consisted of the journeymen, spoken of as *ouvriers* (workmen), and with them can be put the apprentices, who shared their situation.

The social hierarchy was thus governed in this case by the opportunity that a man possessed, or did not possess, to appropriate other men's labor by transforming a fortune into capital and, by this same opportunity, or lack of it, to obtain raw material on the market, to put a product on the market, and to discuss what its price should be. In the 18th century, at least, the antagonism between these two types— between the man who organizes production and sale, because he can appropriate for himself the labor of others and operate on the commodity market, and the man who, possessing nothing but his tools, his strength, and his ability to labor, can only work on the material supplied to him—became a conscious one. In Lyons in August 1744, at a time of strikes and riots, the workers attacked, in a manifesto, "these idlers by condition who today decorate themselves with the title of merchants." They looked back to a time when all were craftsmen, to the time "when every worker was a merchant and every merchant a worker"—meaning the situation, by then much reduced but still in existence, of the *maître-ouvrier-marchand*. They contrasted to the merchant, "who knows how to count, measure, and write labels," the worker, "who alone knows the rules [for making the goods] and who is skillful and industrious," and concluded that "there is no need of merchants in order to establish a regular and stable manufacture."

Thus there existed in Lyons what the socialist theoreticians of the 19th century described by the terms "class" and "class consciousness." The type of hierarchy of crafts I have described above under the name of "artisan" crafts seems to belong properly to the society of orders, whereas, with the "industrial" crafts, we seem to be entering a society of classes in process of formation within the society of orders.

Before concluding that this is indeed so, we should need to carry out in Lyons—where, so far, only the economic relations within the one craft of silkmaking have been studied—an investigation into marriage connections, and in Paris—where marriage connections have been studied—we need an investigation into the economic relations within each craft; for the difference in results may itself result from the difference in the line of investigation followed.

We should also group the towns according to categories based on the predominant function within them. The social hierarchy, even in its lower levels, cannot be the same in the capital, in a center of pilgrimage, in a garrison town, and in a town where trade and industry predominate, like Lyons.

Finally, this question should be asked: In a society of orders, would not the discoverable social relations which resemble or seem to be identical with those of a society of classes be integrated into the whole, constituting an integral and functional part of the society of orders, and would they not develop into relations between orders? This is the fundamental question.

In the present state of knowledge, and for the time being, I believe that what we see here is the formation of the future class society *inside* the society of orders.

In Beauvais the regime governing the manual workers was that of the "free" crafts. After his apprenticeship the "worker in wool" swore an oath before the *juge de police* and thereby "gained his freedom." He could call himself "master" and could carry on his craft, either on his own account or "under another" (but retaining this title). Thus he could work at home, provided he reported this fact to the authorities. He could serve as a workman for a *maître-fabricant* or could himself open a workshop in that capacity. Everything depended solely on his abilities and the amount of money he was in a position to invest. In this way a dual hierarchy emerges: the hierarchy of crafts resulting from the subdivision of the production of cloth, and the hierarchy resulting from the different roles men played in the process of production.

The first hierarchy is made plain through the occupational origins of the master craftsmen, since it can be agreed that, in general, if the sons of masters of a certain craft choose a different craft, this is because the latter will give them a better social status and a bigger reward. It is itself divided into two hierarchies, that of the operations involved in production and that of the product to be made—serge or cloth. The woolen workers of humblest origin were recruited from among the rural workers. The carders were the worst off among them. The sergemakers were above them in rank, since they were partly recruited from among sons of carders. Finally, at the top, were the clothmakers. The sons of day laborers (*manouvriers*), *airiers* (market gardeners), vinegar-makers, and curriers became weavers. Above them were the nappers, for weavers' sons became nappers. The total number of workers was made up of 500 sergemakers and weavers, 250 carders, and 200 nappers and shearers.

The second hierarchy embraced, under the "*fabricants-marchands*" or "*marchands drapiers drapant*"—who were *bourgeois* and are mentioned so that their presence may be kept in mind—the mere "*fabricants,*" who were manual workers. Owning about five looms, they employed carders and spinners, a permanent staff of about a dozen, and sold the cloth they produced to Beauvais merchants. Despite the role they played as organizers, they were principally manual workers, who received no advance payment and possessed no stocks of material; they were dependent on the merchants and led a very modest life. Below them were the *fabricants façonniers,* who had only one loom and one or two spinning wheels and worked with the members of their family and one servant girl. Lower still came the mere *ouvriers,* who worked for a *fabricant* or a *marchand drapier drapant.* Wages were fixed by the seignorial *bailli,* but between 1667 and 1699 they were left to find their own level. Nominal wages were remarkably stable—10 sous a day. Actually, the carders were paid piece wages, on the basis of the weight and quality of the wool they carded. On the eve of the *mortalité* of 1693–94, spinning-women earned between 3 and 3½ sous a day, little girls and old women earned 1 sou, and weavers not "living in" got 9 sous; by comparison, journeymen builders and carpenters got from 18 to 20 sous. They worked about 270 days in the year.

In 17th-century Amiens, textile manufacture brought together about 1,000 "masters," some of whom kept shop (master carders, weavers, dyers, and finishers), and between 3,000 and 4,000 journeymen and apprentices—fewer when trade was bad. The crafts of clothing, foodstuffs, building, metal, and leather numbered between 1,000 and 1,200 small employers and shopkeepers, with the same number of journeymen, clerks, and shop assistants.

Amiens was a town of *maîtrises et jurandes*. "In a society which knew not the individual but recognized only the orders, which knew not juridical equality and respected only privilege, this was the chivalry of the artisan and the symbol of his organic participation in the providential order of society."[2] The craft tended increasingly to become identical with the existence group. A hereditary condition for 30 percent of its members at the beginning of the century, it had become still more so by the end. Moreover, the number of marriages within the craft community increased. In the first half of the century, 43 percent of the marriages in each craft took place between a master and the daughter of another master in the same craft. There were also cases, and they were not rare, of a journeyman marrying a master's widow and of masters marrying their servants. "An interfamilial friendly society, the community also came more and more to resemble an employers' association."[3] The community became above all an affair of the master craftsmen. Animated by a monopolizing spirit, they indulged in violence against the spinners and weavers in the villages. From time to time they secured the expulsion of the itinerant traders who came in from the mountains, the tinkers from Auvergne. They accused the porters and dockers of forming secret societies in order to impose exorbitant payments. They complained of the excessive prices charged by the bakers and butchers. Their fortunes were not large—less than 1,000 livres. It included little ready money and was made up mainly of furniture, linen, tools, the loom, the warps for weaving, and a few pounds of wool and silk. The master usually had a workroom and a shop. He had a big pothanger, and tableware made of pewter. He had several beds, with bedclothes. He did not lack weapons—a musket, a halberd—for his service in the *garde bourgeoise*. He was able, given favorable circumstances,

to acquire a house, a garden, some plots of land, or a municipal office: as weigher of yarn for sayette, measurer, mace-bearing
bailiff (*sergent à masse*). It was rare for him to own any books, and his
elementary education had been neglected. In the period 1660–80, in the
parish of Saint-Martin, which was where the merchants lived, 60 percent of the marriage contracts bore signatures; in the parish of Saint-
Rémy, where the inhabitants were a mixture of *bourgeois* and manual
workers, the proportion was 40 percent; but in the parish of Saint-Leu,
which was "popular" in character, only 20 percent could sign their
names. The parish priests kept charity schools, which were developing
during the second half of Louis XIV's reign.

The journeymen lived in a single room, with mud walls, and kept
themselves warm with fires of peat. They were practically illiterate.
The community of the craft did not function so far as they were concerned, and they tried to form organizations of their own.

In Normandy, in the first half of the 17th century, officials exercising
very subordinate functions or doing clerical work of a very routine
nature seem to have been at a level corresponding to that of the *fabricants:* the *huissiers* in the *bailliages* and *vicomtés*, the *huissiers collec-
teurs de finances*, and the attorneys in the *bailliages*, *vicomtés*, and
élections; the municipal officials of Rouen; the brokers for cider and
other fruit drinks, the sellers and searchers of fruit and counters of
oranges; the *officiers de la grande et petite charrue*, the moneyers in the
Rouen mint.

Markedly lower in the scale, at a level corresponding perhaps to that
of the *fabricants-façonniers* or the master craftsmen, were the *huissiers* in the admiralty of France, the *huissiers* in the department of
waters and forests, and the measurers in the salt storehouses, who
married artisans' daughters with dowries of between 250 and 500 livres.

Finally, at the level of the most modest master craftsmen, carders or
cobblers, and of the journeymen, seem to have been the royal bailiffs
(*sergents*) of the *aides* and *tailles* in the *élections*, those in the minor
centers of the king's authority, the *huissiers-audienciers* in those
courts, the *archers* employed in connection with the *gabelle*, and the
sworn surveyors in the *bailliage*. They married girls with dowries of
200 livres at most, who, being illiterate, signed with a "mark," and
whose parents are recorded with no qualification. These lower court
officials and minor domanial officials thus formed an existence group
with the artisans in a small way of business and the journeymen of the
crafts.

In Orléans in 1789 the making of knitwear was, in principle, organized on the corporative and craft basis. An *arrêt* of the Council in 1769 merged into a single community the crafts of making knitwear with knitting needles and with looms. The *arrêt* provided that two *jurés* should be drawn from the "merchants" and two from the "*fabricants,*" meaning artisans who owned looms. But these descriptions bore little correspondence to reality, owing to the effects of commercial concentration in the industry. Everyday talk distinguished between the wholesalers and the *façonniers,* or workmen. The wholesalers called themselves *fabricants faisant commerce* and wrote that "the jobbing *fabricants* are, strictly speaking, only workmen paid wages by the merchants."

The craft system was moribund, and so was the corporation. Internal conflicts were disrupting the craft, which was in a state of anarchy. The wholesalers seemed to be concerned only to pay the workmen the lowest wages possible, and everything happened as though there was a tacit agreement among them to this end. The workmen were still on the extreme verge of poverty. Very little was needed to unbalance a budget pared to the barest necessities. The life-styles of the wholesaler and the workmen were in utter contrast. The workmen ate wholemeal bread made of a mixture of wheat and rye, while the *bourgeois* ate white bread. The workman wore trousers and a smock, made of hempen cloth in summer and a mixture of wool and hemp—drugget or *poulangis*—in winter, woolen stockings, and caps dyed red (the brightest color). The *bourgeois* wore knee breeches, a jacket, made of woolen cloth or fine linen, and a hat; his stockings were cotton or silk, depending on circumstances and fashion.

The *bourgeois* despised the workman. The wholesalers wrote in a memorandum to the authorities regarding one of the many conflicts in the craft: "Many of these workmen cannot read or write. Most of them are so poor that they are not even listed in the municipal tax roll. Many are in receipt of charity and the bread given by the parish. Who are these 'members of the community' to assert a claim to govern it?" The workmen hated the *bourgeois.* The *façonniers* presented a memorandum to the authorities:

> The poverty to which the workmen have been reduced is due solely
> to the harshness of the knitwear merchant. The knitwear workers,
> in the most cruel distress, seeing the wickedness of the merchants,
> who have reduced what they pay for their work, and being aware that
> they have increased their sales and that the price of all qualities

of wool has fallen by five or six sous, so that it is only pure
knavery done to increase their vile fortunes, do not know what to
do in their wretchedness, treated, as they are, with contempt by
the merchants, who use unbridled insulting language toward them.

Here it may indeed be possible to speak of an antagonism between
bourgeois and proletarian and of a class struggle.

In the countryside

In Beauvaisis in the 17th century, we find at the top of the category of
manual workers a group of large tenant farmers who were also collectors of dues for the *seigneuries*. Some of these even seem to have
been intermediaries between the manual workers and the *bourgeois*.
Between 1694 and 1726, Claude Dumesnil, a tenant farmer at Goincourt-
des-Dames-de-Saint-Paul and also on behalf of some *bourgeois*, cultivated a hundred hectares by means of two ploughmen, two carters, and
a dozen horses. He had 20 cows, 6 pigs, and 225 sheep, worth 2,500
livres in all. He had taken the farm of the receiver-generalship of the
seigneurie and collected two-thirds of the tithe and of the seignorial and
feudal dues. His tenant farms were worth 1,200 livres *tournois* and 40
hectoliters of wheat. He was also the creditor, for 2,691 livres, of
various day laborers and vinegrowers—36 families at Goincourt and 41
in five neighboring villages. He possessed a few works of piety and
also some books on travel and geography. All the members of the
Dumesnil family combined the functions of *laboureurs* and collectors
of dues for the *seigneuries*. In the 17th century all these *laboureurs-
receveurs* were busy gathering tenant farms into large units of exploitation and uniting their families by marriage.

Beneath this group came the ordinary *laboureurs,* corresponding to
the *fabricants* of Beauvais. Each of these cultivated, on the average,
about thirty hectares of land with four horses. He raised a few head of
cattle and a score of sheep. In a good year he made enough to live on
for himself and his family from the first of his three crops.

Lower still, proportionately equivalent to the petty *fabricant-
façonnier* of Beauvais, came the petty *laboureur*. His ownership of two
horses harnessed to a plough gave him this title of *laboureur*, which
was a source of pride to a peasant. He cultivated about ten hectares
and raised a few cattle and pigs and between twenty and thirty sheep.
He owned a house. In order to live, however, he needed also to take up

some small tenancies and to do a second job as grain broker (*blatier*), carrier, or "merchant" sergemaker.

Beneath the *laboureurs* were the successive strata of middle peasants. First ranked the *haricotiers*. A kind of dignity apparently set them above the ordinary workmen in the town, because they lived by cultivating their land and did not need to enter anyone else's service at the time of the grain harvest or the wine harvest. A *haricotier* owned some plots of land and farmed others, cultivating in all between two and eight hectares. He worked with a mare, a mule, or a donkey. He raised a small number of animals—three or four cattle, about ten sheep, a few pigs—and was therefore able to sell a calf, some lambs, a few piglets. But he found it hard to support his family and needed to take on a second job—as cartwright, farrier, cooper, tailor, or weaver—in one or another of the rural crafts.

Beneath the *haricotiers* we come to the vinegrowers of the area around Beauvais. They formed dynasties interlinked by marriage, being an almost endogamous group. They cultivated small vineyards which they owned themselves and also worked occasionally on vines belonging to others. With their work as vinegrowers they combined a little gardening, growing beans and cabbages between two rows of vines. They cultivated a few pieces of arable land.

Beneath the vinegrowers, the *airiers,* or market gardeners, formed the third stratum of the middle peasants. They were landowners on the tiniest scale. They formed endogamous dynasties. Public opinion placed them above the day laborers.

The small peasants were day laborers, proportionately equivalent to the workmen of Beauvais but ranking lower in social esteem. The day laborer was a country-dweller, without any special trade, who worked for others at tasks that might be routine or seasonal or intermittent: tedding, reaping, grape-picking, threshing. He owned a house, a cowshed, a garden, even a few bits of land. He raised a cow, some poultry, and three or four ewes, for the fleece and the lambs. His work on the land did not suffice to maintain his family, so he also worked as a sergemaker, as a weaver of light cloth (*mulquinier*), or as a linen-weaver (as a sergemaker or *mulquinier* in the winter months, as a day laborer in the summer). The sergemaking loom was in the main room of his house, the linen loom in the cellar. Sergemakers and *mulquiniers* were either jobbers, employed by the merchants from whom they bought their woolen or flaxen yarn, or else ordinary wageworkers, who did not even own their looms and received their yarn from a local agent for the merchants, to whom they handed over the length of cloth when completed. In a village of some few hundred inhabitants one might thus find two large tenant farmers, five or six ordinary *laboureurs,* a score of *haricotiers,* and between twenty and fifty families whose members were both day laborers and weavers of serge or linen.

In the Bocage region of Maine in the 18th century, there were, at the very summit of peasant society, *laboureurs fermiers,* who were locally still called *métayers* (sharecroppers), though here the *métairie* was always a farm of more than ten hectares. These *laboureurs* made up about a fifth of the peasant population. They led a relatively comfortable life, with plenty of household chattels, furniture, and linen. Their good position was due to the fact that they enjoyed hereditary succession in their farms. The same farm was let for several generations without a break to the same family. True, the landowner was in principle free to dismiss his tenant when the lease ran out and to give the *métairie* to another man. However, the peasants took a very poor view of such conduct. Decent peasants would not outbid a tenant who had been dismissed by his landlord. Whoever took the risk of doing so might well find one day that his livestock had been slaughtered as they grazed or see, one dark night, his barns mysteriously burst into flames. Accordingly, more often than not the landlord, given the difficulty of finding a new tenant, refrained from dismissing the one he had but let him stay for his lifetime and then gave the lease to his son.

These tenant farmers were highly respected in the countryside. They were independent, had no need to hire themselves out in order to live, and, moreover, were employers of labor. One of them would be addressed as "Maître So-and-so." He maintained a permanent staff of at least two, and during the busiest time of the year he engaged a few day laborers as well. Though he worked with his hands no less than the men employed, he was already an enterpreneur, an organizer, and this gave him a special place in the countryside. He owned little land but was frequently the syndic of his community or the churchwarden of his parish.

On the same level with these *fermiers-laboureurs* must be placed the linen-manufacturers of "towns" such as Mamers, which were actually mere rural market centers. These men owned four or five looms, which they employed a few workmen to operate in the cellars of their houses. They themselves worked all day at their craft, but they had some working capital, some money in hand, which enabled them to buy hemp and hempen yarn. Their situation was comparable to that of the *fermiers-laboureurs*. At Mamers in 1789 there were 48 of these *fabricants*, who employed a total of 308 journeymen, 6 or 7 to each *fabricant*.

The second stratum of the peasant hierarchy consisted of the *bordagers* or *closiers*, who made up three-fifths of the peasant population. They were small peasants who were still relatively independent. They cultivated between five and ten hectares of land. In some cases they were landowners, but mostly they were tenants. They drew an income of 300 to 350 livres from their work. After paying their rent and tithe and the seignorial dues, they still managed to make the minimum needed to keep a family—242 livres, on the average. In a normal year they could get by on what they produced, with the help of their families, from the land they cultivated. They were their own masters and therefore enjoyed a certain prestige.

At the same level as one of these, because his situation was similar, was the *"maître-fabricant à son compte"* in one of the so-called towns already mentioned. These were independent craftsmen, owners of their looms, which they operated in their cellars with the help of members of their families. They wove cloth on their own account, illegally, without affixing any trademark, and despite the inspectors of manufactures they managed to produce and market, fraudulently, thousands of lengths of cloth.

Below them, the fourth stratum was that of the day laborers and foresters, who made up about a fifth of the peasant population.

The day laborers (*journaliers*) owned or leased a house and garden and sometimes a few plots of land, which they cultivated, but the bulk of their resources came from the wages they earned, so that they were the most dependent of all. Their livelihood was a precarious one. If the harvest was good, they found plenty of work. If it was bad, they might be reduced to beggary, and there was indeed no clear line between this category and that of the beggars.

At the same level as these day laborers were the journeymen weavers of the "towns."

The foresters, woodcutters, clogmakers, blacksmiths, and glassmakers were almost as numerous as the cultivators of the land. In the Bocage region of Maine there were some very large ironworks, such as the Comorin works at Champrond, near Montmirail, which was supplied with fuel from the forest of Vibraye. In 1788–89 this works produced from 200 to 500 *tonnes* of iron annually. It employed 15 specialists, who were called *maîtres-forgerons*, and between 100 and

150 woodcutters, charcoal-burners, and carters. Besides the iron-works, there were glassworks. The Lapierre glassworks at Con-trelieux, fueled from the forest of Lapierre, employed 10 "master smiths" and 40 workmen, plus 25 woodcutters in the winter and 10 carters in the spring.

These workmen were always on the move. They lived in shacks and were notorious for their bad behavior, their women, their drunkenness, and their poaching—and also for their unrest, since they were always ready to revolt. The great troubles of 1792 started in the forests of eastern Maine and spread from there into Beauce and central Maine. The journeymen weavers were also very restless, always rebelling against the regulations governing their work. Whenever there was a change in the tariff or the procedure, they made trouble, for, being unable to read or write, they always assumed that they were being cheated.

In 18th-century Lauragais it is noteworthy that it was not the tenant farmers who were at the top of the peasant hierarchy but *"maîtres-valets,"* who, from father to son, cultivated one of the *métairies* of the seignorial *domaine-proche.* The *seigneur* supplied each of these *maîtres-valets* with a house, tools, cattle, a garden, salt and oil for his family's consumption, and wages in grain and in cash. The *seigneur* took the entire crop for himself, so that, economically, the *maître-valet* was a mere wageworker. Socially, however, he and his family enjoyed special prestige among the peasants because, generation after genera-tion, this family worked directly for the *seigneur,* the master, on lands which the latter reserved for them.

In northern Burgundy, peasant society was dominated by a minority of peasants who had made money, the big *"labourers-marchands."* Wearing clogs and a smock (*la blaude*), they became rich by supple-menting their work on the land with trade in cattle and grain, which enabled them to survive agricultural crises without excessive loss. They were often *amodiateurs* of seignorial dues, and they stood to-gether against the poor peasants for abolition of common grazing rights and for enclosures. In 1788 one of them, the tenant farmer of Cîteaux, at Saint-Jean-de-Losne, began to assume the title of *écuyer.*

Directly beneath them was a stratum of specialist village craftsmen. Their numbers, their means of production, and their means of exis-tence seem to have increased considerably in the course of the 18th century. This phenomenon was perhaps due to the diminution of rights of usage in the forests, which were being thinned out and were subject to seignorial encroachments. In this region of ironworks and glass-works there was a shortage of timber, and the peasants, finding themselves increasingly unable to make their wooden implements for themselves, applied more and more to the carpenter, the joiner, and the cartwright. Between 1700 and 1789 the number of village craftsmen grew from 12 to 42 at Renève, from 31 to 57 at Talmay, and from 5 to 20 at Echalot. The number of those whose work was related to building—pit sawyers, carpenters, joiners, masons, and roofers—especially increased. The craftsmen cultivated some small plots of land and raised a few cattle and sheep, but to an ever greater extent the bulk of their resources came from the exercise of their craft. The peasant would willingly become a craftsman, for in his case this would mean proof of having risen in the world. At the same level as these craftsmen were, seemingly, the curates (*vicaires*) of the Catholic Church, who were poor and filled with a spirit of opposition, and the schoolmasters, who also acted as land experts and as bailiffs (*sergents*).

Beneath them was the stratum of small independent *laboureurs,* a social category that was in decline. Debt-ridden and ruined, they were on the way out and tended to become either *laboureurs* working for others or else day laborers.

The lower stratum of the day laborers made up three-quarters of the inhabitants of the villages. They earned 150 livres a year, including their food. Their situation was getting worse because, even if their wages were increasing, the increases did not keep up with the cost of living. Often there was no work to be had. In some villages no more than a hundred days' work was available in a year, and the day laborers had to resort to begging in order to live.

In the northern part of the kingdom, in Flanders, Cambrésis, and northern Hainault, the peasants were in 1789 mostly owners of the land they occupied. They held 32 percent of the land, the nobility 22 percent, the clergy 12 percent, and the *bourgeois* 17 percent. But their holdings were individually small. In Flanders three-fourths of the landowners were peasants. In Cambrésis, near Avesnes, 91 percent of the landowners were peasants. Of these, 70 percent owned no more than about thirty ares, in other words, a house with a small garden, but no fields for cultivation. More than 16 percent had only between one and five hectares; most of them barely two. In order to live independently in Flanders, it was necessary to have five hectares, and in Cambrésis and Hainault ten. The petty proprietors had less than five hectares, the middle-sized ones had between five and ten, and the big ones between ten and forty hectares. Thus, the majority of the peasants would not have been able to survive if, besides their own land, they had not also had some tenant farms.

At the top of the peasant hierarchy were the group of big farmers. These were usually owners of very little land, a mere few hectares, but they were tenants of vast domains. In Cambrésis the tenant farms recall to the historian the *villae* of Gallo-Roman times, for they included a smithy and spinning and weaving sheds and were to a large extent self-sufficient, so that the farmer hardly needed to concern himself with the market, except for selling his surplus product. These large tenant farmers dominated the rest of the population. The small cultivators who had no ploughteams of their own trembled before the man who was in a position to refuse to plough their land or to convey their crops to the market. The cartwright and the farrier solicited the custom of the big farmer. The day laborer lived in daily anxiety, for the farmer might refuse to give him work or to sell him grain and might even cause to be cut off the charity relief payment that the parish allowed him. In general, in Cambrésis, there was one farmer of this type in each village, a sort of kinglet. In Flanders there were several of them, four or five, each individually less powerful but together dominating the village in the same way, and it was among them that the aldermen and the churchwardens were recruited and also the *pauvrisseurs*, that is, the persons responsible for administering public assistance. They paid themselves fees for exercising these functions. They apportioned the burden of the king's taxes, laying it heavily on the poor and lightly on themselves. They assigned themselves the lion's share in common grazing rights and the communal property in general.

In principle, their leases were short—nine-year leases "*à trois, six, neuf,*" that is, terminable at intervals of three years. As in the Bocage region of Maine, however, they managed to keep lifetime tenancies and even to hold them in heredity, so to speak. The fact was that peasant opinion was emphatically opposed to the eviction of tenants. If a farmer took over a tenancy against the will of the previous tenant, the usurper, or the landlord himself, became victims of attempted arson and attacks on his cattle, his trees, his crops, and sometimes even his person. In practice, evictions were infrequent. The tenants were therefore able to limit the amount they paid in rent and to increase their profits, investing their money in the land they cultivated and improving it.

In Flanders, rents for tenant farms were payable in money. In Cambrésis they were payable in kind and were supplemented by "customs" —presentations of chickens, eggs, and fruit and the performance of services by the farmer and his family in the form of cartage, laundry, and so on. In addition, the farmer had to pay a *"pot-de-vin"* in cash, equivalent to one year's rent. He was responsible for paying all the taxes which were assessed on the land, so that he was chargeable for the "twentieths." He also had to bear all the expenses of maintaining the farm.

In Flanders, where 5 hectares were adequate to support a family, a "big" tenant farm meant one of more than 20 hectares. In Hainault and Cambrésis, where 10 hectares were needed for this purpose, it may be supposed that a "big" farm would cover at least 40 hectares. A man who cultivated 20 hectares in Flanders was an employer of wageworkers. For 20 hectares he employed a ploughman, another worker, and a maidservant, all three of whom he provided with bed and board. He also needed day laborers to clean the fields before the harvest, stake the flax, thin out the hops, tobacco, and colza, and help with the reaping and threshing. On extensive farms a shepherd was needed for the flocks, and he would rank highest on the farm after the farmer himself. The farmer and his entire family worked with their hands, too. The farmer's wife went to market, carrying vegetables in a heavy basket. Everyone took part in cleaning the fields. The farmer's sons watched the flocks, even when still children. His daughters were kept busy with household tasks and spinning. The little girls, from the age of six, spent their time spinning and looking after the babies.

The farmhouse of a large farm was usually a building standing alone, of majestic appearance. Its roof was covered with tiles, whereas the other houses in the village were thatched. It was built of brick, whereas the others were made of puddled clay or cob. And it had a big carriage gate and an enormous pigeonhouse in the form of a tower, dominating the scene. The farm buildings were extensive, but the farmer, his family, and his servants lived in conditions of discomfort. Generally speaking, even in the home of a big farmer, everyone lived and slept in one large room, where a wide fireplace provided a certain amount of warmth. In Flanders, above the cellar, a second room, known as *"la salle,"* served both for receiving visitors and for sleeping. The bakehouse was separate. The servants slept in nooks and crannies in the bakehouse, the cowsheds, and the stables.

The farm servants all ate together, along with their master. In the morning they had bread and butter with milk. At noon they had soup

and vegetables with a piece of bacon. In the evening they had bread
and butter with cheese or buttermilk. The master allowed himself one
luxury: coffee, with a little sugar in it.

For everyone the work to be done was tough, the food monotonous,
and hardship habitual. But the big farmer was able in this way to
accumulate savings and become well-to-do, and as a result his descendants could sometimes climb into the *bourgeoisie* by way of law
studies and one of the branches of the legal profession.

Below the stratum of big farmers came that of the independent
laboureurs. These were small landowners who lived by working the
land, adding to their own holding a few plots of leased land or a small
tenant farm. If the land they cultivated was all their own and they thus
had no rent to pay, it was possible for them to live in Flanders on as
little as three hectares. However, only 2 or 3 percent of them were so
situated. Most were simultaneously owners and tenants of land and
lived on at least five hectares in Flanders and on about ten in Hainault
or Cambrésis.

In the Bergues region an area of 5 hectares was equivalent to 12
mesures. The *laboureur* devoted 3 of these to wheat, which brought
him in 12 *rasières* net, after making the deductions for seedcorn and
tithe. Two *mesures* provided 16 *rasières* of oats. Two *mesures* of winter foddering or fallow were set aside for vegetables and fodder crops.
These enabled two or three cows to survive the winter and fatten up on
3 *mesures* of pasture when the fine weather came round again. One
mesure provided barley, for selling. The *laboureur* could take 5½
rasières of his wheat to market. He could feed a horse with his oats and
still have 9 *rasières* left to sell. His cows gave him three calves. He
could also sell a few cheeses and some butter. His oven enabled him to
bake his own bread. With his horse he saw to his own ploughing and
transport and those of the small neighboring *ménagers* as well. He was
self-sufficient and also gained a little money with which to pay his taxes
and to save. He was independent.

His neighbor in the Hazebrouck area or in Walloon Flanders was
even better situated, for he could put a *mesure* of his land under colza,
high-quality flax, or tobacco, the raw materials of several industries,
which sold well and for relatively high prices.

The houses of these *laboureurs* were grouped together. Their walls
had foundations of hard stone, upon which a framework of half-
timbering and lathing was erected. Cob was thrown over this and later
covered with plaster. The roof was of thatch. The interior of the house,

and the food eaten in it, were no different from those of the big tenant farmer.

At the same social level there were a certain number of craftsmen— potters, coopers, clogmakers (there were a lot of these near the forests of Normal and Avesnes), and, at Rimbaucourt, makers of matches. They were all independent entrepreneurs on a small scale, working for themselves, finding outlets for their products by hawking them around. The same applied to those of the *mulquiniers,* or weavers of fine linen, who owned several looms and employed journeymen.

Below them, the third stratum was that of the *ménagers,* who might be owners of land, but of less than 2 hectares in Flanders, or owners and tenants of less than 5 hectares in Flanders and less than 10 hectares in Hainault and Cambrésis. One of them, at Bergues, cultivated 4 *mesures* of land—1 hectare, 76 ares. From his 1 *mesure* of wheat he got 4 *rasières,* after deducting for seedcorn and tithe. From his *mesure* of oats he got 8 *rasières.* One *mesure* of pasture supported a cow during the summer. One *mesure* of winter foddering gave him potatoes and other vegetables and enabled the cow to get through the winter, though only just. If the year was a good one, the *ménager* could sell a little oats, a calf, some cheeses, and some butter, and in this way make what he needed to pay his taxes, his rent, and the expenses of ploughing— for he had to get that task done for him by a nieghboring *laboureur* or the big tenant farmer of the locality. But his wheat sufficed for only half the bread he needed, so that he had to hire himself out by the day to the neighboring farmer or else engage in some craft, together with his wife and children.

These *ménagers* provided most of the craftsmen in the villages: the farrier (who also acted as veterinary surgeon), the cartwright, the mason, the carpenter, the joiner, the thatcher, the tiler, the slater, the weavers, the dressmaker, the shoemaker, the clogmaker. From among them, too, were recruited the little retailers—the sellers of mercery, saddles, tobacco, the keeper of the drinkshop—who were all hostile to the itinerant salesman. Rural industry found among these *ménagers* the labor required for preparing tobacco and, especially, for the making of textiles. During the winter the wife and children spent their days spinning, while the husband wove. An *arrêt* of the king's Council dated 30 April 1776, confirmed by another dated 9 November 1777, authorized them to spin in the unfortified market centers (*bourgs*) and in the countryside. In Flanders they worked with coarse flax, wool, and cotton, in Hainault with high-quality flax. In 1789 there were 46,000 spinning wheels, using coarse flax, between Lille, La Bessée, Le Quesnoy, and Cassel, mainly in the towns and *bourgs;* the weaving of the linen had been left to the peasants. Between Cassel and the Lys, every cultivator had his loom; he sold his linen unbleached, either to the bleacheries along the Lys or in the local fairs. In the villages of the Lille area, 27,000 persons lived by spinning the carded wool "on the little wheel." Tourcoing had cotton spun for its cloth mills in fifty or sixty villages in Pévèle and the Saint-Amand district. Hainault and Cambrésis spun fine flax, provided by the plain of the Scarpe and the neighborhood of Saint-Amand. The little village *mulquinier-ménager,* owner of a warp beam and a loom, received yarn from a wholesale merchant, warped and wove in his cellar, along with his wife and an apprentice, and handed the cloth over to the wholesaler for a flat payment. These men made *toilettes,* that is, cambric and lawn. More than a hundred communes in Cambrésis and Hainault lived by *mulquinerie,* and about ten of them had over a hundred looms.

Below the *ménagers,* the fourth stratum was that of the day laborers. These peasants owned tiny holdings of less than a hectare, often only about thirty ares, with a house and garden. They lived by the work they were able to get from the big tenant farmers and the independent *laboureurs* and by spinning and weaving. Many of them worked in the coalmines of Vieux-Condé, Anzin, and Aniche or as woodcutters and charcoal-burners for the timber merchants, in the ironworks, or in the arms factory at Maubeuge. Their work was precarious: there were many unemployed, so wages were low. In winter, especially, it was hard to find work. And this section of the population increased very fast. On the eve of 1789 contemporaries were denouncing early marriages. Most of the younger men and women of this stratum married between the ages of sixteen and eighteen and soon had children, so that they were often forced to go begging.

The poor

One is always "poor" in relation to somebody else. Furetière wrote, in his *Dictionnaire* of 1690, that the term "poor" was used "of princes and *seigneurs* who are much embarrassed in their affairs and cannot cut the brilliant figure that suits them. A prince who has only 10,000 livres rent is poor, and passes for a beggar."

But this society included two categories of less paradoxical poor: the professional beggars and the people of the lower strata whose resources from time to time fell below the level needed in order to support them in the given social structure.

This society, which was officially Christian, professed the principle of the eminent dignity of the poor. Jesus Christ had come into the world as a poor man and had preached the Gospel to poor men. The Kingdom of God was promised particularly to *them*. The poor, and the poor in spirit, deprived of everything that makes for pride and covetousness in this world, were those who could most easily approach God and enter into his Kingdom. They were assured of eternal bliss. To show respect to them and humble oneself before them was a way of coming closer to Jesus Christ and achieving heaven. Accordingly, the poor by their condition constituted an order in society—the last and lowest, but an order nevertheless. Loyseau described this order of "sturdy beggars," "vagabonds and tramps," who live "in idleness and without care, at the expense of others." The authorities recognized this order, accorded it privileges, and discerned the hierarchy of "estates" that existed within it. In a certain town, by municipal ordinance confirmed by the *bailli,* only the blind and the lame were permitted to beg in the church porches, on account of the role played in the Gospels by persons of their sort. They formed an "estate" that was superior to that of the other beggars, who had to entreat charity farther off. In all epochs and all places one finds at the lowest level of society this order of official and privileged beggars. In 1789, in the north of France, begging was a veritable profession, and an honorable one at that. In the villages there were families of hereditary beggars. They were married and had numerous children. They arranged to be supported by the *pauvrisseur* and taught their children the beggar's trade. They swarmed in the vicinity of the abbeys, which were a reliable source of regular alms.

A certain number of them left the official organization, deserted their own parishes, and became wanderers, vagabonds, and sometimes semi-brigands, organized in gangs that lived by robbing and thieving and by alms extorted by means of threats and acts of intimidation (trees cut down, cattle mutilated, mills set on fire). In Hainault and Cambrésis the *"sommeurs"* called on the big tenant farmers, the parish priests, and the abbeys and extorted money from them by threats of arson. It was a craft, with its own technique. One of them, who did so much of it that he ended by being arrested, sentenced, and broken on the wheel, had in eight years sent twenty-three letters of extortion, each time collecting substantial sums.

The other category of poor people consisted of the persons whose

level of existence was so low that their resources were close to the
biological minimum. From time to time they fell into poverty and might
become uprooted persons, nomads, vagabonds, on a large scale. And
they made up a considerable part of the population. In Amiens between
1625 and 1635, three-fifths of the inhabitants were exempted from the
"poor tax," being themselves too poor to pay it. In the light cloth-
making industry only 155 *saîteurs* (makers of fine woolen lining), out of
1,500 weavers, masters, and journeymen, were taxed. The others must
have been in a state of destitution, since they could not pay at even the
lowest rate, which was three *deniers* a week. The winter of 1621–22
was harsh, and the municipality had to feed the needy: 1,300 men and
women, 2,050 children.

In 17th-century Beauvaisis, in good years, one-tenth of the woolen
workers had to be helped by the Bureau des Pauvres. Their actual
wages were, indeed, always lower than the official wage level fixed by
the seignorial *bailli* at ten sous, from 1640 to 1715. Good weavers and
sergemakers received only nine sous, and those who were aged or not
very good received still less—six or seven sous. Spinning-women were
paid three sous; little girls and old women, one sou. Moreover, their
wages were paid not wholly in cash but partly in wine, meat, and cloth,
plus a few farthings, which gave opportunities for reducing wages still
further. There were about 270 working days in the year. The good
worker thus had seven and a half sous for each day of the year. His
lodging, his obligatory payments, his salt, and the tax to maintain the
army took one sou from him. Wholemeal bread, his basic food, cost
half a sou a pound in good years. Each person needed four pounds
daily. The worker could thus buy thirteen pounds of it each day. If he
had only two children and his wife earned two or three sous at spinning, the family managed all right. If, however, he had many children,
they were in difficulties. Poorly fed, the worker worked in places that
were badly lit, paved, and heated and were damp and airless. Perni-
cious fevers ravaged entire streets. And it took only one illness or one
increase in prices to ruin this precarious livelihood. When the price of
bread doubled, that meant misery. It doubled at Beauvais in 1609,
1618, 1623, 1627, 1631, 1632, 1643, 1647, 1674, 1679, 1699, 1714, and
1720. It trebled in 1649, 1651, 1661, and 1662. It quadrupled in 1693,
1694, and 1710. Moreover, in times of dearth, it was customary to
reduce wages, and, since these were periods of bad trade, unemploy-
ment increased. Many workers had to resort to begging.

In the rural areas of Beauvaisis the day laborers and smallholders were at the mercy of one or two poor harvests. They soon became incapable of supporting their families and head over heels in debt to the farmer and the wool merchant. During *mortalités* they died in great numbers, of hunger or some epidemic. They begged and became uprooted persons, nomads and tramps, and many of them were never able to recover their previous situations. It was among this category that in the Bocage region of Maine, in the 18th century, the *logistes* were recruited—wretched people who installed themselves on the moors and built a place to live in—a mere shack, half-covered with straw and surrounded by stacks of sod, a structure often ruined by rain and hail. They slept on a bed of straw and ferns, the whole family huddled together to keep warm. Without any linen, they were dressed only in rags. These people were no longer even peasants.

In the north in 1789, a large section of the day laborers were obliged to beg as a regular thing. More than 20 percent of the population were regularly relieved by the parish from the poor fund. Begging was an almost permanent resource for widows burdened with children, for old people, and for the sick, and in some villages for all the poor. Even a considerable number of *ménagers,* even farmers who owned two cows, were from time to time obliged to beg in order to make ends meet.

In all the provinces throughout these two centuries, during crises and *mortalités,* "periodical" beggars—workmen, day laborers—reinforced the professional beggars who had left their own parishes. Gangs were formed, which roamed the country extorting money from the big farmers, the parish priests who received tithes, and the *seigneurs.* In broad daylight, hordes of them would surround harvesters, on the pretext of gleaning, and plunder the sheaves. A moral atmosphere of insecurity, anguish, and fear filled the countryside. This was the prelude to the agrarian revolts.

From 1680 onward, writers argued that society was responsible for poverty, that it ought to reform its economy and fiscal system so as to get rid of the problem of the poor, and that, in the meantime, the state had a duty to relieve them. After 1730 the literature devoted to the poor and the beggars became abundant. The writers accused the poor and the beggars of laziness and sloth, of constituting a danger to property and to agriculture—a concern to a society in which happiness achieved through a high standard of living and, therefore, the production of material goods were becoming the essential values, taking the place of the Christian values. The problem was therefore one of training the poor and the beggars to get used to work and of procuring work for the sturdy beggars to do, in the first place by establishing charity work-shops and organizing "field gangs," to be assigned to agricultural labor. Charity offices were to provide immediate assistance and poor persons' savings banks, to give them the opportunity to provide for their future needs. Many of these writers, however, called for rigorous repression of begging and vagrancy, with arrest and internment for stranger beggars and vagabonds, suspected of being thieves and brigands—a dangerous lot.

In this society of orders, social mobility was limited, and rising in the social scale was a slow business, but such changes did happen—as an affair of families, however, rather than of individuals. In Besançon, for example, offices in the *parlement* could be attained, as a rule, only after a gradual climb by a whole family, often involving a halt of two or three generations at each stage. The social ascent took place by mounting from one degree of dignity to the next, in accordance with the con-sensus of the society of orders.

The decisive step was taken when a member of a family succeeded in attaining the rank of advocate, which meant that he had graduated from a university. "Advocate" was a title of some prestige, for the profes-sion was not incompatible with nobility, and many who bore this title did not practice but "lived like nobles." There was a gap between the advocates and, below them, the "practitioners," who had attended grammar classes at high school but had not studied the humanities and had not proceeded to a university. These practitioners were placed in the category of attorneys, *huissiers*, notaries, and other minor law-court officials, a category which, moreover, had its own hierarchy. All of them were "base" (*vils*), since theirs were tasks of procedure and execution; they had no share in judgment or command. There was something mechanical about them, and a certain analogy could be drawn between them and the manual workers. Advocates, however, played a part in stating the law. Theirs was an honorable function.

In the upward march toward offices in the *parlement* there were very few sons, or descendants, of merchants. Generally speaking, it was sons of peasants and craftsmen who became practitioners. Often, they and their sons remained practitioners for two or three generations. But they might become clerks to attorneys, notaries, secretaries to advo-cates or magistrates, clerks in the *bureau des finances*, business agents of noblemen. A practitioner who got on might become a minor official in a law court—a *huissier*, notary, or attorney—and thereby acquire a relative dignity. But a practitioner's son never entered the *parlement* or even became an advocate. A minor law-court official never entered the *parlement,* but the son of such a man might become an advocate and make his way as far as the *parlement.* Historians have recorded 6 of them out of 306 magistrates (1.86 percent). Sons of minor law-court officials became *greffiers* to the *parlement,* deputies to the *procureur général,* and magistrates in subordinate jurisdictions.

The process of social ascent required at least five generations. First, a peasant's or a craftsman's son became a practitioner. Second, the practitioner's son became a minor law-court official. Third, this man's son became an advocate or a magistrate in the financial courts. Fourth, this man's son became an advocate and then a magistrate in a subordinate jurisdiction. Fifth, this man's son became an advocate—and a counselor in the *parlement.*

Often, though, the family remained for several generations stuck at the same stage.

In the *parlement* of Besançon, 3 percent of the magistrates were sons of doctors, big merchants, shopkeepers, ironmasters. In the main, however, lineages rose in the world within the setting of the judiciary: it was to the gown much more than to business or finance that lineages owed their elevation.

Notes

1. G. Lefebvre, *Les paysans du Nord pendant la Révolution française* (1924), chap. 9, p. 307.
2. Deyon, *Amiens, capitale provinciale* (Mouton, 1967), p. 344.
3. Ibid.

Guide to further reading

To the works mentioned after Chapters 4 and 5, especially those by Aulard, Bois, Baehrel, Deyon, Fontenay, Merle, Roupnel, De Saint-Jacob, Sagnac, Sée, Senton, Soboul, and Vénard, add the following:

Abbiatecci, A., et al. "Crimes et criminalité en France, XVIIᵉ, XVIIIᵉ siècles," *Cahiers des Annales* no. 33. Armand Colin, 1971.
Bercé, Yves-Marie. *Histoire des Croquants: Etude des soulèvements populaires au XVIIᵉ siècle, dans le Sud-Ouest de la France.* Paris and Geneva: Librairie Droz, 1974.

Bouchard, Gérard. *Le village immobile: Sennely-en-Sologne au XVIIIe siècle.* Plon, 1972.

Castan, Yves. *Honnêteté et relations sociales en Languedoc, 1715–1780.* Collection "Civilisations et mentalités." Plon, 1974.

Coornaert, Emile! *Les corporations en France avant 1789.* 2d ed. Editions Ouvrières, 1968.

Couturier, Marcel. *Recherches sur les structures sociales de Châteaudun, 1525–1789.* S.E.V.P.E.N., 1969.

Daumard, Adeline, and Furet, François. *Structures et relations sociales à Paris au XVIIIe siècle.* Armand Colin, 1961. (On this highly questionable work, see Roland Mousnier, "Problèmes de méthode dans l'étude des structures sociales des XVIe, XVIIe, XVIIIe siècles," an article written in 1964, now reprinted in *La Plume, la faucille et le marteau* [P.U.F., 1970], pp. 12–26.)

Faure, Edgar. *La disgrâce de Turgot.* Series "Trente Journées qui ont fait la France." Gallimard, 1961.

Goubert, Pierre. *Familles de marchands sous l'Ancien Régime: Les Danse et les Motte de Beauvais.* S.E.V.P.E.N., 1959.

Gutton, Jean-Pierre. *La société et les pauvres: L'exemple de la généralité de Lyon (1534–1789).* Les Belles Lettres, 1970.

Jacquart, Jean. *Société et vie rurale dans le sud de la région parisienne du milieu du XVIe siècle au milieu du XVIIe siècle.* 2 vols. Service de reproduction des thèses, University of Lille-III, 1973.

——. *La crise rurale en Ile-de-France, 1550–1670.* Armand Colin, 1974.

Kleinclausz, Arthur. *Histoire de Lyon.* 3 vols. Lyons: P. Masson, 1939–52.

Lefebvre, Georges. *Les paysans du Nord pendant la Révolution français.* Rieder, 1924.

Lefebvre-Teillard, Anne. *La population de Dole au XVIIe siècle.* Travaux et Recherches de la Faculté de Droit et des Sciences Economiques de Paris, "Sciences Historiques" series, no. 19. P.U.F., 1969.

Leroy-Ladurie, Emmanuel. *Paysans du Languedoc.* Imprimerie Nationale, 1966. (Abridged English translation, *The Peasants of Languedoc.* Urbana: University of Illinois Press, 1974.)

Martin-Saint-Léon, Etienne. *Histoire des corporations de métier.* 4th ed. 1941.

Olivier-Martin, François. *L'organisation corporative de la France d'Ancien Régime.* Sirey, 1938.

Pillorget, René. *Les mouvements insurrectionels de Provence entre 1596 et 1715.* Editions A. Pedone, 1975.

Poitrineau, Abel. *La vie rurale en Basse-Auvergne au XVIIIe siècle (1726–1789).* 2 vols. P.U.F., 1965.

Robin, Régine. *Semur-en-Auxois.* Plon, 1970.

Sheppard, Thomas F. *Lourmarin in the Eighteenth Century: A Study of a French Village.* Baltimore: Johns Hopkins University Press, 1971.

Vénard, Marc. *Bourgeois et paysans au XVIIe siècle: Recherches sur le rôle des bourgeois parisiens dans le vie agricole au Sud de Paris au XVIIe siècle.* S.E.V.P.E.N., 1957.

Zink, Anne. *Azereix: La vie d'une communauté rurale à la fin du XVIIIe siècle.* Ecole Pratique des Hautes-Etudes, Démographie et Sociétés, no. 9. S.E.V.P.E.N., 1969.

7

The Society of Orders
The Catholic Clergy

The ecclesiastical order was the Lord God's portion—those who had devoted themselves to his service, to worshiping and praising him, to sacrificing in his honor and propagating his Word. The order was composed of those persons whom God loved so much that he had given them, by his grace, the capacity to love him, in return, more than anything else, to choose him for their lot on earth, devoting their lives wholly to him—and who had responded to God's grace. They were therefore persons presenting a spiritual character, a quality which was a dignity: the total giving of themselves to the service of God, their protector, master, and lord—a life devoted to God. This spiritual character constituted a sign marking them off from the other members of society. It was well defined by what were called the "irregularities," meaning canonical impediments to the taking of orders. Only the most holy-living of laymen could be received and accepted as clergy. Those who had seriously succumbed to the seductions and temptations of this world were "irregular," incapable of taking orders; for example, persons who, having been baptized, had thereafter committed some crime —heresy, apostasy, homicide, adultery—and this even after doing penance and being reconciled with the Church; persons who had killed someone, even involuntarily, by accident; those who had borne arms, even in a just war; those who, sitting as judges, had caused a criminal to be put to death; those who were "bigamous," meaning married for a second time; and so on. All these actions constituted proof that God had not been, in all circumstances, first and foremost in the thoughts and cares of the guilty or inadequate person, that he had not loved God above all else; and so he could not take orders. The ecclesiastical order thus appeared as a response to God's grace, as a giving of oneself to God for the purpose of exercising on earth the functions associated with the worship of God. It meant consecration to the worship of God, induced by grace and sanctioned by the special graces of this condition.

There were degrees in the graces of God, corresponding to purposes beyond our ken. Men's responses to these graces also varied, in accordance with their free will. There were, therefore, ranks in the ecclesiastical order—a hierarchy of internal orders. The major, or holy, orders were those of bishop, priest, deacon, and subdeacon. The minor orders were those of acolyte, lector, exorcist, porter, and mere tonsured cleric. Membership in the ecclesiastical order must not be confused with function. A bishop could exercise the functions of archbishop or primate; a priest could exercise those of parish priest (*curé*), hospital manager, head of a monastery, penitentiary, or archpriest. But order was fundamentally different from function. It meant a spiritual character, a quality, a dignity attached to one's person which dictated a certain life-style (the tonsure, the long garment, and so on) and rendered one able to fulfill certain religious functions, from which a social element was inseparable. As Loyseau puts it very well, ecclesiastical orders were "true and pure orders, that is, dignities [with] . . . capacity to possess benefices."

"Orders" and "estates" have existed in many societies with nothing Christian about them, and in France they appeared and developed spontaneously within society. It is nevertheless true that in France they owed a great deal to canon law and to the hierarchy of the Roman Catholic Church, which helped political writers to define certain fundamental elements of the concept of an order, namely: a quality attached to the person and constituting a relative dignity; a life-style resulting from this; and, consequently, a capacity to fulfill certain aspects of the social division of labor. The ecclesiastical order thus set apart a whole section of the population, who were recruited from among the lay orders.

The law of the ecclesiastical order

The ecclesiastical order was organized in accordance with its own special law—that of the Church, or "canon law"—with some exceptions which constituted the "liberties of the Gallican Church." The Church distinguished between divine natural law, divine positive law, and human positive law. Divine natural law was the light cast by reason on what we owe to God and to mankind. The rule of right reason was thus the eternal wisdom of God, creator of nature. Divine positive law was that which it had pleased God to ordain for mankind; it was contained in the Holy Scriptures, the Old and New testaments, interpreted by the tradition of the Church transmitted by the Apostles to the bishops, from age to age. The greater part of divine positive law consisted of natural law, as briefly set out in the Ten Commandments, interpreted by the moral precepts of the Old Testament, and given perfect form by Jesus Christ. Human positive law consisted of customs observed by tacit consent and mere usage, together with written constitutions. As regards the Church, it consisted of the canons of the Church councils, mainly the ecumenical ones, the papal constitutions, the ordinances, mandates, and pastoral letters of bishops, the statutes of synods, and the rules of the religious orders.

Natural law and divine positive law were to be obeyed absolutely, for they formed the conditions for salvation. Provided these were not affected, however, any exception might be made where human positive law was concerned. Authority ought to suspend the application of the laws wherever, in its view, the fate of a soul was at stake. For the canonists, law was a rule subject to exceptions in particular cases. A given individual might be exempted from a law without that law's losing its general power and virtue. The pope was able to grant dispensations, for he could legislate *supra jus, contra jus,* and *extra jus* and therefore had the power to issue an "indult," a license to make a particular departure from a general law.

The ecclesiastical hierarchy:
The secular clergy

The clergy, set apart to serve the Lord, after showing their desire to serve God for his own sake, had to have received the sacrament of confirmation and had to be able to read and write. Persons were classed as "irregular," that is, unable to be clerics (to take orders or to fulfill the functions of such orders as they might have taken), if, apart from the crimes or faults listed earlier, any of the following descriptions applied to them: being married to a widow or to a woman who was well known not to be a virgin; having been baptized only when ill; being heavily burdened with debt and embarrassed in business; suffering from physical defects—being deaf, dumb, blind, deformed, voluntarily castrated or otherwise mutilated, epileptic, mad, or possessed by the Devil (even if subsequently cured); not born in lawful wedlock, or legitimized by subsequent marriage of parents; being a slave or a serf (unless his master or lord gave consent); being a monk (unless his superior gave consent); not being of the age required. But there were many dispensations.

The bishop conferred on the new cleric his spiritual character and the outward signs of his new order—the tonsure, the surplice, and the alb—with prayers and church ceremonies. The tonsure was the symbol of renunciation of the world and participation in Christ's kingship through sacrifice of man's most beautiful ornament. The decrees of the Council of Trent obliged all who held benefices to be tonsured and to wear clerical dress, "so as to show the inward worthiness and rectitude of their morals by the outward propriety of their costume." By taking the tonsure, a layman became a cleric, passed under the jurisdiction of the Church, and acquired its privileges. The duty of an ordinary cleric was to take part, wearing his surplice, in the offices of the Church and to carry out the functions of the four minor orders, if those who had taken those orders failed to do so. The ordinary cleric might be married, provided that he did not aspire to a benefice.

The four minor orders were, in ascending order, those of porter, lector, exorcist, and acolyte. The Council of Trent had recommended that they be reestablished in all churches, owing to the importance of everything that impresses the senses: beauty of buildings, orderliness of assemblies, silence, singing, majestic ceremonies. "All of these help even the most spiritual to raise themselves toward God, and they are absolutely necessary for coarse persons, in order to give them a lofty idea of religion and cause them to love the practice thereof." The Council had prescribed that "married clerics be employed, if no others can easily be found," and required that they should at least understand Latin.

The porter had to guard the church day and night, taking care that nothing be taken from it; to open and shut the church and the sacristy;

to look to the cleanliness and decoration of the church; to ring the bells to mark the hours for the various prayers; to ensure that everyone kept to his place and that silence and modesty were observed; to prevent unbelievers from entering the church, disturbing the ceremonies, or profaning the mysteries; and to open the book for the preachers. His functions could be entrusted to laymen.

The lector was responsible for keeping the holy books, reading aloud for the preacher, chanting the lessons, and blessing bread and first-fruits brought to the church. He acted as secretary to the priests and bishops.

The exorcist's task was to exorcise persons possessed by the Devil, by the laying-on of hands; to exorcise catechumens before baptism; to heal the sick; to warn those who were not taking Holy Communion to let others approach the altar; and to pour water for the priest saying Mass. In practice, only priests exorcised, by special commission from the bishop.

The acolyte had to carry the candlesticks, light the candles, prepare the wine and the water for Mass, burn incense, serve the subdeacons at the altar, and carry the Eucharist. It fell to him also to carry messages for the bishops and likewise the pieces of consecrated bread sent as a symbol of communion.

Members of the minor orders did not assume an irrevocable commitment. They could marry, but by doing so they renounced the privileges of the clergy.

The major, or holy, orders were, in ascending order, those of subdeacon, deacon, priest, and bishop. Those who took them were committed for life. Three obligations were common to all of them: to remain chaste, to possess a *titre* (that is, to have an assured livelihood), and to say every day the whole office of the Church, at least in private.

If one of them should marry, the marriage was annulled and a penance was imposed for it. If he had children, they were considered illegitimate and incapable of receiving an inheritance or benefiting from a deed of gift. For a married man to be ordained as subdeacon, it was necessary for his wife to agree and for her, too, to take a vow of chastity and then to enter a convent.

Since it was not "proper that those admitted to the service of God should, to the disgrace of their profession, be obliged to beg or to earn their living in a sordid occupation," the Council of Trent had laid it down that no cleric should be advanced to holy orders "unless it be juridically proved beforehand that he possesses in peace a benefice adequate to support him worthily." A bishop could ordain a man at his discretion, after checking on the ordinand's personal patrimony or guaranteed income, for the needs and advantages of the Church. There were therefore two kinds of ordination: ordination *"avec titre,"* for a particular church and embracing order, office, and benefice; and ordination which was *"vague"* or *"absolue,"* without any *titre* or ecclesiastical office. The doctors of the community and society of the Sorbonne were ordained priests without any *titre patrimonial,* "by right of poverty" alone, *sub titulo paupertatis Sorbonicae.* As far as the regular clergy were concerned, their profession in an approved order served as *titre,* since their monasteries were obliged to support them. Members of mendicant orders were ordained "by right of poverty."

Ordination in all the holy orders was preceded by three announcements during the sermon at the ordinand's parish church, on three successive Sundays, to discover whether he was "irregular"; then by a retreat in a seminary (a practice that became increasingly common during the first quarter of the 17th century); and, finally, by an examination carried out by the bishop or his delegate. Ordination was effected by the laying-on of hands, with the prayer: "Receive the Holy Spirit, so that you may have the strength to resist the Devil and his temptations."

One had to be at least a subdeacon in order to handle the sacred vessels and cloths directly involved in the Holy Eucharist. The subdeacon had to have been tested in all the minor orders, to be at least twenty-two years old, to be educated, and to present testimonials of good conduct from his parish priest and his masters. On the day he was ordained, the bishop warned him: "Up to this moment you have been free to return to the secular condition; but if you receive this order, you will not be able to return. You will always have to serve God, whose service is worth more than a kingdom, to preserve your chastity with his help, and to remain committed forever to the ministry of the Church." The subdeacon had to prepare the water for the service of the altar, wash the altar cloth and communion cloth (the sacred cloth held under the chalice before the offertory, so as to receive the Host and any crumbs that may fall from it), pick up, on this cloth, with the paten, the pieces of the Host in order to place them in the chalice before the consumption, present the chalice and the paten to the deacon for the sacrifice, and place upon the altar the pieces of consecrated bread for the people.

A deacon had to be in his twenty-third year and to have been a subdeacon. He stood in the place of the Levites of old, the Lord's own tribe. He had to serve at the altar, distribute the Holy Eucharist, instruct catechumens, baptize, preach, guard and carry the tabernacle containing the Holy Eucharist, look after the temporal property of the Church and its charitable works; watch over the congregation so as to alert the bishop to any quarrels or scandalous sins; and convey the bishop's orders and accompany him on his journeys.

A priest had to be in his twenty-fifth year and to have been a deacon for at least a year. Priests stood in the place of the seventy elders assigned to Moses in order to help him guide the people, and of the seventy-two disciples of Christ. "Inasmuch as you will henceforth celebrate the mystery of the death of the Lord, mortify your members, with the passions and lusts thereof" (Ritual of Ordination). The functions of bishops being many, they delegated them to the priests who were their assistants and who exercised the same functions as they did, apart from two which were reserved to bishops alone, namely, the confirmation of Christians by giving them the Holy Spirit through the laying-on of hands, and the ordaining of clergy—deacons, priests, and bishops. The bishop consecrated the palms of the priest's hands with "the oil of catechumens," a pure olive oil, so that these hands might be made able to bless, consecrate, and sanctify.

It was necessary for a certain number of the priests of a diocese to live with their bishop in order to help and advise him; these were the "canonical" priests, the canons—those who lived according to a Rule and, together, formed a chapter. Unlike monks, canons did not take a vow of poverty or stability, but they did obey a Rule and live a common life. Or, at least, they resided near the church, and part of their property was made common, constituting the *manse capitulaire,* the chapter messuage destined to provide for common expenses. The canons formed a corporation. Their functions were to celebrate mass, to advise the bishop, and to govern the diocese in the event of there being no bishop. Their privileges were exemption from the bishop's jurisdiction and the exercise of a jurisdiction over their own corporation and, in part, over the diocese. This was the chapter's "officiality" for spiritual and ecclesiastical jurisdiction. Most chapters held a court of temporal justice in their cloister. In Paris it was called *la barre du chapitre,* in Brittany *le régaire.* They sometimes had a provost to administer temporal justice and, almost always, a dean for the spiritual side. The functions of archdeacon, archpriest, and chancellor for the sealing of letters were regarded as chapter dignities. The bishop had a senior cleric, the *primicerius notariorum*, at his disposal for secretarial work, for the clergy were, in principle, the bishop's secretaries and scribes. He had a senior deacon, the archdeacon, who was his chief agent for the administration of the temporal side of his affairs and the exercise of his jurisdiction. He had a senior priest, or archpriest. Vicars general (*grands vicaires*) were entrusted with his voluntary jurisdiction, while "officials" (ecclesiastical judges) were commissioned to look after the contentious jurisdiction. Some were vicars forane, or rural deans, in the countryside. A "penitentiary," or confessor general, received the priests' confessions, and those of laymen in reserved cases, and prescribed penances. Every cathedral church had to have a grammar master to teach the clergy free of charge; this was the *scholasticus* or the chancellor. Every cathedral church had to have an expert in divinity (the *théologal*) to teach the Scriptures. He was supposed to preach on Sundays and solemn festivals and, three times a week, to give a public lecture on the Scriptures. However, these teaching functions were usually looked after by the colleges, universities, and seminaries.

Most of the secular priests were *curés*, that is, in charge of parishes.

The bishops, often referred to as "pastors" or "pontiffs," were the successors of the twelve Apostles. They were established by God in order to sanctify others and lead them to eternal life. They possessed all the spiritual power that Jesus Christ had conferred on his Apostles. The bishop's functions embraced the whole practice of the Christian religion. He had to offer, for and with Christians, the holy sacrifice of the Mass. He had to make men Christians and to nourish them with God's Word, that is, to preach and catechize. The bishop was a doctor of the Church. He had to teach Christians to pray, which meant leading all the public prayers in his church, taking part in all the offices, regulating the entire divine service, and prescribing the form of prayer to be used in families. He had to administer all the sacraments: baptism, communion, penance, marriage, extreme unction. He was the only minister qualified to confirm and to ordain. He had to bless baptismal fonts, the water, the bread, the first-fruits, the bells, the nuptial bed, women who had recently given birth, and so on. These were what were called the bishop's "internal" functions.

The bishop also had to fulfill functions that were called "external." He had to judge sinners and either reconcile them with God or else cut them off from the Church; he had to preserve the Church's purity by preventing the commission of sins and its unity by healing divisions; he had to procure the necessities of life for the poor and, for the wretched, the relief needful in order that they might apply themselves to the care of their souls.

So as to be able to fulfill these duties, the bishop possessed a jurisdiction. He was the sole ordinary and natural judge of everything concerned with the faith. He decided questions of faith or morals by interpreting Scripture in accordance with the Tradition of the Fathers. He had to examine all the books published in his diocese and approve any that dealt with religion; he also had to regulate ecclesiastical administration by means of statutes, mandatory letters, and ordinances in conformity with the general discipline of the Church and the laws of the state. It was for him to dispense from canon law in the cases permitted by that law, in matters like the banns of marriages or the intervals between two ordinations. He could make public appointments of officials or commissioners to assist him in the Church's service. He was the ordinary collator to the offices in his diocese.

The bishop had to judge persons accused of ecclesiastical offenses and punish those found guilty. In the tribunal of penance he judged the sins of those who had voluntarily accused themselves in confession. He also had to judge public sinners, even if they did not want this. It was his responsibility to correct the clergy, who owed him complete obedience. He had the right to settle differences between clergy and laymen.

The bishop was responsible for all the wretched, that is, for persons who were in difficulties and deserved compassion—widows, orphans, the poor, and aged, the mad, imbeciles, wayfarers, pilgrims, strangers. He was therefore in charge of the hospitals and of all charitable institutions.

The bishop had to look after all the temporal affairs of his diocese—tithes, offerings, alms, real estate. He received gifts and accepted endowments. He superintended that part of the Church property assigned for his own messuage.

By virtue of the Concordat of Bologna (1516), when a bishopric fell vacant, the king was obliged to present to the pope within six months the name of a doctor or licentiate in theology or in law who was in his twenty-seventh year at least. If he failed to do this, then, after a further three months had passed, the pope could freely make an appointment. According to the Ordinance of Blois, the king was not to make a nomination until the see had been vacant for a month, until his candidate's life and morals had been investigated by the bishop of the diocese in which he had lived for the previous five years and by the chapter of the cathedral where the vacancy had occurred, and until he had been examined by a bishop and two doctors of divinity. Actually, the king nominated whenever he saw fit to do so. The ecclesiastic nominated sent to Rome the report which had been made on him, together with his profession of faith and a description of the state of his cathedral, drawn up by a bishop. The king dispatched three *lettres de cachet*—one to the pope, one to his ambassador in Rome, and one to the cardinal entrusted with the protection of France.

This cardinal examined the nominee's dossier along with three other cardinals. If all four were able to state that they found him worthy of the appointment, the cardinal proposed him for the first time in the consistory; this was called the "preconization." At the next meeting of the consistory, he presented his report; this was the "proposition." The pope collected the cardinals' votes and issued his decree appointing the nominee, upon which the appropriate papal bulls were dispatched.

When the nominee received them, he swore an oath of fealty to the king. He undertook to remain his faithful subject and servant, to care for his service and the good of the state with all his might, and to take part in no counsel, design, or enterprise prejudicial to them, but, should information of any such come to his knowledge, to tell the king of it. Upon taking this oath, he received letters under the Great Seal recording it, which he caused to be registered by the *chambre des comptes,* together with a letter granting him the revenues that had fallen due while the vacancy continued; thereby he secured the lifting of the *régale* and could enter into possession of his bishopric.

The nominee had to be consecrated within three months. Consecration was the ecclesiastical ceremony that conferred on him the order of episcopacy. It took place on a Sunday in the nominee's own cathedral. A bishop, assisted by two others, carried out the ceremony. The papal bull was read. The nominee swore an oath of fealty to the Holy See. The consecrating bishop examined him as to his faith and morals. He asked him his intentions: did he mean to submit his reason to the sense of the Scriptures, to observe and teach the Traditions of the Fathers and the decrees of the Holy See, to obey the pope according to canon law, to teach his people by word and example, to practice and preach chastity, sobriety, humility, and patience, to show pity and kindness to the poor, and to be devoted to the service of God, holding himself aloof from every temporal concern and all sordid gain? Then the consecrating bishop began the Mass. After the Epistle and the Gradual, he instructed the nominee in his functions. The nominee prostrated himself. The consecrating bishop laid his hands on the nominee's head, saying: "Receive the Holy Spirit"—the essential feature of ordination. The consecrating bishop said the Preface. Then he anointed the head and hands of the new bishop with the holy oil. He handed him the pastoral staff, the ring, and the Gospel. The Mass continued with the reading of the Gospel. After the Mass, the consecrating bishop enthroned the new bishop, installing him in his episcopal chair. The bishop was thenceforth fixed and attached forever to his church, like a wife to her husband or a father to his family. He could never, by his own will, leave the church in which the Holy Spirit had placed him—neither from fear or faintheartedness nor on the pretext of seeking greater perfection. The same applied to a priest.

A bishop whom old age, illness, or some other cause rendered incapable of fulfilling his functions could be assigned a coadjutor by the pope.

The pope could translate a bishop from one see to another for the benefit of the Church. He could agree to the renunciation of his office by a bishop on grounds of incapacity (old age, illness), irregularity, scandalous sin, or the difficulty of a flock who were intractable and incorrigible.

In the event of an episcopal vacancy, the chapter appointed within eight days one or more vicars general to look after the voluntary jurisdiction of the see and an official for the contentious jurisdiction. The chapter wielded all the bishop's powers for ordinary affairs. The king appointed a steward, in accordance with his right of *régale*, to manage the revenues of the diocese.

A bishop could be given the function of archbishop or metropolitan in the chief city of an ecclesiastical province embracing several dioceses. He could exercise the function of exarch, patriarch, or primate in the chief city of a group of provinces.

The bishop of Rome, the pope, was still acknowledged as being superior to all the other bishops, by divine right, a successor to Saint Peter, Prince of the Apostles, and visible head of the Church.

The ecclesiastical hierarchy:
The regulars

The religious was a Christian, a layman in principle (but he could be a cleric), who undertook by a solemn vow to practice throughout his life not merely the precepts of divine law but also the counsels of the

Gospel, concerning himself solely with prayer, fasting, and exercises of mortification, in accordance with a Rule (règle) approved by the Church—whence the name "regular."

Among the religious, distinction was made between the hermits, or ascetics, who lived alone; the monks, who were cenobites, living in community, and were typified by the Order of Saint Benedict, divided into the monks of Cluny, or, "black monks," and the "white monks" of Cîteaux, the Cistercians; the canons regular, such as those of Prémontré, who followed the rule of Saint Augustine; the knights, such as the Hospitallers and the Templars; the mendicant friars—Dominicans, Franciscans, Minims, Hermits of Mount Carmel, Hermits of Saint Augustine—who were officially styled "clercs réguliers;" and the Theatines and the Jesuits.

Their vows consisted in a promise to God to perform some good work which was not a matter of obligation. In order to pronounce these vows, one had to have attained the age of perfect reason. The Council of Trent had fixed the age of profession and of the taking of vows at sixteen, and the Ordinance of Blois confirmed this. In 1768 an edict fixed, for a period of ten years, the age for taking vows at twenty-one for men and eighteen for women. Vows were divided into simple vows and solemn ones. Simple vows could be taken in secret. They bound one's conscience, but a bishop could relieve one of them by commuting one good work into another when performance proved too hard. Solemn vows were pronounced in public, with the formalities required, and between the hands of the person authorized to receive such vows.

The postulant had to recite the formula of his vow in public and sign a written declaration of it, which was registered. Once his novitiate had expired, the postulant, if he was not accepted for profession, had to be put out of the monastery: mere residence for more than a year in a monastery, wearing a monk's habit, could not be accepted as tacit profession.

Those who entered religion were allowed to bring their property with them either wholly or in part. Their parents could make a gift on their account. Novices could dispose of their property before making profession but were not allowed to donate it to the monastery where they were living, owing to the influence that the monastery was presumed to be capable of bringing to bear upon a novice.

The act of profession involved a reciprocal obligation between the monastery and the monk. He could no longer depart from it, but neither could the community expel him, on any pretext whatsoever.

The religious had to continue in their vocation in their own monastery or at any rate in their own *congrégation*. One was not allowed to move from one religious order to another, except for the purpose of a stricter observance and after asking permission from one's superior, even if it turned out that the latter would not grant it. Mendicants could transfer only into the Carthusian Order unless they had special dispensation from the pope, for he alone could transfer a religious from his order into another that was *less* austere.

A religious could appeal against his vows within five years of profession if he claimed that these vows were invalid or that he had been forced to take them. He had to petition a bishop. A papal rescript was not needed. But the religious must not abandon his habit or leave his monastery by his own will.

Religious who broke their vows and went back into the world were declared apostates or runaways. Their superiors had to try to recover them, make them do penance, and then reintegrate them into the community, and secular judges were duty-bound to arrest these runaways if they were recognized and hand them over to their superiors.

The vows taken, aimed at realizing Christian perfection in its fullest form, were vows of obedience, poverty, and chastity. By his vow of poverty the religious renounced external possessions, by that of chastity he renounced his body, and by that of obedience he renounced his will. The religious could add to these some special vows—to serve the sick, train the poor, or teach the young.

Obedience consisted in perfect submission to God's commandments, to the Rule of one's order, and to all the instructions given by one's superior that were not manifestly contrary to the law of God or to the Rule. The religious was even obliged to give willing obedience to his brothers, having neither a will of his own nor attachment to his own opinion.

Poverty meant abandoning all external possessions beyond what was needed to sustain life—only food, clothes, and the simplest of chattels, most like those of the most deprived of God's creatures.

However, religious communities, which were regarded as being similar to great families, could enter into contracts, plead in court, draw up public documents, and initiate judicial prosecutions by the authority of the superior and consent of the community, following the special rules of each institution. Monasteries could receive legacies, but professed religious could not inherit, nor could the monastery in their place; for they were regarded as the first of their families to have died.

The mendicant friars were authorized by the Council of Trent to own houses without ceasing to beg. However, the Capuchins did not wish to take advantage of this permission; they had no certain income and lived only by the alms they were given.

The solemn profession of the religious entailed civil death. The property of the professed went to their legal heirs, unless the professed had made a gift of it before his profession. He could receive a maintenance pension, which was received and used by the monastery. The religious was not allowed to possess anything of his own, neither clothes nor books nor instruments—nothing whatsoever. The religious could not acquire real property. When he died, his superior inherited what chattels he left behind: this was the *dépouille, cotte morte,* or *pécule.* A religious was regarded as comparable to a child in a family, as having had the enjoyment of nothing for himself except by the permission, express or tacit, of his superior, with only precarious usage of it.

The vow of chastity signified renunciation of marriage, since all other faults against this virtue were renounced by every Christian at his baptism. A marriage contracted after profession was null, and any children of it were illegitimate. No women were allowed to enter a monastery. A religious left it only with the permission of his superior and accompanied by another religious. He could travel only with written authority, called an *obédience.*

Most of the regulars were exempt from the jurisdiction of the "ordinary," that is, the bishop. But their exemption had to be based on a formal document—a papal bull or a concordat or arrangement made with the bishop and confirmed in France by royal ordinances and *arrêts* of the Council or the sovereign courts. No regular could preach without express permission from the bishop, nor could he hear a confession without such permission (ordinance of 1695, article 2). If a regular was given a cure of souls, he became wholly subject to the bishop as far as this responsibility was concerned. Regulars were expected to conform to the usage of the diocese in which they found themselves as far as observation of festivals, processions, and other public ceremonies went. The bishop alone could establish or suppress monasteries and devotional communities in his diocese, given letters patent from the king, registered by the *parlement.* The pope alone, or a universal council, could approve or abolish a religious order, with the king's agreement.

The privileges of the clergy

The clergy, both secular and regular, possessed social advantages which marked them off from the laity. They were addressed in honorific fashion. A bishop was called "Most Reverend Father in God, Monseigneur N." and "Your Grace." A priest was called "Venerable and learned person, Messire N." A regular was called "Dom" or "Father" or "Your Reverence." Clerics preceded laymen in the churches and in all religious ceremonies. The corporation of the clergy preceded all the others in political assemblies.

The clergy enjoyed exemptions. According to ecclesiastical law, a cleric could not be prosecuted before any secular judge. He was exempt from municipal responsibilities, from the burdens of guardianship, from arrest for civil debt, and from distraint of his chattels, destined for the service of God.

The cleric was exempt from military service, from serving in the militia, from duties of watch and ward, from having soldiers quartered on him, from the payment to be made for exemption from billeting, and from the taxes levied for the support of troops or the fortifying of towns.

The cleric was exempt from the tolls, subventions, and loans levied by communities. He was also exempt from the personal *taille,* though he had to contribute to what were called *tailles négociales,* meaning the taxes which, in the regions subject to written law, were imposed by the inhabitants upon themselves, by virtue of royal letters patent, for the needs of particular towns.

In the regions where personal *taille* was levied, the parish priests who farmed the tithes did not have to pay *taille* on them, because the collection of tithes of all kinds by them was regarded as something they had a natural right to. Nevertheless, the intendants often taxed them as a matter of course. The incumbent of a benefice was exempt from paying *taille* for a farm of his benefice. In the regions of *taille réelle,* property belonging to the Church was exempt no less than noble property—at least such Church property as was long established and in being before the land survey had been made.

In the regions where the salt tax was levied, clerics were exempt from domiciliary visits. However, the letters patent of 25 January 1724 and 24 March 1727 authorized the captains general of the farms to carry out domiciliary visits at the homes of clerics, nobles, and *bourgeois,* without need of authority from the judges. Several *arrêts* made the same provision where religious were concerned. In the case of convents of nuns, an *arrêt* of the Council dated 19 October 1734, reinforced by letters patent, authorized the agents of the farms to carry out domiciliary visits with the written permission of the bishop or one

of his vicars general or, in urgent situations, with the permission of the
judge, who had to accompany the agents.

Clerics were exempt from paying *aides* on wine they had produced
themselves, whether it came from their benefice or their patrimony.
They were not subject to the "twentieth" if they sold their wine
wholesale, or to the "eighth" or the "fourth" if they sold it retail.

For the wine produced from their benefice, they were exempt from
the *nouveaux cinq sols,* from the *droit de gros et de l'augmentation,*
from the dues for gauging and brokerage for selling wholesale and at
entry to the town, except in the areas where these were paid at the
retail stage, and from the *subvention à l'entrée,* but only so far as their
own household's consumption was concerned.

The wine produced from their *titre sacerdotal* was exempt only from
the *droit de gros et de l'augmentation.*

The surplus wine from their patrimony, where this had come to them
by inheritance or by acquest, was not exempt from any of the *aides,*
unless they were nobles.

Their farmers enjoyed no exemptions except as regards the *taille.*

Ecclesiastical jurisdiction

Ecclesiastical jurisdiction was, in principle, entirely spiritual and based
on the Gospel. The government of the Church was not, in principle, a
"domination" but was founded on charity and tempered by humility.
The bishop's task was to seek men's views and try to persuade rather
than to coerce them. The Church considered that it had the exclusive
right to decide all questions of doctrine relating to faith and morals, to
lay down canons or rules of discipline, to nominate officers to exercise
its jurisdiction, to correct all its sons by imposing penances upon them,
and to cut off from itself any corrupted members, that is, the incorrigible sinners. The Church's jurisdiction could include other powers
if these powers were conceded, expressly or tacitly, by the sovereigns.

All ecclesiastical jurisdiction was, strictly speaking, in the hands of
the bishops. It had been conferred on the Apostles by Jesus Christ and
was communicated to their successors by the laying-on of hands. The
pope, Saint Peter's successor, exercised a jurisdiction of divine right
over all the bishops to ensure that no error should creep into the faith.

Bishops could exercise their jurisdiction either individually or in
council or synod. The Council of Trent had instituted provincial councils composed of the bishops of a province grouped around their met-

ropolitan. These were to be held every three years. Implementation of this decree of the Council of Trent was ordained in France by the Edict of Melun, 1580, and by the edict of 1610 and the declaration of 1646. But the only provincial councils held were at Rheims in 1564 and 1565, at Cambrai in 1565, at Rouen in 1581, at Rheims, Bordeaux, and Tours in 1583, at Bourges in 1584, at Aix in 1585, at Cambrai in 1586, at Toulouse in 1590, at Avignon in 1594, at Narbonne in 1609, and at Bordeaux in 1624.

The ordinary judges were those who possessed jurisdiction in their own right: the pope, the primates, the metropolitans, the bishops, the exempt chapters, the exempt abbots, the monastic priors, the regular abbots. They were allowed to delegate their powers.

The pope could delegate judges to deal with a certain category of cases: apostolic commissioners, among whom were commissioners *in partibus* or *ad partes,* chosen in the region where the parties resided who were appealing to him; apostolic guardians of the privileges of a university (for the University of Paris these were the bishops of Beauvais, Senlis, or Meaux); legates; inquisitors of the faith; visitors of monasteries. These delegates could in turn subdelegate.

Every bishop was supposed to know canon law and be able to sit in judgment. They even had the right to exercise contentious jurisdiction on their own. This was decided by the Council of Narbonne in 1609 and by the assemblies of the clergy in 1655 and 1665. The king had issued corresponding declarations in 1657 and 1666, but they had not been registered by the *parlement.* The lay judges wanted to put the bishops on the same footing as the *seigneurs* who possessed *subordinate* rights of justice and were obliged to have these rights exercised by others.

In fact, the bishop usually entrusted this task to the archdeacon, and the latter therefore usually claimed that the jurisdiction was his. The bishop delegated his powers. For the voluntary jurisdiction, he granted commissions to vicars general (*grands vicaires*) and, for the contentious jurisdiction to priests called "officials."

The "official" was the bishop's lieutenant or vicar. He could also have, to help him, a vice-regent, a promoter of justice, postulant attorneys, *greffiers,* notaries, and apparitors.

The promoter of justice acted as prosecutor. The postulant attorneys were recruited, by virtue of an episcopal commission, among the postulant advocates or attorneys of the presidial courts or other royal tribunals, and they combined both functions. The apostolic notaries were appointed by the pope, while the episcopal notaries received a

commission from the bishop for ecclesiastical matters. In 1691 they
were replaced by the royal and apostolic notaries. The apostolic notary
dealt with documents relating to ecclesiastical benefices: procurations
for resignation, presentations by patrons, appointments, assumptions of
possession, commissions, notifications, summonses, attachments,
interpellations, and so on.

The bishop granted provisions to the office of *greffier* of the officiality. But the *greffiers* for ecclesiastical registries were, after 1595,
royal, secular, and domanial officers. By virtue of the *"édit des petites
dates"* (1553) all documents that might confer a right to a benefice had
to be registered. In 1615 the clergy succeeded in getting the holders of
these offices paid off, and thereafter the bishop could nominate to
them.

In 1637 Louis XIII created comptrollers of applications to resign and
other documents relating to benefices. In 1646 these offices were
abolished, the holders being paid off by the clergy.

The *greffiers* of the ecclesiastical registries were laymen. They had
to be neither officials in church service nor relatives of bankers employed by the Roman Curia. The latter had to be laymen, aged at least
twenty-five, and neither officeholders nor servants of any cleric, and
they had to deposit 3,000 livres as surety.

The ecclesiastical judge had cognizance like any other of civil matters, that is, disputes to be settled, and of criminal matters, that is,
crimes to be punished. The ecclesiastical judge also had to deal with
spiritual matters, affecting all sorts of persons, and personal matters
which affected only clerics *in sacris*. The Ordinance of Moulins, article
40, defined clerics *in sacris* as subdeacons or resident clerics taking
part in offices, ministries, and benefices. The declaration of July 1556
defined them as all tonsured clerics, provided they were benefice-
holders or students. The ecclesiastical judge also had to deal with
disputes between clerics and laymen whenever the cleric was the respondent.

Spiritual matters were concerned with the sacraments and divine
service. They consisted of betrothal (accomplishment or annulment);
marriage, which became null in case of bigamy, religious vows, consanguinity, impotence or other impediment, or refusal to cohabit or
perform conjugal duty, which was a matter of divine right; adultery;
divine service, if it should be disturbed, if the choristers were not paid,
if the statutes of the diocese were not observed, and so on.

The ecclesiastical judge dealt with the spiritual aspect of heresy, that is, stubborn attachment to some dogma condemned by a judgment of the universal Church, as handed down by an ecumenical council or a special council accepted by the whole Church, such as the Council of Antioch, which condemned Paul of Samosata, or by a papal decision accepted by the whole Church, such as Saint Innocent's decision against Pelagius. Heresy entailed deposition for clerics and excommunication and denial of Christian burial for everyone, together with fines and, in accordance with the gravity of the case, confiscation of property, banishment, or death. Apostates were punished more rigorously. The children of heretics were "irregular" as regards eligibility for orders and benefices.

For schism, or separation from the authorized pastors and the community of the Church, the penalties were the same as for heresy. Since the priestly character was indelible, sacraments administered by a heretic or schismatic were still valid, as were those administered by a drunken or unchaste priest, except for the sacraments of ordination.

The ecclesiastical judge dealt with the spiritual aspect of blasphemy—that is, the act of speaking improperly of God and the mysteries of religion—which included perjury. He dealt with sacrilege and all deeds carried out in contempt of religion: profaning of sacraments, churches, and cemeteries; theft from or violence to clerics; sorcery, spells, magic, astrology, palmistry, clairvoyance, and the using of words and "characters" to cure certain ills, inflict certain illnesses, or prevent certain natural consequences. He dealt with superstitions and all practices that were observed under the pretext of religion though neither authorized by the public usage of the Church nor contributing to piety.

The ecclesiastical judge dealt with the spiritual aspect of simony. This consisted in a bargain or transaction concerning a spiritual matter: the buying or selling of the right to preach, to administer the sacraments, ordination, the nuptial blessing, collation to offices or benefices, entry into a monastery. Also treated as simony was the fiduciary arrangement whereby a person received a benefice in order to make the revenues of it available to another or in order to transmit the title to it to someone who did not yet fulfill the required conditions at the moment of collation, so as to keep the benefice in the hands of a certain family. It happened that a family would install a friend of theirs in a benefice rendered vacant by the death of one of their members, to hold it until the child for whom it was destined was old enough to take over; or a soldier might obtain a benefice as a reward for his services and have it occupied by a dependent, who handed over the income to him, keeping only a small pension for himself.

The ecclesiastical judge dealt with the spiritual aspect of homicide, which included murder, dueling, abortion, and suicide. He dealt with concubinage. Laymen who kept concubines were excommunicated after three admonitions. Clerics were not supposed to have women living with them who were under fifty years of age. Clerics guilty of keeping concubines forfeited one-third of the income of their benefices after the first admonition; after the third, they were deprived of their benefices and offices. If they offended again, they were excommunicated.

All usurpations of other people's property were subject to condemnation: robbery, larceny, usury. By the latter term was meant lending at interest. "It is not permitted to derive any profit from lending money or other things which are consumed by use and are estimated in terms of quantity, that is, by number, weight, or measure, such as grain or wine." However, the owner of "*corps certains*"—furniture, a horse, a house—was allowed to lease these out, for such goods have always lost something by the time they are returned, and the rent charged reestablishes perfect equivalence between what was lent and what is returned. Interest in the strict sense was tolerated in the case of delay in repayment beyond the agreed date, on condition that it did not exceed 5 percent, charged from the date when the debt should have been repaid. The lender could charge interest if making the loan had caused him to miss an opportunity for gain (*lucrum cessans*) or to suffer actual loss (*damnum emergens*). Interest was allowed in the case of an association in which everyone shared in profits and losses, as in maritime contracts, insurance, and so on. Interest-bearing loans were permitted when the *rentes* were secured on a principal, a capital, which had been alienated for good, with the *rente* as payment for this. The same applied to life annuities without security, gifts made for valuable consideration, and loans given on security. In all these instances the principle of equivalence between what was lent and what was returned seemed to be safeguarded: "True usury is the profit derived from a mere loan, when, on the expiry of the period of the loan, more is demanded than was lent"—whatever the form employed. Usury was forbidden to all Christians, on pain of deprivation of the sacraments and Christian burial; clerics guilty of it were subject to deposition, and every offender was obliged to pay back the money he had taken in interest.

The penalties, which consisted most frequently of deprivation of the sacraments and imposition of fines, could go so far as excommunication, or cutting-off from the society of the faithful (which implied prohibition of all dealings with the excommunicated person), and interdict, or a ban on the celebration of the Mass or administration of the sacraments in a particular town, province, or kingdom, or a ban on the admission of certain persons to these ceremonies.

The ecclesiastical judge was alone competent to deal with any personal matter of common law that concerned clerics. Laymen were not allowed to take any cognizance of the affairs of the clergy or their morals. The ecclesiastical judge punished violence against the clerics with excommunication and loss of fief or right of patronage. On the other hand, clerics were not allowed to bear arms, even in a just war, or to strike or kill people, even by accident. A cleric guilty of these or other offenses could be reprimanded or forbidden to perform the functions of his order for a certain period. He could be deposed or degraded and thus deprived of all public function—not allowed to say Mass or administer the sacraments—and of all rights, privileges, jurisdiction, benefices, and honors. His benefices were declared vacant and available. He was reduced to the rank of a mere layman. If he nevertheless continued to administer the sacraments, these remained valid, since the priestly character is indelible—but the condemned priest sinned more gravely still by administering them.

In certain special cases, however, namely, the most atrocious crimes, and where it was necessary to maintain public safety, the lay judge could intervene. According to the Ordinance of Moulins, the lay judge was obliged first of all to take cognizance of a special case and send the accused before the ecclesiastical judge dealing with common-law offenses. By the Edict of Melun, 1580, the lay and ecclesiastical judges were to investigate the special case together and then each pronounce his separate judgment. In a number of places, however, the Ordinance of Moulins was still adhered to. The edict of February 1678 and the declaration of 7 July 1684 annulled this provision of the Ordinance of Moulins and ordered that the Edict of Melun should apply throughout the realm.

On the other hand, where purely personal matters were involved, clerics often preferred to go before the lay judge because his decision and its execution were quicker. The ecclesiastical judge had, indeed, no "territory" of his own; and in order to get one of his judgments executed in the territory of a lay judge, he had to obtain a *pareatis* from the latter. Besides, a cleric who was the respondent in a purely personal case was not *obliged* to ask that he be sent before an ecclesiastical judge, even though, in principle, his privileged situation was a matter of public law and he could not renounce it.

Clerics normally went before the lay judge, even as respondents, when the action concerned real property (or was a "mixed" one, that is, concerned with a mortgage), or a contract entered into before a notary, or the acknowledgment of a promise.

The lay judge was alone competent to deal with all matters concerned with benefices—actions both possessory and petitory, as regards the titles and capacities required for the holding thereof. The *arrêt* of 15 June 1626 declared improper the summonsing of persons before the ecclesiastical judge in petitory cases. The same applied where Church tithes were concerned.

As regards spiritual matters, the lay judges claimed, in relation to all sorts of persons, to have cognizance of the crime of heresy,

> because it disturbs public tranquillity by causing differences, for it is morally impossible for there to be concord between persons who, taking religion as seriously as they should, look upon each other as sacrilegious or superstitious. It must not be said that the prince has no rights over the hearts and the opinions of men; he has at least the right to prevent the manifestation of bad opinions; and it must not be allowed that men should speak against the honor of God and the dogmas of religion any more than against the respect due to the ruler, against the fundamental principles of the state, or against good morals.

One could complain against the ecclesiastical judge when there were grounds for claiming that he had exceeded his powers or encroached upon secular jurisdiction and gone against "the liberties of the Gallican Church," and, contrariwise, one could petition against encroachments by a law judge. This procedure was the *appel comme d'abus*. Such appeals were allowed in the *parlement* and also in the king's Grand Conseil. They were recognized throughout the realm, even in provinces not covered by the Concordat, such as Brittany and Provence.

The property of the Church

The property of the Church consisted of all the temporal things consecrated to God for the service of churches—buildings, furniture, lands, tithes, pensions, and so forth. Canon law forbade bishops or any one else to alienate the Church's property, lest the Church be rendered unable to perform divine service and relieve the poor. Alienation meant any transfer of property: by gift, sale, exchange, or mortgage.

Alienations of *seigneurie utile* might be allowed, such as leasing out, for ground rent or on hereditary lease, houses that had fallen into ruin, woods that needed clearing, or an exchange of plots of land so as to effect concentration and consolidation. But these required the approval of the bishop, letters patent from the king, confirmation by the *parlement* (which checked *de commodo et incommodo,* through a local judge commissioned to perform this task), and, for greater certainty, confirmation by the pope.

Since the Church was always acquiring and never alienating, it might have ended up owning *all* real property. Ecclesiastics held in mortmain, so that property once in their possession never left it. However, it was regarded as advantageous that a good deal of land should be on the market. The *seigneurs* were interested in this on account of the dues of *relief* or *rachat* and the *lods et ventes* which they could collect, and the king was interested on account of the *taille.* Ecclesiastics who acquired land therefore had to pay the king a due of *amortissement* and the *seigneur* an indemnity, or else provide him with an *homme vivant et mourant,* at whose death the seignorial dues were paid.

Tithes

Personal tithes hardly existed any more. Real tithes were not levied on "civil" income, such as house rent, houses, or dividends, but only on the "fruits of the earth," both natural and industrial—grain, wine, sainfoin, and so on. Distinction was made between the "great" tithe, levied on grain, wine and other drinks, hay, and all the major "fruits of the earth"; the "little," or "green," tithe, levied on vegetables and herbage of all kinds; and the *dîmes de charnage ou carnelage,* levied on calves, lambs, suckling pigs, and so on. These tithes were divided into ancient and customary tithes; *dîmes novales,* charged on land which had recently been brought under cultivation and made productive (less than forty years earlier); and *dîmes insolites,* charged on new crops.

The tithes were intended to furnish temporal subsistence to the men from whom the people received spiritual nourishment, and so were paid to the clergy—the bishops canons, abbots, priors, and parish priests. But some tithes had been impropriated, that is, were in the hands of laymen. All tithes which had suffered this fate earlier than the

Lateran Council of 1179 were regarded as legitimately impropriated, but it was forbidden thereafter to allow tithes to be lost to the Church in that way.

The *portion congrue* was the stipend that a tithe-owner, such as a bishop, was supposed to pay to the parish priest, either in kind or in money. When paid in kind, it was called *le gros du curé. Arrêts* of the Paris *parlement* fixed the *portion congrue* at 300 livres a year. The declaration of 29 January 1686 made this rate apply throughout France. For Flanders and French Hainault the *portion congrue* was fixed in December 1684 at 300 florins or 375 livres *tournois.* For curates the ordinance of 18 December 1634 fixed the *portion congrue* at 100 livres a year. This was raised to 200 livres in 1775, and the edict of 1786 increased the *congrue* of the parish priests.

The quotas and forms for payment of the tithe were determined by custom, and prescription was acquired by forty years' possession.

The tithe had to be paid before any other debt was discharged. It was collected directly from the fields. If cultivators had their domicile in one parish and their land in another, the tithe they owed was either divided equally between the priests concerned or else each priest took the entire tithe due from what his parishioners produced from land in the other priest's parish; this was called the *dîme de poursuite,* or *de suite,* or *de séquelle.*

The "pope's tenth" was one-tenth of the income from all the benefices. He surrendered it to the king. After the Assembly of Melun (1580), this "tenth" was paid regularly.

Benefices

A benefice was the temporal income attached to an ecclesiastical office. It consisted of tithes and the product of Church property—produce and rents of various kinds. Distinction was made between secular and regular benefices. Secular benefices were bishoprics; chapter dignities—provostships, deaneries, archdeaconries, chancelleries, precentorships, and the offices of *écolâtre* or *capicoul (caput scholae)* and of treasurer, or *chevecier;* canonries (including the regular canonries of Pamiers and Uzès); priories with cure of souls and perpetual curacies; ordinary cures of souls; ordinary priories; and chapels. The regular benefices were abbeys *en titre;* monastic offices endowed with an assigned revenue; conventional priories *en titre;* and the offices of *chambrier,* almoner, hospitaller, sacristan, cellarer, etc.

Collation to benefices

In principle the bishop conferred all ecclesiastical offices, with the corresponding benefice. In fact, however, his right to do this was limited. He shared it, in the first place, with the canons. They elected to dignities. If the bishop's confirmation was needed, the benefice was "elective-confirmative"; otherwise it was "elective-collative," in accordance with usage and the agreements made between bishops and canons.

For cures of souls, the bishop was often obliged to confer office and benefice upon a candidate nominated by a patron. Certain cures were entirely conferred by a chapter, or by monks or nuns. However, after collation by those who possessed no spiritual jurisdiction, like nuns or Knights of Malta, the bishop had to give his *"institution canonique autorisable"* and, therewith, permission to preach and to administer the sacraments.

If a collator failed to fill a vacant office within six months from the day that he was informed of the vacancy, his superior was obliged to appoint someone to it. If *he* neglected to do this, *his* superior had to act, and so on right up to the pope. This was the "right of devolution."

The pope was supposed to have the complete right of disposal of all benefices, by virtue of the plenitude of his power, and to be able to dispose of them even before they fell vacant. An "expectancy" was therefore an assurance which the pope gave to a cleric that he would obtain a benefice. It was conferred by apostolic mandate. A "reservation" was a declaration that the pope was going to appoint someone to a particular benefice when it should become vacant. Both expectancies and reservations had been forbidden by the Council of Trent. By an edict of 1549, however, Henri II had allowed the pope to keep the right of sharing in collation with the bishops of Brittany during six months of the year. In Provence the Concordat of 1516 was to apply, but with allowance of expectancies that the vice-legate of Avignon granted in the pope's name. These two provinces were *pays d'obédience,* that is, provinces where the Concordat did not fully apply. In the regions where the Concordat was fully applicable, the pope could exercise his right of priority over the ordinary as soon as a vacancy occurred.

The pope alone collated to benefices the holder of which died in the place where His Holiness was holding court or within a radius of two days' march round about.

Patronage

In the case of a number of benefices, a patron exercised the right of presentation or nomination, and the collator carried out the institution.

A lay patron had four months in which to present. If his first nominee was considered unsuitable, the patron could present another. He could not be anticipated by the pope. The bishop could not allow an exchange of posts to be affected to his detriment, for this would have been an infringement of the rights of temporal *seigneuries*.

The patron owed protection to his church. In it he walked first in processions, and was the first to be censed and to receive holy water and consecrated bread. If he became poor, his church was obliged to help him. In his own church, the patron went before the *seigneur* who held the power of high justice; and, when he died, his mourning band was painted higher than that of the high justiciar, contrary to what would apply elsewhere.

The privileged universities played the role of patron in relation to their graduates. They presented them, by means of letters to collators, for appointment to such benefices as should fall vacant in the four months of the year that were assigned to graduates. The latter had to be tonsured. The order of preference was: doctors of divinity, college principals, men who had taught for seven years, doctors of canon law, doctors of civil law, doctors of medicine, masters of arts, licentiates, and then bachelors, of the faculties of divinity, law, and medicine, in that order. January and July were the rigorous months, when the order of preference *had* to be observed; April and October were the months of favor, when the collator could make his own choice among the graduates. A graduate described as *rempli* was one who enjoyed a benefice worth at least 400 livres of income; he could never ask for another.

The right of patronage was exercised by those who received from the pope an indult, or concession to nominate to a particular benefice which had just fallen vacant. The indult of the holders of offices in the Paris *parlement,* originally granted by a bull of Eugenius IV in 1434 but then discontinued, had been renewed by Paul III in 1538. By virtue of this indult, the pope allowed the king of France to nominate to any collator he pleased a counselor or other officeholder of the *parlement,* and the collator was obliged to confer a secular benefice on this person. An officeholder could benefit from this right only once in his lifetime, and a collator could be obliged to submit to it only once in *his* lifetime.

If a lay counselor was involved, he nominated someone else who was qualified to be presented by the king. By Pope Clement IX's bull of 17 March 1668, nominees by virtue of an indult could hold regular benefice *in commendam,* and the income that classified them as *remplis* was 600 livres.

If the king's letters nominating someone by virtue of the indult had been made known to the collator, who then refused to confer a benefice, the nominee could ask the executors of the indult to collate him. For the bull of Paul III, these executors were the abbot of Saint-Magloire and, in lieu of him, the archbishop of Paris, the abbot of Saint-Victor, and the chancellor of Notre-Dame; for the bull of Clement IX, they were the abbot of Saint-Denis, the abbot of Saint-Germain-des-Près, and the grand archdeacon of Paris.

The king himself could nominate to benefices in certain cases. On the occasion of his *joyeux avènement* he could nominate to the first prebend that fell vacant in each cathedral; when bishops took the oath of fidelity, he could nominate to the first prebend that became vacant at the disposal of each new bishop; by his right of *régale,* he could nominate during a vacancy in a bishopric.

Conditions for obtaining a benefice

A benefice was not supposed to be conferred on a cleric unless certain conditions had been fulfilled. Secular clergy could not hold regular benefices except *in commendam.* Sacerdotal benefices could be given only to priests: these were cures of souls, deaneries, and priories and abbeys *en règle,* meaning those properly conferable upon regulars and not *in commendam* upon seculars. However, prebends, chapels, ordinary priories, and *commendams* could be given to anyone who was a cleric. By decision of the Council of Trent, one had to have reached the age of fourteen in order to receive a benefice for which only the tonsure was required, sixteen to receive a regular benefice, twenty-two for a benefice that was reserved for a cleric *in sacris,* and twenty-five for a sacerdotal benefice. In France, where the old rule of the Roman chancellery was observed, one had to have reached the age of eleven to receive a cathedral prebend, ten for collegiate prebends, and seven for ordinary priories and ordinary chapels.

Anyone incapable of taking orders was incapable of receiving a benefice. A son was not allowed to succeed to his father's benefice.

In addition, to receive an episcopal benefice, one had to be a doctor or licentiate in divinity or in civil or canon law; and to be given cure of souls in a city or walled town, one had to be a master of arts or to have studied divinity or law for three years.

A benefice could be conferred only if it had been vacated by death, by resignation, or by *dévolut*.

Resignation in favor of a named person was allowed. The rule *de infirmis* of the Roman chancellery prescribed that if a sick man resigned and then died within twenty days, the provision made on the basis of this resignation was void, and the benefice was to be considered as having been vacated by death. However, this rule was no longer observed in France.

It was forbidden by the declaration of 9 February 1657 to keep secret the death of the holder of a benefice and conceal his body.

The rule *de publicandis* was observed. Resignation remained without effect if the resignee did not publish it and if he had not taken possession of his benefice within six months. This rule applied in the case of benefices provided by the Roman Curia; in the case of those provided by the ordinary, the period was one month.

If the resigner was still alive after six months, the resignee could dispossess him, and this power applied for three years thereafter.

Regrès was permitted. This meant return to a benefice which had been resigned, and it was possible to do this in three cases: convalescence from the illness that had motivated resignation; being under the age of twenty-five; and failure to fulfill some condition governing resignation. The Council of Trent had upheld all these cases of *regrès*, but the Grand Conseil would not accept them. However, the *parlements* accepted them.

Dévolut was the right of collation which was yielded to the superior of the ordinary collator in two cases: if the collator had appointed someone unworthy, and if the holder of the benefice, after being appointed canonically, fell into some irregularity or committed some crime entailing deprivation of his benefice. In these two cases the holder retained the right to resign until the *dévolutaire* had signified his taking possession of the benefice.

Provision to a benefice was made in the form of a letter patent from the collator by which he declared that he conferred, upon so-and-so, such and such a benefice, which had become vacant in such and such a way.

If the provision came from the pope, it had to be certified by two *banquiers expéditionnaires en Cour de Rome,* who confirmed that it was in order. If it was a bull, it had to be fulminated, that is, published by the bishop or the official to whom the pope had entrusted its execution. Provision had to receive the *visa* of the ordinary, that is, a letter of approval signed by the bishop or his vicar general, stating that he had found the appointee capable of assuming the benefice in question. The ordinary could reject only persons whose unworthiness or incapacity could be proved before a court.

Possession of a benefice was effected by the appointee's entering the church to which the title of the benefice was attached and occupying the appropriate seat in it—the choir stall or abbot's chair.

The financial obligations borne by benefices

Church property was sacred. It belonged to no individual. The beneficiary had only the administration and usufruct of it. He was required to leave the property in good condition. Though he could live on the income from it, he was responsible for the financial obligations to which this income was subject. In the case of parish churches, the holder of the "great" tithes was responsible for repairs to the choir and chancel. The inhabitants of the parish were responsible for repairs to the rest of the fabric and for the housing of their priest.

Every benefice-holder owed episcopal dues to the bishop: the synodal due or *cens cathédratique,* in recognition of the bishop's suzerainty, a matter of a few *sols* each year; the visitation (or procuration) due, paid in the form of hospitality to the bishop when he came to the parish; and the subsidy, or charitable gift, payable on special occasions, such as when the bishop had to go on a journey to take part in a council. It was not the practice, in France, to give the bishop a quarter of all burial fees or pious legacies.

When a benefice became vacant, the bishop had the right of *déport,* that is, he took the income arising from the benefice while it was vacant, on condition that he fulfilled the office. The bishop had the right to *annates,* which was governed by the old assessments of the Roman chancellery, before the issuing of the bulls on consistorial benefices. He could exercise the right of *dépouille,* though it was customary for the kinfolk of benefice-holders to inherit from them *ab intestat,* without making any distinction between their patrimony and the income from their benefice. Nevertheless, in the diocese of Paris, the archdeacon received the *dépouille* of parish priests: bed, soutane, square cap, surplice, breviary, horse, and traveling-chair or carriage. The *parlement* awarded the *cotte morte* or *pécule,* that is, the savings of a religious who was a parish priest, to the poor of his parish, while the Grand Conseil awarded them to his monastery.

The actual holder of a benefice often had to pay a pension either to the person who had resigned in his favor or to some other cleric, on account of the latter's poverty or incapacity through age or illness. These pensions could be instituted only by the pope, and they were not to exceed one-third of the income of the benefice in money terms.

According to the edicts and declarations of the kings of France, resigners could not keep pensions chargeable on benefices where residence was necessary unless they had ministered there for fifteen years or were ill. The actual occupant had to have for himself at least 300 livres a year.

Pensioners had to wear clerical dress and the tonsure and to recite every day the Little Office of the Blessed Virgin Mary. A pension was forfeited by marriage, irregularity, or crime. It would be redeemed by the holder of the benefice by the pope's authority.

Commendam meant assigning the income of a benefice to someone who was not the holder of this benefice. Only the pope could grant *commendams.* In principle, he did not grant them for bishoprics or convents but only for cures of souls and monasteries and only if the custom of granting them was proved for a period of forty years, with three consecutive beneficiaries.

The Council of Trent forbade the holding of a plurality of benefices with cure of souls. If a benefice was not adequate to support its holder, he was allowed to acquire another ordinary benefice as well, provided that they did not both require him to be resident. The Ordinance of Blois forbade pluralism in respect of benefices with cure of souls. The *arrêts* of the *parlement* declared incompatible all benefices which required residence, such as the combining of a canonry with a cure of souls or with another canonry. Pluralism was allowed where only ordinary benefices were involved.

Certain benefices required residence. The Council of Trent forbade bishops to leave their dioceses without written permission from the pope or the metropolitan and forbade parish priests to leave their parishes without written permission from the bishop. Authorization for absence could be granted for not more than two or three months and only for some reason of clear advantage to church or state. The Ordinance of Blois confirmed these rules. Canons were not allowed to absent themselves for more than three months in the year.

Ordinary benefices—those whose holders did not have cure of souls or obligation to take part in the choir—did not oblige the holder to be resident, nor did abbeys or priories *in commendam* or chapels where only a few masses had to be said.

The liberties of the Gallican Church

The clerical order backed the king in asserting his independence and that of his clergy in relation to the pope, through the "liberties of the Gallican Church." This was an old-established doctrine concerning the relations between church and state, dating from the conflict between Philip the Fair and Pope Boniface VIII. It had been formulated by Jean de Paris, Gerson, Almain, Pierre Pithou, and the brothers Dupuy and by the Sorbonne in its *arrêts,* and it was given new force by the decrees of the Council of Constance and the Council of Basle in the 15th century. It was based on two principles: episcopalism and regalism. According to the former, Christ conferred his power not on Saint Peter alone but on *all* bishops, who were likewise possessed of divine right and were therefore independent of the Holy See. According to the principle of regalism, Christ distinguished between what was God's and what was Caesar's. What was Caesar's was a power no less divine than the spiritual power, held of God like the spiritual power, equal to it, and independent of it.

This doctrine was restated in the declaration of the Assembly of the Clergy in 1682 and was published as an appendix to the edict for the registering of this declaration, issued at Saint-Germain in March 1682 and registered by the *parlement* on 23 March.[1] Promulgated in defense of ancestral liberties based on the Sacred Canons and the Traditions of the Fathers, the declaration, signed by a series of bishops and canons and also by the agents general of the French clergy, recalled in its second article that the pope's plenitude of spiritual power remained as it had been described by the Sacred Ecumenical Council of Constance at its fourth and fifth sessions and that the Church of France did not agree with those who attacked these decrees. In its third article the declaration stated that exercise of the apostolic power should be governed by the canons established by the spirit of God and consecrated by general respect and that the rules, customs, and constitutions received into the kingdom, and the limits "erected by our fathers," should be firmly maintained. In its fourth article the declaration affirmed that, although the pope had the principal part in questions of faith, and his decrees applied to each and every church, his judgment was nevertheless not irrevocable unless the Church consented.

The decrees of 1415 alluded to by the Assembly of the Clergy had declared that the Council of Constance, lawfully assembled in the Holy Spirit, forming an ecumenical council and representing the Church militant, held power directly from God and that everyone, the pope included, was obliged to submit to it in matters relating to faith, the ending of schism, and reform of the Church in either head or members. Moreover, if anyone, even the pope himself, were stubbornly to refuse to conform to the decrees, statutes, and ordinances of the sacred council, or of any other general council canonically assembled, on these points or others having reference to them, he was to be made to do penance and to suffer an appropriate penalty.[2]

Thus, the pope could not act contrary to the laws and customs of the Church in matters of faith, and his decisions required the approval of ecumenical councils.

However, the Gallicans, and even the Paris divinity faculty, accepted, until 1663, that the pope could correct the king if he became a tyrant; and, in serious cases, after the failure of other remedies, such as intervention by the princes of the blood, the great officers of the Crown, or the Estates General, he could excommunicate the king and release his subjects from their oath of allegiance, always provided that his action was confirmed by a general council.

During the Wars of Religion, the papal Curia and the ultramontanists had revived the theory of the pope's direct power in temporal affairs, as formulated by Boniface VIII in the bull *Unam Sanctam,* which was still upheld by Sixtus V (1585–90) and by the Jesuit Mariana (1598). According to them, there was only one society, founded by Christ—the Church. The head of this society possessed authority in all its forms, for all authority came from God, and the vicar of Christ represented God on earth. The pope exercised his spiritual power directly. He delegated his temporal power to the kings and princes, his lieutenants. He instituted them, oversaw them, and, when necessary, judged, deposed, and replaced them. The Roman pontiff was lord over all kingdoms: all were his vassals.

In face of the reaction encountered by these claims, Cardinal Bellarmine had retreated to the theory of indirect power. As he put it, the pope possessed only the spiritual power; but if the temporal power should cause men to stray from their spiritual duties, then the spiritual power could exercise a right of intervention and deposition. It could release subjects from their oath of allegiance.

These theories were held responsible for the murders of Henri III and Henri IV. Therefore, at the Estates General of 1614–15, the third estate proposed the celebrated "Article of the Third Estate," according to which the king could not, for any reason whatsoever, be deposed by the ecclesiastical authority, nor could the oath of allegiance be annulled. The first two orders opposed the adoption of this article, and Louis XIII had it withdrawn. As the 17th century advanced, however, the Sorbonne developed further the old theory of the divine right of kings. Louis XIV convened Assemblies of the Clergy in 1681 and 1682, composed of carefully chosen men. The Assembly of 1682 voted the Declaration of the Four Articles, the first of which repeated the substance of the "Article of the Third Estate": that Saint Peter and his successors, the vicars of Jesus Christ, and even the whole Church, had received power from God only over spiritual things and those concerning salvation, and not over temporal and civil affairs. Consequently, kings and sovereigns were not subject to any ecclesiastical power in temporal matters. They could not be deposed, either directly or indirectly, by the authority of the Keys of the Church, nor could their subjects be dispensed from the submission they owed them or be absolved from their oath of allegiance. This doctrine was to be followed, inviolably, as conforming to the Word of God, to the Tradition of the Holy Fathers, and to the examples set by the saints.

The Declaration of the Four Articles had to be registered in all the *parlements, bailliages, sénéchaussées,* universities, and faculties of divinity and canon law throughout the kingdom, in all the lands and lordships subject to the king. It was forbidden to teach or to write against it. Professors of divinity had to subscribe to this declaration in the records kept by the divinity faculties. The doctrine had, compulsorily, to be taught in the colleges and houses of the universities, at least once every three years if they had only one professor of divinity, and every year if they had several. The professors were obliged to show to the prelates and the king's *procureurs généraux* the notes that they were going to dictate to their students. In order to qualify as a licentiate or doctor, a candidate had to defend this doctrine in one of his theses.

Louis XIV renounced the enforcement of the Four Articles in a letter to the pope dated 14 September 1693, but the bishops and magistrates continued to apply them. The *arrêt* of the Council of 24 May 1766 recalled the inviolable principles of the edicts of 1682 and 1695. The king ordered that the Four Articles be inviolably observed in all his realms and upheld by all the universities, seminaries, and teaching bodies.

The liberties of the Gallican Church were thus based on two fundamental maxims: the power given by Jesus Christ to his Church was
purely spiritual in character, extending neither directly nor indirectly to
temporal matters; and the fullness of power possessed by the pope as
head of the Church was to be exercised in conformity with the canons
accepted by the whole Church, he himself being subject to the judgment of a universal council, in the cases indicated by the Council of
Constance.

The first maxim was based on the New Testament (John 18:36;
Matthew 22:21; Romans 13:1). Its consequences were these. The king
held his temporal power from God alone. There could be no other
judges of his right actions than those that he himself established. No
one had the right to demand of him an account of his government of his
kingdom. The power of the Keys of Saint Peter did not extend to
temporal matters. An excommunicated sovereign could not be deposed
from his kingship. His subjects could not be absolved from their oath of
allegiance, nor could his realms be given to others.

Ecclesiastics could not encroach upon temporal jurisdiction. Legates
a latere were to be dispatched only with the king's consent and must
promise, on oath in writing, to use their powers only at the king's
pleasure and in conformity with the usages of the Gallican Church.
Their bulls would be examined by the *parlement* and be subject to
modification. Nuncios were mere ambassadors.

The pope could legitimize bastards only in relation to spiritual matters, so that they could take orders and possess benefices, but not in
relation to temporal matters. The pope could not provide benefices
in opposition to the rights of lay patrons. The pope could not levy
taxes in France without the consent of the king and the clergy. He
could not alienate Church property.

Without the king's permission, the clergy could not assemble, nor
could bishops leave the kingdom, for "persons consecrated to God do
not cease thereby to be men and citizens, subject like others to the king
and the secular power." Foreigners could not possess benefices in the
kingdom of France, nor could they be superiors of monasteries.

The second maxim was likewise based on the New Testament (Luke
22:15; 1 Peter 2:13). Its consequences were these. "The government of
the Church is not a despotism, which knows no law but the sovereign's
will, but a charitable government, in which power is used only in order
to make reason prevail and in which the authority of the head does not
show itself so long as the subjects do their duty but rises radiant above

everything, so as to make them return to the rules and observe them."

In France, canon law was based on the canons accepted by universal consent of the whole Catholic Church, the canons of the Church councils of France, and the long-established customs of the Gallican Church. It therefore embraced the old corpus of canons of the Roman Church, contributed by Charlemagne, and the decisions of the five synods of Ancyra, Neocaesarea, Gangra, Antioch, and Laodicea, confirmed by those of the four general councils of Nicaea, Constantinople, Ephesus, and Chalcedon, all of which were compiled in 527 by Dionysius Exiguus, to which were added fifty canons of the Apostles, accepted and approved by the Church, some decretals and constitutions of the popes, from Siricius to Hormisdas, forming together the *Codex Canonum ecclesiae romanae,* or *Corpus canonum,* which Pope Hadrian II gave to Charlemagne, who sent it to all the churches of the West. Also to be added were the canons assembled by Gratian; the decretals of the five books of Gregory IX, of Sextus, and of the Clementine literature, or at least those of them that were not contrary to the liberties of France, the ordinances of her kings, and the usages of the kingdom; and, finally, the dogmatic decrees of the ecumenical councils, excluding those relating to discipline.

The new constitutions of the popes during the preceding 300 years were not, however, binding in France unless they were approved by usage. Accordingly only three regulations issued by the Roman chancellery were accepted in France: *De infirmis resignantibus* or *De vigintis diebus; De publicandis resignationibus;* and *De verisimili notitia obitus.* The regulation *Triennali possessore* was observed as a decree of the Council of Basle. Papal bulls that were not couched in the usual style could not be published and executed without letters from the king, after being examined by the *parlement,* and this rule had been confirmed by the *arrêts* of the *parlement* of 15 May 1647, 15 April 1703, 16 December 1716, 1 June 1764, and 11 February 1765. The French were not subject to the censures of the bull *In coena Domini,* 1568, which the pope reissued every year on Maundy Thursday, dealing with the ecclesiastical and civil powers, those who mistreated prelates, sought to restrict church jurisdiction or interfered with it, usurped church property, or tried to subject clerics to taxation; nor were they subject to the decrees of the Congregation of the Holy Office, to those of the Congregation of the Index, or to those of the pope's other congregations or councils. The French were also not subject to the dispensations from natural and divine law, from canons in cases where these prohibited dispensation, or from "praiseworthy customs" and special church statutes which had been confirmed by the Holy See. They were not subject to direct appeal (*omisso medio*), to removal of a case in the first instance, to gifts of French benefices or pensions to foreigners, to bulls on small benefices, or to the reservations provided for in the Concordat, whereby in the *pays d'obédience* the pope conferred benefices alternately with the bishop during six months of the year and with other collators during eight months, but which were abolished by the Council of Trent. All these points made up what were called "the liberties of the Gallican Church," the principal effect of which was to increase the independence and power of the king of France.

Such, briefly summarized, was the juridical organization of this order of the kingdom. We now have to examine its actual relations with society and with the state.

The relations between the clerical order and society

The order of the clergy in France did not recruit from its own ranks, since its members did not have the right to marry and engender a legitimate progeny but drew its personnel from the two other officially recognized orders: the nobility and the third estate. This means that we need to examine the social origin of the members of the clergy and the relations they kept up with the milieux from which they sprang. But such an examination does not exhaust the question, since the members of the clergy entered into relations with other social strata and groups besides those from which they had come, for reasons that were not wholly spiritual, such as the collection of rents and tithes, the cultivation of land, trade, seignorial relations, legal proceedings, entertainment, participation in the administration of fabrics, hospitals, schools and colleges, village communities, apportionments of royal taxes, and so on. Within the clerical order, moreover, the clerics at different levels of the hierarchy had social relations among themselves. Finally, their spiritual functions obviously had an aspect concerned with social relations.

These relations were realized in accordance with the way in which the clerics regarded their estate and caused it to be regarded by the laymen whom they instructed in religion. Increasingly, it was the content of the decrees of the Council of Trent that provided the model for clerical life, shaped the order of the clergy, and determined its relations with the rest of society. The Tridentine decrees were not accepted *en bloc* by a royal edict, although they found their way, in part, into the legislation of the kingdom. Nevertheless, the Assembly of the Clergy in 1615 promulgated them for the clerical order, in response to the wishes of the clergy themselves and the faithful. In this way it amplified the internal reform of the Church and favored the development of a new type of ecclesiastic, for the Church itself was a society with its own purposes, rules, and procedures, which shaped its members, imposed on them a certain pattern of behavior, and determined the behavior of laymen toward them.

At the center of the dogmatic and liturgical work of the Council of Trent was the concept of sacrifice. The priest was seen as the man who, in celebrating Mass, repeated the sacrifice of Jesus Christ on the Cross. He actually brought Jesus himself into this ceremony, and when he consecrated the bread and the wine he transformed them, really and substantially, into the body and blood of Jesus. This victim he offered to God. The Mass was the supreme sacrifice, the sublime prayer, "the sun of all spiritual exercises."

The priest, who repeated the sacrifice of Jesus Christ, was thereby obliged to seek to identify himself with Christ crucified. His own life must be a sacrifice. He must strive for complete Christian purity. More than any other Christian, he must not be of this world but live above it even while remaining within it. He bore a sacrificial and hierarchic imprint. His ascetic way of life must establish the frontier between the profane and the sacred. The world of the clergy was the sacred world. The priest must turn himself into a model of sanctity by prayer, chastity, poverty, refusal to become involved in temporal affairs, and ceaseless preaching of the word of God. For the priest was the man who knew, who possessed the revelation of God contained in Holy Writ, defined by the Tradition of the Fathers and codified by the canons and decrees of the ecumenical councils. This specialized knowledge, taken together with the sacrificial aspect of his life, set the priest apart. But a man could not play this sacrificial role unless he had been called to it by God and felt an inward attraction toward it, unless he had a *vocation*, recognized as such by his bishop. From that followed a whole theory of vocation, which succeeded in setting the sacerdotal world apart from the rest of society.

All this, which conformed to the decisions of the Council of Trent, conformed also to the wishes of the population. The peasants of the *bailliage* of Troyes demanded in 1614 that the priest's life constitute a sermon in itself, that he be resident in his parish, proclaim the glory of God, spread God's word, explain the power of the sacraments, administer them, and provide a pattern of Christian life. However, one may wonder whether, in defining these characteristics of the priest and marking off the sacred world in this way, these *dévots* were not contributing to that desacralization of the profane world which had been in progress since the 13th century.

In any case, while the type of priest defined by the Council of Trent did not cease to develop and become established, right down to the middle of the 18th century (and it continued to exist thereafter), it was increasingly subject to competition from another type, which eventually replaced it. Under the influence of the neo-Stoic movement and the strengthened role of Roman law, together with Cartesianism, there took place in France, from the last quarter of the 17th century onward, a gradual change in social values. This change caused to grow and become predominant the idea of happiness on earth, realized through physical well-being and achievable therefore by the production of material goods. *That* activity came to be seen more and more as what was useful and practical. The morality centered on the bond of love with God and striving to become perfect as God is perfect was reduced to observation of the rules effective for society to function with a view to physical well-being. Thus, the priest increasingly came to be considered, and to consider himself, as a sort of civil servant.

This idea appeared in the first half of the 18th century. The abbé de Saint-Pierre wrote: "Priests are state officials with the task of rectifying morals, that is, causing the citizens to be just and beneficent in their everyday conduct, so as to please God."[3] The idea became widespread among the clergy, even among the upper clergy. The Assembly of the Clergy of 1775 discussed the priest's career as though it were the career of a civil servant. It recommended competitive examinations, promotion by merit, increases in *portions congrues* to keep up with the cost of living, and a decent retirement pension. The parish priests, full of demands, displayed a group spirit, even a real "trade-union" spirit. Some of them went very far in that direction. In the reply to the inquiry of 1774 returned by a curate of Montay-Notre-Dame, who looked after the church of Montay-Saint-Pierre on the other side of the Meuse, we read: "Is it worth crossing the river so many times in the year, winter and summer, night and day, and thereby putting my life at the mercy of the waters, for twenty *écus* a year?"[4] This was no longer the outlook of even the civil servant but that of the trader. The conception of a service performed in return for money replaced that of a vocation to sacrifice by merging oneself with Jesus Christ.

Naturally, the idea passed on from the priests to their congregations. The parishioners of Chaumuzy, in the *bailliage* of Rheims, in their *cahier* for the Estates General of 1789, demanded for "Messieurs les Curés" equality of income, with performance of their functions free of charge to the user and abolition of reliance on perquisites, and retirement at sixty—in short, a career in the public service, of social utility, appropriate to a new type of society, a society of classes.

The numbers of the clergy

The diocese of Paris, apart from the capital itself, must have included, in the 17th century, about 200,000 souls, 420 parish churches, 386 cures of souls, and 840 clergy. To these figures must be added 9 abbeys, 3 monastic priories, 50 ordinary priories, houses of the mendicant and hospitaller orders, and some hermits and recluses, such as those of Mont-Valérien. All together, the clergy must have made up about 1 percent of the population.

In the diocese of La Rochelle, about 1648, it can be estimated that there was 1 priest to 400 Catholics—or, taking the Protestants into account, 1 priest to 430 inhabitants. They comprised between 295 and 302 parish priests, or perpetual curates; between 155 and 170 curates; some chaplains to nunneries or military units; and between 110 and 115 priests who were *habitués* (unbeneficed priests) in the parishes—all together, between 589 and 615 secular clergy. To these must be added the regulars. Their distribution was very uneven. In the plain of Aunis, around La Rochelle, in the marshes of the Charente and the Sèvre, and in the Niortais area there was 1 priest to each parish and to between 500 and 700 Catholics (1,300 in the Ile de Ré); in the plains of lower Poitou, the Pareds district, and industrial Gâtine there were 3 priests to every two parishes, 1 to 450 inhabitants. In agricultural Gâtine, the Thouarsais area, and the district of Layon, there were 2 priests to a parish, 1 to 350 inhabitants; and, in Les Mauges, 3 priests to a parish, 1 to 250 inhabitants.

The diocese of Vannes contained, in 1790, 194 rectors, 261 curates, and 370 *habitués,* with an average of 9 priests to a parish.

Angers in the 18th century had, with the rural areas dependent on it, a population of 35,000, of whom 22,000 lived in the town itself in 1745 and 28,000 in 1787. In 1789 there were 60 monks, 40 friars, 300 nuns, 72 canons, 17 parish priests, 22 curates, 7 priests in the general hospital, others employed by the chapters to look after chapels or serve as deacons, sacristans, etc., some mere wearers of the tonsure, and some seminarists. Altogether, excluding the nuns, 1 in 60 of the inhabitants (men, women, and children) was in holy orders or a member of a religious community.

In the diocese of Narbonne, which had 40,000 inhabitants in 1650, the proportion of clergy in the population must have been 1 per cent.[5]

All together, it can be estimated that, as an average, the male members of the clerical order constituted 1 per cent of the total population. However, on the one hand, the number of nuns was probably higher, and, on the other, the numerical strength of the clerical order declined in the course of our two centuries. The regular clergy found it harder and harder to recruit as the life of contemplation and poverty declined in public esteem. The secular priests also became less numerous. In the diocese of La Rochelle they declined by 10 per cent (from between 580 and 615 in 1648 to between 525 and 560 in 1724) through the gradual disappearance of the *habitués,* those clerics who lived by serving a priory, an almonry, a *commanderie,* or a chapel and by helping the priest in the parishes. As public esteem shifted from the religious and social "estate" to the concept of "function," this type of priest, very numerous in the 16th century, tended to become rare. The number of members of the order thus altered in response to the change in society's values.

> *The relation between the degrees of the clerical order and the hierarchy of orders and estates in society as a whole*

The Council of Trent, faithful to the words of Jesus Christ and to Catholic tradition, had forbidden priests to marry. Therefore, the clerical order did not reproduce itself. Its estates were not hereditary, either directly or by the indirect path of entry into the order after a period of marriage and procreation in each generation. The order was recruited from the ranks of the laity.

The hierarchy of the order was based on spiritual features which were due to divine grace but to which men's wills had to respond. These features were not transmitted by blood, were not innate or instinctive. They could be acquired by God's grace. Thus, the hierarchy became a career. At each of its levels, the office held gave a man a spiritual influence from which a certain power ensued. To each office there corresponded a benefice, which placed appointments and property at the disposal of a man who was not married and who had no acknowledged offspring but who did have brothers and sisters, nephews and nieces. Thus his power became a family power and the property under his control family property, from which the family, the lineage, derived prestige, influence, comfort, or luxury.

Each ecclesiastic attained in the hierarchy of the order a level corresponding to the rank held by his family in the hierarchy of the two lay orders. Each combination of office and benefice tended to be retained: in a lineage, through resignations by uncles in favor of nephews; in a circle of clientages, through the working of the ties of fealty between patron and client, *maître* and *fidèle*, through the influence of services rendered. A slight looseness in the system made possible a certain amount of upward social mobility.

Since the Concordat of 1516 the majority of benefices had been conferred by the king. Increasingly, however, in our period, appointments depended either on a Conseil de Conscience or on the holder of the *"feuille des bénéfices,"* who was himself always a cleric. In the last part of the reign of Louis XIV this role was played by Father La Chaise, followed by Father de Tellier. Under the regency it passed to the Conseil de Conscience, presided over by Cardinal de Noailles, archbishop of Paris, and, in the last years of the rule of Philippe d'Orléans, to a Chambre ecclésiastique, in which sat cardinals De Rohan and De Bissy, Massillon, the bishop of Clermont, and Fleury, the bishop of Fréjus, with the abbé de Thésut holding the *"feuille des bénéfices."* After the regent's death, the task was performed by Fleury and Louis XV's Jesuit confessors down to 1725, then by Fleury on his own. After him came the bishop of Mirepoix (1743–55), Cardinal de La Rochefoucauld (1755–57), Jarente de la Bruyère, bishop of Digne and later of Orléans (1757–71), Cardinal de La Roche-Aymon (1771–77), Marbeuf, archbishop of Autun (1777–78), and Le Franc de Pompignan, bishop of Vienne.

In his last years, Fleury used to take the advice of the Abbé Couturier, superior general of the seminary and congregation of Saint-Sulpice. The practice of consulting the superior general became habitual; and the great seminary was full of sons of noble and powerful families, even princes.

What determined the granting of benefices were distinguished services rendered to the king and relations with families presented at court, with bishops, and with patrons of benefices. Président Filain, who was a *président à mortier* in the *parlement* of Besançon, seeking a benefice for his younger son, reminded the regent, in 1720, that

> the happiness I have had in raising first, with Monsieur our *premier président* (Boisot), the standard for the execution of the wishes of Your Royal Highness and support of the rights of the Crown against the Court of Rome and the rejection of ultramontane principles; the services, for more than forty years, of my late father, *premier avocat général,* and my own services as *président à mortier;* those of my elder son, counselor, and of my son-in-law, also as counselor, and of my two brothers, now dead, who were captains of cavalry in the service of the king, form the basis of my aspirations.[6]

Such were the titles of a young cleric to the obtaining of a benefice.

According to Saint-Simon, the ducs de La Rochefoucauld used to concentrate all the property and wealth of the father upon the eldest son by putting the daughters and younger sons into the Church. The first duc de La Rochefoucauld made his second and fourth sons priests; the elder died as bishop of Lectoure, while the other was content with abbeys and was a chevalier of the Order of Malta. Of the six daughters he had, four were abbesses, the last one a nun. Only the third insisted on having a husband.[7]

The normal line of advance for well-connected younger sons was, first, the Saint-Sulpice seminary; then pensions from abbeys; then rich priories and great abbeys; then, for the most-favored, an appointment as royal chaplain, the functions of *agent du clergé,* and, finally, a bishopric.

The common education given by the seminary and by the Sorbonne, which sent out to the four corners of France bishops and vicars general who were animated by the same spirit, became a powerful factor in unifying the kindgom.

The recruitment of bishops

The kingdom included, at the end of the 18th century, 130 bishoprics, not including the 5 situated in the papal enclaves, the 5 Corsican sees, or the sees of Tournai and Ypres, acquired at the end of the 17th century and lost by the Peace of Utrecht. The population of France in 1790 can be estimated at 26,500,000, according to the figures of the Comité de Révision of the Constituent Assembly. On this basis, there would have been, in the Northwest, Northeast, West, and Center, an average of one diocese for every 300,000 inhabitants and, in the Southwest and Southeast, one diocese for every 110,000. Actually, the differences were even more marked than that. If we accept Necker's estimate, in 1785 France had 25 million inhabitants. On this basis there would have been, in the *généralité* of Lyons, one diocese for 625,000 inhabitants; in that of Tours, one for 450,000; in that of Paris, one for 350,000; in the province of Brittany, one for 250,000; in that of Languedoc, one for 75,000; and in Provence, one for 60,000 inhabitants. The bishopric of Bethléem consisted of the Hôpital de Pantenère, near Clamecy.

Dioceses also differed greatly in the number of parishes they contained. The diocese of Rouen appears to have had 1,388; the dioceses of Chartres, Limoges, Besançon, Clermont, and Bourges, between 800 and 900; but those of Digne, Apt, Ayde, Marseilles, Toulon, Vence, and Grasse, as few as 35.

The income derived from dioceses was no less varied.

The dignities of the dioceses were highly unequal. The bishops of Paris, Beauvais, Rheims, Langres, Laon, Noyon, and Châlons-sur-Marne were peers of France, with precedence over all nobles, other than the princes of the blood, and the right to sit in the *parlements*.

The bishops of Strasbourg, Metz, Cambrai, Besançon, Belley, Toul, and Verdun were still sovereign princes of the Empire.

The archbishop of Narbonne presided *ex officio* over the estates of Languedoc, the archbishop of Aix over those of Provence, the bishop of Autun over those of Burgundy, the bishop of Arras over those of Artois, the bishop of Pamiers over those of Foix, and the bishop of Lescar over those of Béarn.

Some bishoprics conferred on their bishop the title of prince, count, or baron, with the feudal and seignorial rights attached thereto. When the bishop-count of Cahors made his first entry into his episcopal city, the baron de Cessac had to go out of the town to meet him, with his right leg and foot bare except for a slipper, place his foot upon the ground, salute the bishop-count bareheaded and without wearing a coat, and then take his mule by the reins and lead him first to the cathedral and then to the episcopal palace, where he then served him at his dinner table.

Bishoprics were greatly sought after. They were assigned to members of a small group of noble lineages who knew each other and became linked together and who served the king by furnishing him with the military, civil, and religious *cadres* of the monarchy. Most of them belonged to the provincial and rural nobility, with Parisian nobles providing only a minority of the bishops. In families of the *noblesse d'épée*, the eldest son usually received a company or a regiment, while in families of the *robe* it was he who was given the family office. The second son was destined for the bishopric. Everyone knew who was going to be a bishop twenty years on. These young men who were eligible for bishoprics were well prepared for their future positions. Most of them attended seminaries—after the second quarter of the 18th century, the major seminary of Saint-Sulpice. They all took orders, right up to the priesthood. They studied divinity and law seriously and took their degrees—a licence at the least—at the university. All then became vicars general; but, out of about a thousand of these, only four or five each year were promoted to bishoprics. They also obtained canonries, abbeys, and positions as deputies to the Assemblies of the Clergy. Increasingly, during the 18th century, this set of men, who, though mostly born in the provinces, were educated in Paris and became vicar general in one diocese, canon in another, and abbot in yet another, acquired a *national* character; and, as a collective, the leading group of the ecclesiastical order, "the secular clergy of the first order," they constituted a centralizing and unifying force in the kingdom.

According to Norman Ravitch's calculations,[8] in the period 1682–1700, out of 194 bishops, 170 (88 percent) were nobles, 16 (8 percent) were commoners, and 8 (4 percent) were of uncertain origin, probably from families on the way to ennoblement. In the period 1700–1774, out of 240 bishops, 200 were nobles (83 percent), 9 were commoners (4 percent), and 31 (13 percent) were hard to classify. In the period 1774–90, out of 192 bishops, 173 were nobles (90 percent), 2 were commoners (1 percent), and 17 (9 percent) were of uncertain origin. If we try to distinguish between the categories of the nobility, we find that, between 1682 and 1700, out of 170 noble bishops, 83 (49 percent) came from "sword" families, 38 (22 percent) from "gown" families (meaning members of the sovereign courts), 23 (14 percent) from a group of direct agents of the king—*secrétaires du roi, maîtres des requêtes*, officials of the *contrôle général*, governors—and 2 (1 percent) from the *noblesse de cloche*. Between 1700 and 1774, of 200 noble bishops, 137 (69 percent) were from "sword" families, 31 (16 percent) from "gown" families, and 9 (5 percent) from the group of direct royal agents. Between 1774 and 1790, of 173 noble bishops, 130 (75 percent) were from "sword" families, 14 (8 percent) from "gown" families, and 2 (1 percent) were sons of direct agents of the king. In the total for all three periods there remain 74 (14 percent) whose origin is not known.

If we try to classify the noble bishops in accordance with the antiquity of their nobility, we find that between 1682 and 1700, of the 170 noble bishops, 86 (51 percent) belonged to families that had been noble for over 200 years, 24 (14 percent) to families with between 100 and 200 years of nobility, and 21 (12 percent) to families ennobled for less than 100 years. Between 1700 and 1774, of the 200 noble bishops, 119 (60 percent) had 200 years of nobility behind them, 18 (9 percent) had between 100 and 200 years, and 12 (6 percent) had less than 100 years. Between 1774 and 1790, of the 173 noble bishops, 137 (79 percent) came from families with over 200 years of nobility, 6 (3 percent) from families with between 100 and 200 years, and 2 (1 percent) from families of less than 100 years' nobility. Between 1743 and 1770 not a single commoner was nominated to a bishopric. Under Louis XVI only two commoners received episcopal office: Beauvais was appointed to the see of Senez, his nomination arousing the indignation of the aristocrats, and Asseline to the see of Boulogne—during the Revolution. The abbé Beauvais, moreover, had the advantage of being a preacher to the court, a member of the Académie française, a member of the Assembly of the Clergy, vicar general of the diocese of Noyons, and recommended by Mesdames de France, the daughters of Louis XV.

The bishops thus seem always to have been mostly nobles. The change that occurred during our two centuries was that, to an increasing extent, they were *nobles d'épée* and also, to an increasing extent, *gentilshommes de vieille race*. The number of bishops drawn from the *noblesse de robe* continually declined. This may have been among the reasons for the growing antagonism between the *parlement* and the clergy, one of the forms assumed by the struggle between sword and gown, here appearing under the aspect of a conflict between the *noblesse de robe* and the *noblesse "en camail"* ("wearing the mozzetta").

The recruitment of abbots and abbesses

The abbots were also nobles, and usually members of the upper nobility. They held their abbeys, in most cases, *in commendam* and did not reside there. A monk carried out their duties on the spot, with some such title as "prior." At Angers, for example, in the 18th century, the abbot of the Benedictine abbey of Saint-Aubin, attached to the Congrégation de Saint-Maur, was always a great nobleman, destined to become bishop of Rennes, Sées, or Angers. In the Benedictine abbey of Saint-Nicolas we find the noble abbé de Mostuejouls, principal chaplain to Madame, former tutor to the royal children, and titular incumbent also of two abbeys, a priory, and a canonry. His elder brother, the marquis, had inherited the family estates. His younger brother was a canon in the noble chapter of Saint-Julien de Brioude, and one of his sisters was a canoness of the noble chapter of Remiremont. To the Augustine canons of the Order of Sainte-Geneviève was linked the abbey of Toussaint, whose abbot was a nobleman, Le Perrochel, the younger son of a younger son, a former lieutenant of dragoons, nominated in 1783. The abbey most highly esteemed among girls was that of the Benedictines of La Ronceray, which dated from the Middle Ages. All the nuns there were noblewomen, from the high nobility of Versailles. From 1763 onward the abbess was Leontine d'Esparbez de Lussaus Bouchard d'Aubeterre, daughter of a marquis, sister of a marshal of France and minister plenipotentiary in Vienna. In the other religious establishments for girls, created between 1600 and 1660, the Ursulines, Visitandines, Sisters of Our Lady of Calvary, Carmelites, etc., recruitment of the nuns and the mothers superior proceeded in descending order down the degrees of the social hierarchy: the local nobility of Anjou put their daughters into the Convent of the Visitation, while the men of the law sent theirs to the Ursulines.

The recruitment of vicars general

Acceding to the position of vicar general in a diocese opened the path to a bishopric, though only a minority of vicars general actually attained it. Hardly, therefore, had a bishop been nominated than he found himself besieged by young men from all quarters, introduced either by a benefactor, a relative, or a friend or by "Madame la duchesse de" or "Madame la marquise de," competing to secure appointment as vicar general. They were often cousins or nephews of the new bishop and, like him, had emerged from the major seminary of Saint-Sulpice and from the Sorbonne.

There were many vicars general. In 1789 Bishop Boisgelin, at Aix, was flanked by eleven of them; Marbeuf, at Autun, and Royère, at Castres, by thirteen; Cicé, at Bordeaux, by fourteen; Durfort, at Besançon, and Talleyrand-Périgord, at Rheims, by sixteen; Barral, at Troyes, by seventeen; Clermont-Tonnerre, at Châlons, and Phélypeaux, lately archbishop of Bourges, by eighteen; Rohan-Guéménée, at Cambrai, by twenty, one of whom was La Trimouille.

Almost all the aristocratic families of the kingdom had some of their members among the vicars general. A smaller number of commoners of

talent were recruited to cope with the rough work and the administrative details. The great majority of the vicars general were *gentilshommes*. Durfort, at Besançon, had thirteen *gentilshommes* among his
sixteen; at Sens, Cardinal de Luynes had nine out of ten; and, at Cahors,
Bishop Nicolaï had thirteen out of thirteen.

A prelate thus grouped around him, in his provincial town, priests
who were of his own rank and background, talked his language, had the
same tastes, and were seeking or maintaining the same connections.
This group enjoyed prestige; it was imitated, and it influenced local
society, both clerical and lay. It did not necessarily exclude the new
ideas: Lubersac, bishop of Chartres, had among his vicars general the
Abbé Sieyès.

The recruitment of canons

Twenty-one "noble" chapters were reserved exclusively for the nobility. To be received into the noble chapter of Lyons, one had to prove
nobility going back to at least the year 1400 and also had to prove that
one had received "court honors," that is, had been presented to the
king and allowed to ride in the royal carriages. (In 1789 about 1,000
families out of the 25,000 to 30,000 noble families had been "presented.") The important chapters, such as that of the canons-counts of
Strasbourg, were patrons of cures of souls, and their members were
attended by a clientage of chantry priests, for whom they obtained
benefices.

In general, the other chapters included a high proportion of nobles.
Most of the vicars general obtained a prebend in the chapter of their
cathedral. But the local nobility also found additional outlets there for
their younger sons. At Chartres, out of 80 canons, between 35 and 50
percent were petty provincial nobles who remained canons all their
lives.[9] At Angers, among the canons of the cathedral church of Saint-
Maurice, there were in 1789 one who was a tanner's son and another
who was a former schoolmaster and son of a rich merchant of Angers;
but the majority were younger sons of noble families, often very old-
established ones, or else came from the families of notables, nephews
of canons, who were nominated when they were between nineteen and
twenty-three years old. Their dean, César-Scipion de Villeneuve, was a
second son. His elder brother had inherited the château of Tourette-
lès-Vence, and his younger brother was a major in the cavalry. Canon
Charles de Cressy, from a 600-year-old noble family of Normandy, was

a second son, with three brothers in the king's army. Canon Dary
d'Ernemont was supposed to be descended from one of William the
Conqueror's comrades-in-arms. He was a third son. His eldest brother
had inherited Ernemont, another brother was canon of Saint-Waas, at
Arras, and three more were soldiers. Most of the canons came from
noble families of Anjou, Normandy, or Brittany. The chapter did not
include any courtiers' sons; it was not rich enough for that. Six of the
canons were the bishop's vicars general. Seven were doctors of divinity. Almost all were resident and showed regularity and seriousness
in the performance of their duties. The other chapters, in mere collegiate churches, were less sought after. Some of their members came
from the old *noblesse d'épée* or the *noblesse de robe,* but most of them
belonged to families of ordinary "notables"—advocates, notaries,
merchants, wholesalers.

At Castelnau-du-Magnoac, in the diocese of Auch,[10] there was a
collegiate church with twelve canonical prebends, which had been
founded in 1480. Between 1778 and 1786 there actually were twelve
canons there, nine of them being priests in 1778 and six in 1786. The
town was the patron of the chapter. The consuls nominated new canons
to the archbishop of Auch, who conferred canonical institution upon
them. All canons had to be from Castelnau; the chapter refused to
accept anyone from outside. They were recruited from among the good
families of Castelnau, and all were brothers or uncles and nephews;
something like dynasties of canons were formed. But every one of
them was a bachelor, licentiate, or doctor of law or divinity, and in
some cases they taught at the Royal College at Auch. Canonries often
served as means of supporting students at the seminary.

Throughout the kingdom and in the lands and lordships ruled by the
king of France, canons enjoyed an income which, though modest, was
secure, a rank in society, eligibility for distinguished functions, and
dignity and rights of precedence. They form a good example of this
society of close, privileged corporations which one entered by virtue of
birth, influence, or favor. The clerical order was, however, the one that
succeeded best in breaking down provincial particularisms.

The recruitment of parish priests

With the parish priests we step down the social ladder; this seems to
have been true generally in the kingdom and in the lands subject to the

king. In order to become a parish priest, one had to attract the attention of a "patron" or nominator or else obtain the *resignatio in favorem* of a parish priest, usually a member of one's own family. In the diocese of Autun, the bishop nominated to ninety cures of souls, the abbey of Cluny to thirty-five, the cathedral chapter to twenty-six, the prioress of Marcigny to sixteen, the abbot of Saint-Martin at Autun to eleven, and other patrons to three or four: the De Ragny family, the comte de Clermont, the comte de Choiseul, and Madeleine de Castille, who in 1700 founded the parish church of La Boulaye.

Let us take some regional examples. In the diocese of Rheims[11] in 1773 and 1774 an inquiry listed 514 parish priests and 131 curates. Of 537 clerics whose geographical origin is known, 271 came from towns, 163 of them from five "big" towns (Rheims, Rethel, Charleville, Mézières, Sedan) and 108 from 40 small towns and market centers. The 266 others came from the countryside, mainly from the Ardennes and Argonne, out-of-the-way forest areas, with few from the infertile part of Champagne or the vine-growing area.

According to the *titres patrimoniaux* of 100 livres which were settled upon them by their parents or other members of their families, before a royal notary, in the presence of two witnesses, nine (2.4 percent) were sons of nobles; nine (2.4 percent) were sons of "*bourgeois*" of Rheims, Charleville, and Sedan, *rentiers* and "*financiers*"; seventy-three (20 percent) were sons of officials of very varied rank, ranging from the *lieutenant du bailliage* to seignorial officials; thirty-four (9.3 percent) were sons of textile merchants (that is, *fabricants,* petty precapitalist entrepreneurs); eighty-six (23.6 percent) were sons of "*marchands*," meaning ordinary shopkeepers; eighteen (4.9 percent) were sons of schoolmasters and surgeons; fifty-nine (16 percent) were sons of "master" craftsmen (among them, only one urban day laborer, a sergemaker of Rheims); seventy (19 percent) were sons of men described as *laboureurs,* many of whom were, however, quite small cultivators who certainly did not own a ploughteam, and one was a rural day laborer. Among these seventy, there were only four cases in which the whole family participated in settling the income—that is, four cases of quasi-poverty. All the rest, in all the estates, professions, and trades, were comfortably off. The parish priests were recruited elsewhere than from the lowest sections of the people. This was not due to difficulty of access to opportunities for study, since in all the small towns there were Latin schools which the *laboureurs* could attend; and for more advanced studies, there were colleges at Sedan, Charleville, and Rheims. What kept the poor out was the obligation to provide the *titre patrimonial*.

The diocese of Rheims seems typical. At Angers the parish priests were recruited from the town itself or from the area within a sixty-kilometer radius of it. The parish priests were sons of counselors in the *prévôté*, merchants in the iron, charcoal, or grain trades, surgeons, farmers; one was the son of a saddler, another of a weaver and a schoolmistress. Their brothers were advocates, merchants, surgeons, apothecaries, priests. They were educated men, two being doctors of divinity and one a doctor of medicine. After leaving the seminary and being ordained, they spent ten years as curates, often with an uncle who was a parish priest; then they either had to obtain from an uncle or a cousin a *resignatio in favorem* or else had to attract the attention of a patron, for the bishop, the abbots and abbesses, and the chapters were patrons of three-fourths of the cures of souls in the diocese.

In the diocese of La Rochelle, information obtained about a group of between 295 and 302 parish priests or perpetual vicars and between 155 and 170 curates, living in the middle of the 17th century, shows that they were recruited chiefly from among sons of notaries, practitioners, and *laboureurs* and mainly from country-dwellers. Resignations by uncles in favor of nephews were very frequent, and the cures of souls were occupied by veritable dynasties. A young cleric would first acquire a post as chantry priest, with at least 100 livres as his *titre patrimonial,* and then become a curate and, eventually, a parish priest. In the parish of La Verrie, all of the priests, throughout the 17th and 18th centuries, came from only two families.

In the bishopric of Strasbourg in the 18th century the same situation is observable. Chapels and cures of souls were secured from a patron by petty nobles or *bourgeois*. These were then under a moral obligation to confer them on another member of the same family by *resignatio in favorem*. Cures of souls passed from uncle to nephew, from cousin to cousin, from brother to brother.

In the diocese of Autun, between 1660 and 1729, twenty-two *curés* were natives of Autun itself, seventy-five came from market centers and villages in the diocese, and thirty-four came from other dioceses, including three from Provence and one from Lectoure. They were sons of peasants or *bourgeois* in modest circumstances, and some were former soldiers; but all came from families that were comfortably off. In 1714 the *curé* of Gilly-sur-Loire was a former physician.

In the diocese of Rieux, Simon de Boussac, a doctor of divinity, was *curé* of Saint-Laurent de Carbonne from 1666 to 1703. His brother Jean was a doctor of laws and advocate before the *parlement* of Toulouse, while another brother, Durand, was *"garde-sac des procédures"* for that *parlement,* and his sister Marie had married Henri de Lacoze, *seigneur* of Montbel, described as a nobleman. He resigned in favor of his nephew Simon, master of arts of the University of Toulouse. Thus the offices, and the benefices attached to them, were shared out among the families in correlation with their social status and their rank in the social hierarchy. They constituted a sort of prolongation and reinforcement of the status, power, and wealth of families and lineages.

The income of the clerical order

The question of the income of the clerical order is complicated by the fact that members of the secular clergy not only could possess personal property which was derived from their families (and which returned to these families when they died), but could acquire property by using their savings. We also have to distinguish between the nominal holder of a benefice, who received the income from it, and the priest who actually performed the duties in return for a wage.

The bishoprics

The revenues of the bishoprics varied widely. Between 1723 and 1789, according to Norman Ravitch, six bishoprics brought in less than 10,000 livres; thirty-six brought in between 10,000 and 25,000 livres; fifty-four between 25,000 and 50,000; twenty-three between 50,000 and 75,000; one between 75,000 and 100,000; and one, more than 100,000 livres.

Broadly, 1 livre was equivalent to one day's work. In upper Auvergne, out of 229 nobles, only 33 enjoyed an income exceeding 10,000 livres. In the second quarter of the 18th century the bishopric of Bethléem was worth only 1,000 livres a year; that of Vence 6,600 livres; those of Belley, Dijon, Saint-Paul-Trois-Châteaux and Saint-Pol-de Léon, less than 10,000; that of Toulon, 10,700; those of Tulle, Toul, Vannes, and Luçon, between 11,000 and 25,000; those of Rheims, Cahors, Beauvais, Tours, Verdun, Condom, La Rochelle, Lyons, and Montpellier, between 50,000 and 65,000; while those of Cambrai, Metz, Narbonne, Albi, Auch, Rouen, and Toulouse were worth more than

100,000 livres. Paris reached the figure of 162,000 livres, and Strasbourg, 170,000 livres.

In the diocese of Autun, from the beginning of the 18th century onward, the bishop gave up direct exploitation of his property and went over to the system of farming it out.

Charles-Maurice Le Tellier, archbishop of Rheims, Louvois's brother, received as his share of the inheritance of Chancellor Le Tellier, their father, the sum of 800,000 livres, and at his death he left a fortune estimated at between 1,500,000 and 2,000,000 livres.

The monasteries

In 18th-century Angers, the Benedictine abbey of Saint-Aubin received between 58,000 and 68,000 livres every year. It paid out 7,000 livres in taxes, 1,810 livres to the general hospital, 400 livres for relief of prisoners, etc.—all together, 11,000 livres a year. The abbot was paid 20,000 livres. The 27,000–37,000 livres that remained were shared among fifteen monks, each of whom received between 1,800 and 2,400 livres.

The Benedictine abbey of Lesvière possessed three fiefs, a farm, houses, and gardens and drew tithes from six parishes, for a prior and four monks. The prior received 10,000 livres a year.

The income of the Benedictine abbey of Saint-Nicolas was 41,000 livres a year. Its abbot, De Mostuejouls, titular head of two abbeys, a priory, and a canonry, obtained from these sources 50,000 livres a year for himself alone.

The Benedictines of Saint-Serge obtained each year, from fiefs, farms, and slate quarries, between 12,000 and 14,000 livres for the monks as a whole and between 6,000 and 7,000 livres for the abbot.

The abbey of Toussaint gave its Augustinian canons of Sainte-Geneviève 17,000 livres a year. In contrast to this, the Mendicant orders enjoyed only small incomes—the Carmelites, 5,000 livres, from twenty-seven houses; the Cordeliers, 10,000 livres; the Dominicans, 5,000; the Augustinians, 4,000. The Minims and Capuchins actually lived by begging.

The prebend held by a canon of Angers was worth, in the 18th century, 3,000 livres a year, but since it was combined with chapels and priories, each canon enjoyed an annual income of between 5,000 and 6,000 livres *tournois*. Around 1760, the wages of a servant, the cost of lodging two persons, with their expenditure on wine, bread, meat, and fuel, came to 515 livres a year. The canons of Angers were in a position to accumulate fortunes.

The income of the parish priests

Of the ordinary revenues of the cures of souls, the "great" tithes went to the *gros décimateur,* or *curé primitif*–that is, the appropriator—who gave the priest who carried out his duties the title of "perpetual curate" and a share of the "great" tithes called the *gros,* or *portion congrue* if the ordinary revenues—the "little" and "green" tithes, the *"novales,"* the produce or rent of the lands attached to the cure of souls, with endowments and obits—failed to bring in enough to support him. These ordinary revenues were deducted beforehand from the "great" tithes.

The ordinance of January 1629 fixed the *portion congrue* at 300 livres, and the declaration of August 1632 at 200 livres, for Brittany and the areas beyond the Loire, inclusive of the "little" tithes, the lands of the cures of souls, the lands assigned to pay for obits, and so on. By the declaration of 1634 it was fixed at 200 livres everywhere, for parish priests without a curate, and at 300 for those with a curate; the curate was supposed to be paid 100 livres a year. The ordinance of 30 March 1666 raised the *portion congrue* to 300 livres if the priest had no curate, to 400 if he had one. The declaration of 29 January 1686 increased the *congrue* by adding to the priest's 300 livres the *novales,* offerings, honoraria, and various perquisites. The curate was to receive 150 livres, paid by the owner of the "great" tithes and no longer by the parish priest. The edict of May 1768 increased the *congrue* to 500 livres, payable in cash.

In the diocese of Paris[12] in 1666, of 386 cures of souls, 12 were worth less than 300 livres to their priest, 259 produced an income of between 300 and 1,000 livres, 101 an income of between 1,000 and 15,000 livres, and 14 more than 15,000 livres. The parish priests of the plain of France lived well. The *gros* of the *curé* of Issy was 39 *septiers* of grain, paid by the abbey of Saint-Germain-des-Près, the *gros décimateur;* in 1666 these were worth 400 livres, and the priest also had the garden of his presbytery. The *curé* of Antony had 27 arpents of land belonging to his cure of souls, which were leased out for 300 livres a year in 1675, and perquisites as well. The *curé* of Wissous received, in 1671, 332 livres a year. About 1690, Messire Jean Dachery, *curé* of Tremblay-en-France, possessed 52 arpents, leased out for 460 livres, together with the cartage of his wine and timber; to this he added the produce of the tithes, *champarts,* and a *gros* of 538 livres paid by the monks of Saint-Denis. His total income thus came to 1,000 livres. He gave 60 livres to his curate. The *curé* of Coubron lived in a presbytery with a small garden and a small yard. He received both the "great" and the "little" tithes of his parish: a *muid* and a half of wine, three *septiers* of wheat, five *septiers* of rye, four *septiers* of oats—the equivalent of 200 livres a year.

There were thus big disparities between the incomes of the *curés* of the diocese of Paris. We can divide them into the "rich" (with at least 300 livres of income and 6,000 livres of capital), the "middling" (200 and 4,000 livres), and the "poor" (100 and 2,000 livres). A "rich" *curé* could maintain a little household, employing a maidservant, a footman, and one or two farm workers, and entertaining guests. He would be a university graduate from a well-to-do family and would hold another benefice *in commendam.* Such a man enjoyed the comforts of his period. He was in a position to help a nephew take holy orders, to lend money to his parishioners, to give alms to "poor wayfarers," and to support the village school. He paid the wages of a curate or some chantry priests. He was a man of prestige and independence who, when necessary, would stand up to the *seigneur* or the *élu* on his own behalf or on that of the peasants who were his parishioners.

In contrast, there were, in 1755, forty-three *curés* who did not have even the 500 livres regarded as necessary in order to maintain a modest standard of living.

In the diocese of Rheims, out of 573 *curés,* 91 had opted for the *portion congrue* in cash, at 500 livres (after the edict of May 1768, which allowed them to do this), so that we may conclude that the revenue of their cure of souls came to less than this. Forty-two percent of the cures of souls had, according to the terrier of the diocese, a revenue of at least 500 livres, but, with perquisites and *novales,* this revenue might come to 800 livres. The others, the majority, were worth more. Four of them exceeded 2,000 livres in value and must have reached a figure between 3,000 and 4,000 livres.

The *curé* was thus a resident drawer of income from the soil who frequently collected the revenue of his cure of souls "with his own hands," and sold it, but would farm it out if it was very big. He enjoyed relative security.

Within the clerical order, inequality of income was very marked. About 1750 the average annual income of the bishops came to 37,500 livres. The *portion congrue* then still stood at 300 livres. Each priest dependent on this thus had less than 1 percent of the average episcopal income, and a curate had less than 0.4 percent. True, the priest who lived on his *portion congrue* had an income only 22 times less than that of the bishop of Vence, even if it was 566 times less than that of the bishop of Strasbourg.

The poor priests

Beneath the level of the *curés* there were a certain number of poor priests who lived in "*méparts,*" "*familiarités,*" and "*consorts,*" as "*communalistes,*" "*filleuls,*" "*portionnaires,*" "*familiers,*" or "*sociétaires,*" in the dioceses of Clermont, Besançon, Saint-Claude, Dijon, Langres, Chalon-sur-Saône, Mâcon, Autun, and other dioceses in the center and south of France. These communities were numerous—there were seventeen in the diocese of Autun, forty-four in that of Langres, and five in the town of Dijon alone. Founded between the 13th and the 15th centuries, these were societies of priests who had all been born in a particular parish and baptized in its church. They did not live a common life, but they were supported by a common patrimony of gifts, legacies, and endowments. They carried out the obligations laid down in the endowments and sang the offices. They often numbered between eight and sixteen to a community. Such a group did not form a corporation or college, but it had a head, and it recruited new members by a formal procedure carried out before a royal notary in the presence of several witnesses. These communities flourished in the 16th century and in the first half of the 17th. Later their incomes declined and recruitment dried up. By about 1750 they had nearly all disappeared, though the *mépart* of Paray-le-Monial lasted until 1790.

The hermits

Some hermits lived in the woods, others on the outskirts of towns. The latter were "municipal" hermits, installed by the aldermen in premises belonging to the commune and maintained out of municipal funds, on condition that they prayed for the inhabitants. They were allowed to practice a craft. Near Paris, the hermits of Mont-Valérien formed from the end of the 16th century onward a community which also included recluses, shut away forever in their cells. Bishop Jean-François de Gondi imposed in his diocese a regulation to which the isolated hermits were made subject (1644). He obliged them to undergo a novitiate, to obtain the bishop's approval, to wear gray frieze, live in pairs, and attend Mass, with, for the priests among them, daily recitation of the Roman office and, for the laymen, a choice between the offices of Our Lady, of the Cross, and of the Holy Ghost; the illiterates could recite the office of the Virgin's Crown or that of the Crown of Our Lord. The rule of 1677 prescribed for the hermits of Mont-Valérien a costume of white cloth, perpetual abstinence (as in Lent), recitation of the office in common, and the practicing of a craft. Hermits were looked upon with increasing mistrust during the 18th century. After 1730 the bishops of Autun allowed no more of them to live in the *maladrière* of Autun.

Financial obligations

Inequality was aggravated by the burden of charges. More often than not a *curé* had to pay a pension to the predecessor who had "resigned in his favor" and sometimes pensions to more than one such previous holder of the benefice. An edict of 1671 had decided that these pensions must not exceed one-third of the income from a benefice. The *curé* had to pay a "visitation due" to the archdeacon and a wage to his curate, if he had one, and he was required to maintain and repair the choir of his church. Finally, he had to provide his share of the tax assessed by the Assembly of the Clergy. This share was highly variable. In the first place, there were great inequalities between dioceses. Their quotas were fixed, but while the northern dioceses got richer, the southern ones got poorer. Inequality thus increased. In addition, however, each diocese was sovereign as regards the apportionment and levying of the tax from its clergy. The diocesan bureaus were staffed mainly with rich clerics and the biggest tithe-owners, and so the *curés* were taxed proportionately more heavily than the bishops and abbots; often, too, the poor *curés* were taxed proportionately more heavily than the rich ones. There were some amazing disparities. In 1783 the *curé* of Acqueville, in the diocese of Coutances, paid 200 livres in tax on an income of 500 livres, or 40 percent; in 1769 the *curé* of Bussière-Dunoise, in the diocese of Tulle, paid 57 livres on an income of 500, or 11.4 percent; in 1767 the *curé* of Lonlay-l'Abbaye, in the diocese of Le Mans, paid 48 livres on an income of 500, or 9.6 percent; and the *curé* of Vergy, in the diocese of Dijon, paid 72 livres on an income of 500, or 14.4 percent.

During the 17th century the general assemblies of the clergy suggested that abbeys, priories, chapters, and ordinary benefices should be obliged to pay one-third of their income in tax, *curés* one-sixth, and communities one-tenth. However, not much notice was taken of these recommendations.

During the 18th century the quotas were modified as a result of individual measures. In 1729–30 a system of eleven classes was proposed, but it was applied, in 1735, in only eight dioceses that were especially heavily burdened. What was needed was a general revaluation of the values of benefices, but this was never undertaken. The declarations made by the benefice-holders were purely and simply accepted, and they were always too low. Allowing for this situation, a commission of the Assembly of the Clergy proposed in 1755 a progressive system of eight classes of benefice-holders, each paying 25 percent of his *taxable* income. For example, the first class was to embrace ordinary benefices, abbeys, priories, chapels, and monastic offices, each of which would pay a quarter of its declared income. The second class was to be that of bishoprics with incomes exceeding 36,000 livres, cures of souls with more than 1,800 livres, and cathedral dignities with more than 1,500 livres of declared income; they were to pay a quarter of two-thirds of each declared income, or one-sixth. In the eighth class were bishoprics with incomes of 6,000 livres or less, cures of souls worth 300 livres and less, and so on; these were to pay a quarter of a sixth of their declared income, or one twenty-fourth.

This reform, which was applied very unevenly, nevertheless did reduce the share paid by the *curés* and increase that paid by the other clergy. In 1769 in Lyons the curates paid 2 percent of their income, the *curés* 8.25 percent, the archbishop 10 percent, the chapters, monastic offices, and chapels 10.23 percent, the abbeys, priories, and communities 15.03 percent. In the diocese of Bordeaux the reform was applied properly, and in 1781 each class there paid in fact what it was supposed to pay in theory. There was thus an improvement in the situation; but the basis of the system, unchecked declaration of income, was faulty, and fiscal justice was not attained. Discontent persisted among the *curés*.

The life-style of the clerical order

To discuss the life-style of the clerical order could easily lead us into a discussion of the Catholic Renaissance in general, the problems of Jansenism, those of the Catholic "philosophical" movement, and so on. However, we are not writing a history of the Church in France but are trying only to situate the order of the clergy in French society as a whole. It therefore seems appropriate to restrict ourselves to a few characteristics and, in particular, to consider how far the clergy, and especially the priests, matched up to the ideal set by the Council of Trent.

The first half of the 17th century

In the first half of the 17th century we appear to be confronted by a clergy who were in the main poorly educated, even uncouth, and who, in the case of many parish priests, led lives similar to those of ordinary laymen of equivalent rank. This type of cleric gradually declined in numbers. By the 1690s the sacerdotal ideal of the Council of Trent had clearly triumphed, and it remained dominant until the 1760s. In the first part of our period there was still a relatively large number of worldly bishops who spent too much for profane purposes, let their chaplains and staffs traffic in collations to benefices and their servants extort money from persons seeking audience with them, and who took little interest in the recruitment, functioning, or morals of their clergy.

Among the many canons were some who went about in short coats, embroidered and with colored ribbons on them, with a violet mantle, colored stockings, white shoes with silver cavalier-like buckles, loose-fitting shirts, and curled hair descending to their shoulders. They showed little assiduity in their offices and, when they did perform them, gave little attention to the intoning of the psalms, during which they would pursue their conversations; instead, they frequented drink shops, went to brothels, engaged in disputes and brawls, and carried off maidservants.

Many *curés* were not resident and so left the duties of their cure of souls to a cleric who acted for them. *Curés,* chaplains, *habitués,* all failed to teach the catechism or to preach, owing to incapacity; they no longer knew the liturgical formulas, or else they repeated Latin words which they no longer (or had never) understood. They left the sick to die without the sacraments, sold the sacraments, and said masses only if they were paid sufficiently. They celebrated Sunday Mass only irregularly, reducing it to a low Mass and hurrying it through, and usually they did away with vespers. They celebrated without wearing a soutane, with the sacerdotal ornaments flung over their jerkins. Their dislike of hearing confessions was extreme, for they had no idea how to sort out a matter of conscience, and they gave absolution too easily. Lacking respect for God's house, they allowed their churches to fall into dirtiness and disorder.

They saw their parish or their functions as a source of income. What preoccupied them was tithes, *portions congrues,* disputes, and lawsuits. As they had to sell a part of the income that they received in kind, they frequented fairs, trafficked in horses and cattle, became factors and agents for *seigneurs* and *gentilshommes,* engaged in usury, and made money for themselves. They found recreation from these wearying activities in hunting and playing bowls and also devoted themselves to card games with such passion that they spent whole nights over them. They often went to the drink shops, emerging in a scandalous state, which led to brawls, fisticuffs, and fighting with sticks. They took mistresses from among their parishioners, visited prostitutes, or kept concubines in their homes and had children by them. The more responsible ones brought these children up and taught them to serve at the altar; if the children were girls, they gave them dowries and married them off. The inhabitants of the diocese of Autun were so used to all this that they replied to an inquiry in 1645 that some *curés* of this kind led good lives; the parishioners thought that priests were allowed to have concubines.

There were even some priests who were undevout or even atheists, such as Dagonneau of Fontenay, who "may possibly never have told his parishioners that there is a God" (1689), or the famous *curé* of Etrépigny, in the Ardennes, Jean Meslier, who, though he had graduated from one of the best seminaries of the Catholic Counter-Reformation, left at his death a confession of atheist beliefs. However, though it is logical to see a relation between these facts and those previously mentioned, especially since atheism is as natural to man as tuberculosis, they belong perhaps to a different movement of ideas, arising from Cartesianism, mechanism, and neo-Stoicism.

The principal reason for these irregularities doubtless lay in the inadequacy of the training received. Most of these men had acquired only elementary notions about religion, given them hastily by some priest, perhaps their uncle or cousin. Religion in the sense of dialogue, loving intercourse, with the Holy Trinity, and the imitation of Jesus Christ, truly God and truly man, had not become their very life.

From the priests, laxity had spread to the laity. Confraternities were associations of persons who came together in a body within a particular church in order to carry out acts of devotion in the name of some holy patron. They were recognized by written consent from the bishop and letters patent from the king. They had often drifted far from their aim of stimulating religious fervor. In the archdeaconry of Autun these associations were organized in "realms" of men and or women, and the titles of "king" and "queen" were sold by auction or disposed of cheaply, along with the other dignities of the association. At Dompierre-sur-Besbre the "Royaume de Monsieur Saint-Pierre" included king, captain, lieutenant, guidon, ensign, *écuyer tranchant, trésorier des finances,* harquebusiers, and footmen to the king, with twenty-three dignities, first equerry, *maître de camp,* harbinger, winetaster, tenderizer of meat, maker of the king's barge, cook to the king, sergeant in command of a troop, pikeman, first marshal, secretary, and constable. At Neuvry, the "Royaume du Saint-Esprit" had eighty-six dignities, titles, or military ranks. All this served rather to supply a psychological excuse for self-esteem and ambition than to develop humility in accordance with the example of Jesus Christ, "gentle and humble-hearted." The feast day of the saint who was the patron of the confraternity began with a Mass but continued with festivities, a banquet, and dances that had little that was Christian about them.

The recovery, from the middle of the 17th century to the middle of the 18th

From Louis XIII's time onward a gradual recovery is observable. This was one aspect of what has been called the Catholic Renaissance in France. It was due in the first place to a better choice of bishops by the king, his Conseil de Conscience, and the ministers in charge of *"la feuille."* We find thereafter a larger number of bishops filled with a sense of duty, animated even by a truly apostolic zeal, who organize seminaries, repair churches, cause catechisms to be composed and taught, establish schools, purify the forms of worship, and give supervision and guidance to their priests.

The seminaries

The first problem was that of the professional training of the secular clergy, which had never been well looked after. The Council of Trent, by a decree of 1563, had made it obligatory for bishops and chapters to ensure, on a permanent basis, the recruitment of clergy for each diocese through the founding, near the church, of a special college or seminary. Boys were to be admitted from the age of twelve, provided that they could read and write and showed promise of becoming priests. Poor boys were to be preferred, but rich ones would not be excluded, provided they paid for themselves and showed an earnest desire to serve God. The pupils were to wear clerical dress, receive the tonsure, and live under clerical discipline. They were to attend Mass every day and to confess and take Communion every month. They were to be taught grammar, singing, literature, the Scriptures, the art of composing homilies, and the rites and ceremonies of the Church. The bishop, assisted by two delegates from the chapter and two from the clergy of the town, was to administer the seminary, draw up regulations for it, and endow it by means of a deduction from the revenues from all church property, except that of the mendicant friars, and to assign some ordinary benefices to it.

A big effort was made in France, between 1567 and 1614, to establish seminaries. The Ordinance of Blois (May 1579) enjoined the bishops to set up seminaries and called on the sovereign courts to see that this was done. The Edict of Melun (February 1580) ordered bishops to hold provincial councils with a view, among other things, to the creation of seminaries. The cardinal of Lorraine established the first French seminary in 1567 in Rheims, and other establishments followed, at Bordeaux, Valence, Aix, Toulouse, Rouen, Rodez, Agen, at Maillezais in 1601, and then at Luçon, where the seminary was founded by Richelieu in 1611. The bishop supervised these seminaries without the help of the commission provided for by the Council of Trent. He had the power to dismiss the principal. But if he entered into a contract with a religious order for the latter to conduct the seminary, he merely had its accounts submitted to him. Despite the provision of scholarships for poor boys, few pupils came to the seminaries. The first purpose aimed at was to train them in piety and the ecclesiastical spirit. Getting up at half past four in summer and at five in winter, the seminarists made their own beds, cleaned their rooms, and served at table, so as to exercise them in humility. The midday meal was preceded by a reading from some religious work, followed by an examination of conscience focused on the predominant fault, or *examen particulier*. In the evening there was a general examination of conscience. The day began and ended with prayers. Confession was made once a month, and the confessor prescribed the frequency of Communion—fortnightly or weekly. Telling one's beads was much favored. It was compulsory to wear a soutane. The seminarist had to get used to submitting his will not only to God but also to God's representatives, the principal of the seminary and his confessor and director in religious life, and to the rules that they laid down. Between seminarists and principals, feelings of affection and respect were to prevail, but there must be no familiarity: each was to address the other as "Monsieur." Strict chastity was required of all. The seminarists practiced plainsong, took part in church ceremonies, and carried out the duties of acolytes, lectors, subdeacons, and deacons.

Study was regarded as less important than this training but necessary, nevertheless, to equip one for teaching the faithful, serving one's neighbor, and keeping one's end up in controversy. The basis of study in the seminary consisted of the humanities and philosophy; divinity was given only slight attention, however, and dogma was hurried through, church history was not dealt with, and controversy was practiced very little.

By 1614 only six or eight seminaries survived, of mediocre quality; they were attached to colleges. The Wars of Religion, the burning and pillaging of churches and church property that went on, the absence of bishops in forty-three dioceses, and the mediocrity in matters of religion of some of the others were doubtless among the principal reasons for this setback. It was not made up for by the existence of colleges that provided courses in divinity; the Jesuits at La Flèche had 90 students attending these lectures after 1603, while those at the Collège de Clermont had 150.

The great period of the rise of seminaries was 1630–82, and especially 1642–60. Under the influence of the Catholic Renaissance a public opinion was formed which gave support or stimulation to the bishops. Pressure groups like the Compagnie du Saint-Sacrement de l'Autel, and distinguished individuals, like Vincent de Paul, who both inspired these groups and expressed their views, brought about a revival of the movement for founding seminaries.

The Estates General of 1614 urged the bishops to establish seminaries, and the Assemblies of the Clergy repeated the injunction. The ordinance of 1629, due to Keeper of the Seals De Marillac, prescribed the application of article 24 of the Ordinance of Blois, but this ordinance was not registered by the Paris *parlement*. The ordinance of 1666 repeated the obligation laid upon bishops to found seminaries.

These political and legislative moves were stimulated by private persons, both clerics and pious laymen, who were anxious to train priests who would approach the sacerdotal ideal. These clerics and laymen all sprang from the circles of the high *noblesse d'épée*, the magistrates and the lawyers. They tried first of all to get priests who were men of good will to conform to a model based on the principles of the Council of Trent, through life in communities established for this purpose. Soon they began using these communities, in agreement with the bishops, to give candidates for ordination at least the final, purely technical part of a priest's training, by organizing retreats for ordinands. From this stage the bishops passed gradually to the creation of seminaries.

Pierre de Bérulle, son and nephew of magistrates of the *parlement,* having taken the advice, in 1602, of Saint François de Sales, who had just founded at Thonon an establishment modeled on the congregation of the Oratory of Saint Philip Neri, sought to reform the clergy by means of a society of priests. It was with this end in view that, after seeing at Avignon César de Bus, head of the Congrégation de la Doctrine Chrétienne, who informed him of the usages of the Oratory in Rome, and being urged on by his uncle, Président Séguier, he gathered some priests around him in the Maison du Petit-Bourbon, in the rue Saint-Jacques, where the Val-de-Grâce now stands, on 10 November 1611. In May 1613 the Oratory of Jesus Christ received its bull of institution from Pope Paul V, "in honor of the prayers that Our Savior uttered during his mortal life." The members were "pious priests specially devoted to fulfilling with all possible perfection the duties of sacerdotal life." By 1624 the Oratory had forty houses. In 1660 it had sixty-three.

In July 1628 the bishop of Beauvais, Augustin Potier de Gesvres, had suggested to Saint Vincent de Paul that he might concern himself not only with bringing priests closer to the sacerdotal ideal but also with training *future* priests, by means of retreats for ordinands, until it should become possible to establish seminaries. Saint Vincent de Paul saw in this a good way to test the reality of vocations, for vocation was the essential point. In February 1631 the archbishop of Paris asked him to direct, in person, retreats for the ordinands of his diocese, receiving them at the Collège des Bons-Enfants and, in subsequent years, at Saint-Lazare. These were retreats of twenty days' duration. The ordinands were housed and fed free of charge. Each day they heard two talks—in the morning on moral theology, and in the evening on the duties of a priest. After each talk the ordinands, divided into groups of fifteen, discussed the question which had been dealt with. A priest of the mission directed each discussion group and questioned the ordinands. These retreats for ordinands were copied elsewhere.

Even before Saint Vincent de Paul, another disciple of Bérulle and

Saint François de Sales, Adrien Bourdoise, had founded a community of priests which prepared candidates for ordination. Born in 1584, the son of a notary in the diocese of Chartres but soon orphaned, he became a cowherd, then clerk to an attorney, footman to a *président* in Paris, servant to a *curé* at Orléans, and, at last, porter at the Collège de Chartres. Bourdoise formed, while quite young, a high conception of priestly dignity. Porter at the age of twenty-four, in 1608, he taught young clerics and priests and corresponded with *curés* and curates, encouraging them to perform with love and fidelity the obligations of their estate. In 1611 he spent three months in Bérulle's company. He considered establishing a parochial community which could supply priests for a diocese. They would be called to service in the parishes at the command of the bishops and *curés,* would form new communities, in which they would live in the same house, eating at the same table, and would raise up other priests in the ideal of the primitive church. He did not join the Oratory, for Bérulle wished to concern himself mainly with *curés* and curates, who in Paris were persons of condition, and graduates, whereas Bourdoise wished to concern himself mainly with the *plebs* of the clergy, the *habitués.* The Oratory was a *congrégation,* with a head, a rule, a novitiate, houses, and chapels of its own. Bourdoise wanted to form communities that would be wholly dependent upon the *curés.* In 1612, in the first week of Lent, he founded a community of ten priests, and in 1613 he himself became a priest. After 1612 the community was placed under the authority of Messire Froger, *curé* of Saint-Nicolas-du-Chardonnet, doctor and associate of the Sorbonne. The community found lodging wherever it could and often moved on. In 1619 Bourdoise talked with Saint François de Sales, who recommended him to Cardinal De Retz. The latter gave him oral permission to carry on with his work. On 7 December 1620 the community was welcomed into the house in the rue Saint-Victor of the priest Compaing (son of a *greffier* of the King's Council and *secrétaire du roi*), which was later to become the seminary of Saint-Nicolas-du-Chardonnet. On 26 July 1631 the community drew up a formal agreement with Messire Froger. The community, "a parochial family," received into its membership priests who were required to have stayed with it "for at least one whole year, so as to have been trained and exercised, theoretically and practically, in the functions of parish priests and in the manner of living in this community, and who have passed an examination by [the archbishop] and obtained from him . . . authority to hear confessions and perform the other parochial duties in his diocese, with the consent of Messieurs les Curés." The community was approved in letters from the archbishop of Paris, Henri de Gondi, on 24 October 1631, and in letters patent from the king in February 1632, which were verified by the *parlement*. In 1637 a "clerical scholarship" was established, financed by gifts from pious persons, for the maintenance of poor clerics. Bourdoise led the community until 1639. In 1630 Henri de Gondi had entrusted Bourdoise with the task of "causing to be learnt and rehearsed the ceremonies and rubrics both of the Missal and of the Breviary, by the new priests of his diocese." Bourdoise trained in this way over 500 priests, either in retreats preliminary to ordination or in retreats for ordinands.

Saint Vincent de Paul—son of Gascon peasants, bachelor of divinity, secretary and chaplain in ordinary to Queen Marguerite de Valois, abbot of Saint-Léonard du Chaunes, of the Cistercian Order, in the diocese of Saintes—had become acquainted with Bérulle and had stayed at the Oratory. Bérulle had secured for him the cure of souls at Clichy (2 May 1612 to the end of 1613) and then a post as preceptor to the children of Philippe-Emmanuel de Gondi, general of the galleys, brother to Henri de Gondi, archbishop of Paris, Cardinal De Retz, and then, on 1 August 1617, at his request (so that he might spread the Gospel among the poorest and most ignorant of the people, the peasants), the cure of souls at Châtillon-des-Dombes, where he organized a community of *habitués*. Obliged by Bérulle to return, at the summons of the Gondi family, to evangelize the seven or eight thousand peasants on their estates, he began his great work of missions, formation of the sisterhoods of the Ladies of Charity, and visits to the galley slaves, for which he was made chaplain general of the galleys, on 8 February 1619. The Gondis gave him the money to create a society of priests to do missionary work in the countryside, which was established on 17 April 1625, approved in 1626 by the archbishop of Paris, in 1627 by letters patent from the king, and in 1632 by a bull of Pope Urban VIII, and eventually, in 1655, elevated by a papal brief into the Congregation of the Mission. Installed by an agreement made on 7 January 1632 in the former priory and leper hospital of Saint-Lazare, the mission priests, or Lazarists, quickly became active over a wide area.

On his part, Saint Vincent de Paul added to his retreats for ordinands, starting on 16 July 1623 the "Tuesday Conferences of Messieurs de Saint-Lazare," the purpose of which was to "confer with them [the priests] regarding the virtues and functions appropriate to their ministry." These meetings lasted for two hours. Each participant spoke in turn on the subject under consideration. Among those who attended were Jean-Jacques Olier, Bossuet (one of the most assiduous frequenters of the conferences from 1643 onward), the abbot of Roncé, and Pavillon, bishop of Alet. These gatherings were the prototype of the "ecclesiastical conferences."

From societies of priests, retreats for ordinands, and ecclesiastical conferences the transition was easily made to seminaries. In 1624 the archbishop of Paris handed over to Bérulle and the Oratory an already existing seminary, that of Saint-Magloire, in a former abbey adjoining Saint-Jacques-du-Haut-Pas. In January 1642 Father Bourgoing, general of the congregation of the Oratory, reorganized this seminary and welcomed into it fourteen young scholarship-holders, beneficiaries of a donation by Richelieu. Later in the year Richelieu brought Saint Vincent de Paul there, ordered him to create a seminary, and gave him a thousand *écus* for the task. In February 1642 the saint opened, at the Collège des Bons-Enfants, an ecclesiastical school for twelve priests-to-be and also, in an annex of Saint-Lazare, a preparatory school, the Ecole Saint-Charles, which children could attend in order to study the classics without necessarily committing themselves to holy orders. In this way the minor seminary and the major one were brought into existence. Saint Vincent de Paul also founded seminaries at Cahors (1643), Saintes (1644), Le Mans (1645), Agen, Tréguier (1648), and Montauban (1651). The course of study at these institutions, which was of a purely practical character, took between six months and two years.

On 20 April 1644 Jean-François de Gondi officially recognized as a seminary the community formed by Bourdoise at Saint-Nicolas-du-Chardonnet. The period of study was one year. The training was purely practical and concerned with essentials: reading, writing, spelling, plainsong, the sacraments, cases of conscience, and liturgy. Instruction was given by way of question and answer. The principal place in the curriculum was accorded to practical exercises: baptism, carried out with a doll; penance, in which one seminarist played the part of the confessor and another that of the penitent; preaching, when each pupil in turn gave a sermon lasting a quarter of an hour, with variations of tone and gesture, and then was criticized without mercy. Every week the seminarists had a lecture on the Roman catechism, and each Sunday, after vespers, they took the catechism themselves in the church of Saint-Nicolas-du-Chardonnet, under the supervision of the prefect of catechisms; this meant a simple catechism, with explanation of the creed (what a Christian must believe), of the Commandments (what a Christian must do), and of the sacraments, or channels of grace for the reception of faith, hope, and charity. According to Saint Vincent de Paul, the priests turned out by the seminary of Saint-Nicolas-du-Chardonnet were "all ready to serve a parish as a result of having been exercised in that one."

Jean-Jacques Olier, born in 1608, son of a master of requests and intendant of justice at Lyons, after being trained for the priesthood at Saint-Lazare under the direction of Saint Vincent de Paul and after three times declining bishoprics, came in December 1641, with his first two comrades, to Vaugirard, where he began to teach young clerics with a view to making good parish priests of them. In August 1642 Olier became *curé* of Saint-Sulpice, brought his Vaugirard group there, and founded the seminary of Saint-Sulpice. In 1655 he acquired at Issy, from Antoine de Sève, the king's chaplain, the former country seat of Queen Marguerite de Valois and was given Sève's library. He intended Issy to be used as a holiday home for the seminarists and those in charge of them. Two groups soon sorted themselves out among the seminarists of Saint-Sulpice: those who were destined to become parish priests, and the "inner seminary," or "seminary of solitude," those who were to join the community of Saint-Sulpice and become its directors at Issy (except for a period between 1654 and 1658, when they were at the Château of Avron, as guests of Alexandre Le Ragois de Bretonvilliers).

In all the bulls of canonical institution, new bishops were placed under the obligation to found seminaries. In the eighteen years between 1642 and 1660, thirty-six seminaries were founded, and, in the twenty-two years between 1660 and 1682, another fifty-six. At the same time, many "minor seminaries" for the study of the humanities and philosophy were founded. As a result, after 1660, the retreats for ordinands gradually disappeared.

Study at the seminary, which was at first optional, was made compulsory after 1697 in the diocese of Paris for all who aspired to holy orders: nine months of study before entering the subdiaconate and three months before entering the priesthood. Increasing importance was assigned to vocation and the signs thereof: purity of intention, detachment from the world, integrity of morals. Attention was mainly given to training the feelings, and the principal instrument for this purpose was half an hour or an hour of prayer in the morning, in common, after a reading on a subject announced the night before, in

accordance with the method of Saint François de Sales, which Saint
Vincent de Paul had introduced, and following more and more the
method of Saint-Sulpice. Prayer was supplemented, before dinner, by
the reading of a chapter of the New Testament, followed by self-
examination regarding a particular vice or fault; by spiritual readings
taken from the Bible, from the Catechism of the Council of Trent, from
the *De Imitatione Christi,* and from the *Introduction à la Vie Dévote;*
by confession; and by weekly or twice-weekly Communion. Each
fortnight at Saint-Sulpice, each month at Saint-Lazare, every seminarist revealed to one of the directors, outside the setting of confession, his inner disposition, temptations, and difficulties, his progress
and his setbacks. The year began with a retreat lasting between three
and eight days. The directors emphasized the dignity of the priestly
state, as set forth in the Epistle to the Hebrews: Jesus Christ was the
sovereign priest, and priests were by their very character an extension
of his eternal ministry.

To an increasing extent, future priests entered the "major" seminary
after having passed through the "minor" one. Either they received
only a religious education at the "minor" seminary and went on to
study at the neighboring college, or else the "minor" seminary gave
them also a liberal intellectual training, through the humanities and
philosophy. There were two types of major seminary: those to which
men came, after having studied elsewhere, in order to prepare themselves to take orders and carry out priestly functions by obtaining
practical instruction; and those which added, to this, a theological
training, given in the neighboring colleges or divinity faculties but
completed by coaching at the major seminary, as happened at Saint-
Sulpice and at the establishments run by the Jesuits, the Oratorians,
and the Congrégation de la Doctrine Chrétienne. The methods of teaching used were very similar to those of the divinity faculties: at Saint-
Sulpice, half an hour's dictation and an hour of explanation, all of
which was gone over "in conference" under the chairmanship of one
of the more advanced pupils, with questions, objections, and discussion; with the Lazarists, after 1668, the pupils spent half an hour discussing the previous lesson, then another half an hour was devoted to
exercises, and in the last half-hour the teacher explained the next lesson. In both establishments, time was reserved every Saturday for
coaching, revision, recitation, and defense of a thesis by means of
controversy. Examinations on entry and on leaving, and continuous
supervision, were enforced as a means of stimulating and checking on

the pupils' work. Ordination was often refused to those whose work proved unsatisfactory.

As regards the subjects taught, practical considerations predominated, but there was an increasing emphasis on religious feeling. Canon law was not studied. Church history was reduced to a few notions related to divinity and to readings from history during meals. Plainsong, however, was taught with great care, and inadequacy in that accomplishment could result in failure in an examination. The liturgy, which gives expression to dogma, was accorded great attention, and the pupils strove to become filled with its spirit and the significance of its ceremonies and to take part in them with love. The liturgical manual compiled by Beuvelet, a priest of Saint-Nicolas-du-Chardonnet, published in 1654, went through seventeen editions. There were many practical exercises in the administration of the sacraments and the hearing of confessions and also lectures on the Scriptures. At Lisieux, in 1678, aspirants to the diaconate were questioned on the New Testament, and aspirants to the priesthood on the whole of the Bible. However, the purpose was merely to find in the Scriptures elements of spiritual and moral edification that could be used in preaching. Little time was given to theology, and that mostly to moral theology: the Catechism of the Council of Trent, explanation of casuistics, doctrine, and administration of the sacraments. Nevertheless, after 1660, dogmatic and scholastic theology gained ground. The Lazarists used Abelly's manual (1651) in two volumes, the first of which was devoted to dogma. The Oratorians introduced a course on dogma into their curriculum. The future priests were trained to teach the catechisms, and they performed this task in the children's schools. They were exercised in preaching by giving short sermons during meals on Sundays and feast days and even, at Saint-Nicolas-du-Chardonnet, by sermons they delivered from the pulpit on subjects laid down by the prefect, followed by a criticism given by the teacher.

Between 1682 and 1715 eleven more seminaries were founded. At the end of Louis XIV's reign nearly all the dioceses had a seminary, the exceptions being a few of the poorest. The king sought to take the seminaries away from the Oratorians, who were too Cartesian. In 1682 the Jesuits agreed to take charge of the seminaries and associate them with their colleges. Philosophy and theology would be taught in the college, and two or three directors would concern themselves in the seminary with the formation of priests-to-be. The Jesuits made a contract in 1683 with the bishop of Strasbourg for their first seminary, which opened its doors in 1684. However, the Lazarists also took responsibility for seminaries, and other orders, as well, engaged in this work. In Rheims in the 18th century, alongside the Jesuits' seminary, which had very few pupils, there was the seminary of the Canons of Sainte-Geneviève, attended by the majority of the aspirants to the priesthood. At Angers it was the Congrégation de Saint-Sulpice who directed the seminary, and the famous Emery was its superior between 1775 and 1782, before he was summoned to Paris.

The curriculum became more and more theoretical and therefore more and more lengthy. At the seminary of the canons of Sainte-Geneviève, in Rheims in 1774, the course of study took five years, two being devoted to philosophy and three to theology. Canon law made its appearance as a subject of study. Study of the Scriptures was given a new impulse. A Hebrew course was started, first of all in some of the Jesuit colleges; the teachers gave their pupils some ideas of the history of the Bible, the languages in which it was written, the different versions, the various interpretations. The decisive step was taken when Father Bernard Lamy, an Oratorian, published in 1687 his *Apparatus biblicus,* in which he set forth the general content of the Bible and the principal rules for its exegesis. As new editions of the book were produced, he developed his treatment of the origin and history of the people of Israel, the political and religious institutions mentioned in the Bible, information about different versions and editions of the texts, and archaeological data. The manual became a classic and was translated into French in 1696 under the title *Introduction à toute l'Ecriture.* The place given to dogmatic theology (taught in the mornings) was enlarged. The *Théologie de Poitiers* (1708) in four volumes, also called the *Théologie de Bonal,* was definitely a work of dogmatic theology, anti-Jansenist, antiprobabilist, and ultramontane. In this way there was formed in the 18th century a body of clergy who were more intellectual, more disposed to reason, if not more rationalistic, and more aware of their duties, but with a drier and less fervent spiritual life. At Angers, however, the Sulpician Emery wrote, during his period as superior of the seminary, "The first and last aim of this institute is to live for God in Christ Jesus, Our Lord, in such a way that the inward dispositions of His Son may enter into the deepest places of our hearts." He quoted Saint Paul: "I live; yet not I, but Christ liveth in me," and he urged devotion to the Blessed Sacrament and to the Virgin Mary—which shows the limits there are to any generalization.

The training of parish priests was continued throughout their lives in many dioceses, after 1648, by periodical examinations, either during synods or during pastoral visitations, when those who showed themselves inadequate were ordered to study. Another means used was ecclesiastical conferences. Bishop Jacques Raoul de la Guibourgère in 1655 divided his diocese of La Rochelle into forty-one conference areas. In each of these, a vicar forane brought together the priests of between five and eleven parishes for monthly meetings lasting three hours, at which they carried out, in common, study of the subject chosen for that month: Christian doctrine, the sacrament, the divine sacrifice and office, Christ's Sacrifice and the Church, internal oblation and external sacrifice, priesthood of the believers, the Mass, and the Christian life. At the end of each meeting the priests rehearsed the liturgical ceremonies. In the diocese of Paris ecclesiastical conferences were made general after 1666. Each month at such a conference there was discussion of moral theology, casuistics, the rubrics of ritual, catechism, homilies, sermons, and especially the pastoral ideal: prayer and the educating and sanctifying of souls.

This continuous training was reinforced by exhortations from bishops during the annual synods, pastoral visitations by the bishop or his vicar general, annual eight-day retreats in a monastery, and, finally, the priests' individual reading. In the diocese of Sens, Archbishop Gondrin ordered his *curés,* by ordinance of 20 August 1658, to obtain seventeen books and to show them to him when he made his pastoral visitation: the Bible, Carranza's *Summa Conciliarum,* the documents of the Council of Trent, the Roman Catechism, the *Summa* of Saint Thomas Aquinas, Turlot's *Trésor de la doctrine chrétienne,* Saint Charles Borromeo's instructions for confessors, Molina's *Instructio Sacerdotum,* the *De Imitatione Christi,* the *Introduction à la vie dévote,* the works of Saint Gregory, and the works of Saint Bernard. Most bishops worked toward the same end, and after 1729 all *curés* possessed the few indispensable volumes: the Bible, Saint Gregory, Saint Bernard, Saint Augustine, Saint Thomas's *Summa,* catechisms, manuals of theology, works on meditation. Some of them had whole libraries; the *curé* of Saint-Léger de Bourbon-Lancy, for example, left five or six hundred books when he died in 1739.

Results of training

Good results began to show themselves from the middle of the 17th century onward. They were especially noteworthy at the end of that century and in the 18th. The bishops succeeded in securing a greater degree of residence by priests in their parishes and a clearer separation from the world, shown in the wearing of the soutane and short hair. After the end of the 17th century it was exceptional to come upon a priest who was not wearing a soutane. The attitude of priests became serious and modest. Their use of their time included fewer profane occupations and "popular" ways of spending leisure. There was a great deal less hunting, playing of cards and bowls, drunkenness, whoring, concubinage with servants, and taking of mistresses from among the parishioners. There were still cases of *curés* being sent to Saint-Lazare or Saint-Nicolas-du-Chardonnet, being suspended, laid under interdict, or compelled to resign. However, in the archdeaconry of Brie, between 1653 and 1662, only twenty priests were called to order. In the archdeaconry of Paris, in 1672 and 1673, only eleven priests were found deserving of rebuke. In the diocese of La Rochelle during the second half of the 17th century, between 5 and 10 percent of the priests were reprimanded as against 10–25 percent before 1648, while parishioners had become more demanding. Prayer invaded the life of the priest; it included the half-hour of morning prayer prescribed by many bishops, following either the method of the *Spiritual Exercises* of Saint Ignatius or that of Saint-Sulpice, the particular examination, the general examination, and the eight daily offices through the psalms in the breviary.

In the liturgy, the dignity of worship was restored, respect for the grandeur of God was manifested, and religious feelings were shown through the greater honor given to the altar, the beauty of the tabernacles, carved and set off with ornamentation in gold and azure, the sacred vessels made of silver, and the altarpieces decorated with painted columns and figures of saints. The sacraments were accorded great honor. Priests insisted upon penitence, the necessity of contrition, of making reparation, of giving back what belonged to others, of reconciling oneself with one's neighbor, of avoiding occasions for sin. *Curés* preached but rarely; it was the monasteries that provided preachers. In 1697 Cardinal De Noailles enjoined all the *curés* of his diocese to "deliver a sermon at Mass in the parish church and in it to instruct the people as to the principal truths of religion and their duties, in a manner proportioned to their understanding and useful to them." Manuals were published in order to help the performance of this duty. In 1675 there appeared one by A. Gambart, a disciple of Saint Vincent de Paul: *Le missionaire français ou sommaire des exhortations familières sur les 52 dimanches de l'année en faveur des curez, vicaires et ecclésiastiques de la campagne pour l'instruction des pauvres et du simple peuple dans les prônes.* The year 1716 saw the publication of the manual written by Joseph Lambert, prior of Saint-Martin de Palaiseau: *La manière de bien instruire les pauvres et, en particulier, les gens de la campagne.* Catechisms appeared more often. In the diocese of Paris the *curés* used the methods of Bourdoise, as published in 1668 and 1669, which consisted in explaining the three theological virtues of faith, hope, and charity by means of examples taken from biblical history and the lives of the saints, together with an initiation into the liturgy. Each lesson included an outline of the main features, a summary to be recited, and a story. Archbishops, too, composed catechisms—Jean-François de Gondi in and after 1646, Hardouin de Péréfixe in 1672 (*Instruction de la doctrine chrétienne*)—all inspired by Bourdoise's method. In the diocese of La Rochelle, twenty diocesan catechisms were published between 1670 and 1685. Henry de Laval, bishop of La Rochelle, Henry de Barillon, bishop of Luçon, and Henry Arnauld, bishop of Angers, published in 1676 the *Catéchisme ou doctrine chrétienne* known as the *Catéchisme des Trois Henry*. This was threefold in form. There was a short catechism of 27 pages for the younger children; a middle-sized one of 93 pages for children between the age of seven and first Communion; and a big catechism of 382 pages for educated persons and priests. Inspired by Bérulle, Condren, Saint Vincent de Paul, Bourdoise, and Olier, the "Three Henrys" sought to make the religion of believers a life of learning from Christ. They defined the Church as "a holy people, a society, one single body, of which Jesus Christ is the head and every believer a member." They stressed faith, inward worship, the priesthood of believers, and the sacrificial character of the Eucharist. Retreats were organized for laymen in the towns, and missions were sent to the countryside. The confraternities now tried to persuade their members to practice virtue with greater perfection and to lead an exemplary life.

From Christocentrism to anthropocentrism (from the end of the 17th century to the end of the 18th)

Despite all this, many priests were Jansenists. In the 18th century, wills provide evidence that some *curés* who had officially accepted the bull *Unigenitus* remained Jansenist at heart.

As for the Enlightenment, its influence seems to have been felt belatedly. In the diocese of Rheims in 1773, two-thirds of the *curés* were aged between forty and sixty. They had been born between 1713 and 1733 and ordained between 1738 and 1758 or 1760. Twenty percent of the *curés* were over sixty. Consequently, they had received their theological education before the great diffusion of "philosophical" ideas. However, that does not mean that they were unaware of or had remained insensitive to them.

In any case, many of them had been influenced by Cartesianism. In the doctrine that emerged from Descartes, the separation of matter from spirit, the reduction of matter to extension, set up additional obstacles to acceptance of the concept of substance and rendered more offensive to reason the dogmas of the Real Presence and of Transubstantiation. The Cartesianism taught at Saint-Sulpice bears a great deal of responsibility for the apostasy of Ernest Renan. The Saint-Sulpice of Renan's time continued, in its teaching of philosophy, the tradition of the Saint-Sulpice of the *ancien régime*. The teaching of Cartesianism was widespread from 1690 onward. Besides Saint-Sulpice, it was taught also at the Oratory and at the seminary of the Congrégation de la Doctrine Chrétienne, where some priests got their training.

It would appear that the spread of Cartesianism—which (probably quite contrary to what its author intended) favored a mutation of values, bringing to the forefront of social values, of what seemed true, fine, good, and desirable, material wealth, abundance, well-being, and health—helped to bring about a pronounced change in the religious outlook around 1700. Gradually the Christocentrism of Bérulle and the Catholic Renaissance gave way to a form of anthropocentrism. Instead of life led, first and foremost, in and for God, the clergy took to preaching life for one's neighbor—which is good but ought to be only a consequence of a life lived in love of the Holy Trinity. It would appear that this alteration in values may have corresponded to an impoverishment in the culture and spiritual life of the priesthood. In the diocese of La Rochelle, instead of the living unity of the Christian mystery, the teaching consisted of fragmented courses, with morality reduced to cases of conscience, dogma to a dialectic with proofs, objections, and replies, and the Holy Scriptures a separate subject of study. In the ecclesiastical conferences held after 1706 it was no longer a question of studying more thoroughly Christ's sacrifice or the priesthood of believers but of considering intemperance and dispensations. There was less emphasis

on the sacerdotal ideal and more on the limits beyond which transgres-
sion begins. A separation was made between the intellectual and the
spiritual. From the lists of books to be read by *curés*, Saint Bernard,
Saint Gregory, and the *Summa* of Saint Thomas disappeared, and the
utilitarian standpoint prevailed. Sacrifice vanished from the program of
sacerdotal spirituality. Prayer was no longer the movement of the Holy
Ghost in one's soul but meditation upon a work of piety. Less emphasis
was placed on the dispositions necessary for receiving the Eucharist,
and more on the benefits of Communion for the soul. Sunday preaching
dealt with a "practical truth of Christian morality" instead of consisting of a commentary on the Gospels or the Epistles or an explanation of
the articles of the Apostles' Creed or of the requests made in the Lord's
Prayer. The catechism produced in 1716 by Etienne de Champflour no
longer stresses life in imitation of Christ but, instead, the duties of
religion. It was focused on man and his place in a hierarchical society.
It was filled with abstract definitions taken from scholastics, and the
place accorded to the Christian mystery was reduced. "The leading
idea was not the Good News of what God has done and continues to do
for our salvation but what man must do to be saved." It enlarged the
will of man and his power while playing down divine grace. It set forth
these as its purposes: to safeguard the faith by preserving Christians
from heresies and innovations and to inculcate in them a horror
of mortal sin—blasphemy, superstition, impurity, drunkenness, and
greed. The love of God was allowed only a small space at the end; love
of one's neighbor disappeared, being replaced by a code of regulations;
piety was reduced to a means of achieving salvation, with faith as a
means to piety. Love of God, service to God, identification with Jesus
Christ, fell into the background. The catechism had been invaded by a
"bourgeois" spirit of practical utility, quite in line with Cartesianism
and preparing the way for the success of the "Enlightenment." In the
dioceses of Rheims and Rouen the number of ordinations increased
until 1750–60; but then, after 1760, with the falling-off in fervor and the
spread of "philosophical" ideas among the middle classes, the number
of ordinations declined. From an average of twenty-five a year in the
diocese of Rheims between 1747 and 1765 they fell to an average of
eighteen a year between 1765 and 1790. While in 1786 there were
twenty-eight, in 1778 there were only five. The situation of the regular
clergy, especially the contemplative orders, became even worse, as
Christian values were replaced by "bourgeois" ones.

Conflicts between ecclesiastical "estates"

The order of the clergy was divided by a conflict of "estates" between the first and second of its own internal "orders"—between, on the one hand, the *curés,* perpetual curates, and curates, and, on the other, the bishops, canons, abbots and superiors of monasteries, *curés primitifs* (appropriators), and ecclesiastical patrons—a conflict that went on throughout our two centuries, often latent, but with sudden explosions, and intensifying as the 18th century advanced.

The *curés* reproached the bishops for their "episcopal despotism." The bishops claimed, as successors of the Twelve Apostles, to be first in rank in the hierarchical order and to have possessed full and entire jurisdiction from the beginning and by divine right, so that all priests, being inferior to them, ought to be dependent on them, receiving from them all their powers. The edict of 1695 had confirmed the bishops' authority. Parish priests and curates were kept under the strict tutelage of the bishops, who could sentence their subordinates to three months' residence in a seminary without trial. Moreover, bishops could solicit *lettres de cachet* directed against disobedient priests and could have their lawsuits heard by the king's Council.

The perpetual curates, who carried out the functions of parish priests, suffered from their subordinate relation to the *curés primitifs,* who were usually chapters, congregations of canons regular, or the Order of Malta. These communities regarded their perpetual curate as a mere chantry priest, often obliged him to swear an oath of obedience, fined him for negligence, required that he ask permission to expose the Blessed Sacrament or organize a procession, excluded him from the high altar on the major feast days, sometimes permanently, allowing him to say Mass only in a side chapel, and reserved the finest sets of bells in the town for announcing the capitular or monastic offices, to the detriment of those of the parish.

Curés and perpetual curates also reproached the *curés primitifs* and the patrons on whom nomination to cures of souls depended—bishops, church communities, or lay patrons, who kept the tithes and the revenues of the benefices in their own hands—with paying them inadequate *congrues,* and paying them irregularly. The edict of 1786 increased the *portion congrue* to 700 livres, but the communities evaded paying the increase by giving up the title of *curé primitif,* keeping only the patronage of the benefice.

The *curés* felt that their dignity and their interests were injured.

Their discontent grew as the spiritual movement of the Catholic Renaissance and the education provided by the seminaries fostered a higher conception of the dignity of the priest and the *curé*. But their means of action were slight. They were almost completely excluded from the general assemblies of the French clergy, in which the second "order" was represented mainly by vicars general, canons, and abbots. Provincial councils ceased to be convened. Ecclesiastical conferences "resembled a school, or a *lit de justice.*" The *curés* were excluded from the diocesan bureaus which apportioned the burden of taxation between benefice-holders, so as to avoid "the preponderance that the most numerous classes would obtain" (Assembly of 1775). All that was left to the *curés* was the *appel comme d'abus*. There were innumerable lawsuits between *curés* and patrons and between perpetual curates and *curés primitifs*.

The *curés* therefore formed themselves into associations, enlisted the services of advocates, and armed themselves with the ideas of Edmond Richer, the syndic of the Paris faculty of divinity, who in 1611 published *De ecclesiastica et politica potestate libellus*. According to Richer, the power to ordain and create infallible laws lay in the whole community of priests. Jesus Christ had given the keys, that is, ecclesiastical jurisdiction, in common and jointly, to the priestly order as a whole—to the Twelve Apostles and the seventy-two Disciples. The pope was indeed the monarch of the Church, but he did not dominate the bishops, the successors of the Apostles, who themselves held the principal powers of the Church. The bishops were by divine right superior to the priests and so to the *curés;* but the latter, being successors of the seventy-two Disciples appointed by Christ, participating fully in the priesthood of Christ and each appointed to a territory and given charge of souls therein, should share with the bishops in the government of dioceses through synods and in the government of provinces and of the Church Universal through councils. The government of the Church was a harmonious combination of the monarchy of the pope, the aristocracy of the bishops, and the democracy of the *curés*.

The Jansenists, threatened by the requirement to accept the Formulary of Alexander VII and by the progress of episcopal authority, allied themselves with the "Richerists" after 1675. The ideas of Richer were spread by means of a book written by Boileau's brother Jacques, dean of the cathedral of Sens, in 1676, *De antiquo jure presbytorum in regimine ecclesiastico;* by the *Réflexions morales* of the Jansenist Quesnel (1693), which, though condemned by the bull *Unigenitus* (8

September 1713), was reissued many times; by the theological manuals of Louis Habert and Juénin, for use in seminaries (1694); by the *Témoignage de la Vérité* of the Oratorian Vivien de la Borde (1714); and, after 1716, by the books of "Les Trois Nicolas"—Le Gros, Petit-pied, and Travers. Thirty *curés* of Paris appealed to the king to uphold their view that, "in the government of the Church, everything should be decided in common." The Richerist movement underwent phases of virulence and phases of lull but never died out. After 1755 its principles spread among the lower clergy and some bishops. There were conflicts between *curés* and bishops, or between *curés* and chapters, at Sées, Blois, Le Mans, Luçon, Cahors, Lisieux, and Angers in the period 1759–73. At Angers, when municipal elections took place in accordance with the edicts of August 1764 and May 1765, the bishop, Jacques de Grasse, caused "the ecclesiastical order" to be recognized as being constituted by the *curés* and curates instead of by the diocesan bureau, the abbeys, and the chapters, as had been the case from time immemorial, and a *curé* went as representative of the order to the municipal assembly. The advocate Gabriel-Nicolas Maultrot, son of a notary, alderman of Paris, and consultant to the Richerists, produced between 1752 and 1789 the nineteen works forming his *Code crucial,* a systematic encyclopedia of the rights of *curés,* in accordance with the principles set forth by Edmond Richer. This whole movement of ideas was to culminate in what one historian has called "the revolt of the *curés,*" a vast campaign of pamphlets, spontaneous gatherings, and action in the assemblies held in the *bailliages* to compile the *cahiers* of 1789. The *curés* demanded the following: recognition that they constituted a corporation, with the right to be represented in the diocesan bureaus, in synods, and in assemblies of the clergy; government of the Church to be exercised jointly, and *curés* to choose their own curates freely; transformation of the chapters, which should henceforth be made up of former *curés;* and election of candidates to posts as curate, *curé,* or bishop by the clergy and the people or by the *curés* and the canons, with definitive nomination to the post by the *curé,* the bishop, and the king, respectively.

The political organization of the
order of the clergy in France

The clergy of France formed the only one of the orders of the realm that enjoyed, during the 17th and 18th centuries, permanent representation at the king's side, with periodical assemblies, permanent agents, consent to taxation, interventions in religious policy and in the religious life of the kingdom, and protection of the rights and interests of its members. All this applied to the clergy "of France." The so-called *clergé étranger* remained outside this organization; they were the clergy of the territories which had become attached to the royal domain since 1561, with the exception of Bresse and Béarn, where the clergy were counted as being "of France." The *clergé étranger* were those of Artois, Flanders, Hainault, Lorraine, Alsace, Franche-Comté, and Roussillon, along with the benefice-holders of the Saarland, Luxembourg, and the diocese of Speyer.

The origin of the system of representation

The origin of the representation of the clergy was financial. In principle, the clergy were not supposed to pay taxes. Richelieu said, in his closing speech at the Estates General of 1614, quoting the statement by Peter of Blois in 1188: "The real tribute to be obtained from churchmen is prayer." The bishop of Noyon, addressing the king in 1675, declared that the property of the clergy belonged "rather to the Divine Master who is its sovereign owner than to those ministers who are only trustees with responsibility for it," and he added that this property was set apart for services, worship, relief, and instruction related to the salvation of souls and ought not to be diverted from these purposes. The clergy therefore claimed immunity from taxation. And this was what the last Assembly of the Clergy of France was still claiming in 1788: "The liberty of our gifts . . . is the essential point of our immunities."

Nevertheless, there could be exceptions. The Fourth Lateran Council, in 1215, excommunicated anyone who tried to levy a tax on Church property but in its forty-sixth canon inserted this modification:

> If it should happen that a bishop, in agreement with his clergy,
> finds himself faced with a situation of necessity or utility such that,
> the available means having proved inadequate and no constraint
> being imposed, he considers that the Church ought to contribute to
> helping the public utility or necessity, then the laity might receive
> this help with gratitude. However, owing to the imprudence of cer-
> tain persons, the bishop must first consult the Roman pontiff, who
> has to take into consideration the advantage of everyone.[13]

The first general tax imposed on all the benefice-holders of the kingdom was levied in 1188 for the Crusade of Philip-Augustus. It amounted to one-tenth of their income, and every contribution made by the clergy was thereafter called a "tenth." Pope Boniface VIII, in two bulls of 1297 and 1301, authorized Philip the Fair to levy a contribution from the Church of France when the safety of the state was at stake. In François I's time the requirement that the king obtain the pope's consent disappeared entirely. In 1516 a *"département général des décimes"* was drawn up. This was a list of all the benefices, with an estimate of what one-tenth of the income from each would bring. The king sent letters patent to the dioceses for the granting of "a charitable gift equivalent to one-tenth," and he sometimes demanded four of these "tenths" in one year. Diocesan assemblies agreed to the gift, apportioned the burden of the sum required, and undertook the collecting of it.

At the Estates General of Orléans, in 1561, the king revealed that he was in debt to the tune of 43,500,000 livres, of which 19,000,000 was due to be repaid forthwith. In the same year, the Estates General of Pontoise called for alienation of the Church's temporal possessions as a means of meeting this debt. An assembly of prelates, divines, and deputies of the clergy, held at Poissy, made a contract with the king. During a six-year period the clergy would contribute 1,600,000 livres to redeem the domains, *aides, gabelles,* and *rentes constituées* and would hand over everything to the king; during the redemption process the clergy would see to the payment of the *rentes.*

However, the clergy did not provide this money at once, and so the king was forced to carry out a partial alienation of Church property in 1562 and to use the 1,600,000 livres paid to him annually under the contract in order to create fresh *rentes.* The money was thus diverted from its intended purpose, namely, paying off the state's creditors and redeeming the domains and dues of the state. Another assembly of the clergy therefore had to be held in 1567 and a new contract made. Once again all the money paid went to make good the deficit. By 1576 the clergy had paid out 45,000,000 livres, and this had been spent as it was received, without any reimbursement or redemption having been accomplished. Another assembly of the clergy was held in 1579 and a fresh contract made in 1580, but the king had to give permission in advance to the clergy to meet in assembly if, by 1585, the royal debts had not been repaid. This was what happened. At each new gathering the clergy noted that it had not been discharged of its payment of "tenths" and obtained the king's authority to meet again, and these assemblies continued to be held until the *ancien régime* came to its end.

A contract covering a ten-year period was made in 1586. Every ten years an assembly to renew the contract was held—in 1615, 1625, 1635, and so on. These were the Grandes Assemblées, which met whenever the year ended with the figure 5. Petites Assemblées were held to examine the accounts of the *receveurs,* at first every two years, then, after 1625, every five years, with a few irregularities in 1628, 1641, etc. After 1650 they were held whenever the year ended with a zero. The king asked them for extraordinary aids, and they also made contracts with him. Finally, starting in the second part of Louis XIV's reign, the king convened extraordinary assemblies to deal with specially defined questions, first the one in 1682, which adopted the Four Articles of the Gallican Church, and then those of 1693, 1701, 1702, 1707, and 1711. Under Louis XV there were assemblies in 1723, 1726, 1734, 1742, 1747, 1748, 1758, 1762, and 1772; and under Louis XVI there took place in 1788 the last assembly of the clergy of France. In 1719 an *arrêt* of the Council dated 4 November brought a few prelates together to liquidate the *rentes* of the clergy, and so the Petite Assemblée due to be held in 1720 did not take place.

The organization of the clergy of France thus comprised the following: as the general organ of representation, the General Assembly of the Clergy of France; as the permanent organ of supervision, the agents general of the clergy of France; for the collection of the tax, a receiver general of the clergy of France, with provincial and diocesan receivers; and, to deal with disputes about the tax, a *chambre supérieure de décimes* in each province and a diocesan bureau in each diocese.

The General Assembly

The organization of the general assemblies (which were not councils) was provided for by the *règlements* of 1595, 1605, and 1625. Thereafter, only changes of detail were made.

The General Assembly was allowed to meet with the king's tacit permission, for, from 1586 onward, it was provided in each contract made that "His Majesty herewith gives permission for a general assembly of the said clergy on 25 July" of the final year of the period covered by the contract.

During the personal rule of Louis XIV, and subsequently under Louis XV and Louis XVI, however, express permission from the king was needed by virtue of the principle that "no meeting of any kind may be held without royal consent." In October of the year preceding that when an assembly was due, the agents general of the clergy of France went to ask the king where and when the next assembly (which, in principle, was to be held in May) should take place. The king sent a letter to "our very dear and well beloved agents general of the clergy of France." He fixed the date, the place, and the duration of the assembly, the number of deputies, and often the subject of their deliberations, and he commanded the agents general to inform the archbishops. The agents general had the king's letter printed, together with a covering note, and sent it out to the provinces. From 1742 onward the practice was to send the letters of convocation to archbishops only, with as many copies as there were bishops—116 in all.

The number of deputies to be elected was thirty-two for an auditing assembly, sixty-four for an assembly where a contract was to be made, and a figure between these two for extraordinary assemblies.

Election was carried out in three stages. The bishop, or a vicar general, convened and presided over the assembly of benefice-holders of his diocese: delegates of the *curés* and of the collegiate churches, abbeys, and priories. They sat at the bishop's palace and elected one deputy to the provincial assembly; the other representative of the diocese was the bishop himself, *ex officio*.

These diocesan delegates, elected in the first fortnight of March, had to meet as a provincial assembly by 15 March at the latest. In 1614 there were fourteen provinces (archbishoprics or metropolitan sees): Sens, Rheims, Rouen, Bourges, Tours, Bordeaux, Lyons, Vienne, Toulouse, Narbonne, Aix, Arles, Auch, and Embrun. In 1622 Paris was elevated to the status of an archbishopric, with a province made up of the dioceses of Paris, Orléans, Chartres, and Meaux, taken from the province of Sens, so that there were now fifteen provinces. Then, in 1678, the archbishopric of Albi was formed, bringing the number of provinces to sixteen.

The provincial assembly was held, as a rule, in the chief town of the province. At the opening session the archbishop or his vicar general took the chair and, thereafter, one of the bishops. The deputies' credentials were subjected to checking; bishops were allowed to be represented by a proxy supplied with a special power of attorney. After a Mass of the Holy Ghost, the common affairs of the province were examined and a *cahier* of grievances was drawn up; then they proceeded to the elections. Each diocese had one vote. In order to be a deputy of the "first order," one had to be a bishop, and, to be a deputy of the "second order," one had to be *in sacris*, at least a subdeacon, and, according to the regulations reaffirmed in 1715, to have held for two years a benefice that paid at least 20 livres as "tenth"—this benefice to be within the province and not a mere chapel—and to have resided there for at least one year. Dioceses and provinces were required to send deputies on pain of a fine for not being able subsequently to contribute their quota.

Each province sent two deputies to the General Assembly—one from the "first order," a bishop, and one from the "second order," a canon, abbot, or other benefice-holder. Starting in 1619 there were two deputies from each of the "orders" to the Grandes Assemblées.

All the deputies brought with them a power of attorney defining their mandate, which had been established in the provincial assembly and signed so that the province could not subsequently refuse to pay its share. The powers given the deputies contained restrictions which fell into desuetude under Louis XIV, and the Assembly of 1700 framed a standard formula which was thereafter used for the rest of the century. The deputies were empowered to "do, say, manage, and administer whatever they shall think good for the spiritual and temporal welfare and advantage of the clergy in general and that of the said province." The deputies received letters of state from the chancellery; all lawsuits concerning them were suspended while the assembly was in session, and they were exempted from payment for the sealing of their documents.

The king exerted influence on the elections. He caused "undesirable" candidates to be eliminated, after consulting his intendants and also his loyal bishops, by means of a letter sent to the archbishop, and he gave his backing to the candidates he approved, who were almost always elected. Pontchartrain wrote to the archbishop of Arles, on 20 January 1700:

> The king has several particular reasons for desiring that M. the bishop of Saint-Paul-Trois-Châteaux be not sent to the assembly of the clergy, and His Majesty has commanded me to write to you to prevent, through the most gentle means, the choice from falling on him—without anyone knowing that the king has excluded him, unless you are compelled, in which case you can simply declare to those who will form the assembly that it is His Majesty's intention that M. de Saint-Paul-Trois-Châteaux be not delegated.[14]

During the 18th century, however, the government intervened less and less in the elections, and the clerics resisted its interventions more and more. In 1740 the archbishop of Sens refused to send a deputy to the

General Assembly because, five years previously, the king had prevented the one they had then elected from participating. In 1750 several provinces chose with impunity deputies who were well known for their opposition to the reforms of Machault; these same deputies received permission in 1755 to go forward to the assembly of that year. Even so, the court never renounced the practice of intervening in these elections.

Between 1775 and 1788, archbishops made up 30 percent of the representatives of the "first order," and bishops 70 percent. For the "second order," in 1605, out of 40 representatives, 34 were canons, several of these being also abbots *in commendam* or clerical counsellors in the *parlements*. Subsequently, the majority were deans, archdeacons, canons, and, especially, vicars general. There were never more than a very few secular priors and *curés*. The last time a *curé* was elected, in the 17th century, was in 1682. Between 1775 and 1788 the great majority of the mandates of the "second order" went to vicars general—115 out of 128 deputies. The remaining 13 included six kinsmen of bishops and archbishops, who later became vicars general, and six benefice-holders. In 1788 there was one *curé*.

After the personal rule of Louis XIV had begun, to become a deputy to the Assembly of the Clergy for the "second order" was the best way to secure nomination as a bishop. It was the start of a fine career in the Church. This was still the case between 1775 and 1788. In this period the deputies to the Assemblies of the Clergy were all nobles. Dillon, archbishop of Narbonne, chairman of the General Assembly in 1788, exclaimed: "Have not our fathers, our brothers, our nearest kin, fought in Your Majesty's armies?" And, commenting on the refusal to take the oath: "We have behaved like gentlemen."[15]

The General Assemblies of the Clergy of France were usually held in Paris, so that they could conveniently negotiate with the king's Council, on the one hand, and with the Town Hall on the other. On occasion, however, the Assembly followed the king. In 1619 it met at Blois, in 1621 at Bordeaux, in 1640 at Mantes, in 1665 at Pontoise, between 1675 and 1700 at Saint-Germain; then, all through the 18th century, it met in Paris. There, the assemblies met in the monastery of the Grands-Augustins, where the clergy hired a large hall for the meetings, a smaller one for the records, an office for the agents general, and an apartment for the chairman.

The session began with a Mass of the Holy Ghost, in which a general Communion was included. The deputies swore an oath that they would reveal nothing of what was said in their debates. At the beginning of the 17th century they elected several *présidents,* but during the reign of Louis XIV they elected only one, who was actually designated by the king; from 1660 to 1695 (except in 1665) it was the archbishop of Paris, Harlay, and then, from 1700 to 1715, it was his successor, Noailles, both of whom were veritable "ministers for Church Affairs." In 1715 the Assembly went back to its earlier practice of electing several *présidents*—four, six, or eight, chosen from the "first order," with an equal number of archbishops and bishops. The first-ranking *président* held the real power. These *présidents* were always designated in advance, in conjunction with the king, and election constituted a mere formality. The Assembly could name as coadjutor with the *présidents* some person whom it wished to honor: the archbishop of Paris (1747–48) or the first ecclesiastical ministers, Dubois (1725) and Fleury (1725–35). Between 1775 and 1788 the archbishop who was senior in date of consecration presided over the Assembly. However, the court could let such an archbishop know that his election by his metropolitan assembly was undesirable. Archbishop Luynes of Sens and Archbishop Montazet of Lyons were eliminated in this way. In 1785 Archbishop La Rochefoucauld of Rouen had to yield the chair to Archbishop Dillon of Narbonne.

The *président,* or *premier président,* held as representative of the king the effective authority in the Assembly. It was he who received the oath, replied to the addresses, and pronounced the closing speech. Above all, he conferred with the promoters of justice, directed the debates, gave permission to speak, guided discussion, and influenced decisions by the way he presented questions and by the opinions he expressed. He settled many questions on his own, along with the king. He designated the members of the preparatory commissions, and his proposals were always ratified.

The Assembly elected two promoters of justice and two secretaries, for the assemblies which negotiated the contract with the king, and one of each for the auditing assemblies. These persons were chosen from among the deputies of the "second order." The practice grew up of choosing agents who had just retired, while, for the extraordinary assemblies, agents who were still in harness were chosen.

The promoters of justice proposed the agenda, regulated the procedure for deliberations, and looked after the administrative problems of the Assembly. The secretaries called up the provinces to cast their votes in turn, kept the records of the proceedings (revised by a committee), and countersigned all the letters and mandamuses sent out by order of the Assembly. They produced as many copies of the record of proceedings as there were provinces, plus two—one for the use of the *président*, the other for the Assembly's archives.

The Assembly asked for audience of the king, at which it presented its due respects to the queen, the dauphin, the dauphine, and the regent. The king's commissioners came to the Assembly, first to present their respects, then, on their second visit, to set out the king's request for aid.

The Assembly met each day from 7:00 A.M. to 10 A.M. in summer and from 8:00 A.M. to 11 A.M. in winter and often in the afternoon as well. The work of the assemblies was prepared by committees, some temporary and others permanent, the latter being called *bureaux*. There were nineteen committees, one for the contract with the king, one to check the acquittance rolls, and so on—eleven, all together, for financial matters. Others dealt with "matters concerning religion," the drawing-up of the list of grievances, books on doctrine and morals, converted Protestant ministers, acts of violence and robbery committed against clerics, lawsuits, private affairs, and so on. Each committee was made up of an equal number of deputies of the first "order" and of the second, proposed by the *président* of the Assembly and accepted by it. Each committee had a chairman, an agent, and a *rapporteur*, who conferred with the chancellor, the comptroller general, and the state councilors in order to prepare their business.

The proposals of the committees were voted on first within each province and then, by provinces, in the whole Assembly, with the provinces taking turns to be the first to vote. It was enough for ten provinces, each represented by one deputy, to vote in favor of a decision for that decision to be valid. A two-thirds majority was required for acceptance or dismissal of the receiver general and for questions concerned with pensions and gratuities to be decided. At the beginning of the 17th century it was normal for votes to be taken province by province; only where very grave matters were concerned did the Assembly have recourse to voting by individual deputies, who stated their reasons. In the 18th century, on the contrary, voting by provinces took place only on important matters, with voting by individuals only on minor matters and problems of jurisdiction.

The Assembly sent deputations to the king. It negotiated with him through a variety of conferences: preparatory conferences between a few deputies and some state councilors; private conferences with the chancellor; solemn conferences with the Council, with the king's chair at the head of the table. The Assembly had frequent interviews with the *procureur général du roi* in the *parlement*. It drafted edicts, *arrêts* of the Council, and letters patent, subsequently much modified by the Council. It drew up a list of grievances.

The Assembly attended Te Deums, services in memory of deceased princes, and the beginnings of defenses of theses in the Sorbonne or by members of religious orders. The duration of the Grandes Assemblées was restricted by the terms of the king's convocation to four months and that of the Petites Assemblées to two. The Assembly broke up after a solemn audience with the king. It reported on the work it had done and the steps it had taken by sending a circular letter to the dioceses. Starting in 1625, its proceedings were printed. The deputies reported back to their respective provincial assemblies.

The Assembly was in being for only a short time. Between sessions someone had to watch over the execution of the contract with the king and to defend the rights of the Church at large. Accordingly, in 1561 the clergy elected syndics general. These having proved to be excessively good courtiers, in 1579 the Assembly held at Melun replaced them by the agents general of the clergy of France.

The agents general

The agents general were two in number, elected for five years by two provinces, with the provinces taking turns for the honor. Combinations were: Bourges and Vienne, Lyons and Bordeaux, Rouen and Toulouse, Tours and Aix, Sens and Auch, Embrun and Arles, Rheims and Narbonne, and, after 1694, Paris and Albi; usually, that is, one northern and one southern province were paired. The provincial assemblies had to elect priests who held a benefice other than a chapel, who had been in the province for at least two years, who paid 20 livres as "tenth," and who had been resident for at least a year. These conditions were not always observed. The *règlement* of 1715 forbade reelection, by the provinces whose turn it was, of a retiring agent; this practice, frequent in the 17th century, became rare in the 18th. Actually, the provincial assemblies elected clerics who were well connected and were generally promoted to a bishopric when they finished their tour of duty.

The provinces presented their candidates, and the Assembly ratified their election. The king intervened in the choice made. On 30 August

1641 Louis XIII called upon the prior of Saint-Denis, by *lettre de cachet,* to perform the office of agent, as he was dissatisfied with the elections. Under Louis XIV the clergy were always careful to elect candidates agreeable to the king.

The agents whose tour of duty was ending reported to a committee of deputies. Those who were beginning theirs were received by the Assembly and swore an oath. They were presented to the king and to the chancellor, for they were becoming members of the king's Council and even, after 1777, of the Council's *bureaux.* Under Louis XV they received a yearly salary of 5,500 livres, with 1,500 livres for their expenses and 1,500 livres in their capacity as state councilors. The Assembly gave them 90,000 livres as gratuity, for five years. They enjoyed the right of *committimus* to the Great Seal.

The agents of the clergy saw to the conservation of the liberties and privileges of the clergy of France. They therefore followed the publication of edicts, letters patent, *arrêts* of the Council, and the activities of the lawcourts. They supervised the carrying-out of the contract and the maintenance of the guarantees. They received complaints from clerics and brought them to the notice of the Council. In serious cases they took sides with the complainant, whose case thus became that of the clergy of France. They could also bring matters before the *parlement.* They supervised the receiver general of the clergy and his clerks, obliging them to present their accounts quarterly. To these ends they had at their disposal an office with an office manager and clerks, as well as advocates paid by the clergy—three attending on the *parlement* and one on the Grand Conseil—with whom they discussed matters at least once a fortnight, and also a collection of registers and dossiers. All this became in 1748 the Agency General of the Clergy of France. The office manager was Beauvais and then, in 1765, his son-in-law Duchesne, an advocate before the *parlement.* The agents corresponded with all holders of benefices. They had a printing press for the affairs of the clergy and, in the 18th century, their own printer, Simon, who was followed by his widow and then, after 1750, by Guillaume Desprez.

The receiver general of the tenths

The receiver general of the tenths held a commission, not a venal office. Abolished on 26 October 1719, it was reestablished on 9 June 1720. Between 1726 and 1735 the receiver general was called the "intendant of the temporal affairs of the clergy." He was chosen by a two-thirds majority of an extraordinary assembly. He made a contract with the clergy for a ten-year period, pledging all his property and providing a Parisian surety. He swore an oath to the Assembly and was placed under its authority and that of its agents. He was permitted to employ clerks in Paris and in the provinces. He played the role of banker to the clergy, rendering his account to the Assembly. After 1726 he was a member of the king's Council. The receivers general of the tenths were, from 1710 to 1726, Ogier and, from 1726 to 1740, De Sénozan. The latter's nephew, Bollioud de Saint-Jullien, obtained reversion of the commission in 1735 and succeeded to it in 1740. In 1765 the Assembly associated with him his son, aged seventeen, and gave this young man the reversion when he reached twenty-five, in 1773. Ogier's son became *président de Chambre* in the Paris *parlement*. De Sénozan was a lace merchant in Lyons. His son married the daughter of a *président à mortier*, Lamoignon de Blancmesnil.

The diocesan and provincial organs

The agents general of the clergy of France were in contact with the dioceses through the diocesan syndics and the diocesan bureaus, or *chambres des décimes diocésaines*. These were permanent organs functioning in the intervals between sessions of the diocesan assemblies. They began their existence with the *"contrat de Poissy"* and were given legal status by the edict of 1615. Their composition varied. Usually they consisted of the bishop, who presided, and between four and twenty-seven persons chosen for a period that varied from one diocese to another. Depending on the particular diocese, the bishop chose the deputies, or these were recruited by cooption or else were elected, either by all the benefice-holders of the diocese or by an electorate made up of the cathedral chapter, the other chapters of the diocese, the abbots and priors, and the *curés*. In general, the members of these diocesan bureaus, or "commissaries," were chosen from among the canons and other principal benefice-holders in the diocese and were regularly reelected. They chose from among themselves the diocesan syndic. The *curés* were more often than not excluded from the diocesan bureaus. The ordinance of January 1599 and the declaration of 17 August 1750 forbade the levying of any tax from clerics except by virtue of verified letters patent. The Assembly of the Clergy held in 1770 drafted for the diocese of Troyes a regulation which was sanctioned by the *arrêts* of the Council dated 5 March 1771 and 21

October 1775, and extended to the dioceses of Langres, Nancy, and Saint-Dié. It created five classes of benefice-holders and prescribed that one deputy be elected by each class for a period of five years. The classes were: cathedral chapters; collegiate chapters; *curés;* ordinary benefice-holders not obliged to reside and paying at least 50 livres in tenths; and regular communities, of both sexes. The bureau constituted in this way elected a syndic from outside its membership, together with a *greffier* and a diocesan receiver of tenths, for a period of five years.

The diocesan bureau distributed the burden of the diocesan quota among the benefice-holders. It supervised the collection of the money and the work of the receivers. After 1616 it dealt with disputes relating to the tenths; it decided without appeal on matters involving up to 20 livres of the old tenths and up to 30 livres of the "free gift," and it was a court of first instance where sums larger than these were concerned. The diocesan syndic intervened to safeguard all the rights and privileges of the Church. Against the Protestants, he demanded the destruction of those of their places of worship not included in the provisions of the Edict of Nantes. He granted pensions to converted Protestant ministers, and he supported seminaries. The funds for these purposes he obtained by means of additional hundredths, the *sol pour livre* added to the tenths from 1605 onward. The diocesan receiver's was, after 1581, and definitively after 1594, a royal office which could be held by the diocese. The latter nominated a candidate to the king, who gave him letters of appointment. The diocese could own the office and sell it to the candidate. This office conferred the quality of king's counselor, was not incompatible with nobility, and secured exemption from *taille,* from public charges, from obligation to billet soldiers, from *ustensile* and *fourrage,* and from the duties of watch and ward. It was abolished between 1719 and 1723.

Appeal from the decisions of the diocesan bureaus was to the *chambres supérieures des décimes.* Seven of these were set up by the edict of 10 February 1580. Letters patent of 6 February 1586 confirmed their creation and established an eighth, at Bourges. Later, a ninth came into being, at Pau, but the dioceses of Oloron and Lescar failed to send deputies to it, and it ceased to function. The *arrêt* of the Council dated 18 September 1670 ordered that the affairs of these two dioceses be referred to the *chambre des décimes* at Bordeaux.

Each diocese sent to the *chambre des décimes* to which it was attached a deputy who was designated for a five-year period by either the bishop or the archbishop. He had to be a university graduate and in holy orders. The *chambre* associated with itself three counselors from the presidial court or the *parlement* of the town where it sat, choosing these for life. It appointed a promoter of justice to act as public prosecutor. Sessions were held every eight days. Appeals against decisions by the diocesan bureaus were heard, and measures were taken against encroachments by the *parlements* and other judicial bodies. The king's Council could quash the *arrêts* of the *chambre*. It elected a metropolitan syndic with responsibility for vigilance in relation to anything done against the clerical order; however, this syndic seems to have been, everywhere, a somewhat tame and unobtrusive figure.

Provincial receivers of tenths were abolished by the edict of 26 October 1729 and were never revived. Instead, auxiliary bureaus of the general bureau of receipt were established, staffed by the receiver general's clerks, in seventeen provincial "receipt areas" that came to be known as *généralités*—a name which gave rise to confusion with the *généralités* of the royal fiscal system.

The financial functioning of these organs

The diocesan receivers collected the tenths from the benefices in two phases, in February and October, when their bureau was open throughout the month. They had bailiffs at their disposal for the purposes of summons and distraint. They could compel farmers and stewards of benefices to appear before them in person. They reported to their respective bishops every six months. The money they collected went into the provincial treasury, and the provincial receiver could have them arrested for any defalcation. Their wages were proportioned to the price of their office: *au denier 8* (12.5 percent) in 1586, and *au denier 12* (8.33 percent) from 1621 onward.

The provincial receivers, helped by their clerks, concentrated in their hands the money coming in from the province, took measures against slow payers, and rendered accounts every six months to the receiver general and the agents general. Their wages ranged from 300 to 600 *écus,* plus taxations of between 2 and 10 *deniers* per livre (0.80–4.20 percent) on the money they handled.

Finally, the receiver general of the clergy, who was often a former receiver general of the royal fiscal system, assembled all the money and paid it into the Town Hall of Paris for the service of the public debt, or else to the king, if extraordinary subventions were involved. He gave advances to the clergy or to the Town Hall. He was responsible with all his property for the proper conduct of his office. Besides his wages of

12,000 livres, he received interest ranging from 50,000 to 100,000 livres. In the poll-tax roll he figures in the fourth category, on a level with state councilors and the *procureur général* and *avocats généraux du roi* before the *parlement*.

The political functioning of these organs

The clergy succeeded in upholding the principle of its immunity. In France it conserved the principle of the right of subjects to consent to taxation more effectively than the provincial estates did. The clergy gave the tenths, which were levied from the clerics "like the *taille* from the people," in order to pay the king's debts—or rather, in reality, to pay the *rentes* due to the king's creditors, since the king repaid little or nothing of his debts. This was the purpose of the ten-year contracts concluded at the General Assemblies. The clergy also furnished "free gifts," which went straight into the king's coffers to meet war expenses. Nonexistent under Henri IV, these "free gifts" were already large, though irregular, under Louis XIII, and they became regular under Louis XIV, being granted every five years by the Petites Assemblées.

The contracts to pay the ordinary tenths were regarded by the clergy as discretionary and provisional. For them the contracts made between 1561 and 1580 were invalid, since only the Estates General could take on a commitment to discharge the king's debts. The Assembly of Poissy had exceeded its powers, and so had all the cardinals and syndics general down to 1580, being mere private persons without a mandate.

After the Assembly of 1580 the clergy were committed. But the king constantly diverted the sums they gave him to pay off the state debt. Consequently, the clergy owed him nothing more and asked, at every succeeding Assembly, for the matter to be settled and themselves relieved of the obligation to pay the *rentes*. On each occasion the king invoked the necessities of state, and the clergy agreed to pay, while formulating reservations. The royal commissioners took note of these, in the name of the Town Hall of Paris, and promised that if, by Midsummer Day in ten years' time, the king had neither paid his debts nor settled the matter, the clergy would be allowed to hold an Assembly "to deal with their affairs both spiritual and temporal."

The provost of the Merchants of Paris came to the Assembly to request that they continue to pay the *rentes*, as a favor, and to thank them for the renewal of the contract.

The clergy paid out annually 1,300,000 livres, of which 1,202,322 went on *rentes* secured on the Town Hall of Paris. After the declaration of 31 December 1639 they paid the same amount, though the *rentiers* now received only "two quarters and a half" each year, that is, payment for seven and a half months, instead of a full year's payment; the king took the difference, in order to pay the interest on the money he had borrowed from officeholders.

For the "free gifts," the committee of "ways and means" obtained money, over and above the tenths, by taxing the receivers of the clergy, by collecting periodical indemnities paid in return for renouncing Church property which had been alienated during the Wars of Religion, by looking into the payment of *rentes,* and finally, after 1686, by borrowing. In 1710 the committee borrowed the entire amount of the "free gift," intended to redeem the clergy from paying the poll tax—a sum of 24 million. During the fifty-nine years of Louis XV's reign the clergy granted 190 million in "free gifts" and actually paid out 186 million. In addition, they paid 1,300,000 livres every year for the *rentes* on the Town Hall, down to 1719, and then, after the reduction in these *rentes,* 442,650 livres—213,500,000 livres all together, or an average annual payment of 3,618,000 livres. To these figures must be added, however, the clergy's own *rente* obligations and the costs of administration. Actually, the amount paid by the clergy came to 287,954,401 livres, or 4,964,731 livres a year; between 1725 and 1734 they paid 2,688,620 livres a year, but between 1765 and 1774 it was 7,352,108 livres. The reason for the increase lay in the increase in the debts of the clergy, which rose from 32,974,188 livres to 116,979,091 livres in 1775. Since the income of the clergy can be estimated, very broadly, at 60 million, plus between 40 and 50 million in perquisites and tithes, the proportion exacted from them thus increased from one twenty-secondth to one-eighth between the beginning and end of the reign. The royal budget more than doubled in this period, but the burden borne by the clergy trebled.

Under Louis XVI, from 1775 to 1788, the clergy paid out 80,800,000 livres in "free gifts," an average of 5,770,000 livres a year, but with payments of 30 million in 1780, 15 million in 1782, and 18 million in 1785 to meet the costs of the American war and their liquidation.

The clergy kept on borrowing and did not trouble to pay off their own debts, despite the king's help. After 1748 he granted 500,000 livres a year to the clergy for the discharge of these debts. In 1780 he increased the grant to 1 million a year, but this sum was reduced to 700,000 livres

in 1782, and the figure of 1 million was restored only the the year following the signature of peace. The clergy thus received 22,300,000 livres in
all for settlement of their debts. However, they continued to borrow.
Their debts rose to 125,600,000 livres in 1780 and 140 million in 1785.
One wonders whether the clergy were perhaps clinging to their debts,
contracted on the state's behalf and which the state could not pay off,
so as to render permanent the meetings of the Assembly of the Clergy
and the privileges of the clerical corder. The Assembly which met in
1785 said: "Our gifts bind the king. In the contracts which we have the
honor to conclude with him, he undertakes to safeguard our possessions."

The Assembly's participation in royal acts

Thanks to their financial role, the clergy maintained their participation
in the legislative work, the judicial functions, and the executive decisions of the royal government. The clergy asked for, and often obtained, royal edicts, royal declarations by letters patent, and *arrêts* by
the king in his Council, using procedures that were valid for all the
other orders, corporations, and communities of the kingdom. The
clergy may here serve as an example of a fact of general application.

The Assembly received requests from individual clerics; from groups
of clerics, such as those of Marseilles, who had been defrauded of some
of their seignorial rights, or the benefice-holders of Brittany, who had
been hindered in their collection of tithe; and sometimes from laymen,
groups of Catholics such as those of Sancerre, a minority in relation to
the local Huguenots, who did not respect the ban on Protestant funerals being held in public. All such persons sent petitions in writing to
the promoters of justice, who filtered them and put them up to the
Assembly for decision. The Assembly might appoint a committee to
look into serious cases, and on receiving its report the Assembly would
decide whether or not to take steps.

Each province brought its grievances to the Assembly. A deputy
from a given province delivered a report on that province's *cahier*. The
questions arising were distributed among the standing committees of
the Assembly; these examined them, and then their members conferred
with the members of the king's Council before presenting their report
to the Assembly for its decision.

Once this decision was taken, the Assembly delegated some of its
members to confer with members of the king's Council. These were

the "preparatory conferences," consisting of four deputies of the Assembly and a few members of the Council nominated by the chancellor, to study the demands and complaints received, so as to prepare the materials. These were followed by "particular conferences" with the chancellor himself, to settle the affairs. In important cases the clergy obtained "conferences in the Council." The first of these took place on 27 July 1579, with the principal councilors, the chancellor, the superintendent of finance, the comptroller general of finance, the chief minister, and so on.

In 1645 and 1646, for example, we find that conferences were held concerning the "enterprises" of the Protestants. Such conferences took place on 29 August, 12 and 13 September, 21 October, and 21 November 1645. They resulted in six *arrêts* of the Council that were favorable to the demands of the clergy. One series of conferences dealt with spiritual matters, and the clergy obtained *lettres de cachet* enjoining preachers to come and report to the king concerning the doctrine they expounded. Other conferences dealt with encroachments by the *parlements* and other royal judges, who were attempting to take cognizance of monastic vows and the sacrament of marriage. Conferences were held on financial affairs, on the exactions of *traitants* from the peasants (one of these lasted three hours), on dues payments demanded in respect of goods belonging to members of the clergy; there was even a conference at Mazarin's residence, after dinner on 29 January 1646, with the cardinal himself and Bellièvre, Le Bret, and Amelot-Chaillou. Eventually the clergy obtained seven royal declarations.

When the deputies of the clergy reached agreement with the Council, they drafted edicts, declarations, *arrêts* designed to serve as general regulations, and *arrêts* dealing with particular cases, which they had been promised would be implemented. They reported on these and read them to the Assembly, which approved or rejected them. When the drafts were ready, the Assembly entrusted its agents general with the task of getting them executed. The agents tried to obtain the signature of the state councilor concerned and that of the chancellor—signatures which testified, often falsely, that the documents in question had been discussed in Council and were authentic. Frequently, however, the promises made by the state councilors were not kept, and the documents were seriously amended by the king's Council before attaining definitive form.

Besides the conferences, the Assembly had at its disposal the procedure of "remonstrance," in accordance with the duty of all orders, corporations, colleges, and companies to advise the sovereign. For example, on 28 March 1655, as a result of many complaints received regarding the conduct of the Huguenots, the Assembly resolved to ask for an audience with the king "for a remonstrance concerning the Protestants." The agents general were given the task of presenting the request, which was granted. The remonstrance was then drawn up. Before the audience, on 31 March, the archbishop of Sens called on Cardinal Mazarin, to test his reaction to the terms of the remonstrance. The audience took place on 2 April. The Assembly, all members present, gathered at the residence of the archbishop of Narbonne and set off from there, at about three in the afternoon, for the Louvre. They were received by the grand master of ceremonies, who conducted them to the hall where the Council met. Secretary of State Du Plessis-Guénégaud took charge of them there and led them to the Grand Cabinet de la Reine, where they found the king, the queen, the duc d'Anjou, the chancellor, and Mazarin. The remonstrance was read, and the clergy withdrew. On 5 April they received the king's reply: he would order the Council to consider the measures needed to remedy the situation, and he gave permission for a conference. The remonstrance procedure, which enabled the order to make direct contact with the sovereign, was in constant use.

An even more flexible method was what was called "solicitation," an official procedure which resulted in a written report. The Assembly would charge a bishop to "beseech Monsieur the chancellor," to "speak about the matter to Messieurs of the Council," or to "speak about it both to the queen and to Monsieur the chancellor." What was involved here were approaches by individuals (or, more usually, by a small number, perhaps two deputies, one from each of the "orders" of the clergy) constantly and discreetly made in order to prepare the way for conferences or decisions. These approaches were made even where important matters were concerned, such as the execution or annulment of *arrêts*.

The "petition with a view to obtaining an *arrêt*," submitted to a master of requests, examined by a committee of the Council, and either granted or rejected by the chancellor, was established in ritual form, signed by an advocate of the clergy of France. This was a method much in use.

The agents general of the clergy of France acted on requests from individuals or from groups. They received letters from bishops and other clerics asking them to obtain *arrêts* from the Council and to be present at the Council on the day that their petition was brought there, so as to explain their case to the chancellor or to the keeper of the seals. The agents then prepared a *"dispositif,"* that is, a draft *arrêt,* and presented this to the Council, along with the cleric's petition and their own. Throughout this procedure the agents were kept in touch with developments by means of a succession of letters. They were given powers of attorney by the parties to solicit, conclude, and act without the names of the agents themselves appearing in the procedure. A stream of reports and inquiries reached them from the provincial syndics, to which they replied with information, advice, and official documents. They gave an account of all these activities to the General Assembly when their mandate expired, explaining what they had done.

The agents general also acted spontaneously in the name of the clergy of France. In 1690 a priest of Rodez was charged with murder. The *président* of the presidial court considered that it was a case for a royal judge, investigated it, and brought it before the Council. Master of Requests Le Pelletier de la Houssaye having made his report, one of the agents spoke, saying that "it was his duty to make known, very humbly, to the Council, that the Church of France was interested in the injury that the clergy of Rodez would suffer if the *président* was granted his request and that the privilege which he challenged was of concern to all the clergy of the kingdom." He was allowed to intervene, since the common interests of the clergy were at stake in this individual case.

The agents general of the clergy of France also intervened "in the name" of the clergy, as mandatories of the Assembly, a status which the Council recognized. On 3 April 1666 the clergy of France petitioned that "the agents general be regarded as being, in relation to the corporation of the clergy, like the *procureurs généraux* in the sovereign courts ... in whose name actions and defenses are formulated ... but who are in no way responsible for the verdicts that may be pronounced against the corporation." The Council accepted this view, and its *arrêt* provided that the agents general could not be prosecuted or have their property distrained upon connection with the affairs of the clergy.

Actually, in the intervals between sessions of the Assembly, the agents intervened in cases on behalf of the clergy without any mandate from the Assembly. The *règlement* of 1715 (articles 14 and 15) obliged them, in such situations, to consult the advocates of the clergy and those of the Council and the *parlement* and obtain a written opinion. In practice, however, the agents acted freely.

Like any other litigant, they laid before the Council a principal request, in the form of a "petition to the king," which included pleadings and conclusions. The petition addressed the king directly, as embodiment of the law and supreme justiciar, but asked him to give order that the Council pronounce judgment in the sense indicated, for an *arrêt* by the Council was necessary.

The agents general used the *"procédure d'opposition."* They lodged objection to *arrêts* of the Council and royal letters patent in order to get the matter in question reexamined by the King in Council on the basis of new information. This "opposition" took the form of a memorandum which included pleadings and conclusions and which was served by a *huissier des requêtes ordinaires de l'Hôtel du Roi* upon the *grand audiencier de France* and the secretary to the Council.

The agents general proceeded by "request," which was the procedure most favored before the Conseil d'Etat, or Conseil privé. Sometimes they acted on their own, sometimes jointly with litigants. The "request" was signed by two agents and an advocate of the clergy of France. It was a memorandum which quoted facts, documents, and official pronouncements. The agents sometimes "took sides with" a litigant in grave and important cases which involved the general interests of the clergy. They were also accepted as "parties intervening," by ordinances issued on their "request." Finally, by *"jonction,"* they joined the interested party, the litigant, in his case.

The agents general made "representations." This was an oral means, employed in the Council and leading to an *arrêt* issued "upon what has been represented to the King in Council by the agents general of the clergy of France." A "representation" was a veritable counsel's speech. Probably the agents used notes and handed over something in writing to the state councilors, but a "representation" did not give rise to a report by a master of requests or a councilor.

The agents general employed "remonstrances": *"sur ce qui a été remontré au Roi en son Conseil par les agents généraux du Clergé de France."* This formula appears in numerous *arrêts*. In many reports by the agents to the Assembly their "remonstrances" are mentioned. The remonstrances made by the agents resulted in a fresh examination of the matter in question and a report by a master of requests; the King in Council, better informed, and carrying out his duty as justiciar, pronounced a decision.

When the *arrêts* asked for had been obtained, the agents checked on their execution. They caused them to be notified by the Council's *huissiers* to the interested parties, whether these were private individuals or judges or officials of the royal fiscal system.

The clergy of France could also act within the Council through clerics who were state councilors. Besides the chief minister, there were three clerical state councilors in the Conseil d'Etat et privé. From 1627 onward there were always some in the committee specially concerned with the affairs of the clergy and some in temporary committees as well. In 1700 there were seven bureaus, each of six state councilors, to examine contentious questions put before the Council by private persons. One of these bureaus dealt with all church matters; it consisted of one clerical councilor and five laymen.

In addition, all bishops possessed the honorific title of *conseiller du Roi en ses Conseils d'Etat et privé,* and in fact any prelate who happened to be visiting Paris could take his seat in the Council.

Finally, the *parlements* included counselors who were clerics—priests and canons. The Assembly and the agents general thus possessed supplementary means of obtaining information and taking action.

The General Assembly of the Clergy of France enjoyed powers of jurisdiction. The Council devolved upon it all problems relating to the discipline of the clergy or their finances. In 1650 a quarrel broke out between the dean and the chapter of the cathedral of Evreux concerning the nomination of the syndic general and deputies to the *bureau diocésain.* The chapter appealed to the *parlement* of Rouen, the bishop to the king's Council. The Council, by *arrêt* of 19 October 1650, transferred the case to the Assembly for judgment.

A cleric of the diocese of Sarlat, Jean Amarzit, had obtained provision from the Roman Curia to the cure of souls of Saint-Martin de Tayac. The bishop refused his endorsement. Amarzit petitioned the *parlement* of Bordeaux, the bishop petitioned the Council. The Conseil privé, by *arrêt* of 11 July 1670, quashed the *arrêt* of the *parlement,* listing its motivations the *règlements* of the General Assembly of the Clergy in 1645, 1646, and 1666, as well as the royal declarations of 1666, 1667, and 1670. The *règlements* of the clergy thus had force for the Council, like that of manifestations of the royal will.

Thus, the order of the clergy possessed its own representative assembly, a standing executive authority, an administration, an administrative jurisdiction, regulatory and judicial powers, and a whole centralized bureaucracy, tending toward unity, uniformity, and regularity, such as the king certainly did not possess. The clergy preserved in France the principle of representation of the state's subjects and that of consent to taxation, and it provided an administrative model which inspired the work of the Revolution, the Consulate, the Empire, and the Restoration. A true institution of public law, equipped with jurisdictional, disciplinary, and regulatory powers, the clerical order was entrusted, on the other hand, with the defense of the collective interests of the clergy, of the rights, liberties, and privileges recognized by the customary constitution and by royal legislation. It also looked after the protection of individual interests within the framework of recognized collective interests. The individual was sustained, helped, and protected by the order, which, when necessary, took his place so as to defend his rights. The order ensured smooth relations and permanent and easy contact between the king and his subjects, their collaboration in safeguarding particular rights and interests, on the one hand, and, on the other, in subjecting individuals and the order to the general interest. It constituted a sort of hinge between the king and his subjects. The Assembly of 1765 said: "The clergy are, of all the orders in the state, the first: that order which is most concerned with upholding the religion and even the fundamental laws of the kingdom." And the Assembly of 1788 said: "The kingdom of France consists of three orders which cannot and must not be confounded . . . We are French and we are monarchical."

Notes

1. Isambert, vol. 19, p. 379. (For Isambert, see the bibliography at the end of the Introduction to this book.)
2. Joannus Dominicus Mansi, *Sacrorum Conciliorum nova et amplissima collectio*, vol. 27, p. 585.
3. The abbé de Saint-Pierre, *Ouvrages de politique* (Rotterdam, 1735–41), vol. 13, pp. 7–8.
4. Quoted by D. Julia, "Le clergé paroissial du diocèse de Reims," *Revue d'Histoire moderne et contemporaine* 13 (1966): 214.
5. Jean de Viguerie, "Le recrutement des Doctrinaires dans le diocèse de Narbonne au XVIIᵉ siècle (1619–1715)," *Actes des XLIᵉ et XXIVᵉ Congrès d'Etudes religieuses, Fédération historique, Languedoc méditerranéan et Roussillon—Fédération des Sociétés Académiques et Savantes de Languedoc-Pyrenées-Gascogne* (Carcassonne, 1–7 May 1968) (1970), pp. 1–7.
6. Quoted by Norman Ravitch (*Sword and Mitre*, p. 62) from *Archives du Ministère des Affaires Etrangères, Mémoires et Documents, Fonds France*.
7. Quoted by Ravitch, ibid., p. 80.
8. Ibid., pp. 69–86.
9. Michel Vovelle, "Le chapitre cathédral de Chartres," *Actes du LXXXVᵉ Congrès national des Sociétés Savantes, 1960, Section histoire moderne*.

10. Canon Espénan, *La collégiale de Castelnau-Magnoac à la veille de la Révolution* (Auch: Imprimerie Cocharaux, 1930).

11. Julia, "La clergé paroissial," pp. 195–216.

12. Jean Meuvret, "La situation matérielle et morale des membres du clergé séculier dans la France du XVIIᵉ siècle (possibilités et limites des recherches)," *Revue d'Histoire de l'Eglise de France* 54 (1968): 47–68; Jean Desaive, "Les revenus et charges des prêtres de campagne au nord-est de Paris (XVIIᵉ et XVIIIᵉ siècles)," *Revue d'Histoire moderne et contemporaine* 17 (1970): 921–52.

13. C.-J. Héfélé, *Histoire des Conciles*, trans. by H. Leclercq (Letouzey, 1913), vol. 5, pt. 1, p. 1368.

14. G. B. Depping, ed., *Correspondance administrative sous le Règne de Louis XIV*, (1850–55), vol. 4, p. 192, quoted in Ravitch, *Sword and Mitre*, p. 156.

15. Quoted by Michel Péronnet, "Les assemblées du clergé de France sous Louis XVI," *Annales de l'histoire de la Révolution française* 34 (1962): 31–32, n. 51.

Guide to further reading

Durand de Maillane, M. *Dictionnaire de droit canonique et de pratique bénéficiale.* Lyons, 1770.

Fleury, Claude. *Institution au droit ecclésiastique,* ed. Boucher d'Argis. 2 vols. 1767.

Graviers, J. des. *Le droit canonique.* 1958.

Héricourt, Louis d'. *Les lois ecclésiastiques de France.* 1771 edition.

Le Bras, G. *Histoire du droit et des institutions de l'Eglise en Occident. I: Pro-légomènes.* 1955.

Thomassin, Louis. *Ancienne et nouvelle discipline de l'Eglise.* 2d ed. 1679.

Allier, Raoul. *La cabale des dévots.* 1902.

Carrière, Abbé Victor. *Introduction aux études d'histoire ecclésiastique locale.* 3 vols. Letouzey, 1934, 1936, 1940.

Chatellier, Louis. "Société et bénéfices ecclésiastiques: Le cas alsacien (1670–1930)," *Revue historique* 244 (1970): 75–98.

Degert, Abbé A. *Histoire des Séminaires français jusqu'à la Révolution.* 2 vols. 1912.

Desaive, J. P. "Les revenus et charges des prêtres de campagne au nord-est de Paris (XVIIᵉ–XVIIIᵉ siècle)," *Revue d'Histoire moderne et contemporaine* 17 (1970): 921–52.

Ferté, Jeanne. *La vie religieuse dans les campagnes parisiennes (1622–1695).* "Librairie Philosophique." Vrin, 1962.

Julia, Dominique. "Le clergé paroissial dans le diocèse de Reims à la fin du XVIIIᵉ siècle," *Revue d'Histoire moderne et contemporaine* 13 (1966): 195–216.

———. "Le prêtre au XVIIIᵉ siècle," *Recherches de science religieuse* 58 (1970): 521–34.

Laurain-Portemer, Madeleine. "Le statut de Mazarin dans l'Eglise: Aperçus sur le haut clergé de la Contre-Reforme," *Bibliothèque de l'Ecole des Chartes,* vol. 127 (1969), vol. 128 (1970).

Le Bras, G. "Synodes et conciles parisiens," *Revue d'Histoire de l'Eglise de France* 50 (1964): 35–46.

Lefebvre-Teillard, Anne. "Le Conseil archiépiscopal de Lyon," *Revue historique de Droit français et étranger* 48 (1970): 226–51.

Lottin, Alain. "Prêtres et laïcs à Lille à la fin du XVIIe siècle," *Bulletin du Comité flamand de France* 18 (1969–1970): 227–36.

MacManners, John. *French Ecclesiastical Society under the Ancien Régime.* Manchester: Manchester University Press, 1960.

Meuvret, Jean. "La situation matérielle des membres du clergé séculier dans la France du XVIIe siècle," *Revue d'Histoire de l'Eglise de France* 54 (1968): 47–68.

Péronnet, Michel. *Les évêques de l'ancienne France (1516–1789).* 4 vols. Université de Paris-Sorbonne, Centre de Recherches sur la Civilisation de l'Europe Moderne. 1976. (Typescript.)

Perouas, Louis. "Le diocèse de la Rochelle de 1648 à 1724." In *Sociologie et pastorale,* vol. 8. S.E.V.P.E.N., 1964.

Préclin, Edmond. *Les Jansénistes du XVIIIe siècle et la Constitution civile du clergé.* Librairie Universitaire J. Gamber, 1928.

———. "Edmond Richer," *Revue d'Histoire moderne et contemporaine* (1930), p. 329.

Ravitch, Norman. *Sword and Mitre.* Mouton, 1966.

Sauzet, Robert. *Contre-Réforme et Réforme Catholique en Bas-Languedoc au XVIIe siècle: Le diocèse de Nîmes de 1598 à 1694.* 3 vols. Université de Paris-Sorbonne, Centre de Recherches sur la Civilisation de l'Europe Moderne. 1976. (Typescript.)

Schmitt, Thérèse-Jean. *L'organisation ecclésiastique et la pratique religieuse dans l'archidiaconé d'Autun (1650–1750).* Autun: Imprimerie L. Marcelin, 1957.

Sicard, Abbé Augustin. *L'Ancien clergé de France. I: Les évêques avant la Révolution.* Librairie Victor Lecoffre, 1893.

Viguerie, Jean de. "Le recrutement des Doctrinaires dans le diocèse de Narbonne au XVIIe siècle (1619–1715), *Actes des XLIe et XXIVe Congrès d'Etudes religieuses: Fédération historique du Languedoc méditerranéen et Roussillon, Fédération des Sociétés Académiques et Savantes Languedoc-Pyrenées-Gascogne* (Carcassonne, 1–7 May 1968) (1970), pp. 1–7.

———. *Les doctrinaires en France et en Italie au XVIIe siècle et au XVIIIe.* Sorbonne thesis, 1973. (Duplicated.)

Blet, Pierre. *Le clergé de France et la monarchie: Etude sur les assemblées générales du clergé de 1615 à 1666.* 2 vols. Rome: Librairie Editrice de l'Université Grégorienne, 1959.

———. "L'Ordre du clergé au XVIIe siècle," *Revue d'Histoire de l'Eglise de France* (1968).

Cans, Albert. *L'organisation financière du clergé de France à l'époque de Louis XIV.* 1910.

———. *La contribution du clergé de France à l'impôt dans la seconde moitié du règne de Louis XIV (1689–1715).* Librairie A. Picard, 1910.

Coudy, Julien. *Les moyens d'action du clergé de France au Conseil du Roi.* Sirey, 1954.

Egret, Jean. "La dernière assemblée du clergé de France (1788)," *Revue historique* 219 (1958): 1–15.

Lepointe, Gabriel. *L'organisation et la politique financière du clergé de France sous le règne de Louis XV.* Sirey, 1923, 1924.

Péronnet, Michel. "Les assemblées du clergé de France sous le règne de Louis XVI (1775–1788)," *Annales historiques de la Révolution française* 34 (1962): 8–35.

Serbat, Louis. *Les assemblées du clergé de France, 1561–1615.* Champion, 1906.

8

The Society of Orders
The Protestant Order

By virtue of the Edict of Nantes, April 1598, the French Calvinists, "ceux de la religion prétendue réformée (R.P.R.)," were treated as being an order of the kingdom. The king recognized the civil personality of this order and of the corporations it included.

Religious organization

The Edict of Nantes was, in itself, merely one of a number of *"paix de religion"* granted by the king in France since 1562. It particularly resembled the Edict of Poitiers of 1577, whole articles of which it reproduced. The great difference was that this one lasted. Actually, both of the contending parties realized that they could not win and felt exhausted. Furthermore, the religious organization of the minority was accompanied by a political and military organization which ensured their security.

For the Protestants as for the Catholics, the Edict of Nantes was only an unfortunate necessity. "Division in religion" was unacceptable to both. In order to survive, society had to have "one faith, one law, one king." "Difference in religion disfigures the state." It was only a provisional agreement. The king said in the preamble to the Edict: "If it has *not yet* pleased God to permit it [the service of God in France] to be in one and the same form of religion, let it at the least be with one and the same intention." The Catholics expected to convert the Protestants very soon. The Protestants thought that, once they were no longer persecuted, their religion would spread spontaneously and soon win over the majority. They "looked forward to the decay of the Roman religion in the near future... and they did not doubt that their doctrine would quickly make great progress now that it could be espoused without risk to property, life, or expectations."[1] Accordingly, Catholics and Protestants resigned themselves to waiting and meanwhile living side by side, in the same territorial communities but in distinct orders.

The Edict of Nantes, sealed with the Great Seal of green wax on knots of red and green silk, was therefore, "perpetual and irrevocable"—so long as the king's will should remain the same. The Edict granted the Protestants the right to a religious organization of their own.[2] Calvinist worship was restored in all the towns and fortresses where it had been allowed by the Edict of 1577 and where it had been celebrated on 17 September 1577, and also in two suburbs (*faubourgs de ville*) in each *bailliage* or *sénéchaussée*. In the countryside, in the homes of *seigneurs* who held rights of high justice or full "knight's fees," Protestant worship was permitted practically without limit on the numbers participating. In other fiefs the enfeoffing *seigneur* was allowed to welcome to Protestant services not only his *"famille"*—which meant those who were closely associated with him, his *domestiques,* that is, all who lived under his roof on any basis whatsoever—and his peasants, but also persons from outside the fief, though in no larger number than thirty.

There were Reformed churches throughout the kingdom. The big concentrations were in Aunis and Saintonge, in the valleys of the Garonne and the Dordogne, in Béarn, in the Cévennes, in Upper Languedoc, in the Rhône Valley, and in Dauphiné. In the Cévennes, in Upper Languedoc, in Montpellier, Nîmes, Béziers, the Montauban area, and around La Rochelle, the Protestants even constituted the majority of the population. Their churches were much more thinly scattered in the regions along the Loire, in Normandy, and in the regions watered by the Oise and the Marne. All together, according to Samuel Mours, allowing for the emigration which had begun and for conversions to Catholicism (against which have to be set conversions to Protestantism), there must have been, around 1660–70, about 1,200 Protestant churches, with between 700 and 750 pastors, and 1 million Protestants out of 18 million inhabitants. N. Weiss thought that they accounted for 2 million out of the 18.

The warrant containing the secret articles of 2 May 1598 added, in article 34, to the permission given for Protestant worship: "In all those places in which public worship is allowed, *the people may be summoned,* even by the ringing of bells, and there shall be all the usual activities and functions necessary to the practice of this religion, or to *the maintenance of discipline,* such as the holding of *consistories, colloquies, and provincial and national synods,* with His Majesty's permission." An entire hierarchical religious organization was thus recognized and authorized.

Each church had its consistory, entrusted with the "government of the church." A consistory was made up of a pastor and "elders," whose duty it was to watch over the flock, together with the pastor. Elders were recruited by cooptation. The names of those chosen were publicly announced three Sundays running. If no one opposed them, the chosen were publicly received on the following Sunday, after the sermon. Elders were changed every two or three years, or else one-third retired each year. Elders could function as deacons, turn and turn about, or else the consistory appointed deacons. "The office [of deacon] is to collect and to distribute, as recommended by the consistory, the money for the poor, those in prison, and the sick and to visit and care for them." For these tasks the deacons had at their disposal the funds acquired through collections, donations, and legacies. In addition to these responsibilities, the church had to ransom those brothers who had fallen captive to the Moslems of the Barbary Coast.

It was possible for a church to be without a pastor, in which case it was guided by an elder.

A church always maintained a schoolmaster, who read from the Bible on Sundays, at the beginning of the service; he also presided during the week over "public prayers" and performed teaching duties. The pastor himself kept a monopoly of preaching.

The consistory could decide to tax the congregation, distribute the burden of this tax, and levy it. It had the duty of supervising the religious life and morals of the faithful, and in doing so it intervened in civil, everyday life and could exercise "police" powers, either directly or through the *seigneurs* and magistrates.

A colloquy was constituted by a grouping of several churches. Each church could delegate to a colloquy one pastor and one elder. A colloquy held at least one assembly a year, for purposes of regulation and discipline.

A number of colloquies formed a synodal province. The province of Poitou was made up of the three colloquies of Upper, Lower, and Middle Poitou. There were in France sixteen synodal provinces, such as the province of Vivarais, Velay, and Forez, the province of Anjou, Touraine, and Maine, and the province of Saintonge, Aunis, and Angoumois.

Provincial synods met, with the king's permission and in the presence of a royal commissioner, possibly from the Edict of Nantes onward. In any case, the *arrêt* of the king's Council dated 22 August 1626 provided that the Protestants could hold a synod whenever they chose. They had to give notice to the governor or the *lieutenant général* of the province in the month preceding the convocation of the synod so that this magistrate could send a commissioner. In the event of the commissioner's not arriving, the synod had to wait for three days, after which it was free to proceed.

Attendance at the provincial synod was obligatory. The churches of the colloquies concerned each nominated directly one pastor and one elder to represent it at the synod. If no pastor was available, a church could be validly represented by an elder. The deputies received letters of credence from their respective churches. The synod of Poitou comprised between ninety and ninety-two deputies, representing forty-seven churches. Also present at a synod were deputies from adjacent provinces, as observers and for purposes of liaison.

The deputies elected, by a majority of votes, recorded in writing, an "assistant moderator," a secretary, and a "scribe," all of whom were pastors, and an auditing commission, made up of three pastors and four elders.

Provincial synods exhorted the faithful to redouble their prayers and lead a Christian life. God's wrath was manifested in the troubles with which he punished the churches. Everyone therefore ought to humble himself beneath the mighty hand of the Lord and put on sackcloth and ashes, with tears and lamentations. Furthermore, all should refrain from any form of blasphemy and should renounce vanity, luxury, drunkenness, dissoluteness, and every form of defilement.

A provincial synod selected pastors. If the province possessed an academy which prepared men for this function, the "scholars in divinity" who had completed their studies and were able to "*proposer,*" that is, to preach, presented a certificate from their academy. The synod appointed six pastors to examine the *proposant* in Greek, Hebrew, philosophy, and divinity. They investigated his life and morals. If all went well, they had him preach before them twice, once in Latin and once in French, on texts taken from the New Testament and given to him twenty-four hours previously. If these tests proved satisfactory, the pastors laid their hands on the *proposant* in order to instill the Holy Spirit into him, and he was then assigned to a church. Thereafter he could not leave his flock without the synod's permission. As there were not enough pastors for all the churches, the synod often organized a sort of rotation: a pastor brought God's Word to one place for one year, to another place the next. A pastor was paid by his consistory. The synod could suspend or dismiss pastors.

The provincial synod regulated the relief to be given to aged or infirm pastors, the traveling expenses of the delegates it sent to Paris, the honoraria payable to the lawyers who defended its interests, and so on. It could decide on the levying of taxes from the faithful, and it appointed a receiver for these.

The provincial synod made general decisions regarding discipline, baptism, the Lord's Supper, marriage, and burial. It supervised pastors' fulfillment of their duties: the way they preached, administered the sacraments, visited and consoled the afflicted and the sick, and so on. The synod regulated the behavior of the faithful. When in church, they must not talk during the sermon, they must kneel down to pray, and the men must bare their heads when the Word of God was being read and must join in singing the Psalms. Out of church, they must keep the Lord's day holy, refraining from card games, dice, visits to the drink shop, hunting, fishing, and swearing, on pain of excommunication; and at all times they must reconcile themselves with their brothers in Christ, avoid concubinage, aim at modesty and simplicity in dress, renounce all dancing, balls, masquerades, banquets, and carnivals, fast at the prescribed times, and so on.

The provincial synod dealt with particular cases, receiving appeals from the decisions taken by the colloquies and consistories.

The provincial synods could appeal to the king, just like the clergy of France, through the procedures of remonstrance, petition, opposition, intervention, and so on. They sometimes sent a deputy to the court to plead in favor of one of their concerns.

National synods were to be held every three years. Each of the sixteen provinces had to send two pastors and two elders. A national synod was composed, in principle, of sixty-four persons. The synods met regularly at Charenton until the twenty-eighth synod, held in 1644–45. The twenty-ninth and last met at Loudun, from 10 November 1659 to 1 January 1660. The role of national synods was the same as that of the provincial ones, but at the level of the kingdom as a whole. After 1629 and the Edit de Grâce of Nîmes, or of Alais, the national synod appointed two "deputies general" of the Protestants of France to attend upon the king. These were syndics, so to speak, who played a role similar to that of the agents general of the clergy of France, just as the national synod was analogous to the Assembly of the Clergy of France and could employ in relation to the king all the procedures employed by the Assembly of the Clergy.

Organization of justice and administration

The Edict of Nantes allowed the French Calvinists to maintain an organization of justice and administration.[3] The basis of this consisted of the *chambres de l'Edit* or *chambres mi-parties*. In Paris the *chambre de l'Edit* in the *parlement* of Paris was made up of a *président* and sixteen counselors, one of whom was a Protestant. It dealt with all cases, civil and criminal, involving *ceux de la R.P.R.* in the areas subject to the jurisdiction of the *parlements* of Paris, Normandy, and Brittany.

Three *chambres mi-parties*—at Castres, for the *parlement* of Toulouse, at Grenoble, and at Bordeaux—each comprised two *présidents,* one Catholic and one Protestant, and twelve counselors, half of whom were Catholics and half Protestants. The *chambre* at Grenoble dealt not only with cases concerning the Protestants of Dauphiné but also with those of Provence. The Protestants of Burgundy could choose to go either to the *chambre de l'Edit* in Paris or to the *chambre mi-partie* at Grenoble.

All three *chambres* heard without appeal all cases in which Protestants were involved either directly or as sureties. Matters concerning benefices, tithes, patronage of churches, and so on were, however, reserved for the *parlements*.

The powers of these *chambres* included rights of administration and command: "There shall be made in the said *chambres mi-parties* the propositions, deliberations, and resolutions which shall appertain to the public peace, and for the particular state and *police* of the cities where the same *chambres* be" (article 51). The jurisdiction of the *chambres* extended to the execution, nonexecution, or violation of royal edicts when Protestants were involved (article 52).

Political and military organization

Henri IV and Louis XIII tolerated down to 1629 the existence of a political organization of the Protestants in France. In principle this should not have existed, since article 82 of the Edict of Nantes decreed the immediate dissolution of the Protestants' political assemblies and councils and the breakup of all their leagues and associations; it also forbade them to form any such in the future and to levy taxes, erect fortifications, enlist soldiers, or negotiate with foreign powers without the king's permission. But by the warrant of 30 April 1598, which granted *places de sûreté* to the Protestants, the king authorized their general assembly at Châtellerault to appoint a council of ten deputies to sit at Saumur and supervise the execution of the Edict of Nantes until it had been verified by the Paris *parlement*. In fact, the king tolerated the Protestants' political and military organization.

This organization embraced provincial assemblies which elected deputies to the general assemblies. The latter were supposed to meet every three years but actually met more often than that. Sixteen such general assemblies took place between the one at Châtellerault in 1597–98 and the one at La Rochelle in 1620–22. Each provincial assembly had to delegate to the general assembly a *gentilhomme*, a pastor, and an elder—in short, the three orders of the state were to be represented. The proportions were not always respected: the assembly held at Saumur in 1611 embraced seventy persons, of whom thirty were *gentilshommes*, twenty were pastors, and sixteen were elders. The influence of the great Protestant nobles was preponderant in these assemblies.

Councils were set up to ensure continuity between assemblies and check on the execution of their decisions. Provincial councils each consisted of five or seven persons drawn from the three orders, of whom at least one was a pastor and one a governor of a fortress. They received reports and other communications from the Protestant churches and towns and took measures to ensure the defense of fortresses, the recruiting and equipment of soldiers, and so on. Being forbidden by the king, however, they functioned badly. The General Council was a permanent body. It received one deputy from each province and had to include at least four *gentilshommes*, two pastors, and four persons of the third estate.

The deputies general had been authorized by the king in 1601. They were nominated by the general assemblies. The assembly would have liked to have three deputies: one nobleman, one pastor, one member of the third estate, and all elected for one year only. The king wanted the deputies elected for a longer period and with no pastor among them. Eventually it was decided that the assembly should elect six candidates, from whom the king could choose two deputies, nominated for three years. These were to ensure a permanent representation of the Protestants at the king's side.

The warrant of 30 April 1598 accorded *places de sûreté* and garrisons to the Protestants "for their liberty of conscience" and "the safety of their persons, fortunes, and property." It allowed them to keep for eight years all the fortified places, towns, and châteaux they had held with garrisons down to the end of August 1597. The king would draw up a list of these places and sign it. Furthermore, the towns which protected themselves, without any garrison, by means of militias made up of the Protestant inhabitants, might continue to do so. The king allotted 180,000 *écus* a year for the upkeep of the garrisons, not including those in Dauphiné. This sum was to be distributed in accordance with the advice of the Protestants. If the posts of governor or captain of these fortresses fell vacant, the king would appoint to fill them a Protestant certified as such by his colloquy.

It appears that in May 1598 the Protestants must have possessed fifty-eight *places de sûreté* and eighteen *places de mariage,* that is, small fortresses in each of which there was a garrison of only a few men sent there by the *place de sûreté* on which it depended. But the list is certainly incomplete.[4] At the end of Henri IV's reign the Protestants had eighty-four *places de sûreté,* including Châtellerault, Royan, Niort, Saint-Jean-d'Angély, Sancerre, Grenoble, Gap, Lectoure, and Mont-de-Marsan, and eighteen towns which saw to their own protection, including La Rochelle, Montauban, Foix, Nîmes, Uzès, and Pontivy. They had lost nineteen towns through the governor's conversion to Catholicism; these included Mantes, Carentan, Domfront, Sully (Berry), and Tarascon-sur-Ariège.

The governor of a *place de sûreté* was placed under the supervision of the consistory and had to take an oath to the latter not to surrender it without their consent. The governor was appointed by the king, but he had to obtain a certificate from his colloquy that he really was a Protestant and that he lived as a good Christian should. If the colloquy declined to give him such a certificate, that amounted to rejection of the king's appointee, and in such cases the colloquy had to state its reasons.

After the assembly held at Saumur in 1611 the *places de sûreté* were placed under the authority of the provincial councils. They had to check on the condition of the fortresses, sending inspectors to visit them and review the garrisons. The latter were to consist exclusively of Protestant soldiers, and none of these must be a native of the town or its suburbs. The provincial council had to appoint a financial commission for a *place de sûreté,* to draw two-thirds of the amount of money allotted for the garrison, and itself to pay the soldiers and meet the various charges. The provincial council had to draw up the specifications for fortifications and repairs thereto and also had to see to all the business connected with putting out to tender the contracts for the work involved and sending inspectors to check on its performance. Actually, the governors continued to be independent, their loyalty doubtful, the magazines empty, the garrisons deficient, and the fortifications in a bad state.

In 1621 the provinces were grouped in "circles." Each "circle" had its general and was obliged to provide its share of men and money. The eight circles were Ile-de-France; Normandy; Picardy; Champagne; Beauce; Berry; Anjou, Maine, and Perche; and Touraine. But what was always lacking was a head, a "protector," an overall single leadership, despite the (belated) efforts of the duc de Rohan.

The demolition of the political and military organization

This political and military organization had to be demolished if the kingdom of France was not to suffer secession and partition. It went beyond the mere organization of an order, so much in conformity with the customary constitution of the realm, and resulted in the scattering about France of fragments of a Protestant state, with its own government, army, judicature, administration, and church. In fact, it established a federal system, a political dualism, with two different peoples, having divergent interests, and united only by a common head. Where the Protestants held power, as *seigneurs hauts justiciers,* or formed the majority, as in certain towns in the South, they became persecutors. Protestant *seigneurs* sometimes converted their parishes by force. At Nîmes it was hard for Catholic craftsmen to find lodging or work. At Millau the notaries refused to record the legal instruments of

Catholics. At Metz a *curé* was unable to attend one of his parishioners on her deathbed because the Huguenots whose servant she was prevented him. The Protestant *grands seigneurs* were continually in rebellion and drew the general assemblies into their insurrections, opposing the union of Protestant Béarn with the royal domain and the marriage of Louis XIII with the infanta of Spain, maintaining political relations with the United Provinces and England, and trying to facilitate an English invasion. The installation of the Protestants in a Catholic kingdom made territorial secession difficult for them to effect, but they constituted a permanent danger.

The king therefore smashed the political and military organization of the Protestants, in two stages. During the war of 1621–22, which began in connection with the uniting of Béarn with the royal domain, he conquered Poitou, Saintonge, and Guyenne, recovering about eighty *places de sûreté* or *places de mariage* from the Protestants. By the edict of 19 October 1622 he allowed them, as a free concession, to retain the remainder of their *places*.

There were other revolts, which led to the siege and capture of La Rochelle, the campaign in Languedoc, and the sacking of Privas. At the Peace of Alais, in June 1629, the Protestants had to agree to all their fortifications being demolished within three months by the inhabitants themselves. By the Edit de Grâce, given at Nîmes in July 1629, the king declared his wish "to keep them forever inseparably bound to obedience to us, awaiting the time when God's grace and mercy, touching their hearts and enlightening their minds, shall reunite all in the bosom of the Church and dry up the source of these baneful divisions." He therefore granted pardon and amnesty to the Protestants, with free exercise of the two religions, Catholic and Calvinist, full reestablishment of the Edict of Nantes, as registered by all the *parlements* (but not of the warrants and secret articles which had not required registration), and leveling and demolition of all fortifications, "except for the circle of walls" which was, for the men of those days, the distinctive characteristic of a genuine town but which no longer had any military value. The political and military organization of the Protestants thus disappeared completely. They retained their deputies general, but as mere representatives of an order, and the election of these representatives was consequently transferred from the general assemblies to the national synods. The Protestants never rebelled again, remaining loyal to the absolute monarchy until the revocation of the Edict of Nantes.

The destruction of the Protestant order

The destruction of their political and military organization left the members of the R.P.R. organized merely as an order of the realm, and the king could have let them stay like that: organization as an order was perfectly in conformity with the customary constitution of the kingdom of France, and, within the setting of this constitution, it offered only advantages. However, for religious reasons the royal government looked upon its policy of tolerance as only provisional; it resolved to implement the Edict of Nantes in as strict and narrow a fashion as possible, so as to encourage the Protestants to accept conversion. In October 1632 Louis XIII told the Nuncio Bichi, in connection with Montmorency's revolt in Languedoc, where the Protestants remained loyal, that he did not intend to make any concession to them but, on the contrary, would humble them as much as he could, so as to succeed in putting an end to them as soon as possible.[5]

In accordance with the king's ideas, Richelieu had drawn up a plan for use in relation to the synod at Charenton in 1632: to win over some Protestant ministers by means of money, promises, and threats, involve them in discussion with religious, and so convert them to Catholicism; then the other pastors and the Protestant laity would follow their example. After that, the government would proceed by force against any recalcitrants, treating them as disturbers of public tranquillity. The design was revealed too soon, and it failed. Subsequently, Richelieu was preoccupied with the external war.

But the cardinal did not abandon his intentions. He strained theology in order to facilitate conversions. He put forward as his principle the abandonment of everything that was not strictly required by faith, so as to make conversion easier. For example, where the doctrine of purgatory was concerned, it was necessary to leave aside the question of whether real and physical fire was involved and the question of where purgatory was situated; this reduced the matter to the point of faith, namely, the existence of an intermediate state between hell and heaven, where souls suffer temporary purifying pain so as to be able subsequently to go to heaven, and where they can be helped by the prayers and sacrifices of the living.

The cardinal sent Jesuit or Capuchin missions to the Protestants. He gave support to controversialists who were inspired by his principles, such as François Véron, who in 1641 went so far as to challenge the Protestants in their own places of worship. Véron formed groups of laymen, *bourgeois* and craftsmen, who succeeded in convincing Protestants who would have refused to talk with priests. Their method was to point out the contradictions in what the Protestant ministers said— the same method that Bossuet was to use later in his *Variations des Eglises protestantes*.

The cardinal was helped by Chancellor Séguier, the head of the judiciary, who set the royal judges to work. Already in 1633 he applied himself to ousting Protestants from office, obliging them to give up to Catholics the offices they held in the *parlements* and the presidial courts and excluding Protestants from even the minor posts of attorney, notary, and bailiff (*sergent*). Wherever he was compelled to tolerate Protestant officials, he endeavored at least to subordinate them to Catholics. At Castres he gave the presidency of the *chambre mi-partie* to a Catholic; he accorded precedence to Catholic magistrates over Protestant ones, even when the latter were senior; and he gradually excluded Protestants from the distribution of cases requiring reports to be made (for which fees were paid), even though the Edict of Nantes gave them the right to take part in this. He brought pressure to bear on Protestants to decline the competence of the *chambres de l'Edit* and bring their suits before the provincial intendants, in contempt of articles 67 and 68 of the Edict of Nantes. In exchange, he gave Protestants empty dignities, honorific appointments as state councilor, or letters making them *chevaliers ès lois*.

The chancellor sought to prevent Protestant *seigneurs* from purchasing land in strategically important places, with castles and fortified houses. He strove to settle Catholics in the Protestant South, and it was at his instigation that the *parlement* of Toulouse lightened the tax burden borne by craftsmen so as to attract Catholic craftsmen into the area.

The chancellor saw to it that the Edict of Nantes was most strictly enforced, even where religious matters were concerned. He forbade Protestant ministers to preach elsewhere than in the places where they resided, and he had newly built Protestant churches demolished.

This systematic policy was hindered by the prolonged wars, but it never ceased, for it was inspired by the Compagnie du Saint-Sacrement, the secret society founded in 1627 by Henri de Lévis, duc de Ventadour. This society had fifty-three branches in the provinces. Its members included ten bishops; abbots, canons, and *curés;* numerous magistrates, including some of the most highly placed—members of the Council of State and the *parlement,* men like Mesmes, Lamoignon, d'Ormesson, and d'Argenson, as well as officers of the royal household and ambassadors. The Compagnie played a big part in the Catholic Renaissance. Where the Protestants were concerned, it organized missions, a campaign for the propagation of the faith which even involved taking Protestant children away from their families in order to bring them up as Catholics, funds to promote conversions among the common people, and the boycotting of Huguenot craftsmen. Above all, the Compagnie developed a doctrine of strict interpretation of the Edict of Nantes. The principle of this was that the Edict was not at all an edict of toleration but had been signed to enable the king to "reunite with the Church those who had so lightly departed from it." The doctrine was given form in 1642 by Jean Filleau, *avocat du roi* in the presidial court of Poitiers, and then by Pierre Bernard, counselor in the presidial court of Béziers, in his *Explication de l'Edit de Nantes* (1666). A whole documentation of *arrêts* and court decisions unfavorable to the Huguenots was also assembled and interpreted. The method used was this. Take article 27 of the Edict of Nantes, which declared Protestants to be "capable of holding and exercising all estates, dignities, offices, and public charges whatsoever, whether royal, seignorial, or municipal." The question was put: can a Protestant hold office in a town where Protestant worship is not allowed? The answer was: no, for the lesser is included in the greater. The greater, here, is the right to Protestant worship; if that is not present, then the lesser, namely, access to offices, cannot be present. "When the matter was looked into closely, it was found that this article of the Edict of Nantes declares that those of the R.P.R. are merely *capable* of holding offices and public dignities, without there being any necessity for these persons actually to hold them." Consequently, they should not be given them.

By verbal artifice Catholics deprived the terms of the Edict of their substance and even made them say the opposite of their meaning. Members of the Compagnie caused this doctrine, with its principle and method, to be adopted by the *parlements* of Aix, Bordeaux, and Toulouse and by the General Assembly of the Clergy of France from 1654 onward. It was thus able to have the Protestants forbidden the right to possess hospitals of their own (1637, 1653), to have foreign Protestants expelled or locked up, to get the examining boards to exclude Protestants from the functions of notary and attorney, and to cause Protestant women to be refused licenses as qualified makers of household linen (1649, 1656). Even after the Compagnie had been suppressed (1665), their principle and method were still used.

The undertaking was made easier, perhaps, by a certain weakening in Calvinist faith, which some believe they have discerned; by the success among the Protestant ministers of the concept of absolutism sanctioned by divine right; and perhaps also by the decline of the Protestant *gentilhommerie* of the military companies and the increasing influence of magistrates, lawyers, and urban merchants in the consistories. Let us take the example of Mens-en-Trièves, which was attached to the colloquy of Grenoble.[6] This was a large *bourg,* with about 1,200 inhabitants, almost all of them Calvinists, except for fifteen to twenty families living in the outskirts.

Between 1650 and 1685 the influence of the *gentilshommes* declined in Mens, although it was they who had introduced Protestantism there. François de Bonne, *seigneur* of Les Diguières, who settled at Mens in 1573, had made it a center of his religion. In 1650 twenty of the thirty noble families of the neighborhood were Calvinist. Most of them lived in the country, rather modestly. Some were counselors or advocates before the *parlement,* others were officers in the Sault regiment. Only three noblemen figured among the fifty-eight elders of the consistory in the thirty years 1650–1685. The *gentilshommes* were eliminated from the spiritual, moral, and social leadership of the church. Their daughters married sons of notaries, surgeons, *rentiers,* or even merchants.

Beneath them in the social hierarchy came a composite group made up of magistrates, the two castellans, the two vice-castellans, advocates, notaries, attorneys, legal practitioners, doctors and apothecaries, and *rentiers*—the "notables," about fifty families, 12 percent of the population, who occupied 28.5 percent of the seats in the consistory.

Beneath them were the merchants, of whom there were about forty-five families. Commerce here was hereditary in families; in the case of the Richard family, seven of them were merchants at the same time. These merchants formed a close group of brothers and cousins. They made their money from the sale of linen and nails, in Provence and Languedoc. They contributed 28.5 percent of the members of the consistory, including those who remained elders longest (for fourteen or eighteen years). In 1673, out of sixteen elders, six were merchants. One-third of the consuls at Mende, nine out of twenty-six, were merchants. This social group was rising in the world.

Last came the craftsmen, workers in iron, leather, and textiles; they comprised 255 families, making up 66 percent of the total population and 25 percent of the active population. The largest group was that of the ironworkers, who produced nails, locks, and horseshoes. The crafts were family affairs: there were dynasties of nail-makers, locksmiths, and carders. Some well-to-do craftsmen were entrepreneurs employing wage-earners. The craftsmen supplied 36 percent of the members of the consistory, but these were in the main ironworkers, the most highly respected and prosperous of them. Carders, weavers, rope-makers, and curriers, a despised group, were wholly absent from the consistory.

At the very bottom of the scale there were a few *"laboureurs,"* who also were unrepresented.

The most influential persons in the consistory were, at first, men who were in the king's service and proud of their position. Such a one was André Marie, captain and royal castellan of Mens and of the *mandement* of Trièves, the son of a former attorney. He claimed a place of honor in the Protestant church, not only for himself but also for his wife and children. "He is not going to sit in a pew where he will have a servant on one side of him and a clerk on the other, and he did not expect that his wife would find herself among nail-makers and the like ... In view of his office, in which he represents the person of the king, and even if there were five marquises or counts in this place, he considers that he should take precedence of them all." This attachment to the king and to his service, as a source of dignity, was shared by the rich merchants, who had need of order and peace. Possibly there may have been elements here of faith becoming lukewarm and the adoption of a reserved mode of behavior among Huguenots who were submissive and attached to absolutism. The pastors, moreover, were on the whole a mediocre lot. "Among the pastors there was an excellent élite, but the mass of them were very mixed."[7]

From 1661 onward Louis XIV sent into the provinces the commissions asked for by the Assembly of the Clergy in 1654, to inquire into the misdeeds of the Protestants. A commission was made up of a royal intendant, a Protestant *gentilhomme,* and the official of the diocese, who acted as *procureur du roi.* These investigations caused the first wave of emigration by Protestants. After 1665 the commissioners became a permanent body. Appeal from their decisions could be made only to the king's Council.

Rigorous enforcement was suspended for a time by the edict of 1 February 1669, "the second Edict of Nantes." In this the king recognized the legitimacy of the Protestant ecclesiastical organization, the right of members of the R.P.R. to serve on municipal councils and *jurandes,* their right to tax their community in order to meet the expenses of their religious worship, the right of pastors to visit Calvinist patients in hospitals, and the exemption of Protestants from any obligation to contribute to the financing of Catholic worship.

However, the policy of rigorous enforcement of the Edict of Nantes was soon resumed. It was the subject of twelve royal edicts between 1671 and 1679 and then, after the Peace of Nijmegen, at the high point of Louis XIV's reign, of eighty such decrees between 1679 and 1685, applying to the whole of France, together with a great number of *arrêts* by the Council. In 1680 it was forbidden for any Catholic to become a Protestant, on pain of banishment.

In Poitou, where, between 1670 and 1680, two-thirds of the Protestant churches had been demolished and from which a substantial section of the Protestant élite had emigrated, the intendant De Marillac put into effect, from May 1681 onward, the procedure of billeting soldiers, and dragoons in particular, upon the Protestant inhabitants—the so-called *dragonnades.* Billeting was always a harsh experience for the civilian population, owing to the violence, plundering, and exactions indulged in by the soldiers, and in this case it was made even harsher than usual by the incitements against the Protestants which came from above and by the soldiers' certainty that they would not be punished. Some Protestants accepted conversion. On 26 November 1681 the dragoons were sent to Bayonne. On 6 February 1682 Marillac was recalled. The "converts" then retracted their conversions, before notaries. These "relapsed" individuals were thrown into prison, and ten Protestant churches were destroyed.

The Assembly of the Clergy in 1682 addressed a pastoral warning to all the consistories in France, threatening the Protestants with the greatest severities if they remained stubborn. The king sent this warning to his intendants, and it was read throughout the country in September 1682.

After the Truce of Regensburg (Ratisbon), which confirmed Louis XIV's hegemony in Europe, came the great *dragonnade* of 1685, which began in Béarn and in the areas of Montauban and Bergerac. From the Montauban area the dragoons moved on into Upper and Lower Languedoc, Provence, Dauphiné, Lyonnais, and Gex. From the area of Bergerac they advanced into Aunis, Saintonge, and Poitou. Their "sojourns" led to between 300,000 and 400,000 conversions, including over a third of the pastors in the region.

The king was thus able gradually to demolish the Protestants' administrative and judicial organization. On 16 December 1661 an *arrêt* of the Council forbade the *chambres de l'Edit* or the *chambres mi-parties* to send deputations to the king, thereby wounding their dignity and their very status as corporate bodies. An *arrêt* of the Council dated 1 September 1662 merged the *chambre de l'Edit* of Castres with the *parlement* of Toulouse. Another, dated 24 April 1665, referred all matters concerning religion to two commissions in each province, one Catholic and one Protestant. There was therefore no more need for *chambres mi-parties*. The edict of January 1669 abolished the *chambres de l'Edit* in the *parlements* of Paris and Rouen. In Languedoc, under the intendant Bazin de Bazons, the Protestants were excluded from the provincial estates, from the diocesan assessment commissions, and from appointments as consul. The *chambre de l'Edit* ceased to have cognizance of matters concerning the state, nonobservance of Catholic feast days, municipal affairs, and cases of relapse into heresy, apostasy, and blasphemy. The edict of July 1679 swept away the last of the *chambres mi-parties*, those of Languedoc, Guyenne, and Dauphiné, and incorporated their officials in the *parlements*. Cases which had been within the competence of the *chambres de l'Edit* were referred to the *grand-chambres* of the *parlements*, to which those counselors of the *parlements* who were Protestants were not admitted.

The king was also enabled gradually to destroy the Protestants' religious organization. He made it his aim to fragment the R.P.R. of France. A Council *arrêt* of 26 July 1657 forbade the holding of colloquies. National synods ceased to meet after the one held at Loudun on 30 November 1659. All that was left were the separate churches and the provincial synods. Consequently there was no longer, in principle, any national Protestant church, any Protestant "order." The provincial synods, overwhelmed with matters that had previously been dealt with by the colloquies, absorbed in questions of discipline, became less effective politically. The Council's *arrêt* of 5 October 1663 forbade the churches of different provinces to engage in correspondence with each other, so as to prevent a national Protestant church from being kept in existence by that indirect means. Division by provinces had to be strictly observed. On 5 January 1683 a Council *arrêt* forbade consistories to contribute to the maintenance of ministers outside their own areas, thus preventing the rich churches from coming to the aid of the poor ones. This rule fragmented the Protestant communities and drained weaker churches of strength until they died; for although they could survive for a time without a pastor, this situation could not last indefinitely.

The king imposed an increasing degree of supervision by his representatives over the organs of the R.P.R. Already in April 1623 a royal declaration had obliged every synod to accept the presence of one of the king's Protestant officials, whose duty it would be to ensure that nothing was discussed but what the edicts allowed. The *arrêt* of 15 September 1660 forbade the provincial synods to deliberate in the absence of the king's commissioner. A provincial governor usually appointed as commissioner a *gentilhomme* who, though a Protestant, was a *fidèle* of his who would be required to report everything he had seen and heard during the debates. This *arrêt* was confirmed by the declaration of 10 October 1679, which prohibited the holding of any synod without the king's permission and without the presence of a commissioner nominated by the king, who might be either a Protestant or a Catholic, since Protestant commissioners had been accused of conniving at infractions of the rules.

By the Council's *arrêt* of 30 April 1661, consistories and synods could decide on the raising of taxes only if a royal judge was present. The declaration of 21 August 1684 ordained that consistories should meet at no shorter interval than a fortnight, and always in the presence of a royal judge.

The king now considered that he was in a position to annihilate Protestantism in France and, desirous of counterbalancing the triumph won by the House of Austria over the Turks before Vienna in 1683, he revoked the Edict of Nantes by the Edict of Fontainebleau on 17 October 1685. In the preamble Louis XIV declared that he was completing the task begun by his forebears. He claimed that Henri IV had signed the Edict of Nantes "in order to diminish the aversion that existed between members of the two religions, so as to be better able to work, as he had resolved to do, to reunite with the Church those who had so lightly departed from it," but he had died too soon to accomplish his purpose. Louis XIII had granted the Protestants the Edict of Nîmes, in July 1629, with the same intention, but the outbreak of war in 1635 had prevented its implementation. Louis XIV had been too busy with other things, but he made the truce of 1684 so as to be able to turn his attention to the Protestants. "Since the better and larger part of our subjects of the said R.P.R. have embraced the Catholic faith, and since for this reason the carrying-out of the Edict of Nantes and of all that has been ordained in favor of the said R.P.R. has become pointless," the king revoked the Edict of Nantes of April 1598, the *articles particuliers* of 2 May, and the Edict of Nîmes of July 1629.

He banned the public celebration of Protestant worship. All Protestant churches were to be demolished. It was forbidden to Protestants to assemble for worship in any place, even in the homes of *seigneurs justiciers*.

Precautions were taken against propaganda and teaching. All ministers who would not accept conversion were to leave the country within a fortnight. Life was made easier for those who did become converts to Catholicism: they received exemption from payment of *taille* and from the billeting of soldiers; a life pension one-third larger than their previous stipend; dispensation from the three obligatory years of study for those who wished to become advocates or doctors of law, with authorization to appear immediately before the examiners and relief from half of the examination fees; and, finally, the right of reversion for the exemption from *taille* and billeting and the continued payment of half of his pension to a man's widow.

No special schools for Protestants' children were to be tolerated. These children were to be given Catholic baptism within twenty-four hours of their birth. Midwives had to inform *curés* of such births. The children were to be sent by their parents to the Catholic churches, on pain of a fine of 500 livres, and brought up in the Catholic faith. The royal judges and the *seigneurs hauts justiciers* had to see that these laws were obeyed.

Protestants were forbidden to leave the country or send their property out of it, on pain of a sentence to the galleys in the case of the men and imprisonment, with confiscation of property, for the women. Those who had left the country were given four months to return, when they would have their property restored to them. Private worship was permitted:

> in addition, the said adherents of the R.P.R. shall be able, while awaiting God's pleasure to enlighten them like other people, to remain in the towns and places of our kingdom, the countries and lands subject to our authority, and continue to carry on their business and enjoy their property, without liability to being disturbed or interfered with on account of the said R.P.R.—on condition, as has been said, that they do not practice it or assemble on the pretext of praying or worshiping in accordance with the said religion, in any way, on pain of the penalties to their persons and property mentioned above (article 12).

Seventeen other edicts, declarations and *arrêts* of the Council were issued, between 17 October 1685 and the end of January 1686, complementing the Edict of Fontainebleau. The edict of January 1686 ordered that children between the ages of five and sixteen be handed over to their Catholic grandparents, uncles, or other kindred to be brought up in the Catholic faith. If they had no such kin, the royal judges were to entrust them to other Catholics for this purpose. If the father and mother lacked the means to pay for their upkeep, the children would be placed in the *hôpitaux généraux*. In this way it would be made impossible for Calvinism to be passed on to the rising generation, and it would disappear from France.

From the Revocation to the Revolution

French Calvinism, thus proscribed, survived thanks to the institutions of *"le Désert."* It eventually won toleration *de facto* and then, by the edict of 1787, *de jure*.

The problem was to transform into genuine Catholics the "new converts"—those whose conversion had been brought about by the *dragonnades* of 1685 and those who were to become converts later on.

Most of the bishops were for mildness and patience. They considered that a profession of implicit faith in the teachings of the Church was enough; the "new converts" should not be forced to receive the sacraments, especially Communion, for, if they were to take the Eucharist without believing in the Real Presence and Transubstantiation and without having been purged of their sins by a valid confession, that would be the worst kind of sacrilege. Reliance should be placed on instruction and, above all, on prayer.

But it had been necessary to revoke the Edict of Nantes by means of another edict, and the execution of this edict was therefore entrusted to the intendants of the provinces. On the one hand, these administrators continued the policy of *dragonnade* in order to obtain new conversions, and, on the other, they tested the sincerity of the new converts by compelling them to go to Communion. Some of the "new converts" spat out the Eucharist and trampled on it. Those who swallowed the Host became convinced that they had committed the sin against the Holy Ghost, out of weakness, and fell into despair. Forced Communions were abandoned in 1687. Nevertheless, this unbearable violence succeeded in antagonizing many of the "new converts" against Catholicism. It caused them to think that if the priests had agreed to this sacrilege, then the Catholics did not believe in their own teaching and so were hypocrites. Moreover, the government clumsily insisted on such external practices as requiring an oath of adherence to the Catholic faith, recorded in writing, and a formula of abjuration as a condition of marriage.

With their consciences subjected to coercion, the Protestants organized themselves to resist. From April 1686 onward, clandestine assemblies gathered in the Cévennes and in Languedoc. Many Protestants went abroad, to what they called *le Refuge,* but in every generation they left one of their family behind to look after the family property; outwardly Catholic but secretly Protestant, he would, on his deathbed, refuse the sacraments and proclaim his true faith. The Protestants of France created institutions aimed at insurrection. During the wars at the end of Louis XIV's reign they made connections with *le Refuge* and thought in terms of an enemy landing. The revolt of the Camisards and the long war in the Cévennes caused them to appear as traitors in the eyes of the Catholics. In many regions, moreover, Protestantism underwent degeneration. Without pastors and deprived of books by the government's *autos-da-fé,* the Protestants declined into illuminism and prophetism.

Their resistance fixed the king in his resolution to crush them. By the declaration of 8 March 1715, noting that the "long stay in France" of the former Protestants "was sufficient proof that they had embraced the Catholic religion," the king annulled article 12 of the Edict of Fontainebleau. Not a single Protestant was to be left, as such, in France. The regent confirmed this edict by the ordinance of May 1716, which forbade all gatherings of Protestants and all relations with ministers and preachers, and by that of August 1716, which made the exiling of Protestants definitive. Louis XV, by the Edict of Versailles, 14 May 1724, repeated and developed the first eleven articles of the Edict of Fontainebleau and all of Louis XIV's legislation between 1685 and 1715: prohibition of the exercise of any religion but the Catholic and of any assembling for that purpose; a ban on sending children abroad to be educated; schools in all parishes to teach Catholicism, mass every day for schoolchildren, catechism up to the age of twenty; a visit from the priest and reception of the sacraments made obligatory for the sick, with prosecution of anyone who tried to dissuade the sick from taking the sacraments (repetition of the edicts of January 1686 and the declarations of 13 December 1698 and 16 October 1700); only Catholics to be allowed to become officials in the higher courts, *bailliages, sénéchaus-*

sées, prévôtés, hautes justices, the royal household, and the households of the princes; only Catholics to be eligible for the functions of
mayor and alderman or other municipal offices, for the minor judicial
posts of *greffier,* notary, attorney, tipstaff, and bailiff (*sergent*); university degrees to be awarded to Catholics alone, except in the case of
foreigners (repetition of the edicts of 26 February 1680 and March
1707); doctors, surgeons, apothecaries, midwives, and bookseller-
printers must all be Catholics; marriages could be contracted only in
accordance with Catholic rules; underage persons could marry without
the consent of their parents if these had emigrated, and no marriage
could be celebrated in a foreign country without permission from the
secretary of state (repetition of the edict of March 1697 and the declaration of 15 June 1697); archbishops, bishops, *curés,* intendants of provinces, *procureurs du roi,* judges, doctors, surgeons, apothecaries, and
midwives were called upon to see to the application of these measures.
They amounted to total proscription.

The institutions of *le Désert* enabled Protestantism to survive in
France. There had been an especially large number of *émigrés* from the
maritime provinces—Aunis and Saintonge—but nevertheless there
were many "new converts" left in the kingdom. At Florac, out of 1,027
"new converts," only 4 fled the country. Throughout the Cévennes
there were very few who fled. In 1728 a secret census showed that
there were 200,000 Protestants in Languedoc and Dauphiné, almost as
many as before the Revocation. However, by being compelled to
marry in the Catholic church and to have their children baptized there,
and to act as though they were Catholics, they would probably have
been converted in the end.

It was pastors who organized resistance on the spot and created the
needful clandestine institutions. Already in 1681 the Protestant
churches of Dauphiné, Vivarais, and the Cévennes had appointed
commissioners to manage their affairs, fill vacancies in the event of
death, and correspond with Guyenne, Saintonge, and Poitou. In May
1682, when Protestant worship was banned at Montpellier, the pastors
met and arranged for a gathering of sixteen churches in Toulouse on 7
May 1683. These resolved to petition the king and to hold assemblies of
the churches which had been destroyed in Vivarais, Languedoc, the
Cévennes, Guyenne, Saintonge, and Poitou. On 29 and 30 July 1683,
twenty-two churches in Vivarais met together, formed a council, and
organized armed resistance. The "notables" took fright. The
bourgeois of Montpellier deserted the movement. The dragoons had

triumphed. One hundred thirty pastors were arrested. The presidial court of Nîmes condemned to death Isaac Homel, who was broken on the wheel at Tournon on 27 October, 1684. But the conception of the *assemblées du Désert* had been born. In April 1686 clandestine assemblies were held in Languedoc and in the Cévennes.

On 21 August 1715 Antoine Court held in the Lower Cévennes the first *"synode du Désert"* properly so called. In ten years he succeeded in putting the church on its feet again, restoring discipline and purifying faith. From 1721 the three churches of Upper Languedoc, Lower Languedoc, and the Cévennes were functioning, with a colloquy of pastors and elders every six months and a yearly synod. Only two pastors preached, but *prédicants,* accompanied by *proposants,* traveled around the provinces. On 6 May 1726 the first national synod was held in Vivarais. From 1720 onward the Protestants had a representative in Geneva—Antoine Court. A "deputy general of the churches of Languedoc to the Protestant Powers," Benjamin Duplan, visited Switzerland, Germany, the United Provinces, and England, set up committees, and obtained subsidies from governments. In Geneva a group of pastors and teachers constituted L'Hoirie (literally, "the Inheritance"), or Association for Aid to the Afflicted Faithful. Its executive organ was the "Lausanne Committee." Antoine Court went to live in that town in 1729.

The Protestants worshiped in their homes in the evenings, with Bibles and catechisms they received from abroad. From time to time a *prédicant* came by and held a nocturnal assembly in a barn or in the open air. The faithful listened to a reading from the Bible, sang the psalms of Clément Marot, heard a sermon by the *prédicant,* and communicated in accordance with the Calvinist rite.

The synods fought against surrenders of principle. The synod of 1772 forbade mixed marriages, required baptism of children by pastors, in isolated houses or farms, and Calvinist marriage ceremonies, for which the pastor kept a register on strips of paper rolled up in a bag, ordained that the Sabbath day be kept holy, forbade games of chance and dancing, and inflicted penances, including deprivations of the Lord's Supper—but insisted on obedience to the king. In 1728 there were 120 churches in Languedoc and Dauphiné, 47 of which were in the two colloquies of Lower Languedoc and the Cévennes. The faithful were recruited mainly from among the young and the humble folk—coatmakers, wool-carders, shopboys.

The edicts against the Protestants were enforced more and more slackly and spasmodically. In wartime the government was fearful of Protestant risings. This was no imaginary fear. In 1743, during the War of the Austrian Succession, there were revolts in the areas of Castres, Toulouse, and Montauban and in Dauphiné. The government then arrested and hanged a pastor, brought a prosecution against a man who had refused the sacraments at the point of death, having his corpse disinterred and dragged to the garbage dump, and threw some Protestants into prison or sent them to the galleys. Most often, however, the government was content to impose fines for the offense of holding an assembly. Antoine Court was able to come to Nîmes while the war was on and hold an assembly near the Tour Magne on 20 September 1744; it was attended by *gentilshommes,* advocates, doctors, *bourgeois,* rich merchants, craftsmen, and *laboureurs.* In 1746, in Languedoc, the intendant even gave up imposing sanctions and concluded an *entente* with the pastors.

This success was due to the work done by the pastors. First, as novices aged fifteen or sixteen, they traveled about with a qualified pastor on foot, dressed as shepherds and sleeping in barns, caves, and forests. The pastor instructed them, filling them with *l'esprit du Désert:* service to God to the point of martyrdom. They helped him in his tasks of convening assemblies and visiting the faithful.

After a few years spent like this, novices went to Lausanne, to a sort of seminary. Two scholarships to this establishment were instituted in 1728 and then, in 1744, six. They were taught separately and in secret, being given a brief and practical training. Only in about 1749 were they taught a little Greek and Latin. Paul Rabaut never learned these languages. After their apprenticeship they returned to Languedoc, where they were accepted as *proposants;* then, after a few years in the field, they were given the laying-on of hands and became pastors.

The results they achieved were such that the royal declaration of 17 January 1750 repeated that of 1724. The *maréchaussée* and the troops quartered the country. Assemblies were made impossible. *Dragonnades* were resumed, to enforce Catholic baptism of children. There were bloody clashes with the peasants. A price was put on the head of every *prédicant.* In 1752 a *proposant* and a "notable" were hanged. After that, some Protestants emigrated. Others, however, stood firm. There were riots and a Huguenot *jacquerie* in 1753. The government entered into negotiations. The bishops gave up the requirement of a written formula of abjuration and declared themselves content with an oral abjuration made without witnesses. They thus secured Catholic baptisms, and Protestants asked for the rehabilitation of their Calvinist marriages. Eventually, marshal de Mirepoix, governor of Languedoc, made an agreement with Paul Rabaut. The Protestants were not to hold assemblies of more than two or three hundred persons and were not to hold them in the immediate neighborhood of towns or busy roads; in return for this, the governor promised them security, *de facto* toleration. In 1761 there were 80,000 Protestant families in Languedoc, about 350,000 persons all together, with sixteen pastors, seven colloquies, and fifty-seven churches.

The movement that had started in Languedoc spread to other provinces: in 1734 to Limousin; in 1741 to Foix and Béarn; in 1742 to Poitou, Normandy, and Orléans; and in 1750 the *Eglise du Désert* was restored in Saintonge (where assemblies had been held spontaneously since 1733). In the North and Northeast of the kingdom, Protestantism had survived only in the form of domestic worship, in homes scattered here and there; only in 1770 did a revival occur in those parts which was like that in Languedoc.

After 1763 and the end of the Seven Years' War the government and public opinion were increasingly inclined toward tolerance. This tendency was due to the growing influence of the Enlightenment and the change in social values. On both sides, less importance was ascribed to dogma. The pastors belittled the problem of the Eucharist and considered that there was nothing in it to quarrel about. Paul Rabaut envisaged a common religion in which Catholicism, Protestantism, Judaism, and the Enlightenment would all merge. In 1784 the Protestants were widely using the catechism of Vernes, in which the divinity of Jesus Christ was not mentioned. Rabaut-Saint-Etienne defined Christianity thus: "The Christian religion is merely natural religion as revealed to mortals and confirmed by Jesus Christ." He took a rationalist and sensualist line, regarding the passions as necessary and inseparable from human nature. All that his doctrine lacked was God and sin. National synods ceased in 1763. Morals grew lax. Blasphemy, immodesty, and disregard of the rules for baptism and marriage became frequent.

On the Catholic side, the magistrates set about according recognition to Protestant marriages. The *parlement* of Grenoble in 1766 and that of Toulouse in 1769 (after the annulment of the verdict in the Calas case) recognized the validity of marriages made in *le Désert*. After 1769, Protestants were set free from the galleys and their womenfolk from the Tour de Constance. The last occasion when an assembly was surprised by the authorities was at Orange in 1767, and the Protestants arrested were released without trial. At Nîmes, Protestants became advocates, attorneys, and counselors in the presidial court, thanks to conniving grants of "certificates of Catholicity." In 1783 there were nineteen Protestants on the town council. Mixed marriages were frequent. Protestants were even allowed to attend the college run by the Oratorians. Colloquies and synods of each province were regularly held. Pastors were no longer itinerant but were assigned to a particular church. After 1770 assemblies were held openly. In Guyenne, Saintonge, and Poitou there were "houses of prayer" in the midst of towns.

The assemblies of the clergy of France held between 1775 and 1788 and the agents general of the clergy of France called in vain for the enforcement of the laws—the Edict of Fontainebleau and the Edict of 1724.

The new attitudes were given sanction by new laws. In May 1782 a royal declaration allowed *curés* to enter children's names in the parish registers without the parents' having to present a marriage certificate. The General Assembly of the Clergy of France was distressed by this ruling, which reduced the *curé* "to the status of a mere notary."

A prolonged effort, begun by Turgot at the outset of Louis XVI's reign, led to the granting of civil rights to Protestants. In strict law, their marriages were not legal, their wills had no force, and their children were bastards. In 1785 La Fayette, the baron de Breteuil, secretary of state for the royal household, and Lamoignon de Malesherbes began work on a project to change all that. The Paris *parlement* petitioned the king on 9 February 1787 to "ponder, in his wisdom, the most certain methods" for giving the Protestants civil status. In the Assembly of Notables the bishop of Langres, Malesherbes's nephew, spoke in favor of this solution of the Protestant question. Soon after, Malesherbes became keeper of the seals in the government of Loménie de Brienne. The clergy of France were not consulted.

On 19 November 1787 the king issued the Edict of Versailles "concerning those who do not belong to the Catholic religion." It was stated that, while "the Catholic, Apostolic, and Roman religion will continue to enjoy the exclusive right to public worship in our kingdom . . . we nevertheless allow those of our subjects who profess a different religion . . . to enjoy all the possessions and rights that may now or in the future belong to them as property or inheritance, and to carry on their business, crafts, trades, and professions without being disturbed or disquieted on account of their religion." The religious dissidents re-

mained excluded from offices in the judicature, both royal and seignorial, from municipal appointments that had been made offices and to
which judical functions were attached, and from all posts which gave
the right to teach publicly. They were not to regard themselves as
"forming in our kingdom a corporation, community, or special society," and so could not deliberate together or formulate joint demands.
Pastors were not to assume their status officially, wear a special form
of dress in public, or issue any marriage certificates. The dissidents had
to show respect to the Catholic religion and its ceremonies, conform to
police regulations on Sundays and feast days, and contribute to the
costs of repairing Catholic churches.

However, Protestants could contract marriages that had in civil law
the same consequences as Catholic marriages. They were to have the
banns published by the *curés* or officers of justice and notices of them
affixed by the *greffier de justice* on the church door. Objections to
marriages would be signified to the *greffe de la justice*. The judge
would give his ruling on these objections and could grant dispensations
from impediments of kinship up to the third degree, though the Grande
Chancellerie had to rule on closer degrees. The betrothed were to make
their declaration of marriage before the *curé* or the judge, bringing a
certificate that banns had been published and that objections, if any,
had been withdrawn, and also the consents of their parents or guardians; they were to produce four witnesses and declare that they took
each other "in lawful and indissoluble marriage, and pledged fidelity
to each other." The *curé* or the judge would declare them united, in the
name of the law, inscribe the declarations in two registers, with mention of the annexed documents, and have these entries signed by the
couple, if they could sign their names. Marriages previously entered
into could be regularized within one year.

The birth of non-Catholic children would be recorded either by a
certificate of baptism or by a declaration made by the father and two
witnesses, or by four witnesses, before the judge. This declaration
would be entered in two registers and signed by father, witness, and
judge.

Declarations of death were to be made to the *curé* or the judge by the
two closest relatives or neighbors of the deceased and be registered as
above. Administrators of towns, *bourgs,* and villages were to designate
a cemetery for non-Catholics. The bodies of the latter were not to be
displayed outside houses, nor were their funerals to be accompanied by
singing or by prayers recited aloud.

The Lutherans of Alsace and those of the king's subjects who had been allowed the exercise of a religion other than the Catholic religion in certain provinces or towns of the kingdom retained their privileges.

The *parlement* of Paris and the provincial *parlements* registered this purely and simply—with the exception of those of Bordeaux, Besançon, and Douai. The General Assembly of the Clergy of France in 1788 recognized the need for the non-Catholics to be given civil status but would have wished that Catholic baptism had been made obligatory; and, as things were, they refused to allow any participation by the *curé* in the baptism of children of a Protestant marriage, since he had no right to declare such a marriage legitimate. The Assembly noted that the practice of public worship by the Protestants was tolerated, since it was not expressly forbidden.

The Protestants soon completed the process of becoming free citizens. On 23 August 1789 the Constituent Assembly voted the article of the Declaration of the Rights of Man: "No one is to be disquieted on account of his opinions, and in particular not for his religious opinions, provided that their manifestation does not disturb the order established by the laws." On 24 December the Assembly voted for the admission of non-Catholics to all employments, civil and military alike. On 15 November 1790 Rabaut-Saint-Etienne was elected chairman of the Constituent Assembly. He suggested the civil constitution of the clergy, which was repugnant to the majority of French Catholics.

The Protestants' success resulted from the weakening of faith and the sense of religious values. Persecution broke out as soon as the Mountain triumphed in the Convention. Rabaut-Saint-Etienne was guillotined on 5 December 1793. Protestant worship ceased between 1793 and 4 June 1794, for the pastors, forgetful of their sacred character, either fled or else went into politics. The neglect of dogma revealed the weakening of faith, and the weakening of faith led to persecution.

Notes

1. Elie Benoist, *Histoire de l'Edit de Nantes, 1693–95.* vol. 1, p. 61.
2. Articles 6–16 of the Edict; secret articles of 2 May, nos. 1–23.
3. Articles 30–57 of the Edict.
4. Bibliothèque Nationale, MS Dupuy 323.
5. Pierre Blet, "Le plan de Richelieu pour la réunion des protestants," *Gregorianum* 48 (1967): 100–129.
6. P. Bolle, "Structure sociale d'une paroisse réformée en Dauphiné au XVIIᵉ siècle:

Mens-en-Trièves," *85ᵉ Congrès national des Sociétés Savantes, 1960, Section d'Histoire moderne et contemporaine*, pp. 419–32.

7. Samuel Mours, "Les pasteurs à la Révocation de l'Edit de Nantes," *Bulletin de la Société de l'Histoire du protestantisme français* 114 (1968): 67–105.

Guide to further reading

Documents

The Edict of Nantes, the secret articles, and the warrants are printed in Roland Mousnier, *The Assassination of Henri IV* (London: Faber, 1973).

The principal documents concerning the Protestants are given in E. and E. Haag, *La France protestante*, vol. 10 (1858).

Benoist, Elie. *Histoire de l'Edit de Nantes, 1693–1695.* 5 vols.

Isambert, Jourdan, and De Cruisy. *Recueil des anciennes lois françaises.*

Mousnier, Roland, ed. *Lettres et mémoires adressés au chancelier Séguier (1633–1649).* 2 vols. P.U.F. 1964.

Pilatte, Léon. *Edits, déclarations et arrêts concernant la R.P.R., 1662–1751.* 1885.

Secondary works

See the *Bulletin de la Société de l'Histoire du Protestantisme français*, passim.

Allier, Raoul. *La cabale des dévots.* 1901.

Anquez, Léonce. *Histoire des assemblées politique des réformés de France, 1573–1622.* 1859.

Bels, Pierre. *Le mariage des protestants français jusqu'en 1685.* Librairie générale de Droit et de Jurisprudence, 1968.

Benoist, Charles. *La condition juridique des protestants sous le régime de l'Edit de Nantes.* Law thesis, Nancy, 1900.

Dedieu, Abbé Joseph. *Histoire politique des protestants français, 1715–1794.* 2 vols. J. Gabalda, 1925.

Dupuy, Lise. *Les Protestants de Florac de la Révocation de l'Edit de Nantes à l'Edit de Tolerance.* Librairie Protestante, 1968.

Egret, Jean. *La prérévolution française, 1787–1788.* P.U.F., 1962. (Eng. trans. by Wesley D. Camp, *The French Prerevolution, 1787–1788.* Chicago: University of Chicago Press, 1977.)

Jahan, Emmanuel. *La confiscation des biens des religionnaires fugitifs de la Révocation de l'Edit de Nantes à la Révolution.* Librairie générale de Droit et de Jurisprudence, 1959.

Léonard, E.-G. *Problèmes et expériences du protestantisme français: L'urbanisation, l'embourgeoisement, les déviations ecclésiastiques, l'attrait catholique.* 1940.

———. "Le protestantisme français au XVIIᵉ siècle," *Revue historique* (1948), pp. 153–79.

———. *Le protestant français.* 1953.

———. *Histoire générale du protestantisme français.* 3 vols. P.U.F. 1963–64. (Eng. trans., *The History of Protestantism in France.* Vols. 1 and 2. London: Nelson, 1965–67.)

Ligou, Daniel. *Le protestantisme en France de 1598 à 1715.* S.E.D.E.S., 1968.

Miot, Francine. "Les protestants en Aunis et Saintonge depuis la Révocation de l'Edit de Nantes." Pp. 95–100 in *Positions des thèses de l'Ecole des Chartes.* 1964.

Mours, Samuel, "La vie synodale en Vivarais au XVIIe siècle," *Bulletin de la Société de l'Histoire du Protestantisme français* (1946), pp. 55–103.

———. *Les eglises réformées en France.* Librairie Protestante, 1958.

Mousnier, Roland. *La vénalité des offices sous Henri IV et Louis XIII.* Rouen: Maugard, 1945. 2d ed. P.U.F., 1970.

Orcibal, Jean. *Louis XIV et les protestants.* J. Vrin, 1951.

Pannier, Jacques. *L'Eglise réformée de Paris sous Henri IV.* 1919.

———. *L'Eglise réformée de Paris sous Louis XIII de 1610 à 1621.* 1922.

Pouthas, Charles H. *Une famille de bourgeoisie française de Louis XIV à Napoléon.* Librairie Félix Alcan, 1934.

Rebelliau, A. "La Compagnie du Saint-Sacrement et les protestants," *Revue des Deux Mondes,* vol. 17 (1903).

Wemyss, Alice. *Les protestants du Mas-d'Azil, 1680–1830.* Edouard Privat, 1961.

9

The Society of Orders
The Jews

The Jews did not constitute an order in France. They were merely given the status of privileged aliens, as a body or as individuals in the capacity of "new converts"—mainly before 1685. This status was granted them in accordance with the principles of the society of orders and corporations.

In theory there were no Jews in France. The edict of 17 September 1394 had expelled the Jews from France forever. Jews were prohibited from returning to France on pain of death. This edict was renewed on 23 March 1615, when "all Jews, whether disguised or not," were ordered "to quit the realm within a month, on pain of death." Nevertheless, it was in fact possible for Jews to obtain individual permits to stay in France.

There were many reasons for the edicts against the Jews, but three seem to have been of fundamental importance: religious hatred, jealousy, and fear. These feelings were especially widespread among the masses, but they were acutely present even among cultured persons, such as the Oratorian Richard Simon, the Protestants Jacques Basnage, Pierre Bayle, and Jacques Bernard, the Catholic historian Charron (in his *Histoire universelle des Gaulois ou Français*, 1621), and some thirty other historians, from Nicole Gilles in 1492 to Gabriel Daniel, in his *Histoire de France depuis l'établissement*, in 1713.

Religious hatred was vigorous. The representatives of the Jewish people in Jerusalem had not recognized Jesus as the Son of God, God Himself, equal and consubstantial with the Father. They had obliged Pontius Pilate to condemn to death and crucify the Messiah; this was the worst sacrilege, the worst of sins against the Holy Ghost. To Pontius Pilate, when he said to them, "I am innocent of the blood of this just person," they had replied, "His blood be on us and on our children." From this event had been born a relentless hatred by the Christians against the Jews, which, though illogical—since God is love and forgiveness, and the Christian should be perfect, like his heavenly Father—was deep-seated. Most people believed in the legend of the Wandering Jew. In every generation there were Christians who claimed to have encountered this Jew, who had taken part in the sentencing of Jesus Christ and was doomed to wander among the nations until the Day of Judgment.

There was much jealousy of the quick intelligence, sometimes subtle and hair-splitting, frequently found among the Jews. They were charged with having an answer to everything and being able to find good reasons for anything at all. This aptitude of theirs, in conjunction with hard work, frugality, mutual aid between Jews, and skill in business, made them redoubtable competitors who, rich in proportion to their success, became objects of hatred. They were notorious for their usury, which their religious law permitted them to practice in dealings with outsiders and which was often the principal activity permitted to them by the positive law of the country in which they resided.

Finally, they inspired fear. They hated the Christians. The latter believed that, God's curse being upon the Jews, they were helped by the Devil. The Jews were proud, for, regarding theirs as "God's chosen people," they shut themselves off from the rest of the world, immured themselves behind their determination to acknowledge only their own Law. They indulged in voluntary self-segregation. They looked forward to the coming of their Messiah, a conqueror who would give them mastery of the world. They were tormented by a terrible, insatiable thirst for domination; a proud and arrogant people, they would prove unbearable, thought many Christians, if they were ever to become the rulers.

For the moment, they were obliged to dissimulate. Cheating the Christians had become a mania with them. Their hatred was inveterate, their malice ineradicable. Conversion to Catholicism altered nothing, it was thought: Jews remained Jews, an unassimilable race.

Among the people, accusations of ritual murder of Christian children were always current. Even in 1671 the *parlement* of Metz found the Jew Raphaël Lévy guilty of ritual murder and had him executed. It charged the Jewish community of Metz with complicity in the crime, but they appealed to the king's Council, which acquitted them.

Nevertheless, the proscription of the Jews was not complete. A certain degree of toleration, sometimes *de jure,* sometimes *de facto,* was observed. Some Jews became outwardly converted to Christianity while privately maintaining the practices of their own religion. These were the "new Christians" or *"marranes"* (from the Spanish word *marrano*). They were entitled to a privileged status. Others, who had not been converted, might benefit from this, too. Sometimes the authorities quite simply closed their eyes.

The reasons for this toleration were chiefly economic. Toleration increased in proportion as, in the values of this society, what was considered good, fine, and desirable came to be identified more and more with the wealth obtainable from the production of material goods. This tendency was accentuated in Colbert's time. Louis XIV wrote to M. de Baas, governor and lieutenant general of the French West Indies, on 23 May 1671 that he must allow the Jews of Martinique "complete freedom of conscience" and the same privileges as those enjoyed by Christians, because of the expenditure they had incurred in cultivating the land and the advantage the public would receive from this.[1] Colbert wrote to M. de Rouillé, intendant at Aix, on 8 September 1673: "And furthermore, because settlement by the Jews has never been forbidden for reasons of commerce, since, as a rule, commerce increases everywhere that they appear, but rather for reasons of religion, and as at present we are concerned only with commerce, you should pay no attention to the proposals directed against the Jews that will be made to you."[2] Again, addressing M. Morant, also intendant at Aix, on 20 November 1681: "I request you to inform yourself very carefully of the number of Jews in Marseilles . . . As the king does not allow them to be in the kingdom except in those places where they have formal permission to stay, as in Metz, His Majesty is always justified in expelling them whenever he chooses to do so; for this reason you will examine . . . whether the presence of these persons in Marseilles is useful or not." So far as religious considerations were concerned, not a single Jew should have been tolerated in the kingdom, but the interests of commerce imposed a degree of toleration, and it was this that Colbert explained very clearly to M. de Ris, intendant in Bordeaux, on 13

January 1683. A Jew and a Jewess had committed an act of sacrilege. The king could not allow this kind of desecration to occur, and he would have liked to undertake "a general expulsion of all the Jews." But "almost all commerce is in the hands of these people," and so such a measure would be dangerous for the kingdom. Colbert therefore set forth an entire strategy. No new Jewish families should be allowed to settle in France; cases of sacrilege should be used as occasions to expel eight or ten families, from time to time; in this way, within eight or ten years, the Jews would be "gradually expelled from the kingdom; and as this expulsion would be effected gradually, the commerce they carry on would pass into the hands of French merchants, the king's subjects... and we should avoid the disadvantage of seeing taken out of the realm the possessions which these people acquire very rapidly and which they never use as means of naturalizing themselves here."[3]

However, Colbert's cunning strategy remained inapplicable, and the same reason—the Jews' commercial utility—continued to promote toleration in despite of religion. In 1697 the intendant of Alsace, Turgot, explained that the Jews of Metz were indispensable. They smuggled in, from Germany, horses that were needed for the cavalry. They furnished supplies for the army. They sold goods more cheaply than the Christians. They delivered their goods more quickly. It was in the interests of the state to retain them as a *"singularité,"* an element *sui generis,* neither subjects nor aliens.

In 1741 the comptroller general of finance sent out a circular asking the intendants to provide information on the trade carried on by Jews. The intendants were unanimous in replying that the Jews should not be banned from the fairs and markets, for they kept prices low, whereas the corporations tried to raise them to artificially high levels; moreover, they brought about an expansion of trade. This was the opinion of Marshal De Coigny, governor of Alsace, in 1756. In the same year the economist Ange Goudar even recommended introducing Jews into the sector of the *production* of material wealth.

Concern for economic utility thus led the government to tolerate a certain number of Jews, granting them extremely varied types of status.

At the time of the edict of 1394 there were quite a large number of Jews in France, and many of these stayed on, with the authorities pretending to regard them either as "new Christians" or else as vagrants, nomads, *"gens sans aveu."* Many of them even received from the king, on an individual basis, the privilege of remaining in France. In

Paris they went on living in the same districts as during the Middle Ages: on the Left Bank, near the Petit Pont, the rue de la Harpe, the Pont Saint-Michel, the rue Galande; on the Right Bank, in the rue de la Tâcherie, the rue Saint-Bon, and the rue Planche-Mibraye, at the issue of the Pont-au-Change; between the Halles and the Place des Vosges, the rues de la Friperie, de la Toilerie, de la Chausseterie, de la Froma-gerie, Jean de Beauce, des Billettes, des Lombards, and Quincampoix. They were dealers in secondhand clothes and other goods, and moneylenders.

Around 1675 there were also to be found in Paris some Portuguese Jews, who were physicians or students, and Jews from Metz or Alsace, who were peddlers, dealers in secondhand goods, with a few army-suppliers or brokers and some engravers, jewelers, and draughtsmen. They practiced their religion freely. Some, though, in this Parisian setting, became lax in their observances. Richard Simon met between 1670 and 1675 a Jew from Pinerolo, Jona Salvador, with whom he read the Bible, in the library of the Oratory, and also the Talmud. Salvador, who had adapted himself thoroughly to Paris life, avoided submitting to the rigors of the Jewish Law. He carried heavy books about on Satur-day, and he entered the synagogue bareheaded. Generalizing from this man, Richard Simon concluded that, for the Jews, their religion was only outward show and all that moved them was love of money. In fact, however, Jona Salvador was actively engaged in tracking down brother Jews who had gone astray and become *marranes* and in bringing them back to Judaism.

In Guyenne, which was not reconquered from the English until 1453, the edict of 1394 did not apply, and the Jews went on living there, in humble occupations.

Jews continually arrived to settle in France. Some, Ashkenazim, came from the countries of Central Europe to live in Lorraine and Alsace; these were lower-class people of no great education. Others, a more numerous contingent, came from Spain and Portugal. On 31 March 1492 Ferdinand of Aragon and Isabella the Catholic expelled the Jews from their realms. Between 150,000 and 175,000 Jews left Spain; about 50,000 went to Italy, North Africa, and the East, about 100,000 to Portugal, and about 12,000 to Navarre. On 5 December 1496 King Manoel expelled the Jews from Portugal, and those in Navarre were expelled in 1498. The Spanish Inquisition hunted down "new Chris-tians" who still secretly practiced Judaism, and after Philip II's con-quest of Portugal in 1580 it extended its activities to the Portuguese

Jews. There resulted, after the great wave of departures at the end of the 15th century, a clandestine emigration, which went on through the 16th and 17th centuries, to Holland, Africa, and the East.

In France, Jews from Spain and Portugal had already settled in Bordeaux when Louis XI in 1474 granted privileges to all foreigners who should come to that port. When the great efflux from the Iberian Peninsula began, some of the Spanish and Portuguese Jews involved made their way to France. The authorities pretended to regard them as Christians and allowed them to enter. They arrived by sea at Bayonne, Bordeaux, Saint-Jean-de-Luz, Biarritz, Le Vieux-Boucau, La Rochelle, Nantes, and Rouen. Troops of families crossed through the passes of the Pyrenees in litters and carriages. They were still arriving by secret routes, in 1672, at Bidache, Dax, Tartas, Peyrehorade, Labastide-Clairence, Toulouse, Montpellier, and Lyons. These Sephardim were often well-to-do people, educated and even cultured. Many of them stayed in France for only a few years before moving on to Holland, Italy, or Turkey, but others remained and formed communities.

They were treated as Christian aliens and could obtain letters of naturalization. The ordinance of Ys-sur-Tille, October 1535, had provided that foreigners could, on request, be given letters conferring naturalization and privileges. These letters were granted by the king and registered by the *parlements* and the *chambres des comptes*. They were valid only for the reign of the sovereign who had granted them but could be confirmed by his successor. Grant and confirmation were subject to the payment of a sum of money as alms, the product of which was administered by the *grand aumônier* (the king's principal chaplain) and devoted to charitable works. The applicant had to give proof of a lengthy residence in France and to undertake to spend the rest of his life there.

Henri II, by letters patent of August 1550, gave to the "Portuguese merchants," the "new Christians," the right to reside "wherever they chose," with their families, their servants, and their goods, the right to trade freely, to acquire ownership of their houses, to make wills and to make or receive gifts free of charge, and to take their possessions with them in the event of their being expelled. The king dispensed them from the necessity of obtaining individual letters of naturalization. These letters patent were registered by the Paris *parlement* and *chambre des comptes* on 22 December 1550. Henri III renewed them at Lyons on 11 November 1574, and they were registered by the *parle-*

ment of Bordeaux on 19 April 1580. In addition, the king gave a letter of protection to the Spaniards and Portuguese residing in Bordeaux. He ordered that they be not disquieted or slandered and allowed them to remain in Bordeaux "without any inquiry into their way of living"— which meant, in practice, allowing them to practice Judaism behind an outward show of Christianity. Use of the actual word "Jews" was always carefully avoided.

The status thus given did not constitute the Jews of France as communities, but they formed communities spontaneously wherever they resided. In Bordeaux there were about a hundred Jewish families. They observed the outward practices of Catholicism, had their children baptized, attended church services, communicated, and had their marriages and deaths recorded by the *curés* in the church registers. They succeeded in integrating themselves into Christian society. The mother of Montaigne, counselor in the *parlement* of Bordeaux and *seigneur* in Périgord, with claims to be a *gentilhomme,* was a Jewess, the daughter of Pierre de Louppes, or Lopès, a Portuguese Jew who had emigrated to Toulouse; and Montaigne's grandfather, Eyquem, a merchant, may have been himself a *"marrane."* Most of the Jews did, in fact, practice the Jewish religion. They were engaged in trade in silks and jewelry and in maritime enterprises, in the trade in goods from the colonies, for which they were subjected to special taxes. In the days of the League they were accused of having surrendered the city to the enemy. By an *arrêt* of 1597 the *parlement* of Bordeaux sent back to Bayonne those of them who had not lived in the city for at least ten years.

At Bayonne, about 1655, there were 300 Portuguese families practicing the Jewish religion; they lived in the suburb of Saint-Esprit-lès-Bayonne, on the right bank of the Adour, being concentrated in certain streets and in the adjoining hamlets. They did not possess the right to acquire houses in Bayonne itself or to settle or even to spend a night there. Nevertheless, they contrived to rent houses and yards and to sell their goods openly, in violation of the municipal regulations. After 1610 the duc de Grammont, governor of Bayonne, Navarre, and Béarn, was given the responsibility of keeping these Portuguese under His Majesty's protection. The Saint-Esprit community was recognized officially by Louis XIV's letters patent of December 1656, "considering also the great profit that many of them bring to our customs of Bayonne, the income from which they increase by reason of the trade which they carry on there." They thus received the status of a body of foreign merchants.

At Bidache, where the duc de Grammont reigned as sovereign like Louis XIV in his kingdom, the Jews had the right to reside and practice their religion and to become *"bourgeois"* of the town.

The numbers of the Jews gave great concern to the government. Though they guaranteed the rights of the old-established families, they periodically expelled some of the newcomers. This was the purpose of the letters patent of 7 January 1602 for the Spaniards and Portuguese of Bayonne. An *arrêt* of the Council dated 20 November 1684 decreed the expulsion of ninety-six Portuguese families from Bordeaux, Bayonne, Bidache, Dax, and Peyrehorade because they were poor and their maintenance was an expense to the towns named. However, this *arrêt* was never carried out.

There were Jews in Metz before the king was concerned with their affairs. An ordinance by the mayor, 2 July 1562, obliged the Jew Mordecai, his servant, and another Jew named Isaac to leave the city, and this fate was imposed in 1563 on all the Jews living in Metz.

On 6 August 1567 marshal De La Vieuville, governor of Metz, gave permission by ordinance for four Jewish families, those of Mordecai, Isaac, Michael, and Gershom, to remain in the city and carry on business there, especially as pawnbrokers, on conditions which the Jews had offered, namely, to pay 200 *écus* down, and, thereafter, 200 Metz francs every year toward the relief of the poor. Henri III allowed eight families. But these Jews increased and multiplied. From the legal standpoint, the right to reside had been given only to the old-established families, not to the new ones. From time to time the privilege had to be extended from the old families to the new. The duc d'Epernon, as governor, confirmed, by ordinance of 2 January 1603, these eight families and their descendants—twenty-four families in all, and a total of 120 persons—in their right of residence. Henri IV confirmed this decision by letters patent of 20 March 1603—"that they shall continue to reside and be able to carry on trade in accordance with their former franchises, liberties, and customs, lending money with or without security."

As their numbers increased, Louis XIII had to confirm their privileges, on 24 January 1632. However, it was becoming difficult to find employment for them. An *arrêt* of the *parlement* of Metz dated 23 May 1634 allowed them to engage in trade in goldsmiths' and silversmiths' work and also in secondhand goods but forbade them to trade in new goods. Letters patent of 23 September 1657 confirmed the previous ones while extending the Jews' trading rights to new goods.

The corporations of the merchants of Metz opposed the registering of the royal letters. The Jews stated that they wished to trade in new goods only as "merchants from outside" (*marchands forains*), keeping their goods in warehouses, without any display or open shopkeeping. By an *arrêt* of 21 January 1658 the *parlement* of Metz nonsuited the Christian merchants and authorized the Jews to trade in new goods from abroad as *marchands forains*.

The Jews of Metz comprised, by then, ninety-six families, all descended from the families originally allowed to be there, and which were the only ones allowed to reside. They formed a community, with a rabbi, chosen with the king's permission, and enjoyed free exercise of their religion and ownership of the houses in which they lived, though they were forbidden to acquire any other real property. They were confined to a special part of the city, on the right bank of the Moselle.

In Alsace, the king of France, having taken the place of the House of Austria in some of the Alsatian territories as a consequence of the Treaty of Münster (part of the Peace of Westphalia) in 1648, allowed the existing situation to continue. In Upper Alsace the *gentilshommes* had usurped the sovereign right to allow Jews in as they chose, and they exercised this right in return for an annual payment. In the ten former Imperial cities of the prefecture of Haguenau, the magistrates exercised regalian rights in immediate dependence on the Empire. They continued to do so after Münster, but now in dependence on the king. They introduced Jewish families as they pleased and allowed them to reside. In Lower Alsace, in the county of Hanau, the *gentilshommes*, whose lands were formerly in immediate dependence on the Empire, had the right to allow Jews to come in, to send them away, to grant them liberties, or to impose conditions upon them at their pleasure. They levied an annual tax of 12 *écus* on each Jewish family.

Between the end of the 17th century and the end of the 18th the Jews advanced slowly and with many fits and starts from a situation of toleration for a few privileged ones to a situation of citizenship for all. The process began with the official recognition of their existence in the kingdom no longer as "new Christians" but as Jews. The starting point of this evolution can be identified as the Council's *arrêt* of 28 June 1686, which repeated that of 11 January of the same year. It gave foreigners freedom to enter the kingdom and carry on trade there. It relieved foreigners of the need to obtain passports in order to leave the kingdom. It required only mere registration, from all foreigners, of whatever quality, condition, or religion they might be. That was the moment when the Jews of Bordeaux stopped outwardly practicing Christianity and came out openly as Jews. The official recognition of the Jews' right to reside in France as alien merchants did not proceed without some ups and downs. An *arrêt* of the *parlement* dated 22 August 1729 forbade Jews to settle in La Rochelle. An ordinance by the intendant of Languedoc in 1732 forbade the Jews to reside or trade in that province. An *arrêt* of the *parlement* of Grenoble in 1754 ordered Jews to leave the area subject to that court's jurisdiction. However, these spasmodic reactions were inspired by the demands of merchants who wanted restrictions placed on competition by the Jews. This was also the purpose of the Council's *arrêt* of 20 February 1731, which forbade the Jews to carry on trade elsewhere than in the places where they lived—but which thereby gave recognition to their official existence as Jews and implicitly accorded them the right to carry on trade in the places where they lived. In general, there was a growing tendency openly to acknowledge the existence of the Jews and their privilege of residence and commerce.

In 1760 there were in Bordeaux a hundred families of "Portuguese" Jews. Six families of Jews who had come from Avignon, in the Comtat Venaissin, were officially tolerated. Actually, there were twenty-one families of these Avignon Jews in Bordeaux. The "Portuguese" continually called for their expulsion. This was secured by an *arrêt* of the Council in 1722, but the Avignon Jews stayed on. The six families obtained in 1729 a royal charter for the "Jews or New Christians from Avignon residing in Bordeaux," which granted them the same rights as the "Portuguese," and these privileges were extended to all the Jews from Avignon in 1762.

In 1689 the Jews of Bordeaux organized themselves as a Jewish "nation." Thenceforth they refrained from presenting their children for baptism and having their marriages blessed by the *curé*. They formed a *"Sedaca"* in order to assess and collect taxes on themselves and relieve their poor.

In June 1723, by letters patent issued at Meudon, Louis XV, responding to a petition from "the Jews of the said *généralités* of Bordeaux and Auch," acknowledged their right to reside and to live in accordance with their own customs, to possess all kinds of property, to trade, and to make wills. They were not required to take out letters of naturalization. They could not be "investigated in any way on account of their way of life." They had merely to be registered by the local courts. The Jews of the Southwest were thus recognized as Jews and as citizens. These letters were complemented by the ordinance of 15 July 1728 concerning "the Jewish nation of Bordeaux." It provided for the protection of their religion, for it forbade the reception by monasteries, under pretext of religion, of "children of Jews" under the age of twelve. The syndics of the Jewish "nation" of Bayonne had this ordinance registered by the judges of Bayonne on 4 August 1751.

Letters patent of June 1776, registered by the Bordeaux *parlement* on 8 March 1777, declared the "Portuguese merchants" to be "good, useful, and loyal subjects" and confirmed them in all their privileges—this confirmation to apply both to those "who are already settled and domiciled in our kingdom . . . and to those who shall wish to come here in the future . . . We permit them to remain here and to live in accordance with their customs . . . We wish that they be treated and looked upon in the same way as our other subjects, born in our kingdom." Thus, the Sephardim, old-established families and newcomers alike, were, in their capacity as Jews practicing Judaism, to be considered as subjects of the king of France and treated by the law like all his other subjects.

Many of these Jews had integrated themselves in Bordeaux society, as can be seen from the example of the Gradis family. Diego Rodrigues Gradis, expelled from Toulouse in 1685, settled in Bordeaux. His son David prospered in the trade in wine, brandy, and linen. In 1731 he became a *bourgeois* of Bordeaux, a title that three Jews had gained since 1679. He died in 1751, aged eighty-six, leaving a fortune of 400,000 livres. His son Abraham, who was associated with him in his business from 1728 onward, fitted out ships for the king during the wars. He lost thirteen vessels in 1758, the year of the fall of Louisbourg, but when he died in 1780 he left 10 million livres. He enjoyed relations with the baron de Rochechouart; with M. de la Porte, head of the colonial service in 1738; with M. de Rostau, commissioner general for the navy; with marshal De Richelieu, the duc de Lorges, and marshal De Conflans; and with Maurepas and Choiseul. He lent money to all these great personages, and he did not forget that presents serve to maintain friendship. When he was ill, "the *jurats* ordered that the bell not be rung nor the cannon fired from the Tour Saint-Jean, lest the noise disturb him, for his residence was near to the Town Hall." This personage, held in respect by the municipality of Bordeaux, was a practicing Jew, who observed the Jewish Sabbath and protected his coreligionists.

The agent of the "Portuguese" Jews of Bordeaux in Paris, Jacob

Rodriguez Péreire, a member of the Royal Society of London, *secrétaire du roi*, in receipt of a pension from the king as his interpreter for the Spanish and Portuguese languages, was the man who obtained the letters patent of June 1776. These had, moreover, been prepared by Israel Bernard de Valabrègue, the Jew who was the Hebrew expert in the king's library, and by his pamphlet of 1767: *Lettres ou réflexions d'un milord à son correspondant à Paris au sujet de la requête des marchands des Six-Corps contre l'admission des Juifs aux brevets.*

The Jews of the *généralités* of Bordeaux and Auch, who were covered by the letters of June 1723 (and, as regards some of them, by those of June 1776), numbered in the whole Southwest, apart from Bordeaux, between two and three thousand. Those of Bayonne had on 22 January 1698 been given the armorial bearings granted to "the community of the Jewish or Portuguese nation of the Pont-Saint-Esprit of Bayonne." From 25 May 1700 they formed a nation represented by its own syndics. The royal taxes they had to pay were decided by the intendant, and the figure was conveyed to the syndics. The burden was then divided among the Jews by thirteen spokesmen of the community—the three syndics, six notables, and four assistants—who met together as an "assembly of notables." The treasurer of the Jewish "nation" advanced the money to the king, the tax being collected by the *"mande"* or beadle of the synagogue. In addition to the royal taxes, the Jews had to raise the "national contribution" for relief of their poor and gratuities to the "protectors of the nation"—1,000 livres to the duc de Grammont and 1,050 livres to the marquis d'Amon.

Circumcisions, marriages, and deaths were recorded in statements authenticated by a notary and burials by declarations to the superintendent of police, while permissions for burial were granted by the office of the lieutenant of police. The Jews had their own registry office, and legal documents presented by the "Jewish nation" were accepted as evidence by the French courts after 1741. Marriages celebrated in the synagogue were blessed by the rabbi. The Jews ceased maintaining their separate registers of civil status on 2 January 1792. They omitted to register themselves before the royal judge.

The Jewish nation had their own slaughterers, their own cemetery, their own language, festivals, and names—Portuguese or Spanish. In the 18th century they resumed the use of biblical names, and Hebrew reappeared in their liturgy. In everyday life they used a dialect, Ladino, but they used French in social relations. They professed Judaism openly. In 1750 they ceased to be obliged to make a payment to the *curé*, and in 1752 and 1754 their payments to the chapter came to an end. Jewish life was regulated by the *parnasim*, or syndics of the Jewish community. There were three or four *parnasim* elected from among Jews who had resided in the Faubourg Saint-Esprit for six years, had not gone bankrupt, were entered on the poll-tax roll for a payment of at least 15 livres, and were in a position to contribute 200 livres a year to the nation's budget.

The rabbi presided over the rabbinical court. He taught the Talmud Torah and the Law. There were clandestine synagogues from 1600 onward, and from 1684 these existed semiofficially. Observance of the rules regarding food, the ritual bath, circumcision, and the giving of alms was rigorously enforced.

The Jews were still forbidden to practice crafts or engage in retail trade, and they were obliged to complete their purchases in the market by midday.

By the *arrêt* of the king's Council dated 9 July 1718, 480 Jewish families and their descendants were authorized to reside in Metz. Their births had to be registered with the *greffe* of the *bailliage*. They had to pay special taxes and refrain from working on Sundays or Christian holidays. Their pawnbroking activities were subject to regulation. They were allowed to maintain their own slaughterhouses and to elect syndics of their community. The royal declaration of 26 August 1710 obliged them to keep their accounts of banking and commercial activity in French, not Hebrew.

In 1766 they numbered 3,000. The houses in the quarter where they lived had to have five or six stories to accommodate them. They were recognizable by their beards, their black mantles, and the little black band they wore at the neck. They held an assembly every three years to elect their syndics. They had a rabbi and a rabbinical court. They observed various customs and usages, confirmation of which they requested from the *parlement* of Metz after 1743.

From 1769 onward the number of Jews in Metz declined because they were now allowed to settle anywhere in Lorraine. In 1789 they numbered 2,000 out of the 30,000 inhabitants.

A declaration by Duke Leopold of Lorraine, on 20 October 1721, allowed 180 Jewish families to "continue to reside" in that prince's territories, to practice their religion there, to maintain a synagogue, and to engage in commerce. By an *arrêt* of the Council of King Stanislas, 26 January 1753, though the number of families remained fixed at 180, what was meant by "family" was defined, more broadly, as the head together with all the descendants of the male persons living in the same house with him. The Jews of Lorraine formed a single community, with three syndics, appointed by the king and with their headquarters at Nancy. New families could take the places of those that died out. Other Jews were required to leave. An *arrêt* of Louis XV's Council in March 1767 established four licenses for mastership in each craft guild, these licenses to be available to foreigners. Jews obtained grant of these licenses at Sarreguemines, Phalsbourg, Sarrelouis, and Thionville. The Christian merchants appealed to the *parlement* of Metz against the grants, on the pretext that the Jews were not citizens. The case was argued before the *parlement* by Pierre-Louis Lacretelle. He claimed that the Jews were recognized as citizens by the law, since, unlike foreigners, they could inherit from each other and were not subject to escheat. Consequently, they were entitled to the licenses; and, if they were not citizens, they could obtain the licenses by virtue of privilege. Lacretelle's plea made a great impression.

In Alsace a letter from the chancellor, 13 June 1713, had confirmed the "rights and concessions" granted to the Jews. Two rabbis, one for Upper and the other for Lower Alsace, functioned as judges of first instance and as notaries. They heard without appeal all cases concerning spiritual matters and religious ceremonies. The Conseil souverain of Alsace decided on 19 January 1717 that the Jews were not to be allowed to employ Christian servants or to keep drink shops, and on 19 February 1735 it ruled that they must use French or German, not Hebrew, in their receipts, records of loans, etc. In 1780 there were in Alsace about 3,600 Jewish families, numbering 18,330 persons, living in 187 of the 1,000 localities of the province. It was difficult for them to find work. They often fell into poverty and resorted to usury, the receiving of stolen goods, and fraud. Letters patent of 10 July 1784 permitted them to take leases of farms, land, and vineyards, to bring land under cultivation, to exploit mines, to tender for public or private works, and to set up factories. However, they were not to be allowed to acquire ownership of real property, apart from the buildings needed for their personal use. These letters authorized joint action by Jews living in one and the same place if they had common interests. Matters concerning the Jews of Alsace in general could be taken up by the elected "syndics of the Jews." The latter allotted responsibility for payment of taxes and collected them. The Jews were allowed to raise taxes for their own purposes. They were to report their births, marriages, and deaths to the royal judge of the locality. These letters patent thus conferred upon them the status of an order.

In Paris, five Avignon Jews obtained licenses to practice crafts, under the provision of the *arrêt* of the Council of March 1767 mentioned earlier. The "Six Guilds" of Paris, the most highly respected of the merchants, brought an action against them and took the opportunity to call for the expulsion of all Jews from Paris. Nevertheless, the five Avignon Jews held on to their licenses for seven years. In 1774 the case was decided against them; but in 1777 an *arrêt* of the Council granted them the right to carry on trade in Paris.

Thus, in desultory, spasmodic, and sporadic fashion, the Jews had secured the right to legal existence as Jews and then, in that capacity, the status of corporations or orders. In general, the tendency was to treat them more and more like the other inhabitants of the kingdom. On 28 June 1790 the Constituent National Assembly decreed that all those persons known in France as Portuguese, Spanish, or Avignon Jews were to enjoy thenceforth the rights of citizenship. This affected mainly the three or four thousand Sephardic Jews of Bordeaux and Bayonne. On 27 September 1791 the Constituent Assembly declared all the other Jews of France French citizens. These were mainly the Ashkenazic Jews of Alsace, Metz, and Lorraine. Though the law made them all equally French citizens, it was not easy to merge the two groups; at the beginning of the 19th century a marriage between a Sephardi and an Ashkenazi was still regarded as scandalous in Franco-Jewish circles.

Notes

1. P. Clément, *Lettres ... de Colbert,* vol. 3, pt. 2, pp. 522–23.
2. Ibid., vol. 2, pt. 2, p. 679.
3. Ibid., vol. 6, pp. 188–89.

Guide to further reading

Anchel, Robert. *Les Juifs de France.* 1946.

Cirot, Georges. *Les Juifs de Bordeaux, 1550–1789.* Bordeaux, 1920.

Detcheverry, Armand. *Histoire des Israélites de Bordeaux.* Bordeaux, 1850.

Expilly, Abbé. *Dictionnaire géographique, historique et politique des Gaules et de la France, 1762–1766.* 6 vols.

Gaillard, Henri. *La condition des Juifs dans l'ancienne France.* Law thesis, Paris, 1942.

Guyot. *Répertoire de droit et de jurisprudence.* 1784.

Herzberg, Arthur. *The French Enlightenment and the Jews.* New York: Columbia University Press, 1968.

Léon, Henry. *Histoire des Juifs de Bayonne.* 1893.

Malvezin, Théophile. *Histoire des Juifs de Bordeaux*. Bordeaux, 1875.

Nahon, Gérard. *Les communautés judéo-portugaises du sud-ouest de la France (Bayonne et sa région), 1684–1791*. Thesis for the Doctorat de spécialité (3ᵉcycle), Paris, 1969.

Piganiol de la Force, J. A. *Description de la France*. 2 vols.

———. *Description historique de la Ville de Paris et de ses environs*. 10 vols. New ed., 1765.

Privilèges dont les Juifs portugais jouissent en France depuis 1550. 1777. (B.N.: F 26239)

Recueil de lettres patentes et autres pièces en faveur des Juifs portugais contenant leurs privilèges en France. 1765. (B.N.: Fp–1103)

Szajkowski, Zosa. *Franco-Judaica: An Analytical Bibliography of Books, Pamphlets, Decrees, Briefs, and Other Printed Documents Pertaining to the Jews of France, 1500–1788*. New York: American Academy for Jewish Research, 1962.

Yardeni, Myriam. "The Jews in French Historiography of the 16th and 17th Centuries," *Zion: Quarterly for Research in Jewish History*, vol. 34 (1969).

———. "Judaism and Jews as Seen by French Protestant Exiles in Holland (1685–1715)." In *Studies in the History of the Jewish People and the Land of Israel in Memory of Zvi Avneri*, ed. A. Gilboa. Haifa, 1970. (In Hebrew, with English résumés.)

———. "La vision des Juifs et du judaisme dans l'oeuvre de Richard Simon," *Revue des Etudes juives (Historia Judaica)* 129 (1970): 179–203.

10

The Society of Corporations

The kingdom of France and the lands and lordships under the suzerainty of the king of France
were societies of corporations, colleges, companies, and communities—terms that were all
equivalent to each other.

> The origin of corporations has been sought,
> whereas in fact they are part of nature. From
> the greatest corporations, namely, empires,
> to the least, namely, families, we see that
> men, who have always come together for
> self-protection, always under the command of
> superiors, . . . respond to general tranquillity
> with inner tranquillity. It is a chain, all the
> links of which are joined to the first chain of
> all, to the authority of the throne, which it is
> dangerous to break.[1]

Corporations were groups of persons joined
together for their common benefit and at the
same time pursuing purposes of public interest;
examples are universities, academies, craft communities, commercial and financial companies,
and bodies of officers of justice, administration, or revenue. Corporations were persons,
with a name, a seal, armorial bearings, a rank
in society, privileges, obligation to advise
the king and to render to him collective contributions, remonstrances, representations, and aid
of various kinds in the form of the fulfillment of

royal prerogatives by delegation: supervision of weights and measures, watch and ward, fire prevention, apportionment and collection of taxes, and in some cases military service. Corporations were represented in the general assemblies of the inhabitants of towns, participated in the election of municipalities, and drew up *cahiers* of grievances for the meetings of the Estates General.

Corporations were political bodies. They were self-recruiting, approving the admission of new members, whom they received with a ceremony of affiliation that often included an oath. They had their own general assemblies. They elected leaders or officers or else, if they were hierarchical in structure, acknowledged their first-ranking member as leader. A corporation's leaders were assisted by a council, one of whose members acted as *procureur,* or defender of the common interest. A corporation obeyed rules voted by its general assembly, rules which were legally enforceable upon all the members. These rules were supplemented by customs. Corporations exercised disciplinary jurisdiction over their members through their officers.

As moral persons, corporations could make contracts, possess property, and plead in court. They had funds, a "common purse," supplied by admission fees, fines, and taxes on their members, which served to meet current expenses, finance defense of the corporation's interests, and provide alms.

Corporations petitioned the king for letters patent or an *arrêt* by the Council. They intervened in court actions initiated by one of their members or by another corporation. They entered opposition to letters patent, especially when these were about to be registered, and also to judicial decisions to which they had not been party. Such opposition induced the king and his Council to reexamine the question.

Corporations were usually organized spontaneously, but, having as their aim not only the common good of their members but also that of the whole society of which they formed a part, they were closely dependent on the king, who was responsible for the common good of all his subjects. No corporation could exist without royal approval, either tacit or expressed in letters patent creating the given corporation. Corporations existed and acted under the king's authority. He approved their statutes by letters patent and took care that these statutes were not contrary to the laws, to the *arrêts* of the sovereign courts, or to administrative regulations. The officers elected by the corporations frequently had to swear an oath before the administrative authority, *grand officier,* or court of justice on which their corporation was dependent. Any member of a corporation could appeal to the civil courts against the corporation's decisions. The arbitration and disciplinary jurisdictions of a corporation could prepare the way for action by the royal courts, which could also be exercised by *prévention*. The king supervised the day-to-day life of the corporation. He could subject it to measures of tutelage—periodical rendering of accounts, requirement of preliminary authorization. He could suspend some of the monopolies corporations enjoyed. He could reorganize them and could even suppress a corporation that might become a threat to public order or the common good.

The corporations of royal officials

The king's officials formed corporations, or companies. A *parlement*, for example, or a presidial court, a *bailliage,* or a *bureau des finances des trésoriers de France et généraux des finances* constituted a company. A company was a community of magistrates exercising jointly the same set of functions in a defined territorial area and having, as a result, the same responsibilities, the same purpose of public good, and the same procedures, spirit, and interests. A company was not simply a synonym for a corporation; the term implied a certain degree of superiority. Companies were hierarchically related. The *parlements,* the Grand Conseil, the *cours des aides,* the *chambres des comptes,* the *trésoriers de France* were "sovereign companies" or, under the personal government of Louis XIV, "superior companies." The other courts were subordinate companies. All these companies were political bodies, distinguished by their predominant participation in public affairs.

Companies exercised power over their own recruitment. A candidate obtained an office either by purchasing it from the king, if it was a "new creation" or an office "vacated by death," or by purchasing it from the previous holder, who "resigned" in his favor, or else by inheritance, with resignation of the previous holder or even without it if the *droit annuel,* or *paulette,* established in 1604, had been paid. It was the king who instituted the official, by his "letters of provision." But the appointee was not yet an official; he had, so far, only a "right to the office." In order to acquire the order and character of an official, he had to be received; and to obtain possession and exercise of the office, he had to be installed. And the king entrusted the reception and installation of new officials to the corporations of officials themselves.

In practice it was frequent for the candidate, before purchasing an office, to ascertain whether he was likely to be received, since otherwise the acquisition would be useless. Once appointed, the undesirable candidate would have had to sell the office without having exercised it.

The appointee requested the corporation to receive him. The corporation transmitted his request to a *procureur du roi*. The latter caused his deputy to carry out an investigation in the locality where the candidate had resided in the preceding five years. The deputy heard testimony from a priest and four witnesses, officials or advocates who were neither related to nor employed by the candidate. He checked on the candidate's religion (to ensure that he was a Catholic), on his morals, on his loyalty to the king's service, on his family connections, on his marriage contract, on his possessions, on how much he had paid for the office, and on his exact age. The point was to put candidates through a political and social sieve which would not allow entry by persons whose fortune, activities, relations, or sentiments were incompatible with the dignity of the office they sought to fill. The *parlements* did not accept sons of "mechanical" persons or even, in most cases, sons of merchants who had become rich.

The *procureur du roi* might decide to reject the candidate's application because he had been convicted for debt or for some disgraceful offense, or because he had kindred in the corps (father, uncle, brother), or because he lacked sufficient years and experience (one needed to be twenty-five to enter a sovereign court and to have been for four years an advocate in that court), or because he was a Protestant, or led a dissolute life, or had excessively base connections, or practiced a trade that was usurious or mechanical.

If the *procureur du roi* decided that there was nothing to prevent reception, the candidate was examined by the corporation. In a sovereign court or a presidial court, he had to address them in Latin; this served as a test of his general culture. Then he had to explain a law which had been indicated to him three hours previously; this was the test of his legal education. Then he had to explain three passages taken from ordinances and customs "by random opening of the books"; this was the practical test.

If his replies were satisfactory, the court received the candidate, on his taking the oath to serve the king well and faithfully and to uphold his ordinances. In the *parlement* the oath ran as follows: "You swear to fulfill this estate well and faithfully, to administer justice to the poor as to the rich, without distinction of persons, to uphold the ordinances, to keep close and secret the deliberations of the court, and everywhere and in everything to behave as a good and notable member of a sovereign court should do." When this ceremony was completed, the court issued its *arrêt* of reception.

Then the day was fixed for the official's installation. In the case of a presidial court, the new official presented himself, wearing his gown, to the *lieutenant général* who headed the court and was assigned his day. Still wearing his gown, he called on his future colleagues. When the installation day arrived, his letters of provision and his *arrêt* of reception were read. The *lieutenant général* made a speech to him about his new duties and about the need for unity among members of the same corporation and then gave him the fraternal kiss. After that, all the officials came forward as a body to take up their positions, and the newcomer occupied his place among them, declaring that he was taking possession of his office. A minute of the installation was recorded, and thenceforth the newcomer was fully an official.

The corporations of officials wielded disciplinary powers over their members. In the *parlements* and presidial courts an assembly was held on the first Wednesday after the vacation each year to "judge" offenses committed by officials, infringements of ordinances regarding *mores* and the "style of the Palace [of Justice]." Their decisions were conveyed to the chancellor. By means of these assemblies, "the ancient discipline of the *parlements* is kept and preserved." The corporations had the duty of repressing "even the slightest offenses." Therefore, "each year, when the courts resume at Martinmas, the ordinances concerning the responsibility and duty of the officials of the Palace and the discipline of the Palace are read afresh."[2] The *premier président* had to rebuke negligent magistrates. There were instances of *présidents* and counselors whom the *parlement* stripped of their offices and who were also fined, banished, declared incapable of holding royal office, or even sent to prison for revealing the secrets of the court, imposing new *censives* on their *censitaires,* abducting and seducing girls, or committing the crime of *lèse-majesté.* The court even preserved the memory of a counselor hanged for suborning witnesses in 1438 and of another who was beheaded for forgery in 1447. I do not know, though, to what extent these "Wednesday assemblies" were held by the various corporations in the 17th and 18th centuries or the extent to which they resulted in effective sanctions.

The demarcation of competences between courts was seen to by the corporations of officials themselves through suits, either in the *parlements* or, preferably, in the king's Council.

The corporations of officials participated directly in public affairs either through the procedure of remonstrance or through that of opposition to the *arrêts* of the Council and the king's letters patent. These procedures have already been described in connection with the assemblies of the clergy of France. The officials owed the king service of counsel. They themselves considered that, in carrying out their functions, they ought to show loyalty to the king and therefore obedience to him; professional integrity and satisfaction of their consciences, which ruled out passive and unconditional obedience, and so refusal to obey orders that went counter to the purpose of their function, that were contrary to the common good; and respect to the dignity of justice, from which ensued "a just relationship of duties" between themselves and others, and so a balance, an equity to be maintained between the king and his subjects, with, if necessary, protection of the king's subjects from the king, "relief of his people," an equity that conformed to a well-understood *raison d'état*.[3]

This conception of their function thus led the officials to form opinions of the edicts, declarations, and *arrêts* put before them by the king, to suspend their obedience, addressing representations or remonstrances to him in order to secure modifications in what he had decided. The corps of officials issued either *arrêts* for the registration of the royal letters—if need be, with amendments—or else *arrêts* and ordinances containing their observations and remonstrances. The king then deliberated anew with his Council and caused the chancellor and some state councilors to confer with the representatives of the corporation, and he then either amended his edicts, declarations, and *arrêts* or else reaffirmed his decisions and sent the corporation of officials concerned a command to execute them.[4]

As corporations, officially and normally, the various companies worked together with the king and his Council on tasks of legislation, government, and administration. They drew attention to drawbacks in royal decisions and in such cases held up the execution of these decisions. If the king insisted, they usually bowed to repetition of his orders; but in cases which they regarded as highly important, they amended the edicts or even simply rejected them, often with success.

Certain officials formed syndicates and associations, distinct from the corporations and companies, to defend their offices against dangers threatening them. We find, for example, a syndicate of *élus* formed in 1641, at a time when the intendants of provinces, by an administrative revolution subsequently sanctioned by the royal declaration of 16 April 1643, were exercising all the principal tasks in relation to taxation in place of the *élus* and the *trésoriers de France,* apportioning and collecting taxes on behalf of the *traitants* and *partisans,* for even the *taille* had been farmed out. The *élus* and *trésoriers de France* were accused of formalism, delay, favoritism, negligence, and betrayal of trust. They answered with charges of incompetence. The salaries of these officials had been subjected to cuts from 1640 onward, until in 1647 they were completely canceled. In exchange for increases in the dues and commissions they could collect, they had been obliged to pay out large sums—in reality, forced loans—and in 1647 they were no longer paid more than a quarter of the increases.

Accordingly, the *élus* sent representatives to several general assemblies in Paris, on 26 October 1641, then in 1642 and in 1645, and three times in 1649. They formed a "syndicate," with rules (*"les articles du syndicat"*), elected syndics, and a secretariat. In 1649 correspondence had to be addressed to M. Boyrot, "syndic and secretary to the Syndicate of the *Elections* of France, residing in the rue de la Tisseranderie, at the Hôtel de la Mogne, near the Church of the Holy Ghost in Paris." The "companies" of *élus* paid a subscription in March each year to cover the expenses of the "syndicate" and ensure that the syndics were "moderately rewarded."

This syndicate was given official recognition. Several *arrêts* of the Council granted its petitions (on 16 April 1644, 7 January 1645, 27 June 1648). The *chambre des comptes* several times heard statements by the syndicate, as such, in connection with verifications of edicts concerning the *élus.* The *cour des aides* gave authority to the syndicate by its *arrêts* of 16 and 30 January 1643 and 4 January 1644, "and finally by the *arrêt* of approval of the said syndicate in the said court on 15 October 1649." The syndics were often received, as such, by the king and queen in the presence of the whole court and at meetings of the Council.

The *trésoriers généraux de France* avoided using the word "syndicate," but their association for the defense of their professional interests bore many resemblances to that of the *élus.* It was older than theirs. In 1596, after the Assembly of Notables at Rouen, the king decided to abolish the *bureaux des finances.* The latter applied for the maintenance of their rights on condition that they granted a loan to the king. But threats continued, and after 1599 the *trésoriers de France* delegated two of their number each year to stay with the court, with emoluments adequate to the purpose supplied by their colleagues, "so that by their administration we might be able to proceed in step, with information shared by all of us, for the conservation and honor of our companies." In 1648 the representatives were called "Messeigneurs les Députés des Bureaux des Finances du Royaume assemblés en la Chambre du Trésor à Paris." At the request of these permanent representatives, nearly every *bureau des finances* had, after the end of May 1648, a delegate in Paris. The "Paris Assembly" had a secretary. In September 1648 this was M. Le Clerc, *trésorier général de France* at Poitiers. This assembly had a "common purse," supplied by the annual subscriptions of the *bureaux* and by special contributions. The assembly kept in touch with the *bureaux des finances* by means of circulars and dispatches. There seems to have been a sort of "bureau" within the assembly, consisting of six members; for when the *trésoriers de France* were punished with imprisonment on account of one of their circulars, six were put away, and when the assembly had gowns made for its deputies to the court, it ordered six.

When the edicts of 1, 13, and 18 July 1648 abolished the intendants, except in the frontier provinces, and reestablished in their offices the ordinary officials—*trésoriers de France, élus, receveurs généraux et particuliers*—the "Paris Assembly," the council of the syndicate, became a sort of unofficial *conseil des finances*. Its members, who were received by the Conseil de la Direction des Finances, presented proposals to the latter. They were in daily communication with the intendants of finance and with the superintendent of finance and acted as intermediaries between them and the *bureaux des finances*. They supervised the government's measures, to see that they conformed to the declarations of 22 October 1648 and March 1649. They passed on to the *trésoriers de France* the orders and wishes of the superintendent and urged the *trésoriers* to work diligently, as this was the condition for their being maintained in their functions. They concentrated the information needed by the king's Council. They secured the transfer of the powers of the intendants of the provinces to the *bureaux des finances*. The latter became, so to speak, collective intendants: they restored the entire former administration of the revenue and obtained good results. However, the association of *trésoriers de France* did not survive the Fronde. The king reentered Paris on 21 October 1652, and Bordeaux surrendered on 3 August 1653. After the last quarter of 1653 the intendants were slowly and cautiously reinstalled, step by step, in the provinces. Later, the syndicate of the *élus* and the association of the *trésoriers de France* were suppressed by an *arrêt* of the Council.

The corporations of auxiliaries of justice

The auxiliaries of justice were either the minor judicial personnel, such as advocates before the king's Council, notaries, *greffiers,* tipstaffs, bailiffs, and sometimes attorneys, or else lawyers who did not possess the quality of officials, such as the advocates and some of the attorneys. Most of them were subordinate to a court of justice. The *secrétaires du roi* were subject to the chancellor, and the advocates before the Council were subject to the Council and the chancellor.

The *conseillers secrétaires du roi, maison et couronne de France et de ses finances*—or, more briefly the *secrétaires du roi*—were entrusted with the drafting and signing of the letters of justice and of pardon that were dispatched from the chancellery. The king was their direct master, but he delegated his power to the chancellor. They received salaries in their personal capacities but were paid mainly by the charging of fees for the letters they sent off. These fees were paid into a "common purse," and the *secrétaires du roi* shared them out from time to time. For the defense of their interests they were authorized in 1351 by King John the Good to form a confraternity, the headquarters of which was in the church of the monastery of the Celestines. In 1365 the king granted statutes to this confraternity. The *secrétaires du roi* had to attend a mass on 6 May every year at the Celestine monastery, to be present at the funerals of colleagues who had died and arrange for masses to be said for them, to help colleagues who had fallen into poverty, or their families, to give alms regularly to the hospitals and, in times of distress, to the poor, to live like brothers, and to contribute "to the common good of the company."

Alongside this confraternity there was a civil corporation, the Collège des Six-Vingts. As the king appointed more and more secretaries, other colleges appeared, such as that of the Vingt de Navarre, when the chancellery of the kingdom of Navarre was united with that of France in 1620. At the beginning of the 17th century there were five distinct colleges, each with its own statutes but with a common basis. The edict of April 1672 brought about the merging of these five colleges into a single corporation of 240 *secrétaires du roi*. The regulation of 24 April 1672 for the chancelleries gave sanction to the traditions of the separate colleges. The edict of October 1727 fixed at 300 the total number of *secrétaires du roi*.

The Collège des Secrétaires du Roi was a moral person. Its 300 members were all equal but were classified according to the order in which their names had been registered. The corporation was directed by a general assembly, which met on 6 May in the Celestine monastery and also whenever a new member had to be admitted. Six elected *procureurs*, one-third of whom were replaced each year, and one of whom functioned as *procureur syndic*, together with a *greffier* and a treasurer, carried out the assembly's decisions. A *"cabinet,"* composed of the dean and subdean, *procureurs* and former *procureurs*, the treasurer and the *greffier*, met every month to give guidance to the *procureurs*.

A candidate for an office as *secrétaire du roi*, before applying for the office, reached agreement with the *procureurs* regarding the price to be paid and the procedure for payment. Then he negotiated with the person holding the office. The chancellor drew up letters of appointment. The candidate visited all the members of the *cabinet*. This body chose two commissioners who inquired into the religion, morality, competence, and honorable character of the candidate. They received three testimonies on oath, one from a priest and two from officials of the sovereign courts. The *secrétaires du roi* required of candidates that they renounce absolutely all "derogatory" commerce or craft and that they and their parents should have "shut up shop," at least for a considerable time. When this inquiry was concluded with the report of the *procureur syndic,* the assembly balloted. If the vote was favorable to the candidate, this was noted on the fold of the letters of appointment. The chancellor then sealed them and received the oath of the new *secrétaire*. The letters of appointment were registered at the Audience du Sceau.

The new *secrétaire du roi* paid an entrance fee of 1,200 livres to the company, an alms of 100 livres for the Quinze-Vingts, and another of 50 livres for the foundlings. He signed a statement of personal obligation for the company's debts. He swore an oath before the *cabinet* to respect the rules of the company, preserve the secrecy of its deliberations, honor its elders, and live in friendship with all his colleagues and refrain from lending his name in any way to those soliciting favors. Then, at last, he was solemnly installed in office.

The *cabinet* settled disputes between *secrétaires du roi*, dealt with infractions of the statutes, compiled the roster for duty at the chancellery, and designated each month two *secrétaires "populotiers,"* for the *"populo."* On the day after the Audience du Sceau, the *"populotiers"* attended the taxing of the letters that had been sealed and kept a register of the share of this money that was due to the *secrétaires.* Representatives of the *cabinet* were present when the "purses" were made up and subsequently distributed among the members of the company.

The *procureurs* nominated four auditors every month, chosen from among the elders, to supervise the sealing and to check all the letters sealed.

The *cabinet* upheld the privileges and prerogatives of the members of the company: the right of *committimus* to the Great Seal, exemptions, nobility *d'ancienne extraction* transmissible to one's children after twenty years in office, rights in the Great Chancellery and in the subordinate chancelleries, and various rights of precedence. It used all the procedures which have been described in connection with the order of the clergy of France. Sometimes it joined with the other officials of the chancellery to elect a syndic for the whole body.

To cover the costs of lawsuits, upkeep of buildings, refreshments, etc., the *cabinet* had at its disposal the funds from reception fees and fines.

The company came to the king's aid in times of need for the state. It purchased the new offices created by the king—seventy-four in 1622, for 1 million livres, 3 million livres in 1665. During the wars of 1688–1715 there were, besides creation of new offices, increases in salary in return for the payment of a principal and *rentes* secured on the Town Hall of Paris, amounting to 11 million in all. The company had to borrow and also to pay a commission of 1 percent to the notaries who found persons to lend them the money. During the wars of the 18th century the company had to make further efforts: in 1755 and 1758 it paid the king 15 million in exchange for increases of salary of 4 percent, whereas it had to borrow at 5 percent. The company's financial situation grew bad enough for the king to ask nothing of it between 1772 and 1789. It was still 25 million in debt to the public when the Revolution came.

The advocates before the Paris parlement

In order to be an advocate before a *parlement,* and thus before all the courts within its jurisdiction, one had to be at least seventeen years old and, according to the ordinances of 1519 and 1525 and the *arrêt* of the Paris *parlement* of October 1555, to have a degree in civil and canon law conferred by a well-known university where public lectures were given.

After Philip the Bold's ordinance of 23 October 1274, advocates had to swear an oath every year, upon the Gospel, before the *premier président* (or the king, if he was present), that they would plead only just causes. By the *règlement* of the *parlement* dated 13 November 1340 they had to be registered on a roll in the order of their taking the oath. The royal ordinance of 19 March 1345 definitively regulated the exercise of their profession. The names of the advocates were entered on a roll. They had to take an oath to exercise their profession with diligence and honesty, not to accept unjust causes, to warn the court if the king's interests were involved in a case, not to draw up articles that were *"impertinents"* (that is, without relevance to the case), not to invoke false customs, to deal with matters as promptly as possible, without delay or subterfuge, and never to ask for honoraria proportionate to the sums involved in the case but to take as their fee 30 livres at most for a big case and proportionately less for others. Young advocates were not to plead immediately after taking the oath but must for a certain time listen to their seniors at work, so as to learn the rules of their profession and the style of the court.

From 1557 onward, after the ordinances relating to the advocates had been read to them and before they took their yearly oath, the *avocat du roi* delivered an address on questions of discipline to the advocates and attorneys.

There were thus three grades of advocate: the *avocats écoutants,* before their registration on the roll of advocates, during a probationary period which lasted two years; the *avocats plaidants,* the ones whose names were entered on the roll; and the *avocats consultants,* the most senior ones, whom the court consulted and sometimes allowed to sit beside the magistrates on the fleurs-de-lis. Advocates were assigned to their appropriate categories by the *"gens du roi"*—the *procureur du roi* and the *avocats du roi.*

The advocates formed not a corporation or community but an "order," or "bar." From the beginning of the 15th century they had been affiliated, with the attorneys, to a confraternity of Saint Nicholas, to which they paid an entrance fee and an annual subscription for the holding of a church service. The confraternity solemnly celebrated

Saint Nicholas's day, 9 May, and distributed alms. The advocates and attorneys held a general assembly for the defense of their material and moral interests. This assembly was followed by a dinner. The assembly elected permanent representatives to act as go-betweens with the *parlement* and the *gens du roi.*

The advocates also had a special assembly which, from the beginning of the 17th century, elected a *"bâtonnier"* as head of the profession. Originally he was a dignitary of the confraternity, entrusted with carrying the *"bâton,"* that is, the banner of Saint Nicholas. The bar and its *"bâtonnier"* played an increasing role in the recruitment and practice of the profession. It was a senior advocate, the candidate's patron or godfather, who stood surety for the capacity and morality of the candidate and presented him to take the oath. The civil ordinance of 1667 required the establishment of an annual list of advocates, and the *arrêt de règlement* of 17 July 1693 forbade young advocates to sign papers before they had been on this list for two years. It prescribed to the order of advocates the annual compiling of a list of its members, showing the date of reception of each advocate, a copy of this list to be deposited in the *greffe* of the *parlement.* The first such list, containing 240 names, was drawn up on 26 November 1696. Keeping the list up to date was the responsibility of the *bâtonnier.* At the latter's request the *parlement* laid it down, on 5 May 1751, that no advocate might be placed on the list until he had served four years as an *écoutant* and unless he presented a certificate signed by six advocates designated by the *bâtonnier.* In order to obtain this certificate the *écoutants* had to attend lectures on the theory of law, instituted at the beginning of the century.

The *bâtonnier* was elected each year, on Saint Nicholas's day in the summer, by the former *bâtonniers,* being proposed by the outgoing one. He was assisted by a council composed of the former *bâtonniers* and deputies elected, down to 1781, by the body of advocates, unequally divided into eleven "benches," each of which elected two deputies. After 1781 the advocates were divided, equally, into "columns," each of which elected two deputies. Those elected constituted together the body of deputies.

The advocates were obliged to give consultations free of charge, one day a week, to poor litigants, when they sat as a bureau of nine members, assisted by *écoutants,* who had a consultative voice.

The advocates' gains were supposed to be subject to supervision.

The Ordinance of Blois of 1579, in its article 161, prescribed that they must sign all the papers used in their cases and state the payment they received, on pain of a charge of embezzlement. However, when the *parlement* of Paris ordered, on 9 May 1602, the application of this ordinance, the advocates went on strike. Henri IV, in letters patent of 25 May, overruled their withdrawal of services and summoned them to submit; in fact, however, article 161 was never applied.

The *bâtonnier* and his council watched over the advocates' observation of the relevant ordinances, regulations, and usages. They received complaints by litigants against advocates and applied sanctions which might go so far as definitive striking off the rolls of the order. Advocates subjected to a penalty could appeal against it to the *parlement*, but the *parlement* usually upheld the judgment of the order.

The advocates refused to serve before the "*parlement* of Maupeou." The edict of May 1771 made the profession of advocate an office and created 100 offices of advocate before the *parlement*. However, the edict of November 1774 abolished these offices and restored the previous situation.

The advocates enjoyed the dignity of an order. The civil ordinance of 1667 recognized this by according to the twelve most senior members of the profession the privilege of *committimus*. The advocates rejected article 161 of the Ordinance of Blois because it was prejudicial to their dignity. They even claimed nobility by virtue of quality, proclaiming themselves "*chevaliers ès lois.*" They were extremely touchy, always demanding that they be given "more honor" and considering that their "estate" should be "the seedbed of dignities"; and they bore a grudge against purchasers of offices, whom they accused of monopolizing "dignity."

The advocates before the king's Council

Any individual or body could address a petition directly to the Council: "Au Roi et à Nosseigneurs du Conseil." Many of these petitions were, however, of a contentious nature, and litigants presented a great number that were groundless. The king therefore required that petitions be drawn up by advocates before the *parlement* or by *secrétaires du roi*. In the second half of the 16th century the chancellor obliged advocates who wished to practice before the Council to obtain from him "*la matricule,*" that is, the recording of their names in a special register. In 1585 permission to appear as advocates before the Council was held by six advocates, four *secrétaires du roi,* and two referendaries of the Seal of France. The number of advocates before the Council subsequently underwent considerable increase. Protests were made against men combining the functions of *secrétaire du roi* and advocate before the Council, and from 1618 onward these functions were gradually separated. The *règlement* of 14 July 1626 fixed at 100 the list of advocates before the Council. The edict of September 1643 abolished the *matricule* and created 160 venal and hereditary offices of advocate "en nos Conseils d'Etat et privé." The company of advocates before the Council had been formed.

This was not a corporation in the strict sense of the word, since it lacked the capacity to possess real property; but it did present the same characteristic features as the order of advocates before the *parlement.*

In order to become an advocate before the Council one had to have been entered on the roll of advocates before the *parlement* for at least two years. A candidate was received into the order by a sort of cooptation. He negotiated for an office with an advocate before the Council or his heirs. The price to be paid covered the reimbursement of the *"finance"* which had been paid to the king (about 10,000 livres) and also the value of the advocate's "practice," which, under Louis XVI, was determined by two senior advocates before the Council at between 60,000 and 115,000 livres. The chancellor then drew up letters of appointment, which were not sealed, containing the clause: "to be shown to the dean and syndics of the advocates before the Council." He assigned to a master of requests the task of investigating the life and morals of the candidate. The assembly of the advocates before the Council chose a law for the candidate to explain, and they constituted a jury which judged his performance. The candidate made a complimentary speech in Latin, explained the law, and argued about it with the members of the jury. If the assembly decided to receive him, the chancellor had the letters of appointment sealed and the candidate took the oath before him. He was then received and installed by the assembly, to which he swore a second oath to fulfill his office faithfully.

The assembly put forward three names for each of its officers—the dean, four syndics, and a *greffier.* The chancellor selected from these and made the appointments. The ordinary assembly was held every week and dealt with disciplinary matters: breaches of regulations, complaints by litigants against advocates, and disputes between colleagues.

The general assembly drew up regulations for the company within the framework of the general regulations and subject to the chancellor's approval.

The company had a fund which was kept up from reception fees and payments for the documents used by its members. This fund covered the company's expenses: the Mass of the Holy Ghost, services for deceased members, and upkeep of the meeting hall.

The company enjoyed privileges. Its members, being regarded as commensals with the king, possessed the right of *committimus* to the Great Seal. They held the exclusive right to sign petitions, memoranda, deeds, and inquiry proceedings which came before the various sessions of the Council and the jurisdiction of the *requêtes de l'Hôtel*. They alone could produce valid documents, and they composed these for both advocates and attorneys. They signed the petitions and memoranda presented to the Council. However, they did not enjoy a monopoly as pleaders: advocates before the *parlement* could plead before the Council, provided that they were given permission by the chancellor.

Having secured the abolition of an office, created in 1610, of "advocate for the poor," they were required to plead free of charge for poor persons; when they did this, they wrote above their signatures: *Gratis pro Deo*.

All their *actes* and *écritures* were taxed by the king. So as to prevent excessive multiplication of these documents, the *arrêt* of the Council dated 28 June 1738 greatly simplified the procedure. The advocates before the Council rose in revolt against this encroachment on their dignity. However, the argument which had served the advocates before the *parlement* in Henri IV's time had no success with Chancellor Daguesseau. All the advocates before the Council handed in their resignations. They were accepted. The edict of September 1738 abolished the 170 old offices, on the grounds that the behavior of the holders had been "equally contrary to their duty and to the respect due to our authority," and created 70 new ones. The new officeholders sometimes let the old ones use their names and sometimes also signed their *écritures* for them. By a regulation of 17 February 1739, the order of advocates before the Council adopted, in order to put a stop to this practice, the procedure employed for the policing of the crafts and instituted visitations by the bureau of the company, escorted by one of the Council's tipstaffs, who was empowered to confiscate any irregular *écritures* found in advocates' chambers. The regulation was confirmed by an *arrêt* of the Council on 23 February 1739.

The attorneys (procureurs) *before the Paris* parlement

Litigants were represented in court by an attorney (*procureur*). Attorneys were supervised by the court in which they appeared; it examined their capacity, made them take an oath, and entered their names on a special roll. The *présidents* of the courts received the attorneys, thereby creating a clientage for themselves.

The role of attorney could be played by "*solliciteurs de procès,*" who were often attorney's clerks, sometimes competing with the attorneys proper and sometimes acting as touts for them.

By an edict of 1620, confirmed by the declaration of 8 February 1639, the function of attorney before the Paris *parlement* was made a royal office. From 200 their number had increased to 400 by 1771. They were then abolished, and a corporation of advocate-attorneys was created. Though reestablished by an edict of November 1774, their number was reduced to 200. The declaration of 18 February 1776 fixed it at 300.

The attorneys before the Châtelet formed a distinct company. The other attorneys in Paris constituted a community made up of those who exercised "l'état et office de procureur, tiers référendaire taxateur et calculateur de dépens en la Cour de Parlement, Cour des Aydes et des Monnaies, Requêtes de l'Hôtel et du Palais et autres juridictions de l'enclos du Palais." From the 15th century onward they were grouped with the advocates in a confraternity of Saint Nicholas which survived until 1783 as a pious association and mutual-aid society. But the civil community was distinct from the confraternity. It was a corporation to which all the attorneys before the *parlement* were obliged to belong. In order to be an attorney before the *parlement,* one had to be a Catholic, aged at least twenty-five, and to have served an attorney for ten years, for three of these years as chief clerk. The court required that the candidate pass a professional examination, and by the *arrêt de règlement* of 12 February 1717 it assigned to the community of attorneys the task of examining him and looking into his religion, way of life, and morals. The community, if satisfied, issued a certificate of *admittatur,* and letters of appointment were then granted. (The Châtelet saw to its own examination and inquiries.)

The appointee called on the dignitaries of the *parlement* and those of the community of attorneys and swore an oath before the Grand' Chambre. He was then entered on the list of members of the community and took his place on the attorneys' bench with the same rank as his predecessor. After ten years he acquired the quality of senior attorney and certain privileges.

The community provided itself in 1666 with a set of statutes. It was to be governed by four "*procureurs de communauté*" chosen by a limited number of members: the eldest attorney, those who had previously been dignitaries, and six postulants. The *procureurs de communauté* were assisted, on the one hand, by a bureau made up of deputies elected by the senior attorneys, by those of medium-length service, and by the young ones, and, on the other, by a council made up of former governors of the community, together with twelve senior attorneys. All the attorneys could attend meetings of the council ("*les audiences*"), but without the right to speak. Every year at the beginning of the new term, between 20 and 25 November, the leading attorney of the community held a solemn meeting of the council, at which the rules governing the profession were read, and he made a speech on the duties of a good attorney.

The council of the community enforced the king's ordinances and the *arrêts de règlement* of the *parlement* and added to them decisions which it issued "subject to the court's pleasure." It decided delicate points of procedure and issued attested affidavits in the form of decisions. It exercised functions of arbitration and discipline, inflicting penalties on guilty attorneys. It collaborated in the fixing of the fees and honoraria of attorneys by the king or the *parlement,* and it dealt with the payments due to them for the documents they compiled during cases. It provided for the representation without charge of poor litigants. It defended the interests of the attorneys against the tipstaffs, *greffiers, fermiers du roi,* and *solliciteurs de procès.* It provided large sums to help the king in time of war, by means of confirmation of heredity in office, purchase of new offices, and increases in dues. It undertook to raise certain taxes—the poor tax, the poll tax—from its members and to pay over the sums raised.

The attorneys' clerks formed a distinct community, the *royaume de la Basoche,* while the clerks to the attorneys before the *chambre des comptes* formed the *empire de Galilée.* These groupings were officially recognized and protected.

The notaries attached to the Paris Châtelet

These men bore the title of *conseillers du roi, notaires, gardes-notes, et gardes-scel de Sa Majesté au Châtelet de Paris*. They were royal officials who were notaries, that is, they received the declarations of contracting parties and noted them. After they had been assigned the prerogatives of the scriveners (*tabellions*), they engrossed these declarations. Given the title of *gardes-notes* in 1577, they were required to preserve their records. For a long period they had to take their engrossments to the Châtelet to get them sealed with the seal for contracts, or Little Royal Seal, by the *gardes-scel,* but the latter office was merged with their own by an edict of December 1691. In 1696 Louis XIV created twenty *"conseillers du roi, notaires, gardes-scel"* to take charge of the Little Seal. The notaries of Paris bought up these twenty offices, and each of them became a *garde-scel et conseiller du roi*. A little later they acquired for themselves the *greffes* dealing with agreements and arbitrations. In 1693 they were dispensed from *contrôle des actes* by providing the king with 1 million livres against a *rente* of 50,000 livres, and this privilege was confirmed in 1723, in return for a special due payable on the paper and parchment they used. They performed by tradition the functions of apostolic notaries, responsible for drawing up legal documents concerning church benefices. When, in 1691, Louis XIV created offices of apostolic notary, all these offices were bought up by the royal notaries, who then assumed the title of royal and apostolic notaries. Finally, the notaries of Paris were permitted to deal with documents sent to them from all parts of the kingdom.

The notaries of Paris formed a confraternity, authorized by letters from Philip the Fair in December 1308. They had a mass said every week and relieved colleagues fallen on hard times, or their widows and orphans.

The notaries of Paris formed a community. This received candidates for the post of notary, its syndics undertaking inquiries into their morality and capacity and subjecting them to an examination. In order to offer oneself as a candidate, it was necessary to be twenty-five years old and to have worked for a Paris notary for five years as chief clerk (or merely as clerk if one was the son or son-in-law of a notary).

The community was governed by a bureau composed of a dean, twelve delegates, three syndics, and a *greffier*. The dean was the notary who had been longest in service, and he possessed effective authority: he presided over and closed the meetings and made the speeches at them. The community was hierarchically divided into 38 senior notaries, 38 less-senior ones, and 37 youngsters. The 12 delegates were chosen for life, by majority vote of the 38 seniors, the honorary notaries (veterans retired after twenty years in office), 8 of the less senior, and 8 young ones, sitting as an ordinary assembly. This assembly also elected, for a three-year period, the three syndics, one of whom was replaced each year and each of whom became, in turn, the managing syndic. The assembly also elected, for one year, the *greffier,* who became a syndic.

This bureau met every Thursday in the community's room in the Châtelet. It presented its proposals to the ordinary assembly every Sunday, after the notaries' mass. The ordinary assembly had power to make regulations, and it received the accounts of those responsible for the common purse.

The community of the notaries of the Châtelet was a privileged body. Its members were *conseillers du roi.* They were exempt from the burdens borne by commoners, notably from having soldiers billeted on them. They enjoyed the privilege of *garde-gardienne,* being under the king's special protection. The more senior of them enjoyed the privilege of *committimus.* If they were noblemen, the exercise of this profession was not incompatible with their status.

The tipstaffs (huissiers) *and bailiffs* (sergents)

These were, like the notaries, minor officials of the judiciary, but at a lower professional and social level. They were responsible both for maintaining order during court proceedings and for executing the decisions of the court for which they worked. They formed communities: tipstaffs of the king's councils, of the Great Chancellery, of the Paris *parlement,* of the *chambre des comptes,* the *cour des aides,* the *bureau des finances de la généralité de Paris.* At the Paris Châtelet there were communities of bailiffs, *sergents à cheval, sergents à verge, huissiers-priseurs de meubles.* In 1733 the king joined with them some *officiers gardes du commerce,* appointed by commission to carry out arrests. Communities of the same type existed in the provinces, attached to each court of justice. They all included a confraternity (a pious association and mutual-aid society) and a company—a civil body with representatives elected to carry on lawsuits of interest to the profession, of which there were many, against "neighboring" bodies, and also a common purse.

The *"officiers de police,"* or domanial officials

These were occupations that had been made into royal, seignorial, or municipal offices, limited in number and forming privileged communities, for ensuring *"police,"* mainly in the economic sphere. There were many of them, and they were very diverse. We must confine ourselves to a few examples.

The sworn criers had the monopoly of making oral announcements at crossroads and in other public places regarding the prices of goods, lost children, stray animals, funerals, meetings, and so on.

The unloaders of wine fetched barrels from boats. The gaugers and measurers of wine verified their contents. The sworn sellers of wine practiced brokerage. The wine-tasters checked on quality.

The measurers of grain, who had to be present when this commodity was sold, also took note of the total quantity received, so as to check on food supplies, and inspected the quality of grain and flour. The grain-porters carried the goods, when they had been measured and checked, to the bakers and to the houses of private persons. These officials employed day laborers to perform the manual work.

The salt-porters attached to the salt storehouses, who in Paris were called *jurés hanouards,* unloaded salt from boats and conveyed it to the retailers or to those private persons who enjoyed the privilege of *franc-salé*. They assigned the actual carrying to *plumets,* ordinary unskilled workers. The *hanouards* had the privilege, when a king died, of bearing his body from the gate of Paris to the basilica of Saint-Denis.

There were *mouleurs-compteurs* of logs, and porters for firewood; porters and measurers of coal; sworn sellers of sea fish, fresh or salted; sworn sellers of poultry; sworn inspectors of hay; and so on.

All these officials were appointed by the issuing of letters of appointment after they had learned their trade and had been accepted by their corporation. Their graduation from a trade to an office constituted a move upward in society. They were obliged to take an oath.

Each corporation formed an authorized confraternity and a community of temporal interests. The corporation gave itself statutes, which were approved. It held at least one assembly every year. It elected representatives, syndics or attorney-syndics. Over its members it exercised a jurisdiction that was disciplinary, educative, and formative. It had a common purse. It defended its trade either by delegations to the authorities or by lawsuits. It contributed to the public charges either by buying newly created offices or by paying out a principal in exchange for an increase in the dues it could collect.

The universities

The University of Paris may serve as our example. It was a public body composed of persons dedicated to study. As a corporation, they called themselves "members of the university." They consisted of the masters, bound to the university by oath and teaching in one of the establishments attached to it; the students, registered on a roll; the conservators of the university's privileges, apostolic and royal; the university's officials—syndic, registrar, receiver, beadles; its legal advisers—four advocates and two attorneys before the *parlement,* two advocates and one attorney at the Châtelet, and one notary; its twenty-four sworn booksellers and eleven sworn stationers, residing in Paris, Corbeil, Essonne, and Troyes; its two bookbinders, its illuminators, its two scriveners, its *grands messagers.* All these formed the *populus academicus,* or republic of letters.

The university was responsible for secondary and higher education. The primary schools were still in the charge of the bishop, who delegated it to the precentor. In 1675 the primary schools of Paris, some of which taught the rudiments of Latin, had 8,000 pupils.

The university was a federation of colleges which had asked to join it so as to share in its prestige and privileges. Foreign scholars who wished to give public lessons in Paris had to ask the university's permission. Outside the university were the Collège Royal (Collège de France), the Jesuits' college, and the private teachers ("*siffleurs*") who prepared pupils at home for the various university examinations.

As regards the teaching of the "arts" (letters and sciences), distinction was made between the *collèges de plein exercice,* which provided teaching for both scholarship-holders and paying students, and the *collèges ordinaires,* which were merely halls of residence for scholarship-holders who pursued their studies elsewhere.

The university consisted of seven companies: the four "nations" and the three faculties—Divinity, Law, and Medicine.

The "nations" embraced all the arts students. They were divided into "tribes," each including a certain number of dioceses and districts. The four nations were the "French" (France, Spain, Italy, the eastern countries), "Norman," "Picard," and "German" (Germany, Poland, the northern countries). However, the majority of students were French.

Each nation was governed by a *procureur* elected by its members. The *procureur* was provided by each of the tribes in turn, and was, alternately, a *régent* and a licentiate, or bachelor. The nation also elected a *censeur,* to act as syndic. The four nations together made up the Faculty of Arts, but this did not form a distinct body with its own organs.

The faculties of Divinity, Law, and Medicine, which students entered after completing a course of study in a college of the Faculty of Arts, each constituted a corporation. The Law faculty was a "Faculty of Gratian's Decretal," which taught only canon law. Article 69 of the Ordinance of Blois of 1579 had forbidden the teaching of Roman law in Paris, but by an edict of April 1679 Louis XIV decided to add Roman law and French law to the curriculum. The Paris Law faculty consisted of six *docteurs-régents,* selected by competition. After 1656 they were assisted by twenty-four honorary doctors chosen from among the archbishops and bishops, the canons of Notre-Dame, and the magistrates and advocates of the *parlement*. These helpers did not show themselves to be very assiduous, and in 1679 Louis XIV replaced them with twelve *docteurs-agrégés* chosen by competition, who would compete for the place of any *docteur-régent* that fell vacant. The period of study was four years: two years to become a bachelor of law, then one year to become a licentiate, and a final year to become a doctor, after defending a thesis—the *actus triumphalis*. The faculty was governed by a dean, who was elected each year by the college of *docteurs-régents* and *docteurs-agrégés*. The faculty assembly had supreme authority to decide. The dean convened it, presided, put forward proposals, collected votes, and drafted conclusions. He headed the administration, receiving the oaths of the beadles and other officials. He represented the faculty and defended its interests.

The university, formed by the union of the four nations and the three faculties, was a body of teachers and students. Their general assemblies were infrequent and were held mainly for ceremonial purposes. The university was administered by a Council of Eight—the four *procureurs* of the nations, the three deans of the faculties, and the rector, who presided. The rector, the head of the university, was elected by the four *procureurs* of the nations. Thus, the arts men controlled the university. In 1658 the faculties declined to obey the rector whom the arts men had chosen. The *parlement* upheld the customary form of the election but required that, whenever a rector was elected, he must ask for endorsement from all three faculties. In theory the rector was elected for three months, but in practice he remained in office for between one and three years. The rector had to be obeyed by all members of the university. He caused the syndic to convene the assemblies and the council of the university and presided over them. He had judicial powers. He had the right to enter the king's Council to present the university's petitions in person. He attended, enjoying the same honors as the *parlement*, the weddings and funerals of the king and the members of the royal family. During ceremonies he stood on the left of the archbishop of Paris.

The university promulgated statutes or internal regulations which were binding upon all its members, and the faculties and nations did the same. The university had its customs, to which all members were subject. These statutes and customs concerned the discipline of members and the organization of studies. The university possessed disciplinary jurisdiction. The rector gave judgment in the first instance, and a university court, of the same composition as the Council of Eight, heard appeals. The *parlement*, when cases were referred to it, functioned as court of final appeal. The university's jurisdiction included the right of visitation of the colleges.

The university possessed property, could receive gifts and raise taxes ("*bourses*") from its members, and derived fees from the sale of parchment and the work of its public transport service. It appointed to certain ecclesiastical offices and benefices.

The university had the right to plead in court, and so did its colleges, nations, and faculties; it was quick to defend, in all circumstances, the interests of education. The *parlement*, when it was given, for registration, letters by the king which it considered not to be in the interest of education, ordered that these be referred to the university, which would then take steps to oppose them.

The university, fulfilling as it did a special function in society and in the state, enjoyed corresponding privileges. These included apostolic privileges: dispensation from residence for students or teachers who were appointed to a benefice; reservation of one-third of the vacant benefices for clerics who were graduates of the university, with canonries and urban cures of souls monopolized by doctors of divinity; and the privilege of jurisdiction. The university nominated a guardian of its privileges, a judge delegated by the pope—usually the bishop of Senlis, Beauvais, or Meaux. The university had royal privileges which were renewed from reign to reign. So far as their personal affairs were concerned, the students came under ecclesiastical jurisdiction. The university and its members were under the king's protection, which the *prévôt* of Paris was responsible for ensuring. Any act that harmed the person, rights, or property of a member of the university was a "royal case" of breach of the king's protection, which had to be dealt with by the Paris Châtelet. The university, as a corporation, found it easy to obtain letters removing cases to the king's Council, so that it escaped from the competence of the *parlement*. Members of the university were exempt from escheat, from tolls and *traites*, from taxes and subsidies, from *aides* levied on the produce (notably, wine) of their benefices or their patrimonial property. They could either consume or sell this produce in their homes. They were exempt from paying *aides* on the provisions they bought for their own consumption, with the *premier président* of the *cour des aides* functioning as guardian of the privileges of the university in this matter. Members of the university were exempt from service in the watch and in the guard for the city walls, from the obligation to billet soldiers, from responsibilities of guardianship and tutelage, and from other public responsibilities.

In grave situations, and by way of exception, the university agreed to contribute to the public charges and to allow its members to join the army, as happened in 1636. By the *arrêt* of the *cour des aides* dated 4 July 1654, the university remained exempt from paying dues on paper, up to the limit of 30,000 reams, which were allocated by the rector. In 1695 the university was subjected to the poll tax and, in 1710, to the tenth. Acting as a corporation, however, it taxed its members itself and paid the sum raised directly into the royal coffers.

Being entrusted with the conduct of higher education for the common good, the university was watched over by the king, who bore responsibility for this common good. The king was the protector of the university—his "very dear daughter," his "beloved daughter." The university participated in the sovereigns' solemn entries, in the Te Deums for their victories, and in the funeral ceremonies for them or for the members of their family. It had easy access to the king's person, to present him with its compliments, condolences, or requests.

The king reformed the university when it was necessary to adapt it to new circumstances, as Henri IV did in imposing statutes which were registered by the *parlement* and promulgated on 18 September 1600 in the general assembly of the university. Louis XIV appointed in 1667 a commission to reform the University of Paris, but its work came to nothing. The Faculty of Divinity gave itself new statutes, which were approved by royal letters patent in May 1675. In April 1679 the king issued an edict reforming studies in all the Law faculties of the kingdom. He prescribed that Roman law should be studied and initiated the teaching of French law. He forbade *siffleurs* to do more than help their pupils with revision. On 23 June 1679, an assembly of the University of Paris, presided over by two state councilors, supplemented the university's statutes with nineteen articles in conformity with the new edict.

The king intervened in the life of the university. In 1714 he forbade, by *lettre de cachet,* the rector to continue in office and caused a successor to be appointed. In 1765 he imposed his appointee as syndic, by *lettre de cachet,* upon the Faculty of Divinity.

The Collège des Lecteurs Royaux remained outside the university, under the direction of the king's principal chaplain. After 1594 the "king's lecturers" received their wages only on presentation of a certificate of assiduity. The Council's *arrêt* of 18 March 1636 kept the entire direction of the college in the hands of the principal chaplain; but letters patent of 16 May 1772, registered by the *parlement* on 26 March 1773, attached the Collège Royal and its nineteen lecturers to the university.

The Collège de Clermont, run by the Jesuits and subsequently known as the Collège Louis-le-Grand, was never attached to the university but had permission to teach, from the *arrêt* of the Council of 15 February 1618 until the *arrêt* of the Paris *parlement* of 6 April 1762 and the royal edict of November 1764, which suppressed the Society of Jesus in France. The Collège Louis-le-Grand then became a college of the university. Twenty-seven small colleges which were mere halls of residence were merged with it in 1763 so as to train the *régents* who were to replace the Jesuits in their forty colleges in the area subject to the jurisdiction of the Paris *parlement.* In 1766 the king established sixty posts of *docteurs-agrégés* in the Faculty of Arts, to be filled by competition, so as to provide *régents* for the big colleges. At the same time, the king provided the university with the means of granting pensions to its professors emeritus.

The university policed the bookselling trade. By statutes of 1323, in order to become a bookseller one had to prove one's capacity, give surety, and swear an oath to the university, promising to respect its statutes and to submit books to it for examination and correction before putting them on sale.

In 1605, however, the university asked for the aid of the king and the *parlement* in its fight against the circulation of undesirable books. The king prohibited the printing and selling of any book without his permission, contained in letters of privilege reserving to a particular bookseller the monopoly of a particular book. By edict of August 1624 the king attached four official censors to the chancellor's department. These men were usually chosen from professors of the Collège de Sorbonne. Letters patent of May 1618 confirmed the statutes that constituted the bookseller-printers as an autonomous craft, separate from the mechanical crafts and regarded as belonging to the university. The *arrêt* of the Council of 10 December 1725 confirmed bookselling and printing in the status of a distinct art, attached to the university. An apprentice or a master was received by their syndic and community and was then presented by the syndic to the university, which obliged him to take an examination and swear an oath; it then entered him on its registers. The new member could then call himself a sworn bookseller to the university and enjoy its privileges. No book might be published without the king's permission.

The university maintained in every diocese *messagers* who brought students to Paris and carried clothes and provisions for them. They also conveyed money and parcels for the general public. Henri IV, by letters of 9 August 1597, gave the royal *messagers* the right, along with those of the university, to transport parcels and letters for the public at large. After 1647 the king gradually substituted the farmers of the royal *messageries* for those of the university's, merging, *de facto*, services that were properly distinct. Letters patent of 14 April 1719 allowed the university to retain ownership of its *messageries*, but they had to be farmed out at the same time and to the same persons as the royal *messageries*. The university received every year one twenty-eighth of the total amount paid for the farm, and it used this to remunerate the *régents* of the colleges, which made it possible for teaching to be given free of charge.

In this way the king's supervision enabled the autonomous and privileged corporation of the university to provide a state service for the public good.

The Académie française and other royal academies

The academies were learned bodies that resulted from private initiative but had to submit to the king's tutelage in the form of a relationship of fealty—*protecteur-créature*. Starting in 1629, certain men of letters met every week to talk about literature. Richelieu asked them if they "would not like to form a corporation and meet regularly and under public authority." They agreed, since in any case every assembly had to be authorized by the king. The "company" was added to by cooptation during 1634 from among persons who were all exempt from paying the *taille* on one basis or another. Keeper of the Seals Séguier was a member. It began on 13 March 1634 to keep a record of its discussions under the name Académie française. Its existence was authorized by letters patent from Louis XIII in Janaury 1635, which the *parlement* registered on 10 July 1637. The statutes of the Academy were approved on 22 February 1635 by the cardinal, its protector. They were completed and modified by a *règlement* which the Academy itself had prepared and which the king signed at Marly on 30 May 1752.

The Academy formed a corporation: it was one of the "*compagnies réglées*" of the kingdom. Its membership was limited to forty. It was given a seal and privileges and was autonomous, but it was provided with a protector—first Richelieu; then, after his death, Chancellor Séguier; then, after 1672, the king.

After 1668 and the king's return as conqueror from Franche-Comté, the Academy enjoyed the privilege of delivering addresses to the king on occasions of triumph or mourning like "*les autres compagnies supérieures de Paris,*" taking its turn after the high courts of justice and the university. The Academicians were exempt from duties of watch and ward and guardianship. They enjoyed the privilege of *committimus* to the Great Seal, just like "*les officiers, domestiques, et commensaux de notre Maison.*" This privilege was confined to the four most senior members of the company between August 1669 and 5 December 1673.

The Academy kept up its numbers by cooptation, with presentation of candidature, visits to members, and secret ballot. The protector of the Academy had to approve the choice of new recruits. The Academy's members were absolutely equal, with rank determined by seniority alone. They were not paid, but after 1673 they drew attendance money for being present at each of the three weekly meetings.

The Academy was allowed to make regulations within the framework of its statutes. It had an extensive right to own property. It could plead in court. It had three officers, drawn from among its members: a director, to take the chair at meetings, and a chancellor, to keep its seal, these two being chosen by lot every three months, and a permanent secretary, whom it elected and who was housed in the Louvre. It appointed subaltern officials: librarian, conductor of the chapel choir, copyist. The Academy could expel a member for breach of its statutes.

The Academy was obliged to respect the king's authority, the established government, and the laws of the kingdom. Its role was to "give our language definite rules and make it pure, eloquent, and capable of dealing with the arts and sciences."

A fairly large number of provincial academies were formed, taking this one as their model, at Arles, Soissons, Nîmes, Marseilles, and other centers. They were usually affiliated to the Académie française and were often directed by one of its members.

Similarly organized was the Académie des Inscriptions et Médailles, which began in 1663, received a *règlement* on 16 July 1701 and letters patent in February 1713, and was given the title of Académie des Inscriptions et Belles-Lettres by an *arrêt* of the Council dated 4 January 1716. Its task was to study inscriptions and medallions, improve knowledge of Greek and Latin antiquity, and describe the antiquities and monuments of France. The *règlement* of 22 December 1786 assigned to it the purpose of studying history through languages, monuments, titles, and so on.

The Académie des Sciences began in the reign of Louis XIII with casual meetings of men of learning at which Descartes, Roberval, Gassendi, and Pascal were present. Colbert made this group a royal academy. He nominated eight *savants,* who met for the first time on 22 December 1666 in a room in the king's library. A medal was struck on that occasion, bearing the inscription *Naturae investigandae et perficiendis artibus,* which defined the sphere assigned to the new body. Colbert entrusted it with the task of publishing descriptions of all the arts and crafts. Its first *règlement* was dated 26 January 1669. Article 31 gave the academy the mission of examining all the machines for which the king was asked to grant patents of privilege. The government and administration consulted the academy on all technical questions—the making of soda, the management of hospitals, the adulteration of cider, the relation between the price of grain and the price of bread.

Other academies, such as the Academy of Painting and Sculpture and the Academy of Architecture, were given a form of corporate organization that was similar if not identical.

The medical corporations

In some areas the physicians, surgeons, and apothecaries formed a single corporation within which each carried on his particular profession, but in almost every place these three professions were organized separately. The physicians everywhere enjoyed preeminence, however: medicine, surgery, and pharmacy were taught in the faculties of medicine, and physicians were present at the examinations of surgeons and apothecaries.

Physicians

Medicine could be practiced only by graduates of a well-reputed university who were affiliated to the university or college of the place where they wished to practice. Physicians were "scientific persons." Medical practice was not incompatible with nobility. In Lorraine and Roussillon doctors were even ennobled. The only foreign doctors allowed in France were graduates of the universities of Avignon and Pont-à-Mousson.

In Paris the Faculty of Medicine was included in the corporation of the university. It was reformed in 1598. The electoral college elected the dean and chose the professors for the coming year from among its members who were doctors of medicine. In other faculties, such as Montpellier, the professors were chosen by competition. The faculty itself constituted a corporation. It elected a dean to manage its affairs for one year. It held a monthly assembly. It regulated discipline and defended the medical profession. Its students, when they graduated, took the Hippocratic Oath, by which they promised to observe the statutes of the faculty, to behave with decency and gravity, to live on good terms with each other, to have nothing to do with empirics and charlatans, not to attend a patient without being requested to do so, to keep strictly secret whatever they might see or hear in their patients' homes, to sign all their prescriptions, to follow through to the end a treatment once begun, and never to insist that a patient pay a particular fee. During consultations, the most junior physician was to give his opinion first. Juniors were to show respect to seniors, and seniors were to show politeness and good will toward juniors.

The Faculty of Medicine arranged consultations free of charge on

Saturdays, after the Mass of Saint Luke. The edict of 1707 made this practice obligatory in all the faculties and colleges of the realm. It was a matter of usage for physicians to attend the Mass of Saint Luke, not to recommend for the salvation of the body any remedy that might jeopardize the soul, never to lend themselves to an abortion (regarded as murder), and always to observe prudence and modesty in dealings with patients.

In places where there was no faculty, the physicians organized themselves in a medical college, which held meetings, presided over by an elected dean, but never conferred degrees and, as a rule, did not undertake teaching; there were colleges of this kind in Orléans, Troyes, Lyons, Bordeaux, and Lille. One was formed at Dijon in 1626 and another at Nancy in 1752. Physicians were accepted as members after paying the usual visits, passing an examination, and taking an oath. Like the faculties, these colleges always supervised the surgeons and apothecaries, inspecting their work and sometimes providing instruction for them.

The physicians attending the king and the royal family, who received a royal warrant, were thereby freed from the obligation to attach themselves to a faculty or college. The king's principal physician was a *conseiller du roi* and received the oath that had to be sworn by all who were concerned with caring for the king's health.

Surgeons

The barber-surgeons formed a community of the craft type, controlled by *jurés*. It was placed under the authority of the king's principal barber and made a contract with the Faculty of Medicine by which its members were permitted to perform minor operations, phlebotomies, and scarifications, and treat bumps, bruises, boils, and open wounds.

The surgeons, who were regarded as predominantly *manual* workers, were grouped in Paris in a College of Saint Cosmas, which one entered after receiving a *licentia operandi* from two "sworn surgeons" of the Châtelet and taking an oath before the *prévôt* of Paris. The college provided a four-year course of instruction, organized the defense of theses in osteology, anatomy, and surgery, and awarded bachelors' and licentiates' diplomas; its *maîtres* called themselves *chirurgiens de robe longue*. But this college was not affiliated to the university. Nevertheless, it depended on the university's Faculty of Medicine, since it was the dean of the faculty who authorized the provision of corpses for dissection.

The *chirurgiens de robe longue* entered on 1 October 1655 into a contract of union with the barber-surgeons which was confirmed by letters patent of March 1656 and the *parlement*'s *arrêt* of 7 September 1656. However, the Faculty of Medicine having opposed the measure, the *parlement* decided, by its *arrêt* of 7 February 1660, that the new community was to obey the faculty as pupils obeyed their masters. The surgeons were obliged to give up their cap and gown and their maintaining of theses and to remove the word *collegium* from the façade of their amphitheater.

Outside the college and the community were the surgeons of the royal household, who were authorized by royal warrant to practice anywhere in the kingdom. Letters of 6 August 1668 associated with the post of principal surgeon to the king the rights and privileges of the principal barber and gave him authority over the corporation of master barber-surgeons, overriding that of the sworn surgeons of the Châtelet. He was empowered to commission surgeons in the provinces. In 1692 the position of royal sworn surgeon was made an office in the provinces. In 1723, however, the king's principal surgeon was reestablished in all his prerogatives as indisputable head of all the surgeons, responsible for maintaining the charters, statutes, and privileges of the profession.

The statutes of 1699 declared that "surgery is considered a liberal art" (article 24). The surgeons and barber-surgeons attendant on the royal family were attached to the community of master sworn surgeons and barbers. The *arrêt* of the *parlement* dated 11 March 1724 replaced subordination to the Faculty of Medicine with mere tokens of honor and respect. In September 1724 the amphitheater of Saint Cosmas was made the "Royal College of Surgery," with five royal demonstrators appointed by the king. In 1731 Mareschal, the king's principal surgeon, and La Peyronie, who held the reversion of this post, founded the Société de Chirurgie, which recruited by cooptation and carried on scientific work like an academic society.

By letters patent of 23 April 1743 the surgeons of Paris were completely separated from the barbers, the contract of 1655 was annulled, and thenceforth the student of surgery had to equip himself with an arts qualification, just like the student of medicine. The Council's *arrêt* of 4

July 1750 abolished the annual payment and oath which the surgeons had been obliged to offer to the Faculty of Medicine as tokens of subordination. The surgeons had to invite to their examinations the dean of the faculty and two doctors of medicine and give them a place of honor, but the surgeons were to discuss on their own whether to accept a candidate and were themselves to receive his oath. The corporation of surgeons was thus officially recognized as a college.

The statutes of the surgeons of Paris were renewed in May 1768. The royal declaration of 12 April 1772, applicable throughout the kingdom, with a view to preventing confusion between "students of surgery" and "mere artisans," abolished the certificate of apprenticeship while maintaining the obligation to spend a period under instruction from master surgeons, in hospitals or in the army, before beginning regular studies in the college.

Letters patent of 2 July 1748 made the Société de Chirurgie a royal academy, under the presidency of the king's principal surgeon.

According to the statutes of May 1768, the master surgeons of Paris were classed among the *bourgeois* practicing a liberal art. They were separated from the manual crafts, no longer being included in the rolls of the communities of arts and crafts for payment of the poll tax or the twentieth. Their profession was not incompatible with nobility, and it allowed them access to honorable employments. They were exempt from service in the militia and, as before, from duties of watch and ward and all public *"police"* responsibilities.

In order to practice surgery in Paris, one had to be a member of the College of Master Surgeons, which resembled the Faculty of Medicine, though it was not affiliated to the university. This college was headed by the king's principal surgeon, whereas the king's principal physician was not the head of the Faculty of Medicine. The college had a directory of officers, a council which was partly elected and partly nominated by the king's principal surgeon, and a general assembly of master surgeons. It had the status of a moral person, with possessions held as a patrimony, and authority to regulate and protect the profession.

The corporations of surgeons in the provinces were placed under the authority of the king's principal surgeon. They had been reorganized in 1730. After the letters patent of April 1743 their members gave up the barber's trade. The corporations were made into colleges, and their members were accordingly classed among the *bourgeois* notables. They organized themselves in imitation of the Paris college.

Apothecaries

The apothecaries, who were merged with the grocers, had the duty of knowing, keeping, and compounding all substances needed for the art of healing and were everywhere organized in sworn communities. In Paris any apothecary could be a grocer; but in order to be received as an apothecary, one had to be able to read prescriptions and to possess the *Antidotaire Nicolas,* which contained them. The apothecaries elected a *maître* who, accompanied by two physicians appointed by the faculty and two apothecaries appointed by the *prévôt* of Paris, was required to visit twice a year the shops kept by his colleagues. Apothecaries were not allowed to sell their preparations except on a physician's prescription or to give the public "dangerous medicines." All the sworn communities of apothecaries were subject to inspection by the faculty or college of medicine nearest to them.

Louis XIII gave his principal physician full authority over apothecaries practicing in towns or *lieux non jurés,* and he caused the Paris faculty to publish in 1637 the *Codex,* which replaced the *Antidotaire.*

In Paris the statutes of 1638 continued to apply to both apothecaries and grocers. However, those who wished to become apothecaries were obliged to undergo a period of instruction and a searching examination carried out by the master apothecaries, assisted by two doctors of medicine from the faculty. A master apothecary qualified in Paris could practice anywhere in the kingdom. The apothecaries were required to maintain a pharmacy service in the hospitals and to provide medicines free to poor persons.

By a declaration of 14 May 1724 apothecaries were authorized to visit sick persons in the absence of a physician or surgeon. Gradually, from the 15th century onward, the communities of apothecaries had separated themselves from the grocers, and Louis XVI, by his declaration of 25 April 1777, formally removed the apothecaries of Paris from the corporation of grocers and constituted them as an independent corporation under the title College of Pharmacy. Botanic gardens, laboratories, and courses in botany, chemistry, and medical subjects were increasingly made available to persons studying to be apothecaries, who became "pharmacists."

The king even adumbrated a Royal Academy of Medicine. The king's principal physician presided over a royal commission on medicine, set up by *arrêts* of the Council dated 3 July and 28 October 1728, to approve the making and distribution of specific remedies. This commission—composed of the king's principal physician, principal surgeon, and principal apothecary, the dean of the Faculty of Medicine, and representatives, chosen by the king, of the corporations of medicine, surgery, and the apothecary's art—indicated to the king remedies for which he granted warrants of authorization that were valid for three years. An *arrêt* of the Council dated 17 March 1731 gave this royal commission responsibility for reporting epidemics, and one of 10 September 1754 empowered it to state its views regarding any disputes that might arise between the three corporations, of physicians, surgeons, and apothecaries, and also regarding any difficulties affecting the practice, discipline, and limits of each profession, so that the king could make decisions. By a royal declaration of 25 April 1772, complemented by an *arrêt* of the Council of 1 April 1774, the royal commission was made responsible for supervising the distribution of mineral waters. All this came close to the creation of an Academy of Medicine, but such a body did not actually appear.

The communities of arts and crafts

No craft was completely free of regulation in a society such as this. Every craft was, in the first place, subject to the general supervision exercised by the royal or seignorial judges, who fixed wage levels, the number and length of working days, workshop discipline, and often the nature, quality, and size of products and even the procedure for making them, as also the rules governing their sale.

The different categories of craft

Under this overall authority, we have to distinguish between the "free" crafts, the regulated crafts, the sworn crafts, the crafts which had been made into domanial offices, and the federations of crafts.

The "free," or unorganized, crafts were probably still the most numerous in town and country alike. Anyone could practice them, without any examination of capacity or obligatory procedure for admission to the rank of master craftsman and without any entrance fee. They had no statutes, their work was not supervised, and their relations with the public were uncontrolled. These crafts were of all kinds. First and foremost, there was wholesale trade, *"le négoce,"* and overseas trade, activities that required capital, a spirit of enterprise, a taste for risk, and a talent for organizing and doing business. These "crafts" were not regarded as base or mechanical. Nobles could practice them. A definition of them was given in the edict of December 1701: they were the sale of commodities "in bales, crates, or complete pieces, without any open shop being kept or sign displayed." Banking and money-changing were in the same category. In Poitou, mercery, trade in silken cloth, and transport were all "free," and, in Paris, river transport. Nevertheless, the members of these "free" crafts organized themselves in religious and charitable confraternities.

The regulated crafts were those which were regulated by the municipal authority. The municipality laid down statutes for the crafts and enforced their application. It consulted the members of a craft before finalizing the technical articles of the statutes applicable to the given craft and sometimes allowed them to choose the inspectors of their craft. Generally speaking, access to membership in the craft remained unrestricted.

The sworn crafts were to be found in *villes jurées*. The sworn craft was one which had "the right of forming a corporation or community which one entered by taking an oath." They were also called *"corps politiques"* or *"corporations."* In the edicts they were referred to as *"maîtrises et jurandes." Maîtrise,* or mastership, meant the quality that a craftsman acquired when he was received as master in a corporation of craftsmen. *Jurande* meant a position in a corporation of artisans which one acquired by election, entitling the holder to preside over the assembly, admit apprentices and master craftsmen, enforce the statutes and regulations of the craft, and prevent encroachments on the field reserved to the craft; there were between two and four *jurandes* in each sworn craft.

The sworn craft embraced, as a matter of obligation, all those who wished to practice the given trade. Entry into it was subject to an apprenticeship under a master craftsman, service as a journeyman, tests of mastership, payment of entrance fees, and the taking of an oath. The sworn craft drew up its own rules and elected representatives to deal with matters of common concern, enforce observation of the rules, manage the craft's common funds and patrimonial property, and represent the craft in dealings with other crafts and with higher authority. The sworn craft was paralleled by a confraternity with religious and charitable purposes.

Paris was a *ville jurée,* and towns of this order were fairly widespread in northern France. Elsewhere, however, *villes jurées* were somewhat rare at the beginning of the 17th century. Lyons, Montpellier, Bordeaux, and Toulouse were not in this category. In Auvergne the only ones were Clermont, Thiers, and Ambert; in the other towns of that province the crafts were "free," with confraternities only. In Berry the only *villes jurées* were Bourges and Issoudun, and in Roussillon there was only Perpignan. In Béarn there were no sworn crafts at all. In the kingdom as a whole they were in a minority.

Certain crafts had been made into domanial offices in a number of towns, such as the sworn measurers or porters of grain, the sworn sellers of poultry, the sworn porters and measurers of salt, or *hanouards,* the sworn inspectors and testers of beer, and so on. The importance of their functions had caused them to be made direct delegates of public authority; their offices were hereditary but could be sold on condition that the right of redemption remained permanent. They formed a body of administrative officers, exercising, with perhaps greater safeguards for the public, the functions of public interest which were also exercised by the sworn craft. Thus, an edict of 1625 created six offices of sworn inspectors and testers of beer in Paris. In 1629 the Paris community of brewers bought up these offices, and the *jurés* of the community thereafter carried out the inspections for which the officeholders were responsible and which the *jurés* had undertaken before these offices were created. Depending on circumstances, the interests of the public were entrusted either to representatives of the craft or to domanial officials.

There were intermediate cases. In some crafts, the number of members was restricted, and members were appointed by the local administrative authority, which also chose the syndic, although the craft was not an office; this was the case, for example, with the secondhand-clothes dealers of Nevers. At Autun the crafts were "sworn," but certain master craftsmen were allowed to remain outside the craft; and so on.

Some crafts were grouped in federations. Certain federations brought together crafts which, though "adjacent," were distinct and interconnected, such as the different stages of a production process; for example, washers of wool, combers, carders, spinners, warpers, weavers, fullers, shearers, and dyers elected *jurés* in common for the cloth industry in a particular place. Other federations grouped members of the same craft operating in a given territorial area; for example, among boatmen, there was the "Community of merchants using the River Loire and its tributaries,'' consisting of twenty-two corporations, which sent representatives to a general assembly at Orléans every three years.

The organization and functioning
of the sworn crafts

The sworn crafts were corporations regularly organized within the state. Being moral persons, each had a seal, the symbol of its personality and affixture of which committed it. They had armorial bearings, just like physical persons (in the case of the Mercers of Paris, three ships, *argent*, flying the flag of France, with the motto *Gemina gens nota sub axe*), and they struck and circulated tokens bearing their arms in the same way as the clergy of France, the provincial estates, and the municipalities. They had their own banners. Tradition determined their rank in the public ceremonies to which they were regularly summoned: the entries of kings, princes, and governors, Te Deums, fireworks displays, processions, inaugurations of fairs, executions. The Six Corporations of Paris (the clothiers, grocers, mercers, furriers, goldsmiths, and hosiers) possessed the privilege of holding a canopy over the king when he made his first entry into Paris, and in 1643 they were permitted to compliment the king on his coronation.

However, these "persons" were not purely private in character but served purposes of general concern. Their aim was to reconcile the legitimate interests of their members with the common good. The craft had to provide the means of life to the individual craftsman and his family but also to others. Serving the common good was the craft's duty as an "estate." It was necessary to ensure that bread, wine, clothes, and so on should never be lacking, that work should never stop, and that the products of this work should be good and cheap. Craftsmen performed a public service.

Accordingly, the king subjected the crafts to control for the "common benefit," the "common good," the "public good," which was the very purpose of the royal function. From this idea there followed the one expressed in the preamble to the letters of 23 March 1673: the king wishes to reform the abuses of the corporations "so as to keep them within the rules and discipline needed for the maintenance of the estates." The "estates" referred to here were the social conditions and functions which had to be maintained in their customary mutual equilibrium for the sake of the common good.

From this idea there followed, too, an idea that was clearly appreciated from the end of the 16th century and doubtless even earlier. A group of merchants or craftsmen may have been formed spontaneously long since, through necessity, but it does not exist as a corporation until it has been established by the king through letters patent making it a sworn craft. The king alone can transform a craft into a corporation, giving it a statute and granting it immunities and privileges "so as to encourage the craftsmen to perfect themselves in their skill and to serve the public faithfully" (Le Bret, *De la souveraineté du roi,* vol. 4, p. 15).

Instead of royal letters patent transforming a craft into a corporation, the craft might be satisfied with asking the king to give approval to its statutes—approval which in itself implied official recognition of this corporation. The statutes were a reduction to writing of customs resulting from a series of repeated public actions which had not given rise to serious contradictions. The king was, in fact, recognizing a customary constitution.

Finally, if the king did not intervene, the crafts could obtain recognition and approval of their statutes from the *parlement,* the presidial courts, the *bailliages* and *sénéchaussées,* or even from the seignorial administrative judges, the *baillis* of the *seigneuries,* who were all representatives of the king. In these cases, though, the statutes possessed less authority and were not regarded as being perpetual.

The king entrusted the sworn crafts with tasks of public concern which fulfilled two purposes: first, to ensure adequate returns to the members of the craft by protecting them against various forms of unbridled competition and guaranteeing mutual aid; second, to ensure, for the public, continuous service by persons of recognized professional capacity, making and offering for sale in sufficient quantity products of good quality at a just price.

The sworn craft was made up essentially of the master craftsmen, forming a *corps politique,* an "aristo-democracy," governed by an assembly, a council, and a *bureau.* Ordinary assemblies of master craftsmen were held for the election of *jurés* and for approval of their management of the craft during their year of office; extraordinary ones were held for the revision of statutes, the raising of loans, selling of property, etc. The council gave the *jurés* its views on important questions when requested to do so. In the case of the butchers of Paris, the council had twenty-four members: twelve former *jurés* and six experienced and six junior master craftsmen. The bureau consisted of *jurés* to the number of two, three, four, or six, elected by the assembly, approved by the royal judge, and mandated by the community to represent it and act on its behalf. The *jurés* were given different titles in different crafts: *gardes, maîtres jurés, maîtres gardes, prudhommes, visiteurs, syndics*.

The *jurés* could act in the name of the corporation before the king's Council, the *parlement*, the *bailliage* or the *prévôté*, using the various procedures which have been described in connection with the assemblies of the clergy of France and the syndics of the clergy: remonstrances, petitions, oppositions to the king's letters patent or the Council's *arrêt*, interventions, third-party oppositions. In relation to the members of the craft, the *jurés* operated by visitations, searches, and seizures, statements about which they drew up and passed to the officers of justice and police so that they might pronounce judgment and take the necessary steps. The *jurés* had a body of documents at their disposal: collections of statutes, letters patent, Council *arrêts*, and verdicts handed down by various courts.

The sworn craft fulfilled public tasks. It controlled its own recruitment in order to ensure professional competence. Whoever wished to enter the craft had to begin as an apprentice. Apprenticeship took three years, as a rule, but four in the case of apothecaries and five in that of goldsmiths. No master craftsman might take on more than two apprentices; this was to ensure that they were well taught. A contract of apprenticeship was signed with each, and, at the end of his "time," the apprentice was given a certificate.

Some crafts required also a period as a journeyman, following apprenticeship. This took three years in the case of bakers and grocers, six years in that of apothecaries, and eight in that of butchers. Even when this period was not formally required, however, the former apprentices, even if they were sons of master craftsmen, in most instances remained journeymen for a few years in order to perfect their skills. Certain crafts—the locksmiths, joiners, carpenters, blacksmiths, and stonemasons—practiced the *tour de France*. Engagements of journeymen were for one year. Wages were freely agreed upon and were subject to an oral contract. At the end of his engagement the journeyman was given a letter of release.

In order to become a master craftsman one had to be a person of good life and morals, a Catholic (after the revocation of the Edict of Nantes), of the required age (twenty-eight for butchers), and able to prove completion of one's apprenticeship and one's service as a journeyman, where that was necessary, and to pass a professional examination—the *chef-d'oeuvre,* or "masterpiece." In the case of the Paris butchers, the candidate had to "dress" an ox, a sheep, and a calf, that is, to remove the hide, extract the entrails, and prepare the meat for cutting up and cooking, all this in the presence of the bureau of the corporation and eight senior members. In the case of the bakers, the candidate had, in the presence of the six *jurés* of the craft, to use three *setiers* of flour to make various kinds of dough and bread. In the case of the apothecaries, a three-hour examination in theory was carried out by the master apothecaries, assisted by two doctors of the Faculty of Medicine who were lecturers in pharmacy; then the candidate had to identify the various herbs and explain their medicinal use, and finally he prepared five medicaments indicated by the jury. The judgment of this *chef-d'oeuvre* was often performed in the presence of the local *juge de police.*

Candidates for mastership paid a sum of money on acceptance, as their contribution to the common expenditures of the craft, and also an alms for the poor in the hospital, fees for the members of the jury, and a due to the king. Then they swore an oath—first to the bureau of the corporation, then between the hands of the *juge de police.* In Paris, they were presented to the *procureur du roi* at the Châtelet. Their oath bound them "to observe the rules and to show honor and respect to the *jurés* and allow them to make their visitations." Sometimes it was the corporation, sometimes the administrative judge, that delivered the letters of mastership to the new master; in every case, he was entered in the register of the community.

The craft defended the common interests of the master craftsmen. A craft was looked upon as a family property, with the master's authority over his journeymen compared to the domestic authority of a pater-familias. It was generally believed that heredity was the best method of recruitment to the various callings of society. Consequently, where sons of master craftsmen were concerned, the period of apprenticeship was shortened, they were relieved of the need to perform a *chef-d'oeuvre,* and the dues payable on acceptance as master were reduced. However, in many corporations, such as the goldsmiths of Paris, a master's son was obliged to perform a *chef-d'oeuvre* like anyone else. A widow could continue to practice her husband's craft, on the sole condition that she engaged a capable journeyman; she was often given priority in the hiring of journeymen.

The craft sought to reduce competition between master craftsmen as far as possible. A master who had one journeyman was not allowed to obtain a second until all the other masters had one. Enticement of journeymen was forbidden. A master might not have more than two apprentices.

Monopolizing of raw materials was forbidden. Frequently the raw material of a craft—wool, wood, iron, dyestuffs—was divided up and distributed by lot. It was forbidden to resell raw material to another master or to someone working at home.

Each master had to have only one workplace or one stall. Places in public markets were distributed among the masters by lot. Masters were forbidden to engage in peddling. Goods could be advertised through the public criers, but the issuing of handbills for the purpose was forbidden.

Prices were uncontrolled. Masters were not allowed to get together to fix a price. Among the printers of copperplate engravings in Paris, the statutes of 1694 provided for a common purse in which every master was to deposit one-third of his profits. The contents of the purse were shared out among the masters once a fortnight.

The craft sought to reduce competition from other crafts as much as possible. The sworn craft was alone qualified to do a certain kind of work in the given society. It was responsible for doing this work as well as possible. It had the right to have this work reserved for it. The craft therefore fought against persons who tried to meddle in its work: journeymen who, instead of working for a master, worked at home on their own account (*chambrelans, croque-chats, faux ouvriers*). The *jurés* had the right to carry out searches in the houses of persons who gave shelter to these men.

The craft combated encroachments by "neighboring" crafts. There were continual disputes between locksmiths and farriers, chandlers and apothecaries, *grands bouchers* and *petits bouchers*. A lawsuit between the tailors and the secondhand-clothes dealers lasted from 1427 to 1766. The *rôtisseurs* sold all roast meat and had a monopoly of the cooking and selling of poultry, game of all kinds, and kids and lambs. They asserted, against the butchers' opposition, the right to purchase live calves and sheep for their trade, and the *prévôt* of Paris had to compel them in 1648 to get their veal and mutton from the butchers.

The craft sought to ensure that work was carried out honestly, in the interest of the public. In the first place, it shared in the demarcation of functions by the public authorities, with the purpose of preventing intrusion by incompetents, overlapping, and "moonlighting," by means of regulations which had to be changed continually as new techniques were introduced and as public taste changed.

The statutes of the craft included rules concerning materials and techniques to be employed, meticulous regulations aimed at ensuring the quality of the product. The master craftsman put his individual mark on every object that he made. A copy of this mark was kept by the *jurés* of the craft and another copy by the authority of justice and police. There was also a corporation mark: after checking by the *jurés*, a seal bearing the emblem of the corporation would be affixed, at the craft's headquarters, to the end of a length of cloth, for example.

Strikes, combinations, "monopolies," anything that might interrupt work, endanger supplies, or bring about increased prices, were strictly forbidden. Furthermore, in times of dearth and scarcity, wages were reduced by judicial authority.

The craft participated in tasks of legislation, government, and administration. When elections were held in the *bailliages* and *sénéchaussées* for deputies to the Estates General, the craftsmen gathered in their respective communities to elect their deputies to the town assembly, which in turn elected the town's deputies to the assembly of the *bailliage* or *sénéchaussée*. The craft communities compiled *cahiers* of grievances, providing effective representation of the craftsmen.

The craft communities carried out administrative functions on the king's behalf. The boatmen of the Loire ensured at their own expense the navigability of that river and its tributaries. The grocers of Paris acted as keepers of the standard of weight for the royal demesne in the town of Paris, for they were merchants "*d'avoirs de poids*," that is, of goods of high value, which were *weighed,* whereas more ordinary goods were measured. The mercers were the keepers of the standard ell. As a rule, the sworn crafts had the duty of seeing to the fulfillment of the administrative ordinances issued by the judges and *lieutenants de police*. The regulations laid down by these authorities were notified to the communities concerned and had to be entered in their registers; sometimes they even had to be posted in the headquarters of the communities.

Certain crafts which were in continual contact with the public, such as the makers and sellers of wafers and the town criers, had responsibilities in the sphere of information. Each master wafer-maker in Bourges swore, when he was accepted into the craft, that "if anything should come to his notice that concerned the king's service and the welfare of the town, he would warn MM. the mayor and aldermen."

The crafts of the building trade—roofers, carpenters, masons—were assigned the task of fighting fires.

The crafts owed services of watch and ward, but these had been commuted for taxes, so as to ensure that they were carried out by professionals.

The crafts had to pay special contributions of various kinds, voluntary or otherwise, in time of war. In grave situations they even had to perform military service. On 4 August 1636, when the emperor's forces were advancing on Paris, the king summoned the representatives of the crafts to the Louvre and asked for their help. With enthusiasm, they pledged to the king their bodies and their possessions, and the king embraced the syndic of the cobblers. The crafts closed all workshops except those that were strictly necessary to provide food and make arms. The *jurés* of each craft furnished lists of men capable of serving, and all joined up. The crafts taxed themselves to furnish equipment and arms for these forces. This makeshift army was provided with noble commanders and stiffened with some regular troops. The king rode at their head. The Imperialists failed to cross the Oise and fell back in retreat.

Thus, the sworn crafts, like the other corporations of the kingdom, collaborated with the king in legislation, government, and administration. Besides their particular economic function, they fulfilled an increasing number of public functions on behalf of the state, in its place, on its initiative, and under its supervision.

The craft corporations and communities survived without essential change until the reign of Louis XVI. Inspired by the Physiocrats, the Comptroller General of Finance Turgot saw in "the very faculty accorded to the members of a craft to come together and form a corporation" the source of several evils. For the state it meant a shrinkage of trade and "industrious works," since the corporation's monopoly reduced the number of manufacturers. For the workers it meant a loss of wages and livelihood, owing to the reduction in competition. For the townsfolk, it meant the need to deal with workers belonging to different communities even where the simplest kind of work was required, and it also meant worse quality and higher prices than would otherwise prevail. Considering that the "right to work" is "every man's possession, and this possession is the first, most sacred, and most imprescriptible of all," Turgot had it proclaimed that "all persons of whatever quality and condition, even all foreigners," were free "to espouse and practice throughout our kingdom whatever kind of commerce or craft they may choose, and even to combine several," and that "all corporations of merchants and craftsmen, together with all *maîtrises and jurandes*" were to be abolished (Edict of Versailles, February 1776).

After Turgot's departure, the edict of August 1776 modified his reform but did not rescind it. In Paris, twenty-one groups of crafts remained "free," while forty-four new corporations and communities united "occupations which are similar to each other" and which until then had formed separate corporations. The edict opened the new communities to women and girls and to foreigners, who were also freed from liability to escheat. It permitted persons to practice more than one craft and to practice anywhere in the kingdom. It provided for new statutes and regulations, and there was no longer to be any requirement of *chef-d'oeuvre*. On the other hand, confraternities and associations of journeymen were banned.

The king hoped in this way to retain what was good in the old corporative system—internal discipline, authority of the masters over the workmen, aid to the State—together with what was good in Turgot's edict—freedom, emulation, competiton. The edict was definitely to the advantage of the masters as against the workmen. The provisions of the edict of August 1776 were extended to Lyons (January 1777); to the area under the jurisdiction of the *parlement* of Paris, where a certain number of towns were given new craft communities after the suppression of the old ones, with work and enterprise remaining free of regulation elsewhere (April 1777); and to the areas subject to the jurisdiction of the *parlements* of Normandy (edicts of February 1778 and April 1779), Nancy, and Metz and of the *conseil souverain* of Roussillon (edicts of May 1779 and July 1780). Turgot's achievement was thus not ruined.

The commercial corporations: The East India and other joint-stock companies

In principle, wholesale trade, maritime trade, banking, and money-changing were all "free" spheres of activity. Actually, attempts at organization were made in some of these sectors. Numerous towns had corporations of commercial brokers and *agents de change*. The most notable corporations were the companies concerned with shipping, commerce, and colonization. Chartered joint-stock companies had become numerous since the great discoveries of the 15th century. They were necessary in order to assemble capital and reduce competition. In 1604 Henri IV established the Compagnie des Indes, which in 1615 became the Compagnie des Moluques, and which collapsed in face of the enmity of the Dutch. Richelieu initiated several companies which failed owing to the Thirty Years' War. After the Peace of the Pyrenees, letters patent of August 1664 established the East India Company and the West India Company. This was a royal initiative, an operation of national prestige. The king appealed to the need to convert the infidels, to patriotism, to loyalty to the monarchy. He urged the merchants, the nobles, and the magistrates of the *parlements* to subscribe, and he himself put up one-fifth of the capital. He was the principal shareholder and the protector of the companies. But he was using for a purpose of public benefit the old corporative structure, which was customary and so, in its origin, spontaneous.

Here, too, we find the reciprocal relationship of king and society, state and society, with the king utilizing the structures of society for the good of society and the state as he conceived this good. But he was also utilizing the long-established forms of old structures in order to create the conditions for new structures.

The East India Company was, in fact, a moral person, with a name, a domicile, a seal, armorial bearings, and a flag. It was charged with the fulfillment of public tasks, not merely developing overseas trade but also evangelizing and conquering. Consequently, it was given a monopoly. For a period of fifty years it was to enjoy a monopoly of trade in the regions between the Cape of Good Hope, to the west, and the Strait of Magellan, to the east, with commercial privileges: exemption from customs dues and subsidies for goods exported or imported. It was given regalian rights, being allowed to maintain an army and a navy, to declare war and make peace, to conclude alliances and sign treaties. It had a constitution and a government. The general assembly of shareholders made decisions and elected directors to carry them out. Of these twenty directors, nine remained in Paris, while the rest went wherever they were needed. They were mostly merchants, but Colbert represented the king among them. The directors wielded extensive powers. If a difference arose between directors and shareholders or among the shareholders, the parties chose three directors, and this arbitration tribunal gave final judgment in the matter.

This corporation was thus a veritable state. However, it remained subject to the king. He was, in effect, its *seigneur*. The company held its territories of him as a fief, with obligation of faith and homage. The company owed him fealty, counsel, and aid. The king owed the company protection and, consequently, supervision. We have here a very interesting case of the utilization of feudal forms and the sentiment of fealty in order to secure obedience to an absolute monarch on the part of a state organism the power of which was based in distant lands, over which the authority of the king's agents remained very slight.

Furthermore, after 1668 the king appointed to sit among the members of the company's council "commissioners of superintendence" who were to represent the interests of the king and the public. They were entrusted with looking after the common good of the kingdom, while the directors ran the company as a commercial business which had to make money for the shareholders. In practice, previous agreement between directors and commissioners was necessary before a decision could be made. In case of conflict between them, it was for the minister who supervised the company's affairs to settle the matter.

Feudal forms were thus combined with forms of tutelage so as better to ensure the authority of the state. The organization of the company made it possible to carry on the work of colonization without committing a government that had its hands full.

In this way, corporations, integrated into the state and under the absolute authority of the king, secured the common good of every profession or calling. They directed and disciplined the efforts of individuals so as to serve the lasting ends of society. In order that the activity of the corporations should conform to the common good of society and the state, the king supervised them, confirming or correcting their actions. The frontiers between the activities of these corporations often overlapped, and it was the king's responsibility to arbitrate the resulting conflicts, to ensure the common good of the whole realm. But the king did not direct the corporations or regulate their activities. He allowed them to act as "little occupational commonwealths whose citizens themselves conducted their affairs." He obtained their views and allowed their "oppositions" in accordance with the forms and procedures of law. He negotiated with them and did not impose his own decision except in grave and urgent cases. "The corporations are the various links in a chain that extends from families to empires, facilitating relations among men."

Notes

1. "Remontrances du Parlement de Paris sur l'édit supprimant les jurandes, 2–4 mars 1776," in J. Flammermont, ed., *Les Remontrances du Parlement de Paris au XVIIIᵉ siècle* (Paris, 1898), vol. 3, p. 309.

2. Bernard de La Roche-Flavin, *XIII livres des parlements de France* (1617), vol. 11, pp. 643–44.

3. The officials of the presidial court of Montauban to Séguier, 4 May 1633 (Leningrad, Saltykov-Shchedrin Library, Dubrovsky Collection, 108/1, item 1). The *présidents* and

trésoriers généraux de France in the *bureau des finances* established at Caen to Séguier, 24 October 1636 (ibid., item 32).
  4. Bibliothèque Nationale, Clairambault 653, folio 17, recto, 10 January 1595; folio 76, verso, 6 March 1595. Lucien Romier, *Lettres et chevauchées du bureau des finances de Caen* (1910), no. 107, 25 February 1599; no. 116, 23 October 1599; no. 124, 7 January 1601; no. 131, 8 June 1601. *Parlement de Paris*, X 1A 1754, folio 6, verso, 21 January 1598; folio 8 verso, 23 January 1598; folios 67 verso and 68 recto, 29 January 1598; folio 79 recto, 30 January 1598; folio 119, 5 February 1598.

Guide to further reading

François Olivier-Martin's masterly work, *L'Organisation corporative de la France d'Ancien Régime* (Sirey, 1938), gives everything essential, plus a bibliography. In addition, see the following works.

Bluche, François. *Les magistrats du Parlement de Paris au XVIIIᵉ siècle.* Besançon: Jacques & Demontrond, 1960.
————. *Les magistrats du Grand Conseil au XVIIIᵉ siècle (1690–1791).* Les Belles Lettres, 1966.
————. *Les magistrats de la Cour des Monnaies de Paris au XVIIIᵉ siècle, 1715–1790.* Les Belles Lettres, 1966.
————. *Les officiers du Bureau des Finances de Paris au XVIIIᵉ siècle, 1693–1791.* Bulletin de la Société de l'Histoire de Paris et de l'Ile-de-France, no. 97 (1970).
Charmeil, Jean-Paul. *Les trésoriers de France à l'époque de la Fronde.* Picard, 1964.
Cornaert, Emile. *Les corporations en France avant 1789.* 1941.
Lespinasse, R. de. *Les métiers et corporations de la Ville de Paris.* (Series "Histoire générale de Paris.") 3 vols. 1879, 1886, 1892.
Martin-Saint-Léon, E. *Histoire des corporations de métier.* 4th ed., 1941.
Mousnier, Roland, ed. *Lettres et mémoires adressés au chancelier Séguier, 1633–1649.* P.U.F., 1964.
————. *La vénalité des offices sous Henri IV et Louis XIII.* 2d ed., P.U.F., 1970.
————, Goubert, Pierre; Tapié, Victor-Lucien; et al. "Serviteurs du Roi: Quelques aspects de la fonction publique dans la société française du XVIIᵉ siècle," *XVIIᵉ Siècle,* nos. 42–43 (1959).
Yardeni, Myriam. "L'Ordre des avocats et la grève du barreau parisien en 1602," *Revue d'Histoire économique et sociale* (1966), pp. 481–507.

11

The Territorial Communities
The *Seigneuries*

The legal position of the *seigneuries*

The kingdom of France and the lands and lordships under the sway of the king of France were
societies of property-owners grouped in territorial
communities regarded as corporations: villages,
towns, *seigneuries,* provinces.

A *seigneurie* was still in most cases a territorial
community, but the word also signified a form of
real property so important in the eyes of the jurists
of the regions where customary law prevailed that
many of them were inclined to call any and every
form of real property a *seigneurie.*

A form of real property that was still widespread at this time, accounting sometimes for a
tenth of all the land in the regions subject to written law, was the allodial form, the freehold. It
could be defined as "that which belongs so absolutely and independently to its possessor that he
acknowledges no lord of it but God" (Nicolas
Chevrier, *Dauphinois*). In Dauphiné, freehold
had retained from the Roman period the character
of *dominium ex jure quiritium,* for that province
had, under the Romans, always enjoyed the *jus
italicum.* This *dominium* was a right of ownership
that was absolute, exclusive, and perpetual. It
comprised three parts: the *jus utendi,* or right
to make use of a thing; the *jus fruendi,* or
right to collect its fruits; and the *jus abutendi,*

477

or right to divide the thing, alienate it, or destroy it. The owner could concede the *jus utendi* and *jus fruendi* to someone else, but he remained the "bare owner"; those to whom he granted the rights possessed and enjoyed real property that did not belong to them, for they had only *jura in re aliena,* rights in something alien to them. In Dauphiné this natural liberty of the lands of the province had been expressly reserved in 1349 in the deed by which the last independent dauphin, Humbert II, transferred the Dauphiné to the eldest son of the duke of Normandy, the future King Charles V of France. It was confirmed by letters patent of Henri II dated 15 January 1555, by an *arrêt* of the *parlement* of Grenoble on article 383 of the ordinance issued by Chancellor De Marillac in January 1629, and finally by the edict of October 1658. The other regions under written law enjoyed only provincially recognized rights, and landholders there had only precarious and revocable possession, a situation which in the 17th and 18th centuries facilitated the king's attacks on freehold.

The owner of a noble freehold might have powers of justice and might grant land as a fief or a *censive* or lease it to a tenant. Consequently, a noble freehold constituted a *seigneurie.* However, this *seigneurie* was not a fief dependent on a higher *seigneur.* It did not enter into the feudal hierarchy. The owner of a "commoner" freehold could only lease his land to a tenant, for ground rent.

The other forms of ownership of real property, which were by far the most widespread, were the *seigneurie,* the noble fief, and the "commoner" fief or *censive.*

For Loyseau, writing his *Traité des seigneuries* before 1609, *seigneurie* signified "power in ownership." According to him, the word *seigneur* was derived from Latin *senior,* because persons of age and experience were, originally, appointed to offices, and *seigneurie* meant, at first, "office," "magistracy." *Seigneurie* was synonymous with authority and superiority. The *seigneuries* had, as time went by, become property, and the word *seigneurie* had ended by signifying a piece of private property. Loyseau therefore distinguished between two kinds of *seigneuries,* the public and the private. Public *seigneurie* meant possession of superiority and authority over persons and things. This conferred a right to command and public power. Supreme public power was possessed by the state. Public power that was superior but not supreme was lodged in fiefs to which powers of justice were attached. Private *seigneurie* was "true ownership and present enjoyment of some thing," which the *seigneur* could use as he liked; the *seigneurie directe* was that of the feudal *seigneurs,* or *censuels,* and the *seigneurie utile* was that of their subjects who had to pay *cens* to them. The public *seigneur* wielded authority and judicial powers and could compel his subjects to go to war, pay taxes, and so on. The private *seigneurs*, his subjects, retained to the full, however, their personal liberty and their property.

The *seigneurie* in the strict sense of the word—which is the subject of this chapter—was an amalgam of public and private *seigneurie*. It was often called *"terre, fief, et seigneurie."* In this expression, *terre* stood for the demesne that the *seigneur* kept for himself, the *seigneurie utile; fief* meant the *seigneurie directe;* and *seigneurie* meant public *seigneurie* or rights of justice, with the power of command and administration that followed from this. These three elements had to be present for the territorial community called a *seigneurie* to exist. Rights of justice could be detached from a fief and yet leave it still a fief, but they could not be detached from a *seigneurie*. A person who acquired rights of justice, separately, could call himself *"seigneur justicier,"* and a person who acquired a fief by itself could call himself *"seigneur* of such and such a fief." But the only person who could call himself simply *seigneur*— "absolutely, without definition or appendage"—was one who possessed "true and perfect *seigneurie"*: demesne, fief, and justice. The word *terre* designated, on its own, all the revenue derived from the demesne and from the exercise of seignorial and feudal rights. Ownership of a *seigneurie* constituted a social dignity. "There are three kinds of dignities—Order, Office, and *Seigneurie*—and these are the three titles of honor with which we can qualify and accompany our names" (Loyseau, *Seigneuries* [1640], p. 3, par. 7).

The hierarchy of seigneuries

There was a hierarchy of *seigneuries*. The great ones were those which had a title that could imply sovereignty: peerages, duchies, marquisates, counties, principalities. The middle-ranking ones were those that bore a title of dignity not implying sovereignty: baronies, viscounties, *vidamés,* castellanies. The petty or ordinary *seigneuries* were those to which no title of dignity was attached: those with rights of high, middle, and low justice only.

The great *seigneuries* were held as fiefs from the sovereign, with direct appeal to him, while the middle-ranking ones were held as fiefs from the great ones, and the petty ones as fiefs from those of middle rank; thus, the two second categories were held only "mediately" from the sovereign.

The king alone could create *seigneuries* and establish new powers of justice, even if local custom accorded this right to barons and castellans, for no custom could annul the rights of the king.

According to the edict of 1579, in order to be made into a castellany, a *"terre"* had to comprise rights of high, middle, and low justice, the right to hold a fair and a market, the powers of a *prévôt,* and preeminence over the local churches; a barony could be created out of three castellanies held of the king by a single act of homage; for a county it was necessary to have two baronies and three castellanies, or one barony and six castellanies, held of the king by a single act of homage; and a marquisate required three baronies and three castellanies, or two baronies and six castellanies, held of the king by a single act of homage. However, the edict was not always observed.

The great *seigneuries*—peerages, duchies, marquisates, counties, and principalities—were held directly from the Crown and the king and could be held from no one else. Homage for them was rendered in the *chambre des comptes* in Paris. They were honorary sovereignties and shared in the honors of sovereignty. Their armorial bearings were therefore crowned with a crest: in the case of dukes, a coronet of *fleurons;* in that of counts, one of pearls; for marquises, a crenellated coronet; and, for a principality, a simple diadem. The great *seigneuries* were indivisible in the sense that, though part of their demesne could be granted out as fief or *cens,* to the king's disadvantage and without his permission, creating subfiefs or enfeoffed *cens,* no powers of justice could be given therewith.

Duchies, marquisates, and counties created subsequent to the ordinance of the demesne issued in 1566 were subject to reversion to the Crown if there was no male heir descending from the person for whom the fief had been created. The same rule applied to the appanages of the king's sons. However, it did not affect duchies, marquisates, and counties that antedated the ordinance, for they were transmissible to daughters and to collaterals of the original vassal. Furthermore, the king frequently authorized departures from the ordinance of 1566.

Peers of France took precedence of all dukes, marquises, and counts. They had the right to sit and take part in deliberations in the Paris *parlement* from the age of twenty. Cases affecting their honor or the status of their peerages were heard in the first instance by the Paris *parlement,* with all its chambers assembled. Appeals from their courts went directly to the *parlement,* without passing through the courts of the *baillis* and *sénéchaux.*

Middle-ranking seigneurs—viscounts, *vidames,* barons, castellans—had the right to wear their armorial bearings in square form, in contrast to *écuyers,* mere *gentilshommes,* who were allowed to wear them only as escutcheons. However, they did not make use of this right. They crested their arms, like captains, with a helmet that was gilded and open, and could call themselves *chevaliers.* Their *seigneuries* were specially assigned to nobles. They possessed *droit de bailliage,* that is, the right to maintain a higher court for trying major cases, and so employed *baillis* who held assizes for such cases: capital crimes, affairs involving their *domestiques* and those, mainly *gentilshommes,* who were under their guardianship, and complaints against the officers of the ordinary courts and appeals against their sentences—except where the rights of their vassals to whom they had granted all powers of justice were involved, since they could then no longer grant powers of guardianship in the areas affected.

The middle-ranking *seigneurs* had the right to appoint notaries, enforce police measures, and make public proclamations, for they had authority to command as well as jurisdiction. Their police function consisted in making regulations to ensure conditions of tranquillity and convenience for the people. These regulations concerned foodstuffs and the "small-scale trade" for the day-to-day support of people's lives: control of weights and measures, with the *droit de grands poids* (which meant the exclusive right to have in a given town big scales for weighing more than 25 pounds, and to collect 12 *deniers* for every 100 pounds weighed), the *droit des grandes mesures* (meaning the right to appoint surveyors), and the *droit des petits poids et mesures* (the right to keep a standard). They also had power over the sworn crafts, with the right to authorize their establishment in accordance with the edict of 1597, seeing to the election every year of *jurés,* inspectors, and wardens, and to promulgate statutes and regulations for each craft. They were responsible for policing the highways, with the right to levy a toll. They had to see to the upkeep of roads, bridges, crossing places, and causeways, which implied the collection of tolls, known as *barrage* (from the barrier placed across a road), *pontenage, billot* (from the little block of wood hung from a tree), *branchière* (from the branch to which the block was fastened), *coutume,* or *droit de prévôté,* all these expressions signifying the same thing. To these rights was added a right to levy *travers* on all who crossed the *seigneur's* land—this due being payable, however, only by his subjects when they transported goods out of his territory. The middle-ranking *seigneurs* were expected to

keep the roads reliable and free and were therefore civilly responsible
for any robberies that might be committed on them.

The middle-ranking *seigneurs* made the administrative regulations,
but the judges employed by all the *seigneurs* saw to their application.

The middle-ranking *seigneurs* had *droit de notariat,* the right to authenticate contracts with their seals, and the *droit de ban,* the right to
make proclamations by sounding trumpets and having the public crier
read them, and to make *adjudications par décret.*

The middle-ranking *seigneurs* had the right to have a castle or "fortified house," with moats, drawbridges, and towers, and also the right
to prevent anyone from building anything like that on their territory, but they had no right to forbid a village to put walls round itself, if
it had the king's permission.

The petty *seigneuries,* with high, middle, and low justice, present a
picture of great diversity. According to Loyseau (*Seigneuries,* p. 102),
"All *seigneuries* . . . consist principally and formally in their power of
justice"—which is true, provided one does not forget the demesne and
the fief.

Having made these distinctions, we must now first define the law
governing fiefs, *censives,* and seignorial powers of justice in the 17th
and 18th centuries and then bring out some aspects of the actual role
they played in the society of those days.

The law of fiefs

The name "fief" was given to any piece of real property, or anything
regarded as such, which was granted on condition of faith and homage,
that is, in return for fealty and with the requirement of certain duties,
regulated either by the deed of enfeoffment or by custom. The grantor
retained ownership (*seigneurie directe*) while transmitting to the grantee the right to use the property and enjoy its fruits (*seigneurie utile*).
Not all property could be held as fief, but only lands and "*héritages,*"
rights to draw income from the soil, that is, from the property in respect of which the services were due, such as *censives, champarts,
vinages,* impropriated tithes, and so on, together with powers of justice
and also certain offices.

In principle, only nobles could hold fiefs. Commoners, *bourgeois,*
were excluded even if they were advocates, physicians, or professors.
Nevertheless, the king did allow them to hold fiefs on two conditions,
namely, that they paid a tax, the due of frank-fee, equivalent to "one

year's income in twenty,'' or 5 percent, and that they either served the
king in the *arrière-ban* or else, instead, paid a tax proportionate to the
value of the fief. The declaration of 9 March 1700 obliged all commoners acquiring noble lands to record the fact within a year and a day of
the acquisition and to pay frank-fee at the rate of one year of the
revenue expected from their noble property for twenty years to come;
this was confirmed by edicts of May 1708 and April 1751. This tax was
personal; if a father who was paying it died, his son was liable for it the
day after.

Exempt from frank-fee were the inhabitants or *"bourgeois"* of certain towns which had shown special loyalty and zeal in the king's
service: Paris, Périgueux.

In Dauphiné, commoners paid frank-fee in proportion to the period
for which they enjoyed possession of the property or else at each
change of monarch or every twenty-five, thirty, or forty years. However, on 16 May 1693 a declaration relieved all the commoners of
Dauphiné from frank-fee in return for a payment of 330,000 livres. This
exemption was confirmed by an *arrêt* of the Council dated 13 June
1713. On 11 January 1772, however, the *parlement* of Grenoble registered a declaration of 1771 which canceled exemptions.

Also excluded from the holding of fiefs were the *gens de mainmorte*—the Church, ecclesiastical communities, lay corporations, and
communities. Indeed, "with the passage of time, they would be able to
appropriate too large a part of the lands of the kingdom." Besides, they
were exempt from several charges and impositions, and they could not
perform the duties and services of the fiefs. The king could make it
possible for them to possess fiefs, but only by granting *lettres d'amortissement* in return for payment. In the case of fiefs directly dependent
on the king, this amounted to one-third of their value; for "commoner"
lands owing *cens* to the king, it was one-fifth; for fiefs that were held
immediately of the king as subfiefs, it was also one-fifth; and for
"commoner," *cens*-owing lands in the same situation, it was one-sixth.
If a chapter which had received *lettres d'amortissement* for a fief sold it
to a community, the latter had to seek similar permission, for these
lettres d'amortissement were personal. The same applied to a gift or a
legacy: if the donor or the testator did not pay the *amortissement,* then
the Church, as recipient of the gift or the legacy, had to pay it.

A private *seigneur* might also give a *personne de mainmorte* the right
to possess fiefs, in return for an indemnity. Since, like the Church, a
community, ecclesiastical or lay, never died, the *seigneur* would be

deprived of the rights that normally fell to him on the death of one of his vassals. Similarly, since the Church and communities did not sell their lands, the *seigneur* would lose the dues he could normally expect when sales took place (*quints et requints*). Since crimes committed by clerics were not imputed to the Church, the *seigneur* would not be able to confiscate the criminal's possessions. The *seigneur* was indemnified in the first place by a payment, called *profit de fief,* substituted for the casual rights he could have expected to collect and then by the provision of a man "*vivant, mourant, et confiscant*" as a right due to the *seigneur* of the fief in acknowledgment of his suzerainty. The Church or the community nominated an individual to stand in its place as "*vicaire de la mainmorte.*" When this man died, the *seigneur* exacted the dues he would normally have exacted at the death of his vassal if the latter had sold the land or had been found guilty of a crime.

If an individual bought a fief from a *personne de mainmorte,* he had to pay the *quints et requints.* If one *personne de mainmorte* bought a fief from another, the purchaser had to pay a fresh indemnity to the *seigneur.*

Those who had not discharged their due of *amortissement* had to pay the *nouvel acquêt,* a tax of 5 percent on the income from the fief for every year they had possessed it.

In certain cases, women were excluded from the holding of fiefs. They were barred from the Crown of France—the principal fief and source of all the rest. The appanages of the members of the royal family did not pass to girls if there was no male heir but instead returned to the Crown. According to the ordinance of 1566, confirmed by the Ordinance of Blois of 1579 (article 279), should the male line of succession fail, then counties, marquisates, and duchies were to be reunited with the Crown. An edict of 1711 repeated this ruling so far as duchies were concerned. By several of the regional customs, notably that of Paris (article 25), women in the collateral line were barred from succession to fiefs.

A vassal owed "faith and homage" and also *aveu et dénombrement.* "Faith" meant the oath of fealty. It included, either implicitly or explicitly, depending on the province, a promise to do no harm to the *seigneur*'s person, to refrain from injuring him by revealing his secrets or the strength of his forces, not to obstruct his justice, not to damage his property; to seek his advantage; and to help him with counsel and aid "against everyone except the king." In Dauphiné there were fiefs that were held without homage, by "faith" alone. Homage meant a vassal's commitment to being his *seigneur*'s "man," that is, to making himself useful to him. By the custom of Paris (article 63), homage was to be rendered in the following manner. The vassal went to the *seigneur*'s principal manor house or else to some other place designated by the *seigneur*. He asked if the *seigneur* was present, or if there was anyone else there authorized to receive acts of faith and homage. Then, bareheaded and divested of sword and spurs, he knelt on one knee and said to the *seigneur* or his representative "that he bears and renders him faith and homage . . . for the fief dependent upon him." He asked the *seigneur* to consent to receive him. If the *seigneur* was absent or had not appointed a representative, it sufficed to offer faith and homage before the main door of the manor house, after having called upon the *seigneur* three times in a loud voice, and then to notify a neighbor, leaving with him a certified copy of the deed of faith and homage, drawn up by a notary. If there was no manor house, the ceremony was held in some other place designated for the doing of homage.

Faith and homage had to be rendered whenever there was a change of either vassal or *seigneur*. If the vassal was new, he rendered faith and homage within forty days of his taking possession of the fief. If the *seigneur* was new, he had to call upon his vassals to render faith and homage by making general proclamation, informing the individuals concerned and fixing the dates and times.

Faith and homage were supposed to be rendered by the vassal in person, but it was possible for him to excuse himself, and the *seigneur* could accept it from a proxy provided with a special power of attorney in the proper form. Personal excuses regarded as valid were the vassal's illness, absence on public duty, performance of an office, madness, imprisonment, or captivity. Excuses due to reasons that were not personal but which were accepted were the difficulties of traveling because of war, floods, etc. Nuns whose rule kept them in seclusion were allowed to render homage through a proxy.

Faith and homage were due from the holder of the subordinate fief, not from a usufructuary, such as the widow or a younger brother, and they had to be rendered to the holder of the dominant fief, not to the usufructuary.

By the custom of Paris, the age of majority was twenty-five, but under feudal laws boys came of age at twenty and girls at fifteen.

In some cases, faith and homage could be rendered by a community of inhabitants to their *seigneur* in consideration of the fact that they were living on his land, even though they held no *héritage* of him.

Thus, certain feudal forms still survived, but their bearing had been weakened and their symbolism was fading. Faith and homage had formerly entailed the obligation to follow the *seigneur* to the wars, but now military service was owed to the king alone. Faith and homage could make a vassal a liegeman: *ligius ligatus domino suo,* the vassal, bound to his seigneur, promised and undertook to follow him in conflict with any and every adversary. But liege-homage survived only for fiefs that were directly dependent on the Crown. The vassal was thus relieved of his two principal obligations, so that it was clear that "the rendering of faith and homage is today nothing but a ceremony, and fiefs are no longer anything but a shadow of honor, mere skeletons despoiled of the sinews that formerly sustained and moved them" (Boutaric, p. 92). In Dauphiné the process went further. Investiture by the *seigneur*'s giving to the vassal the pen with which he had just signed the deed of sale, or by handing over a document authenticated by a notary, was no longer indispensable, for the Grenoble *parlement* had decided that, fiefs and *censives* being patrimonial, it was the deed of sale, as an instrument agreed to by both parties, that was essential, thereby anticipating articles 1138 and 1583 of the Civil Code. The relationship between man and man and the comradeship of war were disappearing from the background, and the fief was being treated like quiritarian property.

All the same, generally speaking a reciprocal obligation between *seigneur* and vassal did still exist. The vassal owed respect, obedience, and certain *droits utiles,* and the *seigneur* owed him protection and friendship.

"*Aveu et dénombrement* means an exact and detailed description of everything that goes to make up the subordinate fief, both in demesnes and in subfiefs and *censives,* rents, easements, *droits utiles et honorifiques,* preeminences, and prerogatives" (Renauldon, p. 12). *Dénombrement* had to be made in "conclusive" and "authentic" form, on parchment, certified by two notaries or by one notary and two witnesses, and submitted by the vassal within forty days of having been received for faith and homage at the principal manor house of the dominant fief and, if the latter was the Crown, at the Paris *chambre des comptes,* which had the document verified by the judges of the localities concerned. *Aveu et dénombrement* had to be performed, in the forms and within the period laid down, on pain of feudal attachment of the fief.

If the *seigneur* had not reached agreement with the vassal, he was obliged to render *aveu et dénombrement* within a fixed period—forty days by the custom of Paris, three months by that of Anjou, one year by that of Maine, thirty years by the customs of Brittany and Normandy. The vassal had to call upon his *seigneur* to declare that he had received the *aveu*. Should the *seigneur* refuse, the vassal had to "seek the reason for disapproval." If the *aveu* was not disapproved, the vassal then rendered "faith" to the *seigneur,* so as to confirm the stability and rights of the *seigneurie.*

If the *aveu* was rendered to the king, three copies had to be made— one for the *chambre des comptes,* one for the *bureau du domaine,* one for the vassal. The vassal had to obtain from the receiver of the demesne a certificate that he had no grounds for objecting to reception of the *aveu.* The *aveu* was then proclaimed by a royal tipstaff on three successive Sundays as the congregation emerged from High Mass in the parish churches of the fief. A copy was deposited at the *greffe* of the nearest royal court, so that it might be read at three public hearings. If no opposition was expressed, the *aveu et dénombrement* was accepted, by pronouncements of the ordinary royal judge, the *bureau du domaine,* and the *chambre des comptes.*

The *seigneur* received the *droits utiles* of the fief, *quint et requint, relief* and *rachat.*

The *quint* was also called *rachat* in Berry and *lods et ventes* in Anjou and Maine. It was one-fifth of the price of a fief that was sold and was payable to the *seigneur.* Thus, if the fief was sold for 20,000 livres, the *quint* to be paid was 4,000 livres. It was an indemnity due to the *seigneur* for selling the fief without the latter's permission. It was due in case of a sale, of an act equivalent to a sale, or of an exchange for a *rente* redeemable in cash. In the first half of the 17th century the *quint* was not due when exchanges took place, but it was made applicable to these cases by edicts and declarations of Louis XIV and the Council's *arrêt* of 12 December 1724. In the area subject to the custom of Paris it was due, under the revised custom of 1580, from the purchaser, whereas before that it had been payable by the seller. In Normandy the *quint* amounted to one-thirteenth, plus a *droit de rachat.* In Berry it was one year's income.

Acts considered equivalent to sale were: the constitution of a perpetual *rente* secured on the land, because this reduced the value of the inheritance and, consequently, the seignorial dues payable at the next change of possessor; a settlement come to on a contested inheritance, if this involved a change of possessor; and, in general, any change of possessor.

Certain holders of fiefs directly from the king were exempt from paying *quints et requints,* namely, *chevaliers* of the Order of the Holy Spirit, *secrétaires du roi,* and, after the edict of November 1690, members of the *parlement* and the *chambre des comptes.*

The *requint* was one-fifth of the amount of the *quint;* thus, if the *quint* came to 4,000 livres, the *requint* was 800 livres. This was not a generally payable due, since it had to be paid only when a contract expressly stated that the sale was being made *"francs-deniers au vendeur,"* that is, when the purchaser undertook to defray all the seignorial dues involved. This was always the case under the reformed custom of Paris and in the customs of Blois, Meaux, and other places. If a fief worth 5,000 livres was sold *"francs-deniers au vendeur,"* it was sold for only 4,000 livres, and so the seignorial dues to be paid were smaller and the *seigneur*'s interest suffered, since the *quint* was only 800 livres instead of 1,000. A *requint* of 160 livres served to reduce the seigneur's loss. Some customs, such as that of Orléans, expressly excluded payment of *requint.*

Seigneurs habitually remitted part of the *quint* so as to facilitate sales and collect the seignorial dues more frequently. So far as the king was concerned, the receivers of the demesne were instructed to remit one-third of the dues to purchasers who reported their acquisition of real property and paid their dues within three months of their contract. Dumoulin, commenting on article 1 of the custom of Paris, said that, since fiefs had their origin in benevolence and favor, a *seigneur* ought to behave kindly toward his vassal.

Relief et rachat, called *plaît* in Dauphiné and Poitou and *muage* or *muance* in other regions, was payable when a fief changed hands by succession. If succession passed in the direct line, it did not have to be paid, because there was continuity of *seigneurie* and the law looked on father and son, and even grandfather and grandson, as being one and the same person. In the areas subject to the customs of Anjou, Maine, Vexin Français, and Poitou, however, if liege-homage was involved, the *relief et rachat* had to be paid even by a successor in the direct line.

If succession followed the collateral line—brothers, sisters, uncles, aunts, cousins, nephews, nieces—one year's income had to be paid, calculated as the average of the previous three years. *Relief et rachat* was "so called because by means of this due one redeems (*rachète*) the reversion of the fief which ought normally to take place whenever the vassal dies without issue: *relief,* as though the *seigneur* has recovered the fief, or sets it up again (*relevat*) when it has fallen into decrepitude through reversion'' (Guy Coquille, *Institution du droit français,* under "*Fiefs*'').

By certain customs, *relief et rachat* was due when a fief changed hands by gift or exchange, unless the gift was effected by marriage contract or, in advance of inheritance, by an ascendant to a descendant. In the area subject to the customs of Anjou and Maine it was not payable when a fief passed from brother to sister or vice versa.

In Dauphiné and Languedoc there were, in addition to *quint, requint,* and *relief et rachat,* also *introge,* a due paid on entry into the fief, and *plaît,* payable at every change of *seigneur* or vassal, even in cases of gift or exchange, if this had been stipulated in the deed of sale.

The *seigneur* was provided with guarantees in the form of sanctions for nonfulfillment of obligations and of various arrangements.

By *saisie féodale* "the *seigneur* takes the subordinate fief into his hand and power in order to enjoy and exploit it.'' This was carried out when a vassal failed to render faith and homage, *aveu et dénombrement,* or failed to pay the seignorial dues or to fulfill his duties of respect, obedience, and service.

According to the custom of Paris, the *seigneur* was to notify his vassals that they must come and do homage to him within forty days. If they had not obeyed at the end of that period, he could seize the fief and take its produce for himself. If a vassal died, his heir had forty days from the date of death in which to do homage.

If *saisie féodale* was carried out because *aveu et dénombrement* had not been rendered, the *seigneur* was not permitted to seize the produce of the fief but had to appoint a commissioner who would account for this produce to the vassal after he had performed his duty.

In Anjou and Maine the *seigneur* could seize a fief during a period of one year and a day after the day when homage should have been done. After that, he had formally to summon the defaulting vassal, and, during the year and a day following this summons, he could still seize the fief—but not later.

The established practice was for *saisie* to be carried out by authority of the *seigneur*'s judge or, if he had none, by that of the superior judge, even though the *seigneur* was empowered to seize the fief by his own private authority. *Saisie féodale* applied for a three-year period, having to be renewed when this expired. The *seigneur* had to treat the fief like a good *paterfamilias,* not exhausting the soil or deforesting it or taking all the fish from the ponds, etc. He had to discharge all the seignorial dues and pay the taxes imposed in lieu of the *ban* and *arrière-ban.* In addition to the *saisie féodale,* there was the power of *commise,* an act of confiscation by which the *seigneur* acquired ownership of a vassal's fief. This could be invoked in cases of *désaveu* (when a vassal alleged that he did not hold his fief of the *seigneur*), felony, disloyalty, or perfidy, or if the vassal insulted the *seigneur* or committed an outrage against him, struck him, made war on him, accused him of treason, gave him the lie, tried to provoke a quarrel with him, fished in his ponds, snared his rabbits, or lay with his wife or his daughter, being a virgin. But the *seigneur* had to obtain a court ruling. In Dauphiné he was no longer allowed to ask for *commise* if a vassal had alienated his fief without his consent; he had to call three times upon the vassal to do him homage before he could ask for the procedure to be invoked (*chambre des comptes* of Dauphiné, 1698). In short, the magistrates showed themselves more concerned to safeguard property rights than to maintain the bonds between man and man.

Saisie féodale was a sanction. *Retrait féodal,* also called *prélation* or *retenue,* was not a sanction but a safeguard. After a sale, three sorts of redemption of what had been sold were possible. First, conventional redemption: a seller who had sold his heritage was allowed to recover it (*rachat,* or *réméré*) within the period stipulated in the contract of sale by reimbursing the purchaser. Second, *retrait lignager:* this was the right and power accorded by custom to a person to recover a piece of real property, part of the possessions "proper" to his lineage, which had been sold by a kinsman, so as to keep this property in the family. Third, *retrait féodal:* this was the right and power accorded to the *seigneur* to recover, or rather to retain by virtue of his authority over it, a fief held of him which had been sold by his vassal by reimbursing the purchaser for the price he had paid, together with his expenses and fair costs, including ground rent, feudal dependences, and impropriated tithes. "It was desired to compensate *seigneurs* in some way for the freedom that had been allowed to their vassals to dispose of their fiefs without the *seigneurs'* consent, by giving the latter the power to reunite a fief with the demesne or else to choose a vassal more acceptable than the purchaser from outside."

Retrait féodal did not obtain in all the custom areas. It was ruled out by the customs of Toulouse and Cahors as an infringement of common law. Nor did it obtain in all the jurisdictions of every *parlement.*

Almost all *parlements* considered that if a *seigneur* did not wish to invest a vassal whom he disliked but was not in a position to reimburse him for the price paid for the fief, then he could cede his right to do this to a third party. However, this was not accepted by the *parlements* of Toulouse and Grenoble, for whom the *seigneur* had to exercise the right of *retrait féodal* himself or not at all.

The king made little use of his right of *retrait féodal*, which would have enabled him quickly to reunite all fiefs with the royal demesne. The right was denied to the Church by most of the regional customs on the grounds that it could not meet the responsibilities of the fiefs. Where, however, it was permissible to cede one's right of *retrait féodal*, the Church was allowed to use the right on condition that it ceded the recovered fief within a year and a day; otherwise, it went back to the original purchaser.

In the regions of customary law, such as those where the customs of Paris, Anjou, Maine, Touraine, and Poitou applied, the exercise of *retrait lignager* took precedence over that of *retrait féodal*. If someone seeking to redeem a fief in order to keep it in the possession of his lineage found himself in competition with the enfeoffing *seigneur*, the latter had to give way. If the *seigneur* had already carried out his *retrait féodal*, the representative of the lineage could recover the property even from him. If the original purchaser was a member of the seller's lineage, the *seigneur* could not exercise either *retrait féodal* or *retrait lignager*. In the regions of written law, however, the feudal *seigneur* had priority over the representative of the lineage.

A vassal had the right to divide up his fief, sell it, exchange it, give it away, or lease out part of it for rent. By the custom of Paris he had to get the *seigneur*'s consent. Nevertheless, the vassal could "*se jouer de son fief*," that is, he could alienate the land, *cens*, and rents on three conditions: that he continued to render fealty to the *seigneur* for the whole of the fief; that the alienation did not exceed two-thirds of the demesne, *cens*, and rents of the fief (this was laid down in the "new" custom—the "old" one had permitted alienation of the whole fief); and that the vassal retained the feudal dependence or *censive* of the portion he alienated. In this way the purchasers of the two-thirds that were alienated found themselves, by this "*jeu de fief*," bound by faith and homage, or by *censive*, to the one-third that was retained. Consequently, the *seigneur*'s interests were not harmed; for if part of the fief changed hands without his having consented to the alienation, he could still exercise his feudal rights over the entire fief, the alienated part and the part retained alike. If he had consented, he could no longer exercise his feudal rights over the alienated part, which became, so far as he was concerned, a subfief. In fact, the custom of Paris, which was very liberal, released vassals from all restrictions on the buying and selling of fiefs.

The customs of Anjou and Maine forbade division of fiefs. However, a vassal could subinfeudate, creating subfiefs, even if the *seigneur* did not agree, by alienating only one-third of the fief and retaining faith and homage for the part alienated.

If these conditions were not observed, then, under the regime of the customs of Paris, Anjou, and Maine, the *seigneur* could invoke *"dépié de fief."* This meant that, thenceforth, all who held of the vassal some part of the fief which he had alienated, and so had him as their *seigneur direct,* were to hold their land of the original *seigneur,* the *seigneur*-in-chief, directly as a full fief, and the same applied to the *cens*-paying subjects of the fief. By *dépié de fief* the vassal lost his feudal rights, his power of justice, his *seigneurie;* everything returned to the *seigneur*-in-chief, or suzerain.

Thus, in the system of fiefs, the bonds between man and man, the ties of protection and service, had not disappeared, although they were greatly weakened. Their place in society had been taken by direct fealties, bonds between master and *fidèle,* protector and *créature*—relations governed by *mores,* not by law. The fief had become mainly a form of property. Thanks to the right of frank-fee, it was actually accessible to everyone. Where the custom of Paris ruled, trade in fiefs was largely unrestrained, thanks to the *jeu de fief.* A fief was valued more for the social consideration that went with it than for the *droits utiles* that it brought.

The law of censives

A *seigneurie* consisted of demesne, fief, and powers of justice. The fief included "commoner" lands which were leased out, not in return for faith and homage and on condition of rendering the noble services of aid and counsel, but in return for fealty alone and on condition that the soil be cultivated and payment made of *droits recognitifs* and *droits utiles* known as *censive* (or, in Dauphiné, *albergements*). Military service was, in principle, the main condition for the leasing of a *censive.* The *censive* lease was emphyteutic, that is, granted for a long period of time (ninety-nine years). The lessor, the *seigneur foncier* or *seigneur censier*, retained ownership, the *seigneurie directe*. He ceded to the lessee—his *tenancier, sujet, homme, censitaire*, or *albergataire*—the *seigneurie utile*, meaning the right to exploit the land and enjoy its produce, which could be sold or bequeathed (since the *seigneurie utile* itself could be sold or bequeathed, many historians describe it as "ownership"). The lessee had to pay the *seigneur* the *cens* and other seignorial dues and rents. In effect, the lease was granted in perpetuity and was equivalent to sale of the *seigneurie utile*, for the seignorial rent was not redeemable.

It was possible to lease out for *cens*, either by oral engagement or contract in writing, houses, gardens, cultivated land, meadows, woods, rights to use water, to occupy benches or stalls in markets, to use bake ovens, to fish, and so on.

The acquirer of a piece of real property or its equivalent held *en censive* was obliged first and foremost to "acknowledge his *seigneur*," that is, to "declare formally to his *seigneur* that he is in possession of a certain piece of land feudally dependent upon this *seigneur*, holding it subject to payment of such and such dues, which he promises and undertakes to pay" (Boutaric, p. 169). This "acknowledgement" was required at each change of *censitaire* or of *seigneur*. The latter entered these acknowledgments in a register or cartulary, which also contained the *dénombrement* of all the dues derived from the *seigneurie*, the records defining the limits of the area in which he exercised powers of justice and of levying tithe, the laws and usages of the *seigneurie*, the "conditions" (noble, commoner) of the lands and persons constituting it, the leases for *cens*, and so on. This was what was called the *papier terrier* or, simply, the *terrier*. If this *terrier* should be lost or destroyed, a new acquirer of the *seigneurie* could have another compiled, on condition that he obtained *"lettres de terrier"* from the chancellery. He would then call for "acknowledgments" from his tenants. A *terrier* showed the entire makeup of a *seigneurie*.

If there was any dispute as to whether a particular piece of land formed part of a given *seigneurie* and owed *cens*, a single acknowledgment was all that was needed if the *seigneur foncier* was the king or the Church; for deceit or fraud on *their* part was unthinkable. The royal declaration of 1657 even laid it down that, to prove the Church's right to a particular *censive*, the evidence of the *"adminicules"* sufficed. *Adminicules* could be the *rôles de liève*, or "terrier of receipt," that is, the list of tenants who were liable to pay seignorial dues; or the receipts given to previous *censitaires* of the *censive* subject to dispute; or else statements included in public contracts, etc.

In the case of a *seigneur foncier* who was a private person, two acknowledgments were needed to prove his rights, or else one acknowledgment, together with *adminicules,* unless the *censive* concerned lay in an area subject to a custom governed by the maxim: "No land without a lord," in which case all the tenants in the territory under the jurisdiction of the *seigneur foncier* were regarded as being his *censitaires*.

Cens was the fundamental feudal rent, an annual payment which "imports and denotes *seigneurie directe:* it is an acknowledgment of the obedience and subjection of the *censitaire* and of the superiority of the *seigneur.*" *Cens* was normally payable in cash and was normally slight. It could, however, especially in certain areas of written law, be payable in kind and be a little more substantial. In Dauphiné it was payable in kind in 70 percent of cases and high enough to serve as the price of the lease and so not merely as a *droit recognitif.* The first payment, moreover, had to be accompanied by an *introge.* Elsewhere, though, it was actually, above all, the symbol of the *seigneurie directe* returned by the *seigneur foncier,* that is, of his eminent ownership, and also the symbol of his social superiority, the mark of a subject's dependence on him.

The *cens* was a "small due," but it could be doubled. In that case, the primary and basic *cens* was called the *chef-cens* and the additional element the *surcens.*

If it was paid for the *censive* taken as a whole, it was called *gros-cens;* if paid arpent by arpent, it was called *menu cens.*

Gros cens could also mean *cher cens.* According to Renauldon (p. 149), in the custom areas of Orléans, Dunois, and Blois the *cher cens* was almost equivalent to the annual income from the land subject to *cens,* which seems hard to believe.

By common law the *cens* was *quérable,* that is, had to be applied for by the *seigneur foncier* in the place where it was due. But local custom or the terms of a lease might declare it to be *portable,* that is, to be paid at the residence of the *seigneur foncier censier direct.*

Cens was not subject to prescription, for it was a sign of feudal dependence, and that was imprescriptible between *seigneur* and subject. If, however, it had not been paid for a long time, only the arrears of the twenty-nine years before the action for its payment was instituted might be demanded, and this gave rise to the false notion that *cens* became lost by limitation after thirty years. In Dauphiné, though, a territory subject to written law, where jurisprudence tended to treat all property as quiritarian, *cens* was subject to prescription after the passage of six years, this being confirmed by an *arrêté* of February 1708.

Whoever was liable to pay *cens* was also liable to pay another feudal due, namely, *lods et ventes*. These were equivalent, where the *censive* was concerned, to the *quint et requint* in the case of the fief. They were simply "the price paid for the approval and consent given by the *seigneur direct* to a change of occupier" (Boutaric, p. 200). They were subject to common law and similar in nature to the lease for *cens*.

The rate at which they were charged was very variable: a third, a twelfth, a sixth, or a twentieth of the price of the *censive*. The customs did not state whether this payment was to be "*en dehors*" or "*en dedans*" of the selling price. "*En dehors*" meant "over and above." For example, if *lods et ventes* were payable at the rate of one-third "*en dehors,*" and the selling-price of the *censive* was 3,000 livres but the total amount paid was 4,500 livres, then the *lods et ventes* must have come to 1,500 livres. But if the *lods et ventes* were payable at the rate of one-third "*en dedans,*" this meant that they came to no more than 1,000 livres. In the absence of any stipulation in the contract, jurisprudence adopted the solution that favored the purchaser—*en dedans* of the selling price.

Lods et ventes were due in cases of sale but not in cases of exchange, except within the area subject to the jurisdiction of the *parlement* of Toulouse. They were not due to be paid on gifts, except in certain custom areas, where they were charged at half-rate. They were due, however, if the "gift" was made to repay a debt or to discharge a credit, for it was then a disguised sale.

The various customs dealt differently with the question whether *lods et ventes* were due on a sale arising from a redemption, "*la vente à réméré.*" According to Boutaric, by the "common law," meaning the written law, *lods et ventes* were due, since a sale had indeed taken place (Boutaric, p. 215).

Whoever was liable to pay *cens* was liable to pay those rents, not feudal but seignorial or domanial, which were implied in *cens* but could exist independently of the feudal regime. The *seigneur* reserved for himself a very variable share of the fruits of the soil. In the areas where customary law obtained this exaction bore a great variety of names.

For example, in respect of arable land, it was called *champart* in Ile-de-France and Beauce and, elsewhere, *terrage, agrier, agrière* (as in Saintonge), or *tasque*. When charged on the produce of vines, it was called *complant* in Poitou, *terceau* at Chartres, *vignage* at Clermont (Oise) and Montargis, *querpot* in Bourbonnais, and so on. Charged on meadows, it was known in Poitou as *herbaux*. Charged on houses, its names included *hostise* at Blois, *fouage* in Brittany and Normandy, and *festage* in Berry. Charged on the total income of farms and *métairies*, it was known as *bordelage* in Nivernais, etc.

The *seigneurs fonciers* also levied dues which were not derived from the *cens* and were not of the same nature as the lease for *cens* but were purely domanial. They could levy a *"taille"* in certain cases determined by custom. For example, the *seigneur* of Corbière could levy one on the occasion of his wedding, the birth of a child, the marriage of his daughters, his setting out for the wars, his being held in captivity, his traveling overseas, or his acquisition of new lands. Generally speaking, a *taille* was leviable on four classical occasions: when the *seigneur* was knighted, when he traveled overseas, when he had to be redeemed from captivity, and when he married off his daughters.

The *seigneur foncier* could require his tenants to perform *corvées*, that is, days of labor and cartage, within limits fixed by the customs. If the tenants were *"corvéables à merci,"* the obligation amounted to twelve days a year. As a rule it did not exceed three or four days. The *seigneur* had to give his tenants two days' notice of *corvée*. He was obliged to feed them while they were performing it and to let them return home in the evening. He was not allowed to commute *corvées* for money. He might not lay claim to arrears without instituting an action. Past years' *corvées* could not be exacted before this was done: *"arrears of corvées* cannot be accumulated." The king alone was allowed legally to commute *corvées* for money in respect of the lands of his demesne, for *corvées* served the personal needs of the *seigneur*.

Finally came a kind of due which 18th-century jurists of the regions of written law, such as Boutaric, regarded as "extraordinary, exorbitant, and contrary to the nature of fiefs" (Boutaric, p. 287)—namely, *la banalité*. This meant the right possessed by a *seigneur* to compel the inhabitants of his fief to use his bake oven, mill, or winepress. "Most of our writers see the *droit de banalité* as a consequence of the *seigneurs'* violence and abuse of authority . . . I prefer to believe that *banalités* were established through a sort of convention between *seigneurs* and their subjects, as a consequence of the latter not possessing the means, or not wishing, to incur the expense of building mills, bake ovens, and wine-presses for their individual use" (Pocquet, p. 607).

The name was derived from *ban,* an old German word meaning "proclamation," "publication by the crier." However, this term has several meanings, which entail the risk of confusion. The *banalité* must not be confused with the *ban à moissons, à fauchaisons, ou des vendanges,* which was the duty incumbent on the *seigneur* with powers of high justice—to the exclusion of the *seigneurs* with powers of middle and low justice and the *seigneur foncier*—to cause announcement to be made by the public crier at the crossroads, and by the *curé* when he preached in the parish church, of the beginning of the harvests, mowing times, and wine harvests, in accordance with Charles IX's edict of 25 October 1561, article 28 of the Edict of Melun, and article 49 of the Ordinance of Blois, 1579. Nor must it be confused with the *banvin,* which was the *seigneur*'s right to sell by retail the wine produced on his demesne, without competition from his subjects, for forty days after the wine harvest.

According to the custom of Paris, "which we look upon as the common law of the kingdom," *seigneurs* had no right of *banalité* without title, that is, unless there was a contract to this effect between the *seigneur* and the assembly of inhabitants of the fief. Nevertheless, if a *seigneur* forbade "his men" to use any mill, winepress, or bake oven other than his own, and the inhabitants obeyed without protest, then, after the lapse of thirty years, he acquired this right by prescription.

By the custom of Anjou, any *seigneur* possessing powers of low justice could have a *moulin banal* or a *four banal* without need of title if he was *seigneur* of all or part of a *bourg.*

The *banalité* of mill, bake oven, and winepress comprised three elements: the obligation laid upon subjects to do their grinding of grain at the *moulin banal,* their pressing of grapes at the *pressoir banal,* and their baking at the *four banal;* a ban on any construction of a mill, winepress, or bake oven by anyone else anywhere in the *seigneurie;* and a ban on intrusion by neighboring millers, etc., into the territory of the *seigneurie.* The *seigneur*'s right survived so long as he maintained the mill, bake oven, and winepress properly from his own resources.

The *seigneur*'s rights were safeguarded by the *retrait censuel* or *droit de prélation.* This was the equivalent for the *censive* of the *retrait féodal* for the fief, and what has been said of the latter applies to the former. The *seigneur* could recover a *censive* sold by a *censitaire* by reimbursing the purchaser for the price he paid, plus his costs, and could reunite the *seigneurie utile* of the land involved with his *seigneurie directe*. He could make use of this right so long as he had not accepted the purchaser and collected *lods et ventes*. According to Boutaric (p. 229), *retrait censuel* did not apply everywhere, unlike *retrait féodal*. It was applicable in most of the regions of customary law and, in the regions of written law, within the jurisdictions of the *parlements* of Toulouse and Bordeaux. In the last-mentioned area, the *seigneur* was allowed to exercise the right within two months of the day when the contract of sale was notified: this applied, in particular, in Périgord (Edict of Périgord, 25 October 1555) (Renauldon, p. 209).

Renauldon goes further, saying (p. 203): "*Retrait censuel* applies only in certain custom areas, such as Anjou, Maine, Vermandois, Senlis, and some others, but it is not accepted in the area subject to the custom of Paris or in most other custom areas; nor is it accepted by the *parlements* of Grenoble and Provence or in those districts of written law that come within the jurisdiction of the Paris *parlement*." This statement is, on the whole, confirmed by Pocquet (p. 408).

Commise applied to *censives*—not when the *censitaire* merely alleged that his *censive* was not held of the *seigneur*, for that was happening all the time, but in cases where the *censitaire* was guilty of deception and fraud, for example, by concealing the true selling price so as to reduce the *lods et ventes* to be paid, or by forging title deeds, etc. *Commise* also applied if the *censitaire* insulted his *seigneur* and even, in some provinces, if *cens* was not paid for three years running (two years in the case of the Church.)

Acapte and *arrière-capte* were words characteristic of Langudeoc and Guyenne, but they referred to rights that applied everywhere in the kingdom, being the equivalent for the *censive* of *relief et rachat* for the fief. *Acapte* was the due payable when the seigneur died, *arrière-capte* the due payable when the tenant died.

There were some differences from *relief et rachat*. The latter were due only on the death of the vassal, while *acapte* was due also on the death of the *seigneur*. *Relief et rachat* were due only in respect of succession in the collateral line, while *acapte* and *arrière-capte* were due even in respect of succession in the direct line. *Relief et rachat* were of the nature and essence of the fief, whereas *acapte* and *arrière-capte* were not of the nature and essence of the *censive*, being due only when they were stipulated in the lease for *cens*. Like *relief et rachat*, however, they could be *abonnés*, that is, converted into a fixed annual payment.

Saisie féodale could be effected for nonpayment of *cens*, rents, *lods et ventes* (custom of Anjou, articles 1 and 180, 158, and 416.)

The *censitaire* also enjoyed safeguards. By the custom of Paris, he was not subject to *saisie féodale, retrait censuel,* or *relief et rachat.*

Therefore, if he failed to pay his *cens* and rents, the *seigneur* had to proceed against him like any other creditor against a debtor in order to seize the land concerned. This meant that wherever the custom of Paris was applicable the *seigneurie utile* became a very well-protected and free form of ownership, quite close to quiritarian ownership.

Furthermore, the *censitaire* could make use of the right of *déguerpissement* (called in Anjou and Maine *exponse*). If a *censitaire* found that the *cens* and rents to be paid for his *censive* were too burdensome, or if he suddenly discovered that he owed rents he had not been warned of when he purchased it or that his predecessor had left substantial arrears of rent to be paid, then, in the event that he could find no one to sell the *censive* to and was unwilling to hang on to a holding burdened with increasing debt, he could *déguerpir,* that is, inform the *seigneur* in the presence of the judge that he was giving up the holding. The *seigneurie utile* of the land was thus reunited with the *seigneurie directe.* However, the *censitaire* who did this had to pay to the *seigneur* the arrears of rent and feudal and seignorial dues that were due from the *censive* in question. According to the custom of Paris (article 102) he was obliged to discharge only the arrears that had accumulated during his occupation of the *censive,* and not those dating from his predecessor's time as well. Even mitigated in this way, though, *déguerpissement* was an expensive method of getting free of a ruinous commitment.

The forms of ownership surviving from serfdom: Domaine congéable (convenant), quevaise, complant

The *censive* was an essential feature of the fief, so that in Brittany it was described as *fief roturier* ("commoner fief"). Indeed, while a fief was granted on condition of faith and homage and noble services, a *censive* was granted on condition of fealty and "lucrative" or "common" services. The *seigneurie utile* of a *censive* was a true "property," like that of a fief. In regions that were more open to change, such as those subject to the custom of Paris or the areas where written law prevailed, the *censive* had been gradually freed from many of the feudal

and seignorial bond services and turned into something close to quiritarian property. In regions that were remote and closed to outside
influence, much less "perfect" forms of ownership existed, which historians of law have often considered as survivals of serfdom. Brittany
offers good examples, with its *convenant,* or *domaine congéable,
quevaise,* and *complant.*

Domaine congéable was a form of ownership defined not by custom
but by local *usements*—the *usement* of Rohan, recorded in 1580, that of
Broérech (1570), that of Porhoët (1664 and 1683). The *seigneur* owned
the land itself, while the *domanier* owned the "*droits convenantiers,*"
meaning the edifices and surface features of all kinds: buildings and
walls, embankments and ditches, fruit trees, woods, and copses, fruits
of the earth. The *domanier* could sell, alienate, or bequeath his *droits
convenantiers* without seeking permission from the *seigneur foncier* or
could exercise the right of *exponse* (*déguerpissement*); but the *seigneur
foncier* could evict the *domanier* whenever he chose, provided he reimbursed him for his *droits convenantiers*—including the fertilizer he
had invested in the land—after an appraisal carried out by an expert, an
expensive business for which the *domanier* had to pay. Custom to
some degree mitigated this precariousness of tenure. The practice was
to grant *domaine congéable* for a period of nine years, but only in
return for a payment of a very substantial "*droit de commission.*" The
rents and dues payable under this system were very heavy but were
identical in nature with the feudal and seignorial dues payable for *censives* or "*fiefs roturiers*" ("commoner fiefs").

One condition included in the *usement* of Rohan resembled the law
of mortmain. In order to inherit, one had to have lived with the deceased occupier. But, by force of the law of *juveignerie,* it was the
youngest son who inherited, to the exclusion of his brothers. If the
domanier died without issue and there were not collateral relatives
living with him, the *droits convenantiers* fell into *déshérence* and returned to the *seigneur.*

Quevaise applied on the lands of a certain number of ecclesiastical
seigneuries, such as the abbeys of Le Rellec and Béjard and the *com-
manderies* of La Femillée, Pontmelvez, Mael and Louch, and Le Pal-
lacret. *Quevaisiers* were subject to the law of mortmain, that is, there
had to be heirs living with them for the *seigneur* to be able to authorize
inheritance, and the rule of *juveignerie,* by which the inheritance
passed to the youngest son living with the deceased, to the exclusion of
his elders, prevailed in their families. *Quevaisiers* were not allowed to

sell or alienate the land in any way at all without express permission from the *seigneur,* who took for himself a third or a quarter of the selling price. If a *quevaise* was abandoned for a year and a day, the *seigneur* could evict the *quevaisier. Quevaise* gave rise to many *déshérences* and new leases on the same basis, with a very substantial *droit d'entrée* to be paid. The seignorial dues were similar to those borne by *censives,* but heavier.

In the county of Nantes, the system called *complant* applied in the vineyards. The *complanteur* owned the vines, and so long as he tended them he occupied the land, by hereditary right, on condition that he gave the *seigneur* one-third or one-quarter of the harvest, together with dues that were similar to those borne by a *censive.* If, however, he deserted the vines for a period of one year, the *seigneur* could get rid of him.

Leases for ground rent

The freeholder on his land or his *seigneurie,* the *seigneur* on his demesne or *réserve seigneuriale,* which he kept either to exploit for himself by means of wage laborers or to lease out, and the *censitaires* or *albergataires,* if they did not wish to cultivate for themselves their *censive* or *albergement,* could resort to various kinds of lease, which may all be regarded as "leases for ground rent." These leases could apply to cultivable land, dwelling houses, tithes, *champarts,* powers of justice, rights over fiefs and *censives,* or privileges such as those possessed by the wigmakers, etc. A unit of exploitation, a farm or *métairie,* could be leased out as such even if it was made up of *censives* or *albergements* dependent on different *seigneuries* or of fields subject to different juridicial conditions—some being fiefs, others *censives,* others again *domaine congéable* or even fragments of a seignorial demesne. In such cases the price of the lease had to be paid to whoever had formed the unit of exploitation, but the lessee owed the feudal and seignorial dues to various persons, and payment of them was as complicated for him as collection was for the beneficiaries, whose demesnes and *censives* might be scattered in the form of fragments of a number of units of exploitation. The complication was increased by the circumstance that *seigneurs* could become *censitaires* of other *seigneurs* and amalgamate the different *censives* in order to lease them out for ground rent.

True ground rent was *"rente à bail d'héritage."* The possessor of a piece of land could transfer to a purchaser the entire *seigneurie, directe* as well as *utile,* of this *"héritage"* in return for an annual and perpetual rent, which was a deduction from the income arising from the property leased. The right of ownership was not transferred entirely, since the lessee was not allowed to abandon or destroy what he had acquired by lease or to alter the intended purpose of the land, and he was obliged to furnish descriptions of the state of his holding at certain intervals. He had to pay his share of extraordinary expenses, such as repairs to the church tower or the *curé*'s house.

This rent was a perpetual obligation. However, rents chargeable on houses in towns and suburbs could be redeemed at 5 percent (edicts of October 1539 and February 1553). In other cases the contract of lease could provide for redemption, with the lessee redeeming his rent obligation for a period of thirty years by giving the lessor a lump sum equivalent to twenty times the sum that was due annually.

The purchaser, having become *seigneur* of the given piece of land, could in his turn lease out for *cens* the *seigneurie utile* of the land, retaining the *directe* for himself, and bind his *censitaire* to pay the annual and perpetual rent to the previous *seigneur.*

In Dauphiné the lessor could reserve to himself, in the contract of lease, the right to carry out *commise* if the rent was not paid for two or three years. By a *règlement* of the *parlement* of Dauphiné dated 14 July 1600, all persons to whom a *rente constituée* was due could demand repayment of the principal if arrears had not been paid for three years. The period of prescription for arrears was thirty years. It was reduced to seven years in Dauphiné, in February 1708. In 1636 there were 6,000 such *rentes constituées* in that province.

The *métairie* (or *méarie,* or *grangeage*) took various forms. In Gâtine Poitevine, at the end of the 16th century, 95 percent of the sharecropping leases were of the type called *bail à terrage à moitié fruits* (Merle, p. 175). The sharecropper had to pay the *tailles,* tithes, *cens,* and dues borne by the *censives* included in the *métairie.* He had to pay to the *seigneur* a share of all the elements making up the *métairie.* For all the arable land, he owed half the average annual crop—a fixed amount, regardless of what a year's actual crop might be, this condition being all the harder in that it was the sharecropper who provided the seed. For the gardens and the hedgerows he owed a third or a half of the fruit produced. For the farmyard he owed the *"suffrages,"* which meant, for such a lease, six capons, twenty-two chickens, two geese, and one pig. For the meadows and pasture land, the *seigneur* provided half of the *"bêtes aumailles"* (the cattle and horses) and took half of their increase. For the farm buildings, the sharecropper had to pay a sum in cash. Finally, he was obliged to render services—carriage of wine as far as Saintonge and Thouarsais, whenever called upon; workdays to be put in on the *seigneur*'s lands or on building or repairing his *château;* his wife to go and do the washing at the *seigneur*'s residence. This form of lease steadily declined during the 17th and 18th centuries, to disappear completely between 1780 and 1790. It was replaced by the *bail à métayage* properly so called and, to an even greater extent, by the *bail à fermage,* which accounted for 62 percent of all leases in the 1780s.

The *bail à métayage,* properly so called, was an association. It consisted in the freeholder, *seigneur,* or *censitaire* leasing his land to a *laboureur* for cultivation over a period of three, six, or nine years, on condition of a half-share of the produce. The lessor laid down exactly how he wished cultivation to be carried on. Either the lessor provided all the plants and seeds—in Dauphiné this applied in 79 percent of the cases—or else the lessor and the lessee each provided half. In Dauphiné, however, in 42 percent of the cases the lessor reserved for himself the right to take a fixed quantity of the produce, or of the wine, before the share-out. The lessor provided the barn and the cowshed. He required the lessee to perform labor service to supply him with wood and charcoal. In a fourth of the cases *bail à métayage* was accompanied by a *bail à cheptel.*

Freeholders, *seigneurs* of fiefs, *censitaires, albergataires* could all grant leases of land on *bail à ferme,* or *arrentement.* This meant that the lessor entrusted the land to the lessee for cultivation in return for an annual rent. Such leases were usually for a period of between six and nine years. In a third of the cases they were *baux à terrage,* that is, the rent was payable in kind. The lessee sometimes had to pay a *droit d'entrée* as well, the *étrenne* (handsel, earnest money). The lessee had to treat the land with paternal care, that is, he was under obligation not to cut down trees, had to maintain ditches, repair roofs, and so on. Besides the land and buildings, the lessor sometimes provided furniture, implements, dung, and, fairly often, animals for use in cultivating the land he thus farmed out. Quite often, too, the *bail à ferme* was accompanied by a *bail à cheptel.* The latter could take one of three forms: there was the *bail à cheptel simple,* by which the lessor provided the animals and the lessee shared their increase with him half-and-half; there was the *bail à cheptel à moitié,* under which the lessor and lessee each provided half of the animals and shared their increase half-and-half; and there was the *bail à cheptel de fer,* under which the lessor provided the animals and the lessee had to return, when the lease expired, animals to the same value, himself keeping all the profit or bearing all the loss.

A freeholder, *seigneur,* or *censitaire* who fell into debt could pledge a *censive* to his creditor. The creditor to whom it was pledged took the income of the *censive* until the debt had been discharged. The debtor could recover his land at any time by settling the debt and compensating the creditor for any expenses incurred for improving the land. Such pledges were frequent.

A freeholder, *seigneur,* or *censitaire* who sold a piece of real property could agree that the purchaser, if unable to pay the price, in whole or in part, might pay them a rent based on the price or the unpaid part thereof. This rent was treated as equivalent to real property under the customs of Paris and Orléans but as movable property under the customs of Blois, Rheims, Troyes, and Lorraine and as *sui generis* in Dauphiné. It was a perpetual rent, in the sense that the debtor could not be called upon to repay the principal but had the power at any time, without prescription, to redeem his rent obligation. The rate was 5 percent normally, but in Dauphiné between 1679 and 1720 it was higher (*le denier 18* instead of *le denier 20*). Arrears were subject to prescription after five years; following the Council's *arrêt* of February 1708, this was changed to six years.

The law of seignorial powers of justice

A *seigneurie* consisted of a demesne, a fief, and powers of justice. A fief might be without powers of justice in many parts of France, where the maxim prevailed according to which "fief and justice have nothing in common." Under the custom of Paris, fiefs were patrimonial, hereditary, and alienable. Primogeniture was restricted to succession in the direct line, equal sharing of inheritances being the rule for successions in the collateral line. These principles were extended to apply to powers of justice. Thus, in places where this custom and this maxim applied, "fief" and "justice" were often separated. It was possible to hold a fief by faith and homage to one *seigneur* and the powers of justice in that fief by faith and homage to another. By the customs of Poitou, Brittany, and Lower Marche, however, "fief and justice are one and the same." These distinctions, which were accepted as applying to fiefs, were not to be taken as valid for *seigneuries*. A *seigneurie* always had to embrace demesne, fief, and powers of justice.

In law, all seignorial powers of justice were presumed to be concessions granted by the king. "The king alone has power by common law to exercise high, middle, and low justice throughout the kingdom" (Bacquet, p. 6). "All the jurisdictions in the kingdom have their source in the king" (Boutaric, p. 3). No one, therefore, could possess power of justice in any fief, territory, or *seigneurie* in France without specific title, concession, or permission from the king or his predecessors. If the power of justice in a fief, territory, or *seigneurie* was confiscated on the petition of a *procureur du roi*, the *seigneur* was obliged to justify his alleged right to his power by showing title that was adequate and valid. This might take the form of a specific authority in writing; or acts of faith and homage rendered to the king or to another *seigneur*, related specifically to this power of justice and accepted by *chambres des comptes*; or *aveux et dénombrements* accepted without disapproval by the dominant *seigneur* or, in the case of the king, verified by the ordinary judges of the localities concerned, who invited the opinions of those present at three hearings and returned certificates of the outcome; or possession of these powers for a hundred years (treated as equivalent to "time out of mind"), proved by witnesses.

The higher royal judges—*baillis, sénéchaux,* presidial judges—had cognizance, in any case, of a certain number of offenses, to the exclusion of the subordinate judges—*prévôts, vicomtes, viguiers,* etc.—and the *seigneurs'* judges. These were what were called the *cas royaux* and *cas prévôtaux*. The criminal ordinance of August 1670 repeated, defined, and complemented those issued earlier. The *cas royaux* were the crimes of *lèse-majesté,* of sacrilege accompanied by burglary, of rebellion against orders emanating from the king or his officials, of bearing arms (which meant assembling in groups of at least ten persons, armed and come together with a view to violent rebellion), of illicit assembly, sedition, popular disturbance, public exercise of force, counterfeiting, malversation on the part of royal officials, heresy, public nuisance during divine service, abduction by force, arson, rape, peculation, public extortion or oppression, levying of taxes without authority of letters patent, usury, fraudulent bankruptcy, clandestine marriage, adultery, incest, sodomy, parricide, and monopoly. To these were added disputes concerned with honorific rights and the privileges of the Church and "other cases defined in our ordinances and *règlements.*" In general, anything constituted a *cas royal* in which "the majesty of the sovereign, the dignity of his officials, or the safety and tranquillity of the public are violated or concerned."

Cas prévôtaux were distinct from *cas royaux,* but in the old ordinances every *cas prévôtal* was a *cas royal.* The provost marshals and presidial judges had cognizance, to the exclusion of the subaltern royal judges and the seignorial judges, of all crimes committed by vagrants, masterless and homeless persons, or those sentenced to corporal punishment, banishment, or *amende honorable;* oppressive acts, excesses or crimes committed by soldiers, whether on the march, at their staging posts, when gathered together, or when stationed at a particular place; illicit assemblies where arms were carried, or the levying of troops without royal permission; robberies on the highway, burglaries, the carrying of arms, and public acts of violence; sacrilege which involved breakins; premeditated murders; revolts and popular disturbances; and the making, modification, and putting into circulation of counterfeit coins.

The ordinance of 1670, heading 1, articles 7 and 9, completed the rules regarding *prévention. Baillis* and *sénéchaux* were empowered to exercise this right in relation to the seignorial judges; that is, they could take over the investigation and trial of a case when the seignorial judges had failed to deal with it within twenty-four hours.

Seigneurs appointed their own judges. They were not allowed to dismiss those whom they had appointed for valuable consideration or as a reward for services rendered. It was enough for such services to have been mentioned in the letters of appointment for a seignorial judge to be guaranteed against arbitrary dismissal. The jurisdiction of these judges embraced cognizance and decision in matters both civil and criminal; they possessed "the public power or constraint, called in law *imperium,"* to cause their decisions to be carried out. By assignment from the king they had "the right of the sword," that is, the power of command.

The seignorial judges had cognizance of the nobles' own cases, both civil and criminal. Nobles were not allowed to reject the jurisdiction of *seigneurs,* though they could reject that of the subaltern royal judges and have their cases heard, in first instance, by the *baillis* and *sénéchaux* (Edict of Crémieu, article 5, and Declaration of Compiègne, 24 February 1536, interpreting this edict).

Seignorial judges could take cognizance of disputes and suits between a *seigneur* and those subject to his power of justice if they related to the fief, demesne, ordinary or usual dues and payments, leases, subleases, tenures, appurtenances, and dependencies, but "as regards other actions in which the *seigneur* is a party or is concerned, the judge will not be able to take cognizance." A *seigneur*'s judge could take cognizance of arrears of *cens* and of other feudal and seignorial dues arising from *seigneurie directe*. If, however, a vassal involved in a case denied that he was a vassal, or if a *censitaire* involved considered that the *seigneur* was demanding larger dues than ordinarily, he could reject the *seigneur*'s jurisdiction and take his case to that of a higher *seigneur* or that of the king.

All other court proceedings by the *seigneur,* and any cases involving his debts or other interests, fell within the competence of the higher seignorial judge or the king's judge, and not within that of the judge of the *seigneur* concerned, since otherwise he would be both judge and party in his own case.

Powers of justice were patrimonial, venal, and hereditary, being regarded as truly part of one's *héritage.* They were held by faith and homage either mediately or immediately of the king. *Seigneurs* paid feudal profits for them when a fief changed hands. A seigneur could therefore *"vendiquer ses justiciables,"* that is, recall to his court persons subject to his power of justice if they went to another judge than his own. By the terms of the declaration of François I dated 23 April 1537, suits set in motion as a result of disputes arising from the execution of contracts or obligations which had been given the royal seal, on the initiative of a person subject to a *seigneur*'s power of justice, were not to be heard by the king's judge but by the *seigneur*'s. Royal seals did not confer royal jurisdiction, except for the seals of the Paris Châtelet, of Montpellier, and of Brie-en-Champagne. Actions for debt had to be dealt with in the place where the contracting party lived.

There were three grades of *seignorial* powers of justice—high, middle, and low. *Seigneurs* who had power of high justice also had powers of middle and low justice, and those who had power of middle justice also had power of low justice. Customs varied greatly in France. The rule followed by writers was to follow the custom of the *prévôté et vicomté* of Paris, "the capital city of this kingdom . . . and to conduct ourselves according to that." Bacquet's work, for example, was based on articles drawn up by the deputies appointed to reform the old custom of Paris and draft the new one —articles which were not inserted in the new custom.

Seigneurs hauts justiciers had to have *a bailli,* a *procureur fiscal,* a *greffier, sergents* to serve court orders, jailers, prisons, and, if the *seigneurie* in question was very large, *lieutenants du bailli* and an *avocat fiscal.* They could have their own notaries and scriveners if theirs was a *fief de dignité*, if they were castellans or barons, or even, quite simply, if they held deeds entitling them to this privilege, or had possessed it "time out of mind," or their possession of it was recognized by the local custom. The edict of November 1542, article 4, expressly conferred the right to have their own scriveners and their own seal upon all *seigneurs* who were barons or castellans. The customs of Blois (art. 17), Senlis (art. 93), Poitou (art. 375), and Touraine (art. 75) accorded this right to *seigneurs* who were castellans. By article 376 of the custom of Poitou, notaries were to be appointed by the seignorial judges. By the edict of March 1693, seignorial notaries were registered at the *greffe* of the king's courts.

The *huissiers,* who were at once *audienciers* (tipstaffs) and *sergents* (bailiffs), together with the mere *sergents,* were responsible, in civil cases, for serving writs of summons, subpoenas, injunctions, court orders and notices, carrying out seizures of goods, distraints, publications of the sale of chattels, and so on, and, in criminal cases, for personal summonses, search warrants, imprisonments, attachments, and so on. In principle, it was only the sovereign courts and the higher jurisdictions that had *huissiers,* whereas the *bailliages, sénéchaussées,* and lower jurisdictions had only *sergents.*

The *sergents* employed by *seigneurs* served writs throughout the area covered by their *seigneurs'* powers of justice. They were not empowered to act on a decision by a royal judge, serving his writs or carrying out his orders, nor could they summon a person subject to their *seigneur*'s power of justice to appear before a royal judge, these measures being reserved to the competence of the royal *sergents.* Though a seignorial *sergent* could not operate outside the area covered by his *seigneur*'s power of justice, he could do so in any place subject to a power of justice that was subordinate to his *seigneur*'s. Seignorial *sergents* had to be present at court hearings.

Dukes, counts, barons, castellans, and all *seigneurs* with power of high justice had the right to maintain a pillory, a scaffold, and a gibbet—the latter to have eight uprights in the case of a duke, six in that of a count, four in that of a baron or a castellan, and two in that of a mere *haut justicier,* who could, however, erect four uprights if he had an entitlement to do this or else an "immemorial" possession of the right.

The judges employed by *hauts justiciers* had cognizance of all matters of contentious jurisdiction, all cases that were personal, real, or mixed, marriages, successions, sale and purchase of land, loans, financial settlements, etc. They had "the right of the sword," with cognizance of all criminal cases. They could pass sentences of death, mutilation, thrashing, the pillory, the carcan, *amende honorable*, banishment, and branding. They could carry out preliminary investigation of *cas royaux* but had to refer these to the royal judge for trial.

They had cognizance of all cases involving nobles residing in their judicial area and also ecclesiastics (Council *arrêt* of 21 November 1573) and royal officials, provided that the matter did not in any way concern the exercise of their functions as such (Council *arrêt* of 15 April 1644); this provision ensured the independence of the public service in relation to the judiciary. They had cognizance of cases concerning churches, hospitals, leper houses, and communities that were not royal foundations and of the accounts for the upkeep of church fabrics if the interested communities had authorized incoming churchwardens or the *procureur fiscal* to present these accounts. They had cognizance of cases of nonroyal towns and communities established within their jurisdiction, or at least of disputes regarding their property, the accounts of their patrimonial revenues being submitted to the *baillis* and *sénéchaux* and those of their income from tolls to the *bureaux des finances* and the *chambres des comptes*. They had cognizance of cases concerning corporations and companies, guilds, and corporations of attorneys and tipstaffs—provided these were not royal foundations.

Their competence embraced all matters of voluntary jurisdiction: guardianship and emancipation therefrom, deprivation of control over money, separation, permission to alienate the property of minors, division of property (declaration of 24 February 1536; *arrêt* of 8 February 1653 in favor of the accounting officers of Lyons), affixing of seals and compiling of inventories (*arrêt* of 15 January 1579 in favor of the canons of the church of Troyes), opening of closed wills, confirmation of arbitrations between persons subject to the *seigneur*'s justice. However, their capacity to issue warrants was disputed, and *arrêts* were quoted both for and against this.

Their duties included publishing ordinances, edicts, declarations, letters patent, and *arrêts* sent them by the *procureurs du roi*, but registration of these was the prerogative of the royal judges.

Their powers extended to *"police,"* with cognizance of all cases resulting from this, which meant the enforcement of *règlements*. Dukes, counts, barons, and castellans issued *règlements* by public announcement—permissions to begin the wine harvest, to give a theatrical performance, to play the violin, to open a shop, to display emblems and signs of a trade. All holders of powers of high and middle justice enforced the *règlements* and had cognizance of any disputes that might arise from them. They checked on weights and measures, punishing offenders, supervised the highways, admitted candidates for mastership in the crafts, and so on. The establishment of the office of *lieutenant de police* by the edict of October 1699 in no way detracted from their field of competence.

They appointed the subordinate officers of their courts—attorneys, registrars, scriveners, bailiffs. They dealt with malversations by court officials. They could order the execution of decrees, ordinances, or *arrêts* of the *parlement* but could not initiate judicial *règlements* of their own.

They presided over the assemblies of their towns and those of the hospitals in their jurisdiction and accepted the oaths of aldermen.

Seigneurs hauts justiciers were allowed, once in their lifetime, to hold extraordinary assizes to which they summoned all who were subject to their power of justice, so as to "take cognizance" of their *seigneurie*. Some important *seigneuries* also had the right to annual assizes, which had to be attended by all the *seigneurs* and officials.

Seigneurs hauts justiciers had the right to confiscate the property of condemned persons and to take possession of wrecks and all movable things that had no owner and were unclaimed. They had the right of *déshérence,* that is, the right to the property of a man who had died intestate and without kinfolk capable of inheriting.

They alone enjoyed the right to hunt, except in Normandy, where this was reserved to feudal *seigneurs,* to the exclusion of mere *justiciers;* but they could grant permission to hunt to nobles, and holders of fiefs within the sphere of their seignorial justice had the right to hunt in these fiefs. Private persons were not allowed to enclose their land so as to prevent the *seigneur* from hunting. Their right to hunt did not apply after the grain was "in stalk" or, in vine-growing areas, between 1 May and the completion of the harvest.

Seigneurs hauts justiciers were the owners of nonnavigable rivers. They had the right to fish in them and could forbid others to do so. They could prohibit the building of mills. Any islands that were formed, any alluvium that was deposited, any "increases" in the land, became their property.

They had the right of bastardy. If a bastard who had been born and had lived in the *seigneurie* died there *ab intestat* and without issue, the *haut justicier* inherited. In the regions of customary law the *seigneurs hauts justiciers* had the right to take one half of treasure trove if it was found on their land, the finder keeping the other half, and a third if it was found on someone else's land, another third going to the owner of the land and the remaining third being kept by the finder. In the regions of written law the *seigneur haut justicier,* as such, was without any claim to treasure trove, which was divided equally between the owner of the land and the finder of the treasure.

The person who possessed power of high justice in a place was alone entitled to call himself *seigneur* of that place. His pew was situated in the most honorable place in church, in the choir itself. He gave precedence only to the patron of the church, the person who had the right to present to it.

Seigneurs with power of middle justice had to maintain a court with a judge, an attorney, a *greffier,* a *sergent,* and a prison. The judge dealt in first instance with all civil actions—real, personal, and mixed—apart from separations of property between married persons and deprivals of control over money on the part of prodigal sons.

He had cognizance of offenses for which the fine did not exceed 60 *sous parisis* (75 *sous tournois*). He could investigate all other offenses and could arrest all delinquents within the *seigneurie,* hold them for twenty-four hours, and interrogate them and then hand over the case and the prisoner to the *seigneur haut justicier.* When the latter's judge had pronounced sentence, he received the 60 *sous* due to him from the fine imposed.

He could nominate guardians, cause seals to be affixed on property, and carry out inventories of the property of minors.

He could have the lands of persons subject to his *seigneur*'s justice measured and their boundary marks fixed. He could appoint crop-watchers and decide what they should be paid.

He had cognizance of the seignorial and feudal dues payable to the *seigneur moyen justicier* and could fine *censitaires* subject to his jurisdiction for nonpayment of *cens* or dues.

He had cognizance of attachments and distraints carried out in execution of his judgments. However, he could not order the attachment of real property, except in the custom area of Nevers.

A *seigneur bas justicier* had to have a *maire,* a *sergent,* and a prison.

His judge had cognizance of all personal cases arising between his subjects which involved not more than 60 *sous parisis* and offenses for which the fine did not exceed 10 *sous parisis*. More serious offenses had to be referred to the court of the *seigneur haut justicier,* but he took his 10 *sous* from the fine inflicted by the latter's judge. He could arrest anyone accused of a crime but had to transfer him at once to the *haut justicier*'s prison or notify his judge. He could have the lands of his *seigneur*'s subjects measured and bounded, but, if any dispute arose in this connection, it had to be referred to the *haut justicier*. He could order the subjects to pay *cens* and impose a fine for delay in payment; but if they challenged their obligation to pay, he had to refer the case to the *haut justicier*.

Some jurisconsults claimed that whoever possessed a fief or *censive* exercised thereby a power of justice, called *foncière, censière, censuelle,* or *domaniale,* for the safeguarding of his feudal rights or his claim to *cens*. They cited articles 1, 9, and 28 of the "new" custom of Paris, by which a feudal lord could, in the event of a failure to render duties and services, with *aveu et dénombrement,* take possession of a fief that was dependent on him, and also article 74, by which he could seize the "fruits hanging by the roots" for arrears, unpaid *cens,* concealed sales, distraints violated, *aveux* not rendered, and so on. In ɔrder to carry out such seizures of property a *seigneur* certainly needed ᴸo possess power of justice.

The jurisconsults quoted Baldus, who said that "there can be no territory without jurisdiction," and Bartolus, according to whom, "if the Prince grants a castle to someone, he intends to grant it with all the rights that go with it, and, in the first place, jurisdiction and power to command." When the king accepted faith and homage from a vassal, these writers considered that he tacitly granted, along with *censive* of the fief, power of justice *"foncière et censière"* over the produce of this fief, so as to ensure his receipt of seignorial dues and *cens*. They pointed to the *arrêt* of the *chambre des comptes* in 1287 rejecting the claim by the abbey of Saint-Martin-des-Champs to exercise power of high justice over Quinquampoix ("This church has no power of justice other than *la justice du fonds de terre"*) and also the *arrêt* of the *chambre du trésor,* 2 January 1560, refusing powers of high, middle, and low justice to the collegiate church of Sainte-Opportune in Paris— *"fors et excepté le droit de justice foncière."*

Acting on the opinion of these jurisconsults, some *seigneurs* claimed the right to appoint a *sergent* who would carry out distraints by their sealed order alone; and others went so far as to claim the right to maintain a judge, *procureur fiscal, greffier,* and *sergent* and to deal with these cases up to the value of 60 *sous parisis* and fines of 6 *sous parisis.*

Dumoulin, however (article 52, column 78), thought that the custom of Paris gave the *seigneur* the right to distrain only if he possessed a power of justice. In the *arrêt* concerning the abbey of Saint-Martin-des-Champs, the expression *"justice du fonds de terre,"* or *"justice foncière,"* meant, according to him, "low justice"; and, as for the verdict regarding the church of Sainte-Opportune, that had been in-validated by an *arrêt* of 3 August 1586.

Actually, under the custom of Paris, there was no *justice foncière*. It was a tolerated practice for the *seigneur* to whom feudal dues or *cens* were payable to take possession of the fief or *censive* concerned in cases such as those mentioned, acting through a *sergent* holding an order sealed by the said *seigneur;* but this serving of a domanial writ did not confer any jurisdiction upon him—it was merely the action of a master in a private affair, and he was obliged to have it approved by letters from the chancellery, called *lettres de confortemain.* As a rule, in cases like this, the *seigneur* would petition the ordinary judge to grant him an authority to distrain, to be executed by a royal or a seignorial *sergent,* and to appoint a commissioner to take care of the property thus seized.

According to Loyseau, however, in the areas subject to the customs of Anjou, Maine, Touraine, and Blois, *justices foncières* did actually exist. The *seigneurs* seized, on their own authority, lands that were under their *seigneurie directe,* or the fruits of these lands "hanging from the roots," by thrusting into the earth a stick with a wisp of straw attached, called a *brandon;* or else they took the door of the farmhouse in question off its hinges. They appointed *juges guestrés,* with *sergents, greffiers,* and *procureurs,* and arrogated to themselves the right to impose fines. "The peasants, seeing a judge in their village, ad-dressed themselves to him regarding their slightest disputes, especially those that had to do with their lands, such as the fixing of boundary stones, the appointing of crop-watchers, or damage done by animals." These *justices foncières* dealt with real cases in which the fines were assessed at 6 *sous parisis* (7 *sous* and 6 *deniers tournois*).[1] *Justice foncière* was also accepted in Poitou, Brittany, and Normandy.[2]

The actual situation of the *seigneuries*

We have just outlined what was, more or less, the legal position of the *seigneuries* as recognized in the 17th and 18th centuries. We ought now to see what the actual situation was, the usages and practices that in fact obtained, and do this province by province, owing to the extreme diversity of the kingdom and the lands ruled by the kings of France. But there is no room to do that here. We must therefore be content with taking up some problems that were common to several provinces and giving some examples.

The number and extent of the seigneuries *and the* presence of the seigneurs

First, what was, in fact, the density of *seigneuries* and to what extent were *seigneurs* present?

In Lower Auvergne *seigneuries* seem to have been numerous. The region was scattered with châteaux or noblemen's residences, built with turrets and with armorial bearings carved over the doorways. Often a village nobleman was to be found there, an ennobled person, or some privileged individual "living like a noble." Attached to the château would be a *réserve seigneuriale* and a *seigneurie directe,* with a court of justice, a *greffe,* and a prison. Many of the châteaux were in ruins, with seignorial life seemingly extinct. But many still stood, with the owner in residence and seignorial life active. In 1725 there were 400 seignorial families in that region. In Beaujolais, at the end of the 18th century, 87 *seigneuries* were recorded, with 200 fiefs. In Dauphiné, at the end of the 17th, there were 330 *seigneurs* with powers of justice and 213 so-called *"seigneurs" directs* without powers of justice, as well as fiefs.

Seigneuries varied greatly in size. There were some very small ones, covering only a third, a quarter, or even a ninth of the territory of a village, and there were some very large ones. In Dauphiné the duc de Lesdiguières possessed *seigneuries* over seventy-eight communities, the marquis de Sassenage over eighteen, the comte de Saint-Vallier over seventeen. In Beaujolais the baron de Beaujolais had authority over thirty-two parishes in the 17th century and, in 1789, over twenty-six. In the Essonne Valley, near Paris, the *seigneurie* of Villeroy, a castellany raised in 1615 to a marquisate and in 1663 to a duchy, embraced at the latter date forty *terres nobles,* sixteen of which were lands and *seigneuries* held directly by the duke in twelve parishes.

The Polignac family possessed vast *seigneuries* in Velay, and the Latour-Maubourg family in Auvergne.

It must also be noted that a mass of rural nobles held fiefs without powers of justice and were therefore not truly *seigneurs*. In Lyonnais 135 fiefs were listed in 198 parishes, but in a single parish there were 12 fiefs. This meant that there were some tiny fiefs, without powers of justice, which do not enter into calculations of the number of *seigneuries*.

Generally, *seigneuries* were held by nobles or by ecclesiastics. In Dauphiné, of 292 lay *seigneurs* with powers of justice, 212 were nobles, 71 were officials, and 9 were commoners. In Lyonnais and Beaujolais, at the end of the 17th century, officials and *bourgeois* held about 10 percent of the seignorial parishes, nobles 43 percent, and ecclesiastics 27 percent, with 20 percent unaccounted for. In Velay in 1734, of 123 lay *seigneuries*, 42 percent were held by *nobles d'épée*, 14 percent by *nobles de robe*, 37 percent by rural nobles, and 7 percent by commoners.

However, this "distribution" does not really tell us what sort of nobles were involved, for it takes no account of social mobility, of the entry of families of modest origin into the ranks of the nobility and the extinction of old noble families. An upward movement in society went on everywhere, though very unevenly. In the *élections* of Lower Auvergne between 1715 and 1771 there were twenty-one ennoblements—three of these being for military services and fifteen for the exercise of civil functions. Some *seigneuries* thus passed into the possession of persons who, though juridically noble, were not noble socially. In Lyonnais and Velay, commoners and petty nobles fragmented the *seigneuries* of the great nobles and raised themselves up in the social hierarchy. The mechanism of this process is clearly illustrated in Velay by the example of the Polignac family. They began at the end of the 17th century to sell *"petites directes,"* cens, rents, *lods et ventes*. Then they alienated powers of middle and low justice, retaining only the powers of high justice, with title and rank, but having already lost all the rest of seignorial reality. Finally, they sold a power of high justice and the title of baron to a commoner who in 1777 entered the Estates of Velay as a nobleman. This commoner had been the farmer general of the *seigneurie* in question for fifteen years. Once he became *seigneur*, he reconstituted the terrier and squeezed the peasants harder than the Polignacs had ever done. In this way there was formed, in the second half of the 18th century, a "feudal" class of notables, *bourgeois, rentiers,* merchants, owners first of the profits of a *seigneurie* and then of the title of *seigneur,* living side by side with the country *gentilshommes* of old, august families, who were poor, possessing hardly anything but their names.

The extent to which the *seigneurs* were present was uneven, depending on the rank of the owner of the given *seigneurie.* In Auvergne the court nobles were absent, of course—the prince de Conti, owner of the duchy of Mercoeur; the duc d'Orléans, owner of the county of Montpensier and of Combrailles; the marquis de Broglie, owner of Besse, Saint-Saturnin, Saint-Amand-Tallende; the duc de La Rochefoucauld, owner of the barony of Le Luguet—as also were the members of the king's Council, the men close to the government, such as the Lamoignons, the Ormessons, the minister Bertin (who put in an appearance for a few days at Saurier in 1786), the *financier* John Law, and Peirenc de Moras, at the beginning of Louis XV's reign.

The provincial higher nobility were in residence for a few months of the year but were more often to be found at Versailles—families like the Montboissiers, the Montboissier-Canillacs, the Bouillons, the Langeacs, the D'Estaings.

The old nobility of the provinces spent most of the year in their *seigneuries,* but during the winter they withdrew to their town houses in Issoire, Clermont, and Riom. They bought land, supervised the administration of their *réserves seigneuriales,* and carried out their duties as *seigneurs;* examples are the Lastic and Du Crot families.

Many poor *gentilshommes* lived in their *seigneuries* all the year round.

Finally, those townsmen who were *seigneurs* in the country visited their lands only occasionally, as, for example, such *nobles d'office et de robe* as Président De Caldaguès, Président Clary, of the *cour des aides,* Guillaume Chabrol, of the *sénéchaussée* and presidial court of Riom, Pelissier de la Féligonde, of the *sénéchaussée* of Clermont, Grellot de La Deyte, *conseiller* in the *élection* of Brioude; or such ennobled merchants as the manufacturer Dupuy de la Grand-Rive, who in 1736 acquired an ennobling office as *secrétaire du roi* and proceeded to purchase a whole series of *seigneuries* in Livradois.

Those *seigneurs* who were absentees were very willing to hand over the whole of their *seigneurie* to a farmer general. This solution to the problem became increasingly widespread during the 18th century. The farmer general farmed the demesne out to the tenant farmers and sharecroppers. He farmed out the collection of dues separately, in portions.

In this way the *seigneur* lost all contact with his men, his vassals. The farmer general might be a stranger to the province. In 1777 the farmers general of Ravel were the *sieurs* Etienne and Robert Lenoir, *bourgeois* of Paris, men involved in the king's affairs. In most cases, though, the farmers general were Auvergnats, notaries, seignorial officials, advocates, legal practitioners, or merchants.

The example of Auvergne seems to have been typical.

The functioning of the seignorial courts

The actual functioning of the seignorial courts is another problem. They were very numerous, very much mixed up together, with enclaves, and, in certain regions, such as the Paris region, highly unstable. In the kingdom as a whole there were between 70,000 and 80,000 seignorial courts that were fully active—between twenty-five and thirty times as many as the number of magistrates' courts in France on the eve of 1914.

The *prévôté et vicomté* of Paris had 364 seignorial courts in it. Since the locally prevailing maxim was "fief and justice have nothing in common," the courts were multiplied as a result of divisions between heirs and the fragmentations effected by fief-holders for purposes of sale. The number, extent, and limits were extremely varied in the area around Paris.

In Paris itself there was more permanence. Paris had twenty-five *seigneurs hauts justiciers,* possessing powers of high, middle, and low justice. Twenty-three of them were ecclesiastics, with only two laymen—the Grand Chambrier in eight streets and the Bailli du Palais in another eight. There were twenty-four prisons in Paris. The twenty-three ecclesiastics also had seignorial powers of justice in the area around the city, which came within the jurisdiction of their court in Paris, so that appeals from these "suburban" courts were heard by the Paris court on which they were dependent.

The most important of them was the court of the bishop of Paris—archbishop from 1622 onward. His court of Le For-l'Evêque had jurisdiction over 105 streets. He also had courts at Saint-Eloi and Saint-Magloire. His authority extended from the rue Saint-Martin to the Roule, outside Paris. He left to the king most of the territory between the rue Saint-Honoré and the Seine. Enclaves within the area covered by his jurisdiction were constituted by six fiefs with powers of justice, which included Saint-Germain-l'Auxerrois, Saint-Denis-de-la-Châtre, and the Fromentel fief, which, after 1570, was merged with the messuage of Saint-Honoré. Dependent on the court of Le For-l'Evêque were his seignorial courts in the area around Paris—Saint-Cloud, Combs-la-Ville, Mussy-l'Evêque, Créteil, Maisons-sur-Seine, Gentilly, Ozoir-la-Ferrière, etc.

The abbey of Saint-Germain-des-Prés exercised seignorial justice over the Faubourg Saint-Germain, from the rue de la Harpe and the rue de Vaugirard to the Champ-de-Mars and the Seine, with power to hear appeals from the abbey's seignorial courts outside Paris: Vaugirard, Issy, Suresnes, Châtillon, Villejuif, Thiais, Choisy, Parais, Villeneuve-Saint-Georges, Le Breuil, Saint-Germain-Laval, Esmous, and Dammartin.

There were many others of less importance: that of the Temple (the Priory of Saint John of Jerusalem), between the rue du Temple and the rue Vieille-du-Temple; that of the abbey of Saint-Martin-des-Champs, between the rue du Temple and the rue Saint-Martin. The abbey of Montmartre had in 1651 powers of justice in Paris over two houses in the rue de la Heaumerie, eleven houses in the rue de l'Arbre-Sec, twenty-six in the rue Saint-Honoré, eleven in the rue Tirechappe, twelve in the rue Saint-Martin, fourteen in the rue des Petits-Champs, seven in the rue Neuve-Saint-Merry, three in the rue du Moulin, and so on.

When there was an enclosing wall, as in the case of the Temple, the king's officers found it hard to enter, and the place in question became a refuge for all sorts of bad characters.

In the area around Paris the abbey of Saint-Denis dominated the West and North—the Pré-Saint-Gervais, La Villette, Pantin, Belleville, Aubervilliers, La Courneuve, Saint-Ouen, Asnières, Gennevilliers, Neuilly. Outside the ecclesiastical areas of seignorial justice, which were free from fragmentation through succession or alienation, there was a great deal of intermingling, for most seignorial powers of justice were held by members of the *parlement*, state councilors, and *secrétaires du roi*. There were few large areas of seignorial justice belonging to laymen. The most important was the one belonging to the Malon de Bercy family. Nicolas de Malon, as master of requests, held powers of justice in Bercy, Conflans, Carrières, and La Grange-aux-Merciers. In general, though, there was a awarm of little courts, especially in the east of Paris. René Gaillard, *seigneur* of the *seigneurie* of Charenton, had on 16 March 1673 powers of high, middle, and low justice over about thirty plots of land, consisting of two, three, or four arpents each. Instability owing to divided inheritances and sales was the rule.

After the king had settled down at Versailles, the seignorial courts became more permanent and more extensive in the areas they covered. Favorites, princes of the blood, royal bastards, ministers, all established themselves in castellanies near Versailles, at Saint-Cloud, Sceaux, or Chevreuse. These persons, who were very rich, effected a regrouping of fiefs, a concentration of landholdings, and formed large farms for exploitation by entrepreneurs. At the same time they regrouped the seignorial courts and gave them more importance.

Similar disparities occurred elsewhere. In Lower Auvergne, according to the investigation of 1765, the court of the *seigneurie* of Rochecharles had jurisdiction over an isolated church perched on a height. Another such court had authority over twenty persons. The parish of Polhminhac was divided among ten *hauts justiciers*. Eighteen villages of the *subdélégation* of Aurillac had two, three, or four *seigneurs*. Often, though, there was a single *haut justicier* in a parish. Sometimes several *hautes justices* were held by one man: the comte d'Estaing had three, the bishop of Clermont eleven.

In Marche the situation was complex. Between seven and eight hundred "*seigneuries*" were listed, with between three and four thousand fiefs but only three or four hundred seignorial courts, for, except in Lower Marche, "fief and justice have nothing in common." A power of justice was a distinction, an honor. The number of seignorial courts tended to increase during the 17th and 18th centuries, by usurpation at the expense of the count and the king, by subinfeudation, or through sales by the *seigneurs* or by the king himself; Louis XIV, in 1695, during the War of the League of Augsburg, and after a great *mortalité,* sold to Gédéon de Rouffignac, *seigneur* of Sagnat, lieutenant to the marshals of France in Lower Marche, the power of high justice over four *métairies*—eight homes all together. In 1686 he had alienated six royal castellanies to the duc de La Feuillade in exchange for the *seigneurie* of Saint-Cyr, keeping only the right to hear appeals and the feudal suzerainty. The *trésoriers de France,* the *procureurs du roi* in the *sénéchaussée* or the presidial court at Guéret, the intendant himself, were all unable to state the precise number of siegnorial courts. By checking the law books in the archives and the deeds in family papers, we find that there were 250 seignorial courts in Upper Marche, 27 in Franc-Alleu (200 parishes), and 70 in Lower Marche (90 parishes). Lower Marche included, in 1749, 9 "titled" *seigneuries* (1 duchy, 4 marquisates, 4 baronies), 13 castellanies, 12 *hautes justices,* 6 *moyennes justices,* and 5 *basses justices.* Upper Marche included 2 marquisates,

3 counties, 4 viscounties, 5 baronies, at least 200 *hautes justices,* 1 *moyenne justice,* and 1 *basse justice.* The geographical extent of these powers of justice was highly uneven. Every *seigneur justicier* had jurisdiction over his demesne or *réserve,* over the fiefs held of him, and over the subfiefs. There was roughly one power of justice per ten fiefs. Broadly speaking, the minor justices had between 200 and 300 persons subject to them. That of Aigurande-en-Marche covered an area of less than 7 hectares, less than 265 meters wide. That of Maillat measured 3 kilometers by 3, that of Le Monteil 8 by 7, that of Dun-le-Palestel, the biggest, 35 by 20. The areas covered were fairly stable.

In Brittany "fief and justice were one and the same." Power of justice was "inherent in" or "attached to" a fief. Every holder of a fief was a *seigneur* and had power of justice over his fief, over his *seigneurie directe,* including the *domaine congéable,* apart from his demesne. In the *usement* of Broérec the *domaine congéable* was excluded from the *seigneur*'s power of justice. In practice, the *seigneur* also had jurisdiction over waters and woods, markets, auditories, squares, streets, and roads, even though they were not granted out as fiefs. *Justices* were very numerous and were sometimes very small and very changeable, with frequent unions and separations caused by divided inheritances and sales. According to the inquiry of 1711, there were about 3,800 *justices,* 282 being ecclesiastical and 3,518 lay. Of these, 1,500 were *hautes justices.* There were, on the average, 2 *justices* per parish, one of these being an *haute justice;* but there were 3 per parish in the bishoprics of Dol and Saint-Brieuc and 5 per parish in that of Saint-Malo. The rural parish of Corseul boasted 10 *justices,* and that of Pont-Drieux, in 1766, had 19. The town of Rennes was divided up among 27 *justices,* Nantes among 16, Lannion among 10, Tréguier among 7, and Quimper among 6.

The *sub-délégué* of Châteauneuf mentions in 1717 a *justice* the territory of which consisted of a single fief made up of a single *censive.* Many powers of justice, embracing high, middle, and low justice, covered only one-third of a parish, a handful of holdings. But the rural *justice* of Largouêt covered, in 1665, as many as 17 parishes, and in 1749 the number was 28, an area twenty leagues round. It belonged in those days to M. de Cornulier, *président* in the *parlement* of Rennes. The comte de Toulouse, Louis XIV's bastard, possessed, in his capacity of duc de Penthièvre, the *justice* of the town of Guingamp, with fiefs in 56 parishes and the power to hear appeals from 118 jurisdictions. The bishop of Dol had power of temporal justice, or *régaire,* over the town and suburbs, which meant 18 parishes, together with a *régaire* embedded as an enclave in the *seigneurie* of Châteauneuf and another as enclaves in Combourg, with power to hear appeals from 10 fiefs *en haute justice* and 38 *en moyenne justice*.

Seignorial powers of justice were, as a rule, active and flourishing and rendered real services. In Paris, before the edict of February 1674, which merged with the Châtelet most of the area of jurisdiction of the seignorial *justices* in Paris, ordinary hearings were held regularly; in the suburbs, though irregular, they were frequent. In 1606, at Saint-Martin-des-Champs, the court sat every Monday; in 1611, at Saint-Lazare, it sat on Tuesdays and Wednesdays, about a dozen cases being dealt with each time; in 1630, at Saint-Germain-des-Prés, the court sat on Tuesdays and Saturdays, with about fifty cases listed for each sitting, and gratuitous and administrative jurisdiction was available every day; at Le For-l'Evêque in 1645 the court sat five days a week, dealing with twenty-five cases each time.

Among 100 cases heard by a seignorial judge in Paris we find: 20 procedural questions, 18 to do with rent, 10 with guardianship, 10 with the payment of bills, 8 with the payment of feudal dues (mainly *lods et ventes*), 10 with insults, blows, and injuries, 12 with measures of enforcement of the law, and 12 miscellaneous. At the hearing of 13 July 1673 in the court of the abbey of Sainte-Geneviève we note: an appointment of experts to evaluate works and repairs, an order of arrest, a sentence for insults, and settlement of a matter concerned with hat trimmings, five measures connected with preliminary investigations, inquiries, interrogation of witnesses, four sentences to pay various sums, two matters concerned with rent. In short, these courts were much like the magistrates' courts of the Third Republic.

The seignorial courts of Paris also exercised criminal jurisdiction. Death sentences were infrequent, being pronounced for infanticide, bigamy, or robbery. The guilty persons were first strangled and then hanged. The last death sentence found dates from 1664: at Nanterre a husband had murdered his wife when she was seven months pregnant. Exercise of *"justice de sang"* was thus exceptional. Sentences to corporal or disgraceful punishments were less rare; these included banishment, the carcan, thrashing, or public apology, imposed for insults, blows, and injuries or for brawling. The last example found was at Auteuil in 1780.

The seignorial judges of Paris exercised police powers in conformity with the law and jurisprudence of the Paris *parlement*.

In Marche the *justices* were, in practice, all *hautes*. The seignorial judges held assizes, called *"grandes assises"* or *"assises par fief."* These were solemn sessions which the persons subject to the court's jurisdiction were obliged to attend so as to remind them of the court's authority and so that administrative ordinances might be made known; a few important cases, mainly criminal ones, would be tried, and some executions carried out (in effigy, if necessary), so as to produce an effect on people's minds.

Seignorial judges held ordinary sittings at which civil cases, both contentious and gratuitous, and criminal cases were dealt with higgledy-piggledy, all at the same sitting. The frequency of these ordinary sittings was regulated by royal *règlements* and by custom. At Ceilloux, in 1668–70, ordinary sittings took place between four and six times a year; at Saint-Martial-le-Mont, in 1681 and 1687, between three and ten times; at Saint-Maixent, in 1686–89, sixteen or seventeen times; at Chambon-Sainte-Croix, in 1763–73, three or four times; at Sérier and Royère, in 1775–85, ten times; at Saint-Marc and Frougier, in 1789, fourteen times.

At each sitting of the minor courts, two or three cases were dealt with. But at Saint-Germain-sur-Vienne in 1699, at twenty-nine sittings, 171 cases were disposed of; at Dun-le-Palestel, in 1756, 326 cases at twenty-eight sittings; and at Magnac-Laval, in 1775, 312 cases at thirty-two sittings.

Seigneurs were rarely litigants in their own courts; they made up only 8 percent of the total numbers. Most of the litigants were traders and craftsmen, bringing cases against each other, and *laboureurs,* sharecroppers, and tenant farmers suing either each other or the traders and craftsmen. Day laborers and journeymen appeared less frequently. Seignorial justice in Marche was thus much more of a service to the inhabitants of the *seigneurie* than to the *seigneur justicier.*

The seignorial courts of Marche dealt with criminal cases: murders, assaults, insults, sexual offenses, robberies. Investigations took two or three days. Sentence of death was pronounced in grave cases, such as infanticide, but it had to be confirmed by the Paris *parlement.*

The seignorial courts of Marche carried out administrative work to enforce the *arrêts de règlement* relative to the price of meat and of bread, weights and measures, stray dogs, cleanliness of the streets, drink shops, and so on.

But the bulk of the cases concerned the court's civil jurisdiction. On the contentious side there were damage caused by animals, displaced boundary stones between fields, rights of way, tenancies, markets, and contracts. On the noncontentious side there were appointment of guardians, emancipation from guardianship, inventories, checking of guardians' accounts. All these matters were soon disposed of.

Cases concerning feudal or seignorial rights made up only 1 or 2 percent of all the cases brought before a given court during several dozen years: offering of faith and homage, payment of *cens* and rents, *lods et ventes*, recognizances, *banalités, taille aux quatre cas*. (As late as 22 May 1766 a seignorial *taille* was levied on the occasion of the marriage of a *seigneur*'s daughter.)

The seignorial courts thus showed themselves active and useful in Marche. The costs of justice were not high. For restitution of a dowry of 700 livres, expenses were incurred in 1783 to the tune of 31 livres *tournois,* 9 sous, 3 deniers. The sale of two oxen, involving 196 livres, cost in 1789 5 livres, 15 sous. The appointment of a guardian in 1787 cost 19 livres. The royal courts appear to have been a great deal more expensive. In the presidial court of Guéret in 1740 the costs involved in a case concerning a plot of land of three *éminées* came to 643 livres, 13 sous, 3 deniers, and in one concerning a big oak tree in 1780 they came to 272 livres, 15 sous, 9 deniers.

The degrees of jurisdiction seem to have been few in Paris and its neighborhood. Within the area subject to the jurisdiction of the bishop of Paris one could appeal from a seignorial court outside the city to the court at Le For-l'Evêque and from that directly to the *parlement*—only three degrees of jurisdiction. With other seignorial courts, appeal against a sentence pronounced in Paris was to the Grand Châtelet and then to the *parlement*—three degrees of jurisdiction, in serious cases. Death sentences always had to be confirmed by the *parlement*.

In Marche certain *seigneuries* had two degrees of jurisdiction internally—*"le double siège."* The ordinance of Roussillon of January 1564 (new style) decreed abolition of this arrangement (article 24), but it was still in being in the 17th century at the abbey of Grandmont and, down to 1679, in the *justice* of Dognon.

Many of the seignorial courts of Marche were dependent on a higher seignorial court, to which there was appeal from them. In 1723 the high, middle, and low justice of the *seigneurie* of Fougerot was subject in this way to the castellany of La Messelière, and in 1759 the *seigneurie* of Bussière-Poitevine was subject to the *seigneurie* of Magnac. But there were never more than two degrees of jurisdiction before a case went to the royal court.

Once a year the officials of the *sénéchaussées* in Marche could hold a general assize in each castellany, royal or seignorial, and try the cases pending there. This was still mentioned in an *arrêt de règlement* of the *sénéchaussée* of Moulins in 1678 and in an ordinance of the *sénéchaussée* of Guéret in 1684. However, these assizes were held less and less frequently, and they ceased altogether in the 18th century.

Appeals from seignorial courts could be taken to the *sénéchaussées* of Guéret, Le Dorat, or Bellac and then to the presidial courts of Moulins, Riom, Limoges, Poitiers, or Guéret (established in 1635). Most civil decisions made by the seignorial courts were not appealed against to the royal courts. Of all the appeals received by the *sénéchaussées* and the presidial courts, half came from the seignorial courts and half from the royal castellanies. These appeals were put up by *"bourgeois,"* persons described as *"sieur de,"* traders, craftsmen, peasants, and even day laborers, and were directed in some cases against *seigneurs* and their officials. In half of the cases the higher court rejected the appeal, but in the other half the lower court's decision was set aside. It would not seem, therefore, that the royal courts confined their dispensation of justice to certain social groups only.

Appeals to the Paris *parlement* were infrequent as far as civil cases were concerned. As regards criminal cases, there were nine appeals between 1725 and 1750 and six between 1750 and 1780. In these same periods, however, there were forty-five and sixty appeals, respectively, against verdicts given by royal courts. The *parlement* always mitigated sentences pronounced by seignorial courts. In one case it called for additional information and then released the accused.

In Brittany the situation of those subject to seignorial justice was not so good. Fifty-three seignorial jurisdictions in that province came directly under the *parlement:* all the *régaires,* except that of Dol, and some lay courts, such as those of the *duchés-pairies* of Penthièvre and Rohan. In most cases there were between four and eight degrees of jurisdiction, and in seventy-five cases more than five courts were involved. For example, a case proceeding from appeal to appeal might start in the seignorial court at Poirier, go to that at Kerhout, then to the one at Launay-Betloy, from there to the court of Pontrieu, then to the one at Châtelendren; after that it entered the field of royal jurisdiction, starting with the *sénéchaussée* of Saint-Brieuc and going on to the presidial court of Rennes and, finally, to the *parlement.* There were some mitigations. Where criminal cases were concerned, appeal lay *"nûment et omisso medio"* to the *parlement,* and this applied also to verdicts in forest cases and cases relating to administration and offices: guardianships, injunctions, distraints, auditing of accounts, announcements, auctions, adjudications, leases authorized by a judge, inheritances without liability for debts, orders regarding priority in the payment of debts. Finally, *"menées"* were still held. The great seignorial courts and the royal courts held on certain days general sittings which in former times all vassals had been obliged to attend, bringing their men with them, to *"présenter leur menée."* At these sittings the cases still pending in the lower courts were dealt with directly. This obligation had disappeared during the 15th century. However, the vassals of the *seigneurs "ménéants"* still had the right to bring their disputes to the general sittings of the higher courts. They attended on the days assigned for their respective *menées,* being summoned by a special *sergent,* the *sergent ameneur.*

The competence of the seignorial courts of Brittany was more extensive, on the civil side, than in most provinces, owing to the reduction in the number of *cas royaux.* It covered the rendering of accounts for church fabrics (despite *arrêts* to the contrary), impropriated tithes, and matters connected with benefices, such as ordinary tithes, the honorific rights of churches, endowments, and so on. In violation of article 5, heading XII, of the civil ordinance of 1667, it extended to the confirmation and verification of private legal documents and, in violation of article 8, heading XVIII, of the same ordinance, to provisional enforcement in matters of complaint and reinstatement. The competence of these courts was as wide as that of the royal *sénéchaussées.* Despite the restrictions imposed by law, the seignorial courts of Brittany took cognizance of all difficulties arising from the seignorial regime, and, despite what the local "custom" said, even nonfeudal tenants—tenant farmers, sharecroppers, all the inhabitants of a *seigneurie*—were subject to the repressive activity of seignorial justice. The *seigneur* was judge in his own case, even on his own demesne, contrary to article 28 of the new custom, and this held true even if the case concerned not merely unpaid arrears but a challenge to the actual obligation to pay.

In general, the direct profit that these courts brought to the *seigneur* was slight, and they could even be financially burdensome to him. In the end, fines and confiscations contributed little. On 9 March 1665 the accounts of the receiver of fines for the abbey of Sainte-Geneviève in Paris for three quarters showed gross receipts of 57 livres, expenditure of 36 livres, and so a profit of only 21 livres. But the profits from sales of seignorial offices need to be added. At the abbey of Saint-Victor, in 1674, the office of *bailli* was valued at 6,000 livres and that of his *lieutenant* at 3,000 livres, while fines were farmed at 1,200 livres, the *greffe* at 1,200 livres, and the jail at 300 livres. At Le For-l'Evêque the *greffe* was farmed at 1,200 livres and the prisons at 6,000 livres. The costs that the seigneur had to meet were high: removal of dead bodies found, maintenance of children abandoned by their parents, escorting of prisoners, keeping of minutes, searches, rent for the courtroom, rent for prisons, payments to jailers, etc. Criminal proceedings, in particular, were very expensive, especially after the ordinance of 1670. The *seigneur* had to pay in advance the costs of making the arrest, of keeping the accused in custody, and of escorting him to the *parlement* in the event of an appeal. He had to pay for the execution. If his judges had made mistakes in procedure, he was required to have the case tried over again at his own expense. The seignorial officials often absorbed the entire profit of the seignorial court, and in Marche it was considered that all that was left to the *seigneur* was the honor of having his own court.

The *seigneur* had to have a respectable courtroom. At Le For-l'Evêque, in Paris, there were a courtroom, a council chamber, and three other large rooms. When the *seigneur* had no courtroom of his own, he rented the one belonging to a higher seignorial court or a royal court. It could happen, though, even in the area around Paris, that justice was dispensed in a church porch, a cemetery, or a drink shop, or, if the *seigneur* possessed a courtroom, that the judge and public had to share it with pigs and other animals. The *seigneur* had to have a prison. There were some good ones, such as that of Le For-l'Evêque, which in 1664 held about a hundred prisoners and took the overflow from the royal prisons of Paris. Sometimes the *seigneur* rented a royal prison. Sometimes, however, the *seigneur*'s prison either did double duty as a cowshed or was nonexistent. The *seigneur* had to have a *greffe* and keep a register of hearings and of all documents signed by the officers of justice. This was usually farmed by a legal practitioner, a former clerk in some *greffe*.

The *seigneur* had to have officers of justice (*arrêts* of the *parlement* dated 23 June 1516, 19 January 1600, 26 March 1768), whom he appointed by letters of provision but who were "received" by the royal *bailliages* and *sénéchaussées*. In the court of the abbey of Saint-Germain-des-Prés in 1630 there were a *bailli*, his *lieutenant*, a *procureur fiscal*, eleven attorneys, and twelve tipstaffs, together with the personnel of the *greffe* and the prison. These officials had to be capable, honest men of knowledge and integrity, Catholics, aged not less than twenty-five, and laymen. In Paris the seignorial *baillis* were licentiates in law and advocates, and the *procureurs fiscaux* and *greffiers* were attorneys at the Châtelet. In the area around Paris they were mere local legal practitioners who, in the minor courts, were not even graduates. In Marche, thirty-nine seignorial judges were advocates, licentiates in law; thirty had *sieur de* in front of their names, and a few were nobles. They lived in the royal castellanies and the larger *bourgs*. Usually they combined several royal and seignorial offices. Among nineteen *procureurs d'office* we find one *"sieur de,"* three licentiates in law, five royal notaries, and ten legal practitioners. They were usually recruited from the towns, among *bourgeois,* well-to-do traders and minor officials. The *greffiers* were legal practitioners, small peasants, or craftsmen, living in *bourgs,* who knew the rudiments of legal procedure. In Brittany, in the large *seigneuries,* the seignorial officials were advocates who combined a number of jobs: *subdélégués* of the intendant, notaries, *procureurs du roi* in the royal *sénéchaussées, contrôleurs des actes.* They were "received" by the *parlement* and subject to its supervision; they tried cases in accordance with the ordinances and *règlements* of the *parlement,* and their procedures were as regular as in the presidial courts. In the minor courts of the countryside the judges were recruited from among farmers' sons, men who had not studied or obtained degrees and who sometimes were unable to read or write, while the notaries and attorneys were drawn from "the dregs of the people"—tinkers, tailors, beadles. They were at one and the same time farmer, steward, bailiff, notary, *procureur fiscal* here, seneschal there, and sometimes keeper of the drink shop as well.

The seignorial courts were always profitable to the *seigneur* in the sense that they ensured the payment to him of *cens, lods et ventes,* and seignorial dues. In this sense it is not wrong to say that they were everywhere a means of maintaining the feudal and seignorial system—like the entire "public order" of that time. In Marche and Ile-de-France the role of these courts went no further than the application of edicts, ordinances, and customs. The seignorial officials formed a tribunal, not the administration of the *seigneurie.* The administrator was the *seigneur* himself or his farmer general. They made application to the *procureur fiscal,* who gave his conclusions, and the judge pronounced his verdict. But the judge was not a tool of the *seigneur* for exercising oppression. This was not true, however, in Brittany, at least in the minor courts. There the seignorial judges and all the officers of seignorial justice were agents for the exploitation of the *seigneurie*, the *seigneur's* "men of business"—so many intendants and stewards, as it were. The *seigneur* entrusted his seneschal or his *procureur fiscal* with his purchases, with the management of the lands of the *seigneurie*, with the drawing-up or canceling of leases, and with the repairing of mills, supervision of the cutting-down of trees, cartage, and so on, and the seignorial courts always favored the *seigneur* in arbitrary fashion. Seignorial justice became, in Brittany, an instrument of exploitation and exaction.

On the whole it seems that we can say that the seignorial courts provided justice that was equitable, inexpensive, easily accessible, and rapid. Their activity appears to have continued to develop all through the 17th and 18th centuries and to have done so in the general public interest.

The relations between the seigneur and his men

A *seigneurie* often formed a genuine human community. The *seigneur* maintained relations with his men that were based on the mutual obligations of protection and fealty. One can certainly find without difficulty examples of *seigneurs* who were harsh or cruel, abusing their powers. In Lower Auvergne some *seigneurs* were petty tyrants, brutal and sometimes no better than brigands; one of them even used his power of justice to carry out arbitrary arrests and extortions. In Brittany the poor petty nobles, living in manor houses with thatched roofs that were not much different from the homes of the peasants, and rarely going off to serve in the army, had a reputation for idleness, drunkenness, and brutality. The stick seems to have played a big part in their relations with their peasants, and the peasant revolt of the "Torreben" in 1675, known as the Stamped Paper Revolt, offers examples of cruelty by peasants against *gentilshommes* that seem to have been in the nature of reprisals. But a still greater number of examples are to be found, in Brittany, Normandy, Auvergne, and Limousin, in which the *seigneur* appears as the head of the family, the leader of the community, a protector. In many cases *seigneurs* took as godparents for their children their manservants or maidservants, who were drawn from among their peasants. *Seigneurs* signed the marriage contracts of the villagers, stood godfather to the peasants' children, joined in the village festivals. *Seigneurs* wielded important influence in the *bourgs* and communities of inhabitants in their *seigneuries*. They frequently gave directives to the aldermen, *jurats,* consuls, syndics, and principal inhabitants (who, indeed, often asked for them), and these directives were usually followed. The *seigneur* intervened against the agents of the royal fiscal system, the *huissiers* and soldiers sent to collect *taille,* against troops marching through, against men armed by another *seigneur* who invaded his *seigneurie* on an expedition of pillage or vengeance or prestige (there were plenty of such cases well into the 18th century). He gave shelter in his château or fortified house to the peasants and their cattle. He armed those who lived with him, his *domestiques* and servants, his *familia.* He helped his *censitaires,* his subjects, to arm themselves, fired on the attackers with harquebus and musket, and even counterattacked. In time of dearth it was his duty to relieve the peasants' hunger, and in many cases he did indeed do this. This is an aspect of life in the *seigneuries* which has necessarily left fewer traces in the records than leases and loans, and it needs systematic study.

The practice of appointing a farmer general to run a *seigneurie* did not necessarily alter the nature of these relations. It was sometimes the case that the farmer general conscientiously took the place of the *seigneur* in all respects, acting as his representative.

What were the actual man-to-man relations in those areas which still, here and there, retained serfdom and mortmain—Franche-Comté and the Duchy of Burgundy? In 1789 one-third of the Burgundian communities were subject to mortmain and perhaps to serfdom—Autunois, Auxois, Charolais, and Châlonnais, but not the Plain of Burgundy, Mâconnais, Dijonnais, or Châtillonnais, a region depopulated by the Thirty Years' War.

The customaries preserved the principle of serfdom and mortmain. Bouhier, *président* in the *parlement* of Dijon, in his commentary on the custom of Burgundy (1717), expressed approval of mortmain: it tied the peasant to the soil, thereby ensuring good cultivation and consequently guaranteeing revenue to the *seigneurs* and the state, and so it was for the common good.

A *mainmortable* could alienate his property only to other *mainmortables* of the same *seigneurie,* unless authorized by the *seigneur.* He was subject to special seignorial dues. The *corvées* he had to perform were of five or six days in the year instead of two or three days, as in the regions where freedom prevailed. He could bequeath his property only to a *mainmortable* living with him. He could make a will only with the *seigneur*'s permission. If there was no *mainmortable* living with him when he died, his property "fell" to the *seigneur* (this was called *échute*). If the *seigneur* then sold the holding, the purchaser need not be a *mainmortable*, provided that he supplied a man who was of that status. Nevertheless, the tenant who was a *mainmortable* was not a serf, since he had the right of *désaveu*.

The practice of *échute* was still strictly applied, as was shown by the Mauro affair in 1738. Mauro, a *mainmortable* of Charles de Montsaunier, comte de Montal, an *élu* in Burgundy, lived in Paris, where he became syndic of the payers of *rente*, a person both rich and respected. He died in 1738. His kinfolk, who had remained in the fief of Toste, wished to claim the inheritance. But Mauro had not taken the necessary steps to "disavow" his *seigneur*, and the latter claimed the right of *échute*. The seignorial court granted it to him. The provost of the Merchants of Paris and Mauro's heirs appealed against the verdict on the grounds that every Parisian was a freeman. On 29 April 1738 the Paris *parlement* confirmed the verdict of the seignorial court and awarded Mauro's property to the *seigneur*. This *arrêt* set a legal precedent.

The intendants vigorously upheld *mainmorte* until 1750. They opposed enfranchisements, which were not numerous: thirty-six in the 17th century, sixteen in the 18th. After 1750 *mainmorte* came under heavy attack. Voltaire took up the cause of the serfs of the Jura, and Rousseau argued in the same sense in his *Discourse on the Origin of Inequality*, presented to the Academy of Dijon in 1755.

Necker's edict abolishing serfdom on the royal demesne put the *seigneurs* in a difficult position. During the inquiry concerning agriculture carried out among the *curés* in 1779, many of the latter protested against serfdom and *mainmorte* from the standpoint of the improvement of agriculture, and the economists and Physiocrats showed themselves frankly hostile to these institutions.

However, the *seigneurs* wanted money in order to develop agriculture. They kept an eye on successions so as to claim *échutes*. They bothered less about *formariages*, because they thought that marriages made with persons outside the *seigneurie* would lead to *échutes*. Other *seigneurs* emancipated their *mainmortables* but demanded, in return, large sums of money, increased *lods et ventes*, seignorial *taille*, *banalités*, and *corvées*, doubling of the *tierces* (*champart*), the *droit de triage*. And the *tierce* was already much heavier in the regions of *mainmorte* than in those where freedom prevailed.

Mainmorte entailed economic stagnation. The hilly part of Burgundy (the *Côte*), where *mainmorte* was unknown, was a rich region where cultivation was developing. In the 17th century a certain compensation for subjection to *mainmorte* seems to have been constituted by a greater degree of protection given by the *seigneur;* but this protection seems to have diminished in the 18th century, and, at the end of it, the *mainmortables* felt that they were in a humiliating situation.

Seignorial and feudal exactions

Some indications have already been given, in the chapter devoted to the order of the nobility, regarding the relation of the *seigneurs* to the land, that is, regarding the exploitation of the *réserves seigneuriales* and the *censives,* of the *seigneurie,* or of other *seigneuries* which the *seigneur* regrouped, taking over their *seigneurie utile.* The *seigneur* worked his lands either directly, using wage labor, or through share-croppers or tenant farmers. I hope that I may be permitted, in this elementary and, perforce, relatively short work, not to go over the matter again. Let us now examine the problem of how much the seignorial and feudal exactions from the produce of the soil amounted to.

Seignorial and feudal exactions are very hard to calculate. One would need to seek out all the feudal and seignorial dues that were actually levied, using terriers, *cueilloirs,* and account books. Then one would have to determine the ratio between these feudal and seignorial dues and the net product, that is, what the land produced minus the seed corn and the expenses incurred in cultivation, using for this purpose the tax rolls for the "tenth" and the "twentieth." It would mean protracted and arduous work.

Historians have begun by calculating feudal and seignorial exactions per hectare so as to facilitate comparisons. In the area of the present Nord *département* feudal and seignorial dues amounted, on the average, to 8 or 9 livres *tournois* per hectare. But there was extreme diversity. In the village of Broxeele, exactions came to 85 livres per hectare, but in other villages the figure was as little as 1 or 2 livres. In Provence, at Auriol, in 1779, passing from one holding to another we find exactions of 5, 22, 24, 42, 45, and 92 livres per hectare. In the northern part of Gâtinais, in the *seigneurie* of Egreville (now in the *département* of Seine-et-Marne), for an area of 2,600 hectares the feudal and seignorial dues came to 1,766 livres—an average of 12 sous per hectare. In the *seigneurie* of M. de Caumartin, in the same region, for 3,680 hectares the feudal and seignorial dues were 1,610 livres—10 sous per hectare. The rolls of feudal and seignorial dues in twenty-six parishes, covering 29,125 hectares, show 14,727 livres, or 10 sous per hectare, including *champarts* but excluding *lods et ventes*. If the latter are added, we arrive at an average of 12 sous per hectare.

In Upper Auvergne, for an area of 4,500 hectares the feudal and seignorial dues came to 13,595 livres, an average of 3 livres per hectare, with variations from one *élection* to another—3 livres 13 in the *élection* of Aurillac, 2 livres 78 in that of Mauriac, 2 livres 72 in that of Saint-Flour. For 362 hectares of meadowland, the feudal and seignoral dues came to 1,262 livres, or 5 livres 40 per hectare. On 579 hectares of arable land, they came to 1,665 livres, or livres 87 per hectare.

What is perhaps more important is to know what *proportion* of the income from the land was taken by feudal and seignorial dues. In the northern part of Gâtinais, where the average return was 6 livres per hectare, the feudal and seignorial exaction was therefore 10 percent. In that region, Sénac de Meilhan, *seigneur* of Varennes (the parish of Souppes in the old *département* of Seine-et-Marne), enables us, through his *Etat de la terre et seigneurie de Varennes* (1789), to evaluate the seignorial dues at 1,350 livres per year, on the average, for 589 hectares of holdings, or an average of 2 livres per hectare, which is equivalent to 4 or 5 percent of the peasants' income. Those particular peasants were, however, in an exceptionally favorable situation, for there was no *champart* in that *seigneurie* and no tithe (which was, of course, neither feudal nor seignorial).

In Upper Auvergne, in the *élections* of Aurillac, Mauriac, and Saint-Flour, in 1745 and 1746, taking 2,926 assessments, grouped in 125 collections, we find that the net return from the land was 420,581 livres, and the seignorial and feudal rents came to 43,937 livres, or an average of 9.73 percent for the feudal and seignorial exactions. For the period 1780–88, 5,052 assessments in 51 collections give these figures: 740,733 livres net return, with 78,739 livres taken in feudal and seignorial dues, or a feudal and seignorial exaction averaging 10.62 percent. But these results do not take into account *lods et ventes, banalités,* or church tithes. Allowing for tithes, we get 16.41 percent in the *élection* of Aurillac, 19.06 percent in that of Saint-Flour, and 6.08 percent in that of Mauriac. In the plateau of Saint-Flour, a region of large-scale grain cultivation, the feudal and seignorial exactions thus amounted to 20 percent of the net return. Some historians link this fact with the *jacqueries* of 1789 and 1792. One would need, of course, to know, as well, the number of regions where these exactions also came to 20 percent but where there were no *jacqueries*.

In Lower Auvergne the word *cens* was used to cover all dues payable for land. At Boudes, fourteen *seigneuries directes* brought in 150 *setiers* of grain of all kinds out of a total production of 1,000 *setiers*, or 15 percent. At Saint-Géran, La Roche had to pay 100 *setiers*, farmed for 1,514 livres, out of a total net income of 4,938 livres, or 30 percent. At Saint-Jean-des-Olières, in the *élection* of Issoire, the *cens vifs* and the redemption payments for labor service and *corvées* came to 300 *setiers* of grain out of the annual return of 1,600 *setiers*, or 19 percent.

To this, however, must be added the *lods et ventes*, a third or a quarter of the selling price *"en ascendant,"* the due paid by outsiders for the right to reside in the *seigneurie*, the dues paid for use of the *moulin banal* and the *four banal*, the tolls and *leydes*, the *percières*, that is, the *champart* on fallow land when this was brought under cultivation every ten or twenty years, and, finally, the impropriated tithes. For his *seigneurie* of Neschers, of no great extent, Rodde de Vernière received in 1789 between 54 and 60 *setiers* of grain (*mesure de Champeix*) and 1,500 *pots* of wine.

The burden that these exactions represented was made heavier by the system of collection called *pagésie*, which meant that a number of *censives* were lumped together and their occupants made collectively responsible for paying the dues to the *seigneur*. This system was disadvantageous in two ways: it increased the cost of collection borne by the *censitaires*, since, for a *censitaire* who owed 2 sous, the *seigneur*'s farmer would send his tipstaff to one who was better off, and it put the poor in a state of subjection to the better-off, who brought pressure to bear on them.

Altogether, feudal and seignorial exactions seem to have been relatively light in the Paris region and, in general, around the big towns, in regions of large-scale agricultural production for the market. They seem to become heavier and heavier the farther one penetrates into remote areas where circulation was difficult, with poor land and a limited exchange economy. All that, however, is valid only as an overall average. In a region where exactions were light, a particular village or a particular peasant might be heavily burdened, and, in a region where exactions were heavy, a particular village or a particular peasant might bear only a light burden. It is concrete cases, real individual circumstances, that are certainly the most important facts we need to know in order to understand the incidence of political differences.

The seignorial reaction

Some historians have proclaimed, under the name of "seignorial reaction," the occurrence of a vast movement, said to have been a feature of the second half of the 18th century, which involved attempts to increase the burden of already existing feudal and seignorial dues, to revive those that had fallen into desuetude, and to impose fresh ones.

Others have doubted whether this reaction really took place. It must first of all be observed that, in every period, acquirers of *seigneuries* caused terriers to be recompiled, checking on the dues that were payable, and harshly exacted their payment, especially when these acquirers were *robins* or *bourgeois*. In times of economic difficulty, too, years when prices were low, when money was scarce, when there were serious dearths and even *mortalités, seigneurs* would periodically exact with greater rigor and severity whatever was due to them and would look into the question of whether some of their feudal and seignorial rights might have fallen into desuetude and ought to be reactivated. Under these two aspects it would be possible to speak of a permanent seignorial reaction or of periodical seignorial reactions. However, these terms would be inappropriate, since what was involved were circumstances in which *seigneurs* were giving closer attention to their rights, rather than a systematic return to a state of affairs that had formerly obtained, had been weakened, or had come to an end.

Certain facts may serve to support the idea of an effort to bring back to life a system that was on its way into obsolescence. Between 1770 and 1789 an increasing number of *seigneurs* had their feudal and seignorial rights looked into very actively by *"commissaires à terriers,"* commonly known as *"feudistes"*—experts in feudal land law. The *feudiste* was a specialist who approached the *seigneur,* explained his methods, prepared an estimate, and signed a contract with him. He then took up residence in the château, along with his clerks; Babeuf had eight of these in his employment in 1788 and twenty in 1789. He made arrangements with other *feudistes* for them to see to such sections of the work as he could not cover with his team. He sorted out records and checked on inventories, titles, and terriers. Then he went on to the land and checked, plot by plot, on all the details of the estate. He drew up registers arranged in columns and provided plans and maps, for then a mere seven or eight lines of commentary were needed instead of the sixty lines that would have been needed to describe an entire plot.

Then, the *feudistes* endeavored to transform their art into a science. Like the savants and philosophers of the Enlightenment, the *feudistes* of that time sought to discover a single principle governing their art, constant and unvarying forms that would give to a terrier a universal power of conviction. The *feudiste* Aubry de Saint-Vibert, in his book *Les terriers rendus perpétuels, ou mécanisme de leur confection,* which appeared in installments between 1785 and 1787, proposed that, instead of the usual method of surveying an estate, the method of *confins horaires* be adopted, that is, geometrical procedures, with measurement of angles. He suggested that ten registers be compiled instead of the usual eight: *inventaire, atlas radical, indication radicale, terrier radical, cueilloir perpétuel, atlas perpétuel, livre des saisines, indication perpétuelle, terrier perpétuel, livre des recettes.* Babeuf, who worked as a *feudiste* in Picardy between 1779 and 1792, in particular for the marquis de Soyecourt and the comte de Castéja, published in 1784 his *Précis d'un projet de cadastre perpétuel* and in 1789 his *Cadastre perpétuel.*

The third fact was that the *feudistes* and the *seigneurs* were backed by the magistrates of the *bailliages* and *sénéchaussées* and those of the *parlements.* In the appanage of the duc d'Orléans, the duke's council set up a *"chambre du domaine,"* composed of several commissioners chosen from the five *bailliages* of the appanage, in order to receive *aveux et dénombrements* and declarations and to judge domanial disputes. These judges were appointed by royal letters patent.

A certain Boncerf, having published a pamphlet on *Les inconvénients des droits féodaux,* the Paris *parlement,* in its *arrêt* of 30 March 1776, affirmed the need to uphold "the ancient and immutable principles that constitute the solid framework of French society," to safeguard "the property rights of the *seigneurs,*" and to "uphold public order based on justice and law." It ordained the payment of everything that was due to the king as *seigneur* and to private *seigneurs* and forbade any agitation, especially through books and pamphlets, in favor of dangerous innovations. This *arrêt* was binding on all the subordinate judges right down to the Revolution. Thus, the magistracy gave its backing to the *seigneurs* to the very end.

It was possible to speak of a renovation of terriers having been effected throughout the kingdom. The third estate of Auxerre declared in its *cahier* for the Estates General of 1789: "The compiling of terriers has become a task undertaken everywhere in the kingdom by greedy commissioners, for whom this work is an unfailing source of gain." We know that some *seigneurs* required their tenants to obtain a fresh "recognition" every ten years, although, according to the jurisprudence of the *parlement,* this should have been required only at intervals of thirty years. Others insisted on a "recognition" every time there was a change of tenant, whether in the direct or the collateral line. And the dues payable for these "recognitions" were increased. After the Council's *arrêt* of 1666, tenants had to pay 15 sous for the first article and 2 sous 6 deniers for each of the rest. The *arrêt* of August 1786 fixed the payment at 30 for the first declaration in towns and 15 sous in the country. As holdings in the country were extremely fragmented, however, the declarations to be made were numerous, so that, for 50 arpents of land in the *bailliage* of Auxerre, the dues to be paid came to 200 livres. "Recognitions" were formalized at the château in the presence of the *seigneur.* Many peasants were unable to read or write and dared not speak up for themselves. Existing dues were increased or fresh ones imposed. In the event of litigation, it is said that the *parlements* favored the *seigneurs.*

Some *seigneurs* strove to increase the area covered by their *seigneurie directe.* The king and the princes of the blood set the example. By the Council's *arrêt* of July 1781 the occupiers of islands or of "new land" in the rivers Gironde and Dordogne and along the banks of the Médoc were required to show title or else pay *cens* and dues to the king. The *parlement* of Bordeaux came to their defense and began a battle of *arrêts* with the king's Council. Eventually, in 1786, the king agreed not to ask for any payment from those persons in Guyenne whose islands and "new land" were contiguous to their holdings. Elsewhere, however, on the Loire and the Rhône, he imposed *cens,* and all that went with it, upon the islands and "new land," and the *cahiers* of 1789 appealed for the same favor to be shown to them as had been shown to those of Guyenne.

Some *seigneurs* took possession of the commons through *"triage"* of heathland and uncultivated land and *"cantonnement"* of woods. They often seized over a third and sometimes the whole. According to the *cahiers* of 1789, this movement, which had begun about 1770, was accelerating. The *seigneurs* added this common land to their demesnes or else let it out, for *cens* and seignorial and feudal rent, to persons who would cultivate it.

In the duchy of Alençon, the appanage of the comte de Provence, letters patent of June 1786 required the possessors of wasteland or marsh to show title. Those who were unable to do so thought they were fully protected by the custom of Normandy, which stated that, when someone had enjoyed unchallenged possession of a piece of land for forty years, he was to be regarded as its legitimate owner. The comte de Provence subjected them to payment of *cens* and seignorial rents and dues. The Rouen *parlement* supported his victims, in a veritable war of *arrêts*.

The *seigneurs* encroached on the woods in order to obtain timber for building and, especially, for their ironworks. Metallurgy was developing, while the extent of woodland was shrinking, so that the value of woods increased.

Edicts of March 1769, September 1777, and February 1778 forbade *vaine pâture*—that is, the right, when the harvest was over, to let cattle graze in fields which had not yet been brought under cultivation again—in the provinces of Béarn, Franche-Comté, Lorraine, Barrois, the Three Bishoprics, Champagne, Bourbonnais, and the *ban* of Haguenau.

In the Pyrenean valleys the pastures were directly owned by the king, but the local communities had been allowed to use them from time immemorial. *Arrêts* by the Council in April 1776 and December 1785 imposed *cens* and its consequences upon these pastures. Finally, an *arrêt* of 1782 required the payment of one *"barrari"* sheep every year for each of the huts that the peasants possessed in these mountains.

The effect of these measures was to prevent many peasants, and especially the poorest of them, from sending their cattle and sheep to graze in the woods and pastures, on the heaths and uncultivated land. They were at the same time forbidden to collect acorns, fodder, or firewood. The peasants' income sometimes fell by a third. For many it was now hard to find the money to pay their taxes, and for some the consequence was utter poverty.

The *parlements* waged a legal struggle against these measures, and this stimulated peasant revolts. The peasants cut down trees, filled in the newly made ditches that set limits to and enclosed the common lands, and ravaged the crops of the new *censitaires*, so as to force them to throw the land open again and let the peasants' cattle graze on it.

Some *seigneurs* increased the annual payments they required. In Lauragais and in Auvergne, where *cens* was payable in kind, it was sometimes increased by slightly increasing the size of the seignorial container used to measure it. *Champarts* were also increased, often by the same method. Many and protracted were the lawsuits that resulted, and it is said that the *parlements* decided these in the *seigneurs'* favor.

The *seigneurs* demanded payment of dues which they had neglected to exact. In the Limoges area some *seigneurs* required the lump-sum payment of twenty-nine years of arrears of dues which had not been paid for two or three centuries and had perhaps been redeemed by the peasant communities at the end of the 15th century or during the 16th. When dues were payable in kind, some *seigneurs* demanded these not in the months when they fell due but at a moment when the *censitaire* had no grain in store. They then required payment in a cash equivalent and arbitrarily rated the grain at an excessively high price. The peasants were frequently given no receipts or else failed to keep the ones they were given. Some *seigneurs* called on them either to show their receipts for the previous twenty-nine years or else to pay twenty-nine years of arrears. The burdensome effect of these moves by the *seigneurs* was enhanced by the rule that provided for joint responsibility of all the *censitaires* of a *seigneurie* or fief for the payment of seignorial dues; those who were well-off paid for those who could not pay and sometimes found themselves rapidly reduced to the same degree of poverty.

Corvées were substantially increased, especially in the regions north of the Loire and, above all, in Brittany. According to the custom of Brittany, *corvée* could be demanded only for the work of repairing the *seigneur*'s château, but the *seigneurs* of that province added *corvées* for repairing mills, carting the *seigneur*'s wine, grain, or wood to the château, and mowing and winnowing his hay. The Rennes *parlement* supported them in this. In Artois, at Marquion, the tenant farmers complained that the *seigneur* required of them six days of *corvée* in one year, each time to be performed with a cart drawn by four horses—an unheard-of exaction.

Impropriated tithes were increased. Some *seigneurs* demanded payment of them in respect of every kind of produce, though they were properly payable only on grain crops. Lawsuits resulted from this. Some *seigneurs* so intimidated their peasants that they dared not appear before the judge; they then obtained decisions against them by default and, after that, extorted "recognitions" from them, thus obtaining a legal basis for their increased demands.

Some *seigneurs* increased the casual fees payable to them. The king set the example with the rate of frank-fee. In the Limoges area, frank-fee had been payable as one year of income every twenty years. It was increased successively by 10 sous to the livre to a fifth, then by 5 sous to the livre of this fifth, and, after a few years, it was almost double what it had been originally.

All *lods et ventes* were increased, not only because more holdings were subjected to these payments and because there were more changes of ownership, but also because proportionate charges were often substituted for a fixed amount, where that had been the rule. At Anzin, in Artois, "the tenth denier" (10 percent) replaced a fixed rate of 10 deniers (five-sixths of a sou). The abbot of Saint-Pierre de Gand had the right to receive *lods et ventes* of 12 deniers (1 sou.) For this he substituted "the eighth denier" (12.5 percent). In the duchy of Angoulême, the appanage of Monsieur, the king's brother, *lods et ventes* increased from "the 15th denier" (6.66 percent) to "the eighth denier" (12.5 percent). In Lower Vendômois *reliefs et rachats* had ceased to be paid for 150 years. After 1770 the *seigneurs* revived them, and the *bailliage* of Vendôme approved their action.

All seignorial monopolies ("*péages*") were increased, and new ones were imposed in places hitherto exempt. Market dues were instituted in towns and villages previously spared or were extended to additional commodities. *Banalités,* such as mill charges, were made more burdensome, sometimes increasing from a sixteenth to a quarter of the grain ground, or from 5 sous to 11 sous per *mesure,* as at Mesle-sur-Sarthe in 1784. There were cases of extortion pure and simple. At La Baslidonne de Sanerie, in the *sénéchaussée* of Sexte, the *seigneur* insisted on a payment for the use of his bake oven when in fact there was no bake oven in his *seigneurie.* At La Garde-Freinet, near Draguignan, the *seigneurs* exacted a charge for grinding, though they had no mills.

All this forms an impressive picture. Nevertheless, it is made up of facts that are scattered geographically and of cases which, since they struck contemporary observers as being curious may well have been exceptional. To discover which such occurrences were really frequent, current, and happening everywhere, one would need to carry out an overall and systematic investigation, the results of which would then have to be compared with those of other similar investigations covering different periods, so as to establish whether the thirty years preceding the Revolution were really a period of seignorial reaction.

Isolated facts can be interpreted in very different ways. At Buzé-sur-Tarn, near Toulouse, there was a *seigneurie* of which the king had been *seigneur* since the 13th century. The *trésoriers généraux de France* collected the seignorial dues rather irregularly and did not claim the honorific rights at all. In 1770, owing to shortage of money, the king sold his *seigneurie,* which was acquired by a cavalry colonel. This man caused the seignorial seat in the church to be restored, re-erected the gibbet, forbade the peasants to hunt on his land, and levied *champarts* with rigor. He was so harsh that, it is said, the young people of the *seigneurie* were unwilling to remain there and moved away, so that the population of this village failed to increase, while that of all the neighboring villages was growing. In January 1791 the peasants of Buzé accused their new *seigneur* of conspiring, attacked the château, and set it on fire. The National Guard came from Lavaur, a neighboring village, to protect the *seigneur,* and he was able to get away to Toulouse. He was tried by the district tribunal and acquitted of the charge of conspiracy, after which he emigrated.

Here we have a fine case of seignorial reaction, have we not? The only thing is, if it was really through seignorial reaction that the population stagnated at Buzé-sur-Tarn, then, since population increased in all the neighboring villages, the latter must not have suffered any seignorial reaction. If it was owing to seignorial reaction that the peasants of Buzé rose against their *seigneur,* then the peasants of Lavaur, who came to his aid, were presumably not suffering from seignorial reaction.

Until an overall and systematic investigation has been carried out, let us suspend judgment on the question of the alleged seignorial reaction before the Revolution.

The king and the seigneuries

The king swore at his consecration that he would protect the liberties and possessions of his subjects. He was therefore obliged to safeguard the *seigneuries.* Actually, the royal government was concerned mainly with extending the king's authority. It never violated the rights of the *seigneurs,* but, depending on circumstances, it either got round these rights or made use of feudal and seigneurial rights to strengthen the king's power.

An example of the first procedure is provided by the edict of 1674 on the *seigneuries* of Paris. The seignorial powers of justice were a nuisance to the policing of Paris. The enclosed areas they covered were places of refuge for a horde of criminals—thieves, bankrupt craftsmen, and merchants—and in order to effect an arrest it was necessary for a *lettre de cachet* to be sent by the king to the *seigneurs hauts justiciers*. The Edict of Doullens, 16 February 1539, provided for uniting the seignorial courts with those of the king, uniting the *seigneuries directes* of the *seigneurs* of Paris with the king's, and relieving the households of Paris from all feudal dues in return for a tax to be paid to the king. The opposition this edict encountered was so great that it had to be abandoned.

An edict of February 1643 repeated the edict of Doullens, but the death of Louis XIII and the difficulties of the regency that followed caused this one to be abandoned as well.

The Council's commissioners for the reform of the judiciary in 1665, considering that the *seigneurs'* patrimonial powers of justice were the result of usurpations of the king's rights, recommended that they be suppressed. The deliberations of the Conseil de Police, at the Hôtel Séguier in Paris, between 28 October 1666 and 10 February 1667, led to the *arrêt* of 5 November 1666 and the edict of December 1667, reserving the general police authority to the officers of the Châtelet and opening up the privileged localities to them, and to the edict of March 1667, establishing a *lieutenant général de police* for Paris.

There were continual conflicts between the seignorial officials and those of the king, and so the edict of February 1674 merged all the seignorial courts with the presidial court of the *prévôté et vicomté* of Paris. The owners of the seignorial powers of justice thus abolished were to be indemnified for their loss. However, these *seigneurs hauts justiciers* opposed the edict and secured partial restoration of the judicial powers of the archbishop and of the chapters of Notre-Dame, Saint-Germain-des-Prés, Saint-Martin-des-Champs, Montmartre, the Temple, Saint-Jean-de-Latran, Saint-Geneviève, and Saint-Marcel. The area subject to their jurisdiction was to be thenceforth confined, in Paris, to the enclosures of the archbishopric and the various monasteries concerned, and *prévention* by the royal judges of the Châtelet was to be always possible in relation to them. In the district around Paris the *seigneurs* retained their previous jurisdiction. Practically speaking, seignorial courts were done away with in Paris; the jurisdiction of Saint-Germain-des-Prés no longer extended further than to fifty-four shops. These seignorial courts, which had become mere symbols of honor, tiny islets of feudalism, vegetated until the Revolution.

But the king also, and perhaps more frequently, tried to make use of the seignorial institution for his own advantage. *Seigneurie* implied a bond of protection and fealty between the *seigneur* and his subjects. Sentiments of fealty were very strong among the French. The king sought to use them by binding every Frenchman to himself by a personal bond. Since the king was the embodiment of the state, by attaching all Frenchmen to his person he strengthened the power of the state. *Seigneurie* was one of the means he used.

The king employed the theory of the *directe royale universelle*. He tried constantly to reduce the number of allods, the number of "free lands" without any *seigneur*. Such lands were still numerous in Bordelais, Guyenne, Languedoc, Dauphiné, Burgundy, Bourbonnais, Auvergne, Nivernais, and the areas subject to the customs of Troyes, Sézanne, Chaumont, Metz, Verdun, and Langres. The royal government revived the 13th-century thesis that "the king is the enfeoffing *seigneur* of the whole kingdom." The master of requests Auguste Galland wrote in 1629: "The king being universal *seigneur* of all the lands that are in his kingdom, these must be presumed to have been granted by his predecessors and to be subject to his rights, unless a dispensation to the contrary can be proved."[3] The king declared, in the preamble to his edict of August 1692: "We have no right that is better established or more inseparabley attached to our Crown than that of *mouvance et directe universelle.*" The freeholders defended themselves, Caseneuve, a jurisconsult of Languedoc, replying:

> It is therefore the usage of the written law that constitutes the foundation on which the province of Languedoc bases the liberty of its freehold property . . . Now, it is a thing that no one has ever doubted that, according to Roman law, possessions of all kinds are naturally and originally regarded as free and quit of all servitude unless it be shown to the contrary. The provinces of Languedoc and Aquitaine being countries of Roman law, . . . there is no doubt that in consequence all their possessions are allodial.

Caseneuve observed that the liberty of freeholds without title did not prevent the freeholders from being unrestrictedly subject to the king's sovereignty; they were fully his *subjects,* but not his *vassals.*

However, in Guyenne several *arrêts* of the Council, notably that of 30 September 1624, proscribing untitled freehold, brought within the royal *mouvance* an impressive number of freeholds of origin and prescription, which thenceforth were subject to *cens* and *lods et ventes, retrait féodal,* and fealty if they were "commoner" lands, and to faith and homage, *aveu et dénombrement,* noble services, and *quints et requints* if they were "noble."

The edict of January 1629 generalized: "All *héritages* which are not dependent on another *seigneur* are to be regarded as dependent on us, unless . . . the possessors can show good titles relieving them of this dependence." This edict was not registered, but that of December 1641 prescribed that all freeholders must "obtain letters from us and make payment to us for these." There was much resistance, but it was gradually whittled away.

In Languedoc, the Council's *arrêt* of 22 May 1667 allowed presumption of freehold in the case of a "commoner" allod but rejected this in the case of a "noble" one, which was to be seen as an enfranchised fief. Where a "noble" allod was concerned, the freeholder had to produce proof of his enfranchisement, something that it was of course impossible to do. By the edict of August 1692 the king acknowledged presumption of freehold for "commoner" allods in most of the regions where this form of landownership existed, but the possessors had to obtain letters of confirmation, paying in return one year's income. If they had enfeoffed or subjected to *cens* any part of their land, they had to pay, in addition, one-tenth of the capital value of their land, for the king alone "has the right to ennoble both persons and property." In the case of a "noble" allod, the freeholder had to produce proof of enfranchisement.

The distinction was not applied to Bordelais. By a Council *arrêt* of 1670, all its freeholders, noble and commoner alike, were required to present their title deeds, failing which they were to be subject to rendering dues and services to the king.

The king's policy was a great success. The petty freeholders willingly offered their submission to the king, since the *cens* payable was insignificant—one sou or even one denier. As for the *gentilshommes* and the churchmen, their position in relation to the king was weakened by the fact that they were themselves chasing the freeholders in their *seigneuries* and in their fiefs, establishing their *directe* over them. Everywhere *directe seigneuriale* and *directe royale, seigneurie* and fief, progressed at the expense of freehold—both peasant freeholds and those of petty noble families. The *directe royale universelle* grew stronger.

The king frequently also made use of the royal contract of enfeoffment, owing to its flexibility. Implying the king's protection, and therefore supervision, on the one side, and fealty and services on the other, it enabled the king to retain all his potential for intervening and safeguarding the common good, while leaving extensive freedom to new and remote enterprises and giving them the benefit of firm hierarchical structures of the feudal and seignorial type. For example, the undertaking of the Canal du Midi was, juridically, a *seigneurie* held as a fief from the king. Canada was colonized by means of *seigneuries* held as fiefs. The East India Company, established in 1664, was bound to the king by having all its territories, present and to come, granted to it as fiefs, which enabled the king, its protector, to allow the company regalian rights for its conquests and colonizing activity.

Thus the king, embodying the modern state, made use of very old institutional forms, the *seigneurie* and the fief, to develop the power of this entity, the state, and to ensure its authority until the time came when this concept and image had sufficient domination over men's minds for them to believe themselves able to do without the person of the king.

Seigneurie *and society*

The nobles by function and the *bourgeois,* as new vassals and new *seigneurs,* manifested real greed for *seigneuries* and fiefs. They keenly defended, pursued, and revived all feudal and seignorial rights, especially the honorific ones. The first care of an advocate, an attorney, a *conseiller de bailliage,* or a wholesale merchant who had just purchased a *seigneurie* or a fief was to seek royal authority to recompile a terrier (entrusting a notary with the task of investigating the estate as his commissioner), to summon his men to appear before him, obliging the feudatories and *censitaires* to present their title deeds and the feudatories to render faith and homage, and to review the list of his rights.

This gave rise to a great many lawsuits. "You owe me a goose as customary payment." "But I have already sent it to you." "Yes, but it was brought by a servant wearing ordinary dress and not wearing livery with your arms on it, as you ought to have ensured." *There* was sufficient basis for ten years of proceedings, with printed consultations by practitioners, memoranda and pleadings by counsel—all very expensive.

In Burgundy in 1692, Pierre Fijan, *maître des comptes* in Paris, bought the barony of Talmay. Between 1692 and 1708 he spent sixteen years in a litigation with the inhabitants. He usurped the right to levy *taille* and the right to fish, increased the charges for justice, appointed aldermen by means of threats, obliged the communities to carry out building work at his château, made them repair the bridge over the moat and clean the latter out, although his château no longer played any military role, and insisted on expressions of respect from the *curé* in the church. He waged a lawsuit against the inhabitants of the parish over a right to keep a pigeon house. The case lasted ten years and was very costly.

About 1660 a commoner, a retired army officer, came to settle at Barges. He bought a house and some land for 350 livres. He claimed that his purchase included a fief to which certain *censives* belonged, and to establish this claim he began fifty years of lawsuits for the sake of an insignificant revenue.

Everywhere in the recompiled terriers it was above all the honorific rights that were smugly enumerated, or else the powers of justice. Little farms were elevated to the status of fiefs. The fief of Longvic consisted of four *journaux* of land, a single-story house with five rooms, and a farmyard. Madame Bénigne de La Michodière set up there, in 1738, a court of justice with a *procureur d'office,* a *juge-bailli,* and a *greffier.* Five hundred yards away the *seigneur* of Beauregard-Coron established, on his fief inhabited by four families, a seignorial court which held assizes, appointed crop-watchers and guards, and pronounced "verdicts in criminal cases," sentencing people to prison.

The return from feudal and seignorial rights was often very slight. In Paris the house called Le Chauldron, in the rue de la Huchette, was leased out by the Hôtel-Dieu, as *seigneur utile,* at 350 livres a year; to the *seigneur direct,* the religious of Longchamp, it paid a *cens* of 2 deniers. The house called Le Couperet, in the rue de la Bûcherie, bought by the Hôtel-Dieu for 13,500 livres *tournois* in 1646, owed to the *seigneur direct* 12 deniers *parisis* in *cens* and 8 livres 15 *sols tournois* in ground rent.

In the Paris region *cens* was frequently just a few deniers per arpent. A holding at Saclé, consisting of a house, a garden, 100 arpents of arable land, and 2½ arpents of meadow, farmed at 500 livres and with an estimated capital value of 13,000 livres, owed a *cens* of 16 *sols parisis*—that is, 1 livre *tournois*.

Cens entailed *lods et ventes* and other seignorial dues—*champarts, terrages, agrières,* etc. But at Thiais and Avrainville *champart* was only four sheaves per arpent, though the yield per arpent was between

72 and 140 sheaves. Moreover, these dues have nothing particularly feudal or seignorial about them but can be associated with sharecropping or tenancy contracts in societies innocent of fief and *seigneurie*.

These dues were awkward to collect, owing to the motley juridical arrangements. The *métairies* of Gâtine, the tenant farms to the south of Paris, the Burgundian *métairies,* were all made up of plots of land belonging to different fiefs and *seigneurs*. The allocation of feudal and seignorial rights among the various beneficiaries was always a very toilsome business. From the economic standpoint, what mattered was these units of exploitation; and in order to lease them out as *métairies* or tenant farms, the *seigneur* had no need of his feudal and seignorial rights, his powers of justice over the land, or his external marks of respect. In reality, even in regions where feudal and seignorial rights still made up an important part, even as much as one-third, of the income from a *seigneurie,* it would have been to the *seigneurs'* interest to rearrange their lands so as to make their estates coincide with the units of exploitation, merely retaining quiritarian ownership with its simple ground rent arising from sharecropping or tenant-farming leases. *Seigneuries* and fiefs caused the *seigneurs* or get less from their land than they could have got.

But the *seigneurs* clung to their *seigneuries,* fiefs, and *censives* because these possessed symbolic value, "placing" those who owned them in the social hierarchy. They were marks of the social superiority of one man over others. This is well shown in the contract of sale for two arpents of arable land at Sens, 20 April 1616: they are "charged with 2 *sols tournois, as sign and notice of superiority* payable each year to the said prior of Saint-Loup, and also with 12 deniers of rent to whosoever shall have the right to this *in right of superiority.*" Feudal and seignorial rights were a symbol of rank and authority, and, while not despising the income they brought, it was for that, above all, that the contemporaries who were their beneficiaries held fast to them.

For a long time the *seigneurie,* the fief, had constituted a sort of salary for military services, for services of command, justice, and police. And this society continued, even into the second half of the 18th century, to be profoundly military. Its ideal was the sword. Here is the reply of the archbishop of Embrun, Messire Georges d'Aubusson de La Feuillade, chairman of the Assembly of the Clergy, to the deputies of the nobility, on 15 March 1651:

And so it is this nobility, not of blood but of your heroic spirits, which is not buried in the tombs of your ancestors but lives again in the sequence of your generous actions, that has inspired you with the idea of assembling to safeguard your privileges. It is this ancient glory . . . that has been unable to tolerate any longer that all the affairs of *a state that is military by its very foundation,* and of which you form the most brilliant and most powerful section, should be decided without your votes.[4]

The abbé François-Timoléon de Choisy, member of the French Academy, tells us in his *Mémoires:*

My mother, who came of the family of Hurault de l'Hopital, often said to me: "Listen, my son, do not be vainglorious, remember that you are only a *bourgeois.* I know very well that your fathers and grandfathers were masters of requests and councilors of state; but take it from me that in France *the only nobility that counts is that of the sword.* This nation, wholly warlike, has identified glory with arms."[5]

The survival of *seigneuries,* fiefs, and *censives* in the 17th and 18th centuries was first and foremost a survival of ideas and sentiments in minds and hearts. The ruling principle of society was military. Rank in the army and in society was bound up with a hierarchy of landownership. To rise in the hierarchy of landownership through the nature of one's property, even if the commercial value of this property was very little, meant rising in society. And so the hierarchy of landownership was jealously preserved, even if the material interests of the *seigneurs directs* suffered thereby, in that their gains were less than they could otherwise have been. The fundamental principle of French society dominated everything, even economic activity.

Individual property and state property

Seigneuries, fiefs, and *censives* were individual properties which, though it was sought to keep them within the lineages whose economic existence they ensured, were indeed properties, and individually owned. The French doctor Bernier, who had lived from 1655 to 1661 in India at the court of the Great Mogul, ascribed to individual ownership of property the superiority in wealth, solidity, and strength that he perceived in the societies and states of Europe as compared with those of India; writing to Colbert in 1665, he said:

These three countries, Turkey, Persia, and Hindustan, have no idea of the principle of *meum* and *tuum* relative to land or other real possessions; and, having lost that respect for private property which

is the basis of all that is good and useful in the world, they
necessarily resemble each other in essential points . . . All the lands
of that empire are his (the Great Mogul's) property, excepting some
houses and gardens which he gives leave to his subjects to sell,.
divide, or buy among themselves as they shall think fit . . . Far be
it from God's will . . . that our monarchs of Europe should thus be
proprietors of all the lands which their subjects possess. Their
kingdoms would be very far from being so well cultivated and
peopled, so well built, so rich, so polite and flourishing as we see
them. Our kings are otherwise rich and powerful; and we must avow
that they are much better and more royally served. They would
soon be kings of deserts and solitudes, of beggars and barbarians,
such as those are whom I have been describing, who, because they
will have all, at last lose all, and who, because they will make
themselves too rich, at length find themselves without riches or, at
least, very far from that which they covet after, out of their blind
ambition and passion of being more absolute than the laws of God
and Nature permit. For where would be those princes, those
prelates, those nobles, those rich citizens and great merchants, and
those famous artisans, those towns of Paris, Lyons, Toulouse,
Rouen—London, too, if you will, and so many others?

Bernier's idea could be expressed like this. On the one hand, the
Great Mogul, a conqueror, leader of a racially distinct army encamped
in a vanquished country, has seized ownership of the means of production, leaving to his subjects only production goods of secondary importance and consumer goods; even then, if some merchant among his
subjects accumulates a great deal, at his death everything goes to
the Great Mogul. The latter grants precarious tenure of the means of
production to the officers of his army; these alien conquerors, mere
temporary concession-holders, all of whose property will in any case return to the Great Mogul when they die, with no share going to their
children, have no interest in treating with care either the producer or
the means of production. The producers, reduced to a tiny starvation
share in the distribution of goods and having no interest in the means of
production, are no longer concerned to produce and lack the means to
do so, with the result that ruin and misery prevail. On the other hand,
the rule of the Mogul is a mere act of force. The conquerors have no ties
other than those binding them to the person of their leader. With the
inhabitants of the lands temporarily granted to them they have none of
those ties of protection and service, none of those hierarchically ordered obligations of public service, that were characteristic in France

of the *seigneurie,* fief, and *censive.* Should the Great Mogul's army be destroyed and he himself die, everything would break up, whereas in France the structures survived by themselves. When we look at the realities of the India and the France of Bernier's time, his idea seems well founded.

Seigneurie, fief, and *censive* were properties, but hierarchically structured properties, charged with personal or public services and limited in the interest of the social order and the common good. Consequently, they were not the forms of property most favorable to economic production. When concern for happiness through physical well-being, preoccupation with the production of material goods, became dominant in men's minds, there then triumphed in the court of public opinion the quiritarian form of property—absolute, exclusive, perpetual—even before this became, with the Revolution, the predominant form.

Notes

1. Loyseau, *De l'abus des justices de village* (1640 ed.), pp. 12–13.
2. F. Ragueau, *Glossaire du droit français,* ed. Laurière (Paris, 1704), art. "Justice basse et foncière"; Pesnelle, *Coutume de Normandie,* annotated by Roupnel (Rouen, 1759), p. 23.
3. Auguste Galland, *Contre le franc-alleu, sans titre, prétendu par quelques provinces au préjudice du Roy* (Paris, 1629; reissued in 1637).
4. *Journal de l'Assemblée de la Noblesse* (1651), p. 79.
5. Abbé François-Timoléon de Choisy, *Mémoires,* ed. Michaud-Poujoulat, p. 554.

Guide to further reading

Bacquet, Jean. *Traité des droits de justice, haute, moyenne et basse.* 1st ed., 1577. In *Oeuvres,* ed. Claude de Ferrière, 1688.

Bourdot de Richebourg, Ch.-A. *Coutumier général.* 4 vols. 1724.

Boutaric, F. de. *Traité des droits seigneuriaux et des matières féodales.* Toulouse, 1745.

Boutruche, R. *Une société provinciale en lutte contre le régime féodal: L'alleu en Bordelais et en Bazadais du XVᵉ au XVIIIᵉ siècle.* Rodez, 1947.

Chianea, Gérard. *La condition juridique des terres en Dauphiné au XVIIIᵉ siècle, 1700–1789.* Grenoble Law thesis. Mouton, 1969.

Du Breul, Dom Jacques. *Le théâtre des antiquitez de Paris.* 1640.

Fontenay, Michel. "Paysans et marchands ruraux de la vallée de l'Essonne dans la seconde moitié du XVIIᵉ siécle." *Paris et Ile-de-France* 10 (1958): 157–282.

Forster, Robert. *The Nobility of Toulouse in the 18th Century: A Social and Economic Study.* Johns Hopkins University Studies in Historical and Political Science, Ser. 78, no. 1. Baltimore, 1960.

————. "The Noble Wine-Producers of the Bordelais in the 18th Century," *Economic History Review* 2d ser. 14 (1961).

————. "The Provincial Noble: A Reappraisal," *American Historical Review* 68 (1962–63): 681–91.

Giffard, Pierre. *Les justices seigneuriales en Bretagne aux XVIIe et XVIIIe siècles (1661–1791)*. Bibl. de la Fondation Thiers, fasc. 1. 1903.

Goodwin, A. "The Social Origins and Privileged Status of the French 18th-Century Nobility," *Bulletin of the John Rylands Library* 47 (1964): 382–403.

Guyot, P. J. J. G. *Répertoire universel et raisonné de jurisprudence*. 17 vols. 1784–85.

Jousse, Daniel. *Traité de l'administration de justice*. 2 vols. 1771.

Lange, François. *La nouvelle pratique civile, criminelle et bénéficiale ou le nouveau praticien français*. 1681.

Laplace, Antoine. *Introduction aux droits seigneuriaux*. 1749.

Lemercier, Pierre. *Les justices seigneuriales de la région parisienne de 1580 à 1789*. Paris Law thesis. 1933.

Loyseau, Charles. *Traité des seigneuries*. In *Oeuvres complètes*, 1640 ed.

Merle, Louis. *La métairie et l'évolution agraire de la Gâtine poitevine de la fin du Moyen Age à la Révolution*. S.E.V.P.E.N., 1958. ("Les Hommes et la Terre," no. 2).

Pelletier, A. "Babeuf feudiste," *Annales historiques de la Révolution française* (1965), pp. 29–65.

Pocquet de Livonnière, Claude. *Traité des fiefs*. 4th ed. 1756.

Poitrineau, Abel. "Aspects de la crise des justices seigneuriales dans l'Auvergne du XVIIIe siècle," *Revue historique de Droit français et étranger* 4th ser. 39 (1961): 552–70.

————. *La vie rurale en basse Auvergne au XVIIIe siècle (1726–1789)*, Paris Faculty of Letters thesis. P.U.F., 1965.

Renauldon, Joseph. *Dictionnaire des fiefs et de droits seigneuriaux*. 1765.

Rochette, Jean. *Questions de droit et de pratique*. 1613.

Roupnel, Gaston. *La ville et la campagne au XVIIe siècle: Etude sur les populations du pays dijonnais*. Paris Faculty of Letters thesis. Armand Colin, 1922; reissued 1955.

Sagnac, Philippe. *Quomodo jura Domini aucta fuerint regnante Ludovico Sexto Decimo*. Paris Faculty of Letters complementary thesis. 1898.

Saint-Jacob, Pierre de. *Les paysans de la Bourgogne du Nord au dernier siècle de l'Ancien Régime*. Paris Faculty of Letters thesis. 1960.

Sauval, Henri. *Histoire et recherche des antiquités de Paris*. 3 vols. 1733.

Sée, Henri. *Les classes rurales en Bretagne du XVIe siècle à la Révolution*. 1906.

Soboul, Albert. *Le prélèvement féodal au XVIIIe siècle: L'Abolition de la féodalité dans le monde occidental*. Colloques internationaux du C.N.R.S., Sciences humaines, Toulouse, 1968. C.N.R.S., 1971.

Tanon, L. *Histoire des justices des anciennes églises et communautés monastiques de Paris*. 1883.

Venard, Marc. *Bourgeois et paysans au XVIIe siècle, recherches sur le rôle des bourgeois parisiens dans la vie agricole au sud de Paris au XVIIe siècle*. S.E.V.P.E.N., 1957. ("Les Hommes et la Terre," no. 3).

Villard, Pierre. "Les justices seigneuriales dan la Marche." In *Bibl. d'Hist. du Droit et Droit romain*, ed. P.-C. Timbal, vol. 13. Librairie Générale de Droit et de Jurisprudence. 1969.

12 The Territorial Communities Treated as Corporations: Villages and Parishes

The villages and rural *bourgs* of France were natural corporations, communities of inhabitants which organized and administered themselves for the common good. The existence of these corporations was a necessity, so that the communities of inhabitants had no need of letters patent from the king in order to exist legally. Such communities were distinct from the parishes. The parish was the whole body made up of the *curé*, his curates, and the faithful within a defined territory. A community of inhabitants might coincide with a parish, form a fragment of a parish, or embrace several parishes.

The community

The communities of inhabitants were administered by assemblies. These were held in the square in front of the church, under the elms, the oaks, or the lime trees, or in the cemetery, or sometimes in the nave of the church itself, although, since the Council of Trent, this was increasingly regarded as showing disrespect to God's house. The assemblies normally met on Sundays, after the parish mass, but sometimes, if the matter to be discussed was urgent, they met on working days. On the average they met between six and sixteen times a year.

In principle, an assembly required an authorization from the *sei-gneur* or the local judge, but actually this depended on local custom. By the custom of Upper Auvergne the inhabitants could assemble without authorization. By that of Marche they were obliged merely to notify the *seigneur*. In practice, it became less and less usual for authorization to be needed.

The inhabitants were convened by the syndic or, if he was absent, by the churchwarden or the collector of *tailles*. The *curé* announced at the parish mass the day and hour of the assembly and its purpose. An edict of 1634, dealing with *tailles*, obliged him to do this, and it was confirmed in 1646. However, an edict of April 1695, confirmed by the declaration of 16 December 1698, relieved him of the obligation to make any announcements concerning temporal matters. Nevertheless, many *curés* continued to read out, when they preached, the king's ordinances and letters patent, *règlements,* announcements of *adjudica-tions,* and convocations of assemblies. If they did not do this from the pulpit, they would read them out at the church door when the congregation was coming out from mass, or they would have them read by a *sergent de justice*. The holding of the assembly was also announced by the public crier at the crossroads. If it was very important, people were notified by a *sergent* going from door to door. A bell was rung before the actual meeting.

The assembly could not engage in valid deliberation unless it constituted *un peuple,* that is, unless at least ten inhabitants were present. When a loan or a transaction was to be discussed, *all* the members of the assembly had to be present, and when what was on the agenda was alienation of common lands, woods, or pastures or submission to a *droit de banalité* in respect of bake oven, mill, or winepress, unanimity was required. In most communities attendance at the assembly was compulsory, on pain of a fine. But this was not so everywhere; for example, it did not apply in the county of Dunois.

The assembly consisted of heads of households who were entered on the roll of payers of *tailles,* landowners, and persons exercising a craft or function. Consequently, sons living with their fathers had no vote, since they were not taxed separately. Widows who were heads of households had consultative voice (there were thirteen such widows at Ouzouer-le-Doyen in 1681, seven at Moisy in 1689, three at La Jahan-dière in 1697), for they were entered on the roll of payers of *tailles,* and they had a share in the common lands. Actually, any inhabitant who wished went to meetings of the assembly.

The assembly could be presided over the the *seigneur*'s judge or by the *curé*. Almost always, though, the chair was taken by the syndic. He explained the purpose of the gathering, called on speakers, controlled the discussion, and conducted voting, which was by spoken declaration; a report of the meeting, followed by the names of the chief inhabitants, was then drawn up by the judge's *greffier,* the syndic, the schoolmaster, or, if it was desired to authenticate it formally, by a notary. This paper was kept in a chest in the church or in the sacristy.

The names of the chief inhabitants were followed by the words: "And others forming the greatest and soundest part of the inhabitants and peasants of this place." By "greatest" was meant strongest, most worthy of consideration, which might be interpreted not in terms of the number but of the quality of the voters: the churchwarden, the syndic, the principal *laboureurs*. The "soundest" part meant the most reasonable, most conformable to the order desired by God. The whole expression might therefore not signify at all the largest number, the *"pluralité"* or *"majorité"* of the inhabitants; indeed, the word *"majorité"* was an anglicism introduced in the 18th century by Voltaire and Mirabeau.

The report of the assembly's proceedings thus bore the mark of an old rule of canon law which had made its way into the public law of the kingdom. The Third Lateran Council (1179) had provided that if, in a religious community, the largest number of the religious, the *major pars,* had elected a superior who was unworthy, their vote would be null in law and the bishop could designate a candidate put forward by a minority, the *sanior pars,* even if this consisted of no more than a single elector. The idea had developed that the *major pars* ought to mean the most numerous part but that this should also be the *sanior pars*. This idea was still dominant in the 17th century, in canon law as in public law, and it made possible interventions by higher authority—the king, his Council, his provincial intendants, or his commissioners.

The communities of inhabitants participated in the remonstrances presented to the king by the Estates General. For the Estates General of 1614–15 the king's letters to the *baillis* and *sénéchaux* were passed on by them to the judges in the castellanies or equivalent jurisdictions, who communicated them "to the vestrymen or the syndic of the parish, so that they might be published at the sermon after high mass." The *curé* read from the pulpit the order from the *lieutenant général* fixing the date of the general assembly of the *bailliage* and calling upon each parish "to send as deputies two of the most notable of their inhabitants," bringing with them "the *cahiers* of grievances, complaints, and remonstrances that each parish intends to present to His Majesty, with the means to do this." On 21 July 1614, thirty-one inhabitants of the parish of Thiville appointed as their attorney Etienne Belle-non, *laboureur,* to go to Chartres, taking their complaints and remon-strances, and there elect one or two members of the third estate to attend the Estates General, and they provided for his expenses. Each village drew up its *cahier.* The delegates of the parishes assembled in the neighboring town and there drew up the *cahier* for the castellany, representing the views of both the town and the parishes, and this joint *cahier* was taken by the combined delegation to the assembly of the bailliage.

The village communities possessed no powers of justice, being sub-ject to seignorial justice. They attended the *seigneurs'* assizes held in March or May and were there presented with the administrative reg-ulations to be obeyed. Their members expressed their views on each article of these regulations, and the *seigneur's bailli* gave his decision. These assizes survived, however, only in certain provinces— Champagne, Lorraine, Alsace—and in some communities in the Ile-de-France. Sometimes the communities elected their agents at such meetings and took formal decisions.

In the 16th century the community assemblies participated through their delegates in the compiling of local customs. They continued to draw up regulations for rural administration—for defense of the crops and the vines against marauders, for guarding the communal woods, keeping watch against fires, protecting cattle, preserving the bounds of the village, and so on. They appointed guards, crop-watchers, and foresters to enforce these regulations, and sometimes they decided the timing of the harvest or wine harvest or gave their opinion about this to the local judge, who issued the appropriate regulation. They sometimes fixed wage levels, the selling price of straw, and so on. In short, they played a part in legislation, policing, and administration and, by doing so, lightened the burden of the royal administration.

They lightened its burden also by helping in the assessment and collection of taxes. The community assemblies chose the agents re-sponsible for apportioning liability for *taille* and collecting it, or merely for collecting it—the *asséeurs* and collectors responsible for raising the tax charged upon the community. There were many complaints about their partiality and their malversations. The ordinary asembly held in September or October appointed the collectors by majority vote. The only persons exempt from these burdensome functions were the syndic, the churchwarden, the schoolmaster, persons over seventy, the incurably sick, beggars, and fathers of eight children. This assembly also elected the collectors of *gabelle,* who were likewise responsible for raising the amount prescribed. During the wine harvest, the assembled inhabitants estimated, when called upon to do so by the farmer of the *aides,* the average yield of the vines of their territory.

At one time the community assemblies played a part in recruitment for the army. When Louis XIV introduced the militia in 1688, as a territorial force to furnish men for the operational army, the assemblies chose the men who were to compose it. However, the ordinance of 10 December 1691 substituted the drawing of lots for this method of selection.

The village communities relieved the state of an important part of the task of local administration.

The community assemblies decided whether expenditure was opportune, how much should be spent, and the ways and means involved. They made decisions regarding the upkeep or the building of the church, the priest's house, the school, the village hall. The ordinance of 1695 made the inhabitants responsible for the upkeep of the nave, which belonged to them and often served as the village hall, and also the upkeep of the bell tower, the bells, the clock, and the priest's house. Maintenance of the choir remained the *curé*'s responsibility.

The inhabitants maintained the bridges, streets, and roads of their locality by means of the *corvée bourgeoise:* the able-bodied inhabitants had to contribute four days' labor for the upkeep of the community's roads and streets. The assembly issued rulings about all works concerned with the local thoroughfares, drainage ditches, dikes, causeways, and so on.

The community paid the schoolmaster, the clockmaker, the syndic, the crop-watchers, the herdsmen and shepherds, the village crier and messengers, and the midwife.

The community conducted many lawsuits against the *seigneur* regarding rights of use in the woods and also against the tithe-owners and the neighboring communities. These lawsuits were protracted, costly, and ruinous. The peasants were shrewd and stubborn. They appointed attorneys and special delegates, consulted advocates, and often won their cases.

The communities possessed communal property in the form of meadows, pastures, marshes, heaths, moors, salt marshes, woods, and copses, which were used for the feeding of animals, the repairing of buildings and fences, and fuel. They possessed arable land, vines, and houses that were let for the common profit. They possessed *rentes*. Many of these possessions belonged to the fabric, but often the community made use of them as though they were the owners. Sometimes the community had no property apart from what belonged to the fabric. The arrangements for leasing this property were agreed to by the inhabitants themselves, in general assembly. The community's resources thus included the income from these leases, from the felling of the communal woods, and from the ordinary local contributions made by each peasant.

These resources often proved inadequate. The inhabitants then had to decide on extraordinary measures of taxation. It was necessary to obtain letters of assessment from the *élus,* and that was a long and costly business. After royal intendants had been appointed in the provinces, however, the communities could apply to them and quickly obtain the authorizations they needed, free of charge.

When it became necessary to alienate part of the community's property, the alienations were decided on by assemblies of all the inhabitants, for they affected everyone individually.

If the inhabitants lacked common property or this proved insufficient, they had to borrow from the *seigneur* or the *curé* or from a merchant of the nearest town.

The syndic or the churchwarden himself collected the ordinary resources of the community and laid them out on behalf of the inhabitants. If the community's property was substantial, it appointed a *receveur.* The latter, or the syndic, presented his accounts to the assembly, which appointed auditors and, on the basis of their report, gave his acquittance. This, at any rate, they were supposed to do under an *arrêt* of the *cour des aides* dated 27 May 1636, but they did not always comply. Besides, the communities had no budget.

In the northern part of France the community elected a syndic, and in the south it elected consuls. Consuls were magistrates, but a syndic was a mere mandatory agent, a mere attorney for the inhabitants, not a magistrate. He had no judicial or police power, only a revocable mandate. The assemblies chose their syndic freely, without any authorization from the *seigneur.* They elected him by acclamation, usually in December and for one year. Any inhabitant could be chosen. The person so elected was obliged to accept his election on pain of imprisonment. The syndic was relieved of payment of *taille* and exempted from duties of watch and ward. Nevertheless, the responsibility was a heavy one, and consequently many syndics were poor devils, unable to read or write, who were the *créatures* of the richest among the inhabitants.

In small communities the role of the syndic was played by the churchwarden or by the vestryman, the parish agent.

The assembly of the community chose crop-watchers and forest guards for a period of one year. These men were responsible in person and property for the discharge of their duties. They could not refuse to accept appointment. There was no great enthusiasm for these functions, and so they were sometimes chosen by lot. Crop-watchers were chosen to cover the season of the harvest or the wine harvest. Shepherds were appointed to look after the flocks of the community's members. They were held responsible for any loss of animals. They were paid by the inhabitants in proportion of the number of animals owned by each one.

The schoolmaster was chosen by the general assembly from among candidates who had been examined by the *curé* and the notables. The community signed a contract with him for one year or for a number of years. He could be dismissed and the contract annulled. Besides his teaching work, he had to sing in the choir, ring the bell, and accompany the *curé* when the latter carried extreme unction to someone. He was exempt from all burdens and paid a fixed salary, his income being based on the number of his pupils. Classes were held only in the winter months.

The parish

The community of inhabitants and the parish were often hard to distinguish one from the other. Their respective assemblies were frequently made up of the same persons, and the same man acted as agent for both. The *curé* was the head of the parish, sometimes being elected to this position by his parishioners. The latter, in their parish assembly, chose the preachers for Lent and Advent. Parishioners had to provide their *curé* with lodging and furniture, tithe, and perquisites. The parish assembly administered the property of the fabric, that is, the temporalities of the parish, the possessions and revenues assigned for the upkeep of a parish church. The assembly appointed one or more churchwardens, who were to the parish what the syndic was to the community. Often the churchwarden acted as syndic, or as the syndic's helper. The churchwarden was elected for one year, often at the same time as the syndic. His election was monopolized to an increasing degree by the notables, those who paid a certain minimum in *taille*, owing to the duties of assistance to the poor that were incumbent upon the parish. For this reason the churchwardens were chosen from among the well-to-do. They presented their accounts at the conclusion of their period of office.

The fabric received payments toward the upkeep of the church and the expenses of worship. Its income came from gifts, rents paid for land and woods leased out, fees for use of pews and chapels and for funerals, and the results of collections. The churchwardens collected the revenue and looked after expenditures. The parish assembly decided the charges to be levied for pews, made regulations for the sweeping of the church and for interments, and appointed a commissioner for the poor. The churchwarden convened the parish assembly, presided over it, and took the votes. While leaving the place of honor to be filled by the *curé*, he carried out the actual functions to be performed.

In large parishes, the parish assembly owned property that was assigned to the relief of the poor, and the administration of this property was entrusted to a *bureau de charité*, made up of the *curé*, the churchwarden, and some elected notables, with a *procureur de charité* who distributed the income from the property concerned to the school and to individual poor persons. The *bureau de charité* was supervised by the parish assembly. If the property assigned for poor relief proved insufficient, the parish voted special taxes. The parish assembly decided on measures to be taken against epidemics and the enforcement of quarantines. After the edict of 1666 it decided the welcome to be given to religious houses that were installed in the parish.

Thus, the communities of inhabitants and the parishes formed basic local units which brought together the factors essential for the satisfaction of their needs and for participation in public tasks of religion, instruction, poor relief, police, finance, and security.

The types of agent of the communities
of inhabitants

Depending on the province, we find the system of consuls or of *jurats*, three of these generally forming a municipality. Sometimes they were elected, and sometimes they were chosen by the *seigneur* from a list with three names for each post presented by the assembly of the community. They were assisted by the assembly when major decisions had to be taken. This is the system we find in Dauphiné and Provence, where the assemblies were called *"conseils généraux"* or *"conseils particuliers,"* in Languedoc, where they were called *"conseils politiques,"* in Gascony and the Pyrenean districts, where they were called *"assemblées générales,"* and in Quercy, Rouergue, Guyenne, Auvergne, and Burgundy, where two or three aldermen (*échevins*) were appointed *"procureurs"* or *"syndics."*

In the villages of Flanders and Artois we find a mayor and aldermen appointed directly by the *seigneur* or his *bailli*.

A single syndic was the rule in Normandy, Picardy, Soissonnais, Champagne, Ile-de-France, Orléanais, Touraine, Anjou, Maine, Berry, Poitou, northern Limousin, and forty-two places in Brittany. Elsewhere in Brittany the parish and the community of inhabitants were mixed up together: the churchwardens, elected by the parish assemblies, acted as aldermen, consuls, and *jurats*.

In Alsace the *seigneur*'s provost dealt with questions of justice and police, helped by a *Gericht* appointed by the *seigneur*.

The evolution of the communities of inhabitants

The communities of inhabitants were subject, of course, to the tutelage of the state. The governments of the 17th and 18th centuries showed an increasing tendency, down to the reign of Louis XVI, to strengthen this tutelage. The declaration of 22 June 1659 declared quite frankly that the communities and parishes were "to be considered as minors."

The bad financial situation of the communities contributed to justifying and facilitating the encroachments of royal tutelage. At all times the communities of inhabitants suffered greatly from dearths, famines, and epidemics—the *"mortalités"* which killed off some of their producers while increasing the burdens of relief and preventive measures; from the billeting of soldiers in winter quarters or from their passage through, or temporary stationing in, the area—happenings which were accompanied by pillage and violence; and from the damage caused when war, foreign or civil, raged in the provinces, resulting in ruined buildings, fruit trees cut down, and fields deserted and laid waste.

The village communities were therefore from time to time moved to sell to *seigneurs,* judges and magistrates, and prominent townsfolk their possessions, usages, woods, and common lands, often for very moderate sums, without getting the king's authority to do this. Lacking these possessions, the communities were unable to reestablish themselves and feed their cattle, so as to be able to pay the *taille* and improve their land. Accordingly, in 1659, the king restored to the communities of Champagne, in full ownership, the usages, woods, common lands, and other property they had alienated in the previous twenty years. They were to reimburse the purchasers over a period of ten years and, to this end, imposed taxes on themselves by order of the royal commissioner deputed to see to the liquidation of these debts. For the future, the king confirmed the old ordinances under which the communities were not permitted to alienate their usages without the king's permission and a court order. The edict was renewed and completed in April 1667, with application to the whole kingdom. The inhabitants of the parishes and communities had to be restored to ownership of all their lands, meadows, woods, fields, usages, commons, etc., which they had sold or leased out, for *cens* or on hereditary lease, since the year 1620. They had to reimburse the purchasers within ten years and pay interest on any money still not repaid, *au denier 24*. The necessary sums would be levied from the inhabitants, with everyone obliged to contribute, even those enjoying exemptions and privileges. The *seigneurs* who had exercised their right of *triage* since 1630 had to return the land taken to the communities. As regards earlier *triages*, they were to produce their titles, and, if they were confirmed in possession of the land taken, they and their farmers were to be debarred thenceforth from using the other two-thirds of the communal land along with the rest of the inhabitants.

The royal government went ahead with the liquidation and repayment of the debts of the communities. By an edict of 1683 it ordered all the mayors, aldermen, and consuls of the towns, large enclosed *bourgs,* and other communities and parishes of eighteen *généralités* to report the state of their revenues to the intendants. The intendants were to draw up a statement of the ordinary expenditure, with a fixed yearly fund to meet these, to authorize minor expenses, and to refer large expenses to the Council for decision, accompanied by their own opinions. The inhabitants might tax themselves either by adding small amounts to the *taille* or by levying tolls, depending on the intendant's opinion and the Council's decision. Selling and alienation of patrimonial communal property and tolls were forbidden. The communities would be allowed by the king to contract loans, after discussion by the assembly and recommendation by the intendant, in case of plague, or requirement to provide lodging and *ustensile* for soldiers, or rebuilding of church naves. Litigation and the sending of deputations to higher authority were forbidden without the consent of the general assembly of the inhabitants and written authority from the intendant. A declaration of 2 August 1687 confirmed that the edict applied to villages as well as to towns and *bourgs*. The Declaration of Fontainebleau, 2 October 1703, reaffirmed the ban on engaging in lawsuits without the preliminary formalities.

In March 1702 the king, noting that the establishment in the towns of the mayors and assessors provided for by the edict of August 1692 had proved very advantageous, introduced in each parish a perpetual syndic who was to take charge of the affairs of the communities, so reducing to that extent the autonomy they had enjoyed. These *"syndics des paroisses"* were abolished, along with all other municipal offices, by the edict of June 1716. The communities of inhabitants could again elect their own syndics.

It does not appear that the villages were affected by the edicts which first reestablished and then abolished municipal offices, between August 1722 and November 1771, or by Laverdy's reform in August 1764 and May 1765. But the rural communities of inhabitants became the basis of the reform of 1787 creating a hierarchy of provincial and municipal assemblies. This is dealt with in the chapter on the provincial estates and assemblies.

To sum up, down to 1787 the chief care of the royal government was to keep the communities of inhabitants under close tutelage, so as to protect them from themselves and against the oligarchies of well-to-do persons who were in a position to take them over, to the detriment of the common good.

Guide to further reading

Babeau, Albert. *Le village*. 2d ed. 1879.

Babeau, Henry. *Les assemblées générales des communautés d'habitants en France du XIIIe siècle à la Révolution*. Paris Law thesis. 1893.

Bouchard, Gérard. *Le village immobile: Sennely-en-Sologne au XVIIIe siècle*, Plon, 1972.

Clément. "Les communautés d'habitants en Berry," *Positions Thèses de l'Ecole des Chartes* (1890), pp. 45–62.

Denisart, J. B. *Collection de décisions nouvelles et de notions relatives à la jurisprudence*. 1754–56.

Jousse, J. *Gouvernement spirituel et temporel des paroisses*. 1769.

La Poix de Fréminville, Edmé de. *Traité du gouvernement des biens et affaires des communautés d'habitants des villes, bourgs et villages et paroisses.* 1760.

Léonard, E.-G. *Mon village sous Louis XV.* P.U.F., 1941.

Moulin, Léo. "'Sanior et maior pars': Note sur l'évolution des techniques électorales dans les ordres religieux du VIe au XIIIe siècle," *Revue historique de Droit français et étranger* 4th ser. 36 (1958): 368–93.

Prouhet, Dr. "Contribution à l'étude des assemblées générales des communautés d'habitants en France sous l'Ancien Régime," *Mém. Soc. Antiquaire, Ouest* 2d ser. 26 (1902).

Saint-Jacob, Pierre de. *Les paysans de la Haute Bourgogne au XVIIIe siècle.* 1960.

Sheppard, T. H. *Lourmarin in the 18th Century: A Study of a French Village.* Baltimore: Johns Hopkins University Press, 1971.

Zink, Anne. *Azereix: La vie d'une communauté rurale à la fin du XVIIIe siècle.* S.E.V.P.E.N., 1969.

13

The Territorial Communities Treated as Corporations: The Towns

For the French of the 17th and 18th centuries, a town was, first and foremost, an area of security. A town meant a fortified enclosure within which were more or less closely set groups of houses, usually with gardens and parks attached and sometimes fields. Such a place was called a *ville close* or a *bourg clos*. The Hague, capital of the United Provinces, was looked upon as a village rather than a town because it was without walls.[1] Fortification was the essential feature of a town. Inside it was the *"bourgeois"* militia, equipped for war, with its own artillery—the "people" (or at least the well-to-do) in arms. There was, of course, nothing hard and fast about this. Villages were authorized to put walls around themselves in times of insecurity, while yet remaining villages, and Paris was still a town even after Louis XIV had its fortifications demolished.

The second feature of a town was that it was a privileged area. Those of its inhabitants who bore the juridical title of *"bourgeois," "citoyens," "citadins,"* enjoyed various privileges; some of these were honorific, "placing" their holders in the society of orders, while others were fiscal, safeguarding property from the exactions of king or *seigneur*, and yet others were economic, favoring activities that were productive of material goods.

The third feature of a town was that it was an area from which domination was exercised. This was so much so that there was a tendency to call "a town" any seignorial locality where old-established symbols of superiority and authority were maintained.[2] Toward the end of the 17th century this domination became more financial and economic in character. The town appeared as an area in which were concentrated money, cash, *rentes,* bills of exchange, bills payable to order—all the financial resources, some of which constituted capital while others were elements in fortunes that might or might not be transformed into capital.[3]

Three kinds of towns: "Seignorial" towns, *villes de "bourgeoisie,"* and communes

From the juridical standpoint, towns were of three kinds. First, there were the towns which I shall call "seignorial." These were the ones in which the *seigneur* retained most of the powers of administration, exercised through his officers. Paris was typical of such a town. The king administered it through the *bailliage* and presidial court of the Châtelet and his *lieutenant civil,* and through the *parlement.* The town of Paris was a grouping of corporations and colleges, the sovereign courts, the subordinate corporations of magistrates, and the craft guilds. One of these corporations was constituted by the Provost of the Merchants, the aldermen, and the town councilors, to whom the king had granted certain administrative powers. The Bureau de ville and the Assemblée de ville were bodies sharing in the administration and life of the capital.

Next came the *villes de bourgeoisie, villes franches,* or *villes de consulat.* These were the ones that constituted *"corps et collège."* Either by charter or by custom, the most important section of such a town's inhabitants, those who bore the title of *"bourgeois"* of the place in question, formed a body that was endowed with a legal personality and was represented by a group of magistrates and municipal officers, *"le corps de ville,"* an organ that expressed its common will. Examples of this category of towns were Lyons, Marseilles, Toulouse, and Bordeaux.

Finally, there were the towns that were communes. A commune consisted of the inhabitants of a town, confederated and bound together by an oath that was recognized and authorized by the *seigneur* or by the king. A commune was a sworn association—a moral person enjoying privileges and liberties either by custom or by charter. There were communes still in existence at the beginning of the 17th century: Bayonne, Dax, Angoulême, Niort, Saintes, Saint-Maixent, La Rochelle, Noyon, Beauvais, Péronne, Saint-Quentin, Abbeville, Arras, Saint-Omer, Bapaume, Aire-sur-la-Lys, Hestin, Heuchin, Saint-Pol, Montreuil-sur-Mer.

However, the commune was growing weaker. At Niort, Saintes, Saint-Maixent, and Angoulême it was perhaps retained tacitly, after the transformation of institutions that took place during the 17th century. Four communes disappeared: that of Amiens, after the town had let itself be taken by the Spaniards in 1597; that of Saint-Jean-d'Angély, in 1621, and that of La Rochelle, in 1628, after the Protestant revolts; that of Heuchin, on 15 June 1752, as a result of abuses and usurpations, the town being placed under the authority of the officers of the *bailliage*.

The word "*commune*" was used from the sixteenth century onward in the sense of "common people." Furetière gave it this meaning in his *Dictionary* of 1693, and it had this sense in the *Dictionary of the French Academy* also, in its first edition of 1694. In the plural, as *les communes,* it was used for the inhabitants of the rural parishes and sometimes for those of a *bourg* or a village.

The former communes were abolished by the decrees of 4 August 1789. The word *commune* was used by the revolutionaries of 1789, perhaps through the influence of the English language, to signify the third estate ("the commons"). Then the decree of 14 December 1789 gave the name *commune* to the aggregate of the inhabitants of a town or a village. Paris became a commune by the decree of 21 May 1790. The meaning of the word was subsequently extended to the entire territory of an agglomeration.

It is impossible to do without examples. I shall take Paris as my example of a seignorial town, Bordeaux as a random example of a *ville de bourgeoisie,* and Beauvais as a similarly random example of a commune. As a consequence of the king's endeavors, urban institutions came increasingly to be identified, first, with those of the *villes de bourgeoisie* and then with those of Paris. I shall therefore begin with the *villes de bourgeoisie,* taking Bordeaux as my example.

A *ville de "bourgeoisie"*: Bordeaux

The privileges of Bordeaux were confirmed by Henry IV in October 1602. The "*bourgeois de Bordeaux*" were a limited group of privileged persons, recruited by cooptation. One became a "bourgeois" by applying and being accepted by the mayor and *jurats*. It was necessary to be of good repute, to be the owner of a house in the town, and to have lived there for two years in succession. In 1622 the value of the house was fixed at 1,500 livres and the period of residence at five years. Under Louis XIV, candidates had to show possession of an interest in shipping or in certain privileged companies.

The quality of *bourgeois* was hereditary. It was transmitted in the male line to the descendants of the person who had acquired it. But it could be lost by contravention of the rules or if the beneficiary resided for two years outside the limits of the town and its suburbs. The quality of *bourgeois* was attached to one's domicile, to one's participation in the miscellaneous interests of the town of Bordeaux.

The *bourgeois de Bordeaux* were not numerous. On the eve of the Revolution they numbered perhaps 1,500 families—5,000 to 6,000 persons—out of a population of more than 100,000. The title was sought after, even by *gentilshommes*. In 1590 the duc d'Epernon said to a *jurat* of Bordeaux that "he honored highly the quality that the House of Candale possessed in being the first *bourgeois de Bordeaux*." The duke had married Marguerite de Foix, comtesse de Candale. Whether nobles or not, the *bourgeois* of Bordeaux were a group of vine-growers, of crop-growing landowners. They were looked on as the representatives, the attorneys, of the other inhabitants, since they were the ones most interested in the prosperity of the district.

The *bourgeois de Bordeaux* formed a privileged body possessing numerous advantages and powers of jurisdiction and police. By virtue of the privileges granted by Henri II in August 1550, they formed "*corps et collège*." They were exempt from all payment of *taille* or *crue de taille*. Until they had sold the wine from their vineyards, nobody else was allowed to sell his in the town or its suburbs, nor could any wine be subsequently brought in, except from the *sénéchaussée* and diocese of Guyenne. Up-country wines were allowed to be sent down as far as Bordeaux only after Christmas and, even then, not into the town itself. Between Michaelmas and Whitsun the *bourgeois* of Bordeaux had the exclusive right to sell their own wine in the taverns of the town. The *bourgeois* could acquire "noble" lands, even if they were themselves commoners. They enjoyed various other privileges in matters of successions, lawsuits, trade, taxes, and so on.

Above all, however, this body of persons enjoyed political privileges. The mayors and *jurats* exercised powers of "justice and political jurisdiction" over the town and the surrounding area. The latter consisted of:

1.   The *"ancienne banlieue,"* embracing part of Bègles, Talence, and Coudéran

2.   The *prévôté* of Eyzines, including five parishes: Eyzines, Magudas, Le Haillan, Corbiac, and Bruges

3.   The *prévôté* of Entre-Deux-Mers, including nine parishes: Cénon, Floirac, Tresses, part of La Tresne, Artignes, Bouliac, Cérignan, and part of Lormont

4.   The county of Ornon, purchased by the town in 1409, which included seven parishes: Villenave-d'Ornon, the rest of Bègles, part of Martignac, Léognan, Gradignan, Canéjan, and Cestas

5.   The barony of Veyrines, acquired in 1526, with its six parishes: Pessac, Yvrac, Mérignac, Beutres, Illac, and Boulac.

All together, the town possessed twenty-nine external parishes. Between 1591 and 1607 Bordeaux also owned the barony of Montferrand.

None of the inhabitants of the villages dependent on the town of Bordeaux, whether priests, nobles, or commoners, shared in the privileges of the *bourgeois de Bordeaux,* and all were subject to the jurisdiction and *"police"* of these *bourgeois.*

Finally, the town of Bordeaux wielded a sort of moral ascendancy over the neighboring towns of Guyenne, which assumed the title of "god-daughters" of Bordeaux. These were Libourne, Bourg, Blaye, Saint-Emilion, Castillon, Rious, Cadillac, and Saint-Macaire.

The constitution of Bordeaux was oligarchical. The *"corps et collège"* of the *bourgeois* was represented by a series of collegiate bodies, recruited by cooption, which any *bourgeois* might hope to enter when his turn came round. Jurisdiction and *"police"* were exercised by a *"corps de ville"* consisting of a mayor, six *jurats,* a *procureur-syndic,* a town clerk, and a treasurer. The mayor and *jurats* could be advised by a Council of Thirty, a Council of One Hundred, and pensionary councilors.

The mayor was elected for two years by the six *jurats.* There was one *jurat* for each *jurade,* that is, each "quarter" of the town: Saint-Rémi, Saint-Eloi, Saint-Pierre, Saint-Maixent, Sainte-Eulalie, and Saint-Michel. They were elected for two years, half of them being replaced each year, on 1 August. Each *jurat* named his successor as representative of his *jurade.*

The six *jurats* worked with the help of a council of twenty-four notable *bourgeois,* or *"prudhommes,* whom they nominated themselves.

The *jurats* had to comprise equal numbers of *gentilshommes,* advocates, and merchants.

The *jurats* and the mayor were supervised by two counselors of the *parlement*, commissioned to see that the law was respected. Disputes arising from municipal elections were settled by the *parlement*.

The "Thirty Councilors" were appointed each year by the incoming *jurats*, who named their predecessors in office. At the same time, they appointed the members of the "Council of One Hundred." The Council of Thirty was competent to deal with "minor matters," when the *jurats* saw fit to refer them to it, and the Council of One Hundred dealt similarly with more important ones. The *jurats* could combine these two councils to form the Assembly of One Hundred and Thirty "in grave circumstances, when there was need to secure the general consent of the community." In such cases the *parlement* delegated two "*conseillers-députés*" to attend, in accordance with an old custom sanctioned by the *arrêt* of the king's Council of 5 November 1715.

Since the *jurats* did not remain long in office, the *corps de ville* also included some permanent members. By his addresses the *procureur-syndic* drew the attention of the mayors and *jurats* to all measures needed for the good of the town. He was a royal official, appointed by the king, but his name had been submitted to the king by the major and *jurats*. The town clerk was a *greffier*, head of the bureaus and keeper of the papers, registers, and documents of the commune. He recorded the decisions taken by the mayors and *jurats*. He wielded great influence. The treasurer was an official nominated by the *jurats*. The pensionary counselors were advocates who were paid a retainer to give legal advice.

The *jurats*, who were responsible for the town's security, had at their disposal a "watch," commanded by a captain, and twelve *commissaires de police*, who were not permanent.

To control the supply and prices of foodstuffs, the *jurats* had various "*officiers de police*": inspectors of fish, inspectors of taverns, measurers of salt, counters of fish, gaugers, packers, markers of wine, checkers of grain, *sacquiers*, inspectors of rivers, auctioneers, assessors of fish, *auneurs*, refiners, markers of weights and measures, etc.

Being responsible for public education, the *jurats* acted as patrons of the university and subsidized the Collège de Guyenne.

The *jurats* ensured the hygiene of the town through persons appointed to clean the fountains and streets. They appointed "*intendants de haute fuste et de maçonnerie*" from among the master carpenters and master masons to see to the maintenance of public buildings and to put down fires.

They arranged to be represented in Paris, close to the king's Council and the court, by a permanent *"solliciteur."*

On the other hand, the mayors and *jurats* enjoyed financial privileges. They made appointments to all municipal offices "and even drew from this a small benefit for themselves, as their predecessors had always done." They levied various dues, on salmon and sturgeon, for example. They were especially favored with honorific distinctions. The bore the title of "governors of Bordeaux, counts of Ornon, and barons of Veyrines." They were "patrons of the Hôpital Saint-André," "patrons of the Collège de Guyenne," and "patrons of the university." The university respectfully invited them to attend the defending of theses and addressed them as *Sex viri vigilantissimi.* On the occasion of public festivals they processed with an outrider on horseback ahead of them, as well as trumpeters and mace-bearers splendidly arrayed, and were escorted by the soldiers of the "watch," nobly costumed in red-and-white livery. At ceremonies, if *gentilshommes* were present, the *jurats* "took the lead"; at table they sat "above the nobles." They had the right to hang their portraits in the town hall and to retain the title of *citoyen* when they left office.

Before the end of the Hundred Years' War, Bordeaux had been a kind of oligarchical republic, a city-state with its own foreign policy and its own troops, negotiating alliances and truces with foreign powers, great feudal lords, and the king himself. The *jurats* also possessed all "political" jurisdiction, powers of justice both civil and criminal, and fiscal power, with authority to introduce taxes and to collect them.

At the beginning of the 17th century their powers were much reduced. They had lost control of foreign relations and also their financial independence. They were under the tutelage of the *parlement,* the governor, and, soon, the intendant. Nevertheless, they still exercised a number of functions on behalf of the state or in collaboration with the state's agents.

The *jurats* held the keys to the bridges and the towers. They commanded the *"troupes bourgeoises,"* divided into six regiments, one for each *jurade,* with its *jurat* as colonel. The six regiments were made up of forty companies, whose captains, lieutenants, and other officers were appointed by the *jurats* from among the *bourgeois de Bordeaux.* These *troupes bourgeoises* ensured the defense of the town in the king's service—or, if need be, against the king. This was a burdensome duty, for the officers paid for their own equipment and the arming of their men and also for the regimental fifes and drums. Accordingly, they were allowed privileges: exemption from guardianship, from loans and subsidies, and from various municipal responsibilities.

The *jurats* had power to issue police regulations and to punish breaches thereof. This was what was called their "political" jurisdiction. They also took measures to safeguard public safety, order, and hygiene and to care for hospitals, communications, public works, commerce, industry, education, and entertainments.

The *jurats* exercised criminal jurisdiction, but only in conjunction with the *lieutenant criminel* in the *sénéchaussée* of Guyenne, who had the right to remove cases from their cognizance. The jurats dispensed civil justice, not in the town itself, out of respect for the *parlement*, but only in the *seigneuries* belonging to the town, to which the mayor and *jurats* delegated judges and assessors. Litigants could appeal from their verdicts to the *parlement* or to the *cour des aides*.

Thus, the *jurats* were responsible for many functions which after the Revolution were discharged by the state and its direct agents. The *corps de ville* of Bordeaux was still a powerful "intermediate corporation."

The evolution of institutions in Bordeaux

However, the king intended to reduce all the *villes franches* or *villes de bourgeoisie* to unity and uniformity. This intention of his was expressed as early as Marillac's ordinance of 1629, the "Code Michaud": "We desire and ordain that the *corps et maisons de ville* and the manner of their assemblies and administration throughout our realm be brought into line, as far as possible, with the form and manner of our good town of Paris, or as near to that as may be, in the way that has already been achieved in Lyons, Limoges, and other places." The ordinance of 1629 was not registered by the Paris *parlement* and found little application, but the intentions expressed in it remained those of the king's government and guided its policy toward the towns.

The king extended his powers over the nomination of mayors and *jurats* and over their activities. By his edict of 24 September 1620, which took account of the *"mouvements"* going on in the kingdom—a revolt by the queen mother and the grandees, a revolt of the Protestants—Louis XIII postponed the election of a mayor and *jurats* in Bordeaux. Then he put off the election of the mayor *sine die*. There was no mayor for thirty years—no head of the municipality empowered to make decisions. The king himself nominated the six *jurats*, three for two years and three for three. Later, he allowed the customary forms to be resumed, but cooption was thereafter to be effected by reliable persons, "king's men," and the running of the town was left to a coterie, so that Bordeaux was deprived of self-government.

By the Council's *arrêt* of 2 March 1627 it was decided that the *jurats* and the twenty-four *"prud'hommes"* were to nominate twelve candidates, from among whom the king would choose six *jurats*. In the event of complaints against the choice made, the *procureur du roi* in the Bordeaux *parlement* would look into the matter, and the final decision would rest with the king. In 1669 the king ordered that the functions of *jurat* should be exercised alternately by a *gentilhomme* and two merchants and by an advocate and two merchants. On 21 July 1674, however, he reestablished the former balance: two *gentilshommes,* two advocates, two merchants. On 27 December 1683 an *arrêt* of the Council prescribed that nine candidates be elected for each year, three from each order. Each year the king would choose one from each order, and the persons so chosen would stay in office for two years. Half of the six *jurats* would thus be replaced each year.

After the Fronde and the separatist movement of the Ormée, the king perceived the need for "a person of authority to exercise the office of mayor." He reestablished the mayoralty and appointed to it Godefroy, comte d'Estrades, marshal of France, on 30 October 1653. In 1675 Godefroy resigned in favor of his son Louis, marquis d'Estrades. The mayoralty remained in the Estrades family down to 1769. They rarely visited Bordeaux; if necessity arose, however, the position of first magistrate of the town was held by a soldier loyal to the king.

The final blow was delivered by way of venality of the municipal offices, a financial expedient dictated by the War of the League of Augsburg and the War of the Spanish Succession; this resulted in these offices being occupied by men appointed by the king and in no way subject to election.

The edict of August 1692 established mayors *"en titre d'office et héréditaire"* in every town and urban community in the kingdom except Paris and Lyons. In May 1702 an office of deputy mayor was created, and in January 1704 the same was done in relation to the offices of *échevin, consul, capitoul, jurat,* and so on. These edicts were enforced in Bordeaux. Three hereditary *jurats* were appointed, the other three remaining elective. An office as hereditary *jurat* was given by the king, on 3 August 1704, to Etienne Tannesse, advocate and professor of law.

On 10 August 1704 the hereditary office of deputy mayor of Bordeaux was given to Henri de Ségur, vicomte de Cabanac, who in 1707 resigned in favor of his son Joseph.

The king intervened increasingly in the administrative affairs of Bordeaux, imposing his tutelage in the spirit of the declaration of 22 June 1659, which assigned the status of minors to village communities and parishes. The king treated Bordeaux as if the town were a minor. The town's administration was directed to an ever greater extent from Paris, and later from Versailles, through a multitude of Council *arrêts*. Here are some examples. By *arrêt* of 30 March 1654 the king had a statement of the town's debts drawn up and also a list of the commodities and provisions which he was thinking of taxing in order to pay off these debts, and he reserved for himself the decision to be made in this matter. By *arrêt* of 19 January 1669 the king determined the amounts of money to be assigned for cleaning the streets, for the hospital, and for meeting the cost of festivals—Corpus Christi, Midsummer Day, and so on. He laid down the way in which the town's accounts were to be audited, authorized the collection of dues, regulated the rates at which they were to be levied, and arranged for their farming-out. The *arrêt* of 18 July 1670 fixed the rates at 10 livres per ox, 10 sous per sheep, 5 sous per bushel of wheat, 3 sous per bushel of rye, and so on. All these actions were not without their inconvenient aspects, for the central authority was settling questions about which it was insufficiently informed. In 1669 the king abolished the payments made to the *intendants de haute fuste et de maçonnerie,* who were entrusted with fire-fighting. These craftsmen then let houses burn down, in the frequent fires that occurred, due to the pinewood planking, and the king was obliged to reintroduce the payments on 25 February 1679. The sums involved were insignificant, being 30 livres to each of eight craftsmen—four *"de haute fuste"* and four *"de maçonnerie"*—240 livres in all.

The chief representative of the central government for administrative purposes, the intendant of Guyenne, interfered more and more. He acted as comptroller: in 1654 a statement of debts was drawn up in the presence of Sieur Gédéon Tallemant, "conseiller de Sa Majesté en ses conseils, maître des requêtes ordinaires de son Hôtel." The intendant acted as the central government's informer, sending to the Council a report, with his recommendations, on any question that arose, and the Council issued its *arrêts* on the basis of these communications. Thus, on 19 January 1669 the Council made its decision on payments and public works after reading the recommendations of Sieur Pellot, "conseiller de

Sa Majesté en ses conseils, maître des requêtes ordinaire de son Hôtel, commissaire départi par Sa Majesté pour l'éxécution de ses ordres dans la province de Guyenne." The intendant acted as administrator: on 8 June 1677 it was the intendant De Sève who assigned the *octrois*, in the presence of the mayor and *jurats*, and who shared out money among the town's creditors. It was the intendant who, on 27 August 1712, checked the statements of expenses drawn up by the *jurades* and handed them to the town treasurer, and who saw to it that the town clerk kept good records of receipts and expenditures.

Compensation for this growing intervention by the central authority was given to the *bourgeois* in the form of an increase in their privileges. The *jurats* were often in conflict with the *parlement* of Bordeaux, which claimed to exercise general authority over the town. On 3 October 1661 the king granted them a removal: thereafter, the town's lawsuits were to be heard by the Grand Conseil, and those of the municipal officials, their wives, and their children were to be heard by the *sénéchal* of Libourne, with right of appeal to the Grand Conseil.

Above all, the king granted them economic privileges. He protected them from foreign competition. By the Council's *arrêt* of 25 August 1622 it was provided that one had to have resided in Bordeaux for five years in order to be accepted as *"bourgeois."* No foreigner could carry on trade in the town unless he had been so accepted, and no foreigner, even if a *bourgeois de Bordeaux,* could become a sworn broker. Letters patent of 6 February 1628 confirmed this *arrêt.*

The king protected them from competition by vine-growers who were not *bourgeois.* On 30 March 1654 he confirmed that only wine from the vineyards of *bourgeois* might be sold at retail, by *cabaretiers, taverniers,* and other sellers of wine. Any disputes were to be decided by the mayor and the *jurats.*

The king strove to expand maritime trade. We have seen that in 1669 he ensured, for a time at least, that the merchants had the majority among the *jurats.* On 27 June 1671 a Council *arrêt* authorized the establishment of a privileged company of Bordeaux merchants. Nobody was to be accepted as *bourgeois* or as *jurat* unless he had invested 1,000 or 2,000 livres in this company—and so on.

However, in the second phase of Louis XIV's personal government, during the wars of the League of Augsburg and the Spanish Succession, the town was subjected to a crushing burden of venal offices which it had to purchase at great expense.

Bordeaux was thus brought under increasingly close tutelage by the central government, which sought to bring the administration of all towns to a state of unity and even uniformity.

A "seignorial" town: Paris

The town of Paris covered an area that was divided into three parts: *la Cité,* on the principal island; the university, on the left bank of the Seine; and *la Ville,* on the right bank. These three parts were themselves divided into *quartiers.* But the *ville de Paris* was, in essence, not a locality but a grouping of corporations—bodies of magistrates, religious communities both secular and regular, craft guilds. The *corps de ville* was only one corporation among many, and not the most important.[4]

The "police" powers of the king's officials

In fact, the *"police,"* or administration, of the town of Paris was primarily in the hands of the king's officials. In the first place—as with all the towns, whatever their category—Paris was subject to the king's Council and to two ministers: the secretary of state, whose sphere of responsibility included Paris (for matters of security, morality, and administrative disputes), and the *surintendant des finances* or, after 1665, the *contrôleur général des finances* (for all matters concerning finance).

Then, as in all towns where there was a *parlement,* the Paris *parlement* exercised the power of *grande police,* or *police générale.* It protected the town and watched over it. At the end of the 18th century an *assemblée de police* was held every month under the chairmanship of the *premier président.* It was attended by the *présidents* and counselors of the *parlement* and the *lieutenant général de police.* The *parlement,* as "first protector of the capital," inspected all the jurisdictions in Paris. It held "sessions to deal with particular matters." It undertook inquiries. It issued *arrêts* dealing with the shortage of bread, the price of coal, the collapse of a gallery, and so on. It confirmed the ordinances issued by subordinate authorities, such as the *lieutenant général de police.* It sought the opinions of subordinate authorities when it was called upon to register letters patent, as, for example, for the building of a new market for calves or for the use of steam engines to distribute water among houses (1778).

Above all, the real administrator of Paris was the *prévôt* of Paris, a *"police"* magistrate of first instance at the Paris Châtelet. Since the edict of March 1498 "prévôt de Paris" had no longer been more than an

honorific title. The actual functions were carried out by his two assistants, the *lieutenant civil* and the *lieutenant criminel,* who exercised
them together down to 1630, not without mutual conflict; the result was
that vagrants and *"gens mal vivant"* went free and that the price of
foodstuffs was excessive. By the *parlement's arrêt* of 12 March 1630 it
was decided that the *lieutenant civil* should be solely responsible for
matters of *"police"* and should hold a court for this purpose twice a
week, assisted by the *procureur du roi.* If he was unavoidably prevented, this duty would fall to the *lieutenant criminel* or the *lieutenant
particulier.* After the ordinance issued by the *lieutenant civil* Moreau,
on 9 January 1635, every Friday, after the session of the regular police
court, an *assemblée de police générale* was held, under the chairmanship of the *lieutenant civil;* it was attended by the *lieutenant criminel* and
the sixteen commissaries of the *quartiers* whose offices were the
oldest-established, each accompanied by two "notable *bourgeois"* of
his *quartier.* As a result of the declaration of 9 November 1637 the office
of *lieutenant civil* was abolished, and the functions were exercised by
commissioner. The same person was not to hold this commission for
longer than three years. In 1643, after the death of Louis XIII, the office
of *lieutenant civil* was reestablished for Dreux d'Aubray.

However, the *lieutenant civil* was overwhelmed by the number of
cases he had to deal with, and so, by an edict of March 1667, registered
by the *parlement* on 15 March, Louis XIV divided his functions between two offices—that of *lieutenant civil* and that of *lieutenant de
police.* The king was adumbrating a revolution: the separation of justice
from administration. To be sure, the *lieutenant de police* continued to be
a magistrate with a jurisdiction. Nevertheless, the king had separated
justice between individuals from administration, even though the latter
was still to be carried out by a magistrate. The king noted in the edict that
the functions of justice and *"police"* were often incompatible and too
far-reaching for a single magistrate to perform. He therefore divided
them into, on the one hand, contentious and distributive justice, for regulating the affairs of individuals and keeping an eye on their behavior,
and, on the other, *"police"*—"which consists in ensuring the tranquillity of the public and of private persons, in purging the town of whatever
may give rise to disorders, in providing for plentiful supplies, and in enabling everyone to live in accordance with his condition and his duty."

The king therefore abolished the old office of *lieutenant civil du prévôt
de Paris,* reimbursing the heirs of Dreux d'Aubray. He created two
offices, *"en titre d'offices formez,"* of *lieutenants du prévôt de Paris—*

one an office of *conseiller du roi et lieutenant civil du prévôt de Paris* and one of *conseiller du roi et lieutenant du prévôt de Paris pour la police*. Thus, the *prévôt de Paris* was thenceforth to have five principal *lieutenants:* a *lieutenant civil,* a *lieutenant particulier civil,* a *lieutenant criminel,* a *lieutenant particulier criminel,* and a *lieutenant de police*. The *lieutenant civil* and the *lieutenant de police* were to exercise their functions separately and distinctly.

The *lieutenant civil* had cognizance of the receiving of all officials into their offices, of all lawsuits, personal, real, or mixed, and of all contracts, wills, promises, matters concerned with benefices and other ecclesiastical matters, affixing of seals, compiling of inventories, guardianship, *avis de parents,* emancipation of minors, and all other matters concerning contentious and distributive justice within the confines of the *ville, prévôté, et vicomté de Paris*. He took precedence of the *lieutenant de police* in all assemblies but had no authority over him.

The *lieutenant de police* had cognizance of the security of the *ville, prévôté, et vicomté de Paris,* the carrying of weapons forbidden by ordinance, the cleaning of the streets, public places, and *"circonstances et dépendances."* It was his responsibility to give orders when fires or floods occurred. He arranged for the supplying and storing of goods needed for the town's subsistence and fixed the rates and prices for these goods. He dispatched agents along the rivers to see to the collection of hay and the trussing and conveyance thereof to Paris. He inspected and approved the butchers' stalls. He visited the markets fairs, hotels, inns, furnished rooms for let, gaming houses (*brelans*), tobacco shops, "and places of ill repute." He prevented or suppressed unauthorized assemblies, riots, seditions, and disorders. He inspected factories and premises connected with them and supervised the election of the masters and wardens of the "six corporations" of merchants (the mercers, grocers, clothiers, furriers, hosiers, and goldsmiths) and also the issuing of certificates of apprenticeship, the reception of master craftsmen, the reports of the visits carried out by the wardens, and the execution of the statutes and rules of the corporations. He fixed the standards for the weights and scales of all the communities in the town and its suburbs, to the exclusion of all other judges. He took cognizance of contraventions of the ordinances, statutes, and regulations made by the printers, of the printing of forbidden books and pamphlets, and of their sale and distribution by peddlers. He received surgeons' notifications of injured persons. He had to try summarily, on his own, all offenders against the police regulations caught *in flagrante delicto;*

however, if their offenses entailed corporal punishment, he was obliged
to report the cases to the presidial court sitting at the Châtelet. He was
responsible for enforcing all ordinances, *arrêts,* and *règlements* concerning the policing of Paris. He held court in the Chambre civile of the
Châtelet and there received his commissaries' reports and dealt summarily with all matters of police. He had a small room at his disposal
adjoining the Chambre civile.

The first *lieutenant de police* was Gabriel Nicolas, sieur de La Reynie, who subsequently became a state councilor, from 1667 to 1697. In
March 1674 a second office of *lieutenant de police* was created and
linked with the first on 18 April. La Reynie became *lieutenant général
de police.*

The next *lieutenant général de police,* Marc René de Voyer d'Argenson, *conseiller du roi* in the king's Council, made his office a veritable
ministry, from 1697 to 1718. Edicts of 1700 and 1707 transferred from
the Bureau de la ville to him the task of regulating the trade in grain in
Paris and within a radius of eight leagues around it, together with
regulation of the trade in wine, timber, oysters, and other goods arriving by water, and of fountains, water-carriers, bridges, quays, ramparts, the Place de Grève, stages erected for festivals, and craftsmen's
use of the River Seine for washing purposes. Increasingly he took
control of the impressment and recruiting of soldiers, regulation of the
cattle markets of Sceaux and Poissy, supervision of wet nurses,
charities, and hospitals, of loose women, vagabonds, swashbucklers,
and lackeys, inspection of popular celebrations, of actors, jugglers,
buffoons, puppet-masters, and quacks.

The commissaries and inspectors of police in each *quartier* reported
to him daily. There were, after 1586, forty commissaries, sixteen of
whom held the oldest-established offices, and from July 1738 there
were forty-eight. In addition to their inspectors they employed "observers," that is, spies or informers.

The *lieutenant général de police* had no right of inspection over ecclesiastics, who came under the authority of the archbishop; over military officers, who were under that of the marshals of France; over
judicial personnel, who were under that of the chancellor; or over
financiers, who were under that of the comptroller general of finance.
He was, however, obliged to give assistance to all these authorities in
enforcing their orders.

In order to become *lieutenant général de police* one had to be at least
twenty-five years old, a master of requests, and put forward for the

post by the secretary of state responsible for Paris, in agreement with the chancellor. The office was not venal, but it was customary for the incoming incumbent to pay a certain sum to his predecessor, who had resigned in his favor, and he received from the king for this purpose a *brevet de retenue* of 250,000 livres in the 17th century and 150,000 livres in the 18th.

The other *lieutenants généraux de police* were Louis-Charles de Machault d'Arnouville, appointed on 28 January 1718; Marc-Pierre d'Argenson, younger son of Marc-René (18 January 1720); Gabriel Taschereau de Baudry (1 July 1720); Marc-Pierre d'Argenson (26 April 1722); N.-J.-B. Ravot d'Ombreval (28 January 1724); René Héraut (29 August 1725); Claude-Henry Feydeau de Marville, his son-in-law (January 1740); then, starting on 21 May 1747, Berryer, the future minister of marine (1758) and keeper of the seals (1761), etc., who held the post until 1757.

Also involved in the administration of Paris were the Bureau des Finances, the governors of the royal residences, the Direction des Bâtiments, the *bailliage* of the palace, the seignorial judges, and the judges of the appanages.

The *trésoriers de France et généraux des finances* of the Paris Bureau des Finances had among their responsibilities control of the alignment of buildings and of the construction of projecting features, but they exercised this power together with the Bureau de la Ville and also, by article XI of the declaration of 18 August 1730, with the *lieutenant général de police,* who had power of *prévention* in cases of imminent danger relating to houses, in both the town and its suburbs, whose walls adjoined the street. Their functions were gradually encroached upon by the *lieutenant général de police.*

The king's houses—the Louvre, the Tuileries, the Luxembourg, the Palais-Bourbon, the Chancellery, the Hôtel du Contrôle Général, the châteaux of Vincennes, La Muette, and Les Invalides, and the Ecole Militaire—were privileged places, outside the competence of the Châtelet and subject to policing by their own governors, with appeal to the *prévôté de l'Hôtel du Roi.*

The Direction des Bâtiments was responsible for policing the Champs-Elysées, issuing licenses for the stalls and drinking places set up there.

The *bailliage* of the Palace of Justice possessed jurisdiction—civil, criminal, and police—over the courtyards, the new galleries, and the enclosed area of the palace. This old-established jurisdiction was regulated by the edict of October 1712.

The twenty-seven seignorial *justices* of Paris, held by the bishop (later, the archbishop) and by the religious communities, were abolished by the edict of February 1674. These ecclesiastical *seigneurs* thereafter retained jurisdiction only over certain restricted enclosures: the enclosure and courtyard of the Temple, the Commanderie of Saint-Jean-de-Latran (Order of Malta, letters patent of 20 March 1678), the enclosure of the abbey of Saint-Germain-des-Prés (March 1691), the cloister, the parvis, and the area adjoining the cloister of Notre-Dame (the chapter, 14 August 1676), the *bailliage* of Sainte-Geneviève, the *bailliage* of Saint-Martin-des-Champs, and the Oursine fief.

The appanages of the Palais-Royal, granted to Monsieur (the king's brother) by letters patent of February 1692, and of the Luxembourg, with the adjoining land and buildings, granted to the comte de Provence on 25 March 1779, were outside the authority of both the *lieutenant général de police* and the *prévôt de l' Hôtel du Roi*. The prince to whom the appanage had been assigned was responsible for its policing.

The "police" powers of the Bureau de la Ville

By custom, the king relinquished to a college, representing one of the corporations that constituted the capital, a certain number of *"police"* tasks, for instance, the upkeep of bridges, quays, and fountains, control of festivals and celebrations, navigation on the river, supplying the town with wine, grain, and so on.

The Bureau de la Ville originated in the "company of merchants of the river of Paris," whose head was entitled Provost of the Merchants. His headquarters was on the Place de Grève, not far from the principal port of Paris, where the landing places for grain, hay, timber, etc., adjoined one another, and near the great east-west trade route across Paris, traversing the rue Saint-Antoine, the rue de la Verrerie, the market in the cemetery of Saint-Jean, the rue des Lombards, the rue de la Ferronnerie and the rue Saint-Honoré. The building of the Town Hall, begun in 1533 but suspended at the end of Henri II's reign, was resumed in 1606 and completed in 1628.

The town of Paris had long been associated with the royal authority, as was shown by its arms and emblems. The arms of Paris were finally registered on 27 February 1699, in the Armorial Général de France.

The escutcheon of Paris was "gules, on waves of the sea in base a lymphad (ship) in full sail argent, a chief *cousu* azure semy of (scattered with) *fleurs de lys d'or.*" The *fleur de lys*, forming the "*chef de France,*" symbolized the union between the Parisians and the king. The red ground color of the escutcheon recalled both Saint-Denis the Martyr, protector of the royal family and the town, and the noble status of the capital, endowed with all the virtues of the *gentilhomme*— charity, magnanimity, valor, and boldness: first among all the towns of the realm. The silver ship signified the wealth of Paris, its beauty and purity, its loyalty to the sovereign, its service, and the promise of victory.

The motto *Fluctuat nec mergitur* appears on tokens of 1581, 1586, and 1598, though it did not become the official motto of Paris until the Prefect Haussmann so decided, on 24 November 1853. In the 17th century it was merely one motto among others. The tokens struck by order of the Bureau de la Ville in 1611, 1622, 1653, and 1656 symbolize above all the town's submission to the king, its increasing role as an instrument of the royal power. The portrait of the king—Louis XIII, Louis XIV—is frequently seen, together with what had been the royal emblem since Charles V's time: the sun, shown causing a lily to flower or warming and bringing Paris to life with its beams.

The composition of the *corps de ville* and its powers were governed, in principle, by the ordinance of February 1415, which remained legally in force until 1789. At the head of the town stood the Bureau de la ville, made up of the Petit Bureau and the Grand Bureau. The former consisted of the Provost of the Merchants, the four aldermen, the *procureur du roi et de la ville,* the town's *greffier,* and its *receveur.* The Grand Bureau consisted of the Petit Bureau plus twenty-four town councilors, this gathering being also known as the Council de la Ville.

The executive agents of the Bureau de la Ville were the officers of the *quartiers.* Since Charles V's time Paris had been divided into sixteen *quartiers,* the names and limits of which changed from time to time. The Bureau de la Ville seems always to have recognized only sixteen *quartiers,* whereas the Châtelet divided the town in a different way. In 1637, so far as the Châtelet was concerned, Paris consisted of seventeen *quartiers,* three *faubourgs,* and one "*ville,*" that of Saint-Marcel. The Cité was separated from the *quartier* of Notre-Dame. In 1642, according to Delamare, the *quartier* of Saint-André, on the left bank, which had grown too large, was split in two by the creation of a new *quartier*—the *faubourg* of Saint-Germain. In 1673, however, the Châtelet, while recognizing this additional *quartier*—"le Faubourg Saint-Germain des Prés"—merged the *quartiers* of the Cité and Notre-Dame into one, so that there were seventeen *quartiers* in all. In 1680 the Bureau de la Ville redivided the town into sixteen *quartiers*. It established five of these on the left bank, in place of the three of 1673 and the two of 1637. Foreseeing the future extension of the town, it made the *quartiers* stretch out from the center. But the Châtelet kept to the old arrangement, and its "old" *quartiers* were very unequal in size, some containing between ten and twelve streets, while others contained more than sixty; and they were also badly defined, protruding into each other. *Arrêts* of the king's Council dated 14 January 1701 and 14 February 1702, confirmed by the declaration of 12 December 1702, divided *"la Ville et les fauxbourgs de Paris"* into twenty *quartiers*. They were based on the division of 1673, with two of the *quartiers* each split into three. However, a Council *arrêt* of 3 February 1703 restored the division of 1680, so far as the policing of the town was concerned, and this division seems to have prevailed down to 1789, though not without some partial modifications. On a number of occasions, notably in 1729, there were twenty-one *quartiers*. It would appear that the existence of the sixteen *quartiers* recognized by the administration of the Bureau de la Ville was confirmed and that, right down to the Revolution, the two ways of dividing Paris, that recognized by the Bureau de la Ville and that recognized by the Châtelet, coexisted.

In each *quartier* of the Bureau de la Ville there was a *quartinier,* at first elected but later an officeholder, alongside the commissaries of police. By an edict of December 1701 the king created four new *conseillers du roi quartiniers*. The *arrêt* of 14 February 1702 sought to unify the administration by providing that in each *quartier* there should be a *quartinier* and a commissary of police, under the dual authority of the *lieutenant général de police* and the Provost of the Merchants. However, the Council's *arrêt* of 3 February 1703 allowed the sixteen established *quartiniers* to purchase the four new offices, and there were finally no more than sixteen *quartiniers*.

Each of the Bureau de la Ville's *quartiers* was divided into four *cinquantaines;* in each there was a *cinquantenier* (originally elected, but later an officeholder), so that there were sixty-four of these all together.

Every *cinquantaine* was divided into four *dizaines,* each with its *dizainier.* There were sixteen of these to each *quartier*—two hundred sixty-six in all.

The Bureau de la Ville had in its service a number of officials and *commis*—the ten *sergents* or *huissiers,* the architect (or "master of the town's works"), the captain of the guns, the printer, the *maître d'hôtel,* clerks for documents, and a variety of domanial officials: measurers of grain, gaugers of wine, porters, stevedores, carriers of salt ("*hanouards*"), carriers of grain, coal, wine, and timber, criers to announce the arrival of goods, the sale or letting of buildings, deaths, and so on.

Security was ensured by three companies, each consisting of one hundred "*archers,*" who since the time of Charles IX had been armed with harquebuses, as well as with swords, daggers, and halberds. From 1601 on they were called "*archers de la ville,*" and their commanding officer held the rank of colonel.

The "*bourgeois*" militia consisted of 133 companies, grouped in regiments ("*colonelles*"), one for each *quartier.*

Taxes to meet the cost of street-cleaning were collected by *receveurs,* who were "*bourgeois de Paris.*" By an edict of December 1701, however, the king created 20 offices of *receveurs particuliers* and two offices of *receveurs généraux* for the collecting of this money.

Functions of the municipal officials

The Bureau de la ville, presided over by the Provost of the Merchants, heard all commercial cases concerned with goods arriving by water at the ports of Paris; had cognizance of offenses committed by merchants and their agents in charge of these goods; had cognizance of matters concerning the *rentes* secured on the Town Hall; set the rates and prices for goods arriving at the ports; had jurisdiction over the Seine, to safeguard freedom of navigation; determined expenditure on the building and repairing of bridges, ramparts, quays, fountains, and other works in the town; and regulated public ceremonies.

It held court at the Town Hall on Mondays, Tuesdays, and Wednesdays, from 11:00 A.M. until 1:00 P.M. Appeals from its verdicts went straight to the *parlement.*

The aldermen acted as assistants and assessors to the Provost of the Merchants. Each of them had charge of a branch of the administration, for which he was answerable sometimes to the Provost of the Merchants and sometimes to the Town Council.

The Town Council's consent was needed for all important transactions, especially when it was a matter of putting the town under obligation or of selling, buying, or alienating its property.

For loans to the king and the constituting of *rentes* there even had to be a general assembly of the town. This meant bringing together the Town Council, the rector of the university, delegates from the sovereign courts, delegates from the clergy (the bishop, later the archbishop; the chapter of Notre-Dame; the abbots of Sainte-Geneviève, Saint-Victor, Saint-Magloire, and Sainte-Catherine du Val-des-Ecoliers; the priors of Saint-Eloi, Saint-Martin-des-Champs, the Carthusians, and the Celestines), and "mandated" *bourgeois,* six from each *quartier,* with their *quartiniers.* Remonstrances made to the king by this general assembly were treated as being equal in importance with those of the *parlement.*

The *quartiniers* conveyed the orders of the provost and aldermen; had charge of the buckets and iron hooks used for fire-fighting; were responsible for the chains fixed to the corners of the streets, which could be used to bar entry of them—a material sign of the town's liberties; compiled the list of notables; carried out enumerations of the inhabitants of the *quartier;* inspected hostelries; drew up statements of the weapons, grain, and foodstuffs in the *quartier;* established the tax rolls for raising money for loans to the king or to meet the town's needs and for the cleaning and lighting of the streets; ensured the supply of water; and concerned themselves with the measures to be taken to ensure the supply of bread and other foodstuffs.

The *cinquanteniers* and *dizainiers* carried out similar functions: the watch, patrols, chains; listing of the inhabitants and of men capable of bearing arms; listing of stocks of weapons and gunpowder; compiling of tax rolls for levies to meet the cost of public works and the payment of the regiments; exhortation of the communities to come to the aid of the king in his times of financial need.

The Bureau de la Ville dealt with only some of the mercantile cases. There was also, dating from the time of Charles IX, a consular court, held in the cloister behind the church of Saint-Merri. A judge and four consuls were elected each year, the four consuls being chosen by the merchants from among themselves, the judge chosen by them from among former consuls. This tribunal had cognizance of actions concerned with dealings between merchants by bills of exchange, promises, debentures, contracts, or partnership agreements and actions between businessmen, or between them and notaries, about promissory notes payable on demand or at a fixed time.

Privileges of the municipal magistrates

Being provost of the merchants or alderman conferred nobility. By letters patent of January 1577 this nobility was hereditary, provided that the ennobled person and his father had both filled one of these offices and had done nothing incompatible with nobility. The provost of the merchants had the right to the title of *chevalier* and thereby became a member of the higher level of the nobility, was considered a commensal of the royal household, and enjoyed the privilege of *committimus* to the *requêtes du Palais*.

By *arrêt* of November 1706 Louis XIV confirmed all the privileges that had been granted to the provost of the merchants, aldermen, *procureurs du roi, greffiers,* and *receveurs* of the town of Paris. Those of them who were wholesale merchants could continue in business without losing noble status.

In ceremonies the *corps de ville* walked with the *parlement*. The provost of the merchants was on the right of the governor of Paris and preceded the *prévôt* of Paris.

For royal entries and receptions of ambassadors the *corps de ville* rode on horseback. The provost of the merchants was dressed in a cassock of red satin, under a judge's gown, worn open, in the colors of the town, half red and half tan, and a cap of the same, with a broad gold band and a tassel.

The aldermen wore a velvet gown, half red and half tan, with long hanging sleeves and a cap with a gold edging.

The *procureur du roi* appeared in a gown of red velvet, the town councilors in mantles with long satin sleeves, and the tipstaffs in gowns made of cloth, half red and half tan.

Their horses were adorned with bridles of gold.

The municipal magistrates were not paid a salary. The provost of the merchants received, at Easter and on All Saints' Day, a sum of money to pay for two velvet gowns. Each year he received a hundred silver counters in a purse of green velvet, together with paper, ink, sealing wax, gilded copper writing desks, with drawers and secret compartments lines with green satin from Bourges, scales, weights, and eyeglasses made of crystal. The aldermen and all the officials of the Bureau de la Ville received each year a hundred silver counters in purses of green velvet and everything they needed for their work. The town councilors enjoyed the same privileges after 1553, and the *quartiniers* after 1579.

The counters were used for calculations on a table called a *"comptoir,"* which was divided by horizontal lines into six zones. The topmost of these was for thousands, the second for hundreds, the third for tens, the fourth for units, and the fifth and sixth for fractions. As each sum of money was called out, the counters needed to express this sum were placed in the appropriate zones. When all the sums had been recorded, the total amount represented by the counters was calculated, starting from the ones in the lowest zone. The *"comptoir"* was still being used in 1753 by many finance officials and by others in various jurisdictions.

The recruitment of municipal magistrates

In order to be an elector, one had to be a *bourgeois de Paris*. By Philip the Fair's ordinance of 1295, and in accordance with the procedure for admitting *bourgeois* recorded in the registers of the transactions of the Bureau de la Ville, it was necessary to state one's intention of becoming a *bourgeois de Paris;* to find a home in the capital and actually to reside there, with one's family and the bulk of one's property, for at least a year (in fact, for a period that might be as long as thirty years before one was accepted); to produce a certificate from the parish priest showing that one had regularly attended divine worship; to pay the municipal taxes *personally,* this being a favor granted by the Bureau de la Ville to homeowners or principal tenants who undertook to collect the taxes from their neighbors and pay the money over to the *bourgeois* acting as *receveurs;* to serve in the town guard, paying for one's own equipment; and, in consequence of all this, to obtain *"lettres de bourgeoisie."*

The *quartiniers* drew up the list of candidates for the quality of *bourgeois de Paris* in accordance with the criteria set out above and in accordance with the amount of rent paid. As a result, the term *bourgeois de Paris* designated, from one *quartier* to another, persons of differing fortunes and incomes. A lower rent had to be paid in the case of houses used for residence or for the exercise of one of the liberal professions, a higher one in the case of houses used for business purposes. In documents recorded by notaries, we find that, generally speaking, the quality of *bourgeois de Paris* was adopted by minor court officials, domanial officials, merchants, and one out of ten craftsmen. The majority of the master craftsmen, journeymen, porters, and very small-scale homeowners were excluded from the quality. Persons who had migrated to Paris from the provinces, sons of well-to-do peasants or merchants in their home districts, tried to acquire it.

In the registers of the proceedings of the Bureau de la Ville the expression *bourgeois de Paris* sometimes designates *rentiers* "living like nobles" on their *rentes,* without practicing any craft or trade, or *financiers,* handling the king's money.

In memoirs, correspondence, and reports, "*bourgeois de Paris*" is used for persons who were free, not belonging to any profession or corporation, often having retired from commerce or a craft.

All the *bourgeois de Paris* constituted together the "*honnestes gens*" and "*bons bourgeois*" of the town.

The provost of the merchants was elected for two years and could be reelected. The aldermen were elected for two years and could be reelected twice; half of them were replaced each year.

Before an election, the outgoing provost of the merchants, the aldermen, and the *greffier,* accompanied by town councilors and *quartiniers,* went in ceremonial costume to the church of the Hôpital du Saint-Esprit to hear a Mass of the Holy Spirit, so as to secure for the electors the inspiration of the Holy Trinity.

The electoral assembly then gathered in the main room of the Town Hall. It consisted of the provost of the merchants, the aldermen, the town councilors, the *quartiniers,* and thirty-two "mandated" *bourgeois.* These last had been chosen a few days before the election. The *quartiniers* assembled as an electoral section the *cinquanteniers,* the *dizainiers,* and the six *bourgeois* elected for the occasion. The section chose four candidates by secret ballot. On the day for the election of the provost of the merchants and the aldermen, each *quartinier* presented a report of the ballot held in his electoral section. The names of two of the four men chosen were drawn at random for each *quartier,* and these, as the "mandated" *bourgeois,* became the electors of the provost and aldermen.

The electoral assembly balloted. Then a former alderman, with the *procureur du roi,* the *greffier,* and the four ex-scrutineers took the results of the ballot to the king, who received the oaths of the newly elected dignitaries.

In principle, the *dizainiers* and *cinquanteniers* were supposed to be elected by the *bourgeois de Paris* for a period of two years; the *quartiniers* were to be elected by the *cinquanteniers, dizainiers*, and the notables of each *quartier* chosen from a list drawn up by the *quartiniers;* while the town councilors were picked by the provost of the merchants and aldermen from a list of notables presented by the *quartiniers*.

In reality, however, the elections were often only make-believe or even ceased to be carried out at all.

The king was always able to recommend a candidate for the position of provost of the merchants or aldermen by *lettre de cachet,* and he made use of this power. The election of the provost of the merchants and the aldermen took place subject to the king's pleasure, and the report of the ballot was brought to him so that he might "dispose of it according to his will and pleasure." He was prayed to approve the election, "confirming the said privileges of the town." The king declared that the election was agreeable to him, received the oaths of the elected men, and sent them away "to enter upon the exercise of their offices." The king stated that he wished to keep the town in the enjoyment of its privileges. The electoral assembly took care to elect only candidates who could not prove unacceptable to the king.

The procedure of election was maintained as far as the provost of the merchants and the aldermen were concerned. Elections to the other municipal posts ceased to be held, elected persons being replaced by holders of venal and hereditary offices. From the 16th century onward, the posts of town councilor and *quartinier* were conferred by resignation and reversion, from father to son, in the Bureau de la Ville, in the presence of the provost of the merchants, the aldermen, and the town councilors, who voted on the acceptance of the candidates. After 1538 the town councilors formed a community whose interests were entrusted to a *procureur-syndic*. These functions had become, *de facto,* hereditary within a restricted circle.

In the 17th century, venality of office triumphed. In October 1633 an ordinance of Louis XIII, sanctioning a common practice, authorized the *quartiniers* to surrender their posts, by declaration before a notary, in return for payment. Town councilors received the same permission, and their posts were made into offices. This policy was continued by Louis XIV. An *arrêt* of the *parlement* having stated that the posts held by *quartiniers* were not offices, the king, by an edict of July 1681, declared that the posts of the *quartiniers* and, in general, all municipal

posts apart from those of the provost of the merchants and the aldermen, were indeed *offices formés*.

In 1701 the *bourgeois* who acted as *receveurs* for the collection of
taxes were replaced by twenty officeholders who were *"receveurs particuliers"* and two who were *"receveurs généraux."*

The members of the Bureau de la Ville were not all merchants, for
they included a large number of officeholders and also of *rentiers* and
persons interested in the *partis* and *traités* for the royal finances. Between 1598 and 1715 there were twenty-five provosts of the merchants,
who were all high officials—three of them were state councilors, twelve
were *présidents* and counselors of the *parlement*, two were *présidents*
of the *chambre des comptes*, one was a *procureur général* in the *cour
des aides*, another was a master of requests, and three were *lieutenants
civils* at the Châtelet. In the same period, of the 236 aldermen, half
should have been merchants, by virtue of the Council's *arrêt* of 30 June
1615. Actually, 90 described themselves as officeholders, 12 of these
being auditors in the *chambre des comptes*, while 25 were counselors
at the Châtelet, 17 were notaries at the Châtelet, and 7 were *secrétaires
du roi*. In addition, there were 12 advocates, 2 physicians, the director
of the Commerce des Indes (in 1670), the printer-in-ordinary to the
king, Sébastien Cramoisy, the director of the Royal Press at the Louvre
or his proxy, and only 4 merchants out of 111 aldermen. The remaining 125 described themselves as "town councilor" or *"quartinier,"*
and we have no way of knowing whether they were *rentiers, financiers,*
or merchants.

Of twenty-five town councilors elected in August 1614, thirteen were
officials of the sovereign courts: nine were *présidents* and counselors of
the *parlement*, two were masters of requests, and two were *maîtres des
comptes*. Then we come upon a *secrétaire du roi* and two advocates.
The majority of the posts in the Town Council, or "Grand Bureau,"
were thus held by royal magistrates.

Although the Bureau de la Ville was at the king's service, matters
proceeded as though the king distrusted it. From the beginning of Louis
XIV's personal rule we observe a steady decline of the Bureau de la
Ville and a steady increase in the powers and activity of the *prévôté*,
especially of its chief representative, the *lieutenant général de police*.

For a long time the *prévôté* made use of the *quartiniers, cinquanteniers,* and *dizainiers*, who were agents of the Bureau de la Ville,
alongside its own agents, the *commissaires* of the Châtelet. After 1663
the *prévôté* placed under the control of each *commissaire de police* five

"*directeurs de quartier*," each of whom administered a part of the *quartier*, and the *prévôté* seems to have no longer employed, except rarely, the *quartiniers, cinquanteniers,* and *dizainiers.*

After 1702 the Parisians found themselves being dealt with to an increasing extent by the *commissaires* and to a decreasing extent by the *quartiniers.* The latter were loaded with more and more honors. They received the title of "*conseiller du roi.*" In September 1745 they attended for the first time as a body the reception of the king at the Town Hall. They claimed equal status with the town councilors. But they no longer concerned themselves with the cleaning of the streets, with the militia, with the collecting of municipal taxes, or with the listing of houses and inhabitants. They still passed on to the *cinquanteniers* and *dizainiers* the orders of the Provost of the Merchants, but these orders became less and less frequent. The *quartiniers* practically ceased to play a part in the active life of the town, their titles being now purely honorific.

The *cinquanteniers* and *dizainiers* had hardly any functions left to perform; and since they were the recipients of many fewer honors, their offices no longer attracted purchasers. The *cinquanteniers* were supposed to number 64 and the *dizainiers* 266. However, in 1745 there were, respectively, 15 and 67 of them; in 1762, there were 18 and 72; and in 1783, there were 23 and 76. In 1745 the Cité had only one *dizainier* and not a single *cinquantenier.* In 1783 the Town Hall *quartier* had no *cinquantenier.* The town was without officials of its own.

Perhaps the Bureau de la Ville made use of the *commissaires* of the *quartiers.*

Under Louis XVI the provost of the merchants was considered an appointee of the king, and a king's commissioner. The aldermen were recruited from among the most senior of the town councilors and *quartiniers.* Between one's reception as town councilor and one's election as an alderman there had to be an interval of twenty years. Two-thirds of the aldermen, town councilors, and *quartiniers* were lawyers, with advocates before the *parlement* now predominating, and the other third were wholesale merchants. Among the twenty-six town councilors there were always ten members of the sovereign courts. The aldermen were now paid a salary: the first-ranking alderman received, in 1781, 20,900 livres, and the fourth received 15,000 livres.

The *Procureur du roi et de la ville* was an officeholder, whose office was, in 1781, worth 420,000 livres. He was a former secretary in an intendant's office, a reliable "king's man." He was appointed by the provost of the merchants. He corresponded directly with the secretary of state responsible for the royal household. He was an instrument in the hands of the king.

The aldermen did the preliminary work on the town's business, and final decisions were made at the weekly meeting of the Bureau de la Ville. The first-ranking alderman reported on financial matters—debts, recoveries, payment of creditors, sale of the domain. The second reported on public works in progress, the municipal guard, and the ports. The third reported on the fortifications, the public places, and the avenues of trees. The fourth reported on the fountains and the sewers.

The king created organs which were either added to the Bureau de la Ville or had the effect of modifying its composition. The conseil particulier set up in July 1767 included the provost of the merchants, the aldermen, and six members designated by the king from among twelve persons elected by their peers—four by the sovereign courts, four by the *quartiniers,* four by the *"bourgeois."* They remained in office for nine years, in the case of the first Conseil particulier that met, and for six years thereafter. This council had responsibility for new borrowing, selling of town property, *traités,* and new building projects. Over and above this, the king imposed what he had himself decided, "by the king's express command."

After the 1740s, the administrative work of the Bureau de la Ville was reduced to very little, the real work of administration being more than ever carried on by the royal officials of the Châtelet and of the *prévôté et vicomté de Paris.* It is understandable that the king should have desired to bring all the towns of the kingdom into line with his "good town" of Paris.

A "commune" town: Beauvais

As an example of a "commune" town, I shall take Beauvais, which was in the governorate of the Ile-de-France, on the borders of the *généralités* of Paris and Picardy, was the headquarters of a *bailliage* and a presidial court and of a royal *élection,* and was also an important commercial center, with a substantial cloth industry.

Beauvais became a "commune" town because of the presence of a *grand seigneur* against whom the inhabitants leagued themselves in defense of their interests. This *grand seigneur* was the bishop—comte de Beauvais and peer of France. He had long since lost the principal rights of sovereignty (making war, issuing money), but he retained powers of justice, both civil and criminal, and of *police*, which he exercised through his *bailli du comté*. Appeals from the *bailli*'s court went directly to the Paris *parlement*, to which it was immediately subordinate. The bishop-count's rights were based on letters patent of 22 April 1422. He was maintained in his powers of justice by letters patent of 1596 and in his power to make regulations for the *police* of Beauvais by an *arrêt* of 1619.

The town was divided also among other *seigneuries* and *jurisdictions*. The cathedral chapter of Beauvais had *seigneurie directe*, with power of high justice, over part of the town and its suburbs. Other authorities were the Abbey of Saint-Symphorien, the *commanderie* of Saint-Pantaléon, the hereditary castellany of Beauvais, the collegial churches of Saint-Michel and Notre-Dame-du-Châtel, and the abbeys of Saint-Lucien and Saint-Quentin. The most considerable of them— the chapter and the abbey of Saint-Symphorien—were independent of the *comté-pairie*. They were in direct feudal dependence of the king and within the jurisdiction of the *bailliage* of Beauvais. Included in the king's *seigneurie directe*, with power of high justice, were the strongpoints, ramparts, walls, ditches, counterscarp, and fortifications.

The jurisdiction of the *bailliage* of Montdidier penetrated into Beauvais. Appeal from decisions by the judges of the chapter and the fiefs was made to the presidial court at Senlis, and while decisions of the *bailliage* of Montdidier were appealed to the presidial court at Laon.

The royal officials were in a weak position in relation to the bishop, count, and peer. An edict of 1581 established a royal bailliage and presidial court at Beauvais, but letters patent of 1596 expressly forbade the presidial court to concern itself with persons subject to the court of the *pairie*, either by *prévention*, or in first instance, or by hearing appeals. The judges of the presidial court had cognizance only of *cas royaux* and matters concerned with benefices.

Between 1597 and 1616 the officers of the presidial court and the bishop appeared year after year before the *parlement* or the Conseil d'Etat to argue about their rights in relation to each other, and on every occasion the bishop emerged triumphant, thanks to the letters patent of 1596. His power even increased during the 18th century, in the episcopate of Potier de Gesvres (1729–72).

Beauvais had a captain acting for the king, the "*capitaine de la ville*," with a lieutenant. However, this captain was a *grand seigneur*, permanently at court; he transmitted the king's orders to the town all right, but he did nothing to protect it from the bishop, count, and peer.

This relationship of forces, so unfavorable to the king's officials, was of very long standing, and it accounts for the existence of the commune.

The commune of Beauvais was said to date from the time of Louis VI, "the Fat," and to have been confirmed by a charter of 1144, accepted by Louis VII, "the Young." It was regulated by the "Great Composition" of 1276. A charter of King John the Good, in 1352, placed this commune under the king's special protection, assigning to it as particular guardian the *bailli* of Senlis or his lieutenant. Letters patent of Louis XI confirmed the commune again after the siege of 1472 and granted it privileges: exemption from *taille*, right of its *"bourgeois"* to acquire noble fiefs without paying frank-fee (confirmed by *arrêts* of the king's Council in 1634, 1641, and 1655), and exemption from *ban* and *arrière-ban*. These were maintained subsequently in return for the payment of certain taxes.

The town of Beauvais joined the Holy League. When it accepted Henry IV as king, his "edict and declaration concerning the reduction of the town of Beauvais to obedience," issued at Amiens on 22 August 1594, restored its privileges. The privileges of the "town and commune" of Beauvais were confirmed by letters patent of Louis XIII in December 1610. Louis XIV confirmed them again in October 1646, his edict and letters patent being registered by the *parlement* and the *cour des aides*.

In the 17th century the commune of Beauvais was in decline. The essential feature of a commune, namely, the contract of association, had gone. It was enough to have lived in the town for a year and a day, and to have been accepted, to become a *"bourgeois de Beauvais."* The *"issues"* that had to be paid when one left the commune, on pain of remaining subject to its taxes, had also ceased to apply. Likewise, the old distinctions had disappeared; formerly, persons who held a fief of the bishopric or who were *censitaires* or guests of the chapter, were not allowed to be members of the commune, but in the 17th century any of these could become *"bourgeois de Beauvais."*

Nevertheless, the commune retained privileges that ensured it a certain degree of autonomy while bringing it close to the position of the towns I have called *villes de bourgeoisie* or *villes franches*. It had a mayor and aldermen, elected by an assembly of master craftsmen voting by corporations. The *règlement* of 1610 allowed participation in this election to the officeholders, advocates, attorneys, and other lawyers, giving them a vote as though they constituted a corporation. In 1636 the municipality revised the *carte,* or roll of crafts and estates which joined in the choosing of the mayor and aldermen; it listed thirty-one voting groups, as follows:

1. The *présidents, lieutenants,* counselors, *avocat du roi* and *procureur du roi* in the *baillage* and presidial court of Beauvais, the *lieutenant de robe courte,* and the *prévôt* of Angy and the *procureur du roi* in that jurisdiction
2. The *présidents, lieutenants, élus,* and *contrôleurs* in the *élection* of Beauvais, the *président, grènetier,* and *contrôleur* of the salt storehouse, the *avocats du roi* and *procureurs du roi* in the *élection* and the salt storehouse, and the receiver of *aides* and *tailles*
3. The judges and other graduate officials of the patrimonial and ordinary courts in the town and suburbs
4. The advocates and physicians
5. The commissaries, deputies, attorneys, *greffiers,* and notaries of the courts, both ecclesiastical and secular
6. The *huissiers, sergents,* and *archers*
7. The drapers, hosiers, and sellers of dyed cloth
8. The mercers, grocers, lacemakers, button-makers, and makers of sayette (a fine, twilled, fabric)
9. The apothecaries, surgeons, and *inciseurs*
10. The cloth-makers and sellers of wool
11. The nappers and carders
12. The shearers
13. The weavers
14. The serge-makers
15. The wool-combers
16. The tavern-keepers, vinegar-makers, and brewers
17. The bakers
18. The pastry cooks, pork butchers, bacon-sellers, fat-sellers, butchers, and fishmongers
19. The goldsmiths, pewter-makers, lead-workers, and smelters
20. The masons, carpenters, and roofers
21. The ironmongers, cutlers, armorers, furbishers, spur-makers, tinkers, pin-makers, and needle-makers
22. The ironworkers, blacksmiths, edged-tool-makers, and nail-makers
23. The dyers, hatters, knitwear-makers, painters, and glaziers
24. The tanners, tawers, glovemakers, and furriers
25. The shoemakers and curriers
26. The repairers of old shoes
27. The saddlers, packsaddle-makers, and ropemakers
28. The joiners, coopers, and cartwrights

29.	The embroiderers, carpet-makers, jewelers, old-clothes-sellers, and tailors
30.	The turners and basketmakers
31.	The *laboureurs,* vinegrowers, and market gardeners

The commune of Beauvais held assemblies that were irregular but frequent, to decide important questions: in 1617 the establishment of the Minims, in 1627 that of the Ursulines, in 1658 the regulating of the municipal organization, in 1707 the conversion of the *taillon* into *droits d'entrée,* in 1753 the rebuilding of the Town Hall, in 1762 the "free gift" and the regulation of measures. These are merely examples. The composition of these assemblies was variable, being made up sometimes of the honorary officers of the municipality and the principal *bourgeois;* sometimes of deputies from the various estates and corporations and the ecclesiastical communities, both regular and secular; and sometimes, as in 1658, of deputies from the privileged companies and from the *quartiers.* Always, however, the members were persons belonging to a corporation or community. Voting was carried out sometimes by corporations, sometimes by individuals.

Alongside the *corps de ville* and the town assemblies there was an assembly "of the Three Corporations," which looked after the upkeep and management of the institutions of charity and education—the Hôtel-Dieu, the Bureau des Pauvres, and the college; supervision and allocation of the moneys raised for relief of the poor; hygiene; and public buildings. The first of these "three corporations" was the bishop, the second was the chapter, and the third was the municipal officers. The assembly always endorsed the bishop's opinion. In 1662 it took measures against shortages and for the relief of the poor. In 1664 it installed a royal carpet factory. In 1666 it endeavored to save the town from the plague. In 1706 it busied itself with the public fountains. In 1732 it adopted fire-fighting pumps. In 1776 it established a cemetery outside the town.

The commune had judicial powers. It had cognizance, to the exclusion of all other judges, of intrigues and underhand practices in connection with municipal elections, outrages and insults against the *corps de ville,* disputes between the privileged companies of the *bourgeois* militia, military offenses committed by *bourgeois* mounting guard on the ramparts and fortifications, and brawls and insults between private persons.

The bishop possessed the power of *police.* But the *corps de ville* had the right to issue ordinances on its own regarding public celebrations. It supervised the receipts and expenditure of the commune. It allocated the burden of taxes and arranged for the billeting of soldiers. It maintained the roads, causeways, and bridges. It shared in the administration of the hospitals and colleges.

The commune owned property—the Town Hall, and also its patrimonial revenue. This consisted of rents for houses and land, road charges (paid by everyone except the canons, the Hôtel-Dieu, the Bureau des Pauvres, and the nuns of Saint-François); a due levied on all commodities brought in by vehicle or beast of burden (from which the king's forces and the *messagers* were exempt); a due charged on the sale of salt; the *octrois* dating from before 1636 for the upkeep of the·fortifications; the *octrois* introduced after 1636 for payment of the town's debts and consisting of dues to be paid on goods brought in by itinerant merchants and on textile fabrics.

The commune paid the king an annual subvention in place of the *taille.* It paid the *taillon,* sometimes thrice a year, and also a tax in lieu of billeting soldiers, the "free gifts" that the king requested from time to time, the *aides* and *gabelles,* loans to the king, and taxes for the relief of prisoners of war.

The commune of Beauvais steadily declined all through the 17th and 18th centuries. The primary factor in this decline was the venality of the municipal offices. In 1635 the king turned the post of attorney for the commune into an *office formé et héréditaire* (under the title of *"procureur de roi et de la ville"*) and did the same with that of the *greffier de la mairie.* In 1692 all municipal functions became offices— venal, perpetual, and hereditary. An office of mayor and six offices of assessors were created in Beauvais. In 1703 six new offices of councilors and aldermen made their appearance and, in 1708, an additional office of mayor. In June 1717 venality was abolished and elections were reintroduced. Then, in 1722, venality was resumed. Beauvais had fifty-two venal offices allotted to it: two mayors, two assistant mayors, eight aldermen, twelve assessors, two *secrétaires-greffiers,* two *contrôleurs de greffe,* one *lieutenant du roi,* one major, one *procureur du roi,* one *avocat du roi,* and as many as four drummers. In 1724 venality was again abolished. But then, by edict of November 1733, all the municipal offices were revived. However, they did not sell well, and many were still awaiting a buyer in 1747. Accordingly, in August 1747, elections were reintroduced. When the edicts of 1764 and 1765 (Laverdy's reform) were issued, the town of Beauvais asked for and obtained exemption. In November 1771, when the king restored the venality of offices, Beauvais purchased the right to elect its municipal officers and held this until 1789.

The second factor in the decline of the commune was constituted by the attempts of the bishop-count and the royal officials to get possession of the offices.

In 1699 the bishop-count acquired the office of *lieutenant général de police,* which the town had been unable to purchase. (A royal edict had established such posts in all the towns that were centers of royal *bailliages.*) The bishop of Beauvais, Cardinal De Forbin-Janson, whose bid for the office was highest, became *lieutenant général de police* in Beauvais and was authorized to carry out the duties of *bailli du comté.* He also acquired the functions of *procureur du roi* in the sphere of *police* and the posts of *huissiers* and *greffiers* relevant thereto. The king granted to the *bailli du comté* or his *lieutenant* the right to sit and vote in the town assemblies, ranking next to the mayor. Despite its protests, the town had to submit to this.

The officials of the *bailliage,* the presidial court, and the *élections* were envious of the mayor and aldermen. They would have liked to be exempt, as those persons were, from duties of watch and ward, but the king obliged them to fulfill these duties, except when they themselves became mayor or aldermen. After the *arrêt* of 9 July 1698 it was a rule that three of the six aldermen must always be officials of the judiciary. (The rest were merchants or other *"bourgeois".*) When the posts of mayor and assessors were made venal offices in 1692, the town was too poor to buy them. In June 1693 an edict permitted *seigneurs* to buy the offices and exercise them, or have them exercised by an agent, and all Beauvais was in fear that the bishop-count would acquire them. The officials of the presidial court subscribed two-thirds of the price and those of the *élection* one-third in order jointly to purchase the office of mayor, agreeing to occupy this office alternately—the *bailliage* and the presidial court for two years, the *élection* for one year. Nevertheless, from September 1693 to 1704, the *président* of the presidial court, Vigneron d'Hacqueville, was the sole occupant. In 1704 the office was joined with the corporation of the presidial court and the *élection,* and thereafter the alternation provided for was actually observed.

The commune was able to purchase the offices created in 1722 and nominate to the king the persons to be appointed to them. Thus, behind the façade of venality, elections were reintroduced. The merchants launched a vain attack in 1729 on the rule whereby half the aldermen had to be drawn from among the *gens de robe*. The officials of the presidial court, the *élection,* and the salt storehouse and the community of the attorneys obtained a Council *arrêt* dated 2 August 1732 which confirmed the rule. The bishop appealed unsuccessfully for the officials of his *comté-pairie* to be allowed to become aldermen.

When offices were created in November 1733, only three posts of aldermen were bought by private individuals. For the rest, left without buyers, the system of election was reintroduced. In 1747 those of the offices of 1733 not yet taken up were joined to the *corps de ville*. For this, Beauvais had to pay over some *octrois* to the king. In 1772 the town bought the offices that had been created in 1771 and elected persons to fill them.

Broadly speaking, then, election survived. The liberty of the commune's members was limited, indeed, by the obligation to include three officers of the judiciary among the aldermen. It was also limited by the interventions of the king or his intendant. In 1676 the king reduced the number of aldermen by half and filled the post of mayor by commission. In 1691, as the result of an intrigue, the intendant by his own authority installed three new aldermen in place of the three outgoing ones. The Council's *arrêt* of 9 July 1698 maintained in their posts for one year, dating from 2 August 1698, two aldermen due to retire—one official of the judiciary and one merchant; it ordered that one of the two officials of the judiciary to be elected must be M. Walon, an assessor. In 1720 two attorneys were elected as aldermen; the *corps de ville* had their election quashed by the King's Council, for underhand practices, and the Council decided that their predecessors should continue in post. In 1742 a *lettre de cachet* suspended elections and instructed the mayor and aldermen to remain in post until further orders. In general, though, these were sporadic interventions by the tutelary power to safeguard the order and regularity of elections.

More serious were the restrictions on the powers of the commune caused by the presence and activity of the king's officials and commissioners. The captain of Beauvais became the town's governor at the beginning of the 18th century. Marshal de Boufflers became hereditary governor and captain of Beauvais. In 1692, here as everywhere in the kingdom, the captain's lieutenant was transformed into a *lieutenant du roi,* with a hereditary and venal office and the power to convoke and assemble the mayor, aldermen, and inhabitants in order to acquaint them with the orders necessary for the king's service. The first person to be appointed to this office at Beauvais was Jacques Imbert, a Parisian, a protégé of Bontemps. Louis XIV's *valet de chambre*. Above all, the intendant of the province kept Beauvais on a close rein in all matters which did not encroach on the rights of the bishop, count, and peer.

What emerges from this study is that, regardless of the category to which a town belonged, the royal government showed an increasing tendency to treat them all like minors and keep them under ever stricter tutelage. It would have liked to administer them all directly, through its officials and commissioners.

The municipal reform of 1764–65

The municipal reform of 1764–65 was initiated by Laverdy, the *contrôleur général*. Its official purpose was to reestablish order in the finances and administration of the towns; but it was also to establish uniformity in this administration throughout the kingdom, in a lasting manner, by bringing together all the changes previously introduced through *règlements* and *arrêts* in a single law. Actually, there were two main laws: the "Edict of the king containing a *règlement* for the administration of the towns and chief *bourgs* of the kingdom," in August 1764, and the "Edict providing a *règlement* for the execution of the edict of August 1764 in the towns and *bourgs* of the kingdom," issued at Marly in May 1765. The reform did not affect the village communities (even though it mentioned "the towns and other corporations and communities of our kingdom") but only the towns and *bourgs,* which were divided into three categories: (1) those with over 4,500 inhabitants, (2) those with between 2,000 and 4,500 inhabitants, and (3) those with under 2,000 inhabitants.

The reform took municipal power away from the oligarchy of municipal officers, whether they were owners of their offices or were always drawn from the same small set of families, and put real power into the hands of assemblies of notables. All the venal offices of mayors, consuls, aldermen, *jurats,* receivers of public revenues and *octrois,* comptrollers of these receivers, and so on were abolished. The persons concerned were to be reimbursed, and in the meantime they would draw interest at 5 percent on the money they had paid for their offices.

New municipal officers would be elected, two months after publication of the edict in the *bailliages* and *sénéchaussées,* and would form the *corps de ville.* This would be made up, in towns with over 4,500 inhabitants, of a mayor, four aldermen, six town councilors, a *syndic-*

receveur, and a *secrétaire-greffier,* the last two being without the right
to vote. Towns of between 2,000 and 4,500 inhabitants were to have a
mayor, two aldermen, and four councilors, plus the syndic and the
secretary; and in towns and *bourgs* with under 2,000 inhabitants there
would be two aldermen and three councilors, plus the *syndic-receveur*
and the *secrétaire-greffier.*

The mayors were to be drawn from among former mayors or from
among the aldermen and former aldermen. The aldermen were to be
drawn from among the town councilors and must include, in towns of
more than 4,500 inhabitants, at least one graduate. The town councilors
were to be drawn from among past or present notables.

The mayor would be elected for three years and could be reelected
after being out of office for three years. The aldermen would be elected
for two years. There ought always to be two "old" ones and two
"new" ones in office, so two were to be elected each year. They could
be reelected after being out for two years. Councilors would be elected
for four years and could be reelected after an interval of the same
length.

Each town and *bourg* would choose three candidates for the post of
mayor. The names would be sent to the secretary of state concerned,
and the king would select one of them to be mayor. The mayor would
also be chosen by those *seigneurs* who customarily had appointed
municipal officers—by the estates of Burgundy in the counties of Mâcon, Bar-sur-Seine, and Auxerre and by the duc d'Orléans in his appanage.

Persons related to each other up to the second degree of kinship
could not be mayor, aldermen, and town councilors at the same time.

Thus, it became necessary to make one's way up through a succession of grades: notable, councilor, alderman, mayor. The first condition to be fulfilled was to become a "notable."

The assemblies of notables chose, by ballot, candidates for the post
of mayor and the other municipal offices. The notables had themselves
been elected by a two-stage procedure. First, the corporations elected
deputies, who then had to elect the notables. In towns with over 4,500
inhabitants, one deputy each was elected by the principal chapter of
the place, by each secular chapter, by the "ecclesiastical order"
(bishop, *curés,* religious communities), by the "nobles and military
officers," by the *bailliage,* by each of the other jurisdictions (*élection,*
salt storehouse, department of waters and forests, etc.), and by "each
of the other corporations and communities" (the organized crafts). The

last-mentioned might be very numerous and command the majority or might constitute the majority in the electoral body in which the electors voted all together in each category. For this reason, the declaration of Versailles dated 15 June 1766, required that master craftsmen of a particular craft must number at least eighteen in the towns of more than 4,500 inhabitants in order to elect a deputy, and at least twelve in the smaller towns. Otherwise, they must meet together with other crafts so as to elect a deputy jointly. The edict provided that traders, wholesale merchants, and manufacturers were to meet together to elect one deputy.

The deputies elected notables all together, in each category, from among persons aged thirty or over, domiciled for at least ten years in the town or *bourg,* who had held office in their community. In the towns of more than 4,500 inhabitants the notables consisted of the mayor, aldermen, town councilors, and fourteen other notables—one from the principal chapter, one from the ecclesiastical order, one from the nobles and military officers, one from the *bailliage* or *sénéchaussée,* one from the *bureau des finances,* one from the officials of the other jurisdictions, one from the community of notaries and attorneys, two from commensals of the royal household, advocates, physicians, and *bourgeois* "living like nobles," three from the wholesale merchants, merchants who kept open shop, surgeons, and others engaged in the liberal arts, and two from the craftsmen. In towns of between 2,000 and 4,500 inhabitants the notables comprised the mayor, two aldermen, four town councilors, and ten other notables—one from the ecclesiastical order, one from the nobles and military officers, one from the various jurisdictions, one from the notaries and attorneys, two from the commensals of the royal household, advocates, and bourgeois "living like nobles," two from the wholesale merchants, merchants keeping open shop, surgeons, etc., and two from the *laboureurs,* vinegrowers, and craftsmen. In the towns and *bourgs* of fewer than 2,000 inhabitants, the notables would consist of the two aldermen, the three town councilors, and six other notables drawn from the various corporations. For this purpose, the town or *bourg* was divided into three *quartiers*. Each *quartier* sent four deputies, and those twelve elected the six "other notables."

Consequently, in this reform the "three orders" disappeared, as such. "Order" was given less consideration than function, profession, or craft. The nobility were reduced in standing through being merged with the military, who might include commoners, and through having only one deputy and one notable. The clergy were reduced in standing through being represented by two notables, at most, out of fourteen in the "big" towns. In contrast, in these towns the men of law, including notaries and attorneys, were represented by four notables, the liberal professions by two, and the occupations producing material goods by five. Craft, profession, function, and *social* function came before anything else. "Order" disappeared. The word "order" was used only in relation to a section of the ecclesiastics. No distinction of rank was provided for among the notables in their assemblies: each one sat wherever he chanced to be. This reform adumbrated the form of representation of a "society of talents," irresistibly calling to mind the ideas of Domat. It makes one think of the transition from the society of orders to a society of classes and from the state of orders to the *"Etat-gendarme."*

And it was these notables who were to play the essential role. Not only would they elect the officers of the municipality, who would be in charge of the administration of the towns; they were also to supervise these officers and participate in all their major decisions. The officers of a municipality were to meet every fifteen days, without the town councilors, to deal with ordinary business, and once a month with the town councilors to deal with more important matters. Twice a year the municipal officers were to report on their work to the notables and lay before them the receivers' accounts. The notables were to give their views on new buildings and extensions to old ones, on the acquisition and alienation of property, on borrowing, on new *octrois*. They were to decide on the leasing-out of patrimonial property and revenue and to be present in assembly at the *adjudication des octrois* by the officials of the *bureaux des finances* and the *élections*. They were to choose the place where the public funds would be kept, and one of them was to hold one of the three keys to this, the other two being held by a municipal officer and a receiver. They were to decide on what should be done with surplus income, on the sending of deputations to higher authority, and on arrangements for the depositing of deeds and documents; and they were to examine, verify, and approve in March of each year the accounts of receipts and expenditure submitted by the receiver of the previous year and to appoint the collectors entrusted with raising the local tax authorized by the king.

Consequently, the assembly of notables was to have become the essential organ of the municipal administration, with the *corps de ville* as its executive agent. The assembly of notables would have been the culmination of a pyramid of corporations and of functions within these corporations. But what the corporations in question now actually brought together were functions, professions, and crafts and no longer qualities and dignities which were partly hereditary—no longer orders. The reform effected, or consecrated, a veritable revolution toward a different type of society, while reconciling the reward and utilization of individual talents with the necessity of social corporations.

Nevertheless, the state kept a close control over the towns. Contemporaries said that the reform was an episode in the struggle by the royal officials against the royal commissioners, by the *parlements* against the intendants. Laverdy, it was alleged, was the *parlements'* man, and his reform would have greatly reduced the power of the intendants, to the advantage of the *parlements*. This is partly true. The new edicts did indeed delimit the respective roles of the *parlements* and the intendants, whereas previously the intendants obtained *arrêts* from the Council dealing with all matters of administration, just as they liked and as the Council liked. The new edicts certainly strengthened the powers of the officers of the judiciary. But the king and the intendants of the provinces retained, all the same, a preponderant role.

The royal and seignorial justice officials were to be present at the assembly of notables at which, twice a year, the municipality was to report to the notables. The first-ranking official of the royal courts, all the *procureurs du roi,* and the seignorial judges were always to be invited to these assemblies. The discussions concerning acquisition and alienation of property and borrowings were to be confirmed in the royal courts on the basis of conclusions reached by the *procureurs généraux du roi* and the *arrêts* of confirmation, prescribing the way public money was to be spent, were to be included in the king's letters patent. At the request of the syndic or of the municipal officers, the judge of the locality was to compel the receiver, by ordinance, to present his accounts. Accounts for revenue from *octrois* were to be presented every three years to the *bureaux des finances* and the *chambres des comptes*. The general accounts of the receivers, approved in the assemblies of notables, were to be formally presented to the *bailliages* and *sénéchaussées* and communicated to the *procureur du roi* to be "closed, decided, and judged." The *procureur du roi* then had to send the accounts to the *procureur général* so that the latter might, if he found them not as they should be, refer the matter to the Grand' Chambre of the *parlement*. Disputes regarding patrimonial and communal property were to be taken before the ordinary judges of the localities, with appeal to the Grand' Chambre. Disputes regarding *droits d'octrois* were to be decided by the judges who had cognizance of them and, on appeal, by the *cours des aides*.

Thus, the judges were to exercise a serious degree of supervision over the work of the assemblies of notables and over all public finance. Everything was to culminate in the *cours des aides, chambres des comptes*, and *parlements*. The edicts guaranteed the authority of the judiciary over the administration.

But the intendants of the provinces and the *commissaires départis* retained extensive powers. The accounts of the community's finances, seen twice a year by the assembly of notables, were to be handed over to *"l'intendant et commissaire départi,"* who had to send it, with his observations and recommendations, to the *contrôleur général des finances*. The *commissaire départi* gave his opinion on schemes for new buildings or extensions and sent the plans and estimates to the *contrôleur général*. In accordance with this opinion, the king either authorized them or did not, by *arrêt* and letters patent. The *commissaire départi* gave his opinion on the new acquisitions discussed in the assembly of notables, on any alienations of property or borrowings, and on the employment of the municipal revenue, and on the basis of this opinion the king dispatched the necessary letters patent. The *commissaire départi* gave permission for the assembly of notables to be convoked when a new *octroi* had to be discussed. It was the opinion he expressed regarding the assembly's decisions that guided the king in giving or refusing his approval to the use in a certain way of any surplus of receipts. The king would not permit a deputation to be sent to higher authority unless this was recommended by the *commissaire départi*, and that condition applied also to the question of depositing the town's deeds and papers. A summary and certificate of the receiver's accounts had to be sent to the *commissaire départi* for him to transmit, with his observations, to the *contrôleur général des finances*, in order that the latter might present the king every year with a general report on the administration of the towns.

In short, the approval of the *commissaire départi* was necessary if the king was to give his authorization for expenses or receipts. The *commissaire départi* thus exercised influence on decisions before they were finally made, while the judges and courts came into the picture *afterwards*, in order to audit the accounts and deal with any disputes arising. However, clashes might occur in connection with the authorizations needed for the acquisition or alienation of property and borrowings, and these would give occasion for conflict between judges and intendants.

The reform was not applied everywhere. Paris, Lyons, and some other towns, such as Beauvais, were exempt from it. The municipal organization was not introduced in Brittany, Alsace, Lorraine, Flanders, Burgundy, Provence, or Corsica. It was applied with some modifications, not fundamental in character, in Normandy, Artois, Gascony, Dauphiné, Guyenne, Béarn, Lower Navarre, Roussillon, and Languedoc. Elsewhere it was applied in accordance with the edicts.

However, in 1771 the reform was rescinded. Laverdy was very isolated and the object of much opposition. In October 1768 he was replaced at the *contrôle général* by Maynon d'Invau. In December 1769 the Abbé Terray became *contrôleur général des finances*. He had always been against Laverdy's reform, which he claimed had the effect of reducing the king's power. Then Chancellor Maupeou abolished the *parlements* which might have refused to register the edict repealing the reform. The king was in need of money. The edict of November 1771 revoked the edicts of 1764 and 1765 and reestablished the venal municipal offices in all towns other than Paris and Lyons.

These offices found few purchasers. They seemed too expensive to the communities, which showed themselves mulish when it came to buying them up and merging them with the *corps de ville*. On the eve of the Revolution there was complete confusion in this sphere. In a few towns, officeholders were carrying out municipal functions. In others, more numerous, the offices had been purchased and merged and the former municipal organization restored. But even more numerous were the towns where the officers had been neither taken up nor merged. There, the municipal officers were appointed by royal commission, on the intendants' recommendation. The discontented inhabitants accused these commissioners of being the creatures of the *commissaire départi* and regretted the extinguishing of municipal life.

The edict of 1787 will be considered in the next chapter.

Notes

1. Sébastien Mercier, *Tableau de Paris* (Amsterdam, 1782), vol. 1, p. 52.
2. Entry of 13 October 1629, *Minutier central des Notaires parisiens*, Etude LI, file 157. The estate of Gallardon, belonging to Bullion, was described as a *"ville, terre, seigneurie, et baronnie"* because, in this *"place et lieu seigneurial,"* there still stood a great *"motte"* of earth, the base of a former castle.

3. *Les soupirs de la France esclave.*
4. Archives Nationales, H. 1812, folios 4 verso and 5, 18 October 1652: H. 1805, 1636, passim.

Guide to further reading

All the pointers needed are to be found in:

Dollinger, Philippe; Wolff, Philippe; and Guenée, Simone. *Bibliographie d'histoire des villes de France.* C. Klincksieck, 1967.

To this should be added:

Bordes, Maurice. *La réforme municipale du contrôleur-général Laverdy et son application (1764–1771).* Association des Publications de la Faculté des Lettres et Sciences humaines de Toulouse. Toulouse: Maurice Espic, 1968.
Perrot, Jean-Claude. *Genèse d'une ville moderne: Caen au XVIIIe siècle.* 2 vols. Lille: Service de reproduction de thèses, Université de Lille-III, 1974.
Pillorget, René, and Viguerie, Jean de. "Les quartiers de Paris aux XVIIe et XVIIIe siècles," *Revue d'Histoire moderne et contemporaine* 17 (1970): 253–77.
Pillorget, Suzanne. "Lettres inédites de Claude-Henry Feydeau de Marville, lieutenant-général de Police à Paris, à Jean-Frédéric Phélypeaux, comte de Maurepas et de Pontchartrain (janvier 1740–mai 1747)." Thesis for doctorate in history, Université de Paris-Sorbonne, 1972. Typescript.

14

The Territorial Communities Treated as Corporations: The Provinces

The meaning of the word "province"

What is meant here by "provinces" are those stretches of territory distinguished by a common civilization, with a set of customs, traditions, and privileges expressing a moral personality and common interests and endowed with political organs enabling them to form and manifest a common will.

The France of olden times knew many other meanings of this word. Any ecclesiastical circumscription could be called a "province," or this could signify some circumscription—administrative, judicial, or military—defined by the king's government: a *bailliage*, a *sénéchaussée*, an *élection*, a *recette générale*, a governorate. The word could be used for the whole realm, as when the 16th-century poet Passerat writes: "France is the pearl among provinces."[1]

In this book the "provinces" are the regions which constituted natural communities based on ancestral tradition—the tradition of "our own people," "our homeland." Some of these regions bore the name of a Gaulish tribe, such as Auvergne, recalling the Arverni, Anjou (the Andegavi), or Artois (the Atrebates). The names of others went back to the conquest and colonization of Gaul by the Romans: Provence (*provincia*), Orléanais (Aurelianensis), Bourbonnais (Burbo).

Yet others were due to the establishment of later invaders: Ile-de-France (the Franks), Burgundy (the Burgundians), Gascony (the Vascones). Nearly all these names date from before the 6th century A.D., and all had been formed by the 12th. In the 18th century, before the attachment of Lorraine and Corsica to France, Doisy gave a list of 58 provinces:

> Agenais, Alsace, Angoumois, Anjou, Artois, Aunis, Auvergne, Bazadois, Béarn, Beaujolais, Berry, Bigorre, Blaisois (Blésois), Bourbonnais, Bourgogne (Burgundy), Bresse, Bretagne (Brittany), Brie, Bugey, Cambrésis, Champagne, Condomois, Dauphiné, Flandre (Flanders), Forez, Franche-Comté, Gascogne (Gascony), Gâtinais, Gévaudan, Guyenne, Hainaut (Hainault), Ile-de-France, Landes, Languedoc, Limousin, Lyonnais, Maine, Marche, Navarre, Nivernais, Normandie (Normandy), Orléanais, Pays Messin (Metz), Perche, Périgord, Picardie (Picardy), Poitou, Provence, Quercy, Rouergue, Roussillon, Saintonge, Saumurois, Toulois, Touraine, Velay, Verdunois, Vivarais.[2]

The provinces were thus not coterminous with the governorates. Under Henri III there were twelve governorates, and the ordinance of 18 March 1776 listed eighteen first-class *gouvernements généraux* and twenty-one second-class ones—thirty-nine in all.

Nor did the provinces correspond to the *généralités,* those financial and administrative divisions, which numbered twenty-seven under Louis XVI and failed to include Roussillon, Alsace, Hainault, Lorraine, and Corsica, which lacked *bureaux des finances.*

The provinces were themselves divided into *"pays,"* smaller natural units, such as Hurepoix in Ile-de-France or Beauce in Orléanais. There must have been, all together, about three hundred *"pays"* in France.

The contractual nature of the kingdom

The countries ruled by the king of France were bound together by contract. They did not constitute a federation, for the French king's Council was not divided into geographical sections, like the councils of the king of Spain. Nevertheless, the contractual nature of the situation was clear cut. Some of the lands subject to the king were actually outside his kingdom, though with the same sovereign, in Dauphiné called "dauphin," in Provence called "count." Others were within the kingdom but were territories assembled by their dukes and counts, which formed, in the 14th and 15th centuries, states that corresponded to "nations." When the king of France united them with the royal domain, this was done subject to conditions. With these provinces, as with those that had been joined earlier to the royal domain, one principle applied in every case: the *seigneur* represented the common good, but he had to respect the good old customs. And he always did. Sometimes, moreover, he granted charters, which, though legally concessions on his part, were actually contracts. In Dauphiné, Humbert II, dauphin de Viennois, had caused the statutes and privileges of Viennois and Briançonnais to be compiled; and when he ceded his land to the son of the king of France in 1349, the new dauphin swore to respect them, upon which he received the oath of allegiance of his new vassals and subjects. In the case of Normandy, the charter granted to the Normans was dated 1358. In 1451, Charles VII, having reconquered Guyenne from the English, made an agreement with the three "estates" of the province, undertaking to maintain their laws and customs. He did the same in Entre-Deux-Mers and Bazadais. In 1475 Louis XI recovered for the Crown the district of the Four Valleys in Gascony and confirmed the local privileges. The same decision accompanied the annexation of Provence in 1481. François I acted similarly in relation to Dombes in 1523 and to Brittany in 1532. Throughout the 17th and 18th centuries, whenever a district or town was conquered, the act of capitulation signed with the king of France confirmed its privileges, franchises, and liberties, and these were also confirmed in treaties sanctioning such acquisitions, such as the Treaty of the Pyrenees, in 1659, in respect of Roussillon. The king did not allow the countries subject to him to make the renewal of their oath at each change of reign conditional upon a prior oath sworn by the ruler to respect their usages; the only exceptions to this were Béarn and Navarre, which, at the opening of every new reign, sent deputies to the king, who swore, in their presence, to respect "the rights, liberties, and privileges" of Béarn and Navarre, after which the deputies swore fealty to the king.

The personality of the provinces

Each province constituted a person through its distinctive practices and the privileges that guaranteed its customs and special usages. However, a true "moral person" is one that can give expression to a will common to all its members. For that to exist, a province needed to have a representative organ, and, in fact, it always did have one. A sovereign court, a *parlement,* a *chambre des comptes,* a *cour des aides,* a sovereign council, a *bureau des trésoriers de France et généraux des finances,* and, in general, every body of royal officials had to show fealty and therefore obedience to the king, but these magistrates owed to their consciences respect for their own professional integrity and therefore had to refuse to obey orders that ran counter to this integrity. They owed respect to the dignity of justice and therefore had to maintain just relations between the king and his subjects, which meant, if need be, protecting subjects from their king. The sovereign courts always played a certain role as representatives of the king's subjects. One of the reasons why Louis XV did not follow Maupeou and abolish all the provincial *parlements* was that this act would have left the provinces without any protection, thus changing the monarchy into a despotism. Consequently, *parlements,* or at least sovereign councils, were granted to all conquered provinces. Brittany was given a *parlement* at Rennes, Franche-Comté one at Besançon, Flanders one at Douai. A sovereign council of Alsace was established at Colmar, and there were also sovereign councils in Artois and Roussillon.

But the real representative organs were, of course, the provincial estates. François Olivier-Martin prefers to write "particular estates," because, he claims, the expression "provincial estates" was "not used under the *ancien régime."* [3] However, he is certainly wrong on this point. The expression "provincial estates" was in use already in the second half of the 16th century. On 12 October 1576 the chapter of Saint-Pierre de Lisieux mentioned "the congregation and assembly of the provincial estates of Normandy." By the 18th century it had become quite current. True, the jurist Guyot, in 1784, after writing about the "Estates General," goes on to say: "The particular estates are assemblies of the deputies of the different orders of one province or of one town only." [4] But whereas the expression "particular estates" could lead to confusion, "provincial estates" allows of no ambiguity.

The provincial estates played their biggest role in the 14th and 15th centuries as instruments of the French king's struggles against the pope and the English. At that time all the provinces had their provincial estates, convoked by the king, made up of deputies of the clergy, the nobility, and *"les bonnes villes"* and presided over by royal commissioners. These provincial estates voted taxes, raised troops, made alliances with other provinces, and appointed deputies to the Estates General. They presented remonstrances concerning the condition of the province, the royal administration, edicts, and treaties. They allotted the burden of taxes and collected them. They made decisions on public works and on measures to stimulate agriculture and trade. They elected interim commissions and syndics to see to affairs in the periods between their meetings.

Those provincial estates that met periodically underwent gradual decline. After the end of the Hundred Years' War, the king sought gradually to do away with them. Already before 1450 the provincial estates of Limousin, Marche, Anjou, and Guyenne had disappeared. During the 16th century and at the beginning of the 17th the king ceased convoking the estates of the provinces of central France: Maine, Orléanais, Touraine, Berry, Upper Auvergne, Périgord. During Louis XIII's reign, when Richelieu was minister, the royal government endeavored to establish in every province *élections*, that is, bodies of royal officers charged with the task of transmitting to the parishes the orders from the king's Council about the levying of direct taxes, and supervising the collection of these taxes. In 1628 the king created ten *élections* in Dauphiné and forbade the provincial estates to meet. This decision was confirmed by *arrêts* of the king's Council in 1635, 1636, and 1637. The estates of Dauphiné were not abolished; they were merely not allowed to meet without the king's permission—and this was not given again until the eve of the Revolution.

In 1638 the estates of Normandy were suspended. Though reestablished in 1643, they were never again convoked after 1655.

In Provence in 1639 the provincial estates were replaced by an "assembly of communities," which meant a gathering of deputies from "communities of inhabitants," reinforced by two prelates and two *gentilshommes* and presided over by the archbishop of Aix.

During the personal rule of Louis XIV the king ceased to convoke the estates of Lower Auvergne after 1672, those of Quercy and Rouergue after 1673, those of Alsace after 1683, and those of Franche-Comté after 1704.

In 1663 Louis XIV deprived the surviving provincial estates of the power to "oppose," before the *parlement* and the *cour des aides*, the registration of edicts, declarations, and letters patent relating to public affairs.

What were eventually left of the periodically meeting estates were those of Artois, Cambrésis, the Lille district, Tournaisis, Walloon Flanders, Hainault, the Pays Messin, Béarn, Foix, Nébouzan, the Four Valleys, Bigorre, Labourd, Soule, Lower Navarre, Brittany, Burgundy, Languedoc, and, later, Corsica, the little "particular estates" of Mâconnais and Charolais, and the rudimentary ones of Bresse and Bugey.

But "nonperiodical" provincial estates survived more or less everywhere. Even when their estates were no longer convoked periodically, the provinces retained their moral personality and juridical entity. They continued to constitute corporations. They could call upon the king to assemble the men of their three "estates" to consider a particular matter. This practice persisted in all provinces where important matters were concerned, which involved the interests of the king's service, of his subjects, and of the province. The deputies of the province could then meet *"en corps des trois Ordres."*

For many purposes the provinces or *"pays"* elected occasional syndics, levied special taxes, and made use of the procedures of remonstrance or "opposition" before the king's Council. We find, in 1609, 1661, and 1729, meetings of men of the three "estates" of the *sénéchaussées* of Agenais, Rouergue, Quercy, and Armagnac. The district of Lalleu, in Artois, sent deputies to an assembly of its three "estates" in 1698. The Isle of Oléron held such an assembly in 1767, and in 1785 the people of the provinces of Touraine, Blaisois, Orléanais, Saumurois, and Anjou.

The king convoked assemblies of the three estates in areas where there were no periodically meeting provincial estates, in order to initiate "extraordinary" financial measures—new taxes, *droits casuels, cens,* taxes on certain crafts, commutations, on the basis of *sols pour livres,* of domanial dues, redemption of taxes, and so on. Cases of this sort are found in 1694, 1710, 1711, 1772, 1773, 1774, 1782, and 1786.

Certain districts were represented by a permanent syndic who was in continuous contact with the royal administration. In the *"Marches communes franches"* of Poitou and Brittany—a little *pays* consisting of seventeen parishes—the three "estates" were assembled only very rarely, but a standing "interim commission" gave backing to a permanent syndic. The *"Marches communes"* of Anjou and Poitou, torn, so to speak, between the courts of Thouars and Saumur, "opposed" certain royal letters patent and, between 1633 and 1639, succeeded in getting the king to go back on his decisions and obtaining a *règlement* satisfactory to themselves.

This constant collaboration between governors and governed has not been studied sufficiently.

An example: The provincial estates of Languedoc

From Louis XIV's reign until the end of the *ancien régime* the estates of Languedoc were considered to be typical of the provincial estates, and so I shall take them as my example.

The estates of Languedoc met annually. The king convoked them, sending letters on parchment to each bishop, each baron, all the consuls of the towns that had the right to be represented, and also to his officials in the province. In 1704 this assembly had been held for the previous thirty years at Montpellier, in the months of October and November.

The principal role of the estates was to consent to taxation, to distribute the burden, and to arrange for the taxes to be collected. "No tax may be imposed or levied in the province of Languedoc without the consent of the men of the three estates."[5] The estates busied themselves with public works, bridges, causeways, and roads, approving and finding the money for building and repairing these. The estates decided disputes arising from taxation. They drew up and presented to the king a *cahier* of grievances relevant to the common concerns of the province.

"The right to send a deputy to the estates of Languedoc is . . . a property possessed."[6] The rules governing entry and precedence were finally settled in 1612.

As representatives of the nobility, twenty-two barons were members of the estates by virtue of their baronies. The duc d'Uzès sat there not as a duke but as baron de Florensac. The barons were ranked in accordance with their baronies, regardless of the dignities of duke or marquis. The right to be a member of the estates had become "attached to land," possibly because it was the king's custom to write to "the baron of such-and-such a place," without mentioning his family name, or possibly because a baron represented a community, the inhabitants of his *seigneurie* and *fief de dignité*. The twelve baronies of Vivarais and the eight of Gévaudan took turns in attending the estates, so as not to exceed the number twenty-two. However, there were eight dioceses which did not contain a single barony with the right to attend the estates. The diocese of Toulouse was represented by three baronies, and the dioceses of Uzès, Béziers, Montpellier, and Castres by two each. The comte d'Alais ranked first among them, and the vicomte de Polignac second.

A baron who was unable to attend could be represented by a deputy, but such a deputy had to give proof of four generations of nobility on his father's side and to possess a fief in the province, "so that it may not be suspected that its interests are of no account to him."

The highest-ranking nobles were present at the estates. The vicomtes de Polignac were, in 1632, *seigneurs* of thirty-two communities in Velay, Gévaudan, and Vivarais. The Crussol family, to which the duc d'Uzès belonged, were *seigneurs* of thirty-one villages in Gévaudan and wielded great influence. Present, too, were the Lévis family, marquis de Mirepoix, together with the comtes de Rieux, de Bioule, and d'Aubijoux, the marquis d'Ambre, de Calvisson, and de Castries, and the barons de Castelnau de Bonnefous and d'Estrefous. These nobles received payment for attendance, for acting as delegates to the *bureau des comptes,* and for participating in deputations to the court. The right to be a member of the estates increased the sale value of a barony. These nobles formed a ready-made clientage for the Montmorencys and all families holding great offices at court and as governor and *lieutenant général* of Languedoc. Their ways were still somewhat rough in the 17th century. In 1605 one of the Polignacs stabbed the comte d'Apchier in Mende Cathedral because of a quarrel about precedence. In 1620, on the occasion of the wedding of Charlotte de Chambaud, the Catholic and Huguenot nobles of Vivarais slaughtered each other.

The representation of the nobility underwent some changes in the course of the 17th century. In 1632, after the defeat of Montmorency, the lands belonging to the barons who had supported him were deprived of their right of entry to the estates for between ten and twelve years, and this right was transferred to other *gentilshommes.* Then the old order was restored.

After 1684, approximately, when those who acquired baronies were unable to furnish proof of nobility, the king transferred the right to sit in the estates to other lands. Money payments had enabled these persons to buy *fiefs de dignité* but not to become members of the estates.

Some barons sold their right of entry to the estates "when they had obtained from the king his agreement to their resignation 'between His Majesty's hands' and to the transfer of this right to other lands, this having been made effective by a warrant of gift from His Majesty and letters patent in consequence, which have been registered by the estates." New acquirers of baronies had to bring proof of their nobility for four generations, on both their father's and their mother's side.

In 1675 the right of entry to the estates was given to the barony of

Tornac. Thus the nobility eventually came to be represented by twenty-three persons: one count, one viscount, and twenty-one barons, but they still had only twenty-two votes.

The clergy also had twenty-two votes in the estates. They were represented at the beginning of the 17th century by two archbishops and twenty bishops. During the century the king created the bishopric of Alais, detached from that of Nîmes, and then, in 1675, the archbishopric of Albi. The clergy were thus represented by three archbishops and twenty-one bishops, but they still had only twenty-two votes.

The bishops ranked in order of seniority of consecration. Narbonne being the oldest archiepiscopal see, it was the archbishop of Narbonne who presided over the estates. By a Council *arrêt* of 29 September 1687 the archbishop of Toulouse took precedence over the archbishop of Albi because his see was older-established.

These bishops were *grands seigneurs.* In 1628 the archbishop of Narbonne was *seigneur* of nineteen communities, which included Lézignan and Sigeau. He possessed rights of hunting and fishing and various dues even in the royal town of Narbonne. He also owned some "commoner" land. Most of the bishops were of noble stock and formed, from uncle to nephew, episcopal dynasties. They were either from the higher nobility, like Louis de Valois, comte d'Alais, bishop of Agde, or from the local nobility, like Saint-Bonnet de Toiras, bishop of Nîmes, or from ennobled "gown" families, like the De Fossé family at Castres or the Just de Serres family at Le Puy. These bishops were resident and administered their dioceses. Plantavit de La Pause, at Lodève, won a reputation as a man of letters and of learning.

The third estate was represented by sixty-five deputies, with forty-four votes. They were the consuls of certain towns. Of the twenty-eight episcopal towns, twenty sent two deputies but had only one vote each. Apart from Viviers, the episcopal towns sent deputies to the estates each year. There were also seven other towns which sent deputies each year: Castelnaudary, Limoux, Gignac, Valentins, Marvéjols, Pézenas, and Clermont-Lodève. Finally, in each diocese, some small towns, which in certain cases were mere villages, enjoyed the privilege and sent their consuls turn and turn about. In the diocese of Narbonne their turn came round every twenty-four years, in that of Toulouse every eleven or twelve years, in that of Castres every nine years, and so on.

The senior urban magistrate in office acted as spokesman and cast the vote. His colleague who had played this role in the previous year acted as assistant and substitute.

The third estate was represented by an oligarchy. In order to elect municipal magistrates, the inhabitants were divided into categories, or "*échelles*," each of which provided a very small number of electors. These chose the consuls by secret ballot, in concert with the outgoing municipality. By tradition, the offices went to the highest categories and, within these, to a narrow circle of families. The king, acting through the bishop, the governor, or the intendant, often imposed the election of the candidate he preferred.

In all, the estates consisted of 112 persons, with 88 votes—22 for the clergy, 22 for the nobility, and 44 for the third estate. The double representation of the third estate, as compared with each of the others, which was demanded in relation to the Estates General when the Revolution came, had already been realized in the estates of Languedoc.

To our way of looking at things, an assembly like this was not representative at all. At the very least, all the heads of families in each order should have elected the deputies of their order by secret ballot. For the people of Languedoc, however, until the second half of the 18th century, the representative character of such an assembly was not in doubt. "The deputies of the three orders . . . are regarded as an epitome of the province, and the people's proxies"; and Mariotte stresses "the respect and veneration inspired by these fathers of their country when they form this august body."[7]

The claim seems to have been hardly exaggerated. Indeed, according to a very old-established idea, the deputies to the estates came from the *sanior pars,* the best and soundest section of those whom they represented. For a long time, in religious elections, the *sanior pars,* even if very small in number, had weighed heavier than the *major pars,* the majority, unless this *major pars* was also the *sanior pars*. There were a certain number of critieria by which the *sanior pars* could be defined, but it was for a higher ecclesiastical authority—bishop, archbishop, council, or pope—to decide the matter.

From the Church the conception of the *sanior pars* passed to the world of the laity. "*Pluralité*," as people called it ("*majorité*," from the English word "majority," did not become the generally used word until the end of the 18th century), was an idea that was slow to become accepted. A significant formula recurs in documents of the 17th and 18th centuries, in connection, for example, with the elections of representatives of village communities. It was required that "the major and sounder part of the inhabitants" should make the choice. When the idea came to prevail that it was "the majority" that ought to decide, it was still for a long time confined to the majority of a minority, a sort of *sanior pars:* the majority of the heads of families where the communities of inhabitants were concerned; those who participated at various levels in the paying of a proportional tax where the "active" citizens were concerned; and the electors and eligible persons under the Constitution of 1791.

The notion that the bishops, certain barons, and certain consuls constituted the *sanior pars* of the province of Languedoc corresponded to the conception of society as a natural organism. The archbishops and bishops represented the clergy by virtue of the mere fact that they belonged to the "higher order" of the clergy, from which ensued their functions of teaching Christian doctrine, administering the sacraments, and disciplining the clergy and laity. The barons represented the nobility by virtue of the mere fact that they belonged to the higher nobility, holding *fiefs de dignité,* with authority to command, powers of justice and police, the high civil and military responsibilities, from which ensued their quality as representatives of large communities of people. Only certain barons were accorded this quality, and this on account of their baronies, to which it had become attached by the actual movement of life as time went by, just as certain of the body's cells become differentiated and specialized in the course of life. The municipal councils represented the third estate because they were responsible for the order, security, victualing, and, in general, the everyday life of the inhabitants. Only certain towns played the representative role, for the same reasons that applied to certain baronies.

Bishops, barons, consuls, dioceses, fiefs, and towns were regarded as being organs of a living body. Life itself, and the changes undergone by this body from its conception to its youth, maturity, and decline, caused these organs to differentiate, to enlarge, or to wither, giving them their successive functions or determining the intensity and quality of these functions. It was a "spontaneous" organic or organicist conception of society, which found its rational justification *a posteriori* in the philosophy of Aristotle—a biologist's philosophy—and the interpretation of it by his disciples.

The estates of Languedoc met as a single assembly.

> The form in which the estates of Languedoc assemble each year is more praiseworthy than if they were to separate into three bodies, because, when this separation takes place, each order being preoccupied with what concerns itself, without considering how the

public interest may suffer thereby, there never results such great unity or such perfect understanding as when the three estates gather in one and the same chamber and express their opinions all together, as they do in Languedoc—that is, first, one of the bishops, one of the barons, and the deputies of two towns, and then starting again in the same way, until all the deputies have given their opinion.[8]

The singleness of the assembly certainly did give rise to political unity. Nevertheless, the distinctions between the social orders remained very marked. At the mass at the opening of the assembly and at the daily masses, the ecclesiastical deputies were placed on the Gospel side and the king's commissioners and the barons on the Epistles side. Both groups were given pews with backs to them and hassocks to kneel on. The third estate were placed in the middle of the choir, on little benches two feet high with no backs, and they had no hassocks. The king's chief commissioner gave a dinner to the ecclesiastics and barons; after 1664 the third estate was no longer invited. When Louis XIII visited the estates, at Beaucaire in 1622 and at Béziers in October 1632, he spoke and the presiding officer of the estates replied, while "*Messieurs* of the Church and of the nobility remained standing and hatless, and the third estate and the officials of the province knelt."[9]

The king sent commissioners to the estates, to preside in his name, provided with commissions sealed with the Great Seal. This role was played by the provincial governor with one of the *lieutenants généraux*, who took it in turns; the intendant of justice, police, and finance; two *trésoriers de France*, delegated by the bureaus of Toulouse and Montpellier; and a *greffier*. Down to 1664 the king also sent a state councilor or a master of requests.

The estates appointed their officers. These were, in the first place, three syndics general, who had to be advocates. They acted as public attorneys, presenting motions to be discussed, stating conclusions reached, and keeping an eye on everything that might affect the dioceses and communities. Each of them resided at the chief town of one of the three old *sénéchaussées*.

The estates had two *greffiers*, one residing at Toulouse and the other at Montpellier, where the records were kept. They looked after all documents, drew up reports of proceedings, and saw to the despatch of communications. The records included reports of proceedings going back to 1501.

A receiver general, the "*Thrésorier de la Bourse*," collected moneys on the basis of the subdivisions laid down by the estates, and he spent them in accordance with their "schedules of distribution." He received these funds from two treasurers, one stationed in Toulouse and the other in Montpellier.

The estates devoted their first sessions to checking the deputies' credentials. Then they swore an oath to "serve the king and the province faithfully and to reveal nothing, by speech or writing, of anything said or done in the assembly that might be harmful and prejudicial to the assembly or to the individuals composing it."

The formal opening session then took place. The king's chief commissioner handed to the presiding officer the closed letter which served as the commissioners' credentials. This was read aloud by the *greffier* of the province. Then the *"greffier pour le roi"* read the commissions of the commissioners, sealed with the Great Seal, and placed them on the assembly's desk, to be recorded in the *greffe* of the estates.

The king's commissioner next spoke to the deputies about what the king had done during the year to frustrate the enterprises of the enemies of the state and about the various movements of his armies, either to besiege fortresses or to give battle—for the king was the supreme justiciar, and war was the form taken by justice between states.

On the following day the opening mass was said. ("The estates never proceed to deal with any business without having first said public prayers and called upon the Holy Spirit: to this effect they attend a mass next day.") This was followed by a procession of the Blessed Sacrament—a ceremony begun in 1599.

The king's commissioners then visited, as a body, the presiding officer of the estates, to inform him of their orders and instructions.

After that had been done, work began. The commissioners came to the assembly to ask for the province's "free gift" to the king. The governor made a speech, followed by the intendant. The presiding officer replied. The estates discussed what "His Majesty expects from the liberality of his subjects of Languedoc and from their zeal for his service": help in meeting the costs of war and the other expenses of state. Twenty-four hours before the vote was taken, the commissioners went as a body to visit all the bishops and all the barons in order to recommend to them "His Majesty's interests." The chief commissioner summoned to his presence the deputies of the third estate and also, if the bishops and barons were absent, the vicars general of the former and deputies of the latter, "to exhort them to render to His Majesty the aid expected of the province on this occasion."

Whenever the voting concerned a financial question, it took place in a very special way. An absolute majority was required—half of the votes, plus one. Suppose that, on the question of how much should be granted as the "free gift," four motions, A, B, C, and D, have been put down. There are 88 votes. An absolute majority must therefore be 45. Motion A gets 31 votes; B gets 8; C gets 4; and D gets 2. In order to secure an absolute majority, the votes for motions A, B, C, and D must be added together. The 2 votes cast for motion D being essential to complete the absolute majority, this motion will be the one adopted. If motion A had received 30 votes and motion B 15, it would have been motion B that would have prevailed. "It can happen that the view eventually adopted, because it can secure *pluralité,* is a view put forward by a deputy who is alone in advocating it."

The "free gift" all went into the king's treasury, except for a share paid over to the town of Toulouse, which had made a commutation arrangement with the king.

After the "free gift," the royal commissioners asked for a vote on the fixed taxes which were to be used by the province to relieve the king. The commissioners asked for the *aide,* the *crue* of 1548, the *octroi,* the *équivalent,* or due payable on wine, meat, and fish, introduced in 1452, and the *taillon* for the maintenance of the *gendarmerie*—all this being described as the *"anciens octrois et aides."* The commissioners asked for *crues* on the price of salt, to pay the salaries of the officers of the lawcourts and those of the professors at the universities. These taxes, though annually renewed, were not "prescribed," the king asking each year for the estates' consent to them. The estates granted the taxes but always added, as a precaution against "prescription," that this was done *"sans conséquence."* Other oratorical precautions were taken so as not to seem to be encroaching on the royal sovereignty. The estates consented to grant the king his taxes "so as to have the glory of renewing every year their homage to him and also to render their gift more pleasing to their Prince by causing it to emanate from pure liberality on their part."[10]

While the estates were sitting, the king's commissioners checked on the debts of the various communities. Languedoc included, in 1704, 2,500 communities burdened with debt as a result of the passage of troops and the ravages of contagious disease. The deputies interviewed the commissioners about sundry matters concerning the dioceses and communities.

The estates formed a *bureau des comptes,* to audit each year the accounts of the *trésorier de la Bourse*. They allotted the tax obligations for the ensuing year between the town of Toulouse and the twenty-three dioceses of Languedoc in accordance with a scale showing the share that each diocese had to provide. They met all the expenses of the army's staging posts in Languedoc, relieving the royal finances of this charge. They made arrangements, in this connection, for the provision of magazines of all the goods needed, so as to ease the burden falling on the communities.

The estates drew up a *cahier* of remonstrances. Every year this was taken to the king by a bishop, a baron, two members of the third estate, and one of the syndics general, turn and turn about. These deputies were led into the king's presence by the grand master of ceremonies. The governor of the province and the responsible secretary of state presented them. The bishop acted as a spokesman. "Meanwhile, the baron stands on his left, and the deputies of the third estate and the officers of the province kneel." The bishop handed the king the *cahier* of requests, and the king passed it to the secretary of state, to be examined and reported on in the king's Council.

The estates maintained a permanent agent at the royal court to keep track of their business.

When faced with disagreeable royal edicts and *arrêts* of the king's Council, the estates had at their disposal the procedure of "opposition," which they employed before the *parlement* of Toulouse, first of all, and then, after 1664, before the king's Council.

The estates caused their decisions to be put into effect in the province by their offices or by commissioners designated from among their members.

One month after the meeting of the estates, a diocesan assembly, or *"assiette,"* gathered in each diocese, with the task of apportioning to each community the share it had to provide of the taxes voted by the estates. This assembly met, as a rule, in the episcopal town in March or April. At the beginning of the 17th century it was in session for between fifteen and eighteen days. The Edict of Béziers of 1632 and an edict of 1649 restricted the length of the meeting to eight days. As the members of the *assiette* received, to cover their expenses, only a lump sum, fixed in 1634, the gathering lasted, in the 18th century, no more than two days or even just one day.

The estates met the cost of repairs to bridges, causeways, and public roads. They approved all projects for public works and appointed commissioners to instruct the officials concerned. Each diocese taxed itself to finance repairs to the cross-lanes between roads within its territory. The accounts were closed by the estates.

The estates examined the taxes imposed on itself by each diocese to meet its particular charges or its contribution to the expenditure of the estates. They either approved them, by a decision from which there was no appeal, or else ordered that any excess amounts levied be handed back.

The estates heard any disputes arising in the dioceses with regard to the execution of their *règlements* and decisions. Their judgments could be appealed against to the king's Council.

The royal commissioners examined, together with the estates' own commissioners, the taxes imposed by the communities.

The estates decided how much money they would borrow, and they empowered their syndics general to contract the necessary loans.

The estates apportioned the burdens of the *taille réelle* on the different dioceses in accordance with the quantity and quality of "commoner" land they contained, the amount of trade carried on, and the nature of the products involved. A *"cotisation de l'industrie"* was imposed upon factories. Each head of cattle was taxed. A "rate of proportion" was deposited with the *greffe* of each diocese, showing the burden that each community had to bear. The communities taxed their own inhabitants, even the proletarians being required to pay something.

The *assiette* was composed differently in different dioceses, and it did not necessarily include members of all three orders. The king's commissioners subdelegated a member of the estates to preside over each *assiette*. In the diocese of Lodève the *assiette* consisted of the bishop, who, as the dominant *seigneur* of the area, reduced the other members, who were all from the third estate, to a role of mere registration; the principal commissioner, appointed, before the estates broke up, by the chief royal commissioner (this was often the commander-in-chief of the province); the ordinary commissioners, the first consuls of Lodève and Clermont, who had sat as members of the estates, and the bishop's *viguier;* the representatives of the four *"communautés de tour,"* deputies sent by each of the forty-eight communities of the diocese, in turn, at intervals of twelve years (in each community the representative was usually the first consul or the one who had acquired the office of mayor); the *procureur juridictionnel* of Lodève; and the second and third consuls of Lodève. For the opening session, all the communities were allowed to send a representative.

Between the annual meetings the bishop and the commissioners formed a *"bureau diocésain."*

The *greffier* of the *assiette* notified each community of the amount it was expected to raise. The community added to what it owed to the province the amount which the king had authorized it to raise for its own expenditure. The community distributed the burden of taxation among the taxpayers in accordance with the *"compoix,"* a register in which they were all listed, with indication of what each had to pay on his "commoner" property. The community assigned the levying of the taxes to a collector who carried the sums levied to the receivers of the diocese, royal officials who were accountable to the *chambre des comptes* of Montpellier. The diocesan receivers paid the money over to the treasurers of Toulouse or Montpellier, who passed it on to the *trésorier de la Bourse,* who, finally, gave account of it to the estates.

In this way an association was effected, between the king's officials and the representatives of the province, to care for the general interest of the kingdom while protecting the particular interests of the province.

The estates were obliged constantly to fight to maintain the privileges of their province.

In 1628 the duc de Rohan and the Huguenots rose in revolt in Languedoc. The estates of 1628 voted only part of the subsidy asked for by the king so long as the siege of La Rochelle and the war in Italy continued. On 21 November 1628 the king, violating the privileges of the province, increased by his mere authority the *taillon* to be paid by Languedoc, by the amount of 200,000 livres, and charged the *trésoriers de France* in Toulouse and Béziers with the task of distributing the burden over the twenty-two dioceses and collecting the money. After the surrender of La Rochelle the king came to Languedoc, forced Montauban to surrender, issued the Edit de grâce of Alais on 28 June 1629, and in July, by the Edict of Nîmes, merged the *cour des aides* and the *chambre des comptes* of Languedoc and established *élus* in the province, which thus became a *pays d'élections.* Taxes were thenceforth to be decided by the king's Council, and responsibility for payment was to be allotted, and collection carried out, by the *élus,* that is, by royal officials. The syndics of the assembly of the estates and the *parlement* of Toulouse entered a legal "opposition" to the edict. Some bishops and *seigneurs* of Languedoc, who were followed by a number of craftsmen and *laboureurs,* supported the revolt of Gaston d'Orléans, the queen mother, and the duc de Montmorency, governor of Languedoc, against the king and Richelieu in 1632. The assembly of the estates gave its backing to this revolt. After the defeat of Montmorency at Castelnaudary on 1 September 1632, the king deprived six baronies of their right of entry to the estates. The king's action implied that the estates and liberties of the province had no legal existence except by his will and the law of the kingdom of France—that they resulted from toleration, not from right. However, by the Edict of Béziers, 16 October 1632, the king reestablished the estates. But they were to lose the power to discuss taxation: all the old-established taxes became fixed, and all the royal revenues were increased. The estates also no longer had the right to appoint their own financial agent; the post of *trésorier de la Bourse* became a triennial royal office, and its accounts, after being checked by a commission of the estates assembly, were to be submitted to the Paris *chambre des comptes*. In the *assemblées d'assiette,* though the honorary presiding officer was still the bishop, the chair was actually taken by a *trésorier de France,* changed every two years. Royal commissioners were to sign the statements of accounts. The proceedings of the *assemblées d'assiette* were to be reported to the king's Council. The *trésoriers de France* were to check the accounts of the communities. Still, there was no longer any question of introducing *élus*.

During the Fronde, in October 1649, the edict of 1632 was revoked. The estates recovered all their previous powers, in particular the right to discuss the amount of taxation and to appoint the *trésorier de la Bourse*.

When Louis XIV began his personal rule in 1661 he retained the estates because he made of them an effective instrument of royal authority. He made sure that he had agents inside the estates by intensifying practices that had already been employed. The king and his ministers wrote to *seigneurs fidèles* to urge them to persuade the assembly of the estates to agree to the royal requests. As the *seigneurs* could be represented by a proxy, they sometimes sent a blank certificate of procuration to the governor of the province, the king's commissioner. The ministers and the governor promised these *seigneurs* that the king would remember their services. The royal commissioners to the estates reported to the king on the conduct of the *seigneurs,* and the king thanked them by letter. Protracted or outstanding services were rewarded by pensions and *ordonnances de comptant* in favor of the *seigneurs* concerned. Some *seigneurs* of Languedoc held offices, in any case, in the royal household, for example, as *gentilhomme ordinaire de la chambre du roi.* The king appears to have used the same methods in relation to the deputies of the clergy and the third estate.

The final blow to the independence of the estates was the edict of August 1692, which turned the urban magistracies into royal and venal offices, thereby making some of the deputies of the third estate royal officeholders. Generally speaking, the estates remained docile under Louis XIV.

After 1715 the intendants of Languedoc made increasing use of the estates as an internal organ of administration. The estates were, indeed, in frequent communication with the various parts of the province, and problems were studied in its commissions by men of education and common sense who prepared judicious solutions.

The estates initiated the construction of bridges, roads, canals, irrigation channels, dikes, and promenades. They encouraged agricultural and industrial enterprises. The *pays d'Etats* were generally held to be greatly superior to the *pays d'élection.*

The king endeavored on several occasions to extend the range of administration by agents of the central authority. He issued a declaration on 11 February 1764 dealing with the tolls and patrimonial property of the communes. The *parlement* of Toulouse hastened to register this declaration. It ordered the municipal officers of the communes to deposit at its *greffe* a copy of all memoranda and documents which they were going to send to the minister of finance. The *parlement* still held to the old conception of the judicial authority's supervising the administration, and even exercising administrative authority, through its *arrêts de règlement* and *arrêts entre parties*—the conception of a "judicial administration."

The provincial estates protested against the *parlement's* action. They accused it of seeking to interfere in the administration of the communes, in which it had never played any role. They launched an "opposition" to the king's declaration, on the grounds that this—and also the declaration of 21 November 1763, which altered the use to which patrimonial property, the old-established tolls and subventions, were put—amounted to the imposition of a disguised tax. They recalled the fundamental principle of the *pays d'Etats:* "All the aids, ordinary and extraordinary, that His Majesty considers he should obtain from Languedoc can be granted, in accordance with the most ancient, most constant, and most authorized form, only by the assembled estates, which in this part of the kingdom are the real representatives of the people."

Against the *parlement* and the *nobles de robe* the estates drew up, in 1770, a *règlement* aimed at preventing them from getting hold of the baronies which conferred the right of representation in the estates. They proclaimed that heirs, donees, or purchasers of baronies must be engaged in the profession of arms and produce proofs of military nobility on their father's side going back four centuries. Deputies representing barons unable to take their seats in the estates must prove six generations of nobility on their father's side, or at least two hundred years of nobility. On 14 July 1770 the *parlement* quashed articles 7 and 8 of this *règlement*. The syndic of Languedoc complained to the king's Council, invoking the privileges of the province which debarred the *parlement* from any meddling in the deliberations of the estates. On 13 October 1770 the king's Council issued an *arrêt* quashing the *parlement*'s *arrêt*.

The estates came under severe attack on the eve of the convocation of the Estates General of 1789. The king had it announced that the deputies from the *pays d'Etats* were to be nominated exclusively by the provincial estates. However, ideas about political representation had altered under the influence of the Enlightenment, which brought together and concentrated a number of currents of thought: Stoicism, which underlies Roman law, Cartesianism, mechanism, the empiricism of John Locke, Puritanism, and the ideas of the *"monarchomaques"* of the League. The idea of society as a natural organism increasingly gave place to the idea of a society based on a conscious, voluntary, and explicit contract between men who were guided by reason. The representation of citizens should emerge from a free, conscious, motivated, and rational choice made by persons estimated to be those best fitted to defend the interests of their electors and, indeed, the welfare of society as a whole. They should act as though chosen by everyone even if they were chosen by only a section, the majority. A rational decision, the outcome of geometrical reasoning, ought to designate those who should act as representatives, rather than the movement of life itself. Society and the universe were conceived of as mechanisms, put together by, or under the influence of, a sort of clockmaker, the supreme and eternal mechanic, the God of the Deists, instead of being living organisms that emanated from the breath of the Living God, Jehovah, Lord of Hosts, who calls Himself "I Am" and is the God of living men.

On 26 February 1788 the *cour des comptes, aides et finances* of Montpellier, in its remonstrances concerning the edict on the "twentieth," attacked the provincial estates—"an imperfect body, in which the representatives of the orders do not represent them." It also blamed the estates for their pomp and extravagance. On 22 December 1788 it again attacked the form assumed by the estates and, claiming to speak in the name of the public, called for a genuine representation of Languedoc. It declared that the estates were an association of prelates, titled nobles, and consuls, but "the clergy, the nobility, and the people were not there at all." The deputies were persons "lacking character and authority." It denounced the permission given to deputies to be represented by proxy, the perpetual tenure of the presiding officer, the absolute power of the three immovable syndics general, the unsatisfactory distribution of the tax burden, and the excessive amount of borrowing. A little later it characterized the estates as "a body without reality, an assembly without character, an administration without power." On 13 February 1789 the Council quashed the two *arrêtés* of the *cour des comptes* as being *ultra vires* and contrary to justice and propriety.

Nevertheless, the manifestos of the *cour des comptes* unleashed an avalanche of special assemblies, syndicates, and corporate gatherings, which drew up complaints against the estates. The principal merchants of Toulouse observed on 31 December 1788, speaking of the estates, that "nobody delegated them." On 13 January 1789 the nobles of the diocese of Toulouse called for a provincial assembly that should be truly representative. They appointed two syndics of the nobility to communicate their views to all the corporations, ecclesiastical and lay. The chapter of Toulouse Cathedral protested on 16 January 1789 against the estates of Languedoc as being made up of persons who, not having been freely elected by the three orders of the province, could not be either their representatives or their mandatories. On 26 January the *parlement* of Toulouse called for a general assembly of the three orders of Languedoc to be held, in order to form constitutional estates, as in Dauphiné.

On 24 January the king decided to establish electoral colleges in the *bailliages* and *sénéchaussées* for the elections to the Estates General. Languedoc was to be divided into twelve new *sénéchaussées*, each of which should have a number of deputies proportionate to its population. The province would have eighty-four representatives—twenty-one for the clergy, twenty-one for the nobility, forty-two for the third estate.

On 21 February 1789 the provincial estates of Languedoc broke up after their presiding officer protested against the way representatives to the Estates General had been elected. The estates never met again.

The example of Languedoc will, I think, suffice.

The king retained, developed, and in some cases created provincial estates in the conquered provinces. Indeed, the guiding principle followed by the king and his Council in conquered countries was constant: to change institutions as little as possible; to confirm and guarantee the usages, customs, franchises, liberties, and privileges of the province which had been acquired or had been formed out of conquered territories; to endeavor simply to make whatever already existed operate to the king's advantage, gradually increasing taxes and strengthening royal authority; slowly to change the spirit and purpose of the given institutions, through the activity of the permanent royal commissioners, the governor, the intendant, and the judiciary— *parlement* or sovereign council—with the help of the provincial estates. In appearance little was changed, but in fact everything functioned differently. The provincial estates served in the conquered lands as a precious aid in ensuring the loyalty of the inhabitants and winning their hearts for the king of France.

The provincial assemblies

After about 1685, increasingly strong criticism was voiced against the almighty intendants, who were accused of being *créatures* and favorites and of working in a pettifogging way, in complete ignorance of provincial and local realities; against the constant intervention by ministers and their agents in local life and administration; against the tendency to decide all questions in Paris or Versailles, even the expenditure of 50 livres; against the exclusion of the local people from control over those matters that affected them most closely and that they were best informed about.

These criticisms first took shape in the circles of the duc de Bourgogne, dauphin of France. Saint-Simon, in his *Projets de gouvernement résolus par Monsieur le Duc de Bourgogne,* and Fénelon, in his *Plans de gouvernement concertés avec le duc de Chevreuse* (the *"Tables de Chaulnes"*), set out the first drafts for reforming the system. They wanted provincial estates to be reestablished everywhere that they had fallen into desuetude, on the model of the estates of Languedoc, and also periodical meetings of the Estates General. They regarded the privileges "of the various orders and provinces" as constituting "fundamental laws" of the realm. Their ideas were revived by Boulainvillier in 1727, by Montesquieu in 1748, in his *L'Esprit des lois,* and by the marquis de Mirabeau in 1750, in his *Mémoire concernant l'utilité des Etats provinciaux* and, in 1751, in his *Mémoire sur les Etats provinciaux,* which he described as "the people's happiness."

However, a whole current of ideas appeared which was directed against the provincial estates and in favor of new administrative bodies, namely, provincial assemblies. Their advocates criticized the provincial estates as being dangerous to the royal authority and contrary to the spirit of the *"petite patrie,"* the special privileges and the "orders" being based on a conception of social functions which relegated economic concerns to the background.

The marquis d'Argenson wrote, in 1737, a memorandum entitled *Jusques où la démocratie peut être admise dans un gouvernement monarchique.* Manuscript copies of it were read by Voltaire, Rousseau, and the farmer general Dupuis, and in 1764 it was printed. For D'Argenson the government ought to concern itself only with major questions, leaving the "people's officers" to act as its local agents. Bodies of municipal officials should therefore be formed in the villages, *bourgs,* and towns with responsibility for assessing liability to taxation, collecting the taxes, and carrying out public works. The intendant would no longer have to do anything but supervise the municipalities.

It was above all in the thinking of the Physiocrats that the idea of provincial assemblies became most sharply defined. Vivens, with his *Considérations sur les divers moyens d'encourager l'agriculture* (1756), and Quesnay, Louis XV's doctor and the founder of the Physiocratic school, converted the marquis de Mirabeau. In 1757, the marquis reproduced, in the fourth section of his *Ami des hommes,* his memorandum on the provincial estates, but with a quite different introduction. To each order of questions should correspond an order of persons competent to deal with them. There was needed, therefore, a "municipal order," to be responsible for policing "retail trade, production, industry, commerce, and finance." It should be made up of "notables"—the principal landowners, merchants, and craftsmen. From among them should be drawn the deputies to a general assembly of the municipalities of the province. The landowners mentioned here were to consist of all who had the *seigneurie utile* of some piece of land, those who held landed property with *jus utendi* and *jus fruendi*— in other words, the possessors of means of production, regardless of their personal quality. The marquis thus had in mind bodies that should no longer be made up of representatives of the orders, divided according to their "quality," but should consist of representatives of the activities which produced material goods, categorized according to their role in the production process. This change corresponded to a change in values. The production of material goods was becoming the highest social value. From the concept of social "orders," men were going over to that of social "classes."

Mirabeau reiterated his idea in his *Lettres*, published in 1767 and 1768 in the journal of the economists, *Les Ephémérides*. For him, the distinction between "orders" was one that ought to disappear. The government should consult the country landowners, represented in municipalities.

The most thorough scheme was worked out by the Physiocrat Dupont de Nemours for Turgot in 1775, under the title *Mémoire sur les municipalités*. He advocated a hierarchy of assemblies. At the lowest level, parish municipalities were to assess liability for taxation, look after communications, and care for the poor. At the middle level, the municipalities of the *élections* were to allot tax liability between parishes and examine the requests sent up by the village muncipalities. Provincial municipalities would make decisions and formulate views at the level of the province. Every year, the king would gather round himself a "grand national municipality." The distinction between orders would be abolished. Each municipality would recruit its members from among those of the level immediately below it. Village municipalities would be elected by landowners with an income of at least 600 francs a year. The rich would be allowed several votes, in proportion to their income. Thus the idea of a property qualification for electors made its appearance. Everything was to be based on a class of possessors of means of production. This memorandum was not published until June 1787, but Le Trosne expressed similar ideas in his memorandum of January 1779, entitled *De l'administration provinciale*.

This movement of ideas stimulated several experiments by the government. On 6 May 1766 letters patent established in Boulonnais an "administrative body" of eight administrators, charged with responsibility for dealing with current affairs, along with a receiver and *greffier* and twelve councilors (four from each order), meeting once a quarter to decide on important questions. All these men were to be chosen by an electoral assembly that was itself elected: eight deputies from the clergy and the nobility, five deputies from the towns, elected by the "notables," and six deputies from the villages, elected by their syndics. When the personnel of an "administrative body" was renewed, one would need to have been a member of the electoral assembly in order to become an administrator or a councilor. The "administrative body" would supervise the recovery of taxes and would present programs of public works—powers that were kept reduced so as not to alarm the "*financiers.*"

A more significant move was made by Necker, who aimed to cut down the importance of both the intendants and the *parlements*. Council *arrêts* decided to experiment with "provincial administrations"— for Berry, 12 July 1778; for Dauphiné, 27 April 1779; for Upper Guyenne, 11 July 1779; and for Bourbonnais, 19 March 1780. Only those of Berry and Upper Guyenne actually functioned, as Dauphiné refused what was offered to it, and the Paris *parlement* refused to register the *arrêt* regarding the one for Bourbonnais.

According to the *arrêt* of 12 July 1778 the provincial assembly was to be composed on the basis of a compromise between the system of orders and that of classes. It was to consist of the three traditional orders, with twelve members of the clergy, twelve of the nobility, and twenty-four of the third estate; but the *gentilshommes* had to be landowners—they did not enter the assembly by virtue of their "quality" alone but by virtue of that plus their landed property—and the representatives of the third estate (twelve for the towns, twelve for the countryside) had to be landowners. Voting would be on an individual basis, no longer by orders, and the fact that the third estate had twice as many representatives would ensure that it balanced the two other orders. The property criterion and voting by individuals determined that the *class* system would be predominant.

The assembly was to meet for one month every other year. Between its meetings an "administrative bureau" would execute the decisions of the previous assembly. This bureau would consist of the archbishop of Bourges, seven members of the assembly, two *procureurs-syndics,* and a secretary—all, except the archbishop, to be elected by the assembly. The role of the assembly and its bureau was to be the assessment of tax liabilities and the collection of taxes; it was also concerned with constructing main roads, setting up workshops for the relief of the poor, and busying itself with "any other matters that His Majesty may think convenient to entrust to it." The assembly and its bureau could "at any time make whatever representations to His Majesty they may think fit and propose to him measures that they shall believe to be just and useful for the province"—but without holding up the assessment and recovery of taxes. The intendant and the *commissaire départi* could take cognizance of their deliberations. The king's authorization would be needed for all expenditure.

For the first assembly of the province of Berry, Bertin, secretary of state with responsibility for the royal household, convoked sixteen landowners, taken from all three orders: four ecclesiastics (the archbishop, two abbots, one canon), four nobles (two marquises and two counts), and eight members of the third estate, among whom was Soumard, mayor of Bourges, *écuyer* and *seigneur* of Crosses. They met on 5 October 1778 in the great hall of the archbishop's palace and named thirty-two more landowners, who were to form, with them, the first provincial assembly. According to the terminology of the official documents, the assembly was divided into three *"classes"*: twelve ecclesiastical landowners, twelve noble landowners, and twenty-four landowners of town and country. By the *règlement* of 1 November 1778, which remained in force until 1789, the interim "administrative bureau" was to consist of eight persons, two from each *"classe"* (article 22). Debates were to be settled by a majority of votes, *"sans aucune distinction d'Ordre ni de classe"* (article 18). The concept of social class had clashed with that of "order" and had triumphed over it.

All the assembly's work was to be prepared by bureaus. Matters would be discussed by the assembly only after they had previously been examined by one of the bureaus, and on the basis of its report. The assembly set up four bureaus, one for determining the allocation of business, one for taxes, one for public works, and one for trade and industry.

The assembly met again on 16 August 1779, on 22 October 1780, in October 1783, and on 23 October 1786. Its sixth meeting, in 1788, was postponed because the Estates General was to assemble in the near future, and this assembly met no more. It survived in the form of its interim commission. However, the powers of the assembly and of this commission were severely restricted by the *arrêt* of 8 September 1782 (for Upper Guyenne) and that of 23 August 1783 (for Berry). The intendant was assigned the task of conveying all correspondence between the minister, the assembly, and the commission. He dealt with contentious matters affecting assembly and commission. He decided whether public works, the expense of which was to be borne by the communities, were opportune or not and drew up estimates for them. He delivered *ordonnances de comptant* for the services of the province. In short, he intervened constantly to keep control of the provincial administration. The two provincial assemblies vegetated—that of Upper Guyenne and that of Berry alike. They were not backed by the government, and they enjoyed no support from public opinion, for they were not elected but were recruited by nomination and cooptation, and their presiding officer was nominated by the king and was permanent. They seemed to be tools of a king who took no interest in them. The reform of 1787 was not applied, either in Upper Guyenne or in Berry.

The problem of a decentralized provincial administration remained unsolved. In February 1787 Calonne presented to the Assembly of Notables a plan like that of 1775, except that it left all executive power in the hands of the intendant. The notables rejected the authority of the intendant and called for the division into orders to be maintained, since this, they claimed, "formed part of the constitution of the monarchy." Calonne was dismissed in April.

Loménie de Brienne was his successor. In May he revived the project, with modifications. This was the purpose of the edict of June 1787, creating provincial and municipal assemblies, and of the *règlements* of 23 June and 5 August 1787. They fell far short of Necker's scheme, and, though in appearance tending toward a class society, they in fact did more to uphold the division into orders and the authority of the intendant.

Assemblies at three levels were provided for. At the lowest level there were to be municipal assemblies; in the middle, district or *département* assemblies; and, at the top, provincial assemblies. There would be one provincial assembly for each *généralité*. Since the province of Normandy was divided into three *généralités,* those of Rouen, Caen, and Alençon, it would have three provincial assemblies. The second-level assemblies would in some cases, as in Champagne, be based on the *élections;* in others, as in the Ile-de-France and Normandy, they would be based on a new circumscription called the *département* (or, in Lorraine and Alsace, the *district*). Municipal assemblies would be set up for each community of inhabitants, in the villages but not in the towns, since the latter already possessed municipal corporations and the king's intention was not "to change for the moment the form of administration of the established municipalities." The *généralités* of Tours and Bordeaux were huge, embracing several provinces, each of which had its own character—such as, in the *généralité* of Tours, the provinces of Maine, Anjou, and Touraine. Each of these provinces would have its own assembly, subordinate to a general assembly in the town where the intendant resided. In these two *généralités* there would thus be assemblies at four levels.

The new municipal assemblies were to be composed of the *seigneur* of the parish, the *curé,* and other members to the number of three if the community contained fewer than 100 households, six if it numbered between 100 and 200, and nine if there were more than 200.

If the parish was divided between several *seigneurs,* they were to alternate as members of the assembly, succeeding each other in the order of their shares of the parish. The assembly would have a syndic, allowed deliberative voice, who would act as executive officer, and it would elect a *greffier.*

The parish assembly was to consist of persons who paid 10 livres or more in taxes on their land or their persons in the given parish, "of whatsoever estate and condition they may be." With this property qualification for electors, "quality" thus disappeared, being replaced by "fortune." The social structure in "orders" was on its way out.

The electoral assembly was to be held on the first Sunday in August 1787 and on the first Sunday in October in subsequent years. The syndic would preside. The *seigneur* and the *curé* would not be present. Elections would be by ballot, and a simple majority would decide. Any person, noble or otherwise, could be elected if he was not less than twenty-five years old, had resided in the parish for a year, and paid at least 30 livres in taxes on his land or person. One-third of the members of the assembly would be replaced each year. The syndic would be elected for three years and could be reelected for up to nine years in all. All those elected would again be eligible, but only after a lapse of two years.

The *seigneur* was to preside over the municipal assembly or, in his absence, the syndic. The *curé* would sit on the presiding officer's left, and the syndic, when not himself presiding, on his right. The other members would rank according to the date they were elected, not according to their "quality."

The assembly of a *département* or *district* was to have between sixteen and twenty-four members, half of whom would be of the third estate, drawn in equal numbers from town and country. Votes would be cast on an individual basis. If the votes proved to be divided equally, the presiding officer would exercise the deciding vote. This presiding officer, appointed by the king, would always be either a nobleman or a cleric. The assembly would choose from among its members two *procureurs syndics* and an interim bureau.

Only members of municipal assemblies could elect or be elected to the assembly of a *département*. The territory of the *département* would be divided into *arrondissements*, and seats in the assembly would be distributed among these. Members of the assembly would be elected by the electoral assemblies of the *arrondissements*, to which each municipal assembly would send five deputies—the *seigneur*, the *curé*, the syndic, and two elected deputies. The *seigneurs* and the *curés*, sitting by right in their municipal assemblies, would alone be regarded as nobles and ecclesiastics. If a *gentilhomme* were elected to a municipal assembly, he could be elected to the assembly of the *département* only as a member of the third estate; this accentuated the break with the structure in terms of "orders," but it also jeopardized the arrangement whereby the third estate was to have twice as many representatives as the others.

A provincial assembly was to have between twenty-eight and fifty members. The presiding officer would be appointed by the king. One of the *procureurs-syndics* must always be either a nobleman or an ecclesiastic. There would be an interim commission of four, two of whom must always be noblemen or ecclesiastics. The assembly of the *département* would itself designate those of its members who would sit for four years in the provincial assembly. For its initial composition, however, the king would nominate half the members, and these would in turn choose their colleagues. There would therefore be no elected members until 1790.

By the *règlement* of 5 August 1787 the municipal assembly was to be given the task of looking after local interests and executing on its territory orders concerned with the general interests of the kingdom. Acting as agent for the government, the assembly would assign liability for direct taxes and would send to the *élection* the rolls for the *taille* and, to the intendant, the rolls for the poll tax, the tax in commutation of *corvée*, and the local taxes. The intendant and the *élus* would endorse them with the formula for execution, and they would then be passed to the collector, who would be supervised by a member of the municipality. Acting as agent of its community, the municipal assembly would forward to the assembly of the *département* all the communities's proposals or requests. It would maintain the communal buildings and decide on new construction. All its decisions had to be approved by the provincial assembly and authorized by the intendant.

The assembly of the *département* and its interim bureau were to allot the burden of royal taxation among the parishes, give their view regarding the requests put up by the communities, preside over the acceptance of tenders for public works, and evaluate the petitions for rebate submitted by taxpayers. Being entrusted with the care of regional interests, they would discuss the *département*'s needs, send their proposals to the provincial assembly, and, if they were accepted, see to the execution of these proposals.

The provincial assembly was not concerned with executing the orders that the king sent to the intendant. Its responsibility was to look after the interests of the region, discuss all the expenditure each year, decide how much should be borne by each *département* and each parish, and ask the intendant and the Council for authority to commit them. The interim commission had to decide between tenders for public works, direct their carrying-out, and issue mandates for payment. The assembly and the commission had to forward to the minister all proposals of advantage to the province. Reports of them were to be published at once. It was the assembly's duty to examine the accounts of the communities and their requests for discharge, but the final decision lay with the intendant. The interim commission had no right to concern itself with works carried out at the expense of the royal treasury. The intendant continued to be the only executive agent for all matters of general interest. The assembly was still subject to the intendant. It was he who opened and closed its sessions. He was empowered to preside over the assembly and to express his views in it. The *procureurs-syndics* were obliged to submit reports of its proceedings to him, day by day. The intendant could make any checks he chose and could refuse the assembly any information he wished to withhold. He arbitrated in any difference between the assembly and its commission, on the one hand, and the comptrollers general on the other. He gave the Council his comments on each and every discussion that took place. The intendant took the chair in the interim commission when it examined the communities' accounts, the reports by the *procureurs-syndics* on how they had carried out their duties, and the execution of a work which had been paid for jointly by the province and the royal treasury.

This *règlement* was thus even stricter than those which had been issued for the "trial" provincial assemblies of Berry and Upper Guyenne. They all put the assemblies under close and constant supervision. The assemblies were to be reduced to waiting continually for a Council *arrêt* before they could act and to asking permission to spend 50 livres. Actually, the main aim of the reform was to avoid the reestablishment of the provincial estates. It displeased both the nobles and admirers of the provincial estates and the liberal decentralizers who wanted to see each province in possession of its own resources and free to use them as it chose. The reform had been introduced, in fact, to strengthen the centralized authority of the monarchy.

The first members of the assemblies were nominated by Brienne. The promised elections were put off. A majority of privileged persons was designated on the recommendation of the intendants, and so these men were looked on as the *"créatures de l'intendant."* The presiding officer was always an archbishop or a *grand seigneur;* in the Ile-de-France it was the duc du Châtelet. The ecclesiastical members were vicars general, abbots, canons, deans, rarely *curés* of urban parishes, and in no case a country *curé.* The noble members were mainly courtiers, senior military officers, and generals, with almost no *nobles de robe.* In the third estate, the countryside was often represented by town *bourgeois* who happened to own property there. The majority of the third estate's representation was made up of mayors of big towns, advocates, magistrates, a score of wholesale merchants, with only one industrialist, an ironmaster from Soissonnais. The third estate included many *écuyers* and *chevaliers,* so that the arrangement for "double" representation of this estate was negated. Public opinion turned against these aristocratic bodies.

The reform was not imposed in Provence or Hainault. The *parlements* of Besançon, Grenoble, and Bordeaux refused to register it. The regime of 1787 remained unapplied in nine *généralités* out of twenty-six. The *parlements* called for the Estates General to be convened.

At the session of November 1787, Brienne proposed to the provincial assemblies that they agree to an *abonnement* of their "twentieths," with an increase in the amount paid. In this way the royal government would avoid having to get edicts for extraordinary taxation registered by the *parlements.* The latter would be largely deprived of their principal means of political action. They would no longer dare to call for the Estates General. However, the provincial assemblies either declined the *abonnement* or else voted only meager increases. They feared to seem to be acting as accomplices of the comptroller general. The affair nonetheless discredited the provincial assemblies, which had been made to look as' though created merely to facilitate taxation.

The ministers and the comptroller general of finance then ceased to bother any more with the provincial assemblies. They no longer gave either approval to their proposals or sanction to their conflicts with the intendants, and they ended by abandoning them altogether. On 21 September 1787 the consultative assembly of Hainault, nominated by the king, drew up a scheme for the reestablishment of the provincial estates of that province. It was adopted in April 1788. The Council's *arrêt* was issued on 10 October 1788. The *arrêt* of 8 August 1788 had fixed the meeting of the Estates General for 1 May 1789. It suspended the *cour plénière* and stated that there was a need "to assemble the provincial estates in those provinces where they exist and restore them in certain provinces where they have been suspended"; for, the edicts of 8 May 1788 having smashed the *parlements,* it was necessary to try to win over public opinion, and the setback to the provincial assemblies restored the prestige of the provincial estates, provided they became truly representative. By the *arrêt* of 8 August 1788 Brienne urged the former *pays d'Etats*—Auvergne, Normandy, Franche-Comté, etc.—to request that their suspended provincial estates be reestablished. The *arrêt* seemed to proclaim the superiority of the provincial estates over the provincial assemblies. Brienne had not proved able to create a national representation, basing himself on the third estate, by reviving Calonne's plan, with its merging of the orders and its broadly conceived property qualification for electors. This would have meant taking a step toward a class structure, and Brienne had, in fact, stayed with the social structure of "orders."

The failure of the provincial assemblies brought the provincial estates back into favor with public opinion. The king had already allowed these estates to be dispensed from applying the edict of June 1787. After the edict of 8 May 1788, annulling the political power of the *parlements,* the provinces demanded other guarantees. In Dauphiné the movement of revolt on the part of the aristocrats compelled the government to tolerate the spontaneous assembly at Vizille, which met on 21 July 1788. This resolved to reconstitute the provincial estates, but on new foundations. A fresh assembly at Romans reorganized the provincial estates on the basis of a compromise between the structure of "orders" and that of classes. The division into orders was maintained, but the representation of the third estate was doubled and voting was to be on an individual basis. For the elections to the third estate the electorate was restricted to the well-do-do: to be an elector one had to pay between 6 and 10 livres in taxes in the countryside and 40 livres in Grenoble. The powers of the estates were to exceed those of the provincial assemblies. The presiding officer was to be elected. The estates were to have charge of all the administrative and judicial matters connected with taxation and public works, power to act as guardians of the communities, and the right to look into all questions that might concern the province. Every general law had to be submitted to them. But the annual voting of taxes remained the privilege of the Estates General. The estates were to meet every year and to appoint *procureurs-syndics* and an interim commission. The Council's *arrêt* of 22 October 1788 sanctioned these decisions. On 12 December 1788 the estates of Dauphiné assembled. Public opinion everywhere called for provincial estates on the same model. On 27 December 1788 the king's Council announced that the Estates General would organize them in every province.

Notes

1. Edmond Huguet, *Dictionnaire de la langue française du XVIe siècle* (Didier, 1965), vol. 6.
2. Doisy, *Le royaume de France et les Etats de Lorraine, disposés en forme de dictionnnaire contenant les noms de toutes les provinces* (1753), p. 73.
3. F. Olivier-Martin, *Traité*, p. 392.
4. Guyot, *Répertoire universel et raisonné de jurisprudence*, article *"Etat."*
5. Christophe de Mariotte, (*"secrétaire et greffier des Etats de Languedoc,"*), *Mémoire concernant la forme des assemblées des Estats de Languedoc* (1704).
6. Gachon, *Les Etats de Languedoc et l'Edit de Béziers*, p. 20.
7. Mariotte, op. cit.
8. Ibid., p. 1.
9. Ibid., p. 18.
10. Ibid., p. 17.

Guide to further reading

Appolis, Emile. *Un pays languedocien au milieu du XVIIIe siècle: Le diocèse civil de Lodève, etude administrative et économique*. Albi: Imprimerie coopérative du Sud-Ouest, 1951.
Babeau, Albert. *La province sous l'Ancien Régime*. Firmin-Didot, 1894.
Boscary, Gérard. *L'assemblée provinciale de haute Guyenne, 1779–1790*. Law thesis, Paris. 1932.
Braure, Maurice. *Lille et la Flandre wallonne au XVIIIe siècle*. 2 vols. Lille: E. Raoust, 1932.
Cherest, A.-A. *La chute de L'Ancien Régime, 1787–1789*. Hachette & Joly, 1884–86.
Croquez, Albert. *La Flandre wallonne et les pays de l'intendance de Lille sous Louis XIV*. H. Champion, 1912.

Delcambre, E. *Les Etats du Velay des origines à 1642.* Le Puy, 1938.

Dupont-Ferrier, Gustave. "Sur l'emploi du mot 'province,' notamment dans le language administratif de l'ancienne France," *Revue historique* 160 (1929): 241–67; 161 (1929): 278–303.

Egret, Jean. *Les derniers etats de Dauphiné, septembre 1788–janvier 1789.* Grenoble, 1942.

Gachon, P. *Les Etats de Languedoc et l'Edit de Béziers, 1632.* 1887.

Hildesheimer, B. *Les assemblées générales de communautés de Provence.* Pédone, 1935.

Lachaze, Lucien. *Les Etats provinciaux de l'ancienne France et la question des Etats provinciaux aux XVIIe et XVIIIe siècles: L'Assemblée provinciale du Berri sous Louis XVI.* Law thesis, Paris. Arthur Rousseau, 1909.

Lavergne, Léonce de. *Les assemblées provinciales sous Louis XVI.* Calmann-Lévy, 1863. 2d ed., 1879.

Livet, Georges. *L'intendance d'Alsace sous Louis XIV.* Publication de la Faculté des Lettres de l'Université de Strasbourg, 1956.

Mousnier, Roland. "La participation des gouvernés à l'activité des gouvernants dans la France des XVIIe et XVIIIe siècles," *Recueils de la Société Jean-Bodin* 14 no. 3 (1966): 235–97. (With bibliography.)

Olivier-Martin, Fr. "L'action juridique des 'Etats' ou 'Ordres' en dehors des assemblées périodiques en France aux XVIIe et XVIIIe siècles," in *Recueil des travaux d'histoire et de philologie,* 3d ser., fasc. 43. Université de Louvain, 1952.

Pene, Gilbert. *Les attributions financières des Etats du pays et comté de Bigorre aux XVIIe et XVIIIe siècles.* Bordeaux: Bière, 1962.

Prentout, Henri. *Les Etats provinciaux de Normandie.* 3 vols. 1927.

Rébillon, Armand. *Les Etats de Bretagne de 1661 à 1789.* Rennes: Imprimeries Réunies, 1932.

Renouvin, Pierre. *Les assemblés provinciales de 1787.* Faculty of Letters thesis. Paris. Picard, 1921.

Roussot, Jean. *Les Etats du Mâconnais.* Société pour l'Histoire . . . des Anciens Pays Bourguignons, 1938.

Roux, Marquis Marie de. *Louis XIV et les provinces conquises.* Editions de France, 1938.

Saint-Léger, A. de. *La Flandre maritime et Dunkerque sous la domination française (1659–1789).* Lille: Ch. Tallandier, 1900.

Soboul, Albert. *Les campagnes montpelliéraines à la fin de l'Ancien Régime: Propriété et culture d'après les compoix.* Commission de Recherche et de Publication des Documents relatifs à la vie économique de la Révolution, Mémoires et Documents, Vol. 12. P.U.F., 1958.

Vic, Claude de, and Vaissète, Joseph. *Histoire générale du Languedoc.* 3d ed. Toulouse: privat, 1872–1905. (Vols. 11, 12, 13, 15.)

Conclusion to Part One: The Need for a Strong State to Arbitrate and Coordinate in the Interest of the Common Good

The French society of the 17th and 18th centuries was thus still essentially a society of corporations and communities, retaining their own powers, liberties, and privileges. The danger threatening a society of this kind was that particularism, fragmentation, incoherence, and the clash of interest groups might escalate to the point of separatism, civil war, dislocation of the state, and its dismemberment by neighboring powers. In order to survive, such a society needed to have a state that was especially strong.

Historians have sometimes been astonished by the concentration of all powers—legislative, executive, and judicial—in the hands of one man, the king, and by the absence of political organs designed to safeguard individual rights. However, even without considering the independence of the nation in relation to the emperor and the pope—the freedom of the kingdom itself, that basic freedom without which all the others would have been illusory and which called for a strong government—what had to be united inside the kingdom was a hierarchy of *seigneuries,* orders, and corporations—religious, craft, university, intellectual, municipal, provincial—each with its own liberties and privileges. The king's theoreticians tried to define these privileges and liberties as so many advantages granted in return for a service rendered to society, with the king as sole dispenser of such advantages. But those concerned all tried to maintain that their privileges and liberties were rights, derived either from an irrevocable royal concession, from immemorial possession, or from the nature of things. *Seigneurs* and corporations claimed to share in sovereignty. The corporations wanted to issue *règlements* of a legislative character, although, from the beginning of the 16th century, the *parlements* set themselves against this usurpation. Among the *seigneurs,* the princes of the blood and certain grandees claimed to sit in the king's Council and participate in the running of the state, as though the Crown had been given to a family or to a body of aristocrats. They claimed the right to obtain governorships of provinces, to hold these by inheritance, and to exercise in their governorates all the royal powers and enjoy all the attributes of sovereignty. Their aim was to divide up sovereignty, to transform the monarchical state into an aristocratic one, to turn the clock back, and, as it was put in the days of the League, to return to the institutions of Hugues Capet's time, or "even better, if possible."

We need to appreciate the degree of particularity of the provinces, separated by differences of language, custom, and civilization. We need to understand the strength of the bonds of fealty that united the princes of the blood and the grandees with the humblest *gentilshommes,* the king's officials and the *"bourgeois"* of the towns and *bourgs,* and those linking the *seigneurs* with their peasants, bonds which greatly facilitated rebellion. We need to keep in mind the brittleness of the society, always living at the margin of subsistence, in which two bad harvests meant famine and economic crisis, accentuating social conflicts and hurling on to the roads thousands of nomads and vagabonds, who soon became concentrated in the towns, swelling the ranks of the journeymen and small master craftsmen in distress—a mass of people ready to set itself in motion at the first disturbances started by some grandee or the first incitements from a *parlement.* Revolt and civil war were always an endemic threat in this form of society.

When the epidemic of internal troubles was unleashed, when armed bands stalked the roads and barricades were raised in the towns, with aristocratic factions waging war among themselves and against the king, when houses were being set on fire and cattle, harvests, and reserve stocks were being carried off, when women and girls were being raped, when the peasants were being tortured by the soldiers to make them hand over their money—what then became of the rights of individuals? The rights of the strong were well enough safeguarded by the nature of things. The rights of the others seemed for a long time to be safeguarded only by the power of the king. The reason behind the emphasis laid by many theoreticians on the royal sovereignty, and the efforts made to render it as perfect as possible, was that for a long time it seemed to be a condition for survival.

2

The State and the State's Resources

15

The State

In the 17th century, thanks to Jean Bodin's *République* (1576) and Charles Loyseau's *Traité des seigneuries* (1611), two conceptions of the state were brought together: the state as a thing and the state as a sovereign person.

The older of the two, current from the ninth century onward, was the conception of the state as a thing. The state was the *respublica,* "the public thing," the totality of the collective interests of the nation, or, more concretely, as Bodin put it: "A commonwealth is the rightly ordered government of a number of families and of those things which are their common concern."[1] Now, the word "family" has two meanings. It signifies the natural family, those persons who are united by ties of blood. It signifies also "corporation," a term embracing corps, college, craft guild, bodies of officials, universities, the dukes-and-peers as a group, and so on. "The family is a natural community, the guild a civil one . . . The origin of all corporate associations and guilds is rooted in the family . . . Many families and tribes . . . united together . . . formed a commonwealth."[2] Unity, cooperation, are in fact obligatory—if need be, without any division of labor between the "families" but usually with a social division of labor, a specialization which is the condition for excellence in the performance of a social function and for the development of the individual, a division of labor effected through the mediation of corps, colleges, and corporations of one kind and another.

The conception of the state as a sovereign person arose more recently, out of scholasticism, appearing first, it seems, in the 13th century. Sovereignty, as distinct from *respublica,* was needed in order to cause all the families, corps, colleges, and corporations to act jointly, to provide them with the same will, the same purpose, and the same means. Sovereignty implies a free intelligence and will that can be possessed only by a single person (or, perhaps, group of persons)—a head or chief of state.

Bodin and Loyseau brought these two conceptions together. Bodin: "A commonwealth is the rightly ordered government of a number of families and of those things which are their common concern, *with a sovereign power*...Many families and tribes...united together... formed a commonwealth *by means of a sovereign power.*" Loyseau: "The state and sovereignty, taken *in concreto,* are synonymous."[3] Loyseau and Bodin thus ensured the development of the theory of the state as a person.

The state is a person, a juridical person, an entity in law, which unifies the members of the community in a state corporation. The characteristic features of the state are: spontaneity, unity, continuity, and power.

The state is a spontaneous, natural organism, resulting from the needs inherent in human nature, issuing from the natural laws that govern the development of societies, which are necessary facts, independent of man's will. The state comes into being spontaneously, without men thinking about it. When men start to be aware of the state, it has already existed long since.

The state realizes the unity of a plurality of individuals, forming from them an indivisible community, a subject in law which is distinct from and superior to the individuals composing it. The state reduces individual wills to a single will, makes of the members of the community an organic unity of persons, a corporate entity. This single will is expressed by a special organ, an individual, or groups of individuals, given by juridical statute the quality of deciding and acting in the name of the corporation so as to express the latter's profound will, independent of and superior to the wills of its individual members.

The state expresses the continuity of the community. It is immutable, permanent, perpetual, always the same, regardless of its transient membership. Louis XIV gave expression to this continuity on his deathbed: "I am leaving you, but the state will always remain." What follows from this is that decisions or commitments undertaken in the state's name—laws, regulations, contracts, treaties—survive the individuals who decreed them, the government which passed them, and the generation in which they originated. What follows also is that, though the state must have a form of government, it still remains even if the form of government changes.

The essence of the state is domination, "the power to command absolutely and with a coercive authority which cannot be legally resisted." This power is indivisible, but it manifests itself in three great functions, which are inseparable, namely, justice, legislation, and administration, which serve to fulfill the three fundamental tasks of the state: ensuring security from attack from without, ensuring order and regularity within, and creating the conditions for material and moral well-being. Competences varying in number and extent can be grouped under these main headings.

The community comes together spontaneously and entrusts the power to express its single will to an organ in the form of one man or a group of men. In expressing this collective will, the organ makes the community an entity, a juridical person. A day comes when this juridical person gives itself a *statute,* a constitution, which regulates the form of the state, that is to say, determines who the real persons are in whom the state power is embodied for the time being: king, assembly, elected president, dictator, *Führer,* etc. If the wielder of the state is a physical person, two cases are possible: the state can be either a monocracy or, if it is obliged to respect fundamental laws, the rights of corporations, etc., a monarchy. If state power is held by a social group, the state can be an aristocracy (rule of the best) or an oligarchy (rule of the few, usually the richest). If state power belongs to the citizens as a whole, the state is a democracy.

The statute regulates the form of government. It determines which persons are to exercise state power, the procedures they are to follow, and in whose interest they are to act.

We call the fundamental statute of the state the "constitution." Constitutions are usually customary in character. They result from a consensus, a spontaneous and often tacit concordance of wills recognizing the need for the state and submission to the state as the only way of satisfying a large number of collective needs and interests. Such a constitution is an aggregate of customs, together with some written laws, known as the "fundamental laws." Typical of customary constitutions is the British constitution, an aggregate of customs, together with some written laws: Magna Carta, the Petition of Right, the Bill of Rights, etc.

In the 18th century there appeared in the countries of European civilization—the Western world—constitutions that were set out as a written law, fundamental and systematic in character, which imposed certain precise conditions upon the relationship between the state's powers and upon the relations between the government and its citizens. The first constitutions of this kind were those that some of the English colonies in North America gave themselves after their emancipation in 1776, followed by the constitutions of the United States—the Articles of Confederation in 1781 and the federal Constitution of 1787—and the French Constitution of 1791. In the last quarter of the 18th century the European world entered a "constitutional period." Written, systematic constitutions became widespread in the 19th century. By 1914, only Britain and Hungary still had "customary" constitutions. Transition to the written, systematic type of constitution took place when consensus, the spontaneous harmony of wills recognizing necessity, was replaced by contract—conscious agreement, given formal expression, with clauses needing to be set out in the clearest, most detailed, and most finished form. Written, systematic constitutions appeared thereafter to be the only genuine constitutions. "A society in which the observance of the law is not assured or the separation of powers defined has no constitution at all," declares the Declaration of the Rights of Man and of the Citizen (1789), in its article 16.

The word "*constitution*" existed in the French language of the 17th century, but not with the meaning that became general in the last quarter of the 18th. Bossuet seems to have been the first to use the word in the sense of "fundamental law determining the form of government." Von Wartburg claimed to have encountered the word, used to mean "constitutive law which establishes the constitution of a state," in a document of 1488,[4] but this would appear to be an isolated instance.

In the 17th century, "*constitution*" meant "law," "decree," "regulation," or else the arrangement of the universe, a continent, a kingdom, an organism, or the human body.[5] For "constitutive law" the French had an approximate expression—"fundamental laws." This was an approximation, not an equivalent, for, like the British constitution, the constitution of France was customary in character. Further-more, it was not a contract, entered into between the nation and the king and his family, but a statute.

The statute of the French state:
The fundamental laws

The statute of the French state had already been formulated by the jurists of the late 14th century, under the influence of Aristotelian doctrine and scholastic thought. At the end of the 14th century, in the dialogue called *Le Songe du Verger,* the Chevalier du Songe expressed the view of the jurists regarding the "fundamental laws" of the king-dom:

> a king has been ordained and established . . . by the will and ordinance of the people, for any people that is not subject to a king or an emperor may by the law of nations choose and make a king . . . It is ordained by the people's will that kings shall come in either by succession or by election . . . , for everyone when he grants something may set whatever law or condition he pleases. Therefore a people, when it appoints a new king to rule over it, submitting persons and property to him as sovereign, may set a law or condition, provided that this be reasonable.[6]

What is involved, then, is not a contract but a statute imposed on the king by the people.

This theory was made more precise by Jean de Terre-Rouge in his treatises of 1419 on the succession to the throne and the rights of the dauphin, which were printed in Lyons in 1526 and republished by François Hotman in 1585 (*Disputatio de controversia successionis regia*). Transmission of the Crown took place by mere force of custom, imposed on the king. Actually, the custom had been established that consent must be given by the three estates of the realm—clergy, nobil-ity, and third estate—"and by the whole civil or mystic body of the realm" (*totius civilis sive mystici corporis regni*), to which belonged, by common law, the institution and election of the king. The royal dignities belonged to the whole "civil or mystic body of the realm," just as the ecclesiastical dignities belonged to the Church; con-sequently, the head of the realm might do nothing to the detriment or against the will of those to whom these dignities belonged. The organi-zation of the ruling power and the choice of princes was in the hands of the people, and the king was not allowed to alter what had been laid down as the public statute of the kingdom: *"Regi non licet immutare ea quae ad statum publicum regni sunt ordinata."* Therefore, this was not a constitution arrived at by contract but a statute imposed by custom.

The statute was expressed in the "fundamental laws," the chief of which were not written but customary. Royalty was a function of which the king had "a sort of power of administration and use that he enjoys for his lifetime, but of which he is not the owner" (Juvénal des Ursins).

The first of the fundamental laws was the Salic Law, "graven in the hearts of the French" and confirmed by the *arrêt* of Gilles Lemaistre, promulgated by the Paris *parlement* on 28 June 1593. "This is not a written law but one that was born with us, that we have not invented but drawn from nature itself, which has taught us that this is so, and given us this instinct."[7]

The Salic Law was the foundation that ensured the survival of the realm of France. The kingship was not bestowed by election, nor was it bestowed by pure heredity, as in common law, for the king was not the owner of the kingdom, and so the kingship was not hereditary. The kingship was bestowed by right of succession. Males were called to succeed, in order of primogeniture, without any limitation, although consanguinity was normally regarded as ended at the seventh or the tenth degree of relationship.

This law was considered to be to the public advantage. If the king had been elected, what acts of violence, assaults, deeds of vengeance, and murders there would have been, since the laws would have been suspended during the election! If the king had been free to choose the most capable among his sons, what parricides, fratricides, and bloody civil wars would have ensued! The exclusion of females, and of males descended in the female line, was "in conformity with natural law, which, having made woman imperfect and weak in both body and mind, has subjected her to the power of man."[8] The Salic Law thus provided the best guarantee for the tranquillity and well-being of everyone.

This law bound the king. It was not dependent on his will. Rather was it the case that the royal right and power depended on the authority of the law of the kingdom which had disposed of them.[9] Thus, the Salic Law placed the state above the king. Without this fundamental law there would have been no king, and the king could not touch this law. It was a constitutional law, anterior to the ordinary laws, a law which the legislative power had to respect, being unable either to abrogate or to amend it. The French constitution was "rigid," whereas the British constitution remained "flexible." In Britain there was no difference between the constitutional laws and the ordinary ones. Provided the common law and the rights of Englishmen were respected, Parliament—that is, the totality made up of king, Lords, and Commons—could legislate on the constitution just as freely as on any other matter. The king of France could not do this.

In July 1714 Louis XIV made his legitimized bastards, by edict, eligible to succeed to the throne if the legitimate branch of his descendants should die out. He was violating the constitution: it was an act of tyranny. The princes of the blood, the grandees, the *parlements*, all the constituted bodies of the realm, had the right to recall the king to a respect of the fundamental laws and, if need be, to depose him.

In order to avoid greater evils, the authorities kept silent for the time being. However, in July 1717 an edict revoked the one issued by Louis XIV and recalled that the king could not, by his own authority, modify the fundamental statute of the realm—could not dispose of the Crown, which was his to wear only for the good of the state. Underlying this was the idea that, if there was no longer any heir to the throne, the nation recovered the right to dispose of the Crown in favor of whomsoever it chose.

By the Treaty of Utrecht in 1713 the British obliged the former duc d'Anjou, King Philip V of Spain, to renounce the Crown of France. But this renunciation was null and void, for no one who might inherit the Crown could renounce his rights, since these were fixed by the custom of the kingdom. Philip V and his descendants retained all their rights to the Crown of France.

The second fundamental law was constituted by the oaths sworn by the king at his consecration.[10] The king swore two successive oaths: the first to the bishops of France, the second to the Christian people of France. To the bishops he undertook to maintain their canonical privileges, their laws and justice, and to defend them. To the French people the king promised to keep them and the Church in peace, to prevent rapacities and iniquities affecting any of the orders and "estates" of the realm, to preserve equity and mercy in his judgments, and to drive out heretics denounced by the Church.

The king came of age at thirteen. This was the third fundamental law. By Charles V's ordinance of 1374, after their thirteenth birthday, when they entered their fourteenth year, the kings of France were adults, free of tutelage, and capable of governing their realm, "for it has often been observed that these persons anointed by Heaven's special favor are commonly enriched while still young with many virtues and fine qualities which are not to be found in others of baser condition." The ordinance created a juridical fiction: the king, once adult, takes command in person, so that no one may disobey him. The king's majority put an end to the claims of the princes of the blood during regencies and to refusals to obey, which had frequently occurred during royal minorities.

The fourth fundamental law was laid down by the edict of April 1403, confirmed in December 1417. The king's legitimate successor was regarded as being king from the moment of his predecessor's death, provided that he got himself consecrated as soon as possible. It was no longer the consecration that made the king but hereditary vocation alone, as decided by custom. "The King is dead, long live the King." "In France, kings do not die." The *grand maître de France* uttered the first of these formulas on the balcony of the royal bedchamber as soon as the king had breathed his last. He repeated it when the king's body was placed in the vault of the basilica of Saint-Denis. The symbols of royalty—the banner, the sword, the "hand of justice"—were laid beside the coffin. Then they were lifted up again, as the new king was acclaimed. The king wore purple from the moment of his predecessor's death, for which he did not go into mourning. In this way was symbolized the continuity of the royal function, expressing the continuity of the state. Several consequences followed. The ordinances of the late king remained valid after his death without need of express confirmation. The treaties he had signed with foreign princes remained in force, though the new king could denounce them if he chose. Privileges were confirmed, though it was not obligatory upon the king to renew them. The incumbent officials were confirmed in office by *lettres de cachet* or letters patent. The levying of the *don du joyeux avènement* was equivalent to a general confirmation. Louis XIV renounced this *don*. The king did not inherit his predecessor's debts but in practice always accepted them, and so the king's indebtedness committed the state.

The inalienability of the Crown's domain was the fifth fundamental law. The royal domain was treated as being like the domain of the Roman people and therefore untouchable. This was an old-established principle. It was confirmed by the Ordinance of Moulins, February 1566, and that of Blois, May 1579. The royal domain was absolutely inalienable unless the Estates General consented to alienation. This principle was given an international dimension. The king could not cede to a foreign power any part of his kingdom without the express consent of the people of the district concerned and the people of the kingdom as a whole. The domain was inalienable and imprescriptible. Consequently, in 1526, after the Treaty of Madrid, by which King François I ceded the duchy of Burgundy to the Emperor Charles V, the protest made by the Burgundian estates enabled the French king to retain this province. The edict of July 1717 proclaimed that the king was "fortunately powerless" to cede the domain of the Crown.

The sixth fundamental law was the principle of Catholicity. Proclaimed by the Estates General assembled at Blois in 1588, it was confirmed by Henri IV's abjuration on 5 July 1593 and his consecration at Chartres in February 1594. France could entrust its fate only to a Catholic prince.

The king of France was thus in no way a private person. Everything about him was absorbed by his royal function. The normal family "statute" was overturned as far as the French royal family was concerned. The younger sons lost their hereditary rights of inheritance. They could obtain only an inalienable and retractable appanage. The patrimony of the royal family had passed to the Crown. The king possessed nothing of his own. He had no private life. He lived in public. He ate in public. The queen of France gave birth in public. The preamble of the edict of 1607, by which Henry IV joined to the Crown the patrimony of his Bourbon ancestors, proclaimed this law: "Our predecessors dedicated and consecrated themselves to the public, from whom they wished to possess nothing distinct or separate." The king was thenceforth exclusively a public personage, the first servant of the state.

The mystic body of the monarchy

The king held his power by a customary statute. His power was therefore limited by the fundamental laws. But he was the head of a society that considered itself Christian. Christ came to fulfill the old Law, not to destroy it. And in the Old Testament the kings, chosen by God, were anointed. They bore a religious character. This divine choice was not in conflict with the customary statute, for God's choice is exercised through intermediaries. There was an analogy here with the choice of a pope, designated by God and elected, under the influence of the Holy Spirit, by the cardinals. When the pope accepts his election, the Holy

Spirit fills him with the graces peculiar to his estate, and he is the Elect of God.

The anointed king

The king was anointed. This fact was expressed in the ceremony of the anointment at Rheims, the *"mystère du sacre."*[11] The archbishop of Rheims carried this out between the office of Terce and High Mass, before the altar, flanked by the ecclesiastical peers on one side and the lay peers on the other. Near the altar stood the abbot of Saint-Denis, who had charge of the royal ornaments and vestments: spurs, sword, tunic, dalmatic, royal mantle, scepter, and "hand of justice."

The archbishop of Rheims received the king's oath to the Church. Then the king was "raised from his chair by the said bishops of Laon and Beauvais, who, themselves also standing, ask of the people and those round about them whether they recognize him as their king; and, having received the assent of the people and all those present, Monseigneur de Rheims causes him to take the oath to the kingdom . . . which is the holy and sacred bond of the fundamental laws of the state."[12]

The king's oath to the people was thus given after the people had accepted him as king. Consequently, this oath did not represent a condition nor did it sanction a contract. It was obligatory only because the king was the people's first official, their first servant.

The king was then anointed with a mixture of chrism and oil from the Holy Phial. The former was oil mixed with balsam, consecrated by a bishop and used for the sacraments of baptism, confirmation, and ordination. The Holy Phial was a small bottle which had been, so tradition claimed, brought by a white dove to Saint-Rémy, bishop of Rheims, for the baptism of the Frankish King Clovis. The archbishop of Rheims anointed the king in nine places on his body: the top of his head, his chest, between his shoulders, his right and left shoulders, the joints of both his arms, and his two palms. Each time, the archbishop said: "Ungo te in regem, de oleo sanctificato, in nomine Patris et Filii et Spiritus Sancti"—"I anoint thee king, with holy oil, in the name of the Father, the Son, and the Holy Ghost." Everyone present answered: "Amen." This ceremony recalled the anointing of King David by Samuel and that of King Solomon by Nathan; that of Aaron, Moses' mouthpiece, as high priest; that of the priests, kings, and prophets who had ruled over Israel. The result was that "le roi n'est pas pur lai"—

"the king is not merely a layman." He was the leading ecclesiastical personage in the kingdom, "the bishop from without." He received communion in both kinds, like the priests. He could preside over the Council of the Church of France and make laws, ordinances, and pragmatic sanctions concerning the liberties and franchises of the Church of France.

The king as miracle-worker

The outward sign of his sacred character was that the king of France was a miracle-worker. The day after his consecration the king went to Saint-Marcoul for a novena. There, for the first time, he touched "persons suffering from *écrouelles,* the healing of which is specially assigned by God to the king of France." *Ecrouelles* were glandular inflammations due to tuberculosis or scrofula—the "King's evil." On Wednesday, 20 October 1610, and the morning of the following day, Louis XIII touched 868 sick persons, uttering as he did so the sanctified formula: "The king touches you, God heals you." Louis XIV, having been consecrated on Sunday, 7 June 1654, touched on Tuesday, 9 June, 3,000 sufferers from *écrouelles.* Louis XV, consecrated on Sunday, 25 October 1722, waited until 19 November before touching 2,000 scrofula patients. In the 18th century the formula became: "The king touches you, may God heal you." Thereafter the king repeated this ceremony throughout his lifetime, every year on the great feast days of the Church. On each occasion there were some recoveries. This power of the king's gave the French monarchy an extraordinary aura. Sick persons came from the remotest provinces of the kingdom and even from countries whose princes were at war with France—Spain, the Empire. Other rulers took umbrage at this.

In the opinion of contemporaries, the king of France was thus one of God's favorites. Another proof of this special status was, for them, "the long duration of the royal dynasty of France." "We see before us today the lineage of King Hugues, called Capet, which is a most certain proof of God's blessing, for it has never, perhaps, happened before in a kingdom that the male line lasted so long."[13]

> God has given the kings of France so many demonstrations of his grace and favor: by the said holy liquid sent down from Heaven for the baptism and consecration of Clovis, the first king of France to be reborn of the spirit; by the granting of the *fleurs de lys,* so greatly celebrated in Holy Scripture; by their right of precedence over all

other monarchs . . . ; besides the miraculous healing of *écrouelles*
and the conservation of the state over such long period, that he
seems to have wished to raise these kings in glory and honor above
all their fellows.[14]

The "mystery of the monarchy"

At the consecration, after the anointment, the celebrant recalled the
claims of the king of France in relation to England. Then he proceeded
to bless the gloves, the ring, the scepter, and the "hand of justice." By
assuming the ring, the king of France espoused the kingdom. The archbishop of Rheims set it on the third finger of his right hand, "because
on the day of his consecration the king solemnly wed his kingdom and
was by the sweet, gracious, and kingly bond of marriage inseparably
united with his subjects, to love each other mutually even as spouses
do."[15]

The king and the kingdom were united by a kind of sacrament. Just
as husband and wife are to be "one flesh," so must the king and the
kingdom be one. This was the source of the theory of the mystic body
of the monarchy. "The king is the head, and the people of the three
orders are the members, and all together form the political and mystic
body of which the unity is undivided and inseparable, so that no part
can come to harm without the rest suffering thereby."[16]

The consequences of this doctrine were serious. The king, as head,
interpreted the needs and wishes of the body. He sensed, understood,
and distinguished the body's profound will, even when this was hardly
conscious or not conscious at all. This was why, in the Estates General
and in *lits de justice* in his *parlement,* he could make final decisions that
ran counter to the view of the majority. This profound and constant
harmony between the king's will and the real will of his people, this
royal infallibility, so to speak, was what contemporaries meant by "the
mystery of the monarchy." From it resulted the king's power to govern
on his own, to decide matters for himself. He received special graces
from Heaven for that purpose, and nobody could act in his place.

The king by divine right

After the blessing of the gloves, ring, scepter, and "hand of justice"
came the coronation. The archbishop of Rheims held the crown over
the king's head. All the peers supported it. Prayers were said for the

king: "tu contra omnes adversitates, Ecclesiae Christi defensor assistas, regnique tibi a Deo dati"—"that thou mayest be, against all adversities, the helper and defender of the Church of Christ and of the kingdom *which has been given thee by God."*

The king received the kingdom from God. He was king by the grace of God. He was God's mandatory. Indeed, according to Saint Paul, inspired by God, all power comes from God: "Omnis potestas a Deo." The king was king "de par Dieu." For a long time the French thought that he held his kingdom from God only mediately, through the people. However, after two kings of France had been murdered in a space of twenty-one years, (especially after the murder of Henri IV by Ravaillac), and after the Estates General of 1614–15, the idea became established that the king held his powers directly, immediately from God, without the people acting as go-between. This was the theory of kingship by divine right. At the Estates General of 1614–15 the third estate implored the king to proclaim it as a fundamental law of the monarchy that he held his crown only from God:

> That, as he is acknowledged sovereign in his state, holding his crown only from God, there is no power on earth, of whatever kind, spiritual or temporal, that has any right over his kingdom, to deprive it of the sacred persons of our kings, or to dispense or absolve their subjects of the fealty and obedience that they owe them, for any cause or pretext whatsoever. That all subjects, of whatever quality and condition they may be, shall hold this law to be sacred and authentic, as being in conformity with God's Word . . . That the contrary opinion, namely, that it is permissible to kill or to depose our kings, to rise in rebellion against them and throw off the yoke of obedience to them, for any reason whatsoever, is impious, detestable, and goes against truth and against the establishment of the state in France, which depends immediately upon God alone.

The clergy, followed by the nobility, were in agreement as far as the security of the king's person was concerned. "It is not permitted for any reason whatsoever to assassinate kings." Those who assassinated kings were anathema—accursed and damned. That was a divine and theological certainty. The clergy and the nobility also agreed that the kings of France were sovereign—that in the mere administration of temporal things they were dependent immediately upon God, recognizing no other power as higher than themselves. This, too, was a certainty, though only a human and historical one. But the clergy and the nobility considered that when a prince had broken the oath he had sworn to God and his subjects, to live and die in the Catholic religion, it might be proclaimed that that prince had forfeited his rights and that his subjects might be released from their oath of allegiance by the pope or by a council of the Church. The third estate could therefore not say that on this point the "article" it advocated was in conformity with God's word, nor could it impose an oath to hold it as such. The third estate was usurping spiritual authority by judging matters of faith and deciding on dogma. There was danger of a schism. Louis XIII himself withdrew the "article of the third estate." But it was eventually revived, by the declaration of 19 March 1682, and became a law of the state.[17] Apart from that, however, everyone agreed that the king held his powers directly from God.

This theory led to the conception of a power that was responsible only to God. Claude de Morenne, *curé* of Saint-Médéric de Paris, said already in his funeral oration for Henri III:

> God, best of fathers and sovereign ruler, . . . being in Himself an infinite essence, invisible and incomprehensible, causes to appear, for the good and comfort of His human creature, some rays of His divinity, by effects proceeding from secondary causes, establishing to this end kings . . . as His vicars and lieutenants, to rule and govern all kingdoms visibly, while He invisibly inspires their souls with the decisions of His supreme will. There is nothing in this world that represents divinity better than kingship and . . . kings are truly . . . the living and animate images of God.[18]

And André Du Chesne, echoing so many others:

> Now, the kings of France are kings elect and chosen of God, kings after His own heart, kings who, by the divine character that His finger has imprinted on their faces, have the honor to stand at the head of all the kings of Christendom, . . . to be suns, and not inferior stars, . . . to be seas of greatness and oceans of all dignity and amplitude. It is their virtues which, like magnificent degrees, have raised them to this sovereign place of honor, and the gifts which God has specially conferred upon them, and which are not shared by other kings, are the wonders which make them objects of admiration to the kings in the remotest parts of the world.[19]

Such conceptions, having become widespread, could lead to the idea of a power with no limits other than those set by the king's conscience as a Christian and, should this conscience become darkened, or should difficulties pile up, to the practice of a power that would be no longer monarchical but quasi-dictatorial.

The king's sovereignty

The duty of the state was to safeguard order, security, personal property, and individual liberty—the foundations of Western civilization.

> Justice being the first and principal *fleuron* in the Crown of kings, by means of which they remain established in the great states entrusted to them by the will and providence of God, and by which they keep their peoples and subjects in peace, unity, concord, and tranquillity, *enabling them to enjoy in peace the* "héritages" *and possessions that justly belong to them,* and defending them against the force, oppression, and violence of the wicked, to do this being the purpose and true end of the establishment of all empires, kingdoms, and principalities.

So speaks Jean Bacquet,[20] expanding Bodin's proposition that "a family is the rightly ordered government of a number of subjects *and of that which belongs to them,* under the authority of a paterfamilias . . . A commonwealth is the rightly ordered government of a number of families and of those things which are their common concern, with a sovereign power."[21]

The means by which these duties were to be performed were the supremacy and sovereignty of the king, who embodied the state.

The royal supremacy

The king was the supreme suzerain. To his quality as king he added that of *seigneur*—"*seigneur* over all," "enfeoffing sovereign." The Crown of France was the supreme fief, and the king the supreme *seigneur*. All Frenchmen might even be regarded as being his vassals. The king had the rights of a *seigneur* over all the people of France.

As such, he was the protector of all vassals and subvassals, and this gave him the right of constant general supervision. As such, all rights of dispensing justice, with all the powers derived therefrom, were dependent upon him.

The royal sovereignty

If the kingdom of France had been alone in the world, the king's feudal superiority as supreme *seigneur* might have sufficed to ensure the functioning of the state, since the royal domain was by far the biggest domain of all and the king indeed the most powerful *seigneur,* in a position to enforce his will. But it was necessary to secure the independence of the king and the state in relation to foreign powers, especially the pope and the Emperor, who claimed supremacy over all princes. And the jurists of the king's courts and councils found in Roman law the tradition of the prince who held both *imperium* and *potestas, solutus legibus*. The needs of defense against external threat, together with the influence of Roman law, ensured the progress of the idea of sovereignty.

According to Jean Bodin, "sovereignty is that absolute and perpetual power vested in a commonwealth."[22] It is not a tyrannical power, for every sovereign is "subject to the laws of God and of nature, and even to certain human laws common to all nations," and, conversely, "it is possible for a subject who is neither a prince nor a ruler to be exempted from all the laws, ordinances, and customs of the commonwealth." However, "it is the distinguishing mark of the sovereign that he cannot in any way be subject to the commands of another, for it is he who makes law for the subject, abrogates law already made, and amends obsolete law." The power to make law implies also the power to command. In this sense "the Prince is above the law." The laws depend on his pure free will, as is expressed in the definitive formula: "For such is our good pleasure."

Nevertheless, kings must obey divine and natural law, for otherwise they are guilty of "treason and rebellion against God." Kings are also bound to keep their agreements and promises, unless these become unjust through the passage of time and changing circumstances. Kings, finally, are obliged to observe those laws "that concern the king's estate, being, like the Salic Law, annexed and united to the Crown."

He is sovereign who is dependent upon no one, who has "the power to make law binding on all his subjects in general and on each in particular, . . . without the consent of any superior, equal, or inferior being necessary." Law is here understood to include privilege—"a concession to one person or to a small group of individuals."[23]

"In this power of making and unmaking law" are included the following powers: to declare war or make peace; to hear appeals from the sentences of all courts whatsoever; to appoint and dismiss the highest officials; to tax subjects or to exempt them from tax burdens; to grant pardons and dispensations from the rigor of the laws; to appreciate or depreciate the standard, value, and weight of the currency; to compel subjects and liegemen to swear to keep fealty, without exception, to him to whom the oath is due, for the king is the guardian of fealties, which are the very framework of the kingdom.[24]

According to Loyseau, sovereignty

consists in power which is absolute, that is, perfect and entire in
every way, ... fullness of power ... without any (qualifying) degree
of superiority, for he who has a superior cannot be supreme and
sovereign; without any limitation as to time, since otherwise this
would be neither absolute power nor even *seigneurie* but a power
entrusted or deposited; and without exception made of any persons
or things belonging to the state, because whatever was excepted
would no longer belong to the state. And just as there can be no
crown that is not a perfect circle, so there can be no sovereignty if
something is lacking in it.[25]

But sovereign power is limited by the laws of God, the rules of
natural justice, and the fundamental laws of the state. And there is
another limitation which is implicit: sovereignty is based on property.
Seigneurie means all power over property, whether public or private.
La terre seigneuriale means land which is endowed with public *seigneurie*, that is, with public power over property. There are two sorts of
public *seigneuries:* suzerain and sovereign. Suzerainty belongs to those
seigneuries which possess power that is superior but not supreme, and
it is held by the *seigneurs*. Sovereignty, with no superior at all, is the
seigneurie of the state. "Sovereignty is quite inseparable from the
state." "Sovereignty is the form that gives existence to the state." The
state and sovereignty, taken *in concreto,* are even synonymous.
Sovereignty is a property of the state—of the Crown, not of the king. It
is to be respected, like all property. But suzerainty is also a property
and is also to be respected, even by the king.

Loyseau goes on to set a third limitation to sovereignty by enumerat-
ing its rights: "to make laws, to create officials, to decide on peace and
war, to be the last instance for appeals, and to mint money." These five
rights, he says, are inseparable from sovereignty, and to encroach upon
them is to commit the crime of *lèse-majesté*.

There might perhaps also be a sixth right—"to raise money from the
people"—but this is "an irregular undertaking and power."

The sovereign must hold his position "only from God and the
sword"; but "the feudatory prince does not cease to be sovereign,
although his sovereignty be not so excellent or so perfect as that which
depends upon no one else," because he does not owe complete obedience but only faith and assistance in war. Dukes, counts, and princes
are well known to be sovereign, even when they are subjects of the
Empire or of France.[26]

Loyseau thus does not go so far as Bodin. He displaces sovereignty, which in itself is not identical with a seignorial property, and which may embrace more or fewer than the six fundamental rights, depending on circumstances. But then, Loyseau was a seignorial official, *bailli* in the county of Dunois for the duchesse de Longueville, and concerned to safeguard as far as possible the rights and powers of the *seigneurs*. His influence was extensive and still effective with the Paris *parlement* at the end of the 18th century.

According to the state councilor Le Bret, who wrote during the Thirty Years' War, "sovereignty is by its nature . . . to royalty what light is to the sun, its inseparable companion . . . The name and quality of sovereignty should be given only to a perfect and complete sovereignty, one that is dependent only upon God and subject only to His laws."[27]

Consequently, one cannot, in his view, call sovereign the kings of Naples, Sicily, Aragon, Poland, Sardinia, Corsica, the Canaries, Jerusalem, or England, who owe to the Church of Rome liege homage and an annual *cens*. Nor can one call sovereign the rulers in Italy and Germany who are vassals or vicars of the Empire and *domestici* of the Emperor. Nor can one call sovereign those kings whose coronation oaths bind them, in relation to their subjects, to observances which infringe sovereignty, such as the king of Denmark, who may not put any nobleman to death or confiscate his property, and who must leave power in the hands of the senate and jurisdiction without appeal in the hands of the *gentilshommes* of his realm.

But "our kings, holding their scepter from God alone, being obliged to make submission to no earthly power whatsoever and, enjoying all rights that are attributed to perfect and absolute sovereignty, . . . are fully sovereign in their realm. This is why, in their letters, they style themselves: 'By the grace of God, kings of France.' " Pope Innocent III acknowledged that the king of France was dependent on no one in respect of his temporal power, and Clement V revoked the decree of Boniface VIII subjecting the temporal power in France to the Holy See. Finally, the king of France is completely independent of the Empire.

The sovereign king exercises many rights. Sovereignty is exclusively his possession: his wife, brothers, and nephews have no share in it. His consent is needed for the marriage of princes of the blood and *grands seigneurs* of his kingdom. He alone may make, change, and interpret laws. It is a crime of *lèse-majesté* to speak ill of him or to attempt to kill him (that, indeed, is the most detestable of crimes, for "the prince is the spirit animating the body of the commonwealth") or to offer threats or conspire against the sovereign state. The king has the power of the sword over all his subjects; he may judge them and sentence them to death. He has no ownership of his subjects' possessions, to dispose of them without their consent, but he may oblige individuals to give up possessions of theirs in time of war, in order to strengthen a fortified place, enlarging its ditches and widening its avenues, burning its suburbs and "creating havoc." He may do this also in peacetime, in pursuit of the public interest, but only if he pays a reasonable price for the property he needs to take. The king alone may convoke the Estates General and the provincial estates. He has jurisdiction over the Church and can make laws relating to ecclesiastical matters. It is for him to authorize new monasteries and new *congrégations*. He nominates to the pope his candidates for the highest dignities of the Church. The king alone can appoint officials and initiate extraordinary commissions. He alone can make war and peace, create military offices, and nominate to them. He alone can dispose of public funds and appoint finance officials. He alone can ennoble persons, naturalize foreigners, and legitimize bastards. He alone can mint money.

Total obedience is due to him, unless his orders are contrary to God's commandments or to justice and equity. Nevertheless, if, though an order seems unjust, its purpose is the good of the state, as when one is commanded to kill a factious and seditious rebel or to invade the territory of a public enemy, "so as to prevent the accomplishment of his designs upon ours," it is necessary to obey without scruple, for such orders will be seen as either just or unjust "depending on the advantage or disadvantage that may result to the state from their execution." *Raison d'état* justifies everything. The sovereign courts ought therefore to obey edicts imposing extraordinary taxes. "If an edict is intended to meet an urgent need for the public good, I presume to say that any resistance to approving it would amount to mere disobedience."[28]

Le Bret thus went further than Jean Bodin and adumbrated the theory of the totalitarian power of a wartime government.

Absolutism and tyranny

Was not an authority like this in danger of being confused with a tyranny pure and simple? That was not the opinion of contemporaries, who saw the sovereign monarchy as royal but not "seignorial" or tyrannical. According to Jean Bodin:

> Royal, or legitimate, monarchy is one in which the subject obeys the laws of the Prince, the Prince in his turn obeys the laws of nature, and natural liberty and the natural right to property are secured to all. Seignorial monarchy is one in which the Prince is lord and master of both the possessions and the persons of his subjects by right of conquest in a just war; he governs his subjects as absolutely as the head of a household governs his slaves. Tyrannical monarchy is one in which the laws of nature are set at naught, free subjects are oppressed as if they were slaves, and their property is treated as if it belonged to the tyrant.[29]

Bodin considered that aristocracies and democracies, too, could be either legitimate, "seignorial," or tyrannical.

Loyseau said much the same thing:

> Seignorial monarchs . . . have both princely power and also full ownership and private *seigneurie* over the persons and property of their subjects, who consequently are not merely subjects but utter slaves, having neither personal freedom nor any *seigneurie* over their possessions, which they hold only as *peculium* and by forbearance on the part of their seignorial prince.
>
> From this it follows that such a seignorial monarchy is directly contrary to nature, which made us all free men, and it is always introduced by mere force, that is, either by internal usurpation on the part of some citizen or by conquest on the part of a foreigner, to whom the laws of war ascribe such *seigneurie* over the conquered, when, being in a position to kill them, the conqueror instead lets them live on the express condition that they accept such servitude.

Loyseau cites as examples of such "seignorial" monarchies those of the Assyrians, the Medes, the Persians, the Turks, the Muscovites, and the Ethiopians, and he concludes: "These seignorial monarchies are barbarous and against nature...They are unworthy of Christian princes."[30]

Altogether different, says Loyseau, is the monarchy of France, which is royal but not "seignorial" and under which the French are free men. "Royal or legitimate monarchy," as Bodin said, "is one in which the subject obeys the laws of the prince, the Prince in his turn obeys the laws of nature, and natural liberty and the natural right to property are secured to all."[31]

These remarks lead to the delimitation of two spheres of law: that

which concerns the royal function, where the king is sovereign and
therefore absolute, and that which concerns the private life of his subjects, in which they are free and may own means of production as well
as consumer goods. This is confirmed by many preambles to royal
edicts. In them the king often distinguishes between "our affairs"—the
affairs of the king, which are "public and political affairs of our
kingdom"—and the rest, which are his subjects' affairs.[32] Normally
the king does not interfere in his subjects' affairs. He is content to
watch over the observation of the good rules and customs that have
become established. If public safety is at stake, he may intervene in the
sphere of his subjects' rights, but only temporarily. The rights of his
subjects, their liberties, franchises, and privileges, form a protected
sector. All these guarantees were destroyed by the Revolution. The
really absolute regimes were those subsequent to the Revolution, in
which the will of the legislator, the will of the majority, became the
highest law, without any safeguard for the citizens—in the first place
for minorities, but also even for those who had elected the majority.

The concentration of powers

The king of France concentrated in his person powers which it has
become habitual with us to distinguish as the legislative, executive, and
judicial powers. He wielded these powers with unlimited competence,
being able to carry out the modes of action appropriate to every case.

The king was the supreme justiciar. He had the power of the sword.
He could condemn men to death without right of appeal. It was his duty
to punish offenses and to stop them from being committed. From this
judicial power followed his power both to make laws and to annul
them. Making laws included all aspects of the power of command.
"The word 'law' . . . means the rightly ordered command of that person or persons having all power over the rest, without anyone being
excepted, regardless of whether this command affects all subjects in
general *or some in particular* . . . To speak more precisely, 'law'
means the sovereign's command affecting all his subjects in general, or
general matters." The king could command by his bare authority, but it
was seemly for him to consult the *parlements* and the principal officers
of the Crown, who were bound by oath to serve and advise him faithfully. The making of law, which originated in the judicial power, thus
implicitly embraced the executive power as well. The three powers
were merged in the king's person.

There was no limit to the king's sphere of competence. Just as the royal function was universal, so was the royal competence universal. The king was, in principle, able to concern himself with everything within his sphere of rights and also, when the public safety was at stake, outside that sphere. He had the power to take cognizance by himself of any question at all that seemed to him to concern the common good, regardless of whether it was a very small matter or a very big one, provided that it affected security, peace, prosperity, or justice. The king concerned himself, in the first place, more especially with external negotiations, military and naval operations, the defense of the realm, internal order, religion, education, poor relief, the economy, and finance. Without claiming to draw up an exhaustive list, we can say that the royal competence covered legislating on ecclesiastical matters; ordering prelates to hold their synods; levying tenths; authorizing new monasteries and *congrégations;* making appointments to certain benefices; nominating to the pope those who were to be the highest dignitaries of the Church; conferring benefices; appointing officials, by sole right; making peace and war; creating nobles; naturalizing foreigners; legitimizing bastards; minting and exchanging money; granting letters of marque and reprisal; establishing postal services; making orders regarding navigable rivers, highways, forests, woods of full-grown trees, hunting grounds, fortified places, mines, metals, taxes, possessions left ownerless by default of heirs, the property of condemned persons; granting exemptions from taxes, privileges, boons, remissions, pardons, *abolitions;* negotiating through ambassadors; signing pacts, treaties, articles of confederation; disposing of the property of private persons for reasons of public utility; authorizing meetings of the Estates General or of provincial estates; founding universities; instituting fairs and public markets; making general regulations for the policing of the realm; correcting, as the highest instance, the errors of his officials and magistrates; judging appeals, civil petitions, allegations of judicial error, contradiction between *arrêts,* removals from one court to another, deprivations of rights, *règlements de juges.*

Personal rule

The king could govern by himself: it was for him alone to decide. "The sovereign power of command is so unique that it cannot be transferred to anyone."[33] Formally excluded from any participation in power were the wives, children, and brothers of kings, the sovereign courts, and the great houses of the kingdom. "The wives of kings abstain completely from dealing with the affairs of the kingdom."[34]

The person nearest to succession to the Crown bore the title: "By the grace of God, eldest son of France and dauphin of Viennois." "Nevertheless, these titles give him no share in sovereignty while his father lives." The king's sons received mere appanages, without any right or prerogative of sovereignty. These appanages were "inseparable from the Crown" and returned to it if the grantee should die without leaving a male heir.

"Although birth and upbringing make brothers to some degree equal, nevertheless, when their eldest brother comes to succeed to the Crown, . . . [the others] must show him all honor and respect, as their king and *seigneur.*"

The king's sons and brothers were not *soluti a legibus,* "above the law." The king alone was not subject to the rigor of the laws, since he could not execute upon himself the penalties they ordained (Saint Thomas, I, 3, *quaest.* 96). However, his sons and brothers were treated more gently than other people. They were never subjected to death by violence but were punished only by being deprived of property, honors, and dignities. It was a matter of decorum for the king, after having taken note of their prudence and good behavior, to give them employment and admit them to his councils, but "they must await this favor from the pure good will of kings and not lay claim to it as being their due."

The princes of the blood and *grands seigneurs* of the realm were not even allowed to marry without the king's consent. By natural right, marriages were not subject to restraint, but it would be greatly to the public detriment if these persons were to marry unsuitably. The king was the father of the kingdom, the leader, guardian, and protector of the princes of the blood and the grandees, and it was forbidden for children to marry without their father's consent. The purpose of marriage was to strengthen families. Through marriages, crowns became powerful and scepters formidable. "Princes and *seigneurs* of note must not enter into any marriage without the king's permission and without first informing him, so that he may decide whether the marriage will be advantageous and honorable for them and for the good of his kingdom."[35]

The sovereign courts had no right to legislate. The king alone had power to command and to issue edicts and ordinances that would ensure justice and peace and redound to the glory of the state. He alone was empowered to publish such decrees and to oblige people to obey them. He alone could (prudently) modify laws—general, provincial, or municipal—explain their meaning, and interpret them. The sovereign courts had no power over the laws. All they could do was to issue public regulations concerning the forms of justice and police, and that only provisionally and within the limits set by the laws and ordinances already promulgated.

The great houses of the kingdom, such as that of the dukes of Lorraine, had no right of legislation. The king had annulled all the private laws that these great houses had given themselves so as to regulate the order of succession in their families otherwise than as provided by the custom of the places where their possessions lay. The duke of Lorraine was unable, without the king's authority, to order, in contradiction to local custom, that his duchy of Bar should in the future be a masculine fief, so as to prevent girls from inheriting it, as he had done in Lorraine. The duchy of Bar was feudally dependent on the Crown of France, and the duke of Lorraine was not allowed to make laws or to introduce new customs there without the king's consent and the approval of the Paris *parlement,* after it had heard the *procureur général.*[36]

Delegation of powers

The king was not able personally to dispense justice to everyone. He could not personally execute all the laws. And it was necessary that the royal powers be exercised in accordance with the forms of law, which were safeguards both for the inhabitants of the kingdom as individuals and for the general good. The king therefore delegated his powers to certain of his subjects to whom he entrusted the task of dispensing justice in his name and making regulations and ordinances for the execution of laws.

In the first place, the king delegated the sovereign power of command—the regency and government of the kingdom and the guardianship of his children—to his wife or to his mother when he traveled far from France and when it was possible that he might die prematurely while his eldest son was not yet fourteen. The king delegated his powers by letters patent which were verified by the *parlement.* He assigned a council to help his wife or mother fulfill her responsibility.

The king delegated his powers of justice and those derived from them, powers of command by way of *arrêts* and ordinances, to bodies of magistrates and to commissioners. This was a delegation of powers,

not a surrender of them. The kings of France "possess in themselves
the full power of magistracy."[37] The king never transferred his own
authority. He always retained the possibility of settling personally matters that were submitted directly to him, of having removed for his
attention matters that had first been brought before his judges, and of
supervising and directing all magistrates in the exercise of their offices.
The judges in the courts were dispensers, not masters, of the authority
which had been entrusted to them. Their role was simply to execute
the power that the king gave them: they did not own it. "It must not be
inferred that they (the kings) have thereby despoiled themselves of
their sovereign authority, any more than one can say, without great
absurdity, that God has deprived himself of his power because he
makes use of secondary causes for the government and conduct of the
universe."[38] The *arrêts* and judgments of the courts were, accordingly,
drawn up in the form of letters emanating from the king. "By virtue of
the public order of the kingdom, his courts judge in his name and he
judges by means of his courts." This power that the king retained over
his magistrates was "of the essence of monarchy."[39]

The first consequence of this was that the principal officials and
magistrates were unable to oppose the king's commands even when
they thought them unjust. They held their powers from the king alone;
they were his subjects like all the rest of the people, and to resist his
ordinances would have meant setting themselves up as his superiors,
overturning the order of the monarchy.

The second consequence was that the laws were authenticated by
affixture of the royal seal, thus being verified by the chancellor, who
could object to the way they were drafted, and were registered by the
courts after they had verified them and had, if need be, entered remonstrance regarding them; this last was dictated by their duty of counsel
and fealty, while the king's readiness to listen to their remonstrances
was a gratuitous act of good will on his part. Verification, registration,
remonstrance—none of these could set an insurmountable barrier in
the path of the king's will. It was for the king to decide whether to pay
attention to them or to ignore them. He always retained absolute authority of decision, for king and kingdom were one, and their advantage
was common and indivisible. The king was the father of his subjects
and had a father's absolute authority. He held his power from God
alone and was not accountable to his children.

It is from me alone that my courts derive their existence and their
authority . . . The plenitude of this authority that they wield in my

name still remains with me . . . It is by my authority alone that the officers of my courts undertake, not the formation, but the registration, publication, and execution of the law, and that they are allowed to present remonstrances to me, as is the duty of good and serviceable counselors.[40]

The same applied to ministers. The only limit to their power was the king's confidence in them. In principle, however, they had no authority. Their decisions were always decisions taken by the king, to whom they conveyed the "file" of matters to be settled and whose rulings they requested. They were individual instruments of the king for the carrying-out of his decisions. They did not constitute a "ministry" or a "cabinet," a formation with collective responsibility. All that a minister did was to obtain and carry out the sovereign's orders. After 1661 the king was solely responsible for directing and auditing the state's finances, with the comptroller general of finance reduced to a mere executor of his orders. The same was true of the secretaries of state. They were not responsible and were accountable to no one. The only person with responsibility was the king. The king was the sole master of power, and he alone wielded it.

The absolute monarchy and the conception of the universe

The concept of the absolute monarchical state can be justified by more than one ideology. In France in the 17th and 18th centuries it was based on a whole cosmology, theology, and mythology. The absolute monarchy of France was bound up with the deeply held feeling that the king was a creature possessed of supernatural virtue and power, a divine being, a seer capable of knowing and foreseeing what was hidden from other men, and thereby in a position to do good to them. The king was endowed with a holy quality; he was consecrated. This was the instinctive feeling of the masses, and on it came to be erected a whole royal mythology.

The royal mythology

In popular opinion, as in the logic of the political writers, the king was a god. The anointment carried out at his consecration transferred him from the profane sphere to the sacred. This view grew and became stronger as time passed. It was at the beginning of the 16th century that

the royal miracle of touching for the "King's evil" was in full development. Under Henri II we find even in Books of Hours "the prayers that
the kings of France are accustomed to say when they wish to touch
sufferers from *écrouelles*."

The king was, by analogy with Jesus Christ, a priest according to the
order of Melchizedek, "the priest of the most high God," as it was laid
down at the Council of Chalcedon (451 A.D.). The Fathers at Chalcedon hailed the Emperor Marcius: "Long life to the priest, to the
basileus." In the *Life of the Emperor Constantine* by Eusebius of
Caesarea the emperor was called "the bishop from without." The *avocat général du roi* in the Paris *parlement*, the future Chancellor
d'Aguesseau, in his address to the Paris *parlement* in 1699 calling for
registration of the bull against Fénelon's *Maximes des saints*, called
Louis XIV "king and priest in one."

More than that: the king was God. Jesus Christ is the priest *par
excellence* because he is God and so can alone offer to God a sacrifice
that is worthy of Him. By analogy, the king-priest was God. Jean
Savaron, *président* and *lieutenant général* of the *sénéchausée* of Auvergne, declared in 1620 that monarchs were gods in flesh and blood.[41]
On 13 May 1625 the bishop of Chartres proclaimed, in the name of the
Assembly of the Clergy of France: "It is therefore to be known that,
besides the universal agreement of peoples and nations, the Prophets
announce, the Apostles confirm, and the Martyrs testify that kings are
ordained of God, and not only that, but they are themselves gods . . .
No one may deny this without blasphemy or doubt it without sacrilege." A royalist pamphlet of the Fronde period bore a revealing title:
"L'Image du Souverain ou l'illustre portrait des divinités mortelles."
And Bossuet, in his "Sermon on the Duties of Kings," on Palm Sunday, 1662, exclaimed: "You are gods."

From the end of the 16th century onward there developed the legend
of the first healing of *écrouelles* by Clovis. This became an article of
faith. All historians have rejected it, but nevertheless it became embedded in popular belief. Desmarets de Saint-Sorlin included the story
in his great epic, *Clovis ou la France chrestienne*.

Jesus Christ was often depicted by the early Christians in the form of
the sun, even in the form of Apollo, the sun god, sending forth rays as
he arrived in his chariot. By analogy, the king was depicted in solar
form. The sun had been the royal emblem since the time of Charles V.
The cult of the king continued the imperial cult of Constantine in his
role as sun god. The sun cult had been practiced since at least the third

millennium before Christ. The sun was thought of as moving over the cupola of the heavens drawn by four horses—Air, Water, Earth, and Fire. It was the sun that gave out the fire of intelligence. The sun ruled the world. Those who directed men's lives on earth were the sun's representatives. The Christian mystics of the first and second centuries ascribed to Jesus Christ the properties of the sun. The church ascribed them to the Christian emperors and, subsequently, to the Christian kings.

So, then, the king of France was the sun. Nicolas Besongne wrote thus in an official handbook, *L'Etat de la France,* in 1663: "Monarchical government is the order established by nature. For, just as there is but one God in the world and one sun over the universe, so there must be but one king in a realm."[42]

This conception resulted in the royal emblems including a whole symbolism of arch and cupola, representing the heavens, the home of the sun. Arch and cupola were monarchical because they symbolized the vault of heaven. The carriage in which the king rode to his consecration had a domed roof. In the rooms where the king lived, even if there was a horizontal ceiling, the junction of the walls with the ceiling was curved, so as to signify an arch, or, in other words, the heavenly vault. When the king left his residence, the heavens were symbolized by a canopy or a parasol held over his head. The king's bed had a tester over it and was set in a recess which represented the heavenly ambience of the sun that was to occupy the bed. In Louis XIV's bedroom in the Tuileries the recess had a vaulted oval above it, and the room itself a cupola that seemed open to the sky, where Apollo appeared, surrounded by the signs of the zodiac. The Hours attended upon the four horses of his chariot, and the Seasons were shown as though carrying the cupola.

A railing barred the entrance to the royal bed-recess. This must never be touched, for that would be like sacrilege or desecration. The railing marked off a space comparable to the chancel, the part of the choir of a church where the priest stands when serving the mass. This space was sacred. Even if the room was empty, visitors removed their hats and, bareheaded, bowed to the empty bed. Ladies made a deep curtsy; even the princesses, even the queen, did this. Everyone spoke in a low voice.

The king was depicted as an Olympian god or at least as a hero of mythology, one of those divine beings who were the offspring of a god and a mortal woman or of a goddess and a man. Christian dogma was transposed into the terms of pagan mythology. This came easily to men saturated from childhood with classical culture, so that the gods and heroes of Homer and Virgil and Ovid's *Metamorphoses* were familiar figures. Moreover, they had been accustomed to these transpositions by the Christian humanism of the late 16th century and the early 17th century, which did not hesitate even to celebrate the Virgin under the name and with the attributes of Diana, the moon goddess, the huntress unwilling to marry.

It was not difficult to translate this transposition into works of plastic art. The king "is the master or, better, the father of the arts and sciences. It is he who gives them being, helps them to grow, and causes them to flourish among his subjects."[43] Louis XIV's little low-ceilinged apartment in the Tuileries, looking out over the garden, was painted, after Mazarin's death in 1661, by Nicolas Mignard, who decorated it with scenes from the legend of Apollo. "All these paintings taken from the story of Apollo are appropriate to the sun, and, besides, they are emblematic representations of the king's great deeds." It was His Majesty that one was supposed to see in the central picture, in the form of Apollo; that one saw surrounded by an aura of glory; that seemed to be raised above everything else; and that, by force of dignity and lofty qualities, spread light over all the earth and inspired admiration from all parts of the world.

By the four separate pictures which he painted on a background of gold the artist sought to convey four important lessons. *The Punishment of the Cyclopes* shows "in what danger any such rash persons would find themselves whose imprudence might lead them to help and give arms to His Majesty's enemies." *The Story of Niobe* shows the inevitable doom awaiting those who might fail in the respect they owe to the sacred person of so powerful a monarch. *The Punishment of Marsyas* shows the punishment deserved by such crude and presumptuous individuals as might dare to compete in the art of leading the peoples with a prince, who knows how to do this with the prudent harmony understood only by those who have been endowed with it by heaven. And from *The Example of Midas* one can perceive how ridiculous those persons make themselves who, out of ignorance or envy, engage in comparisons to the disadvantage of His Majesty's glory.[44]

Like the Tuileries, the Louvre, Vincennes, Saint-Germain, Versailles, and Marly were all temples of the cult of the royal divinity.

Louis XV followed the same line. Although he extensively altered, after 1738, Louis XIV's interior apartments at Versailles and, in particular, ordered in 1755 a transformation of the king's study, he nevertheless remained faithful to the same symbolism, though he made it less ponderous. In the king's study Boucher painted in 1753, in the middle of the ceiling, *The Sun Pursuing Its Course*. The Seasons, represented by children at the corners of the semicircular arches, recalled the symbolism of the cupola and the vault and carried allegorical emblems of the Virtues. By the king's command, Boucher avoided the "modern" style and kept to the "ancient," out of concern for the royal symbolism as much as to fit in with the features of the décor that had been retained. This royal mythology remained official down to the Revolution and even down to Charles X's reign.

The destruction of the royal mythology

However, even under Louis XV, signs of weakening appeared. When, after his consecration, the king touched 2,000 scrofula victims on 29 October 1722, the formula he uttered was modified. The traditional phrase had run: "The king touches you, God heals you" There was no doubt that God would do as the king said. God's grace was certain. His favor could not fail. It was almost a necessary sequence of events. But the new formula said: "The king touches you, may God heal you." A prayer replaced the recording of divine favor. This was no longer the perfect faith that moves mountains and causes Jesus Christ to perform a miracle, no longer quite that which the Gospel promises: "What things soever ye desire, when ye pray, believe that ye receive them, and ye shall have them" (Mark 11:24).

According to the old belief, the miracle-working power was inherent in the person of the consecrated king. He wielded this power whatever his individual characteristics might be, just as, when an unworthy priest consecrates a host in accordance with the rite, it becomes, beneath the appearance of bread, in substance the body of Christ, despite the priest's unworthiness. But in 1739, when Madame de Mailly became Louis XV's mistress, the king's confessor forbade him to take communion. Louis XV did not perform his Easter duty and dared not touch the sufferers from the "King's evil"—as though their healing was dependent on his personal condition. The notion of the touching of the *écrouelles* as a kind of royal sacrament was becoming blurred.

In 1723 the Marquis d'Argenson, intendant of Hainault, encountered a patient who had recovered three months after being touched by the king. He collected authentic testimonies to the truth of this recovery and sent them to Paris. For this he was sharply rebuked by La Vrillière, the secretary of state responsible for the royal household: proofs were not required, everyone was well aware of our kings' divine gift. Fifty-two years later, however, a certain Rémy Rivière, of the parish of Matongues, having been touched by Louis XVI at Rheims, recovered from the sickness. The intendant of Châlons-sur-Marne, Rouillé d'Orfeuil, heard of this. On 17 November 1775 he sent to Versailles a certificate signed by the surgeon, the *curé,* and the principal inhabitants. Secretary of State Bertin thanked him, asked if there had been any other recoveries, and had the relevant certificates sent to him. "Experimental proofs of the miracle were no longer to be disdained."

Voltaire no longer believed in the supernatural power of the miracle-working king and thought that gradually everyone would cease to believe in it. "The time will come when reason, which is beginning to make some progress in France, will do away with this custom."[45]

There were, in fact, several concurrent causes for this weakening of faith in monarchy, their common source being rationalism, which was operative at least partially and latently.

We observe the controversy waged between the French and their enemies of that time. The kings of England claimed to possess the same power as the kings of France, yet they were Anglican and therefore heretics. Accordingly, Catholic writers denied the validity of the English miracles. They said that the "touching for the King's evil" carried out by the kings of England was either an imposture or an illusion. They agreed that there must have been a collective delusion on a very large scale. Alas, the proofs invoked for the Bourbons were no different from those that applied in the case of the Tudors and Stuarts.

The Habsburgs inspired an attack on this supernatural power that conferred an aureole of prestige upon the kings of France. In 1635 the *Mars Gallicus* of Alexander Patricius Armacanus (Jansenius) sought to show that the gift of miraculous power is given by God gratuitously and so proves neither the sanctity nor the superiority of the beneficiary. Balaam's ass prophesied, but it did not follow therefrom that she had the right to hold supreme power over the race of asses. Pamphlets like this killed wonderment, extinguished sentiment, and gave free rein to dry reason, opening the way to negation.

The influence of Protestantism tended toward skepticism in this matter. For the Calvinists, Jesus Christ alone worked miracles. Denying all the sacraments save two, and refusing to believe that the sacraments operate by themselves, *ex opere operato,* the Calvinists consistently regarded the anointment of the king as a mere symbol and the healing of the "King's evil" as an accident or an illusion. They did not believe that the king was a superman. Besides, if he was really in receipt of special graces from God, he would become a convert to Calvinism. The king was just a sinner like everybody else. They supported absolutism, but only on the basis of Saint Paul's teaching that all power comes from God.

Working in the same direction was the influence of Augustinianism, which became widespread in the 17th and 18th centuries, and of that deviation from it, Jansenism, so strong in France, an expression of which we have just mentioned—*Mars Gallicus.* Conceiving the most lofty idea of the greatness and omnipotence of God and impressed by the weaknesses and miseries of mankind, the Jansenists formed the notion of a terrible God whose designs are unfathomable and whose decrees are beyond our understanding. Without this God, man can do nothing. Man goes wherever his pleasure and gratification lead him, and, since the Fall, they have led him only into evil. His intelligence works in a void and can attain to no reality; his reason, contradictory and various, is a joke; his will, mere impotence. Man is a plaything. Crushing external forces, the fortuitous play of circumstances, habit and custom, these are what guide him, making him turn about like a weathercock with every wind that blows. Egoism, self-regard, individual appetite, these are his driving forces. Man can do nothing about it. But God, the All-Powerful, by his grace causes man to find gratification in the observance of his commandments. God gives this grace to men whom he has chosen from all eternity, whom he has predestined. Christ died for them alone, redeemed only them. They are a very small group. They cannot avoid God's grace, it is imposed upon them. Man is not free, he is God's slave.

This kind of psychology and theology went badly with the idea of the king as hero, the divine king, the king as God. To be sure, one could still claim that the king benefited from special graces, but these were not obvious in the behavior of a Louis XIII, a Louis XIV, or a Louis XV, poor men who could not resist sinning. The Jansenist doctrine was not easy to reconcile with the foundations of the idea of absolute monarchy.

The success of Stoicism, which was so strong in the second half of the 17th century, and the influence of which, through Descartes and

Voltaire, did not fall off until the Revolution, also contributed to sapping the foundations of the absolute monarchy. Stoicism operated both indirectly and through the medium of Roman law, which it underlay. Stoicism contained an element that was fatal to the idea of the king as a supernatural personage, namely, the idea of the identical nature of all men, equal in their free will and their reason, which led to the conception of a society of men equal before the law, free, self-governing, and legislating for themselves. Roman law took over the Stoic idea and treated men as having emerged all equal from the hands of Nature— equally free, equally noble, all children of the same father, all members of one and the same body. Going further, Roman law took in natural law, which it regarded as common to the human race and all the animal creation and as affecting marriage and the begetting and upbringing of children. Civil law confirmed natural qualities and made them more inviolable. Thereby, however, it drew attention, first and foremost, to what is common to all living creatures, their physical, biological qualities, the fact of being male or female, major or minor, over or under the age of puberty, etc., and to those inequalities which result from nature itself. The consequence was a state of mind not very favorable to the supernaturalism of the royal mythology.

Finally, and especially, mechanism and Cartesianism proved fatal to this mythology. Mechanism contributed its demand for experimental reasoning and proof, and Cartesianism a whole logic and metaphysics that were opposed to the supernatural and miraculous. Sharply separating the things of the body from those of the spirit, so that it is no longer clear how the one can influence the other; placing the spirit absolutely outside the realm of nature; reducing matter to geometrical extent—all this meant, in fact, rendering impossible any intervention by the Spirit in the affairs of the world, ruling out any Providence and any miracle, and drying up the springs of those graces that made the king a divine being and miracle-worker. Breaking down reality into minute questions, so as the better to answer them, and proceeding always from what is simplest and apparently most obvious, in order to ascend by imperceptible steps to the most complex, and accepting only what has emerged as perfectly clear and distinct—these methods were contrary to the movement of faith.

In this way the ideological bases of the absolute monarchy were gradually undermined in France.

Notes

1. Jean Bodin, *République*, bk. 1, chap. 1.

2. Ibid., bk. 3, chap. 7.

3. Charles Loyseau, *Traité des seigneuries*, chap. 2, pp. 5, 6.

4. *Französisches etymologisches Wörterbuch* (Leipzig: Teubner, 1940).

5. Loyseau, *Traité des Ordres et simples dignitez*, in *Oeuvres* (Paris, 1610), from the foreword (1609).

6. *Le songe du Verger*, bk. 1, chap. 78.

7. Jérôme Bignon, *De l'excellence des Roys et du Royaume de France* (Paris, 1610), p. 254.

8. Le Bret, *Souveraineté*, vol. 1, p. 4.

9. Poisson de la Bodinière, *Traité de la Majesté royale en France* (1597), p. 6.

10. Théodore Godefroy and Denis Godefroy, *Cérémonial Français* (1649), pp. 59–60.

11. Ibid., pp. 54 ff.: "The modern formulary for the consecration and coronation of Louis XIII, 17 October 1610."

12. Ibid., p. 361.

13. Guy Coquille, *Institution au droit des Français* (1607), p. 2.

14. Jean Richer, *Cérémonies du sacre et couronnement du Très Chrétien Roi de France et de Navarre Louis XIII*, reproduced in Godefroy, vol. 1, p. 412.

15. Godefroy, p. 369.

16. Guy Coquille, *Discours des Etats de France* (1588), in *Oeuvres*, vol. 1, p. 322.

17. Augustin Thierry, *Recueil des monuments inédits de l'histoire du Tiers-Etat*, vol. 1, introduction, p. clxi, n. 1.

18. Claude Demorennes, *Oraison funèbre de Henry III, en l'église Saint-Médéric, le 21 aôut 1589* (Paris: Jamet Mettayer & Pierre l'Huillier, 1595; B.N.: LB 34-816).

19. André du Chesne, *Antiquitez*, pp. 2–3.

20. Jean Bacquet, *Traités des droits de justice haute, moyenne et basse* (1577), p. 1; in Bacquet, *Oeuvres*, ed. Claude de Ferrière (Paris, 1688).

21. Bodin, *République* (1583 ed.), bk. 1, chap. 2, p. 10, and chap. 1, p. 4.

22. Ibid., chap. 8, p. 122.

23. Ibid., chap. 10, p. 211.

24. Ibid., p. 223.

25. Loyseau, *Traité des seigneuries* (1609), chap. 2, no. 8.

26. Ibid., nos. 43, 94.

27. Le Bret, *De la souveraineté* (1632), vol. 1, p. 2.

28. Ibid., vol. 2, chap. 6, pp. 188 ff.

29. Bodin, *République* (1583), bk. 2, chap. 2, p. 273.

30. Loyseau, *Seigneuries*, vol. 2, pp. 17, 18, 62.

31. Ibid., p. 92, and Bodin, *République* (1583), p. 273.

32. E.g., Edict of Blois, January 1551, in Fontanon, *Edits et ordonnances des rois de France* (1611 ed.). vol. 2, p. 58; Declaration of Chantilly, 8 August 1635, in Isambert, vol. 16, p. 458; Declaration of Saint-Germain, 30 November 1635, in Isambert, vol. 16, p. 463; Edict of May 1647, in Isambert, vol. 17, p. 62. Under Louis XV "our affairs" become "the state's needs," "the needs of our state," as against "our subjects," "our peoples" (Edict of September 1759, in Isambert, vol. 22, p. 293; Declaration of 8 July 1759, ibid., p. 288; *Arrêt* of the Council, 21 October 1759, ibid., p. 295). (For Isambert, see the bibliography at the end of the Introduction, above.)

33. Le Bret, *Souveraineté,* vol. 1, pt. 6, pl 42.

34. Ibid.

35. Ibid, pts. 7, 8, pp. 49, 52, 57, 58.

36. Ibid., pt. 9.

37. Gaillard, *Conseil du Roi,* p. 64.

38. Le Bret, *Souveraineté,* vol. 4, chap. 3.

39. Joly de Fleury, *Mémoire sur les évocations* (1766).

40. Louis XV, *Discours de la Flagellation* (1766), in Flammermont, *Remontrances,* vol. 2, pp. 557–58.

41. Jean Savaron, *Traité de la souveraineté du Roy,* p. 3.

42. Nicolas Besongne, *L'Etat de la France* (Bibliothèque Nationale, Lc 2514 a).

43. André Félibien, *Recueil de descriptions de peintures et d'autres ouvrages faits pour le Roy* (Paris: Sébastien Mabre-Craimoisy, 1689), p. 25.

44. André Félibien, *Entretiens sur les vies et sur les ouvrages de plus excellents peintres anciens et modernes,* vol. 2, pp. 494–507.

45. Voltaire, *Essai sur les moeurs,* introduction, p. xxiii.

Guide to further reading

Antoine, Michel. *Le Conseil du Roi sous le règne de Louis XV.* Librairie Droz, 1970.

Batiffol, Louis. *Le Louvre sous Henri IV et Louis XIII.* Series "Châteaux, décors de l'Histoire." 1930.

Blet, Pierre. *Le clergé de France et la monarchie.* 2 vols. Rome: Librairie éditrice de l'Université grégorienne, 1959.

Bloch, Marc. *Les rois thaumaturges.* 1924.

Bodin, Jean. *Six livres de la République.* 1576.

Bottineau, Yves. *L'Art d'Ange-Jacques Gabriel à Fontainebleau (1735–1774).* E. de Boccard, 1962.

Carré de Malberg, R. *Théorie générale de l'Etat.* 2 vols. 1920.

Esmein, Adhémar. *Eléments de droit constitutionnel français et comparé.* 6th ed. 1914.

Félibien, André. *Recueil de descriptions de peintures et d'autres ouvrages faits pour le Roi.* Sébastien Mabre-Cramoisy, 1689.

———. *Entretiens sur les vies et sur les ouvrages des plus excellents peintres anciens et modernes.* 2d ed. 2 vols. 1696.

Godefroy, Théodore, and Godefroy Denis. *Le cérémonial français.* 1649.

Hautecoeur, Louis. *Le Louvre et les Tuileries de Louis XIV.* 1927.

———. *Mystique et architecture: Symbolisme du cercle de la coupole.* A. & J. Picard, 1954.

Joly, Agnès. "Le Roi-Soleil, Histoire d'une image," *Revue de l'Histoire de Versailles* 38 (1936): 213–35.

Le Bret, Cardin. *Traité de la souveraineté du Roi.* 1632.

Lemaire, André. *Les lois fondamentales de la monarchie française.* Albert Fontemoing, 1907.

Loyseau, Charles. *Traité des seigneuries.* 1611.

Mousnier, Roland. "Comment les Français voyaient la Constitution." In "Comment les Français voyaient la France," *Dix-Septième Siècle,* no. 25 (1955).

————. *The Assassination of Henri IV.* London: Faber, 1973.

————. "D'Aguesseau et le tournant des ordres aux classes sociales," *Revue d'Histoire économique et sociale* 49 (1971): 449–64.

Nolhac, Pierre de. *Versailles et la Cour de France.* Vol. 2: *Versailles, résidence de Louis XIV.* Vol. 3: *Versailles au XVIIIe siècle.* Louis Conard, 1925, 1926.

Piganiol de la Force, J. A. *Nouvelle description des châteaux et parcs de Versailles et de Marly.* 9th ed. 2 vols. 1764.

Recueils de la Société Jean-Bodin pour l'histoire comparative des Institutions. Vol. 20: *La monocratie.* Brussels: Editions de la Librairie encyclopédique, 1970.

16 The State's Resources

The resources possessed by the state under the absolute monarchy consisted of the extent of its territory, qualified by the time taken to cross it; the number of men at its disposal, qualified by the problem of the fluctuations in this number; the knowledge that the rulers could obtain of the territory and of what it contained, that is, the problematic of cartography and statistics; the intellectual training of the political and administrative cadres; the means for constructing public buildings, roads, canals, and fortresses and the means of destruction available to the army and navy; and the margin left for taxation by the ratio between production and consumption.

This is obviously not the place to go into the geography, demography, educational system, technology, economy, and finances of the kingdom of France and the other lands ruled by its king. All we are concerned with here is to grasp what resources the king, embodying the state, could draw from these various human activities in order to carry out his mission. Moreover, since full treatment of these questions would necessitate lengthy discussions, I shall confine myself to outlining a few examples of the problems that arise and indicating what calls for study.

The territory of the state

The dimensions of the territory

By the Treaty of Vervins, 2 May 1598, Philip II, king of Spain, gave back to Henri IV his conquests on the frontiers of the Low Countries and in Brittany (Blavet, later Port Louis). He restored the status quo established by the Treaties of Cateau-Cambrésis, signed by France on 2 April 1559 with England and, on the following day, with Spain. By these treaties England ceded Calais to France. Henri II renounced France's claim to the kingdom of Naples and the duchy of Milan; gave back the territories conquered from the Florentines, the duke of Mantua, and Venice; restored the principality of Orange to William of Nassau; and abandoned Savoy, Bresse, Bugey, and Piedmont to Duke Emmanuel-Philibert of Savoy. He retained Boulogne and Boulonnais, reconquered in 1549; Calais, recovered in 1558; and Metz, Toul, and Verdun, occupied in 1552. As pledges of security he kept, in Piedmont, the fortresses of Turin, Chieri, Pinerolo, Chivasso, and Villanova d'Asti, which were so many "gateways" by which to enter Italy and threaten the Spanish military roads. The treaties contained an implicit ratification of the Treaty of Cambrai (3 August 1529), under which François I had released Flanders and Artois from their feudal tie so that the Emperor Charles V might take them over. The territory under the sway of the French king thus extended in those days over an area of 460,000 square kilometers—plus about 4,000 for Calais and the Three Bishoprics or, in all, between 464,000 and 465,000 square kilometers.

Henri IV waged war against Savoy. By the Peace of Lyons, 7 January 1601, he acquired Bresse, Bugey, Gex, Valromey, and the right bank of the Rhône. In July 1607 he merged his private domain with that of the Crown and incorporated in it the principality of Béarn and that part of the old domain of Navarre which lay to the north of the Pyrenees, already covered by the Treaty of Vervins. Thus, at the death of Henri IV, the territory of France amounted to between 470,000 and 471,000 square kilometers. (The France of 1919 had an area of about 550,000 square kilometers.)

Louis XIII, and Louis XIV's government down to 1661, pursued a policy which was not aimed at conquering the "natural frontiers" but at seizing the "gateways" and "avenues" through which hostile armies might gain access to France and at cutting the *"rocades,"* the strategic roads which would enable these armies to move around

France and concentrate in front of the places they wished to attack. The French therefore occupied Artois, Roussillon, and Lorraine in 1634, numerous towns in Alsace, some towns guarding the Rhine bridges between Swabia and Switzerland—Rheinfelden, Laufenburg, Säckingen, Waldshut, Ensisheim—and the sovereign principality of Sedan and Raucourt, in September 1642.

The Treaty of Münster, in Westphalia, 24 October 1648, recognized the French king's sovereignty over the Three Bishoprics. It surrendered to him the possessions of the House of Austria in the Landgraviate of Upper and Lower Alsace, with the counties of Sundgau and Ferrette (except Mulhouse, placed under the protection of the Swiss Confederation), and with the prefecture of the ten Imperial cities (which included Landau, Wissembourg, Rosheim, Obernai, Colmar, and Münster in Alsace). The treaty left some questions unclear: whereas articles 73 and 74 gave the king of France full sovereignty over Alsace, article 87 made an exception in favor of the Alsatian states that were directly dependent on the Empire.

Strasbourg remained a free Imperial city. The king kept garrisons in Breisach and Philippsburg. He handed back Breisgau and the frontier towns commanding the bridges over the Rhine leading from Swabia into Switzerland. The king continued to occupy Lorraine but promised to give it up as soon as the duke had accepted the conditions of peace.

By the Treaty of the Pyrenees, 7 September 1659, the king of France recovered the county of Artois, except Aire and Saint-Omer, and a series of strongpoints in Flanders and Hainault: Landrecies, Le Quesnoy, etc.; between the rivers Sambre and Meuse, Avesnes and Philippeville; further east, Marienbourg, Luxembourg, Montmédy, Thionville, Sedan, and Raucourt. The king acquired Dunkirk, bought from Charles II of England in 1662. He recovered the counties of Roussillon and Cerdagne. He gave up Lorraine to Duke Charles IV but united to the Crown of France the duchy of Bar, the county of Chaumont-en-Argonne, and the *prévôtés* of Stenay, Dun, and Jametz. In 1661 the duchy of Bar was restored to the duke of Lorraine, but it remained a fief in feudal dependence on the Crown of France.

The territory of France then covered about 495,000 square kilometers. To reach the frontiers of 1919 it still needed part of the Nord *département,* most of Lorraine, Montbéliard, Franche-Comté, the duchy of Savoy, the county of Nice, the principality of Orange, the county of Avignon, and the Comtat Venaissin.

Under Louis XIV the extent of this territory changed several times.

By the Treaty of Nijmegen, in 1678, Louis XIV moved, in the north, from an "offensive" frontier, with fortresses scattered far out in front, like advance posts for an attack, to a "defensive" one, which was much more continuous. He gave back Charleroi, Asq, Courtrai, Tournai, and Oudenarde. But he kept Douai, Lille, and Armentières; in Artois, Aire and Saint-Omer; in the region of the Scheldt and the Sambre, Cambrai, Bouchain, Valenciennes, Condé, and Maubeuge; in Flanders, Ypres, Wericq, Warneton, Comines, Bailleul, and Cassel. He annexed Franche-Comté, which had been conquered in 1674. Lorraine, reoccupied in 1670, was given back to its duke, on condition that he ceded Longwy, Nancy, Marsal, and four military roads. The duke refused, and so Louis XIV continued to occupy the duchy of Lorraine.

At that moment, the territory of the French state was almost the same as that enclosed within the frontiers of 1792 and 1814. Twenty-three thousand square kilometers had been acquired, and the territory covered 528,000 square kilometers.

Making use of a practice long established in Europe, Louis XIV caused *"chambres de réunion"* to seek out all the places which had at any time been linked with those that he possessed and over which the latter might still retain rights. In this way he gradually added to the territories dependent on the Crown of France: Courtrai, Dixmude, the county of Chimay, eighty fiefs in Lorraine (including Sarrelouis), Speyer, the town of Luxembourg, the town of Trier, the duchy of Zweibrücken, ten towns in Alsace (including Strasbourg), and the county of Montbéliard. These annexations were ratified by the Truce of Ratisbon (Regensburg) made with the Emperor, Sweden, Holland, and Spain on 15 August 1684. The French state's territory was then at its greatest extent, exceeding 550,000 square kilometers.

The War of the League of Augsburg (1688–97) ended with the Treaties of Ryswick (27 September–30 October 1697). Louis XIV had to give back everything he had taken in the Low Countries since the Treaty of Nijmegen, and also Luxembourg, Trier, Zweibrücken, the county of Montbéliard, the duchy of Lorraine, and all the fortresses occupied on the right bank of the Rhine. The state's territory was reduced to 514,000 square kilometers.

The War of the Spanish Succession was ended by the Treaties of Utrecht, signed on 11 April 1713 with England, Portugal, Prussia, Savoy, and Holland, and the Treaty of Rastadt, signed on 6 May 1714 with the Emperor. The king of France had to give back a certain number of towns he had occupied in the Low Countries, including

Ypres, Dixmude, and Tournai. He also had to cede to the duke of Savoy a series of towns and valleys which were old-established possessions of the dauphin of Viennois on the Italian side of the Alps; but he obtained from Savoy the valley of Barcelonnette, and the frontier was thus stabilized along the Alpine summits. Frederick William I, king of Prussia, ceded to France the principality of Orange, which had already been united with France between 1522 and 1529 and between 1673 and 1697. The total area of the state's territory was not markedly changed. It still covered about 514,000 square kilometers. But as a result of these rearrangements, and of the defense works constructed along the "iron frontier," it had undergone an important change of configuration: there had been a development from the frontier conceived as a zone, possessing depth, to the frontier conceived as a *line*.

The 18th century was a period of territorial stability for France. It no longer increased, except slowly and slightly. Louis XIV, in the instructions he composed during the last two years of his life, recorded the view that it was not possible to advance further on the Continent. He advised that France remain within the frontiers which had been won, that an attempt be made to recover influence in Italy, where the Emperor had been put in possession of the duchy of Milan and the kingdom of the Two Sicilies, and that a maritime war be waged against England, France's "ancient and irreconcilable" foe.

Louis XV followed this policy. By the Peace of Vienna, in 1738, his father-in-law Stanislas, the elected king of Poland, renounced his kingdom and received in exchange the duchy of Lorraine, which was to revert to France after his death—as happened in 1766.

Corsica, coveted by England, was a Genoese possession. It revolted against the republic of Genoa, which yielded to the king of France all its rights of sovereignty over the island on 15 May 1768. On 15 August, Louis XV decreed the union of Corsica with France. On 9 May 1769 the supporters of Corsican independence were decisively defeated at Pontenuovo.

On 28 March 1762 Louis XV obtained the sovereign principality of Dombes by exchange with the comte d'Eu, Louis-Charles, second son of the duc of Maine, for the duchy of Gisors and united it with the domain of the Crown of France.

But, while he took advantage of such limited opportunities as presented themselves, useful for the security of France's frontiers and involving little danger, he obeyed the instructions of Louis XIV in rejecting large-scale territorial aggrandizement. This was why, in the

Treaty of Aix-la-Chapelle (Aachen) in 1748, he declined to annex the Austrian Netherlands, which the Maréchal de Saxe had conquered for him.

Louis XVI followed the same policy. He rejected the advances of Emperor Joseph II, who offered him the Austrian Netherlands if he would help dismember the Ottoman Empire. Louis XVI preferred to surround France with a belt of allied or neutral countries, to serve as "buffer states."

In 1789 all that the kingdom of France lacked, to attain the area of the France of 1919, was the duchy of Savoy, the county of Nice, and the enclaves represented by the principality of Montbéliard and the Comtat Venaissin. The total territory of the state in 1789 was about 528,000 kilometers.

The speed of travel

The real dimensions of a state are given by the ratio between its linear dimensions and area, on the one hand, and, on the other, the time taken to travel over it. It is necessary to distinguish between different "times" taken. For news received by the government and orders dispatched by it, it is the speed of a courier riding at the gallop, changing horses at each post, with a difference between the cases when the courier was himself relieved, handing over to a relay, and those when he was not; for persons, it was the speed of travel of the members of the government and administrators, *conseillers du roi,* masters of requests, intendants, commissioners of various kinds, going out to inspect, investigate, carry orders, and impose the king's will; for troops, it was the different possibilities available to infantry, cavalry, artillery, and supply columns; finally, it was the time needed for the transport over a given distance of heavy goods, such as grain, flour, cloth for uniforms, metals, and building materials. One must, of course, distinguish, too, between movement on foot, on horseback, by pack animals, by various sorts of vehicles, by land, and by water.

Movement by water was used as often as possible to supplement overland travel. It was slow, but, since only one-thirty-fifth as much force is needed to shift a given weight by water as by land, it was indispensable where heavy goods were concerned, such as grain, wine, stones, hay, firewood, and charcoal. It had advantages for travelers, to whom it offered a rest from the bumping, the chaos, and the tribula-

tions of the roads. It also provided the kingdom with transversal communication between east and west—always a problem for France.

The land routes radiated, star fashion, from Paris, the capital. On the
eve of the Revolution there were 40,000 kilometers of roadway in service. After 1740 the technique used to construct them was greatly
improved. The engineers gave them a firm, elastic, permeable sub-
structure composed of pebbles and broken stone.

Travel and transport depended on horses and mules. Even where
movement by water was concerned, recourse was had by preference to
towing by animal power. The "water coaches" were drawn by ordinary horses. There were horses and mules for saddling and for loading
with packs. Between Clermont-Ferrand and Toulouse, transport was
carried on by means of pack-animals, even the transport of wine, which
was conveyed in leather bottles. Between Lyons and Saint-Etienne,
oxen and packhorses transported silk, iron, and steel, though wheeled
vehicles with animals harnessed to them were preferred. For the transport of goods for the market there were two-wheeled and four-wheeled
carts. For travelers there were wagons, which were heavy and slow;
coaches, which were covered wagons without suspension; and then,
later, carriages, four-wheeled vehicles which were covered and provided with suspension on leather straps. After 1737 travelers used
"flying coaches' or "diligences"—"*carabuts*," which were long and
narrow, or "*galiotes*," which were light and fast, or post-chaises,
drawn by post-horses, the quickest and most expensive means of
travel. Postal relay stations had existed since the time of Louis XI.
Postmasters kept horses there, ready harnessed. The traveler could
change horses frequently and so move at a gallop. The *messageries*
were farmed out.[1]

As regards news and orders, express letters, conveyed "*en courant
la poste*," took six days to get from Paris to Strasbourg. Madame de
Sévigné received in October, at Les Roches, near Vitré, a letter from
her daughter, sent from Grignan in Provence, which had crossed
France in nine days. In 1666 a letter took four days from Paris to
London by fast courier, riding via Amiens, Abbeville, Calais, and
Dover. In 1660 a journey from Paris to Irun, in Spain, took five days in
spring and summer, six or six and a half days in autumn and winter.
The distance between Paris and Brussels took, in 1660, forty or forty-
two hours in summer, forty-eight or fifty in autumn and winter. These
were maximum speeds. The frequency of couriers was two per week

between Paris and London and two per month between Lyons and Rome.

For persons traveling on horseback or in vehicles (by coach, for instance) in 1613 it was possible to cover between fifteen and sixteen leagues in a day—that is, in nine hours, in summer. From Paris to Amiens, on the Somme—the strategic frontier until Richelieu's time—a traveler took two days; from Paris to Calais, four and a half days; from Paris to Brussels, five and a half days. From Paris to Rouen the journey took two days, sometimes in a "water coach" drawn by horses hired from the local peasants ("*mazettes*"), sometimes overland so as to cut out the meanderings of the Seine. From Paris to Orléans it took two days, from Paris to Bordeaux seven days, from Paris to Nancy six days, and to Strasbourg eleven days, from Paris to Toulouse between eight and ten days, and from Strasbourg to Orléans thirteen days.

In 1658 a traveler going from Pont-Saint-Esprit to Paris spent five hours in getting to Lyons by "water coach" along the Rhône, or three days if he went by land. From Lyons to Paris via Dijon he took eleven days—between fourteen and sixteen days all together.

In 1718 Zentzner, having to make a fast business trip in July, from Strasbourg to Marseilles, hired a post-chaise, with two horses and a driver. He spent eight hours reaching Lyons. There he embarked on a "water coach" drawn by two horses and went down the Rhône to Avignon in two days. At Avignon he again took a post-chaise and in three days was in Marseilles. His journey, made under exceptionally rapid conditions, had required thirteen days in all.

Madame de Sévigné, traveling by means of two calashes, seven horses, a packhorse to carry her bed, and boats on the Loire, took eight days to get from Paris to Nantes, eight days from Paris to Vichy, a month from Provence to Paris, and another month from Paris to Vitré.

In winter, things could be very bad. La Fontaine, going from Paris to Limoges, wrote to his wife after two days: "I have formed a very good impression of the way we are traveling. We have already covered three leagues without any untoward event. At present we are at Clamart. We are going to have to refresh ourselves here for two or three days." We must, of course, allow for his sense of humor.

In 1692, going from Paris to Dijon, a distance of seventy-five leagues, took eight days in winter and seven in summer. In the 18th century the journey from Paris to Angers took seven days. Matters improved toward the end of the century. In a "*turgotine*" one could get from Paris to Amiens in one day and, in a stagecoach, in 1789, from Paris to Angers in three days.

Louis XIV, moving with his court and some troops in February 1680 from Paris to Châlons-sur-Marne, a distance of 43 leagues, or about 172 kilometers, stopped overnight five times on the way—at Dammartin, Villers-Cotterêts, Soissons, Fismes, and Rheims. He covered between 28 and 30 kilometers a day, and that was very good going. In January 1681, with the same accompaniment, he went from Nevers to Bourbon-l'Archambault in three stages, stopping at Saint-Pierre-le-Moûtier and Moulins-sur-Allier and arriving at his destination on the third day. This gives us an idea of what the army could achieve in normal circumstances. In serious situations, however, the infantry were capable of marching 50 or 60 kilometers a day for four or five days in succession.

For goods, materials, and supplies we need to double the figures given for travelers: from Paris to Lille, four days; from Paris to Orléans, four days; from Paris to Lyons, twenty to twenty-two days; from Paris to Strasbourg, twenty-two days.

Thus, from the standpoint of its government, France was a huge, a gigantic, country. As compared with 20th-century states, the central authority had only a slight grip on the governed. The latter possessed a wide margin of initiative and great freedom of action. Only after 1750 did the progress in means of travel offer possibilities of more rigorous control. But it was not the monarchy that was destined to profit by them.

Knowledge of the territory

Cartography

At the beginning of the 17th century, rulers and administrators could form only a very inadequate notion of the state's territory. Maps were few and of poor quality. The first special map of the Paris region appeared only in 1595 and was highly defective. Not until 1637 did Tassin's map show the wooded areas around Paris, and the map produced by the Academy of Sciences in 1674 was the first to make use of topographical surveys of the region. As regards the Church of France, three dioceses alone had been mapped: Bourges in 1545, Le Mans in 1592, Limoges in 1594.

Encouraged by the state, cartography made steady progress. Maps became available in increasing numbers and were increasingly accurate. But they were still geometrical maps, in which objects were placed in relation to each other planimetrically. Altimetry was neglected, relief being always poorly shown, being represented from imagination, by perspective drawings.

The period from the middle of the 16th to the middle of the 17th century, approximately, was the period of what were called *"descriptions."* Maps showed rivers, mountains, towns, *bourgs,* hamlets, châteaux, ancient monuments, bridges, roads. Sometimes they also showed the boundaries of provinces, *généralités, élections,* and dioceses and were accompanied by lists of place names. They were military, administrative, or pictorial maps, not geographical ones.

Cartography was based on the work of two Flemings, Ortelius and Mercator. These mapmakers knew a few longitudes and latitudes and arranged everything in relation to these indicators. The remaining information was contributed by itineraries such as *La Guide des Chemins de France* by Charles Estienne (1552), descriptions written by travelers, routes for the army's marches, showing staging-posts, and partial surveys made on the ground, especially in the frontier provinces and in regions often traversed by the army.

A corps of royal engineers and geographers existed from the time of Henri IV and Louis XIII. There was one geographer and fortifications engineer for every one, or in some cases two, of the provinces along the frontiers, with *commis* exercising the same craft. They drew up plans of fortifications and maps of provinces. At the beginning of Henri IV's reign, Raymond de Bonnefous was responsible for this work in Dauphiné and Provence. In 1606 his son Jean de Bonnefous had responsibility for Languedoc and Provence, while Jean de Beins was in charge of Dauphiné and Bresse. From 1598 onward Henri IV sought to accumulate plans of all frontier towns and then maps of the coasts. In 1607 he ordered that maps be made of the frontiers of his kingdom. The royal geographer Antoine de Laval worked on maps of the provinces. Sully, grand master of artillery, ordered his lieutenants to compile maps of their respective areas of responsibility, showing bridges that could be crossed by guns, fords, and the roads leading from one town to another. The king had a superb collection of maps, and he was passionately fond of them. The military engineers were subject to the orders of the provincial governors but also to those of the royal geographer. After Antoine de Laval, the man the king relied on for this work was Nicolas Tassin, royal geographer, *commissaire des guerres, conseiller du roi* in 1631. On the instructions of Louis XIII and Richelieu, he abstracted maps, plans, and sections from the surveys made by the engineer-geographers. After him, Nicolas Sanson, a protégé of Richelieu's and Louis XIII's geography teacher, became royal geographer. All the work done by geographers working in their studies was based on the surveys made by the engineer-geographers, whose portfolios were a mine of information. One part of this information remained secret, namely, that which related to the frontiers.

The way in which the engineer-geographers carried out their surveys is explained to us by Jean Tarde, canon of Chancelade, in his book *Les Usages du quadrant à l'aiguille aimantée,* published in Paris by Jean Gesselin in 1621. He says that he is going to draw a map "in the manner of the *maréchaux de camp* when they have to encamp an army," using "a single standpoint, without moving from that place." If he had to draw a map of the country around Sarlat, in Périgord, the engineer-geographer would climb up to some high place from which he could view the country. On a sheet of paper he would mark Sarlat in the middle, draw two straight lines intersecting at Sarlat, and place in the margin a scale divided into quarters of a league. Then, having laid his sheet of paper on a plane table, he would ask a native of the country to point out to him, and name, the towns, *bourgs* and villages and with his quadrant would take a line of sight from Sarlat toward each place that he wished to mark on his map. Using his compasses to define the distances, he would "describe" in this way all the localities, rivers, and streams. Contemporaries were aware that the line of sight is always uncertain. They were never agreed as to the distance between places. Maps made from a single standpoint were always incorrect.

To secure greater precision, they used the "intersection method," with two standpoints. Lines drawn from two places to a third do indeed determine, where they intersect, the exact location of that place. In order to know what sort of triangle was formed by Sarlat, Périgueux, and Bergerac and the distances between the two latter towns and Sarlat, the engineer-geographer took, from Sarlat, two lines of sight, on Périgueux and Bergerac, and then, from Bergerac, a line of sight on Périgueux. This last line cut the Sarlat-Périgueux line at the precise point where Périgueux was. The engineer-geographer verified the accuracy of his work by cross-checking. To check on the Sarlat-Bergerac line, he took a line of sight from Bergerac to Sarlat, which confirmed the location of Sarlat.

In order to complete his map, the geographer had to transfer to his sheet of paper what was shown on all the special maps produced by surveys, together with the rivers, mountains, and forests, which he was able to place through the intersection of lines of sight.

The engineer-geographers used instruments that were many and various. The best of them was the graphometer, which was widely employed in the second half of the 16th century. It included a fixed alidad with sight-vanes, called an *"alidade des stations,"* as its basis, with a semicircle of brass, marked with degrees, on which pivoted a movable alidad provided with a compass, so that sightings could be made. The engineer read off the angle between two directions on the semicircle. This part of the instrument was called the *"observateur."* The second part of the graphometer was the *"rapporteur"* (protractor), a semicircle with graduations on it which corresponded to those on the *"observateur"*; it was provided with a long graduated ruler that enabled the sightings to be transferred to a sheet of paper. Plans and maps could thus be drawn without the need for calculations.

Triangulation could be done with the graphometer. If, in a triangle ABC, one knows the length of side AB and the angles at A and B, it is easy to determine the angle at C and the lengths of sides AC and BC. The engineer-geographer marked off a base, of arbitrary length, on the ground with his measuring apparatus and from each end of this baseline took a line of sight on a third point. He measured the angle made by the line of sight with the baseline. All he then had to do was to reproduce these angles on a sheet of paper, at the ends of a baseline drawn on a reduced scale, in order to find, on the same scale, the position of the point aimed at.

The state possessed many maps compiled from information obtained by these means. The first atlas of France was *Le Théâtre français,* by Maurice Bouguereau, published at Tours in 1594. It included three general maps of France, together with maps of the provinces of Picardy, Vermandois, Lorraine, Burgundy, Dauphiné, Provence, Languedoc, Gascony, Saintonge, and Brittany (the frontier provinces) and, for the interior of the kingdom, maps of Touraine, Maine, Blaisois, Berry, Poitou, and Limousin. Bouguereau was merely an editor, who put together the information supplied by the engineer-geographers and also copied Ortelius, Mercator, the map of France by Postel (1570), etc. The other maps, or *"Théâtres,"* that statesmen had at their disposal were those of La Guillotière (1613) and Jean Leclerc (1620) and, finally, the *"Théâtre"* by Nicolas Tassin, entitled *Les*

*Cartes générales de toutes les provinces de France, royaumes et pro-
vinces de l'Europe* in fifty-six sheets, the first edition of which appeared
in 1633, and others in 1637 and 1648.

From the middle of the 17th century to the beginning of the 18th, the
state was able to draw on the work of cartographers who worked in
their studies on the basis of memoranda. Such cartographers were
numerous, but the principal ones among them seem to have been the
Sanson family. Nicolas Sanson, who was born at Abbeville in 1600 and
died in Paris in 1667, was the founder of a dynasty of cartographers and
a school of cartography. His three sons were cartographers like himself. Nicolas died in 1648 of a wound received while defending Chancellor Séguier during the "days of the barricades." Guillaume and
Adrien, who died in 1703 and 1718, respectively, were prolific mapmakers. One of Nicolas's daughters married Pierre Moulart, *sieur* of
Visé-Marets; their son Pierre, who also became a cartographer, took
the name of Moulard Sanson. He died in 1730, leaving a nephew, Gilles
Robert (1686–1766), who was also a cartographer, and whose son Didier Robert de Vaugondy (1723–89) succeeded his father in the craft.
One of Nicolas Sanson's nephews, Pierre Duval (1618–83), yet another
cartographer, produced a large number of maps after 1645. Another
family of cartographers that should be mentioned was that of Alexis-
Hubert Jaillot (1632–1712) and his sons.

The mapmaking work of the Sansons was "cartography of state,"
civil and ecclesiastical. Nicolas Sanson's activity was inspired by concern to serve the state. At the age of eighteen he published a map of "the
Gauls" which won him Richelieu's favor in 1627. He gave geography lessons to Louis XIII. He worked as an engineer-geographer in
Picardy and later in Alsace. Louis XIII gave him the title of
geographer-in-ordinary to the king, with a pension of 2,000 livres.
Established in Paris in 1645, he developed his work further. It was he
who introduced into maps the boundaries between civil and religious
divisions—archdioceses, dioceses, parishes, abbeys, and other benefices, and governorates, *parlements, chambres des comptes, cours
des aides, généralités, élections,* and *bailliages.* After 1664 he was
helped by Colbert and Le Tellier, who ordered the masters of requests
and *commissaires départis* to search for maps of provinces and *généralités* and to compile memoranda to be sent to Sanson.

Nicolas Sanson's cartography was much more critical and scientific
than has been alleged, even though his maps were not made on the
ground or compiled as a result of travels. He proceeded from a number

of different standpoints, the latitude and longitude of which had been determined by astronomical observations. He based the distances between places on a great body of writings—travelers' itineraries, episcopal visitation reports, etc. He located places by means of compasses, in relation to the determined points. His work in collecting information was immense and conscientious. He created for his maps the groundwork of a projection with sinusoidal meridians, preserving areas. He knew how to center the middle meridian.

His chief maps were, in 1651, *Le Théâtre de France;* in 1658, the *Cartes générales de toutes les parties du monde;* and, in 1665, *La France,* in four sheets, and *Les Gabelles de France.* He also produced maps showing the waterways and roads of France, and so on.

At the end of the 17th century and in the first half of the 18th, the state had at its disposal maps that were much more scientific, having been compiled under the influence of the Academy of Sciences and its activities. The lack of a scheme of geographical coordinates made all previous maps imprecise and often erroneous. The Academy of Sciences, founded in 1666 to play the role of a national center of scientific research, brought about a revolution in cartography. The perfecting of maps required work in two directions: more exact determination of longitudes and, since the Earth is flattened at the poles, measurement of the lengths of the different degrees of the meridian.

The determination of longitudes was hindered by the lack of a chronometer. In the second half of the 17th century, Huygens' pendulum clock, keeping local time, made possible a first step toward the solution of the problem. Under the auspices of the Academy of Sciences a young Italian worked at it. His name was Giovanni-Domenico Cassini; born in 1625, he was the son of a *gentilhomme.* In 1650 he was professor of astronomy at the University of Bologna. In 1664 Pope Alexander VII summoned him to Rome. There Cassini discovered the shadows that Jupiter's satellites cast on the disk of that planet when they pass between it and the sun. In 1668 he published an almanac, *Les Ephémérides des satellites de Jupiter,* to enable longitudes on the planet to be calculated. Louis XIV made him a member of the Royal Academy of Sciences in Paris. The astronomer Picard recommended him strongly to Colbert, who suggested to Louis XIV that he be invited to France for the purpose of improving geographical knowledge. He arrived in France in 1669, was naturalized in 1673, and married a Frenchwoman. He began work at the Paris Observatory in 1671 and there made his discovery of the spots on Jupiter. He died in 1712. Thanks to his observations of the movement of Jupiter's satellites he was able to improve the method of determining longitudes to within a probable error of one kilometer. His method was thus greatly superior to the one based on the lunar eclipses. From 1670 onward, astronomical missions were sent out into the world to measure longitudes by the new methods: Cassini, La Hire, Claude Delisle, Pene, and Nolin took part. It became possible to compile a new map of the world at the Paris Observatory.

In order to establish precise reference points, it was necessary to know the length of the degree of the meridian at the various latitudes. This work was first undertaken by the Abbé Picard, prior of Rillé in Anjou, who became professor at the Collège de France at the age of thirty-five, succeeding Gassendi in 1655. He applied the astronomical telescope to the measurement of angles. Between 1668 and 1670 he measured an arc of the meridian of Paris by means of a chain of triangles. He measured a baseline between Villejuif and the pavilion at Juvisy. Then he triangulated between the Malvoisine farm (at Champeuil, *canton* of Corbeil, in Seine-et-Marne) and the village of Sourdon, near Amiens. Subsequently—using the work done by Giovanni-Domenico Cassini—Picard, Roberval, and Cassini himself surveyed the coasts of France. They presented to the academy and to the king, in 1684, their *Carte de France corrigée par ordre du Roi sur les observations de Messieurs de l'Académie des Sciences.* When congratulating them, Louis XIV could not refrain from saying: "Your work has cost me a third of my kingdom." Indeed, the west coast had been brought in by a degree and a half in longitude to the meridian of Paris, and the south coast by half a degree of latitude toward the North. France was revealed as being much smaller than contemporaries had supposed. The academy caused a map of the *généralité* of Paris to be constructed, by means of a chain of triangles, in 1674, and this was published in 1678. It was the first map based on geodesic surveys and constructed by triangulation. Maps of dioceses were compiled by these new methods.

While the Sansons continued to reissue their maps and to produce fresh ones in accordance with the old methods, Guillaume Delisle (1675–1726) approached the making of maps in a completely new way, in accordance with a scheme of projection. It was he who first depicted the Mediterranean in its exact dimensions, divided into degrees of longitude. He devised the system of conical projection. In 1702 he was a member of the Academy of Sciences, and in 1718 he was the king's principal geographer.

Cartographers compiled information in a critical way, like the Sansons, but also utilized the new methods of Picard and Cassini. Among
them, J.-B. Bourguignon d'Anville (1697–1782) became known, in
1737, by his *Nouvel atlas de la Chine*.

In the second half of the 18th century large geometrical maps began
to appear. They were in part the work of the second Cassini, Jacques,
and his son, César-François Cassini de Thury, who became, at the age
of 22, a member of the Academy of Sciences and later was director of
the Paris Observatory. Jacques Cassini urged that a complete triangulation of the whole of France be carried out. He was given the means to
do this because Comptroller General Orry wanted maps that would
enable the department of bridges and highways to construct the great
roads that were needed for trade. From 1733 to 1742 he worked with
César-François. They marked out the meridian of the Paris Observatory. Commissions of the Academy of Sciences, presided over first by
one Cassini and then by the other, checked the operations. Along the
meridian, at intervals of 60,000 fathoms (rather more than one degree
of latitude), perpendiculars were carried geometrically to east and
west. They constructed a chain of triangles, using eighteen baselines
and 2,000 triangles. They marked out two other meridians—one running from Cherbourg to Bayonne, through Normandy, Brittany,
Poitou, and Gascony, the other from Speyer to Nice, through Alsace,
Franche-Comté, Dauphiné, and Provence—and two perpendiculars to
these meridians, running from the Eastern frontier to the west coast,
from Strasbourg to Brest. This was the origin of the projection known
as "Cassini's": the coordinates of a point are given with reference to a
central meridian and the distance along the great circle through the
position which cuts the meridian at a right angle. The instruments used
were improved. Brass semicircles marked off in degrees were equipped
with telescopic alidads and micrometers to give greater accuracy in the
measurement of angles. The result of this work was, in 1746 and 1747,
the *Nouvelle carte qui comprend les principaux triangles qui servent
de fondements à la description géométrique de la France*.

Aided by the army's engineers, Cassini made a detailed map of Flanders. At the siege of Berg-op-Zoom in 1747 Louis XV had a precise
picture of the terrain before him. Filled with enthusiasm, he decided
that a map of the entire kingdom must be compiled by the Paris Observatory and Cassini. The work began between the Peace of Aix-la-
Chapelle (Aachen), in 1748, and the Seven Years' War, in 1756, which
interrupted it. The first two sheets of the map of France were pub-

lished. César-François Cassini obtained permission to form a private company and appealed to the provincial estates and the authorities in the provinces. Sixty sheets were published after 1760, and 1783 saw the appearance of the *Description géométrique de la France*. When César-François Cassini died, in 1784, only Brittany remained unmapped. His son, Jacques-Dominique, finished the job. The last sheet was published in 1815. At that date the map of France consisted of 182 sheets. Jacques-Dominique had become, under the empire, comte de Cassini de Thury.

The Cassinis' map was a very good one, as a geometrical, planimetrical map. Conventional signs indicated civil and ecclesiastical boundaries, vegetation, forests, together with the walks through them, and main roads. Large towns were shown in plan. Symbols designated churches, mills, and the residences of noblemen, with their names. Rivers were shown. The toponymy was of a remarkably high standard. Local usages and the value of the soil were indicated. The only shortcoming was the absence of relief. Valleys were shown like canyons in a plateau, and mountains by narrow strips of white, marking the crests, with shading for the slopes.

The Cassinis' map of France served as a model for 150 years and aroused emulation in all countries. Among the collaborators of César-François Cassini, Rigobert Bonne invented "Bonne's projection," derived from the conic, which was an equal-area projection. His projection was adopted by most states for half a century. Jean-Louis Dupain-Triel, helped by his brother, Dupain de Montesson, teacher of the future Louis XVI, published in 1781 a map of the rivers and canals of France which was striking in its fineness and detail. He set on foot the great *Atlas Minéralogique* of Guettard. Many maps of all kinds were produced, showing the country by provinces, governorates, and so on.

Depiction of relief remained either absent or poor. The problem of altimetry still awaited solution. The answer was contour lines. But the task of determining levels was hard to accomplish. Barometric measuring was not good enough. What was needed was precise determinations by closed traverse—going all round the heights, taking the altitude at different points, and checking to make sure that the ring closed correctly. The astronomers Bouguer and Clairaut perceived the problem but could not solve it.

Since it was very difficult to construct contour lines by means of the plane table, the engineer-geographers began by making hachures and then drawing curves around these hachures—not without many mistakes.

For the Cassinis, topography was too protracted, detailed, and costly. Attempts were undertaken by others. In the geometrical map of Upper Dauphiné on the scale of 1:86,400 drawn by Villaret between 1749 and 1754, on the orders of General Bourcet, relief was shown, but the mapmaker failed in that he combined horizontal projection of the terrain with bird's-eye views of the hillsides and crests. H.-B. de Saussure drew a map of the Mont-Blanc massif in 1786. In the margin he showed the height in fathoms, determined by barometer, of a certain number of points. He did not dare insert them on his map.

Since the 16th century, sea charts had shown the depths indicated by soundings. The Dutch engineer Nicolas Cruquius, in his 1729 plan of the mouth of the Maas, joined points with the same depth by curves that were ten feet apart. Philippe Buache did the same in 1752 for his physical map and section of the English Channel. Military engineers sometimes used the same method in their levelings for plans of the coasts. The idea formulated by Milet de Mureau in 1749, to mark lines of equal altitude on plans of fortifications, was put into practice in 1761 on Minorca, at Port-Mahon. The theory of it was taught from 1764 onward at the military engineers' school at Mézières. In 1777 Lieutenant J.-B. Meusnier put forward the idea of making a plan with horizontal curves joining all the points at the same height or depth. He applied this method in the roadstead of Cherbourg, with the aid of seven engineer officers. On 20 June 1789 the hydrographic map of the roadstead was completed.

Immense progress had thus been made in the cartographic depiction of the country. This progress had taken place under pressure from the state and in order to meet the state's needs.

Statistics

It was essentially for the purpose of ascertaining the numbers of the population that the state encouraged the progress of statistics. At the beginning of the 17th century the state had only scanty means of estimating the size of the population. There was no general census. Such a method long seemed beyond the bounds of possibility, except for small groups. The state sometimes employed a counting of "households" and applied an arbitrary coefficient for the number of persons living in the same household. Another procedure was to add up the lists of heads of families paying taxes, *taille* or *capitation*, and then multiply the resultant figure by an arbitrary coefficient. In any case, the state could do no more than carry out partial, local enumerations, which it then extrapolated for the rest of the kingdom. More often than not, the state employed a purely qualitative demography, making estimates based on the age of persons getting married, or the density of children playing in the streets, or the rate at which land was cleared for cultivation or was abandoned.

Thus, the state was very badly informed, and its subjects knew even less. Some contemporaries, greatly struck by the *mortalités* of the 17th century, thought, right down to the end of the 18th, that the population of France did not exceed 16 million. When the abbé Expilly in 1772 put forward the figure of 22 million, he was severely criticized. The *philosophes,* Montesquieu, and the Physiocrats all considered that, since the ideas of the Enlightenment were not dominant in France, the population could not but decline. Many even believed that a catastrophic depopulation was taking place. Toward the end of the 17th century, Isaac Vossius thought that France had no more than 5 million inhabitants. The administrators, being closer to reality, were more moderate in their notions, but at least they believed that the population was not increasing. They therefore copied earlier enumerations whenever they could. Only the greatest among them discerned the truth of the matter. Colbert correctly observed the actual shrinkage of the population in his time.

It was only at the end of the 17th century that efforts began to be made to achieve more exact knowledge of the situation. Vauban in 1686 published his *Méthode générale et facile pour faire le dénombrement des peuples,* the substance of which was reproduced in his *Dîme royale* in 1707. Inspired by the example of the government of China, he urged that an annual census could be carried out. He provided a form for such a census in a table with columns, printed in advance: men, women, boys over fourteen, girls over twelve, small boys, small girls, servingmen, and servingwomen. Occupations were shown. His method was put into operation in 1681 at Tours; in 1682 at Douai; in 1685 at Gravelines; in 1686 at Dunkirk, Bergues, Furnes, Bourbourg, and Ypres; in 1688 at Lille, Tournai, Valenciennes, and Tours and in Franche-Comté; in 1693 at Valenciennes; in 1695 in Auvergne; in 1696 in the *élection* of Vézelay and in the *généralités* of Tours, Metz, Brittany, Normandy, Picardy, and Languedoc; in 1697 in western Flanders and on the Isle of Oléron; in 1698 in Dauphiné, Alsace, and Hainault and in the *seigneurie* of Belfort; in 1700 in Provence; and in 1701 in the county of Avignon, the principality of Orange, and Roussillon.

The state was able to find out the rates of birth and death through the parish registers. The Edict of Villers-Cotterets, 1539, had obliged *curés* to keep registers of baptisms, marriages, and deaths. They were often negligent in the matter, but edicts in 1667 and 1673 laid this obligation more rigorously upon them, and the quality of the parish registers improved thereafter. The ordinance of 1737 required greater care in the registering of deaths. Colbert caused monthly summaries of Paris parish registers to be published between 1670 and 1684, and their publication was resumed between 1709 and 1784.

A procedure for working out the total numbers of the population from the birth and death rates was devised by La Michodière, intendant of Auvergne, then of Lyons, and later of Rouen, *conseiller d'Etat,* and provost of the Merchants of Paris. His former secretary in Auvergne and at Lyons, Messance, published his writings in 1766 under the title *Recherches sur la population.*

La Michodière's methods were used by another intendant, Montyon; and his secretary, Moheau, published an account of his work in his book *Recherches sur la population de la France* (1778).

The theory of these procedures was furnished by the mathematician Laplace in the *Mémoires de l'Académie Royale des Sciences,* 1783 (pages 693–702). One had to begin with a locality where the intendant had both parish registers and enumerations or censuses at his disposal. One calculated the average number of births during ten years before the year of the census. By dividing the number of the inhabitants by that of the average number of births, one obtained a coefficient. In another locality, where no enumeration or census had been made but where there were parish registers, one calculated the average number of births over a ten-year period, and then all one had to do was to multiply this figure by the coefficient in order to obtain the approximate number of inhabitants.

This was only a probable figure. For the degree of probability to be high, what must be the order of magnitude of the basic enumeration? Laplace applied the calculation of the probabilities to the calculations already made. For the France of 1781–82 the coefficient 26 gave the figure of 25,299,467 inhabitants. The calculation of probabilities showed that, in order to have a thousand-to-one probability of not being further out than by 500,000 in 25,000,000, it was necessary that the enumeration which served to establish the factor 26 should include

771,469 inhabitants. Actually, the enumeration used, that of Burgundy, exceeded 1 million inhabitants, and so the result, from that angle, was quite respectable. In the case of Paris, the statisticians allowed a coefficient of 30, owing to the large number of celibates in the colleges, universities, and seminaries and among the domestic servants. However, there was a second condition to be observed—that the demographic conditions should remain constant.

The state made a number of attempts at enumeration and census-taking, to an increasing extent as the 17th and 18th centuries advanced.

In the 17th century, there was an attempt at a general enumeration in 1636 and 1637, during the Thirty Years' War. The results of this have survived for the *élections* of Caen, Avranches, and Valognes.

Still available to us also are Terwel's 1657 inquiry, carried out in the parishes between the Aisne and the Meuse to estimate war damage, and the 1659 survey of households in the *élection* of Coulommiers.

Colbert had an investigation underaken by the intendants in 1663 and 1664. From this there survive the enumerations effected in the *généralités* of Tours, Poitiers, Bourges, Moulins, Rouen, Châlons, and Dijon.

The censuses inspired by Vauban have already been mentioned. At the time of the famine of 1693 the intendants listed the number of inhabitants and the quantity of grain available. The results have been preserved for Auvergne, Languedoc, the *généralité* of Alençon, and some regions in the southwest.

The idea of a poll tax (*capitation*) was suggested by Vauban to Comptroller General Pontchartrain. A circular of 31 October 1694 directed the intendants to make inquiries with a view to introducing this tax. A subsequent circular dispatched forms for the enumeration and advice as to how to go about it. These orders were carried out. The intendants of Burgundy, Paris, and Aix sent questionnaires to the *curés* and to the syndics of the communities, and some of the replies received have survived, though the remainder have disappeared. They may have been used by the bookseller Saugrain for his *Dénombrement du royaume,* the first edition of which appeared in 1709.

In 1697 began the great inquiry carried out by the intendants for the duc de Bourgogne. They drew up memoranda which have been preserved but not yet published, except in the case of the *généralité* of Paris. Generally speaking, they are defective. It seems that only Lamoignon de Basville, in Languedoc, undertook a direct census. The rest made use of the number of households, or the poll-tax lists, and estimated the population on that basis. Eight out of thirty-two did not even mention the number of inhabitants in their area.

In 1709 a new inquiry was launched to discover, at a time of famine, the numbers of the population and the size of the country's grain stocks; it was based on the rolls for *taille* and poll tax, supplemented by information obtained on the spot. The results of the 1709 enumeration are preserved in the Bibliothèque Nationale.

In the 18th century, we find the *Nouveau dénombrement du royaume*, by the bookseller Saugrain (1720), and his *Dictionnaire universel de la France* (1726), which gives the number of inhabitants in each parish. On 15 February 1720 it was decided, for the better administration of the realm, that a register be kept in each parish; here would be recorded the number of heads of families, the number of day laborers, and the number of beggars. In 1725 the precious registers of persons liable to pay *gabelle* were established. In 1730 and 1731 there was a general inquiry into stocks of foodstuffs. The crisis in food supplies in 1740–43 led to the inquiry initiated by Comptroller-General Orry in 1745. However, this produced merely an estimate based on the poll-tax records. The Abbé d'Expilly, compiling his *Dictionnaire géographique, historique, politique des Gaules et de la France*, had the *curés* count up all the births, marriages, and deaths in all the parishes of the realm between 1690 and 1701 and then between 1752 and 1763. He sent out printed tables for breakdown of the figures. The intendants helped him. Only the *parlement* of Rouen forbade the carrying-out of the inquiry. D'Expilly received 30,000 replies. He included 7,000 of these in the appendix to volume 3 of his *Dictionnaire* and 8,000 in the appendix to volume 4. The rest have been lost.

In 1762 Comptroller-General Bertin ordered an inquiry from which we still possess the memoranda for the *généralités* of Alençon, Lyons, and Tours. In 1764 Comptroller-General L'Averdy ordered a similar inquiry, from which the memoranda for Auvergne and Languedoc have survived. The questionnaires, inspired by Vauban, covered sex, marital status, and age and had special listings for servants of both sexes, journeymen, apprentices, clerics, religious of both sexes, *gentilshommes,* and privileged persons.

In 1772 Comptroller-General Terray set up the department called *"Statistique de la France."* La Michodière was appointed to head it. By a circular of 4 August, Terray required the intendants to make regular statistical reports on changes in the population. La Michodière distributed forms to the intendants. He centralized the information they supplied, down to 1789, and had calculations made for him by the Abbé Lecoq. He issued annual statements of the population of France from 1770 to 1784. However, the basic documents have not been well preserved in the intendants' records.

Calonne asked the intendants to carry out an enumeration in 1784, but no trace of this remains. The Assembly of Notables and the minister Brienne asked for an enumeration in 1788. On 27 December 1788 Necker told the king's Council that this work had been completed, but nothing of it has survived.

Besides these general enumerations and censuses, there were many partial enumerations, by province or town, and even censuses, such as the one at Meulan on 7 and 8 June 1765.

Great progress was made in this way. The knowledge available to the state was more precise and even led to the formation of genuine statistics. This progress originated first and foremost in the will of the state, which caused work to be done that it needed to meet its requirements. However, the state formed the idea of this work through a change of outlook, and it was this change that gave it the means of realizing its aims.

The first manifestation of this change of outlook was the Cartesian and mechanistic revolution. There was the advance made by mathematics, which was studied to an increasing extent in the colleges, not as yet very much, perhaps, in comparison with other subjects, yet seriously in the 17th century and to a greater degree in the 18th, when excellent teaching manuals appeared, such as those by Bezout and Legendre, simple and clear. Furthermore, it became fashionable to continue to interest oneself in mathematics after leaving college. Elementary works popularized the new physics—in 1671 those of René Bary and Jacques Rohault. In 1674 Bary published his *Parallèle des principes de la "Physique" d'Aristote et de celle de René Descartes*. These writers recommended that study be undertaken on the basis of Nature itself and of experimentation. They urged that everything be reduced to mathematical terms, since mathematics expresses the essence of reality and Nature speaks a mathematical language. Vauban was an engineer. It has even been claimed that Louis XIV and Colbert were inspired in their administrative reforms by the Cartesian and mechanistic spirit, but that remains to be proved.

It must be noted, though, that it was not the French Cartesians who created demographic science. This first arose in Holland and England. Tables of mortality, with calculations of probability of survival, were drawn up in 1662 by Graunt, on the basis of the records of deaths in London. Halley corrected these tables in 1693, using the Breslau records. De Witt published his tables in 1671. William Petty created "political arithmetic" between 1682 and 1691. Davenant published his work in 1699. These writers formulated the first law of demography, the growth of population by geometrical progression. Matthew Hales discovered the period in which numbers were doubled—twenty-five years. All that Malthus had to do later on, to produce his theory, was to relate to these laws the law of diminishing returns.

The new science developed in those countries where the mechanistic outlook had triumphed, the homelands of men like Bacon, Harvey, Halley, and Boyle. No less important, however, were the needs of the state and the rise of precapitalism. The needs of the armies during the Thirty Years' War entailed a continual outbidding of one state by another, so that they all needed to obtain better knowledge of their resources. In 1688 began the long conflict, dominated by the rivalry between France and England, which has been called the second Hundred Years' War. It was in order to calculate the balance of power between the two countries that William Petty created the new science of "political arithmetic." Almost equally great was the influence of the rise of precapitalism. The tables of mortality were necessitated by the successful spread of life annuities and life insurance. Furthermore, precapitalist commercial and industrial enterprise fostered the habit of translating all activity into figures and seeking to define constant relations between economic and social facts. Demographic science certainly owes more to military needs and to precapitalism than to Cartesian or mechanistic science. Vauban, a soldier, the king's engineer charged with the defense and capture of fortresses, who ended his career as a marshal of France and who engaged in statistical studies in order to help the state to make better use of the forces of the kingdom, was accustomed, as an entrepreneur, to make contracts, to calculate numbers of workmen and workdays and quantities of material, and to plan the most economic employment of limited funds.

The population

Changes in the number of inhabitants

In a technological situation in which most of the work of producing material goods was done by hand, manpower was one of the chief concerns of statesmen. What was needed was a numerous population, constantly renewed, from which the state could draw soldiers and workmen for public works without reducing production. The ideal would have been a population that increased slightly but steadily, so as to ensure the supply of soldiers and workmen without compromising the food supply. The state was far from finding such ideal conditions.

Actually, the schema outlined by Malthus in his *Essay on the Principles of Population,* published in 1798, gives an excellent theoretical statement of the relation between food supplies and the number of inhabitants in French society in the 17th and 18th centuries. In that society, population was very elastic and the supply of food very inelastic. As soon as there had been a succession of good harvests, the population grew very fast, in geometrical progression. The supply of food did not keep up with this increase, since it grew, at best, in only arithmetical progression. At this rate, the population would quickly have exceeded the means available for its support. However, even before that threshold was reached, only two or three bad harvests were needed for the food supply to become inadequate and so for dearth, famine, and the consequent epidemics to sweep away, in some places, as much as 30 percent of the population, thus restoring the balance between numbers and food supply. Then the cycle began again.

Short-term changes

The state was thus confronted with a population whose numbers oscillated to a marked degree within short periods in the 17th century and somewhat less sharply in the 18th.

Here are some examples. Between the Aisne and the Meuse, 124 parishes contained 8,133 households in 1636 and 4,036 in 1657. (A factor to be taken into account in this case, though, is the passage of troops through the region.) In the winter of 1650 half the population of certain provinces disappeared. The municipality of Rouen recorded 4,000 victims in fifteen days. In the *élection* of Pontoise in 1694–95, in 46 parishes the population fell from 2,893 to 2,514 households. It increased to 3,176 households in 1709, only to decline again to 2,844 in 1718. At Breteuil, in Beauvaisis, there were 15 deaths in the second quarter of 1693 and 120 in the third quarter of 1694. Births fell from 10 to 5. At Coulommiers there were, in 1570, 6,000 inhabitants, and the priests carried out 240 baptisms. In 1640–42 there were only 200 baptisms each year, and in 1648–53, during the Fronde, there were as few as 165 annually, the population having shrunk to 4,000. Between 1670 and 1680 there was an annual average of 125 baptisms, and the population did not exceed 3,000. In the 18th century these oscillations became less and less extreme. The following figures show the number of households in Tonnerrois:

	ca. 1700	ca. 1713	ca. 1720	ca. 1788
At Argentenay	33	29	33	58
At Lézinnes	110	116	108	200
At Pacy	125	108	118	150
At Vireaux	89	93	97	110

At Saint-Pierre-Eglise, in Normandy, there were, in 1709, 34 baptisms and 54 deaths: the number of the former was 66 percent of the latter. In 1736 there were 59 baptisms and 75 deaths: the number of baptisms was 83 percent of the number of deaths. The oscillation was diminishing.

At Tamerville, in Cotentin, between 1625 and 1643 there was a rough balance between births and deaths. During the Fronde, births declined sharply, while deaths increased. Between 1653 and 1666 the population was reconstituted. The death rate was higher than before, but there was a very high birth rate, for marriages took place at an early age, and there was an excess of births over deaths. Between 1666 and 1680 there were ten years when the death rate was very high. On the average, in each year there were half as many deaths again as in normal times. The victims were especially numerous among those under twenty, which entailed a fall in the number of marriages. Between 1683 and 1711 many old persons died, which meant a fall in the death rate in the next period. From 1680 to 1702 the birth rate rose again, reaching as high as 40 percent per year. Then it fell, once more, between 1710 and 1724. After 1710 the number of marriages increased and, subsequently, the number of births. Two crises occurred, in 1739–43 and 1750–54. These, however, killed off mainly adults and old people. The average age of the population fell. But the crises had the effect of separating couples, and this caused a slight decline in the birth rate. Overall, there was an increase in the population between 1730 and 1770.

Thus, the 17th century was marked by vigorous oscillations in the numbers of the population, large-scale destructions being followed by rapid recoveries. In the 18th century the movement became calmer, with oscillations that were less acute, and the population grew. After about 1750, "*mortalités*" were much less severe. The highest figures for deaths in 1758–59, 1767–68, and 1788–89 were much lower than in the age of Louis XIV. The great *"mortalités"* were being replaced by small, occasional increases in the excess of deaths over births.

Seeking to explain these movements, in 1766 the author of the memorandum *Réflexions sur la valeur du blé tant en France qu'en Angleterre depuis 1674 jusqu'en 1764*[2] put the blame on shortage of foodstuffs and on epidemics: "Various investigations have furnished proof that the years when grain was at its dearest were also those when the death rate was highest and sickness most widespread."

In a period when both harvests and fiscal exactions were normal, the number of births clearly exceeded the number of deaths. Very soon, in the course of a few years, population outgrew subsistence. Prices rose. The humbler strata fed less well than before. The younger generation found it impossible to get work or a place to live and so put off their marriages. The poor took to begging, and the beggars became vagabonds. Then contagious diseases appeared: plague, typhus, cholera, smallpox. Some hundreds of thousands of poor people were carried off, and some thousands of rich ones. The population again fell below the level of available food supplies: prices declined, equilibrium was restored, and the population could start to grow once more. This was an internal demographic phenomenon.

At Auneuil, in the district of Bray, between 1657 and 1676, the average lifetime was twenty-one years. Thirty-five percent of the children failed to live as much as one year, and only 50 percent reached the age of first communion. Those who did attain adulthood died, on the average, at forty-three. In the villages of the Picardy plateau the average lifetime was estimated at twenty. At Beauvais, in the parishes where the textile industry was carried on, the average lifetime did not exceed seventeen or eighteen. The workmen lost 60 percent of their children before the age of fifteen, and the *"bourgeois"* 40 percent of theirs. Well-to-do people died between the ages of forty-eight and fifty-five.

The oscillations diminished during the 18th century because, with improvement in medicine and in food, the average length of life increased. At Auneuil in 1771–90 the death rate, and especially the infant death rate, was reduced. The average age at which adults died was fifty-one instead of forty-three. The average lifetime increased to thirty-two years.

This periodic movement gave rise to serious crises when it was combined with a series of severe winters, in which the seed froze in the earth, and a series of cold, rainy summers, which prevented grain from ripening. The result was famine, followed by a *"mortalité."* Prices rose. In Beauvaisis the price of grain increased by 200 to 300 percent between 1693 and 1694. People who normally ate wheat fell back on to rye, and those who normally ate rye resorted to barley. The prices of inferior food grains rose even more than those of the superior kinds. The lower strata of the population were the hardest hit. In the first year of a crisis, a poor peasant sold his cow and the craftsman his tools. The second year saw the coming of famine. Transport difficulties, especially where transport by land was involved, hindered revictualling and relief. Then "the plague" struck at the people's weakened bodies, with smallpox succeeding it after 1670. Deaths multiplied. Not all were registered: vagrants often died unrecorded. As much as 20, 30, or even 35 percent of the population might be carried off.

If such events happened at a time when the population was increasing, and especially when it was reaching the climax of increase, the consequences were very grave and hard to repair. Cases of this kind were the great *"mortalités"* of 1629–30, 1648–53, 1662–63, 1693–94, and 1709–10, the effects of which were cumulative, each *"mortalité"* occurring before the harm done by the previous one had been mended, so that under Colbert's ministry, and right down to the end of Louis XIV's reign and beyond, the kingdom suffered from a real shortage of manpower. In the 18th century, the crises of 1739–43, 1750–54, 1771–75, and 1779–84 were much less severe than those of the previous century. Food supplies were more plentiful. The famine that killed was replaced by the dearth that wore people down.

Generally speaking, the country districts suffered more than the towns, the workmen more than the *"bourgeois,"* and the grain-growing regions, such as the Picardy plateau, where the textile industry was carried on in the peasants' homes, more than the regions of polyculture and dairy-farming, like the district of Bray. In 1693 and 1694 at Gien the social group comprising the *nobles hommes* and *honorables hommes* lost 17 percent of its members, and the craftsmen and *laboureurs* lost 45 percent of theirs. Young persons (between five and fifteen) were more affected than the old if the population was increasing, but the old were affected more than the young if it was declining. The *"mortalités"* caused a fall in marriages and in conceptions, with the result, twenty or thirty years later, of a sharp decrease in marriages and births—the phenomenon of "empty age groups."

Recovery could be rapid. Auneuil lost 112 of its inhabitants in 1693–94, but this loss had been made up thirteen years later. Often, however, it took longer. Breteuil, which had lost 350 of its people, did not get back to its initial figure as quickly as Auneuil. In some places the losses experienced in the 17th century were not restored until about 1750.

Long-term changes

As regards the long-term trends, the differences observable between regions are great and the uncertainties numerous. Generally, there seems to have been a slow increase in the population from the end of the 16th century until the Fronde years. This growth ceased during the civil war of 1648–53, and then, taking the country as a whole, there was a decline until the end of the century. Recovery seems to have begun in 1698. In 1701–9 the kingdom must have included 19 million people. The first half of the 18th century appears to have been a time of oscillation. Between 1750 and 1770 the increase in numbers was apparently rapid, with annual growth rates of 7.8 to 10.7 percent, which was what probably caused the increase in the price of grain between 1765 and 1775. The overall increase of the population seems to have continued from 1770 to 1778, though more slowly, owing to the misfortunes suffered by the western provinces. Brittany, especially, was ravaged by dysentery, miliary fever, and smallpox; in 1773 this province saw 102,146 burials and only 80,954 baptisms. From 1779 to 1784 conditions were bad throughout the kingdom. In many places there was an excess of deaths over births. Taking France as a whole, there were 5,875,671 births and 5,549,484 deaths. The birth rate stood at about 37.7 percent, the death rate at 36 percent. On the whole, however, the 18th century was an epoch of progress. In 1784, according to Necker, the kingdom had 24,800,000 inhabitants, and in 1790, according to the Taxation Committee of the Constituent Assembly, it had 26,300,000. France had gained, since the end of the 17th century, about 7 million inhabitants—1 million of them by annexation (Lorraine, 834,600; Corsica, 124,000)—or 32 percent in ninety years. That represented an annual growth rate of 3 percent. But several European states had a markedly higher growth rate in the second half of the century.

This increase in the French population resulted mainly from a fall in the death rate, for the birth rate seems to have remained stagnant or even to have declined. The fall in the death rate would appear to have been caused by an increase in food supplies, achieved without any agrarian revolution. Instead of maslin, pure wheat became the principal food grain in the plateaus of the Paris Basin. Wheat is a more nutritious and more digestible cereal than rye, less congesting, less likely to prepare the way for bouts of fever, and calling for less frequent bleeding at changes of season. Maize began to be grown widely in Guyenne, Gascony, and some parts of Languedoc. New methods of bolting made it possible, from the end of the 17th century onward, to get one-third more flour from the same quantity of grain.

The increase in numbers was slow because of relative overpopulation and, undoubtedly, because of birth control. This practice existed among the higher nobility as early as the first half of the 17th century, and it spread in the second half to the magistracy. Among the masters of requests, fathers had between 1 and 7 children between 1661 and 1715, with an average of 3.4 per marriage. Their sons had between 0 and 9, with an average of 3.4, from 1661 to 1677; but between 1688 and 1704 the figures fell to between 0 and 4, with an average of 1.5, because of fifteen cases of only sons. Such a diminution could be caused only by birth control.

From the upper strata of society this phenomenon spread all over France, even into the villages. As early as the end of the 17th century there were, on the average, at Coulommiers and at Chailly-en-Brie, only between 5.12 and 4.95 children per marriage. The intervals between births have suggested to many writers the possibility of voluntary restriction of births. At Coulommiers and at Chailly-en-Brie we find intervals between births of 19, 23, 28, and 37 months. At Rumont, between 1720 and 1790, the intervals were from 25 to 35 months. At Argenteuil, between 1740 and 1790, the intervals were of 22, 30, and 39 months. It was the same in Tonnerrois between 1725 and 1800, and at Villedieu-les-Poêles and Saint-Pierre-Eglise, in Normandy, between 1711 and 1790. However, before concluding that artificial means of birth control were being employed, we need to have more information regarding the employment of wet nurses and the length of the period of lactation, during which a woman cannot conceive.

The quality of the population

We need to go beyond considering the numbers of the population to examine what the men were capable of. Some physical anthropology is called for; bodily shape, height, weight, muscular strength, lung capacity, power of resistance, and so on have to be studied. Few writers have paid attention to these factors.

It appears that the population of France aged early. Arthur Young, in his *Travels in France,* written at the end of the 18th century, describes poverty-stricken country areas where men of twenty-eight to thirty-five were wrinkled and bent like old men, and towns where a man was a greybeard at forty. Montaigne regarded himself at forty as having entered "the approaches to old age." The situation seems to have been analogous to that of most of the peoples of Black Africa in the 19th century, and due to the same cause: intake of food that was inadequate in both quantity and balance, being deficient in proteins and sugar.

This population was often made up of small, puny individuals. Henri Sée draws a grim picture of the Breton peasant as being short, thin, pale, yellowish, half-starved, and alcoholic, but M. Louis Chevalier thinks that in Paris there were plenty of big, strong, fair-haired men.

More precise evidence is provided by the records of the army. Normally the height of a Frenchman did not exceed 5 feet, 1 inch, or 5 feet, 2 inches. If we take a foot to be 32.4 centimeters, an inch to be 2.7 centimeters, and a *ligne* to be 6.6 millimeters, this means that the Frenchman was, at most, 1.66 or 1.67 meters tall. The army wanted no soldiers who were shorter than 5 feet, 3 inches (1.705 meters). If that requirement had been strictly enforced, three-fourths of the nation's males would have been rejected. Commanders even wanted their men to be 5 feet, 7 inches tall (1.813 meters), but these would be "giants." Soldiers were also expected to have a "fine appearance" and a "fine gait."

According to Moheau, the average height of an infantryman in 1774 was 5 feet, 2 inches, 7 *lignes*, or 1.72 meters. However, the dragoons in 1769 are reported to have been 5 feet, 4 inches, 11 *lignes*, or 1.798 meters tall. In wartime there were not enough tall men for the army's needs, and so it had to be content with men of 5 feet, 1 inch (1.66 or 1.67 meters) and even shorter. It was not unusual in the Orléans regiment of infantry to come upon men who were under 5 feet (1.624 meters). The dragoons of Antichamps were sometimes even shorter than the dauphin.

Out of thirty men aged between sixteen and forty-one, twenty-nine were, we learn, less than 5 feet in height (1.62 meters). One would have needed a body of 44,160 inhabitants in order to recruit an infantry regiment of 920 men, and one of 79,600 in order to find the men for a regiment of dragoons with an average height of 5 feet, 3 inches (1.70 meters). The nation was made up mostly of small men.

Soldiers were particularly tall in relation to the general level. At age sixteen, their average height was 5 feet, 1 inch, 3 *lignes*, or 1.658 meters; at twenty, it was 5 feet, 2 inches, 6 *lignes*, or 1,692 meters; and, at twenty-five, it was 5 feet, 3 inches, 1 *ligne*, or 1.718 meters.

The soldiers were exceptionally robust by comparison with the general standard, yet they were far from all being well-built men. The military regulations of 1791 directed that when the order to stand to attention was given, the men's heels must be "brought together, more or less, given that knock-kneed men and those with thick legs cannot make them meet." The regulations also noted that most of the men had "the bad habit of sticking one shoulder forward, holding one side in, or protruding one hip." Since such bad postures are due to muscular inadequacy, we may conclude that these soldiers were puny fellows. *A fortiori*, the number of weak and deformed persons in the nation at large must have been great.

By checking the occupational origin of the soldiers, the historian can form an idea of the differences in height between the different occupational or social categories of the nation. In 1763 the soldiers who came from the craftsman category had an average height of 5 feet, 2 inches, 8 *lignes*, or 1.697 meters; those who came from among the *laboureurs*, vinegrowers, gardeners, and servants had an average height of 5 feet, 2 inches, 9 *lignes*, or 1.699 meters; those from the world of the merchants, wholesalers, manufacturers, "*bourgeois*," and teachers were 5 feet, 3 inches (1.705 meters); and those recruited from the ranks of the *gentilshommes* and the military were 5 feet, 3 inches, 3 *lignes* (1.712 meters). Height was in direct ratio to comfort and abundance of food and in inverse ratio to the amount of manual work done, especially in winter.

This population seems, all the same, to have been very tough, and that is not a contradiction. The writer of these lines was able to observe in his battalion of Chasseurs Alpins the difference between, on the one hand, men's build and their aptitude for gymnastic and athletic exercises, and, on the other, their capacity to march long distances heavily laden and in bad weather. The infantrymen of the *ancien régime* were able to cover twelve leagues a day, four or five days in succession, on foot and carrying their equipment. In 1753 the regiment of Turenne moved from Rouen to Saint-Omer in five days, a distance of 250 kilometers. They had to carry a lot of weight. In peacetime an infantryman's load was between forty and forty-five pounds, and in wartime, with cartridges and several days' rations of bread, it came to sixty pounds. Sometimes they had to carry tents as well, which meant a burden of seventy-five pounds in all. The men's haversacks strained against their chests, leaving a black mark. After 1763 the straps passed over their shoulders. So, the state was able to find, in a population of mostly small and ill-made men, elements capable of serving as soldiers and workmen who could march or work long hours every day for relatively protracted periods. The population was comparatively large, but the frequent, sudden, and often substantial variations in its numbers left the state unsure how many taxpayers, soldiers, or workmen it could count on.

Intellectual training for political and other leadership

How the politicians and administrators were trained is a huge question, which could embrace all aspects and levels of education and also everything that might contribute to sharpening or to distorting men's minds, alongside education and after it: newspapers, learned periodicals, literary magazines, pamphlets, novels and plays "with a message," gatherings in *salons,* and membership in academies, learned societies, literary societies, secret societies, and pressure groups. Apart from considering the way in which the rulers used their heads, how they conceived, judged, and reasoned, we should tackle another huge subject, namely: to what extent did the great currents of thought of the age—the Catholic Renaissance, Augustinianism, Jansenism, the history of Roman law, the formation of French law, the Enlightenment, the Physiocrats—enter into their minds and influence their activity? It is not possible to deal with this whole enormous field here, and we must be satisfied with a few notes.

In the first place, the state had no specialized schools for the training of its magistrates and civil servants of all kinds. The men the state employed in its councils, courts of law, and bureaus had received, as a rule, the ordinary college education, subsequently completed by law studies. Everyone knew a little theology, for the Catholic religion formed a common basis that provided the general views needed regarding the universe, man's destiny, and how he should behave in this world. The sons of some nobles and some magistrates were educated at home by their fathers or by preceptors, as in the case of Chancellor d'Aguesseau, but such an education did not differ essentially from what was given in the colleges.

The humanities

Teaching that corresponded to what we know as secondary and higher education was provided, in the first place, in the colleges of the universities. But future magistrates attended even more commonly the colleges run by the Jesuits, especially the Collège de Clermont in Paris, which became the Collège Louis-le-Grand in 1682 and functioned until 1762, or the Oratorians' colleges, especially the one at Juilly, or the colleges of the Congrégation de la Doctrine Chrétienne. Actually, all of these colleges taught in more or less the same way as the colleges of the University of Paris—"*modo parisiensis.*" The pupil passed through eight forms. First came the secondary forms, where he studied grammar—namely the sixth, fifth, fourth, and third; then came the second form, where he studied the "humanities." The pupil then went on to higher education, in the first form, where he studied "rhetoric." This was followed by a year of "philosophy," in which he studied logic and morality, and another year in which he tackled physics and metaphysics. Having graduated as masters of arts, pupils could proceed to the specialized faculties, where teaching had a vocational bias—divinity, law, or medicine.

Most pupils left college after doing "rhetoric"; Voltaire was such a one. Having been formed by the poets, historians, and storytellers, they gained by their early departure, in that they remained closer to concrete reality. Only those went on to "philosophy" who thought they needed to become licentiates and doctors in the faculties.

The essential purpose of the teaching in the forms from the sixth to the first was to mold man's heart and to exercise and develop his mind. The means employed was the "humanities," the great authors of Latin and Greek literature. One had to steep oneself in them, imitate them, compete with them, surpass them, and, through minor improvements, to give them new life. The metaphor of the bees who collect the nectar from flowers and from it make their honey was constantly used by writers who advocated this mode of education.

The first device used for the training aimed at was the prelection. This was a master's lesson, intended to prepare the pupil for personal reading. The master read skillfully, in order to suggest the meaning of the passage. Then he set forth the argument, that is, the general idea of the passage, and both recalled what had gone before and mentioned what would come after. He then took the passage sentence by sentence, paraphrased it (in Latin), explained obscure points, substituted a simple construction for a more learned one, expanded expressions that were too concise, and clarified allusions. He showed the links of thought by which the sentences were bound together and then considered the passage as a whole once more and brought out what it contained that could be of greatest profit to the pupil.

In the sixth and fifth forms the prelection was concerned mainly with words and patterns, phonetics and morphology. In the fourth and third it dealt with syntax, sentence construction, grammatical correctness, and quantities in verse, and short digressions into mythology and history were introduced. In the second form the "humanities" were based on explication of poetry: formal beauty, appropriateness, and variety of terms, elegance and originality of expression, brilliance and color of images, music of rhythms, all that stimulates feeling and arouses enthusiasm, thus opening up the imagination and the heart. Contemporaries considered that the purpose of poetry was to enrapture the reader. Poets made men better by their moving evocation of human deeds and sentiments, which filled them with *humanitas:* kindness, generosity, benevolence, amiability, gentleness, tact. Homer, Pindar, Aeschylus, Sophocles, Euripides, the Greek Anthology, Virgil, Ovid, Lucian, Martial—these were the great awakeners, who completed the task of drawing the human being out of the savage and the barbarian.

In rhetoric, it was the orators and historians who were entrusted with the work of training: Herodotus, Thucydides, Xenophon, Plutarch, Demosthenes, Caesar, Livy, Sallust, Tacitus, Seneca, and, above all, Cicero, the model, the ideal. The prelection brought out the orator's elocution, the development of his composition, and his oratorical technique, and this led to a "moral" analysis of the passages being studied, from which the commonplaces or general ideas were extracted. The prelection included a study of the writer's erudition, with explanations of history, law, and institutions. History was held to furnish an arsenal of facts and a collection of examples from which one could deepen one's knowledge of the human heart.

The teaching of philosophy was based at the beginning of the 17th century on Aristotle, but in the second half of the century it became thoroughly Cartesian in the colleges of the Oratorians and the Doctrinaires, and indeed Cartesianism infiltrated everywhere.

It appears that the *régents* did not dictate but spoke normally, and the pupils took notes. The passages being discussed were presented on plain sheets of paper without annotations, with wide spaces between the lines, and interleaved with blank sheets, which could be used for the pupils' notes.

After the prelection came the pupil's personal work, known as the *"revue."* He reread the passage and his notes, in the study hall or at home, in tranquillity and silence. He marked the parts he had not understood, so as to have them reexplained to him. He wrote up the master's explanations, copied out the passage, and learned it by heart before he went to bed.

A class began, morning and afternoon alike, with a *recitatio,* a passage declaimed with appropriate gestures. In the grammar classes one also had to recite two or three rules. The best pupils, promoted to be *"décurions,"* heard their classmates recite, for a class might contain as many as two hundred *"écoliers."* The master supervised, questioning two or three pupils at random.

The master then proceeded to test what the pupils had learned from his prelection. This was the *"répétition."* He questioned them at random. He also made the weakest pupils go over their declensions, conjugations, and syntax. He insisted that explanations be given in a clear voice and with perfect pronunciation. This *répétition* took place every day. Each Saturday there was a general *répétition,* covering all the lessons and prelections of the week, and, at the end of each month, a *répétition* of all those of that month; then, in the second semester, came a *répétition* of all the work done in the first. At the beginning of each year the class rapidly reviewed the matter which had been covered in the previous years. Vacations were short—a fortnight for the "grammar" forms, a month for the "philosophy" ones. All the teaching was given in Latin, and the pupils spoke Latin in class.

The master gave homework, to be written in Latin. In "grammar" classes he set his pupils the task of writing a few lines, applying what they had been taught. He dictated what the task was to be, explained the difficulties they would have to overcome, and indicated the words and expressions it would be appropriate to use, which the pupils must group in accordance with the rules of morphology and syntax. Starting in the third form, the master set compositions for the pupils to write. First came letters, which it was indispensable for future secretaries, *commis,* and officials in the king's service to know how to compose. There were treatises on the art of letter-writing. In the "humanities" and "rhetoric" forms the pupil had to compose poems and speeches. He was trained to do this by means of a series of graded exercises: treating one and the same theme now concisely, now amply, now literally, now figuratively; developing a quotation or a fact in eight parts— the preamble, the paraphrase, the case, the contrary, the identity, the resemblance, the example, the evidence, and the epilogue—taking care with the transitions from one to another; transposing prose into verse; altering the meter of a poem; composing in imitation of Pliny, or Virgil, or Cicero. He then arrived at the stage of personal compositions: a panegyric of Saint Dionysius the Areopagite, a eulogy of Trajan, a eulogy of Portia, Brutus's wife, a speech to the Senate on the reasons for and against sending an expedition to America, a speech on the war to be declared against the tyrant Jugurtha.

Every morning the *"décurions"* collected the pupils' homework. While they heard the pupils recite, the master corrected the homework, giving some of it for correction to selected pupils, the *"émules."* They insisted on well-formed letters, regular handwriting, and strict observance of the rules of spelling and punctuation. While the master went on with his correction, the pupils worked. The youngest did exercises in spelling and accentuation; those a little older worked on a task of imitation or translation; the humanists paraphrased a sentence or imitated a commonplace; the rhetoricians wrote a description, an inscription, or an epitaph or translated a Greek speech into Latin or a Latin speech into Greek.

The pupils kept notebooks of *loci communes* or aphorisms, sayings, comparisons, images, definitions, proverbs, maxims, fables, and adages. The compiling of these notebooks called for an effort of intelligence in the choice of documents and in comparing and classifying in accordance with sameness or contrariness of meaning. They formed mines of material for use in reflection on the subjects assigned. Montaigne's essays and Montesquieu's *L'Esprit des lois* both developed directly from notebooks of "commonplaces." This method of work could, indeed, be applied to philosophy, law, or divinity alike.

In the "philosophy" form, lessons were supplemented by disputes on theses. Each day, in class, a quarter of an hour was devoted to expounding a thesis. The remaining three-quarters of the hour were spent in formal argument about it—in Latin, of course. The examination followed the same pattern:

> "I ask you, learned candidate: what is logic?"
> "You ask me, distinguished examiner, what logic is. I answer to the distinguished examiner that logic can be considered in two ways, either according to its name, or according to what it is. Logic, according to its name, is speech. Logic, according to what it is, is a practical skill and science."

The examiner objects:

> "If logic were a skill (*art*), logicians would be craftsmen (*artisans*). But logicians are not craftsmen. Consequently, logic is not a skill."

The candidate makes a distinction.

"If logic were a mechanical skill (*art mécanique*), logicians would be craftsmen. But logic is a liberal art (*art libéral*), and so it is indeed a skill, without logicians being craftsmen."

And so on.

This mode of instruction had its good points. It enabled pupils to become possessed of the best and finest of mankind's achievements. It contributed to the setting-free of what is best in man. It strove to penetrate into the depths of the human heart, even into its most secret corners. It taught a whole method for using one's mind: to look for the thought behind words, so as to avoid rote learning; to look beyond ideas to realities, so as to eliminate empty formulas; to seek the essential character of a reality, so as to avoid empiricism, with its limitations and lack of concentration; to follow up the many different relations between objects and ideas, finding beneath these relations a world that seemed to be harmonious and united around one single center, God. A search for God was undertaken through the beauty of forms and through the spiritual beauty of the great souls who had tried to express themselves in these forms.

Any search may fail. The defect of this mode of instruction was that, apart from what the pupil might be able to find within himself by introspection and outside himself by relations with his schoolmates and his teachers, there was very little observation of reality itself and not much induction from what was observed. The pupil ran the risk, despite his teachers' intentions, of becoming lost among words and formulas. As far as observation of mankind was concerned, the teachers relied on what life and the exercise of a profession could give their pupils. To prepare them to observe things, in philosophy the teaching of mathematics was complemented by astronomy and geographical mathematics. The teachers taught the globe (cosmography), the astrolabe, and the theory of the planets. They taught their pupils how to make an astrolabe, a graduated curve provided with a movable alidad by which to take sightings on various points, and how to use it to carry out astronomical, geographical, and geometrical measurements, measuring the height of a mountain or the depth of a valley. The pupils learned to use Ptolemy's armillary sphere, two or three circles whose right-angled planes helped to determine the coordinates of the stars in relation to the equator and the meridian; to use the arbalest, the astronomical radius or "Jacob's staff," in order to find one's bearings in topography or when at sea; and to use the compass. They constructed rudimentary pieces of apparatus. This was instruction oriented toward practice, as was the instruction in mathematics, in which pupils were exercised in the use of the proportional compasses and in mensuration, surveying, and triangulation. Finally, pupils studied geographical maps and were made to draw such maps.

Law

Most future officials and *grand commis* went on to study law, though a few studied divinity. Turgot considered that only theologians knew how to reason.

Provision for law studies was often mediocre. Numerous universities awarded degrees, as licentiate or doctor, in return for payment. However, students could take advantage of the many private lessons given by doctors of law who were practical men—bishops, masters of requests, counselors in the *parlement,* court chaplains, advocates before the *parlement.* These *"siffleurs"* taught either in their own homes, where they assembled classes of up to twenty, or in those of individual students. Both in the faculty and in private lessons the same method was almost always followed: half an hour of dictation, half an hour of explanation of what had been dictated, half an hour of questions and discussion. Printed "notes on method" gave advice for the students' personal work: revise the dictation and the notes taken during the explanation, write them up, read the passages mentioned and study them, read the codes from which the passages were taken and the books by major authors on the question concerned, and keep notebooks of extracts, classified systematically. In short, the method as a whole was founded on a very good principle: constant reference to the sources and personal, direct study of these sources so as to become imbued with them. Teaching was complemented by discussions, called *"disputes,"* in which students argued against each other in proper legal form.

After 1679 the teaching of French law was added to that of Roman law. In order to become a bachelor in law, it was necessary to study for two years, pass an examination, and take part in a two-hour disputation; to become a licentiate, another year's study was needed, with another examination and a three-hour disputation; to become a doctor, a further year's study, culminating in the explanation of a passage and a disputation lasting four hours.

Theological studies were carried on in the same style but took longer. They were based on learning to explain the Old and New Testaments. Technical instruction for certain functions was gradually developed. The fundamental idea was to apply scientific knowledge to practical work.

Engineering

From early on the colleges made courses in hydrography available to sailors. Then the Abbé Guillaume Denys, once a pupil of the Oratorians at Dieppe, founded a school for pilots there in 1663, with Colbert's backing The minister wished to establish courses in hydrography at all the ports. He employed the Jesuits to this end, and such courses were provided in 1669 in Marseilles, in 1671 in Nantes, and in 1674 at Rennes. An ordinance of August 1681 appointed certified teachers of hydrography who were to enjoy the same privileges as teachers of law. The royal chairs of hydrography were entrusted to Jesuits. The teaching embraced arithmetic, geometry (use of the ruler and compasses, construction of instruments), astronomy, geography, and hydrography. It was conceived on practical lines: how to take bearings, draw charts, navigate, make use of periodical winds and tides, forecast weather changes. In 1720 a repository of charts was established in Paris. An Ecole de la Marine was opened in the Louvre for naval architects. In 1752 the Académie royale de Marine was born.

Next after the sailors, the civil engineers of the department of bridges and highways were provided with a system of technical instruction. A Council *arrêt* of 1716 organized these engineers into a hierarchy. The special school for recruiting and training them began in 1744 as a bureau for mapmakers, which in 1747 Peronnet succeeded in having transformed into a technical school. Its future pupils first had to study grammar at a classical college, in order to acquire order and clarity in their thinking and expression. They then spent two or three years either at a school of architecture, such as Blondel's, founded in 1739, or in the bureau of an engineer in the department of bridges and highways. After that, if they had done well, they presented themselves for the competitive examination for entry to the Ecole des Ponts et Chaussées, where a three-year practical course was provided.

Special military schools were set up, in the first place for the scientific branches. The school at Mézières was opened in 1748 for engineers and engineer-geographers, *"le génie."* A school of artillery was founded at La Fère, and a school of mines in Paris in 1778. For the naval artillery a school for gunnery apprentices was formed in 1766. The royal military school in Paris functioned from 1751 onward, being reorganized in 1777. In all these schools, teaching had a practical bias. Courses of instruction, of great scientific value, were completed by practical work and attachments to military units. At the school of mines, chemistry, mineralogy, hydraulics, and the ventilation and working of mines were taught. At all the special schools the pupils solved many practical problems in the classroom, drew maps, and worked in the laboratory; but three days out of six were devoted to outdoor work: building bridges and fortifications, making gunpowder, practicing maneuvers and shooting. Part of the summer was spent at factories, naval dockyards, building sites. Technical instruction ensured a close union between science and practice, brainwork and manual work.

Summary

The spirit of the humanities, that expression of the Renaissance, was thus gradually complemented, from 1660 onward, by the spirit of the Enlightenment.

A new variety of specialists, the "engineers," increased in numbers. In 1765 the *Encyclopédie* wrote:

> We have three kinds of engineers. There are those for war, who need to know all about the construction of fortresses and how to attack and defend them. Then there are those for the navy, who are expert in matters to do with war and service at sea. And then there are those of the *ponts et chaussées,* who are continually busy improving the main roads, building bridges, beautifying the streets, and making and maintaining canals. All these varieties of men are trained in schools from which they go out into their respective services, starting in the lowest posts and rising, through the passage of time and the acquisition of merit, to the most distinguished positions.

So far, there was no mention of factories in this connection.

Broadly speaking, the magistrates and administrators of the 17th and 18th centuries received a good intellectual training. What was most seriously lacking was an intermediate stage between the basic general training by means of the humanities and the specialized practical training given by actual exercise of a profession or by special schools—faculties of law, divinity, and medicine and central schools of technical instruction: namely, a stage of education in the human sciences that were developing at that time—statistics, demography, political economy. But to an increasing extent, and especially in the second half of the 18th century, many administrators were spontaneously taking steps to remedy this deficiency: men like Montyon, La Michodière, Tourny, D'Etigny, and Turgot, the great "enlightened" intendants. The spheres of justice and *"police"* included a group of able minds who were responsible for the comparative superiority enjoyed by France's government and administration.

Construction methods

The state's primary role was to ensure order and security. It therefore had need of fortresses, both at the frontiers and inside the country. To provide premises for judges, litigants, and court records, to hold arrested persons and convicts in custody, and for the king himself, and for his councils, his ministers, and their staffs, palaces and houses of various kinds were required. For the movement about the country of couriers, magistrates, commissioners, and soldiers and their guns, roads and bridges had to be available. To defend the country and to put down malefactors, rebels, and enemies of the state, weapons were indispensable: cannon, mortars, mines, fougasses, muskets, fusils, pikes, bayonets.

We therefore ought to know, for example, about the methods used in building; the materials—their resistance, their density, the quantities necessary; the pace at which workmen did their work; the tools and machines employed; the time required for different tasks, their cost, and so on.

Technical treatises existed, especially after the foundation of the Academy of Sciences, and from these and from administrative correspondence we can get answers to our questions. It would take too long to deal thoroughly with them. I shall confine myself to some aspects of the construction of fortresses, in which the fundamental principles remained unchanged from the beginning of the 16th century until the 1850s, when rifled gun barrels and steel shells filled with powerful explosives made their appearance.

Belidor, *commissaire ordinaire* for the artillery, royal professor of mathematics in the gunnery schools, member of England's Royal Society and the Prussian royal scientific academy, corresponding member of the Paris Académie royale des Sciences, gives us in his fundamental work, *La Science des ingénieurs dans la conduite des travaux de for-*

tification et d'architecture civile, dédié au Roy, in 1739, a clear picture of the problems confronting the engineers of his time. He wrote six books. The first dealt with the dimensions of revetments needed to resist the pressure of earth and compared Vauban's general cross-section with the previously accepted rules. The second dealt with the thrust of arches and how to determine the thickness of their pillars. The third provided information about materials, their properties, how to divide them and put them to use—lime, brick, sand, mortar, and so on. The fourth studied methods of construction, qualities of wood and iron, ways of calculating the strength of the main elements in a timber frame, the different sorts of building. The fifth discussed the decoration of buildings, the architectural orders, columns, pilasters, and pediments. The sixth gave instruction on how to prepare estimates for building work.

Building the fortress of Ath

Our best plan, though, is undoubtedly to follow Vauban as he went about building the fortress of Ath, in Hainault, between 1668 and 1674. His correspondence with Louvois, the secretary of state for war, the reports of the engineers working at Ath, the letters of the governors of Ath and those of the *commissaire des guerres* who was responsible for providing all that the soldiers and workmen needed—bread, grain, fodder, remounts, equipment, housing—enable us to reconstitute the successive operations involved.

Ath was a medieval town. In the 14th century it had been surrounded by a stone curtain wall, flanked by some thirty two-story towers and with three gates; in front of it there was a wide moat. When Spain ceded it to Louis XIV after the War of Devolution, Vauban set about fortifying the place. The king gave it back to the Spaniards under the Treaty of Nijmegen (17 September 1678). Vauban captured Ath in 1697, during the War of the League of Augsburg, but Spain recovered it by the Treaty of Ryswick (20 September 1697). The Spaniards entrusted its defense to Dutch troops. Reoccupied by the French in 1701, it was taken during the War of the Spanish Succession by the English general Marlborough, on 2 October 1706. By the Barrier Treaty of 15 November 1715 Ath was given to the Emperor Charles VI. Retaken by the French in October 1745, during the War of the Austrian Succession, it was dismantled along with other fortresses forming the Barrier. In 1746, only the main body of the fortress designed by Vauban was left. In 1817, however, after the reestablishment of the Barrier, everything was restored, just as it had been in Vauban's time. When rifled guns came in, the fortress was doomed to obsolescence, and after 1853 it was gradually dismantled. In 1895 all that was left was two mounds, the shapeless remains of the bastions of Luxembourg and Flanders. In 1953 nothing at all remained but the vault of a sluice.

The fortifications of Ath were begun by Vauban immediately after the French troops entered in 1667. In April and May 1668 the royal engineers Montguirault, Deslandes, Poupart, and Saint-Martin arrived at Ath. Peace was signed on 2 May 1668, and Louvois decided to send Vauban to Ath. The chevalier de Clerville was nominally director general of fortifications, but it was Vauban who actually played this role, and in November 1667 a layout by him for the new fortifications of Lille had been preferred to one by Clerville. Vauban arrived at Ath on 16 June 1668 with his "band of Archimedes," his assistants and draughtsmen. Starting on 17 June, he carried out an inspection of the town—with considerable difficulty, because the soldiers were camped in huts along the ramparts, owing to fear of plague. Vauban took levels, made calculations, visited the places where building materials were being prepared, had a plan made of the town, and informed himself regarding the nature and quality of the subsoil, by taking soundings. He drew up five successive schemes. He had been ordered to make use of the old medieval wall, which he was to heighten and thicken, while the ditch in front of it was deepened. However, his soundings showed that the foundations of the wall did not go down even as far as the level of the bottom of the existing ditch. It was not possible to use the old wall, and so it was demolished. Vauban's fifth scheme was completed on 17 July 1668, and the king approved it on 21 July.

The fortification was to take the form of an octagon, with eight bastions. Facing Mont Féron, two sides of the octagon were to be reduced to one straight section, with a flat bastion in the middle. Between the bastions, the curtain was to be protected by a tenail, in front of which would be a demilune with a reduit. The curtains were, indeed, rather long. They need not have exceeded twice the range of a musket, since the curtain was covered throughout its length by the fire from two bastions. The plan also included a further 2,000 fathoms for new buildings and magazines.

Vauban arranged periodical meetings of the engineers and their assistants. He told each of them what he expected him to do. He organized means of supply (a canal, a boat, horses, carts, tools) and amassed materials (quarry stone, lime, sand, bricks, charcoal, wood) until November and the onset of winter.

During the summer of 1668 Vauban had a circular canal dug round the town, to serve to bring materials to the building sites, using the waters of the Petite Dendre and the Villet. He made this canal run where the great ditch was to be, covering half its width. Along the inner side of the canal a berm of earth served as landing place and distribution center for materials. As soon as part of the canal was completed. digging had to be started beside the berm, to make the escarp. In five weeks, two kilometers of a ten-meters-wide canal was in use. It could carry boats containing fifteen to twenty cartloads of stone. In July, Vauban sent out for timber and had ten boats built. They were ready for use by autumn. Orders for twelve more to be built were then given. The service of bringing supplies by boat was put under the command of an engineer. Thanks to this canal, twenty horses and fifteen boats did in one year the work of four hundred horses in two years. The canal cost the king nothing and saved him 250,000 livres.

Vauban reorganized the transport service. He laid down rules for the feeding and resting of the animals. He counted the number of journeys that the carters could make in a day, so as to make sure that they were not wasting their time in drink shops. If they defaulted, he did not dismiss them but put them in prison. He gave the job of controlling the transport service to his nephew, Dupuis-Vauban.

Vauban made contracts for the purchase of tipcarts, wheelbarrows, picks, shovels, and other tools. He explored the countryside around the town to find quarries. The local people concealed them, but a few *patagons* distributed among the peasants, together with his reputation, soon established, as a good payer, removed the difficulties. At the end of June 1668, four quarries were opened. A water-driven pump had to be installed, owing to rain and floods. By the end of July, between twelve and sixteen quarries were being exploited. For one week's building work, between 700 and 800 boatloads of stone, or 16,000 cartloads were needed. At the end of September, Vauban had 4,000 boatloads of stone, or 80,000 cartloads, in store. By the end of the autumn, he had twice as much in store.

Vauban encountered difficulty in finding good *"rocqueteurs"* (stonecutters). Louvois had fifty sent to him from Tournai, together with volunteers from the Royal-Vaisseaux regiment. Vauban arranged for stonecutters to be brought from Limousin, Morvan, and Burgundy. In autumn 1668, fifty quarrymen from Limousin who had signed a contract arrived at Ath. At that time the extraction of stone was being directed by a hundred or so skilled workers. In November, Louvois sent ninety-two workmen from Paris. The local lime was of good quality, so that building work could continue even in winter. By 21 June 1668 Vauban had six limekilns in production. However, he needed twelve in order to accumulate the stock he required, and so, on 4 November, he made a contract with Sieurs Bomare and Cambier.

Two thousand tipcart-loads of sand were obtained from the digging of the canal. But 72,000 such loads were needed for the building of the main body of the fortress, and so Vauban contracted with some civilian entrepreneurs for the additional sand.

Bricks were needed only for the parapets. Vauban had them baked on the banks of the Dendre and brought in by water.

He bought Borinage coal at Saint-Ghislain, eighty cartloads at a time, but he also had mines opened on lands belonging to the king.

Several times during the year he sent an engineer to go with the carpenters into the woods and mark the trees, especially oaks, that would have to be cut down for timber.

The engineers traced the outline of the fortifications on the ground. Using descriptive geometry, they transferred to the ground the line of the polygon to be fortified, the main part of the fortress, or escarp. All the other measurements of the external works were proportioned to those of the great surrounding wall. Thus, the faces of a demilune were equal in length to one-half of the curtain they covered. The width and depth of the moat were determined by reference to the length of the curtain.

The engineers traced the fortifications on the ground with metal semicircles and quarter-circles, a big wooden protractor equipped with a movable arm to measure angles, large wooden stakes or markers, and thick rope. The stakes were driven in at the angles and at intervals along the lines, and the rope, stretched between them, showed the outline to be followed. By 25 July 1668 Lalande, Vauban's assistant, had finished this "trace." It was necessary to knock down thirty houses and to demolish the abbey of Notre-Dame-du-Refuge, outside the medieval walls.

Digging then began. The workmen first dug a big ditch, beginning beside the escarp, on the townward side. They shifted the soil from that side to the place where the escarp, or wall, of the main body of the fortress was to be raised. The soil was placed directly in the spots where it was needed and would remain. All the work was done by hand, everying was carried on men's backs; pickaxes, spades, wheelbarrows, hods, and wooden footbridges were used. The digging was performed by soldiers of the garrison, between 1,600 and 1,800 men all together, but civilian workers were also recruited in the castellany. Vauban sent out circulars and had his appeal for men read out in church on Sundays. Peasants came to enlist for the work, even from the territory under Spanish occupation. They wanted to be paid by the day, but gradually they agreed to payment on a piecework basis, and productivity increased markedly. Vauban recruited three hundred Flemish master navvies, each of whom got through more work than six Walloon peasants.

As soon as the required depth had been reached, and half of the required width, the engineers began laying the foundation of the escarp, or great wall around the main body of the fortress. The neighboring countryside provided the stone and mortar needed. The navvies and the builders worked at the same time on different sectors of the great ditch. To prevent falling débris, the navvies placed fascines, that is, beds of faggots laid alternately this way and that, to strengthen the edges of the ditch. The builders left gaps in the wall where the gates were to be set up.

The navvies then excavated the "outworks," the parts of the fortification beyond the great ditch. The earth was carried either to the embankment of the rampart or to the outer ditch.

After that, the gates were erected, and then the outworks were built up, and the mighty task was completed. However, it took several years for the walls to dry out and the earth to settle.

Vauban wanted to make contracts with entrepreneurs in the building trade for the whole of the building work, but this would have meant taking three years for the task, and Louvois wanted it done in a year. Vauban therefore combined a workshop directly in the service of the king for the construction of three of the bastions, with a contract with civilian builders for the construction of the remaining five. A contract was signed on 23 November 1668 with the entrepreneurs La Touche and Tarade, who undertook to supply the entire revetment of the main body of the fortress within one year and, within two years, all the outworks, bridges, caissons, sluices, and gates.

The escarp was to be ten meters high and three meters thick at the base and flanked with buttresses in the thickness of which arch-shaped openings would be made, the size of an ordinary door. The work involved required 16,000 cubic fathoms of building material, or 128,000 cubic meters. One cubic fathom was equivalent to eight cubic meters, or twenty tipcart-loads of stone. For the escarp wall alone, 320,000 tipcart-loads of stone were needed. On 22 February 1669 the first stone was laid; by the beginning of July 1669 the foundation had been completed to a depth of six meters.

By the beginning of May 1669 the demilunes had been excavated. Vauban made a contract with Paul and Denis for the turfing of all the earthworks.

By November 1669 the navvies had dug out and carried away 75,000 cubic fathoms (600,000 cubic meters) of earth, or a square mass of earth 100 meters by 60 meters. Vauban had employed 400 building workers, 1,560 laborers, 1,020 navvies, 410 stone cutters, 700 excavators, and 100 boatmen and stevedores—about 4,190 workmen in all—together with a large number of soldiers, entire companies being assigned to this work. For their labors the soldiers received, in addition to their pay, one loaf of ration bread per day or a few coins. Nevertheless, a special guard sometimes had to be mounted to prevent the men from deserting the site.

The hardest part of the work was the pile-driving. When the workmen encountered quicksand or sloughs, due to springs, they had to drive wooden piles. These were whole trunks of oak trees, roughly squared, between four and five meters long. They were driven in by means of a rammer, a mass of iron or wood suspended by a pulley from a big tripod. Several men hauled it up by means of a rope and then let it fall on the head of the pile. The piles were set in squares, with their heads at ground level. Over them other piles were laid horizontally, forming a "grid," and the building was erected on this foundation. The whole face of the fortification looking toward Mont Féron had to be provided with such a foundation of piles. In front of the Flanders bastion the soil consisted of mud. Each blow of the rammer drove the piles one meter into the ground; but every time a pile went in, another one came out. Seven rammers were working day and night between June and August 1669.

During the summer of 1669 Vauban began excavating the sluices and designing the gates. In 1670 he installed the sluices, gates, and caissons. On 18 May 1670 the king visited the fortress. In 1671 the gates, temporary bridges, and sluices were completed. An arsenal was built, to store cannonballs and grenades. Three powder magazines were established, each under a bastion. Ramparts of earth were erected along the curtain, with gun emplacements and banquettes in them. During the winter of 1671–72 four rows of lime trees and elms were planted on the ramparts, forming three avenues. In 1672 the great sluice, which was to enable the ditches to be filled with water, was completed.

The main body of the fortress had cost 3,500,000 livres, and the entire complex, 5 million livres.

The undertaking as a whole presents some characteristic features. Working as he did in a civilization based on the resources provided by nature—water and wood—Vauban had to rely on the natural means available in the surrounding area: stone, wood, water. To make use of them, he had to employ a small range of tools and simple machines worked by hand. Everything depended ultimately on men's strength and manual ingenuity. Vauban was served partly by soldiers and partly by civilian workmen, who fell into two categories: a small number of skilled specialists and the rest—peasants acting as laborers—whom they organized.

The overall conception and the supervision of the work was always the responsibility of the royal engineers. They themselves directed the execution of part of the work, *en régie,* while the remainder was entrusted, by contract, to civilian firms.

The direct agents of the state thus appear here as those who conceived plans, drew up programs, assembled resources, coordinated activities, supervised execution, and stimulated enthusiasm. They were the brains and spur of the population. But the level of civilization allowed the state only limited and slow-acting means for carrying out its aims, as compared with those available in the 20th century.

The state's financial resources

There can be no question of dealing here with the state's budget, the fiscal mechanism, the various taxes, and the changes in taxation or of tackling the problems of public credit in their different aspects. My only concern for the moment is to try to discover what margin production offered for fiscal exactions and the extent to which public opinion allowed the state to exploit this margin. It was a narrow margin, and opinion was resistant to taxation.

How the French viewed taxation

Even in the 17th century most Frenchmen thought that the state should meet its ordinary expenses out of the revenue from the royal domain. Resort to taxation should be had only exceptionally, to deal with extraordinary circumstances, such as war.

Furthermore, in a society in which custom had the force of law, in which everything old was revered—because anything whose beginnings were lost in the mists of time, or at any rate went back to very ancient times, proved by its very duration, people thought, that it was a condition of existence—everyone was hostile to increases in taxation, and especially to new taxes. Every innovation was an extortion. Every new tax was a "*gabelle*": the mere word was enough to make men see red and start revolts. The old-established taxes, having become customary, were put up with. The French continually demanded that taxes be brought back, in number and rate, to what they had been in an epoch they regarded as normal. In the 17th century, when the royal myth of Henri IV became established, the French were always calling for a return to the taxes of Good King Henri.

Taxpaying was seen as ignoble. The deduction of a tax from the income of the head of a family was considered a spoliation, a violation of the right of property, an infringement of man's natural freedom, as master of his body, his family, and his goods, to dispose of them as he chose, and, consequently, a mark of subjection that came close to slavery. To pay taxes was degrading. Those who performed the most highly respected social functions, sources of dignity and honor, like the clergy, the nobility, and the magistrates, were therefore exempt from taxation. There were numerous exempt persons, for everyone sought exemption or usurped it, not only because of the universal desire to pay as little as possible, but because exemption was an honor and a sign of rank in society.

This attitude changed in the course of the 18th century. The notion that it was legitimate and necessary for everyone to contribute to the common expenses of society began to displace the old notions about taxes and domain revenues. The universal contribution, it came to be thought, should be subject to consent by the king's subjects, who were free men, and should be moderate in amount. According to Vauban, it should be levied only once on a particular unit of production: if a *seigneur*'s farmer had paid tax on his crop, the *seigneur* ought not to be required to pay tax again on the part of this crop he took as his due. The Physiocrats held that taxation should fall on all owners of land but on them only.

Nevertheless, there was still not much possibility of getting people to agree to a large increase in the burden of taxes. This attitude explains the large number, and the seriousness, of the revolts against taxation. The expressed motive of most popular revolts was the excessiveness, real or alleged, of taxation.

The margin offered by production

The margin of production available for taxation remained a narrow one. France was a mainly rural country. The principal source of taxation was the countryside, agriculture. Whatever might be the relative importance of maritime trade and manufactures, it was the regional and local trade in the produce of the soil that brought about the biggest circulation of money, the means whereby the peasants acquired the cash they needed in order to pay the royal taxes. The king's levies from production here came into competition with those effected by the provinces and the towns and, especially, with those effected, whether in money or in kind, for the payment of seignorial and feudal dues.[3] To determine exactly the margin left by all these exactions, we should need to be able to calculate the gross product and from this deduct the various exactions in order to arrive at the net product. However, the documents required for calculating the gross product are often not to be had. We lack chronological series of records showing, year by year, areas sown to grain, the crops stored in the barns, the vines dressed. Generally, in order to obtain a few dozen usable figures, we have to rely on the chance discovery of a postmortem inventory of a man's possessions, the proceedings of a distraint, a valuation of a harvest, or a settlement of accounts between a farmer and his landlord. It is also hard to ascertain how this gross product was divided—how much went in ground rent, tithe, seignorial and feudal dues, and various taxes, and what the net product remaining was, what the cultivator had to live on. The share taken by the royal taxes depended on the gross product, the other exactions, and the compressibility of the net product.

Records that would enable us to calculate the gross product are often lacking, but, apart from that, the complexity of the factors involved makes such calculation difficult. We have to take into account the amount of money needed to replace old or dead stock, the amount of produce consumed on the spot, the results of the work carried out by the cultivator himself and his family, and many other factors. This calculation is, indeed, so difficult that, always and everywhere, it ends by showing all units of cultivation with a debit balance. Nevertheless, we must make an attempt.

Before doing so, however, let us draw on the impressions and observations of travelers. The English philosopher and politician John Locke traveled in France between 1675 and 1679. He tells us that, being in Bordeaux on Thursday, 15 September 1678, he pushed on as far as Graves. There he saw a family consisting of a poor rural day laborer, his wife, and his three children. The husband earned 7 sous a day, the wife 3 or 3½, "when she could get work." At other times she span hemp to make their clothes, which yielded no money. Their home was "a poor one room and one story, open to the tiles, without window." They had a small vine from which they obtained wine to sell. "The profit of it was very little." Their rent was 12 écus. As the husband probably worked two hundred days a year, we must suppose his wages came to 70 livres. They had to pay 4 livres in *taille,* 6 percent of the man's earnings; they were behind in their payment, and the collector had shortly before seized their frying pan and their dishes. Since their clothes, of hempen cloth, were more or less provided by the wife's work at home, they had 64 livres to spend on the feeding of five persons—not even 8 deniers per day per person. They ate rye bread and sometimes "the inwards of some beast," and they drank water. Their condition was close to starvation. Locke states that the peasants in Saintonge were even worse off than these, who were living near the great commercial center of Bordeaux. What, in a situation like this, was the margin left for taxation? Less than 4 percent, since the total income of the family— the roughly 36 livres they may have obtained for the wine (this being the amount of rent they paid), plus the 70 livres earned by the husband (not reckoning the money that the wife occasionally earned, what was represented by her contribution to the family's clothing, or possible garden vegetables)—would come to no more than 106 livres. The *taille* of 4 livres, even if we assume that this was the only tax they paid, amounted to about 3.85 per cent; they were unable to pay it, and their kitchen utensils were seized for this reason.

M. Jean Jacquart has devoted an excellent doctoral thesis to the countryside of Hurepoix, a district south of Paris, between Beauce and

Brie, which enjoyed proximity to the market constituted by the capital. Trying to determine the gross product, he notes, first of all, that as far as vinegrowing was concerned, one arpent of land yielded, between 1620 and 1630, between 2½ and 5 *muids*. At between 20 and 30 livres a *muid*, the return would be something between 50 or 75 livres and 100 or 150 livres. From this must be deducted 10 to 12 livres for the wine sticks and 4 to 6 livres for manure and the work involved in dressing the vines and for pruning, provining, layering, second dressing, planting the vine sticks, and tying—which cost 25 to 30 livres in 1620–30 and 40 to 45 livres in 1660. Also to be deducted are the costs of the wine harvest—4 sous a day for the cutters, 10 sous for the carriers, and the costs of pressing the grapes, 3 or 4 livres for a good crop, half the amount for a poor one. We get the following picture, for a good crop:

Receipts	Expenses	
100–125 livres	Dressing	25–30 livres
(the price being only 20–25 livres per *muid*,	Materials	10–15
since there was a plentiful supply)	Harvesting	3–4
	Pressing	3–4
	Total	41–53 livres

There remained a gross product of between 47 and 84 livres, equivalent to between five and ten *setiers* of maslin, a mixture of wheat and rye. Consumption of this grain was about three *setiers* per person per year.

For a mediocre wine crop, 2.5 *muids* per arpent, we get:

Receipts	Expenses	
62–75 livres	Dressing	25–30 livres
(the price being 25–30 livres per *muid*,	Materials	10–15
owing to the short supply)	Harvesting	1–2
	Pressing	1–2
	Total	38–49 livres

There was thus a gross product of between 13 and 37 livres, equivalent to between one and four *setiers* of maslin.

When the crop was a poor one (only one *muid* per arpent), the holding showed a debit balance.

On a ten-year average, the wine brought in about 20 livres per year per arpent, which meant the means to buy two *setiers* of maslin, food for one person for two-thirds of a year. As a rule, the vinegrowers cultivated three or four arpents, giving them the means to buy eight *setiers* of maslin and to feed, taking one year with another, two persons throughout the year and a third for eight months of the year.

Cereals were the basic resource, and in certain areas this was practically the only crop. M. Jacquart has studied a farm in Hurepoix, 120 arpents (40 hectares) in size, which was cultivated with one or two ploughs, three or four horses, a carter, a maidservant, a shepherd, and some temporary labor. There was a three-year rotation, with a fallow period and the land divided into three breaks. The first break, of 40 arpents, was devoted to maslin. A good harvest produced 140–80 *setiers;* an average one, 100–20; a bad one, 50–60. For sowing, 26⅔ *setiers* were always needed; the wages of the harvest hands took 13 *setiers;* and threshing cost one-twenty-fourth of the total—7 *setiers* in good years, 5 in average ones, 2 in bad ones. The feeding of one person absorbed 3 *setiers* a year, at two pounds of bread a day. Five persons, with three farm servants, thus consumed each year a minimum of 24 *setiers.* Six more were needed for the harvesters and temporary hired hands.

Thus, when there was a good crop:

Good Soils			Mediocre Soils		
Crop	Expenses		Crop	Expenses	
180 *setiers*	Seed	26.6 *setiers*	140 *setiers*	Seed	25.0 *setiers*
at 7 livres,	Harvest		at 7 livres,	Harvest	
4 sous, plus	hands	13.2	4 sous	hands	12.0
straw for	Threshing	6.9		Threshing	5.8
use on the	Food	30.0		Food	30.0
holding					
	Total	76.7 *setiers*		Total	72.8 *setiers*

Gross product: 103 *setiers* at 7 livres, 4 *sous*—741 livres

Gross product: 67 *setiers* at 7 livres, 4 sous—482 livres

When the crop was an average one:

Good Soils		
Crop	Expenses	
120 *setiers* at 10 livres, 10 sous	Seed	26.6 *setiers*
	Harvest hands	13.3
	Threshing	5.8
	Food	30.0
	Total	75.6 *setiers*

Gross product: 44 *setiers* at 10 livres, 10 sous—467 livres

Mediocre Soils		
Crop	Expenses	
100 *setiers* at 10 livres, 10 sous	Seed	25.0 *setiers*
	Harvest hands	12.0
	Threshing	3.8
	Food	30.0
	Total	70.8 *setiers*

Gross product: 29 *setiers* at 10 livres, 10 sous—304 *livres*

When the crop was bad:

Good Soils		
Crop	Expenses	
60 *setiers* at 16 livres	Seed	26.6 *setiers*
	Harvest hands	13.2
	Threshing	2.3
	Food	28
	Total	70.1 *setiers*

Gross product: a deficit of 10 *setiers* at 16 livres, i.e., a deficit of 160 livres

Mediocre Soils		
Crop	Expenses	
50 *setiers* at 16 livres	Seed	25 *setiers*
	Harvest hands	12
	Threshing	2
	Food	28
	Total	67 *setiers*

Gross product: a deficit of 17 *setiers* at 16 livres, i.e., a deficit of 272 *livres*

The second, or March, break of 40 arpents was devoted to oats. This yielded between 60 and 120 *setiers* on good land and between 40 and 80 *setiers* on the rest. It called for only one or two ploughings, a thin and partial manuring, and 15 *setiers* of seed. The harvest hands employed for the grain crops had to reap and tie the oats for the same wage. For the rest of the work, a small amount of extra labor or a small extra payment was needed. A horse cost six *litres* of oats to feed each day, or eight *setiers* in a year, plus oat straw and grass.

When the crop was good:

Good soils	
Crop	Expenses
120 *setiers* at 4 livres, 12 sous	Seed 15.2 *setiers* Threshing 4.6 Food for horses 32.0
	Total 51.8 *setiers*

Gross product: 68 *setiers* at 4 livres, 12 sous—313 livres

Mediocre soils	
Crop	Expenses
80 *setiers* at 4 livres, 12 sous	Seed 13.5 *setiers* Threshing 3.0 Food for horses 32.0
	Total 48.5 *setiers*

Gross product: 31.5 *setiers* at 4 livres, 12 sous—145 livres

When the crop was an average one:

Good Soils	
Crop	Expenses
80 *setiers* at 7 livres, 9 sous	Seed 15.2 *setiers* Threshing 3.0 Food for horses 32.0
	Total 50.2 *setiers*

Gross product: 30 *setiers* at 7 livres, 9 sous—233 livres

Bad Soils	
Crop	Expenses
60 *setiers* at 7 livres, 9 sous	Seed 13.5 *setiers* Threshing 2.3 Food for horses 32.0
	Total 47.8 *setiers*

Gross product: 12 *setiers* at 7 livres, 9 sous—89 livres

When the crop was bad:

Good Soils	
Crop	Expenses
60 *setiers* at 12 livres	Seed 15.2 *setiers* Threshing 2.3 Food for horses 32.0
	Total 49.5 *setiers*

Gross product: 10 *setiers* at 12 livres, 8 sous—124 livres

Bad Soils	
Crop	Expenses
40 *setiers* at 12 livres, 6 sous	Seed 13.5 *setiers* Threshing 1.5 Food for horses 32.0
	Total 47.0 *setiers*

Deficit of 7 *setiers* at 12 livres, 6 sous—87 livres

Nevertheless, the produce of the March break was more reliable. It did not have to suffer winter frosts, and oats are more resistant to cold, wet springs. It was possible to economize a little on seed and on the horses' food. A small part of the break could be assigned to grow peas, beans, vetches—all vegetables that were sure to find a good market.

The third break was left fallow. The farmer could graze between 100 and 120 sheep there. This flock gave him 60–70 lambs, at 2 livres each, about a hundred fleeces, worth 80 livres all together, and about 10 ewes added by natural increase—say, an overall product of 240 livres.

The break that was left fallow paid the wages of the permanent labor force. An ordinance of 1601 fixed these wages at 15 *écus* for the carter, 12 for the shepherd, 4 for the maidservant. Actually, they were paid a little more than that—80 and 20 livres, respectively. Maintenance of the implements for cultivation and the horses' harness cost 20 livres. The break thus produced a small profit of 20 livres.

To recapitulate. Good soils gave the following gross products (expressed in livres *tournois*):

	Break 1	Break 2	Break 3	Total
Good harvest	741 L.t.	313 L.t.	20 L.t.	1,074 L.t.
Average harvest	467	223	20	710
Bad harvest	−160	124	20	− 16

Other soils gave a gross product of:

	Break 1	Break 2	Break 3	Total
Good harvest	482 L.t.	145 L.t.	20 L.t.	647 L.t.
Average harvest	304	89	20	413
Bad harvest	−272	− 87	20	−339

Over a ten-year period, the good soils provided an average gross product of 746 livres per year, the others one of 408 livres.

Let us now try to calculate the net product.

The farmer owed his landlord either an ordinary rent or else a *rente à bail d'héritage*, which was perpetual and nonredeemable, making the farmer the real owner of the farm. The ordinary rent was more common. An arpent of vine was leased for between 19 and 24 livres in the vineyards of the Seine Valley and for between 8 and 10 livres on the slopes of Hurepoix in the 1620s. An arpent of land cultivated for cereals was leased for 5 to 6 livres on the plateau of Longboyau and for 3 to 4 livres around Boissy-sous-Saint-Yon. For a farm of 120 arpents the farmer benefited from a rebate. He had to pay 480–550 livres on the best soils and 360–420 livres on the others or, in kind, 72 *setiers*, two-thirds in grain and one-third in oats (690 livres) on the best soils, 42 *setiers* (403 livres) on the rest. Ground rent thus constituted a very big deduction.

The farmer owed the Church tithe at the rate of either four sheaves per arpent—3 to 4 percent of a good crop, about 2 *setiers*—or eight sheaves out of every hundred—6 to 7 percent of a bad crop; on the average it came to 100–140 livres, in the case of tithe calculated on the basis of the crop, and 75 livres, calculated on the basis of the number of arpents.

Seignorial exactions seem to have been comparatively light in this district close to Paris. Generally speaking, *champart* no longer existed. *Cens* was 12 deniers *parisis* (15 deniers *tournois*) per arpent. That meant 8 livres for a farm of 120 arpents. In addition, the farmer had to pay a due of 24 livres for 120 arpents. On the average, seignorial exactions came to 3.5 percent on good soils, 7 percent on others.

It is difficult to calculate the amount taken by the state, embodied in the king, as the rolls for the *tailles* in the Paris *élection* have disappeared. From divisions of inheritances we can estimate the *taille* for 120 arpents to have been about 150 livres. Consequently, we get the following results:

Good Soils	Other Soils
1. Ground rent: in money, 480–550 L.; in kind, 690 L.	1. Ground rent: in money, 360–420 L.; in kind, 403 L.
2. Tithe: by area, 75 L.; by crop, 140 L.	2. Tithe, by area, 75 L.; by crop, 110 L.
3. Seignorial exactions: 24 L.	3. Seignorial exactions: 24 L.
4. Fiscal exactions: 150 L.	4. Fiscal exactions: 130 L.
Total: 720–1,000 L. from a gross product of 746 L.	Total: 589–667 L. from a gross product of 408 L.

It is clear that no holding could have met its obligations. And yet the peasants did survive. The fact was that the seignorial exactions and the royal taxes were not always realized. The *seigneurs* granted abatements, and so did the king. Also, the collectors, receivers, and tipstaffs were always complaining about taxpayers whom it was "difficult to reason with." Sometimes, when times were too hard, the populations of entire villages fled to the edges of nearby woods and escaped the enforcement of court orders. The *seigneurs* assembled their tenants, with their cattle, and gave them shelter from the agents of the royal taxation system in their châteaux and fortified houses. Even in the 18th century, in Périgord, cannon had to be used in order to collect the taxes.

The main thing, though, was that the peasants possessed other resources. The best-placed among them, tenant farmers and sharecroppers, sold poultry, eggs, young calves, some fillies, a little butter, and straw. They used their equipment to carry out various agricultural tasks for other cultivators—ploughing, harrowing, carting manure, harvesting. One ploughing of an arpent of land brought in 2 livres, 10 sous, and a manuring was worth 4–8 *livres*. Besides cultivation, they carried on a number of crafts. Jean Hallecour, who cultivated 60 arpents (20 hectares), was also an innkeeper and a master fisherman at Choisy and undertook farm work for others. A small peasant who had a plough and two horses could earn 10 livres a year, and as much again with his carts.

The day laborers, vinegrowers, and small *laboureurs* had their wages from harvest work, haymaking, and, in winter, threshing in the barns. At the rate of one-third of a *setier* per arpent reaped, they could provide the livelihood of two persons by reaping 18 arpents. By looking after a townsman's vines or the garden of his country residence, they could get some money from the "*bourgeois.*" Jacques Mariette, of Orly, dressed 5.5 arpents of vine and looked after Pierre Dupuis's kitchen garden. For that work he was housed, had the use of two arpents of land and a cowshed, and received 80 livres a year, or the means of buying 10 *setiers* of maslin. In addition, a cow produced the family's milk, a few pounds of butter, and a calf each year. If his wife wetnursed a child from the town, she was paid 5 or 6 livres a month— 60–70 livres a year. The day laborer or the vinegrower farmed minor seignorial dues, tithes, and sometimes the cutting of copses. They participated in rural manufacturing industry, making woolen or silk or worsted stockings or carding wool.

In these ways the peasants generally managed to survive. But only a very narrow margin was left for taxation, and great difficulty was experienced in collecting the sums assessed, owing to the unreliability of harvests and the possibility of taxpayers deserting their villages and temporarily taking flight.

A state with extensive political powers but only feeble resources

An additional difficulty was due to the fact that the king's taxes had to be paid in cash. It was often far from easy for the peasant to procure this cash. When the harvest was good, prices were too low, as happened at the end of the War of the League of Augsburg and the beginning of the War of the Spanish Succession. Currency was always tending to become scarcer both because France's armies abroad paid for their purchases in cash and because the circumstance that the ratio of gold to silver was legally lower in France than it was elsewhere led to the exportation of gold. Good coins were also exported and lighter foreign ones imported. All these movements gave rise to the phenomena of inflation.

It was therefore hard for the state to increase taxation to keep pace with the expenditure it considered necessary, to forecast how much a tax would bring in and how it would be paid, and to obtain cash. This was why taxes were assessed on whole communities rather than proportioned to individuals' incomes; why they often retained the character of a request from the state, to be discussed with its agents; and why, in his financial difficulties, lacking a state bank, the king had to resort to "extraordinary measures."

From time to time it became practically impossible, over entire regions, to collect any taxes. The 17th and 18th centuries were, in France, a period when the glaciers advanced—a period with a succession of very cold winters, when the seed sometimes froze in the ground, and of cool, wet springs and summers that were unfavorable to the ripening of grain and grapes. This sometimes resulted in a series of bad harvests and, therefore, increases in the prices of cereals and bread; then came dearth, famine, and epidemics, decimating a poorly nourished population, especially the producers—the peasants and workers. These were what were called "*mortalités.*" They brought on general economic crises; for the urban and rural manufacture of textiles, the principal industry of the time, could in these conditions find only reduced outlets. To avoid contagion, moreover, the towns shut their gates, and fewer markets and fairs were held. Owing to particularly hard climatic conditions, these "*mortalités*" were numerous in the 17th century, when some district or other suffered almost every year.

The great *"mortalités,"* the ones that affected a whole large area of the country, were these of 1627–32, which inflicted a lasting disorganization on France's economy, opening the great recession of the 17th century, that of 1648–53, which coincided with the Fronde, and those of 1661–62, 1693–94, and 1709–10. The most serious aspect of the matter was that these major *"mortalités"* had cumulative effects, for the losses in population and production caused by one of them had not been made up for when the next came on. The consequence was, in Colbert's time, a state of real distress, with a shortage of manpower. In certain villages and *bourgs* the losses in population and property were not made good until the middle of the 18th century. That century was an epoch of less hardship, when periodic famine was replaced by insidious dearth, and, instead of great *"mortalités"* that might carry off as many as 30 percent of the inhabitants, there was a slow exhaustion of men's bodies. Without its excellent institutions, comparatively the most efficient in Europe, its system of overall supervision by the state, its intendants of the provinces, its farmers general, France would never have been able to compensate, to some extent, for these unfavorable circumstances and to withstand so many ruinous wars.

As compared with the big industrial states of the 19th and 20th centuries, the French state of the 17th and 18th centuries was thus the victim of a cruel inadequacy of resources.

The feeling that to pay taxes was degrading, the genuine difficulty often experienced in finding the means to pay them without depriving oneself of necessities, and the view that taxes served mainly to enrich harpies and leeches—the *financiers,* tax farmers, *traitants,* and *partisans*—made taxation the motive, or the pretext, for numerous popular revolts and disturbances. Their frequency, especially in the 17th century, their forms of organization, and the ways in which they began and developed made them almost an institution. From time to time, peasants and craftsmen would rise up against the *traitants,* their agents, and all who took part in the operations and shared in their profits—*receveurs généraux et particuliers, trésoriers* of every kind, and various accounting officers—and also against those who protected them—the intendants and governors. In these antifiscal revolts, the peasants and craftsmen benefited from the connivance of *gentilshommes, seigneurs,* magistrates, and even *parlements* and municipalities. All were affected by the royal taxation system: indirectly when the collection of the king's taxes hindered payment of seignorial and feudal dues and rents; directly when the king tried to tax *all* incomes, without regard to anyone's "quality." The *gentilshommes* armed their *domestiques* and sometimes even their peasants against the royal agents. The *parlements* and presidial courts were lax in their investigations and prosecutions. The municipalities failed to use the urban militias, or else these refused to march. Often the revolts broke out after campaigns of recrimination and incitement by the sovereign courts, which gave the latter some responsibility for the revolts, although, as a rule, they did not participate in them directly. The constituted authorities resolved to act only when rebel bands threatened property or when the government gave them reason to fear that local privileges would be abolished. The taxation system created a permanent opposition to the king's authority, an endemic risk of rebellion, and sometimes provoked the revolt of an entire province, with all ranks of society united against the king's government in defense of the "liberties" and "privileges" of the provincial *patrie*. The Fronde was, in part, a generalizing of these movements. The fiscal problem constantly compromised the authority and functioning of the government.

Notes

1. See the chapter on the royal mail.
2. Published as an appendix to Messance's book *Recherches sur la population*.
3. See the chapter on the nobility.

Guide to further reading

The territory of the state and the speed of travel

Etienne, Charles. "La guide des chemins de France de 1553." Published by Jean Bonnerot in *Bibliothéque de l'Ecole des Hautes Etudes, Sciences hist. et philol.*, vol. 267 (1936).
Livet, Georges. "La route royale et la civilisation française de la fin du XVe au milieu du XVIIIe siècle." In *Les Routes de France depuis les origines jusqu'à nos jours*. Introduction by Guy Michaud. Collection Colloques, Cahiers de Civilisation. Association pour la diffusion de la Pensée française, 1959.
Longnon, Auguste. *La formation de l'unité française*, ed. H. F. Delaborde. Picard, 1969.
Mirot, Léon. *Manuel de géographie historique de la France*. 1st ed. Picard, 1929.
Schrader, F. *Atlas de géographie historique*. Hachette, 1869.
———; Prudent, F.; Anthoine, E. *Atlas de géographie moderne*. Hachette, 1908.
Trénard, Louis. "De la route royale à l'âge d'or des diligences." In *Les Routes de France depuis les origines jusqu'à nos jours* (see Livet). With bibliographies. 1959.
Vaillé, Eugène. *Histoire générale des postes françaises*. 6 vols. P.U.F., 1947–53.

Population

Corvisier, André. *L'armée française de la fin du XVIIe siècle au ministère de Choiseul: Le soldat.* 2 vols. 1964.

Dupaquier, Jacques. "Sur la population française au XVIIe et au XVIIIe siècle," *Revue historique* 239 (1968): 43–79. (Consult this especially for bibliography.)

Esmonin, Edmond. "Quelques données inédites sur Vauban et les premiers recensements de la population," *Population* 9 (1954).

Gilles, Bertrand. *Les sources statistiques de l'historie de France.* 1964.

Lachiver, Marcel. *La population de Meulan du XVIIe au XIXe siècle* S.E.V.P.E.N., 1969.

Le Roy Ladurie, Emmanuel. *Les paysans du Languedoc.* Imprimerie Nationale, 1966.

Levasseur, Emil. *La population française.* 2 vols. 1889–91.

Meuvret, Jean. "Les crises de subsistances et la démographie de la France d'Ancien Régime," *Population* (1946).

Mols, Roger. *Introduction à la démographie historique des villes d'Europe, XIVe–XVIIIe siècle.* 3 vols. Louvain, 1944–56. (Université de Louvain, *Recueil de travaux d'histoire et de philologie,* 4th ser., fascs. 1–3.)

Mousnier, Roland. "Etudes sur la population de la France au XVIIe siècle," *XVIIe siecle* no. 16 (1952).

———. *Paris au XVIIe siècle.* Centre de Documentation Universitaire, 1960–61, fasc. 1.

Reinhard, Marcel; Armengaud, André; Dupaquier, Jacques. *Histoire générale de la population mondiale.* 3d ed. Domat-Montchrestien, 1968.

"Villes et villages de l'ancienne France," *Annales de Démographie historique* (1969).

Cartography

Cassini de Thury. *Description géométrique de la France.* 1783. (B.N.: V-13166)

Crone, G. R. *Maps and Their Makers.* 2d ed. London: Hutchinson's University Library 1962.

Dainville, François de. *Cartes anciennes de l'Eglise de France.* Vrin, 1956.

———. *La carte de Guyenne par Belleyme (1761–1840).* Bordeaux: Delmas, 1957.

———. "De la profondeur à l'altitude." Pp. 195–213 in *Le navire et l'économie maritime du Moyen Age au XVIIIe siècle,* ed. Michel Mollat. IIe Colloque International d'Histoire maritime. S.E.V.P.E.N., 1958.

———. "Le premier atlas de France: Le Théâtre français de Maurice Bouguereau, Tours, 1594," *Actes du LXXXVe Congrès national des sociétés savantes* (Chambéry-Annecy, 1960) (Section de géographie).

———. *Le Dauphiné et ses confins vus par l'ingénieur d'Henri IV, Jean de Beins.* Minard, 1968.

Figuier, Louis. *Vies des savants illustres.* Vol. 4. 2d ed. 1876.

Gallois, Lucien. *Régions naturelles et noms de pays: Etude sur la région parisienne.* 1908.

Libault, André. *Histoire de la cartographie.* Chaix, 1964.

Intellectual training

Charmot, F. *La pédagogie des Jésuites.* Spes, 1943.

Dainville, François de. *Les Jésuites et l'éducation de la société française: La géographie des humanistes.* Beauchesne & Fils, 1940.

————. *La naissance de l'humanisme moderne*. Beauchesne & Fils, 1940.

Dupont-Ferrier, Gustave. *Du Collège de Clermont au Lycée Louis-le-Grand*. 3 vols. De Boccard, 1921.

Lemasne-Desjoberts, M.-A. *La Faculté de Droit de Paris aux XVII*e *et XVIII*e *siècles*. Cujas, 1966.

Mandrou, Robert. *Magistrats et sorciers au XVII*e *siècle*. Plon, 1968.

Mornet, D. *Les origines intellectuelles de la Révolution française, 1715–1787*. A. Colin, 1933.

Mousnier, Roland. *Paris au XVII*e *siècle,* fasc. 3: "La fonction intellectuelle: l'Université." Centre de Documentation Universitaire, 1960–61.

————. *Lettres et Mémoires adressés au chancelier Séguier,* vol. I, introduction, "La psychologie collective des maîtres des requêtes" (pp. 65–111). 1964.

Roche, Daniel. "La diffusion des Lumières. Un exemple: L'Académie de Châlons-sur-Marne," *Annales E.S.C.* (1964), pp. 887–922. (See also a number of other writings by this author.)

Viguerie, Jean de. *Une oeuvre d'éducation sous l'Ancien Régime: Les Pères de la Doctrine Chrétienne en France et en Italie (1592–1792)*. Editions de la Nouvelle Aurore, 1976.

Construction methods

Belidor, B. F. de. *La science des ingénieurs*. Charles-Antoine Jombert, 1739.

Daumas, Maurice. *Histoire générale des techniques*. 3 vols. P.U.F., 1962–68. (With bibliographies.)

Muller, Josy. "Vauban et Ath: Construction de la forteresse (1668–1674)," *Annales du Cercle royal archéologique d'Ath et de la région* 38 (Tamines, 1954). Ducolot-Roulin, 1955

The state's financial resources

Bercé, Yves-Marie. *Histoire des Croquants: Etude des soulèvements populaires au XVII*e *siècle dans le Sud-Ouest de la France*. Librairie Droz, 1974.

Foisil, Madeleine. *La révolte des Nu-pieds et les révoltes normandes de 1639*. P.U.F., 1970.

Goubert, Pierre. *Beauvais et le Beauvaisis de 1600 à 1730*. Imprimerie Nationale, 1960.

Hincker, François. *Les Français devant l'impôt sous l'Ancien Régime*. (Collection "Questions d'histoire.") Flammarion, 1971.

Jacquart, Jean. *Société et vie rurales dans le sud de la région parisienne, 1550–1560*. 2 vols. Université de Lille-III, Service de Reproduction de Thèses, 1973. Reissued as *La crise rurale en Ile-de-France*. Armand Colin, 1975.

Le Roy Ladurie, Emmanuel. *Les paysans de Languedoc*. Imprimerie Nationale, 1966.

Lough, John, ed. *Locke's Travels in France (1675–1679), as Related in His Journals, Correspondence, and Other Papers*. Cambridge, Eng.: At the University Press, 1953.

Meuvret, Jean. "Comment les Français voyaient l'impôt," in "Comment les Français voyaient la France," *XVII*e *siècle,* special issue, 1955.

Mousnier, Roland. *Lettres et Mémoires adressés au chancelier Séguier*. 2 vols. P.U.F., 1964.

————. *Peasant Uprisings*. New York: Harper & Row, 1970.

Pillorget, René. *Les mouvements insurrectionnels de Provence entre 1596 et 1715*. A. Pedone, 1975.

Poitrineau, Abel. *La vie rurale en basse Auvergne au XVIII*e *siècle (1726–1789)*, Aurillac: Imprimerie Moderne, 1965.

Glossary

Abolition	A complete pardon granted by the king, remitting all penalties and closing all investigations into the crime.
Abonnement	An agreement whereby a town or other corporation substituted for its liability to pay a due, the revenue from which was hard to determine, a sum fixed in advance. Such agreements were usually very acceptable to the royal finance officials, since they meant immediate receipt of a definite sum in cash instead of what might or might not prove a larger sum but which would take time and expense to collect.
Adjudication des octrois	Hearing of tenders for the farm of the town's *octrois,* and allotment of this farm.
Adjudication par décret	The decision of a magistrate ordering distraint of a debtor's goods and their sale by auction for the benefit of his creditors.
Agents de change	These persons negotiated bills of exchange on behalf of businessmen.
Agrière	See *Champart.*
Aides	Internal duties charged on certain goods, especially drinks; a sort of excise—the principal indirect tax.
Amende honorable	The public apology for his crime which a convict was sometimes sentenced to make.
Amodiateur	Also spelt *"admodiateur."* Someone who leased a holding, or the collection of various dues, tolls, etc., in a given *seigneurie,* on the basis of sharing the income half-and-half with the *seigneur.*
Appel comme d'abus	This "appeal on grounds of abuse" was a complaint lodged with a *parlement* against an ecclesiastical judge accused of exceeding his powers. If successful, it resulted in the removal of the case from the Church court.

745

Archers.   Each of the king's *compagnies d'ordonnance* was made up of 100 *lances*, and each *lance* consisted of six men— a *gendarme* on horseback, backed by three *archers*, a *valet d'armes*, and a *coutillier*, or page. The word *archer* continued to be used for foot soldiers long after the bow had ceased to be their weapon.

Arpent   A measure of land rather larger than an acre; 25 arpents were equivalent to 35 acres.

Arrêt   Decree.

Asséeurs   Persons elected by a community to apportion responsibility for payment of *taille* and other taxes at grass-roots level.

Assesseurs   "Assessors": used generally for assistants, with special application in various departments, as collectors of taxes, or the lawyer assistants of a *bailli* who was a *noble d'épée*.

Aubaine   If a foreigner died after living in a particular *seigneurie* for a year and a day, his property belonged to the *seigneur*, provided that the latter enjoyed *droit d'aubaine*.

Audience du Sceau   The ceremony of affixing the royal seal to letters and registering them in the chancellery, which was accompanied by the levying of certain fees.

Aveu et dénombre-ment   Every time a fief changed hands, the new holder had to compile and present to his *seigneur* a full description of it, with a list of all the dues to be paid on it—an "avowal and enumeration" of his obligations to the *seigneur*.

Avis de parents   Assemblies of the relatives of a minor—e.g., an orphan—to give their views on what should be done with his property.

Avocats   "Advocates," or "barristers," were of higher education and status than the *procureurs*. The king was represented before the Paris *parlement* by two *avocats généraux* and a *procureur général*, who were spoken of collectively as *les gens du roi*—"the king's men."

Bail d'héritage   Neither a sale nor a lease of a piece of land but its permanent alienation subject to perpetual payment of a certain *rente*.

Bailliage.   The basic traditional administrative division was the *bailliage*, or *sénéchaussée*. Broadly, these divisions were called *bailliages* in the north of France, *sénéchaussées* in the south, but there were exceptions. In the north, Artois, Boulonnais, and Ponthieu, for example, were *sénéchaussées,* while in the south, Labourd was a *bailliage.* The royal *bailli* (or *sénéchal*) was appointed from among the nobility. He had to supervise the royal *prévôts* in his area and to convoke the *ban* and *arrière-ban.* He also had a law court, which was presided over, in his name, by lawyers who were called *lieutenants.* Private *seigneurs* also employed *baillis* to administer their *seigneuries.*

Ban   In Alsace, a territory or jurisdiction (from German *Bann*).

Ban et arrière-Ban   The mustering of holders of fiefs and subfiefs to render military service to the king. Those who could not attend were expected to depute a substitute or pay a tax. Commoners who held fiefs paid "frank-fee" in lieu of performing this service.

Banquiers expédi-tionnaires de la Cour de Rome   Bankers who enjoyed the privilege of negotiating dispensations and the like with the Papal Curia on behalf of individuals who paid them commission.

Bâtardise   A bastard born in a *seigneurie* was subject to the same rule regarding succession as a foreign resident. (See *Aubaine*)

Bordage   A small farm located near the *seigneur*'s residence from which he was supplied with poultry and vegetables.

Bouchers, grands et petits   The *grands bouchers* of Paris had stalls adjoining the Châtelet and the church of Saint-Jacques-de-la-Boucherie. Their rivals, the *petits bouchers,* established themselves on the parvis of Notre-Dame and in other localities, such as the Temple.

Bourg   A small market center in the countryside—an unwalled town.

Brevet de Retenue et de Survivance   A favor granted by the king to the holder of an office which was not hereditary, providing that when he gave up his office he was to receive a certain sum of money.

Brigadier   Under Louis XIII two or three regiments were sometimes formed into a *"brigade"* under the command of the senior *mestre de camp,* who was then called the *brigadier.* Louis XIV made *brigadier* a general officer's rank, to enable poor nobles or commoners to attain this level without passing through the stage of *colonel,* which required both nobility and payment. Today a *brigadier* is a corporal of horse.

Bureau des finances   The group of *trésoriers généraux* and their *receveur général* at the head of each *généralité*.

Bureau des pauvres   A local committee for the administration of poor relief.

Bureau forain   Merchants coming into a town from elsewhere had to report to this *bureau* to arrange for the sale of their goods, subject to the local rules.

Cabaretier   The keeper of a drink shop.

Cahier   Register of grievances or requests sent to the king by provincial estates or other bodies.

Canton   In France today each *département* is divided into *arrondissements* and these, in turn, into *cantons*.

Cantonnement   Partial enclosure, e.g., of a wood.

Capitainerie   The governorship of a royal residence and the lands attached to it: e.g., *la capitainerie de Fontainebleau*. The person appointed to a *capitainerie* had under him a force of guards, gamekeepers, etc.

Capitation   Though a "poll tax" in the sense that everyone had to contribute, this was not a poll tax in the strict sense, because it did not require the same payment from every person taxed; the taxpayers were grouped in categories defined by their estimated incomes.

Cens   This annual payment made to a *seigneur* was the essential mark of "commoner" land, and it entailed the obligation to pay all the other dues—*lods et ventes,* etc.—that were charges upon such land. A holding for which *cens* was paid was a *censive,* and the person responsible for paying it was a *censitaire*.

Cens vifs   The *cens* that were actually being paid, that had not been allowed to lapse.

Chambres des comptes   These were sovereign courts which audited the accounts of the king's finance officials and dealt with claims for exemption from taxation.

Chambrier   In some cathedrals the canon who administered the chapter's revenues was given this title.

Champart   A payment in kind due by a *censitaire* to his *seigneur*— a certain percentage of the produce, which varied from place to place. Also called *agrier,* or *agrière,* and *terrage*.

Chancellerie, Grande   This was the Chancellery that always accompanied the king and, presided over by the chancellor, dispatched letters sealed with the Great Seal. There was also a *petite Chancellerie,* stationary and attached to the *parlement* of Paris, which dealt with matters of minor importance.

Charrue	This "ploughland" varied in area from one part of France to another, being 120 arpents in the Paris region, for example, but 90 arpents in Orléanais.
Charrue, officers de la grande et petite	Officials who weighed the barrows and the baskets, respectively, in which goods were brought into a town for sale, in connection with the levying of tolls.
Chevalier	By this title a higher level of the nobility marked itself off from the mass of noblemen, who were merely *écuyers*. The title was used by holders of *fiefs de dignité*, high officers of the royal household, the chancellor, and so on. Toward the end of the Ancien Régime the younger members of titled families took to calling themselves *chevalier* if they lacked any other title ("Chevalier de X.")
Chevaliers ès lois	This title was claimed by lawyers who wished to assert their equality of status with *chevaliers* in the traditional sense, *chevaliers ès armes*, "knights at arms."
Cinq grosses fermes	The five principal tax farms, which were treated as a unit; also known as the *fermes générales* or *fermes unies,* they were farmed by the group of *financiers* known as the "farmers general."
Commanderie	A benefice belonging to the Order of Malta.
Commis	Sometimes translated as "clerk" or "agent." Whereas a *clerc* was, in principle, holder of a permanent appointment, a *commis* was a temporary appointee and could be dismissed at any time.
Commise	The seizure of a fief on account of private offenses against the *seigneur,* in contrast to *confiscation,* which applied when crimes against public law had been committed.
Commissaire	One who held a temporary, extraordinary commission, serving "at the king's pleasure," in contrast to an *officier,* a permanent official.
Commissaire départi	A special royal agent sent out from the center to somewhere in the provinces to accomplish a particular task. Later known as an intendant.
Committimus	The privilege enjoyed by certain persons of having any lawsuit in which they were involved heard in first instance by the higher courts. There were two "grades"—*committimus du grand sceau* and *du petit sceau.*
Compagnies d'Ordonnance	Toward the end of the Hundred Years' War, King Charles VII raised, by ordinances of 1439 and 1448, a permanent armed force, which became known as the

compagnies d'ordonnance, or *gendarmerie.* The *taille* was originally levied in order to pay for this nucleus of the royal standing army.

Comptant, ordonnances de Orders to pay money to someone without giving a reason for it to the *chambre des comptes.* The king wrote on these orders: "I know why this money is being paid." They were used to finance secret-service work and to reward persons who had served the king well in special circumstances.

Confidentiaire The holder of a church benefice could hand it over to another person, who performed the duties and enjoyed the income, on condition that, when required, he return it to the holder. This was called *confidence,* and the substitute was called a *confidentiaire.*

Confiscation If one of a *seigneur*'s "subjects" was convicted of certain crimes, his property passed to the *seigneur.*

Congrégation A group of religious belonging to the same order, e.g., Benedictines.

Conseil d'en haut So called because it usually met on the upper floor of the palace of Versailles, near the king's apartment. This was the king's highest and most private council. It was also known as the *Conseil étroit* or the *Conseil secret.*

Conseil des dépêches The king's council which dealt with dispatches received from the intendants in the provinces. It was sometimes called the *Conseil de l'intérieur.*

Conseil des finances Also called the *Conseil de direction,* it was responsible for assessing taxes and judging claims and disputes arising therefrom. It awarded contracts for public works and arranged for the farming of indirect taxes.

Conseil des parties Also called the *Conseil d'Etat privé,* this section of the king's Council heard cases transferred to it from the ordinary law courts. It was a royal supreme court of appeal, which Louis XIV aimed to make the ultimate interpreter of the law, taking over the appellate role to which the *parlement* of Paris laid claim.

Conseiller du roi An honorific title attached to a large number of offices, some of them quite humble; it should not be confused with *conseiller d'Etat* ("state councilor").

Conseillers ordinaires These were members of the Conseil d'Etat who served the whole year through, as against those who relieved each other every six months (*conseillers semestres*).

Contrôle des actes This was the function of the *"Enregistrement"*—to

	ensure that all deeds were made out on stamped paper and to register them accordingly.
Contrôleur général	This title was given to the deputy to the *receveur général* in each *généralité*. Not to be confused with the minister called the *contrôleur général des finances* (formerly *surintendant des finances*), sometimes known, for short, simply as the *"contrôleur général."*
Correcteurs	These officials of the *chambres des comptes* checked the accounts of the *receveurs*.
Corvée	Peasant's obligation to do unpaid labor on the roads.
Council	The word Council frequently stands by itself in the text, without specification, particularly in phrases like *"arrêts* of the Council." In such instances, the word refers to the *conseil du roi*, or king's Council.
Cour plénière	In 1788 a "plenary court" composed of high officials was briefly substituted by the king for the *parlements*, for the purposes of registering all acts of the Crown.
Cours des aides	The courts empowered to deal with disputes connected with the taxes called *aides, gabelles*, or *tailles*.
Cousu	The word (literally "sewn") used by heralds to indicate that the "field" and the "chief" of an escutcheon are both of a "metal," or of a "color," a conjunction which is abnormal in heraldic usage—e.g., red and blue, or yellow (gold) and white (silver), adjoining each other.
Crues	These "increases" were additions to the original amount of the *taille*.
Cueilloir	A register of all the *cens, rentes*, and other dues payable to a *seigneur*.
Curé	Chief priest of a parish.
Denier	One-twelfth of a sou. *"Deniers"* was often used to mean "money" in general.
Denier douze, à	"At one denier in every twelve," i.e., "at eight and one-third in the hundred"—8.33 percent. Percentages were usually stated in this manner.
Deniers extra-ordinaires	Revenue, usually raised for war needs, obtained from the sale of new offices or from loans from tax farmers.
"Désert, Le"	"The wilderness," the biblical term used by the Protestants, during the period after the Revocation of the Edict of Nantes, for the remote areas where they continued to worship illegally.
Déshérence	This was the right, possessed by some *seigneurs*, to inherit the property of "subjects" who died without

	leaving legitimate heirs. Cf. English "escheat."
Dévolution	If, when a benefice fell vacant, the bishop let six months go by without filling it, his superior could fill this benefice by *droit de dévolution*. Not to be confused with *dévolut,* the procedure for ousting an unworthy occupier of a benefice.
Directe seigneuriale	The part of a *seigneurie* (in contrast to the *domaine proche* or *réserve siegneuriale*) which was *not* exploited directly by the *seigneur* but leased out in fiefs or *censives.* Not to be confused with *domaine direct.*
Direction des Bâtiments	This institution had charge of a number of buildings, etc., belonging to the king, including the royal carpet manufactory.
Domaine direct	Also called *domaine éminent.* The "supreme ownership" of a *seigneurie* by its *seigneur,* giving him various rights and powers over all the land in it, however this might be exploited. Not to be confused with *domaine proche* or *directe seigneuriale.*
Domaine proche	The part of a *seigneurie* exploited directly by the *seigneur* (cf. the English "home farm"). Also called the *réserve seigneuriale.* Not to be confused with *domaine direct* or *directe seigneuriale.*
Domaine utile	The right to cultivate a piece of land and enjoy its fruits while not possessing full ownership.
Droits	Basically, "rights," but these could be *droits honorifiques* (rights of precedence, and the like, with no financial value), *droits recognitifs* (rights to be recognized as *seigneur* in certain ways, which often meant acknowledgment of one's consequent right to receive payments in one form or another), or *droits utiles*— "lucrative rights," i.e., dues payable in cash or in kind to the *seigneur* by his "subjects."
Echevins	These were town councilors of the highest rank, appointed by the king through the intendant or by the local lord. With the mayor, they formed the executive committee of the municipality. Usually translated as "aldermen." (In some southern cities they were called *consuls.*)
Ecriture	The documents (written consultations, etc.) produced in the course of a case before a court of law, and which served as the basis for payment to the lawyers concerned.
Ecu	The value of this coin, originally 3 livres, was increased by Richelieu to 4 livres 14 sous.

Ecuyer	This title (from which English "esquire" is derived) could be assumed by any noble, in contrast to *chevalier*, which was restricted.
Ecuyer tranchant	The official responsible for carving the meat at the table of the king or other great personages or corporations.
Elections	The *généralités* were divided into *élections*, which originally coincided with dioceses and served as the basic units for tax-paying purposes. They were confined to the provinces that had no "provincial estates," and these provinces were therefore called *pays d'élections*, in contrast to *pays d'Etats*. They were staffed by *élus*, *collecteurs*, and *receveurs*.
Elus	The assessment of *taille* in an *élection* was carried out by officials called *élus*. Though they had originally been "elected," theirs became a venal office.
Engagiste	When a part of a *seigneurie* was temporarily alienated to a creditor, so that he could reimburse himself from its income, he was called the *engagiste*.
Enquêtes, Chambre des	The "chamber" of the *parlement* which heard certain appeals on the basis of reports submitted in writing (*enquêtes*).
Enquêteurs et examinateurs	In every royal jurisdiction there were officials who, under the *lieutenant*, *prévôt*, etc., checked constantly on the observation of administrative ordinances and had power to examine witnesses when investigating breaches of these ordinances.
Enregistrement	An edict of 1693 provided for the establishment of a *contrôleur d'enregistrement* in every town to register all contracts exceeding a certain value and also all wills. This was one of the many *greffes* created by the state in order to have more offices to sell. See *Contrôle des actes*.
Entrées, or *droits d'entrée*	Internal duties on "merchandise in motion"; cf. *Octrois* and *Traites*.
Epargne	The central treasury, or exchequer, into which all revenues were supposed to be paid.
Epices	Payments made to judges by the parties to the cases they heard. Originally they were voluntary gifts of spices, at a time when spices were much sought after and expensive. Later they came to be payments that were expected, and which were made in cash.
Eyminée, also spelt, *éminée*	A tract of land the sowing of which required one *émine* of seed, an *émine* (from Greek *hemina*, a half) being half a *setier*.

Façonnier	A craftsman who makes articles out of materials supplied by the customer.
Fauconnier	An official of the royal household on the staff of the *Grand Fauconnier,* who looked after the king's hawks.
Ferme Générale	The syndicate of *financiers* formed in 1720 to collect *gabelle, aides, traites,* and some other taxes. See *Cinq grosses fermes.*
Fermier judiciaire	A person who "farmed" the collection of fines from those on whom a court had imposed them.
Financier	This meant a moneyed person who was involved in the king's financial business, the word *finances* being in those days normally restricted to the meaning "government finance."
Fleuron	A flower-shaped ornament, e.g., on a coronet.
Forage, Persage, and *Rouage*	*Forage* was a due paid to the *seigneur* by tavern-keepers and other retailers of wine. *Persage* was a due payable when a cask was broached, before the spigot could be inserted. *Rouage* was a due charged on wine sold wholesale and taken away in a cart: it had to be paid "before the wheels began to turn."
Fourrage	The obligation to supply fodder for the horses of soldiers billeted in one's house.
Franc de Germinal	During the Revolution it was decided, by the law of "18 Germinal, year III," that the unit of currency should thenceforth be called the *franc* instead of the *livre.*
Franc-salé	The privilege enjoyed by certain persons of getting their salt free of tax. See *Gabelle.*
Fruitier	An official of the royal household, under the *Grand-Maître,* whose duty was to supply fruit for the king's table.
Gabelle	The tax on salt, a royal monopoly. A large body of officials were concerned in storing and issuing salt. The regulations differed from one part of France to another, some areas being partly or wholly exempt from *gabelle,* and this led to much smuggling of salt across provincial borders. The tax was extremely unpopular, and its name was commonly applied to any tax regarded as new, excessive, and unjust. See *Grènetier* and *Franc-salé.*
Garde-gardienne	Letters by which the king gave certain religious establishments, and also the University of Paris, the right to have any cases they were involved in heard by

	particular courts. Cf. *Committimus.*
Garde-sac des procédures	''Keeper of the bag containing the documents of the case before the court.''
Gardes du corps	Four companies consisting entirely of officers took turns, quarter by quarter, in acting as the king's personal day-and-night bodyguard.
Gâtinais	A province lying between Ile-de-France and Orléanais. Not to be confused with Gâtine, a district in Poitou between Fontenay and Niort.
Gendarmerie	See *Compagnies d'ordonnance.*
Généralités	The thirty-four areas into which France was divided for tax and other administrative purposes. They were governed by thirty-two intendants of justice, police and finance. See also *Trésoriers-généraux de France* and *Elections.*
Grand' Chambre	The most important ''chamber'' of the Paris *parlement.* It heard appeals from lower courts and also dealt with cases affecting the king's rights and with criminal proceedings which involved the principal officers of the Crown. Its *présidents* were called *présidents à mortier* (see *Présidents*).
Grand Conseil	The most important of the special courts. It judged, without appeal, cases transferred to it from the *parlement* by the king himself or those forwarded to it by the *Conseil des parties.* It also dealt with disputes between the *parlements* and the presidial courts.
Grand écuyer	One of the principal officers of the royal household, he fulfilled the functions of the English master of the horse, controlling the king's stables, running a riding school for the king's pages, and so on. He also took charge of the royal postal service. He was referred to at court as ''Monsieur Le Grand.''
Grand-Maître de France	The head of all the services of the royal household and directly in charge of the *maîtres d'hôtel.*
Greffier	Sometimes translated as ''registrar,'' ''clerk of the court,'' or ''recorder.'' Usually a notary, he was in charge of a *greffe,* a place where records of court proceedings were kept, and he was responsible for the registration of all documents involved in cases; he also acted as secretary to the judge. A *greffier hérédital* had hereditary possession of his office. Many corporations had their own *greffes* and *greffiers.* See *Enregistrement.*

Grènetier	The official in charge of the storehouse (*grenier à sel*) from which salt was issued for controlled sale, in connection with the levying of *gabelle*.
Gros et de l'augmentation, droit de	A proportionate tax payable by vinegrowers on the wine they produced, together with certain additions made to it after the tax was first introduced.
Hôpital général	This institution, for vagrants, beggars, and prostitutes, was established on the site of a saltpeter works and came to be known commonly as La Salpêtrière. It was the house of correction to which Manon Lescaut was sent.
Hôtel-Dieu	A hospice for the destitute sick. The one in Paris, adjoining the Cathedral of Notre-Dame, was founded in 800.
Hôtel du Roi	The old name for what later came to be called the *Maison du Roi*—the royal household.
Huissier	The basic duty of the *huissier* was to act as doorkeeper ("usher") in a court of law; the outdoor work of notifying the court's decisions, collecting fines, making arrests, and so on, was carried out by *sergents*. The *huissiers* gradually took over some of this outdoor work while yet retaining their functions inside the court, and *huissier* is often translated as "tipstaff." *Huissiers* whose responsibilities were confined to the courtroom were called *huissiers audienciers*. The word *huissier* was also used for the official whose task it was to receive, announce, and introduce visitors to some high personage.
Inciseurs	These were authorized to lance abscesses and boils.
Journal	The area of land a man was expected to plough in one day.
Joyeux avènement	The king's first entry into a town, usually the occasion for making a special "gift" (*don*) to him.
Juge guestré	Literally, a "judge in gaiters." A rural judge, not a graduate, employed by a *seigneur* to deal with cases concerning land; he held court either in the open air or in a room in an inn.
Largesse	"Generosity in giving." Noblemen were expected to give money away to the poorer commoners on any and every occasion of celebration, commemoration, or the like.
Lettres de cachet	Also called *lettres closes* (in contrast to "letters patent"). These were letters from the king that were

	folded and sealed so that they could not be read without breaking the seal. They were addressed to private persons and concerned matters specially concerning those persons.
Leydes	A due charged on goods brought for sale in a market, as compensation to the *seigneur* for his expenditure on maintaining the market place and providing the weights and measures needed.
Liard	Four of these made one sou.
Lieutenant	*Baillis* and *sénéchaux* were assisted in the exercise of their judicial responsibilities by lawyers. The chief of these was called *lieutenant général,* and he was in turn assisted by a *lieutenant civil* and a *lieutenant criminel,* for civil and criminal cases respectively. There were also a varying number of *lieutenants particuliers,* who presided over the court when their principals were absent. The title *lieutenant général* was also given to the nobleman in the king's confidence who was appointed to deputize for, and often in practice to supplant, the governor of a province.
Lième	A register of all the *cens,* rents, and other dues payable to a *seigneur.*
Ligne	One-twelfth of an inch.
Lit de justice	When the *parlement* declined to register some royal decree which the king was determined should pass into law, he went personally to the *parlement* and, sitting on a pile of cushions called a *lit de justice,* overruled its decision. Once the king had taken his place, the delegation of sovereignty held by the *parlement* was suspended, and so the king's ruling, pronounced in these circumstances, was final.
Lods et ventes	The "mutation fee" charged by the *seigneur* when a *censive* was sold and he did not exercise his right of option (*retrait féodal*). It was usually one-twelfth of the selling price.
Livre tournois	Common unit of money, divided into 20 *sols* and each *sol* into 12 *deniers.*
Louis d'or	The value of this coin varied between 20 and 30 livres.
Maire	The chief administrative officer of a *seigneurie* sometimes bore this title.
Maître	This title was given to any graduate in Roman and canon law and was often used in many other contexts as well, sometimes as a mere expression of respect.

Maître particulier des eaux et forêts	An official in the department of waters and forests who had only a single province under his orders in contrast to a *grand maître,* who had several.
Maîtres des comptes	Top-ranking magistrates in the *chambres des comptes.*
Maîtres des Requêtes de l'Hôtel du Roi	These were originally judges with jurisdiction over officers of the royal household. The king took to using them for special investigations in all parts of the administration, on which they reported directly to him in his Council.
Maîtres d'Hôtel du Roi	These were officials of the royal household, under the orders of the *Grand Maître,* who took turns in acting as butler, supervising the king's table.
Majorat salutaire	This form of entail was so called because it made a "jump" (*saut,* Latin *saltum*) from one line to the other in order to find the eldest member of a family, regardless of the order of legitimate succession.
Maladrière (or *Maladrerie*)	An isolation hospital.
Mandement	This name was given in some areas to a division of a *bailliage* or *élection.*
Maréchal de camp	The lowest rank of general officer. His original function was to precede an army on the march, find suitable locations for camps, and organize the encampment of the troops. Under Louis XIV these duties were transferred to the *maréchal général des logis,* a sort of chief of general staff, and the *maréchaux de camp* thereafter commanded troops. When the rank of *brigadier* was abolished in 1788, *maréchaux de camp* took over command of all brigades and eventually became today's *généraux de brigade.* The rank of *maréchal de camp,* unlike that of *brigadier,* could be held only by a nobleman.
Maréchaussée	The "marshalsea"—the rural armed police force, officered by the provost-marshals, which was largely engaged in hunting down army deserters who had become highwaymen.
Messagers	The officials of the University of Paris responsible for bringing students and their luggage to the capital and ensuring communications between them and their kinfolk at home. The transport network they organized ("*messageries*") was later made available for travelers and parcels not connected with the university.
Mestre (Maître) de camp	The company in a regiment which ranked next to that commanded by the colonel himself was commanded by

an officer called the *maître de camp*, who also acted as second-in-command of the regiment as a whole. The rank was later assimilated to *colonel* and confined to the cavalry.

Mesure A *mesure* was about 44 ares.

Monarchomaques "Opponents of monarchy," the antimonarchical theorists who wrote during the religious civil wars in France in the latter part of the 16th century, developing notions of divided and even popular sovereignty.

Mouleur Firewood was sold according to a special measure called the *moule*, and the official whose task was to check that the right measure was being given was called the *mouleur*.

Mouvance The parts of a *seigneurie* that were leased out were called the *mouvance*. The word was used more generally for "feudal dependence." The part of the duchy of Bar lying west of the Meuse River was within the *mouvance* of the king of France; its duke (the duke of Lorraine) had to do homage for it to the king of France, and this part of Bar was known as *le Barrois mouvant*.

Muid A measure of capacity for grain and liquids, varying in size from region to region. The *muid de Paris* was 18 hectoliters.

Notaires et garde-notes In 1578 the corporation of notaries absorbed the offices of *garde-notes* which had been created only six years earlier, on the pretext of "ensuring the preservation of notarial records," but actually for fiscal reasons—i.e., in order that the king might have additional offices to sell.

Octrois Tolls levied on goods entering a town. The revenues from these tolls were often farmed.

Palais de justice Seat of a *parlement*. In Paris the Palais also housed the *chambre des comptes, cour des aides,* and *cour des monnaies*.

Parties casuelles The revenue derived from payment of the annual due from officeholders called the *paulette,* and from the forced loans exacted from them from time to time.

Partisans Tax farmers whose form of contract was called a *parti*.

Patagon A silver coin struck in Flanders and Franche-Comté.

Pénitencier A priest entrusted by the bishop with the absolution of certain reserved cases.

Placard A public proclamation.

Placeage, Pesage, Mesurage, and *Aulnage* *Placeage* was paid for a place in the market where goods or cattle were to be displayed for sale. *Pesage,*

	mesurage, and *aulnage* were dues payable when goods or cattle were measured and weighed.
Police	This word covered many functions beyond the modern conception of "police work"; for example, it referred to regulation of wages, prices, weights and measures, and so on. It is sometimes translated simply as "administration."
Populo	The list of fees accruing to the king for the affixing of his seal in the chancellery; it was compiled monthly.
Pot	A liquid measure, in some areas one-three-hundredth of a *muid*. A *pot* of wine was, literally, a particular quantity of wine, but the expression *pot-de-vin* also came to be used for a small sum of money paid over and above the nominal price of some commodity and later signified a bribe, or "hush money."
Pouillé	The terrier of an abbey or other ecclesiastical property.
Poulangis	A coarse cloth woven in Burgundy out of a mixture of woolen and hempen yarn.
Prédicant	A lay preacher in the Protestant community.
Président	The presiding judges of the sovereign courts were called *présidents,* and the highest-ranking among them were *premiers présidents.* The judges of the *Grand' Chambre* of the Paris *parlement* were called *présidents à mortier,* from their distinctive headgear, resembling a mortar with a pestle in it.
Prévention	The power possessed by certain royal judges to "take over" any case from the seignorial court within whose competence it would normally have fallen. The pope also had the power of *prévention sur l'ordinaire,* by which he could confer a benefice before the bishop in whose diocese it was included had acted to fill it.
Prévôt	This title was held by the lowest-ranking of the royal judges, who presided over civil courts of first instance, dealing with cases not important enough to be reserved for the *bailliages* and *sénéchaussées.* In some parts of France these judges were called *châtelains* ("castellans"), *vicomtes,* or *viguiers.* The *prévôt de l'Hôtel* (*du Roi*), later called the *grand prévôt de France,* had jurisdiction over cases arising within the royal household. The *prévôts des maréchaux* ("provost marshals") acted as military police, under the orders of the marshals of France.
Prévôt des marchands de Paris	The provost of the merchants was head of the municipal government in the capital.

Procureur	This word was used to mean "attorney," "legal representative," or "proxy." A *procureur du roi* acted as public prosecutor in a royal court of law. In the jurisdictions of private *seigneurs,* his equivalent was called *procureur fiscal.* The *procureurs* in general were lawyers practicing like the English "solicitors" or French *avoués* of today.
Prud'hommes	"Upright, honest men."
Quint et requint	"A fifth plus a fifth of a fifth." This was the due payable to a *seigneur* when a fief was sold—the equivalent of the *lods et ventes* payable when a *censive* was sold. If, for example, a fief was being sold for 100,000 livres, then 20,000 plus 4,000, i.e., 24,000 livres, had to be paid to the *seigneur.*
Quinze-Vingts	"Fifteen score." A home for blind men, originally founded by Saint-Louis in 1254 for 300 knights captured by the Saracens whom the latter had returned after putting out their eyes.
Rachat et relief	If a fief or *censive* was bequeathed to a person who was not a relative in the direct line of succession, one year's income from the fief or *censive* had to be paid to the *seigneur.*
Rasière	A measure of capacity, equivalent to a little over 70 liters.
Régale	The king's right to enjoy the revenues of a diocese during any period when it had no bishop.
Régie générale	This institution, whose officials were called *régisseurs généraux,* dealt with certain minor *aides,* such as duties on playing cards. When some revenue-producing activity was administered directly by royal officials instead of being farmed by *financiers,* it was said to be *en régie.*
Règlement de juge	Decision by a higher authority determining what judges were to deal with a certain case.
Relief	See *Rachat et relief.*
Rentes	Though used sometimes to mean "rents," the word usually signifies annuities or interest-bearing bonds received in return for a loan or a capital investment. A *rente constituée* was derived from purchase of the right to draw the revenue, or part of it, from a piece of real property. *Rentes sur le domaine royal* were pensions paid out of the revenues from Crown lands. The word *rentier* came to be used generally for a person living on unearned income in the form of regular cash payments.

Rentes sur l'Hôtel de Ville The king borrowed money on the security of the revenues of his capital city. The "Town Hall" in question here was that of Paris.

Robe, Grande This term was used for the higher stratum of the *noblesse de robe,* or *"robins,"* those who served in the king's Council or the sovereign courts. Not to be confused with *robe longue,* which meant the same as *robe* alone, i.e., the world of "the gown" as contrasted with that of "the sword," persons belonging to the latter being referred to as *de robe courte.*

Sacquier The official at a port who supervised the loading and unloading of goods transported in sacks, notably salt and grain.

Secrétaires des commandements Members of the clerical staff of the king or some other great personage who were authorized to sign letters on his behalf when "commanded" to do so.

Secrétaires du roi These were not, as such, personal secretaries to the king but persons who had purely clerical duties as assistants to the chancellor in drafting and dispatching documents. There were hundreds of them, and the office was much sought after because it conferred noble status. Their formal title was *notaires et secrétaires du Roi, Maison et Couronne de France.*

Seigneurie directe, utile See *Domaine direct, utile.*

Septier (or *setier*) A measure of capacity used for both liquids and solids. In different parts of France it varied in amount from one-twelfth to one-twenty-second part of a *muid.*

Sergent An official responsible for enforcing the decisions of a law court—making arrests, distraining, serving summonses, etc. The word is sometimes translated as "bailiff" or as "catchpole." Some *sergents* carried a rod or a mace and were then called *sergents à verge* or *sergents à masse.* See *Huissier.*

Soiture A measure of meadowland, the area that a man could mow in one day.

Sol Another form of sou, used in the names of certain taxes—*nouveaux cinq sols, sol pour livre,* etc.

Sol (sou) tournois This was worth 12 deniers, whereas the sou *parisis* was worth 15.

Subdélégué After 1637 each *élection* was headed by a *subdélégué,* who was appointed and removed by the intendant.

Subvention à l'entrée A tax payable on goods entering a town, originally introduced by the king to pay for the cost of maintaining troops in winter quarters in these towns. In some cases the right to levy it was later granted to the town itself, to raise money for its own needs.

Surintendant des finances This minister had supreme oversight of the king's finances. After the downfall of Fouquet, in 1661, the title was changed to *contrôleur général des finances.*

Tabouret The folding stool on which some privileged ladies were on certain occasions permitted to sit, instead of standing, in the royal presence.

Taille The tax levied by the king (originally, to pay for the *compagnies d'ordonnance*) from all commoners. The word was also used for special exactions levied by private *seigneurs* from their commoner "subjects" on certain occasions.

Taille réelle In parts of southern France the *taille* was levied not only on the persons of commoners, as elsewhere, but also on what were classed as "commoner" lands, even if these were owned by nobles.

Taillon A tax, additional to the *taille,* raised to provide extra resources for military purposes. The name meant "little *taille.*"

Terrage Another name for *champart.*

Tour de Constance The prison near Nîmes where the wives of Protestants were imprisoned.

Traitant The *financiers* who undertook to provide the *deniers extraordinaires* for war needs, farming the special taxes imposed for this purpose, entered into a contract called a *traité de ferme* and so were known as *traitants.*

Traites foraines Customs duties charged on goods conveyed from one province to another.

Trésoriers généraux de France The *trésoriers de France* were originally the officials responsible for collecting the revenues from the royal domain—the king's *finances ordinaires.* There was one such *trésorier* over several *bailliages* or *sénéchaussées.* For the collection of *taille* and other taxes—the king's *finances extraordinaires*—divisions called *généralités* were created, corresponding to the areas for which the *trésoriers* were responsible. The men at the head of these *généralités* were called *généraux des finances.* Later, the offices were combined under the name *trésoriers généraux de France.*

Triage, droit de The *seigneur*'s claim to take one-third of the common lands if these were divided up.

Usement	The area where a certain usage or custom was current.
Ustensile	The furniture that hosts had to provide for soldiers billeted on them. This obligation was later commuted into a tax payable in cash.
Vidame	The nobleman appointed to administer and protect the temporal possessions of a church or monastery.
Viguerie, viguier	Equivalent to *prévôté* and *prévôt*.
Vinage	A due levied by *seigneurs* on wine produced in their *seigneuries* or transported across them.

Index

Abbots and abbesses, 297, 325–26, 332–33, 336, 356
Abduction, 61–66
Absolute monarchy, 670–77. *See also* Monarchy
Académie Française, 455–57
Académie des Inscriptions et Belles-Lettres, 457
Académie Royale de Marine, 720
Académie des Sciences (Academy of Sciences), 457, 689,
    694–96, 722
Academies, 455–58, 461
Academy of Architecture, 457
Academy of Painting and Sculpture, 457
Acapte and *arrière-capte,* 498
Acolytes (ecclesiastical), 7, 282, 284–85
Advocates: grades of, 440; hats of, as sign of rank, 9; before
    king's Council, 442–45; living like nobles, 228; before
    Paris *parlement,* 439–42; and social ascent, 239, 250, 278–79
Agents general (of clergy), 367–69, 376–78
Aguesseau, Henri François d', 35, 444, 671, 713
Albergements. See *Censives*
Albrecht VII, archduke of Austria, 116
Aldermen: in Beauvais, 595–97; and municipal reforms of
    1764, 598–600; in Paris, 584–90
Alès de Corbet, Pierre Alexandre, 216
Allods, 542–43
Alsace, 683
Amboise, Ordinance of, (1555), 135
Anet, Ordinance of, (1547), 141
Anne of Austria, 118
Apothecaries, 462–63, 468–69
Apprentices, 8, 468–69
Arc, Philippe Auguste de Sainte-Foix, chevalier d', 194–95,
    197

765   Archbishops: in estates of Languedoc, 614–16; function of,

282, 291; and General Assembly, 362, 364–65; in society of orders, 7, 24; taxes on, 337

Archdeacons, 288, 297, 364

Argenson, Claude de Voyer d', 92

Argenson, Marc René de Voyer d', 577, 628

Argenson, René de Voyer d', 66, 91–93

Aristocracy, 42–44. *See also* Nobility

Armies, 43. *See also* Militia

Armorial bearings: East India Company's, 474; form of, 114–17; and heralds, 118–19; in Paris, 579–80; on property, 116–17; registering of, 119–20; royal, 116–17; of *seigneuries,* 480–81; sworn crafts', 466; as symbols of rank, 113, 122, 480–81; usurpation of, 135; wearing of, 114–18, 125. *See also* Nobility

Armorial Général, 119–20

Army, 196–97, 711–12

Arnauld d'Andilly, Robert, 100–101

Artisans. *See* Craftsmen

Artists, 229, 232–33

Artois, Charles Philippe, comte d', 182

Ascetics, 292

Assemblies, provincial: composition of, 629–31, 633–34, 636; failure of, 637; functions of, 634–36; models established for, 630–32, 635; proposed, 628–29; structure and organization of, 632–34

Assembly, 38. *See also* National Assembly

Assembly of the Clergy, 247, 397–98

Assembly of Notables, 196

Ath (fortress), 723–29

Attorneys, 9, 435–36, 509

Aubert, Georges, 241

Aubert, Jean-Baptiste, 242

Aubrey de Saint-Vibert, Charles-Louis, 535

Aubusson de La Feuillade, Georges d', archbishop of Embrun, 546

Audiger, 94

Augustine, Saint, 292

Aumale, Ordinance of, (1540), 133

Authority, 14, 32, 79–80, 85–89. *See also* Monarchy, powers of

Auxiliaries of justice, 437–49

Aveu et dénombrement, 486–87, 512, 535

Ayrault, Pierre, 88

Babeuf, François Noel (called "Gracchus"), 535

Bacquet, Jean, 66, 507, 659

Bailiffs (*sergents*), 448–49, 508, 513

Bakers, 468–69

Banalités, 496–97, 532, 539

Barber-surgeons. *See* Surgeons

Barnave, Antoine, 36–45

Barons: in estates of Languedoc, 612–14, 616–17; and powers of justice, 508–9; in seigneurial hierarchy, 481; in society of orders, 7, 26, 28

Bary, René, 703

Basoche. See Royaume de la Basoche

Bassompierre, François de, 100

Bastards, 23, 204, 511, 651

Bautru, Nicolas, comte de Nogent, 106

Beauvais, 590–98, 604

Beauvillier, Paul, duc de, 17–18, 174

Becdelièvre family, 149

Béchameil de Nonteil, Louis, 148

Beggars, 274–75, 277–78

Beins, Jean de, 690

Belidor, Bernard Forest de, 722

Benefices (ecclesiastical), 304–11, 314, 316; and church recruitment, 321–22, 331; notaries and, 447; and Protestants, 388; and tax, 359–60

Benoist (de Vaubuzin), Jean, 203

Bernard, Pierre, 395

Bernier, François, 547–48

Bérulle, Pierre de, 343–46, 353–54

Besongne, Nicolas, 672

Bethman family, 237

Béthune, François-Gaston, comte de, 108

Bichi, Cardinal Alessandro, 393

Bignon, Armand-Roland, 65

Birth control, 710

Birth and death rates, 699–700, 705–10

Bishops: absences of, 310, 314; and apostolic power, 311–12; appointment and consecration of, 289–91; and canons, 287–88; in Catholic Renaissance, 340; and church property, 303; confer benefices, 305, 309, 316, 329; conflict

of, with lower clergy, 356, 358; in
Conseil d'Etat et privé, 379; dignities
of, unequal, 323; Domat on qualities
of, 33; dress of, 8; dues to, 309; duties of,
288–89, 291; in estates of Languedoc,
614, 616–17, 620–21; and Genēral
Assembly, 362–65; incomes of, 331–32,
334, 337; jurisdiction of, 296–98;
numbers of, 322; and ordination, 286,
288; recruitment and social origins of,
322–25; and regional organs, 369;
and religious orders, 292–94; royal protection of, 651; and seminaries, 341,
343, 347, 351; in society of orders,
7–8, 24, 282, 285; subject to king, 314;
and taxes, 336–37; and tithes, 303–4;
worldly behavior of, 332
Blois, Declaration of, (1577), 130, 289,
292, 310
Blois, Ordinance of: of 1567, 132; of 1579,
62–63, 65–66, 91, 135, 341–42, 442, 497,
652; of 1588, 132
Bodin, Jean, 48, 85–86, 88, 645–46, 659–64
Boileau, Jacques, 357
Bologna, Concordat of, (1516), 289
Boniface VIII, Pope, 662
Bonnaffé family, 237–38
Bonne, François de, 396
Bonne, Rigobert, 697
Bonnefous, Jean de, 690
Bonnefous, Raymond de, 690
Booksellers, 454–55
Bord, François-Philippe Loubert, baron
de, 195–96
Bordeaux, 565–74
Bossuet, Jacques-Bénigne, bishop of
Meaux, 394, 648, 671
Boucher, François, 474
Boucherat, Louis, 175
Bouillon, Henri de la Tour d'Auvergne,
duc de, 51
Boulainvilliers, Henri, comte de, 122
Bourdoise, Adrien, 344–46, 353
Bourgeoisie: in Beauvais, 592–94; de-
fined, 236–37; Domat on function of,
31; domination of, in society, 39; dress
of, 263; ennoblement of, 215; fortunes of,
250–51; living like nobles, 214–21, 226,

233–34, 238–39, 243, 245; in Paris,
587–88, 590; recruitment of clergy from,
329; relations of, with nobility, 205–6;
Saint-Simon condemns, 21; social strati-
fication and mobility of, 239–53; in
society of orders, 8; surgeons as, 461;
tax exemptions of, 483; titles for, 123;
and town status, 564, 565–74; values and
life-style of, 237–39, 247–48. *See also*
Merchants
Bourgogne, Louis, duc de, 17–20, 75
Bourguignon d'Anville, J.-B., 696
Boutaric, François de, 4
Bouthillier, Claude, 105
Bread prices, 276
Brienne family, 182. *See also* Loménie de
Brienne
Brittany: seigneurial justice in, 520,
524–25, 527–28; seigneurial ownership
in, 500, 538
Brun, François, 90
Buache, Philippe, 698
Building. *See* Construction methods
Bullion, Claude de, 105
Bureau de la Ville (Paris), 579–82, 585–86,
588–90
Bureaux des finances, 435–36
Burgundy, 529, 531, 653
Butchers, 468–69

Cabinet des Titres, 120
Cadenet, marshal de, 154
Calais, 682
Calas case, 407
Calvinists, 388, 396, 402. *See also*
Protestants
Canada, 544
Canal du Midi, 544
Canon law, 283, 289, 296–302, 350
Canons (ecclesiastical): absences of, 310;
confer benefices, 305; duties of, 287;
in France, 315; and General Assembly,
364; incomes of, 332–33; life-style of,
338; recruitment and social origins of,
327–28; regular, 292. *See also* Chapters
Capet, Hugues, 641, 655
Capuchins, 293, 332
Cardinals, 7–8, 24, 290

Cartesianism. *See* Descartes, René
Carthusian Order, 293
Cartography, 689–98
Cas: prévôtaux, 505–6; *royaux,* 505–6
Caseneuve, Pierre de, 542
Cassini family (cartographers), 694–98
Castellans and castellanies, 7, 480–81, 508–9
Catechisms, 353, 355
Cathedrals, 288
Cattel, Martin, 114
Censives (albergements): in fiefs, 109, 482–83, 486, 491; law of, 492–99, 501; and leases, 501–4; as private property, 549; rates of, 738; and seigneurial exactions, 533, 538, 545; and seigneurial justice, 511–12
Census (population), 698–703
Chalais, Louis-Jean-Charles, prince de, 144
Champarts, 482, 496, 533, 538, 738
Chancellors of France, 14, 23, 153–55
Chapters (of canons), 287–88, 297, 358
Charity, 278, 289
Charles II, king of England, 683
Charles V, Emperor, 653, 682
Charles V, king of France, 130, 478, 651
Charles VII, king of France, 43, 608
Charles VIII, king of France, 130
Charles IX, king of France, 133, 497
Chartered companies, 473–75
Châtelet (Paris): and administration of Paris, 574, 578, 580–81, 588, 590; appeals to, 523; attorneys before, 445; notaries attached to, 447–48; and police, 541; and royal jurisdiction, 507; and surgeons, 459–60; and sworn crafts, 469; and the university, 453
Chérin, Louis-Nicolas-Henri, 121, 154, 196
Chevalier, Louis, 711
Chevaliers (knights), 7, 9, 14, 124, 130, 136–38, 481
Cheverny, Philippe Hurault, comte de, 51
Chevrier de Saint-Maurice, François de, 119
Children, 88–91

Chirurgiens de robe longue, 459–60
Choiseul, César-Gabriel de, 182–83
Choisy, François-Timoléon de, 547
Chotard, Jean-Baptiste, 177–78
Churchwardens, 558
Cinq-Mars, Henri Coeffier Ruzé d'Effiat, marquis de, 65
Cistercians, 292
Civil code, 84–85
Class (social), 6, 36–40, 44–45, 259
Clement V, Pope, 662
Clergy: administrative model of, 380; agents general of, 367–69, 376–77; antagonism between *parlements* and, 325; Assemblies of, 311–13, 317–18, 336–37, 342; and benefices, 304–8; bishops' responsibility for, 289; communities of, 344–46; crimes committed by, 484; Domat on, 33, 35; dress of, 8; Enlightenment influence on, 353–55; in estates of Languedoc, 614; financial commitments and immunities of, 372–74; functions of, 37; hierarchy of, 112, 120, 282, 284–85, 320–21; income of, 13, 331–37, 373; internal conflicts among, 356–58; "irregular," 281, 284; life-style of, 337–58; numbers of, 319–20; ordination of, 286–87; political participation by, 374–80; political representation and organization of, 358–67, 379–80; privileges and exemptions of, 294–96; and Protestant civil rights, 408; qualities and disqualifications of, 281–84; receive tithes, 303; regional organization of, 369–72; "regular," 291–94, 319–20, 355; relations of, with society, 316–19; religious offenses of, 300–302, 379; Saint-Simon on, 24–25; social origins and recruitment of, 316, 320–31, 340; in society of orders, 7–9, 11, 14, 24, 37, 281–82; taxes on, 336–37, 359–61; and town elections, 601; training of, 340–53; vows and commitments made by, 292–94. *See also particular ranks and offices.*
Clovis, king of the Franks, 654–55, 671
Coats of arms. *See* Armorial bearings

Code Michaud (1629), 75, 570
Coigny, Jean-Philippe de Franquetot, marshal de, 416
Coislin, Armand du Cambout, marquis de, 155
Colbert, Charles, marquis de Croissy, 177, 206
Colbert, Jean-Baptiste, 18; and Académie des Sciences, 457; and Cartesianism, 703; and East India Company, 474; and engineering training, 720; and Jews, 415–16; and property, 547; on population, 699–701, 708; and reduction of nobility, 147
Collège de Clermont (later Collège Louis-le-Grand), 454, 714
College of Heralds, 118
Collège des Lecteurs Royaux, 454
Collège Louis-le-Grand. See Collège de Clermont
College of Master Surgeons, 461
College of Pharmacy, 462
Collège Royal (Collège de France), 450
College of Saint-Cosmas, 459–60
Collège des Six-Vingts, 437
Commerce, 190–93
Commoners: claims by, to noble status, 135, 138; and dueling, 143; ennoblement of, 127; and holding of fiefs, 482–83; in military service, 193, 195–97; use of armorial bearings by, 114–16. See also Bourgeoisie
Communes, 564–65
Communities: domestic, 78–83; tacit, 79–83
Communities of inhabitants: administration of, 551–59, 561; property of, 555–56, 559–60; reforms affecting, 561; revenue-raising by 560–61; and royal tutelage, 559–61
Compagnie des Indes (later Compagnie des Moluques), 473. See also East India Company
Compagnie du Saint-Sacrement, 93, 140 394–95
Compagnie du Saint-Sacrement de l'Autel, 342

Companies, 431, 434–35; commercial, 473–75. See also Corporations
Compiègne, Ordinance of, (1763), 91
Complant, 500–501
Condé family, 174, 182
Confraternities (clerical), 339–41, 353
Congrégation de la Doctrine Chrétienne, 348, 354, 714–15
Conseil: de Commerce, 247; de Conscience, 340; d'Etat et privé, 379; de la Guerre, 196–98; des Parties, 34, 155; du Roi (see King's Council)
Constable of France, 141–42
Constituent Assembly (National Assembly), 39, 410, 427
Constitution (state), 647–51
Construction methods, 722–29
Conti family, 174, 182
Convenant, 500
Convents, 295. See also Nuns
Corporations: of academies, 455–58; of auxiliaries of justice, 437–49; commercial, 473–75; of crafts, 254, 263, 463–73; definition and organization of, 429–31; and fiefs, 483; and judicial power, 509; medical, 458–63; of royal officials, 431–37; the "six," 240, 242, 576; and the state, 645–46; universities as, 450–55; villages and parishes as, 551–62
Corsica, 685
Corvées, 496, 529, 533, 538
Costar, Pierre Coustard, called, 106
Coston, Jean, 249
Council of Orders, 21
Country, 264–74
Counts, 7, 26, 32, 480, 508–9
Counts-and-peers, 156
Cour des aides, 1, 135–36
Court (royal), 153–58. See also Monarchy
Court, Antoine, 405–6
Courts of law: appeals, 523–25; and Beauvais, 591, 596–97; officials of, 526–28; in Paris, 540–41; profits and costs of, 525–27; and reformed municipal administration, 602–3; and royal power, 669; seigneurial, 517–28. See also Justice; Parlements

Coyer, Gabriel-François, 147, 191–93
Crafts, craftsmen: and apprenticeship system, 468; and *bourgeoisie,* 236–37; and class consciousness, 259; competition among, 470–71; corporate organization and duties of, 463–73; in country, 264–70, 273; dress of, 263; earnings of, 260–61, 263; fortunes and possessions of, 261–62; free, 255, 260–61; literacy among, 262; marks of, 471; master, 468–71; and merchants, 259; organization of, 254–55, 263; Protestant, 396–97; ranks of, 240–41, 243–44, 254–60, 262; recruitment of clergy from, 330; responsibilities of, 471–72; in society of orders, 8; and tax revolts, 740; and town elections, 600–601. *See also individual crafts and occupations*
Cramoisy, Sébastien, 588
Créatures, 105–10
Crime and criminals: clerical, 484; poor and, 275, 277–78; and powers of justice, 505–6, 521–22, 540–41; and punishment for gentlemen, 11–12; religious, 298–302
Cruquius, Nicolas, 698
Cuperly, Catherine, 241
Curés. See Priests
Customary law: and *censives,* 495; and disposal and recovery of fiefs, 487–89, 491–92; and domestic communities, 80–81; and paterfamilias, 87; and primogeniture, 72–74, 172; of property in southern France, 78; and *retrait lignager,* 68–69; and seigneurial fealty, 485, 487; and seigneurial justice, 513
Customary reservation, 70–71

Damien family, 247
Danse family, 245
Dauphiné: leases in, 502–4; seigneurial rights in, 477–78, 484, 486, 490, 494–95; size of *seigneuries* in, 514–15
Deacons, 7–8, 282, 285, 287, 349
Death sentence, 521
Declaration of the Four Articles (1682), 313
Decorations, 232–34. *See also individual orders*

Delisle, Guillaume, 695
Demoiselle (title), 9
Denys, abbé Guillaume, 720
Derogation, 131–34
Descartes, René (and Cartesianism), 344–45, 677, 703, 715
Descent. *See* Lineage
Desmarets, Nicolas, 18
Dioceses, 322–23, 369–73. *See also* Bishops
Directe royale universelle, 542–43
Divorce, 60. *See also* Family; Marriage
Doctors (medical), 458–62
Domain, royal, 651–52, 659. *See also* Monarchy
Domaine congéable, 500
Domanial officials, 449–50, 465
Domat, Jean, 29–36, 82, 601
Dominicans, 292
Doullens, Edict of, (1539), 541
Dowries, 81, 83, 205–6, 241, 244, 262. *See also* Marriage; Wives; Women
Dubos, abbé Jean-Baptiste, 122
Du Bourg, Georges, 99
Du Chesne, André, 658
Duels, 11, 120, 139–41, 143–46
Dukes, 7, 23, 26–27, 31–32, 156, 480, 508–9
Dukes-and-peers, 21–23, 32, 73, 155–56, 175, 203–4, 206–7
Dumesnil, Claude, 264
Dumoulin, Charles, 73
Dupain de Montesson, 697
Dupain-Triel, Jean-Louis, 697
Duplan, Benjamin, 405
Du Plessis family, 51–53
Dupont de Nemours, Pierre-Samuel, 629
Du Verger family, 56–57

East India Company (French), 474–75, 544
Ecclesiastical order. *See* Clergy
Echute, 530
Ecole de la Marine, 720
Ecole des Ponts et Chaussées, 720
Ecole Royal Militaire (Paris), 195–96
Ecuyers (esquires), 10, 122, 136, 138, 218, 222
Education, 713, 719–21
Effiat, Marie (de Fourcy), 65

Elections (provincial), 610, 632
Elus, 435–37
Emery, Jacques-André, 350
Emperor, Holy Roman, 660
Empire de Galilée, 446
Encyclopédie, 721
Endogamy, 13. *See also* Marriage
Enghien, duc d', 95, 105
Engineering, 720–29
Enlightenment, 353–55, 713, 721
Entails, 75–77
Epidemics, 709, 740–41
Equality, 36–38, 41, 44–45
Esquires. See *Ecuyers*
Estates, provincial, 609–27, 663
Estates General of France: and administrative reforms, 627; Barnave on, 44; composition, 113; Domat on, 31; elections to, 151, 202; and ennobled voters, 216; and *gentilshommes'* corporate sense, 199, 201; and hierarchy of orders, 6, 13–14; and king, 656–57, 663; and marriage law, 62; and provincial assemblies, 636–38; provincial deputies in, 609; and royal domain, 653; and seminaries, 342; and social class, 37–38; and taxes, 638; and tensions within nobility, 205; transformed into National Assembly, 39
Estienne, Charles, 690
Estrades family, 571
Etigny, Antoine Mégret d', 722
Exactions (land), 531–33
Exarchs, 291
Exorcists, 7, 282, 284–85
Expilly, abbé Jean-Joseph, 699, 702

Faith and homage. *See* Fealty
Family: defined, 49, 645, 659; and domestic communities, 79–83; as fundamental social group, 48; importance of, to *bourgeoisie,* 239; as *maison,* 93–95; as *ménage,* 83–91; and paterfamilias, 85–91, 659; and *retrait lignager,* 68–69. *See also* Lineage; Marriage; *Ménage*
Famine. *See* Food supply; *Mortalités*
Farmers: living conditions of, 271–73, 732; methods and activities of, 184, 271–74;

productivity of, 731–39; rights and duties of, 270–71; social position of, 264–74
Farmers-general, 215, 217, 219, 516–17
Fealty: and East India Company, 474; and feudalism, 108–10, 486; Louis XIV and, 107–8; and monarch, 542, 660; nature of, 99–105, 110; and *protecteurs* and *créatures,* 105–7, 110; in *seigneuries,* 484–89, 492, 499, 542, 544
Fénelon, François de Salignac de La Mothe, archbishop of Cambrai, 19, 627, 671
Feudalism, 108–10, 486, 493–94, 534–35
Fidèles. See Fealty
Fiduciary substitutions, 74–77
Fiefs: defined, 482; disposal and recovery of, 487–92; elevation to status of, 545; and fealty, 108–9, 482–86; and freehold rights, 478; inheritance of, 73–74, 77, 484, 488–89; law of, 482–92; and leases, 501, 503; and nobility, 127, 482; number of, 515; and powers of justice, 504–5, 512, 519; as private property, 549; taxes on, 482–84. *See also* Property; *Seigneuries*
Fijan, Pierre, 544
Filain, Président, 322
Filleau, Jean, 395
Financiers: living like nobles, 216–21; in society of orders, 7; sons of, in military service, 193–95, 197
Fontainebleau, Edict of: of 1609, 120; of 1645, 128; of 1685, 400, 402–3, 408; of 1750, 131
Food supply, 705, 707–11, 740
Fortresses, 721–23
Fouquet, Nicolas, vicomte de Vaux, 106
Four Articles. *See* Declaration of the Four Articles
Franche-Comté, 529
Franciscans, 292
François I, king of France, 45, 507, 608, 653, 682
François de Sales, Saint, 343–44, 348
Frank-fee, 482–83, 492, 539
Franks, 15–16. *See also* Clovis, king of the Franks

Frederick William I, king of Prussia, 685
Freehold. *See* Property, freehold
Freemasons, 198, 220
French Revolution, 44, 665
Frérage, 77
Friars, mendicant, 292–93, 332
Fronde, 13, 107, 200, 202, 209, 742
Furetière, Antoine, 48, 274

Galilée. See *Empire de Galilée*
Galland, Auguste, 542
Gallican declaration (1682), 24
Gardes du corps, 197
Gassion, Jean, marshal de, 105
Gaudemet, J., 80
Gaulmin, Gilbert, 63
Gauls, 15–16
Gautier, Jean-Etienne, 51
Gayet de Sansale (of Lyons), 163
Gendarmerie, 197
Genealogy. *See* Family; Lineage
General Asembly of the Clergy: agents
	and receiver general of, 367–69; con-
	stitution of, 361–67, 369, 372; political
	function and procedures of, 372, 374–
	80; powers of jurisdiction of, 379; and
	Protestants, 408, 410
General Assembly (of nobles), 201, 209
Généralités, 371
Gens de lettres. See Learned men
Gens du roi, 440–41
Gentilshommes: and antagonism within
	the nobility, 202–6; coats of arms of,
	8, 10; in commerce, 190–93, 229; as
	court nobles, 154; deprivation of no-
	bility of, 12; and derogation, 169–70;
	Domat on qualities of, 33; and duels,
	139–41, 143–46; and equality process,
	38; farming methods of, 183–84; and
	fealty, 105; Frankish origins of, 16;
	in hierarchy of nobility, 122–24, 153,
	165–66, 203; means of living of, 170,
	181; as members of *gardes du corps,* 197;
	membership of, in *parlements,* 164, 188;
	military service by, 188, 191, 193–98;
	and newly ennobled, 129–31, 216; as of-
	ficeholders, 160; origins of, 216; poverty
	of, 167, 169, 189–92; and precedence,

125; privileges of, 10–11, 25; and proof
	of status, 136–38; and property entails,
	75; in provinces, 158–59, 183; and right
	to work, 133–34, 169–70; rights and cor-
	porate sense of, 198–201; role of, in pro-
	duction, 189–90; and *seigneuries,* 10,
	516; in society of orders, 7–10, 13–15,
	25–26, 35–36; tax exemptions of, 199;
	trials of, 199; wealth of, 13. *See also*
	Nobility
Glassmaking, 11–12, 134
Glucq, Claude, 163
Goldsmiths, 468–69
Gondi family, 345–46, 353
Goudar, Ange, 416
Gradis family, 423
Grain (cereal), 733–37, 740
Grand Conseil, 302, 308, 310
Grande Ecurie, 118
Grandees (the *grands*). *See* Nobility
Grocers, 471. *See also* Apothecaries
Groulart, Claude, 179–80
Guibert, François-Apollini, comte de,
	196–98
Guyot, P. J. J. G., 35, 121–23, 132, 138,
	609

Hall of the Nation, 39
Harvests, 733–37, 740
Henri II, king of France, 45, 135, 305,
	418, 478, 671
Henri III, king of France, 127, 129, 313,
	418, 420, 658
Henri IV, king of France: and advocates'
	strike, 442; and Beauvais' status, 592;
	becomes Catholic, 653; condemns duel-
	ists, 120; establishes Compagnie des
	Indes, 473; and fealty, 99–100; and
	Jews, 420; and magistracy, 45; mur-
	dered, 313, 657; and University of Paris,
	453, 455; and Protestants, 389–90, 400;
	territorial acquisitions of, 682
Heredity, 6, 13, 15, 25. *See also* Inheri-
	tance
Heresy, 298–99, 302
Hermits, 292, 335–36; of Mount Carmel,
	292; of Saint Augustine, 292
Holy Spirit, Order of, 26, 153, 155

Homage. *See* Fealty
Homel, Isaac, 405
Honnêtes hommes, 49
Honor. *See* "Point of honor"
Hospitallers (knights), 292
Hotman, François, 649
Household. See *Maison;* Royal household
Hozier family, 119, 147
Huguenots. *See* Protestants
Huissiers. See Tipstaffs
Humanities, teaching of, 713–20
Humbert II, dauphin, 478
Hunting rights, 510
Husbands, 85–91
Hydrography, 720
Hypergamy, 13. *See also* Marriage

Imbert, Jacques, 597
Independence of opinion, 40–41
Indults, 306–7
Industrialists, 231–32
Inheritance: Argenson's provisions for, 91–93; and customary reservation, 70–71; and domestic communities, 82, 84; and fiduciary substitutions, 74–77; and invalid marriages, 65; and lineage, 66–77, 91–93; and majorat, 77; among nobility, 167, 171, 188; and primogeniture, 72–74, 187; and *retrait lignager,* 69, 78; of *seigneuries,* 480, 488–89, 500, 510–11. *See also* Legitim; Primogeniture; Property
Innocent III, Pope, 662
Intendants (of provinces): abolished, 436–37; and census, 701; and education, 722; and provincial administration, 624, 627, 635; Saint-Simon's proposals on, 28, 627; and town administration, 569, 572–73, 602–4
Isabella, Infanta, 116

Jacquart, Jean, 732, 734
Jansenism, 353, 357, 676
Jansenius, Corneille Jansen, called, 675
Jaunet, Claude, 51
Jesuits, 292, 342, 348–50, 450, 454, 714, 720
Jews: antipathy toward, 413–15; conver-
sions of, 414–15; expulsions of, 420; immigration and settlement of, 417–22; "nations" of, 422–24; numbers of, 419–20, 422, 425–26; occupations of, 417, 419–21, 425; officially recognized, 421–23, 426–27; and property rights, 426; religious observances of, 417, 419, 423–25; social integration of, 423–24; status, rights, and privileges of, 413, 416–27; tolerated, 415–16
Joint-stock companies, 473–75
Joseph, Father (François Joseph Du Tremblay), 101
Jourdain family, 247
Journeymen, 8, 468–70, 473
Judges: ecclesiastical, 297–302; and king's powers, 669; and municipal reform, 602–4; and precedence, 125; in seigneurial courts, 527–28; and seigneurial powers, 505–8, 511. *See also* Courts of law
Juge d'armes, 119
Jurats (town), 567–71, 573
Justice: and appeals, 523–25; costs of, 523, 526; Domat on, 33; ecclesiastical, 296–302, 379; and *seigneuries,* 480–81, 492–93, 504–13, 517–28, 540–41; and sovereignty, 659. *See also* Auxiliaries of justice; Courts of law; Judges

Keepers of the seal, 153
King. *See* Monarchy
King's Council (Conseil du Roi): advocates before, 442–45; and Assembly of Clergy, 374–78; and corporations of officials, 434; in Domat's social order, 31; magistrates predominate in, 20; members of nobility in, 160–61, 641; and provinces, 607, 610–11, 620, 622, 625, 627, 638; Saint-Simon's reform proposals for, 21; and society of orders, 13; and sworn crafts, 468; and *trésoriers,* 436. *See also* Monarchy
"King's evil" (*écrouelles*), 665–66, 671, 674–76
King's men (*gens du roi*), 9
Kinship, 29. *See also* Family; Lineage
Knights. See *Chevaliers*

Laboureurs, 8
Lacretelle, Pierre-Louis, 426
La Flèche (school), 196
La Michodière (demographer), 700, 702, 722
Lamy, Bernard, 350
Land: Barnave on, 42, 44; *bourgeois* ownership of, 245–46, 251–52; inheritance of, 67–74; leases for, 501–4; management of, by nobility, 183–86, 531; productivity of, 731–39; seigneurial exactions from, 531–33; taxation on, 730–31. See also *Censives;* Fiefs; *Seigneuries;* Sharecropping leases
Languedoc provincial estates: composition and representation of, 612–16, 621, 625–27; dissolved, 627; meetings, 616–21; restrictions on powers of, 622–26; revolts in, 622–23; and taxes, 619–23
Laplace, Pierre-Simon, marquis de, 700
La Reynie, Gabriel-Nicolas, sieur de, 577
La Rochefoucauld family, 322
La Rochefoucauld, François de, 238
La Roque de La Lontière, Gilles André de, 123, 132, 134, 152–53
Lateran Council (1215), 61
Latour-Maubourg family, 515
La Tullaye family, 149
Laverdy, Clément Charles François de, 561, 598, 602, 604
La Vrillière family, 205–6
La Vrillière, Louis II Phélypeaux, seigneur de, 175–76
Law, 660–61, 665–68, 719–20
Laws, fundamental, 649–53, 657
Lawyers, 28, 32–33, 35, 526–27. *See also* Courts of law; Justice; *and individual offices*
Lazarists, 345, 348–50
Learned men (*gens de lettres*), 7–8, 227–29
Leases, 501–4, 531–33, 544–46
Le Bret, Cardin, 662–63
Le Clerc, François-Joseph, seigneur de Bussy, 170
Lectors, 282, 284–85
Lefebvre, Georges, 250, 252

Legitim, 65, 70, 73, 188
Le Grand, abbé Joachim, 203
Le Laboureur, Jean, 203
Letters of provision, 431
Letters patent, 430, 434, 468
Lévy, Raphaël, 415
Liancourt, Jeanne, duchesse de, 105
Liberties, church, 316
Liege-homage, 486, 488. *See also* Fealty
Life-expectancy, 707
Lineages: and church hierarchy, 321, 331; defined, 48–49; and *fidèles,* 105; and marriage, 58–66; and property, 66–77, 490; records of, 50–51; and social differences, 223; social function of, 49–50
Literacy, 262–63
Livres de raison (account books), 50–51, 58, 170
Locke, John, 732
Lods et ventes, 495, 498–99, 532–33, 539, 545
Loménie de Brienne, Etienne Charles, comte de, 196, 635–37
"Long robe," 7–8
Longueville, Catherine de Gonzague, duchesse de, 5
Lorraine, Louis de, 118
Louis XI, king of France, 43, 418, 608
Louis XIII, king of France: and Académie Française, 456; and apothecaries, 462; on armorial bearings, 114, 118; and Article of Third Estate, 313; and Beauvais privileges, 592; and Bordeaux administration, 570; denounces misalliances, 59; and divine right, 658; and ecclesiastical jurisdiction, 298; on the family, 86; and fealty, 99, 101–2, 105; and Jews, 420; and Languedoc revolt, 622–23; and Paris officials, 587; and Protestants, 389, 392–93, 400; and provincial estates, 610, 617; revokes ennoblements, 130; and seigneurial courts, 541; territory of, 682; touches subjects to cure king's evil, 655; treaty of, with duc d'Orléans (1637), 103; use of royal arms by, 116
Louis XIV, king of France: and armorial

bearings, 115, 118; author of *Mémoires pour l'Instruction du Dauphin,* 107; and bastard sons, 22–23, 651; and Beauvais privileges, 592; and Bordeaux town, 573; and Cartesianism, 703; and cartography, 695; on continuity of state, 647; death of, 16–17, 19; and Declaration of Four Articles, 313; and declaration on registering entails, 76; and decline of fealty, 107–8; divinity of, 671–72; and duc de Bourgogne, 17–18; and dukes-and-peers' powers, 207; and East India Company, 474–75; edicts of, against dueling, 142–43, 145; and ennoblement, 25, 45, 127–28, 150; and General Assembly of the Clergy, 363–66; and higher nobility, 158; and Jews, 415, 419; and notaries, 447; and Paris administration, 575, 587–88; and Protestants, 397–400, 403; and provincial estates, 610, 623–24; renounces *don,* 652; and social order, 20–21; territory of, 682–85; travels of, 688; and the University of Paris, 451, 454

Louis XV, king of France: and agents general of clergy, 368; and cartography, 696; edict of, against dueling, 146; and Jews, 422; and Protestants, 403; and provincial *parlements,* 609; and royal arms, 117; and royal bastards, 23; and royal symbolism, 673–74; and royal touch, 674; territory of, 685–86

Louis XVI, king of France, 20, 408, 462, 472–73, 675, 686

Louvois, François-Michel Le Tellier, marquis de, 723–26

Loyalty. *See* Fealty

Loyseau, Charles: on *bourgeoisie,* 237; on clergy, 282; on hierarchy of nobility, 152–53; life of, 4–5; modern use of, as historical source, 152; on nobility of letters, 227; Paris *parlement* invokes, 4, 35, 36; on poor, 275; on powers of justice, 513; on right to armorial bearings, 114; on *seigneuries,* 478, 482; on sovereignty, 661–62, 664; on state, 645–46; views of society of, 4–16, 22, 35,

39–40; works of, 4–5, 645

Lutherans, 410. *See also* Protestants

Luynes, Charles, duc de, 154

Lyons, 604

Mably, abbé Gabriel Bonnot de, 122

Magistrates: Barnave on refractory nature of, 43; barred from trade, 133; companies of, 431; in Domat's social order, 31, 33, 35; education of, 721; ennoblement of, 26, 45, 206; living like nobles, 222, 224–26; preeminence of, 10, 14, 16, 36, 45, 88; Protestant, 394; in ranks of nobility, 160–62, 164, 206–7; and Saint-Simon's reforms, 20, 26–28; support seigneurial rights, 535. See also *Parlements*

Mailly, Louise Julie, comtesse de, 674

Main, la, 21

Mainmorte. See Mortmain

Maison (household), 48–49, 84, 91–95

Majorat, 77

Majority, age of, 485

Malesherbes, Chrétien Guillaume de Lamoignon de, 408

Malta, Knights of, 305

Malthus, Thomas Robert, 704–5

Manual workers, 253–74. *See also* Crafts and craftsmen

Maps. *See* Cartography

Maréchaussée (marshalsea), 142

Marie, André, 397

Marillac, Michel de, 75

Mariotte, Christophe de, 615

Marly, Edict of, (1730), 66

Marquises, 7, 24, 26, 32, 480

Marriage: abductions and clandestine, 61–66, 88; among advocates, 228; within *bourgeoisie,* 241–44, 248, 257; and canon law, 60–62; civil law on, 62–66, 90; and clergy, 284–85, 294, 316, 320; by consent, 61–65, 88; among countrymen, 264–65, 274; early, 274; among ennobled *bourgeoisie,* 215–16, 221; and family fortunes, 188; Jewish, 424, 427; and lineage, 58–66, 90; and lineal property, 66–67, 187–88; among manual

workers, 253, 255–57, 259, 261–62; of
minors, 65; misalliances, 59–60; within
nobility, 204–6, 209, 216; among office-
holders, 222–23, 225–27; and population
changes, 706, 708, 710; and Protestants,
407–9; registers of, 63; and social
hierarchy, 152, 156, 161, 164, 182; and
younger children, 188. *See also*
Divorce; Family; Inheritance
Marshals of France, 153. *See also* Tri-
bunal of the Marshals of France
Marx, Karl, 40
Mathematics, 703
Matricule, la, 442–43
Maugars, André, 106
Maultrot, Gabriel-Nicolas, 358
Maupeou, René Nicolas Charles Augustin
de, 604, 609
Mauro affair (1738), 730
Mayenne, Charles de Lorraine, duc de,
99–100
Maynon d'Invau, Etienne, 604
Mayors, 561, 567–71, 595–600
Mechanistics, 677, 703–4
Medicine, 458–63
Melun, Edict of, (1580), 301, 303, 341,
497
Ménage, 48–49, 81–91. *See also* Family
Merchants: as *bourgeois,* 236–37; cor-
porations of, 473; and craftsmen, 257–
60, 263–64; ennoblement of, 247; for-
tunes of, 245–47, 249; ranks of, 240–
42, 244–46, 248–49, 251, 257; recruit-
ment of clergy from, 329–30; in society
of orders, 7–8, 26, 223–24; style of
living of, 247–48; wholesale, 229–32
Meslier, Jean, 339
Mesnard, Paul, 19
Messance (demographer), 700
Metropolitans, 291, 297, 310
Meusnier, J.-B., 698
Mignard, Nicolas, 673
Military Merit, Order of, 232
Military schools, 195–96
Militia, 555
Minims, 292, 332
Mining, 189
Ministers of state, 153, 670

Mirabeau, Victor Riqueli, marquis de,
116, 553
Monarchy: absolute, theory of, 670–77;
and age of majority, 651–52; and
appointment of bishops, 289–91; Barnave on, 43–44; and Beauvais authority,
591–92, 595–98; and benefices, 307, 310,
321; and church property, 303; and corporate nobility, 198, 200–201, 204; and
corporations, 430–31, 434, 475; and
court nobles, 153–54; delegation of
powers of, 668–70; divine right of, 313,
656–58; and East India Company, 475;
and ennoblement, 126–28, 132; fealty to,
542–44, 608–9; and fundamental laws,
649–53, 657; and General Assembly of
the Clergy, 361–67, 376, 380; mystic
consecration and religious status of,
653–58, 670–77; and nobility, 43; and
Paris administration, 574–82, 586–87;
and personal rule, 666–69; and
physicians, 459; power of, 640–42, 647,,
650, 653, 665–70; and powers of justice,
505, 507, 540–41; and provinces, 607–
11, 617–20, 622–24, 627, 629–31, 636;
and provincial nobility, 209–10; public
status of, 653; and revolt, 641; and royal
touch, 655–56, 671, 674–75; seigneurial
property and claims of, 536, 539–40;
and *seigneuries,* 480, 491, 493, 540–44;
and sovereignty, 659–65, 669; and succession, 650–52, 667; and sworn crafts,
472; symbols of, 671–72; and tax on
clergy, 360; and tax collection, 740–
42; and temporal power and church
liberties, 311–15; and town administration, 570–73, 598, 602–3; and University of Paris, 453; and village communities, 559–61
Monasteries, 292–93, 332–33
Money (currency), 188–89
Monks, 24, 284, 292, 305
Monnier, Sophie de, 116
Montaigne, Michel Eyquem de, 419
Montesquieu, Charles de Secondat, baron
de La Brède, 43, 122
Montrésor, Claude de Bourdelle, comte
de, 103

Montyon, Jean-Baptiste Antoine Robert
    Auget, baron de, 722
Morenne, Claude de, 658
Morgan, Jacques, 246
Morgan, Jean-Baptiste, 246–47
Mortalités, 740–41
Mortmain, 529–31
Morvilliers, Jean de, bishop of Orléans, 59
Motte family, 245
Moulins, Ordinance of, (1566), 75–76,
    79, 91, 298, 301, 652
Mours, Samuel, 384

Nantes, Edict of, (1598), 383–84, 389, 392,
    394–95, 398, 400–402
National Assembly, 39
"Nations" (university), 450–51
Necker, Jacques, 630, 632, 703, 709
Needs (social), 33–35
Nicolaï family, 54–55
Nicolaï, Catherine, 95
Nijmegen, Peace of, (1674), 115
Nîmes, Edict of, (1629), 400–401
Nobility: Arc's military proposals for,
    194–95; assemblies of, 200–203, 209;
    barred from gainful employment, 12,
    132–33; church rights of, 191; claims to,
    investigation of, 135–39, 148;
    corporate sense of, 198–202; court and
    higher, 153–59, 182, 192, 194, 196–97;
    degrees of, 122–24, 152–66; derogation
    of, 131–35; diversity and conflicts
    among, 202–10; in Domat's social order,
    35; dress of, 8; entry to, by office,
    130, 149–50, 163, 221–27; in Estates
    General, 199–200; in estates of Langue-
    doc, 613–14; fortunes and incomes of,
    13, 166–68, 173–74, 331; and Fronde,
    107; at General Assembly of Clergy,
    364; inheritances in, 167, 171; judicial
    status of, 121; and land management,
    184–86; limited by fiscal policy, 148;
    lineages of, 51–58; marriage among, 156,
    204–6; means and style of living of, 166–
    98; membership in, 11–12, 36, 126–31,
    137, 148–51, 202, 215–16, 220–21, 229–
    32; merchants admitted to, 247–48; in
    military state, 547; and monarchy, 43;

numbers and distribution of, 147–52;
    privileges of, 124–26; in provinces, 156–
    59, 172, 183–87, 209; punishments
    appropriate for, 126; quality of, 121–22,
    127, 136, 148, 198; recruitment of clergy
    from, 323–27, 329; revocation of, 127–
    29; rights of, to armorial bearings, 114,
    120, 124–25; right of, to fiefs, 482; right
    of, to receive salutes, 10; rights of, to
    occupations, 132–34; and rule of primo-
    geniture, 170–71, 187; in Saint-Simon's
    proposed reforms, 21–22, 25–29;
    seigneurial holdings by, 515–16, 543;
    and seigneurial jurisdiction, 506; social
    functions of, 37; in social hierarchy,
    120–21; social standing of, 147–66; in
    society of orders, 7–11, 14, 16, 24, 37,
    112–213; tax exemptions and obligations
    of, 11, 25, 37, 125, 172, 186–87; and
    town elections, 600; in trade and indus-
    try, 191–93, 464; transmitted through
    mother, 131; trials of, 198–99; usurpa-
    tion of, 135–38, 148, 203. *See also
    individual ranks*
Noblesse: de cloche (*noblesse munici-
    pale*), 130, 150, 163; *dormante,* 170;
    d'épée, 160–61, 165, 204–5, 207, 325;
    de race, 123, 127, 130, 132; *de robe*
    (*robins*), 27, 159–65, 204–7, 218
Notaries, 447–48
Nuns, 24, 305, 319–20, 326, 485

Officeholders (officials), 221–27
Officers, military: court nobility as, 154,
    192, 194, 196–97; Domat on qualities of,
    32–33; opened to *gentilshommes,* 191,
    193, 196; ranks of, 34; Saint-Simon on,
    27; social sources of, 193–97
"Officials": ecclesiastical, 297; royal,
    431–37
Olier, Jean-Jacques, 140, 346–47, 353
Olivier-Martin, François, 609
Oratory of Jesus Christ (Oratorians), 343,
    348–49, 354, 714–15
Orders and decorations. *See* Decorations
Orders, religious, 292–94
Orléans, Ordinance of, (1560), 75, 91, 115,
    132, 135

Orléans family, 182
Orléans, Gaston, duc d', 103
Ormesson, André d', 58
Ormesson, Olivier Lefèvre, seigneur d',
    58–59
Oudenarde, Battle of, (1708), 17

Papon, Jean, 79
Parage, 77
Paris: administration and powers of,
    574–90; arms of, 579–80; *bourgeoisie* in,
    240–41, 587–88, 590; customary laws of
    seigneuries in, 485, 489, 491–92, 499,
    504, 513; defenses of, 582; division of,
    into *quartiers,* 9, 580–83; Jews in, 417;
    mapped, 689, 695; municipal magis-
    trates in, 584–87; and municipal re-
    form, 604; officials of, 575–78, 582–90;
    police in, 541; powers of justice in, 507,
    512–13, 541; seigneurial courts in, 517–
    18, 521, 523, 526; Six Corporations of,
    466; taxes in, 583, 585, 589; town status
    of, 563–65, 570; University of, 450–55,
    458, 460–61
Paris *parlement:* advocates before, 439–
    42; on armorial bearings, 117; attorneys
    before, 445–46; authority of, in Paris
    administration, 574–75; and benefices,
    306, 310; and craft communities, 473;
    and ennoblements, 130; and hierarchy
    of orders, 13–14, 36–38; invokes Loy-
    seau, 4, 35, 36; members of, in nobility,
    159–63; and Protestant cases, 388; and
    seigneurial courts, 521, 523–24, 531;
    and seigneurial property rights, 535;
    sentences by, for dueling, 144; social
    composition of, 160–63, 207–9; and sur-
    geons, 460; titles of members of, 9; and
    trial of peers, 126, 480; and University,
    452–54; wearing of hats by members of,
    207
Parishes, 323, 551, 557–58
Parlements: admission to, 278–79, 431–
    43; and agents general of clergy, 368;
    antagonism between clergy and, 325;
    clerical members of, 379; and corporate
    nobility, 201; and dukes-and-peers, 155;
    and ecclesiastical jurisdiction, 297, 302;

and hierarchy of orders, 13–14, 161;
    incomes and fortunes of members of,
    177–80, 188–89; internal discipline in,
    433; and Louis XIV's sons, 22; and
    marriage law, 63–64; Maupeou
    abolishes, 604, 609; nobility of members
    of, 160, 163–65; and papal power, 315;
    power of, 641; and Protestant cases,
    388; in provinces, 609; and provincial
    estates, 624–25, 627; recruitment from
    nobility to, 149, 188; and royal power,
    665; Saint-Simon's proposed demotion
    of, 28; and seigneurial courts, 524, 527;
    and seigneurial land claims, 538; as
    sovereign companies, 431–34; and
    sworn crafts, 468, 473; and town admin-
    istration, 569–70, 573, 602. *See also*
    Magistrates; Paris *parlement*
Partisans, 216
Pastors (Protestant), 386–87, 389–90, 397,
    404–6, 410
Paterfamilias, 85–91, 94, 659
Patriarchs, 7, 291
Patrons (ecclesiastical), 306–7, 329–30
Pays, 607, 611
Peasants: as *bourgeoisie,* 252–53; grazing
    rights of, 537; lawsuits by, 555; living
    standards of, 732, 739; possessions of,
    269–70, 732; relations of, with
    seigneurs, 528–29, 532; revolts by,
    537, 641, 741–42; and seigneurial extor-
    tions, 536–40; social position of, 8,
    265–67, 269–70, 274; taxation of, 187,
    732, 738–41
Peeresses, 155
Peers, 23, 126, 156, 480. *See also* Nobility
Pellisson, Paul, 106
Penthièvre family, 182
Pérard family, 252
Perche, Pierre, 249
Petty, William, 704
Pharmacy. *See* Apothecaries
Phélypeaux family, 55–58
Philip II, king of Spain, 682
Philip IV, king of Spain, 115
Philip V, king of Spain, 651
Physicians, 458–59, 462–63
Picard, abbé Jean, 695

Pinon, Charles, 178
Pinon, Jacques, 179
Pinon, Jean, 179
Plague, 707–8. See also *Mortalités*
"Point of honor," 139–46
Poitiers, Edict of, (1577), 383–84
Police, 541, 568, 580
Police, officiers de, 449–50
Polignac family, 182, 515
Poll tax (capitation tax); and census, 701–2; clergy and, 373; and nobility, 148, 151, 167–68, 187, 189; universities pay, 453
Pontchartrain family, 57, 701
Poor, the, 274–79
Popes: and appointment of bishops, 290–91; and benefices, 305–10, 314, 316; and Gallican church liberties, 311–12, 314–15; jurisdiction of, 297–98; relations of, with bishops and clergy, 357; relations of, with French king, 311–14, 662–63, 666; and religious orders, 293–94; supremacy of, 291, 312, 660; and tax on clergy, 360
Population, 319–20, 322–23; changes in, 704–10, 741; figures, 709; measurement of, 698–704; physical characteristics of, 710–13
Porters (ecclesiastical), 7, 282, 284
Portugal, 417–20, 422
Postal service, 687
Pothier, Robert Joseph, 35, 66, 82
Power, 39–43. See also Monarchy, power of
Precedence, 9, 14, 125
Prelates. See Bishops
Premiers présidents, 14
Présidents, 14, 32
Priests (and *curés*): associations of, 357; commitment and vocation of, 291, 317–19, 343, 347; communities of, 346; and community assembly, 552–53, 555, 557; conflict of, with upper clergy, 356–58; dress of, 8; duties of, 287–88; and Enlightenment philosophy, 354–55; and equality process, 38; and General Assembly, 365; incomes of, 333–36, 356; life-style of, 338–39; and marriage

laws, 61–64; means of, 252; moral laxity of, 338–39, 352; numbers of, 319–20; pensions of, 336; qualifications for, 287; recruitment and social origins of, 328–31, 341; reformed attitudes of, 352; Saint-Simon on, 25; social and civic role of, 318–20; in society of orders, 7–9, 282, 285; and taxes, 336–37; and tithes, 304; training of, 341–53, 355; unfrocking of, 12. See also Clergy
Primates (clerical), 7, 282, 291, 297. See also Archbishops
Primogeniture: among nobility, 167, 170–72, 187; and property inheritance, 72–74, 167, 172; and royal succession, 650
Princes, 7–9, 14, 22, 32–33, 204
Princes of the blood: and conflict among nobility, 209; dignity of, 32; and king's personal rule, 667; marriages of, 156, 667; privileges of, 155–56, 641; in provinces, 156–57; and regencies, 652; seigneurial property of, 536; in society of orders, 7; titles of, 124
Princesses of the blood, 155–56
Priors, 297, 364
Prisons, 526
Procureurs, 437–39, 445–46, 602
Productivity, 731–35
Professions, 228. See also *individual crafts and professions*
Property: Barnave on, 41–43; *bourgeois* ownership of, 245–46, 251; confiscation of, 510; and customary reservation, 70–71; and domestic communities, 80–82, 84; ecclesiastical, 302–3, 309, 321, 331, 359–60; as election qualification, 629; and fiduciary substitutions, 74–77; freehold, 477–78, 542–43; Jews and, 426; lineal, 66–77; and majorat, 77; and primogeniture, 72–74; private and state, 547–49; recorded in *livres de raison,* 50; redemption of, 67–69, 78; and rights of paterfamilias, 87–88; in southern France, 78. See also Fiefs; Inheritance; *Seigneuries;* Wealth
Protecteurs, 105–7, 110
Protestants: barred from *parlements,* 432; behavior of, 386–87, 397; campaigns

against, 393–400, 403–6; church organization of, 385–88, 399–400, 408; civil rights of, 408–10; clandestine practice of religion by, 404–7: coerced to become Catholics, 401–3; destruction of places of worship of, 370; distribution of, 384; emigration of, 397, 403–4; General Assembly and, 376; increasing tolerance toward, 407–8; and justice and administration, 388–89; numbers of, 319, 385, 407; persecution of Catholics by, 391–92; political and military organization of, 389–92, 398–99; proscription of, (1685), 400–404; recognized by Edict of Nantes, 383–85; revolts and suppression of, 392–93, 406; in Revolution, 410; and royal divinity, 675–76; social composition of, 396–97. *See also* Calvinists; Synods
Provence, Louis Stanislas Xavier, comte de (Louis XVIII), 182
Provinces: assemblies in, 628–38; contracts between kingdom and, 607–9; defined, 606–7; estates in, 609–11, 627–28, 636, 638–39; nobility in, 157–59, 172; *parlements* in, 609; particularity of, 641; property rights in, 478; and Saint-Simon's reforms, 28
Provost of the Merchants (Paris), 582–88
Proyart, abbé Liévin-Bonaventure, 20
Pucelle, abbé René, 163
Punishment. *See* Crime; Prisons
Pyrenees, Treaty of the, (1659), 608

Quevaise, 500–501
Quints et requints, 487–88

Rabaut, Paul, 406–7, 410
Rabbis, 424–25. *See also* Jews
Racine, Jean, 49
Racine, Jean-Baptiste, 49
Rapin, René, 93
Ravaillac, François, 657
Ravitch, Norman, 324
Readers (ecclesiastical), 7
Rebellion, 537, 641, 741–42
Receiver general (and provincial) of the clergy, 368–73

Relief et rachat, 487–89, 498–99, 539
Religion: crimes and offenses against, 298–301; freedom of, 410. *See also* Catholic Church; Jews; Protestants
Religion Prétendue Réformée (RPR). *See* Protestants
Religious orders, 88, 91. *See also individual orders*
Renan, Ernest, 354
Rents. *See* Leases
Retrait: censuel, 497–99; *féodal,* 490–91, 498; *lignager,* 67–69, 78, 490–91
Revolt. *See* Rebellion
Richelieu family, 51–53
Richelieu, Armand-Jean du Plessis, Cardinal duc de: and the Académie française, 456; and aristocracy's decline, 43; on clergy's taxes, 359; and fealty, 101–2, 105; fortune of, 174; initiates chartered companies, 473; lineage of, 52–53; and marriage alliances, 59; and nobility's means, 189–90; as protector, 105–6; reforms nephew's household, 94; and seminaries, 341–46; and suppression of Protestants, 393
Richelieu, Louis François Armand de Vignerot du Plessis, duc de, 53–54
Richer, Edmond, 357–58
Roads, 687
Robins. See Noblesse de robe
Rodriguez Péreire, Jacob, 423–24
Rohan, Henri, duc de, prince de Léon, 391
Rohault, Jacques, 703
Roman Catholic Church: and *censives,* 493; collection of revenues by, 369–72; ecclesiastical jurisdiction of, 296–302; and fiefs, 483–84, 491; hierarchy of, 282; and kings of France, 653–55, 657–68; liberties and temporal power of, 311–16; and marriage, 60–63; and property, 302–3; and Protestants, 391–92, 401–4, 406–10; and relative power of clergy, 357–58; "Renaissance" of, and reforms in, 340, 342, 352–54, 357, 395; and tithes, 303–4. *See also* Clergy; Canon law
Rousseau, Jean-Jacques, 530

Royal College of Surgery, 460
Royal household (*Maison du roi*), 94. *See also* Monarchy
Royaume de la Basoche, 446

Saint Benedict, Order of, 292
Saint-Germain, Claude-Louis, comte de, 196
Saint-Germain, Declaration of, (1679), 143
Saint-Germain, Edict of: of 1640, 128; of 1669, 133
Saint-Lazare seminary, 343–48, 352
Saint-Louis, Order of, 131, 196–97, 232
Saint-Michel, Order of, 25, 232–33
Saint-Nicolas-du-Chardonnet seminary, 346–47, 349, 352
Saint-Pierre, abbé Charles Irénée Castel de, 318
Saint-Simon, Louis de Rouvray, duc de: and Bourgogne's plans, 19–20; on duels, 145; on the ennobled, 215–16; personality of, 17; political writings of, 20; and provincial reform, 627; reactionary reform proposals of, 20–23; on social structure, 16–29, 35
Saint-Sulpice seminary, 347–48, 350, 354
Saisie féodale, 489–90, 499
Salic law, 650, 660
Salons, 217–19
Salt tax, 295
Salvador, Jona, 417
Sanson, Nicolas (and family), 691, 693, 695
Saugrain, Claude-Marin, 701–2
Savaron, Jean, 671
Schomberg, Henri de, comte de Nanteuil, 100–101
Scientists, 228–29
Secrétaires: du roi, 437–39, 442–43; "*populotiers*," 439
Secretaries of state, 153, 670
"Secretaries to the king," 25
Seduction, 62–64, 66
Sée, Henri, 711
Séguier, Pierre, duc de Villemor, 23, 105, 154, 394, 456
Seigneuries and *seigneurs:* armorial bearings of, 116–17; and community assemblies, 552; defined, 479, 492; dues and obligations owed to, 492–99, 500, 530–34, 536–40, 545–46, 738, 741–42; expansion and encroachments by, 536–38; farming-out of, 516–17, 529; and fealty, 109, 484–87, 492; *financiers* acquire, 220; fortunes derived from, 175, 178–79, 181; hierarchy of, 27, 479–82; holders of, 515–17; as individual properties, 547–49; and inheritance, 67, 480, 488–89, 500; jurisdiction of, 297, 480–82, 492–93, 497, 541; and land management, 184–86, 531; and leases, 501–4; legal position of, 477–513; in military society, 547; monarchy and, 480, 491, 493, 540–44, 641; and mortmain, 529–31; and new enterprises, 544; number and extent of, 514–15; and powers of justice, 504–13, 517–28, 540–41; prosecution of rights of, 544–46; reaction and revival of property rights of, 534–40; relations of, with men, 528–31; and sovereignty, 661. *See also Censives;* Fiefs
Seminaries, 340–41, 346–51
Serfdom, 529–30
Sergents. See Bailiffs
Sharecropping leases (*métairies*), 12
"Short robe," 7
Simon, Richard, 417
Société de Chirurgie, 460–61
Soldini, abbé (Louis XVI's confessor), 20
Sons. *See* Primogeniture
Sorel, Charles, 104
Sovereign. *See* Monarchy
Sovereignty, 645–46, 659–65. *See also* Monarchy
Spain, 417–18
Stamped Paper Revolt (1675), 528
State: Barnave on power of, 41, 43–44; conceptions of, 645–47; Domat on obligations to, 30; duty of, 659; fealty to, 108; and fundamental laws, 647–53; territorial dimensions and possessions of, 682–86
State Council (*Conseil d'Etat*), 9–10, 24
Statistics, 698, 703–4
Stoicism, 676–77

Subdeacons, 7–8, 282, 285–86, 298, 347
Sublet de Noyers, François, 105
Succession, 65. *See also* Inheritance;
   Monarchy, succession to; Property
Surgeons, 459–63
Sword, right to wear, 10
Syndicates, 435–37
Synods (Protestant), 386–88, 392, 400,
   405, 408

Taille: army officers exempted from, 131;
   and census, 702; clergy exempted from,
   252, 295; and community assemblies,
   552; diocesan receivers exempted from,
   370; due to *seigneurs,* 496; farmed out,
   435; *négociales,* 295; and newly
   ennobled, 128–29; nobility exempted
   from, 11, 25, 37, 125, 172, 199; *per-
   sonelle,* 186; and productivity, 738; and
   proof of nobility, 136; Protestant converts exempted from, 401; *réelle,* 173,
   186, 295, 620
Talent, men of, 221, 227
Talon, Omer, 65
Tametsi decree, 61, 63, 64
Tarde, Jean, 691
Tassin, Nicolas, 689, 691–92
Taxation, taxes: attitudes to, 730–31;
   clergy and, 336–37, 359–61, 369, 380;
   collected by syndicates, 435; and
   Estates General, 638; on fiefs, 482–84;
   Jews and, 421–22, 424–26; and poor,
   276; principles of, and methods of col-
   lection, 729–42; within Protestant
   church, 385, 387, 389, 400; in provinces,
   610–12, 619–23, 629, 634, 636; and re-
   volts, 741; tenant farmers and, 271–73;
   universities exempted from, 453. *See
   also* Poll tax; *Taille*
Teaching. *See* Education
Templars (knights), 292
"Tenths," 360, 368–73
Terray, abbé Joseph Marie, 604, 702
Terre-Rouge, Jean de, 649
Texier family, 237
Theatines, 292
Third Estate: Article of, (1615), 313; Barnave on rise of, 44; forms National

Assembly, 39; and gainful employment,
   11; income of, 13; and king's divine
   right, 657–58; and social equality, 38–
   39; in society of orders, 7, 9, 12–14
Tipstaffs (*huissiers*), 448–49, 508–9
Tiraqueau, André, 72
Tithes, 302–4; and law of *censives,* 493;
   and law of fiefs, 482; and Protestants,
   388; seigneurial, 532, 538
Tonsure, 7–8, 11, 282, 284. *See also*
   Clergy
Torcy, Jean-Baptiste Colbert, marquis de,
   18
Touch, the king's, 665–66, 671, 674–76
Toulouse, Louis Alexandre de Bourbon,
   comte de, 19, 22–23
Tour de France, 468
Tourny, Louis, marquis de, 722
Toussaint de Saint-Luc, Father
   (Toussaint Le Bigot), 147
Towns: *bourgeoisie* and, 8, 236, 250–51,
   482, 565–74; "commune," 590–98;
   community organization in, 563–605;
   craftsmen in, 255–64; features and types
   of, 563–65; may confer nobility, 11;
   and municipal reforms (1764–65), 598–
   604; privileged, 8; royal and central
   intervention in, 570–73, 598, 602. *See
   also names of individual towns*
Trade: Barnave on, 42–43; corporate organization of, 463–65; magistrates and,
   133; men of law and, 133–34; limitations
   on nobility's engaging in, 132–35
Traitants, 216
Transport, 686–89
Travel, 686–89
Trent, Council of: and benefices, 305, 307–
   8, 310, 316; and catechism, 348–49; and
   clergy, 284–85, 292, 316–18, 338, 340,
   343; and ecclesiastical jurisdiction, 296–
   97; and marriage laws, 61–63, 66
Trésoriers: de la bourse (Languedoc), 617,
   620, 622–23; *de France,* 435–37, 623
Tribunal: de la Connétablie, 142; of the
   Marshals of France, 141–44; *du point
   d'honneur,* 142
Tristan family, 169
Tull, Jethro, 184

Turgot, Anne Robert Jacques, baron de
l'Aulne: abolishes craft corporations,
472–73; abolishes *maîtrises et jurandes*,
254; and education, 722; establishes
equality of duties, 36–37; and Protestant
civil rights, 408; and provincial
assemblies, 629; on wholesalers, 230

Unigenitus bull, 353, 357
Universities, 306, 450–55. *See also* Paris,
University of
Usury, 247, 300, 339
Utrecht, Treaty of, (1713), 651

Vagabonds and tramps, 8, 275–76, 278,
641
Vair, Guillaume du, 88
Valabrègue, Israel Berard de, 424
Vassals, 485–92, 507, 525. *See also*
Feudalism; Fiefs
Vauban, Sébastien Le Prestre de,
Marshal: and construction of Ath for-
tress, 723–29; on numbers of nobles,
147; on population, 699, 701, 704; on
taxation, 730; training of, 703–4
Vendôme, Louis Joseph de Bourbon, duc
de, 17
Ventadour, Henri de Lévis, duc de, 394
Vernet, Joseph, 51
Véron, François, 393
Versailles, Edict of: of 1704, 145; of 1723,
120; of 1776, 254, 472; of 1787, 408
Vicars general (*grands vicaires*), 288, 291,
297, 326–27, 364

Vidames, 481
Viennois, Humbert II, dauphin de, 608
Villages, 551–62. *See also* Communities
Villeroi, François de Neufville, duc de,
Marshal, 145, 152
Villeroy family, 173–74
Villes jurées, 464–65
Vinages, 482
Vincent de Paul, Saint, 342–43, 345–48,
353
Viscounts, 26, 481
Voltaire, François Marie Arouet, called,
530, 553, 675, 714
Vossius, Isaac, 699
Vows. *See* Fealty
Vows, religious, 292–94
Voysin, Daniel François, 18

Wartburg, Walther von, 648
Wealth, 40–42, 44
Weapons, 125
Weiss, N., 384
West India Company, 474
Wholesalers, 229–33
Widows, 552
Wills, 74–75. *See also* Inheritance
Wine, 733–34
Wives, 67. *See also* Dowries; Marriage;
Women
Women, 81, 86–87, 484. *See also* Wives
Workers, 8. *See also* Crafts and craftsmen

Young, Arthur, 710